P9-APX-374

FUNDAMENTALISMS OBSERVED

THE FUNDAMENTALISM PROJECT

VOLUME

1

FUNDAMENTALISMS OBSERVED

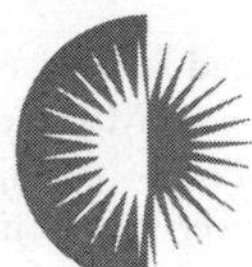

EDITED BY
Martin E. Marty and R. Scott Appleby

A study conducted by
The American Academy of Arts and Sciences

The University of Chicago Press
Chicago and London

Martin E. Marty and R. Scott Appleby direct the Fundamentalism Project. Marty, the Fairfax M. Cone Distinguished Service Professor of the History of Modern Christianity at the University of Chicago, is the editor of *The Christian Century* and the author of numerous books, including the multi-volume *Modern American Religion,* also published by the University of Chicago Press. Appleby, a research associate at the University of Chicago, is the author of *"Church and Age Unite!" The Modernist Impulse in American Catholicism.*

The collection of essays in this volume is based on a project conducted under the auspices of the American Academy of Arts and Sciences and supported by a grant from the John D. and Catherine T. MacArthur Foundation. The opinions expressed are those of the individual authors only, and do not necessarily reflect the views of the American Academy or the supporting foundation.

The University of Chicago Press, Chicago 60637
The University of Chicago Press, Ltd., London

Printed in the United States of America

00 99 98 97 96 95 94 93 92 5 4 3 2

Library of Congress Cataloging in Publication Data

Fundamentalism observed / edited by Martin E. Marty and R. Scott Appleby ; sponsored by the American Academy of Arts and Sciences.
p. cm. — (The Fundamentalism project ; v. 1)
Includes bibliographical references and index.
ISBN 0-226-50877-3
1. Fundamentalism—Comparative studies. I. Marty, Martin E., 1928– . II. Appleby, R. Scott, 1956– . III. American Academy of Arts and Sciences. IV. Series.
BL238.F83 1991 vol. 1
291′.09′04 s—dc20
[291′.09′04] 90-24894
CIP

∞ The paper used in this publication meets the minimum requirements of the American National Standard for Information Sciences—Permanence of Paper for Printed Library Materials, ANSI Z39.48–1984.

CONTENTS

INTRODUCTION

The Fundamentalism Project: A User's Guide

Modern religious fundamentalisms receive attention in *Fundamentalisms Observed,* as they will in five subsequent projected volumes.

Modern, like the other two words, resists easy definition. It would not be possible to pursue the project if the scores of scholars involved with it had to agree on its meanings and usages. Yet consistently in these pages "modern" is a code word for the set of forces which fundamentalists perceive as the threat which inspires their reaction. Modern cultures include at least three dimensions uncongenial to fundamentalists: a preference for secular rationality; the adoption of religious tolerance with accompanying tendencies toward relativism; and individualism.[1] From this perspective fundamentalisms are recently developed forms of traditionalisms, forms which agents of liberal cultures had not expected to see rise or flourish. They appeared at first to be residues, vestiges, or throwbacks, not active elements in an emerging and unsettling set of global changes. In these pages, however, it will become apparent at once that fundamentalists do not reject all features of the ways called modern. Rather, they exist in a type of symbiotic relationship with the modern, finding, for example, technology, mass media of communications, and other instruments of modernity congenial to their purposes.

Religious, like the noun *religion,* equally eludes precise definition, but readers will see that the scholars tend to include in their use, among others, at least these elements: religion has to do with what concerns people ultimately, and provides them with personal and social identity. Religion leads adherents to prefer myth and symbol, along with rite and ceremony, over other forms of expression. And religion tends to imply some sort of cosmic or metaphysical backdrop and to stipulate certain behavioral correlates.

The present point in adducing the term is to suggest that while there may be such a things as a "fundamentalist mentality" which finds its expression in various ideological or scientific forms, here the prime interest has to do with fundamentalisms in which the religious dimension is foremost. In cases where it is epiphenomenal—the

1. Robert Booth Fowler, *Unconventional Partners: Religion and Liberal Culture in the United States* (Grand Rapids, Mich.: William B. Eerdmans, 1989), p. 4.

author of an essay on Japan, for instance, sees religion associated with political fundamentalism—the association must be very close and vivid.

Fundamentalism is at least as controversial an issue for definers as are the other two terms, which are less central to the present project, so it demands more attention.

Let it be said at the outset that the directors of the project have assured all authors herein that in this introduction and in all that follows, they will make it emphatically clear that "fundamentalism" is not always the first choice or even a congenial choice at all for some of the movements here discussed. Most of the essayists take some pains to say why they are uneasy with the term, and they say so often, with evident awareness that some of their colleagues who specialize in the same topics will criticize their assent to use the term. We have asked them to keep their apologias brief, since we would elaborate here.

Among the reasons for insistence on a single term are these:

First, "fundamentalism" is here to stay, since it serves to create a distinction over against cognate but not fully appropriate words such as "traditionalism," "conservatism," or "orthodoxy" and "orthopraxis." If the term were to be rejected, the public would have to find some other word if it is to make sense of a set of global phenomena which urgently bid to be understood. However diverse the expressions are, they present themselves as movements which demand comparison even as they deserve fair separate treatment so that their special integrities will appear in bold relief.

Second, when they must communicate across cultures, journalists, public officials, scholars, and publics in the parts of the world where these books have their first audience have settled on this term. Rather than seek an idiosyncratic and finally precious alternative, it seemed better for the team of scholars to try to inform inquiry with the word that is here to stay and to correct misuses.

With those two reasons goes a third: all words have to come from somewhere and will be more appropriate in some contexts than in others. Words which have appeared in these paragraphs—"modern," "religious," "liberal," and "secular"—are examples. It is urgent in all cases that these terms be used in such ways that they do justice to the particularities of separate realities, something which we are confident readers will find the present authors responsibly undertaking to do.

Fourth, having spent two of the five years set aside for research and study comparing "fundamentalism" to alternatives, we have come to two conclusions. No other coordinating term was found to be as intelligible or serviceable. And attempts of particular essayists to provide distinctive but in the end confusing accurate alternatives led to the conclusion that they were describing something similar to what are here called fundamentalisms. The prefix "ultra-" or the word "extremist" did not connote enough. When scholars made suggestions for replacements such as "revolutionary neotraditionalist Islamic (or Jewish, or Christian, or whatever) radicalism" and were then asked to define these alternatives, they came to describe pretty much what the other authors were calling "fundamentalism."

We early came to an agreement, then, that the authors could take some pains to mention any uneasinesses they had with the term, with the assurance that we editors would ask readers constantly to think of what we here call "fundamentalisms" as being equal to "fundamentalist-like" movements. It will be appropriate in virtually every case to picture individual quotation marks surrounding the term and then proceed with the inquiry and the reading.

If people cannot agree on cross-cultural terms like the chosen one, "fundamentalism," they are also not likely to agree on all features of its definition. Readers of these essays will find, however, that the authors have certain elements of definition in mind, without which they would not know what to seek. Someone proposed Ludwig Wittgenstein's concept of "family resemblances," and it seems appropriate.

To anticipate a key feature separating "fundamentalism" from, say, "traditionalism" or "conservatism," we take an observation from one essay in this book.[2] The coauthors say that the members of the movement they observe "no longer perceive themselves as reeling under the corrosive effects of secular life. On the contrary, they perceive themselves as fighting back, and doing so rather successfully."

Fighting back. It is no insult to fundamentalisms to see them as militant, whether in the use of words and ideas or ballots or, in extreme cases, bullets. Fundamentalists see themselves as militants. This means that the first word to employ in respect to them is that they are reactive (though not always reactionary). These essays make clear a feature which in our inquiries to date have struck us with surprising force and have appeared with astonishing frequency: fundamentalists begin as traditionalists who perceive some challenge or threat to their core identity, both social and personal. They are not frivolous, nor do they deal with peripheral assaults. If they lose on the central issues, they believe they lose everything. They react, they fight back with great innovative power.

Next, they *fight for*. It will become clear that what they fight for begins with a worldview they have inherited or adopted and which they constantly reinforce. If there are assaults on the most intimate zones of life, such as the family, they will respond with counteraction in support of such an institution. Along with this go certain understandings of gender, sex roles, the nurturing and educating of children, and the like. They will fight for their conceptions of what ought to go on in matters of life and health, in the world of the clinic and the laboratory. While some fundamentalists may be passive for a time, just wanting to be left alone, when the threat grows sufficiently intense, they will fight for a changed civil polity. If nothing else works, as a last resort they may fight for territory, or the integrity of their social group, by using the instruments of war.

Fundamentalists *fight with* a particularly chosen repository of resources which one might think of as weapons. The movements got their name from the choice: they reached back to real or presumed pasts, to actual or imagined ideal original conditions and concepts, and selected what they regarded as fundamental. The verb includes a clue: fundamentalists are selective. They may well consider that they are adopting the whole of the pure past, but their energies go into employing those features which will best reinforce their identity, keep their movement together, build defenses around its

2. Samuel C. Heilman and Menachem Friedman, "Religious Fundamentalism and Religious Jews: The Case of the Haredim," chapter 4.

boundaries, and keep others at some distance. These chosen practical or doctrinal fundamentals, to use terms which appear in these essays, often turn into icons, fetishes, or totems in the rituals of those who employ them.

Fundamentalists also *fight against* others. These may be generalized or specific enemies, but in all cases, whether they come from without or within the group, they are the agents of assault on all that is held dear. The outsider may be the infidel, the agent of antithetical sacred powers, the modernizer; but he or she may also be the friendly messenger who seeks compromise, middle ground, or a civil "agreement to disagree." The insider as threat is likely to be someone who would be moderate, would negotiate with modernity, would adapt the movement. Many of the fundamentalists here described spend more energy focusing on the moderate or the apostate than on the polar opposites of their movement.

Fundamentalists also *fight under* God—in the case of theistic religions—or under the signs of some transcendent reference in the minority of instances, such as Buddhism and Confucianism. Particularly potent are those fundamentalisms whose participants are convinced that they are called to carry out God's or Allah's purposes against challengers.

Those five references to fighting suggest what no doubt every reader of this book knew before opening it: that they are dealing with topics which elicit great passion both from fundamentalists and from those who would oppose or even seek merely to understand them. That being the case, the people who hosted the scholarly conferences which were the platforms for inquiry behind these chapters and the directors and editors have taken special pains to see that the greatest possible measure of fairness be present and demonstrated.

In this first volume, two approaches are webbed: the historical and the phenomenological. The chapters in every case include narratives which feature the steps taken by movements as they reacted and as they transformed their conservatisms into fundamentalisms. The authors put in brackets their own presuppositions, an approach which does not mean that they successfully leave them behind, but that they become aware of them, take them into consideration, and do some compensating for them.

The goal in every case is to come up with essays in which the people described therein would recognize themselves in the portrait and see that efforts were made to deal fairly with them. Why not have fundamentalists write chapters? There is no proscription against such an endeavor, but the scholars commended to us, people with coordinating skills and willingness to see each fundamentalism in the context of others, were not such fundamentalists. Some were "participant-observers" in the movements they describe; many are coreligionists who do not share the fundamentalist reactive aspect. For this volume, which seeks to understand the fundamentalists' perceptions of an external order that often developed in contrast to the normative order prescribed by the religious tradition, it was the responsibility of each contributor to take the interests of the fundamentalists into consideration. Subsequent volumes, with different aims, will more closely reflect other perspectives, some necessarily less empathic than the ones represented here.

In mentioning this important matter of varying perspectives on a controversial subject such as fundamentalism, it is appropriate to state clearly that the positions and interpretations put forth in this collection of essays are those of the individual authors and do not necessarily reflect the views of the American Academy of Arts and Sciences. In undertaking this project, the principal purpose of the Academy is to bring together scholars with the best credentials in the several areas and cultures under study, and to ask them to present as inclusive and fair a presentation as possible.

In this first volume, although relatively little direct comparing yet goes on, each author addresses a set of common questions. When and under what circumstances did the group or movement form? Did it evolve from, or inherit conceptual or material resources from, an earlier tradition? Does the history of the movement include episodes of activism and, conversely, of withdrawal from public life? If the group or movement is reactive, against what is it reacting? What is the group's vision of a just order? What are the specific economic, political, religious, social goals of the movement? Are strategies in place for achieving these goals? In addressing these questions authors were concerned particularly with the religious character of these fundamentalisms. Was there a charismatic founder? If the group or leader appeals to a sacred text or tradition, how is this source interpreted and applied? How does the movement understand history and human freedom under God?

In providing answers to these and similar questions, the emphasis is on introducing readers of the series to the phenomenon in fourteen separate accountings which offer a balanced, if not always uncontroversial, overview. Rather than attempt direct comparative or synthetic statements at this stage, the authors were asked to confront readers with the rich textures of the separate experiences, thus doing justice to the several fundamentalisms which, by definition, could not agree with each other. They were also asked to summarize in their essays the background material necessary for a nonspecialist understanding of these separate experiences. This volume may serve, then, both as a series of fresh interpretations and as a necessary source of reference for users of the entire series and for subsequent project authors who will focus more exclusively and exhaustively on certain of the themes introduced here.

Accordingly, there are several ways to conceive of these books as useful, that is, as suited to readers.

While published by a university press, each book is intended to be accessible to what publishers call a "trade market." This means that it is aimed at the informed, if not professional, readers in what in the academic world would be called the various humanities and social scientific disciplines, as well as the sciences. The assumption is that the task of understanding fundamentalisms is urgent for citizens at a time when these movements are so frequently catalysts in an unsettled world. At the same time, reading the books might enlarge one's picture of how some very different people live and who they are. To that humanistic end, we have pressed the scholars to write clearly, to keep formal technical terminology to a minimum or in every case to explain it.

Of course confronting cultures alien to one's own experience, an act which must go on in the present circumstance, means coming to terms with apparently remote and arcane terms and people. (There are enough names like Indira Gandhi and Anwar Sadat in the chapters to sustain one through unfamiliar patches.) Momentarily there may be an assault on the eye as one first confronts untranslatable and hard to transliterate words and names, but readers are encouraged to read on: after a few pages, if we are at all successful, they will find themselves at home in the succession of fourteen disparate thought worlds. It takes a bit of doing, but here the effort toward clarity and vividness ought to be apparent.

Just as at one extreme these are to be compared to trade books for a general literate public, they are designed at the other to be attractive to libraries as *encyclopedic* works. We have tried to organize the chapters in sufficiently similar ways to make this encyclopedic use apparent for reporters, students, public officials, or anyone who wishes to make some sense immediately of movements which are part of the day's news and which might have determinative roles in trends and events which will concern us all.

Despite the necessary heft of such volumes as these, they also are designed to have *textbook* possibilities. All the essays look ahead to the strange new world that is unfolding at the century's end. Even as they were being written, sudden and drastic changes in Central and Eastern Europe, in Central and South America, in Africa and the Pacific island worlds presented new opportunities for fundamentalisms. When change came to the Soviet Union and exposed to view the durability of Islamic religion in the socialist republics that seventy years earlier had become part of a system which repressed religion, it was clear that the religion of various peoples was a bond for social identity and an agent for new expression. One scholar observing ethnic clashes said that the whole scene was "fundamentally religious." That point is controversial. It is less controversial to say that the religions which are so forceful are "fundamental" or fundamentalist. That being the case, a new generation of college and university students finds reason to assess the role and power of fundamentalisms around the globe. Many will be doing business with nations in which fundamentalisms are potent and even guiding forces. Some of them may even be fending off military and terrorist movements by fundamentalist extremists some day.

Textbooks which provide access to such a world are in place, and as editors we have tried to keep utility for such purposes in mind. In this introductory volume we have commissioned essays that reveal the sweep and scope of fundamentalist movements. Some of the authors were given a daunting assignment in a relatively short space: provide an overview of a particular type of religious fundamentalism in a large region (e.g., in North America, or in Latin America, the Sunni Arab world, the Indian subcontinent), while others enjoyed the relative leisure of focusing closely on one movement or nation (e.g., in Israel, Japan). Even though the authors were given such ambitious assignments, however, the volume is hardly comprehensive, even in general terms, of the range of fundamentalist-like movements around the world. The project volumes taken together will not exhaust the phenomenon; however, many of the essays which will appear in subsequent years should help fill in the gaps. At the same time, the appeal of these volumes as textbooks will lie less in their coverage of events behind the most recent headlines and more in their promise of providing tools of conceptualization and analysis for these and other developments in years to come.

Finally, these are also scholarly *monographs*, specialized studies in which appropriate experts draw on years of experience to present, often for the first time, their subjects of specialty for readers who have a coordinating and synoptic view in mind. As such they are to be stimulants toward more scholarship. The Fundamentalism Project is preparing supplementary bibliographies and rosters of scholars to advance such a cause through the years after the publication of these books.

Readers might find it attractive to begin their own coordinating work with this first volume, which can stand on its own. They might start asking what fundamentalisms have in common with each other and where and how they differ, as we have done in the concluding essay to this volume. They will thus anticipate the subsequent volumes. The second and third of the books will describe the effects of fundamentalisms around the world, effects on, for example, family life and education, mass media, constitutionalism, economies, and military programs. A fourth volume will attempt to account for the surprising rise of modern religious fundamentalisms by examining the dynamic of movements across a spectrum from separatist to accommodationist. This will be followed by a fifth book whose authors will finally be charged to delineate common features among fundamentalisms. The last volume will discuss the public policy implications which motivated the American Academy of Arts and Sciences to charter this scholarly inquiry.

The Fundamentalism Project issues from the world called Western, the sphere in which the "modern," "liberal," and "secular" achievements were most readily experienced, and where fundamentalisms had appeared to be recessive, if not waning. It has become increasingly clear to participants in this study that their inquiry is occurring at a time when not only Marxist polities and ideologies are being questioned from without and within. The West also finds its programs and conceptual schemes in disarray. The rise of these fundamentalisms also on Western soil, where the very term itself was patented seven decades ago, suggests something of the degree of such disarray. In a way, the voices of the fundamentalists reproduced in these chapters are challenges to those who have held non- and counterfundamentalist understandings of reason, practice, and politics. They help force critical examination of beliefs and presuppositions and thus in a way are a mirror for the Western academy, a window toward the future to be shared by antifundamentalist and fundamentalist alike.

ACKNOWLEDGMENTS

We thank first the advisers who began planning and conceptualizing The Fundamentalism Project in meetings at the House of the American Academy of Arts and Sciences in Cambridge, Massachusetts: Gabriel Almond, William Bouwsma, Stephen R. Graubard, D. Gale Johnson, Edward H. Levi, Franklin Long, Ernst Mayr, Everett Mendelsohn, Roy Mottahedeh, Joel Orlen, Richard Pipes, Fazlur Rahman, A. K. Ramanujan, Erica Reiner, Tu Wei-ming, Frank Westheimer and Marvin Zonis participated in the final and most definitive of these sessions in December 1987. Subsequently, Nancy T. Ammerman, James Barr, Leo Beranek, Harvey Brooks, Gerhard Casper, James S. Coleman, Shireen T. Hunter, T. N. Madan, and Abdel Azim Ramadan joined an executive committee formed to oversee the subsequent planning phases of the project.

Also contributing in significant ways to the process of identifying and recruiting scholars and clarifying themes for this first volume were Joel Carpenter, Jay Dolan, Wendy Doniger, Bruce Lawrence, Robert McKinley, and Emmanuel Sivan. Many other scholars contributed to this volume through written responses and criticisms of particular essays after they were presented during a public conference; those not mentioned by name here are acknowledged by the authors in the endnotes.

Joel Orlen, executive officer of the American Academy of Arts and Sciences, merits a second word of thanks for his leadership and encouragement in advancing the project from stage to stage.

In skillfully steering the editors through the various phases of volume review and production Alan Thomas of the University of Chicago Press was unfailingly patient. He was ably assisted by Claudia Rex, Jennie Lightner, and Barbara Anderson.

We are grateful to University of Chicago professors Franklin I. Gamwell, former dean of the Divinity School, and Bernard McGinn, director of the Institute for the Advanced Study of Religion, for providing intellectual stimulus, office space, and the semi-annual use of Swift Lecture Hall. The Divinity School also hosted a graduate seminar, led by the Project directors, during which students drawn from throughout the university discussed and dissected early drafts of the essays. Graduate students David Spesia, David Westerberg, Tim Nelson, and Kent Gilbert contributed hundreds of hours of photocopying, proofreading, and research assistance. Doctoral candidates J. E. Llewellyn, Jeffrey Kaplan, and Laura Grillo checked sources and made valuable editorial suggestions. Mr. Kaplan also prepared the glossary. Patricia A. Mitchell put in many long and careful hours compiling the index and preparing the final manuscript for publication.

In such an endeavor as this, there is usually one person without whom there would be no project. In this case that person is Barbara A. Lockwood, who performs with extraordinary skill and grace the duties of office manager, secretary, and research assistant. The editors are happily in her debt.

CHAPTER
1

North American Protestant Fundamentalism

Nancy T. Ammerman

As fundamentalism re-emerged in the United States in the late twentieth century after a period of apparent hibernation, no two words better captured its public image and agenda than "Moral Majority." In 1979 independent Baptist pastor Jerry Falwell declared that people who were concerned about the moral decline of America were a majority waiting to be mobilized. He set out to accomplish that task, and for the next decade conservative voters were registered, rallies were held, and legislators elected. Ronald Reagan came to see religious conservatives as an important constituency, speaking at their rallies and inviting their leaders to the White House. And in 1988, politically active conservative pastors again had the ear of Republican George Bush.[1] By 1989 Falwell could declare his mission was accomplished, that conservative consciences had been raised; he could return to pastoring his church and leading his growing Liberty University.

Pastoring churches and establishing schools had long been the more likely strategies of people who called themselves fundamentalists. Not all saw politics and social change as their mission, and many had discounted such activities as useless, even counterproductive. At the same time that some fundamentalists were lobbying in the White House, others were waiting anxiously for the Rapture, the time when they would be transported to heaven. A new book had appeared that set 1988 as the date for this eschatological event, and many were convinced by its claims that the Jewish New Year, Rosh Hashana, would be the appointed time.[2] Like many dates before it, this appointment with the End Times went unkept, but believers were reminded again of how important it was to be "Rapture ready" and to seek the salvation of others.

Fundamentalists in North America could be found in both camps—waiting for the Rapture and lobbying in the White House. In both cases believers were drawing on a distinctive view of the world that had emerged about a century earlier. They were willing to argue that certain beliefs were "fundamental," and they were willing to organize in a variety of ways to preserve and defend those beliefs.

A Brief Introduction and Definition

In the last quarter of the nineteenth century, many leaders in American Protestantism were actively seeking ways to adapt traditional beliefs to the realities of "modern" scholarship and sensibilities. They were met head-on, however, by people who saw the adaptations as heresy and declared that they would defend traditional beliefs from such adaptation. In the first two decades of the twentieth century, they produced a number of publications that furthered this defensive cause. Among the most important was a series of short scholarly essays issued over a five-year peiod (1910–15) and entitled "The Fundamentals"—a name that was being widely used as the designation for the threatened beliefs. In 1920 Curtis Lee Laws, editor of the Northern Baptist newspaper *The Watchman Examiner*, wrote that a "fundamentalist" is a person willing to "do battle royal" for the fundamentals of the faith.[3] It was both a description and a call to action, and the name stuck.

During the 1920s fundamentalists actively fought against modernism in their churches and against evolution in their schools. They lost those battles but retreated and reorganized into a network of institutions that has housed much of the conservative wing of American Protestantism ever since.

However, the name fundamentalist is not synonymous with "conservative." It is, rather, a subset of that larger whole. Fundamentalists share with other conservative Christians their support for "traditional" interpretations of such doctrines as the Virgin Birth of Jesus, the reality of the miracles reported in Scripture (including the Resurrection of Jesus from the dead), and the eventual return of Christ to reign over this earth. In spreading these teachings, conservatives tend to support the more supernatural interpretation of events, while liberals tend to seek naturalistic explanations.

In American society such conservatism in religion is widespread. Seventy-two percent of Americans say the Bible is the Word of God, with over half of that number (39 percent of the total) saying that it should be taken literally. Almost two-thirds say they are certain that Jesus Christ rose from the dead. Nearly three-fourths say they believe in life after death.[4] And almost half (44 percent) could be called "creationists," since they believe that God created the world in "pretty much its present form" sometime in the last ten thousand years.[5]

Not all these people, however, are fundamentalists. Even within conservatism there are a number of significant divisions. Among other things, not everyone agrees on that most central of doctrines—how people are saved, that is, how they make themselves acceptable to God. One branch of conservative Protestantism places primary emphasis on the historic creeds of the faith and membership in a church that confesses those beliefs. People are baptized (initiated) as infants into a community of faith.[6] These "confessional" churches are often conservative, but they are not often the home of fundamentalists.[7]

Fundamentalists are more often found in the other, much larger, branch of conservative Protestantism that identifies itself as "evangelical." These are people for whom only an individual decision to follow Jesus will suffice for salvation. They are concerned not only about their own eternal fate but also about the destiny of those around them. They seek to "win souls for Christ" by their words and deeds, testifying to the necessity of a life-changing decision to become a Christian. They often speak of that experience as being "born again." It is an experience that gives them a sense of personal and intimate communion with Jesus and often shapes their lives and conversations in noticeably pious ways.

But even within the evangelical branch there are significant subdivisions. Almost all black Protestants belong here, for instance, but they have developed independent traditions over two centuries of segregation that have made them quite distinctive from many white evangelicals. Blacks hold to many of the conservative doctrines of other evangelicals, and three-fourths of black churchgoers are in one of the black Baptist or Methodist denominations. They are likely to hold Scripture in high regard and to emphasize the necessity of being saved.

These churches were born out of the Great Awakening and the later southern revivals, and they have retained much of that evangelical heritage. But the distinctive style of African American worship and the distinctive relationship of African Americans to society make the label *fundamentalist* less than apt. Theirs is a style of worship that is distinctive not for its doctrinal content but for the way in which it celebrates a separate ethnic tradition. C. Eric Lincoln has described the function of separateness as protecting the black believer from distortions that whites might introduce and as reinforcing and enhancing the very characteristics of African American worship belittled in white society. He claims that "black ethnicity denies the relevance of white styles of worship for black people and sanctions the ritual patterns developed in the churches of the black experience."[8] Theirs is not, then, a religiously based separation from a secular world but a racially based separation in which church and community are bound tightly together. In Lincoln's words, "in the black community the Black Church is in a real sense a universal church, claiming and representing all Blacks out of a tradition that looks back to the time when there was *only* the Black Church to bear witness to 'who' or 'what' a black [person] was."[9] When a black preacher speaks, he or she speaks for more than a mere congregation. In that sense, black evangelicals have yet to experience the modern secularization that has separated religious institutions from the political and economic mainstream. Theirs is not a rebellion against modernist compromises. Although they share many beliefs with other evangelicals, those beliefs function quite differently in their very different social world.[10]

Pentecostal and charismatic Christians in North America also belong in the evangelical family but are a distinct group within it. Beginning with the Pentecostal revivals near the turn of the twentieth century, new denominations such as the Church of God, the Church of God in Christ, and the Assemblies of God were formed, in which "gifts of the spirit" (such as speaking in tongues and healing) were emphasized as evidence of the believer's spiritual power. By the 1960s an emphasis on the Holy Spirit's power had also found its way into many mainline denominations, with prayer and healing groups meeting around the country in the parish halls of Catholic, Episcopal, Presbyterian, Methodist, and many other local churches. The *Christianity Today*–Gallup poll estimated that only about one-third of the nation's twenty-nine million charismatics are in traditional Pentecostal denominations.[11] Whatever their denominational location is, charismatics tend toward becoming "evangelical" in their insistence on a personal experience of salvation. But their religious experiences go considerably beyond the "rebirth" noncharismatic evangelicals claim.[12]

Another group sometimes called "evangelical" or "fundamentalist" is the Church of Jesus Christ of Latter Day Saints, the Mormons. This group's reverence for its scripture, their disciplined way of life, and their aggressive evangelism sometimes cause them to be referred to as "fundamentalist." The term, "Protestant Christian fundamentalism," however, is not appropriate in the case of the large majority of Mormons. While they share some religious and social characteristics with fundamentalists, they are certainly not Protestant. They accept few of the traditional doctrines Protestant fundamentalists hold sacred, and their adoption of a unique sacred text, *The Book of Mormon*, sets them firmly at odds with Protestant fundamentalists.[13] In fact in recent years Mormons have experienced a fundamentalist movement within their own ranks, in groups seeking to purify their tradition and return to orthodox interpretations of their scripture.

These groups occupy the same general religious territory as fundamentalists. They are all conservative and evangelical, but they are still distinct from each other and from fundamentalists. Mormons have their own scripture, African Americans are defined more by race than by doctrine, and Pentecostals trust the revelatory power of experience more than do the more rationally oriented fundamentalists who seek to confine revelation to Scripture alone.

While we may be able to identify these other distinct subgroups, it is less clear that we can identify fundamentalists as distinct from evangelicals in general and on what basis that might be done. During most of the first half of the twentieth century "fundamentalist" and "evangelical" meant roughly the same things. People might use either name to describe those who preserved and practiced the revivalist heritage of soul winning and maintained a traditional insistence on orthodoxy.

But as orthodox people began to organize for survival in a world dominated by the non-orthodox, two significantly different strategies emerged. Seeking a broad cultural base for their gospel, one group saw benefits in learning to get along with outsiders. They did not wish to adopt the outsiders' ways, but they wanted to be respected. They began, especially after World War II, to take the name "evangelical" for themselves. Billy Graham can be seen as their primary representative.[14] The other group insisted that getting along was no virtue and that active opposition to liberalism, secularism, and communism was to be pursued.[15] This group retained the name "fundamentalist." To this group we now turn our attention.

Central Features of Fundamentalism in North America

Evangelism. When fundamentalists describe how they are different from other people, they begin with the fact that they are saved. They clearly affirm their kinship with other evangelicals on this point. Much of their organized effort is aimed at seeking out converts. They invite the "lost" to church, broadcast evangelistic messages over radio and television, print millions of pages and record millions of words on cassette tapes—all aimed at convincing the unconvinced that eternity in heaven is better than the eternal damnation in hell that surely awaits the unsaved. Preachers proclaim the hopeless conditions of lives not entrusted to Jesus. And individual believers invest much in prayer and testimony directed at the eternal fate of their families and friends. Evangelism and the salvation of individual souls remains at the heart of the message fundamentalists proclaim to American society in the late twentieth century.

Inerrancy. Fundamentalists also claim that the only sure path to salvation is through a faith in Jesus Christ that is grounded in unwavering faith in an inerrant Bible. As fundamentalists see the situation, if but one error of fact or principle is admitted in Scripture, nothing—not even the redemptive work of Christ—is certain. When asked what else makes them distinctive, fundamentalists will almost invariably claim that they are the people who "really believe the Bible." They insist that true Christians must believe the whole Bible, the parts they like along with the parts they dislike, the hard parts and the easy ones. The Bible can be trusted to provide an accurate description of science and history, as well as morality and religion. And only such an unfailing source can be trusted to provide a sure path to salvation in the hereafter and clear guidance in the here and now. As Kathleen Boone has pointed out, fundamentalists imagine "themselves either steadfast in absolute truth or whirling in the vortex of nihilism."[16]

Such contemporary use of ancient texts requires, of course, careful interpretation. Studies of fundamentalists invariably point to the central role of pastors and Bible teachers in creating authoritative meanings out of the biblical text.[17] Fundamentalists live in communities that are defined by the language they use and the stories they tell. Community leaders, teachers in Christian schools, and Christian media personalities give shape to the way ordinary believers understand their world by offering interpretations that give the infallible text its concrete human reality. The more people are immersed in this fundamentalist community of discourse, the more easily they accept the Bible as completely accurate. They are more likely to question the validity of science than to doubt the unfailing Word of God.[18]

Some aspects of modern science, of course, are *not* questioned (the earth's roundness and orbit around the sun, for instance). The interpretive task fundamentalists undertake, then, requires a careful balancing of facts about the world presumed by moderns to be true with the assumption that the Bible contains no factual errors. Phrases that seem to indicate a modern view of the solar system (such as "circle of the earth") are highlighted, while statements clearly reflecting an ancient view (such as references to "waters" above and below the earth) are said to be poetic and not intended to be "scientifically precise."[19] Likewise, moral teaching in Scripture that seems to condone slavery or polygamy must be neutralized. Such teaching is neither endorsed as eternally relevant (with the notable exception of patriarchy) nor rejected as a mistake of ancient writers. Rather, such practices are deemed irrelevant to salvation, to be accepted if in keeping with the cultural custom and abandoned if not.

Within any social arrangement individuals can live fully Christian lives by virtue of their personal relationship with Jesus.

Because this idea of inerrancy is so central to the identity of fundamentalists, it is an idea that receives considerable attention and development. Theologians and church leaders worry about all the nuances of interpretation and arrive at various theories that seem best to support the Bible's truthfulness. They often argue vociferously among themselves, but their worrying rarely affects the people in the pews. The primary affirmation of ordinary believers is simply that the Bible is a reliable guide for life. It contains systematic rules for living that have been proven successful over six thousand years of human history. Fundamentalists are confident that everything in Scripture is true, and if they have questions about a seemingly difficult passage, they know that prayer, study, and a visit with the pastor are guaranteed to provide an answer.[20]

Premillennialism. Fundamentalists do not simply read the Bible to learn history or moral principles. They also expect to find in Scripture clues to the future destiny of this world, what will happen in the End Times. From the beginning of the fundamentalist movement, traditionalists who were concerned about Scripture and doctrine were closely linked with people who were concerned about interpreting the Bible's prophecies. The legacy of that connection is that today most fundamentalists are "pre-tribulation dispensational premillennialists." The ideas that go with that label are almost as complicated as the label, but one of the most important is the idea of the Rapture. For fundamentalist readers of Scripture, one of the most central stories is Jesus' description of how it will be when the "Son of Man comes" (Matt. 24:37–41). "There will be two men in a field; one will be taken, the other left; two women grinding at the mill; one will be taken, the other left." Combined with words in 1 Thessalonians (4:15–18) about being "caught up in the air to meet the Lord," a picture of heavenly escape is created. True believers will one day soon simply hear the heavenly trumpet and disappear into the sky, leaving those around them bewildered. That is the Rapture for which they seek to be ready. If the Rapture does not come before death, believers have, of course, the "hope of heaven" after death. But the Rapture might come first, meaning that even those with no reason to expect death do not know how long they have on this earth. The belief in an "any moment" Rapture, then, lends both urgency to the evangelistic task and comfort to persecuted believers.

While the Rapture is perhaps the most central feature of fundamentalist eschatology (that is, their beliefs about the climax of history), it is nearly overshadowed by the emphasis on prophecy that accompanies it. Believers are not content to know that Jesus is coming for them; they want to know when and what will happen next. For these clues they turn to the apocalyptic books of Daniel (in Hebrew Scripture) and the Revelation (at the end of the New Testament). Here there are great images of destruction and horror preceding the ultimate triumph of God. Believers interested in prophecy dissect these images to create a systematic scheme (often pictured in elaborate charts) that chronicles the "Tribulation" of the earth following the departure of believers, the rise of a world ruler (the Antichrist), and the final battle (Armageddon) in which the forces of good and evil will meet. Only then will Christ establish a kingdom of peace and righteousness on this earth. That fundamentalists believe Christ will have to return before the millennium (one-thousand-year reign on earth) makes them "premillennialists" (in contrast to the more optimistic "postmillennialists" who thought human effort might usher in the reign of God). That they think the Rapture will happen before the upheavals of the Tribulation makes their position "pretribulation." (There are also "mid" and "post" tribulation positions, but they are less popular.) That they divide history into such clear-cut periods, separated by climactic acts of God, is at the heart of being "dispensationalist."

Dispensationalists take their name from a reading of history that divides time into distinct periods (usually seven) in which salvation is "dispensed" in unique ways. The period from the time of Jesus' death until the Rapture is known as the "Church Age," in which salvation is by grace, obtained through belief in Jesus. Both before and after this age, salvation is granted differently. Therefore scriptures addressed to people in different ages may not apply to our own. Likewise, Scripture addressed to God's earthly people, the Jews, is distinct from Scripture addressed to God's heavenly people, the church. Sorting all of this out requires a good deal of effort, and many fundamentalists turn for help to the Scofield Reference Bible (1909) or the more recent Ryrie version (1978). Both contain extensive footnotes explaining the true intent of each passage of Scripture.

It is in these interpretations of prophecy, then, that fundamentalists depart most dramatically from a literal reading of Scripture. Prophetic words do not mean what they seem to mean to the uninitiated. Weeks are really sets of seven years, armies coming from the north refer to Soviet forces, "Tubal" is Turkey, and so forth. In these prophecies, believers discern a kind of secret road map to the unfolding of human history. They can cross-reference Scripture and the nightly news. They only occasionally set dates for the Rapture—they are, after all, repeatedly warned against that in the Bible—but they are constantly watching for the signs that it might be soon. And they distrust claims to orthodoxy made by people who do not take prophecy seriously.

Strict inerrancy, then, is taken by fundamentalists as demanding a premillennial interpretation of Scripture and attention to its "inerrant" prophecy alongside its inerrant history, science, and moral teaching. In this view, the truth of Scripture can be "proved" by its accurate predictions of future events, as well as by its practical advice about salvation and Christian living. The systematic derivation of facts and principles that is at the heart of fundamentalist interpretation lends itself to the systematic outlining of history and future found in dispensationalism.

Separatism. The conservative orthodoxy and evangelism of fundamentalists clearly do not make them unique. As we have already seen, there are many nonfundamentalist conservatives. Even inerrancy and premillennialism are not fully sufficient defining characteristics. Among nonfundamentalist evangelicals there are inerrantists and premillennialists, but those views are both less dominant and held less dogmatically in nonfundamentalist circles of evangelicals. And more importantly, few nonfundamentalist evangelicals would insist that eschatology is a critical test of faith. The ultimate characteristic that has distinguished fundamentalists from other evangelicals has been their insistence that there *can be* tests of faith. Fundamentalists insist on uniformity of belief within the ranks and separation from others whose beliefs and lives are suspect. The fundamentalist, then, is very likely to belong to a church with strict rules for its own membership and for its cooperative relations with others. It is likely to be an "independent" church, since so many of the denominations are seen as infected with apostasy and compromise. The true believer will also adhere to strict rules for her own life, shunning any person or practice that might reduce the effectiveness of her life's witness to the message of salvation. When confronted with unbelief, doubt, error, or sinful ways, fundamentalists weigh the possibility that direct confrontation might avert a brother or sister from eternal damnation. If pickets at the doors of a movie such as "The Last Temptation of Christ"[21] will keep even a single soul from the fires of hell, then the effort is worth it. But if confrontation is likely only to drag the believer down to the level of the sinner, better to avoid the situation. Even if the believer might be able to witness to his buddies while they are drinking after work, the possibility for misinterpretation of his presence (or even slipping into sin himself) is too great to risk. He would rather lose his friends than his soul. Simply getting along, not making waves, accepting the ways of the world, is not characteristic of those evangelicals who deserve (and claim) the label "fundamentalist."

The Emergence of Fundamentalism in North America: Retrieval of a Past

That a movement would insist on its separateness and opposition to the world around it is of course not surprising when that movement was born in conflict and eventually relegated to the margins of North American religion by those perceived to be in power. Much of what fundamentalism is today can be seen in conflicts that emerged in the latter part of the nineteenth century, largely in the urban, northeastern centers of United States and Canadian culture.

The World from Which They Came

When today's fundamentalists speak of tradition or orthodoxy or "what Christians have always believed," they are most likely referring, even if unknowingly, to ideas, images, and practices that were prevalent in the late nineteenth century. It was a period that shaped them more than they often realize. Their "traditional" family, for instance, is the middle-class family form that had emerged from nineteenth-century industrialization with its "two spheres" for men's and women's work.[22] "Traditional" music in fundamentalist churches is likely to bear a copyright from the late nineteenth century. The doctrines they emphasize as most important were the ones they had to defend against "modernism" during that period. Even the informal network of organizations they prefer over formal denominational structure was characteristic of most of nineteenth-century Protestantism.

More subtly, the way fundamentalists think about the nature of truth reflects the view of science prominent in the era before the changes to which they responded. That view of science was in fact part of what they sought to preserve, namely, a way of looking at the world undistorted by human theory and open to God's design. In 1895 A. T. Pierson, speaking at a prophecy conference, put it this way: "I like Biblical theology that . . . does not begin with an hypothesis, and then warp the facts and the philosophy to fit the crook of our dogma, but a Baconian system, which first gathers the teachings of the word of God, and then seeks to deduce some general law upon which the facts can be arranged."[23]

Fundamentalism's systematic, rational approach to finding and organizing the facts of Scripture reflects the nineteenth-century scientific world from which the movement emerged.[24] George Marsden argues that both the theology and the science of fundamentalism reflect the "Baconian" view of the world to which Pierson referred in speaking of a system constructed by gathering "facts" drawn from the Bible and scientific data to be harmonized with these biblical facts. For scientists of the early modern period, such as Francis Bacon (d. 1626), the task of science was the discovery of the Laws of Nature. They understood the world to be organized by rational principles established by an all-knowing God and "truth" as objective and available to the "commonsense" reason of the sincere seeker. In this view, human senses apprehend facts, and reason discerns the underlying order in them. The task of science, then, is to catalog, organize, and derive theories about the true facts of the universe. By the late nineteenth century, the Baconian system was still the dominant scientific orthodoxy of the day, at least among ordinary, educated folk. It was no accident that Mr. Pierson knew something about Francis Bacon.

However, marshaled against this system by the late nineteenth century were various intellectual forces, one of the most influential of which was the legacy of the eighteenth-century German philosopher Immanuel Kant. The intricacies of Kant's critiques of pure and practical reason were lost on popular scientific culture in America, but they created a thought world accessible enough to challenge the Enlightenment's wholesale confidence in human reason and commonsense induction. By placing the subject at the center of the process of perceiving and knowing the world, Kant had called the entire scientific enterprise into question. Objective truth is always filtered through subjective experience and perception, he argued, and thus scientific knowledge is always shaped by the cultural and historical context in which it emerges. We cannot know "absolute realities." The "thing-in-itself" can never be apprehended but comes to us only through the welter of our sensory experiences. The order we perceive, the forms and categories through which we understand, are not demonstrably present in the natural world itself but are instead inherent in the ability of the human mind to reason.

And just as science depends on human reason, so also does moral philosophy. Kant held that an act is morally right not because of its consequences or because it conforms to any law but because it originates in a good will. The moral agent, then, must be autonomous, acting in terms of her own will, not God's. And the measure of her actions is their universalizability. We must be able to use our reason to choose actions that are good not only for our own benefit or that of our group but as a rule for all to live by.

Kant's ideas were but one element of an intellectual revolution that began to take shape in the nineteenth century, a revolution against which fundamentalists would eventually mount a counterforce. In the world of biology, Darwin proposed his theory of evolution and natural selection in *On the Origin of Species by Means of Natural Selection* (1859). In place of an orderly catalog of existing species presumed to have been created at one time in their current forms, Darwin proposed a scheme of changing, emerging, and disappearing species. Things natural, he argued, are not as they seem to be to the Baconian commonsense observer. They have a history unseen to the naked eye. The competition among species for dominance in a territory can rarely be perceived directly. Likewise, the shifting balance among creatures and their environment is not readily apparent. Nor is the static observer likely to perceive the changes from generation to generation that produce whole new species. Darwin's theory of the relationships between simple and more complex organisms led him to propose that even *Homo sapiens* be seen as part of this natural, evolving order and thus as the product of natural selection (rather than a special creation). It was a theory that would make Darwin the fundamentalists' symbol of all that was wrong with modern science.

The world of society and politics was also transformed in the wake of the Enlightenment. New democratic governments and the new science of sociology began to challenge the assumption that traditional social forms reflected and followed the divine order of reality. As people experienced the upheaval attendant upon forging new political structures, they learned firsthand that human beings have a role in shaping their destinies. The French and American revolutions were built on premises of human freedom that challenged older notions about status, participation, and the role of the church. The Constitution of the United States of America was unprecedented in the annals of political philosophy in its claim that the full rights of citizenship inhered not in the accidents of birth but in the dignity of human nature itself.

Just how broad the human role in society might be was the concern of a generation of sociologists from Auguste Comte (d. 1857) to Emile Durkheim (d. 1917). Comte proposed that humanity had passed from a stage dominated by theology and superstition into a stage dominated by metaphysics, that is, an effort to understand the abstract forces that rule society and nature. The final stage to come, however, would be one of reason and philosophy, a stage in which philosopher-sociologists would rule in enlightened fashion. Religion in its traditional forms would soon be left completely behind. Durkheim provided less speculative, but no less unsettling, analyses of human behavior. His study of suicide, for example, illustrated the power of social forces to shape even so individual an act as that. Likewise, Durkheim argued, religious rituals are the expression of a group's solidarity: the very gods the group worships are projections of its own deeply felt sense of identity. While he acknowledged certain useful functions performed by religion, he held out no illusions about its nature. The morality we accept as divinely bequeathed is shaped by the very social worlds we have created and live in. In Durkheim's words, society is a reality sui generis, as potent in its unseen effects as the force of gravity.

Finally, even the inner world of the soul came under the scrutiny of science. Under the watchful eye of psychoanalysts, the battle in the depths of the subconscious was fought not between God and Satan but between id and superego. Even the human personality was not what it seemed to be to the commonsense observer. It was driven by unseen forces to actions, fears, and dreams with meanings far beyond their apparent import. The human personality is shaped not by a unique act of divine creation but by interactions and traumas in the young child's life. The individual is a bundle of contradictory impulses, created and re-created by human effort. Lives were to be changed on the psychiatrist's couch, not at the mourner's bench.

In every area of intellectual life, then, nineteenth-century scholars were challenging two basic premises at the heart of traditional Christian orthodoxy. First they proposed that hidden forces and ancient natural processes have created and sustain human life. These are neither the commonsense, discoverable laws of a static Nature nor the cataclysmic action of an invisible God. Second, although these processes may be hidden from the naked eye, they are not, as the theists believed, beyond human manipulation and control. The moral code emergent from these challenges to Christian anthropological assumptions was direct and unadorned: We have no one to blame for our destiny but ourselves. Neither the natural origin of, nor the human manipulation of, the social, political, psychological, or biological realms conformed to previous notions about God's creation and ordering of the world. The new scientific worldview posed, in short, a challenge that could not go forever unmet.

But no aspect of nineteenth-century intellectual life proved more challenging than the turning of a scientific eye on the Scripture itself. Around midcentury, German scholars had begun to study the Bible with the same critical tools being used to uncover the origins and meanings of other ancient texts. They analyzed its literary forms and its historical contexts and speculated about who really wrote which book and when. One of the most influential theories to emerge bore the names of German scholars Wellhausen and Graf. It asserted that the books of Moses (which contain accounts of the earliest Hebrew history) were in fact among the latest to be written in the Old Testament period, coming after the preaching of the prophets in the eighth century B.C.E. Even the history recounted in Scripture was not, according to them, what it appeared to be. These biblical scholars had great confidence that they could unravel all the apparent mysteries of Scripture. For some, angels became phosphorescence and the Transfiguration of Jesus the product of sleepy disciples and a beautiful sunset. Visions and miracles were recounted in modern terms. Biblical books were redated and stories compared to other ancient literature. Some of these interpretations have survived, while others fell quickly by the wayside. Their method of interpreting, however, became so accepted by the end of the century that "exegesis" and "criticism" became synonymous.[25]

The message of the new biblical scholars was that the Bible is neither the unique "word of God" nor the historical document it seems on the surface to be. Critical study disclosed that it is both much more and much less than it seems to the commonsense, faithful reader. It is more in that it is a record of human experience situated in particular cultural and organizational contexts. Ideas reflected in Scripture are part of a long history of ideas about the nature of the world and of human relationships with the divine. When and where they are recorded matters as much as the idea itself. Stories may have been recorded in an era very different from the one they describe, and they reflect the concerns of that later era along with the history of the earlier one. Biblical books bearing one author's name may draw from several oral traditions or have been composed by an anonymous school of disciples. Thus, Moses is no longer seen as the sole author of the Pentateuch, nor Isaiah as the single author of one seamless book. There is simply more to the Bible than meets the eye.

Yet with contextualization came the realization that the Bible was also less than it had seemed to be. If other cultures had also composed creation and flood narratives for their epics, and if time-bound authors with time-conditioned intentions had composed the Judeo-Christian epics, then perhaps the words of the Bible are to be considered as something less than an exact and fully authoritative divine revelation. Perhaps they are only perceived as such, accepted by believers but elusive of any absolute proof. Such implications of nineteenth-century biblical criticism would prove unsettling to the churchgoing Bible believer.

The cultural upheaval that occurred during this period was not, however, simply the handiwork of academicians. New attitudes and values were born of social and economic dislocations as well. The end of the agrarian base of the United States economy had been foreshadowed before the Civil War; after the war, change occurred rapidly. The industrial work force quadrupled before the end of the century. Railroads and telegraph lines made transportation and communication easier and precipitated economic expansion wherever they were built. Iron and steel were being manufactured at a record pace; new inventions—from electricity to telephones—were changing the face of the nation. It was an age of vast growth in wealth, with huge fortunes accumulating to men who would later be dubbed "robber barons."

Alongside the industrial boom, the forces of immigration and urbanization were transforming the social landscape, especially in the northeast.[26] Between 1890 and 1920, 17.6 million immigrants entered this country, over half of them from countries where Protestantism was not dominant.[27] In 1890, four out of five New Yorkers were already either foreign-born or the children of foreign-born parents. These immigrants brought new languages and customs, but also new religious traditions. There had been Catholics and Jews in the United States almost from the beginning, but they had been everywhere a minority. The ethos of the country had confirmed Protestantism as a sort of unofficial state religion. But now that was being challenged by the realities of a new religious pluralism. Those who held orthodox Protestant beliefs could no longer assume that their views were shared, even by other religious people.[28]

These challenges from science, from society, and from the new biblical studies warranted responses by the theologians and church leaders of the time. As the century wore on, some sought to redress the ills caused by unprecedented urban crowding and poverty through the Social Gospel movement. These church people wedded modern convictions about the human capacity to shape nature and society to the doctrine of postmillennialism, which held that human efforts at righteous living would inaugurate the thousand-year reign of Christ. Accordingly, they elevated fair labor practices and provision of decent health care to the spiritual status of church-going as evidence of righteousness. Walter Rauschenbusch (d. 1918), Washington Gladden (d. 1918), and Horace Bushnell (d. 1876) were the most effective champions of the Social Gospel, and they encouraged Christians to take responsibility for the betterment of this world as a direct and necessary step in ushering in the next.[29]

Another approach to the new sociocultural conditions, often adopted alongside the Social Gospel, addressed the challenges to Scripture by devising new interpretations of old doctrines. Each of the inherited Christian beliefs deemed unsupportable in the light of modern science—the miracle stories, Jesus' bodily resurrection and virgin birth, the creation narratives—were to be taken as allegory, myth, symbol, but not as literal truth. By the 1890s, many Protestant seminary faculties were dominated by such views, and some denominations (most notably Presbyterians) began to make efforts at officially revising their historic creeds. Older beliefs about the Virgin Birth or Resurrection would be reinterpreted to make them palatable to the modern mind. In this modernizing approach, science was taken to be a reliable source of truth to which Scripture would have to adapt.

Bold innovation was also a noticeable response on the American religious landscape. New movements interpreted the signs of the times and offered creative answers to the age-old questions posed by philosophy and religion. Some of them heralded a coming millennium that would bring an end to the age. Within Protestantism, such "adventist" movements flourished. William Miller was not deterred from his predilection for predictions when Jesus did not, in fact, return in 1844, and his followers rallied to become the Seventh Day Adventists. Similarly, when Charles Russell's prediction of the end did not materialize in the early years of the twentieth century, the prediction was reinterpreted, and the Jehovah's Witnesses formed to pass on the prophecy. At about the time Miller waited upon the Rapture, Mormons retreated across the western frontier to form their earthly Kingdom in the desert. By the 1890s, they were content to take their place within American society, seeking converts outside Utah and deepening America's religious pluralism and variety. Concern with the coming divine kingdom—in this world and in the next—was the driving force for these new movements. All adopted some new version of the millennium as their response to the challenges of this age.

Probably the most dramatic religious innovation of the day, however, was Pentecostalism. An emphasis on the power of the Holy Spirit had been nurtured for a quarter century in the Keswick and Holiness movements that were spread by hundreds of evangelists from their bases in England and in New Jersey. These movements were a natural outgrowth of the revivalist piety of the day, and they nurtured many future fundamentalists as well. Millions of enthusiastic participants had prayed that they might be emptied of sin and self and filled with God's Spirit. They had gathered around the country in prayer meetings and revivals, businessmen's groups and ladies' circles. But the revival on Azusa Street in Los Angeles in 1906 brought a new dimension to the Holiness experience. There the power of the Holy Spirit was manifest in new ways, especially in the practices of speaking in tongues and healing. People filled with the Spirit spoke in unknown tongues as they believed had happened on the New

Testament day of Pentecost. They also invoked divine power for the healing of physical infirmities, just as first-century Christians had. The news of the revival traveled quickly, as did the practices. Within twenty years several new denominations had been formed, groups in which such ecstatic religion was fostered.[30] Their response to their own longings for God's presence in an increasingly alien world led them into new experiences beyond the revivalist Protestantism from which they had come.

Each of these religious innovations, traced in barest outline here, can be seen as a response to the religious and social chaos of the late nineteenth century. Although many of the groups placed great emphasis on the strict interpretation of Scripture and a morally rigorous lifestyle, each also signaled a significant departure from the past, claiming some new truth as its revelation. Fundamentalists, too, would respond to that chaotic social environment, but their stated purpose would be restoration rather than innovation. They would take the materials of that nineteenth-century social and religious world and create a new synthesis of tradition that would carry them well into the next century.

A Developing Ideology for Fundamentalists

Those who would eventually claim the name "fundamentalist" were, then, also responding to the changes around them, but their response was not, overtly at least, innovative or adaptive but instead, an attempt to restore the purity of the faith. Among conservative Protestants there was a growing sense that adaptation constituted nothing less than heresy. If Jesus was not a virgin-born worker of miracles who physically rose from the dead, then how could he be other than a hoax? If the Second Coming of Jesus was not imminent, wherein lay their hope? And if the Bible could not be trusted to report the history of Israel and of the church, could it be trusted in matters of salvation? Their answer was a resounding condemnation of compromise and a clear affirmation of the orthodoxy they knew.

Their affirmation, however, was different in kind from the affirmations of the generations that had preceded them. Their times would demand that the defense they mounted be innovative in its own right. Previous generations had accepted the Bible as true and had assented to orthodox dogma in a world where most, if not all, sources of cultural authority upheld those beliefs. Never again would that be the case. Those who would affirm the historical reliability of the Bible would forever after be forced to defend their affirmation. *Fundamentalism, then, differs from traditionalism or orthodoxy or even a mere revivalist movement. It differs in that it is a movement in conscious, organized opposition to the disruption of those traditions and orthodoxies.*

Tradition, orthodoxy, and revival exist within an ongoing, stable system. Fundamentalism exists in the midst of change. Clifford Geertz describes this difference in the Islamic societies he has studied as the difference between "being held by" one's beliefs and "holding" those beliefs, between having faith and having reasons.[31] In a culture in which there is a great deal of stability and agreement on the way life should proceed, beliefs are part of the fabric of life. To be part of one's culture and to affirm those beliefs are inseparable. In such situations, one is held by beliefs about ultimate reality. But once that culture is disturbed by change or outside intrusion or mobility, beliefs lose their taken-for-granted character. They must be consciously held.

Fundamentalist beliefs about the Bible therefore reflect both continuity and discontinuity with the patterns that existed before them. While it is true that most Christians before the nineteenth century had accepted Scripture as a reliable record, it was not until the latter part of that century that a doctrine defending the inerrancy of the Bible became central to Christian belief.

The New Fundamentals: Inerrancy

The story of the emergence of the doctrine of inerrancy is a mirror on the changes that convulsed the nineteenth-century Protestant world and eventually produced fundamentalism.[32] The scholarship that laid the foundation for a fundamentalist defense of Scripture was developed during the nineteenth century at Princeton Theological Seminary. At the beginning of the century, Archibald Alexander had set out to defend orthodox Calvinism against, on the one hand, the more subjective and individualistic interpretations coming from the revivals of the Second Great Awakening and, on the other hand, the naturalistic assumptions of Deism. He addressed the former by insisting on the authoritative character of the Bible (as over against experience). He addressed the latter by asserting that everything in the Bible was in accord with scientifically verifiable truth. He assumed that science could uncover nothing that could contradict Scripture. The reader rightly led by the Spirit and the scientist rightly led by reason were bound to arrive at the same conclusions.

Alexander's student and successor at Princeton was Charles Hodge. It was he who went even further in applying Baconian science and Scottish Common Sense Realism to the study of Scripture. Scripture became a "storehouse of facts." Just as the scientist begins with facts, so does the theologian. Common Sense Realism, in turn, asserted that those facts were directly apprehended in the words of Scripture. One should not look for the ideas behind the words; truth is contained in the words themselves, words whose meanings are true and changeless, words that have the power to change lives. Hodge was able to ignore or dismiss the budding new German methods of biblical study, continuing to assume that sincere believers reading the biblical text would arrive at the same facts and the same orthodoxy.

That assumption ceased to be plausible by the time Hodge's son, Archibald Alexander Hodge, took over his father's post in theology in 1878. Working with the younger Benjamin B. Warfield, he set out to defend orthodoxy against the new challenges present in historical critical study of the Scripture. Warfield, especially, studied the critics carefully and addressed them directly. Still grounded in the Common Sense perspective, he looked to the Bible itself for proof of its authority and reliability. If the Bible claimed to be inspired, it could be trusted to be telling the truth, because it was, after all, inspired (a circular argument not likely to convince the unconvinced).

If his commonsense proof for inspiration was something less than formidable, his defense against critics was quite the opposite. To prove the Bible to be in error would require, he argued, that the critic prove that a disputed statement: (a) was in the "original autographs" (the original texts untainted by copying and transmission errors—long ago lost and thus unavailable for inspection); (b) was intended to mean what the critic says it means; and, (c) was really in conflict with a proven fact of science. Thus the orthodox interpreter had at least three lines of defense. The "scientific" facts could be wrong. The interpretation of Scripture could be wrong. Or the discrepancy could be due to errors introduced by human scribes and not present in the original.

The *original* writings of Scripture, then, took on for Hodge and Warfield an increasingly supernatural aura. Those original autographs had to be inerrant. While human interpretations and errors may have crept in between our versions and the original, human reason could bring the texts into line with "true" science. Thus, for Warfield, ironically, it was reason that must precede faith, reason that could sort out and prove the propositions of Scripture. Unlike his predecessors, Warfield could no longer assume that Scripture would prove itself. He maintained his confidence that human reason would in the end triumph, with true science and true faith ultimately pointing toward salvation and the kingdom. But it was no longer assumable that the "facts" of science and the "facts" of Scripture would be in harmony.

Warfield's successor, J. Gresham Machen, carried the rational defense of Scripture that Warfield and Hodge had formulated into the arena of the modernist-fundamentalist controversies of the 1920s. He would eventually find his old seminary too liberal and leave it to found a fundamentalist school, Westminster Theological Seminary, in Philadelphia. But the battling Machen clearly stood on the shoulders of the Princeton scholars who had preceded him. And those scholars represented the nineteenth century's move from commonsense acceptance of the Bible's inspiration to a rational defense of it. They were no longer "held by" their scriptures, but had to "hold" doctrines about them.

By the end of the nineteenth century, then, both scholars and ordinary believers were working out ways to defend the reliability of the Bible.

The New Fundamentals: Dispensational Premillennialism

As it happened, many of the same people who were seeking to defend Scripture had also been captured by the notion that Jesus might return "at any moment." They had been going to "prophecy conferences" at the same time that they had been going to Bible conferences; and many who were becoming "inerrantists" were also becoming "dispensational premillennialists."

The idea of dispensations in history had first been worked out in the earlier part of the century by John Nelson Darby, a British member of the Plymouth Brethren. Darby was evidently the first to promulgate the idea that the Rapture would take place before the tribulation, not at its end. Most previous expositors had understood the "catching up" of the church as part and parcel of the Second Coming, rather than a prelude to it. The idea of an imminent departure of the church caught on, spreading throughout both England and America. It was extensively developed over the next half century in conferences and popular writing, so that by 1909, C. I. Scofield could publish a King James Version of the Bible completely annotated with dispensational interpretations.

Another of the dispensationalist ideas that made it so popular was its prediction of the total ruin of this age and the apostasy of the church. As they saw it, things would only get worse until Christ returned. The Age of the Church was only a "great parenthesis" in history between climactic acts of God, and the corruption of the Church was a signal that God was about to intervene with some new means of salvation. As believers watched the changes in belief and morality that unfolded around them, dispensationalism offered an explanation that placed those events in cosmic context.

Not all of those who emerged as defenders of the Bible were also dispensationalists, but almost all dispensationalists were ardent defenders of literal Scripture. There was enough overlap between the leaders and concerns of the two movements to give the budding fundamentalist movement a strong premillennial flavor that has endured.[33]

As the twentieth century began, then, the stage was set for a fundamentalist movement. Old orthodoxies were in disarray, and new ideas defending them had begun to emerge. Out of the ideological ferment of the previous quarter century fundamentalists would create their identity.

A Developing Organization

No movement, of course, consists solely of ideas. Those ideas must find some material form in persons, groups, publications, political activity, and the like. And those organizations are likely to have characteristic social locations, places where they make sense, places where people and ideas can come together. The places where fundamentalist ideas made sense, and therefore the locations for most early fundamentalist organization, were the urban centers of industrialized Canada and the United States—Boston and Toronto, New York and Chicago. People living in the countryside might still enjoy uniformly Protestant traditionalism, but people in cities could have no illusions about unanimous agreement on religious basics. Urban life disrupted the sense of religious continuity and tradition present in other times and places. It was in the cities that the challenge to Protestant ideas and hegemony was most clear.

Cities not only meant pluralism of belief and lifestyle; they also meant a complex division of labor. Industry and commerce occupied their niches, with public affairs and education increasingly distinct as well. Religion, too, began to be seen as serving specific, discrete functions. Its role in education diminished, as many Protestant colleges and universities became independent of their religious parents. As the nation moved from village to city, the church moved from village green to side street. It was not that religion disappeared or was unimportant, but it was separated from public economic and political life.[34]

It was also in the cities that organizational structures were taking shape that could become the carriers of a social movement. The activities that gave birth to and sustained fundamentalism were Bible teaching and preaching and their dissemination in written form. Those activities took place in largely urban settings and gradually became distinct as an identifiable movement. In those early days, fundamentalism borrowed one organizational form, revivals, and created another, Bible and prophecy conferences. It was in those activities that leaders emerged and constituencies developed. Here ideas met the test of audience response, and ideologues worked out their compromises. As changing cities pushed people toward changing ideas, organizational structures emerged to shore up the faithful and rescue the perishing.

Early Organization: Urban Revivalism

Revivals had of course been an accepted part of the American religious scene for one hundred and fifty years.[35] The first and second Great Awakenings had created and sustained this form of emotional religious gathering, whose aim was to make people experience visible signs of God's power. Sometimes the preacher was as learned as he was passionate; sometimes he was unlettered and sensationalist. Sometimes, as in the First Awakening, revivals took place in the small towns of New England and the mid-Atlantic. Later, in the Second Awakening, gatherings moved south and west onto the frontier. But always the emphasis was on individual decisions to accept God's offer of salvation, with refusal painted as having the direst of eternal consequences. Sinners could look forward to judgment "in the hands of an angry God" (to use Jonathan Edwards's phrase). The results of such preaching were visible changes, whether in transformed lives of individual converts or in renewed zeal among Christians. Whole communities were sometimes transformed. By the middle of the nineteenth century, the "awakening" had been institutionalized in the form of the "revival" and had moved largely to cities as its base. Even on the frontier, the "camp meeting" had become a regularly scheduled annual event rather than an unpredictable moving of divine spirit.[36]

Among the most prominent practitioners of the emerging urban revivalism was Charles G. Finney.[37] Not only was he a remarkable revivalist himself, he became a systematizer of the methods he practiced. He was the first to articulate the goal of revivalism as "winning souls" and the first to set out a step-by-step method for achieving that goal and calculating its success. He urged his followers to use "any means" necessary to produce the powerful excitements that would result in revival. He matched means and results like a scientific experimenter. He also urged preachers to avoid complicated theological arguments in favor of words directly from the Bible, expressed in plain talk understandable by ordinary folk. Both the results (individual decisions about salvation) and the message (plain truths from the Bible) were therefore democratized and taken outside the realm of institutional religion.

Finney was followed by Dwight Moody and Billy Sunday, each of whom further developed the organizational system of revivalism in the direction of business-like structures. Throughout the period, these preachers were touring the cities of America, offering a message of salvation from despair and hell. Revival preachers spoke to the worries of the day—unbridled business, the abuse of alcohol, unassimilated (Catholic) immigrants—and offered a ritual of purification that was both individual and communal. As drunkards, Catholics, and greedy businessmen repented of their ways, the community was reassured that their Protestant God was still in charge.[38] The community of common sentiment and rhetoric they created was the womb from which a fundamentalist movement would emerge.

What the urban revivalists accomplished, then, was significant both for its religious consequences and for the organizational structures to which it gave birth. Here were gatherings in which people of nearly every Protestant denomination participated. No one congregation or denomination sponsored them; rather, sponsorship required cooperation. Therefore evangelism and Christian practice became more important than denominational tradition and dogma. If the participants could agree on the need for personal salvation, they would leave the details of doctrine for other times and places. At midcentury, such a lack of concern for the specifics of doctrine still seemed possible, since most of American Protestantism could agree that personal salvation and piety were paramount.[39] Revivals, then, provided a meeting place that transcended denominational lines, bringing together potential allies in a fight that they did not yet know they would face.

Revivals also required the active participation and support of laity. Ordinary Christians gathered for weeks in advance to pray and study. They recruited potential converts and taught those converts about being Christian. They embraced a religiosity that called them to personal holiness and evangelistic fervor. Many became part of the Keswick and holiness movements, where they learned to seek a "second blessing" that would transform them from mere "carnal Christians" to spiritual ones. Christianity in this tradition was not to be the specialized province of the learned clergy but the lifeblood of the ordinary person in business and home and school.[40]

Revivals were also a natural activity for those concerned about prophecy and the End Times. Millenarians who eagerly awaited the Second Coming of Christ were also anxious to save as many souls as possible before that time came. When new coalitions were later built, evangelists and premillennialists would be among the contributors.[41] Nineteenth-century revivals provided them with an early common ground.

It is no accident that during the nineteenth century, revivals moved increasingly toward an urban setting. The kind of systematic, large-scale efforts they became was part and parcel of the urban, industrialized, world. It took a city to provide the base of support necessary for such efforts. It also took a city to provide the moral grist for the evangelist's mill. It was in cities that the ills of the day were most visible and that individuals seemed most in need of salvation, most disconnected from any source of grace. And it was in cities that Christians could organize to encounter those needs. Revivals, then, had created a climate of evangelism and piety that permeated all of nineteenth-century Protestantism. They had also democratized religious practice and provided a meeting ground outside established religious structures for people not otherwise linked. Until well after the Civil War, revivals were much too widespread in practice to be characterized as unique to any movement or branch of religion. They were simply part of the religious life of the day. But their location in cities placed them strategically close to the upheavals out of which fundamentalism would arise, and their transdenominational structure laid the groundwork for alliances out of which a movement would emerge.

Early Organization: Bible and Prophecy Conferences

Bible conferences and prophecy conferences, unlike revivals, were more nearly unique to the branch of Protestantism out of which fundamentalism would grow. They have precursors in the camp meetings and holiness groups and even in the Bible lecture series some prominent churches hosted. But by the last quarter of the century, conservatives were developing their own organizational form. These were gatherings of people with specific concerns that took them beyond evangelism or personal piety. They wanted to explore the teachings of the Bible and discover its truth for themselves. These were occasions of the "head" as much as of the "heart."

The most famous of the Bible conferences, initially dubbed the Believers' Meeting for Bible Study, began in 1875. Eight years later it moved to a new location at Niagara-on-the-Lake, Ontario, and adopted its more commonly known name, the Niagara Bible Conference.[42] It was a series of one- or two-week summer retreats featuring some of the leading Bible teachers and preachers of the day. Here gathered J. H. Brookes, William Eerdman, C. I. Scofield, A. T. Pierson, and A. J. Frost, Presbyterians and Baptists all. They and their listeners came together to worship and fellowship and study, enjoying the beauty of the setting. There were as many as five addresses each day, sometimes including a Bible reading. This practice consisted of consecutive readings of passages selected to illustrate a point or doctrine. Except for a brief introduction or conclusion delivered by the teacher, the attempt was to let the "facts" of Scripture speak for themselves.

Leaders found in Bible conferences an opportunity to develop among themselves a coherent program of biblical emphases. By 1890, for instance, they were ready to adopt Brookes's statement of Fourteen Points of essential Christian doctrine.[43] As the challenges of modernism began to be clear, Bible conferences were places to share ideas and encouragement. Those who attended found messages and spokesmen that gave expression to their yearnings. The 1875 conference was soon followed by similar conferences throughout the country, most notably Dwight L. Moody's summer retreat at Northfield, Massachusetts, begun in 1880. Closely related to these, however, were other gatherings called specifically to study the prophetic portions of the Bible. Many of the leaders in Niagara were also instrumental in calling the first International Prophecy Conference in 1878. It was held at the Holy Trinity Episcopal Church in New York City and was followed by further conferences in 1886 (Chicago), 1895 (Allegheny, Pennsylvania), 1901 (Boston), 1914 (Chicago), and twice in 1918 (in

Philadelphia and New York). These were meetings for those seriously interested in the details of eschatology. Speakers sometimes adopted the style of a scholar presenting a research paper, although many simply preached. They looked at the sorry state of the world around them and likened it to words they found in Scripture. They counted days and months from one historic event to another and argued over dates and interpretations about what would come to pass before and after Christ's return.[44]

In these early days premillennialists who gathered for prophecy conferences were part of the growing coalition of conservative Protestants ready to oppose liberal innovations in their churches. These meetings, along with Bible conferences and revivals, gave them a growing sense of identity, a core of leadership, and readily accessible ideas for interpreting the dilemmas they faced.

Early Organization: Bible Institutes

The first Bible Institute grew directly out of efforts to train laity, not clergy. In the 1870s, the Chautauqua movement had begun as a summer effort to train Sunday school workers, but the idea was soon expanded into year-round courses aimed at wider audiences. In 1886 Dwight L. Moody gave his support to a Bible training school in Chicago, run by Miss Emma Dryer. It would become the Moody Bible Institute and later provide pastoral, as well as lay, leadership for the fundamentalist movement. In its early years, however, it was primarily aimed at training ordinary Christians to be effective evangelists in the cities where they lived. By the turn of the century a dozen such schools were in existence.[45]

In 1908 a Bible Institute was formed in Los Angeles, with the financial backing of oil millionaires Lyman and Milton Stewart. This institute quickly became a leading center of premillennial thought and published *The King's Business*, a leading dispensationalist journal of the day.[46] These two organizations were prototypes of the training institutions fundamentalism would need. As more seminaries came under the dominance of historical-critical methods, conservatives needed places they could trust for pastoral training. Bible institutes and Bible colleges filled that need. They emphasized practical evangelistic skills and techniques for uncovering the facts of Scripture. By founding institutions for the training of clergy, people concerned about the Bible were taking another step in the direction of a separate identity.

Early Organization: The Printed Word

These Bible believers who emphasized the importance of the Word of God were also enthusiastic producers of their own words. This, too, helped to give shape to their movement. If they were not physically gathered in one place listening to the words of their leaders, they could nevertheless share the inspiration of those moments in newspapers and pamphlets and books.[47] Millenarians could turn to J. H. Brookes's magazine *Truth,* or (after 1894), to the journal *Our Hope,* edited by Arno Gaebelein. And in 1886 William E. Blackstone's book *Jesus Is Coming* began its long reign as one of the most popular of prophetic books.

As efforts to communicate among scattered believers grew, the Bible League of North America added a new voice. Formed in 1903, this organization immediately began producing *The Bible Student and Teacher.* In the beginning its leaders and contributors were largely conservative Presbyterians. But as the apparent threat of modernism grew, so did its coalition of supporters. Ten years after its founding, reflecting the increased militancy of the day, the name was changed to *Bible Champion*.

During that same period, two of the most influential publications in fundamentalism first appeared. In 1909 Oxford University Press published the *Scofield Reference Bible*. From the ideas that had developed over two generations of conferences and writing, C. I. Scofield created an annotated Bible that would become the standard reference point for fundamentalists for most of the century. Where there had been competing notions about the details of Christ's return, now a consensus began to emerge as increasing numbers of people accepted Scofield's interpretations along with the literal Scripture they revered.

One year later the first of twelve paperback volumes appeared, a series entitled *The Fundamentals*.[48] It was a project conceived and financed by the same Stewart brothers who had helped found the Bible Institute of Los Angeles. The aim was to produce intellectually sound, popularly accessible defenses of the Christian faith. The preface to the fifth volume noted that these testimonies were being presented so "that the unbelief, which in pulpit and pew has been paralyzing the Church of Christ, may be overcome, and that a world-wide revival may be the result." The volumes would be distributed broadly to pastors, seminary professors, YMCA workers—three million of them in all.

The ninety essays they contained ranged from defense of Scripture to doctrinal apologetics to personal testimonies. Although articles on the Bible were clearly central, the overall tone was surprisingly uncontroversial and the quality of the writers quite high. Many had earned doctoral degrees and distinguished teaching posts. They could tackle an inflammatory topic like socialism with even-handedness and conclude that the "church leaves its members free to adopt or reject Socialism as they may deem wise."[49] Even though a number of prominent dispensationalists were among the authors, for instance, little of that doctrine was actually contained in the volumes. The series seemed to be important not so much because it broke new ground, as because it pulled together ideas that characterized conservative Christians at the historical moment when they recognized that they would have to fight to preserve their faith. And of course it suggested what those conservatives might call themselves.

Fundamentalism as a Social Movement, 1915–25

By 1915 the stage was set for fundamentalism to emerge with its own distinct identity. The upheavals of the late nineteenth century had produced a ready audience of followers. Those followers were involved in urban revivals, Keswick holiness groups, the study of premillennial prophecies, and zeal for missions. In all of those activities they had a core of leaders whose ideas would soon be brought together into a fundamentalist movement. They had already worked out the elaborate but accessible defense of the faith that would serve them in the years ahead. In addition those leaders were operating within an increasingly broad but distinct organizational network of schools, conferences, and publications. What might have happened in the face of increasing challenges to traditional faith was a gradual withdrawal from mainline denominations and from secular United States culture. What did happen was a spectacular period of conflict between fundamentalists and those institutions.

New Ideological Concerns

World War I triggered, among other things, intense interest in prophecy. Three International Prophecy Conferences were held between 1914 and 1918. Speakers examined the apocalyptic character of the times in light of the premillennialist teachings developed over the previous decades. Germany, the birthplace of biblical critical methods, seemed a natural target for a cataclysmic war against evil. At war's end the League of Nations evoked fears of the worldwide government dispensationalists had come to expect as part of the Tribulation. And the growth of communism raised the specter of a world without God, again hinting of a Tribulation to come.

Perhaps neither the League of Nations nor communism would have seemed so threatening had they come exclusively from overseas. But the League of Nations was being promoted by the United States's own president, and in the Red Scare of 1919 communists were seen around every corner.[50] It seemed to many to be a time to shore up the lines of defense. Conservatives sought bastions of true belief, and they found few indeed. Even their own denominations seemed to have stepped onto a precarious slippery slope leading directly from doubts about the Bible to godless communism. In the postwar years, liberal Protestants were enthusiastically embracing international ecumenism, hardly a trend to please those concerned about national and doctrinal distinctives. To protect Christian civilization was essential, and there was apparently no one to do it.

The chaos and tensions of the times drew believers outward, while the strength of the organizational structures they had built pushed them along. In this particular time, their message matched the needs of the culture. Those who rallied to the cause, calling themselves fundamentalists, sought to restore the true and sure belief that would keep the nation strong.

Organizing for Battle

In 1919, instead of holding another prophecy conference, conservatives, led by Reuben A. Torrey, issued a call for a World Conference on Christian Fundamentals, with an eye toward forming a permanent organization that would contend for the faith.

Over six thousand people gathered in Philadelphia that year, and from their meeting came the World's Christian Fundamentals Association (WCFA). This umbrella organization was never very successful; in the coming years believers were too busy to build a new organization. They were busy fighting battles on two fronts—education and religion itself. The WCFA journal, *Christian Fundamentals in School and Church*, edited by William Bell Riley, offered support for the effort.

Modernism in the Denominations

The most dramatic battles in the churches occurred in the Northern Baptist and northern Presbyterian denominations.[51] These two denominations had supplied the bulk of the leaders and participants in the Bible conference and prophecy movements of the previous decades. These were also the denominations for which the future was contestable. Other groups, such as the Congregationalists, were so thoroughly dominated by modernists that no battle was possible. Still others (like the southern Presbyterians and Southern Baptists) were so thoroughly conservative as to make prolonged controversy unlikely.[52]

Trouble in Northern Baptist circles had been brewing at least since 1913. In that year, a liberal professor at the University of Chicago Divinity School was forced out of the local ministerial association. Conservatives were so dismayed by trends at the university that they organized the Northern Baptist Theological Seminary as a more orthodox alternative. But 1919 proved to be a year that precipitated much more widespread conservative reaction. In that year, Harry Emerson Fosdick, the noted liberal Baptist and associate pastor of the First Presbyterian Church in New York, was the Northern Baptist convention speaker. To make matters worse, a new journal was launched under liberal control. And worse yet, the convention voted to participate in the Interchurch World Movement, an ecumenical fund-raising effort. The conservatives were outraged.

In the years between 1920 and 1925, organized coalitions of fundamentalists repeatedly assaulted the structures of the Northern Baptist Convention. They held preconvention rallies and sought to devise a conservative creed that would become a test of faith. They documented heretical teaching in the denomination's schools and pushed for (and got) a committee to investigate these charges. To protect the orthodoxy of their missionaries, fundamentalists offered a very large gift from a friendly donor, a gift conditional upon the missionaries' assured conservatism.

The militancy of fundamentalist Baptists met with one difficulty, however. The structure of the denomination left little room for enforcing orthodoxy. Since it was a convention based on voluntary cooperation among local congregations, there was no doctrinal court of appeals. This structural impediment, combined with appeals for toleration from some considered quite conservative themselves, slowed the fundamentalists considerably. The militants, led by Riley of Minneapolis, Shields of Toronto, and Straton of New York, countered by organizing the Baptist Bible Union, but they suffered a major setback in 1922. Riley's proposal that the New Hampshire Confession be adopted as a creed was defeated by a two-to-one margin in favor of a proposal making the New Testament the only ground of faith and practice. By 1926, militant

Baptist fundamentalists knew that the battle was lost, and they turned their attacks toward the moderate leaders who had crafted the compromises and argued for tolerance.

Among Presbyterians, of course, church structure is different. The adoption and enforcement of creeds is possible. And when Fosdick launched a frontal assault on Baptist conservatives with his 1922 sermon "Shall the Fundamentalists Win?" Presbyterian conservatives responded with "Shall Unbelief Win?" In 1923, at the insistence of fundamentalists, the General Assembly of the Presbyterian Church instructed its New York presbytery to bring its ministers (meaning Fosdick) into line. This proved a brief victory, however. The Judicial Commission ruled that since Fosdick was a Baptist, they had no way to judge him. Fosdick, not surprisingly, refused their offer to transfer his membership into the Presbyterian fold.

Throughout these years of controversy, fundamentalist Presbyterians were repeatedly thwarted by compromises. After apparently winning one battle, they would lose another. They won reaffirmation of the 1910 and 1916 statements of the fundamentals of the faith, a five-point declaration which included inerrancy. But a commission appointed to study the spiritual state of the church reported back in 1926 and 1927 that there ought to be enough room in the Presbyterian church for liberals and conservatives alike.

This position was vigorously opposed by no less a mind than Princeton's J. Gresham Machen. He argued that modernist compromises had so changed the basic Christian faith that it was no longer recognizable as the same religion held by orthodox believers through the previous nineteen centuries. He urged those who truly held modernist beliefs simply to declare that they were no longer Christian and withdraw from the churches. His argument was persuasive enough that popular publications such as *The New Republic* agreed with him. It was not that the publishers favored conservatism, only that they saw the modernists as having departed in significant ways from the beliefs formerly called Christian.

Neither Machen nor the editors of *The New Republic,* however, were in power in mainline Protestant denominations. Liberals had, by the middle of the decade, assured themselves that they could beat back the attacks of fundamentalists. Minor battles in the Methodist, Episcopal, and Disciples of Christ denominations had all resulted in liberal victories. Combined with victories among Northern Baptists and northern Presbyterians, liberal leaders felt firmly in control. Fundamentalists, meanwhile, were left to assess the damage and chart a course for their future.

Evolution in the Schools

At the same time that fundamentalists were battling modernism in their churches, they had joined forces with others to battle Darwinism in society. Ever since evolutionary ideas came to prominence in the previous century, they had been fought by conservatives who saw each biological species (especially humanity) as a unique creation of God, accomplished in a historical period recent enough to be recounted in the pages of Scripture. World War I, however, gave a new urgency to the ideological battle. Marsden argues that fundamentalists saw in the war the ultimate manifestation of a "survival of the fittest" mentality.[53] If one believes that the strong are destined to displace the weak, then war on one's neighbors is only natural. The war became, then, a struggle between Christian civilization and German barbarism. The presumed German acceptance of evolution (and the role of German scholars in producing the historical-critical method of interpreting Scripture) was linked in conservative minds with German aggression. Just as America was called on to defend Christian civilization against that aggression, so Christians were called to attack the ideas at the root of Germany's sin—evolution.

Fundamentalist concern about evolution might have remained a matter confined to religious circles had not William Jennings Bryan chosen in 1920 to take up the cause. For the next several years, anti-evolutionism became a national fad. It drew together denominational conservatives and dispensational premillennialists, northerners and southerners, farmers and city dwellers. Fundamentalists organized rallies, and Bryan spoke. People throughout the country became convinced that the future of civilization depended on banishing this atheistic and harmful dogma from the schools. And premillennialists who had thought political action useless in the face of an imminent Rapture found themselves obsessed with seeking social change.

In twenty states as diverse as New York and Georgia, activists introduced bills in their legislatures seeking to prohibit the teaching of evolution.[54] In the Northeast those efforts never got very far. In many of the southern states there were real fights, but in most cases newspapers and universities were able to rally support among the educated public for freedom of thought. In two border states, Kentucky and Texas, the fights were especially bitter; and in Kentucky it took religious intervention to work out a compromise.[55] Yet in neither state did a law against evolution succeed. But in Oklahoma, then Florida, followed by Tennessee, Mississippi, Louisiana, and Arkansas, the outcome was the reverse. In these states anti-evolution forces got laws on the books with relatively little effort. For many in those regions, teaching evolution was simply inconceivable. Outlawing it was not difficult to do.

Nor would enforcement have been much of a problem in Tennessee had it not been for the intervention of outside forces. Whether John Scopes tested the law on his own or was induced to do so is not nearly as important as what happened after he was charged with the crime of teaching evolution in the public schools of Tennessee. The American Civil Liberties Union sent in a team of lawyers headed by Clarence Darrow to defend him, and the anti-evolutionists dispatched William Jennings Bryan. The result was a highly publicized clash between new and old, between science and religion, between city and country. Scopes was convicted as charged, but "in the trial by public opinion and the press, it was clear that the twentieth century, the cities, and the universities had won a resounding victory, and that the country, the South, and the fundamentalists were guilty as charged."[56]

In the days following the debacle in Dayton, Tennessee, anti-evolutionists organized furiously,[57] but their efforts were increasingly radical and marginal to the larger culture. Leaders began to fight among themselves. J. Frank Norris and Thomas T. Shields were tarnished by scandal. The racism of others was all too apparent. The

Bryan Bible League, the Supreme Kingdom, and the Bible Crusaders were all formed —and largely fizzled—in those years, unable to rally the nation against evolution or modernism. As Baptist and Presbyterian fundamentalists lost battles inside their denominations, they began to organize schismatic groups. After 1925 fundamentalism lost its credibility and with it the ability to rally national, or even denominational, support for attacks against the enemies of Christian civilization.

In the battles of the 1920s, people in the United States sought for themselves cultural symbols that would make sense of the world as they now knew it. The cultural upheavals of the previous fifty years had climaxed in the Great War. And the anxieties of the war had lingered in the crises of the years immediately following it. With its millenarian and anti-evolutionist allies, fundamentalism offered a vision of civilization restored. For a few years, early in the decade, many Protestants found that vision appealing. But after 1925 it became clear that whatever image America chose for its new self, it would not be the fundamentalist version of a restored Christian civilization built on an inerrant scripture.

Fundamentalism Transformed and Organized, 1925–75

What may have appeared as the demise of a movement may better be seen as its transformation. After 1925 the culture ceased taking fundamentalists seriously as social and religious reformers. The crusade against evolution had been discredited in Dayton. Over the next few years, both Northern Baptists and Presbyterians would repulse fundamentalist attempts to impose doctrinal restrictions. People who remained concerned about the health of their civilization would no longer gain a wide public hearing and would have to adopt other means. And having lost their fight to control the denominations, they would have to find other organizational bases from which to express their concerns. But fundamentalists had already built organizational structures that served to smooth the way into a new era of diminished visibility and diminished social activism.

An Ideology for Outsiders

The story of the decades following 1925 is, then, a story of reorganization; but it is also a story of transformation. Until 1925 fundamentalists had thought of themselves as the restorers of Christian civilization and of orthodox religion. They had always assumed that the territory they desired to possess was rightfully theirs and only temporarily occupied by strangers. They were the true keepers of the heritage. However, after 1925 it became painfully apparent that neither mainstream religion nor the larger culture was willing to acknowledge their ownership. They had become outsiders.

Now that they were outsiders, their view of mainstream culture and religion changed. As insiders, they had been concerned with modernism as a perversion of the true faith to be purged from religious life. Now they proclaimed that the denominations were hopelessly apostate, no better (and perhaps worse) than the secular world. As insiders to the culture they had fought evolution as a dangerous idea to be purged from the schools. Now they saw the entire culture dominated by non-Christian influences. They became convinced that all of society had come under the sway of ideas that excluded God, ideas they saw as forming a pattern and an ideology that they eventually termed "secular humanism."[58]

The designation of external forces as secular humanism began in the earliest days of the movement. When fundamentalists argued against Germany during World War I, they were likely to cite German philosophies that elevated human reason above divine law. Evolution, as well, was deemed dangerous because it substituted human wisdom and progress for divine action. Not until after World War II, however, did fundamentalist writers gather all the scientific, political, and philosophical influences together under one umbrella. In his 1946 book, *Remaking the Modern Mind,* Carl Henry wrote of the "secular philosophy of humanism" with its tenets of progress and human goodness.[59] He, and later others, would argue that Christians should be socially and politically active in an effort to re-establish Christian claims in a civilization now dominated by secular humanism.

In the face of that fact, the primary strategy adopted by fundamentalists during these years was the effort to save individual souls: the "call to evangelism" was the overarching theme of the period after 1925. If the culture and the denominations cannot be rescued, the reasoning went, then individuals must be the focus of mass evangelism and personal witnessing. Fundamentalism may have lost its public relations battles and waned as a social and political movement, but it remained lively as a force in the lives of a vast segment of the country's population. Even if orthodoxy was not welcome in the seats of cultural power, the gospel message of individual transformation and piety was quite welcome in the everyday lives of people in many areas of the United States.

For those who remained true believers, fundamentalism offered a comprehensive and satisfying explanation for the complexities of life. If the condition of society seemed to be deteriorating, then the Rapture must be near. If there were choices to be made, then the Bible surely had the answers. Where others might be preoccupied with change and adaptation, believers could rest assured in unchanging truth. While no one could know with certainty what the future might hold, believers were proud to sing that they "know Who holds the future." Individual lives in disarray were put right by the clear rules and discipline of a fundamentalist lifestyle. While a changing, ambiguous world tossed lives and expectations about like flotsam, fundamentalists claimed an anchor in the storm. Just as their grandparents had sought scientific facts in Scripture, so these new generations sought principles to live by. Just as they continued to be sure that true science and true belief could not be in contradiction, so they also held fast to the assurance that right living demanded obedience to the rules of Scripture and to the earthly authorities Scripture commended to the believer.[60] People who chose fundamentalism chose a life of certainty in the midst of an uncertain world.

Organizations for Outsiders

Maintaining such a strict way of life and traditional way of believing demanded a great deal of people who were now outsiders to the larger culture. The movement remained alive, indeed thriving, in part because its institutional structure was so strong. The work of the last generation had paid off in laying a foundation for this new phase in fundamentalism's history. Building on that foundation, both new and expanded structures emerged. It was a time of active reorganization.

New Denominations and Independent Churches

By the 1930s it was apparent that the major northern denominations were dominated by modernism, and there was little to be done to stem the tide. Fundamentalists began to face the painful, sometimes bitter, choice of separation.[61] What emerged over that decade were three basic patterns of affiliation. Some churches remained within the now-liberal denominations as a continued witness to the conservative heritage. Those churches, however, increasingly existed at the margins of their own denominations, often participating equally in the emerging network of more independent, fundamentalist organizations. Other groups of churches broke away to found new, conservative denominations. Still others chose the path of complete congregational independence.

Existing in a kind of parallel relation to these three northern paths were the large southern denominations in which conservatism still held sway. The southern churches had joined the rest of the movement in the fight against evolution, but they had been little affected internally by either that fight or the other doctrinal disputes of the twenties. The Southern Baptists and southern Presbyterians had also been little affected by the teachings of dispensationalism. To these inhabitants of a rural, Protestant world, neither their church nor their culture seemed much in need of rescue. Neither dispensationalism's gloomy forecasts of religious decay nor fundamentalism's aggressive defense of Scripture seemed appropriate. Nor did it seem necessary to organize institutions that would replace or supplement existing denominations. Southern churches shared a traditional, orthodox conservatism with their northern fundamentalist friends, but there was as yet little overlap in their organized activities. The primary connection between southern conservatives and northern fundamentalists was in the person of J. Frank Norris, sometimes known as "the Texas Tornado" for his rhetorical style and incendiary personality. He pastored the First Baptist Church of Fort Worth from 1909 until his death in 1952 and during most of that time acted as a gadfly in his own Southern Baptist Convention. He never gathered much of a following in that denomination, but he did what he could to work with Northern Baptist leaders in fostering aggressive fundamentalist cooperation. He supported the Baptist Bible Union in 1923, and began his own "seminary" (actually a Bible institute) in 1939. In 1950 disgruntled Norris followers formed the Baptist Bible Fellowship—perhaps the most influential of the new denominations and quasi-denominations emerging out of the period.[62]

The new denominations formed by groups of fundamentalist churches were largely Baptist and Presbyterian. Earlier Northern Baptist discontent had led to some defection to the Southern Baptist convention. As the early controversies over liberalism brewed, individual churches in southern Illinois and in Arizona requested affiliation with the more conservative southern body, while state conventions in Oklahoma and Missouri that had been dually aligned with the two denominations dropped their northern connections.[63]

Some of those who stayed with the Northern Baptists to lead the 1920s battles eventually withdrew to form the General Association of Regular Baptists in 1932.[64] This group was the successor to the Baptist Bible Union but was almost exclusively northern in membership. These were the most separatist of the Northern Baptists, being unwilling to associate themselves any longer with the "apostasy" they had seen grow during the 1920s. A decade later, a larger group was ready to leave the denomination, becoming, after 1947, the Conservative Baptist Association.

Among Presbyterians, the schisms were led by Machen and his student Carl McIntire. In 1933, after already having formed Westminster Seminary and having proposed a separate mission board, Machen inspired the beginnings of the Orthodox Presbyterian Church. But in the next several years, several additional schisms followed. Indeed, in 1937 even McIntire left to form the Bible Presbyterian Church.

Those who chose more complete congregational independence often argued that the only biblical form of church organization is the local body. Any organization beyond or above that level violates Scripture. Some of the churches banded together for fellowship and some cooperative ventures in the Independent Fundamental Churches of America, formed in 1930, or the Baptist Bible Fellowship. The IFCA had its strength in the upper Midwest, while the BBF began to make inroads in the South. Many of the IFCA's members were not Baptist in background, so it offered a meeting ground with the broad interdenominational flavor of the earlier Bible and prophecy conferences. Another successor to those meetings was McIntire's American Council of Christian Churches (ACCC), formed in 1941 in direct response to the Federal Council of Churches (an ecumenical, mainline organization) and the National Association of Evangelicals (a moderate evangelical organization). It too drew together a number of the new fellowships and denominations.

Local fundamentalist churches ranged, during this period, from tiny groups on the outskirts of cities to huge metropolitan edifices. They offered to their members an ideological home. When the rest of the world seemed to be living by the wrong rules, believing the wrong things, church was the place where everything made sense. It offered them a way to understand the Bible and rules by which to live their lives. It also offered friendships and potential marriage partners, even support for hard times and help in finding jobs. There might be activities on nearly every night of the week—some evangelistic, some educational, and some just plain social. To become a fundamentalist was to join a group—a local, visible, supportive community. Living in a hostile world required nothing less.[65]

The radically local sentiments of these churches revealed at least some kinship to the "Landmark" movement in nineteenth-century Southern Baptist life (which survives in organized form in the American Baptist Association). That movement argued, among other things, that only members of a given local church could partake of the Lord's Supper in that church, and only adult baptism by immersion in a Baptist church would count for church membership. They also argued against national missions organizations, preferring that local churches conduct their own local evangelizing.

On the issue of missions, however, the new fundamentalist independent churches differed from their Landmark cousins. These churches were eager to do mission work beyond their own locale and quite willing to organize to make that possible. The form of organization they chose, however, was designed to protect their local autonomy and help them ensure that no heretical missionaries would receive their support. The organizations through which they chose to do mission work were agencies that were as independent as the churches they served, but they provided the kind of extended network of support needed by such independent local churches.

Independent "Denominational" Agencies

Churches that shunned mainline denominations were not left without organizational support. For nearly a century, people concerned about evangelism and Scripture and prophecy had been coming together in the revivals and conferences that had fed the activist movements of the twenties. In the 1930s, they simply took those forms one step further, expanding them and creating a loose network of church support and extension that replaced denominational affiliation.

Among the earliest American and British efforts at overseas mission work, in fact, were organizations based in transdenominational evangelical coalitions. Just as nineteenth-century revivals were supported by groups beyond denominational lines, so mission work brought together sometimes disparate groups who shared an evangelistic zeal. Perhaps the most famous extradenominational mission agency, having survived since 1865, is the China Inland Mission. As the century wore on, however, independent agencies became less the rule and more the exception as much mission work came under denominational auspices. In the early twentieth century, American Protestantism, basking in the glow of its Reform era, postmillennial hopes, was eager to evangelize the world.

By the 1930s, however, the mainline denominations were struggling to keep a missionary force in the field. Liberalism did not lend itself to enthusiastic proselytizing, and money was getting tight besides. In 1933 conservative Presbyterians (led by Machen) were so disgusted by their denomination's mission effort that they organized their own rival board.[66] That move only hastened the brewing schism in the denomination. And when fundamentalists left that and other denominations, they often took their missionary zeal with them. They invested that zeal in dozens of independent mission agencies that did work throughout the world. At the very time that denominations were struggling, fundamentalist mission efforts were growing by leaps and bounds.[67]

At the local level, evangelism and missions often took the form of the evangelistic crusade led by an independent traveling evangelist. Carrying on the traditions of Billy Sunday and his predecessors, preachers such as Bob Jones, Sr., and John R. Rice pulled together the conservatives in a community for an all-out effort at soul winning.

They would later shun the similar but more ecumenical efforts of Billy Graham, preferring to keep their evangelism unsullied by liberal associations.[68]

Special efforts were also directed at youth, especially college students. During this period, Youth For Christ (which gave Graham his start) and Inter-Varsity Christian Fellowship were thriving fundamentalist ministries. In 1951, Bill Bright started his Campus Crusade for Christ, and within ten years they were located on forty campuses in fifteen states. With their simplified Four Spiritual Laws version of the gospel, Campus Crusade workers sought out student leaders as well as student derelicts. They urged youth to follow God's "wonderful plan for your life," offering them fellowship and purpose in exchange for the experimentation and loneliness often characteristic of young adulthood.[69] Smaller groups like Word of Life and Young Life targeted younger teens with camps and special programs. These "parachurch" youth organizations were joined in the late 1940s by efforts to begin Christian day schools as well.[70]

Another of the institutions in this growing network of independent agencies were the summer Bible conferences. An outgrowth of the Bible and prophecy conferences of the previous generation, these gatherings were half vacation, half revival. By 1941 there were at least fifty different sites in operation, spread from Winona Lake, Indiana, to Redfeather Lakes, Colorado, to the Atlantic City Boardwalk.

Proliferation of Bible Colleges and Institutes

If it had not already become clear that mainstream educational institutions would not serve the needs of conservatives, the defeats of the 1920s made it clear. Many Protestant colleges and universities had now been under secular control for a generation or more. Denominational seminaries were now heavily influenced by historical-critical study of Scripture and liberal theology. The struggle at the Princeton Seminary between Machen and his colleagues was a kind of last stand on the education front. When Machen lost at Princeton and left to found Westminster in 1929, the last major conservative stronghold seemed undone. By the 1940s, there would be virtually no evangelical/fundamentalist presence in major American educational institutions.[71] On the one hand, fundamentalists had shunned scholarship as unimportant in the quest for souls. On the other hand, a liberal cultural establishment had shunned fundamentalists as obscurantist and obnoxious. The gulf between the two camps was growing.

Fundamentalists, however, had already begun establishing educational institutions of their own. The Moody Bible Institute in Chicago and the Bible Institute of Los Angeles were already in place and thriving. A few of the evangelical colleges of the nineteenth century, most notably Wheaton College (also in Illinois), retained their conservative orientation. Wheaton was a school with broad interdenominational ties, and its leaders had moved during the nineteenth century from centrist evangelicalism to aggressive fundamentalism.[72] During the 1930s Wheaton was a mecca for bright young scholars who would shape the next generation.[73] Much further south, the Dallas Theological Seminary became the center for dispensationalist thought. But after the 1920s the need for new institutions grew. All over the country Bible colleges and institutes sprang up. In 1930 there were at least fifty institutes considered to be "true to the faith."[74]

Within the next generation, many of the institutes became four-year colleges, some accredited, some not. The Bible colleges were usually designed to give their students a broad base of learning—from the sciences to history and mathematics—carefully kept within the guidelines of an inerrant Scripture. The subjects of the liberal arts and sciences were taught, but with a particular conservative flavor. While these schools were less numerous than Bible institutes, their total enrollment doubled during the financially troubled decade of the 1930s.[75] Those that remained Bible institutes were more narrowly defined organizations designed to teach specifically religious skills and interpretations. Evangelism techniques, Bible-teaching skills, and explorations of doctrine were at the heart of their curriculum. They began with (and continued to include) training for Christian laity. But they also trained pastors and missionaries. They taught much more than on-site or in-residence programs. They held weekend workshops in churches, supplied guest preachers, and sponsored various other extension programs. In 1937 Moody Bible Institute enrolled nearly fifteen thousand people in its correspondence programs. Bible institutes became effectively the new denominational headquarters.

These new institutions of course had to develop new bases of financial support and student body recruitment. The increasing number of independent churches and parallel independent agencies provided that. They were also helped by an increase in the circulation of published fundamentalist communications and by innovations in the media through which that communication was received—innovations and growth which Bible institutes, in turn, helped to introduce and sustain.

Publishing and Broadcasting

A distinctive fundamentalist publishing network had begun to take shape with the organizations and materials of the previous generation. A number of national, transdenominational magazines and journals already existed, as well as large publishing houses for conservative books and Bibles. Many Bible institutes had their own magazines and other publications. As with other nondenominational institutions, growth in publications followed on the heels of conservative defeats. As fundamentalists could no longer trust or enjoy the materials they received from their denominations, they sought out new suppliers. Many of the beneficiaries of this new market were publishing arms of Bible institutes, most notably Moody's huge Colportage Association. Houses such as these were only too happy to produce the Sunday school literature, books, and periodicals needed to educate the growing segment of independent churches and new denominations. Continuing in the tradition of newspaper and magazine publishing were John R. Rice's *The Sword of the Lord* (a millenarian monthly), *The Sunday School Times,* and magazines from many of the Bible institutes. Among the most widely circulated of these was probably the *Moody Monthly*. These publications kept ideas and leaders before the people, and they advertised the schools, books, and trinkets that were the material and intellectual substance of fundamentalist culture.

Fundamentalists had always been anxious to use the technologies of the modern age in the service of the gospel. Revivalists had developed thoroughly modern business organizations to support the delivery of their message. They met in large halls equipped for the task, and they delegated various responsibilities for the rationally organized business of winning the most souls most efficiently. It was only natural, then, that they would leap at the chance to move beyond personally delivered messages and printed words. When radio came on the scene, revival preachers were quick to seize the opportunity. During this era, the most popular religious radio program (indeed perhaps the most popular radio program of any kind) was Charles Fuller's "Old-Fashioned Revival Hour." Beginning as the "Radio Revival Hour" in 1934, Fuller's program featured a skillful combination of music and straightforward gospel preaching. By evoking the rituals of old-fashioned religion, he obviously struck a responsive chord for many displaced people. In his first anniversary broadcast, he talked about the many letters he had received from "heart-broken, heart-hungry humanity, some contemplating suicide, yet hundreds have come, cheery and full of thanksgiving that they have received comfort and new hope and strength from hearing God's Word again, and hearing the songs they used to sing 'back home' with Mother."[76]

While "official" religious slots on the networks were distributed free to "official" representatives selected by the Federal Council of Churches of Christ, fundamentalist preachers were grudgingly willing to buy time, often on independent stations, for programs that sometimes proved more popular than the official ones. A dozen or so major national programs were joined by hundreds of local ones. They included revival-style preaching, Bible study classes, gospel music, and personalities with whom listeners came to identify in the peculiarly intimate way fostered by broadcast media.

By the early 1950s, a new medium—television—had emerged, and fundamentalists were again eager experimenters. Revivalists such as Graham, Rex Humbard, and Oral Roberts were the pacesetters, adapting their usual style and format to the demands of the small screen. By the 1960s, conservatives were convinced of the power of the broadcast media to create national audiences for their message. When in 1960 the Federal Communications Commission began to allow paid time to count toward stations' public service requirements, the desires of the stations and the desires of the preachers dramatically coincided to produce a surge in conservative (paid) broadcasts that soon pushed mainline (free) broadcasts into near oblivion.[77] Broadcast ministries slowly began to replace revivalists and their Bible institutes as the "denominational" centers of the movement.

All these institutions made possible the continuation of an evangelical view of the world, even in a time when the culture and the rest of religion seemed hostile to it. This vast, seemingly invisible, institutional empire provided a home for those who had become outsiders to the religious and cultural mainstream. These same institutions also provided the base from which revival spread into the mainstream during the 1950s and from which a reform movement would rise again in the 1970s.

Political Radicalism

Becoming outsiders, however, meant for *some* fundamentalists a move toward political and cultural radicalism. The 1930s saw the rise of what S. Ahlstrom calls "demagogues of the right."[78] Men like Gerald Winrod and Gerald L. K. Smith toured the country preaching a message of conspiracy and hatred. Winrod had been active in the anti-evolution and fundamentalist movements of the 1920s, developing close ties to the leaders and organizations of those causes. Based in Wichita, Kansas, he formed his Defenders of the Christian Faith, an organization to combat the teaching of evolution and other perceived threats to Christianity. By 1934 there were sixty thousand subscribers to his journal. He saw the political and economic crises of the 1930s as primarily spiritual in character, signs of the coming End Times. And by the middle of the decade, he had concluded that the Antichrist would be a Jew. He was convinced that "a Jewish elite had played satanic roles in a divinely directed drama now drawing to a close. The modern version of this plot provided an 'exact parallel' to Bible prophecies about the last days."[79] That conclusion led to his prediction of an alliance between Hitler and Stalin—both anti-Semites—his declaration that Roosevelt was really a Jew, and his adoption of *The Protocols of the Learned Elders of Zion* as the centerpiece of a comprehensive theory about a Jewish conspiracy to rule the world.[80] Such preachers, using ideas never far below the surface of American politics, gave voice to the sentiments of the most marginalized and disenfranchised in the American population.

This anti-Semitism was in stark contrast to the pro-Zionism of most premillennialists. Believing that the Jews would play a decisive role in the unfolding of the End Times, dispensationalists were eager to see a Jewish state and were protective of Jewish people.[81] During the 1930s, many fundamentalist publications and mission societies began to become aware of the situation in Europe and sought to alert their readers.[82] These were people who believed that God had promised to "bless those who bless the Jews," people who placed evangelism ahead of political or ethnic considerations.[83]

Later, in the 1950s, a few visible fundamentalist leaders took up the banner of radical anticommunism. Carl McIntire, founder of the ACCC, had picked up this theme in the early days of the fundamentalist movement, but during the Cold War era his concerns found a wider hearing. His accusations against church leaders earned him a place among Senator Joseph McCarthy's helpers. He assembled lists of communist sympathizers among the clergy and charged that the Revised Standard Version of the Bible was the product of a Red plot. His organization also helped to launch the careers of Billy James Hargis and Major Edgar Bundy, among the most visible of the anticommunist crusaders of the 1950s and beyond. Both Hargis and McIntire spread their message through popular radio broadcasts. These radical leaders were joined in 1958 by the John Birch Society in a growing crusade dominated by conspiracy theories and active in secular politics.[84]

Communism, of course, was not the only enemy identified by leaders on the radical right. For the John Birch Society communism is the chief enemy, and blacks and Jews are welcomed as members. Hargis, however, was instrumental in linking white racial concerns with anticommunism and concern for religious orthodoxy. For the various Ku Klux Klans, blacks and Jews symbolize the greatest threats to white Christian civilization. And for the later Christian Identity movement, any group not white, Christian, and American cannot claim God's blessing as a "chosen race." Some, who are today known as "Survivalists," are so convinced of an immanent threat that they are physically and militarily prepared for the siege. A small core of radical activists and a somewhat larger core of sympathizers have kept alive a continuing strand of fundamentalist religion that is tied to a wide variety of racial and political conspiracy theories.[85] Such conspiracy politics, however, were not representative of American religious conservatives of the time. Evangelicals were much more concerned about supporting the next Billy Graham crusade than about routing communists from the Eisenhower cabinet.

Even fundamentalists were unwilling to tolerate the political rhetoric and activities of McIntire and his associates. The Orthodox Presbyterians, the Evangelical Methodists, and even the Independent Fundamental Churches of America all withdrew from the American Council of Christian Churches in protest over McIntire's agenda. While evangelicals were clearly against communism, they were also jealous of their growing acceptance in American culture. The Billy Graham who regularly visited the White House could hardly be expected to embrace the conspiracy politics of the radical right.

Strains Within

All was not well, however. Fundamentalists still had to come to terms with what sort of outsiders they would be: loyal opposition or separatist minority party? During the 1930s and well into the 1940s, the terms "fundamentalist" and "evangelical" could be used interchangeably, but by the end of that decade, the words began to have distinct meanings that reflected the division over how to relate to culture. Carl Henry, who would become evangelicalism's leading spokesman, put the dilemma this way in 1948: "Evangelical Christianity is once again, as in the early days of church history, a minority movement in a universally antagonistic environment—that much is certain. What is not so clear is . . . is evangelicalism's only message today the proclamation of individual rescue from a fore-doomed generation? Or has this evangel implications also for the most pressing social problems of our day?"[86] The choice facing the movement was between cultural relevance and cultural separation.

The quintessential separatist was Carl McIntire.[87] He had followed Machen from Princeton to Westminster in 1929, but their differences soon became apparent. Most important was dispensationalism. McIntire wanted a movement that would be, on the one hand, completely free of the corruption of (Presbyterian) denominational affiliation, and on the other hand, open to dispensationalists of all denominational backgrounds. The result, in 1937, was his founding of the Bible Presbyterian Church and Faith Theological Seminary. Four years later he attempted to organize the transdenominational dispensational group he envisioned into the American Council of Christian Churches. His choice of name and of tactics reflected his militant opposition to the mainline churches. He was willing to paint vivid pictures of vast conspiracies inspired by Satan and aimed at destroying true belief. His Manichaean rhetoric identified a number of enemies of God, from apostate churches to communist-inspired politicians. He was a natural for his role as leader of the Christian anticommunist crusades in the 1950s.

Perhaps the best representative of the more accommodating wing of the movement is Harold Ockenga, who, along with radio preacher Charles Fuller, founded Fuller Theological Seminary in 1947. For Ockenga there was a growing sense that fundamentalism had to learn to speak in terms the larger culture would understand and respect. Learning was highly valued (Ockenga boasted a Ph.D.), and conspiracy theories were not. What separated him from McIntire was not so much the content of their beliefs about the Bible or evangelism or eschatology as the style of their relationship to the culture. Ockenga described his goals for Fuller in terms that reveal his position. It was to be an institution "fully committed to the authority of Scripture and *fully positive* in its testimony."[88]

In 1942, one year after the ACCC was formed, Ockenga was part of the formation of the National Association of Evangelicals, a group designed to pull together the loose coalition of extradenominational agencies and conservative denominations that had been forming. While at first they thought of their effort as a duplication of McIntire's, it slowly became clear that the name they had chosen—"evangelical"—was designating a group increasingly at odds with the "fundamentalists," who sought more militancy.[89]

Throughout the 1950s and 1960s, the rift grew. Militant fundamentalists, disenchanted with evangelical Billy Graham because he was willing to involve "apostate" denominations in the planning and leadership of his evangelistic crusades, declared their separation from his work in 1956. Graham, perhaps realizing that he no longer needed to fear the disaffection of such separatists, acknowledged the rift and removed his name from the list of members of the cooperating board of the *Sword of the Lord*.[90] A decade later, the Graham organization would actually exclude McIntire from their 1966 Berlin Congress on World Evangelization.[91] Perhaps the break became symbolically most apparent with the 1963 changing of the guard at Fuller Theological Seminary. Older fundamentalists who insisted on strict inerrancy as a test of faith resigned or were demoted, while newer evangelical faculty sought a broader agenda.[92]

As North American fundamentalism entered the 1970s, it could draw on a rich (and sometimes bewildering) legacy of ideas, organizational forms, and relationships to the larger world. Its nineteenth-century position as keeper of orthodoxy had given way in the early part of the twentieth century to a battle defending that orthodoxy against modernism, a battle that was both religious and cultural. With defeat in that battle, fundamentalists had withdrawn into separate territory to assess their potential as outsiders. Some had used their organizational and evangelistic skills to build an impressive religious empire rivaling the mainline denominations in institutional strength. Still expecting that Jesus might return at any moment, believers put their energy into saving souls from a decaying civilization. Some became convinced that the evangelistic task demanded some accommodation and cooperation with the ways of the world, and they slowly began to shun the name "fundamentalist." Others insisted on separatism as the only legitimate position for the defenders of truth. And a few radicals ventured into the political arena in pursuit of the kind of ideological cleansing perceived necessary to preserve America's Christian heritage.

Re-emergence as a Social Movement: 1976 and Beyond

For fifty years, fundamentalism had been largely invisible on the American political scene. A few fundamentalists had joined the anticommunist crusades of the fifties, but most had remained relatively inactive in politics, preferring instead to put energy into the churches and institutions that made their view of the world possible. Evangelism and missions far outweighed social reform on their agendas. However, a number of things happened in the sixties and seventies to mobilize fundamentalists again as a social movement. In some ways the culture itself pulled fundamentalists into the public arena; in other ways, internal changes pushed them outward.

The World from Which It Came

One cannot speak of the 1960s in the United States without speaking of rapid social change. When John F. Kennedy spoke of "New Frontiers," he could hardly know just how new they would seem. The civil rights movement, simmering since the mid-1950s, burst into the national consciousness in the early years of the sixties. Televised scenes of marchers being beaten and churches being bombed began to mobilize the conscience of the nation. Legislation moved through Congress mandating that relationships between blacks and whites change. A century of legal segregation and three centuries of servitude were to be replaced by equal rights and equal opportunity. Such a revolution brought, of course, counter-revolution and protest from traditional whites in the North and South. It also brought the assassination of the Reverend Dr. Martin Luther King, Jr., the most visible leader of the cause. And his death was followed within months by the assassination of Robert F. Kennedy. Along with John F. Kennedy, shot five years earlier, two more champions of justice had fallen victim to the chaos of the times.

Not only were the relationships between blacks and whites changing; so were the roles of men and women. Women lashed out at the "feminine mystique" that had kept them imprisoned in domestic roles. Bras were burned and new language invented, with "Ms." becoming the symbol of liberation from conventions that tied women's identities to men's. Both men and women in the counterculture youth movements preached new sexual mores under the slogan, "Make love, not war." Old rules were being overturned as fast as they could be questioned by students on college campuses or demonstrators in the streets.

Their protests were given a special moral urgency by the war in Vietnam. Convinced that their government was pursuing a misguided, even malevolent, policy, students sought to end the war. They burned their draft cards, fled to Sweden and Canada, and marched in the streets of nearly every American city. Americans who supported the war could not understand the defiance of the students, and the students could not understand the unquestioning obedience of many of their elders. The students urged everyone to "question authority" as a matter of course. The war would not end until well into the 1970s, but the legacy of division and distrust it spawned would go on much longer. As the 1960s faded into the 1970s, even less radical folk were faced with the disconcerting reality that not all presidents were trustworthy. As the scandals of Watergate unfolded, people who had supported a "law and order" president were confronted with a president who broke the law. The rules of morality and leadership they had presumed to hold simply did not seem to apply.[93]

This seeming disintegration of society lent extra urgency to the evangelistic task. Such chaos could only mean that the Rapture was near. Such rapid change is the stuff of which sermons are made. And it is the stuff of which converts are made. The changes experienced in the culture were often experienced by individuals as an intolerable shaking of the foundations. From burned-out hippies to disillusioned liberals to ordinary seekers, they made their way into fundamentalist churches. One of the hippies-turned-fundamentalist interviewed by Steven Tipton put it this way, "One person tells you to do one thing, and the next person says to do the opposite. 'Get a job, get a haircut.' Or 'Turn on, tune in, drop out.' Or 'Support the President,' and someone else says, 'Impeach Nixon' or 'Stop the War,' or whatever it is, you know. It makes you crazy. What do you do? It's typical of the world. You're in confusion. In the Lord the Word shows you what to do, and you can rest in it. You don't have to be gray."[94] In fundamentalist churches, they found answers and order, love and stability.

If the culture as a whole was in some disarray, that seemed doubly true in the South. Just as the northern United States and Canada had experienced industrialization, urbanization, and immigration in the last quarter of the nineteenth century, so the southeastern United States was experiencing those same forces a century later. From the Depression onward, people were leaving their farms; but the pace quickened after World War II. At first they were more likely to go to northern cities than to southern ones, but after about 1960, the Sun Belt had its own attraction. In the 1940s the South had been two-thirds rural, but by 1960 less than half of the people lived in the countryside. During that same period, gains in education and in an industrial base had laid the foundation for the growth that would follow.[95] By 1980 well over 10 percent of the South's urban population had been born outside the region.[96] Air conditioning and cheap labor made it the region of choice for corporate moves and new ventures. For the first time, migration in from other regions outstripped migration away from southern small towns and farms. The presence of newcomers and the diversity of cities created a pluralistic environment never before seen in the South. Alongside radical change in racial norms, southerners found themselves in a world they hardly recognized. The beliefs taken for granted in their small traditional communities had to be defended if they were to survive in this new world.[97]

The rapid social change of the 1960s, then, created fertile ground that fundamentalists were only too happy to plow. Increasing numbers were anxious to hear a message about God's truth and God's plan for the future. They looked around them at the chaos of the times and wondered what they could count on, where the dependable rules were. A young convert reflected on her life left behind, "There are no lines, I guess, there. You are totally free. And now I realize that lines are definitely better because you'll go too far, as much as you think you won't."[98] It was a good time for a revival.

But a social movement is more than a revival. The transitions of the sixties and seventies pulled fundamentalists not only into new fields for evangelism but also into new institutional and political action. The entire country, but especially the South, was ripe for a fundamentalist movement, and fundamentalists would become vital players in some rather massive political realignments.

The sixties revolution had in fact pulled the entire U.S. polity toward new partisan alignments. The Democratic Party's hold on the South disintegrated with that party's embrace of civil rights.[99] And working-class whites outside the South also began to drop their Democratic allegiance. Both northern and southern Democrats became more interested in moral and lifestyle issues than in traditional party interests and loyalties—interested enough to vote for Republicans who caught their fancy.[100] There were political choices to be made, and people were searching for the grounds on which to make them. At least some people began to wonder if churches might help them in that process.

Meanwhile, the U.S. government itself was creating a certain alarm in the minds of fundamentalists. The retreat from Vietnam raised fears that the nation might no longer enjoy its world supremacy. Fundamentalists cared deeply about that possibility, partly because they feared the growth of communism, but also because they saw American military and economic might as guarantors of their ability of evangelize the world. For fundamentalists the United States has always been the "city on a hill" ordained by God as the light to the nations. From the beginning they had been committed to foreign missions, and now they wondered if the light of the gospel might go out because it would have no great chosen nation to carry it.

Their fear for the future of the country was intensified by the 1963 decision by the U.S. Supreme Court that outlawed prescribed prayers in public schools. It seemed impossible that in this Christian nation children should be told not to pray in school. Over the next decade, the evidence mounted in the minds of fundamentalists that the nation was being run by people intentionally hostile to their beliefs and determined to stamp out all vestiges of traditional religion in the coming generations.[101] The attacks on home and school and church seemed so systematic that they surely must have come from a single ideological source, identified in Tim Lahaye's popular 1980 book, *The Battle for the Mind,* as secular humanism. Among the developments fundamentalists found alarming:

> First, a constitutional amendment was proposed that could have been interpreted so as to prevent women from fulfilling their biblical role as submissive wives, serving primarily in the household.
>
> Second, the family was further attacked as social agencies and legislatures sought to define the limits of physical punishment permitted in a father's attempts to discipline his children.

> Third, the IRS began to take on the task of investigating the finances of religious agencies and determining what "counted" as true religion (at least for tax purposes).
>
> Fourth, civil rights arguments began to be extended to those (especially homosexuals) whose lives were deemed grossly immoral by fundamentalists.
>
> Fifth, not only could children not pray in school, they were also being taught "values clarification" and other "humanist" ideas that undermined the unwavering beliefs and traditions their parents held dear.
>
> Sixth, even Christian schools could not do their work without government agencies imposing certification restrictions that seemed to strip them of their theological power.
>
> And finally, Roe v. Wade. All the forces seeking to destroy traditional families and moral society seemed to converge in a court ruling that abortion was a matter of private choice.[102]

The courts and schools and legislatures seemed to be daring fundamentalists to come out of their separatist institutions to defend their right to exist.

While fundamentalist churches were enjoying the revival brought their way by increasing numbers of seekers, they were also being pulled out of their institutional subculture by broader concerns. There was a growing sense that if "God's people" did not stand up for their principles, the nation might forever be lost. And if those same people did not stand up against an aggressive government in this generation, there *might not be* another generation of believers. The sense of urgency coming from the culture was matched by the momentum of institutional strength coming from within. In the late nineteenth century, conservatives concerned about the drift of the culture into modernism had created new institutions to support their cause. In the late twentieth century, those institutions were already in place. They were, in fact, thriving.

Working-class fundamentalists of the 1930s and 1940s had given birth to a generation of middle-class children. Southerners moving to cities were also moving into greater economic resources. The people inside fundamentalism simply had more money to give to their churches, money that helped to fuel the institutional boom.[103] They could afford to pay tuition to Christian academies and to send donations to television ministries. They could afford to build churches that provided services attractive to a wider and wider audience. And they could afford to get involved in politics.

Nowhere was this surfeit of organizational power more apparent than in the television ministries.[104] Television is an enormously powerful medium for raising money, and evangelists were constantly being pushed along by the sheer power of the resources available. They not only raised money to stay on the air and preach the gospel; they also raised money for whatever enterprises their imagination and charisma could create and sustain.[105] Like the urban revivalists before them, these preachers built quasi-denominational complexes of institutions to extend their mission. There were colleges (CBN University, Liberty University, and the like), hospitals (most notably Oral Roberts's City of Faith Hospital), publishing houses, missionaries, and even amusement parks (Heritage USA being the most prominent).

Although these institutions were thriving, they were, ironically, irrelevant to the dominant culture. The standards of achievement in the two spheres were simply different, with success inside fundamentalist ranks going largely unnoticed on the outside. After two generations of separation, fundamentalists were beginning to realize just how isolated they were. They were tired of being ignored.[106] Their resentment can be heard in Jerry Falwell's assessment of the age. "We are living in a society today that is quite sophisticated and very educated. Ours is indeed a clever generation, but one that is suffering because men are doing what is right in their own eyes and disregarding God's immutable laws. If a person is not a Christian, he is inherently a failure."[107] As the culture pulled fundamentalists outward, then, their own economic and institutional strength, combined with a certain sense of cultural isolation, provided the fuel with which they could generate a movement for change.

The Movement Organized: Christian Academies

Following World War II, a few conservative churches began to organize their own day schools, but the movement accelerated rapidly during the 1960s. Some outsiders saw the move toward private church-sponsored schools as merely a retreat from integration—and some of it was clearly that—but the motivations were much larger.[108] Fundamentalists had concluded that the public schools were actively hostile to their children's faith. Now that they had the resources, they took matters into their own hands. Between 1965 and 1983, enrollment in evangelical schools increased sixfold, and the number of schools reached about ten thousand. In addition, perhaps as many as one hundred thousand fundamentalist children are being taught at home.[109] Usually sponsored directly by one or more congregations, these schools draw primarily on the children of members. They offer parents the opportunity to surround their children with knowledge that is in harmony with their beliefs. A mother in a northeastern city explained why she wanted her daughter in the church's academy: "I think she is going to have less options thrown at her in a Christian school than if she was in a public school, where there might be a few more things that she might have to choose about. I would rather control her environment as much as possible while she is young, until she is old enough to be let go."[110] She knows that the Bible will be a textbook in every classroom, with each subject shaped by a conservative point of view. History is "Christian History," and economics is strictly free enterprise. Biblical words and examples even show up in spelling and math. Even more important, Christian schools operate in the kind of disciplined atmosphere that reinforces belief, and they provide a supply of Christian friends and role models that give those beliefs plausibility.[111]

A number of publishers have begun providing complete curricula. Among the most widely used are the materials of the Accelerated Christian Education series. Publishers and school administrators are proud to claim that children in Christian schools compare very favorably on standardized tests with their public school counterparts. Private schools appear to have become an entrenched part of the fundamentalist way of life. It is one of the ways in which they "proclaim themselves as guardians of American culture. Caught in a world whose complexity tends to render people impotent, evangelicals have chosen to delimit their world in order to gain control over it."[112]

The Movement Organized: The New Christian Right

The other major effort of 1980s fundamentalists in gaining control over their world was an active entry into politics. It is ironic that the attention of United States news media was first turned toward the political potential of conservative religion, not by fundamentalists themselves, but by Jimmy Carter, who better fits the label "evangelical." Far from attempting to make his religion his political agenda, Carter was a strict adherent of the traditional Baptist belief in the separation of church and state.[113] And it soon became abundantly clear to fundamentalists that Carter shared few of their foreign or domestic policy positions.

But it was the "Year of the Evangelical" in 1976, and the year of the nation's bicentennial. The nation (or at least the intellectual and political elite) suddenly discovered that conservative religion had not disappeared after 1925 and that a good many people were willing to vote according to their moral consciences. When southerners gave their Baptist favorite son a trip to the White House, the pundits imagined that conservative, religious folk had newly arrived in politics. While the pundits were not quite right about this "new birth," it was true that 1976 gave evangelicals and fundamentalists a new sense of efficacy. The national attention paid to them and to the nation's moral roots boosted their growing interest in political affairs.

In truth, a political alignment of religious people, concerned about conservative social issues, was both older and newer than the 1976 election. At least since the early 1970s people identifiable as religious conservatives had been coalescing around an agenda of family-related issues. They did not yet know they were a movement, and 1976 only served to further awaken them to the inefficiency of following traditional religious or political labels. Jimmy Carter might be a Southern Baptist, but he was not their man. A true political movement awaited the organization of new vehicles for carrying their concern.

That organization came in 1979. A group of pastors of huge "superchurches" decided that the time had come to organize to promote morality in American life. With the help of conservative political organizers Richard Viguerie and Ed McAteer, they put together a nonpartisan political organization that they called Moral Majority. Its head was to be Jerry Falwell, with other board members James Kennedy (Presbyterian from Florida), Greg Dixon (independent Baptist from Indianapolis), Tim LaHaye (conservative ideologue from California), and Charles Stanley (Southern Baptist from Atlanta).[114] Other conservative religious political groups were being organized as well—the Religious Roundtable, the American Coalition for Traditional Values, and Christian Voice—but it was the Moral Majority that caught the imagination of the public (and the news media), becoming the symbol of a revitalized, politically potent fundamentalist movement. The group built on two primary organizational bases: the network of independent churches in existence since the 1930s and the television fund-raising mechanisms developed to a fine art in the 1970s. With pastors as the primary organizers, the movement spread quickly into their spheres of influence, often large suburban churches. And with television preachers and their direct-mail fund raising lists also available, the net was broadened further.[115]

The strategy adopted by the Moral Majority involved the full range of political activities. They distributed information through newsletters, seminars, and the broadcast ministries. They registered voters and lobbied Congress. And they trained and encouraged conservatives in the fine art of running for office. No public office or bureaucratic position was too low; as political organizers, they realized that their crusade must begin from the ground up. And like the network of independent churches on which they built, Moral Majority activities were often out of public sight, varying in form and emphasis from one location to another.

The numerical strength of the movement has never been quite clear.[116] To the extent that they represent people of strictly fundamentalist religious beliefs, the constituency is clearly quite small. In at least some local elections, religious supporters indeed seem the only ones interested in Moral Majority candidates.[117] To the extent that a moral coalition is being built, however, its size might be much larger. On some issues, Moral Majoritarians do represent majority opinion, while on others they are a tiny minority. Sometimes their position represents the majority, while their reasons for holding that position are far removed from the mainstream. Attempts to define empirically a coherent platform of issues held by any broad segment of the public have consistently had mixed results. In the heady early days of the movement, Falwell and other leaders (with ample help from newspeople) took generous credit for conservative political victories. In retrospect, such credit was probably misplaced.[118]

Over the years, New Christian Right activists have learned how to play the political game. They are less likely to expect instant electoral success or legislative revolutions. They have convinced enormous numbers of voters that involvement is important, and the high commitment of those voters may outweigh their relatively small numbers. These are voters who not only cast ballots but have joined Moral Majority, Concerned Women for America, and other local groups. Many of these new activists are preachers, whose influence (often indirect) can be widely felt. Even more widely felt are the messages of Christian broadcasters who in varying degrees support political involvement.[119]

Those who are connected to the political activities of this movement receive a regular flow of information about letters they need to write to Congress and phone calls that need to be made in support of a bill. Conservative groups generate the vast majority of the religiously based constituent pressure felt in Washington. The conservative religious lobbies are also learning to play the political hardball that makes an impact on policy. They are learning the slow, painstaking process of developing contacts, researching issues, drafting legislation. While their efforts were at first ill-timed and ineffective, with experience they could count the demise of the Equal Rights

Amendment to the United States Constitution and the success of "equal access" legislation (for after-hours religious activities in public schools) to their credit.[120]

Fundamentalist Ideas in the Political Arena

The issues around which fundamentalists have attempted to rally support have ranged from gun control and the Panama Canal to drugs and pornography. The fight against evolution had already been revived in new form as an effort to institute the teaching of "scientific creationism" alongside evolution. Other public school issues included efforts to reinstitute prayers in the classroom and initiatives against the many forms of secular humanism to which conservatives feared their children were being exposed. Tim LaHaye called it "The Battle for the Mind." And the legal strategies adopted were premised on viewing secular humanism as a religion (a premise given some legitimacy by reference to it as such in a 1961 Supreme Court opinion).[121] But the central theme of the fundamentalist foray into politics was protection for the "traditional family, the basic unit of society." By this was meant a legally married man and woman, with their children, preferably supported solely by the husband's labor. From this flowed the movement's opposition to gay rights, pornography, the Equal Rights Amendment, and laws designed to protect abused wives and children. For the nation to be strong, its families should be constituted according to God's rules, rules including the headship of men and the necessity for physical discipline of children.

Concern for the family was most acute, however, on the issue of abortion.[122] Evoking images of holocaust, pro-life speakers and writers decried the immorality that led to unwanted pregnancy in the first place, the greedy doctors who make a living destroying life, and the morally bankrupt government agencies and courts that allow such a practice to flourish. Stopping the slaughter of innocent unborn babies became the rallying cry that mobilized many previously inactive conservatives.

Abortion was also the issue that tested the limits of fundamentalist activism. In 1988 a group called "Operation Rescue" arose as a vehicle for the promotion of civil disobedience in opposition to abortion. The group not only picketed abortion clinics but sought to prevent women from entering. They sat down, formed human blockades, and pleaded with those who came and went. When clinics obtained court orders against them, they were not deterred, and many went to jail. During that summer's Democratic National Convention, Operation Rescue demonstrators filled Atlanta's jails, many giving only Jane or John Doe as identification. While leaders of the New Christian Right sympathized with their cause, most drew the line at civil disobedience. Jerry Falwell declared himself their "cheerleader" who was himself not yet ready to go to jail. Mainstream fundamentalists, then, would stick to standard political means, while this new group explored more radical measures.

The abortion issue not only divided fundamentalists into differing tactical camps, it also united fundamentalists and other religious conservatives who had otherwise shunned each other as doctrinal inferiors or heretics. Catholics especially, long seen as allies of the Antichrist by many fundamentalists, were embraced by those active in the pro-life movement. Other issues brought together other unlikely coalitions: feminists joined the fight against pornography; Mormons were active in fighting the ERA; Jews of course were partners in supporting Israel. Falwell was adamant that such partnerships were essential, boldly asserting that the Moral Majority was committed to "pluralism." Claiming that they were not simply fostering "born again" politics, he asserted that "the acceptability of any candidate could never be based upon one's religious affiliation. Our support of candidates is based upon two criteria: (a) the commitment of the candidate to the principles that we espouse; (b) the competency of the candidate to fill that office."[123] This organization was an attempt to find a common moral ground on which conservatives could agree. It was an attempt to maintain purity of belief alongside cooperation with those of different beliefs.

Finding common ground of course called for significant ideological and organizational innovation among fundamentalists. It meant playing a secular game by secular rules.[124] It also meant that Falwell and his organization quickly became anathema for believers like Bob Jones, who declared him "the most dangerous man in America" for his practice of forming coalitions with unbelievers. For a generation, fundamentalists had built their identity around "separation." They had built separate institutions and tried to live separate lives. They refused to drink or dance, gamble, or smoke. They dressed modestly and were careful about their associates. These were people who had condemned Billy Graham for cooperating with Lutherans and Episcopalians; they could hardly be expected now to embrace cooperation with Catholics and Mormons. Evangelism, true belief, and right living had been seen as the only legitimate strategies for Christians anticipating the Rapture and surrounded by a corrupt world. Christians who got involved in politics were in this view doomed to be sullied by the dirty world into which they went.

The task Falwell faced was convincing fundamentalists that they ought to be involved and explaining to them how they could do that without jeopardizing their Christian witness. He did so by appealing to the missions instinct ingrained so deeply in fundamentalists. He turned their own concerns back against them, saying, "We must stop being so negative and critical of everyone who is trying to reach people with the Gospel but does not wear our label."[125] He pointed out that Jesus had commanded them to preach the gospel to every nation, a command they could not carry out if that nation were communist—a good reason to support a strong military and a conservative foreign policy. As a "chosen nation," America had had a special role in spreading the gospel—a good reason to keep America free and morally upright. Quoting Hebrew Scripture about the need for repentance and righteousness in the nation had long been a staple of fundamentalist preaching: "Only by godly leadership can America be put back on a divine course. God will give national healing if men and women will pray and meet God's conditions."[126] Falwell took those revival sermons and gave them new implications. He did not want to give up on saving souls, but he also wanted to save the nation. He wanted to see both "spiritual revival and political renewal in the United States."

The political renewal sought by Falwell and his supporters is strongly reminiscent of the return to Christian civilization sought by fundamentalist reformers in the earlier part of the century. Families are important because they are the basic unit of that civilization, and secular humanism is the enemy because it represents the ideological and cultural core of the institutions that now dominate society. This struggle between fundamentalists and their enemies is a very real contest to see who will define the terms of American culture.[127] Secular humanists (many of whom of course are not very secular at all) are the intellectual and bureaucratic elite (the "knowledge class") who hold the reins of power in American society. They have gained their positions through formal education and credentials—education and credentials fundamentalists less often have. Their business requires the free flow of information and ideas, and they have the power to declare that pluralism is required in American democracy and that separation of church and state implies the exclusion of religion from public life. Television, news, and the arts, along with the educational system, uphold a religion-neutral (or religion-absent) view of society. Fundamentalists are convinced that America must have a pro-religion culture, one in which they have a stronger voice in shaping the values and images that guide society. Theirs is an ideological battle for control of the way America will view its past and its future.

The ideological battle fundamentalists wage pits them against powerful cultural enemies and forces them to re-evaluate their own way of relating to the outside world. In the 1980s the ideological balance in fundamentalism subtly shifted away from premillennial pessimism toward an optimism about social reform more suited to postmillennial visions. Activists were reviving the myths of Christian civilization and godly dominion that have been widely shared throughout this nation's history. They were not yet ready to give up their premillennial ideas, but they were willing to say that eschatological ideas were "not significant" in explaining their political involvement.[128]

This entry into a public crusade for moral reform marked an important new phase in fundamentalist life. After several decades in which its primary activism was individual evangelism, fundamentalists were again seeking collective change. While sparked by a certain desperation about the future of Western culture, the movement nevertheless exhibits the kind of optimism present in earlier efforts to restore Christian civilization. It has drawn on its ideological roots of evangelism and mission, its image of America as the "city on the hill," while suppressing its heritage of dispensational premillennialism. And it has drawn on its organizational roots in independent churches, agencies, and broadcast ministries, while creating new organizational forms to accommodate the broader public coalitions necessary to achieve new goals.

New Battles on the Religious Front

The same political savvy that began to be apparent in the New Christian Right's moral crusade was present in the religious battles of the 1980s. The issues sounded like a rerun of the twenties—biblical inerrancy against liberalism—but the strategies were distinctly new. Carefully planned grass-roots campaigns resulted in fundamentalist victories in the Lutheran Church, Missouri Synod, and in the Southern Baptist Convention. As far back as the 1940s, some Missouri Synod Lutherans had worked to bring progressive change into their very conservative denomination. During the 1960s, talk of possible Lutheran denominational mergers led some scholars to reevaluate their interpretations of historic Lutheran confessions in light of what fellow Lutherans believed. It just as quickly led others in the denomination to resist. Missouri Synod Lutherans differed from other Lutheran groups on both adherence to the confessions and on views of Scripture. Since at least the 1920s, they had been using "inerrant" and "infallible" to describe Scripture, while other bodies generally rejected those terms.[129]

During the sixties, conservatives began to organize. They presented resolutions condemning teachings at Concordia Seminary in Saint Louis and started a newspaper, *Christian News*. That paper was later followed by *Affirm* as a voice of the conservatives. In 1969 they actively campaigned (something unheard of before) for the election of J. A. O. Preus as president of the Synod. He won, unseating an incumbent, and the controversy emerged into the open. Opposing forces were led by John Tietjen, the newly installed president of Concordia. In 1970 the investigations of Concordia began. Over the next four years, Preus and the seminary exchanged numerous demands and refusals. The conservatives joined fundamentalists of earlier generations in insisting that the inerrancy of Scripture is the foundation of all other beliefs, including the historic Lutheran creeds. Like their nineteenth-century predecessors, they worried about "evil geniuses like Darwin, Marx, and Freud."[130]

Because Preus was taking such an active role in the governing of the school, the Association of Theological Schools put the seminary on probation in 1972. But the following summer, at the Synod convention in New Orleans, Preus received full authorization to proceed with the purification of the denomination, with special attention to the seminary. Moderate forces responded by organizing "Evangelical Lutherans in Mission" and publishing a new paper, *Missouri in Perspective*. They held rallies throughout the country, signaling a new phase in the controversy. In February of 1974, most of the students and faculty of Concordia Seminary left the campus to form "Seminary in Exile" (Seminex). At the same time the fracture of the denomination's mission efforts into rival programs was underway. Over the next several years, the moderate dissidents were systematically forced out, eventually to form a separate denomination, the Association of Evangelical Lutheran Churches. Their departure completed the conservative purge.

During the same period, Southern Baptist conservatives had been worried about their denomination, and since the early 1970s they had begun to organize. They established a "Baptist Faith and Message Fellowship" (named for the doctrinal statement of the denomination) and started a newspaper, the *Southern Baptist Journal*. Theirs was a renewed emphasis on the inerrancy of Scripture, along with a strong dose of dispensational premillennialism.[131] They knew that they feared the liberal drift they saw in the seminaries and colleges and disliked the social activism that seemed to be present in some agencies. Like their northern counterparts half a century earlier, they insisted that an infallible Bible had to be the foundation for all other beliefs.

The kind of cultural homogeneity that had made a southern fundamentalist movement impossible before had been broken by three decades of rapid change. The South had urbanized, its racial mores had been disrupted, transplants from the North were arriving daily, and tradition was generally in disarray.[132] Southerners now knew that liberals existed in their midst whom they were willing to oppose. They were now more likely to join political movements such as the Moral Majority and more likely to turn their Southern Baptist conservatism into Southern Baptist fundamentalism. In addition, their rising levels of income and urbanization gave them resources and opportunities for mobilization that had not been there in earlier eras. Southerners were both more concerned and more able to fight to defend the orthodoxy they remembered.

They wrote letters, offered resolutions, and otherwise voiced their dismay at the perceived abandonment of tradition. They also withheld their dollars, preferring to support unofficial seminaries and missionaries untainted by the denomination's liberal drift. But their protests went largely unheard until a Texas judge, Paul Pressler, gave them some lessons in politics. He looked at the denomination's constitutional structure and discerned that the convention president, always thought to be an honorific position, actually held the key to changing policy. Agencies, including seminaries, are run by their boards of trustees; and those trustees are elected by the "messengers" (delegates) who attend the annual convention meetings. However, the process by which trustees are nominated begins with the president, and nominees are almost never turned down. Pressler and fellow Texan Paige Patterson gathered a small group of prominent pastors who took on the task of organizing their states. Working largely unnoticed, they held informational meetings and rallies, convincing pastors and lay people that they should make a trip to the annual convention to vote for a conservative president. In 1979, in Houston (Pressler's hometown), Adrian Rogers was elected, beginning an unbroken string of fundamentalist victories.

By appointing only strict inerrantists and by passing conservative resolutions that could be used as policy guidelines in the denomination's institutions, fundamentalists began to put their stamp on the nation's largest Protestant denomination. Slowly the new trustees began to take office, a few more each year; and by 1987 denominational agencies were beginning to feel the results of the movement. A seminary president was forced from office, as was a Baptist editor in Georgia. Professors began to seek other employment rather than live with doctrinal restrictions. The publishing house agreed to produce a commentary series based on strict inerrancy. Mission efforts began to turn away from educational and health concerns toward single-minded evangelism and starting new churches. And the social concerns agencies of the denomination turned firmly away from issues of separation of church and state, hunger, racism, and violence toward abortion, school prayer, and the political agenda of the New Christian Right.[133] The leaders of the movement exulted that theirs was the biggest conservative victory ever in the fight against liberalism.

New Variations on the Fundamentalists: Reconstructionists

One of the people who celebrated along with Judge Pressler at the conservative Baptist victory was Dr. Gary North, head of a small Texas conservative think tank. In 1986, North interviewed Pressler for a tape to be distributed through his "Dominion

Tapes." His purpose was to draw on Pressler's experience as an example for other conservatives who wanted to organize grass-roots opposition to bureaucracies dominated by humanists and liberals.

Unlike Pressler, however, North belongs to a movement of orthodox Christians called *reconstructionists,* who seek to pose a direct threat to "the modern bureaucratic State." In their view, "Christians are called by God to exercise dominion."[134] The two primary texts on which their ideas are built are Genesis 1:26–28 (God's command to the newly created humanity to "subdue" the earth and have dominion over it) and the "Great Commission" of Matthew 28:16–20 (Jesus' charge to the disciples to "teach all nations" the things he commanded).

The movement evidently grew out of the orthodox Presbyterian views nurtured at Machen's Westminster Seminary and its southern counterpart in Jackson, Mississippi. There Calvinist scholars continued to write about the necessity of restoring Christian civilization and the eventual victory of God over the forces of Satan. In 1965, Rousas John Rushdoony, a California pastor and evangelist, formed Chalcedon ministries. His associates began publishing a newsletter and later a journal (the scholarly *Journal of Christian Reconstruction*) in which the issues confronting Christianity were explored. For a time the journal was edited by North, Rushdoony's son-in-law, but in the late 1970s he left to form the Institute for Christian Economics in Tyler, Texas. In the early 1980s, an attempt was made to form a denomination for reconstructionists, with a divinity school in Tyler to serve it. That attempt failed, but the publications of both the California and the Texas groups, along with materials originating in New York, Florida, Tennessee, Mississippi, and Georgia, have continued to inspire groups outside the strictly Calvinist, Presbyterian circles in which the elites reside.[135]

The intellectual and theological foundations of the movement are clearly Calvinist. The "golden age" to which reconstructionists look is not the nineteenth century but the seventeenth. Their heroes are the Puritans of Massachusetts who dared to establish civil law based explicitly on biblical principles. John Cotton's 1641 "Abstract of the Laws of New England" serves as a respected point of reference.[136] They also look fondly to Calvin's Geneva in the century before and to the strict Calvinists who fought Presbyterian liberalism earlier in the twentieth century. J. Gresham Machen and Cornelius Van Til, of Westminster Seminary, are admired as warriors against secularism.

Van Til developed the idea of "theonomy," or submission to the rule of God. Those who are the Elect have the ability to understand all of life in the light of God's laws; those who live in the darkness of "autonomy" (reliance on human judgment) can produce no true knowledge at all.[137] Non-Christian schools then, are shunned, with the argument that the entire system of public education is dominated by secular humanist assumptions. Christian schools are seen as essential, a necessary step in preparing a citizenry that understands God's laws. Not only must children be properly trained in history and morality, but more advanced learning needs correction as well. The intellectual elite of the movement is active in producing publications that will redirect knowledge in all areas of life, from psychology and history to mathematics and philosophy.[138]

Reconstructionists are, then, concerned about bringing all of life under God's rule. In this they criticize and hope to undermine institutions that they see as usurping

God's rightful place of lordship. Chief among the culprits for them is the modern state. In their view, it has grown far beyond its legitimate boundaries and must be brought down, like a tyrant, by its subjects. The only legitimate function of government is keeping the peace, with other functions constituting idolatry. The modern state, as reconstructionists see it, has substituted itself for God. Citizens have been tricked into trusting the State to care for them, rather than reserving that role for God. "Our once Christian-based civil government has become idolatrous by arrogating to itself the God-like power of permeating every aspect and sphere of citizens' lives."[139] North writes, "Civil law is not supposed to make men good; it is supposed to restrain external evil."[140]

Such a stance does not, however, mean that reconstructionists are uninterested in government or unwilling to obey its laws. The spread of civil disobedience in opposition to abortion (especially through Operation Rescue) was denounced by reconstructionist clergy as it was by other fundamentalists. In the January 1989 issue of the *Chalcedon Report,* Rushdoony wrote in opposition to the "lawless protest" of Operation Rescue's demonstrators. While strongly arguing that abortion is a sin and unjustified under any circumstances, he also argued that Christians are obliged to obey the civil law. To seek change through protest and revolution is to violate the Christian presupposition that change comes only through God's power.

Arguing for obedience to the law does not, however, mean that reconstructionists are indifferent to the content of those laws. They are intensely interested because they see all law, government, and social action as inherently religious. Rushdoony writes, "Every law structure or system is an establishment of religion. There can be no separation of religion and the State."[141] All such institutions attempt to mold the moral life of the culture, and all make assumptions about where the power for change lies. For those reasons, reconstructionists will even denounce a document such as the 1988 Williamsburg Charter on the role of religion in public life. Because it is framed in terms that could be acceptable to unbelievers, writer John Lofton sees "the faith of the secular humanists [as] the foundation of this document."[142] For reconstructionists there is no neutral ground, no sphere of activity outside God's rule. One is either following God in all areas of life or not following God at all. One is either engaged in godly politics or is participating in the anti-God structures that now threaten the home, the school, and the church.

That sense of threat from active anti-Christian structures seems to have spurred this movement into action. They fully agree with fundamentalists that government is controlled by the religious faith of secular humanism and that humanism is being thrust upon ordinary people through the schools, in programs that restrict traditional family values, and even in intrusion into church life. They also agree with fundamentalists about the chaotic character of today's world. An April 1989 southeastern regional conference was titled "Judgment and the Christian in a World Disintegrating." In the absence of God's law, the world is in their view "disintegrating." Reconstructionists also agree with fundamentalists in tagging communism as an enemy, alongside chaos and secular humanism. The newsletter contains regular news reports of religious persecution in eastern bloc countries and regular columns warning against being taken in by liberal ideas about "social justice" or a "moderate" PLO (Palestine

Liberation Organization). The enemies reconstructionism has identified are the same enemies fundamentalism has been fighting all along.

The newsletter also warns against the tendency of "Caucasian Christians" to condemn themselves for racism. Regular writer Otto Scott points out that it was "Caucasian Christians [who] stopped the Amerindians of Central America from conducting their enormous human sacrifices, who ended the Hindu practise of forcing widows to sit in the midst of flames that consumed the cadavers of their husbands, who halted the slave practices of Black Africa, who lifted (though briefly) hideous despotisms in many parts of the Orient . . . [and] sacrificed their lives in a great Civil War to free black people from slavery." He also argues that blacks in South Africa are much better off than in some black-ruled countries in Africa.[143] Scott made a similar effort in an earlier column to picture Spain's General Franco as a friend of the Jews.[144] This revisionist history does not appear to be aimed at a racist vision of the future (described as "composed of every race, assured by God of eternal life and eventual victory"). Rather, reconstructionists, like other fundamentalists, are rewriting the "secular humanist" catalog of "sins" and attempting to reclaim the goodness of the American experience.[145]

Reconstructionists disagree with some other fundamentalists, however, about the role of religion in public life. For reconstructionists, pietism and separatism only play into the hands of the humanists who wish to keep Christians neutralized. Like the activists of the New Christian Right, reconstructionist preachers and writers urge believers to become informed and get involved. But they urge involvement with a large measure of caution against the corrosive compromises built into the political process.[146]

The potential corruption of the political process is to be countered by keeping a clear eye on the scriptural laws that should shape all areas of life. The social order they would foster would be "non-neutral," a religiously based rule of law. For reconstructionists, in fact, laws are not just abstract principles but detailed guidelines that are as true today as when first handed down by God. Rushdoony's *Institutes of Biblical Law* outlines the plan, based on the covenants and law of Hebrew Scripture. Civil government is to be the servant of God, enforcing God's laws. Among the more controversial of Rushdoony's extractions from biblical law is the the suggestion that habitually rebellious children are to be put to death. And it is this wholesale adoption of Mosaic law that most troubles some younger followers who no longer call themselves reconstructionist for that reason. While they wish to see biblical principles guiding government, they do not believe that the details of Hebrew law can be implemented today.

Implementing any biblical principles in today's society requires, of course, a group willing to believe change is possible. This is a program dependent on a hopeful eschatology. Reconstructionists shun the pessimism of premillennialists and the escapism of the dispensationalists. The newsletter advertises a book purported to expose the "true origins" of Scofield and his ideas, in the hope that many dispensationalists will "turn from the system." Recent converts from older fundamentalist groups speak of being rescued from "Rapture fever." Theirs is now a "victory orientation": they expect that God will bless the preaching of the gospel with a steady addition of believers.

Through the faithful living of those believers, the Bible will eventually become the dominant force in the culture. Christians will win. They will not use force or political power to restrict nonbelievers; they will simply participate with God in a victory God has promised.

The process will be aided by God's judgment as well. Reconstructionists are quite sure that a nation which so routinely breaks all of God's laws (especially through the murder of millions of babies by abortion) can expect the punishment God promises those who break divine law. Using the energies of the universe, God's providence will bring lawlessness, humanism, socialism, and the other "isms" to destruction. Whatever stands in the way of Christian influence will be destroyed, clearing the way for God's people to rule. They look to Scripture (especially the history of Israel) as a model for God's blessing and cursing. (Deuteronomy 28 is the usual source for a view of God's judgment.) Those who obey are promised both spiritual and material prosperity, while those who disobey will be either slowly or suddenly destroyed.

Like their premillennial cousins, then, reconstructionists wait for a dramatic change in history. But they are not merely waiting. Because they anticipate having a role in the change, they seek to train while they wait. Their strategy "seeks to remove the political and institutional barriers to God's law in order to impose the rule of God's law . . . In most instances, this must be a 'bottom-up' program."[147] People who know God's laws begin at the grass-roots level to challenge a system they see as wrong. They practice in judging all of life and the people they meet by the biblical standards that will prevail in the coming time of dominion. And despite their insistence that God is the sole agent of redemption, they support any political program that will reduce taxes, take away the power of the government bureaucracy, and otherwise limit the state. They also work for laws that embody Christian morality.

The reconstructionist emphasis on grass-roots organizing to counter humanism with biblical government has found a growing audience. Its most natural home is in orthodox Presbyterian circles, but activist Baptists and charismatics are discovering their kinship with Rushdoony and North as well. Even Falwell has declared himself to be a Calvinist, and presidential candidate Pat Robertson asserted that he sees the United States Constitution as based on Calvinist principles. Robertson reportedly reads Rushdoony's publications (and is commended in them); for Falwell the direct links are less clear. Some local Moral Majority leaders have also been active in reconstructionism, but Falwell himself has not endorsed the program. For both fundamentalists like Falwell and charismatics like Robertson, the push to be active in the world has precipitated a reevaluation of theological roots that brings them closer to the ideas of a Christian social order that are explicit in the Calvinism of Christian reconstruction. In turn the reconstructionists recognize their kinship with some activist fundamentalists and recommend organizations like Christian Voice and Eagle Forum to reconstructionist readers.[148]

One of reconstruction's allies from the Pentecostal tradition is Bishop Earl Paulk of Chapel Hill Harvester Church in suburban Atlanta. Declaring his Pentecostal heritage entirely too dour, he gives a message of "kingdom now."[149] His worship services, televised in most of the major markets of the United States and throughout the world, are a mixture of charismatic enthusiasm, highly polished music and art, and prophetic pronouncements about Christian duty. His huge congregation is divided into twelve geographically based "covenant communities" whose members help each other find jobs, care for children, and monitor political and community affairs. The church's new buildings include a Christian shopping mall, and their school draws pupils from throughout the city. They dare to preach victory over sin, no matter what form that sin might take. They have tackled problems of safety at a nearby shopping center and regularly assist gays and lesbians in becoming "straight."[150] Members of this congregation are "reconstructing" their individual and community lives in some rather dramatic ways. And through a network of affiliated churches in other parts of the world, Bishop Paulk's message of Christian victory is heard widely indeed.

The influence of reconstructionism seems in fact to be largely through its secondary effects. Few are willing to adopt the program in all its Mosaic strictness. But growing numbers of activist fundamentalists and Pentecostals are finding a "dominion" theology compatible with their desires and activities.[151] They are realizing that their premillennial views sit uncomfortably alongside their activism, and a postmillennial system provides them with a logical rationale for working toward change.

Conclusions and a Look toward the Future

Out of the intellectual and social changes of the late nineteenth century came a movement that sought to defend the truth of Scripture. Developing a doctrine of inerrancy and adopting dispensational premillennialism, the movement provided for its followers an explanation for the apparent decline of Christian civilization and a language in which to describe their traditional orthodoxy. The movement thrived in the industrialized and pluralistic cities of the northeastern United States and southern Canada and came to flower in the chaotic years following the First World War. In religious and political battles during the 1920s, fundamentalist leaders sought to reassert their place as spokesmen for the culture.

When they lost those battles, fundamentalists began the process of taking their place alongside many other moral communities in the American cultural mosaic. They became outsiders to the spheres of influence in politics, education, and the press, but they built a lively subculture where conservative religion thrived for five decades. Its religious, educational, and missionary institutions provided a home for fundamentalists who sought to maintain their purity of life in the midst of a culture they saw as dominated by secular humanism. Their primary relationship to that outside culture was in aggressive evangelism, in seeking individual converts whose lives would be changed despite the deteriorating world around them. By the 1970s, however, the culture was again undergoing a moral upheaval, and the time was ripe for the message of certainty preached by fundamentalists. But they did not respond with a message of individual salvation alone. They had begun to see the benefits of being a more active participant in the public arena from which they had retreated. Threatened by secular humanism—not just as a deceiver stealing individual souls but as an aggressive institutional opponent encroaching on the territory they had created—they were ready to fight back.

In fighting back, late-twentieth-century fundamentalists have again created new institutions to embody their concerns. Building on the network of independent agencies and churches created since 1925, this resurgent movement has added organizations for political mobilization and influence. In addition, it has captured two major denominations and can draw on their institutional strength. This organizational base is likely to serve fundamentalists well in the decades to come, whether or not conservative religion remains a visible public force. Fundamentalism is likely to remain a force in North American culture for the foreseeable future. It has built an infrastructure that is unlikely to wither, and it draws on ideas still familiar to most as symbols of the culture. For individuals, fundamentalist churches provide a haven where life makes sense. In chaotic times and places, when individuals and communities are searching for moorings, the certainty and clarity of fundamentalism often seems appealing. Drawing as it does on a biblical heritage that is deeply ingrained in the culture, fundamentalism asserts a claim to be the rightful interpreter of the stories that shape American identity, and it offers a subcultural system in which those ideas can be nurtured and sustained. In revivals and local pulpits, the message of individual salvation will continue to contain a healthy mixture of exhortation to righteous living, and the righteous living espoused by fundamentalist preachers will continue to shape the vision of a good society held by those who listen.

Whether fundamentalism will remain a visible and active force in the larger culture is not yet clear. The political structures in place and the experience accumulated would seem to predict a continued role for fundamentalists as participants in political life. Once built, institutions tend to have a life of their own, shaping the actions of those who inhabit them. In addition, the ideas being borrowed from "dominion" theology offer a plausible rationale for continued public involvement in a way that neither evangelism nor premillennialism ever has. It seems entirely likely that fundamentalists may take their place in the public arena alongside other previously silent minority groups. Even though they may argue that only their particular Christian view has legitimacy, they will be doing so in the context of a pluralistic democracy in which their voices will be heard and weighed against many others.

Fundamentalism in the United States, then, has been shaped by a variety of cultural, ideological, organizational, and political forces. Ideologically fundamentalists have always combined a heavy emphasis on widely held traditional symbols with significant additions from newer systems of thought. They have also drawn clear boundaries between themselves and the rest of the culture, emphasizing distinctive ways of living and unambiguous conceptions of truth. And they have been equally clear that those outside their fold needed to change, although just how that change would take place has varied over time. At times they have been content to wait for divine intervention; at other times they have sought change one soul at a time; and at still other times they have taken matters into their own political hands.

Organizationally fundamentalists have been masters of innovation. After losing their places in existing institutions, they created a new infrastructure and have entered their current period of activism from a strong organizational base. The organizations have proven effective both in sustaining a separatist subculture and in mobilizing an activist movement. Since they have now created specifically political institutions, political involvement is likely to continue, whether it is highly visible or not. Jerry Falwell can retire and disband the Moral Majority without affecting the hundreds of local organizations that have been spawned by his efforts.[152] Once having created an organizational home, fundamentalism has proved able to enter and leave the public arena as circumstances demand.

Fundamentalism has been most politically active and culturally visible in times following periods of major cultural unsettlement. These have also been times when the power of government was expanding, and fundamentalists offered both a cultural re-ordering and a protest against an expanding state. The mix of active and passive, individual and political responses has seemed to depend on the degree of the threat fundamentalists perceived, the degree of potential responsiveness in the culture, and the strength of fundamentalists' own organizational resources. But what they are able to accomplish in the larger culture is limited by the pluralist assumptions of American and Canadian culture and law. They can offer their vision of a good society and demand to be heard. During certain periods their message may be adopted by a wide following, but fundamentalists in North America cannot impose their way of life without the consent of the governed.

Notes

1. One strategy meeting of conservative ministers with Bush included Presbyterian James Kennedy and Southern Baptist Convention president Jerry Vines, both pastors in Florida. See S. Hastey and M. Knox, "Bush Meets with Evangelicals, including Southern Baptists," *Baptist Press*, 4 August 1988.

2. The source of the prediction was a book called *88 Reasons Why the Rapture Will Be in 1988*, written by engineer Edgar C. Whisenant and published by the World Bible Society in Nashville. While admitting that he could not know the "day or hour" of the Lord's return (due to multiple time zones), he nevertheless was sure that he could calculate "the year, the month, and the week of the Lord's return" from the Bible's many "end time" prophecies (p. 3).

3. George M. Marsden, *Fundamentalism and American Culture* (Oxford: Oxford University Press, 1980), p. 158.

4. George Gallup, Jr., *Religion in America: 50 Years, 1935–1985* (Princeton: The Gallup Report, 1985).

5. George Gallup, Jr., *Public Opinion 1982* (Wilmington, Del.: Scholarly Resources, 1983).

6. J. D. Hunter makes this distinction between confessional and "born again" evangelicals in "Operationalizing Evangelicalism," *Sociological Analysis* 42 (1982): 363–72.

7. The notable exception, of course, is the Missouri Synod Lutheran Church, taken over by fundamentalists in the early 1970s, to be discussed below.

8. C. E. Lincoln, *Race, Religion, and the Continuing American Dilemma* (New York: Hill and Wang, 1984), pp. 92–93.

9. Ibid., p. 96.

10. On the black church, see E. F. Frazier, *The Negro Church in America*, and C. Eric Lincoln, *The Black Church since Frazier* (bound together; New York: Schocken Books, 1973); and J. R. Washington, Jr.,

"The Peculiar Peril and Promise of Black Folk Religion," in David E. Harrell, Jr., ed., *Varieties of Southern Evangelicalism* (Macon, Ga.: Mercer University Press, 1981), pp. 59–69.

11. See K. S. Kantzer, "The Charismatics Among Us," *Christianity Today,* 22 February 1980, pp. 245–49.

12. Meredith B. McGuire, *Pentecostal Catholics: Power, Charisma, and Order in a Religious Movement* (Philadelphia: Temple University Press, 1982); Mary J. Neitz, *Charisma and Community: A Study of Religious Commitment Within the Charismatic Renewal* (New Brunswick, N.J.: Transaction Books, 1987); and Joseph H. Fichter, *The Catholic Cult of the Paraclete* (New York: Sheed & Ward, 1975), offer helpful accounts of the charismatic movement.

13. For overviews of Mormon history and practice, see Jan Shipps, *Mormonism* (Urbana: University of Illinois Press, 1985); and Thomas O'Dea, *The Mormons* (Chicago: University of Chicago Press, 1964).

14. On Billy Graham, see William Martin, "Billy Graham," in *Varieties of Southern Evangelicalism*, pp. 71–88. On the development of evangelicalism since the 1940s, see George M. Marsden, *Reforming Fundamentalism: Fuller Seminary and the New Evangelicalism* (Grand Rapids, Mich.: Wm. B. Eerdmans, 1987); and J. D. Hunter, *Evangelicalism: The Coming Generation* (Chicago: University of Chicago Press, 1987).

15. Jerry Falwell, *The Fundamentalist Phenomenon* (Garden City, N.Y.: Doubleday-Galilee, 1981), contains a discussion of the contrasts from his point of view.

16. Kathleen C. Boone, *The Bible Tells Them So* (Albany: State University of New York Press, 1989), p. 24.

17. Cf. Alan Peshkin, *God's Choice: The Total World of a Fundamentalist Christian School* (Chicago: University of Chicago Press, 1986); and Nancy T. Ammerman, *Bible Believers: Fundamentalists in the Modern World* (New Brunswick, N.J.: Rutgers University Press, 1987).

18. On fundamentalist ideas about the relationship between science and religion, see also S. D. Rose, *Keeping Them Out of the Hands of Satan* (New York: Routledge, 1988).

19. *The Proceedings of the Conference on Biblical Inerrancy* (Nashville: Broadman Press, 1987) contains a number of interesting examples of fundamentalist modes of interpretation. See especially Robert Preus, "The Inerrancy of Scripture," pp. 47–60. For a discussion of more "everyday" processes of interpretation in a fundamentalist congregation, see Ammerman, *Bible Believers*, chap. 4; and Boone, *The Bible Tells Them So*.

20. On the role of the fundamentalist pastor, see Ammerman, *Bible Believers*, chap. 7; and Boone, *The Bible Tells Them So*, chap. 6.

21. The 1988 film by Martin Scorsese depicts Jesus as doubtful about his mission and subject to human lusts.

22. See Hunter, *Evangelicalism*, chap. 4, on the history of the "traditional" family.

23. Quoted in Marsden, *Fundamentalism and American Culture,* p. 55.

24. James Barr makes this point as well in *Fundamentalism* (Philadelphia: Westminster Press, 1978), pp. 270ff.

25. Robert M. Grant and David Tracy, *A Short History of the Interpretation of the Bible*, 2d ed. (Philadelphia: Fortress, 1984), pp. 110ff.

26. Martin E. Marty, *The Modern Schism* (New York: Harper and Row, 1969).

27. James S. Olson, *The Ethnic Dimension in American History* (New York: St. Martin's Press, 1979), p. 206.

28. Martin E. Marty, *Righteous Empire* (New York: Dial, 1970); and Robert T. Handy, *A Christian America* (New York: Oxford University Press, 1971).

29. Williston Walker, *A History of the Christian Church*. (New York: Charles Scribner's Sons, 4th ed., 1985).

30. On Jehovah's Witnesses, see James A. Beckford, *The Trumpet of Prophecy* (Oxford: Basil Blackwell, 1975). On Mormons, see Jan Shipps, *Mormonim*. On the history of Pentecostalism, see Robert M. Anderson, *Vision of the Disinherited* (New York: Oxford University Press, 1979). And on Seventh

Day Adventists, see Gary Schwartz, *Sect Ideologies and Social Status* (Chicago: University of Chicago Press, 1970).

31. Clifford Geertz, *Islam Observed* (Chicago: University of Chicago Press, 1968), p. 17.

32. This discussion is based largely on J. D. Pulis, "Jerry Falwell and the Moral Majority: A Case Study of the Relationship between Theology and Ideology" (Ph.D. diss., Emory University, 1986). See especially chap. 3.

33. Ernest R. Sandeen argues in *The Roots of Fundamentalism* (Chicago: University of Chicago Press, 1970) that millenarians were the driving force in the movement. Marsden, in *Fundamentalism and American Culture*, offers a more cautious account of their role, as does Timothy P. Weber in his history of premillennialism, *Living in the Shadow of the Second Coming* (Chicago: University of Chicago Press, 1987).

34. Marty, *Modern Schism*.

35. On revivals, see William G. McLoughlin, *Modern Revivalism: Charles Grandison Finney to Billy Graham* (New York: Ronald Press, 1959); and Donald Dayton, *Discovering an Evangelical Heritage* (New York: Harper, 1976).

36. John B. Boles, "Evangelical Protestantism in the Old South: From Religious Dissent to Cultural Dominance," in Charles R. Wilson, ed., *Religion in the South* (Jackson: University of Mississippi Press, 1985), pp. 13–34.

37. Razelle Frankl, *Televangelism: The Marketing of Popular Religion* (Carbondale, Ill.: Southern Illinois University Press, 1987); and McLoughlin, *Modern Revivalism*.

38. S. Sizer, "Politics and Apolitical Religion: The Great Urban Revivals of the Late Nineteenth Century," *Church History* 48, no. 1 (1979): 81–98.

39. T. L. Smith, *Revivalism and Social Reform* (New York: Abingdon, 1957).

40. Marsden, *Fundamentalism and American Culture*, chaps. 8–9.

41. Sandeen, *Roots of Fundamentalism*, pp. 174ff.

42. Descriptions of these conferences can be found in Sandeen, *Roots of Fundamentalism*, pp. 135ff; Marsden, *Fundamentalism and American Culture*, p. 62; and Weber, *Living in the Shadow*, pp. 26–28.

43. Sandeen, *Roots of Fundamentalism*, chap. 6.

44. Ibid., pp. 148ff.

45. Charles J. Ratcliff, "A Study of the Social Objectives of the Member Schools of the American Association of Bible Colleges" (Ed.D. diss., University of Cincinnati, 1979).

46. Marsden, *Fundamentalism and American Culture*, pp. 35, 119.

47. Norman F. Furniss, *The Fundamentalist Controversy* (New Haven: Yale University Press, 1954), chap. 4.

48. *The Fundamentals*, A. C. Dixon, general editor (Chicago: Testimony Publishing, 1910–15).

49. Professor Charles Erdman of Princeton Seminary, "The Church and Socialism," in vol. 12 of *The Fundamentals*.

50. Robert K. Murray, *Red Scare: A Study of National Hysteria, 1919–1920* (New York: McGraw-Hill, 1955).

51. On the battles, see Furniss, *Fundamentalist Controversy;* Stewart G. Cole, *The History of Fundamentalism* (1931; reprint, Westport, Conn.: Greenwood Press, 1971), pp. 65–131; Sandeen, *Roots of Fundamentalism*, pp. 250–66; and Marsden, *Fundamentalism and American Culture*, pp. 164–95. Furniss and Cole include discussions of related controversies in the Methodist, Episcopal, and Disciples of Christ denominations.

52. Furniss includes the Southern Baptists and southern Presbyterians. Marsden, in *Fundamentalism and American Culture*, p. 165, and B. Primer, "The failure of southern fundamentalism" (Paper presented to the Southwestern Historical Association, Houston, Tex., 1980), make the point that southern conservatism was still thoroughly entrenched.

53. Marsden, *Fundamentalism and American Culture,* p. 149.

54. Sandeen, *Roots of Fundamentalism*, pp. 76–100.

55. John L. Eighmy cites the role of E. Y. Mullins, president of the Southern Baptist Theological Seminary, as important in mediating the dispute. *Churches in Cultural Captivity: A History of the Social Attitudes of Southern Baptists,* rev. ed. (Knoxville, Tenn.: University of Tennessee Press, 1987), p. 126.

56. Marsden, *Fundamentalism and American Culture,* p. 186.

57. Cf. Sandeen, *Roots of Fundamentalism,* pp. 57–71; Marsden, *Fundamentalism and American Culture,* pp. 189–90.

58. This term was popularized by Tim LaHaye in *The Battle for the Mind* (Old Tappan, N.J.: Revell, 1980).

59. Cited in Marsden, *Reforming Fundamentalism,* p. 78.

60. The worldview of ordinary fundamentalists is discussed at length in Ammerman, *Bible Believers,* chap. 4.

61. See Marsden, *Reforming Fundamentalism,* pp. 41ff.

62. The story of Norris's path toward schism is told in M. G. Toulouse, "A case study in schism: J. Frank Norris and the SBC," *Foundations* 4 (1981): 32–48.

63. Robert A. Baker, *The Southern Baptist Convention and Its People* (Nashville, Tenn.: Broadman Press, 1974), p. 356.

64. On fundamentalist denominations, see G. W. Dollar, *A History of Fundamentalism in America* (Greenville, S.C.: Bob Jones University Press, 1973), pp. 213ff.

65. Fundamentalist congregational life is discussed in Ammerman, *Bible Believers,* chap. 6, and in Boone, *The Bible Tells Them So,* chap. 5.

66. Marsden, *Reforming Fundamentalism,* p. 41.

67. The best discussion of institutional growth in this period is found in Joel A. Carpenter, "Fundamentalist Institutions and the Rise of Evangelical Protestantism, 1929–1942," *Church History* 49 (1980): 62–75.

68. Dollar, *History of Fundamentalism,* pp. 250ff.

69. See Bill Bright, *Come Help Change the World* (Old Tappan, N.J.: Revell, 1970).

70. Dollar, *History of Fundamentalism,* pp. 257ff.

71. Marsden, *Reforming Fundamentalism,* p. 22.

72. Marsden, *Fundamentalism and American Culture,* pp. 28–32.

73. Marsden, *Reforming Fundamentalism,* pp. 45–47.

74. Cited in Carpenter, "Fundamentalist Institutions," p. 66.

75. Ibid., p. 68.

76. Quoted in D. P. Fuller, *Give the Winds a Mighty Voice* (Waco, Tex.: Word Books, 1972), p. 110.

77. Frankl, *Televangelism,* pp. 68ff.

78. Sydney E. Ahlstrom, *A Religious History of the American People,* vol. 2 (Garden City, N.Y.: Doubleday Image Books), p. 418. This politically radical segment is the only aspect of fundamentalism mentioned by Ahlstrom in describing this period. Until the late 1970s, most historians treated fundamentalism similarly. Its existence as a vital religious sector was ignored.

79. Leo Ribuffo, *The Old Christian Right* (Philadelphia: Temple University Press, 1983), p. 114.

80. See Ribuffo on Winrod and Smith. On the political radicals of this period, see also Marsden, *Fundamentalism and American Culture,* p. 210; Gary K. Clabaugh, *Thunder on the Right: The Protestant Fundamentalism* (Chicago: Nelson-Hall, 1974), p. 83; and Erling Jorstad, *The Politics of Doomsday: Fundamentalists of the Far Right* (Nashville, Tenn.: Abingdon Press, 1970), chap. 1.

81. Weber, *Living in the Shadow,* chap. 6. See also H. Lindsey, *The Road to Holocaust* (New York: Bantam Books, 1989) for an explanation of why premillennialists should not be anti-Semites.

82. W. R. Glass, "Fundamentalism's Prophetic Vision of the Jews: The 1930s," *Jewish Social Studies* 47 (1985): 63–76.

83. Nancy T. Ammerman, "Fundamentalists Proselytizing Jews: Incivility in Preparation for the Rapture," in *Pushing the Faith: Proselytism and Civility in a Pluralistic World,*

ed. Martin E. Marty and Frederick E. Greenspahn (New York: Crossroad, 1988), pp. 109–22.

84. Clabaugh, *Thunder on the Right;* Jorstad, *Politics of Doomsday;* Phillip Finch, *God, Guts, and Guns* (New York: Seaview, 1983).

85. Finch estimates the total membership of such organizations at about one hundred thousand.

86. Quoted in Marsden, *Reforming Fundamentalism*, p. 69.

87. On McIntire, see Jorstad, *Politics of Doomsday*, pp. 27–36; and Marsden, *Reforming Fundamentalism*, pp. 65ff.

88. Quoted in Marsden, *Reforming Fundamentalism,* p. 220; italics mine.

89. Marsden's *Reforming Fundamentalism* is the story of this shift as seen in the life of Fuller Theological Seminary.

90. Farley P. Butler, Jr., "Billy Graham and the End of Evangelical Unity" (Ph.D. diss., University of Florida, 1976), p. 160.

91. Dollar, *History of Fundamentalism,* p. 210; Falwell, *Fundamentalist Phenomenon,* pp. 129–31.

92. Marsden, *Reforming Fundamentalism,* pp. 220ff.

93. Robert Wuthnow cites these factors of national upheaval and self-doubt in "The Political Rebirth of American Evangelicals," in *The New Christian Right,* ed. Robert C. Liebman and Robert Wuthnow (Hawthorne, N.Y.: Aldine, 1983).

94. Steven M. Tipton, *Getting Saved from the Sixties* (Berkeley: University of California Press, 1982), pp. 37–38. See also R. S. Warner, *New Wine in Old Wineskins* (Berkeley: University of California Press, 1988).

95. J. C. McKinney and L. B. Bourque, "The Changing South: National Incorporation of a Region," *American Sociological Review* 36 (1971): 399–412.

96. R. W. Stump, "Regional Migration and Religious Patterns in the American South" (A paper presented to the Society for the Scientific Study of Religion, 1985).

97. Nancy T. Ammerman, "The New South and the New Baptists," *Christian Century* 103, no. 17 (1986): 486–88.

98. Quoted in Ammerman, *Bible Believers*, p. 41.

99. B. Johnson and M. Shibley, "How New is the New Christian Right?" (Paper presented to the Society for the Scientific Study of Religion, Savannah, 1985); E. Rosenberg, "The 'New Federalism,' The 'New Racism,' and the 'New Right': Are Southern Baptists Still Captive of the Old Culture?" (Paper presented to the Religious Research Association, Chicago, 1988).

100. See L. J. Lorentzen, "Evangelical Life-Style Concerns Expressed in Political Action," *Sociological Analysis* 41 (1980):144–54.

101. This view is supported by Richard J. Neuhaus in *The Naked Public Square* (Grand Rapids, Mich.: Wm. B. Eerdmans, 1984), and in several essays included in Neuhaus and Michael Cromartie's *Piety and Politics: Evangelicals and Fundamentalists Confront the World* (Washington, D.C.: Ethics and Public Policy Center, 1987).

102. Jorstad provides a helpful expanded list of the issues concerning fundamentalist activists in *The New Christian Right, 1981–1988* (Lewiston, N.Y.: Edwin Mellen Press, 1988), pp. 6–8.

103. W. D. Sapp makes this point about Southern Baptist growth in "Southern Baptist Responses to the American Economy, 1900–1980," *Baptist History and Heritage* 16 (1981): 3–11.

104. Jeffrey K. Hadden, "Religious Broadcasting and the Mobilization of the New Christian Right," *Journal for the Scientific Study of Religion* 26, no. 1 (1987): 1–24.

105. On the technology and structure of television fund-raising, see Razelle Frankl, "Television and Popular Religion: Changes in Church Offerings," in David G. Bromley and Anson D. Shupe, Jr., eds., *New Christian Politics* (Macon, Ga.: Mercer University Press, 1984), pp. 129–38. Such fund-raising power almost inevitably invited corruption. The lavish lifestyle of Jim and Tammy Bakker eventually overstepped the bounds of what would be permitted by the courts.

106. This insight was suggested by Joel Carpenter in conversation, May 1988.

107. Jerry Falwell, *Listen America!* (New York: Doubleday, 1980), p. 53.

108. V. D. Nordin and W. L. Turner, "More Than Segregationist Academies: The Growing Protestant Fundamentalist Schools," *Phi Delta Kappan,* February 1980, pp. 391–94.

109. D. B. Fleming and T. C. Hunt, "The World as Seen by Students in Accelerated Christian Education Schools," *Phi Delta Kappan* 68, no. 7 (1987): 518–23.

110. Quoted in Ammerman, *Bible Believers,* p. 176.

111. For descriptions of Christian academies, see Peshkin, *God's Choice;* Ammerman, *Bible Believers,* chap. 10; and Rose, *Keeping Them Out.*

112. Rose, *Keeping Them Out,* p. 10. A similar argument is made in Ammerman, *Bible Believers,* pp. 195ff.

113. E. Brooks Holifield, "The Three Strands of Jimmy Carter's Religion," *The New Republic,* 5 June 1976, pp. 15–17.

114. Falwell, *Fundamentalist Phenomenon,* p. 188.

115. Hadden, "Religious Broadcasting," and Liebman, "Mobilizing the Moral Majority," in *New Christian Right,* ed. Liebman and Wuthnow, pp. 50–74.

116. Attempts to assess that strength include S. Rothenberg and F. Newport, *The Evangelical Voter* (Washington, D.C.: The Institute for Government and Politics, 1984); J. H. Simpson, "Support for the Moral Majority and Its Sociomoral Platform" in Bromley and Shupe, *New Christian Politics,* pp. 65–68; and S. D. Johnson and J. B. Tamney, "The Christian Right and the 1984 Presidential Election," *Review of Religious Research* 27, no. 2 (1985): 124–33.

117. See, for example, S. D. Johnson and J. B. Tamney, "Factors Influencing Vote for a Christian Right Candidate" (Paper presented to the Society for the Scientific Study of Religion, Louisville, 1987), and James Guth and J. C. Greene, "The GOP and the Christian Right: The Case of Pat Robertson's Campaign Contributors" (Paper presented to the Midwest Political Science Association, Chicago, 1987).

118. Hadden makes this point in "Televangelism and the Future of American Politics," in Bromley and Shupe, *New Christian Politics,* pp. 151–68.Estimates of strength varied widely from exaggerations immediately following the 1980 election to a series of debunking studies, including Johnson and Tamney's "The Christian Right and the 1980 Presidential Election," *Journal for the Scientific Study of Religion* 21, no. 2 (1982): 123–31; and James Guth's "Southern Baptist Clergy: Vanguard of the Christian Right?" in Liebman and Wuthnow, *New Christian Right,* pp. 118–32. However, by 1984 the assessment changed again to account for the organizational strength that accrued to the movement over time. Johnson and Tamney's "The Christian Right and the 1984 Presidential Election" and Guth's "Political Activism Among a Religious Elite: Southern Baptist Ministers in the 1984 Election" (Paper presented to the Society for the Scientific Study of Religion, Savannah, 1985) were no longer debunking.

119. Frankl, *Televangelism,* chap. 9, analyzes the differing contents of the various programs.

120. A. D. Hertzke, *Representing God in Washington* (Knoxville, Tenn.: University of Tennessee Press, 1988), chap. 3, is an excellent analysis of religious lobbying strategies and accomplishments.

121. Jorstad, *The New Christian Right,* p. 28.

122. Mary J. Neitz, "Family, State and God: Ideologies of the Right to Life Movement," *Sociological Analysis* 42 (1981): 265–76.

123. Falwell, *Fundamentalist Phenomenon,* p. 191.

124. A point made by Arthur E. Farnsley, "The Relationship of Belief to Institutional Location in Moral Decisionmaking: The Case of the Southern Baptists" (Paper presented to the Association for the Sociology of Religion, Atlanta, 1988), and by M. A. Cavanaugh, "Secularization and the Politics of Traditionalism: The Case of the Right-to-Life Movement," *Sociological Forum* 1 (1986): 251–83; and F. Lechner, "Fundamentalism and Sociocultural Revital-

ization in America: A Sociological Interpretation," *Sociological Analysis* 46 (1985): 243–60.

125. Falwell, *Fundamentalist Phenomenon*, p. 221.

126. Falwell, *Listen America!* p. 15.

127. Donald Heinz, "The Struggle to Define America," in Liebman and Wuthnow, *New Christian Right,* pp. 133–48.

128. Hadden, "Religious Broadcasting," pp. 1–24.

129. K. E. Marquart, *Anatomy of an Explosion: Missouri in Lutheran Perspective* (Fort Wayne, Ind.: Concordia Theological Seminary Press, 1977), is a conservative account of the controversy. F. W. Danker, *No Room in the Brotherhood* (Saint Louis: Clayton Publishing, 1976), provides an account by a member of the Seminex faculty. A very detailed report and a more objective analysis of the controversy can be found in L. A. S. Hayes, "The Rhetoric of Controversy in the Lutheran Church—Missouri Synod with Particular Emphasis on the Years 1969–1976" (Ph.D. diss., University of Wisconsin, Madison, 1980).

130. Marquardt, *Anatomy of an Explosion*, p. 138.

131. H. L. Turner, "Southern Baptist Cosmogony and Eschatology: Mechanisms for Coping with Twentieth Century Societal Stress" (Paper presented to the Religious Research Association, 1988).

132. On the relationship between southern social change and the Southern Baptist Convention, see N. T. Ammerman, *Baptist Battles: Social Change and Religious Conflict in the Southern Baptist Convention* (New Brunswick, N.J.: Rutgers University Press, 1990).

133. Nancy T. Ammerman, "Southern Baptists and the New Christian Right" (Paper presented to the Society for the Scientific Study of Religion, Louisville, Ky., 1987).

134. See Gary North, *The Theology of Christian Resistance* (Tyler, Tex.: Geneva Divinity School Press, 1983), pp. 60ff.

135. See A. P. Jones, "The Imperative of Christian Action: Getting Involved as a Biblical Duty," *Journal of Christian Reconstruction* 8, no. 1 (1981): 86–131, for a list of recommended publications.

136. Reprinted in *Journal of Christian Reconstruction* 2, no. 2 (1975–76): 117–28.

137. M. A. Cavanaugh, "Puritanism by Way of Mind Cure: Christian Reconstructionism and Religious Differentiation" (Paper presented to the Association for the Sociology of Religion, Atlanta, 1988).

138. Cf., for example, Gary North's *Foundations of Christian Scholarship* (Vallecito, Cal.: Ross House Books, 1979).

139. T. Rose, "On Reconstruction and the American Republic," *Journal of Christian Reconstruction* 5, no. 1 (1978): 34.

140. Gary North, "Comprehensive Redemption: A Theology for Social Action," *Journal of Christian Reconstruction* 8, no. 1 (1981): 19.

141. Rousas J. Rushdoony, "Biblical Law and Western Civilization," *Journal of Christian Reconstruction* 2, no. 2 (1975): 5.

142. J. Lofton, "The Naked Public Neuhaus," *Chalcedon Report* 283 (February 1989):12.

143. O. Scott, "Caucasian Self-Hatred," *Chalcedon Report* 283 (February 1989): 2–3.

144. *Chalcedon Report* 273 (April 1988): 8–9.

145. Although the goal seems to be abolition of all racism, one cannot read these revisionist versions of white history without being reminded of the rhetoric of more radical right-wing groups.

146. Volume 8, no. 1, of *Journal of Christian Reconstruction* is a symposium on social action, while volume 5, no. 1, was on politics. See especially articles by A. P. Jones in the former and by R. Walton and Gary North in the latter.

147. North, *Theology of Christian Resistance,* p. 63.

148. Jones, "The Imperative of Christian Action."

149. See P. Thigpen, "What's the Fuss about 'Kingdom Now'?," *Ministries Today*, July/August 1988, pp. 33–39, for a theological treatment of Paulk's preaching.

150. For a description of the ministry to homosexuals, see Scott Thumma, "Straightening Identities" (M.Div. Honors Thesis, Emory University, 1987).

151. Based on the author's interview with one of the movement's leading pastors.

152. D. Shribman, "Going Mainstream: Religious Right Drops High-Profile Tactics, Works on Local Level," *Wall Street Journal,* 26 September 1989, p. 1.

Select Bibliography

Ahlstrom, Sydney E. *A Religious History of the American People.* Garden City, N.Y.: Doubleday Image Books, 1972.

Ammerman, Nancy T. *Bible Believers: Fundamentalists in the Modern World.* New Brunswick, N.J.: Rutgers University Press, 1987.

———. *Baptist Battles: Social Change and Religious Conflict in the Southern Baptist Convention.* New Brunswick, N.J.: Rutgers University Press, 1990.

Anderson, Robert M. *Vision of the Disinherited.* New York: Oxford Press, 1979.

Baker, Robert A. *The Southern Baptist Convention and Its People.* Nashville, Tenn.: Broadman Press, 1974.

Barr, James. *Fundamentalism.* Philadelphia: Westminster Press, 1978.

Beckford, James A. *The Trumpet of Prophecy.* Oxford: Basil Blackwell, 1975.

Boone, Kathleen C. *The Bible Tells Them So.* Albany: State University of New York Press, 1989.

Bright, Bill. *Come Help Change the World.* Old Tappan, N.J.: Revell, 1970.

Bromley, David G., and Anson D. Shupe, Jr., eds. *New Christian Politics.* Macon, Ga.: Mercer University Press, 1984.

Clabaugh, Gary K. *Thunder on the Right.* Chicago: Nelson-Hall, 1974.

Cole, Stewart G. *The History of Fundamentalism.* 1931. Reprint. Westport, Conn.: Greenwood Press, 1971.

Danker, F. W. *No Room in the Brotherhood.* Saint Louis: Clayton Publishing, 1976.

Dayton, Donald. *Discovering an Evangelical Heritage.* New York: Harper, 1976.

Dollar, G. W. *A History of Fundamentalism in America.* Greenville, S.C.: Bob Jones University Press, 1973.

Eighmy, John L. *Churches in Cultural Captivity: A History of the Social Attitudes of Southern Baptists.* Rev. ed. Knoxville, Tenn.: University of Tennessee Press, 1987.

Falwell, Jerry. *Listen America!* New York: Doubleday, 1980.

———. *The Fundamentalist Phenomenon.* Garden City, N.Y. Doubleday-Galilee, 1981.

Fichter, Joseph H. *The Catholic Cult of the Paraclete.* New York: Sheed and Ward, 1975.

Finch, Phillip. *God, Guts, and Guns.* New York: Seaview, 1983.

Frankl, Razelle. *Televangelism: The Marketing of Popular Religion.* Carbondale, Ill.: Southern Illinois University Press, 1987.

Frazier, E. F. *The Negro Church in America,* and C. Eric Lincoln, *The Black Church since Frazier.* Bound together. New York: Schocken Books, 1973.

Fuller, D. P. *Give the Winds a Mighty Voice.* Waco, Tex.: Word Books, 1972.

Furniss, Norman F. *The Fundamentalist Controversy.* New Haven: Yale University Press, 1954.

Gallup, George, Jr. *Public Opinion 1982.* Wilmington, Del.: Scholarly Resources, 1983.

———. *Religion in America: 50 Years, 1935–1985.* Princeton: The Gallup Report, 1985.

Geertz, Clifford. *Islam Observed.* Chicago: University of Chicago Press, 1968.

Grant, Robert M., and David Tracy. *A Short History of the Interpretation of the Bible.* 2d ed. Philadelphia: Fortress Press, 1984.

Handy, Robert T. *A Christian America.* New York: Oxford University Press, 1971.

Harrell, David E., Jr., ed. *Varieties of Southern Evangelicalism*. Macon, Ga.: Mercer University Press, 1981.

Hertzke, A. D. *Representing God in Washington*. Knoxville, Tenn.: University of Tennessee Press, 1988.

Hunter, J. D. *American Evangelicalism: Conservative Religion and the Quandary of Modernity*. New Brunswick, N.J.: Rutgers University Press, 1983.

———. *Evangelicalism: The Coming Generation*. Chicago: University of Chicago Press, 1987.

Jorstad, Erling. *The Politics of Doomsday: Fundamentalists of the Far Right*. Nashville, Tenn.: Abingdon Press, 1970.

———. *The New Christian Right, 1981–1988*. Lewiston, N.Y.: Edwin Mellen Press, 1988.

LaHaye, Tim. *The Battle for the Mind*. Old Tappan, N.J.: Revell, 1980.

Liebman, Robert C., and Robert Wuthnow, eds. *The New Christian Right*. Hawthorne, N.Y.: Aldine, 1983.

Lincoln, C. E. *Race, Religion, and the Continuing American Dilemma*. New York: Hill and Wang, 1984.

Lindsey, H. *The Road to Holocaust*. New York: Bantam Books, 1989.

Marquart, K. E. *Anatomy of an Explosion: Missouri in Lutheran Perspective*. Fort Wayne, Ind.: Concordia Theological Seminary Press, 1977.

Marsden, George M. *Fundamentalism and American Culture*. Oxford: Oxford University Press, 1980.

———. *Evangelicalism and Modern America*. Grand Rapids, Mich.: Wm. B. Eerdmans, 1984.

———. *Reforming Fundamentalism: Fuller Seminary and the New Evangelicalism*. Grand Rapids, Mich.: Wm. B. Eerdmans, 1987.

Marty, Martin E. *The Modern Schism*. New York: Harper and Row, 1969.

———. *Righteous Empire*. New York: Dial, 1970.

Marty, Martin E., and Frederick E. Greenspahn, eds. *Pushing the Faith: Proselytism and Civility in a Pluralistic World*. New York: Crossroad, 1988.

McGuire, Meredith B. *Pentecostal Catholics: Power, Charisma, and Order in a Religious Movement*. Philadelphia: Temple University Press, 1982.

McLoughlin, William G. *Modern Revivalism: Charles Grandison Finney to Billy Graham*. New York: Ronald Press, 1959.

Neitz, Mary J. *Charisma and Community: A Study of Religious Commitment Within the Charismatic Renewal*. New Brunswick, N.J.: Transaction Books, 1987.

Neuhaus, Richard J. *The Naked Public Square*. Grand Rapids, Mich.: Wm. B. Eerdmans, 1984.

Neuhaus, Richard J., and Michael Cromartie. *Piety and Politics: Evangelicals and Fundamentalists Confront the World*. Washington, D.C.: Ethics and Public Policy Center, 1987.

North, Gary. *Foundations of Christian Scholarship*. Vallecito, Calif.: Ross House Books, 1979.

———. *The Theology of Christian Resistance*. Tyler Tex.: Geneva Divinity School Press, 1983.

O'Dea, Thomas F. *The Mormons*. Chicago: University of Chicago Press, 1964.

Peshkin, Alan. *God's Choice: The Total World of a Fundamentalist Christian School*. Chicago: University of Chicago Press, 1986.

The Proceedings of the Conference on Biblical Inerrancy. Nashville: Broadman Press, 1987.

Pulis, J. D. "Jerry Falwell and the Moral Majority: A Case Study of the Relationship between Theology and Ideology" (Ph.D. diss., Emory University, 1986).

Rose, S. D. *Keeping Them Out of the Hands of Satan*. New York: Routledge, 1988.

Sandeen, Ernest R. *The Roots of Fundamentalism*. Chicago: University of Chicago Press, 1970.

Schwartz, Gary. *Sect Ideologies and Social Status*. Chicago: University of Chicago Press, 1970.

Shipps, Jan. *Mormonism*. Urbana: University of Illinois Press, 1985.

Smith, T. L. *Revivalism and Social Reform*. New York: Abingdon, 1957.

Tipton, Steven, M. *Getting Saved from the Sixties*. Berkeley: University of California Press, 1982.

Walker, Williston. *A History of the Christian Church*. 4th ed. New York: Charles Scribner's Sons, 1985.

Warner, R. S. *New Wine in Old Wineskins*. Berkeley: University of California Press, 1988.

Weber, Timothy P. *Living in the Shadow of the Second Coming*. Chicago: University of Chicago Press, 1987.

Whisenant, Edgar C. *88 Reasons Why the Rapture Will Be in 1988*. Nashville: World Bible Society, n.d.

Wilson, Charles R., ed. *Religion in the South*. Jackson: University of Mississippi Press, 1985.

CHAPTER
2

Roman Catholic Traditionalism and Activist Conservatism in the United States

1. Roman Catholic Traditionalism

William D. Dinges

On 30 June 1988, under a tent-church constructed in the shadow of his flagship seminary in Ecône, Switzerland, eighty-three-year-old French Archbishop Marcel Lefebvre consecrated four priests to the Roman Catholic episcopacy.[1] The consecrations were necessary, according to the archbishop, because of the "apostasy" and "iniquity" of the See of Peter in capitulating to the influences of "Liberalism, Communism, Socialism, Modernism, Zionism" that had been "demolishing" the Roman Catholic faith in the wake of the Second Vatican Council (1962–65). Lefebvre intimated that the climactic events of the day had been foretold by prophesies of the Virgin Mary concerning corruption and apostasy in the Church in the twentieth century: "she speaks of a prelate who will absolutely oppose this wave of apostasy and impiety."[2]

As a result of the unauthorized consecrations, Archbishop Lefebvre, his new bishops, and all members of his priestly fraternity, the Society of Saint Pius X, were excommunicated, thereby provoking the first major schism in the Roman Catholic Church since the separation of the Polish National Catholic Church of America at the turn of the century. However, in the context of the turmoil and conflict besetting Catholics in the postconciliar era, the dramatic consecrations at Ecône were not an isolated event but the culmination of a two-decades-long confrontation between a movement of self-proclaimed "Roman Catholic traditionalists" and the magisterium (episcopal teaching office) of the Church.

While the confrontation between traditionalist Catholics and the magisterium has often been portrayed in the media as little more than a nostalgic campaign to save the "old Mass," the Latin Tridentine form of the liturgy that had been mandated by a papal edict (*Quo Primum,* 1570) issued by Pope Pius V in the wake of the Council of Trent (1545–63), the nature of the conflict is in fact both more complex and profound, challenging both the meaning and validity of the Second Vatican Council itself and, ultimately, the power and authority to define Catholic identity and lay claim to the "true Church."

The emergence of a "traditionalist" anticonciliar movement spearheaded by a "rebel" archbishop indicates the scope of the conflict that has divided Catholics in the postconciliar era: the public challenge to hierarchical authority is not confined to liberal or progressive elements or to "dissenting" theologians but can also be found among those who hold positions of hierarchical leadership and who claim the high ground of Catholic orthodoxy. The rise of the traditionalist movement also illustrates how Catholicism's troubled encounter with modernity has spawned movements and ideological orientations closely paralleling those associated with Protestantism's own fundamentalist reactions to the modern world. Indeed, Archbishop Lefebvre's brand of Roman Catholic traditionalism is a militant and organized reaction against the intellectual and cultural inroads of modernism long resisted by leadership elites in the Church. Traditionalism seeks to arrest and reverse religious change among Catholics and to preserve the ideological, organizational, and cultic patterns altered, abandoned, or discredited in the postconciliar era. Traditionalism is also a protest against the blurring of Catholic identity and the loss of Catholic hegemony in the social, cultural, and political sphere.

The Second Vatican Council: Conservative Opposition

With the unfolding of the conciliar reforms, the term *aggiornamento* (updating) came to signify for many conservative Catholics a radical and "contradictory" departure from many of the doctrines, disciplines, and symbols of spiritual reality that were held to constitute the essence of the Roman Catholic faith. In the wake of the Council, the time-honored "eternal truths" taught by Christ, entrusted to the Apostles, codified as "objective" theological knowledge, sanctioned in solemn terms by centuries of tradition, Church law, and solemn pontifical pronouncements, and defended with the blood of martyrs appeared substantially altered by the very authority consecrated to their preservation. Furthermore, anxiety over the inherent dangers of aggiornamento was dramatically reinforced by "excesses" accompanying the implementation of the reforms (especially in the area of the liturgy) and by the climate of conflict, polarization, and institutional dysfunction that followed in the wake of the Council.

By the late 1960s, a new form of "underground church" began to appear among Catholic populations. This time, however, the phrase referred not to small, unauthorized groups of liberal laity and priests meeting to celebrate the most ancient of the Church's public rituals but instead, to groups of self-proclaimed Roman Catholic traditionalists whose far-flung rebel congregations and "wildcat" parishes were clinging tenaciously to the traditional forms of the sacraments and devotional piety, to "pure" and "unadulterated" doctrine and discipline, and to what they viewed as Catholicism's core sacramental ritual—the Latin Tridentine Holy Sacrifice of the Mass. By the mid-1970s, the traditionalist movement had emerged as a worldwide phenomenon, a reactionary Catholic subculture whose defense of the Tridentine liturgy had come to symbolize the repudiation of aggiornamento.

The rise of the traditionalist movement itself, however, did not go uncontested, even in the climate of ecclesial pluralism and tolerance following the Council. Catholic progressives chided traditionalists for their "separation anxieties" in refusing to give up the old Mass[3] while more serious accusations of disobedience and malfeasance came from the hierarchy. In the wake of their open refusal of the mandatory implementation of a new rite of the Mass *(Novus Ordo Missae)* in 1971, traditionalist Catholics were made the object of Church discipline and censure. Episcopal authorities warned of the dangers of anticonciliarism and potential schism in the traditionalist cause. Catholics who attended unauthorized Masses in traditionalist chapels were instructed that they were not fulfilling their Sunday obligation. Traditionalist priests over whom bishops exercised more direct juridical authority found themselves suspended, "retired," or subject to other disciplinary sanctions. By the mid 1970s, Pope Paul VI himself was intimating that traditionalist Catholics who had chosen open rebellion by holding fast to preconciliar forms and who were resisting aggiornamento were "outside obedience and communion with the Successor of Peter and, therefore, outside the Church."[4]

The Scope of the Movement

Catholic traditionalism today is an international, segmented, and loosely organized montage. Although not as large as other postconciliar phenomena, such as Catholic Charismatic Renewal, traditionalism has grown steadily in the last quarter century. Precise numbers, however, are difficult to ascertain. Vatican estimates place the number of active traditionalists worldwide at sixty thousand to eighty thousand.[5] These figures can be considered low; and they do not include many sympathetic supporters of the traditionalist cause who remain unaffiliated. Traditionalism is also generally understood to be both larger and more militant in Europe (especially France) than in the United States, where there are some ten to fifteen thousand active participants.[6] An additional clue to the scope of the movement can be adduced in part by the size of Archbishop Lefebvre's priestly fraternity, the largest and most media-visible traditionalist organization. As of 1986, Lefebvre had ordained some 250 traditionalist priests. His Society of Saint Pius X operated a worldwide (twenty-three countries) network of schools, priories, and religious foundations including 339 churches and 6 seminaries (Switzerland, West Germany, United States, France, Australia, Argentina) with over 250 candidates studying for the priesthood.[7]

Adding to the difficulty of determining the scope of the movement is a definitional problem. Some traditionalists dislike the term because it assumes a pluralism in Catholic modes of belief and practice—an assumption they reject pointedly. Nor have all self-proclaimed traditionalists been supporters of Archbishop Lefebvre, either before or after his official break with the Vatican. A small number of traditionalist Catholics are also linked with the Old Roman Catholic Church or with religious orders that have no licit canonical status. Others are devotees of visionaries or self-proclaimed popes who have ordained priests and bishops lacking any qualifications whatsoever. By more centrist standards, these "traditionalist" elements are peripheral to the movement and will not be discussed here.

Forms of Traditionalist Dissent

Over the past quarter century, Catholic traditionalist dissent in the United States has found expression in a variety of different forms. Many of the ex officio traditionalist parishes that formed in the wake of the Council were first located in homes, hotel rooms, and meeting halls until suitable facilities could be found. These parishes are ministered to by individual priests who remain unaffiliated with any official traditionalist organizational structure. While many of these priests are either officially on leave, or have been suspended by their local ordinary, they have remained active in the ministry and have maintained a traditionalist support base ranging in size from a few dozen to several hundred parishioners.

Traditionalist dissent has also found an outlet through independent publishing initiatives. In the United States, Hugo Kellner, Father Lawrence Brey, William F. Strojie, and Solange Hertz are among the better-known traditionalist apologists who have produced an assortment of anticonciliar literature.[8] Internationally, one of the most prolific traditionalist apologists is Michael Davies, an Anglican convert to Catholicism. Mr. Davies has written a multi-volume apologia of Archbishop Lefebvre and published numerous essays and monographs on wide-ranging subjects related to Catholic doctrine, liturgical reform, and the defense of the Tridentine rite.[9]

The Remnant, published by Walter Matt in Saint Paul, Minnesota, is the oldest traditionalist journal in the United States. In the decade following the Council, *The Remnant* came to play an important role in linking the nascent traditionalist movement in the United States with its European counterpart. Although unaffiliated with any traditionalist organization, Matt's paper developed a reputation as the unofficial voice of Archbishop Lefebvre in the United States before the latter established his own headquarters and publishing sources in this country.[10] Although clearly aligned with the traditionalist cause, Matt has remained an independent and tempered voice within the movement, rejecting the more strident traditionalist attacks on the papacy, organizing petition drives for the reinstatement of the Tridentine mass, and sponsoring Remnant Forums that bring traditionalist Catholics together in a show of solidarity and support.

Aside from the independent chapels and anticonciliar publishing initiatives, traditionalist aspirations have also found expression in quasi-ecclesial organizations such as the Catholic Traditionalist Movement, Inc. (CTM), the Orthodox Roman Catholic Movement (ORCM), Catholics for Tradition, Roman Catholics of America, Traditional Catholics of America, Union Catholica Trento, the Saint Pius V Association, Liqa Katholisher Traditionalisten (LKT), and Archbishop Lefebvre's Society of Saint Pius X.[11] I have chosen to discuss two groups that played key roles in initially mobilizing traditionalist discontent in the United States—the CTM and ORCM—and the work of Archbishop Marcel Lefebvre and his Society of Saint Pius X. These organizations have been among the most visible traditionalist initiatives—although the work of the former two organizations has been largely overshadowed by the latter. They are also representative of the religiocultural ethos that constitutes the essence of the traditionalist cause célèbre, namely, a return to the Church of the Counter-Reformation.

Catholic Traditionalist Movement, Inc. (CTM)

In spite of Archbishop Marcel Lefebvre's pre-eminence as the embodiment of the traditionalist cause, his efforts in mobilizing traditionalist dissent were preceded by nearly a decade by those of Father Gommar De Pauw, a forty-six-year-old Belgian-born professor of theology and academic dean at Saint Mary's Major Seminary in Emmitsburg, Maryland.[12] On 15 March 1965 De Pauw launched the first self-proclaimed traditionalist initiative with the publication of the "Catholic Traditionalist Manifesto."

De Pauw's "manifesto" was in fact a tempered document that merely amplified the growing uneasiness in conservative Catholic quarters over the tremors of aggiornamento, especially in the all-important area of liturgical reform. The manifesto complained that liturgical changes were being "subtly extorted" from the bishops by a well-organized minority of self-appointed liturgical experts who had failed to consult the "average Catholic." While concessions were made to certain "spiritual advantages" of partial vernacularization, De Pauw warned that changes in the liturgy were "dangerous" harbingers of a broader scheme that would eventually lead to the "Protestantizing" of the Roman Catholic faith. The manifesto urged that the Latin form of the Mass not be abandoned, that any further vernacularization be halted, and that components of preconciliar Catholic identity be re-emphasized: belief in the Real Presence of Christ in the Eucharist, obedience to the Pope, celibacy, distinctive clothing for priests and nuns, and "unadulterated doctrine."[13]

In conjunction with the public release of his manifesto, De Pauw also formed the Catholic Traditionalist Movement organization (CTM)—later incorporated in the state of New York as a nonprofit educational organization. The CTM had no formal membership at the time, but De Pauw publicly claimed the support of several thousand Catholics, the endorsement of some thirty American bishops (including Cardinal Spellman of New York), and the support of Cardinal Alfredo Ottaviani, the aging, arch-conservative Vatican Prefect of the Congregation for the Doctrine of the Faith.

Although De Pauw launched his Catholic traditionalist movement with little initial public controversy, this situation changed rapidly. Within three weeks after the release of the manifesto, Archbishop Lawrence Shehan of Baltimore notified De Pauw by registered mail that he was to dissociate himself from the CTM or leave the archdiocese. According to Shehan, De Pauw's organization "conflicts with the teachings of Vatican II."[14] De Pauw ostensibly consented to Shehan's order and removed himself as head of the CTM. In his technical absence, a "Father X" directed the CTM from the basement of a New York home.[15] However, the Baltimore priest continued on as "spiritual leader" of the movement and spoke and wrote freely on its behalf. In July of 1965, Archbishop Shehan transferred De Pauw to a Baltimore parish, effective the following summer. Outraged and convinced that he was being publicly humiliated for speaking out against the Council, De Pauw requested permission from Shehan to attend the final session of Vatican II as *peritus* (advisor) to Bishop Blaize Kurz, a German-born Franciscan missionary bishop and close friend of the De Pauw family who had been living in retirement in New York City. De Pauw then traveled with

Kurz to Rome in August of 1965, where he again contacted Ottaviani and received assurances from the cardinal that there was nothing wrong with his CTM efforts to preserve tradition.

By his own account, De Pauw was subsequently incardinated into the diocese of Tivoli, Italy.[16] He returned to New York in early January of 1966 and assumed his post as head of the CTM—announcing at a public press conference that he was no longer under Shehan's jurisdiction, that he had the "personal blessings" of the Holy Father, and that he would continue his campaign against the liturgical and theological innovations that were "Protestantizing" the Roman Catholic Church.[17] On January 28, Shehan suspended De Pauw from his priestly functions and ordered him to return to Baltimore immediately. De Pauw refused, in spite of a Vatican ruling that his incardination process had not been properly expedited and that he was therefore still under Shehan's authority.[18]

As a self-proclaimed defender of Catholic tradition battling "modernists" and "liberal-inspired innovators," De Pauw traveled extensively across the United States, lecturing to capacity audiences and appearing on radio and television broadcasts. In the context of the mounting conflict over aggiornamento, the "rebel priest" became an immediate cause célèbre on the Catholic right. He received effusive praise in the editorial pages of *The Wanderer* as a heroic and "much maligned" cleric who had been "smeared" by the liberal Catholic media while progressive Catholics were openly thwarting both the Council mandates and the authority of the hierarchy with impunity.[19] With De Pauw on the lecture circuit, members of the CTM picketed chancery offices, distributed copies of the manifesto, paid for its publication in newspapers, and conducted surveys purporting to show widespread negative reaction among American Catholics to Vatican II changes. By the late summer of 1967, however, De Pauw's criticism of aggiornamento had escalated dramatically, as had his attacks on the Church's magisterium. On 15 August, one month before the first postconciliar Synod of Bishops met in Rome, De Pauw sent a twelve-page letter to Pope Paul VI warning that traditionalist patience in the United States had "reached the breaking point." The CTM leader demanded that the Pope declare an end to "the interregnum of Vatican II," admit that the Council had been a "horrible mistake," and establish a separate Latin rite in the Church. De Pauw also gave notice that CTM supporters no longer considered themselves part of a "conciliar Church" that had "completely betrayed the tradition and beliefs of the Church of our Fathers." The CTM leader vowed that, if need be, traditionalist Catholics would carry on their "spiritual resistance movement without the hoped-for papal approval."[20]

Gommar De Pauw remained a controversial symbol of traditionalist discontent with Vatican II throughout the latter 1960s. His visibility in the deepening controversy over liturgical reform was further highlighted in late 1967 when a furor arose over the implementation of an all-English liturgy and the alleged mistranslation of the canon of the Mass. With the implementation of the *Novus Ordo* rite in 1969, De Pauw was among the first to charge that the new liturgy was "schismatic, sacrilegious, heretical, and possibly invalid." According to De Pauw, the American bishops were excommunicating themselves by making a Mass mandatory that "destroys the whole basis of the Roman Catholic religion."[21] De Pauw's efforts to "save the Mass" and mobilize the opposition to aggiornamento on the Catholic right were handicapped, however, by his conflict with ecclesial authorities. His public defiance of Cardinal Shehan cost him the support of more moderate Catholic conservatives who had grown increasingly concerned by the late 1960s with what many perceived as the accelerating deterioration of magisterial authority, especially in the context of the wholesale repudiation of *Humanae Vitae,* Pope Paul VI's 1968 encyclical reaffirming the traditional proscription of artificial birth control (against the recommendations of a theological commission he had appointed to study the question). Conservatives expressed fears that De Pauw's unauthorized actions, heroic as they were, were but another example of how the "Protestant principle" of private judgment was eroding authority in the postconciliar Church.[22]

Aware of such criticism, and having failed to legitimate his efforts through Vatican channels, De Pauw tried to circumvent the authority of the American hierarchy in 1967 by affiliating with an organization known as the Sovereign Order of Saint John of Jerusalem, Knights of Malta (OSJ), headquartered in Shickshinny, Pennsylvania. This effort, too, proved unsuccessful when De Pauw was forced to acknowledge that the Shickshinny OSJ was not the legitimate successor to the original Maltese Order. De Pauw's faux pas with the OSJ had important ramifications for the fledgling traditionalist movement in the United States. Henceforth, the CTM founder vowed, he would never again associate with any other group on behalf of the traditionalist cause, thus closing the door to cooperation with other traditionalist leaders and organizations.[23]

In June 1968, De Pauw and his supporters purchased a former Ukrainian Orthodox Church in Westbury, Long Island. De Pauw stopped serving CTM chapels in several other states. He began broadcasting a weekly radio Tridentine Mass in October of 1970. While he continued his public speaking and writing on behalf of the traditionalist cause (and does so today), the traditionalist initiatives of the "rebel priest" were eventually eclipsed by other organizations.[24]

The Orthodox Roman Catholic Movement, Inc. (ORCM)

While Father De Pauw's CTM, Inc., initiatives were among the first to organize resistance to Vatican II and to work for retention of the Latin Tridentine liturgy, a traditionalist organization with a national network of chapels and Mass centers did not come into existence in the United States until nearly eight years after the close of the Council. In January 1973, Father Francis Fenton, a fifty-five-year-old priest pastor in Bridgeport, Connecticut, with several lay supporters organized the Orthodox Roman Catholic Movement, Inc. (ORCM).

Fenton served as a diocesan priest in the Bridgeport Diocese from 1963 to 1968. He then secured a leave of absence from his bishop in order to devote greater time to writing and lecturing on behalf of the John Birch Society, on whose board of directors he served.[25] In 1970 Fenton began holding traditional Latin Masses in a private home in Sandy Hook, Connecticut. In 1972 he and a small group of traditionalist supporters purchased a chapel in Brewster, New York. Another chapel was later purchased in Monroe (Stratford), Connecticut, to become the national headquarters of the ORCM.

From its inception, the ideology of the ORCM was more explicitly anticonciliar than had initially been the case with Gommar De Pauw's CTM, indicating in part the degree to which traditionalist Catholic dissent had become radicalized by the early 1970s. The goal of the ORCM was to "preserve the Roman Catholic religion as it had existed historically up to and including the pontificate of Pope Pius XII" and to provide the "means whereby all those who wished to practice that religion could do so."[26] In practical terms, these objectives were to be accomplished by establishing a national network of chapels and Mass centers committed to retention of pre-Vatican II Catholic religious forms and coordinated by the ORCM office in Monroe.

Fenton's long-standing involvement with the John Birch Society and his friends and acquaintances among its Catholic membership proved a natural conduit for promoting and expanding a national network of ORCM chapels. Within three years of its founding, the organization had twenty different Mass locations throughout the United States; by 1978 the number had reached twenty-eight, and there were ten additional priest members. The ORCM also published numerous anticonciliar pamphlets and a newsletter *(ORCM News)* featuring articles by ORCM-affiliated priests assailing Vatican II and the leadership of the establishment Church. Fenton's editorials typically blended right-wing political themes with denunciations of the Second Vatican Council and the Church's hierarchy, along with discourses on preconciliar Catholic piety and doctrine.

The most widely distributed ORCM tract was a twenty-one-page booklet entitled "Holding Fast." Written by Fenton, the publication soundly denounced the Second Vatican Council, the *Novus Ordo* Mass, and erring bishops. Charges of "communist" and "Masonic" subversion in the Church were raised, along with doubts—already circulating in some traditionalist circles—as to whether or not Paul VI was a legitimate pontiff.[27] These anticonciliar themes were also repeated in an address given many times by Fenton entitled, "The Roman Catholic Church: Its Tragedy and Hope." Fenton's grim assessment of postconciliar Catholicism included allegations that Rome had been "massively infiltrated and subverted" by its enemies and was in their hands and under their control: "The result is the heresies, the sacrileges, the blasphemies, the disarray, the chaos we behold on all sides."[28]

On 16–18 April 1979, the ORCM held its first national convention in Chicago. While organization officials publicly praised the convention as a success, internal tension over Fenton's John Birch affiliation, his autocratic authority within the organization, financial problems, and the addition of another priest to the ORCM board of directors precipitated a leadership crisis that could not be resolved.[29] As a result, Father Fenton left the ORCM, moved to Colorado Springs, Colorado, and established another traditionalist organization called the Traditional Catholics of America, Inc. (CTA). The CTA retained control of those chapels served by ORCM priests who remained loyal to Fenton. Father Francis McKenna, O.P., who had assisted Fenton in the establishment of the ORCM and who was pastor of the Monroe ORCM church, assumed leadership of the organization and continued to publish a newsletter *(Catholics For Tradition)* and maintain a network of traditionalist chapels.

Archbishop Marcel Lefebvre

Marcel Lefebvre was born in Tourcoing in northern France on 29 November 1905. His father, a rigid disciplinarian with monarchist political views, was a textile manufacturer whose business suffered bankruptcy at the beginning of the Great Depression. Marcel, one of eight children, studied for the priesthood in his own diocese. He then attended the French seminary in Rome, where he was strongly influenced by its monarchical Integralist rector, Father Floch, a supporter of Action Française, a far-right, anti-Semitic, anti-democratic movement that was condemned by Pope Pius XI. Lefebvre was ordained on 21 September 1929. He was then appointed to the working-class parish of Marias-de-Lomme. Three years later, he joined an older brother in the Holy Ghost order and was subsequently sent to Gabon, where he served as the rector of a seminary and in various missionary apostolates in French Equatorial Africa. Lefebvre returned to France in 1945 to become head of the training school of the Holy Ghost Fathers at Mortain. Two years later he returned to Africa, was consecrated a bishop, and was named Vicar-Apostolic of Dakar by Pope Pius XII. In 1948 Lefebvre was appointed apostolic delegate for the whole of French-speaking Africa, a task at which he labored for the next eleven years. Lefebvre returned to France in 1959 and became bishop of the diocese of Tulle. In 1962 he was honored by the Pope with the title of Archbishop of Synnada in Phrygia.[30]

Between 1960 and 1962, Archbishop Lefebvre served on the Central Preparatory Commission charged with producing the schemas presented at the Second Vatican Council. In 1962 he was also elected superior-general of the Holy Ghost Fathers. Lefebvre's opposition to the new theological currents animating Vatican II was evident during the Council.[31] He was a founder of the International Group of Fathers *(Coetus Internationalis Patrum)*, an organization of conservative prelates maneuvering to uphold tradition against the liberal-progressive elements pushing for change. Lefebvre sided with conservatives in all of the major Council debates and refused to sign the conciliar documents on the Church in the Modern World *(Gaudium et Spes)* and the Declaration on Religious Liberty *(Dignitatis Humanae)*.[32]

In 1968 Lefebvre resigned as head of the Holy Ghost Fathers in a dispute with members of the Chapter General over reform of the order in keeping with the Council directives. He then moved to Rome to retire but by his own account was sought out by a group of young men who were looking for someone to direct them in traditional priestly formation.[33]

Lefebvre guided his first seminarians to pursue their studies at the University of Fribourg. He abandoned this course of action, however, when he became convinced that the university—like the Church itself—was "infected" with modernism. He then acquired permission from Bishop Charrière of Fribourg to establish a house for seminarians in that location in June 1969. With the approval of Monsignor Adam, bishop of Sion, Lefebvre obtained a large house belonging to the canons of Saint Bernard in the canton of Valais, Switzerland. This property became the Ecône seminary, opening formally on 7 October 1970. The following month, Bishop Charriere canonically established Lefebvre's priestly fraternity as the Fraternité Sacerdotale de Saint Pie X (the Society of Saint Pius X)—named after the Pope known as the "scourge of modernists."

During the next three years, Ecône's reputation as a traditionalist seminary adhering to the Tridentine rite, to Thomistic theology, and to a general repudiation of the reforms associated with Vatican II, spread rapidly. In the fall of 1974, in response to the archbishop's escalating critique of the Council and continuing use of the (then prohibited) Tridentine liturgy, and in response to pressures for the French bishops who opposed Lefebvre's "rebel seminary," the Vatican announced that an investigation ("Apostolic Visitation") of Ecône would take place. On 21 November, in reaction to the "scandal" occasioned by remarks made by the two Belgian priests who carried out the visitation, Lefebvre issued an acerbic "Declaration" denouncing the "neo-Modernist and neo-Protestant" tendencies that were contributing to the "demolition of the Church, to the ruin of the priesthood, to the destruction of the Holy Sacrifice of the Mass and the Sacraments, to the disappearance of religious life, and to naturalist and Teilhardian teaching in universities, seminaries, and catechetics, a teaching born of Liberalism and Protestantism many times condemned by the solemn Magisterium of the Church." Lefebvre renounced the new Mass as the pre-eminent symbol of all postconciliar trends opposed to "orthodoxy and the never-changing Magisterium." Vatican II was "entirely corrupt"; it "comes from heresy and results in heresy, even if all its acts are not formally heretical." Fidelity to the true Church and the salvation of souls could only be assured by a "categorical refusal" of the Council and its "reformation."[34]

For the next two years, the tensions between Rome and Ecône remained high. On 6 May 1975, the Commission of Cardinals investigating Lefebvre condemned his Declaration as "unacceptable on all points" and "impossible to reconcile" with fidelity to the Church, the Pope, and the Council.[35] Although publicly rebuked by the Pope and ordered to close his seminary and to disband his priestly fraternity, Lefebvre refused, ordaining thirteen seminarians in June of 1975 and twelve more in June 1976. Three weeks later (22 July 1976), Lefebvre was officially suspended *a divinis*.[36]

In spite of his suspension and public censure for "contumacious insubordination," communication between Lefebvre and the Vatican remained open throughout the next twelve years. The archbishop corresponded with Pope Paul VI and his successors, answered various doctrinal queries from the Congregation for the Doctrine of the Faith, and appeared for discussions with Vatican officials, notably Cardinal Franjo Seper, prefect of the Congregation for Doctrine of the Faith, and later (1981) with his successor Cardinal Joseph Ratzinger.[37]

While discussions with the Vatican proceeded without resolve, Lefebvre's priestly fraternity steadily expanded its international network of publishing enterprises, chapels, schools, priories, and seminaries. Society priests both generated and capitalized on the anticonciliarism of the 1970s and on earlier traditionalist initiatives that had been undertaken in the period immediately after the Council. Lefebvre's priests pressed traditionalist Catholics for support on the grounds that the Society was the only "realistic potential" for the traditionalist cause—in light of its founder's episcopal credentials and ability to ensure a long-term supply of "valid" traditionalist priests.[38] The society began its work among American Catholics in 1973–74 when several of Lefebvre's American seminarians returned to the United States and established chapels in East Meadow, New York; Houston, Texas; and San Jose, California. Father Clarence Kelly, one of five Americans ordained by Lefebvre in 1973, began a periodical, *For You and For Many*. In 1978 the society began publishing *The Angelus* from its center in Dickinson, Texas.

Following the election of Pope John Paul II (1978), the atmosphere in Rome with regard to the "Ecône affair" turned more conciliatory than had been the case during the pontificate of Paul VI. The new pope, conservative on matters of Church orthodoxy, signaled a desire to reach accommodation with Lefebvre as part of a broad campaign to curtail "unfavorable tendencies" associated with liberal-progressive interpretations of aggiornamento. Lefebvre met personally with John Paul II on 18 November 1978. In all subsequent negotiations (conducted primarily by Cardinal Joseph Ratzinger), the archbishop pressed in one form or another demands for the reinstatement of his priestly fraternity, independence from diocesan bishops (through the establishment of an independent prelature), and the right to continue use of the Tridentine Mass and the preconciliar liturgical texts. The Vatican, in turn, demanded an apology from Lefebvre for his public disobedience, explicit acceptance of the Second Vatican Council and the *Novus Ordo Missae* (Lefebvre was personally to use this rite on occasion), and a halt to violations of canon law in performing confirmations and ordinations in various dioceses without permission of the local bishop.[39]

However, while appearing publicly irenic and willing to reach some accommodation with the Vatican, Lefebvre continued to equivocate on his position on Vatican II, reasserting on the one hand that the Council was "schismatic,"[40] while holding on the other hand that he would adhere to its decrees only "as interpreted in accordance with tradition"—which he assigned to himself the right to define.[41] Lefebvre also continued publicly attacking "modernist" and "Masonic" influences among the hierarchy and denouncing the new liturgy as a "bastard rite"—although the tone of his public and private discourses on all these matters varied. While Lefebvre disavowed the more extremist "sede vacantist" traditionalist position and rejected the view that the new liturgy was "intrinsically" invalid (which would have closed the door to any further negotiations with the Vatican), he left no doubt among his supporters that the hierarchy was in error with regard to the conciliar reforms, that the new Mass was a "Protestant" rite, and that the Church had "always forbidden the faithful to assist at the Masses of heretics or schismatics, even when they are valid."[42] Lefebvre and the priests of the society categorically refused any use of the new liturgical texts.

Although the expectations of rapprochement were high with the election of John Paul II, negotiations between Lefebvre and the Vatican remained in a state of impasse throughout the early 1980s. In 1983, Lefebvre retired as superior general of the society and chose Father Franz Schmidberger, a German priest, as his successor. However, on the occasion of the ordination of several priests of the society in October of that year, Lefebvre increased his pressure on the Vatican by intimating that in order to "safeguard the Catholic priesthood which perpetuates the Catholic Church," he would consecrate a successor—with or without papal permission.[43] Lefebvre's threat of episcopal consecrations was followed in October 1984 by a Vatican indult permitting worldwide use of the Tridentine liturgy, albeit under carefully restricted conditions.[44] The archbishop, however, rejected this overture as no more than a Vatican "enticement" intended to marginalize the traditionalist movement. He continued to warn his supporters against any rallying to the "liberals" and "modernists" who were governing the postconciliar Church.[45]

Lefebvre again publicly threatened consecrations three years later, this time during the 29 June 1987 ordinations at Ecône. His decision to risk excommunication was now being prompted in part by his age (eighty-two) and declining health. All that was needed were "signs from Providence." These signs came, according to the archbishop, in the form of the Pope's ecumenical meeting in Assisi in October 1986 and in the Vatican's reply (February 1987) to Lefebvre's written objections to the Council's "novel doctrine" of religious liberty.[46] Lefebvre visited the Vatican the following month (14 July). Two weeks later he received a letter from Cardinal Ratzinger proposing official recognition for his Society of Saint Pius X, its own seminaries with the Tridentine liturgy, and a cardinal-visitor to perform ordinations. Accordingly, the cardinal-visitor would "guarantee" the orthodoxy of the Society's seminaries and would have the final word on who was ordained.

In October, the Vatican announced that the conservative Canadian cardinal Edouard Gagnon would make an apostolic visitation to Ecône. Gagnon's visitation lasted from 11 November to 8 December 1987. His thirty-page report went to Pope John Paul II the following January. In February Lefebvre received a letter from Cardinal Ratzinger informing him that a Vatican commission had been appointed to study a "regularized legal status" for the society. Negotiations between Lefebvre and Cardinal Ratzinger continued for the next several months, culminating in the signing of a 5 May 1988 protocol granting Lefebvre much of the substance of his previous demands: official recognition to the Society, semi-independence from diocesan bishops, and permission to continue use of the Tridentine liturgy. Differences over the interpretation of Vatican II documents and other matters related to reconciling the traditionalist cause were to be thrashed out by a panel of two Lefebvre followers and seven Vatican delegates. On the critical issue of a successor, Lefebvre received permission to consecrate one bishop. For his part of the agreement, the archbishop was required to profess fidelity to the pope, to pledge to have a "positive attitude of study and communication" concerning Vatican II reforms which did not appear to him as easily reconcilable with tradition, and to recognize the validity of the new Mass and respect the discipline and ecclesiastical laws of the Church.[47]

The long-sought solution to the "Ecône problem" proved short-lived, however. Lefebvre promptly withdrew his assent to the protocol the following day. Insisting that the Vatican was stalling and had not collaborated effectively, Lefebvre demanded a 30 June date for consecrations (no specific date had been set in the 5 May agreement). He pressed again for a papal mandate to consecrate more than one episcopal successor—lest the Society continue to find itself vulnerable with but a single bishop to insure its perpetuation.[48] Above all, however, Lefebvre made it clear that he had absolutely no intention of compromising nearly two decades of struggle and persecution on behalf of the traditionalist cause by now turning control of his priestly fraternity over to agents of "modernist Rome" whose goal was to "reabsorb us within the Conciliar Church."[49] On 25 March 1991, at the age of eighty-five, Lefebvre died in a hospital in Martigny, Switzerland. Before his death Lefebvre chose Rev. Franz Schmidberger to succeed him as head of the Society.

Traditionalist Ideology

Catholic traditionalism does not present a completely uniform ideology, although it stands united as a worldview opposed to theological modernism. Not all self-proclaimed traditionalist Catholics share exactly the same positions with regard to the Second Vatican Council, the authority of the pope, or with respect to the new liturgy. Nor is there complete consensus with regard to what constitutes the proper mode of dissent vis-à-vis the Church's magisterium. Serious conflicts over these and other issues have divided traditionalists, dissipated their organizational resources, and prevented the emergence of a unified international movement.

Furthermore, there are many affinities between conservative and traditionalist anticonciliarism and their respective positions on a number of social and political issues. Also, ideological motifs emphasized by particular traditionalist groups often highlight concerns or orientations specific to them. For example, themes lionizing the status of the priesthood are especially pronounced in the literature of the Society of Saint Pius X; allegations of a "communist conspiracy" were prominent in the literature of the ORCM under Father Fenton's tutelage.

Traditionalist ideology must also be viewed as dynamic and developing in a dialectical and progressively radicalized manner in response to social and religious change, to the reactions of Church authorities to the movement, and in response to organizational needs accompanying the problem of legitimating dissent.

In spite of a lack of complete uniformity and consistency, however, there are distinctive characteristics that differentiate traditionalist ideology from other religious orientations in the postconciliar Church and that give expression to the movement's fundamentalist ethos. These characteristics include tendencies toward a highly cognitive-doctrinal religiosity marked by objectivism, dogmatism, and literalism. Traditionalist ideology is also exclusivist and elitist, separatist in its action orientation, and deeply imbued with a conspiracy sense of social causality. Traditionalist ideology also manifests clear affinities with many right-wing political orientations.

Integralism as a Precursor of Traditionalism

Catholic traditionalism developed in a diffuse and segmented manner in the wake of the Second Vatican Council. The movement cannot be traced along a unitary line of growth as is the case with Catholic charismatic renewal, nor can traditionalism be reduced to a single historical or social cause, although the rise of the movement is clearly related to the crisis of reform and authority attending the Second Vatican Council. Like Protestant fundamentalism in its formative years, traditionalism has been fueled by the quest for a lost religious identity, by heightened anxiety surrounding rapid social and religious change, by the loss of contact with the Catholic past, and by the erosion of certitude in matters of faith and morals.

The signifying feature of traditionalism is that it is a movement of *religious* protest, a reaction against what is perceived as the spread of false *doctrine*. As such, traditionalism both illuminates the nature of the crisis of Catholicism in the culture of modernity and functions as an organized and coherent response to it. In particular, traditionalism gives heightened expression to the staying power of prior religious identities and orientations that were once normative for many Catholics. The roots of traditionalism are not to be found in the repudiation of Vatican II and the ensuing postconciliar crisis, per se, but in the legacy of an earlier response on the part of Church leadership to tensions created by the pressures of modernity, most notably in the form of Catholic Integralism.

At the beginning of the twentieth century Integralism was an expression of a campaign of Roman curial officials against the heresies of the modern age, including the historical and textual studies of the Bible, Darwinian evolution, liberal democracy, and widespread European anticlericalism. The Integralist reaction to modernity was distinguished by its condemnation of all theological liberalism, its "authoritarian heteronomy" regarding the magisterium, its singular imposition of scholastic philosophy, and the championing of "Christendom" models of the social order. Integralism represented the static categorization of tradition, the defense of objectivism in the face of subjectivism, the conversion of discipline into doctrine (and doctrine into dogma), and the construction of images of a heretical conspiracy among deviant insiders.[50]

In 1907, Pope Pius X condemned a "movement" known as "Modernism," declaring it to be "the synthesis of all heresies." Modernism was, in fact, a self-conscious, if inchoate and loosely organized, attempt by certain European Catholic exegetes, historians, philosophers, and theologians to construct a viable synthesis between the ancient faith and modern (post-Kantian) thought. Although the individuals implicated in the aftermath of the condemnation (most of them priests) arrived at various, often contradictory, conclusions and appropriated a host of methodological perspectives, they did share a principled repudiation of the categories and methods of the neoscholastic system of thought buttressing papal authority in Rome. Each modernist did, to one degree or another, stress the need to develop a new apologetic for Catholic belief that would not appeal exclusively, as did the neo-scholastic system, to a supernatural, "extrinsic," once-and-for-all "deposit of faith," but also to an ongoing human experience of the indwelling spirit of God in the individual soul and in history—an error labeled "vital immanence" by Pius X. In essence modernism involved the complete acceptance of historical consciousness by certain Catholics, so that all dogmas and practices were viewed as products of particular historical periods and in need of periodic revision.[51]

Postconciliar traditionalism draws heavily on this Integralist legacy in its blanket denunciations of all vestiges of liberalism and modernism in the Church, in treating tradition in a static and ahistorical manner, in absolutizing (selective) magisterial pronouncements, in anti-ecumenism, and in promoting the exclusive use of categories of scholastic theology and social conservatism. Traditionalist Catholics have also found in the Integralist warnings about internal subversion and conspiracy in the Church a ready-made and authoritatively articulated explanation for negative developments in the wake of the Council.

The role of the Second Vatican Council in the rise of the traditionalist movement is complex. One aspect of the Council reforms that facilitated the rise of traditionalist dissent was the mere pace of change itself. With the possible exception of the consolidation and centralization of power and authority in the Curia in the late nineteenth and early twentieth centuries, change in the Roman Catholic Church in the previous two centuries had been relatively slow, making it easier to argue that reform and innovation, when they did occur, were a consequence of the "development" of doctrine. With the Second Vatican Council, however, change in Catholic ecclesiology and theology accelerated dramatically, a fact that in itself helped spread suspicion about the "radical" nature of aggiornamento. Institutional declension following the Council in the form of rebellious clergy and laity, catechetical disorder, and turmoil in the Church's corporate prayer life also provided opponents of reform with a seemingly empirical rational for repudiating it—indicating both a low tolerance of gaps between the ideal and the real, and a proclivity for measuring conciliar change against a myth of a golden age associated with the Church of Pius XII.

More directly relevant, however, to the rise of traditionalist dissent was the manner in which aspects of aggiornamento raised the specter of "contradiction," thereby calling into question fundamental categories of Catholic religious self-understanding, the credibility of hierarchical authority, and the core of Catholicism's supernaturalist assumptions. The conviction that Vatican II contradicted previous Church teachings is an ubiquitous motif in traditionalist literature and public pronouncements. It is also the informing assumption that has led to the conclusion that the conciliar Church is a "schismatic Church," not because it changed, but because it did so in a manner that "breaks with the Catholic Church that has always been."[52] This contradiction motif animates the traditionalist assertion that they have not left the Church, the Church has left them.

The centrality of a contradiction motif in traditionalist ideology is a partial expression of the inherent difficulties of change in the Roman Catholic Church in light of the dominance of scholastic theological presuppositions which posit revelation as a complete, unified, consistent, absolute, and immutable "sacred deposit." There is also a conviction that this sacred deposit had been handed down intact generation after generation, that only the words and descriptive metaphors changed, and that what appeared to be new could be explained as merely a difference in terminology.[53] In the wake of the Council, scholastic theology seemed to yield to situationist theology; previously condemned modernist propositions on ecumenism and religious liberty were endorsed, and a collegial and participatory form of leadership displaced, at least temporarily, the authoritarian style. Forbidden books, oaths against modernism, and other artifacts of Catholicism's antimodernist network were dismantled. Ideas once linked with "Protestant" thinking on the priesthood of the baptized, the nature of the Church, and the primacy of the Bible found, with some modification, official endorsement and legitimation in postconciliar theology. In the crucial area of the liturgy, the emphasis on increased lay participation, on the use of the vernacular, on the communal and meal aspects of worship, and on a more prominent role for Scripture had conspicuous antecedents in the liturgical reforms initiated by Luther, Cranmer, and other "heretics."

In other words, what had once been linked in the most solemn pontifical manner with error, heresy, and conspiracy to destroy the Catholic church (first in the form of Protestantism, later under the hydra-headed guise of modernism), now appeared mandated by the very agents commissioned to protect the sacred deposit. In light of this perception of contradiction, the struggle of the "remnant faithful" to maintain truth and tradition can be seen as an attempt to maintain cognitive integrity in response to the dissonance created by change.

Ideological motifs emphasized by traditionalist leadership elites are not always and at every point the same as those motivating the involvement of the movement's rank and file.[54] It should be noted, therefore, that the following discussion of traditionalist ideology is derived primarily from analysis of the pronouncements of leadership elites.

"Correct Belief"

Public perceptions notwithstanding, Catholic traditionalism is not a campaign motivated by nostalgia for bygone ritualism. Nor is traditionalism first and foremost a struggle over the disciplinary or canonical status of dissident clergy and their supporters. Neither a disciplinary or juridical problem nor a form of naïveté or ignorance, Catholic traditionalism is a radicalized and self-conscious antimodernist ideology. Traditionalism did not arise unaware of the new intellectual or theological order; it stands in opposition to that order, defending a worldview and governing assumptions of religious experience that have been decisively penetrated by the theological, cultural, and scientific currents of modernity. Among its intellectual and clerical elite in particular, traditionalism is a repudiation of historical consciousness, the "anthropocentric turn" toward the subject, and other relativizing tendencies that characterize contemporary consciousness and much modern theology and that are reflected in one fashion or another in key documents of Vatican II.

The fundamentalist dynamic within Catholic traditionalism, however, is not to be found exclusively in the *content* of its antimodernist hermeneutical framework; it lies rather in the *saliency* of "correct belief" itself in traditionalist self-understanding and in the *manner* in which these beliefs are held and understood.

One of the distinguishing characteristics of fundamentalism is the tendency to make the cognitive dimension of religion foundational and determinative. As scholars like James Barr and George Marsden have suggested, fundamentalism is not distinguished by the specific content of its orthodoxy (i.e, the "five fundamentals"), or necessarily by its epistemological presuppositions per se (i.e., pre-Kantian empirical rationalism, dispensational millennialism, a Newtonian worldview, or "Princeton theology") but by the priority of "correct belief" itself. The fundamentalist orientation therefore is not an emotional one but a strongly rationalistic one where religion is based on a standardized, objective knowledge of God. Fundamentalism seeks to be a "true science," a "truth-oriented" version of Christian evangelicalism. For the fundamentalist, "holding right views" and uniformity of belief is normative for all other elements of religious self-understanding. It follows, therefore, that doctrine is not the historical product of Christian experience but what *determines* Christian experience, that religious truth is a fixed body of eternally valid propositions, that religions are contraposed ideological entities, and that the theological task is apologetic rather than exploratory or critical.[55]

Catholic traditionalism manifests this same highly cognitive religious orientation in its anxious concern for doctrinal truth and uniformity. Among traditionalists, it is correct belief that is the primary basis of religion and the sole and definitive norm for all other forms of Catholic religious self-understanding. Catholicism is an exclusive deposit of doctrinal and moral truths. Adherence to correct doctrine—under the code name "tradition"—defines who is and who is not a "true Catholic." Traditionalist institutional initiatives in the form of schools and seminaries are promoted as the only authentic expression of the true church because only they adhere to sound doctrine. Effective and experiential modes of religiosity such as those associated with Catholic charismatic renewal are derided as "weird," false, "Protestant," and entirely unacceptable. Catholic social activism on behalf of peace and justice as well as movements of liberation theology are berated as Marxist and politicizing. For traditionalist Catholics, it is orthodoxy, not orthopraxis, that ensures salvation.

The priority of correct belief in traditionalist religious self-understanding and the corollary campaign against the teaching of false doctrines animates all traditionalist writings and public pronouncements and is the movement's real *casus belli* with the Church's magisterium. The matter of correct doctrine is also at the heart of the traditionalist repudiation of the Second Vatican Council and all of its reforms. While conservative Catholics have sometimes lacked enthusiasm and manifested certain anticonciliar themes, they have generally not repudiated the Council, per se, but have alleged that "distortions" and "excesses" surrounding its implementation have been a primary cause of postconciliar dysfunction.[56] Cardinal Ratzinger, the current prefect of the Congregation for the Doctrine of the Faith (formerly the Holy Office), has repeatedly insisted that Catholicism's postconciliar malaise cannot be attributed to the Council—which is "in strictest continuity with both previous councils" (Trent and Vatican I)—but to certain "distortions" and "misinterpretations." Resolution of the current crisis necessitates an end to the "arbitrariness and thoughtlessness" of these interpretations and a return to the "authentic" meaning of the texts.[57]

Traditionalists, by contrast, have consistently rejected this "strict constructionist," "improper implementations" thesis and instead laid blame for Catholicism's "auto-destruction" unequivocally on the Council itself. While deprecating Vatican II because of its "ambiguities" and "time bombs," the more distinctive traditionalist position is that the Council broke radically and decisively with the Church's previous teachings and embraced error, falsehood, and heresy—a view readily transformed into the assertion that Vatican II was a "schismatic" council. The practical consequence of the infusion of doctrinal "errors" into the Council documents has been to sow confusion among Catholics and weaken the Church's ability to promote absolute doctrinal conformity.[58]

Archbishop Lefebvre's position on Vatican II is typical. According to Lefebvre, the Council assimilated into the Church the "false principles" of Protestantism, liberalism, and modernism unleashed by the Reformation and the French Revolution—directly in documents like the "Declaration on Religious Freedom" and indirectly through ambiguities in other texts. In his eyes, the motto of the French Revolution—"Liberty, Equality, Fraternity"—has been embraced in the form of religious liberty, collegiality, and ecumenism in the postconciliar Church. Catholicism's current malaise is the logical fruit of this capitulation to the "poison of heresy." The proper response to the Council, therefore, is for Catholics to recognize that the proximate cause of the crisis in the Church is more than a wrong interpretation of the Council and that it flows from the Council itself.[59]

The priority of correct belief in traditionalist religious self-understanding is also evident in the controversy over liturgical reform and the implementation of the new rite of the Mass *(Novus Ordo Missae)*. Unlike conservatives who have assailed the new liturgy for its ritual flatness, aesthetic banality, and "desacralizing" aspects,[60] the traditionalist case commences from the perception of doctrinal error: the new Mass is dangerous and bad because it is theologically polluted, a "Protestant" and "bastard" rite that no longer conveys the Eucharistic doctrines of the Church as they were articulated by the Council of Trent. In accordance with the theological dictum *lex orandi, lex credendi* (the law of prayer expresses the law of belief), the new Mass is to be rejected because it presents a different and heretical faith.[61]

Traditionalism and Liturgical Reform

The complex process that brought Catholic worship into conformity with the Council's call to reform the liturgy began with Pope Paul VI's approval of the Constitution on the Sacred Liturgy *(Sacrosanctum Consilium)* on 4 December 1963 and ended with the promulgation of the *Novus Ordo Missae* on 3 April 1969. The Pope approved the instruction putting the new liturgy in effect on 18 October 1969. Significant liturgical alterations in the Roman Catholic Church between the Council of Trent and Vatican II had been few in number and little more than piecemeal initiatives to raise lay enthusiasm. The initial changes between 1963 and 1969 continued this pattern of modifying and adapting the Tridentine rite, with congregational responses to the priest's prayers, the singing of contemporary hymns, some vernacularization, and the celebration of the Mass from an altar facing the people. Structurally, however, the Mass up to the late 1960s remained virtually indistinguishable from the liturgy of the four previous centuries. The *Novus Ordo* Mass, by contrast, constituted an entirely new rite of worship. Its changes represented a shift away from hierarchy, tradition, conformity, and the rigid maintenance of the boundary between the sacred and the profane. The new liturgy was simplified and shortened. Many of the baroque accretions and archaic ceremonialisms that had characterized the Tridentine Mass were dropped. The new rite broke with the pattern of rigid and precise rubrics in favor of variations and options. Communicants took the Eucharist standing up and in some instances under both species. The number of Scripture readings was expanded. The most dramatic feature of the new liturgy was the manner in which it responded to the call for the laity to be "knowingly, actively, and fruitfully" (1.11) involved in the Mass.

Much of the initial opposition to liturgical reform on the Catholic right centered around the manner in which it had been imposed (by liturgical experts "out of touch" with ordinary Catholics) and its alleged "horizontalizing" and "desacralizing" tendencies.[62] However, the more radical critique of the traditionalist opposition came to focus primarily on issues of doctrinal defect. This traditionalist doctrinal critique of liturgical reform escalated dramatically in 1968 when a furor arose over an alleged mistranslation of the canon of the Mass, the eucharistic prayer that contains the rite of consecration.

In 1967 Father De Pauw was among the first to bring public attention to the possibility that the all-English canon contained serious doctrinal error.[63] With the introduction of the *Novus Ordo* Mass in 1969, the issue of doctrinal error in the Church's corporate worship carried over into the attack on the new *Ordo,* which also contained the "false canon" and was in itself a new rite of worship. With the campaign against the false canon and the new Mass, traditionalist anticonciliar and anti-hierarchical rhetoric escalated dramatically. Pope Paul VI, in particular, became a frequent target of traditionalist vilification. Both he and the bishops of the Church were castigated for "contradicting their legitimate teaching authority" by endorsing and promoting the liturgical reforms.[64] Traditionalists also intensified their denunciations of conservative Catholic "compromisers" whose own defense of the papacy had hardened in the wake of the near universal repudiation of *Humanae Vitae*. By accepting the new *Ordo,* conservatives had deserted the "true faith" and abandoned the cause of orthodoxy. Conservatives for their part rejected the argument that the new canon invalidated the Mass, relying on the conviction that that Christ's promise to be with His Church "all days" precluded such a grievous error. They urged support for the new liturgy because it had been imposed by "legitimate authority."[65]

By the 1971 deadline for the mandatory implementation of the new Mass, traditionalist Catholics were concluding that the issue of holding to the Tridentine rite or accepting the *Novus Ordo* was the dividing line between themselves and the "apostate" Church. As a traditionalist priest wrote, "This matter of the Mass may well be the final test of orthodoxy, the auto-da-fé of the latter times, which will differentiate the true remnant Church and its faithful from the growing body of apostates who have affiliated with the religion of the beast."[66]

The controversy on the Catholic right over liturgical reform following the Council included an ideological shift from issues of aesthetics and errant discipline and vague allegations over its allegedly Protestant character to the more serious matter of the possibility of doctrinal error. The concern with doctrinal deviation came increasingly to characterize and define the traditionalist position, both in reference to the Council itself and in terms of its specific reforms. The controversy over the new Mass in particular came to play an analogous role to the evolution controversy in Protestant fundamentalism; for traditionalist Catholics, the *Novus Ordo* Mass became the preeminent symbol of modernist inroads into the Church and a concrete and powerful issue around which to mobilize an anticonciliar movement.

Objectivism

In conjunction with a highly cognitive doctrinal orientation, traditionalist religious self-understanding is also marked by tendencies toward extreme religious objectivism and a heightened sense of supernaturalism. This type of extreme objectivity in the religious sphere means that the human person experiences religion as "something outside of himself." Eternal truths are deposited in forms that stand apart from any other source of religion. They are superimposed, concretized, codified, fixed, and entirely outside the mediation of history or culture. In Protestant fundamentalism, the Bible is the most tangible and authoritative locus of this objectivist approach to sacred reality. The Bible is without error or imperfection and is the "only true testimony" of divine truth. Because the Bible is objective, unmediated, and superimposed, it is a closed hermeneutical circle; the Bible interprets itself. Implicit in this orientation is the understanding that faith is an object of knowledge (rather than trust), and that in religious matters, the human person is not a "world-producing being."[67]

Similar objectivist orientations in Catholic traditionalism are reflected in the presentation of the Church as an institution essentially unaffected by human experience and, therefore, one that "cannot change." Faith for Catholics is certain, objective, and devoid of any human subjectivity; faith is something to which one merely "submits." In theological discourse, truth is not produced by the human mind but is something that "comes from the outside." According to Archbishop Lefebvre, the human person does not construct or create this truth but merely "receives it."[68] The traditionalist presentation of the "deposit" of faith is that of a "fact" which is divorced entirely from subjectivity, historical contextualization, or social and cultural settings—in contrast to the "subjectivism" and "naturalism" that now permeate the theology and ecclesiology of the postconciliar Church. The supernatural therefore is taken as a self-contained and superimposed realm that dominates all life and that works through miracles and extraordinary events.

These tendencies toward heightened objectification are especially evident in the controversy over the liturgy—again pointing to the centrality of this issue in the etiology of the traditionalist movement. Traditionalist pronouncements present the Tridentine Mass as a liturgical rite essentially devoid of any subjective and/or culturally determinative elements. It is the "Mass of all time." The *Novus Ordo* rite, by contrast, has been "artificially fabricated" and constitutes a "horizontal" rather than a vertical mode of worship.

This objectivist view of ritual among traditionalist Catholics has obvious parallels with the fundamentalist view of Scripture: as the Bible is "timeless and eternal," the Tridentine rite is the "Mass of all time"; as God's perfection is revealed in the Bible, so it is revealed in the "spiritually perfect" Tridentine liturgy; as an inerrant scripture propounds Christian life, theology, faith, and morality in uniform manner, a "perfect" and universal Tridentine liturgy promotes Catholic doctrinal and disciplinary uniformity; as an inerrant scripture promotes a sense of security and enduring permanence, so does the unchanging Holy Sacrifice; as the Bible cannot change, neither can the Tridentine rite.

Tendencies toward heightened objectivism are also apparent in the traditionalist extension of dogmatic infallibility (a Catholic equivalent to "inerrancy") over a wide, but highly selective, array of magisterial pronouncements. It should be noted, however, that while traditionalism gives expression to a cognitive form of religiosity concerned with "correct doctrine," the primary source from which it is derived is not the same as that of Protestant fundamentalism. The traditionalist movement is not a campaign on behalf of the literal inerrancy of Scripture, although tendencies toward literalism are present in traditionalist biblical hermeneutics. Instead, traditionalist norms for correct belief are derived primarily from magisterial pronouncements, especially those associated with the Council of Trent, the philosophico-theological system of Saint Thomas Aquinas mandated for the Church by Pope Leo XIII in 1879, and the papal and curial antimodernist broadsides of the past two centuries—rather than from the broader historical range of Catholic ecclesiology and theology. These pronouncements are presented as entirely dogmatic and inerrant or infallible. Traditionalist proclivities toward extreme objectivism are also accompanied by a legalist orientation.[69]

Elitism and Exclusivism

Traditionalist ideology is also characterized by elitist and exclusivist orientations marked by a categorical distinction between the "true" and "false" Church and the repudiation of all ecumenical initiatives or efforts that "compromise" Catholicism's status as the one "true Church." Under the banner of restoring the "Christian order," traditionalist apologists like Archbishop Lefebvre call for the return of Catholic hegemony over the entire social and political realm.

Much of the imagery revealing traditionalist self-perception combines themes of self-deprecation with the quest for holiness and spiritual heroism. These motifs are situated in a context of eschatological and apocalyptic urgency. Traditionalists portray themselves as a beleaguered "remnant faithful" holding fast to the pure and unadulterated faith during a time of widespread apostasy and "Divine chastisement." They are "the little people of God" whose holy resistance and preservation of the "true Mass" will save the true Church. As Father Fenton has said: "Are we not, then, although but a remnant, blessed beyond measure for, unworthy though we be, are we not today cast in the sublime role of being God's human instruments for the preservation and defense of our divine faith."[70]

The elitist and exclusivist orientations among traditionalists are also expressed in the determination to monopolize all religious reality. Thus, traditionalists do not promote their cause as one option within a pluralistic Catholic ecclesiology but as the only acceptable Roman Catholic alternative to the modernist-inspired conciliar Church. The affirmation of traditionalist identity is often juxtaposed against the "errors and deviations" of the post-Vatican II Church, while the traditionalist view of the patrimony of faith is presented as something pristine and uncorrupted—implying that traditionalists, and traditionalists alone, have continuity with the one true church. Within this elitist-exclusivistic framework a doctrine of double-election is at work: Catholicism is the one true religion; traditionalists are the only true Catholics.

Elitist and exclusivist impulses also find expression in the traditionalist antipathy toward all ecumenical initiatives and movements toward inter-religious dialogue.[71] The Second Vatican Council's embrace of the principle of religious liberty has been repeatedly denounced by traditionalist apologists as a "false ecumenism" and a "scandal" that lends credibility to "false religions" while eroding Catholicism's "fighting spirit." Ecumenical initiatives and calls for collaboration with people of other religions in building a better world are held to undercut Catholicism's exclusivistic claims and to contradict what the Church had previously taught on this matter.[72]

Action Orientation

Traditionalism is also an action-oriented ideology. It is a position that seeks not merely to state an ecclesiology within the Catholic tradition but to discredit and eliminate all others. Traditionalist rhetoric is dominated by the imagery of spiritual warfare and mission. The campaign to save the "true Church" is cast in "holy war" combat symbolism that situates the traditionalist cause within the broader framework of a cosmic battle for truth and righteousness. Traditionalist Catholics are the true "soldiers of Christ" warring against theological modernists, against the "scourges of the age," and against the powers of evil and error that now occupy positions of power and authority in the Church. As partisans of a heavenly cause, traditionalists are assured of final victory and God's assistance on their behalf. While the use of this holy war symbolism is not an explicit system of doctrine within the movement, it serves as an important mode by which traditionalists organize their perceptions of crisis in the Church and culture at large and by which they mobilize to do battle against the "powers of darkness."

In light of its antimodernist ethos, the traditionalist campaign against a host of contemporary "isms" (i.e., liberalism, naturalism, existentialism, subjectivism) that have "infected" Catholic theology and ecclesiology is hardly surprising. More noteworthy and distinctive, however, is the traditionalist proclivity for opposition to *all* partisans of error in the Church, including attacks and recriminations against their conservative coreligionists and against those in the highest positions of hierarchical authority.

While criticizing the hierarchy (especially bishops and episcopal conferences) for managerial and theological incompetence and/or doctrinal and disciplinary laxity,[73] conservative Catholic groups and organizations have generally insisted on submission to the Church's magisterium, especially as this authority is exercised in and through the papacy. One of the hallmarks of conservative groups such as Catholics United For the Faith (CUF) and Opus Dei is their profession to "think with the Church" in upholding hierarchical authority.[74]

Traditionalists, by contrast, have been both more strident and more openly and explicitly anti-magisterial as a dissenting and sectarian-like counter-Church movement. Traditionalists have bitterly denounced establishment Church leadership for "conspiring with the enemies of the Church,"[75] "giving away the Church,"[76] acting as a "fifth column of Satan,"[77] and for a host of other "errors" and "deceptions" that have lead Catholics "into the apostate religion of humanism."[78] Traditionalists have also openly attacked papal authority in the implementation of Vatican II aggiornamento, especially in the area of liturgy reform.

It should be noted, however, that although the traditionalist critique of magisterial authority has often been bitter and recriminating, it is not a repudiation of the nature of that authority, per se; nor does it question that magisterial authority exists by divine will, or that popes in the postconciliar era have been true popes. The exception to this position is that taken by sedevacantist (from the Latin *sede vacante*, "vacant see") traditionalists, a highly radicalized fringe element who have refused to recognize the popes since Pius XII as valid popes, asserting instead that all recent popes are deposed, excommunicated, or improperly elected, and that the chair of Peter is therefore vacant. Principal among this sedevacantist segment are priests ordained bishops by the former Vietnamese archbishop Pierre Martin Ngo-Dinh-Thuc.[79]

Although a minority position among traditionalist Catholics, the sedevacantist position has precipitated considerable conflict within the movement. Archbishop Lefebvre has previously admonished his supporters to dissociate themselves from any cleric claiming to be a bishop not recognized by the pope and not to assist at the Mass of any sedevacantist priest.[80] In 1983 Lefebvre went so far as to expel nine priests from his own society who had assumed a sedevacantist position and would not "pray for the Pope."[81] Throughout his imbroglio with the Vatican, Lefebvre maintained that while he acknowledged the legitimacy of the papacy, he challenged only certain acts and orientations of John XXIII's successors in failing to defend the faith and "what the Church has taught for two thousand years."[82] When the hierarchy uses the institutions and authority of the Church to "endanger" the faith, it is the proper duty of Catholics "to disobey and keep the Tradition." However, with his decision to consecrate episcopal successors without Vatican authority and attendant charges that Rome was now occupied by the Antichrist,[83] Lefebvre clearly moved closer to the sedevacantist position he had previously repudiated.

The traditionalist attack on their right-wing coreligionists follows allegations that conservative Catholics have failed to challenge the hierarchy in the face of the "decomposition" of the Church, a failure attributed to a lack of nerve and a misguided "papolatry" that reflects a "distorted sense of obedience."[84] Traditionalist leaders have also berated conservatives for "neutralizing" opposition to Vatican II reforms by draining off traditionalist support into organizations controlled by the hierarchy.[85] Hard-line traditionalists have also refused any cooperation with conservative Catholic groups, especially where the latter have undertaken petition drives for the reinstatement of the Tridentine liturgy.

The most significant aspect of traditionalism as an action-oriented ideology, however, is not its inflammatory rhetoric or holy war imagery, but its tendencies toward separatism. Traditionalist Catholics have not been content merely to decry the influence of modernists or the auto-destruction of the postconciliar Church, nor have they opted for the ultramontanist solution to the tensions surrounding the meaning of

Vatican II, as have many conservative Catholic groups and individuals. Instead, traditionalists have sought to remedy through separatism what they could no longer decisively influence from within—through the establishment of a network of parallel ecclesial structures: schools, parishes, chapels, seminaries, and foundations outside official Church channels. This organized and separatist institutional aspect of traditionalist dissent gives social expression to the movement's schismatic character. It has also led to traditionalism accruing deviant status within the postconciliar Church and to the disciplinary action taken against the movement's participants. This separatist-sectarian dynamic within traditionalism received its fullest expression in Archbishop Lefebvre and his priestly fraternity and is the principal reason why Vatican concern with the traditionalist cause has focused heavily on the initiatives of the French archbishop and his society.

"Conspiracy Against God and Man"

A fourth distinctive feature of traditionalist ideology is its predilection for conspiracy and subversion theories of social causality. The conviction that the "enemy is in the Church"[86] and that Catholicism's postconciliar malaise is the consequence of conspiracy and subversion "done deliberately by the enemies of Christ" who intend to "wipe out his Church"[87] is a persistently recurring theme in traditionalist literature, sermons, and public statements.

While sharing the view in conservative Catholic circles that postconciliar transformations and tensions are the result of bureaucratic insurgency and the machinations of theological neomodernists, traditionalist interpretations of the pressures of aggiornamento tend to be more extremist, conspiracy-oriented, and imbued with apocalyptic imagery. Sociological explanations of postconciliar conflict and tensions among Catholics are derided as too mundane and prosaic, portraying a "secular" bias that lacks insight into the current eschatological dimensions of the struggle between good and evil occurring in the Church. As Father Fenton noted, " Surely a more logical explanation . . . is that the destruction of the Church which we are witnessing today is by no means an accident but that it has been planned that way. 'An enemy has done this.' There is no question, to my mind, but that the Roman Catholic Church is here and now in an advanced stage of planned destruction."[88]

Generally speaking, themes of conspiracy and subversion were not prominent in conservative sectors at the beginning of the Council deliberations, save for long-standing anxieties that the hierarchy would succumb to a resurgent neo-modernism through the influence of liberal *periti* (theological advisors). However, as traditional patterns and symbols of Catholic identity became destabilized, and as the radicalized anticonciliarism of traditionalists became a more isolated and marginalized position, conspiracy theories became a more prominent feature of the attack on the pope, the Council, and the New Mass.

The conspiracy web that eventually came to animate the traditionalist position drew its inspiration and legitimacy primarily from earlier papal warnings against the peril of the "virus" of modernism in the Church, especially Pius X's antimodernist broadside *Pascendi Gregis* (1907) solemnly warning Catholics of the threat to the faith "in the very bosom and heart" of the Church itself. Catholicism's long-standing antipathy to Freemasonry and communism also provided traditionalist Catholics with ideological material for anticonciliar conspiracy theories. In 1968 Tito Cassini, an Italian Catholic journalist, published *The Torn Tunic,* attacking liturgical renewal and protesting that changes in the Mass were linked to the influences of "Marxists and Masons."[89] In the United States, Gommar De Pauw was among the first to charge that the Church had entered a time of severe trial during which "diabolical-oriented advisors" had infiltrated the highest echelons of the magisterium as allegedly predicted at Fatima.[90] Allegations that Vatican II was part of a "diabolic communist conspiracy" against the Church were also a prominent and persistent theme in the writings and public pronouncements of Father Fenton and in other ORCM literature.[91] And promulgation of the new liturgy quickly became linked with lurid apocalyptic foreboding regarding the "final savage onslaught to destroy the last vestiges of God's Holy Catholic Church,"[92] with the "sign of the anti-Christ,"[93] and with the onset of an apocalyptic era in which the "forces of hell have broken upon earth and Satan is deceiving the Nation."[94]

The most prominent conspiracy theory to circulate in traditionalist quarters centered around allegations of Masonic influences among the hierarchy.[95] These charges became a full-blown part of the traditionalist ideological repertoire in the mid-1970s, when published accounts first appeared in Europe charging high-ranking Vatican prelates with membership in Masonic lodges.[96] In addition to Satanic, communist, and Masonic allegations, traditionalist conspiracy theories have also been interwoven with anti-Semitic motifs, although the latter are a less prominent feature of traditionalist ideology.[97]

Whether or not the pervasiveness of conspiracy theories among traditionalist Catholics reflect paranoid tendencies within the movement remains to be demonstrated. As a social movement stratagem, such theories have obvious ideological utility in legitimating traditionalist dissent; they focus attention on the occupant of ecclesial office rather than on the nature of the authority of the office itself. Such an emphasis is paramount for Catholics protesting in defense of orthodoxy. The pace and scope of aggiornamento also greatly facilitated the tendency to equate conflict and dysfunction in the Church with conspiracy, especially in an institution that had long been perceived as static in its disciplinary, doctrinal, and ritual forms. Furthermore, the parallels between widespread cultural and social dysfunction in society at large and dysfunction within the Church itself—the one crisis reflecting and reinforcing the other—also facilitated conspiracy thinking. The thesis developed by Catholic Integralists in the nineteenth and twentieth centuries that developments since the Reformation were a long chain of events let loose by Satan to destroy the Church, along with turn-of-the-century magisterial antimodernist pronouncements, also reinforced the credibility of conspiracy views of aggiornamento. So did, at the level of popular Catholic folk piety, apparitions of the Virgin Mary (Fatima, La Salette) allegedly warning of a period of widespread apostasy in the highest echelons of the Church. These revelations and supernatural messages—which were also interwoven with biblical forebodings over the Great Apostasy foretold by Saint Paul (2 Thess. 2:3), the coming "chastisement," and the era of the Antichrist—provided traditionalist Catholics with a transcendent verification of the link between postconciliar turmoil and certain "punishments foretold by Mary."[98] Prophesies and apparitions have also provided traditionalists with a contemporary form of Catholic dispensationalism that divides Church history into discrete periods and that situates their dissent within a historical eschatological framework that both tests the endurance of their faith and fidelity to the true Church while simultaneously legitimating their dissent from those who occupy the positions of authority within it.[99]

Right-Wing Politics

As was the case with Protestant fundamentalism during its first generation, postconciliar traditionalism also remains a movement primarily concerned with the struggle for power, authority, and the plausibility of a religious worldview within an ecclesial body rather than a world-transforming type of sectarianism. As such, the traditionalist movement does not have high visibility with regard to issues of public policy, nor is traditionalism an organized force in the political realm. The traditionalist approach to social and political issues is characterized primarily by the advocacy of a militant piety and spiritual crusades against the evils of the age. In the United States, traditionalist Catholics are more clearly a "remnant faithful" than a moral majority. In France, however, Archbishop Lefebvre's supporters have been openly allied with French monarchist-nationalist tendencies and the reactionary movement of Jean-Marie Le Pen.[100]

Although traditionalism is primarily a movement of religious dissent, traditionalist ideology is nonetheless clearly permeated with a right-wing sociopolitical agenda, including standard condemnations of homosexuality, pornography, abortion, feminism, socialism, rock music, the Supreme Court decision on prayer in school, and other forms of "moral depravity" pervading modern society. Although themes of messianic nationalism are absent from traditionalist literature and public pronouncements, anticommunist and Cold War themes have been pervasive. (The John Birch Society connections with the ORCM membership have already been noted.) Traditionalists also deprecate liberation theology, Vatican II-inspired involvement in peace and social justice initiatives, and Catholic advocacy of human rights as a "modernist agenda" that reduces salvation "to economic and social well-being."[101]

Reactionary right-wing themes emphasizing authority, social hierarchy, and obedience, as well as condemnations of liberalism, the democratic ethos, the "rights of man" associated with the legacy of the Enlightenment and the French Revolution, and the political and cultural ethos of modern liberal democracy are especially prominent in the writings and public statements of Archbishop Lefebvre. All such values, according to Lefebvre, are inimical to the Catholic religion.[102] The archbishop's social agenda—which reflects in many ways the turbulent religiopolitical contours of French Catholicism's struggle with the legacy of 1789—calls for the restoration of the "Christian Social Order" understood as the re-establishment of Catholic hegemony in the social, cultural, and intellectual spheres.[103] The traditionalists repudiate the Vatican II theology affirming the pilgrim nature of the Church and encouraging tolerance and collegiality. They reject individualism and permissivism at the moral level and of liberalism at the political level. Traditionalism's call for the return of Catholic hegemony also gives expression to the longing for an all-encompassing religious culture in which religious values dominate all spheres of life, a position that repudiates the notion of a proper "secular" sphere of thought or action. The gathering of traditionalist Catholics around Mass centers and schools is one sociological manifestation of the quest for this "total" Catholic experience.

Class Conflict and Status Politics

While traditionalism's ideological roots lie in the problems posed by theological modernism, Catholicism's Integralist legacy, and the perception of contradiction stemming from the reforms of Vatican II, the causes of traditionalist discontent also include conflict stemming from alterations in the Catholic social structure and role status relationships within the Church. In this regard, Catholic traditionalism as a religious movement gives expression to the elective affinities between ideas and social class interests.

Much of the discontent on the Catholic right following the Council has been directed against pressures brought to bear on Catholicism's authority structure by the spread of professionalism, bureaucratism, and the influence of an emerging new knowledge class within the Church's administrative infrastructure. In populist-like symbolism pitting "simple laymen" and "folk Catholicism" against insensitive liberal "bureaucratic tyrants" and "professional elites," both conservative and traditionalist Catholics have denounced the influence of these "experts" on Church decision-making and on the public image of Catholicism. The traditionalist critique, the more radical of the two, derives from the suspicion of a modernist conspiracy of elites bent on undermining the traditional faith of the Catholic rank and file.[104]

More germane to the rise of traditionalism as an organized social movement, however, is the shift in class and role status relationships affecting laity and clergy in the wake of Vatican II. It is significant that while lay initiatives have been the primary impetus behind the formation of many postconciliar conservative Catholic interest groups, clergy have been the primary architects of virtually every major traditionalist organization. Clerics maintain key positions of power and authority within the traditionalist movement and are its chief ideologues and apologists. Clergy also constitute the core of traditionalism's organizational and administrative infrastructure—most conspicuously in the case of Archbishop Lefebvre and his priestly fraternity. Furthermore, traditionalist priests have made themselves perpetually relevant to the central objectives of the movement through their advocacy of pre-Vatican II clerically centered ecclesial and sacramental forms as the only proper means of saving souls and identifying the true Church.

While reflecting pre-Vatican II dominant-subordinate patterns of clerical-lay relations, clerical prominence in the traditionalist movement also gives visibility to interest group agendas resulting from role status loss accompanying liturgical reform. In the preconciliar Catholic social structure, priests were generally perceived as spiritual virtuosi. Their high social status rested in role incumbency (specialized control over a cultic enterprise) rather than in individual charisma.[105] The priesthood received its highest status affirmation in the monopolistic power to "offer" the Mass and "change" the bread and wine into the Body and Blood of Christ. With some ethnic exceptions, lay-clerical relationships were marked by codes of special etiquette, the observance of social distance, and deferential behavior on the part of many laity. Clerical status was further enhanced by the manner in which the priesthood came to be tied in the Catholic consciousness to superior access to the truths of revelation and to the veneration of the sacred itself. This bonding of social role and sacred cultus found popular catechetical expression in the teaching that by showing reverence and honor to the priest, Catholics were actually showing "reverence and honor to Christ Himself, for the priest is in a very true sense another Christ."[106]

Vatican II implicitly demythologized aspects of clerical life and status by offering egalitarian theological premises for lay-clerical relations. The Church was no longer to be defined exclusively in terms of clerical prerogatives. Laity were to become more integrated into Catholicism's institutional life. The most important change affecting Catholic lay-clerical distinctions occurred in the area of the liturgy. Laity were now given a more active part in what had been an exclusive clerical preserve for centuries. Liturgical reform thus introduced a new division of labor in Catholic ritual, providing laity with greater operational access to the cultic basis of clerical status. In the *Novus Ordo* Mass, emphasis shifted from the model of an individual priest standing between Christ and the community as an exclusive spiritual mediator, to that of the priesthood and ministerial character of the community itself. Laity offered the Mass "not only through the hands of the priest but also with him" (*General Instruction,* Art. 11, 62).

These shifts in the dispersion of sacred charisma raised ambiguities about the role of the priest as one who possessed exclusive mediational and sacramental power. Many priests found themselves marginal men whose identity had come to lack clear purpose or a meaningful rationale commensurate with the discipline associated with clerical life.[107] In the years immediately following the Vatican II, the high number of departures from the priesthood, the change in attitudes among Catholic parents with regard to a priestly vocation, and dramatic declines in the number of seminarians also reflected declining clerical status, especially in industrialized nations like the United States.[108]

The status politics of clerical prominence in the traditionalist movement are made most conspicuous in a key theme in the traditionalist attack on liturgical reform: the New Mass is illegitimate because it falsely shifts the focus of worship from the isolated role of the priest as intermediary to the collective participation of the entire worshiping community. Thus the role of the priest as one who exclusively offers sacrifice loses hierarchical status and instrumental significance. Accordingly, the priest is denigrated to the role of a "presider," a "president," one of several "ministers of the assembly" who "sums up" the prayers of the congregation and whose position is minimized, therefore depriving the priest of "the reason for his existence, and importance." This diminishing of the priest's proper role in the new liturgy (and in other aspects of Catholic life) is the result of "an exaggerated concept of the so-called lay priesthood."[109]

The symbolic defense of preconciliar clerical role status vis-à-vis resistance to liturgical reform is a prominent theme in the writings and public statements of Archbishop Lefebvre and the priests of his fraternity. Lefebvre decried liturgical reform for bringing about the "ruination" of the priest by permitting greater lay participation. According to the archbishop, the modernist-inspired "democratic agenda" and "wave of laicism" in the postconciliar Church have caused the priest to be reduced to the equivalent of a "Protestant functionary" and to lose his proper status in the Catholic economy of salvation.[110] In his 1976 ordination sermon, Lefebvre remonstrated:

> By this idea of power bestowed on the lower rank on the Holy Mass, they [liturgical reformers] have destroyed the priesthood! They are destroying the priesthood, for what is the priest, if the priest no longer has a personal power, that power which is given to him by his ordination, as these future priests are going to receive in a moment? They are going to receive a character, a character that will put them above the people of God! Never more shall they be able . . . to say, "We are men like other men." This would not be true. They will no longer be men like other men! They will be men of God. They will be men, I should say, who almost participate in the divinity of Our Lord Jesus Christ by His sacerdotal character.[111]

Concern with maintaining clerical role status is also reflected in the archbishop's equation of the essence of the Church with the hierarchical priesthood, in his establishment of traditionalist seminaries as the exclusive instrumentality for "saving the true Church," and in his disparagement of the seminary training of establishment Church clergy.[112] Whatever its theological merits, the traditionalist campaign to save the "true Mass," spearheaded by a priestly fraternity, is also a stratagem for maintaining the clerical power and status threatened and marginalized by postconciliar reform. The traditionalist campaign strives to preserve the ritual basis of this power. Because the preconciliar Mass was central to the Catholic economy of salvation and served as the cultic basis of the "true priesthood," the strident defense of the Tridentine liturgy was a logical reaction to the perceived threat to clerical power.[113]

Structural Polity

Also relevant to understanding the rise of the traditionalist movement is a sociological analysis of the relationship between norms and values within the structure of Catholic polity. Where social systems tend toward differentiation, the structure may allow normative change without simultaneously appearing to challenge basic values. However, in systems in which all social and normative rules are thought to be part of a comprehensive order, alterations in or challenges to norms are likely to be interpreted as efforts to subvert fundamental values. Although conflict is less likely to occur in less differentiated systems, the conflict will be more intense and value oriented once it surfaces; any protest against norms will likely be interpreted as a protest against values.[114] Religion is especially vulnerable to conflict of this nature because it is a comprehensive meaning system.

Catholic traditionalism did not begin as a distinct social movement but emerged out of diffuse conservative Catholic discontent with aggiornamento. Father De

Pauw's "Traditionalist Manifesto" was, in spite of its hyperbolic title, a document relatively moderate in tone and typical of conservative Catholic anxiety at the time. The views expressed in the CTM Manifesto were not overtly anticonciliar and did not represent a wholesale repudiation of Vatican II or a full-blown conspiracy theory of aggiornamento. Nor was Archbishop Lefebvre's public position on the Council prior to 1970 one of complete denunciation, although his early repudiation of collegiality provided a means for rejecting any majority decisions in advance.

Within a relatively short period of time, however, traditionalist dissent over aggiornamento and its implementation became linked with a challenge to hierarchical authority. In the United States, this first occurred in the context of Father De Pauw's canonical conflict with Cardinal Shehan; later it occurred with Archbishop Lefebvre's refusal to close his seminary and stop ordaining priests and his administering sacraments in violation of Canon Law.

While the specific juridical controversies of Father De Pauw and Archbishop Lefebvre were important in contributing to the radicalization of traditionalist dissent, the broadly based traditionalist resistance to liturgical reform presented the most direct and open challenge to magisterial authority. The tension over liturgical reform was acutely exacerbated by the mandatory implementation of the *Novus Ordo* Mass and the prohibition of the Tridentine rite after 1971. Between April 1969 and November 1971 the Tridentine and *Novus Ordo* rites co-existed in the Church—with the later replacing the former with varying degrees of speed from diocese to diocese. Under this two-rite arrangement, Catholics opposed to the new liturgy could continue their traditional devotional pattern (provided they could find a parish with a Tridentine liturgy in suitable proximity). However, once the *Novus Ordo* Mass became mandatory, this option was no longer available. Those who would not give up the old Mass faced the choice of openly defying the hierarchy by attending the now illicit Tridentine liturgy (in chapels established by traditionalist groups) or foregoing Mass altogether—an unacceptable option for the orthodox committed to the sacramental necessity of the Church in the economy of salvation.[115] By virtue of their own religious self-understanding, traditionalist Catholics now found themselves without an exit option. Ironically, the kind of authoritarianism and hierarchical order extolled by traditionalists thus made their manner of resistance and rebellion a zero-sum game. With the prohibition of the Tridentine liturgy, anticonciliar dissent took on a deviant status in the postconciliar Church, leading to a further radicalization within the movement, the emergence of full-blown conspiracy theories, public and unrestrained attacks on the hierarchy, and the establishment of institutions for the perpetuation of a counter-Church movement. Ironically, the prohibition of the Tridentine Mass after 1971 also transformed the core symbol of Catholic corporate unity and mystery into a sign of dissent and resistance not only to the reforms of the Council but to the Church's own authority structure.

De-Objectification

A final but critical factor relevant to the rise of Catholic traditionalism concerns the problem of religious objectification and the preservation of supernaturalism in the culture of modernity. Objectification—identifying spiritual realities with material objects or historical events—is essential to all religious life and indeed to all cultural life. Without this process, collective identity, shared experience and worship, and continuity of tradition are not possible. Objectification also provides a critical means for articulating and preserving the boundary between the sacred and profane. However, one danger inherent in objectification in religious matters is that religious symbols (i.e., texts, doctrinal pronouncements, ritual actions) can come to be perceived as acting autonomously and as ends in themselves. This objectivist fallacy heightens when cultural situations that give rise to symbols and support them change and cease to give them plausibility, or when symbols are subject to new interpretations via the advancement of science, historicism, and the relativizing tendencies associated with modernization. As secularization makes inroads into religious consciousness, religious symbols may become subject to more arbitrary and extravagant manipulation, or in the fundamentalist response, they come to be justified solely by virtue of what is perceived as their divine origin. Symbols are then taken as irreducible to any aspects of the empirical world. The transcendent is then understood as a reality that enters the world primarily in the form of miracles and special acts of revelation which are encoded in fixed creedal and dogmatic propositions and frozen in liturgical rites and other symbolic forms. These supernaturally guaranteed truths are "inerrant" and "unchanging" because they are taken as unconditioned by their historical, social, or cultural contexts.[116] "Objectification" runs rampant.

As the history of evangelical Christianity illustrates, the "disenchantment" of the world and the de-objectification of religious symbols caused by the dynamics of modernization stimulated counter tendencies toward a hardened objectification of religious realities. Theologians and biblical exegetes provoked a crisis in the late nineteenth century by employing scientific and historical-critical methods that had the practical effect of undermining the objectivity of the Bible and thus challenging evangelical religious self-understanding. The fundamentalist response to these developments was an exaggerated, objectivist view of Christianity as a codified, propositional, fixed, and unalterable revelation—a position that precluded the integration of new theological concepts and religious symbolism aimed at bringing the Christian faith into harmony with the new historical era and intellectual order.

The rise of Catholic traditionalism illustrates a similar dialectic, where religious objectivism and reification have intensified in response to the perceived attempt by liberals and modernists to break the link between religious symbols and "objective" reality. Liturgical reform is again instructive. For many Catholics, the full experience of the Tridentine Mass—the theology of "mystery" expressed therein, the use of an archaic language, the ritual signs of the cross, kisses, bows, and upheld hands—revealed and "objectified" a salvific religious sphere standing over and against the mundane patterns of everyday experience. And the 450-year tenure of the Tridentine rite strengthened the conviction among most Catholics, who knew little about the historical development of the liturgy, that the Mass in this form constituted a permanent, superimposed symbol of the Church's own divine reality and ahistorical, immutable character.

With the rapid change in the liturgy between 1964 and 1969, this objectivist mentality was subject to severe erosion. Many Catholics were left with the impression that what they had viewed as heaven-sent and absolute in form and structure was permeable and subject to redefinition and cultural and territorial variation. Changes in Catholicism's core corporate ritual also suggested the troubling possibility that other constituent elements of the Church were not objective, superimposed "givens," but that they too had been (and could be) sociologically and historically constructed and reconstructed.[117] Thus Vatican II and its attendant liturgical reform initiated a crisis of de-objectification for Roman Catholics. Core constituent symbols of sacred reality and religious self-understanding were de-objectified by those who sought to make them relevant to the modern age. This produced a hostile anticonciliar reaction: a broad spectrum of doctrines, customs, and modes of discipline that could be taken as authoritative but contingent rather than definitive were now insistently described as "inerrant" or "infallible." Thus the rise of Catholic traditionalism gave vivid expression to the effort to maintain a categorical and objective distinction between the natural and the supernatural in an age for which such a distinction had become increasingly tendentious.

Conclusion

The June 1988 schism of Archbishop Lefebvre opened a new chapter in the traditionalist campaign against "neo-modernist Rome." In spite of their excommunication, the archbishop and his supporters remained undaunted in their struggle for truth and tradition, taking refuge in their own marginalized institutions and remaining convinced of their eventual exoneration with the restoration of the "true Church." Predictably, traditionalists have condemned the excommunication as "meaningless" and as another indication of the Vatican's "cruel persecution" of their cause.[118] In a spirit of exalted defiance, the excommunication was welcomed. In a 6 July 1988 open letter to Cardinal Gantin, prefect of the Congregation for Bishops, superiors of the society expressed their delight in being repudiated by the "adulterous spirit" of the "counterfeit church": "we ask for nothing better than to be declared outside of this impious communion of the ungodly."[119] For his part, Archbishop Lefebvre continued to legitimate his consecrations on the grounds of "necessity" and the eschatological urgency of the times and to profess astonishment that two decades after the Council, Catholics were still being deceived "in the name of obedience (Satan's masterstroke)" and were not heeding Saint Paul's warning: "Even if an Angel from Heaven came to tell you anything other than what I have taught you, do not listen to him."[120] Among his more enthusiastic supporters, the aging archbishop continued to be held up as a prelate "raised up by providence," a modern-day Athanasius who in times of similar general "blindness in heresy" (Arianism), was excommunicated but subsequently exonerated and eventually canonized.[121]

In the aftermath of the schism, the Vatican attitude toward traditionalists remains lenient and flexible, suggesting that it is the defiance of papal authority and juridical norms, not traditionalist views or beliefs, per se, that is the more important Vatican concern. In proclaiming Lefebvre's excommunication (while not explicitly extending it to his followers) and denouncing his "incomplete and contradictory" notion of tradition, John Paul II established a Vatican commission to work toward reconciliation of those connected with the Society—along the lines of the protocol rejected by Lefebvre—and admonished Catholics to show respect for those Catholics attached to the Latin liturgical tradition by a "wide and generous application of the 1984 indult."[122]

Shortly after the schism, eight traditional priests from different movements met with John Paul II, Cardinal Ratzinger, and Cardinal Mayer and were encouraged to found a priestly society as a means for keeping the "traditions of spirituality and apostolate" to which traditionalist Catholics were committed. On 18 July 1988, the Society of Saint Peter was founded at the Cistercian Abbey of Houterive (Canton of Fribourg, Switzerland). The superior and his two assistants were former members of Archbishop Lefebvre's Society of Saint Pius X. The immediate goal of the new order was to create an international seminary in Europe that was Thomistic in theological orientation and traditional in spirituality and liturgy but, unlike Ecône, in communion with Rome. Traditionalists dismissed the new organization as nothing more than a Vatican ploy to divide their cause.[123]

While the excommunication of Lefebvre has created some cases of personal crisis among those who support the archbishop in all respects but who reject justification of the consecrations on the grounds of necessity,[124] there is little indication that the schism has precipitated a mass exodus of the archbishop's supporters.[125] Given the worldwide scope of the society's organizational infrastructure and episcopal mechanism for self-perpetuation, the traditionalist movement is unlikely to disappear. Schools operated by the society will continue to function as an important source for recruitment into the movement's clerical ranks.

While it is not declining dramatically, there is also no evidence that the traditionalist movement à la Lefebvre is spreading rapidly—although anticonciliarism remains a strong neoconservative tendency within the Church.[126] A movement claiming legitimacy as the "true" Roman Catholic Church while simultaneously asserting that the See of Peter is occupied by the Antichrist is inherently self-limited. Nor is the trauma of change that initially galvanized the traditionalist movement as acute now as it was in the first decade following the Second Vatican Council. What have been interpreted as the restorationist initiatives of the current pontificate are also likely to constrain any dramatic increase in traditionalist Catholic ranks, because such initiatives work to mollify disenchanted conservatives from whom the traditionalist movement has drawn it rank and file.

Traditionalism qua Fundamentalism

Like Protestant fundamentalism, Catholic traditionalism is an antimodernist worldview rooted in adherence to religious and epistemological categories that have lost much of their plausibility and privileged status in the wake of institutional and intellectual change and adaptation. Traditionalism shares with Protestant fundamentalism tendencies toward a highly cognitive doctrinal religiosity marked by an objectivistic, dogmatic, legalistic, and dichotomous cognitive style. Traditionalism manifests the fundamentalist tendency to absolutize the cognitive aspects of religion and to reify constituent symbols of religious identity. Objectivity in the religious sphere is taken as a closed hermeneutical circle unalloyed by human interpolation of any kind. Traditionalism also follows the fundamentalist pattern of holding that theological liberalism or modernism can never be accommodated to the "true faith," that liberalism and Christianity are genetically distinct, that liberalism can never be orthodox, and that those who advance liberalism in the name of orthodoxy are merely trying to subvert the Church from within.[127]

Like its Protestant counterpart, Catholic traditionalism is also marked by militancy, exclusivism, a "church against the world" ecclesiology, separatist tendencies, and conspiratorial-eschatological interpretations of social change. In both the Protestant and Roman Catholic traditions, the rise of a self-conscious fundamentalist movement draws attention to the problems of one sociology of knowledge resisting displacement by another, to the inherently dialectical manner in which social reality is constructed, and to many of the negative effects of modernization and secularization on contemporary culture and on religious sensitivities. However, it should be noted that although it is antimodernist in its theological orientation and in high tension with society at large, the sectarian impulses in traditionalism do not preclude the use of many aspects of modern bureaucratic organization and mass media communications technology to further their organizational efforts. It is also worth repeating that traditionalism, like fundamentalism, gives expression to both a selective retrieval of the broad spectrum of Catholic experience and to ideological innovation based on that tradition.

The causes of Catholic traditionalism also have many affinities with those of Protestant fundamentalism: the extension of earlier theological orientations, the reaction against new epistemological and hermeneutical frames of reference that decisively penetrated each tradition, widespread social and cultural crisis linked to the loss of religious identity and discipline, the erosion of traditional forms of authority, and the crisis of faith brought about by the relativizing of sacred realities by strategic elites within the respective traditions.

Although similar in content and cause, Catholic traditionalism and Protestant fundamentalism also differ in their respective forms and structures. While the fundamentalist movement developed in a gradual and diffuse manner in evangelical Christianity, the rise of Catholic traditionalism was precipitated primarily by a specific event: the Second Vatican Council. Catholic Traditionalism has also been more preoccupied with the problem of legitimation than had been the case with Protestant fundamentalism. The traditionalist emphasis upon ritual practice rather than biblical texts is also a differentiating characteristic.

Fundamentalist Orientations and Fundamentalist Movements

One must distinguish between a fundamentalist *orientation*—which may be a latent ethos in any religious tradition—and a separatist fundamentalist *movement*. Fundamentalist orientations do not mean, ipso facto, fundamentalist movements. It is the latter, not the former, that have the more serious sociocultural implications both in the area of public policy and within the development of specific religious traditions themselves.

Traditionalist and conservative Catholics share many ideological affinities: a cognitive defiance of many aspects of modernity, fears of internal threat and subversion, the tendency to view liberal or progressive Catholics as modernists working to destroy the faith, and an "authoritarian heteronomy" that treats the ecclesial magisterium in the same manner as Protestant fundamentalists treat the Bible. Both conservative and traditionalist Catholics also favor right-wing political agendas, ethical rigorism, and the maintenance of strict boundaries between the sacred and the profane.[128]

Conservatism, however, is a valuable and necessary component in all religion. As John Coleman has noted, authentic conservatism in the Roman Catholic experience cherishes the traditional symbols, rituals, and spirituality that have constituted Catholicism's rich religious heritage. Authentic conservatism resists fads and too-quick adoption. It seeks to conserve the Church's historical discipline and orthodoxy. It does so, however, while respecting the Church's necessity to change and adapt.[129] Organizations such as Opus Dei, Catholics United for the Faith, and others that have often been identified as "fundamentalist" by liberal Catholic critics[130] do not, in fact, constitute fundamentalist movements—although they express certain fundamentalist tendencies and orientations. As demonstrated in the essay by James Hitchcock below, these movements are generally norm-oriented and strict-constructionist in their approach to the documents of the Second Vatican Council. While their piety is often militantly ascetic and while they view the meaning of the Council in terms of "internal" and "spiritual" rather than structural reform, they do not represent an outright disavowal of change. Nor, more importantly, have conservative Catholics set up counter-Church institutional structures. Nor, politically, is the profound moral conservatism of conservative Catholics allied, as in the case of traditionalists, to a reactionary and antidemocratic political ideology that extols the virtues of the ancien régime.[131]

Traditionalism as a fundamentalist phenomenon, by contrast, is a more radicalized orientation. Traditionalism petrifies doctrines, disciplines, and modes of Catholic religious identity while seeking to monopolize the entire religious economy. Where conservatives extol an authoritarian and hierarchical Church, traditionalists want a counter-revolutionary one—as is clearly evident in Archbishop Lefebvre's vehement denunciations of the legacy of the French Revolution and the entire modern experiment. It is thus that Catholic traditionalism reveals its essentially sectarian character.

As Troeltsch[132] and others have observed, Catholicism has historically expressed itself through a synthesis of culture and intelligence—in spite of the predominance of its Greco-Roman cultural heritage. Through its "church-like" proclivities it has sought to come to terms with different intellectual and spiritual needs of different constituencies situated differently within social structures. Throughout its history, the Church has struggled to develop a powerful and credible synthesis of culture and the Gospel that can support and enhance both culture and religion. In so doing, Catholicism has struggled with the tensions inherent in maintaining the integrity and prophetic stance of the tradition while simultaneously developing it. Traditionalism exaggerates the sect-like patterns and doctrinal complex that became a more prominent feature of Catholicism's institutional life during its troubled engagement with contemporary culture and thus reduces the Church to a sectarian aspect of the broader culture.

As previously noted, Catholic traditionalism did not begin as a discrete movement, but emerged out of, not independently from, conservative Catholic discontent. Traditionalists should not, therefore, be seen as a fringe element of antiquarian malcontents but rather as a "hard" expression of religious orientations that were already present in the Catholic right. Fundamentalism may thus be more properly viewed as a highly radicalized and deviant form of conservatism rather than as a genetically distinct religious orientation—suggesting the aptness of Harry Emerson Fosdick's observation that fundamentalists are really "mad conservatives."

2. Catholic Activist Conservatism in the United States

James Hitchcock

Confronted by a demand from police that they cease blocking the doors of a building, the demonstrators refuse. Systematically the police begin moving in, prodding some to walk to vans, carrying or dragging others who have become limp. Eventually several hundred people are arrested, many of whom as a matter of principled tactic refuse to give their names. Most are imprisoned overnight, and some are later tried and given brief jail sentences for disorderly conduct or resisting arrest.

Such scenes occurred countless times, in all parts of the United States, during the 1960s. The demonstrators were activists of the left, many of them college or university students. However, the episode described above took place in 1988, in Atlanta. One of those arrested, far from being a radical student, was a sixty-one-year-old man named Austin Vaughan, the Roman Catholic auxiliary bishop of New York. Vaughan and his fellow protestors were participating in an action of Operation Rescue, a national organization that sponsors anti-abortion protests employing tactics of civil disobedience. Many of those participating in the protest had earlier decided to refuse to move when ordered to do so by police.[133]

Bishop Vaughan was the first Catholic bishop ever arrested in the United States and in fact was taken into custody six times during 1988–89. Following his example, seventy-three-year-old retired Auxiliary Bishop George Lynch of Raleigh, North Carolina, was also arrested several times during the same period, while Bishop Albert Ottenweller, seventy-three, of Steubenville, Ohio, and Bishop Paul Dudley, sixty-two, of Sioux Falls, South Dakota, were each arrested once. Approximately five thousand people were arrested in Operation Rescue during 1988; despite the common impression that abortion is primarily a Catholic issue, many of the participants were evangelical or fundamentalist Protestants. Ironically, the most dramatically militant expression of conservative Catholic moral belief is in fact an ecumenical movement, organized and headed by a fundamentalist Protestant named Randall Terry.[134]

Bishops courting arrest by deliberately violating civil laws and practical cooperation between Catholics and traditionally anti-Catholic Protestant fundamentalists are developments which could not have occurred in American Catholicism before 1965. The surprising religiopolitical coalitions formed in the past twenty-five years lend weight to Robert Wuthnow's judgment that contemporary American religious life is no longer divided by denominational boundaries but according to ideological ones.[135] The ecumenical character of Operation Rescue suggests that the political agenda of conservative Roman Catholicism in the United States is neither unique nor distinctive. The major concerns of conservative Catholics are shared by conservatives in many religious denominations, with whom conservative Catholic activists often make common cause. And although conservative Catholics are identified publicly with the movement to outlaw abortion, they have been unable to agree completely among themselves as to the precise content of their political agenda beyond this central issue. Most disapproved of the tactics of civil disobedience during the 1960s, for example, and many still do. National Right to Life, the largest anti-abortion organization in the United States (officially nonsectarian), omits any mention of Operation Rescue from its official publications. And while Catholic bishops have been arrested in acts of civil disobedience, other prelates have expressed disapproval of all illegal acts.

While most anti-abortion activists have concentrated on education and political action—on changing public opinion and changing laws—those engaged in direct action justify their strategy in terms of both immediate and long-range effects, arguing that it delays, and possibly prevents altogether, the death of fetuses. Indeed Operation Rescue members see themselves as warriors in a pitched battle with the forces of death and darkness and employ militant rhetoric in describing their mission to block abortion clinics: a "rescue" is a military "skirmish"; targets are "hits"; protesters are "troops"; both sides use "spies." Similarly, the "Siege of Atlanta" refers to the five months following the 1988 Democratic National Convention—a period during which Operation Rescue burst upon the national scene and in which 1,307 people were arrested in actions against abortion clinics. Former Benedictine monk Joseph Scheidler, a national anti-abortion leader and the executive director of the Pro-Life Action League in Chicago, has perfected the "rescue method" and written a book on it. His moral view is absolutist: "We are going to win because we are right. They are wrong. We are good. They are bad. It's that simple."[136]

Such activism is intended to capture the moral imagination and serve as a powerful witness. Bishop Vaughan contends that the acceptance of abortion on demand has corrupted American society. As Bishop Dudley explained, "We honestly believe that life is precious, and that life is being snuffed out in this building."[137] Despite the dramatic clerical participation in Operation Rescue, the witness given in this and other manifestations of conservative Catholicism since about 1970 has been primarily inspired and led by Catholic laity, with participants often troubled by what they regard as clerical caution or indifference.

In fact conservative Catholic activists believe that large segments of the clergy have been misled by liberal and modernist ideas in the Church during the past generation. Lay men and women have stepped into the breach. Although most rank and file conservative Catholics hold traditional views about the role of women in society, activist Joan Andrews has won the admiration of many of them. Raised on a Tennessee farm, the child of a devout Catholic mother and a Protestant father who later became a Catholic, Andrews was a college student in the late 1960s, and became involved in protests against the Vietnam War. The antiwar protest led to her participation in a number social protest movements, but it was *Roe v. Wade,* the 1973 Supreme Court decision legalizing abortion, that confirmed in her a self-conscious and enduring commitment to the cause of preserving fetal life.[138] Subsequently she was arrested numerous times while demonstrating at abortion clinics. In 1986 she entered a clinic in Pensacola, Florida, and unplugged a machine used in certain types of abortions. Arrested on a variety of charges, she was offered probation if she would agree to stay away from abortion clinics, which she refused to do. She was then sentenced to five years in a maximum security prison. As a protest against what she regarded as the illegitimacy of her sentence, she refused to cooperate with certain established prison procedures and was kept for long periods in solitary confinement and was refused permission to attend Mass. She also claims to have been subjected to various kinds of harassment and humiliation by prison guards. Andrews, thirty-eight at the time of her imprisonment, soon became a martyr of sorts in the eyes of anti-abortion activists.

Once a political liberal, Andrews refused to support Ronald Reagan for the presidency in 1984 and 1988, despite his anti-abortion stand. She is, however, a religiously conservative Catholic who found praying the rosary her chief consolation in prison, distributed rosaries and religious medals to her fellow prisoners, and objected to some anti-abortion activists accepting contraception as an alternative. She complained that the prison chaplain was "more of a social worker than a nun." Until Bishop Vaughan became involved in Operation Rescue in 1988, Catholic leaders, including the bishops of Florida, had refused to support her, and at one point the Florida Catholic Conference circulated a memorandum stating that she had been dealt with fairly by the state government.[139] Such splits between the hierarchy and conservative laity have been a common feature of recent Catholic history.

Andrews was released late in 1988. Her style of activism draws upon the methods of the political radicalism of the 1960s, informed by the model of the pious Catholic hero, pursuing God's will in the face of all obstacles. Yet her activist methods, if not her cause, distance her from the majority of those who would describe themselves as conservative Catholics.

Historical Context

Conservative Catholics share a basic interpretation of the history of the Church in the United States. For example, it is held that for the masses of Catholic immigrants who poured into the United States in waves from 1820 to 1920, the underlying meaning of the Catholic faith was not much in dispute: the Church's doctrines were believed to be clearly formulated in creeds, works of speculative theology, and popular educational materials, and its system of discipline and governance was firm and effective. Catholics might have disputed among themselves, sometimes bitterly, over political and economic issues or over church matters which did not involve doctrine, such as finances or the actions of particular church leaders, but seldom about the meaning of their faith. In its doctrines, its rituals, and its moral norms, the Catholic Church was thought to provide its members with a basis for unity which transcended their particular differences. This view of an internally stable American Catholic community, while challenged by liberal historians, is an important element in the conservative Catholic worldview.

However, conservatives recall that the specter of heresy did appear in two controversies at the beginning of the twentieth century. In 1899 Pope Leo XIII condemned a tendency among certain bishops and priests in France and in the United States that he labeled "Americanism." Those presumed to be "Americanists" protested that their enthusiasm for the civil and religious liberties protected in the U.S. Constitution did not imply a challenge to formal church teaching but was merely an affirmation of a particular way of relating Catholicism to American culture. Pope Leo charged, however, that the admirers of the American experiment had absolutized the principle of the separation of church and state and had placed undue emphasis on the active virtues at the expense of passive virtues such as humility, piety, and contemplation. And in 1907, Pope Piux X condemned modernism (see above), of which there were relatively few American proponents.[140] Neither Americanism nor modernism had a wide popular base in the United States. Yet the issues they raised were to return, in somewhat different form, a half-century later. Some conservative Catholics, for example, posit an underground survival of modernism in certain religious orders and seminaries for the training of priests, from around 1910 to around 1960, when ideas carefully nurtured below ground became once more open. There is little evidence for such deliberate preservation.[141]

In the decades following the condemnations of Americanism and modernism, American Catholic theological or ecclesiological innovation beyond the parameters of neo-scholasticism was rare, and Catholics developed instead a tradition of social thought and action, represented in the 1930s and 1940s by figures such as the laywoman Dorothy Day, co-founder of the Catholic Worker movement, and John Ryan, a priest whose writings and extensive lobbying for a minimum wage, federal aid to dependent children and the unemployed, and other social welfare programs anticipated aspects of the New Deal. Although Day and Ryan represented different approaches to Catholic social action and especially to the role of the federal government in such action, both grounded their philosophies and programs in the papal social encyclicals of the era.[142]

In the generation after World War II, a system of thought called "neo-Thomism," itself a reinvigoration of the neo-scholasticism which had enjoyed intellectual hegemony in the Roman Catholic Church throughout the nineteenth century, informed American Catholic self-understanding. On one hand, neo-Thomism was a renewal of the medieval synthesis of Catholic thought and action: it was presented as a unified vital system comprehensive of the entire range of Christian dogma and practice; it celebrated the supernatural life of the Church in the sacraments and in the community of saints in heaven; and it envisioned the world as a fertile valley awaiting the planting and nurture of Catholic idealism. On the other hand, neo-Thomism was more flexible intellectually than neo-scholasticism: as it developed in phases in the twentieth century, it proved itself capable of incorporating biblical as well as traditional images, metaphors, and theologies; it encouraged historical, archaeological, and linguistic studies; and it served, for a core of American priests, as the theological and philosophical point of departure in their attempts to more deeply involve the laity in the social and religious work of the Church (Catholic Action) and to explore the inherent link between the celebration of the Eucharist (the primary Catholic liturgical act) and the work for social justice.[143]

For these American priests and for others like them around the world who had been experimenting within the neo-Thomist framework, Pope John XXIII (1958–63) "opened windows" after the long Counter-Reformation period during which the Church had maintained itself as a fortress protected from the world. To a great extent the significance of his pontificate was in its style and emphasis—he embraced leaders of the Jewish and Eastern Orthodox communities, he warmly greeted non-Catholic observers to the Vatican—rather than in substantial changes that occurred before his death in 1963. However, he was primarily responsible for the convening of the Second Vatican Council, the twenty-first ecumenical gathering of Catholic bishops. The Council possessed in effect supreme legislative authority in the Church, although its decrees also required papal approval. At that time and afterwards it was widely perceived as having effected a revolution in the Church.

Conservative Catholics point out that Vatican II proclaimed no new Catholic doctrines, and that it explicitly designated itself a "pastoral" council, meaning that its chief purpose was to make the Church more effective in its ministry to the modern world. To this end it addressed itself systematically to a series of questions involving every aspect of Catholic life. In general conservative American Catholics were surprised and somewhat taken aback by the Council's actions, since they understood the identity and solidity of the Church to be based on precisely those things which non-Catholics found most difficult to understand, most "scandalous." (For example: Catholics did not practice birth control and tended to have large families; priests accepted the teaching that celibacy was essential to their ministry; few people questioned the wisdom of saying the Mass in Latin). Despite the important leadership of American theologians and bishops on seminal questions such as the discussion of religious liberty, conservative American Catholics perceived the Council as a triumph of bishops and reforming theologians from a swath of European territory extending from Austria through Germany and France to the Low Countries.

The impact of the Council was such that the label *conservative* came to refer to those who de-emphasized or denied any radical or revolutionary aspects of the Council and instead stressed the continuities with previous Catholic thought and practice. To those Catholics, substantial change did not seem warranted: in their eyes, the

American Church was healthy, even vigorous. In the great urban centers Catholics had, in the postwar period, learned to manipulate the levers of local politics and in time became a powerful force in the national Democratic Party. Until the 1960s, however, Catholics were probably not proportionately represented in the higher levels of major American industries. Under such conditions there was an inevitable leakage of Catholics away from the Church, especially in those areas where there were proportionally few of them. On the whole, however, conservatives argued, the degree to which the immigrants "kept the faith" was, given the pluralist and increasingly secular character of American society, surprising and impressive. Keeping the faith involved of necessity a rather high degree of self-consciousness concerning those beliefs which set Catholics off from other people—from major doctrines like the meaning of the Mass and the authority of the Pope through practices like abstaining from eating meat on Fridays. By 1960 the United States had one of the highest rates of Catholic church attendance in the world, and by most other signs the Church was flourishing.[144] To conservatives after the Council, Vatican II had threatened the theological foundations of such self-conscious faith—and had thus plunged American Catholics into a crisis of religious identity.

In its nature fundamental Catholic doctrine is held to be unchangeable, in the sense that nothing which has been officially and solemnly taught can later be repudiated. All change must be "development," that is, new ideas are seen as a legitimate unfolding of earlier teachings or a process of extending those teachings in new directions. In every one of its decrees the Council laid down far-reaching principles which did indeed seem to proclaim a new era in the history of the Church. However, in each case the Council fathers also reaffirmed traditional principles which it insisted could not be negated. These were stressed by conservative Catholics as they tried to discern elements of continuity between the pre-Vatican and the post-Vatican churches. What follows is a summary of the attitudes conservative Catholics have taken toward the Council in the twenty-five years since its close.

The Nature of the Church. The Council moved away from the prevalent emphasis on a strictly hierarchical, primarily institutional model and described the Church as a community guided by the Holy Spirit. It revived the idea of "collegiality," long neglected, by which authority inheres in the whole body of the bishops, not in the pope alone, a model which by implication could be extended to other levels of Church life. However, as conservatives reminded the liberals, the Council also reaffirmed that the Church is indeed a hierarchical institution and that the Pope may exercise his authority without the prior approval or ratification of the bishops.[145]

Liturgy. The Church's official rituals, especially the Mass, constitute its liturgy ("public work") and are regarded as the heart of Catholic life. Vatican II called on the laity to become full participants in the liturgy, not mere spectators. In practice this quickly led to the praying of the Mass in the vernaculars (something the Council itself cautiously authorized but did not mandate, conservatives pointed out) and the abandonment of particular rituals now deemed outmoded. And conservatives emphasize that at the same time the Council explicitly urged that the Church's liturgical traditions (including, for example, Gregorian chant) be honored and preserved. Unauthorized changes in the liturgy were forbidden.[146]

Ecumenism. For the first time Catholics were encouraged to approach other religions—mainly other Christian groups, but extending even beyond them—in an open and positive spirit. On the practical level organized worship with other Christians was permitted for the first time. But while acknowledging that all faiths partake of divine truth to some degree, conservatives emphasized the conciliar declaration: "For it is through Christ's Catholic Church alone, which is the all-embracing means of salvation, that the fullness of the means of salvation can be obtained."[147]

Religious Life. The term "religious" has been used in Catholicism to designate those who have consecrated themselves to God in a special way, mainly through established religious orders such as the Franciscans or the Sisters of Mercy. The Council encouraged these communities to reexamine themselves to judge whether they had been faithful to their original purposes and whether any changes might be warranted which would make their ministries more effective. But it also unambiguously affirmed the importance of formal hierarchical structure and traditional virtues like obedience.[148]

The Role of the Laity. In describing the Church as the "People of God," the Council gave wider scope to the role of the laity, who were treated not as mere passive supporters of the work of clergy and religious but as themselves active participants in the Church's mission. But conservatives maintained that the Council did not indicate that the Church was now to be regarded as a democracy. Nor did the Council emphasize the role of the laity in the Church's governing structure.[149]

Religious Freedom. Along with ecumenism, the one conciliar decree which seemed to represent a palpable leap forward from previous Church teaching denied that coercion was legitimate in matters of belief, since belief must be a free action, and respect for the dignity of the person requires such freedom even when it may be misused. But conservative Catholics argued that, in context, the decree appeared to address itself not to internal Catholic affairs but to the role of religion in the larger society.[150]

The Church in the Modern World. Gaudium et Spes (Joy and Hope) was the Council's longest decree and seemed to embody and comprehend the others. Here the Council fathers reached out to the modern world sympathetically and compassionately, willing to learn from the world where it was appropriate, determined not to condemn but to help. But at the same time, conservatives pointed out, the world was diagnosed as radically deficient in spiritual understanding, a lack which only the Gospel of Christ could provide.[151]

In their sustained reaction to Vatican II, which included resistance to the relaxation of previous ecclesial and symbolic boundaries between Catholics and non-Catholics, conservative Catholics began to discover a resonance with fundamentalist

Protestants, who also rejected official ecumenism (as institutionalized in associations such as the National Council of Churches). The first sympathy between conservative Catholics and Protestants was precipitated by what both saw as symptoms of a widespread moral crisis of American society—legalized abortion, a mushrooming divorce rate, increased drug use, and the acceptance of the sexual revolution. Conservatives on both sides of the denominational line began to realize that, as far as these issues were concerned, they had more in common with conservative counterparts on the other side of the line than they did with their liberal coreligionists. This in turn led to the discovery of a theological basis for such conservatism—a traditional view of religious truth and of religious authority. Both Catholic and Protestant conservatives believe that God's Word has been revealed to humanity and must be obeyed. Both regard the Bible as directly inspired by God. As a result, both accept as necessary for an authentic Christian the doctrines that Jesus is truly God and man, that He was born of a virgin, and that He rose from the dead bodily. The great dividing line in modern Christianity came to be seen not as between Protestants and Catholics but as between those who accept these traditional teachings and those who reject or compromise them.[152]

Catholic Separatism: The Dilemma of Conservative Catholicism

For conservative Catholics, then, the Council posed a major problem of spiritual and psychological adjustment. Small groups of conservatives, many of them looking for leadership to the French archbishop Marcel Lefebvre, either rejected the Council openly, arguing in various ways that its decrees were not authentic and binding, or maintained an ambiguous attitude toward the decrees. In earlier times it had sometimes been possible for Catholics to appeal from the authority of a general council to the authority of the Pope (or vice versa), but Vatican II permitted no such strategy, because the succession of popes from John XXIII to John Paul II affirmed the Council at every opportunity, without the slightest hesitation. Thus those who reject the Council must of necessity reject the Pope as well. Unlike conservatives in most other religions, Catholics suspicious of the direction in which their church is moving have no place to flee. To join another faith or to found one's own splintered remnant of the Catholic Church is to deny the Catholic principle, which demands unity under papal authority. In this study, then, the term "conservative Catholic activists" is used to designate those who have remained in full communion with the post-Vatican II Roman Catholic hierarchy and who engage in religiously motivated activism in an attempt to be faithful to the "authentic traditions" of the Church (in contrast to those whom they usually call "liberals" or "modernists")—and to an "authentic reading" of Vatican II. Thus conservative Catholics must find ways to validate Vatican II's actions, whatever misgivings they may have about its results. Furthermore, their dissent from liberal Catholicism on religious matters often takes place within the local church structures, whereas their dissent from liberalism and secular humanism on sociopolitical matters may be expressed through a variety of extra-ecclesial organizations.

For many years a recurring issue in American politics has been the interpretation of the Constitution. There is a split between those who believe it should be understood narrowly and as far as possible as the framers intended, and those who see it as embodying broad principles to be boldly applied in each age. The conservative-liberal split in Catholicism is of a similar nature, between those who read the texts of Vatican II carefully and cautiously—as "strict constructionists"—and those who see the Council not as the definitive word on the modern church but merely as the beginning of a continuing process by which the Church seeks to update itself. Yet the conservative Catholic program suffers from the dilemma of any movement which undertakes to defend what has been attacked: to some extent it permits its enemies to define its agenda. Most conservative Catholics took their beliefs for granted until, sometime after Vatican II, they realized that many of those beliefs were being called into question. Issues like the ban on artificial means of contraception, or the exclusively male celibate priesthood, loom much larger than they might otherwise for the simple reason that they have been important rallying points for Catholic liberals. Conservative Catholics have been deliberately and even stubbornly countercultural in making a firm stand at precisely those points where Catholic teaching is most strongly attacked.

Conservative Catholic Political Activism

Many conservative American Catholics are politically quiescent, far more concerned with problems in the Church than with those in the larger society. Many hold that the religious problems must be solved before the Church can become a unified and effective voice in public life. Conservative Catholic activists reject this line of reasoning. And while not as sharply defined (in terms of a single movement) as in some other countries, conservative Catholic activists in the United States are well organized and in some ways highly effective. Their political activism is well organized and effective because they have joined, or formed, groups that depend on ecumenical membership. Conservative Catholic activists were, for example, members of the Moral Majority, founded by the Baptist minister Jerry Falwell, which disbanded in 1989. They were also allied with conservative Protestants in court cases designed to correct what they view as prejudicial interpretations of the First Amendment to the Constitution, as in a 1986 Alabama case charging that "Secular Humanism" had in effect been established in the public schools.[153] Indeed, to the degree that conservative Catholics can be said to have a public agenda, it is broadly speaking the agenda of the New Right, an agenda which at almost every point brings them into alliances with conservative Protestants and Orthodox Jews.[154]

Conservative Catholic activists in state and federal legislatures define their political concerns as pro-family, meaning that government policy should strengthen the traditional nuclear family in any way it can and refrain from actions which might weaken it. (For example, although it is not yet a prominent issue, some conservative Catholics favor revision of the tax laws so as to encourage large families.) The strength of the family is seen as based on religious values and on strict sexual morality which encourages marital fidelity; Catholic activists on state and local levels are thus particularly active in opposing pornography and in monitoring public standards of decency.[155]

The issue which by far has most effectively mobilized Catholic political activity since 1970 has been legalized abortion. The anti-abortion movement tended to bifurcate toward the end of the 1980s, with the more moderate part placing its hopes mainly in legislation and court decisions and with an increasingly militant wing favoring direct action. Many conservative Catholics who disapproved of tactics of civil disobedience during the 1960s have been willing to justify them against abortion.[156] Although anti-abortion activists usually insist that they are "single issue" people, and that this is the source of their political strength, most espouse a general moral conservatism which includes a whole range of what are sometimes called the "social issues." A sample agenda would include these positions:

1. The federal government should not finance abortions either at home or abroad and should not pressure recipients of foreign aid to limit the size of their families.
2. Contraceptive and abortion services should not be provided through the public schools or other public agencies.
3. Divorce should be more difficult to obtain, and no fault divorce should be abolished.
4. Government should not fund massive day-care programs for small children, lest it encourage mothers to abandon their responsibilities.
5. Sex-education programs should include clear affirmations of traditional sexual morality. (Some would argue that there should be no such programs at all.)
6. Pornography should be outlawed, and laws against it vigorously enforced.
7. The practice of homosexuality should not be a legal right.
8. Nondenominational prayers should be allowed in the public schools. (Most conservative Catholics send their children to religious schools, but they view this as an important symbolic issue for the entire country.)
9. Court decisions drawing a sharp line between church and state should be relaxed.
10. Private religious schools should be aided by the government in the form of direct subsidies, vouchers which would allow parents to choose the schools their children attend, or tax benefits to those with children in private schools.
11. Laws against euthanasia should be strictly enforced. (There is considerable suspicion about living wills and other measures viewed as promoting either euthanasia or suicide.)[157]

Conservative Catholics tended to support the Reagan-Bush administration throughout the 1980s, while remaining cautiously skeptical about its genuine commitment to the social issues. (Anti-abortionists, for example, thought that President Reagan was not as aggressive on the issue as he should have been.) By demonstrating an ability to attract votes and by working assiduously within the Republican Party, conservative activists were able to have a significant influence on federal appointments during the Reagan administration, especially in key agencies such as the Department of Health and Human Services, the Department of Justice, and the Department of Education.[158]

Most conservative Catholics were more suspicious of George Bush than they had been of Ronald Reagan, judging that Bush's elite New England Protestant background rendered him insensitive to their own concerns, a judgment which seemed borne out early in his administration when he bluntly stated his opposition to all public aid to private schools, but then seemed to retract in the face of strong criticism. Two Bush nominees for federal office were forced to withdraw following strong opposition from anti-abortionists.[159] Nonetheless, the confidence conservative Catholics placed in the Republican Party of the 1980s seemed at least partially vindicated at the end of the decade when a Supreme Court with three Reagan appointees handed down a decision significantly restricting the legal right to abortion and hinted at its willingness even to reverse its 1973 decision making abortion legal.[160]

Social and Cultural Disposition

There is no systematic study of the social roots of American Catholic conservatism, but it appears to have its base in the American middle class. Many working-class Catholics, especially of the older generation, are religious conservatives by habit and conviction. However, to become an articulate religious conservative requires some measure of education and some degree of comfort with the world of organizations, meetings, manifestos, and public controversy. Most Catholic activists have at least a high-school education, and many are college graduates. The Catholic conservative movements profiled below are supported financially largely by the donations of their members, with occasional larger infusions. Two industrial fortunes—derived from beer and pizza—have been identified as supporting such movements to a significant degree.[161] There is no striking geographical pattern to the movement, except that it naturally tends to be strongest in places where Catholics are numerous, primarily the Northeast and the urban Midwest and California to a lesser extent. (However, it is far less prominent in traditionally Catholic Louisiana and the Southwest.)[162] Rank and file members of the conservative Catholic groups described below were for the most part educated in the Catholic parochial school system of the 1940s and 1950s. Most are not intellectuals. However, the hard-core conservatives who provide the leadership to the various groups tend to come from an elite educational background.

Conservative Catholics are an alienated group in that they deplore certain directions in which they believe both their church and the larger society are moving. However, such alienation is for the most part to be taken at face value—it does not appear to conceal other, unacknowledged kinds of alienation such as loss of economic or social status. Conservative Catholic activists are by temperament rather tenacious, more willing to engage in combat than are their conservative coreligionists. Entering into contemporary religious battles usually requires the warrior to accept minority status and to be seen as a rather troublesome and divisive person. While some conservatives may enjoy this status, at least consciously the movement looks forward to the day when it will once again define the mainstream, and when the battles will no longer be necessary.

Conservative Catholics acknowledge that their principal quarrel is with modernity itself, mainly as it has developed in the West, and most hold a view of history in which earlier societies are considered far more pervasively religious than present societies. The glorious epoch was the Middle Ages, when Christendom was identified with papal temporal and spiritual authority. Depending on their predilections and on the degree of their knowledge of history, conservative activists disagree mildly among themselves about precisely when the decline set in.[163] However far back the roots of modernity may be traced, few American Catholics had any direct experience of its severe religious consequences until the 1960s. Although Church leaders in the earlier decades routinely warned against secularism, materialism, and the general decay of public morals, on the whole, Catholics growing up before of Vatican II lived in a remarkably stable world, based on a broad moral consensus. For most conservative Catholics, therefore, the watershed experience of modern history was the general cultural phenomenon called "the sixties," although many would claim that what happened then was merely the inevitable unfolding of the logic of earlier periods. Catholics who hold this view are vulnerable to the charge of nostalgia, of thinking that the previous period was a golden age. However, judging by the criteria conservative Catholics think important—including the stability of the Church itself and sexual behavioral norms—the change from 1960 to 1990 was indeed measurably dramatic.

Technological change plays little role in the corruption of society as conservative Catholics see it; indeed, they have accepted advanced technologies and have readily adapted them for their purposes. Many regard television as a major corrupting force, but only because of the content of the programs, not because of the medium itself. The major technological threat, so far as conservative Catholics are concerned, is now in the field of bio-engineering (especially in vitro fertilization and test-tube babies); characteristically, it is the applications rather than the technology itself which they find objectionable.[164] Most conservative Catholics have ambivalent attitudes about the theoretical sciences: while science in and of itself is true and good, scientists draw inferences from it which are invalid.[165]

In diagnosing the evils of modernity which they reject, conservative Catholics emphasize the guidance of explicit doctrinal formulas as a test of authentic faith—and as the standard by which to judge "right reason." Heresy has been treated as the worst of sins, on the grounds that bad conduct is correctable in the light of true belief but false belief recognizes no principle of correction. Conservative Catholics thus differ from fundamentalist Protestants in that they identify the essential failure of modern culture not mainly as the loss of religious faith but as the decline of reason. In this view the sickness of modernity is not excessive reliance on rationalism (although they acknowledge that there can be such a thing) but instead the triumph of subjectivism and irrationalism (existentialism and psychoanalytic theory are, for example, customary targets).[166] Reason leads one to the threshhold of faith, and the basic principles of the moral law, as well as most of its applications, can be known from reason alone. (Thus, in principle the abortion question is not exclusively or even properly a religious issue at all.)

In short, conservative Catholic activists fight a war of ideas before all else, and objectionable behavior is understood as the inevitable outcome of wrong thinking. Accordingly, Catholic orthodoxy is perceived as vulnerable precisely in its head, so it is no surprise that the universities have become the centers of heresy and liberal dissent. On campus, subjectivity and individualism are celebrated, and this too has tended, in the eyes of conservatives, to undermine traditional truth.[167] Indeed, the heart of the conservative Catholic worldview is the belief that eternal verities exist, some specially revealed by God through the Bible and the Church, others knowable by human reason, and they remain unchanged and unchangeable. Put another way, conservative Catholics believe that the universe is governed by a sacred order and that it is the duty of human beings to conform to that order. The Catholic Church is regarded as one of the very few institutions in the world officially committed to this view of truth. Conservative Catholics thus believe that the sacred texts and traditions containing this definitive truth, reflecting as it does the objective moral order, must be authoritatively interpreted by the magisterium, headed by the bishop of Rome. They believe that certain actions—primarily the sacraments of the Church—are sacred in a unique way and involve the believer's extra-historical participation in this eternal order. They believe that by virtue of their ordination priests are given sacred powers beyond human comprehension.

Conservative Catholic activists are aware that they hold a view of reality which once existed in the Western world in a variety of forms but for the most part no longer does. Thus, they realize that new organizational forms and apostolates are necessary; indeed, the predominantly lay character of the activist groups reflects the shared conviction that structures of the post-Tridentine church, largely elite and clerical, have eroded beyond recognition in the recent, tumultuous generation.

This conviction is evident in the emergence of a corps of activist Catholic laywomen who fit the classic definition of the volunteer. Some are aware of the paradox that in becoming activists on behalf of their goal of a stronger family, they tend to fall into the same pattern of semiprofessional activity outside the home that they otherwise deplore, but they do not see any present alternative. They differ from career-oriented women in hoping that eventually social and political conditions will change in such a way as to make their activism no longer necessary.[168]

In 1984, for example, a group of women in Saint Louis began circulating a petition in support of official teachings under attack, and eventually it was signed by approximately forty thousand American women and presented to Pope John Paul II. From this grew an organization called Women for Faith and Family, intended to serve as a voice of traditional Catholic women who believe that the hierarchy pays too much attention to organized feminists. Thus when the bishops of the United States announced that they would prepare a "pastoral letter" on the role of women in the Church, the group argued through letters, petitions, and appearances at the bishops' "listening sessions" that the majority of Catholic women do not feel oppressed and regard the Church as their true spiritual home. In this they found themselves diametrically opposed to other women who expressed themselves as pained by what they called the "oppressive patriarchy" of historical Catholicism. Conservative Catholic women not only oppose abortion but also favor public policies that would encourage mothers to remain at home with their small children (e.g., tax credits that would render it economically unnecessary for mothers to pursue full-time employment).[169]

Conservative Catholic women also believe that contraception damages women's spiritual and even physical health, and several organizations—the Couple to Couple League (Cincinnati) and the Family of the Americas Foundation (Covington, La.), for example—promote natural family planning, including periodic abstinence from sexual activity.[170] Conservative Catholic women of the Family of the Americas Foundation organized a pilot program designed to reduce pregnancy among high school girls by teaching and advocating sexual abstinence before marriage. The program, federally funded, was challenged on the grounds that it violated the separation of church and state, but the Supreme Court upheld the grant.[171]

The Crisis of Authority

As traditional religious beliefs erode before modern pressures, it might be assumed that fidelity to those beliefs would be strongest among religious professionals—people employed by the Church, specially trained and living within a relatively protected ecclesiastical environment. Conversely, it might also be assumed that those most likely to doubt traditional beliefs would be lay people immersed in the world, with only voluntary ties to the Church as an institution. However, the dominant pattern in Catholic conservatism is the reverse of that expectation. Those groups that fight militantly on behalf of what they regard as endangered beliefs are overwhelmingly lay in membership. It is not unusual that at gatherings of outspokenly conservative Catholics, there is scarcely a single priest or nun present. In fact, although conservative lay people do see the secular world as dangerous to their faith, their immediate battles are more often with their own clergy, whom they believe have betrayed that faith. The most dramatic changes since the Second Vatican Council—the Mass celebrated in the vernacular, the abandonment of many traditional religious practices such as Friday abstinence from meat, the reformulating of traditional doctrines, ecumenical relations with other religions, a more flexible approach to moral questions, deeper involvement in social and political issues—could not have taken place without eventual clerical encouragement and support. A capsule summation of conservative complaints in the United States would read somewhat as follows: "Our worship is no longer a truly sacred action, and liturgical rules are widely ignored. Our children are not being taught authentic Catholic doctrine in the schools. Everywhere people are given dubious or distorted ideas about what the Second Vatican Council really taught. Most of those responsible for such abuses are priests and religious.

When confronted, they adamantly refuse to change. Complaints to the bishop either go unheeded or are summarily rejected. In some cases the bishop himself is actively sympathetic to dissenting clergy."[172]

Conservative Catholics often appear, therefore, to be anticlerical, a stance usually thought of as leftist and opposite to what might be expected of them. The fact that priests and religious are, ironically, often more secularized than their lay counterparts reflects the very intensity with which religious elites confronted the changed ecclesiastical circumstances of the Vatican II era; the crisis of religious identity was for them directly personal and professional and weighed more heavily on them than on most lay people. As a result of the Council, far more priests and religious began studying for advanced degrees than was formerly the case, because Catholic belief was now seen to be in crisis and had to be completely rethought. There was a great increase in the number of priests, religious, and lay people formally certified as experts in religious education, liturgy, and other aspects of church life. Diocesan bureaucracies grew as new offices—worship, social justice, personnel—were created and the new professionals were placed in charge of them. Priests and religious in the ranks have repeatedly, over a quarter of a century, been summoned to official meetings designed to acquaint them with the latest ideas, and ecclesiastical bureaucrats continuously formulate policies aimed at steering frontline clergy in appropriate directions. The professionalization and specialization of ministries in the Catholic Church that occurred in the wake of the Council reinforced in those priests and sisters the momentum away from a vertical faith and toward a corresponding interest in public issues.[173]

Meanwhile, due in part to their detachment from the institution of the church on a daily basis and their relative lack of exposure to the teaching of the conciliar theologians, many lay people adhered to traditional beliefs more closely than did the clergy and women religious. Conservative activists believe that a moderate liberalism has become the conventional wisdom in most clerical circles and regard the professionalization of the clergy with considerable suspicion.[174]

Although most conservative Catholics would not deny that professional competence has a legitimate place, most also believe that it is now greatly overvalued. The classic concept of church authority is one in which the official teacher (pope or bishop) consults his advisors but ultimately issues an authoritative pronouncement on the basis of official Church teaching. In doing so he is believed to be guided by the Holy Spirit. Conservative Catholics think that bishops have now ceded much of their authority to the professionals and in some cases have allowed themselves to be intimidated by their own bureaucrats. Thus postconciliar Catholic life has been in continuing tension, sometimes erupting into open conflict, between people who are lay in a double sense—they are not clergy, and they are also not trained professionals in any religious field—and professionals who show many of the characteristics of what has been called the "new class": relatively well educated, articulate, and self-consciously progressive, exercising a kind of authority which owes less to office itself than to professional expertise. Conservative lay people found themselves in the anomalous situation of telling bishops that the latter have ceded their authority to their own bureaucrats and that they ought to reclaim it, which is rather like royalists telling kings to be less cooperative with parliamentary structures. Many bishops were not receptive when the disgruntled laity prodded them to take firmer stands.

During his pontificate John Paul II has enjoyed the enthusiastic admiration of conservatives alienated from their local churches, who have frequently appealed to him as the ideal combination of orthodox intellectual and tough-minded ruler. In so doing they have even appealed to the conciliar call for a stronger lay voice in church affairs. (They have thus been forced to devise a kind of theory of a lay church. It is not, however, held with comfort and is regarded as reflecting an emergency situation prevailing until such time as the clergy return to their senses.) American Catholics, perhaps more than any other national group, have bombarded the Vatican, over a twenty-year period, with complaints about the entire range of Catholic issues. The photocopy machine and the tape recorder have proven a great boon to conservatives, who have been able to send Rome copies of confidential letters, speeches, position papers, and other documents supporting their claims about "the true state of the American Church."

Counter-Institutions and Organizations

A revealing paradox relative to the conservative Catholic movement in the United States is the extent to which, in its efforts to preserve an age-old faith, it has been compelled by circumstances to operate through institutions which are new. This has occurred mainly because, from the conservatives' standpoint, established institutions were to a great extent captured by liberals after the Second Vatican Council. The conservative Catholic movement may be better organized and more effective in the United States than in any other country for a similar paradoxical reason—although conservatives insist that the Church cannot be democratic, they have learned the lessons of American democratic organization. Few of the institutions they control can claim official endorsement, but they operate on the assumption that faithful Catholics have a right to make their voices heard. And although many of these institutions and groups were formed in response to what is perceived as a strictly ecclesial malaise and continue to focus on its symptoms and treatment, conservative Catholic activists have emerged from these institutional homes to do battle on public issues such as abortion.

Catholics United for the Faith

Probably the single most important conservative organization in the United States is Catholics United for the Faith, founded in 1968 to support the Pope following the intense attack on *Humanae Vitae,* the encyclical restating the traditional opposition to artificial means of contraception. International in scope, with chapters in Australia, New Zealand, and parts of the third world, the organization has a membership of approximately twenty thousand, with headquarters in New Rochelle, New York. The national center consists of a board of directors, national officers, and staff members—together numbering about twenty-five people.[175]

CUF, as it is commonly called, can be regarded as an authentically populist organization, a lay apostolate whose members describe themselves as "ordinary Catholics." The rank and file are often recruited because of dissatisfaction with the Catholic schools—dissatisfaction with the substance of the curriculum, problems with educational content and method, and with the philosophies and theologies said to be informing them. CUF has no official ecclesiastical standing, and clerical participation is minimal. Often there is no priest or nun present at local CUF meetings. Despite its populist character, CUF's founder, H. Lyman Stebbins (d. 1989) was a Yale graduate, a convert from Episcopalianism, and a former Manhattan stockbroker. CUF was born in a press conference he held in Washington, D.C., on 26 September 1968, to oppose the public dissent against *Humanae Vitae* by forty-four priests. Stebbins's successor, James Likoudis, is a former college history professor. Stebbins set a rule for his group that members should not publicly criticize church authorities, including bishops, a rule which some other conservatives regard as overly confining and which in fact local CUF members often ignore.[176]

There are about 150 local chapters, where much of the actual work of the group is carried out. Such chapters form after individual Catholics in a particular town or diocese discover others like themselves disturbed over the direction of the Church in their area, and they come together for mutual support. This banding together leads to the preparation of a list of grievances (complaints about parish liturgies, parochial education, diocesan policies, and sometimes, the political and sociomoral utterances of Catholic leaders), followed by a visit to the bishop or other diocesan officials, a visit which the people often find unsatisfactory for resolving their problems.

Liberals, including some bishops, sometimes characterize CUF members as "self-appointed watchdogs of orthodoxy," and CUF activists have been chief among those sending material to the Vatican concerning irregularities in the American Church. In addition to religious education, liturgical practice is a chief concern. The CUF activists object to all deviations from Vatican-mandated rules and rubrics, as well as what they regard as a general spirit of irreverence in the celebration of the Mass. They also tend to scrutinize sermons very carefully and to analyze their theological content. The "canon within the canon" for CUF members is *Humanae Vitae*. Assent to the teaching of the encyclical is "a unique litmus test of one's orthodoxy and, thus, of belonging to the church at all."[177] Paul VI's ban on artifical birth control is an appropriate litmus test precisely because it was widely rejected and because many clergy claimed it was not strictly binding. Thus those who disobey its moral teaching signal an unwillingness to acknowledge full papal authority and the supernaturalist worldview supporting it. As the CUF journal *Lay Witness* put the matter in 1980: "Those who begin doubting the church's teaching on contraception generally go on to deny her teachings on a whole host of other subjects such as abortion, the indissolubility of marriage, pre- and extra-marital chastity, and so on."[178]

CUF's Catholicism is not, however, uncritically obedient and has been rather critical of bishops who have overlooked, or connived with, open liberal dissent. There was indeed a measure of irony in the fact that CUF was successful in provoking the ban on the popular catechism *Christ Among Us* in 1986. The group organized to overturn an episcopal imprimatur granted the book years earlier, in this case appealing over the bishop's head to Rome. "In this case, the Holy See gave ex post facto vindication of CUF's campaign."[179] Ironically, many CUF members would readily admit that they lack the education of some of their liberal opponents and that they hold no official position in the ecclesiastical structure but would justify their activities both in terms of Vatican II's call to the laity and on the grounds that no one else is available to perform the tasks they have undertaken.

CUF sees itself as having a positive as well as a negative function. Part of conservative Catholics' dissatisfaction with the postconciliar Church has been with the perceived neglect of traditional devotional practices, such as group recitation of the rosary, days of recollection, and novenas (prayers said over a nine-day period for special intentions), as well as traditional devotional literature. CUF meetings usually include some of these devotions, and the organization provides its members with the kind of traditional religious guidance which they seek, conscious of the irony that at one time this task would have been unquestionably performed by the clergy.

CUF also provides its members with intellectual resources to use in their local fights, including periodic detailed critiques of particular catechisms or other books which the group deems objectionable. It sponsors both national and local conferences at which appropriate speakers address the members. In 1988 the organization cosponsored publication of a series of new catechisms which it hoped would replace many of those previously in use.[180]

Opus Dei

Opus Dei (the work of God) is an international, predominantly lay organization founded in Madrid in 1928 by Monsignor Escriva de Balaguer y Albas. It claims seventy-two thousand members worldwide, with approximately three thousand in the United States. Pope John Paul II has been a strong supporter of the group, and in 1982 he made it a "personal prelature" under its own bishop and thus independent of ordinary ecclesiastical authority throughout the world. The prelature of the Opus Dei develops its apostolates through two sections, a masculine one and a feminine one. For ruling the prelature, the prelate has the assistance of two councils (one for each section). The prelate is elected in a general congress summoned to that end. The candidate has to be a priest with no less than five years of experience. His position lasts for life and must be confirmed by the Pope. The General Council helps the prelate in ruling the Male Section. The Female Council is ruled by the prelate with the general secretary vicar, the vicar for the Women's Section and the Central Office, which is similar to the General Council of the Male Section and with analogous functions. All the directors of these organisms are named for a period of eight years. Members are divided into four grades: *numerarii* ("numeraries," celibate priests and laity who constitute the leading group of the movement); *agregati* (celibate priests and laymen engaged in the coordination of external work); *supranumerarii* ("supernumeraries," priests and laity who work in their profession according to the ideals of the movement); and *cooperatores* (the rest of the cooperators, among whom there are also non-Catholics). It is estimated that 2 percent of its members are priests. There are Regional Councils, subject to the General Council, which is presided over by a general president (the prelate).[181]

As a religious movement inside the Roman Catholic Church, Opus Dei represents a new historical model which differs from unions, associations, and lay organizations, and from traditional religious orders and congregations, tertiary orders, and secular institutes. Clergy and religious live their priestly mission and consecrated life inside the movement. They constitute a new kind of clergy, neither secular nor regular, because they are integrated into and at the service of the movement. In fact the novelty of the movement consists of the perfect integration of priests, religious, and laity in a united organization which constitutes itself as a convergence of two historic developments: the development of the movements of lay apostolates and the development of the movements of spirituality of the religious and the priests.

Opus Dei prides itself on having anticipated the age of the laity begun by Vatican II, and its primary emphasis is on lay people achieving holiness in their professional lives. Opus Dei members live and work in the world in the belief that unaided human reason does not produce full truth and knowledge. The individual self is not the ultimate reference point in thought. This repudiation of a strictly rationalist approach to reality leads to a suspicion of much of contemporary speculative theology. At the same time Opus Dei fosters the development of dynamic religious elites as guardians of spiritual values and moral authority. It tends to establish houses near major universities (for example, at Columbia in New York City), and most of its recruits hail from the professional classes—doctors, lawyers, engineers, and businessmen.[182]

The viability of new movements like Opus Dei marks the beginning of a sensitive alteration in the balance of forces inside the social body of the Church. Joseph Comblin has described Opus Dei as both typical and atypical. It is an atypical movement "because of its social elitism, its very strict system for recruiting new members, its discipline of secrecy which it practices systematically, though maybe in an unconscious way." Yet it is also representative of the new model: "because of the intimate integration between priests and laity, which changes the status of priest and laity, because of the emphasis on spirituality and personal formation, because of the centralization of spirituality around the laity, because of the will always repeated—and emphatically proclaimed—of being withdrawn from any political or social option, because of the will—also emphatically proclaimed—of being withdrawn from any social class distinction."[183]

The movement does not openly enter into the kinds of battles which energize Catholics United for the Faith—the fact that Opus Dei in the United States also has its headquarters in New Rochelle does not reflect a connection between the two groups—and its leaders deny that it has a covert public agenda. Opus Dei has nonetheless been categorized by its critics as a rigidly conservative group associated with Integralism and with hidden political and religious agendas which intersect, in part because it was perceived as linked with the Franco government in Spain. Yet over half of its worldwide members live and work in Latin America, where bishops have supported its apostolic work, mostly because of the evident papal favor it enjoys.[184]

Claims of secretiveness and of political involvement aside, the organization is often criticized in liberal Catholic circles because its fusion of modern lay professionalism with traditional forms of piety and spiritual discipline, including a concept of firm obedience to religious superiors, is perceived as a strategy in an undeclared war against liberalism. Some young adult members of Opus Dei in the United States have been active in Operation Rescue and in legal and political coalitions fighting abortion on demand such as Americans United for Life—although not openly as Opus Dei members. Indeed Opus Dei draws much of the time and energy of its members inward to the organization itself.

The Blue Army

Woven into the fabric of modern Catholic piety are strands of apocalyptic expectation. Since the early nineteenth century there have been a series of reported appearances of the Blessed Virgin Mary in Europe, the most important of which were those at Lourdes in France in 1858 and at Fatima in Portugal in 1917. Lourdes is mainly associated with the healing of the sick, with thousands of miracles reported over almost a century and and half. The Virgin's alleged appearance at Fatima, however, occurred during World War I, and the message reported by the three children who claimed to have seen and talked with her had to do with the world's need to repent of its sins, with dire warnings of the terrible consequences which would otherwise follow. Devotees of Fatima believe, among other things, that the Virgin there foretold World War II, and that an aurora borealis in 1939 was one of the immediate signs which she promised. Devotion to Our Lady of Fatima reached its peak during the 1950s, when it was closely associated with anticommunism. Fatima devotees prayed regularly for the conversion of Russia to Christianity and believed that only such an occurrence could avert a third world war.[185] The Blue Army, with headquarters in Washington, New Jersey, was founded shortly after World War II to promote this type of devotion to Our Lady of Fatima. It claims a membership of twenty million worldwide and five million in America.[186]

The Second Vatican Council, while still encouraging devotion to Mary, seemed also to be guiding Catholics' attention in other directions. Anticommunism itself began to wane. Whereas Fatima devotions could be said to have been part of the mainstream of popular piety for forty years, after about 1965 they came more and more to be a kind of specialized interest. The Blue Army retains a huge membership by Catholic standards, but it has been relatively inconspicuous. Meanwhile, disputes have arisen among Fatima devotees about who has been faithful to the authentic message. Several alleged appearances of the Virgin took place during the 1980s, in various parts of the world. By far the best known was at Medjugorje in Yugoslavia, which has attracted thousands of pilgrims from all over the world, many of them not Catholics. Some of them have reported that they came as skeptics but went away as believers. Many devotees of Medjugorje regard this alleged appearance as yet another warning given by Mary that the world must repent of its sins or be chastized. However, the messages as reported have been rather diverse and do not seem to constitute as unified a body of belief as those of Lourdes and Fatima.[187]

Belief in Marian apparitions demonstrates the firm commitment which most conservative Catholics have to a supernatural view of reality. It is a tenet of their faith that God can and does intervene directly in human affairs, and can and does do so through the mother of Jesus. Most conservative Catholics, while remaining open to the possibility of doubt in any particular case, think that it is necessary to believe that such things can in principle happen. They also regard such events as real, not as due merely to the power of the human imagination.

Given their view that the world is going through a period of exceptional infidelity, in which religious doubt and contempt for traditional morality are blatant, many conservative Catholics find the apocalyptic aspects of such devotions intellectually and emotionally satisfying, as indicating that God has allowed things to deteriorate radically as a prelude to chastising the world. However, on the whole such speculations are not central to the conservative Catholic worldview (as they are to the traditionalist worldview). Most conservatives struggle to reverse trends which they regard as still within their power to influence.

There are a number of other conservative Catholic organizations worthy of mention. *The Cardinal Mindszenty Foundation,* named for a Hungarian prelate persecuted by the Communists after World War II, was founded in 1958. Its traditional religious beliefs are articulated in the context of a strong anticommunism. Communism's official atheism and its persecution of religion are seen as modern manifestations of evil. The foundation lists approximately sixteen thousand members, and has its headquarters in Saint Louis.[188] *The Saint Joseph Foundation* was established in 1985 to assist conservative Catholics in making use of the Church's own legal and administrative machinery to achieve their goals. It has brought action through official Church structures on matters such as the closing of churches or their radical remodeling. In 1989 it began an action aimed at requiring an American archbishop to withdraw his *imprimatur* (permission to publish) from a series of textbooks in sex education widely used in Catholic schools.[189] *The Latin Liturgy Association* (two thousand members, headquarters in Meadville, Pa.) was founded in 1972 to promote the use of the new Mass in Latin, that is, acceptance of the liturgical changes of Vatican II while taking advantage of the fact that Latin is one of the languages in which the new liturgy may be celebrated. (Celebrating the new Mass in Latin has the advantage of preserving Gregorian chant and other traditional music.) *The Traditional Mass Society* linked to the international group Una Voce ("one voice") has its headquarters in San Juan Capistrano, California. It was founded to promote the use of the Latin Mass which in practice was almost abolished after Vatican II.[190]

The *Catholic League for Religious and Civil Rights,* founded in 1973, is unusual in having been directed throughout most of its history by a Jesuit priest. Modeled on the Jewish Anti-Defamation League, it exists to fight what its members regard as anti-Catholic prejudice. With twenty-five thousand members and headquarters in Milwaukee, the league is especially opposed to the liberal, secular worldview inherited from the Enlightenment—a worldview that portrays the Catholic Church as a reactionary, repressive institution seeking to impose its own outmoded moral code (as on abortion) on modern democratic societies. The league is vigilant in discerning signs of this prejudice in the mass media, the educational system, and other mainstream American institutions. The league also fights for public aid to private schools, arguing that such schools are denied aid because of their Catholic affiliation. While open to all Catholics, and while it has received some support from liberals, on the whole the ethos of the organization can be called conservative. Catholics who disagree with the Church's position on abortion are unlikely to support the league.[191]

The Wanderer

The distilled essence of conservative Catholicism in America, served up undiluted in a strength even many professed conservatives do not find entirely palatable, is the newspaper *The Wanderer,* published in Saint Paul (Minn.), with a circulation of 37,500.[192] Founded in 1867 for German immigrants, the newspaper began publishing in English in 1930. Until the time of the Second Vatican Council, when Catholic doctrines and practices suddenly came into dispute at the popular level, the paper was read mainly by Catholics of German extraction. Since then, however, it has become the principal voice of militant, unreconstructed Catholic conservatism in the United States. Throughout its history *The Wanderer* has been owned by the Matt family of Saint Paul. Its major internal crisis came shortly after the Council, when the editor, Alphonse J. Matt, Jr., made the decision to support the legitimacy of the new Mass authorized by the Council. This led to a break with his uncle, Walter Matt, who founded *The Remnant* for people who were suspicious of liturgical change or who rejected it outright. In the process *The Wanderer* lost a considerable number of subscribers and is often scornfully dismissed by those who call themselves traditionalists.

The Wanderer is the most graphic example of the pattern whereby conservative Catholics who regard themselves as defenders of the authentic faith often find themselves at odds with local church authority. Since at least the mid-1970s the paper has been increasingly critical of American bishops both individually and collectively, and it is no exaggeration to say that by the end of the 1980s, the editors had come to regard the working majority of the bishops as a major obstacle to the authentic revitalization of the Church.[193] By contrast, the paper appeals constantly to papal authority, and sometimes to other Vatican offices, as expressing the true meaning of Catholicism, a meaning which is being systematically undermined in the United States. What sets the paper apart from the movement as a whole and causes it to be held at arm's length by many who agree with it in principle is an unrelenting aggressiveness, a tendency to do battle even with those who might otherwise be allies.

However, the paper's political orientation reflects that of the Catholic conservative movement. Abortion has been its chief social concern, and it has given a great deal of publicity to Operation Rescue, while frequently criticizing anti-abortion leaders whom it regards as overly cautious or compromising. A regular weekly column informs readers of pending legislation or other political developments affecting abortion and urges them to write to the appropriate public officials. Other preoccupations in the political sphere encompass the familiar New Right agenda—opposition to pornography and legalized homosexuality, support of prayer in the schools. The paper has been militantly anticommunist and regularly publishes articles about religious persecution in Communist countries; it has also consistently supported the Reagan-Bush policies in Central America.

Yet *The Wanderer* is in another way characteristic of the mentality of conservative Catholic activism and thus instructive about its nature: political concerns and involvement, including militant activism, proceed from a profound sense that religion is in crisis. Lay activism in the public sphere is necessary because the duly constituted religious authorities (of "Catholic Christendom") have abdicated. *The Wanderer* regards itself as being near the front of the armies which are doing battle for the soul of the Catholic Church. The chief enemies in the struggle, hedonism and infidelity, have imbued the Church and infected the ecclesiastical organism. Until the Church—the supreme custodian of the world order and interpreter of the eternal law (as expressed in divine revelation, natural law, and civil codes)—is righted, there is little hope for a return to previous standards of public morality.

Wanderer readers are regarded as loyal and militant, and periodically the paper urges them into letter-writing campaigns, as in the spring of 1989, when rumors circulated that the Vatican would allow girls to formally assist priests at the altar in the celebration of Mass. A regular column in the paper publishes items from parish bulletins or diocesan newspapers sent by readers to illustrate corruption in the Church at the local level.[194]

In addition to *The Wanderer* there are a number of other periodicals devoted to the dissemination of a conservative Catholic ethos. Most recent among them is *30 Days,* founded in 1988 as the English-language edition of an Italian journal published by the international Catholic movement *Communione et Liberazione* (Communion and Liberation). The core of the Italian movement encompasses about fifty thousand university students; there are only a few hundred members in the United States as of this writing. As the name indicates, the group stresses the unity of the Church and a concept of liberation distinguished from its purely political forms—primarily liberation from sin. In Italy the organization has sometimes been controversial, because it has in part been defined in contrast to earlier Catholic lay movements considered predominantly liberal. Like Opus Dei, Communion and Liberation asks priests and laity, in the words of Pope John Paul II, an ardent advocate, "to live your ecclesial membership within the context of your adherence to the movement." Indeed the pope has recognized Communion and Liberation as a "privileged instrument" in support of "the attempts of your brothers and sisters to express [Christian] culture in ever more incisive forms of civil and social responsibility." John Paul II sees the movement as a vanguard in "the work of overcoming the division between the Gospel and Culture" and has praised the membership as "the first witnessess of that missionary impetus with which I have charged your movement."[195]

The periodical *30 Days* has, accordingly, an international perspective on Catholic affairs. Its editor is an American Jesuit, Father Joseph Fessio, who founded and runs Ignatius Press to publish conservative Catholic literature, especially European theology. He also founded, and at one time directed, the St. Ignatius Institute of the

University of San Francisco, a "college within a college" devoted to traditional Catholic education, on the premise that existing Catholic institutions were no longer offering that kind of education.[196]

As the voice of Communion and Liberation, *30 Days* opposes secularization in politics and culture and espouses the view of the movement's founder, Monsignor Luigi Giussani, that human liberty can find its complete expression only "in a community in which all are Catholics." Produced in the slick professional style of popular newsmagazines, the monthly is a compendium of conservative Catholic concerns and thus provides insight into the worldview and its political principles. Editorials and interviews demonstrated the apocalyptic backdrop of the magazine's religiocultural critique. In one issue, for example, speculation on the secret messages of Fatima led to the claim that in spite of the liberalization and "apostasy" of the Vatican II Church, the fall of communism in Eastern Europe was due to the intercession of the Virgin. Anticommunism remained a strong staple even after the fall of the Berlin Wall.[197]

Although Fessio's American edition reports on events and trends in world Catholicism, developments in the United States receive special notice. *30 Days* is vehement in support of pro-life crusaders. In early 1990, for example, the editors ran a series of articles on Bishop Vaughan's participation in Operation Rescue and in defense of his quoted remark that New York governor Mario Cuomo, a Catholic, risked "going to hell" because of his support of abortion.[198] In its first year, *30 Days* gained thirty-three thousand subscribers in the United States.

In 1972 Fessio was instrumental in bringing into English publication *Communio*, an international journal begun by the late Swiss theologian Hans Urs Von Balthasar, who was a favorite theologian of John Paul II. The *Communio* movement has given consistent theological affirmation to traditional Catholic beliefs, while exploring contemporary problems and contemporary modes of expression. To some extent it has functioned as a counterweight to dissenting scholarship, especially as expressed in the progressive theological journal *Concilium*. The American edition of *Communio* has seventeen hundred subscribers and is published in South Bend, Indiana.

Two other conservative Catholic periodicals issue from South Bend, although with no official connection to the University of Notre Dame. *Crisis* (7,500 subscribers) was founded in 1982 by a coalition of orthodox Catholics and political neoconservatives, sometimes held together in uneasy alliance. *Fidelity* (circulation 22,000) was founded in 1981. Its mission has to a great extent been one of religious exposé, focusing on particular dioceses, religious orders, or educational institutions. Articles tend to be detailed and aim at revealing scandalous situations showing lack of fidelity to Catholic principles. The magazine is unusual in conservative circles in that beginning in 1988, it has also trained its investigative guns on targets on the Catholic right. Through much of 1988, it was the center of an emotional controversy precipitated by a series of articles claiming that the alleged visions of the Virgin Mary at Medjugorjge (Yugoslavia) are inauthentic. It has also warned against what it regards as cultish aspects of certain fringe Catholic movements.[199]

Along with their commitment to print journalism, conservative Catholics have no principled opposition to modern technology and, like their Protestant counterparts, have tended to use the electronic media more effectively than their liberal coreligionists. The national Catholic television network is the Eternal Word Network (EWN), a cable operation emanating from a convent of cloistered Poor Clare (Franciscan) nuns in Birmingham, Alabama. It was established by an unlikely person—Mother Angelica, the prioress of the community, whose members are supposed to have only minimal contact with the outside world. She became interested in this apostolate after appearing on Protestant television programs and concluding that Catholics needed something similar. Mother Angelica's style is Southern and informal, laced with homey humor and sudden outbursts of fervor or affection.[200] A common format on EWN is the talk show, which features guests firm and devout in their Catholic faith. It includes theologians, activists in various organizations, people engaged in charitable work, and people with inspiring personal stories to tell. There is little overt controversy, but from time to time both the guests and Mother Angelica herself enlighten viewers as to official Church teaching and warn against corrupting social and religious influences In 1988, after trying unsuccessfully to develop a national television network of their own, the American bishops voted to affiliate with Mother Angelica's operation, but she terminated the affiliation in 1990 after disputes about programming.

The Conservative Alliance Tested: The Charismatic Movement

In the late 1960s there appeared in the United States a new movement, first called Catholic Pentecostalism, then "the Charismatic Movement," a phenomenon which centered on belief in the direct inspiration of the Holy Spirit in the lives of individuals, an intensely personal and emotional piety, and the formation of closely knit groups of people who have had similar experiences.[201] At first conservative Catholics tended to be highly suspicious of this new movement, seeing it as merely one more example of the "Protestantizing" of the Catholic Church. Direct inspiration by the Holy Spirit was viewed as merely a rationalization for following one's own impulses without respect for religious authority. Newly formed charismatic groups were thought to be rivals to the main body of the Church. Specific practices, such as speaking in tongues, were considered bizarre and possibly pathological.

The mainstream of the movement, however, became increasingly conservative in its beliefs. While not abandoning the idea of direct inspiration by the Holy Spirit, Catholic charismatics in the 1970s and 1980s emphasized that such inspiration must always be tested against the teachings of Scripture and the Church. Yet in other ways Catholic charismatics resembled Protestant evangelicals, in relying on Scripture authoritative guidance for life and in the formation of structured communities resting on hierarchical authority, obedience to authoritative teaching, and a strict personal morality, especially with regard to sexual behavior. Catholic charismatics soon began to be in the forefront of those who see in contemporary Christianity a massive crisis of belief and fidelity.[202]

Catholic charismatics have been more effective than many other conservative movements, because they have generated a formidable spiritual dynamism. At its peak the Charismatic Movement attracted over twenty thousand people annually to a summer conference at the University of Notre Dame, and as many as three million American Catholics are estimated to have participated in charismatic activities at one time or another. (These numbers had declined slightly by the end of the 1980s).[203] One center of the Catholic charismatic movement, the Word of God Community of Ann Arbor, Michigan, is a "covenant community" whose members live together—unmarried people in communal houses, families in separate houses clustered together—with most of their religious and social activities carried on within the community. It has about fifteen hundred members, many recruited as students at the University of Michigan.[204] Catholic charismatics believe that such communities, while not essential to living an authentic Christian life, may be one of the few viable alternatives to what they see as a pervasively secular society. (Many members of covenant groups do work outside the community in business and professional careers). The Word of God Community publishes the periodicals *New Covenant* and *Faith and Renewal* (circulation twenty thousand and fifteen thousand, respectively), aimed primarily at other charismatics but having a somewhat wider readership. The journals focus on practical spiritual and organizational advice, as well as on social and religious issues. Both can be viewed as becoming more overtly Catholic over the years. Also operated by the community is a book publishing house, Servant Books, which publishes books oriented toward charismatics but also publishes others of a more general religious nature. It is one of the most important publishing houses within conservative Catholicism.[205]

Suspicion of Catholic charismatics in the wider conservative Catholic community waned as it became apparent in the 1970s that Catholic charismatics were drawn not only to a style of personal and emotional piety no longer present in their parish churches but also, increasingly, to an emphasis on objective religious truth, the reality of the supernatural, and an ordered and disciplined approach to life based on explicit moral and religious principles. Thus a significant development over the past decade has been the close cooperation, especially on moral and social issues, between conservative and charismatic Catholics, both of which oppose abortion on demand, pornography, and the perceived moral and cultural deterioration of American society.[206]

Thus styles of worship and piety may diverge from group to group in the vast and complex American Catholic Church, but Catholics on the political right have demonstrated repeatedly the capacity to put aside differences in eschatology and theology in order to form coalitions with one another—and with conservative Protestants. The ability of conservative Catholics to work within the system—whether "the system" is the institutional church or the American political order, or even the American tradition of civil disobedience—is secured by the principled refusal to allow doctrinal differences and/or particular apocalyptic scenarios to diminish their influence on the sociopolitical mainstream. Although conservative Catholics do share a sense that their valued way of life and belief is threatened by the compromises and facile adaptations of their liberal coreligionists, they are ultimately loyal insiders, ultimately unable and unwilling to repudiate the Church from which they came and by which they are nourished spiritually—even as they attempt to correct its many recent errors and redirect its path.

To those who seek "family resemblances" to fundamentalism, perhaps the salient characteristic of conservative Catholic activism in America is this willingness to collaborate with outsiders. Such willingness reflects the assumption that by their own efforts, conservative activists can reverse or modify historical trends set in motion by the penetration of secular modernity into the Church and into American society. This assumption is not shared by the separatist Roman Catholic traditionalists, who may more accurately be described as representing a Catholic variant of fundamentalism. Nonetheless, as students of religious fundamentalism have pointed out, those who try to remain faithful to traditional religion even as they partake of the benefits and travails of modernity frequently seem to be the most innovative adapters. The dominantly lay character of conservative Catholic activism suggests that people feel surfeited with the world in their daily lives and want to find oases of the spirit (at a time when, ironically, many clergy may feel stifled in a predominantly religious environment). Hence the paradox by which cloistered monks are less likely to be religiously conservative than computer programmers or business executives. Indeed, Catholic conservatism in the 1990s is not simply an attempt to preserve or even to recreate the preconciliar Church. In the coalitions and alliances it has formed and in its predominantly lay character, this conservatism is a new and unprecedented brand of American Catholic activism, one that has significantly altered the religious landscape of America.

Notes

1. All had been ordained by Lefebvre and were members of the Society of Saint Pius X. The consecrations were also attended by Bishop Antonio de Castro Mayer of Campos, Brazil, a long-time supporter of Lefebvre. Mayer was also excommunicated for his part in the consecrations.

2. The alleged apparition to which Lefebvre referred was that of "Our Lady of Good Fortune" in Quito, Ecuador (4 February 1634). For Society of Saint Pius X documentation pertaining to the consecrations, cf. *The Angelus* 11, July 1988, and Francois Laisney, *Archbishop Lefebvre and the Vatican: 1987–1988* (Dickinson, Tex.: Angelus Press, 1989).

3. Cf. "Temptations to Idolatry," *America,* 24 March 1973, p. 262.

4. Remarks made by Pope Paul VI on 24 May 1976 to the Consistory of Cardinals. Quoted in Michael Davies, *Apologia Pro Marcel Lefebvre,* vol. 1 (Dickinson, Tex.: Angelus Press, 1979), p. 176.

5. *Latin Liturgical Association Newsletter* 32 (March 1989), p. 4.

6. Figures based upon the author's research in the early 1980s. Cf. William D. Dinges, "Catholic Traditionalism in America: A Study of the Remnant Faithful," (Ph.D. diss., University of Kansas, 1983).

7. Society figures in *The Angelus* 9, August 1986, p. 5; July 1988, p. 52. The Society "Letter of Superior General" (27 November 1989) lists 205 active priests and 280 seminarians. For a current listing of traditionalist chapels in the United States (of which there are 264) cf. *Our Lady of the Sun Mass Directory* (Peoria, Arizona, 1989 [annually]). For a more extensive international listing of traditionalist chapels, schools, religious houses and foundations, publications, and organizations, see Professor Radyko Jansky's *World-Wide Catholic Traditionalist Directory* (Saint Louis, Missouri), published quarterly since 1970.

8. Hugo Kellner, "Some Proposals for a

Reform of the Church Adopted to the Eschatological Situation of Our Time" (16 October 1964); Lawrence Brey, "Operation Michael: A Letter to Three American Traditionalist Spokesman" (30 November 1967); "The *New Ordo* Mutilation," *The Voice,* 13 June 1970; "Advisory to Traditionalists" (1 January 1976). William F. Strojie has published a series of anti-Vatican II "Letters" and "Papers" with titles such as "The New Mass Invalid Because of Defect of Intention" (1972) and "The Enemy Within the Catholic Church." Cf. also, by Strojie, *From Rome to Ecône* (1977); *A Short Dictionary of Vatican II Words and Phrases* (1978); and *Popes of the Revolution: A Council of All Believers* (1980).

9. Cf. Michael Davies, *Liturgical Revolution: Cranmer's Godly Order* (New Rochelle, N.Y.: Arlington House, 1976); *Liturgical Revolution: Pope John's Council* (New Rochelle, N.Y.: Arlington House, 1977); *Sacrifice and Priesthood in the Catholic Church* (Devon: Augustine Publishing Company, 1977); *Apologia Pro Marcel Lefebvre,* 3 vols. (Dickinson, Tex.: Angelus Press, 1979–83), p. 198; *Pope Paul's New Mass* (Dickinson, Tex.: Angelus Press, 1980); *The Roman Rite Destroyed* (Augustine Pamphlet, 1978); *The True Voice of Tradition* (booklet) (Saint Paul, Minn., Remnant Press Reprint, 1978). Mr. Davies also contributes numerous articles to *The Remnant* and speaks and writes regularly on behalf of the traditionalist cause.

10. In 1975, Archbishop Lefebvre personally thanked Matt for publishing information about his traditionalist efforts "that otherwise would remain unknown to our American friends." Cf. *The Remnant,* 11 October 1975, p. 14.

11. The number and variety of such organizations that have arisen in the past quarter century preclude any exhaustive treatment here. Cf. Jansky, *Directory*, for a complete listing.

12. Gommar De Pauw was born in Flanders, Belgium, in 1918. After graduating from the College of Saint Nicholas, Belgium, he entered the diocesan seminary at Ghent. At the outbreak of World War II, De Pauw fought with the Belgium infantry. He was taken prisoner at Dunkirk but escaped and returned to the seminary. He was ordained in 1942 and joined members of his family in the United States in 1949. In 1952, De Pauw accepted a chair of moral theology and canon law at Mount Saint Mary's Seminary in Emmitsburg, Maryland. The following year he received a Doctor of Canon Law degree from The Catholic University of America. Cf. *Sounds of Truth and Tradition* (hereafter *STT*) (1974), pp. 23–26.

13. *STT* (1973), pp. 1–3.

14. *The Wanderer,* 15 April 1965, p. 12.

15. This "Father X" was probably De Pauw's brother, Father Ademar De Pauw, a Franciscan priest stationed in New York at the time.

16. Incardination is a canonical rule that binds priests to obey and serve the bishops to whom they are attached. De Pauw's incardination in the Tivoli diocese was reportedly "arranged" by Cardinal Ottaviani, who introduced De Pauw to Bishop Faveri of the Tivoli diocese. Accordingly, Ottaviani dropped Cardinal Spellman's name as a De Pauw supporter. Cf. *STT* (1974); (1979); also *Commonweal,* 21 January 1966, p. 458.

17. De Pauw had had a brief audience with Pope Paul VI on 1 December 1965. For De Pauw's account of this meeting, cf. *STT* (1979), pp. 11–21.

18. Copy of a letter from Bishop Faveri to Cardinal Shehan, author's file. De Pauw continued to insist that he had been legally incardinated into the diocese of Tivoli and could therefore, ignore directives from the Archdiocese of Baltimore. His appeal to the curial office with jurisdiction over incardination controversies proved unsuccessful. On 30 September 1966, the Sacred Congregation of the Council ruled that De Pauw was still incardinated in the Archdiocese of Baltimore and therefore "legally subject" to the authority of Cardinal Shenan. Abstract copy from a Decree of the Sacred Congregation of the Council in Rome, 30 September 1966.

19. Cf. Walter Matt, "The Case of Fr. De Pauw—Smear vs. the Truth," *The Wanderer,*

20 January 1966, p. 4; also 13 January 1966, p. 4, and 31 March 1966, pp. 4, 29.

20. Copy of De Pauw's letter to Pope Paul VI, 15 August 1967. Author's file.

21. *STT* (1967), p. 16.

22. Cf. "A Final Word on the De Pauw Case," *The Wanderer,* 5 October 1967, pp. 1–3; *Triumph,* June 1970, p. 25. De Pauw reacted angrily to this loss of support (including *The Wanderer*'s refusal to publicize any of his CTM activities) by asserting that the real reason the paper dropped him was because of pressures of financial backers among the Church establishment.

23. De Pauw was especially critical of Archbishop Lefebvre's traditionalist initiatives in the United States. De Pauw assailed Society priests for "taking over" traditionalist strongholds that he and other American traditionalist priests had built up, especially the opening of a Society chapel near his CTM headquarters on Long Island. De Pauw also resented Archbishop Lefebvre's refusal to support publicly the CTM. Besides deriding Lefebvre for soliciting money from "anti-Paul VI Catholics," and acting like a "de facto pope," De Pauw also charged that Lefebvre's "schismatic antics" in ordaining priests in violation of Church law caused the Tridentine Mass to become a symbol of rebellion, thereby precluding any possibility that Paul VI would grant traditionalists permission to use the old rite. Cf. *STT* (1977), pp. 33–40.

24. Gommar De Pauw continued to produce various traditionalist publications *(Sounds of Truth and Tradition)* and other media materials relevant to the traditionalist cause. On De Pauw's role in the rise of the Traditionalist Movement, cf. also William D. Dinges, "In Defense of Truth and Tradition: Catholic Nationalism in America, 1964–1974," Working Paper Series, University of Notre Dame, Cushwa Center for the Study of American Catholicism 17, no. 2 (1986).

25. Fenton joined the John Birch Society in 1958. He was appointed to its national board of directors in 1964.

26. Cf. Francis Fenton, *Holding Fast* (ORCM, Inc., 1977), p. 1.

27. *Ibid.* Over 80,000 copies of this booklet were eventually distributed by the ORCM.

28. Francis Fenton, "The Roman Catholic Church: Its Tragedy and Hope." This address was also printed in booklet form by the ORCM.

29. Dinges, "In Defense of Truth and Tradition."

30. For biographical material on Lefebvre, cf. Davies, *Apologia,* vol 1., esp., 1–24; also, *The Angelus* 11, July 1988, pp. 6–21.

31. Cf. Marcel Lefebvre, *A Bishop Speaks: Writings and Addresses, 1963–1975,* trans. U. S. M. Fraser (Edinburgh: Scottish *Una Voce,* 1976); Marcel Lefebvre, *I Accuse the Council!* (Dickinson, Tex.: Angelus Press, [1976] 1982).

32. Cf. Daniele Menozzi, "Opposition to the Council (1964–1984)," in Giuseppe Alberigo, Jean-Pierre Jossua, and Joseph A. Komonchak, eds., *The Reception of Vatican II* (Washington, D.C.: Catholic University of America Press, 1987), p. 325–48.

33. Cf. Milan Mikulich, O.F.M., "The Lefebvre controversy in Perspective," *The Wanderer,* 18 August 1977, pp. 4 and 6. Mikulich claims that Lefebvre himself actively sought out seminarians.

34. Lefebvre, *Collected Works,* vol. 1 (Dickinson, Texas: Angelus Press, 1985), pp. 34–35.

35. Cf. Davies, *Apologia,* vol. 1, p. 57–58.

36. This suspension was an order forbidding Lefebvre to offer Mass, preach, or administer the sacraments, thereby depriving him of the canonical authority to exercise his priestly powers.

37. Much of this material is documented in Michael Davies's three volumes on Lefebvre. Documentation on events since 1987 can be found in Francois Laisney, *Archbishop Lefebvre and the Vatican, 1987–1989* (Dickinson, Tex.: Angelus Press, 1989).

38. Cf. *For You and For Many,* (National Newsletter of the Society of Saint Pius X, January, 1978).

39. Laisney, *Archbishop Lefebvre and the Vatican.*

40. Interview in *Le Figaro,* August 1976. Quoted in Menozzi, "Opposition," p. 339.

41. Cf. Menozzi, "Opposition."

42. Cf. Marcel Lefebvre, "The New Mass and the Pope," pamphlet (8 November 1979).

43. Marcel Lefebvre, "A Public Statement on the Occasion of the Episcopal Consecration of Several Priests of the Society of St. Pius X," 19 October 1983.

44. Pope John Paul II granted bishops authority in October 1984 to allow Catholics to return to the use of the old Mass. However, those desiring the Tridentine liturgy were to secure permission of the bishop and make it "publicly clear beyond all ambiguity" that they were in no way connected with groups that impugn the lawfulness and doctrinal integrity of the new liturgy. This Vatican "pastoral consideration" was widely rejected by professional liturgists. The action reversed Pope Paul VI's decade and one-half prohibition of the Tridentine liturgy and disregarded a 1980 worldwide survey in which the bishops of the Church overwhelmingly rejected any need for the old Mass. Cf. *Notitae Sacra Congregation Pro Sacramentis in Cultu Divino* 17 (1981), pp. 587–609. According to John Paul II, the Tridentine liturgy was reinstated because "the problem [of the attachment to the traditional liturgy] continues." *The Wanderer,* 10 January 1985.

45. Cf. Lefebvre's remarks to a conference of Society priests at Nicholas du Chardonnet, Paris, in *The Angelus* 10, July 1987, pp. 2–9, 27.

46. *The Angelus* 10, July 1987, p. 13.

47. Cf. Laisney, *Archbishop Lefebvre and the Vatican,* pp. 76–82.

48. Lefebvre also protested that he had never been allowed to see Gagnon's report and that the Vatican had not agreed to any of the candidates he had previously submitted for consecration. He also objected to the fact that the headcount on the commission would include only two traditionalists. Cf. Laisney, *Archbishop Lefebvre and the Vatican,* pp. 90–93.

49. 24 May 1988 letter from Lefebvre to Ratzinger in Laisney, *Archbishop Lefebvre and the Vatican,* pp. 114–15.

50. For treatments of Integralism, see Lester Kurtz, *The Politics of Heresy: The Modernist Crisis of Roman Catholicism* (Berkeley: University of California Press, 1986); Gabriel Daley, "Catholicism and Modernity," *Journal of the American Academy of Religion* 53, no. 3 (1985): 773–96. Also Daniel Alexander, "Is Fundamentalism an Integrism?" *Social Compass* 32, no. 4 (1985): 373–92.

51. Cf. R. Scott Appleby, *"Church and Age Unite!" The Modernist Impulse in American Catholicism* (Notre Dame: University of Notre Dame Press, 1991).

52. Cf. Lefebvre, "Reflection on the Suspension à divinis," Angelus Press, 29 June 1976.

53. Cf. Kurtz, *Politics,* p. 42.

54. On ideological differences between leadership elites and social movement participants, cf. John Wilson, *Introduction to Social Movements* (New York: Basic Books, 1973).

55. On this emphasis on cognitive religiosity in fundamentalism, cf. George Marsden, *Fundamentalism and American Culture* (New York: Oxford University Press, 1980); James Barr, *Fundamentalism* (London: SCM Press, 1977).

56. Cf. James Likoudis and Kenneth D. Whitehead, *The Pope, the Council, and the Mass: Answers to the Questions Traditionalists Are Asking* (West Hanover, Mass.: Christopher, 1981).

57. Joseph Cardinal Ratzinger, *The Ratzinger Report: An Exclusive Interview on the State of the Church,* trans. Salvator Attanasio and Graham Harrison (San Francisco: Ignatius Press, 1985), pp. 27–45.

58. For examples of traditionalist attacks on the doctrinal integrity of the Council, cf. Marcel Lefebvre, *I Accuse the Council* (Dickinson, Tex.: Angelus Press, 1982); Christopher Hunter, "Vatican II: The Council of Contradiction," *The Roman Catholic,* November 1980, pp. 7–16; Ursula Oxford, "The Hidden Enemy of the Church," *The Voice,* 13 November 1972. A more tempered traditionalist critique of the Council can be found in Michael Davies, *Pope John's Council:*

Part Two of Liturgical Revolution (New Rochelle, N.Y.: Arlington House, 1977). Cf. also William D. Dinges "*Quo Vadis,* Lefebvre?" *America,* 11–18 June 1988, pp. 602–6.

59. Lefebvre, *I Accuse the Council!* Also by Lefebvre, *Liberalism* (Dickinson, Tex.: Angelus Press, 1980).

60. Cf., for instance, James Hitchcock, *The Recovery of the Sacred* (New York: Seabury, 1974).

61. Traditionalist polemics against the new Mass include "Is the Holy Sacrifice of the Mass Being Destroyed in America?" (True Mass Tapes, Inc., n.d.); Walter M. Matt, "Questions about the New *Ordo Missae* "*Remnant Supplement* (1970); William Strojie, "The New Mass Invalid Because of Defect of Intention" (Sheridan, Oregon) (1972); "The Great Deception" (Angelus Shop Reprint no. 10., n.d.); Patrick Henry Omlor, *Questioning the Validity* (Reno, Nev.: Athanasius, 1969); *In Defense of the Faith* (Massapequa Park, New York: Confraternity of Traditional Catholicism, 1974), esp. 4, on "The *Novus Ordo Missae,*" pp. 29–125.

62. Hitchcock, *Recovery;* also Dietrich von Hildebrand, "The Case For the Latin Mass," *Triumph,* October 1966, p. 15.

63. De Pauw claimed the American bishops were "automatically excommunicating" themselves and the priests who follow them by making the all-vernacular Mass mandatory. De Pauw's letter of 25 December 1967, author's file, p. 21.

64. "The Liturgy of Heresy—Some Important Observations Concerning the English Canon," *The Reign of Mary Newsletter* (Coeur d'Alene, Idaho, n.d.); also William Strojie, *Pope, Council, and Chaos*, Lebanon, Oregon.

65. Cf. "Tridentine Mass Still Permitted?" *Homiletic and Pastoral Review* 8 (May 1973).

66. Lawrence Brey, "The Final Test of Orthodoxy," *Pro Multis* (author's file, n.d.). The traditionalist attack on the new *Ordo* linked promulgation of the Mass to a sinister conspiracy to destroy the Roman Catholic faith and replace it with a "humanistic" and "Protestantized" commemorative rite. These views and the anti-papal rhetoric that accompanied them were crystallized in the early 1970s in a book written by a Louisville priest, Father James F. Wathen. In *The Great Sacrilege* (Rockford, Ill.: Tan Books, 1971), Wathen castigated Pope Paul VI for committing the "great and unspeakable sacrilege" of promulgating the new Mass. Wathen denounced the new *Ordo* as a denial of the Catholic theology of the priesthood and a contradiction of the Catholic doctrine of the Mass as a propitiatory sacrifice. He also linked postconciliar institutional dysfunction to the promulgation of the new liturgy. Readers of *The Great Sacrilege* were reminded that popes had used their authority in "wicked and destructive ways" in the past and that such abuse could be rightfully challenged, especially in matters regarding Church discipline. Wathen also reiterated conspiracy themes that had been germinating in traditionalist circles. According to Wathen, "The Revolution" had infected the postconciliar Church. Priests who said the *Novus Ordo* liturgy did so because their minds and will were controlled by "Masonic Masters." True Catholics were advised to divorce themselves from any connection with the "Great Sacrilege" and to return to the "true Mass."

67. Barr, *Fundamentalism,* p. 313. Cf. also Peter Berger, *The Sacred Canopy* (New York: Doubleday Anchor, 1967).

68. Cf. especially, "Neo-Modernism or the Undermining of the Faith," in Marcel Lefebvre, *An Open Letter to Confused Catholics* (Herefordshire, England: Fowler Wright Books, 1986), pp. 120–28.

69. Thus, for instance, use of the Tridentine rite is defended by traditionalist apologists on the grounds that no episcopal authority has the power to abrogate Pope Pius V's *Quo Prium* because this document grants an indult to all priest to freely and lawfully use the *Missale Romanum* "in perpetuity"; nor, accordingly, has Pope Paul VI "definitively" revoked *Quo Primum* according to canon law. (The bull *Quo Primum Tempore* was promulgated by Pius V on 9

July 1570 to consolidate and codify the Roman rite of the liturgy. The document was contained in all subsequent revisions and re-editions of the *Missale Romanum*. Traditionalists have argued that because *Quo Primum* ordered use of the Tridentine Mass "in perpetuity," and because the document is "irrevocable," the Tridentine rite cannot be lawfully prohibited.) See Wathen, *Great Sacrilege,* pp. 37–45.

70. Francis Fenton, "The One True Church," *ORCM News,* 27 October 1975, p. 4.

71. Cf., for instance, Marcel Lefebvre, "To Remain a Good Catholic Must One Become a Protestant?" in *A Bishop Speaks,* pp. 73–81, and Lefebvre, "Searching and Dialogue, Death of the Missionary Spirit," in They Have Uncrowned Him (Dickinson, Tex.: The Angelus Press, 1988), pp. 175–83. Also, "A Recent History of the Vatican's False Ecumenism," *The Angelus* 12, February 1989, pp. 26–27.

72. Cf. Lefebvre, *Open Letter To Confused Catholics,* 78–89; Also Franz Schmidberger's "Letter to Friends and Benefactors," no. 34, 21 February 1988, and Francois Laisney, "Letter to Friends and Benefactors," 1 February 1989. Archbishop Lefebvre, in particular, has been especially adamant in denouncing the "errors" of Vatican II with regard to religious liberty, "false ecumenism," and the loss of Catholic hegemony in the social and political realms. Lefebvre has rejected all Vatican initiatives toward non-Catholic and non-Christian traditions, denouncing, for instance, John Paul II's 1986 visit to the Jewish synagogue in Rome and his ecumenical "prayer meeting" in Assisi as "scandal on an unprecedented scale" and as encouraging "false religions and praying to false gods." Cf. the "Declaration" by Lefebvre and Bishop De Castro Mayer to the French bishops and the press in *The Angelus* 10, January 1987, pp. 2–3. Lefebvre claimed that his decision to consecrate was provoked by the Vatican's response to his *dubia* regarding the Vatican II Declaration on Religious Liberty and by Pope John Paul II's inter-religious activities at Assisi. Cf. Lefebvre's sermon at Ecône, "Bishops to Save the Church," Society reprint, 29 June 1987.

73. Cf., for instance, George Kelly, *The Battle For the American Church* (New York: Doubleday, 1979); James Hitchcock, *Catholicism and Modernity: Confrontation or Capitulation?* (New York: Seabury, 1979).

74. This position has not precluded conservative groups from publicly attacking individual bishops. See, for instance, Penny Lernoux's discussion of the Hunthausen affair in *People of God: The Struggle For World Catholicism* (New York: Viking, 1989), p. 231.

75. *The Voice,* 10 February 1968, p. 6.

76. *Maryfaithful,* March–June 1978, p. 2.

77. *The Voice,* 10 February 1968, p. 6.

78. *In Defense of the Faith,* p. 27; Also, Francis Fenton, "The American Bishops," *ORCM News,* 4 January 1978, p. 6; and Father Robert McKenna, "From the Pulpit," *ORCM News,* 14 May 1976, p. 6.

79. Thuc was elevated to the archiepiscopal See of Hue in 1960. He attended the Second Vatican Council but was denied a visa to return to Vietnam (he was a brother of Ngo Dihn Diem). Thuc continued to live in Rome. In 1968 Pope Paul VI forced his retirement. Thuc moved to Toulon, France. He first gained notoriety in 1975 for giving episcopal consecration to a self-styled seer of Palmar de Troya in Spain named Clemente Dominques. Clemente subsequently "consecrated" dozens of "bishops" and went on to declare himself pope. Thuc was excommunicated for consecrating Dominiques but later was absolved (1978) after repenting for his "mistake." However, Thuc was again convinced by a group of ultratraditionalists to agree to consecrate some bishops. In 1981, he conferred episcopal consecration on one French (May 7) and two Mexican priests (October 17) without authorization. These "bishops," in turn, consecrated a number of North American traditionalist "bishops." On 25 February 1982, Thuc issued a declaration that the Holy See was vacant. Cf., Michael Davies, "The Sedevacantists," *The Angelus* 6, February 1983, pp. 10–12.

80. Lefebvre, "The Pope and The Mass" (Society of Saint Pius X).

81. These priests were led by Father Clarence Kelly. Kelly was among the first American priests ordained by Lefebvre at Ecône in 1973. Kelly served as superior of the Society in the United States from its beginnings. Lengthy litigation followed Lefebvre's dismissal of Kelly and his priest supporters over the disposition of property of those churches which had been a part of the Society before the schism. Roman Catholics of America headquarters are located in Oyster Bay Cove, New York.

82. Lefebvre, *An Open Letter,* p. 138.

83. Cf., Lefebvre's 29 August 1987 letter to his future bishops in *The Angelus* 6, July 1988, p. 38.

84. Father Clarence Kelly, "The Catholic Thing to Do," *For You and For Many,* November/December 1976, pp. 1–6.

85. Cf., for instance, Rama Coomaraswamy, "The Pope, The Council, and the Mass: CUF and the Big Lie," *The Roman Catholic,* May 1981, pp. 4–11. For a conservative response to traditionalists, cf. Frank Morris, "What Do Conservatives Really Want?" *The Critic* 36, no. 3 (Spring 1978): 18–26; Kirby Whitehead, "The New Protestantism," *Homiletic and Pastoral Review* 79, no. 9 (June 1979): 18–28.

86. Archbishop Lefebvre, "1978 Ordination Sermon," *The Angelus* 1, August 1978, p. 3.

87. "The Great Deception" (Yorba Linda, Calif.: Angelus Shop Reprint, n.d.).

88. Francis Fenton, "An Open Letter to Priests," ORCM Reprint, 15 November 1977, p. 3.

89. Tito Casini, *The Torn Tunic: Letter of a Catholic on the Liturgical Reform* (Rome: Tipografia Sallustiana, 1967 [Hawthorne, California: Christian Book Club of America, 1968]), p. 12.

90. In *Sounds of Truth and Tradition* (1980), p. 11.

91. Cf., Francis Fenton, "Incredible!" *ORCM News,* 14 May 1976, p. 3; Also, *ORCM News,* 14 June 1974, p. 4; and 8 July 1979, p. 4.

92. *The Voice,* 13 November 1971, p. 3.

93. Ibid.

94. Letter from Father McKenna, *The Remnant,* 30 November 1970, p. 13; also, McKenna's "Return to Bethlehem," *Catholics For Tradition,* 31 December 1981, pp. 1,7. For an early expression of traditionalist conspiracy thinking, cf. Hugo Kellner, "Some Proposals for a Reform of the Church Adopted to the Eschatological Situation of Our Time," 15 October 1964 (author's file).

95. In *The Great Sacrilege,* Wathen had advanced the "Masonic Masters" theme, as did a tradition-minded West German bishop, Rudolph Graber, in his *Saint Athanasius and the Church of Our Time,* trans. Susan Johnson (Bucks, England: Gerrards Cross, 1974). Conspiracy themes are also prominent in Father Clarence Kelly's *Conspiracy Against God and Man* (Belmont, Mass.: Western Island, 1974). Kelly's book concerned the "Great Conspiracy" inaugurated by Freemasons and Marxism threatening the survival of Christian civilization. See also "The Liberal Conspiracy of Satan Against the Church and the Papacy," in Marcel Lefebvre, *They Have Uncrowned Him,* pp. 145–63.

96. Charges against Archbishop Bugnini first appeared in a traditionalist publication called *Sí Sí no no* (Velletri, Italy) edited by a retired Italian traditionalist priest named Francesco Putti. See also Michael Davies's discussion in his *Pope John's Council,* pp.158–72; and see "Masons in the Vatican?" *The Remnant,* 18 August 1978, pp. 11–17. For a repudiation of these charges, see Father John Flanagan, "Charges of Freemasonry in the Hierarchy Shown to be False," *The Wanderer,* 3 May 1977, p. 8. The first prelate so named was Archbishop Annibale Bugnini. Bugnini was an obvious target for traditionalist vilification; he had headed the commission charged with carrying out the reform of the liturgy (Consilium for the Implementation of the Constitution on the Sacred Liturgy) and was one of the principle architects of the *Novus Ordo* rite. It was Bugnini who had "destroyed" the Tridentine liturgy. Traditionalist allegations against the Archbishop Bugnini were soon

followed by similar charges against other high-ranking Vatican prelates, including Cardinal Jean Villot, (Vatican secretary of state), Archbishop Agostino Casaroli (secretary of the Church's Council for Public Affairs), and Cardinal Leo Suenens (Brussels, Belgium). The list of Masonic conspirators was first published in the United States by the ORCM. See Father Robert McKenna, "Our Vindication: Masonic Prelates in the Church," *OCRM Reprint,* 1977.

97. These motifs link the Second Vatican Council with alleged "Zionist influences" and the propagation of "Jewish ideas" in the postconciliar Church. They follow themes from a 700-page tome entitled *The Plot Against the Church* (1962) which appeared under the pseudonym of Maurice Pinay (printed in Italian) and which was distributed by anonymous sources at the beginning of the Council. *The Plot* contained a hodgepodge of materials purporting to show that a "Jewish conspiracy" (behind the influences of communism and Freemasonry) would employ a "fifth column in the hierarchy" to bring about "shameful reforms" during the Council that would lead to the destruction of the Roman Catholic Church and "Christian civilization." More vitriolic allegations accusing Pope Paul VI of being a "trained Jew" and associating the Second Vatican Council with a "Jewish-Masonic" conspiracy were advanced in a 1971 book by Joaquin Saenz y Arriaga, a Spanish Jesuit traditionalist priest (excommunicated in 1972), entitled *The New Montinian Church.* Anti-Semitic themes linking Vatican II with "Zionist influences" and "Jewish ideas" were also propagated by traditionalist sources in the United States, notably through a Louisville, Kentucky, publication called *Veritas.*

98. Cf. Lefebvre's "Ordination Sermon," *The Angelus* 10, July 1987, pp. 10–14. For current traditionalist thinking on alleged Marian prophecies, see Brother Michael, "The Mystery of the Third Secret of Fatima," *The Remnant,* 15 June 1986; 15 July 1986.

99. Cf. Yves Dupont, *Catholic Prophecy: The Coming Chastisement* (Rockford, Ill.: TAN Books, 1970). Traditionalist dispensationalist theories have also been derived from the prophecies of Anna Katarina Emmerick, a nineteenth century stigmatized Augustinian nun. See Carl E. Schmoeger, C.S.S.R., *The Life of Anne Catherine Emmerich* (1870 reprint) (Los Angeles, Calif.: Maria Regina Guild, 1968).

100. Cf., *National Catholic Reporter,* 20 May 1988, p. 17; *New York Times,* 30 October 1988.

101. Lefebvre, *Open Letter To Confused Catholics,* p. 166.

102. Ibid. Cf. also Lefenvre, *A Bishop Speaks.*

103. Marcel Lefebvre, *They Have Uncrowned Him: From Liberalism To Apostasy, The Conciliar Tragedy* (Dickinson, Tex.: Angelus Press, 1988).

104. Cf. Thomas Molnar, *Ecumenism or New Reformation?* (New York: Funk and Wagnalls, 1968); James Hitchcock, "The State of Authority in the Church," *Cross Currents* 20 (1970): 341–81.

105. Max Weber, *The Sociology of Religion,* trans. Ephraim Fischoff (Boston: Beacon Press, [1928] 1963).

106. John O'Brien, *Understanding the Catholic Faith: An Official Edition of the Revised Baltimore Catechism* (Notre Dame, Ind.: Ave Maria Press), p. 252.

107. David P. O'Neill, *The Priest In Crisis: A Study In Role Change* (Dayton, Ohio: Pflaum Press, 1968).

108. Cf. Andrew Greeley, *The American Catholic: A Social Portrait* (New York: Basic Books, 1977); Dean Hoge et. al., *Research On Men's Vocations to the Priesthood and Religious Life* (Washington, D.C.: USCC Office of Research, 1989).

109. Cf. Gommar De Pauw, "Catholic Traditionalist Manifesto" and "The New Mass," *STT,* Spring 1975, pp. 25–44. Also Eugene Bartkowiak, "They're Destroying the Priesthood," *The Voice,* 12 April 1976, p. 13; Francis Nugent, "Why We Refuse the Novus Ordo Mass," pamphlet, n.d.

110. Cf. Lefebvre, *A Bishop Speaks,* esp. pp. 163–90; Marcel Lefebvre "The Holy Sacrifice of the Mass," *The Roman Catholic,* 1978, pp. 17–23.

111. 1976 Ordination Sermon in Davies, *Apologia,* vol. 1, p. 205.

112. Lefebvre, *A Bishop Speaks.* Cf. also, Lefebvre's lecture to his seminarians in Zaitzkofen in February 1987 in *Verbum* 27 (Summer 1987): 5, and *Open Letter To Confused Catholics*, pp. 31, 57, 62–66, 116.

113. The fact that Catholic laity have also defended clerical role status via defense of the Tridentine liturgy does not belie the point but attests to the staying power of preconciliar theological positions within the postconciliar Church and demonstrates that social roles do not exist in isolation from one another. Roles involve reciprocal relationships. Redefining the role of "Father" after Vatican II forced many lay Catholics to make a troubling reassessment of their own religious self-understanding and responsibilities to the meaning and mission of the Church. Cf. William D. Dinges, "Ritual Conflict as Social Conflict: Liturgical Reform in the Roman Catholic Church," *Sociological Analysis* 48, no. 2 (Summer 1987): 138–58.

114. On the role of structural characteristic in social conflict and the distinction between norm- and value-oriented movements used in this paper, see Neil J. Smelser, *Theory of Collective Behavior* (New York: Free Press, 1962).

115. William D. Dinges, "The Quandary of Dissent on the Catholic Right," in Roger O'Toole, ed., *Sociological Studies in Roman Catholicism: Historical and Contemporary Perspectives* (Lewiston, N.Y.: Edwin Mellen Press, 1989), pp. 107–27.

116. On religious objectification, see Berger, *Sacred Canopy.*

117. Cf. Dinges, "Ritual Conflict," pp. 138–58.

118. Comment by Denis Roch, a Society priest, in *The Globe and Mail,* 9 July 1988, p. 3.

119. "Open Letter to Cardinal Gantin" (6 July 1988) in Laisney, *Archbishop Lefebvre and the Vatican,* pp. 156–59.

120. Cf. "True and False Obedience" in Lefebvre, *Open Letter to Confused Catholics,* pp. 134–41.

121. Michel Simoulin, "Some Simple Reflections Which We Make Without Bitterness," in Laisney, *Archbishop Lefebvre and the Vatican,* pp. 254–59; also Michael Davies, "The True Voice of Tradition" (Reprint, Remnant Press, 1978).

122. Laisney, *Archbishop Lefebvre and the Vatican,* pp. 145–49. The Pope appointed Paul Augustin Cardinal Mayer, previously prefect of the Congregation for the Sacraments and of the Congregation for Divine Worship, president of the commission instituted in accordance with the terms of *Ecclesia Dei.*

123. Laisney, *Archbishop Lefebvre and the Vatican,* p. 263.

124. Cf. Michael Davies's remarks in *The Remnant,* 31 August 1988.

125. The largest defection of a group associated with Lefebvre was that of about twenty French monks led by Dom Gerard Calvet, prior of the Traditional Benedictine Monastery of La Barroux in France (*New York Times,* 4 September 1988, p. 8).

126. Cf. Mennozi's conclusions on this issue: "Opposition," pp. 347–68.

127. These were among the central charges of J. Gresham Machen in his fundamentalist classic, *Christianity and Liberalism* (Grand Rapids, Mich.: Wm B. Eerdmans, 1923).

128. Cf. Michael Cuneo, "The Smoke of Satan Within the Temple of God: Pro-Life Activism and the Pursuit of the Sacred," *Pro Mundi Vitae* 1 (1987): 4–27.

129. John Coleman, "Who Are the Catholic Fundamentalists?" *Commonweal,* 27 January 1989, pp. 42–47.

130. Cf., for instance, Lernoux's treatment in *People of God.*

131. Cuneo sees the political agenda of conservative Catholic groups in North America as organized primarily around the anti-abortion movement.

132. Ernst Troeltsch, *The Social Teachings of the Christian Churches,* 2 vols., trans. Olive Wyon (London: George Allen and Unwin, 1931).

133. For accounts in the Catholic press,

cf. the *National Catholic Register*, 28 August 1988, p. 1; 2 October 1988, p. 1; 16 October 1988, p. 1; 13 November 1988, p. 1; 27 November 1988, p. 1; 29 January 1989, p. 1; *The Wanderer,* 1 April 1989, p. 1; 3 August 1989; 20 April 1989, p. 1; 4 May 1989, p. 1; 11 May 1989, p. 1; 20 July 1989, p. 1; 27 July 1989, p. 1.

134. Cf. Randall A. Terry, *Operation Rescue* (Springdale, Pa.: Whitaker House, 1988).

135. Robert Wuthnow, *The Restructuring of American Religion: Society and Faith Since World War II* (Princeton: Princeton University Press, 1988), pp. 3–4.

136. Quoted in the *Chicago Tribune*, 20 May 1990, sec. 5, p. 9.

137. Quoted in *The Wanderer*, 15 June 1989, p. 1.

138. Richard Cowden-Guido, ed., *You Reject Them, You Reject Me: The Prison Letters of Joan Andrews* (Manassas, Va.: Trinity Communications, 1988), especially pp. 16–21, 28–30, 99, 196, 222.

139. Ibid., pp. 112, 116.

140. Thomas T. McAvoy, C.S.C., *The Great Crisis in American Catholic History, 1895–1900* (Chicago: H. Regnery, 1957); John Ratté, *Three Modernists: Alfred Loisy, George Tyrrell, William L. Sullivan* (New York: Sheed and Ward, 1967).

141. Ralph M. Wiltgem, S.V.D., *The Rhine Flows into the Tiber* (Devon, England: Augustine Publishing House, [1967] 1978).

142. Cf. Joseph McShane, S. J., *"Sufficiently Radical": Catholicism, Progressivism, and the Bishops' Program of 1919* (Washington, D. C.: Catholic University Press, 1986); Mel Piehl, *Breaking Bread: The Catholic Worker and the Origin of Catholic Radicalism in America* (Philadelphia: Temple University Press, 1982).

143. Cf. William M. Halsey, *The Survival of American Innocence: Catholicism in an Age of Disillusionment, 1920–40* (Notre Dame: University of Notre Dame Press, 1980).

144. *Religion in America: 50 Years 1933–85* (The Gallup Report, no. 236, May 1985), p. 32.

145. Austin P. Flannery, ed., *Documents of Vatican II* (Grand Rapids, Mich.: Eerdmans, 1975), pp. 350–436.

146. Ibid., pp. 1–40.

147. Ibid., pp. 452–70.

148. Ibid., pp. 611–23.

149. Ibid., pp. 766–98.

150. Ibid., pp. 799–812.

151. Ibid., pp. 903–1001.

152. Problems remain, however. Conservative Catholics would not, as a matter of principle, participate in a Eucharist in a Protestant church, and in general they believe that even the best-willed Protestants have only a part of the truth, being especially lacking in an understanding of the whole sacramental system. Also ignored for the time being is the fact that the Catholic Church tolerates practices like drinking, smoking, dancing, and gambling, which many conservative Protestants regard as sinful. However, when the historical authenticity of Scripture is directly questioned by liberal Protestants or by liberal Catholics, conservative Catholics defend it vigorously.

153. *Smith vs. Alabama* (1986–87). The plaintiffs' contention was upheld by a Federal district judge but was overruled on appeal.

154. It may be significant that few conservative Catholics advocate that the sale of contraceptives to adults be made illegal, nor are they inclined to oppose conservative Protestants on the issue of legalized gambling, which most Catholics regard as tolerable.

155. For example, Morality in Media (New York City), an anti-pornography group, was founded by a Jesuit priest.

156. Although it is sometimes viewed as a "Catholic issue," the anti-abortion movement has increasingly attracted conservative Protestant support. Most anti-abortion organizations—American Life League (Stafford, Va., near Washington), Americans United for Life (Chicago), Human Life Foundation (New York City), Human Life International (Washington), and the Pro Life Direct Action League (Chicago)—were founded and are still directed by Catholics

but welcome, and to some extent receive, Protestant support. The largest anti-abortion group, National Right to Life (Washington), has had several Protestant presidents.

157. Cf. Paul Weyrich, "A Conservative Manifesto for the 1990s," *Crisis* 8, no. 7 (July–August 1990): 43–7. Weyrich, a conservative Catholic, is the founder and director of the Free Congress Foundation, a Washington think tank.

158. Conservative Catholics in important positions in the Reagan administration included: William Bennett, Secretary of Education; Patrick Buchanan, of the presidential staff; Frank Shakespeare, ambassador to the Vatican; William Casey, director of the Central Intelligence Agency; Donald Regan, first Secretary of the Treasury, then White House chief of staff. Conservative Catholics also held numerous upper- and middle–level positions in major departments of the government, and most believed that they had never before had such access to the levers of power.

159. The nominees were Richard Fiske to the Justice Department and Robert Fulton to the Department of Health and Human Services.

160. *Webster vs. Reproductive Health Services,* issued 3 July 1989.

161. For some years the largest private Catholic philanthropic agency in the country was the DeRance Foundation of Milwaukee, established by an heir to the Miller brewing company. In 1985 the foundation suffered severe internal troubles, stemming from problems within the family of its founder and head, Harry John. See the *National Catholic Register,* 1 June 1986, p. 1; *National Catholic Reporter,* 30 May 1986, p. 4; 1 August 1986, p. 28; 29 August 1986, p. 1. Thomas Monaghan, founder of Dominos Pizza and owner of the Detroit Tigers baseball team, also funds Catholic causes. See the *National Catholic Register,* 22 May 1988, p.l.

162. Catholicism in the United States is a major exception to the familiar sociological thesis that urbanization and industrialization weaken religion. Most Catholic immigrants to America came from peasant stock, but they adapted successfully to the urban milieu, and the Church flourished precisely in the great industrial cities of the continent. Cf. Jay P. Dolan, ed., *The American Catholic Parish: A History from 1850 to the Present,* 2 vols. (Mahwah, N. J.: Paulist, 1987).

163. On this point cf. Kelly, *Battle for the American Church,* pp. 25–50.

164. An exception is John Senior, a convert to Catholicism who is a professor of comparative literature at the University of Kansas. During the 1970s Senior and several other professors directed a special liberal arts program there at Pearson College, several hundred of whose students became Catholics. Senior's book *The Restoration of Christian Culture* (San Francisco: Ignatius Press, 1983) rejects most of modern culture, including most technological developments.

165. For a characteristic statement of this distinction, cf. Stanley Jaki, O.S.B., *Chance or Reality and Other Essays* (Lanham, Md.: University Press of America, 1986).

166. Cf. Kelly, *Battle for the American Church,* pp. 35–55.

167. Ibid., pp. 57–98.

168. Cf. Stephen Clark, *Man and Woman In Christ* (Ann Arbor, Mich.: Servant Books, 1980). Clark is one of the principal leaders of the Catholic charismatic movement.

169. *Voices* is the newsletter of Women for Faith and Family; it is in private circulation.

170. Nona Aguilar, *No Pill-No Risk Birth Control* (New York: Rawson, Wade, 1980.

171. *Chan Kendrick, et al., vs. Margaret Heckler* (1988).

172. For a discussion of these positions, see James Hitchcock, *Catholicism and Modernity* (New York: Crossroad, 1979), pp. 96–125.

173. Cf. R. Scott Appleby, "Present to the People of God: The Transformation of the Roman Catholic Parish Priesthood"; Patricia Byrne, "In the Parish but Not Of It," in Jay P. Dolan, ed., *Transforming Parish Ministry: The Changing Roles of Clergy, Laity,*

and Women Religious (New York: Crossroad, 1989).

174. Appleby, "Present to the People of God," pp. 70–85.

175. Membership figures have been supplied by the organization.

176. M. Timothy Iglesias, "CUF and Dissent: A Case Study in Religious Conservatism," *America* 156, no. 14 (April 11, 1987): 305.

177. Ibid.

178. Ibid.

179. Ibid.

180. *Faith and Life* (San Francisco: Ignatius Press). The work is multi-volume, extending through grammar school.

181. On the central government, members, ends and organization of Opus Dei, see J. Jacques Thierry, L'Opus Dei: *Mythe et réalité* (Paris: Hachette, 1973). The book was also published in English under the title *Opus Dei: A Close-up,* tr. Gilda Roberts (New York: Cortland, 1975). On the strategy followed by the movement, see Peter Hertzel, *Ich verspreche euch den Himmel: Geistlicher Anspruch, geselschaftliche Ziele und kirchliche Bedeutung des Opus Dei* (Dusseldorf: 1985), pp. 123–142.

182. John Coleman, "Who Are the Catholic Fundamentalists?" p. 46.

183. Joseph Comblin, "Movimientos e ideologias en America Latina," in *Fe cristiana y cambio social en America Latina* (Salamanca: Ediciones Sangueme, 1972), pp. 105–110.

184. Cf. Pablo Deiros, " Catholic Fundamentalism in Latin America," unpublished paper, 1988.

185. The children of Fatima revealed two "secrets" (warnings) which Mary had allegedly given them, with a third secret to be hidden until 1960. In that year Pope John XXIII reportedly opened the envelope which contained the secret, but Church authorities never made any public announcement about its contents. This episode, along with other, more sweeping, changes in church and society, combined to undermine interest in the Fatima message on the part of many Catholics.

186. Warren H. Carroll, *1917: Red Banners, White Mantle* (Front Royal, Va.: Christendom, 1981). There is a split between *Soul* magazine, published by the Blue Army, and *The Fatima Crusader*, published in Fort Erie, Ontario. The *Crusader* contends that the world has not been properly consecrated to Mary, as she reportedly requested at Fatima.

187. Mark Miravalle, *Heart of the Message of Medjugorjie* (Steubenville, Ohio: Franciscan University Press, 1988); Lucy Rooney, S.N.D., and Robert Faricy, S. J., *Medjugorje Journal* (Chicago: Franciscan Herald Press, 1988). For a skeptical analysis of the phenomenon by a conservative Catholic, see E. Michael Jones, "Medjugorje: The Untold Story," *Fidelity* 8, no. 9 (Sept. 1988): 18–41.

188. Figures supplied by the organization.

189. The series is titled *New Creation* (Dubuque, Iowa: William Brown, 1986).

190. Information supplied by the organizations.

191. Besides its newsletter, the Catholic League has published a number of pamphlets, such as Robert A. Graham, S.J., *Pius XII's Defense of the Jews and Others, 1944–45* (n.d.).

192. For historical background of *The Wanderer*, see Philip Gleason, *The Conservative Reformers: German-American Catholics and the Social Order* (Notre Dame, Ind.: Notre Dame University Press, 1956), pp. 4, 176. Information about the split with the *The Remnant* has been provided by *Wanderer* staff members.

193. Thus, following a 1989 meeting between the Pope and the archbishops of the United States, the paper asked in a headline, "Will the U.S. Bishops Join in the Catholic Restoration?" (23 March 1989) and indicated its doubts that they would.

194. In 1988, *The Wanderer* began introducing an element into conservative American Catholicism which had been largely absent, except during the brief ascendancy of *Triumph* magazine after Vatican II. A *Triumph* veteran, Gary Potter, began writing a

weekly column titled *Intra Urbem Extraque* (Inside and Outside the City) which, among other things, and without using the name, began expounding the classic theory of Catholic Integralism. Potter has begun a renewed search for a genuinely Christian society, detecting signs of it in Argentina, for example (21 July 1988; 20 July 1989), and among the Carlists of Spain (6 July 1989). He has also recalled (28 July 1988) the French political theorist Charles Maurras, whose movement Action Francaise was condemned by the Vatican in 1929 and has often been called fascist. Potter left the paper in 1990.

195. Pope John Paul II, "Continually Renew the Discovery of Your Charisma: To the priests participating in a course of Spiritual Exercises promoted by Communion and Liberation. Castelgandalfo, 12 September 1985," in "The Idea of Movement: Three Speeches of Pope John Paul II to Communion and Liberation" (San Francisco: Thirty Days, 1989), pp. 18–20.

196. Cf. Bill Kenkelen, "Fessio: An Absolutely Orthodox Ultracrusader," *National Catholic Reporter,* 30 March 1990.

197. Alver Metalli, "The Secret of Fatima and Apostasy in the Church," *30 Days in the Church and in the World,* March 1990, p. 3. Also cf. Stefano M. Paci, "Miracle in the East?" *30 Days,* March 1990, pp. 6–14. The magazine also published a letter from Sister Lucia, one of those to whom the Virgin appeared at Fatima, confirming this interpretation.

198. Patrick Riley, "Will God Damn the Governor?" *30 Days,* March 1990, pp. 22–24. Also, cf. Richard Cowden Guido, "The History of Operation Rescue," *30 Days*, October 1989, pp. 30–34.

199. *Fidelity* 7, no. 9 (1988): 18–41, no. 10 (1988): 20–40. These criticisms initiated an extensive controversy in the magazine which was still continuing two years later.

200. Her life is an unusual one—she is the daughter of an abusive father who left his family but was eventually reconciled with them; in her later years, Mother Angelica's own mother became a nun at her daughter's convent. Daniel W. O'Neill, *Mother Angelica: Her Life Story* (New York: Crossroad, 1986).

201. The literature on the Charismatic Movement is extensive. Cf. Mary Jo Neitz, *Charisma and Community: A Study of Religious Commitment within the Charismatic Renewal* (New Brunswick, N.J.: Transaction Books, 1989); J. Kerkhof, ed. *Catholic Pentecostalism* (Staten Island, N.Y.: Alba House, 1977); Edward O'Connor, C.S.C., *The Pentecostal Movement in the Catholic Church* (Notre Dame, Ind.: University of Notre Dame Press, 1971): René Laurentin, *Catholic Pentecostalism*, trans. Matthew O'Connell (Garden City, N.Y.: Doubleday, 1977).

202. Cf. Ralph Martin, *A Crisis of Truth* (Ann Arbor, Mich.: Servant Books, 1982).

203. Statistics supplied in correspondence to author by Servant Books.

204. Cf. *Pastoral Renewal* 11, no. 1 (July–August 1986): 1; *New Covenant* 18, no. 7 (February 1989): 17–19, 25–26.

205. One of the few American Catholic colleges whose move toward liberalization has been reversed is the Franciscan University of Steubenville, Ohio, which under a charismatic priest-president became heavily charismatic in spirit and at the same time firmly orthodox. The university was guided in new directions by a charismatic (in a double sense) Franciscan president, Michael Scanlan. His autobiography is *Let the Fire Fall* (Ann Arbor, Mich.: Servant Books, 1986).

206. The Word of God Community sponsors an annual conference, "Allies for Faith and Renewal," attended by conservatives from a range of religious denominations, one of the rare places where Roman Catholics, Eastern Orthodox Christians, and Southern Baptists, for example, talk to one another sympathetically about common concerns.

Select Bibliography

1. Roman Catholic Traditionalism

Alberigo, Giuseppe, Jean-Pierre Jossua, and Joseph A. Komonchak, eds. *The Reception of Vatican II*. Washington, D.C.: Catholic University of America Press, 1987.

Davies, Michael. *Liturgical Revolution: Cranmer's Godly Order*. New Rochelle, New York: Arlington, House, 1976.

———. *Liturgical Revolution: Pope John's Council*. New Rochelle, N.Y.: Arlington House, 1977.

———. *Pope John's Council: Part Two of Liturgical Revolution*. New Rochelle, N.Y.: Arlington House, 1977.

———. *Sacrifice and Priesthood in the Catholic Church*. Devon: Augustine Publishing Company, 1977.

———. *The Roman Rite Destroyed*. Augustine Pamphlet, 1978.

———. *The True Voice of Tradition*. Booklet. Saint Paul, Minn.: Remnant Press Reprint, 1978

———. *Apologia Pro Marcel Lefebvre*. 3 vols. Dickinson, Tex.: Angelus Press, 1979–83.

———. *Pope Paul's New Mass*. Dickinson, Tex.: Angelus Press, 1980 .

Dupont, Yves. *Catholic Prophecy: The Coming Chastisement*. Rockford, Illinois: TAN Books, 1970.

Graber, Rudolph. *Saint Athanasius and the Church of Our Time*. Trans. Susan Johnson. Bucks, England: Gerrards Cross, 1974.

Greeley, Andrew. *The American Catholic: A Social Portrait*. New York: Basic Books, 1977.

Hitchcock, James. *The Recovery of the Sacred*. New York: Seabury, 1974.

———. *Catholicism and Modernity: Confrontation or Capitulation?* New York: Seabury, 1979.

Kelly, Clarence. *Conspiracy Against God and Man*. Belmont, Mass.: Western Island, 1974.

Kelly, George. *The Battle For the American Church*. New York: Doubleday, 1979.

Kurtz, Lester. *The Politics of Heresy: The Modernist Crisis of Roman Catholicism*. Berkeley: University of California Press, 1986.

Laisney, Francois. *Archbishop Lefebvre and the Vatican: 1987–1988*. Dickinson, Tex.: Angelus Press, 1989.

Lefebvre, Marcel. *A Bishop Speaks: Writings and Addresses, 1963–1975*. Edinburgh: Scottish *Una Voce,* 1976.

———. *I Accuse the Council*. Dickinson, Tex.: Angelus Press, [1976] 1982.

———. *An Open Letter to Confused Catholics*. Herefordshire, England: Fowler Wright Books, 1986.

———.*They Have Uncrowned Him: From Liberalism To Apostasy, The Conciliar Tragedy*. Dickinson, Tex.: Angelus Press, 1988.

Lernoux, Penny. *People of God: The Struggle For World Catholicism*. New York: Viking, 1989.

Molnar, Thomas. *Ecumenism or New Reformation?* New York: Funk and Wagnalls, 1968.

O'Brien, John. *Understanding the Catholic Faith: An Official Edition of the Revised Baltimore Catechism*. Notre Dame, Ind.: Ave Maria Press.

Omlor, Patrick Henry. *Questioning the Validity*. Reno, Nev.: Athanasius Press, 1969.

———. *In Defense of the Faith*. Massapequa Park, New York: Confraternity of Traditional Catholicism, 1974.

O'Neill, David P. *The Priest In Crisis: A Study In Role Change*. Dayton, Ohio: Pflaum, 1968.

Ratzinger, Joseph Cardinal. *The Ratzinger Report: An Exclusive Interview on the State of the Church*. Trans. Salvator Attanasio and Graham Harrison. San Francisco: Ignatius Press, 1985.

Whitehead, Kenneth D. *The Pope, The Council, and the Mass: Answers to the Questions Traditionalists Are Asking*. West Hanover, Mass.: Christopher, 1981.

Wilson, John. *Introduction to Social Movements*. New York: Basic Books, 1973.

2. *Conservative Catholic Activism in the United States.*

Aguilar, Nona. *No Pill–No Risk Birth Control*. New York: Rawson, Wade, 1980.

Clark, Stephen. *Man and Woman In Christ*. Ann Arbor, Mich.: Servant Books, 1980.

Cowden-Guido, Richard, ed. *You Reject Them, You Reject Me: The Prison Letters of Joan Andrews*. Manassas, Va.: Trinity Communications, 1988.

Dolan, Jay P., ed. *The American Catholic Parish: A History from 1850 to the Present*. 2 vols. Mahwah, N. J.: Paulist, 1987.

———. *Transforming Parish Ministry: The Changing Roles of Clergy, Laity, and Women Religious*. New York: Crossroad, 1989.

Flannery, Austin P., ed. *Documents of Vatican II*. Grand Rapids, Mich.: Wm. B. Eerdmans, 1975.

Hauke, Manfred. *Women in the Priesthood? A Systematic Analysis in the Light of the Order of Creation and Redemption*. San Francisco: Ignatius Press, 1988.

Hitchcock, James. *Catholicism and Modernity*. New York: Crossroad, 1979.

McAvoy, Thomas T., C.S.C. *The Great Crisis in American Catholic History, 1895–1900*. Chicago: H. Regnery, 1957.

O'Neill, Daniel W. *Mother Angelica: Her Life Story*. New York: Crossroad, 1986.

Senior, John. *The Restoration of Christian Culture*. San Francisco: Ignatius Press, 1983.

Thierry, J. Jacques. *Opus Dei: A Close-up*. New York: Cortland, 1975.

Wiltgen, Ralph M., S.V.D. *The Rhine Flows into the Tiber*. Devon, England: Augustine Publishing House, [1967] 1978.

Wuthnow, Robert. *The Restructuring of American Religion: Society and Faith Since World War II*. Princeton: Princeton University Press, 1988.

CHAPTER
3

Protestant Fundamentalism in Latin America

Pablo A. Deiros

On 13 December 1974, in the presence of 2,500 lay men and women, leaders of the Chilean evangelical community signed a declaration of support to the military junta, which was published in the Santiago daily, *El Mercurio*. General Pinochet, president of the junta, then attended the dedication of the new cathedral of the Methodist Pentecostal Church at Jotabeche Street.[1] This document, entitled *Declaración de la Iglesia Evangélica Chilena* (Declaration of the Chilean Evangelical Church) proclaimed that:

> The uprising of the Armed Forces, in the historical process of our country, was a response from God to the prayers of all believers who saw Marxism as the most powerful expression of evil and darkness. Any government is legitimate if it responds to the will of the majority and satisfies the needs of the Nation; ours is so because it satisfied the need to be delivered from a Marxist system, enslaving and foreign. This system which, it is true, was born on a constitutional base, became illegitimate in trampling the institutions that supported it, even against the will of most of the Chileans. . . .
>
> The Holy Scriptures, the sole rule for faith and practice, tell us: "Let every person be subject to the governing authorities. For there is no authority except from God, and those that exist have been instituted by God" (Rom. 13:1). We Evangelicals, have always been subjected to all the authorities that have ruled our Nation, and we recognize then, as the utmost authority of this country, the Government of the Military Junta, which, in liberating us from Marxism, came to give an answer to our prayers.[2]

In his words of introduction to the signing, held in the Plenary Room of the Diego Portales Building, Rev. Puentes Oliva said:

> Today, we halt on our way to give testimony of our gratitude to God for having delivered us from Marxism through the uprising of the Armed Forces, which we recognize as the rampart raised by God against atheistic impiety. But we

are convinced that Marxism can only be totally defeated by the gospel of Jesus Christ, since he alone can change the heart. Because of this fact we are here, to support our government in the courageous and determined struggle against Marxism and to offer our spiritual assistance that comes out of a living experience which can totally change our country. . . .

The Evangelical Church is present, and aligns itself with its governors, so demonstrating the unity which in the diversity of institutions we marvelously keep. Because Evangelical unity is not the product of a cold structure, but of the warmth of the faith in our Lord Jesus Christ. . . . And He, our Lord, will deliver our nation from the Marxist hate, from the hypocrites of our society, and from international calumny.[3]

In effect, the statement linked the coup of 11 September 1973 with the work of God, interpreting it as "a response from God to the prayers of all believers who saw Marxism as the most powerful expression of evil and darkness."[4] Accordingly, the signers categorically rejected "the disgraceful declaration made against our country by the United Nations," when, after sending a fact-finding team to Chile to investigate the truthfulness of repeated reports of torture and brutality, it accused the junta of failing to uphold minimal human rights after the overthrow of a constitutionally elected government.[5] On 14 September 1975, the "first Protestant *Te Deum* in the Republic of Chile" was held in honor of General Pinochet.[6] The sermon was delivered by a distinguished and well-known Chilean Pentecostal leader.[7]

In a meeting room packed with people of different ages, a Guatemalan preacher jumps and screams in unknown "tongues" as he lays hands on several elderly women kneeling in front of him. As they are touched by the preacher, they fall back to the floor. Later they will declare that they have been healed of diverse minor infirmities. Charismatic ceremonies like this one in a rich suburb in Guatemala City are testimony to the growing popularity of revivalist religious groups in Central America. From the pulpits, radios, or rented stadiums, preachers proclaim their message to receptive and growing audiences.

From March 1982 to August 1983, General Efraín Ríos Montt held the presidency of Guatemala. During his presidency Ríos Montt retained his post as elder of El Verbo Church, a Guatemalan mission of the California-based evangelical network, Gospel Outreach. Each Sunday, dressed in civilian clothes, the illustrious elder preached a sermon broadcast through the State television channel, even as the government he headed conducted the most repressive anti-insurgency campaign in Guatemala's history, marked by thousands of violations of civil and human rights. In the first four months of his rule, according to figures culled by Amnesty International, 2,600 civilians were killed in the purges. In the months following the March 1982 coup, Amnesty International also received reports of the torture of people in custody, including both Guatemalan and foreign Protestant church workers. The agency implicated in these instances was the army secret unit.[8]

As Guatemala was approaching its presidential election in 1990, two candidates nominated for the office had strong support within the fundamentalist evangelical community. One was the engineer Jorge Serrano Elías, who had finished third in the

1985 election. The other was Ríos Montt, attempting to return to power after his 1983 overthrow. He was the principal opposition candidate seeking to prevent the re-election of the Christian Democratic Party.[9] In January 1991, Serrano won a smashing victory after Ríos Montt was disqualified from the election.

Amid El Salvador's wasteland of violence the evangelical presence grew in the 1980s. The Central American nation of 5 million experienced tremendous upheaval and bloodletting during the decade. Thousands of Salvadorans fled the country, or lived there in fear. The Protestant population of about 250,000 manifested signs of a revival. Local churches affiliated with the Central American Mission (now CAM International), for example, boasted of a 30 percent growth rate during 1980 compared to a 4 percent increase in 1979. Converts came from all levels of society: guerrillas, army officers, and soldiers. The Assemblies of God has an estimated 100,000 members in both missionary and national churches in El Salvador, or almost half of the Protestant population. In only five years (1980–85) Assemblies churches grew from 20,000 to 80,000. Other large Protestant groupings include independent Baptists, United Pentecostals, Apostolic Pentecostals, and the CAM churches.[10]

Throughout Central America in the 1980s, scores of organizations were dedicated to full-time evangelism. Fundamentalist missions were a multi-national, multi-million-dollar enterprise. By 1979 there were more than 53,500 North American overseas missionaries working with agencies which grossed nearly $1.2 billion in income.[11] Most of these missionaries were representatives of the conservative and fundamentalist agencies, which used crusades, door-to-door witnessing, radio programs, and social assistance programs. Nicaragua's evangelicals were estimated at 3.2 percent of the population in 1979, but by 1983 they were over 12 percent. Guatemala claimed the distinction of having the highest percentage of Protestants per capita in Latin America, with over 25 percent. If the present growth rate continues, by the end of the century it will be the first country to have at least half the population evangelical. In one year the Assemblies of God in Guatemala grew 44 percent. For the past fifteen years the Church of God (Cleveland, Tennessee) has planted on the average of one church in Guatemala every five days, and they have been doing the same in Costa Rica for the past ten years.[12]

Indeed, as the above vignettes and statistics suggest, evangelical Christianity has become both a religious and a political power in Latin America. In terms of religious affiliation, the recent growth of "evangelical" groups (a broad term including also fundamentalist and Pentecostal churches) has been phenomenal. In all of Latin America, there are 481 million people, of whom 60 million now belong to evangelical churches. Penny Lernoux reported in 1988 that "every hour 400 Latin Americans convert to the Pentecostals or other fundamentalist or evangelical churches," and predicted that by the end of the 1990s, in the countries most susceptible to Protestant Christian mission activity, such as Guatemala, half of the population will belong to the spectrum of evangelical-Pentecostal-fundamentalist churches.[13] In Central America alone, evangelical Christians numbered only 30,000 fifty years ago; by 1990, they had grown in number to between 5 and 6 million, or approximately 20 percent of the 27 million people in the region. They are organized in more than 650 independent groups, and 120 separate identifiable Protestant denominations. In Guatemala alone these groups represent approximately 30 percent of the population of 8.5 million, or over 2.5 million people.

Religiously, the evangelical churches are in a struggle with Roman Catholicism for the soul of Latin America. Yet across this broad Protestant spectrum one must make distinctions: between indigenous churches and North American missions; between those oriented to political action and those whose apolitical orientation carries its own political implications; and among the varieties of Protestantism decribed by the words *fundamentalist, evangelical,* and *Pentecostal.* This essay will attempt to examine the fundamentalist impulse as it has emerged in both indigenous churches and those planted by missionaries, and as it informs churches and missions that might otherwise be described as evangelical and Pentecostal.

At the same time, it must be asserted that many evangelical organizations and churches are not fundamentalist (some, as we shall see, oppose fundamentalism vigorously), and even among those church agencies that once were aligned with fundamentalist missions, there are notable defections. World Vision, for example, is one of the world's largest evangelical service organizations, with branches in every Central American country except Nicaragua (where it ceased operation in 1979). Its annual expenditures in the region exceed $10 million. Prior to opening its first Central America branch in Guatemala in 1976, World Vision had been active promoting seminars and pastoral conferences. Despite its conservative fundamentalist background, it was among the first to offer support for the new Latin American theologians who urged greater social responsibility. Over the last years, the organization, headquartered in Monrovia, California, has placed greater emphasis on social outreach through local educational and community development programs, and has tailored its theology accordingly.[14]

Although the complexity of the Latin American religious scene makes it difficult to isolate fundamentalism, the 1980s did witness an unambiguous resurgence in its influence. North American Protestantism was polarized between fundamentalism and liberalism—in many cases forcing mainstream evangelicals to lean one way or another—and denominational missionary agencies reflected the changes. By capturing the presidency of the Southern Baptist convention, for example, fundamentalists were able over the course of the decade to gain control of the appointments to its governing boards, seminaries, and agencies—and over one of the largest evangelical missions to Latin America. (In 1985, 1,276 missionaries, working with national denominations, reached 900,000 church members.)[15] Meanwhile, the largest missionary presence in Latin America, the Pentecostal Assemblies of God, based in Springfield, Missouri, disseminated its own distinctive variation on the evangelical worldview through the 67,375 ministers serving 81,836 churches and another 25,715 students training for the ministry in 145 Bible schools. With 10 million members in the region in 1984 (6 million in Brazil), the Assembly of God accounted for approximately 1 of every 4 evangelicals in Latin America.[16]

Although Southern Baptist and Assembly of God missionaries would disagree vehemently on a host of religious and theological matters, they appear to many observers of Latin American politics as participants in a new religious movement that has been a bulwark of dictatorial regimes, and amenable to the aims of anti-Marxist leaders in the region, who consider the movement as a means to combat revolutionaries, among them the most radical followers of liberation theology. Ríos Montt's was not a lone voice in Central America sermonizing on behalf of the new policies towards "communist sympathizers": preachers throughout the region urged the peasants to support "the divine elected authorities." "We were taught that Satan had triumphed in Nicaragua . . . and that the [Guatemalan] guerillas were sinners and, because of that, they starved in the mountains and were killed," reported a former student of the Guatemala City Seminary of the Central American Mission (based in Dallas, Texas). "Liberation theology is not biblical. It is extremist and degenerate," warned Alfred Kaltschmitt, an elder of Ríos Montt's church. "The devil uses it to inculcate extremism in the church and to promote revolution."[17]

The Protestant Presence in Latin America Before 1960: A Brief Overview

One of the most remarkable features of Latin American religious history prior to the contemporary era was the endurance and the stability of the Roman Catholic Church. Throughout the colonial period (1492–1808), the Church remained unchallenged and monolithic in its dominance of public religion. Having integrated the local Indian cultic practices of a previous era into Catholic ritual, church officials breathed the spirit of *Romanitas* into the structures of Spanish and Portuguese colonial administration, and Catholic cultural hegemony became an inevitable fact of life. Three centuries thus passed between the beginning of Roman Catholic evangelization and the introduction of Protestant Christianity. Apart from isolated cases, Protestant penetration did not begin until the first third of the nineteenth century.[18]

The advance of liberal ideas from France and the growing political and economic influence of the Anglo-American powers fostered such penetration. More than fifty years before Max Weber developed his thesis, Latin American liberals already regarded it as self-evident that Protestantism was more compatible with capitalism than was Catholicism. Imbued with the ideas of the British political economists, they promoted the notions of self-help individualism and what they regarded as the capitalist ethic, in direct opposition to their native Catholicism. They anticipated the material and moral advances of the Latin American republics and considered a drastic curtailment of Catholic influence an essential prerequisite. Thus nineteenth-century liberal political leaders tacitly supported the introduction of Protestantism because of their ideological commitment to the international liberal-modernist movement and to its concomitant economic system, capitalism. These liberals saw in Protestantism an ally with which to confront the regalist and clerical order inherited from Spain, and looked to the Protestant countries as their political models. The United States, a nation with no established Church and a religion that seemed to encourage reason and individualism, was considered a monument to the successful repudiation of dogmatic authoritarianism and provided an attractive model of the linkage of capitalist enterprise and political liberty.[19]

With the struggles between church and state that followed Independence, the power of the Roman Catholic Church began to wane, and Protestantism made inroads into Latin America. During this period (1808–50), Roman Catholic relations with the State were marked by acrimony. As a zealous defender of conservatism, the Church firmly opposed liberalism and its British and North American exponents, who nonetheless found in many of the new Latin American governments an enthusiastic welcome. The church thereby lost the support of the liberal states, which, in an ongoing effort to restrict the religion's sphere of influence, introduced civil registration and marriage, secularized cemeteries, abolished tithes, and expropriated the church's lands. In spite of these troubles, however, Catholicism retained the loyalty of the masses. And in some countries adjustments in the relations of church and state did not extend to complete disestablishment; in these cases, the Church continued to have structural links with the state.[20]

Because it was thus planted in a culturally hostile environment, Protestantism grew very slowly during the first decades of its presence. It appeared on the continent via three routes. At the beginning, it was an importation brought by European immigrants who came to the continent as part of the colonizing efforts of liberal governments. Leaders such as Bernardo O'Higgins in Chile, Domingo F. Sarmiento in Argentina, and Benito Juárez in Mexico saw in Protestantism an ally against ignorance and superstition and against the excessive power of the clergy, and welcomed European immigrants to their countries. At midcentury, dozens of groups settled on the continent. In Argentina, for example, German Lutherans arrived in 1843 and were soon affiliated with the Prussian state church. Today their descendants form part of the German Evangelical Church of the River Plate. The Waldensians, spiritual descendents of the French merchant of Lyon, Peter Waldo, arrived in Uruguay from Italy in 1856, but in 1859 crossed the River Plate to establish colonies in Argentina. To the south, in the Chubut Valley, a group of Welsh Protestants settled in 1864, bringing with them their own pastor. By 1897 this community had grown to 2,372 members. These immigrants tended to settle close to each other in order to preserve their ethnic, cultural, and linguistic identity. They generally did not engage in proselytizing.[21]

A second path of early Protestant penetration in Latin America was the work of the American and British Bible societies. Many evangelists traveled throughout the continent following a common pattern: "First a Bible, then a convert, then a church."[22] A third, later pattern of penetration came with missionary activity fostered by the Protestant churches of Europe and North America. Many of the missions came late to Latin America because Protestant missionary societies of the period considered the Latin American countries to be already Christianized. As late as 1910, for this reason, the continent was not included in the agenda of the World Missionary Conference held in Edinburgh. The needs of the area, however, were increasingly recognized, and in 1916 Latin America was officially considered to be a mission field by the Congress on Christian Work in Latin America, which met in Panama that year. By then, missionary efforts, though limited, were sixty years old.[23]

Guatemala's history reflected these patterns. The liberal reform period reached its zenith in Central America with the ascent to power in 1871 of Justo Rufino Barrios in Guatemala, with liberals already in power in El Salvador and Honduras. Viewing Protestants as a convenient ally against the Catholic hierarchy and the rural oligarchy, Barrios invited the Presbyterian Church to send proselytizers in 1873. Slowly a new phase of Protestant expansion began, through conversion rather than immigration, as first the Presbyterians and later the Methodists, Baptists, and Seventh Day Adventists arrived.[24] By similar patterns elsewhere, Protestantism gained a foothold in Latin America toward the close of the nineteenth century and, through the establishment of mission churches and institutions, began to develop and grow in size.

Latin American Protestant Typology

In the twentieth century, Protestant missionary penetration in Latin America has occurred most regularly and effectively in the urban areas. As is well known, the rate of urban growth in Latin America, especially in the last fifty years, has the characteristics of a real explosion. The annual rate of demographic growth has been almost 3 percent. In 1950, for example, three-fourths of the population lived in cities of less than twenty thousand people; by 1975, only half that number did. In 1960 only six cities numbered more than half a million people; a decade later, largely because of migration from rural areas, thirty-six cities had grown to that size.[25]

Those who migrated to the towns in this surge entered a "social vacuum," a milieu marked by the absence of social norms or values. The weakening of traditional social controls and the situation of anomie, characteristic of modern urban life, led to an acute crisis of personal identity in the lives of the new urban dwellers, some of whom embraced the possibility of new religious affiliations, including conversion from Catholicism to Protestantism. In response to this crisis, a new nationalistic spirit, a greater maturity, and a firmly accented sense of identity have led to the configuration of a Latin American Protestantism.[26]

TABLE 3.1
URBAN POPULATION IN LATIN AMERICA

	In 1985[a]	In 2000[a]	Area[b]	Density[c]
Mexico City	16,901	27,872	522	23,356
Sao Paulo	14,911	25,354	451	33,062
Buenos Aires	10,750	12,911	535	20,093
Rio	10,116	14,169	260	38,907
Lima	5,447	9,241	120	45,392
Bogota	4,711	7,935	79	59,633
Santiago	4,700	6,294	128	36,719

Source: *The World Almanac and Book of Facts* (1990), p. 774.
[a]In thousands.
[b]In square miles.
[c]Population per square mile.

This Protestantism presents itself, paradoxically, as something both typical and unique, a voice to be heard matched by a will to make its own contribution to the development of Christianity. On the surface, it is strikingly heterogeneous. The different churches or denominations on the continent generally tend to reflect three influences: the social environment in which they are developing, their particular ecclesiastical and theological tradition, and their overseas links. By examining Latin American Protestantism's history, theologies, ideological patterns, attitudes toward ecumenism, and its various relations to the Roman Catholic Church, one may construct a typology that is faithful to the heterogeneous character of the tradition in the twentieth century and at the same time instructive in isolating the fundamentalist impulse in contemporary Latin American life.[27] Thus it is possible to characterize Protestant Christianity in Latin America in three broad categories: mainline Protestantism, Evangelical Protestantism, and Pentecostal Protestantism.[28]

Mainline Protestantism is also called *historical Protestantism,* because it is related to the churches of the Reformation. On the other hand, it also represents Latin American ecumenical Protestantism. The most important expression of mainline Protestantism is found in the ethnic communities of immigrant origin that came to the continent during the second half of the nineteenth century. These immigrants included German Lutherans, Scottish Presbyterians, English Anglicans, Italian-French Waldenses, members of Dutch and Swiss Reformed churches, and some Welsh Baptists. They settled on the continent as colonists and kept the religious practices and traditions they brought from Europe without a stress on evangelistic outreach.[29] Missionaries of these groups, mostly from the United States and Europe, followed the settlers. With them, the historical churches opened themselves to the native community.

However, today's most characteristic form of Latin American Protestantism is *Evangelical Protestantism.* Evangelicalism in Latin America corresponds to a current inside the great Protestant confessions associated with the "free church" tradition. Free churches are autonomous and independent of the state. The majority of these ecclesiastical institutions came from Europe, were established or emerged in the United States, and reached Latin America through missionary work. So influential are these denominations that "evangelical" is today practically synonymous with "Protestant" in Latin America. (The term *evangelical* is often used in Latin America in reference to all Protestants irrespective of their denominational affiliation.)[30] This evangelical Protestantism is fundamentally conservative in doctrine and firmly committed to zealous proselytism in the name of the gospel.[31]

In this sense the term *evangelical* is not primarily confessional; it is purposive. Evangelical churches are voluntary associations of like-hearted and like-minded individuals, united on the basis of common beliefs for the purpose of accomplishing tangible and well-defined objectives. One of the primary objectives is the propagation of their worldview, which they consider to be normative for all humanity. Evangelical Protestants are characterized by their emphasis on the authority of the Bible in all matters of faith and practice; on personal conversion as a distinct experience of faith in Christ as Lord and Savior, which sets the Christian apart from the non-Christian;

and on the practice of evangelization as the fundamental dimension of the mission of the Christian faith.[32]

In discussions of the roots of Latin American evangelicalism, one must distinguish between two different kinds of missions sponsored by religious organizations overseas, especially in the United States. In general, both of these types of missions depend heavily either on denominational boards or nondenominational societies in the home country. Most of the churches that came to the continent as part of the modern missionary movement belong to the tradition of the historical free churches. They represent the historical free churches of the evangelical Anglo-American tradition, with some denominations of British origin and some others of American origin. Within this group are found Baptists, Methodists, Presbyterians, Congregationalists, Disciples of Christ, and Seventh Day Adventists. Other churches in this group belong to more recent denominations, such as the Christian and Missionary Alliance, the Church of the Nazarene, and the Evangelical Free Church. Historically these churches have provided the most organic and influential evangelical presence on the continent.

However, the post–World War II era witnessed the rise to prominence of several independent missions, also known as "faith missions." These are nondenominational and interdenominational foreign missionary agencies, whose governing concept requires that they look to "God alone" for financial support. Their growth and impact in the first half of the century was not as great as that of the denominational groups. Today, however, they represent a sizable portion of overseas missionary personnel in Latin America. Most of these missionary agencies have their headquarters in North America and are affiliated with independent fundamentalist churches there. They share the characteristic emphases of other evangelicals and are theologically conservative, but they also embrace a dualistic worldview in which the fundamentalist church is the lone force of good, battling myriad forces of evil—at times even represented by certain groups of nonfundamentalist evangelicals. Separatist in their relationship to structured denominations, these faith missions and their supporting agencies are opposed to the ecumenical movement on the grounds that it is either apostate, or theologically liberal, or concerned with social action rather than with the prior (to fundamentalists) proclamation of the gospel of redemption. Most of the Latin American churches founded by these nondenominational agencies consider themselves to be fundamentalist.[33]

The nondenominational groups arrived on the continent in significant numbers after the Second World War, when the North American missionary agencies diverted missionaries from the fields being closed in Asia and Eastern Europe. The most active of the nondenominational fundamentalist missions were those which supported themselves "by faith," that is, through the new independent fundamentalist churches of the United States imbued with an antidenominational missionary spirit.

A third expression of Latin American Protestantism is *Pentecostalism,* represented either in autochthonous Pentecostal movements that emerged from the evangelical denominations or in movements that originated in the missionary work of European and American Pentecostals in the first decades of the twentieth century. A recent development within the broader Latin American Pentecostalism is noted by the term "charismatic movement" or "charismatic renewal movement," which has drawn members from classic Pentecostalism as well as from both the historical and missionary churches.[34] Unlike classic Pentecostalism, many of these churches evince, for various reasons, an openness to ecumenical dialogue.[35] Pentecostalism in general is the fastest-growing Christian movement in Latin America, a fact attributable in part to its adherents' characteristic attitude of constant testimony and religious militancy that translates into a zeal for winning souls.[36]

Beneath this heterogeneity, however, lie important tendencies and traits common to all three groups. Although terminologically more precise, the tripartite division of Latin American Protestantism cannot account for the dynamics of religious and ecclesiastical reality. In actual practice, each of the groups is characterized by a mode of religious behavior and belief best described by the general term "evangelical." Many of the missionaries of the historical churches, for example, imparted an evangelical ethos to converts which determined the quality of their religious life more than doctrinal or confessional particularities did. And apart from their distinctive understanding of the doctrine of the Holy Spirit, Pentecostals share the doctrinal and ethical convictions and, more important, the abiding sense of the meaning and necessity of a personal experience of redemption, of their non-Pentecostal evangelical counterparts.

Latin American Protestantism is indeed marked by the "puritan-pietistic-evangelical complexion" of global evangelical Christianity, the historical roots of which are in the Pietist movement in continental Europe, the Puritanism of seventeenth- and eighteenth-century England, and the Great Awakening of eighteenth-century America. Pietism itself represented a significant effort to reform the Protestant heritage, and its influence has lent a distinctive cast to the evangelical Christianity practiced in Latin America. At times, for example, the pietistic tendency has led to subjectivism and emotionalism and has fragmented the church through enthusiastic separatism. Pietism has also been the force behind the development of legalistic moral codes and in extreme forms has served to diminish the perceived value of Christian traditions. Pietism has also inspired powerful renewal in the Church by witnessing to the indispensability of Scripture and by advocating lay Christian ministry and mission work. The puritan-pietistic-evangelical character of Latin American Protestantism in general has also served to promote religious freedom and cooperation among believers. Central to this character is the insistence that individuals not rest until they find intimate fellowship with God.

These trends have typified the recent history of Protestantism in Latin America. Its adherents share similar sociological backgrounds as well as ideological concerns which transcend denominational boundaries.[37]

The Development of a Fundamentalist Impulse

Within this shared puritan-pietistic-evangelical ethos, there is a discernible impulse toward fundamentalism, not only within faith missions that bear the name *fundamentalist* but also within certain segments of the Pentecostal movement. This impulse takes a variety of forms, but its conveyors tend to lend greater weight to the "hard" (oppositional or divisive) edge of the puritan-pietistic-evangelical ethos—its legalistic morality, a fervid and exclusionary emotionalism, and of more recent origin, a pronounced sympathy for political candidates and positions on the right wing of the Latin American spectrum.

A pattern of development within the rise of evangelical churches in the twentieth century encouraged the emergence of a fundamentalist impulse within these churches. In the first phase of this development, while they struggled to formulate a missionary strategy for the continent, denominationally affiliated institutions grappled with larger theoretical issues raised by modern religious thought. The divisive nature of the new European and North American intellectual trends lent a fanatical and intolerant tone to the debates about them in the Latin American seminaries and churches. The debates became an occasion by which many of the institutions defined themselves over against foreign liberal trends and toward a fundamentalistic rejection of open-ended adaptations to modernity. Among the debates most significant for the future of evangelical religious life were those centering on the "modernist-fundamentalist" and "Social Gospel" controversies imported by the North American missionary agencies.[38]

Both controversies served as catalysts for reaction in Latin America, for a deepening of the fundamentalist impulse within the missionary presence on the continent. The churches belonging to historical, mainstream Protestantism, more affected by the modernist trend, continued founding schools and centers for social help and widened the ministry of those already existing. The more conservative and fundamentalist churches increased their missionary personnel and developed their ecclesiastical structures in response. The fundamentalist missionaries believed not only in the verbal inspiration and infallibility of the Bible but also in a whole series of evangelical doctrines which they presented *in toto* to their congregations as a package, and almost as a type of spiritual inoculation against the disease of modernism ravaging their co-religionists north of the border.[39] The growth of both types of churches was rather rapid in the first three decades of the twentieth century, and by 1936 the Protestant community had reached 2,400,000 believers, of which the vast majority were native Latin Americans.[40]

For example, the Plymouth Brethren, a fundamentalist evangelical denomination (known in Latin America as Hermanos Libres), had its beginnings in Argentina as early as 1882, when Mr. J. H. L. Ewen began his evangelistic travels in the first horse-powered "Bible Coach." This method of spreading the Gospel, as well as the use of tents and open-air meetings, became characteristic of Brethren expansion across the country. Other missionaries in subsequent years came from the Commonwealth countries and the United States. The first decade of the twentieth century saw a phenomenal increase in their missionary activity. By 1911 there were 38 missionaries in the country. Many of their converts were from among the recent immigrants from Europe, and Italian family names were common among them. By 1915 there were at least 40 local assemblies, and their number was increasing rapidly. During these years the numbers in attendance at the open-air meetings were unusually high. At times there were as many as 700 present (in contrast to today's mere handful as the Brethren persist in this approach). In the third decade of the twentieth century the growth of the Brethren continued at an even more accelerated pace. During the 1930s, tent evangelism continued, sometimes for 34 nights straight, with over 350 present nightly. Group baptisms became the norm, and membership in the churches increased. The churches preached an uncomplicated message of salvation directed to the individual; the message often depicted the church as saved, the world as fallen, and "theology" (read "modernism") as liberal and morally bankrupt. The encouraging signs of growth continued up to the beginning of World War II, when the British missionaries felt the pressures of hostilities and a tighter economic situation.[41]

A second stage in the development of a fundamentalist impulse followed upon these reactions to North American controversies but was a reaction to events occuring at home. The economic and political crisis in Latin America in the wake of the worldwide depression interrupted the advancement of such foreign missionaries and left the continent in the hands of its native religious leaders. The continent's "Year of Crisis" of 1930 brought about the destruction of the Latin American liberal state and gave way to the appearance of de facto governments. In the nineteenth century, a pact had been established between Latin America and the central powers (namely, England and the United States), wherein Latin America was placed in a type of neocolonial dependency, now no longer Iberian but English and American. At the end of the century, Latin America had structured its economy in terms of this dependent relationship on London and New York, the new economic capitals of the world. Consequently the landholding Latin American oligarchy bore the brunt of the economic collapse of 1929. In 1930 a stage in the political and economic history of Latin America thus ended, for by that time the neocolonial pact between the Latin American bourgeois oligarchy and the United States and England had run its course. The classical liberal bourgeois project was deemed a failure.

There followed the emergence of the Latin American military class as a political force, whose ideals and lifestyle actually differed little from those of the oligarchy. "Liberalism" was transformed into a more conservative "neo-liberalism" and began to strenuously defend Latin American Christendom under the guise of "Western Christian civilization." A series of military governments seized power and established dictatorial regimes, often associated with the clerical elites and the landholding and bourgeois oligarchies. The prevalent ideology was Fascism, with a strong nationalistic, statist, and authoritarian emphasis.

Neo-liberals came to power in Brazil, for example, in 1930, at a time when the economy was bankrupt because of a big drop in the world market price of coffee, and a semi-paralyzed industry was laying off workers by the thousands. In Argentina, a military coup d'état pulled down the democratic government of Hipólito Yrigoyen. Venezuela started its petroleum boom. Velasco Ibarra took charge of the government of Ecuador, and Rafael Trujillo initiated his rise to absolute power as president of the Dominican Republic (1930–61). In 1932, the "Socialist Republic" in Chile came to an end because of a military coup, and Bolivia and Paraguay were involved in the Chaco War. In Mexico, Plutarco Elías Calles was losing power, while in Peru the military became the true rulers. In 1933, the government of Gerardo Machado y Morales in Cuba came to an end, and Fulgencio Batista, a sergeant of the Army, began to manipulate the power which he would hold in later years.

During the 1930s, Christianity struggled to adapt to this time of political and economic transition and uncertainty.[42] The economic crisis of the early 1930s produced drastic reductions in North American Protestant missionary budgets and personnel and in the subsidies available to the national churches. The immediate result was to add a much greater responsibility to the national churches, both in terms of finance and in leadership, as Latin American leaders came to assume the decision-making role in the historical churches as well as in the autonomous Pentecostal churches.[43]

However, the trend toward nativism did not transform the fundamentalist "faith missions," in which the individual missionary tended to retain the leadership of the church. Although still relatively small in size and influence, these missions provided a culturally significant element of continuity amid the political restructuring of various countries throughout the 1930s and 1940s. And in the historical churches, the trend toward native Latin American leadership was interrupted when a new generation of North American missionaries arrived in the aftermath of the Second World War.

This postwar infusion of missionaries came at a time of heightened nationalism in Latin American countries that created a hostile environment for foreigners in some quarters. Nationalism in this context is a politico-ideological movement that has sought to restore the notion of peoplehood through the rediscovery of indigenous culture, the redistribution of the land (agrarian reform), and the nationalization of national resources. An important force in the recent history of Latin America, it has brought together large sectors of the continent in a joint effort against national oligarchies, their political representatives, and foreign economic interests. It has taken different forms in post-World War II Latin America, but a common denominator has been an anti-American animus.

This anti-Americanism affected the work of foreign missionaries, denominational and nondenominational alike, who were identified in the postwar era with expansionist ideology (often perceived in the oft-stated American expressions of "manifest destiny"), and were forced to defend their own national ideals as if they were defending the Gospel itself. The North American missionaries in turn often interpreted the anti-Yankee attitude as due in part to the influence of Cold War communism. In response, the missionaries proclaimed the Christian gospel as the best defense against all evils, especially communism.

The emergence of the communist world and its attempt to foment social and political revolutions in every land also worried the Latin American ruling elites at the time. They feared that Marxists would succeed in inspiring the dispossessed to make greater demands and to organize nationalist movements in defense of their rights. Hence the shared fear of a common enemy forged an incipient alliance of sorts between the ruling oligarchies and the evangelical missions. Rulers moved to make certain controlled concessions and to grant benefits to the missions in the hope that they would help to curtail any popular movements of violent revolution.

TABLE 3.2
GROWTH OF INDUSTRIAL LABOR FORCE IN BRAZIL

Year	Number of Workers	Growth Percentages
1920	275,512	
1940	718,185	183.54
1950	1,177,644	50.75
1960	1,509,713	29.20

Source: Instituto Brasileiro de Geografia e Estatistica, *Anuário Estadistico,* 1956, 1962.

At the same time that this alliance between certain evangelicals and ruling elites was forming, the economic and social transformations attendant upon rapid industrialization began to occur. Between 1920 and 1940 in Brazil, for example, the number of industrial workers almost tripled; by 1960, it was almost twice as high as it had been in 1940. The assumption that the diffusion of Protestantism has been roughly parallel to the processes of industrialization and urbanization, and that the largest concentrations of fundamentalist Protestants are found in areas where these processes have been most intensive, is supported by figures on the growth of the industrial labor force and its distribution within Brazil. It was particularly in southern Brazil, where the growth of the industrial labor force was higher, that fundamentalist missions and churches grew most rapidly during those years.[44]

In this period of industrialization millions of peasants throughout Latin America left their villages to escape poverty, lack of opportunity, and guerrilla and military violence, or simply to seek a better life in the cities. This migration changed the balance of Latin America's population in those years from rural to urban: from 1950 to 1980, the share of the population living in urban areas doubled from 30 percent to approximately 60 percent.[45]

Religious patterns were dramatically affected by industrialization and the corresponding migration to the cities. For those who migrated, the conditions of anomie produced the possibility of religious change. Uprooted from families and religious traditions, living in slums and at the mercy of criminals and sometimes governmental predators, the urban poor became a fertile seedbed for evangelical proselytism. The weakening of traditional social controls, the sense of confusion and helplessness in the anonymity of city life, the shock of new social values sometimes accompanying the adaptation to industrial work, the absence of familiar community loyalties and of the encompassing paternalism still characteristic of rural employment—all these conditions favored the growth of an acute crisis of personal identity for the migrants. Under such conditions, the exchange of old religious values for new ones was (and remains) likely to occur.

In addition, economic and political centralization was accompanied in Latin America, as elsewhere, by a de-Christianization of culture. To Catholic and non-Catholic observers alike, traditional Roman Catholicism, increasingly perceived as a church of the elite, appeared impotent in the face of the challenges posed by creeping secularization. Associated in the popular mind with an exaggerated ritualism and formalism, the Roman Catholic Church had been oriented to a rural ministry and suffered, in this time of dislocation, from a dearth of well-trained clergy capable of adapting to the quite different pastoral challenges of urban life. Meanwhile, prominent members of the Catholic hierarchy, seemingly content to enjoy the benefits of a long-standing alliance with the ruling class, remained aloof from the crisis.

Thus the postwar processes of urbanization, mechanization, popular education, and migration, along with the dwindling appeal of traditional Catholicism, created favorable conditions for the development of a populist religious movement. The new urban dweller, recently arrived from a rural area, forced to adjust not only to the routines of factory labor but to crowded living conditions and to the personal and familial disorientation attendant upon displacement, was often without benefit of pastorally effective clergy. As with any crisis or moment of decision, the migrant was presented with new possibilities for creating identity. Evangelicals responded to this opportunity with notable vigor and enthusiasm.[46]

Pedro Gutiérrez's experience in Argentina perhaps exemplifies thousands of cases. Gutiérrez had spent thirty-five years of his life in a small town in the province of Tucumán. In 1950, encouraged by the populist propaganda of President Juan Perón, he moved to the city of Buenos Aires with his wife and two children, to become an industrial worker. President Perón had just launched an industrial program oriented to light and middle industry. Like many others, the Gutiérrezes settled in a small apartment in the urban belt around the big city. They left their parents, friends, and the simple lifestyle of rural people far behind them. They also left behind their Roman Catholic faith and their religious practices. One day, as Pedro's wife talked with a neighbor, she was given a tract and heard for the first time about the "evangelical faith." Among other things, she was encouraged to leave the "paganism" of the Roman Catholic religion and to embrace the new faith in the power of the Holy Spirit. She was promised not only salvation but also health, prosperity, and a life of peace and happiness. To satisfy her curiosity, the following Sunday she and her children went to a Pentecostal church in the neighborhood. That night, she publicly expressed her confidence in the Gospel that was preached and was received into the community. Two months later she was baptized in the new faith. The next step was to take her husband along with her. Today, Pedro is a Pentecostal pastor. His old Catholicism is something of the past, of his "old life" as he says, before he came "to know Jesus." Once politically affiliated to the Peronist Party in his native town in Tucumán, Pedro had served there as a labor union delegate. Today, however, he believes that politics is "something dirty" and contends that political commitment is "not convenient for a Christian pastor." However, in the 1983 presidential elections, Pedro voted for the Radical party candidate, Dr. Raul Alfonsin, and in the 1989 elections he voted for the Peronist Party candidate, Dr. Carlos Menem.[47]

Nondenominational fundamentalist missions were among the agencies responding most effectively to the plight of such displaced families. Buoyed in organizational terms by the large numbers of missionaries available as a result of the closing of the mission fields in China and in ideological terms by the anticommunist rhetoric and crusading spirit of the Cold War, fundamentalist patterns were reinforced by the almost absolute dominion of the missionaries over the doctrinal, pastoral, and administrative leadership of the independent churches. The number of Protestant missionaries in Latin America increased from 3,821 to 6,451 between 1945 and 1961, and the majority of them were nondenominational fundamentalist. In 1958, for example, the total number of missionaries from all the Protestant groups and denominations which worked in Latin America reached 5,431 (25 percent of the world total). Of these, 3,182 belonged to nondenominational or faith missions. This surge coincided with a general increase of interest in Latin America and a better knowledge of its moral and spiritual situation; for example, the mission literature reflects the fact that international evangelical missionary organizations were self-consciously rejecting the stereotype of the Latin American missionary as mere anti-Catholic fanatics.[48]

Evangelical Growth, 1960–90

By the early 1960s, then, the religious contest for the soul of Latin America was established between Roman Catholic and evangelical Christians. The growth of evangelicalism over the next three decades was at least in part a result of the changed circumstances in the Catholic community, but this is not to suggest that evangelicalism, much less nondenominational fundamentalism, has carried the day. A careful assessment of the Roman Catholic capacity to cope with the new conditions of life in Latin America must take account of the fact that, despite low levels of attendance at the Catholic Mass, the observance of some elements of folk religion survives and flourishes, with families preserving veneration for saints, and with feast days continuing to form familiar demarcations in the domestic calendar. Furthermore, the process of secularization and of "Catholic drift" has not taken place in a synchronized pattern but has varied in different regions of the continent.[49]

Nonetheless, traditional patterns of religious observance and cultural life waned among important segments of the Catholic population beginning in the 1960s. Institutions were less successful in regulating the traditional lifestyle of the individual, and the fact of change became more widely accepted as normal and necessary. Similarly, the functional differentiation typical of a modern society increasingly served to compartmentalize daily life in Latin America. In more developed countries, such as Argentina, Brazil, and Chile, society no longer functioned as an undifferentiated whole. The nuclear or reduced family accordingly lost its traditional functions. With the materialistic expectations of better economic circumstances, with the advent of a suburban lifestyle, with the acquisition of secular ideas through the process of bourgeoisification, and for some, the attraction of Marxism, the secularization and de-Christianization of certain segments of the populous seemed to be accelerating.

In response to these trends, the Roman Catholic Church made significant efforts to retain proletarian aspirants for social transformation who might otherwise have regarded the espousal of Marxism as requiring the rejection of Catholicism. For example, the pervasive use of Marxist rhetoric and the adoption of radical social idealism, which characterized a wing of Latin American Catholicism after the Medellin Conference (1968), was reinforced by the prominence of Catholic priests serving as spokesmen for programs of political liberation and for liberation theology. During the 1970s, many priests and women religious submitted their pastoral methods and degree of identification with the people to a critical re-evaluation in the light of the Gospel and the Church's social teaching. Their reflection led them to redirect many of their activities and to re-adapt their lifestyles to be more in harmony with that of the poorest classes.

The crowning achievement of liberation theology thus far has been methodological. As a result of this new way of doing theology, grass-roots Christian communities have developed throughout Latin America. Traditional Catholics consider them outrageous innovations. Military regimes in Brazil, Argentina, El Salvador, and other countries have monitored them closely. They are very numerous: some three million Latin American Catholics (at least one million of them in Brazil) take part in these communities. However, in spite of the fact that liberation theology has arisen mostly out of praxis and is intended to enhance praxis, it has not affected deeply the religious beliefs and practices of the majority of Latin American Roman Catholics. Although this expression of Catholicism has yet to enlist the masses of Catholic faithful, its demonstrated attraction to the poor of Latin America can hardly be overestimated.

Another development leading to the greater acceptance of evangelical Protestantism was the wave of ecumenism that washed over the religious landscape in the late 1960s. Before Vatican II, in the early 1960s, evangelicals were still regarded as religious deviants in many parts of Catholic Latin America. Converts tended to keep their religion to themselves because of the fear of being rejected by their neighbors and employers. In some cases, open persecution frustrated any proselytism and religious prejudice characterized evangelicals as heretics and agents of "Yankee imperialism." These conditions continue to exist today to a significant degree. But a pluralistic spirit, promoted in part by the entry of the Catholic Church into ecumenical dialogue as a result of Vatican II, was accompanied, by the end of the 1960s, by a cultural opening to Protestantism. Perhaps the most striking harbinger of this new openness was the treatment of the faith by the mass media, which provided and disseminated generally accurate information that helped to diffuse popular opposition.[50]

The peculiar conditions of traditional Catholicism in the aftermath of Vatican II and the rise of liberation theology thus helped, ironically, to prepare the ground for the evangelical growth and development of the 1970s and 1980s. The limited number of priests, coupled with the impression that some of them appeared more interested in secular than religious pursuits, created opportunities for pastoral work by evangelical pastors. The lack of sufficient Catholic priests to serve the burgeoning population was increased by the fact that they, unlike evangelical pastors, are expected to spend long years in theological study. This experience also has alienated them culturally from their people. In contrast, poor people have been attracted by the evangelicals' daily work among the people, their constant emphasis on the social benefits of strict morality, and the way conversion can transform neighborhood misfits into upright community leaders.

This pattern may be contrasted to the increasingly foreign character of the Catholic priesthood in Latin America. As the enormous population growth of the twentieth century overtook the manpower resources of the Church, the ratio of priests to people has radically declined, and the size of parishes has increased. Foreign priests have therefore been introduced in large numbers, and at all levels of the Church: some as parish priests, some in the specialized ministries. Many came early in the 1960s, in response to the appeals by Pope John XXIII and Pope Paul VI for more clergy to undertake work in the developing world. Their presence assisted the integration of Catholic immigrants, but it has not helped to lessen the cultural dislocations associated with the more important internal migration and urbanization of peoples. It has also provided grist for the anti-Catholic rhetoric of fundamentalist preachers. The Roman Catholic Church, particularly in the cities, has been accused, with great effectiveness, of being exclusively at the service of the well-to-do social classes, or more preoccupied with its own interests than with the real spiritual and material needs of the masses of poor people trapped in misery. It is often seen simply as an institution that affords too much importance to structures and not enough to its apostolic mission.[51]

However, the impact of the Catholic struggles should not be exaggerated. Most of those who go to the cities do not change their patterns of religious practice; most retain the orthodox, or nominal, folk Catholicism of their rural origins. For every person who changes allegiance there are several who do not. Taking refuge in the familiar rituals of Catholic worship is in fact the typical response to the conditions of anomie. The situation remains an unstable one, and it varies according to the particular conditions in each country. What is clear is that for most of the new urban population, the sacred and the secular are not yet so divorced as they are in the urban societies of the developed world. Thus personal religious crises lead less often to atheism or agnosticism or simple indifference; rather, the individual searches for a new communal expression of religion. Evangelical Protestantism has obviously benefited from this circumstance, as have new Roman Catholic forms, such as the ecclesial base communities and the charismatic movement. Protestant evangelizing efforts will likely continue to result in marked numerical growth at the expense of the Catholic congregations in urban areas that are not secularized.

During the same era, on the other hand, evangelical church growth has been spurred by the disappearance of a climate of popular prejudice against Protestants in certain countries. The evangelical presence is generally accepted and valued by significant segments of the populace in Guatemala, Nicaragua, Brazil, Chile, and (to a lesser extent) Argentina, in large part because of the benevolent influence that evangelicals have had through educational and philanthropic works.[52] David Martin has recently argued that by establishing hospitals, schools, orphanages, and networks for mutual support—in effect, by "the autonomous creation, ex nihilo, of a system for welfare and for educational advance"—evangelicals have mobilized the lower strata of society and affected the collective psyche "so much so that they alter their social position."[53]

The Appeal of Pentecostalism

Since the 1960s Pentecostal churches have been most successful in identifying themselves as the true "churches of the disinherited" for those seeking an alternative either to Catholicism or to radical secular politics, which sometimes serves as an alternative expression of individual disorientation. The label "Pentecostal" is not particularly helpful if it suggests an exclusive affinity with either the European or the African experience of revivalism. Certainly the Pentecostal groups reveal classic manifestations of a common rejection of institutionalized religion, and they tend to be egalitarian both in organization and in their interpretation of spirituality. But, unlike the historical churches, the Pentecostal churches are class-based organizations and are often protest movements against the existing class structure.[54] These churches have often been at variance with the surrounding social structure in terms of organizational rules and traditional symbols, which they consider as belonging to the upper classes. They refuse an accommodative attitude to traditional values. Moreover, Pentecostals have flourished in places where there is cultural change, in the anomie of the urban areas, and in the rural districts where economic change has resulted in disturbance of traditional relationships. Recent Pentecostal advances have been made among sections of the working population of the lower strata—especially in areas or groups of marked social dislocation, where Pentecostalism appears as a "lower-class solidarity movement."[55]

Pentecostalism has emerged from diverse backgrounds and assumes quite different forms in Latin America. This charismatic renewal is in fact most distinctive from its classical expression in its adaptability and willingness to include believers of different doctrinal and ecclesial persuasions.[56] In Chile, it is a descendant of the national Methodism of the early twentieth century. In taking on its own life apart from the mother church, Pentecostalism has proven to be divisive as well as dynamic and has appealed primarily to the lower strata of the population. The movement today is self-supporting, strongly missionary, and steadily growing.[57] Pentecostals arrived in Brazil in 1910 with two Americans of Swedish origin. They began the work of the Assemblies of God, which has seen an impressive growth in that country. Another interesting Pentecostal denomination in Brazil is the Christian Congregation, which emerged as a result of a spiritual revival among the Italian immigrants living in Sao Paulo.[58] Neo-Pentecostalism took root in Argentina in 1964 and spread throughout the continent quickly, cutting across denominational and confessional barriers.

Pentecostalism in various forms has met with success in Latin America in part because it compares favorably among the lower classes with both traditional Catholicism and historical Protestantism. Much has been written about "the Latin American character," whose traits include innate warmth and hospitality, resignation in the face of periodic natural calamities, a flexibility of spirit producing tolerance, enchantment with charismatic personalities, individualism, and a distinct turn to emotionalism and mysticism. Particularly in Pentecostalism, these traits have found channels of expression. In contrast with the Pentecostal type of service, the average meeting of historical Protestant churches is often described as colorless, tasteless, and boring. The sermon too often deals not with religious expression and life but with the "grammar of religion," namely, the doctrines which are not infrequently a verbal substitute for the real life experience. Similarly, the hymns are many times foreign importations, in which the words are didactic rather than lyric (expressing a sentiment of the heart, as in Spanish and Portuguese poetry and song). The utter lack of group pageantry, drama, and participation make these services seem more like a session in a lecture hall than a corporate worship of the Most High. On the other hand, in place of the Catholic Church's technical-theological language, which only the clergy understands, Pentecostals have a highly significant system of communication. All may receive the gift of tongues—a more ecstatic experience than reciting the abstract phrases of a specialized language. Much of Pentecostal liturgical dancing and group participation in prayer is a form of folk drama. Pentecostals do not have the miraculous wafer to offer the people, but they can offer the promise of miraculous healing, not only as the gift of God but as proof of a measure of faith and of the fact that God has responded to the people's attempt to communicate with Him. There is great emphasis upon group participation in prayer and singing, and the sermons are generally on the intellectual level of the people, with plenty of opportunities for men and women to respond, not only verbally but by signs of the indwelling of the Spirit.

The charismatic leader, unfettered by traditional ecclesiastical structures, easily commands an enthusiastic band of followers. Individualism, too, finds fulfillment in the Pentecostal understanding of the Christian faith. In many Pentecostal churches, at the top of the ecclesiastical structure is either a group of men or a single strong personality who dominates the group. The strength of this structure is, however, the full participation of almost everyone and a gradation which depends largely on function rather than background. Since the people come largely from the same general socioeconomic class, there is not the same tendency for the rich or well educated to stifle the development of the more humble people, as is the case in many churches of the more historical denominations.

In this regard it is not surprising that converts have often been drawn from a rootless and disconnected subculture, from people whose extended family networks disintegrated in the rush to the cities and who therefore had lost much of the social infrastructure needed to survive there. An example of these recent trends is found in the growth of Pentecostal churches in northeastern Brazil. Common to all of them is the fact that the followers constitute part of an underprivileged mass of people, many of them former Catholics, whose socioeconomic situation has made them receptive to the message of local preachers. The message invariably contains the promise of a better life predicated upon immediate conversion, part and parcel of which is the adoption of an ascetic way of life. Buoyed by emotional exaltation and messianic expectations, eager to proclaim the rebirth of the self by engaging in forms of behavior intended to repudiate the weaknesses and sins of one's former life, the members of such churches have proven capable of remarkable success in ordering their lives socially and to some extent economically. The pastors of local Pentecostal churches facilitate these personal and social transformations, often acting as public representatives of the unemployed and dispossessed seeking honest work.[59]

Pentecostal communities served as an alternative to social and economic dislocation in Central America as well. In the mid-1980s, in the wake of the Latin American debt crisis that kept the majority of the population in poverty and threatened the middle class, Jimmy Swaggart Ministries poured millions of dollars into the building up of Assembly of God church communities—constructing handsome sanctuaries for central congregations, Bible institutes to train a new national church leadership, and "Jimmy Swaggart schools, to provide children with hot meals, clothing, education, and spiritual growth."[60] In this effort, Swaggart was joined by an indigenous core of national leaders, theologically and pastorally prepared in the theological institutions founded by the pioneer missionaries and economically supported by foreign resources.

The Assembly of God succeeded in Brazil and in Central America because it developed indigenous leadership and did not depend solely on the North American missionaries. Pentecostals expected every church member to actively evangelize and encouraged many to become open-air preachers, Sunday school teachers and deacons, and organizers of satellite churches in nearby neighborhoods and villages. The pastor president of a "mother church," like other "apolitical" evangelical pastors in Latin America, supported the political machine in order to obtain building and parade permits, neighborhood improvements, and government jobs for church members. In the 1980s, tension arose between high-profile North American televangelists on missionary crusades (like Jimmy Swaggart) and local evangelical leaders, who felt that the popular mass ministries were reduplicating or competing with their own long-term community-building efforts.[61]

Parachurch Ministries and Media Evangelism

To this picture of Latin American evangelicalism one must add the presence of parachurch organizations and ministries that had been intent on winning Latin America souls since the planting of the first faith missions, but which were now quick to adapt and to learn from the successes of Pentecostalism. In the 1960s and 1970s, these North American agencies paved the way for a new generation of high-profile media evangelists from the United States. Their work led to an adroit blending of the fundamentalist world view of the faith missions, the commmunity-organizing methods of the Pentecostals, and the right-wing politics of the American televangelists in the mass evangelization campaigns of the 1980s.

Among these agencies was the Institute of Church Growth, founded by the missionologist Donald McGavran in the early 1960s. McGavran, a Disciples of Christ missionary who had worked in India, was the first dean of the Fuller Theological Seminary School of World Mission in Pasadena, California. He was dedicated to the principle that missionaries should encourage "people movements" of entire tribes or other "socially homogenous units." He researched the most effective methods of evangelization through empirical testing and predicated church growth upon racial, linguistic, and class insularity. Like other church-growth experts after him, McGavran was something of a marketing specialist, equipped with statistics of average annual growth rates and intent upon establishing church communities that reflected the local culture.[62]

Similarly, the Latin American Mission (LAM), an agency that offered support services to other missions and churches, developed new strategies to evangelize the region. By the early 1960s, the agency had developed pandenominational campaigns, had fully incorporated Latin Americans into its inner circle, and was riding the crest of anticommunist sentiment. *Evangelism-in-Depth* was a LAM campaign in the 1960s for "total mobilization" of the evangelical populations in Latin American nations.[63] Other evangelical leaders joined para-ecclesiastical organizations such as Campus Crusade for Christ, Youth for Christ, World Vision International, and Operation Mobilization. The 1960s and 1970s saw the proliferation of these para-ecclesiastical evangelical organizations to complement media outreach (radio, TV, books, movies) among select groups—children, women, prison inmates, businessmen, and students.

The most enduring and successful of these organizations operating in Central America has been Campus Crusade for Christ, founded by conservative evangelist Bill Bright. Door-to-door "personal evangelism" and street-corner "mass evangelism" of youth teams has characterized the work of Alfa y Omega (the name of the organization in Latin America). After two years (1978–79) of intense evangelization, for example, the organization claimed sixty-four thousand new converts nationwide in El Salvador alone. The movement is noted for its dogmatic and uncompromising theological positions. In the Central American context, the political resonance of their approach is inescapable: converts are readily perceived as potential voters. Explained Leonel Motta, Campus Crusade's regional director for Central America, "the struggle in which we are engaged, not only on Central America but in the whole world, is an ideological one."[64] Campus Crusade sees itself as recruiting "shock troops" to turn back communism and liberation theology in the region and to discredit liberal pastors. For the office director in Costa Rica, "the theology of liberation people are nothing more than masked communists. They're a bridge between faith and communism."[65]

Like other parachurch agencies, Campus Crusade was run in a top-down, corporate manner by the man who founded it. In his initial campus ministry at UCLA in 1951, Bright provided students a new "family" away from home, middle-class standards, and a model of upward mobility. Christianity was to be advertised and marketed. Bright's extraordinary success in attracting contributions from wealthy businessmen reinforced his tendency to see his ministry as specially ordained by God and to rule his expanding organization in an authoritarian manner. In the 1970s and 1980s, Campus Crusade adopted a mass-media approach to evangelism—known as "saturation evangelism"—which, unlike McGavran's approach, did not make exceptional efforts to adjust its message to local situations.[66]

In the late 1970s and early 1980s, under pressure from indigenous pastors, many of these California-based missions and parachurch agencies, including World Vision, the Wycliffe Bible Translators, and Campus Crusade for Christ, internationalized their administrative structures and increased revenues.[67] They also turned to Latin Americans to lead the rallies carried on television and radio.

Luis Palau (b. 1934), an Argentinian-born former waiter and now an evangelist hailing from the Plymouth Brethren tradition, presides over an evangelistic association with headquarters in Portland, Oregon. As a mass evangelist, he belongs to a transconfessional family that emphasizes the proclamation of the Gospel in terms of an oral testimony of the facts of the Christian message oriented toward the conversion of the individual. Palau owed his initial prominence to the Overseas Crusade Ministries (OCM), an American mission agency with ambitious goals for the evangelization of Latin America (Guatemala would be "50 percent evangelical by 1990.")[68] As part of its effort to train Latin American leaders, OCM brought Palau to the United States, where he married and became a United States citizen. From Overseas Crusades, however, Palau returned to Latin America to pursue Evangelism-in-Depth, by capturing public attention in rallies and over the airwaves while churches mobilized their members to go from door to door. He consciously imitated the methods of Billy Graham and became "a Latin face for the latest in North American-style, market-oriented evangelism."[69]

Under the general motto of *Festival de la Familia* (Family festival), Palau has organized religious crusades throughout the continent. The Palau campaign held in September 1982 in Asunción, Paraguay, for example, attracted the attention of the Paraguayan press, radio, and television. Attendance at rallies totalled 155,000, and more than 10,000 people made professions of faith in response to the evangelist's preaching. A number of churches have reported that their congregations have doubled in number since the campaign. Similarly, in November 1982, evangelicals in Guatemala celebrated the hundredth anniversary of their arrival in Guatemala with an outdoor meeting with Palau, who shared the platform with Ríos Montt. The size of the crowd, estimated at five hundred thousand, testified to the appeal of Palau's simple biblical message: his interpretation of the Bible is literal and based firmly on his belief in inerrancy. To a biblically based worldview and ethos he contrasts certain "pernicious" trends subsumed under the banner of "secular humanism," a force in Latin American culture that he believes is responsible for eroding churches, schools, universities, governments, and above all, families. Through his messages, books, and articles published in *Cruzada* (the magazine of his evangelistic organization), Palau fights the enemies which he considers to be offspring of secular humanism: evolutionism, political and theological liberalism, lax personal morality, sexual perversion, socialism, communism, and any weakening of the doctrine of the absolute, inerrant authority of the Bible.[70]

Although he claims to be apolitical, Palau has courted the favor of the authorities, among them Alfonso López Michelsen in Columbia, Alfredo Stroessner in Paraguay, Ríos Montt in Guatemala, and Fernando Belaúnde in Peru. His pattern has been to hold a prayer breakfast for the president of the regime as a prelude to broadcasting his talk show and rallies over government-controlled networks. In Bolivia, for example, the Summer Institute of Linguistics introduced Palau to army dictators Hugo Banzer (1971–78) and Juan Pereda Asbún (1978). Over government airwaves, Palau exhorted Bolivians to obey their government because it was ordained by God. Eventually, under another army dictator, Luis García Meza (1980–81), Palau's call for a "new emphasis on morality" was sponsored by a regime linked to right-wing violence and the cocaine trade.[71]

Alberto Mottesi, an Argentinian of Baptist roots, now residing in the United States, has staged similar evangelical rallies, particularly in Central America. Mottessi is convinced that simple evangelism is inadequate without sustained efforts to attenuate the erosion of Latin American culture and the traditional family. Thus he has held numerous workshops for religious leaders and has mastered the use of various forms of communications media in disseminating his message of social and religious conservatism both to these leaders and to local congregations in the region. Omar Cabrera, a Pentecostal preacher, has enjoyed similar success. In 1979 he founded an evangelistic movement called *Visión de Futuro* (Vision of the Future), which in only five years recruited 135,000 members in 35 preaching centers.[72]

Defining the Fundamentalist Impulse

An impulse toward fundamentalism exists in each of the wings of evangelicalism discussed above: in the influence and missionary activity of certain independent North American faith missions; in an attitude that has developed in a segment of the autochthonous Pentecostal churches as part of their particular historical experience; and in the parachurch organizations, many of which are headed by prominent American-based televangelists.[73] Fundamentalism in Latin America is not, then, simply an institutionalized movement but also an ideological trend within some churches that are otherwise referred to as evangelical or Pentecostal. Although there are some local churches that consider themselves to be fundamentalist, most will use the term as an adjective rather than as a noun. Accordingly, "fundamentalist" is perhaps best understood as a distinctive way of being a Christian in the modern world that finds expression in some popular sectors of the evangelical churches in Latin America, among people who have been exposed to the dissolution of modern life without being able to find in the culture of modern society the spiritual resources to confront the enormous doubts which the contemporary world presents.[74] Thus fundamentalism in the Latin American context is less an interdenominational distinction than an intradenominational line of identity cutting across historical, evangelical, and Pentecostal churches. Moreover, fundamentalist evangelicals consciously set themselves apart from conservative and liberationist evangelicals.

Liberationists are clustered in mainline Protestant churches, including the transplanted Protestant immigrant churches, the established denominations of Protestant migrants, and the missionary denominations.[75] They forge links with the World Council of Churches (WCC), the Latin American Council of Churches (CLAI), and various para-ecclesiastical organizations that represent the Protestant ecumenical movement in Latin America. Liberationists take their name from their adherence to or sympathy with the theologies of liberation of the continent, which have been quite influential in mainline Protestantism. Because they are ecumenical theologies, a good portion of them have been developed within Latin American Protestant circles.[76] Liberationists subscribe to the traditional tenets of evangelical Christianity, although they are critical of that tradition, especially of interpretations of it that stifle or underemphasize the Christian commitment to social and political justice. Liberationists, also known simply as "liberals," represent the extreme evangelical left in Latin America, and are vehemently opposed by fundamentalists.[77]

Conservative churches and individuals are representative of neo-evangelicalism in Latin America. They subscribe to *The Lausanne Covenant*, the 1974 document produced by the International Conference on World Evangelization held in Lausanne, Switzerland.[78] Conservative evangelicals insist on the ethical and political relevance of the Christian faith, emphasize its intellectual respectability, and develop their convictions inside and along the lines of the evangelical denominations. They may express their faith in a radical political and ecclesiastical language,[79] but they remain faithful to the core of evangelicalism, namely, its obedience to the authoritative character of the Christian Scriptures. Though critical of the accommodation of today's culture and churches to wealth, power, militarism, and unjust social and economic structures, they will not abandon their ecclesiastical or denominational commitment to their Anabaptist, Wesleyan, or Calvinistic roots.[80] Conservatives are often branded as "liberals" by the extreme right, and as "fundamentalists" by the extreme left. Fundamentalists will criticize conservatives because, in their affirmation of the authority of the Bible, conservatives do not share an inerrantist hermeneutic (the belief that the the Bible is literal and correct, and that it can therefore be interpreted without error). Liberationists, on the other hand, charge that conservatives are not committed to social justice, or will not take the radical, revolutionary measures necessary to obtain it. Accordingly, conservatives are at the center of the spectrum of evangelical Christianity and in tense dialogue with both extremes.

Fundamentalism is today identified with the recent wave of radical conservatism influencing faith missions and Pentecostal churches across the continent and sponsored by the parachurch organizations of mass evangelists such as Palau, Cabrera, and Mottesi. Many of the churches with this tendency hold membership in the Latin American Evangelical Confraternity (CONELA), formed by disgruntled delegates to the Consultation on World Evangelization, held in Pattaya, Thailand, on 16–27 June 1980, under the sponsorship of the Lausanne Committee on World Evangelization. Led by two executives of the Luis Palau Evangelistic Team, this splinter group felt that the newly organized Latin American Council of Churches (CLAI) was too closely related to the World Council of Churches, and therefore did not represent them. Claiming that they spoke for the majority of the Latin American Protestant churches—which, according to them, were "conservative and . . . faithful to the Bible"—202 delegates representing 98 different evangelical denominations established the Confraternity during meetings held in Panama on 19–23 April 1982. The Confraternity disavowed "any relations with the World Council of Churches . . . [or] with the Latin American Council of Churches (CLAI). . . . " Their constituency would come, they claimed, from "Evangelical Christian Churches who are faithful to Biblical authority, without denominational distinctions, and whose principles are in harmony with the tenets which spring from the Protestant Reformation of the Sixteenth century."[81]

The new confederation's leaders defined their separatist identity by denouncing CLAI and liberation theology; they also set themselves, albeit less openly, against the Lausanne Covenant. They feared that evangelicals pursuing its call for "social responsibility" were compromising their faith with left-wing ideology. Palau executive Bill Conard charged that "Leftist ideologies are penetrating the church, and there is no united defense of the biblical gospel, nor offense as to how to apply biblical principles in our churches and life. CONELA offers a real solution to this impasse."[82] CONELA claimed to represent twenty million evangelicals and incorporated existing associations, such as the Evangelical Council of Venezuela (CEV), and proceeded to organize new ones in countries where they were lacking, including Mexico, the Dominican Republic, and Panama. But while delegates from eighty-four denominations attended CONELA's founding conference, three-quarters of the 4.2 million church members represented directly belonged to the Assemblies of God in Brazil. Unfortunately for CONELA, the more fundamentalist churches tended to be very difficult to organize. Their reason for existence was splitting off from social activist and ecumenical churches, after all, and they distrusted any attempt to organize them into something larger.

The North American mission establishment, including Campus Crusade for Christ, Overseas Crusade Ministries, and the Palau organization, joined sixty-one other parachurch agencies at the founding conference. Media organizations and mass evangelists—at the mercy of government fiat for their access to airwaves and coliseums—were attracted by CONELA's outright conformist stance toward political authority.

For CONELA and for evangelical preachers such as Palau, Mottesi, and Cabrera, the church exists for the proclamation of the Gospel; it is the place where people are turning to God in repentance. It also provides a base from which to roll back the incursions of a secular culture. These preachers consider themselves to be fundamentalist. Selectively open to interdenominational cooperation, they reject out of hand any association with the ecumenical movement. In successive campaigns Luis Palau has, for example, succeeded in involving the majority of the non-Roman Catholic churches in a concerted evangelistic effort directed at nominal Catholic populations. These mass evangelists call for a streamlined Protestantism bolstered by a return to an inerrant and infallible Bible, to a core of fundamental doctrines, and to a traditional, premodern moral code which they describe as the authentic expression of a Christian ethics.

The organizations and churches aligned with these and other fundamentalist preachers share certain attitudes and behaviors which set them apart from fellow evangelicals. These include a distinctive understanding of the role of the Bible in ordering and sustaining both the religious community and the political culture, an eschatological vision that promotes withdrawal from direct political action, and in continuity with these, an ultraconservative ideological profile.

The Centrality of the Bible

The Bible occupies a central place in the life of Latin American Protestantism as the sole authority for faith and practice.[83] The Latin American adherence to biblical inerrancy reflects both the acceptance of tenets imported from the nineteenth-century inerrancy movement in the United States and an appreciation of the Bible as the germinative factor of evangelical Christianity on the continent. Both evangelical and Pentecostal churches owe their lives and identities to the Bible; accordingly, much of their energy goes to preserving and solidifying the place of that foundation stone. Inerrancy provides the possibility of protecting that foundation from any attack and guarantees the stability of the community on a commonly accepted ground of authority.[84] To this emphasis on inerrancy North American faith missions added the anti-historical bias that characterized American Protestantism during the late nineteenth and early twentieth centuries.[85] This ahistorical approach in Latin America derived not from a consciously held contempt for tradition; rather, it was the result of a long-standing policy in fundamentalist-staffed seminaries and institutes of avoiding "mainstream" twentieth-century biblical criticism in the historical and theological education and training of pastors and other church leaders. This "historylessness" allowed fundamentalist missionaries and preachers to rather straighforwardly identify their reading of Scripture with that of the apostolic church of the New Testament—and thereby to denigrate what they term to be the errant "interpretations" of their evangelical (not to mention Roman Catholic) rivals for the allegiance of the masses.

This pointed allegiance to a supreme and unquestioned source of religious authority is best considered in the light of evangelical Protestantism's twentieth-century struggle for existence against almost universal opposition as a religious minority in Latin America. Evangelicals sought a source of absolute authority that would undercut the tradition-based claims of Roman Catholicism. They found it in the Bible, which, as the commonly recognized Word of God, they proposed to place directly in the hands of the Spirit-guided individual believer as his only necessary guide to faith and practice. Fundamentalists seized upon this historical impulse by emphasizing "no creed but the Bible" and the right of "private judgment" under the inspiration of the Holy Spirit in its interpretation, with the beliefs and practices of primitive Christianity as normative and authoritative.[86] "Primitive Christianity" became the Latin American fundamentalist model for imitation; however, fundamentalists sought not a complete return to this sacred past but an appropriation of its values, doctrines, and ethos for a contemporary "crusade of faith."

Although mission fundamentalists did not presume to adopt uncritically the worldview and customs of the *ancient* past, they did adopt the worldview of the *recent* past—the North American past. And as faithful heirs of the theology and traditions taught by the missionaries during the Cold War—the formative period for the indigenous pastors of today—many Latin American fundamentalists continue to identify with the American way of life that characterized fundamentalist churches in the United States during the 1950s. Thus the fundamentalist claim to return to the "fundamentals" of the Christian faith and their "selective retrieval" of primitive Christianity is characterized by a literal understanding of the Bible according to the patterns established in the conservative Protestant churches of North America at the beginning of the century and renewed during the Cold War. As we have seen, faith missions developed a bold strategy to mobilize their membership in a drive for new converts in the wake of the Cuban revolution. Promoting the faith as an ideological alternative to communism for the 1960s led to an era of aggressive proselytization that increased the ranks of fundamentalists and made them a force to be reckoned with. The crucial element in this surge was spiritual conversion to the truths of the Bible presented, in typical fundamentalist fashion, by cloaking the evangelical mission in the images of an "American" patriotism—a united North-South spiritual front against atheistic communism. In the nineteenth century, the theme had been manifest destiny, with missionaries as the bearers of enlightenment. In the Cold War era, it was anti-communism, and evangelicals represented the last hope of freedom. These themes continued, in a different vein, to characterize Latin American fundamentalism in the 1980s as the region became a staging ground for confrontations between the ideologies of the United States and the Soviet Union.[87]

It should be noted that, in the "Cold War crusade" fortified by an inerrant Bible, the non-negotiable "fundamental" was not a particular doctrine, but the system of inerrantist hermeneutics itself; however, the hermeneutical issue is presented as a theological question. What other evangelicals may regard as issues open to discussion, critical analysis, and ongoing interpretation, fundamentalists defend as theological tenets not subject to discussion. In this defense, inerrancy becomes in part a means of appealing to the common biblicism of all Latin American evangelicals; however, fundamentalists evince an absolutistic view of Scripture which sets them apart from other evangelicals. They are convinced that their purchase on the truth is, like the truth itself, complete and absolute, unqualified by partial understanding or error. In this certitude lies the essential requirement for effective opposition to antibiblical forces such as communism and secular humanism.

Thus organizations such as Alpha y Omega (Campus Crusade for Christ) have expended considerable energies in contrasting Christian identity with other possible identities infected by modernism, liberalism, biblical criticism, Marxism, liberation theologies, ecumenism, humanism, and any corruption of pure Christianity through the "inventions and contrivances of clever men" (Eph. 4:14). Fundamentalist polemicists seek to prove that these alternate identities are incompatible with the system of biblical Christianity.[88]

Fundamentalist Eschatology and Ideology: The "Oppressed Conscience"

In fundamentalist discourse the inerrant Scripture discloses the drama of salvation history unfolding in dispensations of human history. Premillennial doctrine teaches that the kingdom of Christ will be inaugurated in a cataclysmic way and that divine control will be exercised in a supernatural manner. The return of Christ will be preceded by signs, including wars, famines, earthquakes, the preaching of the Gospel to all nations, a great apostasy, the appearance of the Antichrist, and the great tribulation. These events will culminate in the second coming of Christ, which will result in a period of peace and righteousness when Christ and his saints will control the world. This rule will be established suddenly, through supernatural methods, rather than gradually over a long period of time by means of the conversion of individuals.

Through the footnotes written by Cyrus I. Scofield to his Scofield Reference Bible (in Spanish) and the influence of evangelical denominations such as the Plymouth Brethren, most Latin American premillennialists became dispensationalists, dividing history into an elaborate system of dispensations of innocence, of conscience, of civil government, of promise, of law, of grace, and of the kingdom. Dispensationalism became the theological backbone of Latin American fundamentalism.

In the eschatological understanding of dispensationalists and premillennialists, the world will go from bad to worse. There is no hope for progress in history. This message can have no attraction for the rich and powerful, but it has an extraordinary seduction for the dispossessed, who are able to transfer their frustrated earthly expectations to a glorious eschatological future of plenty and satisfaction. Man is conceived as the object of history and not the subject of it. God's action in history is consistent with a pattern which has been determined outside history and which will be determined by forces other than human action. The historical-social vision of fundamentalism is thus informed by a historical determinism.

The dominance of the premillennial view continued during the post-1960 evangelical boom; fundamentalists became macroconsumers of the eschatological musings of books like *The Late Great Planet Earth,* by Hal Lindsey, which interpreted the world through the eyes of the American Republican press, attacked the enemies of fundamentalism, and was permeated with a naive but aggressive American nationalism.[89] According to this eschatological vision, the present generation is living in the "last days." The basic reason for this conclusion is that the historical social and religious condition of the interpreter is understood as the one which faithfully reflects the truth of God.

This type of eschatology is replete with heroes and villains, agents of God and Satan; hence, it helps not only to identify the enemies of fundamentalism but also to mythologize them, to elevate them to the status of cosmic provocateurs, worthy opponents of the righteous. Fundamentalists of the Cold War era, for example, wed the standard polemical arguments of the Reformation to a premillennial dispensationalist doctrine that portrays the Catholic Church as the harlot of Revelation 17. The totalitarian system of dispensationalism, fed by its doctrine of apostate Christendom, marked out both friends and enemies, with the Roman Catholic Church being the first enemy to be denounced and condemned.

The center of the debate was accurately described by W. Stanley Rycroft as the opposition of "religion" and "faith."[90] The Roman Catholic religion was interpreted as a form of idolatry, superstition, and magic. Behind these denunciations was a more general rejection of religion as something transmitted and inherited with the culture, as a set of observances, as ritual and ceremony, as mediated through institutions, sacraments, and priesthood. Faith was described, on the other hand, as immediacy, as personal participation and spontaneity. The contrast was frequently expressed in fundamentalist preaching by rhetorically opposing a living to a dead religion. Personal conversion meant a liberation from the whole religious-social structure and implied the immediate abandonment of the Roman Catholic Church and all allegiance to its doctrine and practice.

The idea that Catholicism, unlike Protestantism, has encouraged a low moral sense remained a central theme in anti-Catholic Protestant fundamentalist preaching well into the 1980s. It carried clear social implications, not only for improving the quality of family life but also for creating the community of reasoned moral order that Latin American reformers depicted as prevailing in Protestant countries.[91]

Eschatological considerations also lent a certain drama and urgency to the fundamentalist refusal to compromise with other kinds of outsiders, especially fellow evangelicals who supported the Christian ecumenical movement.[92] The sense of eschatological urgency nonetheless led Latin American fundamentalists to join forces with one another and with nonfundamentalists in massive crusades of evangelization, most of them sponsored by fundamentalist organizations in the United States. An important precedent was set in the mass evangelization and saturation campaigns described above (especially in the efforts of the Latin American Mission to mobilize evangelical believers in Central America during the 1960s). To that purpose it was necessary to set aside doctrinal disputes. Because fundamental theological principles seemed threatened by this initiative, however, the promise of greater outreach and new converts was not in itself sufficient incentive for many fundamentalist pastors. Many church leaders felt that LAM's approach would debase cardinal tenets of the faith or diminish the importance of correct biblical interpretation. To overcome these qualms, LAM explained its strategy in terms of biblical principles such as the Great Commission to spread the gospel in advance of Christ's return—principles which, for most churches, outweighed the requirement of strict doctrinal purity. The churches also had to grasp the political dimensions of their mission. In an eschatological Cold War vision, LAM hinted that the spread of communism in the region was a sign of impending doom and that evangelicals had a special role to play in countering the menace.[93]

For evangelical leaders both in Central America and the United States, the call was compelling. With the support of major missionary boards, the cooperation of national denominations, and an enthusiastic response from local churches, the stage was set for Evangelism-in-Depth. The first campaign was in Nicaragua in 1960, followed closely by campaigns in Costa Rica and Guatemala. The crowds were enormous for the various rallies. In Guatemala in 1962, the campaign combined open-air rallies with door-to-door evangelism and reached 250,000 homes and more than a million people. The congregations of evangelical churches swelled that year by over fifteen thousand. Staged with similar cooperation from the local churches, the regional campaigns in the 1970s and 1980s by Palau, Mottessi, Cabrera, and others successfully imitated aspects of this method.[94]

The type of religiosity promoted in these mass rallies and in the neighborhood church communities to which the newly converted flocked, confirmed believers in a "vertical" faith often divorced from the variety of possible social or political implications of Christianity. This is not, however, to suggest that these churches were simply apolitical, for congregants were encouraged to depend upon charismatic leaders for guidance in political matters. This mentality in turn fostered an uncritical justification of the established political order—an attitude with antecedents in classical Protestant religiosity. Fundamentalist leaders have tended to refuse to accept direct responsibility for social processes and limit the social accountability of their flock to voting, or merely to abstract sympathy toward a particular party. They have also promoted the doctrines of laissez-faire capitalism and the ideological liberalism dominant in the West—a seemingly incongruous attachment, given their support for right-wing regimes. This is expressed in several causes or principles that capture the allegiance of fundamentalists, including the right of private property and the acceptance of the benefits and institutions of social aid.

Nonetheless, religion itself belongs to the individual, private sphere. Of course when a person becomes a Christian he or she should demonstrate a distinctive quality of life. By her industriousness, honesty, respect for the law, and sobriety she will become an asset to society. "But every intent to relate faith and Christian doctrine to the public sphere is considered an 'intrusion' which violates both the 'lay' character of the public sphere and the 'spiritual' purity of the faith."[95]

This attitude of political quiescence has roots in the minority complex typical of the Protestant denominations in Latin America. Evangelicals have understood themselves to be a "sacrificed and disciplined minority."[96] Prior to the 1960s they felt themselves to be overwhelmed by the Roman Catholic Church, which held fast to the majority of the population, used politics to increase its power, and opposed dissent to prevent any significant participation by Protestants in the centers of power. In the contemporary period, the evangelicals most susceptible to both indigenous and imported fundamentalism are those who have inherited this "oppressed conscience." They belong to those sectors of the Latin American population that live most concretely the drama of Latin America: the misery, the exploitation, the oppression by those forces which have usurped power, whether they are political, military, economic, or religious.[97] As such, they are afraid of any change, of anything that could menace the fragile stability of their world. The way to maintain a sense of security for themselves is to develop a conservative, almost reactionary, character.[98] The oppressed conscience of many fundamentalist evangelicals is reinforced by the ecclesiastical organizations of which they are members. These institutions supply sociocultural structures which give a sacred character to this state of oppression and so freeze the oppressed conscience, "because they proclaim and require their faithful to believe that they find themselves in institutional structures which are marked with the seal of the will of God."[99]

The oppressed conscience is reinforced by the religious convictions characteristic of Protestant fundamentalism. A dualism reminiscent of Anabaptist theology, with a strong emphasis on the idea of separation from the world and a corresponding estrangement from political power, is at the root of the apolitical interpretation of the principle of separation of church and state. The public sphere is understood as purely lay in character, and consequently it has nothing to do with the spiritual purity of the faith.[100] This transcendental, vertical vision of the Christian faith, which confines the believer within the narrow frame of the local congregation (as a refuge from the world), ends with the complete alienation of the Christians by pushing them outside the framework of society.

Fundamentalist eschatology contributes to the apolitical attitude and to the oppressed conscience. Dispensationalist and premillenial theology presupposes the vision of a fallen world, whose sinfulness is reflected in its structures and way of life.[101] The immediate result of the dispensationalist interpretation of history and its corresponding hermeneutic is the alienation of the church from the world. In this way, politics is understood as a "thing of the world," a practice of fallen men. In this way, the internal development of society is left to those who want to dedicate themselves to this "dirty work."[102] Missionaries, for example, as foreigners and because of strategic considerations, were forbidden by their boards to be involved in politics at all.[103] On the other hand, Protestants of immigrant origin were more concerned with their own material survival than in any historical project. As immigrants in any part of the world, those who came to Latin America were indifferent toward the political process and were afraid of any involvement that could endanger their dreams of a new beginning in the New World.

Fundamentalists tend to consider evangelism—in its narrower or "spiritual" sense—to be the only legitimate activity of the church and remain wary of current trends toward church involvement in political affairs. They fear that such involvement may lead the church away from its central evangelistic mission into a substitute religion of good works, humanitarianism, and even political agitation. They see in the church a unique, divine institution which, while still very much in the world, does not dare to identify itself institutionally with social and political movements that are either overtly or covertly antireligious, or which advocate violence and hate as a means of achieving supposedly Christian ends.[104] While believing that revolutionary wars are on some occasions justified as a last resort, fundamentalists consider Saint Paul's injunction as the Christian norm: "If possible, so far as it depends on you, live peaceably with all" (Rom. 12:8; see context Rom. 12:14–13:7). That the Christian message focuses primarily upon the inward transformation of lives through faith in Jesus Christ rather than on the mere outward restructuring of human institutions is basic to the fundamentalist's beliefs. Such a position, while not necessarily incompatible with genuine social concern, has in many cases left the fundamentalist churches in Latin America without an effective program of social action. This attitude has been adopted by many Pentecostal groups, as expressed in what Lalive d'Epinay called the sociopolitical "strike."[105] This means that Pentecostalism teaches its initiates withdrawal and passivity in sociopolitical matters, limited only by the commandment to be submissive to authority. In this way, fundamentalist and Pentecostal churches tend to be defenders of the status quo instead of promoters of change.

Because fundamentalists place the end of history outside of history, their social conscience is subdued, and their organizations reinforce this oppressed conscience by supplying a sociocultural structure which attributes a sacred character to the state of oppression. The fundamentalist churches do not just form part of those structures which contribute to the maintenance of the state of oppression, but they reinforce human alienation by claiming divine right. Any claim for justice or liberation from oppression is transferred to a remote eschatological future. As a well-known evangelical hymn puts it: "*Si sufrimos aquí, Reinaremos allí, En la Patria Celestial.*"[106] The kingdom of God is not a part of the historical world. Injustice, oppression, and other evils will disappear with the second coming of Christ. In the words of a fundamentalist magazine: "We believe that the second coming of Christ will put an end to misery and pain, to wars, infirmities, and death, and will open the way to the establishment of a kingdom of peace and justice, so longed for by man, and which only a God of love can establish."[107] In the meantime, the correct political attitude is one of submission to established authorities. As a neo-Pentecostal leader has advised:

1. Cultivate the mental consciousness that all authorities are instituted by God.
2. Recognize that both subjection and rebellion are essentially attitudes more than actions.
3. Trust God that he will change those authorities who are not just. There are many unjust rulers, officials, administrations, laws, rules, ordinances, and restrictions in our countries. And God knows each one of them. They exist under his permission to fulfill his purpose. When that purpose has been accomplished, they can and will be taken away.[108]

Among fundamentalists, the most commonly quoted biblical text with regard to politics is Dan. 2:21 (RSV): "He changes times and seasons; he removes kings and sets up kings; he gives wisdom to the wise and knowledge to those who have understanding." The future of Latin America is under the direct control of God; the Kingdom of God has nothing to do with a historical project. This is particularly true for the mass of Pentecostal believers. Speaking in tongues is the desperate cry of those who cannot make themselves heard in the daily language of society. Visions and eschatological expectations provide a politically acceptable means of expressing the tension of frustration and hope in which the Latin American lower classes must live.[109]

The direct social implications, such as they are, of fundamentalist preaching, are found in the emphasis on the individual over the society. The decisive justification for the missionary enterprise is the intrinsic possibility for individual fundamentalists to transform Latin Americans, creating in them new patterns of behavior and ethical norms. The new converts pass from their old lives to new ones, from condemnation to salvation. Economic, political, and social structures remain outside the religious experience of the individual. The individual, however, is expected to produce social change through Christian testimony to a lost society. Consequently in this conception, the individual is the touchstone upon which all social and religious change in Latin America depends.[110] This notion leads to an expectation of the predominance of spontaneous over intentional change. An overriding conviction imparted by the missionary movement is that the social, political, and economic transformation of Latin America will occur spontaneously and in the degree to which the number of conversions and the process of evangelization occurs. Many slum inhabitants in the large Latin American cities, this argument goes, need a religion that can serve as a refuge in a society perceived to be in a state of permanent and progressive disintegration in order to deal with fear, threats, repression, hunger, and death. Fundamentalism provides that kind of religiosity. Therefore deliberate action is frustrated by a purely religious phenomenon.

The divisive character of this ideology is evident in the fact that religious differences between the diverse Protestant groups are based not only on theological convictions but, very significantly, on ideological presuppositions which come to the surface as the various groups are confronted with the challenges and turmoils of the political and social process in Latin America. Also, inter-ecclesiastical differences have given way to intra-ecclesiastical differences. This means that sometimes it does not matter so much whether one is a Baptist or a Methodist as whether one is for the "left" or the "right" in political issues, or for commitment or noncommitment in social matters.

With their insistence on a literal interpretation of Romans 13, Latin American fundamentalists have advocated submission to any political regime, even to dictatorships.[111] One striking political consequence of fundamentalist millennialism has thus been its ready exploitation by authoritarian regimes or simply by those in power. Rightist dictators in Guatemala, Chile, Brazil, and Argentina have indicated appreciation of the attitude described above: fundamentalists are good citizens.[112]

Even in cases of flagrant violations of human rights by military dictatorships, fundamentalists have consciously rejected any critical attitude toward the existing order. In Argentina, for example, Christian fundamentalists were among the primary religious supporters of the military junta that ruled from March 1976 to December 1983, in spite of the many credible testimonies of open violations of human rights. Fundamentalists were also popular with the government of General Augusto Pinochet in Chile, because of their political conservatism and emphasis on passive acceptance of authority—in contrast to socially activist Catholic groups inspired by liberation theology.[113] In the years following the establishment of an alliance between the Pinochet regime and a highly visible segment of the Chilean churches, political repression tightened, not only in the form of the abrogation of all political parties but also in the reported imprisonment, torture, and in many instances, execution of hundreds and even thousands without trial, without regard for the most basic human rights, and without respect for world opinion, which openly and vehemently condemned such actions.[114]

In a media event evoking both this pattern of internal Pentecostalist support for Pinochet and the close connection of fundamentalist Pentecostals to their North American counterparts, American Pentecostalist Jimmy Swaggart visited Santiago in early 1987, defended the regime of Pinochet, and congratulated him for having expelled "the devil" (leftists) in the 1973 coup. Angry Chilean Catholics subsequently denounced the Chilean fundamentalist churches as "Reagan cults" and warned that fundamentalists had converted approximately 10 percent of the Chilean population, including fifteen thousand members of the armed forces.[115]

Protestant fundamentalists offered similar support to the military regime in Guatemala and to United States policies in the region. In 1982, the largest known crowd of evangelicals in the history of the Western world, 750,000, gathered together in Guatemala City to listen to Luis Palau and celebrate the one-hundreth anniversary of the gospel in Guatemala. The celebration of the centennial was the occasion for a show of support for Ríos Montt, whom Palau and associates considered to be "the anointed of God."[116] Ríos Montt had come to power on 23 March 1982, as president of a military junta, through a coup d'état. A former Christian Democratic Party candidate for the presidency in 1974 and the brother of a Roman Catholic bishop, Montt discovered in 1978 the Word Evangelical Church (Iglesia Evangélica El Verbo), a Guatemalan branch of the evangelical organization Gospel Outreach, of Eureka, California. Soon after becoming an evangelical, Montt became an administrator of a Bible school for children and a member of the council of elders of the Verbo Church. He was working in his office at the Verbo Christian Day School when the officers who plotted the coup invited him to come to the presidential palace in 1982. A journalist present at a Sunday service in the Verbo Church on 4 April 1982 described the following event: "All together, hand in hand, with their heads bowed, they said a special prayer on behalf of their brother Efraín, for his pious example to be understood by millions of his fellow citizens, for Guatemala to be a light to everybody, a lighthouse to humankind, a new Israel. Coincidence? The most important Guatemalan newspaper has issued the first number of a 'Christian Supplement' addressed to the 'one Million and a half Evangelicals who are in Guatemala' (over seven million inhabitants)."[117]

This open ideological commitment went hand in hand with an anti-Catholic attitude in the fundamentalists' tacit support of the government's widespread and systematic repression and persecution of Catholic priests and catechists. The message of personal salvation, preached with charismatic zeal, was interwoven in the Guatemalan case with both a virulent anti-Catholicism and anticommunism. Riós Montt forces in the region exploited these attitudes in legitimating their violent opposition to social change; sectors of the Roman Catholic Church openly committed to peace and social justice were indiscriminately suspected of communism and subjected to repression; many were executed.[118]

Dictatorships have not, then, posed a problem to Latin American fundamentalist evangelicals, provided that they were allowed to perform their proselytizing work and enjoy a certain level of access to media and to those in authority. In accounting for the tendency of fundamentalists to support anticlerical and anti-Marxist regimes, attention must be given both to the influence of the religious right through the North American missions, parachurch agencies, and visiting televangelists, and also to the indigenous factors that make fundamentalist evangelicalism appealing to Latin Americans.

The ideological pattern of Latin American Fundamentalism has in part been inherited from North American missionaries. Cultural penetration has been recognized as one of the most characteristic features of North American missionary work in Latin America. Together with the investments and the activities of American businessmen in the Latin American countries came the growing activities of United States fundamentalist missionaries. One observer has noted that "the crisis in Central America since 1979 has forced a sharper political definition of groups such as Campus Crusade, and the U.S. foreign policy establishment has actively enlisted their cooperation. The link between evangelical growth and the administration's political offensive is made vivid by the flow of money, the design of organizational strategy and the production and marketing of doctrinal materials. The link is forged of ideology, history and worldview, not of conspiracy. 'Good against evil' translates easily into 'communism versus American-style capitalism' to build a strategic consensus."[119]

The activities of the religious right in Latin America were interpreted by some commentators in the light of the objectives of the so-called "Santa Fe document" prepared for President Reagan by a group of his advisers influential in determining U.S. policy in Central America. The document avers that "The United States must seize the ideological initiative. . . . The war is for the minds of mankind. . . . U.S. foreign policy must begin to counter (not merely react against) liberation theology as it is utilized by the 'liberation theology' clergy. The role of the Church is vital to the concept of political freedom. Unfortunately, Marxist-Leninist forces have used the Church as a weapon against private property and productive capitalism, infiltrating the religious community with ideas that are less Christian than Communist."[120]

In October 1983, hearings were held on Capitol Hill by a Senate subcommittee investigating terrorists and "Marxism and Christianity in Revolutionary Central America." Among those called before the subcommittee was a representative of the Council for Inter-American Security, the think tank which developed the Santa Fe report. The recommendation of the report, and of the representative, was that the United States government formulate policies to counter liberation theology and provide support for "counter-insurgents"—right-wing guerrilla movements.[121]

North Americans of the religious right were deeply involved in the Nicaraguan contra war. In the 1980s Pat Robertson's Christian Broadcasting Network was among the biggest contributors, raising millions of dollars for food, medicine, clothing, vehicles, and other aid for Nicaraguan "refugees" who also happened to be contras, or for Miskito Indians drawn into the armed struggle. In January 1982 the Nicaraguan government undertook a massive relocation of eight thousand Miskito Indians from the area along the Honduran border to the interior of the country. While the Nicaraguan government justified this relocation because of the danger of raids from Honduras into the Miskito camps and the defense of the national territory, international controversy ensued. The government claimed to have documented evidence of the participation of Catholic deacons and Moravian pastors in armed counter-revolutionary activities.[122]

In 1984, alliances between armed counter-revolutionary activity and pastors of various churches were reported, and the most active areas of the "fundamentalist sects" were described as havens of "Contras, right-wing guerrillas. . . . A kidnap victim taken to a Contra camp in Honduras, who later escaped, related how the prisoners were told that if they joined the sects they would not be harmed. Reports of this kind have inflamed historical tensions between Catholics and non-Catholics."[123]

In the case of Nicaragua, two fundamentalist principles collided—anticommunism and support for the regime in power—and the former survived, with the help of the Americans. In 1987, in El Salvador and Guatemala, support for the regime and anticommunism were once again linked. Leftist Salvadorean and Guatemalan guerrillas prohibited evangelical church workers from entering villages and towns they captured, because "evangelicals quiet down people," a rebel spokesman complained, "they teach them to be agreeable, to wait for God to solve their problems and give them justice. We believe that their message has been carefully devised, that it is a part of a psychological war undertaken by the United States in the name of the Salvadorean army."[124]

Robertson had also been a strong supporter of Ríos Montt, lobbying in 1983 for "mercy helicopters" to Guatemala during the congressional ban on arms transfers.[125] In addition Robertson lent a measure of credibility both to Ríos Montt's self-description as a "chosen man" and to his weekly broadcasts on Guatemalan radio that promoted his political and military programs with frequent references to the Bible. Robertson told his American television audience that "Ríos Montt is a beautiful man. . . . We're in constant battle for religious freedom and I'm very thankful to say we're winning. By the way, the people in Guatemala are thrilled that Ríos Montt is their leader. . . . So let's pray for this man and for all of Latin America."[126]

While American evangelicals did not raise the one billion dollars which Ríos Montt said he expected from them, they did play an important public relations role for the general. Wealthy North American congregations were courted both by the Guatemalan government, which hosted numerous visits by American evangelicals, and by the White House, which set up a spring 1982 meeting between Ríos Montt's chief adviser, Francisco Bianchi, and Jerry Falwell, Pat Robertson, and James Watt. In response the American churches promoted the new Guatemalan model in their publications and church bulletin inserts and through their prayers and sermons.[127]

More subtle than the CBN material support to the conflict in Central America was the subliminal communication that "God is an American"; it served to undermine any challenge to North American hegemony as the work of the devil. Some very popular televangelists in Latin America reinforce with their preaching the idea that the American way is synonymous with Christianity. Preachers such as Pat Robertson and Jimmy Swaggart were quite successful in the 1980s in promoting the notion that, "the American system is the expression of Christian ideas," and that the formation of the United States was the "single most important" event since the birth of Christ.[128]

Conclusion

It is certainly true that Latin American fundamentalists for over a generation were prepared by North American missionaries to accept the linkage between conservative, anti-Marxist policies and the Gospel of Jesus Christ. Missions were the vehicle for a foreign culture which was mixed with evangelical preaching. Consequently, Latin American fundamentalism is saturated with values, ideas, and norms of behavior similar to those which dominate North American society, and the result is a complicity, conscious or unconscious, between Latin American and North American fundamentalism. Social and political criticism is reduced to the evils of individual behavior, such as alcoholism, smoking, drugs, dancing, gambling, etc. Not only are social, economic, and political oppression not denounced as opposed to Christian principles but they are sometimes sanctified and justified with Christian arguments.[129] Fundamentalism may therefore be seen as a channel of cultural and ideological penetration from the United States that serves, intentionally or not, to alienate fundamentalists from the often harsh sociopolitical reality of their fellow Latin Americans.[130] It may also be defined in terms of the forces against which it reacted during its formative period; that is, by its anticommunism and anti-Catholicism.

But the fundamentalist impulse in Latin American evangelicalism has also been a product of indigenous forces and a popular movement in its own right. Protestantism in Latin America has in general served as a protest against the *Hispanidad* values of traditional society and as a rejection of the influence of the Catholic Church. These values were closely associated with the characteristic individualism of the Spanish soul and the idea of a Christian society based on the alliance of the Catholic Church and the State. In this scheme of things, the Church was allied to what remained of Hispanic traditionalism, and because it appeared as the most authentic and stable embodiment of Hispanic virtue, it was also allied to the landholder society whose conservative politics put the Church at variance with the liberalism of the urban elites. As an alternative to the Roman Catholic religious monopoly, the Protestant denominations have achieved a following within small sections of the educated classes and within the aspiring middle sectors. They are the churches of a rising middle class, or of the masses of poor people. Yet the evangelical churches did not bring a message of liberation from oppressive political alliances but instead from Catholic *spiritual* hegemony. Even when the twentieth-century advance of the evangelical movement was predominantly through the introduction of social benefits (schools, hospitals, social welfare institutions, etc.), which carried with them an implicit ideology of liberalism, it was understood that the gradual transformation of society would take place by means of the correction of faults at the individual level.

Ironically, fundamentalism enjoys a popular base also because of its cultivated stance of suspicion and distrust of the very elites who ensure stability. The anti-intellectualism of certain segments of Latin American evangelicalism is one expression of a pervasive, fundamentalist anti-elitism, a reaction against the higher learning of the elites in government and religion: reason is set in unflattering contrast to revelation, and the arcane matters of modern science juxtaposed to the clear truths of the Bible. In Chile, for example, among Pentecostals higher formal education for both ministers and laity is frowned upon; schisms have occurred in some denominations when some members have tried to introduce schools. The preference for the poor, ignorant, and uneducated has wide and indisputable currency among the Chilean Pentecostal churches. Any kind of learning beyond the literacy needed to read the Bible is frowned upon, and educated members who show intellectual interests or ambitions are watched with considerable suspicion.[131] There is a somewhat general impression that to be a good and pious minister, theological education is not necessary, and that an intellectual pastor is deficient in piety.[132] "For the Fundamentalist Christian the powers of theology are one of the major dangers to faith, because modernity comes into Christian thinking through them."[133] Academic theology endangers the authority of the Bible. Biblical criticism throws shadows on God as the author of the Bible and questions the affirmations of the sacred text. It is considered a profane exercise to subject the Scriptures to any scientific study or to use the tools provided by the applied sciences to the analysis of the Bible.

In fundamentalist evangelical churches, the basis for reliable knowledge is common sense rather than abstract reasoning. Knowledge is not the product of the subject who knows but something objective to be possessed. The most secure truths are those which are apprehended through personal experience. Truth is not built up through theories but is directly apprehended. It objectively and irresistibly affects the senses, which are passive organs. To deny this understanding is for the fundamentalists a matter of artificial speculation that confounds common sense.[134] The most important truths of religion are those that have to do with the supernatural world and the future. These realities, however, cannot be apprehended through the senses. To know what is true, a precise revelation from the other world is necessary. The Bible is the authoritative and inerrant means for the revelation of these truths. Theology and human reflection are fallible and confusing. Common people do not need those human resources. They can approach the inerrant Scripture and capture its truths through common sense. Theological reflection is for an elite who demean the Bible through their futile attempts to know the truth.[135] Fundamentalist seminaries and theological institutions, together with an abundant production of literature, are "intellectual" efforts dedicated to popularizing and ennobling the faculty of common sense possessed by all. Intellectual discipline is targeted toward the defense of the faith and against the menaces coming from the world of science.[136]

This commonsense, anti-elitist mentality makes fundamentalist evangelicalism more appealing as a more popular grass-roots movement than its rival for the loyalty of the masses, liberation theology. The latter movement began among religious professionals, and its modest claims to success thus far are based on the demonstrated appeal of base communities, especially in Brazil. Their congregational nature developed in part out of conscious imitation of successful evangelical models in the region. Liberation theology is also hampered by its necessary and formal ties to the hierarchical structure of the Catholic Church, predicated upon an institutionalized rather than a charismatic approach to religious authority. In contrast are the flexible structures and leadership roles of independent fundamentalism. The autocratic pastors of the faith missions and the high-profile foreign missionaries mask a deeper and more prevalent trend toward the formation of independent churches by native Latin American religious leaders, the needs of the local village or community uppermost in their minds. Accordingly, the worldview and ethos of fundamentalist evangelicalism tends to correspond more directly to the needs and experiences of the Latin American lower classes. For liberation theology:

> The underlying dilemma is that the liberation agenda often contradicts the ways in which the poor make sense of their lives and find ways to endure. While it is tempting for sympathizers to glorify moments of rebellion, the religiosity of the poor tends to operate on the basis of euphemization—ritualizing and symbolizing injustice in such a way that it can be handled without setting off unmanageable confrontations between classes and ethnic groups.
>
> Liberation theology destroys euphemisms. It demystifies social inequalities and makes situations explicit by telling people to face up to their oppression, get organized, and do something about it. But can the people so bestirred defend themselves from the resulting political backlashes? Central America is

> littered with the remains of progressive church movements, often determinedly nonviolent, whose participants are now dead or in refugee camps. Encouraging the poor to insist on their rights means throwing away the protective cloak that surrounds religious activities. It means forsaking the church's role as a sanctuary from oppression. Now evangelicals are restoring that haven with a new set of euphemisms.[137]

Indeed, Latin Americans do have "ample experience with sociopolitical visions" and have "learned the consequences of confronting the power structure."[138] In coping with that power structure and with the limited economic opportunities it offers, fundamentalist evangelicals have concentrated on the areas of life that fall under their aegis, namely, family, neighborhood, school, church. In that sense, David Stoll suggests, these Christians are addressing the most intimate aspects of life in innovative ways that may have a long-term effect on paternalistic Latin American culture:

> Stage figures like Jimmy Swaggart, jumping with the electricity of the Holy Spirit, dramatize converts' attempts to defend themselves against a world which has spun out of control by struggling for mastery over themselves. Empowered by collective religious enthusiasms, converts ritualize their refusal to allow the "world"—especially traditions like drunkenness—to exercise its sway. . . . One way of understanding [this] power is by recognizing women's role in evangelism. Though the focus is usually on the male-dominated apparatus of missions, churches, and revivals, most converts are made slowly out in households. . . . Many churches begin essentially as groups of abandoned women who decide to join a new social group led by a few family-oriented males. . . . [these churches] redefine men's goals to coincide with the child- and subsistence-centered aspirations of their mates.[139]

Because it is proving itself capable of responding to the immediate concerns of the lower-class masses, Protestant evangelicalism, fundamentalist-style, will continue to grow in numbers in Latin America, both from the continuing activity of missionaries and from the rise and growth of independent local churches. The political slant of these numbers is difficult to anticipate. Latin Americans are looking for ways of expression in the context of few opportunities for sociopolitical participation. The recent past has borne out Lalive d'Epinay's prediction that "if the possibilities for social and political participation open to popular classes are reduced, opportunities for the diffusion of Pentecostalism will grow in the same proportion."[140] The Dutch social scientist Juan Tennekes came to the same conclusion in his study of Chilean Pentecostalism after the 1973 coup d'état. "Now that all legal opposition has been proscribed, the only avenue open is that of religious protest; now that there are no other organizations that may operate as communities, the search for religious community will be greater than ever," he wrote. "Pentecostalism, therefore, will be strengthened. . . . For the Chilean people, crushed in fire and blood by its own armed forces, religion will become the only legally accepted form of expressing its problems, doubts and hopes."[141]

As long as the present conditions of oppression, poverty, and injustice persist, such analyses will continue to carry a measure of truth. Today most evangelicals continue to belong to the lower and lower-middle social classes. The participation of these social classes in the transformation and control of the political process in Latin America has been minimal. The adaptation of the traditional lower-class mentality to a religious society that is other-worldly in its orientation has deepened the apolitical orientation.[142] However, if the religious zeal and pious faith of Latin American fundamentalists experiences a shift in theological orientation, perhaps in the wake of worsening economic and social conditions, their direct influence on social and political processes on the continent could be immense.

Notes

1. Pedro Puentes Oliva, *Posición evangélica: un documento que define posiciones* (Santiago, Chile: Editora Nacional Gabriela Mistral, n.d.); Humberto Lagos Schuffeneger, *La función de las minorías religiosas: las transacciones del protestantismo chileno en el período 1973–1982 del gobierno militar* (Louvain-la-Neuve, Belgium: Cabay, 1983), pp. 78–97. Cf. also Brian Smith, "The Catholic Church and Political Change in Chile: 1925–1978" (Ph.D. diss. Yale University, 1978). For a sociological interpretation of the Chilean Pentecostal commitment to the military regime cf. Christian Lalive d'Epinay, "Reflexiones a propósito del pentecostalismo chileno,"*Concilium* 19 (January 1983): 101–5; Humberto Lagos Schuffeneger, "Relaciones iglesias evangelicas-gobierno: Chile 1973–76" (Thesis for Licenciado en Ciencias del Desarrollo, Instituto Latinamericano de Doctrinas y Estudios Sociales/ ILADES/, Santiago, Chile, 1977); and especially, idem, *La libertad religiosa en Chile: los evangélicos y el gobierno militar,* 3 vols., research report sponsored by Vicaría de la Solidaridad del Arzobispado de Santiago and UNELAM, Santiago, Chile, 1978 (Mimeographed). Cf. also Hans Jürgen Prien, *Historia del cristianismo en América Latina* (Salamanca: Ediciones Sígueme, 1985), pp. 1097–98.

2. It has been said that government pressure was brought to bear on the signers. It must be pointed out, however, that the Declaration was made through the office of an independent Presbyterian pastor, Rev. Pedro Puentes Oliva, who was a staff member of the General Secretariat of the junta, the same person who made the public presentation of the document, published it, wrote the preface, and directed the drafting committee of the introductory text. He visited church leaders with the text of the statement and indicated the government would be displeased if they did not sign. It should also be borne in mind that there was at least one bishop—Lutheran bishop Helmut Frenz—who took strong exception to the Protestant statement and disassociated himself from it. There were some other leaders who refused to sign. Rev. Oscar Pereira, a Baptist pastor and teacher at the Baptist Theological Seminary of Santiago, told the author he had participated in the meeting ignorant of its real intentions. When he realized the ulterior purposes of the Declaration, he did not sign it. Also missing from the list of signers is the name of Rev. Isaías Gutiérrez, a respected Methodist pastor who served at the time as executive secretary of the Chilean Bible Society. Cf. Puentes Oliva, *Posición evangélica*, pp. 30–31.

3. Ibid., pp. 26–27. Cf. Schuffeneger, *La función de las minorías religiosas,* pp. 82–84; idem, "La libertad religiosa en Chile," vol. 1, p. 33; and Prien, *Historia,* pp. 1097–98. Cf. also "Fuller Information on Chile Protestant Statement Sought," *Ecumenical Press Service* 42 (23 January 1975): 2; and "Origins of Chilean Protestant Statement Disclosed," *Ecumenical Press Service* 42 (27 February 1975): 6.

4. "Fuller Information," p. 2.

5. Ibid.

6. Cf. Schuffeneger, *La función de las minorías religiosas,* pp. 119–21; idem, "Relaciones iglesias evangélicas-gobierno," pp. 59–61; idem, *La libertad religiosa en Chile,* vol. 3; Prien, *Historia,* p. 1098.

7. Schuffeneger, *La función de las minorías religiosas,* pp. 119–20; idem, "Relaciones iglesias evangélicas-gobierno, " p. 60. The sermon was divided into three parts, each with a connotation of thanksgiving to God for the past, present, and future, respectively, of the Chilean people and the Protestant community. The "Te Deum," commented the preacher, was a debut for the Protestant Church of Chile, inasmuch as it marked "the first time" it had "officially received the highest authority of the nation." Even so, he insisted that the moment was not a "protocol" performance, but a service of thanksgiving. Prien, *Historia,* p. 1098.

8. Amnesty International, *Amnesty International Report 1983* (London: Amnesty International Publications, 1983), pp. 140–43. Cf. especially Amnesty International, *Massive Extrajudicial Executions in Rural Areas Under the Government of General Efraim Ríos Montt* (London: Amnesty International Publications, 1982); and Amnesty International, *Torture in the Eighties: An Amnesty International Report* (London: Amnesty International Publications, 1984), pp. 158–61.

9. "Dos evangélicos candidatos a presidente," *NotiCONELA* (January–March 1989): 2–3.

10. Garry Parker, "Evangelicals Blossom Brightly Amid El Salvador's Wasteland of Violence," *Christianity Today* 25 (8 May 1981): 34.

11. Samuel Wilson, ed., *Mission Handbook: North American Protestant Ministries Overseas* (Monrovia, Calif.: Missions Advanced Research and Communication Center, 1981), pp. 29–30.

12. Peter Wagner, *Spiritual Power and Church Growth* (Altamonte Springs, Fla.: Strang Communications, 1986), p. 29. Cf. also *Estudios Teológicos* 7 (January–June 1980): 1–157.

13. Penny Lernoux, "The Fundamentalist Surge in Latin America," *The Christian Century,* 20 January 1988, p. 51.

14. Cf. Enrique Domínguez, "The Great Commission," *NACLA: Report on the Americas* 18, no. 1 (1984): 21.

15. "1985: The World in View," *Commission* (May 1986): 31–42.

16. Assemblies of God Division of Foreign Missions, *1984 Annual Report;*idem, *1985 Annual Report.*

17. Chris Hedges, "Las Iglesias evangélicas logran conversiones en América Central," *La Nación* (Buenos Aires), 25 July 1987, p. 9.

18. Cf. Pablo Deiros, *Historia del cristianismo: con énfasis sobre los evangélicos en América Latina* (El Paso: Casa Bautista de Publicaciones, 1985), pp. 229–30; and idem, *Historia del cristianismo en América Latina* (Mexico City: Facultad Latinoamericana de Estudios Teológicos, 1986), pp. 172–74.

19. José Míguez Bonino, *Doing Theology in a Revolutionary Situation* (Philadelphia: Fortress Press, 1975), pp. 11–12; idem, "The Political Attitude of Protestants in Latin America," *Noticiero de la Fe* 37 (July 1972): 4; and Jean Pierre Bastián, *Breve historia del protestantismo en América Latina* (Mexico City: Casa Unida de Publicaciones, 1986), p. 88. Cf. also Roberto Craig, Carmelo Alvarez, and José Míguez Bonino, *Protestantismo y liberalismo en América Latina* (San José, Costa Rica: Departamento Ecuménico de Investigaciones, 1985); Israel Belo de Acevedo, *As cruzadas inacabadas* (Rio de Janeiro: Editora Gemeos, 1980), p. 95; Prien, *Historia,* pp. 406–9; Deiros, *Historia del cristianismo en América Latina* (1986), pp. 172–74.

20. Edward Norman, *Christianity in the Southern Hemisphere: The Churches in Latin America and South Africa* (Oxford: Clarendon Press, 1981), pp. 7–13.

21. Waldo Luis Villalpando, ed., *Las Iglesias del transplante protestantismo de immigración en la Argentina* (Buenos Aires: Centro

de Estudios Cristianos, 1970), pp. 16–17; Prien, *Historia,* pp. 716–21; Acevedo, *As cruzadas,* pp. 98–100; Deiros, *Historia del cristianismo en América Latina* (1986), pp. 235–37. Cf. also John E. Baur, "The Welsh in Patagonia: An Example of Nationalistic Migration," *The Hispanic American Historical Review* 4 (1954): 468–92.

22. W. R. Read, V. M. Monterroso, and H. A. Johnson, *Latin American Church Growth* (Grand Rapids, Mich.: Wm. B. Eerdmans, 1969), p. 40. Cf. also Prien, *Historia,* pp. 710–16; Acevedo, *As cruzadas,* pp. 96–97; Deiros, *Historia del cristianismo en América Latina* (1986), pp. 178–82; idem, *Historia del cristianismo* (1985), pp. 237–40; and Creighton Lacy, *The Word Carrying Giant* (South Pasadena, Calif.: William Carey Library, 1977), pp. 115–23.

23. Acevedo, *As cruzadas,* pp. 97–8; Prien, *Historia,* pp. 761–69; Deiros, *Historia del cristianismo en América Latina* (1986), pp. 183–203; idem, pp. 240–49; Justo L. González, *Historia de las misiones* (Buenos Aires: Editorial La Aurora, 1970), pp. 327–439.

24. Deborah Huntington, "The Prophet Motive," *NACLA: Report on the Americas* 18, no. 1 (1984): 5.

25. Cf. United Nations, Department of International Economic and Social Affairs, *Demographic Yearbook: Historical Supplement,* Special Issue (New York: United Nations, 1979), pp. 308–26; United Nations, Department of International Economic and Social Affairs, "Patterns of Urban and Rural Population Growth, Series A," *Population Studies,* no. 68 (New York: United Nations, 1980), pp. 13–16; James W. Wilkie, *Statistical Abstract of Latin America,* vol. 22 (Los Angeles: UCLA Latin American Center Publications, 1983), pp. 86–96.

26. Deiros, *Historia del cristianismo en América Latina* (1986), pp. 210–19; Acevedo, *As cruzadas,* pp. 147–51; Prien, *Historia,* pp. 800–8; Deiros, *Historia del cristianismo* (1985), pp. 250–52.

27. Christian Lalive d'Epinay classifies Latin American Protestantism into five types: (1) the transplanted Protestant immigrant churches, (2) the established denominations of Protestant migrants (or "the interjected migrants' church"), (3) the missionary denominations (or "traditional Protestantism" as the term is used in Latin America), (4) the established conversionist sects or "Protestantism of sanctification," and (5) the conversionist sects (Pentecostalism and "faith-mission" churches). This typology is based on two variables: "the sociological type of the mother church (ecclesia, denomination, established sect, conversionist sect) and the form and sphere of penetration. Cf. Christian Lalive d'Epinay, "Los protestantismos latinoamericanos: un modelo tipológico," *Fichas de ISAL* 3, no. 24 (1970); also in idem, "Les protestantismes latinoaméricans: un modéle typologique," *Archives de Sociologie des Religions* 15, no. 30 (1970): 33–58. For Rubem Alves there are two types of Protestantism in Latin America: conservative and revolutionary. See Rubem Alves, "Función ideológica y posibilidades utópicas del protestantismo latinoamericano," in *De la iglesia y la sociedad* (Montevideo: Tierra Nueva, 1971), p. 4. José Míguez Bonino presents a similar ideological interpretation with a historical, social, ecclesiastical approach. Cf. Míguez Bonino, "Political Attitude," pp. 4–7. For a critique of these different approaches cf. Orlando E. Costas, *Theology of the Crossroads in Contemporary Latin America* (Amsterdam: Rodopi, 1976), pp. 30–40. From a different perspective, Read, Monterroso, and Johnson have classified the churches of Latin America as five basic types: (1) the churches which are related in a direct manner to the faith missions; (2) the Pentecostals; (3) newer denominations (non-Pentecostal indigenous churches, as well as the churches related to newer denominations abroad); (4) the Seventh Day Adventist Church; (5) churches of the traditional denominations. Cf. Read, Monterroso, and Johnson, *Latin American Church Growth,* p. 58.

28. Costas, *Theology of the Crossroads,* pp. 40–45. Cf. also Samuel Escobar, "Identidad, misión y futuro del protestantismo latinoaméricano," *Boletín Teológico* 3–4 (1977): 2–3; idem, "Qué significa ser evangélico hoy?" *Misión* 1 (March–June 1982): 18, 35; Orlando E. Costas, *El protes-*

tantismo en América Latina hoy: ensayos del camino (1972–1974) (San José: Costa Rica: Publicaciones INDEF, 1975), pp. 8–11.

29. Julio de Santa Ana, *Cristianismo sin religión* (Montevideo: Editorial Alfa, 1969), p. 44; Thomas J. Liggett, *Where Tomorrow Struggles to Be Born: The Americas in Transition* (New York: Friendship Press, 1979), p. 59. For a thorough study of these churches see Villalpando, ed., *Las iglesias del trasplante*.

30. "Evangelical" is here the translation of the Spanish *evangélico*, the preferred self-designation of the many Christian groups in Latin America with some connection to Protestantism. Escobar, "Identidad," p. 2; idem, "Qué significa?" pp. 15–16. Orlando Costas says: "The socio-theological category of 'evangelical' is usually designated by such terms as 'pietism,' 'conservatism,' or 'fundamentalism,' but these are terms that have too many negative social, political and theological connotations and are not necessarily accepted or appreciated by the newer breed of Latin American evangelical church leaders and theologians. These leaders have often protested at the way certain groups of evangelicals persist in considering all those who are nor part of their respective branch of evangelical Protestantism to be 'liberals,' 'modernists,' etc. " *Theology of the Crossroads*, p. 48, n. 65.

31. Escobar, "Que significa?" p. 15. Escobar states: "In Latin America the majority of Protestants describe themselves as 'evangelical.' They constitute a dynamic and growing religious minority. " Samuel Escobar, "El problema ecuménico en América Latina," *Misión* 4 (September 1985): 78.

32. Costas, *Theology of the Crossroads*, pp. 40–47. Cf. also idem, "La teología evangélica en el Mundo de los Dos Tercios," *Boletín Teológico* 19 (December 1987): 20; and José Míguez Bonino, "Cristianismo en América Latina," *Orientación* 19 (January 1971): 9–10.

33. Kenneth Strachan called the attention to this independent missionary movement in *The Missionary Movement of the Non-historical Groups in Latin America* (New York: Latin American Cooperation Committee, 1957).

34. This movement is known in America as "neo-Pentecostalism" in both its Protestant and Roman Catholic versions. On Pentecostalism, and especially neo-Pentecostalism in Latin America cf. Wagner, *Spiritual Power and Church Growth*.

35. Costas, *El protestantismo en América Latina hoy*, pp. 10–11. Cf. also Wagner, *Spiritual Power*, pp. 131–46.

36. González, *Historia de las misiones*, p. 438; and Wagner, *Spiritual Power*, pp. 11–12. The bibliography on Latin American Pentecostalism is vast. Cf. Walter J. Hollenweger, *El pentecostalismo: historia y doctrinas* (Buenos Aires: Editorial La Aurora, 1976), pp. 143–58; Christian Lalive d'Epinay, *El refugio de las masas* (Santiago: Editorial El Pacífico, 1968).

37. Costas, *Theology of the Crossroads*, p. 47; Escobar, "Identidad," p. 3; Kenneth S. Latourette, *Desafío a los protestantes* (Buenos Aires: Editorial La Aurora, 1957), p. 78. Justo González notes the pietistic, individualistic, and missionary profile of this evangelical Christianity that was born at the end of the seventeenth century and was developed throughout the eighteenth century. González, *Historia de las misiones*, pp. 197–98. Emilio Castro has noticed that "in the past . . . Evangelical perspectives on spirituality (and theology) basically came from theologians of the North Atlantic region," but today they are coming from all over the world. Cf. Emilio Castro, "Ecumenism and Evangelicalism: Where Are We?" in *Faith and Faithfulness: Essays on Contemporary Ecumenical Themes—A tribute to Phillip A. Potter* (Geneva: World Council of Churches, 1984), p. 9. Cf. also J. Van den Berg, *Constrained by Jesus' Love: An Inquiry Into the Motives of the Missionary Awakening in Great Britain in the Period Between 1698 and 1815* (Kampen: J. H. Kok N.V., 1956), pp. 116ff., 122; F. Ernest Stoffler, *The Rise of Evangelical Pietism* (Leiden: Brill, 1965); pp. 6ff.; idem, *German Pietism During the Eighteenth Century* (Leiden: Brill, 1973); Bernard Semmel, *The Methodist Revolution* (London: Heinemann, 1973), pp. 81ff.

38. As Nancy Ammerman details in her treatment of these controversies in this vol-

ume, American fundamentalists opposed modernism in its sociopolitical as well as its theological and ecclesiological expressions. The sociopolitical expression of modernism was known as "the Social Gospel." Social gospelers rejected the fundamentalists' exclusive focus on saving the souls of individual sinners in favor of collective action to save society as a whole by eradicating unjust social structures. Achieving a better life on earth replaced the concern for the afterlife, and it was expected that Christ and Christian values would conquer the world. Progress could be seen in the advance of political democracy, the movement for world peace, and efforts to end racial and social discrimination. Walter Rauschenbusch, the American father of the Social Gospel, interpreted the evangelistic commitment of the church as any enterprise for the betterment of the quality of life in social terms. Theological modernism, on the other hand, questioned the uniqueness of Christianity and shed light on biblical and Christian thinking by comparing it to similar, or parallel, features in other (usually ancient) religions.

39. Deiros, *Historia del cristianismo en América Latina* (1986), pp. 210–11.

40. For an evaluation of the galloping expansion of evangelical Christianity in Latin America cf. Read, Monterroso, and Johnson, *Latin American Church Growth,* pp. 48–60. Cf. also Stanley W. Rycroft and Myrtle M. Clemmer, *A Factual Study of Latin America* (New York: Commission on Ecumenical Mission and Relations of the United Presbyterian Church USA, 1963).

41. Arno W. Enns, *Man, Milieu, and Mission in Argentina: A Close Look at Church Growth* (Grand Rapids: Wm. E. Eerdmans, 1971), p. 145–50.

42. From Europe, the influence of Jacques Maritain revived the ideal of a New Christendom among Catholics, and the movement called "Catholic Action," officially defined as the participation of the laity in the apostolate of the hierarchy, was encouraged by the clergy as part of a larger campaign to regain the influence lost since the time of the Independence. Politically, Christian Democratic parties formed in response to the new challenges. Christian Democracy was successful with the election of Rafael Caldera to the presidency of Venezuela in 1968, and of Eduardo Frei in Chile in 1964. Frei has been the great intellectual advocate of Christian Democracy. His writings owe much to the thought of Maritain and to the Latin American neo-Thomists. His rejection both of liberal capitalism and of Marxist collectivism is rooted in the papal social encyclicals. Frei's Christian Democracy resembles a version of the "Christendom" ideal, since his social polity is to be based firmly in Christian principles. Cf. Eduardo Frei, *Sentido y forma de una política* (Santiago: Editorial del Pacífico, 1951), p. 8.

43. Cf. Thomas J. Liggett, *The Role of the Missionary in Latin America Today* (New York: Committee on Cooperation in Latin America, 1963), p. 15.

44. For an exhaustive analysis see Emilio Willems, *Followers of the New Faith* (Nashville: Vanderbilt University Press, 1967), pp. 68–82. For the ecology of Protestantism in Chile, see pp. 86–93.

45. Cf. Norman, *Christianity in the Southern Hemisphere,* pp. 62–63.

46. This was the challenge of the evangelical movements, conferences, congresses, and evangelistic crusades sponsored by the independent churches and missions that took place since 1948. For a thorough discussion of this issue see W. Dayton Roberts, "El movimiento de cooperación evangélica: de San José 1948 a Bogotá 1969," in *Oaxtepec 1978: unidad y misión en América Latina* (San José, Costa Rica: Consejo Latinoamericano de Iglesias, 1980), pp. 45–64.

47. As personally told to the author in various conversations during 1988 and 1989.

48. Cf. Read, Monterroso, and Johnson, *Latin American Church Growth,* p. 47. Thomas J. Liggett says that "there has been a marked increase in the number of 'faith missions' and non-church-related missions since the end of World War II."; Liggett, *Role of the Missionary,* p. 15.

49. Cf. David Martin's introductory es-

say in Thomas Gannon, ed., *A General Theory of Secularization* (London and New York: Macmillan, 1988).

50. Latin American Protestantism has inevitably assumed "a permanent posture of contradiction, rectification, and alternative to Iberian Catholicism, and that this posture has profoundly conditioned its own form of thought and emphases, as well as its negations and oppositions. Out of this tension are derived both the vigor and validity of the Protestant presence and also its limitations and liabilities." Gonzalo Castillo Cárdenas, "Protestant Christianity in Latin America: An Interpretation of Today's Situation," *Student World* 57 (1964): 62.

51. These perceptions were courageously recognized by the Latin American bishops in the Conferences of Medellin (1968) and Puebla (1979). Cf.*III Conferencia General del Episcopado Latinoamericano, La evangelización en el presente y en el futuro de América Latina: Documento de Puebla* (Buenos Aires: Conferencia Episcopal Argentina, 1979), p. 59.

52. David Martin, *Tongues of Fire: The Explosion of Protestantism in Latin America* (Oxford and Cambridge, Mass.: Basil Blackwell, 1990), p. 45.

53. Ibid. Education occupied first place with regard to direct evangelization and church planting in the missionary strategy of most of the evangelical groups, at least among mainline or historical Protestant churches. The goal was to win the upper-middle class and the Latin American intellectuals. To that end, education was considered to be the adequate means. Cf. Deiros, *Historia del cristianismo en América Latina* (1986), pp. 215–16.

54. Willems, *Followers of the New Faith,* p. 218.

55. Cornelia Butler Flora, *Pentecostalism in Colombia: Baptism by Fire and Spirit* (n.p.: Associated University Presses, 1976), p. 93.

56. Costas, *Theology of the Crossroads,* pp. 77–80. On the charismatic renewal movement in Latin America, cf. Wagner, *Spiritual Power,* pp. 131–46.

57. Deiros, *Historia del cristianismo en América Latina*(1986), pp. 219–22; Prien, *Historia,* pp. 823–24, 828–29; and Lalive d'Epinay, *El refugio de las masas.* For a brief history of the movement and a description of its main characteristics, cf. Arturo Chacón, "The Pentecostal Movement in Chile," *Student World* 57 (1964): 85–88. Cf. also Lalive d'Epinay, "Reflexiones a propósito del pentecostalismo chileno," pp. 87–105; and Ignacio Vergara, *El protestantismo en Chile* (Santiago: Editorial del Pacifico, 1962).

58. Hollenweger, *El pentecostalismo,* pp. 119–62; Deiros, *Historia del cristianismo en América Latina*(1986), pp. 219–21; Prien, *Historia,* pp. 825–27; Willems, *Followers of the New Faith;* Emilio Willems, "Religious Mass Movements and Social Change in Brazil," in *New Perspectives on Brazil,* Eric Baklanoff, ed., (Nashville: Vanderbilt University Press, 1966), pp. 205–32; and Walter J. Hollenweger, "O movimiento pentecostal no Brasil," *Simposio* 2–3 (June 1969): 5–41. According to a recent study of the Brazilian Institute of Geography and Statistics, nearly 10 percent of the 140 million inhabitants of Brazil belong to 4,077 evangelical churches. The majority are Pentecostal, the fastest-growing evangelical group in Latin America. Cf. Lernoux, "The Fundamentalist Surge," p. 51.

59. Martin states, "Pentecostals constitute a much more extensive engagement with the poor and are the first popular manifestation of Protestantism. What is interesting is the way the flexibility and variety brought about by fragmentation both enables them to stay popular (in the sense of reaching the mass of the people) and to create offshoots which can be offered either to those who are ready for mobility or to those already in the middle class. *Tongues of Fire,* p. 53.

60. David Stoll, *Is Latin America Turning Protestant? The Politics of Evangelical Growth* (Berkeley: University of California Press, 1990), p. 109.

61. Cf. Gary Nigel Howe, "Capitalism and Religion at the Periphery," in Stephen D. Glazier, ed., *Perspectives on Pentecostalism: Case Studies from the Caribbean and Latin*

America (Washington, D.C.: University Press of America), pp. 125–41.

62. McGavran insists that "a principle and irreplaceable purpose of mission is the (numerical) growth of the church." Donald McGavran, *Understanding Church Growth* (Grand Rapids, Mich. : Wm. B. Eerdmans, 1969), p. 32. Cf. also Arthur Glasser, "Church Growth and Theology," in A. R. Tippett, ed., *God, Man, and Church Growth* (Grand Rapids, Mich.: Wm. B. Eerdmans, 1973), p. 52; John H. Yoder, "Church Growth Issues in Theological Perspective," in Wilbert R. Shenk, ed., *The Challenge of Church Growth: A Symposium* (Elkhart, IN: Institute of Mennonite Studies, 1973), p. 44.

63. Cf. Stoll, *Is Latin America Turning Protestant?* pp. 119–20, 177, 275.

64. Quoted in Deborah Huntington, "God's Saving Plan," *NACLA: Report on the Americas* 18, no. 1 (1984): 31. Campus Crusade showed the film *Jesus,* for example, to more than 100,000 Central American viewers in the first half of 1983.

65. Ibid.

66. Stoll, *Is Latin America Turning Protestant?* p. 92, discusses "Explo 85," a technological extravanganza bringing together 300,000 Christians in 90 local conferences via satellite hookup.

67. Ibid. "Wycliffe's U.S.-origin income alone increased from $18 million in 1978 to $48 million in 1985, while World Vision's—boosted by famine in Africa—soared from $39 to $232 million. . . . The volunteer nature of these organs meant that they fielded large numbers of personnel. On $105 million in global income in 1984, Campus Crusade supported 16,000 full-time and associate staff."

68. J. Montgomery, "DAWN is About to Break on Guatemala, " *Global Church Growth,* March–April 1984, p. 351.

69. Stoll, *Is Latin America Turning Protestant?* p. 122. Stoll notes that Palau's meetings were designed for television. When he appeared before half-empty stadiums, for example, the audience was directed to sit behind the evangelist, to give the cameras out on the playing field the impression of a full house.

70. Cf. Luis Palau, *Luis Palau: Calling the Nations to Christ* (Chicago: Moody Press, 1983).

71. On this campaign, cf. Stoll, *Is Latin America Turning Protestant?* p. 122.

72. On Motessi's campaign for the National Council of Evangelical Pastors, cf. Kate Rafferty, "Gospel Air Power in Central America," *Religious Broadcasting* (National Religious Broadcasters), April 1984, pp. 22–23.

73. As, for example, the Central American Mission, founded by Cyrus I. Scofield, the author of the well-known annotated Bible that carries his name. This Bible was published in Texas in 1908 and has had extraordinary influence in shaping Latin American fundamentalism. Cf. Nancy Paredes Muñoz and Pedro Carrasco Malhue, "La Biblia anotada de Scofield: instrumento del fundamentalismo," *Taller de Teología* 8 (1981): 27–44.

74. Jorge Pixley, "El fundamentalismo," *Estudios Ecuménicos* 3 (June–August 1985): 35.

75. The first group includes those state churches that came from Europe and retained a linkage with the home city. Such is the case with the Anglicans, some Lutherans, Scottish Presbyterians, and Dutch Reformed Protestants. Protestants of "the interjected migrant's church" represent churches of immigrant origin but not connected with the state, such as Waldensians and Congregationalists. Methodists, Baptists, and Presbyterians are among the missionary denominations.

76. Some Protestant avant-garde ecumenical groups like Church and Society in Latin America (ISAL) and theologians like Rubem Alves and José Míguez Bonino have been attracted to these ways of doing theology. Cf. Costas, *Theology of the Crossroads,* p. 73. Cf. also Julio de Santa Ana, *Protestantismo, cultura y sociedad* (Buenos Aires: Editorial La Aurora, 1970), pp. 111–15.

77. Orlando Costas, in his *Theology of the Crossroads,* presents a thorough study of this

type of Christianity, which he calls "Mainline Protestantism." Cf. also José Míguez Bonino, "Visión del cambio social y sus tareas desde las iglesias cristianas no-católicas," in *Fe cristiana y cambio social en América Latina*, ed. Instituto Fe y Secularidad (Salamanca: Ediciones Sígueme, 1973), pp. 199–202.

78. Williston Walker, Richard A. Norris, David W. Lotz, and Robert T. Handy, *A History of the Christian Church*, 4th ed. (New York: Charles Scribner & Sons, 1985), pp. 706–7. The Lausanne Covenant affirmed: "the divine inspiration, truthfulness and authority of both Old and New Testament Scriptures in their entirety as the only written Word of God without error in all that it affirms, and the only infallible rule of faith and practice." Further, "evangelism and socio-political involvement are both part of the Christian duty." Most of the approximately two hundred members of the Latin American Theological Fraternity support this position.

79. An example of this is the "Jarabacoa Declaration" signed by a group of evangelical theologians and politicians as a result of a Consultation on Theology and the Practice of Power, held in Jarabacoa, Dominican Republic, in May1983, under the auspices of the Latin American Theological Fraternity. Cf. Pablo A. Deiros, ed., *Los evangélicos y el poder político en América Latina* (Grand Rapids, Mich.: Nueva Creación, 1986).

80. Cf. C. René Padilla, ed., *Hacia una teología evangélica* (San José, Costa Rica: Editorial Caribe, 1984). Cf. also Gabriel Fackre, *The Religious Right and Christian Faith* (Grand Rapids, Mich.: Wm. B. Eerdmans, 1982), pp. 5–7; and Kenneth Kantzer, "Unity and Diversity in the Evangelical Faith," in David F. Wells and John P. Woodbridge, eds., *The Evangelicals* (Nashville: Abingdon Press, 1975), p. 39.

81. Cf. Roger Velázquez, "CONELA," *Pastoralia* 4 (July 1982): 78–83.

82. Quoted in Stoll, *Is Latin America Turning Protestant?* p. 134.

83. Cf. Rolando Gutiérrez Cortés, "Espíritu y Palabra en la comunidad evangelizadora," in *América Latina y la evangelización en los años* 80 (n.p.: CLADE II, 1979), p. 190. Costas says that "the heart of evangelicalism is its faithfulness to the Reformation's formal principle of biblical authority and its material principle of salvation in Christ through faith." Orlando E. Costas, "Evangelical Theology in the Two Thirds World," in Mark Lau Branson and C. René Padilla, eds., *Conflict and Context: Hermeneutics in the Americas* (Grand Rapids, Mich.: Wm. B. Eerdmans, 1986), p. 314. Cf. Emilio Antonio Núñez, "Herederos de la Reforma," in *América Latina y la evangelización en los años* 80 (n.p.: CLADE II, 1979), pp. 168–70.

84. Kenneth Kantzer has suggested that "the formal principle of biblical authority is the watershed between most other movements within the broad stream of contemporary Protestantism and the movement (or movements) of twentieth-century Protestantism known as fundamentalism." Kantzer, "Unity and Diversity in Evangelical Faith," p. 39. Latourette has called attention to the rapid growth of the fundamentalist movements "which appealed to the illiterate or semi-literate masses of the lower income strata." He adds: "Emotional, with an unquestioning faith in the inspiration and inerrancy of the Bible, and demanding an unequivocal and personal morality, they caught the ear of the dispossessed and offered a door to a richer life." Kenneth S. Latourette, *Christianity in a Revolutionary Age*, vol. 5, *The Twentieth Century outside Europe* (Grand Rapids, Mich.: Zondervan, 1976), p. 239.

85. North American fundamentalists tended "to ignore the developments which had taken place in Christianity in the Old World after the first century." Kenneth S. Latourette, *A History of the Expansion of Christianity*, vol. 4,*The Great Century: Europe and the United States* (Grand Rapids, Mich.: Zondervan, 1978), p. 428.

86. Roger Mehl has called attention to this feature of sectarian Protestantism. "Whether the sect evolves towards personal revelation or biblical literalism, it attempts to satisfy the same fundamental demand,

that is, an immovable certainty." Roger Mehl, *Tratado de sociologia del protestantismo* (Madrid: Studium Ediciones, 1974), p. 262. Cf. also Ernest R. Sanden, *The Roots of Fundamentalism* (Chicago: University of Chicago Press, 1970), p. 103.

87. According to *The Evangelist,* a magazine of the Latin American Mission: "The earthly religion of the reds cannot be fought with the hollow traps or dead traditions of Romanism. Only a supernatural, evangelical faith can save Latin America." Quoted in Rubén César Fernández, "Fundamentalismo a la derecha y a la izquierda," *Cristianismo y Sociedad* 69–70 (1981): 33.

88. Justo L. González says: "much of our Protestantism was formed in the illusion that it had no history. The missionaries who brought it to us passed on to us the vision of a simplistic return to New Testament Christianity. For many of them 'history' and 'traditionalism' were the same thing; and both of them were opposed to the radical obedience to the sole authority of the Scriptures. We were taught that the 'great apostasy' of the Roman Church consisted precisely of its attachment to tradition, and that only by setting aside more than fifteen centuries of history could we truly understand what the Scriptures were telling us." Justo L. González, "Apuntes en pos de nuestra propia historia," in *Lectura teológica del tiempo latinoamericano* (San José, Costa Rica: Seminario Bíblico Latinoamericano, 1979), p. 127.

89. Hal Lindsey and C. C. Carlson, *La agonía del gran planeta Tierra* (Maracaibo, Venezuela: Editorial Libertador, 1972).

90. W. Stanley Rycroft, *Religion and Faith in Latin America* (Philadelphia: Westminster Press, 1958). Cf. José Míguez Bonino, "Análisis de las relaciones del protestantismo con el catolicismo romano hasta 1960," in *Lectura teológica del tiempo latinoamericano* (San José, Costa Rica: Seminario Bíblico Latinoamericano, 1979), pp. 195–201.

91. For a discussion of anti-Catholic attitudes, cf. Scott Mainwaring, *The Catholic Church and Politics in Brazil, 1916–1985* (Stanford, Calif.: Stanford University Press, 1986).

92. By the beginning of the 1950s, Latin American Protestantism was divided into two lines of action: one emphasized civilizing and cultural works and the other emphasized evangelization. The former trend is represented by the churches that became associated with the World Council of Churches, created in 1948 by missionary Protestant denominations in conjunction with European Protestant denominations and some Eastern Orthodox sects. The latter trend is comprised of denominations and faith missions of the conversionist type, which reject any form of ecumenism, although some of them have international links with evangelical associations. Theological polarization, resulting from the importation of foreign theological controversies irrelevant to Latin America, has led fundamentalists to resist any attempt to cooperate with other evangelicals, particularly those linked to the ecumenical movement. However, they have not hesitated to align themselves with North American fundamentalists. This relationship permanently estranges them from churches and individuals who are theologically evangelical, but who are related to denominations belonging to the World Council of Churches. Míguez Bonino, "Cristianismo en América Latina," p. 10.

93. Fernández, "Fundamentalismo," p. 35.

94. Cf. Deborah Huntington and Enrique Domínguez, "The Salvation Brokers: Conservative Evangelicals in Central America," *NACLA Report on the Americas* 18, no. 1 (1984).

95. Míguez Bonino, *Doing Theology in a Revolutionary Situation,* p. 38.

96. Samuel Escobar, "El reino de Dios, la escatología y la ética social y política en Américo Latina," in *El reino de Dios y América Latina,* ed. C. René Padilla (El Paso: Casa Bantista de Publicaciones; 1975), p. 133.

97. Christian Lalive d'Epinay, "Latin American Protestantism in a Revolutionary

Context," *The Lutheran Quarterly* 22 (February 1970): 31–33.

98. Ibid., p. 32.

99. Ibid., p. 33.

100. Samuel Escobar states that "the Evangelical groups that most spread across our countries adhere to a kind of radical or Anabaptist Protestantism." Escobar, "El reino de Dios," p. 131. The outcome of this separatism is, in the words of Christian Lalive d'Epinay, a kind of "social strike." Lalive d'Epinay, *El refugio de las masas,* pp. 163–80. Míguez Bonino, "Political Attitude," p. 4.

101. Escobar, "El reino de Dios," p. 138.

102. Cf. Carl F. H. Henry, *Evangelical Responsibility in Contemporary Theology* (Grand Rapids, Mich.: Wm. B. Eerdmans, 1957), p. 33. Julio de Santa Ana says that "fundamentalism has insisted so much in the otherworldliness of Christianity that has came to lose sight of the social dimension of the Gospel." Santa Ana, *Protestantismo, cultura y sociedad,* p. 112. Cf. also Israel Belo de Azevedo, "A redoma e o horizonte," *Simposio* (1967): 67–108. Also cf. Jorge Lara-Braud, "Protestants and the Process of Integration," in Samuel Shapiro, ed., *Integration of Man and Society in Latin America* (Notre Dame and London: University of Notre Dame Press, 1967), pp. 209–10.

103. Rubem Alves, "El destino manifiesto y la empresa misionera," in *Lectura teológica del tiempo latinoamericano* (San José, Costa Rica: Seminario Bíblico Latinamericano, 1979), pp. 217–19. Cf. also Emilio E. Castro, "El pensamiento teológico en América Latina," *Cuadernos Teológicos* 10 (April–June 1961), p. 97; and Charles F. Denton, "La mentalidad protestante: un enfoque sociológico," in René Padilla, ed., *Fe cristiana y Latinoamerica hoy* (Buenos Aires: Ediciones Certeza, 1974), pp. 76–77.

104. Santa Ana, *Protestantismo, cultura y sociedad,* pp. 111–13; and Hiber Conteris, "El rol de la Iglesia en el cambio social de América Latina," *Christianismo y Sociedad* 3, no. 7 (1965): 55. In fundamentalism, there is an individualistic emphasis on the interpretation of the Christian faith. Cf. Acevedo, *As cruzadas,* pp. 156–57.

105. Cf. Lalive d'Epinay, *El refugio de las masas,* pp. 163–80. The mission of the church is understood as being that of changing individual lives and building up the strength of the ecclesiastical institution. Society will improve only to the extent that there is an increase in the number of transformed people. Azevedo, *As cruzadas,* p. 157. This is the characteristic emphasis of those denominations that share the "Billy Graham perspective" of social change. Cf. Billy Graham, *World Aflame* (Garden City, N.Y.: Doubleday, 1965), p. 182. Cf. José Míguez Bonino, "Fundamentos teológicos de la responsabilidad social de la iglesia," in *La responsabilidad social del cristiano: guía de estudios,* ed. ISAL (Montevideo: Iglesia y Sociedad en América Latina, 1964), pp. 23–24.

106. "If we suffer here, We will reign there, In the Heavenly Kingdom."

107. Israel Leito, "Frente a una tarea gigantesca en América Latina," *El Centinela* (September 1979): 9.

108. Don Basham, "El cristiano y el gobierno secular," *Vino Nuevo* 2 (September–October 1977): 22.

109. Escobar, "El reino de Dios," pp. 137–39.

110. Míguez Bonino observes: "The main emphasis of the Protestant proclamation in Latin America has been undoubtedly the call to individual conversion conceived in terms of the theology and practice of the Anglo-American evangelical revival. . . . Against the background of traditional Roman Catholicism, Protestant preaching emphasized the need of a personal encounter with Jesus Christ, a living experience of forgiveness and conversion and the evidence of a new life expressed in the proclamation of the Gospel," in "Protestantism's Contribution to Latin America," *Lutheran Quarterly* 22 (February 1970): 93.

111. To a great extent this is because traditional evangelical faith has had an antiworld theology. The world was and is conceived as a negative reality by definition. See

Lalive d'Epinay, "Reflexiones a propósito del pentecostalismo chileno," pp. 94–95. The impact of secularization that is a massive social phenomenon and depends on the social process is interpreted as a crisis of the faith. People have to decide between accepting the world and abandoning their faith or keeping their faith and forsaking the world.

112. Christian Lalive d'Epinay, "Le cas du protestantisme en América Latine," *CIRA* (1972), p. 19. History shows that Protestant groups in Latin America have seldom intervened directly in politics but have acted to defend or obtain certain rights of a religious character, such as religious freedom. This attitude began to change with the success of the Christian Democrats in the 1960s. Christian Democratic parties have been established in all the nations except Cuba, Haiti, Honduras, and Paraguay. In 1958, a Christian Democratic party, COPEI, became the second-largest party in Venezuela. In 1964, the Christian Democratic candidate, Eduardo Frei, was elected president of Chile, and the following year the party gained control of the lower house of congress. With the advance of Christian Democracy, Chilean Protestants began to develop a greater interest in politics. But it was the historical churches rather than the fundamentalist groups which then underwent a degree of politicization—parallel to that taking place at the same time in the Catholic Church.

113. Orlando E. Costas, *Christ Outside the Gate: Missions Beyond Christendom* (Maryknoll, N.Y.: Orbis Books, 1984), p. 50. Cf. also Chacón, "The Pentecostal Movement in Chile," pp. 87–88; Humberto Lagos Schuffeneger and Arturo Chacón Herrera, *Los evangélicos en Chile; una lectura sociológica* (Concepción, Chile: Ediciones Literatura Americana Reunida and Programa Evangélico de Estudios Socio-Religiosos, 1987), pp. 37–48, 49–50.

114. For a penetrating theological analysis of the Chilean coup, cf., among others, "El reino de Dios sufre violencia (Mt. 11, 12), en Chile," *Misiones Extranjeras* 22–23 (July–October 1974): 569–629. Orlando E. Costas concluded that "such public behavior either reflects a historically and politically naive posture with an ethically inconsistent, spiritualistic, and privatistic missiology, or represents a morally and missiologically apostate gesture. Having refused for years to translate the liberating thrust of the gospel into the socio-political sphere, Chilean Protestantism had now decided to do so. But it had made this translation in terms that could only evoke memories of the Evangelical Church of Nazi Germany against whom the Confessing Church of the Barmen Declaration was forced to turn," Costas, *Christ Outside the Gate,* p. 51.

115. On Swaggart's support of Pinochet, cf. Plutarco Bonilla, "Comunicación y evangelio," *Pastoralia* 9 (July 1987): 8–9.

116. Virgilio Zapata Arceyuz, *Historia de la iglesia evangélica en Guatemala* (Guatemala City: CAISA, 1982), pp. 172–73. On the support of evangelical fundamentalists to Ríos Montt, cf. Bastián, *Breve historia,* p. 169; Jorge Pixley, "Algunas lecciones de la experiencia de Ríos Montt," *Cristianismo y Sociedad* 76 (1983): 7–12.

117. Quoted in Jean Meyer, "Cincuenta años de radicalismo," *Vuelta,* no. 82 (September 1983): 17.

118. Penny Lernoux says: "While Catholics were being slaughtered, U.S. fundamentalist churches, including Ríos Montt's church, the California-based Gospel Outreach, received the army's blessings to evangelize among the Indian population. Even after the military ousted him for abusing the principle of separation of church and state, Ríos Montt continued to enjoy the support of Pat Robertson." Penny Lernoux, "The Fundamentalist Surge," p. 52. Also, cf. Phillip Berryman, *The Religious Roots of Rebellion: Christians in Central American Revolution* (Maryknoll, N.Y.: Orbis Books, 1984), pp. 218–19.

119. Huntington, "God's Saving Plan," pp. 24–25.

120. Trevor Beeson and Jenny Pearce, *A Vision of Hope: The Churches and Change in Latin America* (Philadelphia: Fortress Press, 1984), p. 260.

121. Stoll, *Is Latin America Turning Protestant?* p. 143.

122. Laura Nuzzi O'Shaughnessy and Luis H. Serra, *The Church and Revolution in Nicaragua*, Monographs in International Studies, Latin America Series, no. 11 (Athens: Ohio University, Center for International Studies, Latin America Studies Program, 1986), pp. 21–22.

123. Beeson and Pearce, *Vision of Hope*, pp. 264–65.

124. Hedges, "Las iglesias evangélicas," p. 9, quotes a Salvadoran rebel named "Roberto."

125. For details, cf. Donna Eberwine, "To Ríos Montt, With Love Lift," *The Nation*, 26 February 1983.

126. Quoted in Beeson and Pearce, *A Vision of Hope*, p. 264.

127. Stoll, *Is Latin America Turning Protestant?*

128. Quoted in Beeson and Pearce, *A Vision of Hope*, p. 264.

129. Brazil, however, provides an interesting and striking exception to this general rule. After early rejection of the idea of political action by "preachers baptized by the Spirit," leading Pentecostals like Manoel de Melo, Levy Tavares, and Geraldino dos Santos decided, in the 1960s, that political and social justice was an important aspect of Christian service. Hollenweger, *El pentecostalismo*, p. 128–29.

130. Cf. the illuminating analysis of Rubem Alves, "El destino manifesto," pp. 207–28.

131. A minor split which occurred in a provincial town of the central valley in Chile was originated by a small group of "educated" members of the Iglesia Metodista Pentecostal who attempted to open schools and to "promote the cultural development of the congregation." These attempts were thwarted by the local junta, and since the promoters refused to conform to the "authoritarianism" of the local pastors, the split became inevitable. In Brazil and Argentina, however, this general trend has been modified. There has been much less resistance to formal education, and the Pentecostal churches have used both journalism and broadcasting extensively in their campaigns of conversion. The leaders of Brazilian Pentecostalism show more sophistication and familiarity with the use of such mass media as press and radio than do their Chilean brethren. The literature of the Pentecostal movement in Brazil is impressive. For example, Emilio Conde of the Assembly of God is the author of several books. Many leaders are gifted writers who publish abundantly in periodicals and religious tracts. Bishop Eurico Mattos Coutinho, a former Presbyterian who became the founder and leader of a Pentecostal church, recorded revelations he received from the Holy Spirit and published them in a volume of considerable literary quality. Many of these writers and lecturers, however, were educated outside of their denominations in institutions of higher learning, frequently in Protestant seminaries which they attended before becoming leaders of Pentecostal congregations. Willems, *Followers of the New Faith*, pp. 117, 120.

132. Most of the best-known fundamentalist Latin American ministers and evangelists have no formal education and have never been in a seminary. For a critical analysis of theological education in Latin America cf. Hugo Zorrilla, "Aspectos críticos en la educación teológica en América Latina," in *Lectura teológica del tiempo latinoamericano*, pp. 238–46; Osvaldo L. Mottesi, "Educación teológica y coyuntura histórica," in ibid., pp. 247–54; Hiber Conteris, "La educación teológica en una sociedad en revolución," in Justo L. González, ed., *Por la renovación del entendimiento: la educación teológica en la América Latina* (Río Piedras, Puerto Rico: La Reforma, 1965), pp. 95–125; and Wilfred Scopes, ed., *The Christian Ministry in Latin America and the Caribbean: Report of a Survey Commission of the International Missionary Council* (Geneva: Commission on World Mission and Evangelism of the World Council of Churches, 1962).

133. Pixley, "El fundamentalismo," p. 33. As Míguez Bonino has said: "The Latin American Protestant has never had a very deep consciousness of theological problems (he rather has a certain prejudice against any theological discussion), while he shares with every Latin American his scarce

sense of historical tradition" (Míguez Bonino, "Análisis de las relaciones del protestantismo," p. 204). As Míguez Bonino has also said, Latin American Protestantism has not created anything in theology; it simply reflects the trends already existing in other places. José Míguez Bonino, "Main Currents of Protestantism," in *Integration of Man and Society in Latin America*, ed. Samuel Shapiro (Notre Dame and London: University of Notre Dame Press, 1967), p. 191. According to Lalive d'Epinay, "it is interesting to know that words such as 'debate,' 'discussion,' 'critique,' have a derogative sense in Evangelical spheres." Lalive d'Epinay, "La iglesia evangélica y la revolución latinoamericana," *Cristianismo y Sociedad* 6 (1968), p. 28.

134. Personal and subjective experience is the means to acquire knowledge through inspiration. Preaching is not doctrinal but experimental. All of their faith rests upon a personal experience which becomes valuable in revelation, and revelation itself is understood as an experience. Certainty is the result of experience. Mehl, *Tratado de sociológia*, pp. 261–64.

135. In turn, "common sense" is nothing more than the transmitted set of interpretations and explanations shared by most fundamentalists on certain biblical issues. These issues are relatively defined with regard to historicity, ethical character, and theological meaning. Each problem has a definite solution, and each question a particular answer. The trust placed on the certainty of this knowledge, based on common sense, is rooted in the feeling that it is the result both of one's own personal experience and of the accumulated experience of the past. Cf. Lalive d'Epinay, *El refugio de las masas*, p. 194.

136. Pixley, "El fundamentalismo," pp. 33–35.

137. David Stoll, "A Protestant Reformation in Latin America?" *The Christian Century* 107, no. 2 (17 January 1990): 45.

138. Ibid., p. 46.

139. Ibid., p. 47.

140. Lalive d'Epinay, "Reflexiones a propósito del pentecostalismo chileno," p. 104.

141. Juan Tennekes, *La nueva vida: el movimiento pentecostal en la sociedad chilena* (Amsterdam: published by the author, 1973), p. 130.

142. As Lalive d'Epinay has concluded: "(1) social class determines a particular level of political knowledge, but (2) inside each social class, the fact of being a Protestant is related to the fact of having much less information than other groups of the same class" (Christian Lalive d'Epinay, *Religión e ideología desde una perspectiva sociológica* [Río Piedras, Puerto Rico: Ediciones del Seminario Evangélico de Puerto Rico, 1973], p. 54). Cf. idem, "La iglesia evangélica," p. 29. Also, the laws of many countries on the continent did not give opportunities for evangelicals with political vocations to look for positions in the government. According to the second article of the Constitution of the Argentine Nation, "The Argentine Nation supports the Roman Catholic Church." Another article establishes that the president and vice-president of the nation have to be Roman Catholics. The constitutions of several Latin American countries have not until recent times established a separation of church and state. Cf. J. Lloyd Mecham, *Church and State in Latin America: A History of Political-Ecclesiastical Relations* (Chapel Hill, N.C.: University of North Carolina Press, 1966); and Frederick B. Pike, ed., *The Conflict Between Church and State in Latin America* (New York: Alfred A. Knopf, 1964). In three cases—Brazil, Uruguay, and Chile—the separation of church and state was attained without political upheaval.

Select Bibliography

Berryman, Phillip. *The Religious Roots of Rebellion: Christians in Central American Revolution.* Maryknoll, N.Y.: Orbis Books, 1984.

Branson, Mark Lau, and C. René Padilla, eds. *Conflict and Context: Hermeneutics in the Americas.* Grand Rapids, Mich.: Wm. B. Eerdmans, 1986.

Costas, Orlando E. *Theology of the Crossroads in Contemporary Latin America*. Amsterdam: Rodopi, 1976.

———. *Christ Outside the Gate: Missions Beyond Christendom*. Maryknoll, N.Y.: Orbis Books, 1984.

Enns, Arno W. *Man, Milieu, and Mission in Argentina: A Close Look at Church Growth*. Grand Rapids, Mich.: W. B. Eerdmans, 1971.

Fackre, Gabriel. *The Religious Right and Christian Faith*. Grand Rapids, Mich.: Wm. B. Eerdmans, 1982.

Flora, Cornelia Butler. *Pentecostalism in Columbia: Baptism by Fire and Spirit*. n.p.: Associated University Presses, 1976.

Graham, Billy. *World Aflame*. Garden City, N.Y.: Doubleday, 1965.

Henry, Carl F. H. *Evangelical Responsibility in Contemporary Theology*. Grand Rapids, Mich.: Wm. B. Eerdmans, 1957.

Lacy, Creighton. *The Word Carrying Giant*. South Pasadena, Calif.: William Carey Library, 1977.

Latourette, Kenneth S. *Christianity in a Revolutionary Age*. Vol. 5: *The Twentieth Century Outside Europe*. Grand Rapids, Mich.: Zondervan, 1976.

———. *A History of the Expansion of Christianity*. Vol. 4: *The Great Century: Europe and the United States*. Grand Rapids, Mich.: Zondervan, 1978.

Liggett, Thomas J. *The Role of the Missionary in Latin America Today*. New York: Committee on Cooperation in Latin America, 1963.

———. *Where Tomorrow Struggles to Be Born: The Americas in Transition*. New York: Friendship Press, 1979.

McGavran, Donald. *Understanding Church Growth*. Grand Rapids, Mich.: Wm. B. Eerdmans, 1969.

Mecham, J. Lloyd. *Church and State in Latin America: A History of Political-Ecclesiastical Relations*. Chapel Hill, N.C.: University of North Carolina Press, 1966.

Norman, Edward. *Christianity in the Southern Hemisphere: The Churches in Latin America and South Africa*. Oxford: Clarendon Press, 1981.

Pearce, Jenny. *A Vision of Hope: The Churches and Change in Latin America*. Philadelphia: Fortress Press, 1984.

Pike, Frederick B., ed. *The Conflict Between Church and State in Latin America*. New York: Alfred A. Knopf, 1964.

Read, W. R., V. M. Monterroso, and H. A. Johnson. *Latin American Church Growth*. Grand Rapids, Mich.: Wm. B. Eerdmans, 1969.

Rycroft, W. Stanley. *Religion and Faith in Latin America*. Philadelphia: Westminster Press, 1958.

Rycroft, W. Stanley, and Myrtle M. Clemmer. *A Factual Study of Latin America*. New York: Commission on Ecumenical Mission and Relations of the United Presbyterian Church U.S.A., 1963.

Shapiro, Samuel, ed. *Integration of Man and Society in Latin America*. Notre Dame, Ind.: University of Notre Dame Press, 1967.

Semmel, Bernard. *The Methodist Revolution*. London: Heinemann, 1973.

Shenk, Wilbert R., ed. *The Challenge of Church Growth: A Symposium*. Elkhart, Ind.: Institute of Mennonite Studies, 1973.

Strachan, Kenneth. *The Missionary Movement of the Non-historical Groups in Latin America*. New York: Latin American Cooperation Committee, 1957.

Stoffler, F. Ernest. *The Rise of Evangelical Pietism*. Leiden: Brill, 1965.

———. *German Pietism during the Eighteenth Century*. Leiden: Brill, 1973.

Tippett, A. R., ed. *God, Man, and Church Growth*. Grand Rapids, Mich.: Wm. B. Eerdmans, 1973.

Turner, Frederick C. *Catholicism and Political Developemnt in Latin America*. Chapel Hill: University of North Carolina Press, 1971.

Wagner, C. Peter. *Spiritual Power and Church Growth*. Altamonte Springs, Fla.: Strang Communications, 1986.

Wells, David F., and John P. Woodbridge, eds. *The Evangelicals*. Nashville: Abingdon Press, 1975.

Willems, Emilio. *Followers of the New Faith: Culture Change and the Rise of Protestantism in Brazil and Chile*. Nashville: Vanderbilt University Press, 1967.

Wilson, Samuel, ed. *Mission Handbook: North American Protestant Ministries Overseas*. Monrovia, Calif.: Missions Advanced Research and Communications Center, 1981.

CHAPTER

4

Religious Fundamentalism and Religious Jews: The Case of the Haredim

Samuel C. Heilman and Menachem Friedman

The premise of this collection of essays is that religious fundamentalism, a term historically associated with versions of American Protestantism and more recently employed to describe certain expressions of Islam, exhibits generic characteristics which apply to various religious settings. Hence not only Christianity and Islam but also Hinduism, Buddhism, Judaism, and other religions may be found to have fundamentalist variants. Moreover, an understanding of each of these versions of fundamentalism, so the argument runs, will shed light on the phenomenon as a whole.

While we are not prepared to assess the merits or flaws of this argument, nor do we yet share a universally agreed upon definition of "fundamentalism," we are prepared to describe and analyze a segment of Jewry that has been denoted by many who are concerned with such categories and definitions as fundamentalist. These Jews are often called "ultra-Orthodox" (i.e., beyond merely Orthodox), but we prefer the term *haredim* for those who in many cases visibly distinguish themselves not only from non-Jews but also from most of their coreligionists by way of their dress, attitudes, worldview, and the character of their religious life. These Jews move in an opposite direction from the one chosen by most others who have sought to retain a Jewish way of life in the contemporary world.[1] One might say these Jews believe in the *fundamental* truths of their religion which they assume are unchanging. To these Jews their religion as practiced today is part of an unbroken tradition that began with Abraham, Isaac, and Jacob, was established by Moses at Sinai, and continued through the Prophets and later still the leaders of the Great Assembly, the Jewish elders, the rabbis, sages, and codifiers. Together these historical figures represent a continuous chain linking the Jew of today with his forebears, his tradition, and God. To these Jews the past is the great teacher: today is never as great as yesterday, and the best that tomorrow can promise is a return to the great days of yesteryear.

Yet while this characterization may help one understand in a preliminary way what is fundamentalist about these Jews, it does not really comprehend a crucial feature of their existence: a refusal to endorse or legitimate contemporary Western culture. Governed by what these Jews call (in a Yiddish-accented Hebrew) *chukos ha goyim* (the laws [ways] of the Gentiles [i.e., other nations]), this culture is at worst anathema and at best a disappointment to those who are the subject of this essay. And their entire life is devoted to fortifying their own way of traditional Judaism, a process which for many requires some form of opposition to the *chukos ha goyim*.

Ironically—and this is perhaps what makes this relatively small group, a minority of a minority of a minority (that is, approximately 30 percent of Orthodox Jewry, which itself is only about 15 percent of the approximately twelve million members of world Jewry),[2] so fascinating—these haredim find themselves not in some isolated, backwoods enclave where they might live their lives in quiet isolation. Rather, they struggle to maintain their traditions and opposition to modern Western culture in the capitals of this very culture. They are most concentrated in New York City, the quintessential modern megalopolis, and in the two largest metropolitan areas of Israel, an exemplar of a modern state.[3] Precisely this effort to join the battle between tradition and modern Western culture in the precincts of the West, and the haredim's apparent success in maintaining their way of life in this environment, is what calls our attention to them. How have these few succeeded in apparently overcoming the demands of the dominant host culture, and what is the nature of their success? These two questions must stand behind everything else we say about them. But first we must answer a more basic question.

Defining the Haredim

To answer the question, Who are the haredim? it is necessary first to locate these Jews historically. But even before that, a word about the term *haredim* is required.

Language abhors a vacuum. When something which people perceive to be real exists but lacks a term to denote it, a term is somehow formulated. If the expression succeeds in capturing an essential element of the unnamed reality, it comes to signify it. In time, however, the term itself may absorb the reality. And then, as the retelling of an experience may become more real than the event it seeks to recount, the term may acquire a life of its own which masks the reality it was meant to denote.

Such is the case with the Hebrew term *haredi* (*haredim* in the plural). In Isaiah 66:5: "Hear the word of the Lord, you who tremble [*haredim*] at His word," the term is used to describe those, along with the poor and the contrite in spirit, to whom the Lord will pay heed. They get His particular attention because they offer Him theirs. Speakers who are familiar with this verse as read in the synagogue several times a year trace contemporary usage to this source.

For a time *haredi* was used, especially by speakers of Hebrew, to denote any Jew who was punctilious about his religion. Gradually over the last fifty years it has increasingly come to designate those Jews who in their style of life, worldview, ethos, and beliefs went beyond what most people seemed to understand by "orthodox," a word that by itself was problematic and was often exchanged for the term "religious" in English or *dati* in Hebrew. In some circles the term "ultra-orthodox" seemed to work, and in the English-speaking world it still serves as a marker, but like "orthodox," it is a term that came from a language foreign to Jewish experience and thus could not precisely capture the essentials of the people it was meant to signify. Something more was needed, and the biblical term *haredi* provided it.

But what does *haredi* really mean? What does it mean today to be one of those "who tremble at His word?" Are they still perceived as the "special ones" to whom God offers His attention? And does it mean the same thing to all those who use it?

While aware of the meanings packed into the term, these Jews do not always refer to themselves as *haredim*; hence it is a term more commonly used for reference by outsiders. Rather, they often merely call themselves, in Yiddish, *yidn* (Jews), or more specifically, *erlicher yidn* (virtuous Jews), those who observe the Torah and its commandments.[4] That is, the names they choose for themselves emphasize their conviction that they are very simply the true Jews, and not some separate sect called *haredim*. And so if they are indeed haredim, then it must mean that to them there is something essentially Jewish about being haredi and something essentially haredi about being Jewish. To the haredim, this truth is beyond question.

Operationally haredim may be defined as a radical segment of those Jews who over time have come to be called "Orthodox." Accordingly, any discussion of the historical emergence and contemporary meaning of haredi Jews and Judaism must begin with a brief survey of the ideological panorama in which Orthodoxy first appeared. Strictly speaking, the term *Orthodox* is inappropriate because what distinguishes those Jews who have come to be called "Orthodox" is not *doxa,* belief, but rather practices and a way of life punctiliously attached to ritual. It denotes a population that is generally identifiable as championing tradition and ritual *orthopraxis* in the situation of modernity.[5]

As an organized and identifiable movement, Orthodoxy emerged in the last third of the nineteenth century in Europe, particularly in central and western Europe, the precincts of Ashkenazic Jewry, as a reaction and opposition to the changes and reforms sweeping through Jewish life. All around the Jews the old order of life was eroding. Venerable truths and established customs were being undermined by new ideas and orders. Following upon the age of reason came the troika of forces which shook the world order: industrialization, urbanization, and mobility. As a consequence, the future became more important than the past, and change rather than stability became the hallmark of existence. In the industrial age and the urban environment, traditions were rapidly outdated, and faith was expected to give way to reason.

Political and economic changes accompanied these forces. After centuries of dominance, feudal society and its privileges passed away. This was a movement, in the words of Henry Sumner Maine, "from Status to Contract," from a society organized around people's tribal and familial ties to one ordered by "the free agreement of individuals."[6] Edicts of tolerance, political upheavals, and revolutions spread like a wave eastward across the continent. Traditional authorities of all sorts found their control eroded. In this new age people were "citizens," and all citizens were at least in principle deemed equal. What one did was far more important than who one's ancestors were. In this atmosphere, parochial orientations yielded to cosmopolitanism, and universalism threatened to eclipse provincialism. People began to look beyond the horizon of family, tribe, village, and traditions, and thought of themselves increasingly as individuals. Goal-oriented rationality, the engine of industrialization, informed the behavior of those who adapted to the new order.[7] In all of this the character of life inexorably changed.

Ashkenazic Jews, who found themselves dispersed among those who were undergoing these transformations, discovered that they could not escape their effects even in their ethnic enclaves, and even though in many quarters they were considered a pariah people. Although they had been for generations separated from the host cultures among whom they lived, Jews found—in some places more than others, but everywhere to some degree—that the ramparts of tradition that had enclosed them in ghettoes were crumbling, and with them the foundations for a world ruled by the eternal yesterday of traditional Judaism.[8] In spite of the fact that they held onto a despised faith in an overwhelmingly Christian civilization, the Jews had more to gain by these changes than many others, precisely because they were neither bonded to place nor part of the landed aristocracy or Christian nobility that had based its authority and power on ascription. And gain they did. This process was referred to by both historians and contemporaries of the time by a variety of terms: naturalization, civic betterment, amalgamation, assimilation, and (most commonly) emancipation.[9]

After emancipation, the Jews were no longer to be treated as a separate corporate group whose leaders spoke for and served as intermediaries between the governing powers of the host societies and individual Jews. As society moved from status to contract and individuals became freed from formal community controls and began to fend for themselves, so, too, did the Jews. This had repercussions within the Jewish domain as well. While in traditional (pre-emancipation) Jewish society "the observance of the Jewish tradition could and would be enforced by the organs of the Jewish community," which had been a kind of tribal, quasi-familial order, the *new* Jewish community which emerged *after* emancipation, the modern one "was denied the right to impose its will concerning thought and action on the individual."[10] It was voluntary. The result was, as historian Jacob Katz concludes: "Everywhere the individual gained a certain amount of freedom in evolving or absorbing ideas and determining his conduct accordingly. Jews also gained this leeway in their relation to the community and the traditional values represented in it."[11]

Where individuals were freed from formal community control and sanction, the Jewish community had to exercise its authority informally, through social norm, mores, custom, or folkway. What was once perceived as fate now became a matter of choice.[12] People had to *choose* to remain within the bonds of tradition; they could not count on formal mechanisms to keep them within it. And of course once religion became a matter of choice, it had to make itself attractive in the marketplace of ideas and possibilities available to the individual. Often that meant that Judaism had to do away with its restrictive and parochial tendencies and present itself as more in tune with the times.

To be sure, the process that led to this choice did not happen all at once. The winds of change that began as light breezes in the eighteenth century and ended up as tempests in the twentieth moved gradually and unevenly eastward across Europe, arriving relatively late in Poland, Russia, and the pale of settlement where the great bulk of Ashkenazic Jewry had settled.[13] Moreover, these changes were met in distinct ways by different communities; and in any given place, reactions of Jews were by no means the same. An increasingly mobile Jewry was becoming increasingly differentiated in its response to the new conditions of Jewish existence. While German Jewry seems to many to have been the archetype for Jewish emancipation and enlightenment, the experience there was by no means the absolute paradigm for all other Jewish communities. Galician, Lithuanian, Russian, Hungarian, French, Dutch, Moravian, Bohemian, Italian, English, Scandinavian, American, and finally Palestinian-Israeli Jews each had their own special and diverse responses to modernity.[14]

Although these different reactions and the circumstances that led up to them constitute an important concern for the historian who would no doubt want to be quite careful about delineating and analyzing the complexity and nuances of the variations, we may for our purposes consider these reactions as falling roughly into three broad categories: *assimilation, acculturation,* and *contra-acculturation.*

At one extreme were those who chose to assimilate. Although it is a complex phenomenon, assimilation may be defined operationally as a process in which strangers or newcomers so thoroughly learn the ways of the host society (which accepts them) that they become for most practical purposes indistinguishable from members of that society. In the most extreme cases, the assimilated—who commonly constituted a minority before they joined the mainstream—abandon or forget completely their original identity and patterns of culture and take on ways that are new.[15] Jews who took this option "found Jewry too narrow, too archaic, and too constricting. They all looked for ideals and fulfillment beyond it."[16] To such cosmopolitan Jews, who broke away from their tribal ties and the venerable authority of the tradition, there were in principle "no intermediate loyalties between the individual and humanity as a whole."[17] Those who completely assimilated ceased to be Jews.

But not everyone chose the assimilationist option. *Maskilim,* Jews who sought to embrace enlightenment *(haskalah)* and the opportunities of emancipation without necessarily abandoning their attachments to Judaism and Jewish life, opted for another alternative. In the parlance of sociology, maskilim could be described as promoting culture contact with the world outside the Jewish world but eschewing complete absorption. They advocated acculturation, the achievement of "continuing competence in the [host] culture," but not assimilation.[18] In practice this meant learning to become literate in the language of the host society, moving beyond exclusive attachment to the local Jewish community (for example, having friends or political loyalties that were not only Jewish), getting a university education, and perhaps pursuing a profession that was not strictly speaking bound up with Jewish concerns, and thus sharing in the values and ethos of the non-Jewish world. It meant becoming pluralistic in attitude at the very least and often becoming so in practice as well. Capturing the essence of this attitude, the eighteenth-century German *maskil* Moses Mendelssohn urged his fellow Jews to: "comply with the customs and civil constitutions of the countries in which you are transplanted, but at the same time, be constant to the faith of your forefathers."[19] In a popular aphorism of the haskalah, the late eighteenth-century thinker and early maskil, Naftali Herz Wessely, suggested that a Jew "be a person when you go out and a Jew in your home."[20]

The bicultural option the maskilim selected engendered opposition. While to their traditionalist opponents the essential thrust of their action was to advance excessive movement away from Jewish parochialism, their assimilationist counterparts considered them still too powerfully bound to Jewish loyalties. In time, however, many of the aspects of acculturation that the maskilim had sought to encourage were mandated by the state. For example, in the late eighteenth century, Emperor Josef II of the Hapsburg Empire issued an Edict of Tolerance which offered Jews rights and privileges, provided they would become good citizens who would learn the German language and be actively involved in the economy and society around them. In Russia, at the beginning of the nineteenth century, the rulers sought to encourage the Jews to acculturate themselves by trying to create new types of religious leaders (and rabbinical schools) who would be learned in the Russian language and secular education. In these two places, major centers of Jewish population, the state and its absolute rulers were quickly making the same sorts of efforts as the maskilim to bring the Jews out of their insular world. This was particularly true in the sphere of education, which became increasingly a matter of public rather than parochial control; the state, as we have pointed out, demanded instruction in the language of the host country. And the demands of industrialization and modernization tacitly encouraged career patterns that required Jews to learn skills, acquire training, and make a life for themselves beyond the precincts of the ghetto. Finally, the army drafted young citizens of all backgrounds and thus severed them from their tribal and familial connections at a crucial point in their development.

Perhaps because they had been at the forefront of culture contact, the maskilim were often caught up in the sweep of history and the allure of the emergent new civil society. Many experienced severe difficulty in holding fast to their Jewish ties. Numerous maskilim or their children—including Mendelssohn's—ultimately embraced the most extreme form of assimilation: they stopped being Jews.[21] And in the retrospective light of history, maskilim became, for many of those who opposed them and who cared little about the nuances that differentiated one from another of those who associated themselves with contemporary non-Jewish culture, nothing less than full-fledged assimilationists.

Yet the pluralistic ideal of the haskalah did not disappear. It influenced a variety of other Jewish movements that sought to make their peace with the changing conditions of modern society without capitulating to complete assimilation. And its basic premise—that culture contact with the world beyond the Jewish world could be beneficial for the Jews (and for their host cultures)—remained influential (both positively and negatively) in much of what Jewish life became.

The haskalah and its original ethos of acculturation affected diverse elements of Jewish life. For example, it set the stage for a renascent Hebrew and developing Yiddish literature that was to take its place in modern literature. By writing about contemporary matters in those ancient and time-honored Jewish languages, one could remain bonded to Jews while also fostering links to contemporary society. In the sphere of political life, the haskalah nurtured in some (albeit a small minority at the outset) the idea of secular Zionism, a political ideology that merged Jewish nationalist aspirations with the modern secular notions of liberalism, socialism, and the nation-state. Not only could an individual Jew be like all other people, a citizen like all other citizens yet still a Jew, a Jewish state could also become like all other states without losing its specific Jewish character.

But the haskalah also affected religion. In that domain, some attempted to reach an accommodation with the host society through a process of compromise which minimized the strains and conflicts that came from being a Jew in a Gentile world.[22] Some of these Jews wanted merely to re-form Judaism, to make it fit in with the times. To many "reform" Jews, no part of Jewish life seemed more irreconcilable with the emancipation, enlightenment, and the acculturation to which they aspired than traditional ritual practice and prevailing Jewish images. Aesthetic standards and refinements derived from the host culture's Protestants—whose religious style began to become for many Jews, particularly in the Germanic countries, the most important frame of reference—were applied to synagogue architecture, liturgy, education, and personal style or appearance. Functionally this meant shaving off beards, donning fashionable clothes, remaking the synagogue so that it was more in line with Gentile places of worship, and generally omitting parts of the traditional way of Jewish life that appeared irreconcilable with the new position of Jews.

This, then, was the first aspect of Judaism subject to reform. Religion became for many reformers something separated from ritual praxis—a fundamental break with the prevailing creed of traditional Judaism where being a "good Jew" meant punctiliousness in observing the commandments and the associated ritual practices. To the reformed Jew, if "good Christian" was synonymous with "good person," so too was "good Jew," as long as excessive Jewish ritualism gave way to a general morality. The emphasis throughout, however, remained on entering fully into the mainstream of modern society and the host culture, but doing so as a re-formed Jew. In Germany this emphasis characterized such prominent figures as Holdheim, who wanted to cancel the ritual of circumcision and move the Jewish Sabbath from Saturday to Sunday. It also characterized the well-known historian and philosopher Abraham Geiger, who crystallized the major features of German Orthodoxy.

Although less extreme than the reform Jews, others, like Zechariah Frankel of Breslau, also sought acculturative "changes that were not in conflict with the spirit of historical Judaism," changes that "could be made validly in the light of biblical and rabbinic precedent."[23] They were conservative in the changes they were willing to make, but they were, like their reformist counterparts, absolutely convinced that change was indispensable.

In sharp contrast to those who opted for acculturation in one way or another were those Jews who, repelled by the values and ways of the world outside their own, wished to contra-acculturate, "to stress the values in aboriginal ways of life, and to move aggressively . . . toward the restoration of those ways."[24] In the face of culture contact—especially after the state laws mandated it—and seeing how many of those who had sought to accommodate themselves to civil society had fared, these Jews sought steadfastly to retain their tribal and traditional ties. Wedded to yesterday and distrustful of what today or tomorrow offered, they saw the acculturative trends of the haskalah and the charm and substance of the non-Jewish world as potentially harmful and illegitimate, as a recipe for extinction. Still attached to the idea of a "Chosen People," they repudiated pluralism, and many turned their backs on the world outside their four cubits of Jewish existence.

Generally those who would emerge as the most traditionalist Orthodox—those who would serve later as the role models for the haredi—rejected as much as possible the attractions of the host cultures to which former Jews flocked; while on the other extreme, the more modernist Orthodox sought to retard the movement outward by demonstrating the capacity of historic Judaism to harmonize its teachings with modern conditions.

Those who considered themselves modern Orthodox accepted the substance of their host cultures and also tried inductively to create some synthesis of Judaism and contemporary civil society. They eschewed the implicit contra-acculturation of Orthodoxy, avoiding the rejectionism and social insularity it fostered. Those Jews wished to be *of* as well as *in* the host culture and contemporary society and refused resolutely "to be identified with ghetto conditions"; but at the same time they would not abandon the Jewish attachments embedded in Orthodoxy.[25] Although they looked upon Jewish life as providing them with ultimate meaning and value, they viewed the demands of both cultures they inhabited as legitimate. They sought to accept the authority of the past, while still maintaining some modicum of personal autonomy in an age that increasingly emphasized it. By placing a premium on reason, science, and secular education, they tried to follow in a temperate way the path of culture contact embarked upon by the maskilim. At the same time, by punctiliously maintaining strong ritual and communal links to the traditional Jewish community, law, and faith, they also hoped to resist the assimilationist forces which had swept away their forebears. Whatever compromises they made they considered to be *religiously* insignificant. Major figures in this mode included such German Orthodox rabbis and thinkers as Samson Raphael Hirsch and Ezriel Hildesheimer; the latter established a new modern Orthodox rabbinical seminary in Berlin.[26] To be sure, this modern Orthodoxy often required segmentation or compartmentalization of their lives and led to what would in time become an ongoing quest for wholeness, a way to unite their modern (secular) citizenship with their ancient (religious) tribalism—but that is another story.[27]

During the early years, however, "Orthodox" was the term most often associated with those who rejected modern culture and lifestyles, the traditionalists who supported contra-acculturation or at least a very decelerated and grudging acculturation to Western society. As such, the term and in a sense the movement are products of the struggle against reform and religious change, and are reactionary and negational in character. To some, including those who do not share the entirety of this point of view, this sort of Orthodoxy continues to "represent 'true Orthodoxy' in its purest form," and "all other forms are compromises and, therefore, less authentic."[28] Indeed to this day the struggle for the spirit of Orthodoxy goes on between those who assert that it must remain staunchly contra-acculturative and those who argue that only a modernized Orthodoxy that allows for acculturation without assimilation provides the wherewithal for survival in a world that does not allow for total isolation from other ways of life.

Those who chose contra-acculturation tended to look upon anyone who embraced or gave legitimacy to a modern culture, which to them remained essentially anti-Jewish, as a potentially contaminating influence. All efforts were made to remain separate not only from aspects of such an outside culture but also from those people or things that, passing near or through their world, carried contaminating elements of that foreign culture. But that foreign (modern) culture surrounded them on all sides, and they found themselves increasingly dependent upon it, economically and politically. Economically, the moderns' philanthropy helped support those who stayed in the precincts of the holy; politically, the moderns, who had contact with the non-Jewish world, provided needed intercession for those still in the ghetto. This often made those who chose modern, outward life options more powerful and those who remained Orthodox weaker and suppliant, an image that, it was feared, might cause the young to abandon the ancient ways for the new ones. Accordingly, the contra-acculturationists had to be constantly concerned with protecting themselves, their way of life, and most particularly their impressionable young from its incursions. Hence, in addition to investing energy in building a positive culture, replete with injunctions of what was permissible, they had also to absorb themselves with maintaining their separatism by delineating what was to be avoided. This became one of the primary concerns of their educational system, which aimed to shelter the young from the undermining attractions of modernity.

As such, much of the warp and woof of life among the contra-acculturative Orthodox was (and to this day remains) concerned with gatekeeping. Keeping the outsiders out and insiders in became for many who ensconced themselves in the tradition a constant accompaniment to the preservation and enhancement of that tradition. It constituted in essence an effort to remake the world in defiance of the situation of modernity. And though the battles would be fought on all fronts, schools were the front line.

Categories of Orthodoxy

To say that Orthodoxy even from its earliest days was a movement that negated assimilation and reform and distrusted acculturation, and that it was more or less divided into two parts, between those who were confirmed in their contra-acculturation and those who wished to engage in a kind of tempered or tentative acculturation, is not enough. It does not really convey fully the landscape that would be called "Orthodox."

That landscape was already going through a series of remarkable transfigurations in the early years of the nineteenth century, and some would say beginning in the closing years of the eighteenth century. Jews with an attachment to tribal and ritual patterns of existence whose ways of life would later have been called Orthodox were becoming divided among *Hasidim,* followers of a spiritualist and charismatic movement that began in Podolia, Volhynia, and Galicia and spread through much of Eastern Europe, and *Misnagdim,* Jews—many of them of Lithuanian origin—who opposed the practices of Hasidism and maintained instead a rigorous and unyielding attachment to the letter of Jewish rabbinic law.

Both movements created institutions that separated youths, especially males, from their families and local communities and created a cadre of followers who owed their highest allegiances to, and became dependent upon, the leaders of these institutions. Thus, the Misnagdim created yeshivot like the pioneering one in Volozhin, Lithuania, which took in young men in their early teens (and in some cases even their pre-teens), separated them from their families and local communities, and socialized them into a way of life dedicated to Jewish learning and subordinated to the views of the *rosh yeshiva*, the school dean and guide who in every respect was *in loco parentis*. Similarly, the Hasidim originated the *rebbe*'s court into which young disciples flocked, often leaving home and family in order to learn the ways of Hasidism and to immerse themselves in its spirit.[29] In both cases a new voluntary and somewhat separatist community, whose members were dedicated to a totalistic involvement in some form of Judaism and willing to subordinate themselves to a rabbinic (and increasingly charismatic) authority, evolved. Although in their origins both of these communities were engrossed in building institutions and articulating practices which stressed the positive and constructive phase of their culture, they in time found themselves locked in battle, first with each other and later with assimilationist and acculturationist Jews and Judaism.

In general, Hasidism began in the second half of the eighteenth century in Volhynia and Podolia (southeastern Poland) as a kind of folk religion based on feeling, piety, and human attachments. While this is not the place to review its growth, a few words about its origins and essentials are necessary in order for the reader to understand how it later fit in with the contra-acculturationist Orthodoxy of the haredim.

There are varying explanations for the emergence of Hasidism. Some argue that it was a reaction to the despair that fell over much of Jewry following the collapse of the messianism stimulated by followers of Sabbatai Zvi, and others suggest that it was a response to the Chmielnicki pogroms, a kind of reaffirmation of Jewish life in the face of these losses in the seventeenth century. Still others see it as a people's movement that emerged as a backlash against the rabbinic (i.e., Misnagdic) scholars' contemptuous treatment of ignorant masses in Eastern Europe, where Hasidism first emerged. Undoubtedly there is some validity to all these explanations.

In its essentials, Hasidism embraced principles set forth in the early eighteenth century by its fathers Israel ben Eliezer, "Baal Shem Tov" of Podolia, and his disciple and successor, Dov-Baer, "the Great *Maggid*" of Mezerich in nearby Volhynia, and their followers. The essentials included an assertion that true piety consists not in great learning or in the rigorous formalistic observance of the ritual but in prayer. "The love of God is not to be attained by intellectual power or learning, but by the outpouring of the soul in prayer."[30]

Within a generation the Hasidim spread their influence by gathering adherents among the folk of Jewish eastern Europe—Poland, Galicia, Ukraine, White Russia, Hungary, and Romania, and even to some extent Lithuania, the heartland of their opponents. The Hasidim also maintained an attachment to, and belief in, the extraordinary power of individual spiritual contemplation of, and encounter with, God. Such contemplation was exemplified in their rebbe, or leader, who was considered a *tsaddik*—a perfectly righteous man. The rebbe was not just a model of the redeemed Jew; he was also a charismatic intercessor with God. In the words of Mordechai of Lakhovich (1742–1810): "The Tsaddik cannot deliver any religious teaching unless his soul is first bound to the soul of his dead Master, which is in turn bound in heaven to the soul of *his* Master, and so on up to the Kabbalists, the Prophets, and right to our Teacher Moshe and then back again: from Moses to Joshua to the Elders, and right down to his Master, and from his Master to the Tsaddik."[31] In short, the tsaddik was one in line with the Prophets and Moses. Like them, and because of his connection with the Master and the secrets of the *kaballah,* he could work miracles. The emergence of the rebbe marked both a return to the extraordinary times of the prophets and a revolutionary breakthrough from legalism to a new kind of Judaism. It represented *radical continuity and radical change* at the same time. This paradox would continue play a role in Hasidic Judaism into the present age.

The rebbe became all-important and closeness to him crucial for all Hasidim. They could share in his charisma. As Wolf Rabinowitsch explains: "[In the mind of the ordinary Jew] tsaddikism—the belief in the Tsaddik as the 'true foundation of the world' and the material effectiveness of his prayer and blessing and his power thereby to help the individual Jew in time of need . . . became the principal doctrine of Hasidism."[32] While there were some rebbes who disavowed the extraordinary claims made on their behalf by their Hasidim, in every case the rebbe played a crucial role in defining the nature of his brand of Hasidism so that in time the movement and its various incarnations became indistinguishable from its rebbes.[33] And in each court the rebbe became a "the unifying agent binding his adherents together into a single, close-knit society.[34]

The rebbe acted as a model for his followers. If his tradition stressed long earlocks and beard, in strict adherence to the biblical injunction not to cut off the "hair on the sides of your head or the edges of your beard" (Leviticus 19:27), or encouraged the wearing of a special sash around the waist during prayer to separate the higher and lower parts of his body, or if it emphasized the elite's wearing of white stockings or a fur hat, they would do this too.

Indeed the attachment to the rebbe, to the style of life he evolved, and of the followers to each other among the various Hasidic groups, led to a "tendency of the Hasidim to segregate themselves from the rest of the community."[35] At first the separation was simply a consequence of the desire to be close to the rebbe, but in time it evolved into an end in itself, a desire to be separated from non-Hasidic opponents as well as from assimilated secular and general society.[36] To the extent that it worked, such separatism intensified the special character of Hasidic life. And it became an important theme in haredi existence: true believers, the faithful, separated from the masses.

Some have argued that Hasidism nurtured revolutionary religious tendencies in its willingness to supersede the letter of the law with spirit and in its emphasis on personal redemption (particularly of the tsaddik or rebbe) which could determine the destiny of the group. In the words of one Hasidic master to his disciples, for example, "every Jew is also in himself a kind of Messiah, [i.e., a revolutionary,] for every Jew is obliged to think and know that he is unique in the world, and that no other person like him has yet existed in the world. . . . Every single person is something new in the world and must in this world perfect his character."[37] With attitudes such as this, Hasidism may have set the stage for some of the individualistic and revolutionary actions of Jewish modernity.[38] On the other hand, by creating separate communities which made totalistic *Jewish* demands on its members, Hasidism also conformed to what would become an essential element of contra-acculturative Orthodoxy. Yet whatever the revolutionary implications of the concept of Hasidism, in practice Hasidim were always very much a part of nonassimilated Jewry—Orthodox Jews.

Hasidim, however, were not all alike by any means. Almost from their beginnings in the nineteenth century they were divided into sects or courts, each of which followed its own rebbe, who took his title from the community in which he asserted authority. Hasidim disagreed about the gifts and abilities of their respective rebbes; they also disagreed about the best ways of effecting salvation and arousing the spirit.[39] They were divided over the benefits of studying mysticism as opposed to studying Hasidic lore or even Talmud.

After a rebbe's death, some of his followers would choose as his successor the one of his favorite disciples with whom they felt most spiritual affinity. The deceased teacher's disciples would usually continue to propagate their master's doctrine, founding an independent dynasty of their own, alongside that of their master. This was the way the movement spread and branched out. Often the transfer of leadership upon the death of a rebbe led to a schism in the group and the emergence of a new sect. In time these differences evolved, in certain cases and respects, into often unbridgeable ideological disputes. Thus, in the past, a follower of the rebbe from Munkacz, Chaim Eliezer Shapiro, looked upon the disciples of the then rebbe of Belz, Aaron Rokeach, as misguided at best and heretical at worst. And even today followers of, for example, the rebbe of Lubavitch, Menachem Mendel Schneerson, see the disciples of the rebbe from Satmar, Moshe Teitelbaum, in similar negative ways. The disputes were internal to Hasidism and led to sectarianism of the most vehement sort, a sectarianism that helped establish patterns of communal partition that would characterize Jewry from then until now. They honed the process of struggle of Jews against other Jews.

But even before the divisions among Hasidim expressed themselves, there were conflicts with Misnagdim. The Hasidim looked upon the strict and inflexible adherence to the letter of the law by certain rabbis—those who in their opposition to Hasidism would come to be called *Misnagdim* (opponents)—as an obstacle to true religiosity. For their part the Misnagdim disdainfully looked upon Hasidism as folk beliefs and practices carried on by the unschooled. In contrast to early Hasidism, Misnagdic Judaism, with its emphasis on talmudic learning, particularly of the rigorous sort practiced in Lithuania, the heartland of Misnagdic opposition, remained an elite religion, based on knowledge and scholarly orientations. Misnagdim generally "held to their view that Hasidism discouraged the study of the Talmud and thereby had an adverse effect on Lithuanian talmudic scholarship."[40] They further considered the Hasidim to be perverters of Judaism who made their own emendations and deletions to a tradition that the Misnagdim believed was subject only to rabbinic interpretations.[41]

The conflicts were heated and intense. Thus, for example, Y. Rivkind, a native of Amdur, a village in Lithuania where the dissension was especially sharp, wrote in his memoirs that he recalled that Misnagdim "were traditionally believed to go into mourning and sit *shiva* when a member of the family became a Hasid."[42] The groups differed over the proper text and style of prayer, over the nature of the knife which was obligatory for ritual slaughter, and over a variety of practices that in retrospect seem minor only if one forgets how relatively minor were the matters which distinguished the early Christians from the Jews, or which led to other major religious schisms.

Thus an important legacy of this Hasidic-Misnagdic conflict was the intensification of the idea of schism or division. Out of the conflict there emerged in the modern era once again the idea of separate Jewish communities, each of which considered the others to be corruptions of genuine Judaism. These were separations which were born of ideological and practical differences but which evolved into communal and political ones. Thus the Misnagdim were for a long time in charge of the *kahal*, the autonomous Jewish community recognized by the state authorities. This led Hasidim to "struggle to free themselves from the jurisdiction of the official kahal," but in time "the essentially religious character of this struggle was thus almost completely overshadowed by secular issues, such as embezzlements of public funds by the leaders of the kahal and the like."[43] That is, once set on the road of schism, ideological differences diminished in importance and personal and political ones took over. This was true in the conflicts between Hasidim and Misnagdim and also in the internal dissension among Hasidim.

The more successful the Hasidim became in spreading their doctrines and ways—and they were very successful—the more severe the Misnagdim became in their opposition to them. For example, one group tried to excommunicate the other and to prohibit any contact with them, even trying to prevent their dead from being buried in Jewish cemeteries. Or they might declare the ritual slaughter of the other's meat not kosher and therefore forbidden. And if the Hasidim were moved to support their interpretations of Judaism by their attachment to their charismatic rebbes, the Misnagdim had to implicitly create a charisma for their rabbi and his authority. Thus while the Misnagdic rabbi, or *rav,* had originally based his authority on scholarship, the competition with Hasidism in the modern marketplace of ideologies and voluntary associations inevitably transformed the Misnagdic rav into a quasi-rebbe. To the followers of the rav, his scholarship endowed him with charisma and turned the relationship that they had with him into something that at times approached the relationship that Hasidim had with their masters. The idea of devotedly following a *gadol,* a great, became firmly established among both groups of Jews. It was an idea that would remain embedded in the character of Jewish life and play a growing role in the years to come, particularly among haredim.

Orthodoxy and the Struggle Against the Modern Secular World

But something else would intervene in Jewish history that would affect contra-acculturative Orthodoxy; namely, the rapid pace of acculturation which made the differences between Hasidim and Misnagdim seem trivial in comparison. For while Hasidim and Misnagdim argued over how to practice Judaism and which rituals to emphasize, over whether to pray in one style or another or ritually slaughter animals with one sort of blade or another, and over whether the rebbe or the rav was correct, their acculturating brethren were ceasing to practice rituals altogether and had abandoned all sorts of religious masters. Both Misnagdim and Hasidim became allies in a contra-acculturationist campaign that sought to reverse the erosion of Judaism as they understood it. In this campaign, Hasidic-Misnagdic disputes paled in comparison. We say "paled" because they did not evanesce altogether but were simply neutralized by the overwhelming problems of contending with the rapid pace of assimilation and cultural change that crashed against the crumbling walls of the Jewish ghetto. These Hasidic-Misnagdic divisions would, however, re-emerge when the Orthodox population felt secure enough about their survival in the face of modern secular culture. That would come later, beginning in the last quarter of the twentieth century, when Hasidim and Misnagdim would try to draw distinctions among themselves within the domains of haredi contra-culture.

At the outset, the continuing battle against those who were perceived to be abandoning Judaism served to bring together the two erstwhile adversaries. By the 1850s there were "friendly relations . . . even between the Geonim of Lithuania [champions of the Misnagdim] and a Hasidic tsaddik." Even in Lithuania, both sides—the Rav and the Tsaddik—came to realize that in the light of the trends toward assimilation there was no place for disputes between them in religious matters, despite great differences in their respective interpretations of Jewish teaching.[44] Now Hasidim and Misnagdim and all varieties of Orthodox Jews found more that bound them together than divided them.

Thus, recalling the two pre–World War II generations in Amdur, Y. Efron could write "the difference between the Misnagdim and the Hasidim has become less pronounced, there were Hasidim that prayed and studied in misnagid synagogues and batei midrash."[45] By 1922 a Hasidic leader, Moshe of Stolin, had founded a yeshiva that merged elements of both Misnagdic and Hasidic approaches to Judaism. "The yeshiva was called Beth Israel and the main subject taught was *Gemara* [Talmud], the aim being to achieve a synthesis of Lithuanian talmudic scholarship with the spirit of Karlin Hasidism."[46] Hasidic rebbes and their followers were beginning to act more like Misnagdim, emphasizing Torah study and yeshiva learning, while the latter absorbed some of the spirituality of hasidism and the charismatic elements of leadership. Rav and rebbe both became spiritual leaders and champions of the struggle against assimilation and for increased Jewish scholarship *(da'as Torah)* with which this war could better be fought. What both shared more than anything was an animosity to the culture of non-observant and assimilation-oriented Jews. The seeds for a society of scholars attached to the tradition and anxious *(haredim)* about the future of Judaism were being sown. When the conditions were right, they would begin to bloom in the form of countless yeshivot and academies of Jewish study in which the haredim would find themselves.

What were these places? Among the most important was the Etz Chaim yeshiva in Volozhin, Lithuania, established in 1803 in Lithuania by Rabbi Hayim Volozhiner, a disciple of the famous Rabbi Eliahu, the Gaon of Vilna. Then came the yeshivot in Mir, founded in Grodno, White Russia, in 1815 by Rabbi Samuel Tiktinski and headed later, in the 1880s, by Rabbi Yom Tov Lipman. Slobodka, founded in 1882 in Lithuania and headed by Rabbi Nathan Zvi Finkel, became the pre-eminent yeshiva, and many of the boys who had studied in Volozhin went there when the latter was forced to close its doors. There would be others, like the Kaminetz and Hebron yeshivot (which later transplanted themselves to Israel and America when little or nothing remained for Jews in Europe).

Implanted in both Hasidim and Misnagdim was the element of a contra-acculturative Orthodoxy. Certainly the Misnagdic emphasis on the letter of the law and its devotion to the eternal review of sacred texts as well as its dependence on the ultimate authority of the rav, the rabbi-scholar who could best interpret the law and text, lent itself to opposition against the compromises and pluralism that characterized contemporary secular culture. And Hasidism, which at its outset seemed so revolutionary and unfettered in its approach to Judaism, also carried within itself the seeds of unyielding religiosity and contra-acculturation. Soon after the passing of the first generation of tsaddikim, with their revolutionary fervor, it too had established the supremacy of rabbinic authority. In place of the Misnagdic rav it placed the Hasidic rebbe. Both *rebbe* and *rav* acted as restraints on individual innovation on the part of their followers and disciples. Indeed, the rosh yeshiva, the rabbinic head of a Misnagdic or Hasidic institution, often demanded exactly the same sort of submission from his students. Both demanded stringent and steadfast attachment to traditions and beliefs. Both were striving for religious renewal and vitality in a world which was sapping this sort of Orthodoxy. And because both had succeeded in building separate communities—in the yeshiva or rebbe's court—they could more easily and single-mindedly pursue their goals. Separate from the lay population, they had less need to make compromises with modern reality and contemporary society.

Thus, the struggle against assimilation once more strengthened the hand of the gadol. He became the guide for those who would swim against the tide of contemporary secular culture. His pronouncements now were not only about what the law or piety demanded; they were also about the evils of secular life. The gadol came to be called the *admor,* an acronym for the Hebrew honorific: "our master, teacher, and rabbi."

Practiced in struggle against Jewish opponents, both Hasidim and Misnagdim displayed the same stubborn power of resistance in meeting the second onslaught—this one of acculturation—as they had in meeting the first. They used the mechanisms they had exercised in the previous battle against each other. These were separatism, emphasis on stringent attachments to dogma and ritual, and devotion to a rabbinic leader whose authority was absolute and unyielding, coupled with a deprecation of those who did not share their views and way of life. They found supporting documents in Scripture, talmudic and rabbinic texts, all of which convinced them that they were the true and truly virtuous Jews. But the struggle was difficult, for much in the outside world was attractive, and so these Jews forever fretted about the erosion of their religious life.

The Legacy of Eastern Europe

There is one last element in this mix that forms the background for contemporary haredi life: Eastern Europe. Both Hasidim and Misnagdim shared a common view of the ideal Jewish society. This view was the world of Eastern European Jewry as it existed prior to the erosions of it brought about by the forces of enlightenment and emancipation. To be sure, the formal ideal was a far earlier version of Judaism, a biblical or talmudic one. But Eastern Europe represented a world that had found a way to express its continuity with that sacred past. In a sense it was through the prism of Eastern European Jewish life that the ancient Jewish heritage could best be viewed by many of those who filled the ranks of Hasidism and the yeshiva world.[47] This was a world with its own clothes—the long black caftans and broad-brimmed black hats, knickers, and white shirts—its own language, Yiddish, and a variety of customs, all of which gradually had become interwoven with Jewish life. Hence, when the Orthodox who struggled against the erosions of contemporary society and acculturation imagined a world before these erosions began, it was always the world of Eastern Europe. But of course it was not the real Eastern Europe, which always had its share of heretics and Jews whose dedication to matters Jewish was less than total. Rather, the Eastern Europe of the Orthodox imagination was an idealized image of a perfectly Jewish world.

Following the Nazi fire storm and the absolute destruction of what was left of that Jewry, this idealization was enhanced even further. By the 1950s, when people were beginning to emerge from the numbness that the Holocaust had engendered, many

Jews, including those who were not themselves Orthodox, thought of the world of Jewish Eastern Europe in these terms. They acted as if that place at one time was a totally Jewish universe, sanctified by tradition and pristine in its connection to Judaism. Thus, Eastern European Judaism became for many—even for those who had never seen it—the incarnation of authentic religion. It became mythical, and the characters who filled it became larger than life. To the Orthodox, and particularly the haredim, the rabbis became perfect heroes and the maskilim perfect villains.

The upheaval of Europe, because of political and institutional as well as technological and instrumental changes, was affecting all corners of life, including those who sought to insulate themselves from the upheavals.[48] As mobility became ever more possible, even the most insular and traditionalist of Jews found themselves moving around. This served at the same time to sharpen feelings of sympathy for other Jews who shared similar worldviews and antipathy for those who did not. Not only did reform movements in Judaism become pan-national, trends toward Orthodoxy and traditionalism did too. Old boundaries and loyalties were redrawn. In time, among the Orthodox, and particularly the contra-acculturationists, there arose a cadre of heroes and eminences who spanned local borders. Thus, in the first half of the nineteenth century men like Rabbi Moses Sofer of Pressburg (Austria-Hungary), and, in the beginning of the twentieth century, Rabbi Meir Israel HaCohen (Kagan), known by his pen-name, "the Hafetz Haim," Rabbi Chaim Soloveitchik from Brisk (Lithuania), Rabbi Chaim Ozer Grodensky of Vilna (Vilnius, Lithuania), and Rabbi Avraham Alter of Ger (Gora Kalwaria, Poland) were transformed in lore and legend from parochial leaders to universal haredi heroes whose worldviews and judgments took on a symbolic importance far greater than they could ever have hoped for when Jews were still immobilized and localized in their various ghettoes. We shall return to this last point again in greater detail.

Contra-acculturative Orthodoxy—the international society of haredim, as we know it today—was shaped in large measure by all of this. Thus, it reflects an attachment to traditional Judaism (and in particular the version of it practiced in Eastern Europe) and a rejection of emphasis on the freedom of the individual. But haredim society also carries the memory of all of the former struggles between Hasidim and Misnagdim, and against the haskalah and modern secular culture (the conflict which muted all other dissension), along with a need to remain separate from contemporary Jews of all other stripes. The contra-acculturative Orthodoxy of the haredim is, in short, formed by opposition and sectarianism overlaid on continuity.

Active and Passive Orthodoxy: A Definition of Haredi Fundamentalism

The essential element that united the contra-acculturationists—Hasidim and Misnagdim alike—was the confidence that Jewish life and tradition was an alternative superior to anything that non-Jewish contemporary culture could offer. The conviction that a society and culture shaped and controlled by infidels could nor provide anything of lasting value that would supersede what Judaism offered was the keystone of contra-acculturationist Orthodoxy; it would explain their later rejection of secular Zionism, as well as their renunciation of all efforts at reform by those Jews who displayed no attachment to the Jewish tradition and ritual but rather seemed to them to be following *chukos ha goyim*. Turning away from that contemporary Gentile culture and its acculturationist imitators was at the same time a way to separate themselves from its threats and a renewed confirmation of their ancient rituals and faith.

At first there seemed to be two options for those who sought this way of life. One was a passive approach. This tactic required a resolute attachment to the status quo and a steadfast refusal to accept erosion as an objective, inevitable phenomenon, along with a denial of the process of secularization and acculturation to modernity: Ignore everything and anything of the *chukos ha goyim* that tries to impose itself on the Jewish domain. Stay the course and do not change anything. This attitude was perhaps most dramatically articulated in the slogan made famous by Rabbi Moses Sofer, known as the Hatam Sofer and a major rabbinical influence of the last generation, who asserted: "The new is prohibited by the Torah."

The passive approach essentially emerged out of a conviction that Judaism was a totalistic system which had no need of outside influences. The fully engaged Jew did not require the cultural riches of the host societies; what his own heritage endowed him with was enough. Those who looked upon Judaism in this way were tacitly saying that the attractions of the host societies which the maskilim were so taken with were vanity. But rather than openly denigrating and attacking the attractions, those who chose the passive option simply enclosed themselves in tradition.

To be sure, ignoring the modern world is not the same as remaining ignorant of it. The former requires a conscious choice as well as an effort and an outlay of cultural energy or resources and is only possible in the situation of modernity; the latter requires absolutely nothing, but is only possible in another time. After the enlightenment and political emancipation, ignorance became impossible. Choosing to ignore modern culture, however, paradoxically became an option available only in modern times, when religion became a matter of choice.

Those who chose to turn their backs on modern life, or at least refused to celebrate it or grant it moral legitimacy, might be termed "traditionalists." Traditionalism is positive in its continuing emphasis on the advantages and benefits of maintaining the tradition. In its *passive* form it assumes that simply by living an exemplary life strictly guided by the demands of the tradition one can at the same time fulfill one's own obligations and also attract followers from among those who may have abandoned the tradition or who know nothing about it. The opposition to secular and modern culture remains implicit in passive traditionalism, but the guiding dynamic of the traditionalist way of life is not negating the modern secular world but rather affirming the traditionalist one. It does not see itself in an active Kulturkampf with modernity. But it *does* see itself as outside the flow of events and separate.

For example, the yeshiva in Volozhin, Lithuania, was founded not in order to actively do battle with *chukos ha goyim* but simply to train young men from throughout the world of Eastern European Jewry in the ways of Jewish tradition. Drawing its students from a variety of locations, it separated them from their parents and steeped them in sacred texts while exposing them to great rabbinic masters. Volozhin simply wanted to sequester its students, foster their resocialization by exposing them to teachers in the Torah academy, and ignore the world outside. The yeshiva did not want its students to be concerned with any of the demands of practical existence—*tachlis,* as they called it in Yiddish-Hebrew. Nor did it want students exposed to the secularized maskilim, so it prohibited study in any language other than the Holy Tongue and Yiddish. The people of Volozhin sought to preserve religion and prevent erosion by keeping to themselves. Volozhin epitomized the passive approach to traditionalism, even as the *choice* to attend it was an expression of a mobile modern world's new possibilities.

Some among those who took a traditionalist attitude and rejected modern secular culture concluded that passively ignoring the outside world was insufficient, because that world would inevitably intrude upon them. They sensed that the modern world demanded competition for hearts and minds. And the best defense was an offense. They advocated an *active* traditionalism that attacked acculturation and wherever possible opposed *chukos ha goyim.* To justify their stand they could point to the collapse of Volozhin. Forced by the local authorities to provide its students with instruction in the vernacular, Volozhin was stymied. Rather than comply with what they saw as the first step toward acculturation, the yeshiva had closed its doors. And if the example of Volozhin was not enough, the activist traditionalists could point as well to the rapid erosion of Jewish life in Western Europe and other places where assimilation seemed to be sweeping up Jews by the thousands. This demonstrated that passive opposition to acculturation was insufficient. The activists moved beyond traditionalism and toward what may be called active contra-acculturation, or something akin to what today is called "fundamentalism." As those Jews demonstrate, fundamentalism as such is not identical to traditionalism, in that it is not content with mere emphasis of the positive elements of tradition but focuses equally, or even more intensively, on the negative aspects of modern secular culture. Fundamentalism is thus essentially a movement of active and aggressive opposition.

Much of the thrust of this fundamentalism is caught up in its negational character. The opposition is to a *particular kind of culture* and its interpretation of life's meaning and obligations. Fundamentalism advances alternative, and in its view superior, life options, but it advances them not simply by example, as the passive traditionalists do, but by attempting to remake society in such a way that even those who do not initially share its point of view will come to the conviction that the old-time religion is normative for all. Only by this approach, these activists believe, can they truly safeguard their way of life. The approach argues that if a place like Volozhin wants to keep its doors open it must, whenever possible, go out and do battle against the forces which would change it, for without such aggressive action Volozhin and places like it which are passively traditionalist will in the end have to close their doors.[49]

To be sure, remaking the world requires struggle and conflict, especially because the nonreligious are at first blind and are often resistant to religion. Thus, the fundamentalists may at times be forced to be perceived as the enemy before they can be understood to be the true friends who will lead the blind to see the light. There are of course various strategies to be used. There is the approach of aggressive contention, epitomized today among the Jews by the followers of Satmar Hasidism—one of the major Hungarian strains and emblematic of the most uncompromising rejectionism—who refuse to make any compromises in their struggle for Judaism. And there is the approach of the agents provocateurs, embodied nowadays in Lubavitch Hasidism, which appears at first glance to be tolerant of other ways, only to subtly bring about a change in the people it harnesses to its way of life. (It is no accident that Satmar and Lubavitch not only differ in approach but also view each other as having betrayed the true way, of not being properly haredi, and therefore as illegitimate in many respects.)[50]

If contra-acculturative activists wish to missionize in or change modern society, passive traditionalists would like it to go away. This conceptual liquidation of the legitimacy of the modern world represents the juncture between passive traditionalism and the more activist fundamentalism. Both reject part or all of the modern world, but while passive traditionalism does so by emphasizing its positive involvement in the tradition, its activist counterpart does so by an emphasis on what it refuses to become. And for activists there must be constant vigilance, for until the final victory over the contemporary world, invasion by contemporary values and the consequent erosion of fundamental Torah beliefs remains possible. So the activists must be especially on guard; they are *haredim,* worried and anxious over any further erosion of their way of Jewish life by compromise and cultural adaptation. The true haredim tremble and cannot be content to be simply passive in their traditionalism; they must be active in their Kulturkampf, ever demonstrating the religious "truth" to the majority who are enticed by the hedonistic pleasures of contemporary culture and who thus submit to desire. We shall see this theme again and again in what follows.

In a sense, fundamentalism uses tradition as a vehicle for denying the legitimacy of all other ways of life. As such, in the dynamics of its existence, it becomes as dependent upon modernity as upon tradition. That is because modernity provides it with something to oppose and thereby shapes its character. Modernity determines which aspects of the tradition fundamentalists will emphasize. In other words, active contra-acculturative Orthodoxy (fundamentalism) becomes an archetypal counterculture. It is *against* more often than it is *for,* because it is overwhelmed by its sense of having to preserve tradition against intrusions and assaults from the outside.

Ironically, like other aspects of the pluralist modern world, fundamentalism presents itself as an alternative. Thus fundamentalism takes traditional values and places them in active competition with modern ones. And in places like the yeshiva, it takes traditional knowledge and makes it a counterwisdom to the knowledge that comes from secular learning.[51] In fundamentalist hands the yeshiva is no longer simply a place for scholars: it becomes a frontline battle station in the war against *chukos ha goyim.* As such, not only Misnagdim need yeshivot. Hasidim also need them—even the modern and more moderately Orthodox need them (although this last group's institutions—often called "day schools" and [in Israel] *yeshivot tichoniyot*—are far less aggressive in their contra-acculturation because the modern Orthodox who fill them are similarly moderate).

To be sure, the contra-acculturative activists (who believed that the fate of their souls depended on their fidelity to the Jewish law and way of life) were from the beginning fascinated by contemporary culture. Precisely because they too could feel its attractions—if not always consciously—did they struggle so aggressively against them. Thus, for example, contra-acculturative activists were and continue to be obsessed with sexual expression precisely because that is one of the most attractive aspects of modern life. Accordingly, they are most militant in combating the inroads of modern culture and society in that sphere because they realize intuitively that modern culture is aided in its efforts by the inherent libidinal desires of all people. So from their beginnings the haredim stressed "modesty" in women's dress and were scrupulous about having married women (whose capacity to arouse they never doubted) cover or even shave their hair in order to avoid even the unconscious desires that could elicit the anathema of adultery. To this day, the neighborhoods of the haredim are plastered with signs warning visitors, particularly the women among them, to be "modest" in their dress. And even today all pictures—in television, magazines, posters, and the like—that suggest sexuality must be carefully controlled (although sometimes the controls themselves serve to focus on precisely what is meant to be denied, and thus these Jews often make one realize that even the very young and the very old are still sexual objects). In a sense the sexually repressive nature of the contra-acculturative society proves the Freudian assertion of the power of the libido. But that libidinal pleasure must be repressed and redefined as iniquity—precisely, the iniquity which powers the modern world.

It is in this sense that haredim, who represent traditionalism in its most radical form, view those who have compromised with contemporary culture as being "weak." They are weak in that they have not been able to repress their (libidinal) desires which naturally tend toward the attractions and pleasures of this world. To the haredim, all moderns implicitly or explicitly are governed by *taivoh,* lustful desires. The arena of sexual expression displays the psychological dimension of the Kulturkampf. Accordingly, fundamentalism in general and the Jewish case in particular should be considered as a psychological, and not just a social, conflict. It is an effort to champion repression as a desirable option for the modern person.

But because the attractions of contemporary culture are so powerful, many Orthodox Jews have managed more today than ever before to find ways of entering the situation of modernity and the spirit of the times while still keeping strictly within the letter of the law. Thus, for example, the very wigs and long dresses that were in principle meant to hide the woman's sexuality in many cases have become quite the opposite: stylish and attractive exemplars of the best in contemporary fashion, even as they cover a woman's head and body completely, thus fulfilling the law. Today, many an Orthodox wife wears wigs and clothes that make her altogether handsome. And even the most aggressive contra-acculturationists have wives who, while wearing dark kerchiefs over shaved heads and black stockings over naked legs, find ways to express their sexuality in the earring studs or flowery dresses they wear, or even in the way they swing their hips.

This trend among the modern Orthodox has led haredim today even more than in the past to become partisans of the stringent, rather than the lenient, interpretations of Jewish law. In Hebrew this is called choosing the *chumra* rather than the *kula*.[52] The espousal of stringencies led and continues to lead haredim to adopt customs that were often beyond the demands of the law but were aimed to anticipate and prevent even the hint of compromise with modern culture. And if one group chose one interpretation of the demands of Jewish law, another group—in order to demonstrate its greater piety—would find an even stricter interpretation. Haredi culture continues to move in the direction of increasing chumra. Thus there continue to be calls to do away with wigs in favor of shaved heads and kerchiefs, and there are frequent efforts to shun material pleasures. That is, the chumra has inserted an ascetic strain into Judaism. In the haredi world, increasingly, the one who turns his back on the pleasures that modern life has to offer, he who embraces the chumra even when an easier, more lenient option is available, is portrayed in many circles as the true haredi, the finest Jew.

Precisely because it often makes exorbitant demands on the practitioner, the chumra also serves to differentiate and separate him from most others. It allowed and continues to allow him to express a deeper religious commitment. It thus became yet another way in which the haredim could distinguish themselves from the *chukos ha goyim,* a crucial matter for those who stress survival above all other elements of Judaism, a matter which, as we shall argue later, is of great importance to haredi culture.

Still, where modernity seemed not to undermine the worldview, even the contra-acculturationists were attracted to it. One of the most striking ways that the fascination with contemporary life displayed itself was in the manner in which those Jews would in time learn to embrace and use the most sophisticated and modern forms of technology and become consumers of modern products and the like, as long as those aspects of modernity seemed to have no significance beyond the instrumental. And where their instrumental advantage could enhance religious life, technology was positively adored. Such a selective involvement with modernity would require a nuanced understanding and a developed capacity for compartmentalization. It would require the redefinition of certain items of modern technology in traditionalist terms. Thus a timer would become a "shabbos clock," a device for turning electricity on and off on the Sabbath, something that, although it was otherwise prohibited by law, now became possible. Or a knowledge of computers and modems would allow haredi women to find employment without leaving the shelter of their homes and the surrounding community. Thus, the editor of one of the most aggressively traditionalist newspapers in Israel's haredi press could prepare his publication, which rails against modern Zionist culture and *chukos ha goyim,* more efficiently on a personal computer, and the most sophisticated electronic equipment available could be sold in Manhattan's Forty-Seventh Street Photo, a firm owned and staffed by Satmar Hasidim, among the most aggressively contra-acculturationist traditional Jews.

To be sure, there were haredim who worried that even this apparently innocent use of tools of the modern world could lead to *chukos ha goyim*. Thus, video recorders with which the special occasions of haredi Jewish life were chronicled could become tools for viewing prohibited films. And the search for material pleasure could undermine aspirations for spiritual and religious purity.

From the beginning, activist contra-acculturationists sought new ways to do battle with the outside world, to undermine secularism, and to delegitimate even the mildest forms of acculturation. Indeed, to those activists, those most properly called haredim, it was precisely the acculturationist Jews, who believed they could make some compromise with contemporary non-Jewish culture and pursued some modus vivendi with it, who represented the greatest enemy: the acculturationists were after all nothing more than goyim, crypto-Gentiles, people who lived by *chukos ha goyim*.

But the haredim encountered a problem in the case of some Jews who seemed to have both a fidelity to the tradition and an association with the general culture. These moderate acculturationists included not only the earliest maskilim but even more, as time passed, the modern Orthodox who sought to be part of both the secular and the traditionally Jewish worlds, and even those who were willing to accept the externals and superficial patterns of behavior of the emergent civil society while (at least to themselves) deliberately rejecting many of the values and ideological assumptions of that world.[53] And it included as well the religious Zionists, who believed they could be citizens like everyone else but in a distinctively Jewish modern state, without having to meaningfully compromise their fidelity to Orthodox Judaism.

Thus, while all these acculturationists thought they were not subverting Judaism—indeed many believed they were saving it by adapting it and themselves to changing times and circumstances—the contra-acculturationists, and particularly the haredim among them, were convinced that the acculturationists were undermining the future by uprooting the past. Moreover, they worried that the unsophisticated and uninformed might come to believe these adaptations of Judaism were legitimate. Thus, many of the heroes of moderated acculturationists—people like the maskil Moses Mendelssohn and chief rabbi Abraham I. Kook of Palestine, or most of the leaders of religious Zionist parties—became anti-heroes for the haredim. Haredi Judaism portrayed those Jews as creating an ideology of mediocrity in which failure to struggle against the eroding effects of contemporary culture was the greatest sin.

The Contemporary Emergence of Haredim: Radical Activist Traditionalism

While all these trends have their roots in the various streams of Orthodoxy and the Hasidic-Misnagdic encounter of earlier generations, traditionalism—and particularly its activist and contra-acculturationist form, haredi Judaism—has become more radical since the end of the Second World War and the rise of a new Zionist-Jewish state in Israel. Why?

Although European Jewry experienced profound change following the emancipation and the haskalah, there still remained robust enclaves of traditional and Orthodox Jewish life in Europe right up to the eve of destruction in the Shoah (Holocaust). The most Orthodox had until the very end for the most part refused to go either to

America, which they considered a place that swallowed up Jewish life (the *trefe medina* [unkosher state], they called it), or Palestine, which they often saw as a holy land being desecrated by socialists and infidels. But after the war they had no choice, and they migrated both to the West and to Israel. Those who came were survivors in a double sense: most recently of a physical annihilation by Nazis and their sympathizers, and before that, of a cultural obliteration by the champions of acculturation.

Many of the survivors came to their new addresses with a conviction that they—the last remnant—would not be wiped out because they had a sacred obligation, especially to their dead kin who had paid with their lives for staying in Europe, away from the iniquities of America and Palestine. This obligation was *to recreate their traditional experience*. They felt that they could and should resurrect the world they recalled, in a recollection that was now ringed by a halo of nostalgia and survivor guilt; they felt that they needed to prove their spiritual worth to account for their survival. They would now resurrect the dead Jewish world and give it a life even more potent than before. This was a revolutionary idea, dressed in the garments of putative continuity.[54]

In America, particularly in Brooklyn but also in parts of the Lower East Side of Manhattan, and in later years in Queens and parts of Rockland County in New York state, and later in all sorts of far-flung places, Hasidic courts were reassembled by the survivors. Among the major ones were Satmar, Lubavitch, Bobov, and Vizhnitz Hasidim. Lithuanian-style yeshivot were established, some in the late 1920s and some in the 1930s, but many more in the 1940s and in the postwar period. While many were established in the New York area, where most Jews lived, there were important schools that tried to once again isolate themselves from lay communities and chose places like Lakewood, New Jersey, Philadelphia, Pennsylvania, or Cleveland, Ohio, and even those that were in New York sometimes tried to set themselves up in places separate from the center in Brooklyn and the Lower East Side of Manhattan.[55]

Those who came to America focused their energies on the building of *mosdos,* institutions that would permit the re-establishment of Orthodox Jewish life in America and at the same time serve as a protective institutional barrier within which they could remain insulated from American culture. To remain independent, all the institutions needed was to present themselves in religious terms. Moreover, America offered advantages in that it not only allowed the building of these institutions but also provided tacit financial support by allowing donations to religious institutions to be tax deductible.

Many of the Orthodox Jews who came to America after the Holocaust found a Jewry that was growing in affluence, ready to give to Jewish causes, and weighted down with enough survivor guilt to give money to the rebuilding of institutions paralleling or named after villages and communities of European Jewry—even if the donors did not share the Orthodox worldview and philosophy of the institutions they were supporting. (Probably the givers were convinced, as were most American Jews, that Orthodoxy was dying out and these were its last remnants.)[56]

The American Orthodox, even the most activist contra-acculturationist among them, could not, and did not want to, fight America, their new haven. They tried instead to ignore its culture whenever possible—even to the extent of traveling through it inside their own buses—and saved their energies for the struggle to keep other, non-Orthodox Jews at bay. In America, the haredim, such as they were, withdrew from intra-Jewish organizations as much as possible, maintaining only the ties they needed to attract funding for their institutions. They vilified the Reform and Conservative Jews and were privately contemptuous of those who called themselves modern Orthodox. They refused to join most intracommunal Jewish organizations. Agudat Israel sympathizers took over the organized rabbinical association (Agudas Ha Rabonnim) that was made up of Orthodox rabbis who were not affiliated with the more mainstream Orthodox Rabbinical Council of America.[57] And the most insular groups organized their own separate rabbinical union. Hence, they were called "ultra" Orthodox. Their positive efforts concentrated on building and maintaining their institutions and causes, an effort that sometimes caused them to check their criticism of the non-Orthodox benefactors.

In America the contra-acculturative Orthodox thus focused on making money, the ultimate American power, and limiting the influence of non-Orthodox Jews in Jewish life, particularly in determining matters of personal status (deciding who was a Jew, or who was married or divorced). The money, the result of an open society which provided many economic opportunities never before available to those who remained Orthodox, would provide independence and help support the Orthodox way of life. For some this meant developing strength in the diamond trade, for others real estate, the garment industry, and during the last twenty-five years, the electronics business. Living in a community of people who trust one another and adopt a no-nonsense approach to business (which, somewhat like the Protestant ethic, reinvests profits and limits spending to necessities and giving to charity), these Jews placed no inherent value on money apart from what it could accomplish in terms of maintaining their Jewish way of life. In America they succeeded as never before.[58]

Moreover, to keep America responsive to their needs, these Jews (like all their coreligionists) were especially careful to vote at election time, making it increasingly certain that the parties and candidates knew that they voted in high numbers and en bloc. In this last regard, they allowed themselves to be publicly identified as *Jewish* voters—so much so that candidates seeking Jewish votes often still have themselves photographed with haredim, hoping that this will symbolize their attraction for Jewish voters of all stripes.[59]

In the Land of Israel and later in the new Zionist state, Orthodox Jews who arrived after the Second World War also tried to recreate and resurrect their traditional experience. To these Orthodox Jews—even those who shared similar Hasidic or Misnagdic affiliations—their American counterparts were not really haredim; they were Americans. They read American newspapers, worked with Americans, spoke English, and had subtly been swept up by America and the *chukos ha goyim*. They could not really overcome so powerful a cultural giant as the American way of life. True haredim, the Israelis maintained, fought relentlessly against all outside influences, including the host society, and did not allow themselves to be assimilated by the modern world even in the quest for funds for their institutions. In fact, the Israelis would argue, only the ongoing struggle against everything that led to acculturation could keep one haredi. Of course even Israeli haredim were only relatively more isolated than their American counterparts: they spoke Hebrew, listened to the radio, and were touched by general Israeli culture. Yet this was not the same as in America where the general culture was dominated by *chukos ha goyim*. But how had the Israeli haredim created a situation different from the one confronting the Americans?

To answer this question it is necessary to understand something about the framework into which the Israeli haredim and their more passive contra-acculturationist supporters entered when they arrived immediately before and after the Shoah. Because Israel had been the Holy Land, the place to which the Messiah would one day return and bring about the final redemption, a large number of very pious Jews had begun to return to await that day even before the days of secular Zionism. There had been Orthodox Jews in the Land of Israel before those postwar days. Indeed, they had been part of what was called "the Old Yishuv," the pre-State settlement that was established in the Holy Land during the late eighteenth and early nineteenth centuries and that antedated the waves of secular Zionist immigration in the late nineteenth and the twentieth centuries. Those Orthodox Jews came to live a fuller Jewish life and to observe those rituals and laws that could be carried out only in the Holy Land. They were relatively few in number, and they lived a kind of passive traditionalist life.

But as the new brand of active Zionists, ignited by socialist and revolutionary ideas that emerged out of Jewish emancipation and haskalah, came to the Land of Israel, they seized the political initiative and overwhelmed the small group of Jews who had come to the Holy Land to passively await the Messiah and live their lives by the strict dictates of Jewish law. The Zionists transformed those Jews into an increasingly marginal and powerless community. In the process they created a deeply held feeling of resentment in the precincts of Holy Land Orthodoxy. This resentment would be part of the legacy of the relationship between the secular Zionists and those who saw themselves as rooted in the traditionalism that characterized the Old Yishuv.

There were in fact two grounds for the discomfort of the Jews of the Old Yishuv with the Zionists. First, they looked upon them as heretics and unbelievers, which indeed many were, even though a large number had grown up in Europe in religious homes, and some were even former yeshiva boys. A central element of the Zionists' unbelief was their conviction that they could by their own actions bring about the redemption that a return of the Jews to their homeland would portend. The Orthodox Jews of the Old Yishuv were convinced that exile would end only when God decreed it, and they could never bring themselves to believe that God would use as his instruments of redemption such unbelievers as Theodore Herzl and the other secular Zionists.

The second ground for the opposition of the Orthodox Jews of the Old Yishuv to Zionism was the Zionists' assertion that one could be a complete Jew by being a Zionist, and that it did not require a scrupulous attention to the letter of Jewish law. This was once again the same problem that Orthodox Jews had had with maskilim in Europe. Zionists were simply a version of maskilim. They were a particularly dangerous version because they really did wholly devote themselves to being Jewish, but their view that being Jewish was being a pioneer who takes his destiny in his own hands was very different from the one that traditionalist Orthodoxy held. The latter found itself fighting against secular Zionism over the meaning of such basic principles as diaspora and redemption.

But while this philosophical argument was evolving, the Zionists were becoming increasingly powerful. They were supplanting the approximately fifty thousand Jews of the Old Yishuv as representatives of the Jewish presence in Palestine. This made the Jews of the Old Yishuv feel increasingly that even though they were in the Holy Land, they were still "in diaspora among the Jews."[60] That is, they were powerless Jews, subject to the *chukos ha goyim,* except the goyim now were Jews. After the Balfour Declaration on 2 November 1917, in which the British mandatory authorities declared that they "looked with favor" on the idea of a Jewish state in Palestine, the Zionist dream seemed on the verge of becoming a reality. Accordingly, the tension felt by the Jews of the Old Yishuv and their sympathizers became even greater.

Let us summarize the differences between the new Zionists of what would be called the "New Yishuv" and the traditionalist Orthodox Jews of the Old Yishuv. First, the Zionists were in the majority not Orthodox Jews.[61] On the contrary, as we noted earlier, many arrived with socialist and atheistic convictions, zealous to create a new sort of Jew, a person who would be "normalized" through his enfranchisement in the world of nations only when he had his own state. Second, since they were revolutionaries, the Zionists were skeptics and heretics, ready to throw off the yoke of received authority (they had left the rabbis behind in the yeshivot), while the people of the Old Yishuv still lived by the wisdom of received authority and rabbinic sages. Third, unlike the Old Yishuv Jews, who waited for Heaven to take the first step in bringing about redemption, the Zionists were going to redeem the land and themselves through their own efforts. They were not counting on miracles from God: they believed *themselves* to be the miracle workers. Fourth, they chose to resurrect Hebrew from its role as an ancient language used only in sacred texts and make it the lingua franca of a reborn people. Meanwhile, the Jews of the Old Yishuv spoke Yiddish, the language of exile, and used Hebrew only for writing and sacred study. Fifth, the Zionists dressed and acted like moderns, working the land as farmers, building Tel Aviv on the sand dunes outside of Jaffa, and draining the swamps in the Jezreel Valley. But the Jews of the Old Yishuv preferred garb and grooming that seemed part of medieval Europe and not modern Israel. They dressed in the black symbolic of their mourning over the exile and lived in the holy cities of Jerusalem, Safed, Tiberias, and Hebron where they spent the day in study and religious activity. Finally, while the Old Yishuv lived on handouts—what was called the *chaluka* (literally, the distribution)—from Jews living abroad who worked rather than engaging in sacred study and holy waiting for the Messiah, the modern Zionists wanted no handouts and were determined to amass their own fortunes. They looked upon the Jews of the Old Yishuv as representing everything they had decided to abandon in their quest for a new nation: passivity, powerlessness, and mendicancy. So the Zionists offered a paradigm of a new Jew, a revolutionary new model who had thrown off the burden of the past, while the Orthodox of the Old Yishuv represented the oppressed and repressed, the outdated and shabby.

Of course the Jews of the Old Yishuv did not think of themselves in that way. On the contrary, they considered themselves protectors of the heritage of Judaism. Reacting to the portents following upon the Balfour Declaration, they saw a need to organize themselves or risk being overpowered by Zionism and Zionists. On 9 November 1917, a move was taken to form what would become "Knesset Yisrael," the Council for the Jews of Palestine, the site of the largest concentration of traditionalist Jews of the Old Yishuv.[62] This organization subsequently divided as a result of reverberations of the Hasidic-Misnagdic splits, cults of personality oriented around various charismatic rabbis, and ethnic differences among the Orthodox. The result was a new organization, the Eda Haredis, made up largely of yeshiva students who were extremely anti-Zionist. Unlike many of the members of the Old Yishuv who sought to find some modus vivendi with the Zionists, the Eda Haredis eschewed the passivity of the Old Yishuv and espoused an activist and aggressive struggle against Zionism and all it represented. It singled out the chief rabbi of the Yishuv, Abraham I. Kook, as a traitor to the cause of true Judaism because he was cooperating with the infidels and heretics of the Zionist cause.[63] From then on, the Eda Haredis would represent the most confrontational and radical of the traditionalists. They sought to define what it meant to be haredi.

For a long time the Jews of the Eda Haredis were a small minority, no more than 9,000 people out of about 175,000 Jews by the end of the 1920s. They lacked even the most basic tools for the modern political struggle. Many had no education beyond their exposure to sacred texts and had no idea how to use modern methods of organization. They could not supplant the Zionists in dealings with the British; they had no voice in the international councils. They fumed on the margins.

Besides these weaknesses, the Eda Haredis confronted an ever more successful Zionism. Even the most traditional Jews were becoming excited by the possibility that after two millennia of exile, Zionism might succeed in establishing a Jewish state. Many of the young people of the Old Yishuv found themselves lured by the prospect of becoming pioneers and builders, even if it was in a state that at best ignored and at worst denigrated traditional Jewish religion, a state that declared that labor establishing a Jewish settlement was far more important for Jewish survival than ritual praxis or Torah scholarship. Moreover, the Eda Haredis seemed an affront to Jewish solidarity, something that to many Jews—including traditionalists—seemed crucial if the British were ever to agree to a Jewish state. While a few of the Eda Haredis kept the faith and fought against Zionism for a time, most of the Orthodox exhibited feelings of doubt about their capacity to survive Zionism. When the farmer seemed a greater culture hero than a Torah sage, those who revered the sage must surely have felt themselves beleaguered.

In the meantime, at least at the beginning of the twentieth century, European contra-acculturative Orthodoxy was relatively more powerful. Yet, as we have already noted, it was also struggling against modern secular trends, including Zionism. Because it was larger, it could more easily carry on the Kulturkampf, creating institutions like the yeshiva at Volozhin, institutions that attempted to reinforce totalistic Jewish involvement using scholarship and the walls of the yeshiva as a bulwark against the corrosive impact of acculturation. But Volozhin closed. And even when other similar institutions managed to stay open, they had to permit their graduates to be reabsorbed into Jewish society, where they would be compromised by the needs of earning a living in the modern world. But of course European Jewry's greatest defeat came at the hands of persecutors who physically annihilated Jews and Jewish institutions. And then came the Second World War and the end of all Orthodoxy in Europe.

Even before, during the late 1920s, Orthodox Jews had begun to come in greater numbers to the Land of Israel, particularly as life there became an increasingly viable option. Many of these Jews had been affiliated in Europe with Agudat Israel, the union of Orthodox Jews that had been founded in May of 1912 in Silesia but had from its beginnings been a fragile amalgam of all sorts of Orthodox Jews who were united only in their opposition to reform efforts in Judaism. The Agudists, whose main raison d'être had been to act in ruling forums as a voice for providing for the religious needs of Jews, an activity that often brought them to loggerheads with Reform and other non-Orthodox Jews, had acted as a political party in Poland (and had even served in the Sejm, the Polish parliament). Through this experience Agudat Israel had found a way to reach an accommodation with some aspects of modernity; it had learned to be part of the modern political system. To the activist contra-acculturationists like those of the Eda Haredis, Agudists (with whom, until the 1940s, they remained organizationally affiliated) were accommodationists and compromisers, not truly haredi Jews, even if they were fighting the good fight against non-Orthodox Jewry and *chukos ha goyim*. When some of them came to Palestine in the 1920s, ready to accommodate to the British as they had to the Poles or Germans (for example, allowing English to be taught in their schools), the Jews of the Eda Haredis counted these new Jewish immigrants among their antagonists. And yet the Agudists were not like the Zionists; they were really Orthodox Jews. They often dressed in the long black caftans, wore beards, and were scrupulous in their observance of Jewish law. It was very hard to convincingly portray them as proponents of the *chukos ha goyim*.

Agudat Israel was a variegated organization, embracing all sorts of Orthodox Jews in Europe: Hasidim, Misnagdim, modern German neo-Orthodox, and even some religious Zionists. These were uncomfortable allies, who remained united only so long as they shared a common enemy. When they came to the Land of Israel, however, they did not share a common enemy. While some opposed Zionism, others did not. And in the Jewish environment of the Yishuv, old rivalries between Hasidim and Misnagdim, temporarily dormant, began to reawaken.

The religious Zionists could not feel comfortable with Jews who considered the only legitimate activity in Israel to be religious activity and Jewish scholarship. Land had to be tilled, settlements had to be guarded against Arab marauders, and the nation had to be built. On the other hand, there were those among the Orthodox who felt that only religious activity could truly protect Judaism. In 1939 a group representing this latter point of view, a group whose sentiments put them much closer to the Eda Haredis than anyone else, was established under the name Neturei Karta, an Aramaic term denoting "Guardians of the City." They took their name from the Talmud story of two scholars who, sent by Rabbi Judah the Prince to supervise a community, asked to see the city guards. Upon meeting them, they told the armed guards, "You are not the city's guardians but its destroyers. The scholars who study the Torah are the true guardians of the city [*Neturei Karta*]." To the Jews in 1939, the message was the same: the armed Zionists were not the true guardians—the scholars in the yeshivot and the haredim were. By 1945 the Neturei Karta and the Eda Haredis became twin forces leading the most aggressive contra-acculturation forces and the battles for traditionalist Orthodoxy. They sought to define what was truly Jewish, and what was truly Jewish was haredi.

These two groups were the only ones among the Orthodox who publicly opposed the establishment of the State of Israel as a Jewish state. These objections were publicized both in the Land of Israel and abroad. Of the two, Neturei Karta was the more active in its opposition, demanding, for example, that their members not accept Israeli identity cards, which the entire population of the newly constituted state was expected to have and hold. They refused to be conscripted in the universal draft, even going so far as to stage demonstrations which called for the Jews to surrender to the Arab armies. Later, in the early years of independence, there were other struggles against the state, including efforts to ban cars on the Sabbath from certain main thoroughfares that skirted Orthodox neighborhoods in Jerusalem, or to close social clubs that allowed mingling of the sexes and swimming pools that permitted mixed bathing. Even more in recent years, these groups have played roles in, for example, closing a bathhouse in a neighborhood adjacent to theirs, or having what they considered lewd posters removed from bus shelters in Jerusalem.

Yet, even as the two groups became more extreme and aggressive, they did not at the outset represent large numbers of people. Many of those who came just after the war found that while they might not sympathize with the Zionists' methods, they were happier to be with Jews than with Nazis and other anti-Semites. In Palestine before statehood in Israel, and then in the first years of statehood, important Hasidic community leaders succeeded in revitalizing their courts, often with help at the start from secular Zionists who looked on them with some guilt as a last remnant of a destroyed world which they, the secular Zionists, had abandoned to its death.

But if there were sympathies between the secular Zionists and the Orthodox survivors of the European extermination, they did not last very long. Already in 1943, the "Teheran Children's Affair" was emblematic of the tensions that would persist. In this affair, Polish children, uprooted from their Orthodox Jewish homes by the war in Europe, were smuggled to Palestine via Teheran, Iran. In Teheran, they were handed over to counselors from Zionist youth organizations. Rumors swiftly spread throughout the Orthodox world that the counselors had prevented the children from observing their religion. The rumors served to rally the Orthodox in the Land of Israel. Later, in the 1949 "Operation Magic Carpet," when thousands of pious Yemenite Jews were airlifted to Israel and the arriving children had their earlocks cut off, or in extreme cases were separated from their religious parents—all in the name of Zionist nation building—the Orthodox Jews had the same sort of reaction. The loudest objections came from the haredim, who tried to rally their passive counterparts to activity.

The point in both cases and others like them was simple: Zionism cannot be ignored; it must be actively opposed. In the most extreme expression of this attitude, the Satmar Hasidim explained that the Holocaust itself was divine retribution for the great sin of Zionist activity, and was thus an example of the dangers of trying to hasten the redemption by the heretical acts of infidels and sinners.

Agudat Israel, whose representatives, M. D. Lowenstein and I. M. Levin, had signed the Israeli Declaration of Independence, with Levin serving as Welfare Minister in the new Israeli government, could not continue to represent those Orthodox Jews who were outraged by Zionism. In many ways the Zionists were the most dangerous models, for they were both unapologetically secular and undeniably Jewish and as such represented the synthesis that traditionally oriented Orthodox Jews considered untenable. And when the State of Israel came into being, the dangers of Zionism were even more definitive because they were not just theoretical, they were actual.

Agudat Israel became a-Zionist in reaction. This meant that it did not embrace Zionism, because it could not share in the aspirations of the secularists or the maskilim who were part of the Zionist cause. But it was also not ready to be aggressively anti-Zionist. It sought a passive traditionalism in which it would treat the Zionists as it had treated the Polish parliament: with respect for its power and an interest in safeguarding Jewish religious concerns. So Agudat Israel accepted the concept of "living in exile among the Jews," but it did not choose to take the haredi stance of active conflict. This was left to the Eda Haredis and the Neturei Karta. The question would be: which group would end up speaking for contra-acculturative Orthodoxy in Israel? Would it be the passive traditionalists, the largest group, who looked to Agudat Israel as its voice, or would it be the more radical activists, the Eda Haredis and the Neturei Karta?

The Development of Haredi Culture in Israel

Who was coming to Israel from among the most traditionalist Orthodox? Despite the fact that the Old Yishuv was a traditional religious center, the Land of Israel was not attracting graduates of Lithuanian yeshivot like Volozhin. These institutions were still cultivating a separate elite of scholars in Europe, a cadre of young men who had to answer only to the authority of the sacred texts and their teachers in the rarefied atmosphere of the yeshiva. They did not want to leave the protective and sacred environment of the yeshiva, either for the real world of European Jewry or for the putatively holier Land of Israel. But some came nevertheless, because the situation in which their yeshivot found themselves in Europe was weakened. Revolutionary change in Russia after the First World War and political shifts throughout Europe had not only closed Volozhin, they had also made life harder for many other similar institutions.

Thus by the 1930s, three major European yeshivot partially relocated in the Land of Israel: Slobodka moved in part to Hebron, the Novardok yeshiva (Beit Yoseph) moved to Tel Aviv and its sister city B'nai Brak, and the Lumzah yeshiva went to Petah Tiqwa. It was no coincidence that the institutions did not go to Jerusalem, the capital of the Old Yishuv. The institutions were in effect riding in on the same tides that accounted for rising Zionism. Zionism in a sense had prepared the ground on which the new institutions would be planted. Tel Aviv and Petah Tiqwa were after all creations of Zionism.

The yeshiva students who came at this time eschewed the strict separatism of the Eda Haredis. On the contrary, the Lithuanian yeshivot in the Land of Israel encouraged cooperative relations between its students and the new Zionists. Many of the students hoped to be absorbed into the economic framework of the new Yishuv after marriage, an inevitable departure from the closed world of the yeshiva. The students from the Lithuanian yeshivot could not follow the path of increasing separatism forged by the Old Yishuv extremists after the Balfour Declaration and the British occupation. Instead they saw the secular Zionist "yishuv" as an integral part of their future.

The guardians of tradition in the Old Yishuv therefore did not welcome the yeshivot. Paradoxically, the existence of the new Lithuanian yeshiva in Hebron threatened them more than the immigration of secular Zionists. The Hebron yeshiva represented an alternative model of traditionalist religious Judaism. This model possessed different standards from those of the Old Yishuv on issues such as deviation from tradition, adaptation to modernity, and separatism. For example, most of the yeshiva students had shaved faces, longer hair, and no sidelocks and wore modern dress. And in contrast to accepted Jewish tradition, they remained unmarried to a relatively late age.[64] These were not merely external differences but also expressed a different mentality and relationship to the modern Jewish surroundings. While the Old Yishuv remained contra-acculturationist and Orthodox, the yeshiva world as transplanted to Israel was ready to make some compromises with acculturation.

A second element of the traditionalist Orthodoxy to come to the Land of Israel was those who were not yeshiva boys but the proletariat, the simple laborers who were part of Poalai Agudat Israel (PAI), the "Workers of Agudat Israel." Founded in Poland in 1922, PAI was a kind of labor union of Orthodox Jews sensitive to their status as workers and as Orthodox Jews in an unsympathetic world. It was at the same time critical of the petit bourgeois establishment of Orthodox Judaism and especially of their mother movement, Agudat Israel. Obviously influenced by the socialist revolutions in Russia, members of PAI considered Agudat Israel lax in the fight against the exploitation of Jewish workers. And yet the members of PAI were Orthodox Jews, no matter what their sympathies were with workers. Hence, their relations with Agudat Israel, in spite of its championing of the Orthodox way, were deeply ambivalent.

Nowhere was this ambivalence more vivid than in the emerging Zionist new Yishuv in Palestine. Here the PAI, which began its activities in 1933, felt sympathy for the Orthodox religiosity of Agudat Israel on the one hand, but shared the socialist, labor and settler aspirations of the Zionists on the other. In the eyes of some of the more conservative elders of Agudat Israel, this made PAI members dangerously anti-traditional. And indeed in many ways they were. So from the start, PAI represented a splintering of the contra-acculturationist Orthodox community. And fragmentation meant weakness.

Like other Zionist movements, PAI members established two groups for preparing potential settlers for the new Jewish state. These groups reflected the twin ideals of the movement: a concern for safeguarding Orthodoxy and a focus on the Jewish worker. The first of the settlement groups was a Noar Ha'agudati (Agudist youth) branch in Kfar Sava. The second was an Ezra Orthodox youth group in Gadera. Later, in 1944, both of them joined together to form Kibbutz Hafetz Haim, named for Rabbi Israel Meir Hacohen.

The two embryonic groups expressed the alternative to traditional religious practice in two ways. First, affected by their labor movement concerns, their approach was far more universalist, in contradiction to the Eastern European Orthodox practice of separatism and particularism. They tried to recruit followers from all Jewish quarters, thereby establishing a model for a pan-Orthodox movement and a broad-based haredi culture in Israel. Second, in contradistinction to the other secular labor movements, they expressed a new religiosity, more stringent and more willing to cut against the grain of modern acculturation. They were more religiously demanding than modern Orthodoxy and its articulated acculturative religious Zionism, and even more stringent than many of the Agudat Israel followers. This stricter, more haredi, religiosity was reflected in a greater awareness of, and care about, the minutiae of religious custom and law among the PAI than among the other groups. Moreover, this was accompanied by a reluctance to seek formalistic or technical means for bypassing religious restrictions and a stress on the need for stringencies *(chumra)*. The PAI were very simply haredim. Thus, it is easy to understand how Rabbi Israel Meir HaCohen (Kagan) (1838–1933), the "Hafetz Haim," was chosen as the eponym for the group. The Hafetz Haim, especially through his writings on the evils of gossip and rumor, represented on the one hand a moral consciousness and sensitivity (and the labor movement sensibility). On the other hand, he was also the author of the legalistic and exacting *Mishna Brura*, the single most influential book of codes and legal interpretations of the previous generation. For most Orthodox Jews this text has become the handbook for daily religious conduct, the sourcebook for stringency, and the classic expression of the haredi sensibility.

In their haredi inclinations, the PAI pioneers were also influenced by another sage, Rabbi Avraham Yishayahu Karelitz (1878–1953), known widely by his nom de plume, "the Hazon Ish." An autodidact who sought anonymity at first, the Hazon Ish was first known only to the world of the Lithuanian yeshiva through his many books. Arriving in the Holy Land in the summer of 1933, he moved to B'nai Brak, where he lived a modest, rather ascetic life. And yet in spite of a desire for personal anonymity, he found himself playing an increasingly active role in what would become the increasingly active development of haredi culture in Israel.

A claim can be made that the wider popularity of the Hazon Ish began when he came into contact with the haredi vanguard of PAI over the Judeo-legal questions regarding the Jewish sabbatical year 1937–38. According to the Torah (Exod. 23:10–11, and Lev. 25:1–7), Jews are obligated to refrain from working the earth in the Holy Land or reaping its fruits during the entirety of every seventh year. Obviously the requirement to allow land to lie fallow for an entire year is one of the most difficult ritual obligations for farmers to fulfill. In fact, because of the nature of planting cycles and their overlap with a Hebrew calendar year, farmers could actually sometimes lose a harvest for two years.

To the secular Zionists who were reclaiming their ancient land by planting it, making the dessert bloom and the swamps disappear, such a ritual obligation was a double anathema: it forced Jews to revitalize what they considered anachronistic and superfluous laws, and it also threatened the success of the new Yishuv, which depended both symbolically and in fact upon the harvests. No one among the secular Zionists ever seriously entertained the idea of observing this law. But to the Orthodox, failure to fulfill the sabbatical prohibitions represented secularization of the Holy Land. The sabbatical year was a test to see if the secular and religious could co-exist in a single national entity.

For the religious Zionists, the sabbatical year presented a real dilemma. They turned to rabbinic scholars for solutions which would permit farmers and their Jewish workers to work their lands without transgressing the Jewish law. Only in this way could they participate fully in the Zionist enterprise without having to compromise their religious principles. The most widely acceptable dispensation which would allow the farmers to continue to work the land was what came to be called the "sale allowance." According to this rabbinic procedure, farmers could formally sell their land to non-Jews (who were not bound by the rules of the sabbatical) for the duration of the year, working it then as tenant farmers. Thus the produce legally belonged to non-Jews, although they would not really reap the profits. At the end of the year, the land would be repurchased. This was of course a legal fiction, because the intention was not to really sell the land to non-Jews. In fact, the intention was just the opposite: to find a way to keep the land under Jewish control. Rabbi Abraham Y. Hacohen Kook, then rabbi of Jaffa and the surrounding settlements, gave the most latitudinarian interpretation of the "sale allowance" for the 1909–10 sabbatical, thus finding an option that Zionist and religious Zionists could both accept. Since then the "sale allowance" has been named for him, and to this day it is renewed every seven years by the state Chief Rabbinate.

The PAI haredi pioneers faced an existential dilemma in the sabbatical year of 1937–38. Dissatisfied with the "compromising" Kook sale allowance, they sought some alternative dispensation, one that reflected their greater attachment to ritual stringency. As Agudists, moreover, they refused to recognize the legitimacy of a Zionist chief rabbinate. Thus they turned to the Hazon Ish, a recognized legal scholar and dedicated Orthodox Jew, for an impartial but rigorous answer. His decision, while it permitted some slight and agriculturally insignificant work, essentially delegitimated the sale allowance. This decision was freighted with symbolic significance.

It demonstrated undeniably that Zionist and Orthodox aspirations for the Land of Israel were antithetical to each other. To observe the law of the sabbatical, the secular Zionists argued, meant to give up the active settlement process. To be a good Jew, the followers of the Hazon Ish countered, meant that one could not choose the Zionist path.

For the PAI pioneers, the Hazon Ish had one more word. He said that precisely the difficulty of the sabbatical prohibitions represented the genuine pioneer challenge; the true heroism of the Agudist pioneer demanded of him a measure of sacrifice in order to maintain the sanctity of the Land of Israel. Thus, the PAI could be greater pioneers than the compromising religious Zionists who had accepted the sale allowance and gone on with their farming. This was a strikingly clear articulation of the haredi identity which would stand in contrast to the Zionist identity. The haredim were developing a countercultural hero—the stringent and heroic adherent to Torah—who was an alternative to the farmer-soldier secular Zionist pioneer.

But the PAI were accepting land from the Zionist Jewish National Fund; they were organizing kibbutz training groups. To other haredim, this sort of venture was too much of a compromise with the unbelievers. Paradoxically, even as the PAI became more stringent by following the Hazon Ish's dicta, their compromises with the Zionists threatened the activist haredim by posing a way to acculturate to Zionist modernity. By the 1940s many of the haredim of the Land of Israel thus began to paint PAI as an independent and renegade movement that sought to dictate a false path for Agudat Israel and its sympathizers.

In response to PAI's deviation from the policies of Agudat Israel, an alternative movement, Zairei Agudat Israel (ZAI, Agudat Israel Youth), was formed to represent the true heroic Zionism. Organized in the wake of the Teheran Children's Affair, ZAI emerged from the same social framework as PAI. These youths were also confronted with the crumbling of the traditional framework as a consequence of emancipation and enlightenment. Like PAI, ZAI also aimed to attract youth from all currents of Orthodoxy, not only the Hasidic or Misnagdic stream. Its leadership included German and Hungarian immigrants, Gur Hasidim, and graduates of Lithuanian yeshivot. In the Land of Israel, the focus of its activities was organizing students in haredi schools in an attempt to combat the abandonment of religion as a result of exposure to the surrounding secular Zionist culture. In this context ZAI attempted to establish schools for the refugees that reached Israel, hoping to avoid another Teheran Children's Affair. A long-term objective was to establish a kibbutz that would bring into being an exemplary model of social and religious life. Yet despite this pioneering attitude, ZAI remained militantly anti-Zionist.

This position led to tension between ZAI and PAI, which tended to work more closely with the Zionist institutions. However, for all of its opposition to Zionism, ZAI remained Israel-centric and thus sharply criticized the focus of its parent organization, Agudat Israel, on European Jewry and its neglect of the Land of Israel in its activities before the war. ZAI, moreover, stressed the centrality of the Land of Israel to Jewish life after the Holocaust.

In some ways, ZAI went too far for its constituency. It repeatedly questioned the policies of Agudat Israel and the religious Zionists, effectively cutting off those organizations as sources for its membership. Secondly, its Israel-centrism led to ZAI members raising the Zionist accusation of Jewish passivity in the Holocaust, a position that essentially indicted those Jews, including the Agudists and other contra-acculturative Orthodox, who had remained in Europe to face annihilation rather than come to the Land of Israel when confronted with destruction. They also questioned the actions of rabbis and sages before and during the Holocaust.

To be sure, ZAI, like other Orthodox groups, held the sages in high regard. They too were a young guard who sought to express their zeal, choosing to do so in a haredi way. They were deferential not only to the Hazon Ish, whose influence was on the rise, but also to Rabbi Yitzchak Zeev (Velvele) Soloveitchik of Brisk, who had fled to the Land of Israel at the beginning of World War II and who, like the Hazon Ish, filled no formal public role but exercised influence by virtue of his reputation as a scholar and religious zealot. Both the Hazon Ish and Velvele Soloveitchik were well suited to be generic haredi leaders, for they had no particularistic affiliation. As a new generic haredi group the ZAI were the young champions of these generic sages.

In addition to the two rabbis, the ZAI cultivated leaders of the great Hasidic courts: Gur (Rabbi Avraham Mordechai Alter), Belz (Rabbi Aaron Rokeach), Vizhnitz (Rabbi Elazar Hager), who arrived as refugees from the Nazis and who also were made generic haredi heroes. ZAI were making universal haredi leaders out of men who once had been rabbis for particular groups, including sages from the world of the Lithuanian yeshiva of Mir, Rabbi Eliezer Yehudah Finkel, and from Ponevezh, Rabbi Joseph Kahaneman. But not every sage could be the same sort of hero.

The differences between Rabbi Kahaneman and the Hazon Ish exemplify the two emergent images of the haredi Jew in the Land of Israel. Kahaneman was educated in important Lithuanian yeshivot and later became the rabbi of Ponevezh and established a yeshiva there. During the war he escaped to the Land of Israel and re-established the Ponovezh Yeshiva in B'nai Brak. By this act he sought to renew and replant the ancient heritage of Lithuania on the new-old soil of Israel. He could essentially reinvent Ponovezh in Israel. And he did. Starting with seven students, by the 1950s it had developed into one of the largest and most important yeshivot in Israel. Kahaneman was able to nurture his institution and the kind of contra-acculturative Orthodoxy it fostered. In the effort he adapted to a "division of labor" between the yeshiva world that remains focused around Torah learning and ritual activity, and the Jewish lay world that provides financial support. In this effort, Kahaneman did not hesitate to turn to the left-wing socialist leadership or to Western Jewry as a whole, for support. He based his claims for financial assistance on the traditional arguments, but also invoked four additional reasons for support: (1) the nostalgic and romanticized feelings of Jews toward the world of their childhood that was destroyed in such a brutal manner; (2) the guilt feelings that began to develop in many that rebelled against religion and tradition, especially after that world had been abandoned and subsequently destroyed in the Shoah; (3) the consequent emotional need of many to eternalize the memories of their dead loved ones in a traditional religious framework like the yeshiva, a setting that seemed at least on the surface to mirror the one lost in the Holocaust. The yeshiva Rabbi Kahaneman symbolized and headed was to the non-Orthodox Jew a living museum. It was also helpful to his cause that Rabbi Kahaneman was a benign personality who presented a tolerant public face, an attitude that represented a change in the image of the yeshiva from a hostile institution to a valued cultural icon.

Unlike this founder of an institution and builder of bridges, the Hazon Ish exemplified instead the ideal of the spiritual dimension of Torah study. In 1940, under the guidance of the Hazon Ish, a Kollel Avrechim (yeshiva for young married scholars) opened in B'nai Brak. It was meant to provide an environment for those who wished to dedicate themselves to lifelong Torah scholarship, a place where no compromise and minimal contact with the real world outside was necessary. During most of its existence it was called Kollel Ha Hazon Ish, and it served as the model for all of the *kollelim* (post-graduate yeshiva institutes) that were established during the 1950s and later.

The Kollel Ha Hazon Ish was an important catalyst for the development of a haredi society in the West and the Land of Israel, for it would provide a cadre of people devoted exclusively to the sacred texts and uncompromising sages. They would intensify Jewish life in the rarefied atmosphere of the kollel and contemplate with scorn at all those who were either passive in the face of the acculturative and heretic trends of Zionism and modern life or who actively took part in it. The people of the kollel, and in particular the young men who were its students, would in time join Agudat Israel and focus it upon the yeshiva as a spiritual and social center of haredi life. These active traditionalists became the soul of the traditionalist Orthodox community in Israel and the world. They would serve as the conscience of those who remained opposed to modern secular trends. Instead of those who modeled their approach on Rabbi Kahaneman, or even the PAI, these Jews would become the guardians of the haredi way of life. It would, however, take several more years for them to become self-assured and politically powerful enough to take over the spirit of the haredi world.

With the end of the Second World War and the establishment of the new State of Israel two years later in 1948, the haredi element in general found itself overwhelmed by the Zionist fever that overtook all elements of the Jewish world. At this time the haredim had no illusions. They knew that a Jewish state would not only be secular in nature but would also be controlled by the militantly antireligious socialist party. And yet at the same time that the haredim felt overwhelmed by Zionism and the new state, they were articulating a counterculture that was being defined more and more by its opposition to the modern secular Israeli state. Preservation of the tradition in the face of modern secularity became the moving force behind haredi life. Through their continuing and growing struggle with this modern secularity, traditionalists developed a finely tuned self-image of themselves as a separate group (the Orthodox believers and true Jews) and an increasingly conscious, open articulation of their role. Those who differed from them were as seen as straying from the authentic or legitimate path.

The haredim became increasingly pre-occupied with the struggle, sometimes even neglecting the very elements of the culture they were presumably defending. Yet ironically the modern secular reality continued to define the "battlegrounds" on which the militant struggle took place. The forces of tradition had to respond to whatever moves were made by the modernists, to continually prove themselves in the face of modern Israeli culture and society. Thus, the ideological concerns of the community were determined by, and in response to, developments from without.[65]

Outside of Israel some traditionalist Orthodox Jews not only defined themselves in opposition to modern secularity but began to define themselves most distinctly by their opposition to Zionism and delegitimation of the State of Israel. Thus, while the Satmar Hasidim, for example, were making their peace with contemporary America as they developed successful diamond and electronics businesses and institutions of learning and worship in New York, they were expressing their haredi side through unremitting opposition to Zionism, often publicly articulated during the 1970s and 1980s in full-page anti-Israel ads in *The New York Times*. Some might even argue that this extreme antagonism to Zionism and the State of Israel was a compensation for the compromises they made with modern secularity in America. After all, many of these Americans were out in the business world while the new generation of Israeli haredim were studying Torah in yeshivot and kollelim for longer periods of their lives.

From Weakness to Strength: The Revitalization of the Haredim

During the late 1940s and the 1950s, haredim in America were involved in the quiet process of rebuilding themselves. This meant establishing yeshivot and Hasidic courts and easing many Holocaust survivors—the immigrants who were the lifeblood of this Orthodoxy—into America. It was a time to have children and make money, start businesses, and to take measure of what was and was not possible in the new American environment, so different from the Europe they had just fled.

In pre-State Israel the reality the haredim confronted was more turbulent. In the feverish time of the establishment of the new state, the haredim seemed to be barely holding on to their followers. Not only was secular Zionism apparently a great success, but among those who considered themselves Orthodox there were disputes and serious differences of opinion about how to respond to the Zionist success in establishing a state. The Neturei Karta, who had recently taken control of the Eda Haredis, took a public stand against the establishment of a Jewish state—not a very popular position in those days.[66] Agudat Israel, on the other hand, was not ready to take such an extreme stand and therefore hesitated to enunciate any public reaction. It was caught in a bind, because on one side an important part of its leadership was committed to an anti-Zionist ideology, while on the other, many people recognized the errors in Agudat Israel's prewar refusal to maintain relations with the Zionists, especially in light of the human cost that this refusal had taken in the Holocaust. Had Agudat Israel adopted a stronger pro-Zionist stand in favor of a Jewish settlement in Israel, perhaps many Jews who perished in Europe might have decided that they could live an authentic Jewish life in Israel and might have emigrated earlier and thus saved their lives.

Consequently Agudat Israel began negotiations with the Jewish Agency, the parent body of the new Israeli government, with regard to its participation in the united Jewish effort to establish a Jewish State and help absorb new immigrants. Only as part of the system, Agudat Israel leaders reasoned, could they struggle successfully against attacks on Orthodoxy, such as the Teheran Children's Affair or later in the tragedy of the Yemenite children in Operation Magic Carpet, and thereby contribute to establishing a true Jewish presence in the Land of Israel. Moreover, cooperation with Zionist representatives was necessary in the efforts to rehabilitate world Jewry after the Shoah and to resettle in Israel the thousands of Jews expelled from Muslim countries (most notably Egypt, Syria, Iraq). (After all, many of those Jews were traditionally oriented and represented souls to be saved and young Jews to be educated in the ways of Torah.) In those days, then, Agudat Israel evolved its strategy of being a-Zionist, negotiating with the Israeli government as it had with the Polish one, yet keeping aloof from the enthusiasms of Zionism. The organization's guiding principle remained the conviction that it alone could provide for the religious needs of its traditionalist members; therefore its growing network of contacts with the governing authorities was absolutely necessary.

The Agudat Israel approach seemed to work fairly well. It could point to dramatic successes in its negotiations with the Ben-Gurion government (Prime Minister Ben-Gurion was himself a confirmed unbeliever). Agudat Israel representatives walked away with an agreement signed by the Zionist leadership, including David Ben-Gurion, which safeguarded the Sabbath as the national day of rest in Israel, provided a religious public educational system and allowed private religious education as an option, maintained *kashrut* in a variety of public and government sponsored institutions, confirmed the religious Orthodox control of matters of personal status (such as who was married, who divorced, who genuinely converted to Judaism), and later granted exemption from the universal military draft to yeshiva students. To be sure, the agreement did not completely satisfy Agudat Israel, because it contained no real obligations, only a declaration of intent. But the agreement articulated the outlines of the basic concerns of haredi culture.

One of the key concessions Agudat Israel won from the Zionist Israeli government was achieved almost unwittingly during the War of Independence. Yeshiva students were exempted from army duty. As we shall argue below, this allowance would in the long run serve as one of the pillars of the haredi world. To be sure, even before the Declaration of Independence and during the arduous battles for Jerusalem in the War of Liberation of 1947–48, the leaders of the Eda Haredis–Neturei Karta declared that yeshiva students should not even report for temporary duty in the army. This position was not based only on the premise that it is forbidden to aid the Zionists, but also on the claim that Torah study also contributes to security no less than bearing arms. This was, after all, what the Neturei Karta were—Torah guardians of the city. In actuality, most of the yeshiva students were drafted in one way or another during the War of Independence and a majority fought in what was essentially a civilian army.

At the outset the question of army service and subjection to the universal draft centered on the Orthodox Jews of Jerusalem, where many of the students were from

Old Yishuv yeshivot. In those institutions, there was a combination of youths and married men, many of whom lived off contributions that came from abroad. There are no data on their numbers, but most estimates put their number at between 150 and 200 heads of families. Those people never saw themselves as part of the Zionist entity that had evolved around them and never expected that they would be required to perform some type of public service in order to be exempt from armed service. Their small number, the assumption that they were part of a residual old world remnant that would continue to decline in the years ahead, the feeling by the Israeli government that they were part of a quickly receding past, and the desire of the new leaders to prevent an ugly confrontation with the Eda Haredis led to a de facto agreement to completely exempt yeshiva students from army service.

But what seemed a concession to the past became an inducement to the future. In fact, the exemption would in time serve as an incentive for increasing numbers of haredi young men to find their way to the yeshiva in which they would spend many years. It was also an incentive for Hasidim, whose essential character had often stressed piety over scholarship, to now also organize yeshivot and become a society of scholars rather than exclusively a society of piety.

After the exemption became accepted practice, haredi young men *(avrechim)* would marry, start a family, and pass their army years protected inside the yeshiva-kollel walls. They would do so with the tacit permission of the state and the approval of the haredi world which had nothing but praise for a person who dedicated his life to Torah learning (and chose not to be swallowed up by the *chukos ha goyim* of the Zionist army). Moreover, the longer the avrechim stayed in the ivory tower of the yeshiva-kollel, the more they would be confirmed as uncompromising contra-acculturationists. It was the crucible of haredi culture.

In America, the yeshiva-kollel would do the same, although the pressures to get out and work were greater because there was no draft to avoid and no tacit legitimation of an alternative Jewish identity implied by one's involvement in American society. In America the risks of leaving the yeshiva were less. Nevertheless, American Orthodoxy moved to the right as a result of the yeshiva-kollel boys who, when they were out in the community, still carried with them the values and worldviews of their yeshiva days. But they were not as religiously stringent as their Israeli counterparts. Indeed, if Americans wanted their sons to be truly dedicated to Orthodox Judaism, many sent them to a yeshiva-kollel in Israel.

Israel was also different in that the Israeli government unwittingly helped to support a network of feeder primary schools which would serve as a conduit for young boys who would ultimately attend the yeshiva-kollel. In the pre-State period Agudat Israel and its members had set up a variety of independent Orthodox schools. After the establishment of the State and in the interests of coalition building, the government recognized the Agudist schools and made them eligible for state funding. This meant a huge influx of tax funds would be available for those institutions that had until then lived off donations for the most part. Within one year the number of students in haredi institutions increased by at least 50 percent, and they were often filled with immigrants from Muslim countries who were traditional in orientation but who lacked their own school system. Over the years the haredi independent school system has steadily continued to grow. And during that time it has received 70–90 percent of its budget from Israeli taxes.

Not only did the school system now provide a separate and well-supported educational environment for haredi youth, it also furnished an arena of employment for graduates of that educational system.[67] Males could serve as teachers. And because the haredi school system rigorously and absolutely separated the sexes in its institutions, it also provided a workplace for women teachers. The haredi woman was coming into her own.

In Europe the Orthodox had already established educational institutions for women, a great break with tradition, which suggested that women's capacity for Jewish study was limited. Among the most prominent of those institutions was the Bais Ya'akov Teachers Seminary founded in Krakow, Poland, in 1917 by Sara Schnirer and with the support of Agudat Israel.[68] That institution, a branch of which had set up a teachers' seminary in Israel, was now geared up to provide instructors for the haredi school system.

There were some who had at the outset worried about the development of the Bais Ya'akov schools, seeing in them a modernist and maskil trend. Teaching women Torah was revolutionary in the Orthodox world. The belief in some quarters was that "women who are educated and work outside the home bring back with them new ideas and new perceptions of themselves as complete human beings."[69] With these notions, they might upset the traditional order of Orthodox family life in which the woman was essentially subservient to the demands of being a wife and mother. Indeed in some quarters the Bais Ya'akov girls were definitely viewed as overly modernist. But in Israel, they fostered a trend that in many ways strengthened the haredi way of life.

Although in the past marriage had provided the reason for a man to leave the yeshiva to support his family, during the 1950s marriage—particularly to a Bais Ya'akov graduate—enabled a man to remain within the yeshiva-kollel framework. The new teachers from Bais Ya'akov seminaries were encouraged to support their families and allow their husbands to continue study of the Torah. The main proponents of the ideal were the Hazon Ish and Abraham Joseph Wolff. In the Bais Ya'akov teachers seminary in B'nai Brak, Wolff taught that a wife who aids her husband in learning Torah will share his reward in the world to come. Girls began to look for kollel boys to marry.

The new ideal was not welcomed by many parents. Although they wanted their daughters to marry haredi yeshiva students, as had the Orthodox for generations, they expected the men to eventually seek a profession, with which they could support a family. But the young who sought to outdo their elders found the new arrangement a way of asserting their independence without undermining tradition. They could be more stringent in their dedication to religion by enabling the males to study longer in the Torah academy while providing women with a far more responsible position in the Torah world than they had ever had before. A girl did not need to be a fishmonger or grocer—as perhaps her grandmother might have been in Europe—to enable her husband to study Torah. She could be a respected teacher in a haredi or other religious school system (drawing a respectable salary from the educational institutions which were receiving state aid). Despite parental opposition, that type of marriage became the norm by the late 1950s, both in Israel and abroad.

After the pattern was established, marriage no longer represented a transition from the sealed and ideal world of the yeshiva to the real world of compromise. Now it was simply a life-cycle event that occurred within the framework of the sealed and insular yeshiva-kollel world. After marriage a young man and his wife could remain committed institutionally and ideologically to maintaining a separate and religious stringent, haredi, lifestyle. And they did.

A Society of Scholars: Institutionalizing Separatism

In a world in which modernity and secularity were constantly assaulting tradition, those who sought to maintain the strictures and patterns of tradition needed a sanctuary. In the past they could depend on ghettoes which not only kept the Jews out of mainstream culture but also protected them from what some on the inside perceived as the destructiveness of the outside world. If life in the Pale of Settlement in Russia kept the Jews subservient, it also guaranteed that they would remain dominated by a Jewish order. But the ghetto walls had been breached and broken, and since the emancipation and enlightenment the ghettoes had been places Jews left behind. While haredi society, in its championing of contra-acculturation, had tried wherever possible to reconstruct the ghetto, living in neighborhoods where Jewish life was most intense and intimate, this was not always possible, especially during the extraordinary dislocations of the twentieth century when mobility rather than stability became the rule.

In the diaspora—America, Australia, and Western Europe—the Orthodox, and particularly the haredim, located themselves in separate communities. In Israel this was more difficult, for at least two reasons. First, as Jews even the Orthodox were often swept up by Zionism and therefore wanted to be part of the great return of their people to their ancient homeland. Accordingly, while their Orthodoxy might have pushed them to separatism, their Jewishness drew them toward participation in the larger society, which after all was a Jewish society. Second, Israel and the Yishuv were relatively small societies, and at the outset their settlements, even in the big cities, were small. Hence, even if Orthodox Jews were located in a particular neighborhood, the secular Zionist world found ways to penetrate its margins and sometimes its heart. This was the case in Jerusalem of the 1950s in a controversy over a secular Zionist youth center, the Moadon Ha Meriva, which conducted its activities on the Sabbath right inside Mea Shearim, one of the haredi neighborhoods near the center of Jerusalem. Haredim wanted to close the center, while secular Zionists wanted it to remain open. The complications of the issue are vividly captured in the following account by a man who is today editor of one of the most militant and activist haredi periodicals:

> The *chiloinim* [secularists] of then were brothers, literally members of the family, cousins. All were from the same family (which incidentally caused some

> extremism in certain elements of the secular). They lived together with us. There was not yet the ghettoization of living conditions that is so developed today. Within the Hungarian houses, inside Mea Shearim, one could hear a radio on Shabbat![70] This came from the [secular] neighbor who lived within the Hungarian houses, the son of Moishe who went bad. This was *not* some secularist who invaded Mea Shearim. The sons of Mrs. Shosha came on Shabbat morning with big cigarettes to the alleys of the synagogues and stood tall, and the boys who carried a holy book cowered off on the side against the wall. But this was already gone by the time I was growing up, but it was typical of the days leading up to the rise of the state. This [chiloini] was already a member of the Haganah or Etzel [Zionist military organizations], he was a *chevreman* [a regular guy]. And if he was not one of those smart guys, he had stayed in the yeshiva.
>
> There was a great crisis. Out of full classes in Yeshivas Etz Chaim there remained only a smattering of students.
>
> When I was a boy, there were still large numbers of chiloinim who were on my street. I remember that Moadon Ha Meriva [the center of dissension] was near what today is Yeshivas Slonim, and it was a place where they wanted young boys and girls to mix together! And who do you think wanted to allow this abomination—an outsider? No, these were local boys who wanted to open it.[71]

For haredim, then, the challenge was to find some place where they could remain protected from the invasions of the culture they were struggling against. One way, of course, was to expel all non-haredi elements from their neighborhoods. This was done with increasing vigor during the 1970s and 1980s. And it was done by surrounding the foreign element, be it a non-Orthodox resident or institution, and squeezing it out by a war of attrition that included economic sanctions, violent harassment (broken windows, flat tires, etc.), and political pressure. The sanctions became possible only because the haredi world in Israel, buoyed by the concessions of the government, had grown in size and confidence.

A second mode of separation from the secular world, the yeshiva, was tacitly supported by the State of Israel, particularly by the exemption of its students from the military draft. Within their walls, as young men and aged sages reviewed the ancient texts and hallowed traditions, time seemed to stop and stability reigned. There yesterday still remained regnant over today and tomorrow. After the Second World War, Misnagdim of the Lithuanian yeshivot and Hasidim alike created institutions of Jewish learning *(mosdos)*, and transformed themselves into societies of scholars who discouraged compromises with the world outside the yeshiva and became the hard core of the new haredi world.

By the late 1960s, the scholars had taken over the major leadership of the haredi world, the rabbinical courts of the Eda Haredis, and were also becoming the persons whose certification of food as kosher was the most authoritative. Thus the uncompromising scholar rapidly became the symbol of the ideal Jew to the haredi world.

Increasing Radicalization: The Rise of Active Haredim

As the number of haredim grew, so did their needs and demands. Agudat Israel found itself forced constantly to find new religious needs of its constituents that it could "fix" in the government. And it had to find constituents who would participate in the Zionist system by voting for Agudat Israel at election time. For Agudat Israel and the passive traditionalists, maintaining a balance between ideological opposition and instrumental cooperation became a key feature of existence. Only thus could the party exert influence in the coalition politics that was a constant feature of every Israeli government. This was not easy.

Extreme elements, the most actively contra-acculturationist, like the Eda Haredis, called upon its supporters to refrain from voting, for even such a seemingly benign act gave legitimacy to the heretics whose presence in the Holy Land was a sacrilege. To maintain a following, Agudat Israel, on the other hand, had to show its supporters that by not voting they might engender other sacrileges, and they had to demonstrate their achievements. These included garnering funds for mosdos and assuring that religious matters were not slighted by the state, something the Eda Haredis always claimed.

Among the first to arise in the new state were: (1) the education of new immigrants, especially those from Islamic countries who were now in refugee camps; (2) universal army or national service for women; and (3) Sabbath observance in areas near haredi neighborhoods in Jerusalem. On the first point Agudat Israel lobbied for funneling new immigrants into the haredi schools. On the second, they led the battle against forcing religious girls to serve in what the haredim viewed as the licentious environment of the army, where sexual relations between unsupervised boys and girls were a constant danger. They could not exempt the girls, as they had the boys, for girls did not go to the yeshiva-kollel to become clergy. On the third point, the haredim fought to close or cordon off their neighborhoods to prohibited car traffic on the Sabbath. The closing of Sabbath Square, a main intersection of Jerusalem which bordered on Mea Shearim, a haredi stronghold, became the focus of many of those concerns in the early years.

The conflicts provided an important political lesson for the haredi Jews. They learned that in a democratic state, the power of the majority is limited when it confronts an opposing minority willing to fight an issue at any cost. In order to preserve tradition, the haredim were, ironically, using modern methods and the modern political system. With every victory the haredim became more dominated by their activist wing, who were ready to fight every issue with unremitting zeal. The activists made it their business to pick fights with modern culture wherever they encountered it. Struggles were mounted against the drafting of girls for the Israeli army, on behalf of deferments for yeshiva students, and later against archeological digs that seemed to desecrate ancient Jewish cemeteries, bus shelters trimmed with posters that haredim found too explicit sexually, the operation of a Turkish bath near a haredi neighborhood, and the presence of certain heretical books in particular neighborhood shops. The list was endless, driven only by the need of the haredim to be increasingly stringent in their Judaism and by the party's need to demonstrate their indispensability.

In time Agudat Israel took its cue from the Neturei Karta–Eda Haredis, whose members were increasingly seen as the heroes of the haredi struggle. And when the police arrested them or beat them back, sometimes bloodying a few heads, the activists became martyrs. Those who marched away in handcuffs or were seen running out of the way of billy clubs were most frequently the yeshiva boys. The yeshiva-kollel avrechim distinguished themselves in the community by their stringency. The process was one of unremitting and escalating intensity.

The public and often violent deeds of the activist traditionalists have been described as acts of protest, with elements of verbal and physical violence. In actuality it is rare for Neturei Karta to initiate demonstrations. Generally the demonstrations develop spontaneously, and as a result of Neturei Karta's subsequent rabble-rousing they become wild and violent. Stones are thrown, barricades are erected, and occasionally some glass is broken or someone is roughed up. However, when we consider the use of violence in activities of zealots, it must be remembered that the haredim's use of violence is quite limited. Of course it is true that stoning a passing car could lead to a catastrophe, but in fact that hardly ever happens. When it did happen that a driver was badly injured by a stone, the haredi leadership was seized with anxiety, came to visit the injured party in the hospital, and apologized.

The complex relationship of the haredim to physical violence is connected to their minority status and their dependence on the surrounding society. Should their level of violence reach a certain point, they realize, they are likely to feel the iron hand of repression. Indeed, an Israeli haredi who throws stones on the Sabbath will not be forced to desecrate the Sabbath by being made to ride in an Israeli police car if he is arrested. (This is not the case in America, as some haredim discovered when they tried to stone a New York City bus that passed through their Brooklyn neighborhood on the Sabbath and were promptly hauled to jail in the police car.) But if he goes too far, he may be punished more severely than he can tolerate.

But there are other reasons why haredim limit protest violence. Haredim in general, and even the activist zealots among them, see themselves as the legitimate expression of traditional Jewish society and the bearer of its values. The physical injury or perhaps the death of another Jew, even if he is an atheist, is perceived as an unjustified and particularly strong deviation. The use of violence with the intent to kill by any extreme ideological group, be they religious fundamentalists or political extremists, is vested with a dimension of sovereignty. It implies the desire to direct history. The great majority of passive traditionalists who consider the Jewish people to be in exile and thus neither able to nor permitted to take their historical fate into their own hands by seeking sovereignty, are not prepared to direct history—even if their activist-fundamentalist counterparts outside the haredi world may be. Violence is far too directive for a people who sees itself as outside of history, awaiting a millennium. So, although violence sometimes seems to get out of hand, it has thus far been relatively circumscribed and benign.

Leadership of the Sages

And who was prompting the activists? Who was molding the ideal as haredi society grew in the State of Israel? Key to much of the process were the sages, the yeshiva heads and Hasidic rebbes, whose influence was growing exponentially as the time men spent in their institutions of learning increased. Increasingly those who were not endowed with personal charisma became enhanced with the charisma of office that flowed from their position as heads of major Hasidic dynasties or yeshivot. As such, they were preceived as all-knowing because they had *da'as Torah,* knowledge of the wisdom of the Torah, a wisdom that borders on divine inspiration. With *da'as Torah,* the sages were able to make all sorts of demands on their students.

The sages—they were always men, and usually aged men—based their authority on a time-honored Jewish tradition of venerating the elders. And in addition they now headed increasingly powerful institutions. As more Jews looked to them for guidance, adjudication, kashrut supervision, and education, their authority consolidated. The rabbis—particularly those who were now generic leaders—felt themselves to be bound only by the Torah and not by the dictates of the Zionist state. And because even the socialists viewed Israel as a Jewish state, upholding Jewish values, the State of Israel could not permit itself to punish rabbis that rebelled against the laws for religious reasons.

In the framework of Agudat Israel, an effort had been made to give formal institutional expression to the growing body of pan-local generic haredi rabbinic leaders. Formally established in 1912, Moetzet G'Dolay Ha Torah (the Council of Torah Sages, the rabbinical advisory board of the party) included from the outset rabbis who represented the various streams of traditional Orthodox Jewry that were ready to be included in the party. It included Hasidic leaders, yeshiva heads, respected adjudicators, and renowned Talmud scholars. Moetzet G'dolay Ha Torah was to emphasize the common and unifying elements of both the Jewish people and their rabbinic leadership and to downplay what divided the traditional Orthodox community (for example, the Hasidic-Misnagdic split) which through Agudat Israel sought to represent all of European Jewry.

From the outset Moetzet G'dolay Ha Torah was supposed to represent a definitive and unrestricted religious leadership. The council would protect Agudat Israel from the modern and acculturative Orthodox left. All decisions it made would be binding on all *erlicher yidn,* for no one questioned the sages and still called himself haredi.[72]

The Torah council also served as a protection for Agudat Israel from those on its traditionalist right flank. Thus, though there might be some activist traditionalists who opposed Agudat Israel's contacts with the more modern elements, the presence of the rabbis on the Moetzet G'dolay Ha Torah served to offset any efforts to delegitimate it. They gave the new organization a legitimacy which contact with modernity and the West might have otherwise taken away from it. Moetzet G'dolay Ha Torah was thus a crucial element in the emergence of Agudat Israel. The party needed its *g'dolim* (sages) to negotiate the narrows between left and right in traditionalist Orthodoxy. Everything seemed to be converging to give enhanced power to the aged sages.

The sage was important also to the young activist haredim. These radicals, like the Neturei Karta, claimed to operate according to the fundamental wishes of the sages. With this legitimation, neither Agudat Israel or any other passive traditionalists could object to their aims. Thus, the passive traditionalists in a sense became ideological hostages of their activist, extremist, fundamentalist right wing. That is, they could not deny the activists' claims to be defending the ways of the Torah. So even if Agudat Israel and the more passive traditionalists were not comfortable with the aggressive approach the radicals used, they could not denounce the aims of their actions. However, the radicals were not completely free also since they needed a sage to support and defend their aims.

In many ways the sages can also be considered passive traditionalists. They were not ready to go out on the streets to fight against the modern world either. They sought to enclose themselves in scholarly communities. They were dealing with academic questions, talmudic legalisms. But the young radicals whom they instructed were not tempered by independent, traditional community standards. The traditional community with its customs had after all been remodelled by the events of modernity—revolution, sweeping migration, the Holocaust, and the rise of a new state and society. The only guides left were the scholars and their books. The radicals, lacking a true sense of the way things always had been done (for the past was after all gone), instead put the scholars' words into practice and drew the scholars into the struggle. This often made the rabbis uncomfortable with their followers, especially when the latter engaged in violent, unbecoming zealotry. Occasionally the sages found themselves in the position of being forced to support extreme actions that had been neither approved by them nor discussed with them. Nevertheless, in principle and often in practice, the opinion of the sages became law for the haredim.

This was an extraordinary reversal of history. The haredi world had found a way of bringing to center stage the very rabbis whom the secular and modern world had tried to relegate to the junkyard of history, or at the very least to the obscure and marginal academy of Jewish learning. Old men with long grey beards who spent their lives steeped in often recondite and archaic texts, who, like all academicians, could afford to ignore reality, were suddenly called upon to direct the behavior of people living in the modern world.[73] In a modern state, they had to deal with new questions and dilemmas every day. The haredim had brought the sages back from a symbolic death; and they had brought them back to a life more powerful than they had ever known before. The Moetzet G'dolay Ha Torah was no mere legal authority; it was a moral compass and politico-religious authority. No mere local rebbe or yeshiva head, no unsung scholar of some unread text, the new sage was a public leader in competition with modern leaders of other groups—including the state leaders.

To be sure, there were problems in the councils of sages. In the past the Moetzet G'dolay Ha Torah had been asked to offer opinions only on rare occasions, and then only on issues of principle. And the matters were often academic, particularly in Europe, where Jewry remained an increasingly fragmented diaspora community. In Israel, however, the Moetzet G'dolay Ha Torah was asked to render practical decisions which could become politically consequential, particularly when Agudat Israel became a key player in the coalition politics of Israeli life. The need to take a unified stance on matters of policy rather than principle served to emphasize the differences among the rabbis who sat on the council. Suddenly the old divisions among Hasidim, and between them and the Misnagdim, once again became salient. The old rivalries and conflicts, muted for the battle against *maskilim* and modernity, now were again discernable. And now the sages found themselves facing each other in a standoff.

Thus, the followers of one of the Hasidic rebbes who sat on the council would not abide by a majority opinion of the council if this meant denying the point of view of their particular rebbe. How, after all, could a hasid who believes his own leader is endowed with charisma, an intermediary to God, a man with divine inspiration, disavow his rebbe's point of view and accept the decision of a Misnagid or some other Hasidic rebbe? He could not. And could a yeshiva head of the Lithuanian Misnagid persuasion abide by a Hasidic ruling that he opposed in principle? Never. Collective decisions became increasingly difficult for the councils of sages. As the haredi Abraham Lazerson once explained, from the perspective of da'as Torah there is no possibility of winners and losers, no rule of majority and minority where the former imposes its will on a dominated minority; there is only a series of valid points of view.[74]

When the rabbis became snared in their own rivalries, their followers—those moved to react to developing events in the modern world—became the de facto leaders. And thus, even though the disciples invoke the authority and da'as Torah of the sages as their guiding principle—and the sages remain silent, for they cannot speak in a single voice—it is really the young activists who hold the power. And as young activists they are far more likely to take extreme and often radically uncompromising positions. With the paralytic silence of the sages, which passes as acquiescence, and the support of the passively contra-acculturationist, the fundamentalists carry the day.

The Sephardi Element

In Israel of the 1950s, there entered into the political and ideological framework one more element: traditionally religious Jews from Muslim countries. Sometimes called Sephardim, and at other times Edot Ha'Mizrach (ethnics from the east), the Jews from Muslim countries, most of them North African and largely from Morocco, were committed to a traditional kind of Judaism. Obviously, after the Teheran Children's Affair and the separation of many Yemenite children from the tradition, haredi Jews decided the Sephardim belonged in the haredi camp.

But without the history of the tensions and strains with acculturation and assimilation that had formed Ashkenazic (European) Orthodoxy, the Sephardim could not be considered part of European Orthodoxy. Thus, they were neither Hasidim nor Misnagdim. They were neither acculturationist nor contra-acculturationist. Nevertheless, when they came to Israel, clearly a cultural enclave of the West in spite of being situated in the Middle East, they experienced a culture shock of major proportions. Many, seeking to make it in a new world, abandoned the strict observances of their forebears even as they remained emotionally attached to tradition. Torn from a cultural milieu and social reality in which tradition, Jewish observance, and folkways were concentric and simultaneous, they developed a kind of hybrid marginal culture which made it possible to go to a strictly traditional Sabbath service on Saturday morning and then attend a totally secular event like a football game the same afternoon, without being troubled by feelings of duplicity. They could look upon the pronouncements or blessings of holy rabbis or upon the actions of political leaders with nearly equal veneration. In fact, the two often coincided. The Sephardim became secular Israelis who nonetheless maintained ties to the folk tradition which was also Jewish tradition.

Because they were not secular, and certainly not Hasidic, a small minority of the Sephardim were absorbed into Lithuanian Misnagdic-style yeshivot. They learned Yiddish, dressed in the black of the haredi world, and began to take positions that characterized that world. In Israel, they would become the venerated holy men and leaders of the first group of Sephardim.

More Sephardim who followed the religious vocation were absorbed into a series of specifically Sephardic yeshivot which were modeled on, but separate from, the parallel Ashkenazic institutions. Their teachers, however, were not Sephardim but rather Ashkenazi haredim. In time there was a Sephardi educational structure, pan-local (i.e., made up of people who were national or even international religious leaders) in character. Those who controlled the structure saw natural allies in the Lithuanian yeshivot which were also pan-local. Indeed, some of the controlling elements were Lithuanians themselves. But at the time that all this happened the haredi world was in its phase of increasing localism, in which a balkanization was occurring, with each group claiming its leaders to be predominant and seeking funds from all sources for its special institutions and projects. In the face of these developments, the Sephardim found themselves powerless, for they did not have a fully developed local structure which could compete for funds and symbolic power in the haredi world. They had jumped into the haredi world of the yeshivot without the previous history and institutions (established in Europe) to fall back on in the era of haredi balkanization in the late 1970s.

When the money began to flow from the Israeli government coffers—particularly in the last fifteen years, as the Likud party tried to cement political alliances for the purposes of coalition politics—the haredi Sephardim, without a party apparatus and their own institutions, found themselves last in line. In the atmosphere of localism and economic need that developed in the surge of the Sephardi religious population, who were quickly becoming the majority of Israelis, the Sephardim found it necessary to form their own interest group, which in time would emerge as a full-blown party: Shas Torah Guardians, with its own Council of Torah Wise Men (Moetzet Chachamay Ha Torah). For many years before this, the haredi Sephardim had counted themselves as Agudat Israel supporters.

There was another element which helped precipitate a Sephardi-haredi break. In 1977, secular Zionist Israel ceased being a single large left-leaning block when the Likud and its traditionalist supporters came to power on the strength of Sephardic voters. Now Orthodox Jews were offered an alternative coalition partner, who did not resonate with secularity the way the socialists had. Agudat Israel—the third party which gains from the contention of the other two, what Georg Simmel called the *tertius gaudens*—at once began to find a place for itself in the political penumbra of the Likud, and shared in its spoils.

Yet as Agudat Israel became less of an outsider to the corridors of power, it also found itself setting the stage for its own undoing. When members of Agudat Israel became chairs of the all-powerful Knesset Finance Committee, it was harder for them to rail against the enemy Zionist state since they were part of it. But there was something else which directly affected the Sephardi element. As the Likud had demonstrated by unseating the once all-powerful Labor coalition, everything was suddenly up for grabs. Establishment parties were in danger. Furthermore, the Sephardim inside the Agudat Israel world had not missed the spoils lessons of the Likud victories in national Israeli politics. The period of their novitiate was over.

For a long time Sephardim were recruited to study in Lithuanian yeshivot and become part of Agudat Israel, while the laity grudgingly supported non-haredi political parties. But with the rise of Sephardic political power under the Likud government and at the initiation of several rabbinic figures—most prominently Ovadia Yosef, the former Rishon Le Zion (Sephardic chief rabbi), and Eliezer Schach, head of the Ponovez Yeshiva—the traditionalists among the Sephardim formed a new organization, the Shas Torah Guardians, which ran candidates for the eleventh Knesset.

Rabbis Yosef and Schach each had their own reasons for forming the party. Yosef keenly felt betrayed by the political powers which had not supported his bid for another term as chief rabbi. His ouster, moreover, could be portrayed as an affront to all those who looked upon him as a holy man. It was another case of Ashkenazim holding down Sephardim, a pattern that had characterized most of the first twenty years of the State. Moreover, he and his supporters had been deprived of the spoils that were flowing to the yeshivot. Schach, on the other hand, worried that Sephardic Jewry was becoming too much influenced by the Hasidic trends within Agudat Israel; he wanted an ally who would help pry funds loose from the burgeoning Hasidic institutions.

Furthermore, as a staunch Misnagid, Schach had become troubled by the tacit alliance with the Hasidim. He saw the emphases that the Sephardim placed on holy men and their blessings as something too close to Hasidism. Encouraging the formation of a separate party for the Sephardim was one way to demonstrate to the powers of Agudat Israel that they needed to pay more attention to the non-Hasidic elements in the party or else risk losing ground. In short, after three decades of power in Israel, the contra-acculturative Orthodox were beginning to splinter again into Hasidic and Misnagdic camps and a third, Sephardic, camp. Of course that the parties should be subject to the decisions of rabbis and sages was consistent with traditional patterns.

Shas victories in the eleventh Knesset were dramatic—the haredi echo of the Likud displacement of Labor—and they came at the expense of Agudat Israel. The four seats Shas gained in 1984 doubled the number lost by Agudat Israel. At the same time, Shas generally adopted principles similar to the Agudists. But because they emerged in the context of a Zionist state and lacked the historical baggage of the Agudat Israel and its role as a diaspora party, they could more easily engage themselves with Zionism and Israeli political life. As chief rabbi, Ovadia Yosef had after all been a functionary of the Zionist state, and many Shas supporters served in the Israeli army. Shas people, aggressive in their support for Jewish law and tradition, were not quite sure what their relationship to the Jewish state should be. Moreover, because many of their supporters were acculturated Jews, people who were very much part of Israeli secular culture even as they maintained strong folk ties to Jewish tradition, they could run on a populist platform that advocated a general return to fundamental Jewish values without becoming caught up in the minutiae of religious legislation that often characterized the Agudat Israel campaigns and limited its potential supporters in the population at large. Thus, even as they engaged in a Kulturkampf against contemporary culture, Shas leaders campaigned on television (the major haredi party to do so), directing their appeal to all voters. To be sure, it was an odd appeal, filled with scenes of the blowing of ram's horns, religious songs, and even blessings by rabbis who promised divine deliverance for those who voted for Shas.

No doubt the seeds of the disintegration of the Shas connection with Agudat Israel, which reached its peak on the eve of the 1988 elections in Israel, could already be seen in Moetzet G'dolay Ha Torah by careful observers. Here particularism had begun to grow, ending the relatively brief period of pan-localism that had characterized the early days of Moetzet G'dolay Ha Torah. How and why?

While as individual rabbis the sages were only consulted on the "great questions," as had also been the case in the early days of the Moetzet G'dolay Ha Torah's existence, they were now in the small State of Israel confronting and contending with one another about all sorts of small, everyday matters of politics. While acting as a council which had to consider political realities and finding themselves dealing with mundane and everyday political matters, they were plunged into the little contests that turned them into little men. The scramble for funds intensified the rivalries and conflicts. This forced them to compromise or else remain immobile and indecisive. So now they were no longer a council that was symbolic of the pan-local, the universal, Jewish community; they were instead representatives of different interest groups. Rabbis left the Council of Sages. Rabbi Eliezer Schach of the Ponovez Yeshiva walked away. Rabbi Simcha Bunim Alter, the rebbe of the Hasidic court of Ger, and Rabbi Moshe Hager, leader of the Vizhnitz Hasidim, remained as the representatives only of Hasidim, and Ger and Vizhnitz Hasidim, while a large group, were by no means the only Hasidim on the scene. With the Lithuanians out, the Moetzet G'dolay Ha Torah ceased to function as a pan-local body.

All this set the scene for the situation which confronted Israel on the eve of the 1988 Knesset elections in which haredi Orthodoxy found itself divided between Hasidim and Misnagdim, and between Shas and Agudat Israel supporters. Moreover, it was a situation in which old conflicts—between Hasidim and Misnagdim and within Hasidism—once set aside, had begun to reappear. The Moetzet G'dolay Ha Torah was immobilized. Moreover, there still remained those who saw in Zionism the great Satan and chose to remain outside the electoral process altogether.

Into this cauldron, two new elements were added on the eve of the elections for the twelfth Knesset. The first came out of 770 Eastern Parkway in Brooklyn, New

York, world headquarters of the Lubavitch (ChaBaD) Hasidim. Here Menachem M. Schneerson, the rebbe and a man in his eighties, decided that his followers and supporters, who in the past had never formally endorsed a particular Israeli political party, should now vote for Agudat Israel. The purported reason for this move was the rebbe's concern that the haredi world was becoming fragmented. Others, however, offered less generous reasons for the move, among them Schneerson's desire to have Agudat Israel press for a change in the Israeli law defining who is a Jew in order more closely to align the law with halakha. This was a concern particularly important to recent Lubavitcher ideology. Yet another reason for the Lubavitcher formal endorsement of Agudat Israel was, according to some, the desire of the Hasidic rebbe to challenge the Misnagdic Rabbi Schach in response to recent efforts by the latter to reduce Lubavitch influence in the haredi world, efforts directed at preventing Lubavitch from advertising its programs in the haredi press. Whatever the true reasons for the Lubavitch move, its actions galvanized the haredi world. Suddenly, the old Hasidic-Misnagdic antagonism was again public and salient.

Rabbi Schach demanded that Agudat Israel separate itself from Lubavitch influences, disallowing advertisements for it in its newspaper, but the Ger Hasidim, a dominant element in the party, were not ready for this sort of a boycott. Schach left the party, and Lubavitch—until now political neutrals—became its boosters.

But what is Lubavitch? On its face, it is a Hasidic sect. But from its inception it was different in its philosophic doctrines, with pan-local features that sought to attract all sorts of Jews. It was therefore never altogether bounded by its particular location—whether in the pale of settlement or in Brooklyn. It was from the start interested in Jews far afield from its origins. With its origins in czarist Russia, at a time when that regime was on the verge of falling, Lubavitch Hasidism found itself often exiled to places far from its origins—to eastern Siberia, the Caucasus, Buchara in Central Asia—where it had to learn to keep the fires of its doctrines and Judaism ablaze. Lubavitch thus molded itself from the outset to serve Jews of all sorts under all conditions.

The activities in America must be seen in this light. They began with the arrival in 1940 of the previous rebbe, Joseph Isaac Schneerson, and become more intensive under the influence of the present rebbe, his son-in-law, Menachem Mendel Schneerson, who has expended his energies on university campuses. Having himself experienced life at the university at the Sorbonne, he saw the need to protect Judaism on the campus. But in this context Lubavitch found itself with a double dilemma. First, it confronted directly the question of who is a Jew, for many of its targets on the campus for Jewish renewal were the products of mixed marriages. Second, it also seemed to some on its haredi right to be undermining its haredi stance by having such direct and unmediated contact with the non-Orthodox.

Both of these dilemmas could be solved by actions in the Israeli elections. To make the issue of who is a Jew a primary matter would solve their problem on the campuses, because it would allow Lubavitch activists to sidestep the problem of offspring of mixed marriages by simply stating that Israel would not accept their Jewishness. And so, of course, they could not either. Second, it would show their critics on the right that they, Lubavitch, were more concerned with the principles of Orthodoxy than any other group. Their critics of course included Rabbi Schach and the Lithuanians. This led them to try to take over the Agudat Israel party over this issue.

There was one other religious reason for their activity: the matter of messianism. The Lubavitcher rebbe, who at eighty-six has no obvious heirs, is at the same time the center of the movement—particularly among the new recruits to Lubavitch who belong to no Hasidic tradition—and the source of concern about its continuity. Messianism may be a solution to the problem of continuity. To say "we want Messiah now," as the Lubavitchers do, solves the Lubavitch problem while simultaneously raising tensions with other particularisms. The activist messianism promoted by the rebbe and which focused around him led to conflict, which broke into the open, with the sectors of the haredi community, most prominently Rabbi Schach and the Lithuanian world.

Shaken by the split within the community that once had to choose between it and not voting at all, Agudat Israel was being reconstituted. It managed to attract Lubavitch, hold on to Ger and Viznitz Hasidim (the largest groups), and even return the Poaley Agudat Israel to the fold. On the other side, however, it lost the Sephardim and was about to lose many of the Lithuanians. Rabbi Schach and the Misnagdim wanted a party to oppose Lubavitch, which now seemed poised to claim Agudat Israel for itself. Shas, increasingly an independent entity and highly identified with Sephardic Jews, could no longer serve this need. Accordingly, on the eve of the elections, the Misnagdim, at the instigation of Rabbi Schach, formed a new party: Degel Ha Torah. Its supporters would be the Misnagdim as well as those Ashkenazic haredi Jews who felt alienated from Agudat Israel.

There was one other element of support for the new Degel Ha Torah party: the old Tzieray Agudat Israel, the youth wing of the party founded in the early 1940s by yeshiva students who gathered around the great rabbis of the day, most prominently Rabbi Abraham Isaiah Karelitz (the Hazon Ish), and encouraged the mythos of Torah scholarship as the primary source of leadership. In the 1950s this youth wing of Agudat Israel were the representatives of the world of the yeshivot out of which they had come. But in the 1980s they were no longer youth. They were grown up, and their rosh yeshiva, Rabbi Schach, was in his nineties. Together they were ready to create their own political party. This was Degel Ha Torah, and it too would seek its share of the spoils, both pecuniary and ideological.

Ironically enough, the party included Belzer Hasidim, proving that even in the world of ultra-Orthodoxy, politics can make strange bedfellows. The Belzers, a growing Hasidic court, had estranged themselves from many in the contra-acculturative and anti-Zionist haredi world, like the Eda Haredis and Satmar Hasidim, by accepting funds from the State Ministry of Education for their growing educational institutions. This had earned Belzer Hasidim many adversaries in the precincts of ultra-Orthodoxy, for whom such compromises were freighted with theological and ideological significance. Many haredim argued that those who take money from the Zionists give them legitimacy in return.

Degel Ha Torah offered a way to prove that they were not hurt by this enmity, for a victory of the party would once again demonstrate the Belzers' power and support in the ultra-Orthodox world. It would also be an important show of power for their new rebbe, who after many years in waiting was a leader of one of the fastest growing Hasidic groups which was searching for increased influence and power.

So this was the haredi line-up as the Israeli voters went to the polling booths. For those who used to vote only for Agudat Israel, there was now Agudat Israel, dominated by the Hasidim (especially Ger) and endorsed most prominently by Lubavitch, and Degel Ha Torah, the party of the Misnagdim and Belzer Hasidim. And for the Sephardi voter who wanted the power of the holy men behind him and wanted to restore the pride to his heritage—who in the past might have voted for Agudat Israel, the pro-Zionist National Religious Party, or even one of the major secular Zionist parties—there was Shas. And of course for the Neturei Karta and the most extreme haredim (such as the Satmar [of Hungarian origin] Hasidim), there was the option of not voting at all.

Thus, the elections for the twelfth Knesset represented not only a contest for the parliament but also an arena in which other rivalries and enmities within the Orthodox and ultra-Orthodox world could be played out. The foreground of contention would be the Israeli elections, but the background, the deeper structure of contention, was less concerned with Israel and more concerned with a test of strength between timeworn antagonists—Misnagdim and Hasidim, and the new contenders, the Sephardim of Shas.[75]

The Political Crisis of Spring 1990

In the early spring of 1990, a number of factors converged in Israel to create a situation that would bring into sharper focus the various trends within the haredi world in general and within its Sephardi element in particular. Although a detailed review of the Israeli political process is not necessary here, a sketch of certain basic facts must serve as a background. First, the National Unity government in Israel, established as a result of the elections for the twelfth Knesset, began to disintegrate over the question of the peace process in the Middle East. With the deterioration of the coalition between the two major parties, Labor and Likud, each of its political leaders began to seek alternative alliances to form a parliamentary majority. These alliances were possible only with the minor parties, the largest single block of which were the haredi ones.

Foreseeing the imminent collapse of the National Unity government, the Labor party under Shimon Peres began even before the political crisis to explore contacts with the haredim and came to an informal understanding with leaders of Agudat Israel and with Arye De'eri, who they believed represented Shas. This understanding was based primarily on agreements that would help these two haredi parties finance their various institutions. With its firmly established institutional infrastructure, Agudat Israel was always in need of ongoing infusions of money. While many Agudists argued in public that their discussions with Labor came because of disillusionment with Likud over ideological matters such as its refusal to support changes in state laws that supported greater ritual and religious observance, their main problem was Likud's previous refusal to deliver all the financial assistance it promised in its original coalition agreements following the 1988 elections. They came to the agreement with Labor even though Labor made no ideological concessions on matters of ritual and religious law.

The informal agreement between Labor and Shas also had an ideological and financial dimension. While Shas, like Agudat Israel, cared about enhancing the influence of religious and ritual matters in the state laws, their new ideological concern had to do with the Middle East peace process. This concern with peace must be understood in an historical and social context. Like all groups, Sephardim are not a monolith. Not only were there differences between the pragmatic and the ideological tendencies, there were and remain differences in social class. These are reflected in two general worldviews within the population supporting Shas. One is associated with the Sephardi upper strata and establishment. These were people who when they lived within the Muslim world—particularly in North Africa—had been urbanized businessmen who were relatively integrated into the parallel non-Jewish urban merchant class. Their counterparts in Israel and abroad were political moderates who encouraged a peaceful resolution of the Arab-Israeli conflict. Rabbi Ovadia Yosef, the spiritual (and patrician) head of Shas, and Arye De'eri were much influenced by this point of view. This became most evident in a trip they took in late summer of 1989 to Cairo to meet with President Mubarak of Egypt, after which they came back expressing the dovish position that when Jewish blood was in danger of being spilled, territory would have to be ceded to the Arabs.[76] Rabbi Yosef tried to defend this in a haredi rabbinic forum. This position obviously put them closer to the Labor than the Likud camp; and it had the effect of creating for Shas a distinct haredi political face that took a far more involved and responsible position in Zionist state affairs than had ever before been the case.

The other point of view in the Shas population was that of the lower strata, those who lived in the ghettos of Casablanca and Fez, Marakesh, and elsewhere, as well as in villages of the Atlas Mountains. They took a more traditional xenophobic and chauvinist perspective that divided the world between Jews and their enemies, among them Arabs. Their contemporary counterparts expressed this attitude in an abiding skepticism about peace with the Arabs in general and particularly with Rabbi Yosef's dovish stance upon his return from Egypt. This made that stance far more politically precarious and weakened its expression in Shas circles.

But in addition to the ideological factors that put at least part of Shas closer to Labor were financial considerations. Even more than Agudat Israel, Shas, as a new party, needed large amounts of money to establish and support its own emergent Sephardic infrastructure. Too long had they been the last and the least to get their share of funds for their haredi institutions. Peres and Labor promised money; they needed coalition partners, and Arye De'eri, who saw in this a chance to be in charge of disbursing funds and therefore a key figure in the next government, accepted the Labor partnership in principle.

But these informal agreements were written in sand rather than etched in stone, for they ignored basic divisions within the haredi world in general and the Sephardi-Shas world in particular. First, there was the small Degel Ha Torah group. Rabbi Eliezer Schach, its mentor—and the progenitor of Shas—had in the past expressed opinions that suggested he might be inclined toward dovishness. This included a statement that suggested that holding onto "territories" was not essential for Jewish identity; Jewish peoplehood was created in the wilderness and maintained for generations in the Diaspora. While many interpreted this to mean that Schach was ready to cede territory conquered after 1967 to the Arabs, others understood that Schach was talking about all of the Land of Israel, including the Zionist state. While the Labor party hoped that Schach would also join them in a coalition, based on ideological grounds (a willingness to cede territory) and financial agreements, they ignored, at their political peril, the fact that the Schach people retained a fundamental antagonism to secular Zionism as represented historically by the Labor party, and were unwilling to enter a coalition with their Hasidic-Agudist adversaries.

There was also the tension in Shas between the already-cited upper and lower strata of its supporters. While the upper strata inclined toward an alliance with the Labor party, their counterparts in the lower strata saw such affiliations as a betrayal of their loyalties. For them this meant a coalition with a party that embraced the Arabs, for whom they had no sympathies, and a party that had long excluded them from power and influence.

In the days following the informal agreements, as Labor ministers made pilgrimages to Rabbis Schach and Yosef, forces opposing the agreement began to raise their heads. In the inner corridors of power, negotiators were discovering that Rabbi Schach was far from ready to make a deal with Labor. This in turn had implications for the negotiations with Shas. For as the Labor people soon realized, there was yet another division within the Sephardi Torah Guardians. This division we may call the B'nai B'rak—Jerusalem split. B'nai B'rak, the locale of Rabbi Schach's Ponovez Yeshiva, represented those Shas members who held an allegiance to their rosh yeshiva, Rabbi Schach, and were altogether unwilling to break from his political stance, which was daily growing clearer and clearer in its antagonism to a coalition with the Labor party. Jerusalem, on the other hand, represented the forces in Shas that felt greater loyalty to Rabbi Yosef, who lived there and who tended toward an alliance with the Labor party. While this split had been relatively mild in the past, these matters of party politics suddenly threw the divisions into bold relief. Rabbi Peretz, minister of the interior, a supporter of the B'nai B'rak school of thought, unexpectedly resigned from Shas and openly expressed his disagreement with Rabbi Yosef and his inclinations toward Labor. Seeing this, Rabbi Yosef and his Jerusalem group realized that they could not bring Shas into a deal with Labor without tearing their party in two. Things stood in limbo.

To resolve the matter, Degel Ha Torah used the occasion of its first annual convention as a forum for Rabbi Schach to address his followers and offer his guidance on the coalition talks. The entire nation realized now that whatever Rabbi Schach would say at this occasion would effect the Degel Ha Torah party and tip the balance in favor of one or the other of the major political parties who were in a dead heat. What only sophisticated political observers understood as well was that it would also affect the B'nai B'rak faction of Shas and therefore Shas as a whole.

Over twenty thousand converged on Yad Eliahu Stadium, the site of basketball tournaments, the High Temple of Israeli secular culture, to listen to the words of the aged sage. Among the rabbinic notables was Rabbi Yosef, whose presence on the dais signaled that whatever Rabbi Schach said would be binding on Yosef as well. A noted scholar of haredi culture was enlisted to offer interpretation and commentary on national television to allow the Israeli people to understand the meaning of the speech. Schach had the ears and eyes of millions who never before had been exposed to the words of such a man nor present at such a religio-political ritual gathering. And here in a speech that lasted less than ten minutes, he turned his followers against all associations with Labor and secular Zionism.

Speaking first in Hebrew, he implied that the large crowd had not come to hear politics but to "be strengthened by hearing words of Torah." He would speak "a few just and honest words, without any political implications." Although what he said was in fact freighted with political significance, this assertion gave a symbolic and cultural importance to his remarks: this would be one more salvo in an ongoing Kulturkampf. "We live in a terrible and awful time," he proclaimed. "The wars we are fighting [against those who oppose tradition] did not begin today; they began already at the time of the First World War, and only the Master of the Universe knows what else is expected." The battle, however, was far from lost, for "the Jew cannot be destroyed. He may be killed but his children will continue to cleave to the Torah." For Schach, the Jews who had become like Gentiles were epitomized by those who lived in kibbutzim, the crown jewel of Labor Zionism. The kibbutzim were overwhelmingly secular—places "which know not what Yom Kippur or Sabbath is"—and therefore the people in them were essentially non-Jews. "If there is no Sabbath observance and no Yom Kippur, in what is a person to be considered a Jew?" There could be no compromises and certainly no alliances with those quasi-goyim identified with the kibbutzim. Although Schach did not mention the political coalition talks directly, he made clear the connections between what he said and the agenda of the day. "What makes me happy," he explained, "is I see that there is a public that wants to hear the word of God without politics. Some turn to Labor, some turn one way and others the other, but what do we have from Labor? Is Labor something holy? Have they not separated themselves from our past, and seek a new Torah?" In the passion of his remarks, Rabbi Schach had switched to Yiddish, the language of his allies and insiders. The nation needed a translator, as did even his ally Rabbi Yosef, for whom Yiddish was a foreign tongue. Yet one thing was clear when Rabbi Schach was finished: Degel Ha Torah would not cut a deal with Labor, and, as they soon would discover, neither would Shas.

Shimon Peres had found individual defectors from the Likud who would join him in the government and with Agudat Israel, whose Council of Torah Sages had already agreed to join Labor; he would be able to have the minimum of sixty-one seats in the Parliament to become prime minister. Agudat Israel was pleased with the results at

Yad Eliahu, for this meant they would be the sole haredi power in the government and that they would have control over funds. But some elements in the Agudat, cognizant of the haredi Kulturkampf, were disturbed with the implications of an affiliation with secular Zionist and dovish groups. A representative of Poaley Agudat Israel, Abraham Verdiger, and Eliezer Mizrachi, associated with ChaBaD and Rabbi Menachem Mendel Schneerson of Brooklyn, found themselves at odds with the Agudat-Labor alliance. Verdiger was a well-known hawk and Schneerson opposed any territorial compromise.

As Peres declared his intention to present his majority government to the Knesset, these two members defected from their party in favor of their principles. The sixty-one seats were now fifty-nine; Labor was out. Haredim had remained haredim and the balance of power swung to the Likud. While the haredim recognized that the Likud, in the words of Rabbi Yosef, also had members who "ate pork," that is, who did not identify with the highest demands of Jewish ritual, they nevertheless found them the lesser of the two evils and joined, some more reluctantly than others, the coalition which in May resulted in a right-wing, Likud-controlled government. By 1990, even Agudat Israel had joined the Likud coalition.

The Haredim Today

The burst of activity engendered by the Israeli elections illustrates the situation of the haredim today. The haredim is a group of largely passive, contra-acculturative Jews, survivors of a spiritual and physical onslaught against their way of life. Anxious about the continued existence of their way of life, they are now often drawn along by an activist and more radical wing, a cadre of young men who are products of the postwar world and who have been part of the society of scholars forged in the yeshiva-kollel. The hard core is attached to a stringent interpretation of the law which enables them to be heroic opponents of the modernist world. But, it is their struggle with that modernist world that encourages their stringency and a remodeling of the past which makes it thinkable. Starting anew after the Holocaust and in a new Israel, they have refashioned the past in the present. In a sense they have put their reborn tradition into active competition with the modern world and have thus thrust themselves into the thick of contemporary life.

What is the way of life the haredim present as an option? If the modern world emphasizes pleasure and ease, they emphasize duty and challenge. If the modern world stresses the need to change, they stress the need to remain loyal to the past. But, as moderns, they invent that past—a past that has in reality been torn away by the events of history and can only be imagined in its recreation: it is a past which is improved and enlarged, a tradition enhanced beyond anything that ever existed. That is the heroism of the contemporary haredi: he has radically outdone his forbears even as he exalts their greatness in his rhetoric. The elders and sages are greater than the present generation, but it is the present generation that directs history in that veneration.

Over the last half century, the numbers of the haredim have grown. This is in part because of their birthrate, which, at about 4.6 children per family, is far greater than the average of 2 children for the average Diaspora Jew and 3 for the average Israeli Jew. It is also because of the success that the haredim have had in holding on to their own in their institutions and neighborhoods (in Israel, primarily in Jerusalem and B'nai Brak; and in America, in Kings, and parts of Queens and Rockland, counties of New York). While the haredim still account for a small minority of Orthodox Jews, who themselves account for about 12 percent of American Jewry and about 20 percent of Israeli Jewry, probably slightly more than half a million people,[77] they no longer perceive themselves as reeling under the corrosive effects of secular life. On the contrary, they perceive themselves as fighting back, and doing so rather successfully.

Nothing so encourages this attitude than victories over the modern world, and nothing better symbolizes such victories than the turning of young people or heros of that secular world toward the tradition. Indeed, the activists often point with pride (for the benefit of their passive public, which needs to be constantly reminded that only active and aggressive traditionalism will save the day) to the numbers of young Jews who have abandoned secularity and attached themselves to the haredi way of life. Every returnee is treated as a victory over the forces of darkness. The very public turn of the Israeli movie star Uri Zohar, once a favorite of modern Israeli society, to the haredi world is an event freighted with symbolic meaning for the haredi world; it signals the victory of the Old Yishuv over Zionism.

In the fastest-growing wing of the haredi yeshivot are those which cater to the newly Orthodox. Long after the haskalah seemed to have won the day, the haredim can point out that people are seeing that the real light comes from the traditional way of life. This has of course strengthened the yeshiva heads.

Because of these perceived victories, haredim often find themselves willing to be even more aggressively contra-acculturationist than in the past. In a sense the principle of allowing certain compromises out of a desire for peace with those in charge, be they Gentiles or Jews who follow in the the ways of the Gentiles, has been nullified. That code of conduct applied when the Orthodox sensed they were in decline. Now that they feel that their hand is stronger politically, demographically, and symbolically, they no longer need to make the compromises or take the passive stance that seemed advisable in earlier times. This means that the religious right wing, the actively traditionalist, have become the ideological leaders and are no longer the radical fringe. They set the agenda in the political parties or they determine the style of life that is acceptable on the haredi street. They no longer have to fume on the margins.

But the haredi world is beginning once again to become fragmented. The old divisions among Hasidic groups, and between them and Misnagdim, are returning with vigor. Each accuses the other of being too compromising, lenient, modern, Zionist. The competition for economic resources and political prizes sharpens the splits even more. In the last years, many of the battles have been fought in public. The outbreak of fistfights between the supporters of Satmar and those of Belz Hasidim several years ago—both in the streets of Jerusalem and New York—had their origins in conflicts over relations with Zionism and control over lucrative kosher food certifications. The recent political and ideological battles between Rabbi Schach, current head of the Ponovez Yeshiva, and Rabbi Schneerson, leader of the Lubavitch Hasidim, were central to the competition between Agudat Israel and the newly formed haredi political party, Degel Ha Torah. Those were simply two of the most public such battles. Other less visible ones go on all the time.[78]

And then there is Shas and the Sephardim, who are now the third-largest party in the Knesset. Its supporters are that peculiar mix of secular Israelis who still hold onto folk beliefs about the efficacy of religion and holy men. Some of them constitute the most fertile field from which newly Orthodox Jews blossom. Reacting against the tensions of maintaining the dualism of their life, some of them support extremist religious politics even though they are not ready themselves to be haredim. And in the meantime, their leaders hover between political pragmatism and religious fervor. Some make political deals, while others see in all events the hand of God or even the millennium approaching.

Thus Shas found it possible to take positions of power in the Israeli government after its victories in the last two Israeli elections. The ideology it espoused was purely haredi at the manifest and public level. But in its practical implementation of that ideology, Shas often found itself divided between its pragmatist wing, symbolized by the current Israeli interior minister Rabbi Arye De'eri, a young man in his thirties, and its ideological wing, symbolized by absorption minister Rabbi Yitzhak Peretz. Peretz is a sermonizer; in a particularly memorable statement, he accounted for the death of some youngsters from the Israeli city of Petah Tiqwa in a train-school bus accident by explaining that the disaster was divine retribution for the fact that Petah Tiqwa allowed cinemas to be open on the Sabbath in violation of Jewish law.

But in spite of all the differences between them and the two sorts of Shas constituencies they symbolize, both men subordinate themselves to the head of the Council of Torah Sages—the Shas counterpart to the Moetzet G'dolay Ha Torah—Rabbi Ovadia Yosef. That sort of approach to authority and avoidance of ultimate supremacy is distinctively haredi.

Nevertheless Shas succeeded in becoming the third-largest party in the Israeli Knesset in the last election, because its electors were not themselves haredim but rather non-European Jews who revere the holy even as they live the profane life. They can support the holy, however, as long as it does not overstep its bounds. Thus, while Shas may on the one hand represent a new incursion of haredi culture into contemporary life, in its effort to remain powerful it will probably have to mediate its ideological purity, forged in its leaders' experiences in Lithuanian yeshivot during the last thirty years, by a dose of realpolitik. Moreover, the rise of the haredi political power only serves to fragment the haredi world further. What was once a struggle among Hasidim, and between them and Misnagdim, between Zionists and anti-Zionists, is now also a struggle between the Shas brand of haredi culture and the other groups. And in this struggle there are complications of ethnicity that were far more muted in the earlier struggles.

Thus today's haredim are a varied lot, ever more aware of their divisions even as they taste the victories of growing political strength. Once again, as in the days when the conflicts between Hasidim and Misnagdim first broke out, ideological differences are often superimposed on personal and political rivalries. And in the meantime, the number of haredim of all varieties increases, straining their financial resources. Ironically, this growth makes them far more dependent financially on the non-haredi world. They live off donations and even more the direct grants and welfare payments from the State of Israel.

Moreover, the stronger they get, the potentially more powerful the backlash against them from the non-haredi world becomes. Once the non-Orthodox perceive that in this Kulturkampf they could lose, they are likely to pull out all the stops in the battle. This might mean drafting yeshiva boys into the army, decreasing financial grants to haredi educational institutions, and changing the political system to diminish the power of the religious parties in coalition politics. Such changes would suddenly force even the activists to change tactics and make compromises. This in turn could signal a radical change in haredi existence, making Israeli haredim much more like American haredim: passively contra-acculturationist. How imminent such changes are it is difficult to say, but that such changes are possible is beyond question.

Conclusion

Fundamentalist Jews—contra-acculturative activists, as we call them—did not and do not act as they do because they have an historical consciousness. What they have, rather, is a commitment to a particular constructed image of an idealized past. The past—destroyed by the Holocaust—can only remain an image. And as an image it can be painted as altogether different from what it was in reality. That is what today's haredim have done. Their struggle against contemporary culture and all sorts of opponents colors and shapes their interpretations of the past and visions of the future.

Accordingly, haredim have become particularly dependent upon the authoritative interpreters of that history. The authoritative interpreters—rabbis—become the arbiters of what happened in history and what the genuine definition was of the ideal. They become the catalysts for action, even if they cannot control its direction or outcome. And because haredi fundamentalism is an oppositionist and negational movement, the interpreters (rabbis) are constantly recalibrating or reassessing their evaluation of precisely what the tradition was and what the sacred texts mean in order to confront and compete with modern society and culture. The Kulturkampf which fundamentalism represents is therefore a struggle not only over what must be done in the present but over what was done in the past. This becomes particularly important in those battles which contra-acculturative activists have with acculturationists. Thus, the former are often in battle with other modern Orthodox Jews over precisely what the halakha demands. And they struggle with Zionists over who and what is a Jew. And everyone reinterprets history all the time. And they also clash with one another.

The spectacle of haredim questioning the legitimacy of one another's leaders and worldviews which so captures the attention of the non-Orthodox is really nothing new. What makes it seem new is that for a time it seemed that the haredi world was becoming unified, particularly in its promotion of generic sages. But while the generic sages are important in the battle against secular culture, they are of no use in the struggle for dominance within haredi culture.

As the haredi world grows by dint of its great birthrate (birth control being one of the aspects of contemporary civilization that all traditionalists eschew), and as it therefore competes for scarce economic resources—resources crucial for maintaining its scholars and institutions—there will undoubtedly be increasing tensions within the haredi world. While American traditionalists will probably not feel this as quickly, for they are wealthier (not having abandoned *tachlis,* practical reality, as much as their Israeli counterparts) and have proportionately fewer people living on stipends in yeshiva-kollelim, they also may find themselves becoming more passively contra-acculturationist. If their counterparts in the Israeli haredi world weaken, the passive contra-acculturationists in America may find themselves gradually slipping into acculturation. In the end, how different will the Satmar Hasid working at an electronics shop in Manhattan be from any other American ethnic?

The fundamentalism train is pulled by the Israeli locomotive. That locomotive is traveling very fast on rails maintained by someone else. When those rails fall into disrepair—as well they may if the Israeli public tires of supporting the haredi world—the whole train could derail. That is why haredim of all stripes have taken increasing interest in the political life of the Zionist state; they have a great deal riding on it.[79]

The criticism which contra-acculturative activism expresses about modern society and culture always carries within it a grain of optimism that repair is possible (although only the activists are prepared to bring it about; the passivists await some deus ex machina which will bring about the millennium). Hence, fundamentalism must be viewed as generated by a short-range pessimism in its practical activities but as sustained by a long-range optimism—a messianic optimism—about the ultimate resolution of the conflict between contemporary culture and the idealized culture of the tradition. The contra-acculturationists believe that yesterday is better than today and that however bleak things may appear today, tomorrow will always bring us back to the golden days of yesteryear. They believe that ultimately the modern world, secular society, Zionist Israel, and Jewries of all sorts that fail to follow the strict paths of Orthodoxy will crumble of their own inner corruption. One by one those who wish to be saved will return. When such repair has taken place, the Messiah will come. Whether they are correct or not is one of the great questions that only the future can answer.

Notes

1. If our description of these Jews serves to shed light on more than this specific case, yielding insights on the more general matter of fundamentalism, this will be a welcome by-product of our effort, though it is not necessarily our primary aim. Nevertheless, at the outset some comments about the applicability of the English word "fundamentalism" to them are in order. First of all, these Jews do not use the term "fundamentalist" to refer to or describe themselves or their variant of Judaism. Strictly speaking, "fun-

damentalism" is a term that is etymologically inappropriate for them, borrowed as it is from a Christian religious context.

2. The answer to the question of numbers is necessarily vague, because there is no totally accurate census of Jews in general. In the United States, where the single largest population resides (slightly more than five million), the national census does not ask questions about religion, and thus any count of Jews is based upon estimates made on the basis of Jewish institutional affiliations, estimates that probably underrepresent the unaffiliated while doubly counting the affiliated in some cases. Census figures for the Soviet Union and other Eastern bloc countries are problematic, because they may count as Jews people who do not so identify themselves, while missing others who have kept their Jewish religious affiliations undisclosed.

If it is difficult to count Jews in general, it is even harder to count Orthodox Jews, because there are no universal criteria for defining who is Orthodox. These figures too come from estimates based upon affiliation and in the case of Israel, from poll results in national and local elections.

3. There are *haredim* in other places—Western Europe, Australia, South America, and even South Africa and the Soviet Union—but these represent a very small proportion of the total.

4. Cf., for example, Solomon Poll, *The Hasidic Community of Williamsburgh* (Schocken), in which he cites the fact that these people call themselves *shayner yidn*, "nice Jews." Or see Amnon Levy, *The Haredim* (Jerusalem: Keter, 1989), who points out that they call themselves "the nation of the Torah," "the Jews of the Torah," or "the Jews who observe the Torah and its commandments" (p. 19).

5. For a full discussion of contemporary Jewish Orthodoxy, cf. Samuel Heilman and Steven Cohen, *Cosmopolitans and Parochials: Modern Orthodox Jews in America* (Chicago: University of Chicago Press, 1989).

6. Henry Sumner Maine, *Ancient Law*, 5th London ed. (New York: Henry Holt & Co., 1885), pp. 164–65.

7. This is what Max Weber called "*zweckrationalität*."

8. Cf. Jacob Katz, ed., *Toward Modernity: The European Jewish Model* (New Brunswick, N. J.: Transaction Books, 1987).

9. Cf. Jacob Katz, *Out of the Ghetto: The Social Background of Jewish Emancipation 1770–1870* (New York: Schocken, [1973] 1978).

10. Katz, *Toward Modernity*, p. 1.

11. Ibid., p. 2.

12. Cf. Peter L. Berger, *The Heretical Imperative* (New York: Doubleday, 1979), p. 3.

13. We say "unevenly" because there were early contacts with the outside cultures even in the farthest reaches of the east, in the Pale of Settlement. However, by and large these were isolated and limited to people who in one way or another had traveled or had contact with travelers. But when communities as a whole are considered, it is possible to state that generally emancipation and enlightenment began in western Europe (and America which was at first only an outpost of German Jewry) and moved eastward rapidly only after the First World War and the Soviet revolution.

14. Cf. the essays by Israel Bartal, Emanuel Etkes, Michael Silver, Michael Graetz, Joseph Michman, Hillel J. Kieval, Lois Dubin, Todd Endelman, and Michael A. Meyer in Katz, *Toward Modernity*.

15. On assimilation, cf. Leonard W. Doob, *Becoming More Civilized* (New Haven: Yale University Press, 1960), p. 265. E. A. Sommerlad and J. W. Berry write of a process in which "the minority group changes its identity to that of the host society," in "The Role of Ethnic Identification in Distinguishing Between Attitudes Towards Assimilation and Integration of a Minority Racial Group," *Human Relations* 23 (1) (1970): 24.

16. Isaac Deutscher, *The Non-Jewish Jew and Other Essays* (New York: Oxford, 1968), p. 26.

17. J. H. Randall, Jr., *The Making of the Modern Mind* (Boston: Houghton Mifflin, 1940), p. 377.

18. Melville Herskovits, *Man and His Works* (New York: Knopf, 1949), p. ix.

19. J. L. Blau, *Modern Varieties of Judaism* (New York: Columbia University Press, 1966), p. 27.

20. This aphorism was later quoted and made well-known again by the Hebrew essayist and poet Yehuda L. Gordon. Although he was deservedly famous for the phrase, however, he was not simply advocating acculturation with it—the message most frequently assumed to be the primary one embedded in the aphorism. He was also reminding people to remain Jewish in spite of their acculturation. As Aharon Zeev Ben-Yishai suggests, Gordon "was also disappointed in the Jewish *maskilim,* particularly the young, who were carried away by the assimilationist trend, rejecting indiscriminately and forsaking Jewish values and the Hebrew language which Gordon loved without reservation." *Encyclopedia Judaica* (Jerusalem: Keter, 1972) vol. 7, pp. 801–2.

21. Of Mendelssohn's children, "two turned Catholic, two Protestant. Two remained Jews—but last generation Jews." Abraham J. Karp, "Ideology and Identity in Jewish Group Survival in America," *American Jewish Historical Quarterly* 65 (June 1976): 312.

22. E. W. Burgess (*International Encyclopedia of the Social Sciences,* vol. 1 [1930]) defines accommodation as this kind of social adjustment, while G. E. Simpson calls it a "process of compromise." We write here of a "Gentile" world because most of these processes historically occurred first among those Jews who found themselves surrounded by Christians and not among those in the Islamic world.

23. *Encyclopedia Judaica,* vol. 6, p. 80; vol. 5, p. 901.

24. Herskovits, *Man and His Works,* p. 531.

25. Leo Jung, "What is Orthodox Judaism?" *The Jewish Library,* 2nd ser. ed. L. Jung (New York: Bloch, 1930), p. 115.

26. For a full discussion of Hildesheimer, cf. David Ellenson, *Tradition in Transition* (Lanham, Md.: University Press of America, 1989).

27. For the modern Orthodox story cf.: Heilman and Cohen, *Cosmopolitans and Parochials.*

28. Chaim I. Waxman, personal communication November 1988. Cf. also his *America's Jews in Transition* (Philadelphia: Temple University Press, 1983).

29. On the yeshivot, cf. Shaul Stampfer. And on the move to the rebbe, cf., for example, Wolf Zeev Rabinowitsch, *Lithuanian Hasidism,* trans. M. B. Dagut (New York: Schocken, 1971) who writes, "there must have no doubt been many young Lithuanian Jews who . . . made their way to Mezerich [where the Hasidic leader Rabbi Dov Baer lived] to hear the new doctrine there." And he continues, quoting Solomon Maimon, a witness to the unfolding of early Hasidism: "Young men would leave their parents, wives, and small children and travel in groups to visit these great 'Rebbes' and to receive instruction from them in the new doctrine" (pp. 9, 10).

30. Rabinowitsch, *Lithuanian Hasidism,* p. 3.

31. Ibid., p. 154.

32. Ibid., p. 52.

33. "R. Shelomo of Karlin . . . expressed the opinion that God counted the miles traversed by the hasid on his journey to the Rebbe and recorded them to his credit, [but] R. Moshe used to say that he would be called to account for every step that a Jew took to come to him" (Rabinowitsch, *Lithuanian Hasidism,* p. 173). And there were differences between ChaBaD (Lubavitch) and Karlin hasidim over the power of the *Tsaddik.* In the beginning ChaBaD sought to diminish it, while Karlin did not.

34. Rabinowitsch, *Lithuanian Hasidism,* p. 191.

35. Ibid., p. 16.

36. Thus, for example, in the 1920 will and testament of Reb Yisrael of Stolin the rebbe wrote: "I counsel my sons not to meddle in communal affairs or in any worldly matters, especially not in money cases or matters concerning the secular authorities." Rabinowitsch, *Lithuanian Hasidism,* p.104.

37. Rabbi Aharon, the Second of Stolin (1902–1872) quoted in Rabinowitsch, *Lithuanian Hasidism,* p. 99.

38. Cf. Gerschom Scholem, *The Messianic Idea in Judaism and Other Essays on Jewish Spirituality* (New York: Schocken, 1971). Indeed, the appeal which the tales of the Hasidim have for modern literature and the modern imagination may have something to do with this revolutionary and personalistic character. Martin Buber surely understood this when he took those tales and retold them for the modern reader. Cf. Martin Buber, *Tales of the Hasidim* (vols. 1 and 2).

39. For example, Reb Aharon (of Karlin) urged that every one of his disciples should "shut himself up in solitude in a special room for one day every week and spend the time in fasting, repentance, and study of Torah. . . . And if possible, he should shut himself up alone everyday," while others preached joyfulness. Some Hasidim emphasized prayer nearly exclusively, while others—notably ChaBaD Hasidism—introduced something of Lithuanian Talmudic scholarship into hasidism, viewing Hasidism as a complement to rabbinism rather than a protest, and noting that both required study. Rabinowitsch, *Lithuanian Hasidism,* pp. 18, 22.

40. Ibid., p. 85.

41. This attitude toward the unschooled Jews was not new in Judaism. Even in Talmudic times, the rabbis distinguished between *haverim,* those who were part of the academies of learning, rabbis who knew and properly interpreted the law, and the *am ha'aretz,* the simple folk who based their practices and beliefs on custom and everyday wisdom rather than scholarship. The Misnagdim were simply the latest version of the *haverim* who in turn looked upon Hasidim as *am ha'aretz.*

42. Quoted in Rabinowitsch, *Lithuanian Hasidism,* p. 148 n. 46. Cf. also M. Wilensky, *Hasidim u Mitnagdim.*

43. Rabinowitsch, *Lithuanian Hasidism,* pp. 52–53.

44. Ibid., p. 181.

45. *Grodner Opklangen,* vols. 5–6 (Buenos Aires, 1951), quoted in Rabinowitsch, *Lithuanian Hasidism,* p. 142.

46. On the deradicalization of Hasidism and a growing emphasis on Torah study like that of the Lithuanian yeshivot, cf., Mendel Piekarz, *Ideological Trends of Hasidism in Poland during the Interwar and the Holocaust* (Jerusalem: Bialik, 1990), pp 37–156. Rabinowitsch, *Lithuanian Hasidism,* p. 218.

47. There is a marvelous picture that captures this. In an illustrated Passover *haggadah* sold by and popular among many haredim, this text, which is read during the traditional meal, or seder, portrays the Israelites marching out of Egypt dressed as if they came from a small village in Poland. And of course Moses looks like a Hasid.

48. Cf. Jacob Katz, *Out of the Ghetto,* for a fuller discussion of the process.

49. To be sure, battles against the encroachments of the outside culture were more easily fought against Jews who championed acculturation than against the Gentiles whose culture was encroaching. The latter, after all, had guns.

50. Satmar Hasidism today must be understood on two levels. The first is as a particularistic Hasidic sect established by Rabbi Yoel Teitelbaum in the early years of the twentieth century in Satu Mare, Hungary, which moved in the late 1940s and re-established itself in Brooklyn and with outposts throughout the Jewish world (including Israel). At another level, however, Satmar represents the worldview of a particular brand of Hasidism which subsumes a whole panoply of Hungarian, anti-Zionist, extremist insular Orthodoxy, which includes various Hasidic sects such as Munkacz, Debritzin, and the Reb-Arelach as well as non-Hasidim like the Eda Haredis. Lubavitch, on the other hand, is among the earliest of Hasidic sects. It is known by its Hebrew acronym ChaBaD (which stands for the Hebrew words: Wisdom, Understanding and Knowledge) and was established in White Russia at the end of the eighteenth century by Rabbi Schneur Zalman of Liadi, one of the disciples of the Maggid of Mezerich. It also represents today an Orthodoxy deeply engaged in Jewish outreach and, in spite of an

anti-Zionist ideology, is very much involved with Israel and Israeli politics.

51. Cf. S. Heilman, *The People of the Book: Drama, Fellowship, and Religion* (Chicago: University of Chicago Press, 1982), in which Talmudic *lernen* is opposed to secular learning.

52. Cf. Menachem Friedman, "Life Tradition and Book Tradition in the Development of Ultra-Orthodox Judaism," in H. E. Goldberg, ed., *Judaism Viewed from Within and from Without* (Albany: State University of New York Press, 1986).

53. Many of the modern Orthodox were at the outset German Jews, those who found themselves in a host culture whose treasures beckoned them far more than the peasant culture that surrounded Eastern European Jewry beckoned them.

54. The notion of survivor guilt and of resurrecting the dead to greater power than they ever had in life is of course an old one. It was most dramatically elaborated in Freud's famous essay, *Totem and Taboo* (London: Routledge and Kegan Paul, 1950).

55. Cf. William Helmreich, *The World of the Yeshiva* (New York: Free Press, 1982), especially pp. 18–51, for a full and fine treatment of this history.

56. Cf., for example, Marshall Sklare, who in the original version of his book *Conservative Judaism* (New York: Schocken, [1955] 1972) wrote about a dying Orthodoxy, but who in the new, reissued "augmented" version was forced to recant and describe the unexpected vitality of postwar American Orthodoxy.

57. Cf. Jeffery Gurock, "Resisters and Accommodators," in *American Jewish Archives* (November 1983), pp. 112–14.

58. Perhaps the most famous of them are the Reichman brothers of Canada, owners of Olympia and York Real Estate Development Corporation, one of the Fortune 500 corporations, and haredi Jews.

59. For a fuller discussion of some of these issues cf. Samuel Heilman and Menachem Friedman, "The Haredim in Israel: Who Are They and What Do They Want?" *American Jewish Committee Research Report,* 1990. See also Samuel Heilman, *Defenders of the Faith: Life among the Ultra-Orthodox* (New York: Schocken, forthcoming).

60. Cf. a pamphlet by Nathan Birnbaum, *In Gulos by Yidn* (In exile among Jews) (Warsaw: 1922).

61. There were a small number of Orthodox Jews who were Zionists, but their impact on Zionism would not be felt until much later.

62. The Orthodox made Jerusalem, the place of the Western Wall and the ruins of the Holy Temple, the focus of their attention. The Zionists built Tel Aviv out of the sand dunes near Jaffa and drained the swamps in the Galilee.

63. Rabbi Kook, himself a very pious man and yeshiva scholar, had evolved a highly nuanced ideology that suggested that even the secular Zionists could be instruments of God's redemption because their heresy was the result of temporary errancy. In the end of days, as redemption, approached, he was sure they would come around to the truth. Indeed, when in the days following the 1967 war there seemed to be a mass Israeli recognition of miraculous and eschatological events, Rabbi Kook's son, Rabbi Zvi Yehuda Kook, took up this theme again, and many of his disciples formed the nucleus of what would become the Gush Emunim movement (Cf. chap. 5).

64. This was because they saw marriage as inevitably ending their yeshiva existence and forcing them to go out and get a job. The Jews of the Old Yishuv who lived off the dole from abroad took it as a given that they could marry and still remain in the yeshiva and therefore married at the age of eighteen or nineteen, as demanded by Jewish tradition.

65. Deborah R. Weissman, "Bais Ya'akov: A Women's Educational Movement in the Polish Jewish Community: A Case Study in Tradition and Modernity," M.A. thesis, New York University, p. 17.

66. When one speaks about Neturei Karta and the Eda Haredis, one is tempted of course to ask how many people these organizations actually represent. This is dif-

ficult to answer, since, for example, membership in one organization does not preclude membership in the other, and thus Agudat Israel supporters could also be boosters or participants in Neturei Karta. People slip from one to another of these groups easily. Clearly there are more supporters than members in Neturei Karta and the Eda Haredis. To determine, however, how many are in the hard core one needs to look at the numbers of haredim who do not vote. Not voting is the litmus test for membership in the most extreme organizations. Those who do not vote express thereby their unwillingness to offer even symbolic legitimacy to the modern Zionist state. And they also thereby distinguish themselves from the rank and file of haredim who at the very least enter the political process, by far the majority. There are about fifty thousand eligible voters who come from haredi neighborhoods.

67. For all of its struggles against Arab enemies and large-scale immigration during its formative years, Israel was for a long time a great success. It flourished and found many ways to reach economic well-being, something that assisted the haredi institutions more than any donations from abroad ever had during the days of the Old Yishuv.

68. Cf. Weissman, "Bais Ya'akov."

69. Ibid., p. 21.

70. The use of a radio is prohibited on the Sabbath.

71. Field interview, Samuel Heilman, 7 May 1989. While the informant mixes up some historical sequences, his view captures the haredi perspective.

72. Their decisions, while based on *da'as Torah* were directed primarily to followers of Agudat Israel.

73. We are indebted to Haym Soloveitchik for this insight.

74. Abraham Lazerson, "*Da'as Torah* as a Foundation in our Lifeways," *Ha Modia,* 17 Ellul 1980.

75. For a fuller discussion of the entire election, cf., Samuel C. Heilman and Menachem Friedman, "The Haredim in Israel: Who Are They and What Do They Want?" *American Jewish Committee Research Report,* 1990.

76. This is based on the Jewish ethical and legal principle of *pikuach nefesh.*This principle places the saving of life above nearly all other religious demands.

77. See n. 1.

78. For example, a rivalry between two Hasidic sects erupted at a wedding between the offspring of the leaders of the sects, because the rebbe of one sect allowed Minister Ariel Sharon to sit at the head table at the wedding reception This tacit recognition of the Zionist regime by paying honor to one of its ministers became the focus of a fight that was also rooted in an otherwise muted rivalry between the sects that were being joined by the marriage.

79. Cf. Asher Arian, *Politics in Israel* (Boulder, Colo.: Westview Press, 1990).

Select Bibliography

Arian, Asher. *Politics in Israel.* Boulder, Colo.: Westview Press, 1990.

Blau, J. L. *Modern Varieties of Judaism.* New York: Columbia University Press, 1966.

Cohen, Steven. *Cosmopolitans and Parochials: Modern Orthodox Jews in America.* Chicago: University of Chicago Press, 1989.

Deutscher, Issac. *The Non-Jewish Jew and Other Essays.* New York: Oxford University Press, 1968.

Doob, Leonard W. *Becoming More Civilized.* New Haven: Yale University Press, 1960.

Friedman, Menachem. "The Social Significance of the Shemita Polemic." In J. Hacker, ed., *Jerusalem: Shalem,*455–80. Jerusalem: Ben-Zvi Institute, 1974.

———. "Religious Zealotry in Israeli Society." In S. Poll and E. Krausz, eds., *On Ethnic and Religious Diversity in Israel,*91–111. Ramat-Gan, Israel: Bar-Ilan University Press, 1975.

———. "Back to the Grandmother: The New Ultra-Orthodox Woman." In *Israel Studies: The Review of the Jerusalem Institute for Israeli Studies,* 21–26. Jerusalem: Spring, 1978.

———. *Society and Religion: The Non-Zionist Orthodoxy in Eretz-Israel, 1918–1936.* 2nd ed. Jerusalem: Yad Ben-Zvi, 1982.

———. "Haredim Confront the Modern City." In P. Medding, ed., *Studies in Contemporary Jewry,* vol. 2. Bloomington: University of Indiana Press, 1986.

———. "Life Tradition and Book Tradition in the Development of Ultra-Orthodox Judaism." In H. E. Goldberg, ed., *Judaism Viewed from Within and Without: Anthropological Studies.* Albany: State University of New York Press, 1986.

———. "The Haredim and the Holocaust." *The Jerusalem Quarterly* (Winter 1990): 86–114.

Friedman, Menachem, with J. Shilhav. *Growth and Segregation: The Ultra-Orthodox Community of Jerusalem.* Jerusalem: The Jerusalem Institute for Israeli Studies, 1986.

Heilman, Samuel, and Steven Cohen. *Cosmopolitans and Parochials: Modern Orthodoxy in America.* Chicago: University of Chicago Press, 1989.

———. *Defenders of the Faith: Life among the Ultra-Orthodox* (New York: Schocken Books, forthcoming).

Helmreich, William. *The World of the Yeshiva.* New York: Free Press, 1982.

Katz, Jacob. *Tradition and Crisis.* Glencoe: Free Press, 1961.

———. *Out of the Ghetto: The Social Background of Jewish Emancipation 1770–1870.* New York: Schocken, 1973.

Katz, Jacob, ed. *Toward Modernity: The European Jewish Model.* New Brunswick, N. J. Transaction Books, 1987.

Liebman, Charles S., and Eliezer Don-Yehiya. *Civil Religion in Israel: Traditional Religion and Political Culture in the Jewish State.* Berkeley: University of California Press, 1983.

———. *Religion and Politics in Israel.* Bloomington: Indiana University Press, 1984.

Levy, Ammon, *The Haredim.* Jerusalem: Keter, 1989.

Rabinowitsch, Wolf Zeev. *Lithuanian Hasidism.* Trans. M. B. Dagut. New York: Schocken, 1971.

Schiff, Gary. *Tradition and Politics: The Religious Parties of Israel.* Detroit: Wayne State University Press, 1977.

Sivan, Emmanuel, and Menachem Friedman, eds. *Religious Radicalism and Politics in the Middle East.* New Haven: Yale University Press, 1988.

Waxman, Chaim I. *America's Jews in Transition.* Philadelphia: Temple University Press, 1983.

Webber, Jonathan. "Rethinking Fundamentalism: The Readjustment of Jewish Society in the Modern World." In L. Caplan, ed., *Studies in Religious Fundamentalism.* Albany: State University of New York Press, 1987.

CHAPTER
5

Jewish Zionist Fundamentalism: The Bloc of the Faithful in Israel (Gush Emunim)

Gideon Aran

Gush Emunim in Historical Context: An Overview

During the mid-1970s, public attention in Israel turned to a band of skullcapped and bearded young men, assault rifles on their shoulders and rabbinic texts in their hands. They spent their nights in the territories conquered and administered by the Israeli Defense Forces since the 1967 war. There they skillfully outmaneuvered or aggressively attacked soldiers and then compelled them to join in an ecstatic Hasidic dance. Joined by their wives and numerous babies, they pitched tents as they repeated the sermons of an aging rabbi. In the mornings, they marched through Arab towns, waving Israeli flags, breaking windows and puncturing tires. Meanwhile, within the State of Israel proper, other group members convened with senior officials and conspired with tycoons, and traveled hundreds of miles in a dilapidated pickup truck to recruit supporters, sometimes napping in sleeping bags along the road. They preached morals and rebuked the nation for its moral shortcomings via the TV cameras which were immediately attracted to them. They covered the public squares of large cities with placards, lay down in front of the vehicles of visiting foreign ministers, and shouted their anguish through loudspeakers to disrupt the prime minister's daily routine. Between, and even during, these campaigns, they studied the Torah intensively and prayed with great devotion.

Initially the phenomenon was described as lunatic, esoteric, episodic, and marginal. Observers expressed their amazement or disdain. In time, however, it became clear that the phenomenon was not merely something exotic but possessed depth of content and influence. All the characters in this original band have since become very familiar to the Israeli public. For nearly a generation, they have time and again risen to the top of the national and regional agenda.

These several hundred true believers constituted the future leaders and cadres of the central religiopolitical radical movement in Israel, the Gush Emunim (Bloc of the Faithful). The movement has borne this name with pride since its official founding in the wake of the Yom Kippur War.

The chief public manifestation of the Gush Emunim (hereafter GE) is its settlements, the earliest and most important of which were founded contrary to government decision and against the will of significant segments of the Israeli public. The proliferation of settlements surrounding and penetrating hostile Palestinian population centers has transformed the status, landscape, and atmosphere of the Territories. The settlements represent a planned effort to force the inclusion of this area within the boundaries of legitimate Israeli control.

My research began with the movement's birth and continued throughout its early growth. For this purpose, I spent much time in the Territories, accompanying the activist-believers in the hills and the desert. While conducting participant observation, I served as a driver, arms bearer, and bodyguard for several of the movement's leaders. As such, I became a confidant and an intimate witness to GE activities, both formal and informal, public and discreet.[1] As a companion to Rabbi Moshe Levinger on his nighttime forays through Arab villages and refugee camps, I witnessed the combination of asceticism and stubbornness that have been a model for GE and its symbol to the outside world. More than anyone else, Levinger has imprinted his personal seal on all decisive—and controversial—measures taken by GE. The history of the movement reflects his own personal career over the past twenty-four years. Outside the movement he is known as an accomplished troublemaker, while within it he is considered the inspiration of the most radical elements. Rabbi Levinger bears the torch so far ahead of the camp that he often detaches himself from the rest. When the charismatic power of his blunt statements or his hysterical or histrionic outbursts fail to motivate, this *enfant terrible* does not hesitate to force *faits accomplis* on the movement. At times he has worked alone at his own discretion, following a path which others considered both undesirable and unfeasible. Nevertheless, he has always succeeded in imposing an ex post facto commitment on the entire movement, which has recognized his path as the official one. Even GE members who oppose Rabbi Levinger are greatly impressed with his consistency, dedication, and self-sacrificing manner. They find it difficult to withstand his enthusiastic demands, original interpretations, far-reaching forecasts, and heroic personal example. In the secular-dovish-liberal camp, he is pejoratively called "Khomeini." More than once, the Israel Press has chosen him "man of the year," and once even "man of the decade."

During the mid-1970s I spent many long hours with Rabbi Levinger, strolling alongside the canyons that lead from Jerusalem to the Dead Sea. As he faced the barren expanses, he fervently predicted that they would one day be filled with mothers and babies, with engineers and farmers, and especially, with Torah scholars. He would point to the desolate hillsides and declare confidently that settlements would be established at their peaks, complete with synagogues, factories, and offices. At a time when GE didn't even have a single vehicle, he sketched out a network of highways crisscrossing the Territories. When the movement treasury could not pay its telephone bill, he spoke of investments of hundreds of millions of dollars. Later GE drew up a systematic program for settling Greater Israel. When this agenda was first revealed, in a stifling, crowded cellar, it aroused only ridicule. Nevertheless, despite the active opposition of prime ministers and defense ministers, and of elites and substantial sectors of the Israeli public, today Jews have settled every one of the locations we passed on our moonlight walks.[2]

GE prides itself on its historical-scale impact. Once it emerged in recognized form in the mid-1970s, GE became involved in direct-action politics, which included violent attempts to sabotage international agreements based on Israeli withdrawal from Sinai and the West Bank. By means of mass rallies and illicit settlement attempts, ingenious parliamentary and extraparliamentary maneuvering, and skilled manipulation of public opinion and of the establishment authorities, GE pursued the objective subsumed under the slogan "The Whole Land of Israel," meaning in practice the annexation of the territories governed by the military since 1967. The movement is largely responsible for the fundamental change in the Territories represented by over eighty thousand settlers in more than 120 settlements.[3] Recent Cabinets also share this responsibility, since their support was essential for furthering the movement's cause. This in turn has been another measure of GE's success.

Through such activism, GE aroused considerable opposition in the country and created both an ideological and a tactical conflict among Israeli Jews. This resulted in physical clashes in which the esctatic cadres of the movement and their supporters belligerently confronted leaders of the state, high officials, agents of law and order, and adversary groups. All these clashes grew out of provocations perpetrated by relatively few activists. While dramatic actions such as illegal settlement brought GE into direct conflict with the police and military, they also split the Israeli populace into two camps. GE had staged confrontations with local Arabs in which the true believers behaved with less restraint, beginning with acts of vandalism and harassment against the indigenous population and ending with wounding and killing.

This violent stream of GE activism found its logical conclusion in the plot to blow up the sacred Islamic mosque and shrine on the Temple Mount in Jerusalem. The act was to have been the crowning achievement of the "Jewish Underground in the Territories."[4] The activist group involved in the planning was small and included hardcore members of GE close to the movement's leadership and in sympathy with its platform and mood. Subsequently this group earned the sympathy of a considerable portion of activist-believers. Their goal was to end what they felt was Islam's contamination of the holiest Jewish site, in preparation for the final redemption. This covert initiative was interrupted by the Israeli secret services in 1984. A scholarly simulation game conducted at the Harvard Center for International Affairs analyzed the possible outcomes of such a scheme, had it succeeded. Some experts believed that it might have triggered World War III. The cell of activist-believers had in fact taken such a possibility into account. The heads of the Underground foresaw that the bombing of the "abomination" would arouse Muslims to a jihad, sweeping all mankind into an ultimate confrontation. This they interpreted as the "War of Gog and Magog," with cosmic implications. Israel's victorious emergence from this longed-for trial by fire would then pave the way for the coming of the Messiah.[5]

Mythic and Historic Origins of the Movement

GE has accorded its own chronicles the status of sacred history. Like all mythology, the story of the movement's origins has a dramatic narrative structure. The present is only an episode in the legendary annals of the movement, a connecting link between the glorious beginning and the longed-for end, the two foci of classic myths. GE's eschatological vision of the future foresees Israeli sovereignty over all the Land of Israel within its maximum biblical boundaries (from the Euphrates River in Iraq to the Brook of Egypt), and centers on the rebuilt Temple as the focus of both religious and national life. Meanwhile, competing myths of origin also circulate within GE, enveloping the original historical kernel with heroism and magic.

One popular version attributes the founding of the movement to a sermon delivered by its spiritual leader at the Merkaz Harav Yeshiva (Talmudic academy) in Jerusalem in May 1967. As the story goes, in an emotional and ceremonial address marking Israel's nineteenth Independence Day, Rabbi Kook the Younger raised several tenets of the messianic mystical system (hereinafter called "Kookism") which would come to constitute the spiritual base of the revolutionary Jewish-Zionist drive of GE. Employing powerful rhetoric, Rabbi Z. Y. Kook expounded a series of fundamentals, including his "incontestable" claim that redemption is already underway, its manifestations national-political but not yet necessarily religious-ethical. The realization of messianism, he continued, is not a function of a return to explicit faith in God and to fulfillment of halakhic precepts, but rather a phenomenon which precedes and conditions such return. The current State of Israel embodies the very fulfillment of the messianic ideal, precisely as it was envisioned by the Prophets. Therefore, he concluded, reinforcing the Israeli Army is a vital religious and spiritual matter, at least equivalent to glorifying the Torah by increasing the number of yeshivas.[6]

Normative Judaism would have considered this message audacious. But the activist-believers of GE have learned Rabbi Kook's words by heart. A tape recording of his speech has long served as a focal point of movement festivals. At one point, the rabbi's stammering whisper suddenly becomes an outburst of weeping. He cries out in yearning for parts of the Land of Israel "which were torn from the live body" with the territorial partition of 1948, specifying Hebron, Jericho, and Shechem (Nablus). This utterance surprised his audience, coming as it did before any sign of the impending war and at a time when the issue of the integrity of the Land of Israel was not on any public agenda whatsoever. Several weeks later, when Shechem and Jericho were conquered and the rabbi's students made their pilgrimage to these sites, they imparted a prophetic quality to the sermon. GE believes its birth to have taken place at this moment of revelation.

An alternative opening to the movement saga occurred in the wake of the Six-Day War, known in GE's idiom as the "War of Redemption." In spring 1968, Rabbi Levinger and about ten Torah scholars and their families celebrated the Passover seder at the Arab-owned Park Hotel in the heart of Hebron and remained in the area as squatters. Later this group became the spearhead of settlement efforts in the Territories.[7] They had come to the hotel claiming to be Swiss tourists, deceiving the local population and maneuvering around the Israeli government by exploiting squabbles among cabinet ministers. That night they introduced, as they say, "new facts in the field and changed the map of Israel." Since then, this pioneering vanguard has clung to the City of the Patriarch Abraham despite political opposition, harsh physical conditions, and difficult security problems.

Yet another "sacred moment" came after a five-year period of hibernation and in the aftermath of the October 1973 Yom Kippur War. As part of the Kissinger initiative for a disengagement agreement with the Syrians, Israel was obligated to withdraw several kilometers in the Golan Heights. Popular opposition to this "defeatist" measure was expressed mostly through sit-ins in front of the prime minister's home. There the original GE core group met its future periphery, primarily members and former members of the religious Zionist youth movement Bnei Akiva. Also among the protesters were the future allies of GE, the Land of Israel Loyalists,[8] most of whom were secular veterans of the right-wing undergrounds of the pre-State period (the Irgun and the Stern Group) and representatives of the activist faction of the labor movement hailing from veteran cooperative settlements and kibbutzim, which inherited the legacy of the Palmach (the elite troops of the Hagana, the militia which became the core of the Israeli Defense Forces after independence). In this milieu the core that would form GE discovered its affinities with other groups and seized upon the opportunity to form coalitions. GE also realized its public appeal for the first time and became captivated by the charm of what it called "flirtation" with secular Zionists. The core group rejoiced in the feeling that it had expanded dramatically and was now poised at the center of the national and world stage.

Shortly thereafter a series of events occurred which together constitute the best-known starting point for GE: the breakthrough of settlement in Samaria. The movement's few official publications speak of the Elon Moreh settlement group's success following eight attempts to establish a foothold in the Territories as the "Hanukkah miracle of our own day," while adversaries call it their "original sin." Government orders to evacuate the activist-believers led to violent confrontations with the army and finally to a showdown ending in compromise, called the Kaddoum Affair, that enabled the movement to establish the first Jewish settlement in the Nablus region (December 1975).

Other important settlements took root in the wake of the 1973 Yom Kippur War. Within the state, demoralization and anomie prevailed, while outside of it, Israel lost prestige and endured pressures for concessions. Young people licked their war wounds and protested the establishment's "national blunder." A United Nations decision denounced Zionism as racism. In Sebastia, an abandoned Ottoman railroad station located near the ruins of the ancient capital of biblical Israel, GE members began to settle. They considered the site to be the sacred heart of the Promised Land as well as a bridgehead for penetration into the heart of a Palestinian population thought to manifest an extreme national consciousness. Sebastia was a formative and decisive moment in the movement's history. It is GE's counterpart to the storming of the Bastille in 1789 and Khomeini's landing at the airport of Meharabad in 1979: this place and event symbolized the movement's historical progress. Since then, Sebastia has served as a reminder of devotion and sacrifice, and the Elon Moreh group which settled there has taken on the role of supreme moral authority because its members mapped out GE's ideological, political, and operative front with their own bodies. After consolidating their settlement at the original site, they migrated to a new location, then another, and then another, each time provoking conflict with the establishment and with the local population as they came closer to the final objective—the Casbah of the Arab city at the foot of biblical Mount Gerizim.

Two years prior to this dramatic settlement, during a February 1974 conference at kibbutz Kfar Etzion in the Territories, the name *Gush Emunim* was coined and immediately broadcast and perpetuated by the media. Torah scholars began leaving the confines of the yeshiva and engaging in external activity, joining already active settlement groups and cooperating with veteran politicians who suddenly realized that the existing political systems, especially that of the National Religious Party (NRP), were too restricting and decadent for them. Thus GE gradually shed its identification with the young guard of partisan religious Zionism and developed its organizational and ideological autonomy and formally incorporated the Elon Moreh settlers, whose contribution to the merger was a fierce fighting spirit and operational experience.

In these recountings of GE origins activist-believers and researchers alike have overlooked the fact that shortly after the establishment of the State of Israel, when no one would have entertained the notion of the conquest of the Territories, there were unmistakable portents of GE on the horizon. Many of the religious and social characteristics of Jewish-Zionist radicalism in Israel emerged in embryonic form during the early 1950s through the phenomenon known as *Gahelet* (literally, "the embers")—the Pioneer Torah Scholars' Group. Gahelet was a group of students at a school belonging to Israel's neo-orthodox stream, which was then at its lowest ebb. Possessed of a naive, intense enthusiasm for traditional religious Judaism, coupled with feelings of inferiority and envy with regard to the modern secular Zionist world, these young people sought to participate in the dynamics and achievements of that world. They developed a strikingly original and ambitious worldview that differed significantly from both religious and secular-national perspectives, and they sought religious validation for their initiative in a father-son team of rabbis. Thus, over twenty years before the public emergence of GE, and ten years before the "rediscovery" of the Territories, members of Gahelet appropriated the doctrine of Rabbi Kook the Elder, transforming it from the esoteric and quietistic dogma of a small and marginal circle into a gospel which spread throughout Israel to serve as a platform for the ensuing activism. By adopting Rabbi Kook the Younger as their spiritual leader, members of Gahelet propelled him from the status of a forgotten, ridiculed figure at the margins of the Torah and Zionist worlds into an outstanding Israeli personality with a magnetic influence on a broad circle. GE thus had its beginnings in the work of about a dozen fourteen-year-olds. Today, every one of them has a position in the gallery of spiritual authorities of the radical Jewish-Zionist movement.[9]

The War of Redemption: June 1967

Given these competing and overlapping moments of origin, one must nevertheless isolate June 1967 as the critical date perceived by the activist-believers as the start of a revolutionary era, the zero point of the movement's calendar, in which the national and religious reckoning begins with the birth of redemption.[10] The Six-Day War and its results had a startling impact on Israeli society. Its significance lay not only in the fantastic, unexpected dimensions of the victory itself but also in the shock of moving, in the space of a few days, from the brink of national destruction to unprecedented heights of strategic achievement. It was in this dramatic reversal that the force of the event lay, not least from a religious point of view. Even many secular Zionists described their euphoria in religious terms. Although religious Zionists, among whom the Kookist youth were prominent, were subject to the amazement and confusion affecting all Israelis, they had at their disposal a unique theology and a consequent outlook which enabled them to interpret the extraordinary experience rapidly and effectively.

The Kookist youth treated the anomic results of the radical upheaval of 1967 by integrating them within the existing messianic-mystical approach taught at Mercaz Harav yeshiva. It was a perfect match yielding a clear and convincing interpretation of the revolutionary circumstances which also corroborated and expanded the Kookists' religious conception. Those potential activists who had lacked self-assurance were now filled with confidence in their faith and themselves. They described the "shock" of victory sensed by most Israelis as the impact of a "burst of light," which the public was not yet capable of containing and appreciating. Thereafter activist-believers employed the term "light" incessantly, fully aware of its kabbalistic connotations of divine abundance, while stressing that it appeared in various combinations in the titles of most of Rabbi Kook's works.[11] Several of the most outstanding Kookists, including Rabbi Levinger and Hanan Porat, were overcome by great enthusiasm, accompanied by an intensification of traditional religious conduct, such as deep devotion to Torah study and prolific production of a new genre of religiopolitical homiletics. An ecstatic frenzy of activism followed.

Documents from that period reveal that some of the Kookists believed that they had undergone a profound mystical experience. At their meetings, they built upon this shared sense to consolidate a joint intellectual and social framework, although not as yet an organizational one. One important milestone was the spontaneous conference of rabbis and yeshiva students from the Merkaz Harav school of thought, several months after the fighting ended. Some considered this conference to be the genesis of GE because it was the first to address explicitly the critical connection between original Kookism and the territorial issue which had recently risen so dramatically to the center of Israeli consciousness. Prevailing circumstances presented the Whole

Land of Israel to the harbingers of GE as an ideal focus for their messianic-mystical conception. From this point on, the Jewish radicals had a cause—the Territories—in which to invest their religious energies and simultaneously develop their potential political powers. Their theology, which was revolutionary in any case, was now augmented by a new component which penetrated toward the center; it thus acquired additional dimensions and an unexpected vitality and attractiveness. The integrity of the land, in turn, was accorded an intense significance, which raised its importance inestimably.

A spirit which would characterize GE began to develop at such increasingly frequent and gradually institutionalized meetings of Torah scholars, who participated either actively or as close observers of what they called the "liberation of the Patriarchs' legacy." This spirit imbued intense all-night discussions by the core group in formation. The meetings produced a series of publications which appeared in standard establishment forums but were innovative in content and in style. These publications attest to a transition of the group from a period of emotional personal confessions sparked by a powerful trauma to a period marked by a relatively stable mood and a well-ordered dogma. Hence the central ideas and values of the GE were formulated about eight years before the movement consolidated and made a public impact. The ideas and values were expressed in a pastiche of realpolitik analyses, Zionist clichés, moral preachings and biblical injunctions, and citations from the Talmud and later rabbinic authorities. The two major themes linking these sundry sources together were the Messiah and the boundaries of the Land of Israel. A new Jewish-Zionist language emerged, focusing on redemption and territory and leading to unprecedented religiopolitical behavior.

The postwar meetings produced operative initiatives that were initially few in number and modest in scope. The first Israeli settlement in the Territories was Kfar Etzion, which enjoyed government assistance and national consensus because it was a case of children returning to the kibbutz their parents had fled in a previous war. Moreover, the site was considered vital from a strategic point of view, as part of the Jerusalem complex. A short time later, Levinger's group drove in stakes in Hebron. After struggles and compromise the government reluctantly established a special enclave for his group outside the boundaries of the Arab city. After an initial brief period of development, this settlement, Kiryat Arba, remains a small, unstable urban community. This is in a nutshell the history of the settlement of the Territories during the period between the two wars.

The Six-Day War transformed the Whole Land of Israel from a distant dream, from an object of contemplation and yearning, into an immediate physical and political reality. Thus a messianic principle thousands of years old was inadvertently realized in one fell swoop. (Actually only one element of the vision of redemption was fulfilled, but people naturally tended to view this element as the all-encompassing vision itself.) Perception of the conquest of the Land of Israel as a critical event in the process of redemption far exceeded all proportions of its original religious significance and gave rise to a messianic dynamic supported by an extensive culture and reflected in discernible behavior. Esoteric and passive doctrine and folklore were now channeled into messianic political activism.[12]

At the same time two trends were taking place in Israeli society in general, also in part in response to the 1967 war. First, there developed among Israelis a more explicit and intense nationalism.[13] Second, Israeli society experienced a wave of what could be called "Judaization" after nearly a century of Zionism. This reaction hinged on a number of factors, including demographic growth in the proportion of traditionally minded Jews (especially immigrants of Middle Eastern origin), a popular surge in feelings of guilt and remorse upon realizing the dimensions and significance of the Holocaust, and of course the symbolic significance of the military victory.

Evoking in one sense the historical memory of the destruction of European Jewry or Jerusalem's destruction and in another sense the meta-historical eschatology of redemption, the war forced Israelis to re-confront their relationship with Jewish peoplehood and with Judaism itself. This meant rediscovering a positive relationship with both the past of the Jewish people and the present-day Jews of the Diaspora. Terms such as "eternal unity," "common fate," and "destiny" were revived in the process. Nationalism and statehood, permeated by the values of modernism and secularity, were suddenly placed in a new proximity and sympathy with the values of religion and tradition. This in turn led to a renewed identification between the two value systems but also a heightened consciousness of their differences.

The war reconnected the State with the Land. The rediscovery of the ancient Promised Land was perhaps no less significant than the rediscovery of Jewishness. The return to the Land of Israel, or, more specifically, to the territories severed from the state at its establishment in 1948 and considered to be the cradle of religion and nationhood, brought secular Zionism closer to Judaism. In the land of the Bible the Israelis have met the Israelites. The return to cherished landmarks and longed-for vistas, pregnant with rich cultural associations, reawakened a long dormant impulse associated with the mystique of the land. The famous photograph of a weeping paratrooper kissing the stones of the Western Wall is a symbol of the unforeseen emergence of religious motifs in contemporary Israel.

The Land of Israel Movement which formed around this mystique was primarily an intellectual trend, the lot of a limited circle of poets, professors, journalists, and retired politicians and military officers. These people were articulate and unimpeachably committed to the cause of reclaiming the land but lacked the temperament and skills required for logistic and tactical activity and for the mobilization of the masses. It is no wonder, then, that they tried to bring the core of activists who would comprise GE under their aegis, as their "troops" or their executive arm. These intellectuals and publicists inspired much of the post-1967 activist and expansionist Zionist ideology, lending a certain sophistication and solemnity to the message which core activists had presented until then in a religiously transparent and politically crude manner. Later, the Land of Israel Movement formulated the secular-national aspect of the ideology of the activists who would form GE, thus supplying the activist-believers with the resources they sorely lacked because of the naiveté of their yeshiva background: brilliant rhetoric, an arsenal of expert arguments in the spheres of strategy, economics, and politics, and a reservoir of financial and moral support.

Because its membership included establishment figures and celebrities, the Land of Israel Movement imparted a certain legitimacy and a measure of respectability to the activists and to the general concept of settlement. By focusing exclusively on the integrity of the Land of Israel, the movement succeeded in uniting followers of ideological and political camps separated by heretofore unbridgeable gaps—right (revisionists) and left (the Kibbutz Meuhad movement), religious and secular. Future members of GE studied this unforeseen matchmaking and learned to exploit it. Activist-believers later enlisted the aid of functionaries from all shades of the parliamentary spectrum, among whom the common denominator was the territorial sentiment first aroused by the Land of Israel Movement.[14]

Between the wars there was also a series of changes affecting the national-religious camp in Israel—the soil from which GE sprouted. The most important upheaval in the realm of Zionist neo-orthodoxy took place within its educational system, which grew in size and stature.[15] The system was based on yeshiva high schools—hybrid, elitist boarding schools which combine high academic standards with equally high ethical demands and ambitious religious studies, primarily concentrating on the Talmud. The result is an exclusive total institution, within which the authority of the rabbis is unchallenged and halakha (Jewish law) is exempt from questions of practical applicability. The counterpart to this system is the national religious youth movement, Bnei Akiva, which displayed extraordinary moral momentum during a period of general decline in ideological tension. This movement has over 30 educational institutions and some 150 branches all over the country. Like the national-religious camp in general (Mizrachi, Hapoel Hamizrachi), Bnei Akiva had tended to educate students for a religious and political middle ground by promoting a humanist-socialist outlook in the style of its "historical allies," the labor parties. However, after 1967, Bnei Akiva youth gravitated toward right-wing parties and toward higher yeshiva education and deemphasized pioneer objectives in a kibbutz—which had been until then the pinnacle of the educational path of this youth movement.

A new type of institution was created in the same spirit for graduates of these systems: the Hesder yeshivas. These offered an alternative path to standard compulsory army service. Over a period of five years, by special arrangement with the Israeli Defense Forces, young men divided their time between concentrated periods of Torah study in the best Orthodox tradition and combat service as soldiers and officers in the infantry or armored corps. In general they maintained outstanding levels of both military and scholarly achievement. Like settlements in Judea and Samaria, the Hesder yeshivas are perceived as a spearhead in the fulfillment of national objectives, but at the same time, they tend to become more isolated and even alienated from the national environment while the level of their self-imposed religious standards increases. Today, there are about fifteen such institutions with nearly fifteen hundred students aged eighteen to twenty-three. Many of the Hesder yeshivas are being established at

GE settlements, where they supply militant cadres for the movement. In a sense they are armed militia devoted to the interests of Jewish radicalism.

In the developments following the Six-Day War, a new breed of religious Jew emerged in Israel, one well-rooted in, and proud of, his religiosity and at the same time eager to excel in service to the life of the nation. One manifestation of this new phenomenon was the rise of the young guard in the National Religious Party. These young people (today aged fifty and up) rebelled against the established leadership of religious Zionism and rid themselves of its old mentality. Their protest centered on a demand to express their views not only regarding issues recognized as traditionally religious, such as observance of dietary laws on Israeli Navy ships, but also regarding secular matters, primarily questions of foreign and security policy. They were no longer content to take a back seat to secular Zionism and sought to introduce initiatives and assume leadership in society and state affairs. In doing so, they abandoned the classic religious-national stand, characterized by moderation and political pragmatism, in favor of an openly ideological, hawkish stance. They also contributed to the early stages in the development of GE; NRP Young Guard personalities were among its most outstanding proponents. Subsequently, however, the activist-believers broke through conventional political party lines and established themselves as the counterforce, even to the more extreme politicians.

The Impact of the Yom Kippur War: October 1973

These developments may have been necessary conditions for the appearance of GE, but they were not sufficient ones. During the first six years after the Six-Day War, virtually nothing occurred which could be viewed as the beginnings of the movement. On the contrary the complacency and stagnation prevailing in all aspects of life in Israel weakened the early momentum and the embryonic manifestations of movement organization. Something more was needed to bring the potential of Jewish-Zionist radicalism to fruition. Once again it was a war. The Yom Kippur War of 1973 was the catalyst for the eventual formation of GE.

Immediately after the 1967 battles, Rabbi Kook had refused to sign the charter of the Land of Israel Movement, because, as he claimed, the "true whole Land of Israel" was still not in Israel's hands. But he did publish a proclamation identifying the land by its full biblical borders and declaring that a person should even risk his life for its conquest and settlement. Only after the 1973 war was this statement disseminated and popularized; overnight it became the manifesto of GE.

Ironically, an event which might have otherwise signaled retreat in the messianic process led instead to the surge of the messianic movement. The Yom Kippur War resulted in the loss of certain territories considered part of the Whole Land of Israel, followed by the threat of losing additional territories conquered in the Six-Day War. Simple logic suggested that these developments would perhaps create an insurmountable problem of interpretation for religious activists, contradicting their formula that Israel's territorial, military, and political achievements reflect and serve cosmic progress. Messianic fulfillment was long considered an absolute certainty based on the linking of the messianic phase with specific geopolitical signs. Now there was an unambiguous change on the historical side of the equation; hence one could expect a parallel change on the spiritual side. However, the opposite result occurred. Instead of feeling disappointment and abandoning their messianic strategies, the activist-believers now appeared to have even greater confidence in their Kookist method and proceeded to apply it without compromise.

Was the famous law of cognitive dissonance at work here?[16] This social-psychological paradigm has been employed to explain other paradoxes in the history of messianism: the momentum which transformed Christianity from just another marginal sect to a universal religion gathered only in the wake of the Crucifixion; similarly, the incarceration and conversion to Islam of Shabbetai Zevi, the Jewish Messiah of the seventeenth century, led to an additional pulse of messianic ecstasy among the masses.[17] The success of religion in such cases depends on its ability to supply the faithful with an explanation of the frustrating incident in terms of the faith itself, by providing an interpretation corroborating belief with events ostensibly contradicting it. The "embarrassing blunder" is integrated into the overall scheme of things so that it becomes the axis of a new phase of religion. A complex theology develops around such historical episodes, rendering their crisis potential a source of inspiration for religious revival.

From the outset, Kookism was a religious reaction to the victory of modern nationalism in Judaism. The rabbi's messianic-mystical method is an original variant of a religious phenomenon which tries to come to grips with the secularity confronting it by converting the latter into its revelation. According to this conceptual strategy, the existing lay order in Israel—particularly its statist pioneer version, as reflected in hawkish policies and settlements à la the Greater Land of Israel—is but a crude and provisional embodiment of the supremely sacred and thus appears as sinful and heterodox only to those of limited faith. Such ultranationalism is in fact an expansion and exaltation of the old religion, a return of true Judaism to its full and original scope, which transcends conventional Orthodoxy.

According to GE, secular Zionism has a function in the messianic plan and is therefore vital and sacred. There is a Jewish mission which only Zionism can fulfill, but once it realizes its destiny and exhausts itself and its secularity, its latent religiosity will come to light. In the final accounting, modern secular Judaism will be exposed as episodic, exactly like Orthodox Judaism. After these two—antitheses of one another—complete their role, they will make way for a new Jewish entity which will emerge from their synthesis: religious-national revolutionary Judaism.

This quasi-kabbalistic interpretation could account successfully for the Six-Day War and its outcome. Initially, at least, the results of the war could not be perceived as anything but a mighty victory for secular Zionism and a powerful proof of the justice of the ways of secular nationalism (particularly the labor movement's version). GE, however, found a lofty religious message in it. Moreover, the historical irony of the situation in which the victory of the new "Israelism" brought it into contact with the old Judaism, provided support for the Kookist outlook. But now in the Yom

Kippur War, proud Zionism suffered a mighty blow. Failures in the battlefield were perceived as the result of ideological and moral decay. Zionism itself described the situation as an intense crisis. The Kookists proposed a religious explanation to suit the upheaval, rendering faith even more compelling and encouraging than it had been before. Borne on this exegetical layer of its peculiar doctrine, the radical Jewish Zionist movement took off.

Thus, the perceived post-1973 decline of classic Zionism reinforced faith and impelled believers to activism. At their disposal were additional explanations from the repertoire of the messianic legacy, all contributing to the movement effort: withdrawal from the Territories in the wake of a cruel war is a crucible, a trial in which God tests Israel; it is a signal from above that we have not done our part below within the framework of the overall scheme, in which, determinism notwithstanding, there is an active role for mankind. These are the "pangs of the Messiah," the trials and tribulations which emerge before redemption, heralding and conditioning its fulfillment. Activist-believers recalled an obscure legend about the existence of two Messiahs: Only when the first one, the son of Joseph, falls in battle will his successor, the son of David, arise to complete the job.[18] One Kookist rabbi, a significant spiritual authority for GE, described the future of secular Israel as that of a soldier falling in the desert after a fierce and heroic war. Now faithful Israel must take the torch from the corpse and ascend the mountain to carry on the mission of redemption.

Only in this context could GE launch an assault on Zionism, aiming to inherit its legacy in the name of Judaism. Movement propaganda portrayed the post-1973 situation as fraught with danger and the movement itself as the savior of the nation. The activist-believers appealed to both sides in the crisis: they prescribed settlement in Judea and Samaria as both a strategic and a moral solution. GE offered itself as a "Zionist and Jewish response." Members believed, and continue to believe, that GE is answering a divine call by responding to the needs of an errant people who cry out for a determined leadership to supply it with spiritual guidance and rehabilitate its sagging morale. In their eyes the cruel war confirmed and accelerated the messianic process and revealed the weakness of the Christian civilization which had penetrated the "Westoxicated" State of Israel.[19] Similarly, the nation's leaders were "hesitant," "cowardly," and "overly concerned with the goyim." In place of Zionism conceived as a "solution of the Jewish problem," or as a "safe refuge," GE offered "Torah Zionism" and a "Zionism of Redemption." The movement presented itself as a candidate for national leadership while claiming to be simply the executor of the genuine national will.

During the first few months after the war, GE became part of the rising tide of protest movements against the political establishment. These protests were initiated primarily by demobilized soldiers with a heroic aura and Zionist commitment who felt betrayed and confused. GE was unique among these proto-organizations in its unambiguous analysis and positive and concrete program. While the solutions suggested by this naive grass-roots awakening targeted the civil and administrative spheres (e.g., the demand to change the electoral system), and its criticism focused on particular personalities (demanding the resignation of Prime Minister Golda Meir and Defense Minister Moshe Dayan), the protestors who called for a cultural revolution would soon become the founders of GE. The Yom Kippur War was thus more than a trigger for the movement's appearance; it created a crisis of ideology and authority in Israel which GE sought to address.

The Charismatic Formative Phase: 1974–77

By 1974 GE already had in place an elaborate ideology, a defined set of objectives, and a core group of highly talented and devoted members. But it took at least another year to develop full self-awareness as a movement, a year characterized by intensive activity and spiritual tension. As the circles of activists and supporters stabilized, GE gradually developed organizational systems, operational methods, and a distinctive ethos. The activist-believers sensed that a movement was in formation and that they were "making history."

That period was characterized by great enthusiasm; everything was new. GE sent out feelers to the government and the public, clarifying its own motives to others and to itself. Between and during "campaigns," movement leaders met in innumerable marathon conferences, engaging in soul-searching and heated debates on a vast spectrum of operative questions and guiding principles: Shall we encourage members to refrain from striking Jewish policemen? Is it permissible to insult IDF generals? Shall we condemn our comrades who toyed with the notion of assassinating Secretary of State Kissinger? Shall we go as far as suicide in applying the precept of "devoting one's life" to the land and the people? Do we welcome delegations of well-wishers and supporters from kibbutzim, even if they travel to us on the Sabbath? Shall we cooperate closely with personalities and groups of questionable moral fiber for purposes of settling the Territories? Shall we continue to pursue a political line despite the reservations of yeshiva rabbis? Shall we temporarily suspend our sharp differences of opinion with the prime minister and express solidarity with him as he faces the president of the United States and the nations of the world? Is the "Brook of Egypt," which the Bible delineates as the southern boundary of Israel, Wadi El-Arish, in the center of the Sinai peninsula, or is it the Nile, far to the west? The political context for GE was a frontal confrontation with the government, left-wing parties, and spontaneous citizens' initiatives. While pressures mounted in the international arena for disengagement of the opposing forces as a step toward the eventual return of territories occupied since 1967, the Israeli public was in turmoil and the Israeli government was plagued by in-fighting which undermined its authority. GE exploited this situation expertly.

Initially, GE activity took the form of protest demonstrations, primarily against the postwar disengagement agreement with the Syrians and the interim agreements with Egypt, brokered by the United States. At that time the movement focused primarily on Sinai, as well as on the Golan Heights, where the settlement of Keshet was founded (1974).[20] Later the center of gravity shifted to the West Bank and to the insidious or forcible creation of "facts in the field." During the sensational settlement attempts at Elon Moreh in the Nablus region, the settlement of Ofra, near Ramallah, took root far from the limelight and became the first Jewish settlement in Samaria (1975). These two settlements produced leaders of the movement, joined by the hard core of settlers who had never ceased aggressive efforts to penetrate the heart of Hebron. Subsequently other settlements joined the GE system in the Territories, including Maale Adumim, which began with a dozen families in tents on an exposed desert mountaintop and is now a relatively large urban center, a bedroom suburb of Jerusalem.

These new points of settlement, although few in number and small in size, were of crucial significance to GE's progress in that they broke down the psychological and political barriers against settlement in the Territories and increased public awareness regarding the integrity of the land. Furthermore, they bolstered the movement's self-confidence considerably, reinforced its cadres, improved methods and means through trial and error, concentrated resources, and helped create a movement heritage. Later they would supply guidance and support and provide a model and bases for subsequent settlement campaigns.

After these initial successes, GE devoted the following two years (1976–77) to preparing the infrastructure for the expansion and consolidation of settlement. Besides countering government opposition, GE devoted its energies to recruiting face-to-face, exploiting existing networks of the young religious national sector. This is why, for example, a settlement core group may comprise former congregants of a particular synagogue in central urban Israel. Both recruitment and buildup of commitment and solidarity were carried out primarily through home meetings, at which veteran members address groups of ten to twenty persons, primarily young couples. Meetings took place every evening throughout Israel. In addition to campaigns in the field and lobbying in the Knesset, these meetings remained a central activity of the movement. In these meetings the second wave of settlers was recuited. Naturally this group was less homogeneous and generally less motivated and qualified than the pioneer settlers were. Nonetheless, by early May 1977, the movement boasted about a dozen groups prepared to settle in the Territories.

During this period, the movement encouraged sympathetic media coverage of its persistent acts of settlement in the Territories, and attempted to exacerbate rifts in the Knesset. The movement also embarked on propaganda campaigns that consisted mainly of lectures at any available forum, including secondary schools, community centers, kibbutzim, and of course various religious institutions, such as yeshivas and synagogues. These activities were accompanied by the "muscle flexing" of mass rallies and events designed to broaden the popular base of GE, increase its self-confidence, and exert pressure on decision makers. Such events included festive assemblies of hard-liners—not all of them Orthodox—as well as colorful marches of primarily Orthodox youth and families with children, who spent a day or two walking across Judea and Samaria. Among these campaigns were the Hakafot (Torah scroll processions, accompanied by singing and dancing) held during the 1975 Sukkot (Tabernacles) school vacation, in which many of the participants experienced a spiritual uplift while hiking through the desert and confronting the troops. In the Land of Israel March on Independence Day, May 1976, nearly twenty thousand people, armed to the teeth, participated in a kind of peripatetic picnic in the barren hills and Palestinian villages in Samaria. Such operations were timed to coordinate with impending settlement attempts and to serve as a source of recruitment and moral support.

The years 1974 to 1977 constituted GE's formative period: the behavioral patterns established then have endured despite changing circumstances. It was a period of purity in which a complete and consistent worldview was established along with the characteristic qualities of the movement. The movement achieved maximum spiritual and operative momentum. Even in celebrating its considerable strategic achievements on the occasion of its tenth anniversary, GE referred for guidance to those charismatic days which they termed "the Sebastia Era." If GE experienced a golden age, this was it.

Legitimation and Institutionalization, 1977–82

The political upheaval of May 1977 took GE by surprise, but the movement, seeking to collect on the victorious Likud's promissory note, immediately embarked on a massive settlement campaign. The new prime minister, Menachem Begin, reacted negatively, however, to the movement's initiative. Despite the government ban and intervention by the army and police, GE dispatched several of its settlement groups which were already on the alert. After a few weeks' honeymoon between the movement and the government—during which still unauthorized settlements were accorded official sanction—a bitter conflict ensued. But in time, relations between GE and the establishment stabilized and became characterized by mutual ambivalence: Begin admired GE, but insisted on maintaining the initiative, control, and credit for himself. GE, in turn, complained, but realized that it couldn't hope for a more convenient administration. One hand of the government gave to the movement generously and encouraged it, while the other admonished it. In turn GE acknowledged the government but violated its instructions and provoked and criticized it.

Movement leaders soon realized that GE was in a trap. On the rise of the hawkish right-wing parties to power, the movement found itself in an unfamiliar situation. First it lost something of its uniqueness. Mounting nationalist sentiment in the Israeli government and the public dimmed GE's centrality and aura. The movement also missed its identity as an opposition force. In the new political reality, it enjoyed a certain legitimacy which proved somewhat embarrassing to the radicals. Thus, despite its obvious advantages, the institutionalization of the movement's relations with the administration and its new role as an integral part of the Israeli political system was at best a mixed blessing.

The movement felt somewhat superfluous: its work was being accomplished by the government, which established settlements in the Territories, set up electricity lines, paved roads, and encouraged people to settle there en masse. Yet the government also continued to uphold its commitment to law and order, democracy, and the peace process, which now appeared to threaten Israeli sovereignty in the Territories.

The ostensible contradiction in the government's behavior was paralleled by a curious irony within GE: as settlements proliferated and expanded at an unprecedented pace, the movement seemed to be deteriorating, lurching from one crisis to another.

The most dramatic event of the years 1977–82 centered on the Elon Moreh settlement venture and reflected the delicacy and ambiguity of GE's relations with the new government. The establishment of a Jewish settlement on a site near Rujeib village overlooking Nablus was a GE reaction to the disclosure of plans for autonomy for the Arabs in the Territories, perceived as opening the door for a Palestinian state in Judea and Samaria. GE set up this settlement in the heart of a territory considered to be in danger of losing its Jewish control at a speed which effectively prevented any possible countermeasures by either Israelis or Arabs. When local residents recovered from the initial shock, they appealed to the Israel Supreme Court, which ruled that the settlement indeed violated their rights and robbed them of their property. The court decided that the land was to be returned to the owners (October 1979). Fearing a precedent which might jeopardize annexation of the Territories, GE demanded changes in legislation which entailed violation of the American-engineered Israel-Egypt accords.

The movement threatened violent opposition to evacuation and exerted considerable pressure on the government, with the tacit cooperation of some cabinet ministers. In the end, however, faced with a determined stand by Prime Minister Begin and with increasing disapproval by the general public, the Elon Moreh settlement group left quietly, but not without exacting a price, namely, a government promise to reinforce settlement in the Territories and remove any remaining legal obstacles. When the government dragged its feet on the promise, settlement leaders began a well-publicized hunger strike in front of the Knesset. The government responded with a public declaration of a "settlement offensive" and massive appropriation of Arab-owned land, thus temporarily stilling settlers' demands.

The incident reflected GE's animosity toward the Israeli legal system, which they perceive as a manifestation of all that is negative in secular Zionism. The Supreme Court of Justice is considered by GE to epitomize the liberal-universalistic world view and seen as engaging in a petty and superficial legalism under the pretense of enlightenment. GE's own illegalism, on the other hand, is presented as legitimate because motivated by utter loyalty to the nation and a deep understanding of its "genuine" needs. Especially revealing in this respect were the official declarations of the Torah-centered settlers' representatives, who inadvertently undermined the pleadings of their own attorneys. They claimed that the crucial factor in determining the site of a settlement in the Land of Israel is certainly not civil law or even strategic interests but rather the religious mandate: "Elon Moreh is the very heart of the Land of Israel in the deepest sense of the word, a divine promise and an ancestral heritage as formulated in the Torah. Thus security considerations (concerning proposed settlement sites), while sincere and important in themselves, are of no significance to us. Hence we reject them, as they render settlement conditional and provisional, whereas it should be axiomatic and eternal."

During this period, GE's charismatic elan began to wane somewhat. The movement looked back nostalgically on the days when its hallmark had been spontaneity and enthusiasm. As in other movements, institutionalization of achievements inaugurated a decline. Routinization and consolidation were expressed both within the settlements and at higher GE levels. The situation at the settlements was reflected in the luxurious villas which replaced the narrow, dilapidated caravans, inciting reproof of bourgeois values and decadence. On the intersettlement level, a wide-reaching network of sophisticated institutions developed. Above the local authorities, which functioned as municipalities in every respect, was the Council of Settlements, a body of delegates of all Jewish settlements in the Territories. In Hebrew the council was called Moetzet Yesha, the latter word both an acronym for "Judea, Samaria, and Gaza" and a term meaning "salvation." It is a rather democratic and pluralistic institution comprising personalities and communities which are not necessarily identified with GE. The movement still considers itself as the moral authority which provides the council with guidance and decides certain issues, but the council is becoming more autonomous and is thus a potential rival to GE. As a sort of parliament of Jews in the Territories, the council functioned, and continues to function, as a lobby in Israeli politics and as an administrative authority with a considerable degree of autonomy. It has developed diverse executive organs, such as an investment company and newspaper, as well as systems of commerce, advertising, recreation, transportation, and the like.

Specialized GE institutions arose in the Territories at this time, many of which have continued to support the movement and its activities. Of particular significance is the educational system, from kindergarten through *kollel* (a yeshiva for family men over twenty), which trains future members of the movement. The educational system is also a major supplier of jobs. In fact, a high percentage of settlers earn their living from organizations revolving around the GE axis.

The pride of GE's branch institutions is undoubtedly Amana, the Jewish settlement organization in the Territories. When founded in 1976, it was only an appendage of GE, described by the movement's leadership as "a by-product which should be left by the wayside as we press onward." Gradually, Amana became a dominant and nearly independent organization because of the increase in the scope of its activities and achievements. This was reflected partly in its growing prestige and budget, accompanied by a rise in professional expertise and formalization. The latter development underscores the deterioration in the cohesiveness and stability of GE's leadership, which was unstructured from the outset. Amana evolved an original settlement model, which is increasingly emulated outside the Territories as well. This is the "community settlement," characterized by homogeneity, intimacy, and strict social and moral control, as well as by political tension, a high level of involvement in the community, righteous behavior patterns, and dedication to the cause of Greater Israel. It aims at combining the radical ideology of GE with an ecologically improved quality of life, social exclusiveness, and a high cultural level. This combination makes the settlements attractive, especially because the majority of settlers commute daily to jobs in central Israel, despite the high value attached to living in the Territories. Every family lives according to its taste and means as an economically and socially separate, independent unit. Along with a capitalist laissez-faire regime, there are elected bodies responsible for public affairs. Community settlements are run on a semi-cooperative basis, in which there is cooperation in municipal but not economic affairs. The end product is a kind of hybrid of a village and a suburb.[21]

At this writing many of the GE leaders and activists can still be found on the government payroll as rabbis, teachers, students, soldiers, Interior and Defense Ministry officials, and even as functionaries of the Ministry of Religious Affairs. Ironically, in the new reality of the Territories, much of the anti-establishment activism is essentially financed by the government itself—a situation regarded as scandalous by GE critics. The government provides GE members with the economic base and the necessary free time, not to mention the legitimation, for their religiopolitical activism.

The extent of GE's institutionalization over the past decade is clearly reflected in the administrative sphere (for example, the movement has a proper headquarters, with a permanent staff, representatives abroad, etc.) and in the political sphere: personalities identified with the movement can be found in various parliamentary factions, such as the NRP, Tehiya, and Morasha.[22] Movement leaders maintain regular close contact with factions in the major parties, such as the Likud. In this new situation, there are some areas of partial overlap between movement institutions and those of the government itself, including such sensitive issues as finances and even security. The Interministerial Committee for Settlement, headed by Ariel Sharon, and the Settlement Department of the Jewish Agency, headed by Herut functionary Matti Drobles—the well-financed and well-staffed bodies responsible for settlement of the Land of Israel—work in full cooperation with GE, so much so that the movement's cadres are often perceived as civil servants.[23] The IDF has established organic units of settlers, with their own arms and command, who deal with their Palestinian neighbors both within and outside of the limits of their military authority. Sometimes it is difficult to distinguish between state affairs and GE affairs. Even their rhetoric has begun to sound similar.

A new type of movement leader, less expressive and more task oriented, emerged in response to the process of institutionalization in the late 1970s and early 1980s. Some of the new leaders moved up from the periphery of the movement, while others constitute a new generation of members altogether. Although no less radical, they seem much more practical. Leadership positions are assumed by Uri Elizur, Pinhas Wallerstein, Uri Ariel, Israel Harel, and many more heads of local councils and other bureaucratic bodies, most of which are not Torah-centered. Although this younger group initially accepted the authority of GE's spiritual leaders and founders, such as Moshe Levinger and Hanan Porat, they gradually became the alternative to these founders, largely on the strength of their record of successful, pragmatic action based on a policy of accommodation with the government and other sectors of Israeli society. At the same time, the Kookists are losing their majority among the settlers. Moreover, an increasing number of non-Orthodox and not even particularly hawkish

Israelis are moving into Judea and Samaria. A mass of settlers is emerging which cannot even be identified with GE. This is another of the unforeseen results of the movement's success.

Consolidation, Crises and Contradictions, 1982–87

As GE became routinized and firmly rooted, it underwent a series of crises beginning with the Camp David Accords of 1978, which were received with utter shock. The activist-believers' confusion was exacerbated by a feeling of betrayal. They abandoned their illusions as they realized that the evacuation of Sinai would be a consequence of the accords. GE was totally committed to the Movement to Stop Withdrawal from Sinai, which it led and manned.[24] The activist-believers set up fortifications on the rooftops of the town of Yamit. It took a major IDF force to remove them in April 1982, following difficult physical confrontations which, miraculously, did not end in casualties. The movement's frustration, beyond the very act of withdrawal from parts of the Land of Israel, was aggravated by the vast gap between its ambitious objectives—to obtain the signatures of more than a million sympathizers and to assemble a "critical mass" of at least one hundred thousand active opponents of withdrawal—and its actual accomplishments, which fell far short of previous achievement levels. The movement's disappointment was acute indeed. This was the first time that it faced an overt test, having put all its energies into an issue and its prestige on the line. Then, following the Yamit Affair, the movement became for a time isolated and despised, even by its former friends, after it attempted to sabotage the longed-for peace with the Arabs and even to raise a hand against the army and drag it into an internal political dispute. Only a few months later, the 1982 Lebanon War broke out, bringing in its wake more disappointing results for GE: the government representing nationalism and a hard-line approach lost its authority, the peace camp grew more powerful, and Palestinian opposition in the Territories not only was not eliminated but even increased in intensity.

These setbacks provided the background for a series of terrorist attacks against Arab institutions and personalities in the West Bank, including the booby-trapping of cars of Palestinian mayors and the wounding of several of them (June 1981) and the murder of three students at the Islamic College in Hebron and the wounding about thirty more (July 1983). Members of the Jewish Underground in the Territories were tried, found guilty, and sentenced to prison (April 1984). Their capture came just in time to prevent the destruction of five Arab-owned buses by explosive devices set to go off during the rush hour; their capture also led to the discovery of the plot to blow up the mosques on the Temple Mount. The twenty-seven defendants charged with conspiring in this plot were the very flesh and blood of GE.

These events placed the movement in a situation it had never experienced before, suffering condemnation and banishment from the outside and a deep schism within. The general public and the movement itself began to question the limits of religious national extremism: in certain situations, may this Jewish violence also be directed at Jews? A rift developed between two camps within the movement. Some said that GE should publicly avow full identification with its jailed companions, whereas others demanded that the movement dissociate itself even from public efforts to gain a presidential pardon for them. The rivalry between the two groups was and remains fundamental and intensive. It represents a split between those who remain loyal to the radical trend characterizing the earlier phases, some of whom became even more extreme, and the broad strata which joined GE subsequently without any commitment to the original messianic-mystic position. The controversy extended to questions of the desirable degree of democracy in the decision-making processes within the movement, of whether it is advisable to elevate support for the cause above the risk of alienating fellow Jews, of the possibility of temporarily foregoing oppositionist activism in favor of educational and publicity activities until a new generation emerges, of the nature of human rights for local Arabs and of the wisdom of an a priori rejection of any accommodation with the Palestinians. Members even disagreed on the desired degree of influence of religious considerations on political decisions.

In this time of testing, a measure of the early complacency and optimism of the activist-believers was replaced by a mood of humility and sobriety and a heightened sensitivity to the moods and tendencies within the movement and the public at large. The new sensitivity was reflected, in turn, in a willingness to adopt less dramatic and more subdued patterns of activity. This phase lasted from 1984 to the end of 1987. These were not years of spectacular events and the relative calm was used to strengthen the movement's hold on the Territories and on power centers within Israel. There were signs that the tension of political and religious radicalism was abating—until the next crisis.

Coping with the Intifada, 1987–

This essay was completed during the third year of the Palestinian national uprising in the Territories. The Intifada returned GE to the headlines. Since it began, the settlers have shifted their focus from confrontation with the Israeli government to confrontation with the neighboring Arab population. The threat to law and order and to the values of Western democracy was compounded by a threat to coexistence with local Arabs and to their rights and well-being. In these confrontations, GE again acted through parliamentary and extraparliamentary channels and also adopted an aggressive, reactive, or provocative "sacred vigilantism."[25] A significant number of Palestinians have been wounded or killed by activist-believers.[26]

As time passed, the Intifada became somewhat routinized. Even if it changed appearance from time to time in an attempt to instill new vitality, it nonetheless became more stable and institutionalized. Thus, like the Arabs of the Territories, the Jewish settlers, too, learned to live with the uprising. Moreover, GE cadres claim that their struggle in the present crisis reinforces their faith and entrenches their hold on the Territories. Nevertheless, especially at the inception of hostilities, the Intifada engendered a certain anomie in Israel, especially in the Territories, and the Jewish radical settlers sought authoritative guidance. GE assessed the confrontation with the Palestinian uprising in the Territories—as it did all other issues—according to religious principles. These supply motivation and legitimation for emergency initiatives. On this front as well, the activist-believers operated within a moral space they themselves defined, situated between kabbalistic values and halakhic norms. The former determined overall tendencies and spirit, whereas the latter mapped out the details and restrictions. Movement members and leaders sought answers from their rabbis, who convened in 1989 to discuss "Life in Judea and Samaria during the Intifada according to Torah Law." They considered broad theoretical issues, such as the question of whether the situation in the Territories can be defined as war, and if so, whether the war is mandatory or optional, with entirely different rules applying to each situation. Their responses have significant practical implications. For example, if the situation is indeed considered a state of war, then it is permissible to impose collective punishment, such as blowing up the homes of parents of Arabs who harm Jews. This strategy was based on the biblical account of Simeon and Levi, the sons of Jacob, who slaughtered all the inhabitants of Shechem in retribution for the rape of their sister Dinah. Nevertheless, this case was subject to various interpretations. Even within GE circles, a lively debate developed concerning the relevance and validity of such precedents, its participants fully aware that the ensuing conclusions demanded implementation in the field.

Another question asked which authority is empowered to make decisions about methods of coping with the Intifada—the government or the institutions of activist-believers in the Territories? In general there is a tendency to recognize the authority of the government, which is considered to be the "kingdom of Israel," although some have challenged this view. In practice, the settlers undertake numerous paramilitary activities at their own discretion; some even anchor them in ideology. For example, premeditated GE initiatives were proscribed by the rabbis, but spontaneous reaction to attack was deemed permissible. Furthermore, some GE members readily engaged in reprisals against Arabs, but acknowledged the government's right to prohibit (or permit) the use of lethal force in the reprisals. Movement discussions focus on biblical precedents and halakhic decisions, in which parallels abound. Settlers in the Hebron region, for example, cite the deeds performed by David in the same region even before he was anointed king of Israel some three thousand years ago. David's handling of Nabal the Carmelite remains a source of imitation in crafting contemporary rules of behavior toward stone-throwing Palestinians. In any case, the sanctioning of an operative step by settlers is not based on the severity of the circumstances but rather on the measure's contribution to the religious-national struggle interpreted within the scriptural and Kookist frameworks. Consequently it has been deemed permissible to burn down Arab shops along the road to a settlement if such a measure increases the security of Jewish passers-by.

GE members constantly consult religious authorities in the Territories and elsewhere regarding norms of conduct in specific situations: In reaction to stone throwing, should settlers shoot Palestinians to kill or only to wound? Under what circumstances does one recite the Hagomel blessing (thanking God for deliverance from danger) after traveling through Arab villages—if one escapes injury altogether, or only if one is actually wounded? The local newspaper of one leading GE settlement served as the forum for a rabbinic dispute probing the issue of "whether one may violate the Sabbath to provide medical assistance to a wounded Arab terrorist."

Despite its outbursts of enthusiasm, GE subjects itself to rigid religious discipline in taking such measures. Even under the harshest of conditions, the activist-believers rarely diverge from the guidelines and constraints of a defined code of ethics, whose rules are determined by the application of precedents in the spirit of Talmudic principles. The precedents retrieved from sacred history are largely viewed ahistorically, creating the basis for a rather flexible and selective interpretation, by which different authorities may issue different instructions to the religious public. Consequently the opinions of rabbis identified with the hawkish line espoused by Torah-centered settlers may clash with those of other religious authorities. The halakhic interpretations diverge and even contradict one another, primarily over the two basic issues underlying all GE's endeavors. These issues have become especially acute since the outbreak of the Intifada: (1) considering the public controversy regarding the settlers' activities, does the integrity of the Land of Israel take precedence over the integrity of the Jewish people, or vice versa? (2) as the maintenance of a stalwart hold on the Territories entails the sacrifice of human life—and may escalate violent international conflict—is the integrity of the Land of Israel superseded by the commandment to save lives, or is it so important that it even justifies warfare?

Similarly, the public debate between supporters and opponents of GE—and the broader conflict between sectors upholding Jewish settlement and Israeli sovereignty over the Territories at any price and those who favor withdrawal from the Territories in exchange for an arrangement with the Arabs—emerges as a confrontation between two camps of rabbis. Many ultra-Orthodox authorities in Israel side with the more dovish camp, while the GE activist-believers generally appeal to "their own" rabbis, who predictably provide them with a seal of Torah approval. However, there are also rabbinic disputes within the movement. A forum of GE rabbis, most of whom were settlers themselves and all of whom were followers of the Rabbis Kook and associated with Merkaz Harav yeshiva, convened largely in response to the exigencies of the Intifada. One issue they considered was the status of television news teams covering events in the Territories: as they disgrace Israel before the Gentiles and incite Palestinian aggression, do the media fall in the category of *moser* and *rodef* (informer and pursuer), for whom halakha prescribes the death penalty? Moreover, a stormy debate arose among rabbis in the Territories in 1989 following the public remarks of certain Torah-centered settlers, convicted of firing at Palestinians, who called for "distinguishing between one kind of blood and another." These remarks evoked a reaction from a former chief rabbi of Israel who is now very close to GE circles: "Anyone who claims that we should differentiate between the punishment of a non-Jewish murderer and a Jewish one is correct, although we need not state everything publicly before the world."[27] As a sequel to this affair, which began with a violent reprisal campaign in an Arab village by Jews who sought to settle in Nablus, the magazine of the Judea and Samaria settlers published a debate on the question of whether the Commandment "Thou shalt not kill" applies to the killing of Arabs.

Another instance of the application of a precedent from biblical history and the codex of the Middle Ages to solve current political problems arising from the Intifada occurred when a group of Torah-centered settlers organized to offer sanctuary to several Palestinians who collaborated with the military administration in the Territories. The collaborators claimed that the authorities used the information they provided and then abandoned them to the vengeance of radical Palestinian resistance groups, which condemned them to death for treason. The extension of aid to these Arabs was no trivial matter but rather a far-reaching measure which demanded rabbinic sanction. The senior authorities in the Territories, headed by Rabbi Levinger, decided that one should "extend a hand to a friend." However, this does not mean that GE recognizes the existence of "good Arabs." Actually, many settlers object to housing the collaborators in Jewish settlements, even on a temporary basis. They also express reservations about the intentions of some collaborators to convert to Judaism. The mandate for GE assistance to these Palestinians is limited to its benefit to the Jews in an emergency situation, that is, its contribution to the struggle for Jewish settlement in the Territories. The initiative is explained as follows: "During the conquest of Canaan in the time of Joshua, the Israelites were loyal to the peoples which aided them at risk to their own lives. Similarly, we should repay such assistance in kind today as well, remaining true to the heritage of our forefathers and following the example of their concern for Rahab, the harlot of Jericho (Josh. 2:2)."

At this writing, in early 1990, GE activity continues to intensify the acuity and tragedy of the Intifada. Even more important, perhaps, is its input to the infrastructure from which the Intifada emerged in the first place. To a great extent, GE has planned, initiated, and even implemented the attempted reconstitution of the West Bank as Judea and Samaria.[28] GE continues to be a highly influential factor in determining the rules of the game in the Territories. Along with their enemies, the PLO "shock committees," GE remains the most militant and effective protagonist in the battle over the Territories.

Before the Intifada erupted in late 1987, it appeared that GE had nearly achieved its objectives. The situation of de facto annexation of the Territories was already considered "irreversible."[29] By spring 1990, however, GE appeared to be farther than ever from achieving its objectives. It was no longer the same movement that it was fifteen years ago, when it appeared to be on the verge of taking Israel by storm. Nevertheless, it is still too early to eulogize the movement. For example, after a period of decline, there are signs of a renewed upswing in the recruitment of settlers.[30] The argument can also be made from the movement's history that the current conflict may in fact reinvigorate the cadres of GE if it is seen as underscoring their centrality in the eschatological drama they believe is being played out in the Territories.

Gush Emunim: Descriptive and Analytical Themes

Ideology and Theology

In many studies of Israeli society and of religious-political extremism, the rise and devlopment of GE is connected to that of the Likud, and the crystallization of Jewish fundamentalism is linked to the stance of the revisionist extreme right.[31] While these assertions are not groundless, they should nonetheless be examined in light of several basic facts. The teachings of Rabbis Avraham and Zvi Yehuda Kook were conceived and cultivated by their disciples in the historic epoch of Labor's hegemony. GE's symbolic system owes much to the pioneer Zionist legacy identified with the left. GE burst onto the scene years before the upheaval which brought the "Nationalist Camp" to power, reaching the peak of its enthusiasm and self-confidence under a Labor Government. While the Israeli Government was under the stewardship of Rabin and Peres before 1977, GE laid the foundations of its politics and settlement tactics and established its organizational patterns and modes of struggle. The movement's ideology was fully developed by then and has hardly changed since. Under Labor the number of active supporters who identified with GE's initiatives and the scope of the spiritual awakening GE elicited in various strata of the nation and its elite cadres reached a peak. It is not surprising, then, that to this day GE wishes it could return to that time.

The depiction of GE as the fruit of Jabotinsky's legacy and of the Begin-Sharon regime stems from a tendency among most researchers to focus on the movement's present appearance and extrapolate to its past, assuming that the explanation of its early emergence and growth is to be found in recent circumstances, and implying that it has always been as it is today. The picture thus obtained is not only incomplete but also distorted. In contrast this essay provides a description and analysis of the Jewish-Zionist radical movement from the mid-1970s to the early 1980s—the "classic" period of GE—and focuses on the movement's *hard core*. GE's allies and its circles of followers and supporters—which are by no means homogeneous—are a vital element in completing the picture. However, the movement's periphery contains little which may be considered permanent and tangible and is not as coherent or vigorous as the center.[32] At times, the movement's center opposed the periphery or lacked one altogether. Such instances were eventually shown to be critical periods during which GE achieved impressive results. The center differs from the periphery not only in the extent of its delineation and intensity; it is not simply "more of the same." The center is substantially different from the periphery and largely also considers itself to be a reaction to it.[33]

GE has been an activist core group of observant Jews, mainly yeshiva students, teachers and graduates—young people who number at most several thousand. GE retains many characteristics typical of schismatic and even deviant fringe groups. Yet, with the passage of time, it has achieved a certain centrality in Israeli life, reflected in its disproportionate salience in public consciousness. For nearly twenty years, GE has played a decisive role in determining the agenda of public debate in Israel. Moreover, the movement has been an obstacle to possible arrangements between Israel and the Palestinians and Arab states. People in Israel find themselves arguing about the movement; Israeli society is thus debating with itself. The bitter and sometimes violent arguments about GE, both pro and con, contain several of the fundamentals of Israel's key cultural-political discourse. Although the movement is extra-establishment or anti-establishment and poses a challenge to the center,[34] it essentially expresses the innermost impulses and inclinations of the establishment itself, constituting a cross section of Israel's central complex of ideas and values.[35] This is no accident. From the outset, GE directed itself toward the fragile, sensitive points of Israeli existence, thereby exposing and intensifying the tensions which comprise it. This orientation has constituted yet another source of GE's power.

Some elements of GE ideology are familiar to the public because they were translated into easily assimilated slogans ("Withdrawal from the Holy Land—Over Our Dead Bodies"), as well as acts which speak for themselves, primarily *fait accompli* settlements. Curiously, despite the movement's propaganda efforts, GE has never published a binding and systematic program. The closest the movement came to it was an incidentally composed, amateurish position paper, published during GE's early days, when it had burst into the public arena in the aftermath of the Yom Kippur War. For some reason, the document was only hesitantly released; in any case, it was shelved a short time later. Viewed historically, this document may be considered the movement's articles of establishment (notwithstanding its having been titled "Appendix"). This, GE's only unequivocal and comprehensive statement of faith in over twenty years, may effectively serve as the movement's manifesto to this day. The following excerpts are indicative:

> *Aims:* To bring about a great awakening of the Jewish People towards full implementation of the Zionist vision, realizing that this vision originates in Israel's Jewish heritage, and that its objective is the full redemption of Israel and of the entire world.
>
> *Background:* The Jewish People is now engaged in a fierce struggle for survival in its land and for its right to full sovereignty therein. Yet we are witnessing a process of decline and retreat from realization of the Zionist ideal, in word and deed. Four related factors are responsible for this crisis: mental weariness and frustration induced by the extended conflict; the lack of challenge; preference for selfish goals over national objectives; the attenuation of Jewish faith. The latter is the key to understanding the uniqueness and destiny of the people and its land.
>
> *Principles of Action:*
>
> (a) Education and publicity (a link with Torah and Jewish ethics; love of the Jewish People and the Land of Israel; Zionist consciousness and the vision of redemption; national missions and fulfillment).
>
> (b) Love of Israel.
>
> (c) *Aliyah* [Jewish immigration to Israel].
>
> (d) Settlement throughout the Land of Israel.
>
> (e) An assertive foreign and security policy.
>
> "Let us be strong on behalf of our people and the cities of our God, and the good Lord will do what is best.[36]

When GE leaders are asked to epitomize the main thrust of their enterprise, they recite the formula "revival of the sacred," an example of the idiosyncratic, homiletic language used in internal discourse among the activist-believers. To the general public, in contrast, they employ another language which is public relations oriented, less religious, and more nationalistic, declaring their focus to be "the restoration of Zionist fulfillment." Naturally the movement denies any dissonance between these messages, claiming that both amount to the same thing. They argue that these two aspects of Jewish renaissance, religious and national, are predicated on the prevention of withdrawal from the territories GE considers liberated, or even redeemed. Even people who are not affiliated with GE refer to the disputed areas of the West Bank as Judea and Samaria, reflecting another facet of the movement's success, one which is no less significant than the two billion dollars and more invested in altering the Territories' infrastructure.[37]

One of the movement's principal strategies is the biblicization of the Territories, which are easily accessible to Israelis, just across the former border, only a few minutes from their homes. The area includes Shechem (Nablus), Hebron, Anatot, Shiloh, Beit-El (Bethel), and other well-known sites mentioned in the Holy Scriptures which denote the ancient land of the Patriarchs. This is the heart of the "sacred Jewish geography"—the arena of GE activity, where the movement cadres make their homes.

Recently in light of international, regional, and local political developments perceived as capable of establishing a Palestinian state in the disputed areas, the ground is beginning to shift under the feet of the activist-believers. Signs of frailty and confusion are emerging, along with pain and even some cynicism. But even if certain settlers have lost confidence, and in certain peripheral circles there are second thoughts about compromise and dialogue, the GE leaders are still strong in their views and consistent in their declarations. Movement leaders remind the public of Judea and Samaria's vital importance to Israel from both the strategic and national points of view. At the same time GE is attempting to rekindle the torch of faith by stressing the religious significance of Judea and Samaria. Even if the volume is far lower this time, the same slogans are being used, primarily quotations from the rabbis who served as the movement's spiritual founders:

> The Land of Israel within its biblical borders has a lofty internal quality. Every bit of its territory, every clump of earth, is the holy of holies, as the Torah declares. This holiness is also derived from the nature of redemption. Redemption means sovereignty over the entire Promised Land. Therefore, any declaration or deed by any government in the world, including that of Israel, which contests our hold on the Territories liberated in the holy war, has no validity and is considered null and void. In contrast, all weapons of the army which conquers and defends our land are of spiritual value and are as precious as religious articles. An IDF rifle and tank have the same value as the prayer shawl and phylacteries; soldiers are as important as Talmudic scholars, and settlers are a particularly saintly group.[38]

GE's battle cry is "not one inch" and its watchword is "do or die."[39] Conquest and settlement of the Land of Israel is a divine precept;[40] some activist-believers believe it to be a select precept which outweighs all others. Furthermore, the religious importance of the entire Land of Israel derives from its mystic-messianic value. Conquest and settlement are perceived as an essential step toward ultimate religious fulfillment. Some maintain that it constitutes redemption itself, or at least a critical element of redemption, guaranteeing its eventual consummation.

Salvation and Aggression

At least in the movement's early phases, its extremist politics primarily constituted a peculiar expression of intra-religious dynamics. The tactical, logistic, legal, and administrative act of holding on to Judea and Samaria is, to GE members, simultaneously a magical act. The sophisticated initiatives to "eliminate the boundary" which separates the two parts of the Holy Land functioned as a symbolic act meant to hasten the consummation of the messianic process. It served as a ritualistic bridge between the two levels of the believers' consciousness: between their inner world dominated by the exhilarating religious reality of redemption and the frustrating outer world in which they must face a historical reality only partially redeemed.

GE views the world in the light of redemption. All pragmatic or moral considerations must be judged according to one messianic criterion: will the matter at hand delay or hasten the process of complete redemption? This is especially true with respect to sovereignty over Judea and Samaria, perceived as the key to salvation. Settlements in the Territories are an objective of religious yearning. According to the activist-believers, establishment of a settlement in the heart of the Palestinian population, an act intended to promote annexation of the Territories, is considered a sacrament.[41]

GE perceives settlement in Judea and Samaria not only as restoration of the Zionist spirit but also as *tikkun*—the kabbalistic concept of healing, repairing, and transforming the entire universe. According to the mystical-messianic conception prevailing in GE, national changes are both a reflection of and a means to celestial changes. Consequently the movement's activism on the national level is an axis for a cosmic revolution, with universal implications. This formula solves the inherent paradox in GE's message, as reflected in a claim of Rabbi Levinger:

> Settlement of the entire Land of Israel by the Jewish People is a blessing for all mankind, including the Arabs. Jewish settlements in the midst of local population centers are motivated by feelings of respect and concern for the Palestinians' future. Consequently if we meet the Arabs' demand for withdrawal, we will only encourage their degeneration and moral decline, whereas enforcing the Israeli national will on the Arabs will foster a religious revival among them, eventually to be expressed in their spontaneous desire to join in the reconstruction of the Third [Jewish] Temple. We [the Israelis] must penetrate the casbahs of cities in Judea and Samaria and drive our stakes therein for the good of the Arabs themselves.[42]

Although aggressive, GE has never openly embraced an ideology of violence. Instead it advocates peaceful coexistence with local Arabs. Nevertheless, the actual implementation of this cosmic vision has time and again demonstrated its potential for motivating and rationalizing a kind of religious violence. Activist-believers committed acts of sabotage and murder against the very Arabs who, according to GE's idiosyncratic interpretation, will voluntarily lend a hand in the redemption of the Jews. Several times the Torah-centered settlers addressed the local Hebron Arabs in a seemingly conciliatory tone. In summer 1976, Rabbi Levinger drew up a leaflet distributed among the Arabs of the Casbah by his trigger-happy disciples: "All in all, we have come to cleanse you of the air of murder to which you have become accustomed and introduce an air of understanding and friendship. We have not given up hope of breaking the wall of hatred between the two nations. We extend our hand in peace. Please do not reject it."

Rabbi Levinger heads a group which has settled permanently in the Old City of Hebron, while other GE members are ready to move into the Old City of Shechem. The GE hard core is becoming more obsessive in its aspiration to migrate from the territorial-demographic periphery to the heartland. In autumn 1989, I again observed Rabbi Levinger, still walking alone, submachine gun in hand, seeking provocations in the narrow, dark alleys of the Palestinian neighborhoods whose residents know him well and focus all their hatred of Jews on him.[43] He has become more involved than ever in incitement and riots, including the breaking of windows, the burning of shops, and even gunfire. Levinger was recently indicted for allegedly firing at close range, killing a local Arab shoe salesman and wounding his client. He was said to have then uttered a stream of cries and curses as he ran amok through the marketplace, overturning vegetable carts. In the courtroom, Levinger denied the charges: "I didn't kill anyone. More precisely, I, a person who is considered to be a bearer of the flag of Israel, wish that I had been privileged to kill a son of Ishmael."[44]

At that same time, Levinger's partner in the GE leadership, Hanan Porat, delivered a Rosh Hashanah sermon at a synagogue in a settlement, citing the following biblical verses: "O clap your hands, all ye peoples; shout unto God with the voice of triumph. For the Lord most high is terrible; he is a great king over all the earth. He shall subdue the people under us, and the nations under our feet." (Ps. 47:1–4). He asked rhetorically: "What are the nations around us rejoicing about? Is this some kind of masochism? Our neighbors are rejoicing not only because of God's greatness but also because of the very fact that they have merited being subdued beneath our feet. Subjugation to the once and future kingdom of Israel causes happiness in the Whole Land of Israel."

In these troubled times, Torah scholars in Judea and Samaria are again examining their religiopolitical mores, relying on the same formulas: "What appears at present to be realization of Israeli interests in Judea and Samaria essentially guarantees general salvation and obviously must be considered to be in the Palestinian interest as well. We are responding to the call for responsibility and human love. If we succeed [in movement campaigns], the Arabs will soon recognize the moral-religious value of the Jew and will thank him for all his endeavors among them." This is what the activist-believers contend as they join forces in an attempt to suppress the Palestinian uprising in the Territories. GE resorts to deterrence and retaliation, involving humiliation, beatings, and even shooting, while it seeks to win public approval and convince the IDF and the government to adopt harsher measures in dealing with the rebels.

The Territories, Mysticism, and Nationalism

The Territories stand not only between Israel and her neighbors but also between Israel and herself. The problem is not only strategic-political but also cultural: the Territories constitute a bone of contention regarding Israel's survival and the core of her identity. The question concerns the very life of the nation, physically and symbolically. The Territories have been the axis around which the new brand of Israeli nationalism has revolved and the hub of a new form of religion in Israel. They have been a focus for asserting extremism in nationalism and in religion and have bound the two extremisms into one. Through the acquisition and possession of these territories, the religionization of nationalism and the nationalization of religion take place.

GE embodies the essence of trends toward growing nationalism and increased religiosity, and has played a key role in initiating and sustaining the relationship between them. In according the Territories a mystical-messianic value, GE has pushed both conventional nationalism and normative religion in this direction. The movement embodies a Jewish revivalism conducted in the manner of ultra-Zionist activism: a genuine religious movement which adheres to an extreme politics of ethno-nationalism, GE calls for and militantly implements a Zionist renaissance. It thus signifies a Zionist and Jewish revolution and implies a revolution *within* Zionism and *within* Judaism. Behind the innovation in nationalism lurks an innovation in Judaism: GE introduces a novel religious conception which transcends and confronts Orthodoxy. As such, it challenges Israeli identity no less than it threatens Palestinian being.

GE's interests appear to be exhausted by matters of foreign policy and security. The movement's uniqueness in the Israeli political scene and the source of its political efficacy stems from its concentration on one issue alone—the boundaries of Israel. The activist-believers are obsessed with boundaries. Latent within their struggle over the territorial boundaries of the state, however, is a battle over the boundaries of Judaism. GE strives for nothing less than a radically new conception of Judaism: the annexation of land is but a medium for the appropriation of national secular values, an attempt to control the determination of Judaism and Jews. Behind the geopolitical definition of disputed parcels of land is an issue involving the definition of a controversial identity. The struggle over the definition of the boundaries between the two parts of the land—the "small" country within the 1948 borders and the "greater" one within the 1967 borders—is simultaneously a battle to define the boundary between the Land of Israel and the State of Israel. These two concepts respectively symbolize the collectivity's particularistic or primordial definition, on the one hand, and its civil, universalistic one, on the other hand.[45] This appears to cover the division between religious Judaism and secular Israelism. More appropriately, it indicates the boundary between two conceptions of Judaism: Orthodoxy, which is non- or anti-Zionist versus radical religious Zionism. In fact, this is yet another manifestation of the tension between two familiar trends of Jewish religiosity: the normative (halakhic/rabbinic) versus the kabbalistic (mystical/messianic).

At the forefront of the battle to expand Israeli colonization and extend Israeli sovereignty over the Territories, GE is essentially striving to win hearts and minds, to include more Israelis within its own version of Judaism. The compulsive preoccupation with the exact location of international boundaries is simultaneously an attempt to negotiate and ultimately eliminate the boundaries between secular and observant Jews. Thus, the desire to erase the Green Line and control the Whole Land of Israel is also a desire for a "complete" Judaism which would transcend the differences between the religious and secular worlds.

From Religious Politics to Political Religion

GE is among the most resourceful, determined, and efficient groups in Israeli politics. To elucidate GE's national and international significance, however, it is essential to understand it as a religious phenomenon.[46] True, by now the movement's politics have virtually assumed a life of their own, complete with a clear national ideology devoid of celestial theological premises. In particular, a security and foreign policy has emerged which many find persuasive even without polemical quotes from religious texts. And at times the movement has succumbed to inertia, and certain of its vested interests have grown stronger, including personal, organizational, sectorial, and even economic interests of a sort.

By self-definition GE is a religious movement of professed, practicing believers. Many of their leaders are religious scholars, even clerics; some could be called religious virtuosi.[47] The movement's motives and objectives are religiously defined and its members' experiences expressed in religious terms. Its activities entail considerable religious commitment and enthusiasm.[48] To gain a full understanding of the movement's structure and dynamics, political science in its narrow sense will not suffice. Derived from energies released by an experience reminiscent of Hasidic worship, GE's activism is structured on a ceremonial paradigm shaped during the genesis of the movement, when its logic was more expressive than instrumental. This activism is rationalized in terms of an esoteric kabbalistic dialectic, while in its constraints, it adheres to rabbinic decisions grounded in halakhic law. After all, as the activist-believers themselves claim, hunger strikes before the Knesset building and even lobbying among minor apparatchiks in the Knesset cafeteria are tantamount to prayer and study of the Torah.

We may thus consider GE a renewal or revivalist movement, and also a *teshuva* movement, that is, a movement of return to the bosom of religion. As such, it is noteworthy among contemporary religious resurgence movements because it is manifested not in the crossing of religious-nonreligious boundaries—attracting the secular to join the traditionally religious—but rather in transforming the already religious into people with a proud, active, high-voltage religion, manifested in aspirations to apply the sacred in realms which transcend traditional boundaries.[49] The totality of

GE's activity, including facets which appear absolutely indifferent to religion, is charged with religious valuation and interpreted through religious reasoning. One central tenet of GE is to leave nothing outside the boundaries of religion. Nothing remains religiously neutral, especially politics. The activist-believers religiously experience and conceptualize primarily that which appears to be extra-religious. In fact, the movement ascribes the highest religious significance to those very notions and actions by which it became celebrated as ultra-political.

GE's success is partially due to the leadership crisis and ideological vacuum in Israel in the 1970s and the state of melancholy which prevailed in Israel in the aftermath of the Yom Kippur War, but it is also an authentic and original attempt to revitalize traditional Judaism, which finds itself in a crisis brought about by the reality of secular, modern Israel.[50] It is a Jewish movement which bears the flag of Zionism, its competitor. Notwithstanding the widespread expectation that the movement would become progressively secularized over the years, GE has instead manifested signs of religious radicalization.[51] Along with its extreme nationalism, GE has displayed a tendency to move deeper into religion, which is ultimately incompatible with Zionism. GE's religious ethic is a bold and effective response to the existential distress of the Orthodox Jew in Israel. It represents a clearly religious problematic and an attempt to resolve it which, although religious, pursues the secular options of political activism.

Thus, GE is radical in at least three senses. First, in settling the Greater Land of Israel, it disregards, as a matter of principle, Arab rights and interests. Second, it consistently, although indirectly, strives to impose religion on secular sectors, using power to dominate state and society and make them abide by the movement's particular norms. Third, the subtlest and deepest sense of GE's radicalism refers to the symbolic system which shapes its worldview. GE's revolutionary notion of Judaism presents Zionism as an integral component of religion, if not its axial one. GE claims that just as there is no Zionism that is not religious, there can be no Jewish religion that is not Zionist. Moreover, it argues that Zionism is the core and essence, the critical criterion of Judaism. The traditional definition of Judaism is broadened to encompass nationalism, perceived as an elevation and perfection of conventional religious Judaism. These three levels of GE radicalism coalesce in the perception of ultimate sanctity in a militant regional policy. According to the activist-believers: the more hawkish, the more Jewish.[52]

Rather than religious politics, then, GE represents a political religion. But it is necessary to distinguish it from what social scientists commonly envision when they refer to quasi-religious, totalistic, and absolutistic political systems (e.g., Marxism, fascism).[53] In contrast, notwithstanding its central tenet of nationalism, GE is a religious system par excellence, organically linked to a definite political outlook and style. Jewish fundamentalism was born of the dashed hopes of religious Zionism.[54] GE offers its unique solution to the Israeli public at large and believes its solution can accommodate secular Israelis as well. This is so despite the fact that traditional religion and modern nationalism in GE's mystical-messianic system do not meld in a synthesis.

Rather, religion usurps modern nationalism and presents nationalism as its own manifestation.

Modern Nationalism as a Religious Dilemma

For more than fifteen years, GE has not only dominated the headlines but has also made inroads into major realms of Israeli institutional life. The movement's effects may be discerned in new norms of disrespect for law and order and conditional obedience to official authorities;[55] in the introduction of a conservative and puritanical trend in public morals, which has nevertheless contributed to the brutalization of social relations; in the reinforcement of hawkish tendencies in foreign policy and in the challenge it presents to Israel's liberal, democratic regime. The effect is reflected and enhanced by the nature of Israeli discourse, which constitutes ideas and values transposed from the domain of religion, even when addressing strategic issues.

Israel is essentially a modern secular society, yet religion, which appeared to be a passing and marginal phenomenon, has become a political and moral factor that can no longer be dismissed. Religion has been rather successful not only at promoting its own interests but also at imposing itself on Israeli life in general, as reflected in the legal, governmental, and cultural spheres. This success has been so phenomenal that the Israeli religious camp—which is by no means homogeneous or unified—purports to redefine the central symbols of Israeli society. It bids for practical and especially spiritual leadership and tries to monopolize the legitimation of the Jewish-Zionist national entity. This process of suffusing politics with religious meanings is enhanced by the passivity or implied consent of various nonreligious sectors, and sometimes by their conscious cooperation. After all, Israel defines itself officially not only as a state of Jews but as a Jewish state, and most of its citizens—including nearly all secular Jews—accept it as such.[56]

The Zionist political entity presents Orthodoxy with a religious dilemma: a sovereign but secular Jewish state is a painful contradiction. Graver still, elements in Jewish Orthodoxy find it difficult not to interpret modern Israel as a materialization of the messianic vision so pivotal in religious tradition. However, the religious ideal, having become a reality after thousands of years, was ostensibly realized by infidels in a sinful enterprise. GE is an effort to resolve this paradox.[57]

One attempt to grasp the essence of the Zionist revolution defines it as the demystification of Jewish messianism.[58] The most recent brand of Jewish messianism represents a process of its *re*mystification and its simultaneous imposition on realpolitik. GE plays a key role in this transformation. It has proven itself to be a creative and potent response to the identity crisis of orthodox but modern Israelis who seek to preserve their religiosity within a Zionist framework and their Zionism within a religious framework. These Israelis find it difficult to continue leading their lives according to the Torah in a modern, secular world without a renewed confirmation of their ancient faith. They are caught in the tension between their new commitment to a progressive nation-state, on the one hand, and their traditional obligation to observe halakhic commandments and their profound need for immediate holy communion, on the other. GE enables them to combine a compelling religiosity with an appealing nationalism. In their activism, they can at the same time draw fully on their Jewishness and their Zionism and extract the essence of both identities. Moreover, GE members have reached a stage which allows them to pretend to be more religious than the ultra-Orthodox haredim and more patriotic than pioneer kibbutzniks.

Fundamentals and Action

At the foundation of religious renewals combined with activist politics, some observers argue, is a rationale which is essentially civil, economic, or class-related. Religion in turn constitutes a system of symbols available for expressing such mundane distress and effective for recruiting forces to alleviate it. At times, however, the nature and significance of the experience underlying the radical initiatives is perceived by the activists as religious, whereas the language used by these believers is likely to sound patently political. In the case of GE, it is evident that the movement's religiosity is not exhausted in rhetoric and appearance. Religion, in this case, is not merely an ancillary factor providing at most a rationalization and perhaps a partial motivation for processes whose logic is principally extra-religious.

Although the believers do refer to the systematic and somewhat abstruse ideas of the theoreticians, it is doubtful whether such elevated conceptions in their original form actually motivated them or shaped movement life: the effective meaning of the message is found on the popular homiletic level and at the nexus between the social nature of the movement and the sacred texts ascribed to it.

A vast system of commentary mediates the formal sacred text of GE and the student cadres.[59] Analysis of a symbolic system must be accompanied by a description of the specific interpretation a given movement accords that system. There are several versions of Rabbi Kook's philosophy; the Kookism characteristic of the Jewish-Zionist radical camp is nourished by only one of them. At issue is a particular collection of essays written by Rabbi Avraham Itzhak Kook, edited and transmitted by his son, Rabbi Zvi Yehuda Kook, and cultivated by a certain coterie at Merkaz Harav in Jerusalem from the early 1950s. In the 1970s they were expressly proclaimed as the platform of GE activists.

It is also important to trace the manner in which a system of ideas and values was converted into the ideology of a movement: who imbibed from whom, when, and where. Modern research employs the important category of "networks."[60] These play a decisive role in GE, so much so that Israelis with a religious and political view identical to that of the movement and possessing all the required talents and motivation to become leading figures among the activist-believers were rejected by the inner circles despite all their efforts, simply because they didn't belong to the "good old boy" network.

Concentration solely on doctrinal analysis overlooks important ritualistic and experiential dimensions of the phenomenon, as well as those motivational and institutional structures which mediate theory and action. The public pronouncements of the journals and pamphlets published by GE can indeed create an image of an intellectual movement. However, deep within its somewhat academic discourse lies a myth of a decidedly fantastic nature. A powerful, authentic, and profoundly religious experience nourishes the discourse. A direct continuation of discourse is action, which is highly effective despite its ritualistic basis. Viewed from close range, experience at one end and action at the other overshadow the abundance of words in the middle and lend them their contextual meaning.

Judaism, like Islam, places less emphasis on religious doctrine and hierarchy and more on religious experience, especially religious ritual. Fundamentalism intensifies both religious experience and rituals which are themselves intertwined: ritual institutionalizes and anchors a primary experience, reawakening it each time to provide a living reinforcement of faith.[61] While exciting powerful emotions among its adherents, GE's faith is expressed in and supported by ritualistic behavior. Compulsive, shrewd, original, daring, and generally aggressive, GE's activism is also a kind of religious ritual. It is through activism, the acting out of its unique religiosity, rather than doctrinal "fundamentals," that GE's unique spirit is revealed. The radical Jewish ethic is channeled into political activism, and this creates new energies and content which in turn reinforce the ethic. The often spectacular and extralegal operations typical of GE contribute to its private and public image as much as an explicitly stated worldview. Mass rallies on one side of the Green Line and unbudging settlements on the other serve an instrumental as well as expressive function; they are the *modi operandi* of the struggle to advance GE's cause. When the believers trudged through desert sand dunes at night to bypass police roadblocks, when they ripped up a government order while reciting Psalms, it was then and there that GE perfected its techniques of organization and action. At that point its leadership patterns and folkways were set as well; its cadres were mobilized, tested, and forged, its rousing slogans were invented and tried out, new chapters were written in messianic Zionist mythology, and original interpretations of the Torah were entertained.

Fundamentalism is also associated with high drama—and with hatred, jealousy, revenge for past insults, and occasional moments of hysteria and euphoria. Envy of the Yishuv's secular pioneer settlers and fighters on the one hand, and competition with the scholarly excellence and halakhic observance of students at Lithuanian yeshivas on the other, youthful rebellion, the desire to overturn the inferior status once imposed on religious Israelis by the Labor Party's Socialist hegemony, exaltation and intoxication in the feeling of having succeeded in creating hard geopolitical facts impelling the government to act or motivating the entire nation—all these are integral components of the system which drives GE forward.

Indeed the activist-believers have been motivated by a sense of participation in a great historical enterprise, or even a metahistorical one, which has brought them close to the ultimate satisfaction of the kind yearned for by any mystic or messianic believer. When Rabbi Zvi Yehuda Kook delivered a sermon and wept in front of hundreds of enthusiasts celebrating the establishment of a new settlement on the road to Jericho, or when squatters wrapped themselves in prayer shawls and screamed while holding onto the territory with bleeding fingers during a confrontation with the soldiers who came to remove them from a hill overlooking Ramallah, the activist-believers experienced what they believed to be a true revelation. It is of such elements that GE—and fundamentalism—are made.

Zeroing In on the Movement

Some observers have implied that GE has become characteristic of Israeli society as a whole, a conclusion which might well enjoy widespread appeal. Oversimplified and overdrawn views of the situation in Israel and the surrounding region are usually linked to one of two approaches, in which GE is either glorified or demonized. Equating the movement with political maximalism—or, for that matter, with religious orthodoxy—means that large, if not central, sectors of the Israeli population are fundamentalist. Furthermore, according to the political terms many observers use, we may view the proponents of the Likud and those national or religious groups to the right of it as a fundamentalist bloc. As a result of this simplistic picture of Israeli society, the depiction of GE loses shape. For example, the movement's schismatic and innovative character, especially in the religious sense, is thus overlooked. The failure to recognize Jewish radicalism as a unique and compact framework deflects the reader from considering how GE managed to become so influential in Israel. A cohesive core group of fervent, dedicated, and talented true believers can imprint its mark on history, especially when it gives vent to widespread moods in society and manipulates its central values.

The standard concept of radicalism, Jewish or other, overreaches itself. Throughout the literature on GE, skullcapped and bareheaded Jews are casually interchanged or massed together; they are seen as alternatives and sometimes speak for each other, as if it were irrelevant that some of them happen to eat pork and never saw a Torah scroll in their lives, while others are yeshiva teachers and students who don phylacteries every morning. For the former, the Land of Israel is of strategic value; for the latter, it is of redemptive value.[62] It is especially absurd to discern within the ranks of the religious revival nonreligious personalities such as Rafael Eitan (former Chief of Staff), Yuval Ne'eman (professor of physics and MK), Avraham Yaffe (head of Israel's Nature Reserve Authority), and Moshe Tabenkin (a poet and kibbutznik). All of these men are secular to the core, yet rank among the leaders in the roster of fundamentalists proposed by prominent GE watchers. Is that simply because they oppose withdrawal from disputed territory and to that end have joined in a coalition with GE?[63] No less absurd is the tendency to ascribe to GE the masses of lower strata Israel—young Oriental Jews with little income, education, and prestige—even though, statistically speaking, these are people who support annexation of the Territories and a hard line toward the Arabs.

The liaison between believers and secular Israelis is important in understanding GE's political mechanism; as an expression of GE's fundamentalist nature, however, it merits careful examination. Secularity and secular organizations, sectors, and persons undoubtedly play a key role in the understanding of fundamentalism. However, evaluation of the significance of these secular elements demands that we view them as separate, competitive, and complementary factors. The partnership whose effects have been so crucial has only limited content: the success of this partnership is perhaps guaranteed by its limitations. Secular Israelis do not share the Kookists' mystical-messianic belief and certainly do not emulate their observance of Torah commandments. The alliance held only for aspects which the movement deliberately highlighted in its quest for mass appeal: settlement, security, and other values of pioneer Zionism.

The blurring of GE boundaries and its identification with surrounding secular bodies also reflects the movement's natural tendency to present itself as popular, heterogeneous, and as embracing the majority of Zionists. GE is perceived as the vanguard of the national ideal (or rather as an actor which consistently underscores the potential inherent in this ideal, thereby unavoidably exposing the "genuine" face of Zionism). This public image of GE derives from both its self-image and its public relations efforts.

The Jewish radicals transmit a dual message which is clearly characteristic of other religiopolitical radicals as well: at one level of its attitude toward the surrounding environment, the movement arrogantly emphasizes its uniqueness and its advantages over all others, whereas at the propagandistic and more apologetic level, GE presents its normal and conventional side and with a certain feigned innocence attempts to obscure the differences between it and other movements perceived as legitimate and even between it and its attackers. Moreover, in the effort to rehabilitate their public image, the activist-believers liken themselves to the stalwart idealists who later found their place in the national pantheon. The movement cadres placed themselves at the end of a glorious chain, among whose links are not only the Maccabees (165 B.C.E.) but also the heroes of modern Jewish history—all of them secular. They remind us that Herzl, visionary of the Jewish state, was mocked in his day as a dreamer and an incurable optimist, that Ben-Yehuda, reviver of the Hebrew language, was known as unbearable fanatic in his own community, that Ben-Gurion, who established Jewish sovereignty, was perceived as working against all odds. Some eighty years after the legendary *halutzim* of the Second Aliyah period, who drained the swamps and built the frontier kibbutzim, GE calls them mystics, no more realistic or rational than the Torah-centered settlers of Judea and Samaria. Yet these are the very people who became a model for Israelis to this very day. The movement not only stresses its similarity to these Zionist founding fathers but actually boasts of being their direct successor. GE perceives itself as the heir apparent of secular Zionism even while it reconstructs and revives religious Judaism in a generation in which both are in crisis.

It is claimed that fundamentalists may be distinguished by their quest for immediate and complete social change based on a model which "substantially contradicts the prevailing myth" under which existing institutions legitimize their power. However, fundamentalism is far more subtle than this implies. Despite all their innovation, religious radicals—certainly no less than secular radicals—appropriate elements from the old myth as well for various reasons, including the realization that otherwise the alternative they propose would be less acceptable to the people. Besides, parts of the old myth are themselves so assimilated into radical conceptions that they become untraceable and unremovable. The old myth has a key function in the fundamentalist breakthrough.

GE draws its legitimacy and its revolutionary thrust from symbols originating in significant chapters of not only the Bible but also the history of the pre-State Yishuv, on which all Israelis are reared. Just as it was difficult for the ultra-Orthodox in Israel to invoke the Torah to disqualify the GE cadres as Jews, since the latter observed all its commandments meticulously, it was similarly difficult for the Israeli Labor establishment to invoke the "pioneer spirit" to disqualify the GE cadres as Zionists, as the latter were the first to volunteer for all missions on behalf of the collectivity, just like those very pioneers who created the national ethos, an ethos which was once considered totally secular in nature.

Jewish-Zionist radicalism is thus rooted in the glorification and revitalization of elements taken from the prevailing myth in Israel, so much so that even the most sophisticated sworn enemies of GE have had difficulty in contradicting its avowed pretension to be the loyal successor of Judaism or of Zionism. One source of the movement's potency is its arousal of pangs of conscience among Orthodox Jews of lesser piety and its function as surrogate fulfillment for the nonreligious who have already abandoned the ideals of ***halutziut*** (self-sacrifice in the service of society and the nation).

A Community and Counterculture

Political-religious radicalism ultimately aims at shaping a different society, based on the image of a revolutionary old-new man. The movement establishes a heretofore unknown and unprecedented religious type, although it often presents itself as pristinely original or traditional nonetheless. Schematically speaking, it is common to say that Judaism recognizes three types of God-fearing persons: the ***talmid hacham*** (Torah scholar), the ***tzaddik*** (righteous man), and the ***hasid*** (saint).[64] GE adds an additional pietist model: the settler. There is thus a new form of worship, namely, Zionist ultra-activism.

This factor intensifies a significant difference between GE and the diverse shades of orthodoxy on the one hand and the various types of political hawks on the other. There is a thin but decisive line between GE and the overall "Land of Israel loyalist camp," and between GE and the "Sharon camp," or even Rabbi Meir Kahane's Kach group.[65]

The narrower and sharper definition of Jewish-Zionist fundamentalism, one which zeroes in on those who identify themselves as GE members in the full sense of the term, focuses attention on the cadres which yearn for the immediate renewal of the Chamber of Hewn Stone, as charted by the Old Testament blueprint. This hard core of the movement comprises young, Ashkenazic, native Israelis, the well-educated children of middle-class families raised in the ambience of the establishment-oriented Bnei Akiva youth movement.[66] The stalwart members of GE are either products of the yeshiva world or are very close to it and are subject to the influence of the personalities and doctrines intimately linked to Merkaz Harav or its affiliated schools.[67] At most they number no more than a few thousand.

TABLE 5.1
POPULATION CHARACTERISTICS (%)

	GE Settlers	All Israeli Jews
Adults Under 45	93	35
Native Born	68	53
Orthodox Observance	92	20+
Post–High School Education	66	13
Higher Yeshiva Training (men)	35	3
Ashkenazic Ancestry	82	40

The group is both homogenous and close-knit. Compared to other movements, GE is unique in its intimacy. This is not merely a function of its relatively small size. GE members fall into a close age range (the inner circle consists of individuals who were twenty-five to forty years old when the movement burst onto the public scene) and belong to a minority sector of the country. Since childhood most of its members have grown up in the same milieu—the same neighborhoods, schools, summer camps, army units, songs, jokes, and newsletters. They share not only the same abstract values but also the same formative experience and normative behavior. They are intensely interrelated in a manner characteristic of family ties. It would not be an exaggeration to say that the leaders and active members of the movement, including their wives and children, know each other personally. In fact the women and children are an integral part of the movement.

GE is not essentially a secret society or underground organization, unlike some well-known fundamentalist bodies in the region. Nevertheless, it is closer to the sectarian variation of fundamentalism than the mass-anonymous type, despite its popular faces—or phases—which have made it appear to be an alternatively expanding and contracting ("accordion") collective. Like several other religious-political activist frameworks, GE is more than just a movement. It is a whole culture as well as a self-sustaining community. The hallmark of an activist-believer is not confined to a religious viewpoint or political stance; it also emerges in an encompassing system of behavioral norms which regulate all aspects of life, from housing patterns to leisure-time activities. True believers also have their own folklore.

Religious radical behavior may be discerned not only in distinctive contents but also in characteristic forms (as well as certain moods). Activist-believers favor certain literary genres, specific dress codes, and a particular brand of humor. A distinct type of beard, for example, is an inseparable feature of a Jewish radical's appearance. Linguistically GE is recognizable in a particularly revealing inflection and vocabulary: a rare mixture of talmudic-based Yiddish expressions uttered with an Ashkenazic-Diaspora accent, along with a native Israeli vernacular borrowed from the IDF's lexicon, filled with expressions of heroism, advanced technology, and simple congeniality. GE runs on its own schedule (for example, it tends to turn day into night); it has a particular taste in interior decoration and music, and reflects a typical range of livelihoods, not to mention a specific repertoire of books, children's names, and other identifying features. One can easily identify typical GE patterns of family and interpersonal relations, techniques of recruitment and conversion, mechanisms of decision making and social control, and the like.

These features render GE a collectivity which fulfills most social functions in its own peculiar manner. Among other characteristics, even the everyday, trivial aspects of life in GE are laden with halakhic and messianic tension, on the one hand, and civil-Zionist tension, on the other. In certain respects, the activist-believers constitute an entity unto themselves, geopolitically as well as socially. They represent an exclusive, almost autonomous, framework with its own institutions of leadership and administration, maintenance and economy, entertainment, communication, etc. To some extent they even have a self-sufficient mechanism of security. Most important of all is their separate, effective system of socialization. GE is cultivating a second and third generation of cadres via a comprehensive educational apparatus and tight social control. The movement provides a quasi-"total institution" environment which envelops all aspects of life in the collectivity from birth onward (significantly, the birth rate itself is high). Institutionalization and transmission of the radical legacy to future generations constitute another classic problem of activist-believers.

GE's society operates alongside Israeli society: half dependent and half independent, apart from the public and the establishment but competing with it and aspiring to lead it. The Jewish fundamentalist enclaves, especially the settlements, are ghetto-like, with all the advantages this allows for leading a religious life in a secular world. At the same time, the settlements are both a bridgehead for assault and a model of an alternative life-style. GE is more than just an intellectual current or pressure group; it is actually a countersociety.[68] In concentrations of Jewish Zionist radicalism, one may even discern an essential withdrawal from the world into an alternative, protected space, a kind of physical and/or psychological emigration.

Therein lies the distinction between Jewish radicalism in the guise of GE and the Land of Israel Movement, on the one hand, and Tehiya, Zomet, Moledet, and the right-wing contingent of Likud on the other. The latter, while calling themselves movements, are really parliamentary factions and mechanisms for extraparliamentary pressure. The Land of Israel Movement is merely a circle of literati and a current of ideas. In contrast, GE has a religious-messianic character and bears the stamp of a true movement in that it exhibits collective behavior. This behavior is characterized by charisma and ecstasy, romanticism and heroism, ritual singing and dancing, prayer and Torah study, as well as by physical confrontations with agents of law and order. All of these behaviors serve also as revolutionary media employed by GE.

Gush Emunim in the Spectrum of Fundamentalism

The Concept and the Israeli Model

When the Shi'ite revolution broke out in Iran, GE was already some five (or twelve) years old; GE reached its peak about five years before we first learned about the group of Sadat's assassins and about the suicide terrorists in Lebanon. These events in the Middle Eastern Muslim world accorded the term "fundamentalism" its present connotation and popularity. Only subsequently was the term associated with GE, initially by its opponents of course. GE naturally rejected this label, with its connotations of intransigence and obscurantism. Moreover, GE resents all descriptions which do not imply its uniqueness and exclusiveness as the possessor of the Truth, not to mention its distaste at the very comparison with Islam, which they consider inferior to Judaism and hostile to Israel. Thus it is ironic that GE's bitter domestic opponents have labeled the movement "Israeli Khomeinism." Notwithstanding the discomfort of the radical Jews, we must examine whether there is any heuristic value in the analogy. After all, even impartial observers have detected an element of fundamentalism in GE.[69]

Rather than uncritically reject or accept the association between GE and fundamentalism, this study considers it as an hypothesis to be examined. In certain respects, GE is an ideal case for studying fundamentalism. The movement is compact; its clearly-delineated boundaries and relatively small dimensions allow for complete circumscription and detailed analysis. Moreover, it constitutes a complete, cohesive and homogeneous social system, with distinct features. Since the movement's inception, its history has been relatively well-documented; we also discern a closing point or at least a certain decline. Finally, the movement allows for examination "from within." Despite GE's notoriety, its members are outgoing and friendly, eager to present their side of the story and to cooperate with researchers.

A wide variety of empirical and conceptual context appears relevant to the study of this movement; from millenarism and mysticism, through nativism and irridentism, to colonialism, terrorism, proto-fascism and many others. Recurring motifs within GE locate it, however, on the spectrum of modern fundamentalist movements: obsession with authenticity in response to the challenge posed by drastic change in social environment; reliance on ancient holy writ as a source of authority and a guide to behavior, with a tendency toward unequivocal, binding interpretation; sharp distinction between the collective of the elect, pure, and faithful, and all others, who are considered infidels and the embodiment of evil incarnate; an oppositional, if not hostile, stance towards the prevailing culture, the religious establishment, and other religious groups; authoritarianism and absolutism; an apocalyptic or utopian and simultaneously restorative perspective; and finally, an emphasis on moralism.[70]

Many of the features ascribed to fundamentalism may be found in social movements or sects in general, in various manifestations of extremism, dogmatism, and schism, and not necessarily in a religious or modern context. Several scholars assert that there is nothing new about fundamentalism. For example, it is claimed that Islam has historically been a chain of revivals, in which contemporary radicalism in the Middle East is only another link. Consequently fundamentalism is perceived as a sui generis phenomenon only when arbitrarily removed from the context of Muslim history.[71] According to a similar principle, there is also a tendency to assess GE as yet another radical Jewish movement. Proponents of this view are apparently undeterred by the fact that the past eighty generations of Diaspora life were virtually unaffected by religiopolitical radicalism. Looking back some nineteen hundred years they declare the zealots in the State of Israel in the 1970s to be a direct continuation of the *kana'im* (zealots) who were active in the Land of Israel on the eve of the destruction of the Temple.[72] The partisan insinuation behind this analogy is clear. Is it any wonder that GE's opponents in politics and in the media have adopted it eagerly?

Radicalism and Traditional Norms

Fundamentalism is a unique phenomenon which is by definition both religious and modern. Fundamentalism begins in a collectivity that invariably travels a secular-religious continuum toward the more pious extreme. The collectivity may include either formerly secular persons who became religious (typically such people are regarded as having returned to their original source; in Judaism, they are called *baalei teshuva*) or persons who were already religious in a conventional and somewhat routine sense and subsequently became particularly devout. Fundamentalists in Israel are a kind of "born-again Jews."

Fundamentalism involves an intensification of piety. In Judaism, this phenomenon is primarily reflected in a strict interpretation of religious law and elaboration of the details thereof.[73] Even within Orthodoxy, there is some room for flexibility; in the case of GE, however, activist-believers fulfill certain religious precepts which are not practiced by their parents and comrades—nearly all of them Orthodox—because of the easing of religious tension in Israel during the previous generation. For example, while it was customary among vast sectors of the national-religious public to fast only one or two days a year—Yom Kippur and perhaps the Ninth of Av—Jewish fundamentalists observe at least four additional fast days which are of secondary, if not questionable, significance (such as the Fast of Esther). They conform to norms which had effectively become only optional, such as reciting morning prayers with a *minyan* (quorum) at sunrise, as well as those which prevail only in pockets of pietistic culture, since they are not explicitly stipulated in the Torah, such as wearing socks with one's sandals on the Sabbath and holidays. GE goes even farther in applying Orthodox norms: for example, separation of the sexes in education and entertainment has been extended as far back as early childhood, married women are covering more of their hair and their dresses are getting longer, and so forth.

At the same time, GE also ascribes greater importance to detailed, comprehensive knowledge of these norms and their sources through a kind of professional training which itself constitutes observance of a religious precept—Torah study. This practice likewise invites increasing extremism; moreover, its intensity may be assessed according to proven indicators, such as the number of pages of *Gemara* (the Babylonian and Jerusalem Talmuds) studied each day, or the number of hours per week devoted to study. Twenty years ago, no one would have believed that young, nationally minded, modern Israelis would spend eighteen hours a day in a yeshiva, even long after they matured and became family men. In parallel, their children also study at yeshiva throughout their school life. For the youngest among them, they even recently established a *heder* (an early childhood class concentrating almost exclusively on religious materials and using obsolete, demanding, and stringent methods). In recent generations, this institution has disappeared from the landscape of Jewish society, except in tiny exotic enclaves, such as Mea Shearim. Among national religious circles in Israel, the heder has been replaced by a modern state educational system, as prescribed by law. Until recently, the future GE cadres rejected the concept of the heder, which they ridiculed as a "fossilized remnant" of Diaspora Jewish life. According to these criteria, GE members tend to resemble the ultra-Orthodox haredim. Some of the haredization which also denotes Jewish-Zionist fundamentalism may be detected in the next aspect of religious extremism as well.

In addition to strict interpretation and elaboration, there is an expansion of the scope in which religious law is applied. From the individual's point of view, this means that more aspects of his life are regulated by religious values and norms. One critical step in this direction is the shattering of the "privatization" which characterizes contemporary religion by the acceptance of Judaism's relevance outside the spheres of home, family, and leisure time.[74] Observance of dietary laws, refraining from Sabbath violation, and selecting one's mate or friends according to the extent of their orthodoxy are deemed insufficient. Even business decisions are to be made according to Talmudic regulations. The extension of the application of religious law most relevant to the present study is the injunction that civic or political behavior be guided by halakha. GE activist-believers accept rabbinic decisions regarding the political party to vote for in Knesset elections. As a corollary to such decisions, support of another parliamentary faction—especially those from the liberal-dovish center or left—is deemed a violation of divine law. The culmination of the process of expansion of the scope of the law is reached when all affairs of the collectivity are conducted according to the Torah. This, of course, is the climax or epitome of the fundamentalist vision.

These ritual and normative aspects of religious radicalization are generally accompanied by structural elements, such as exclusivity and segregation, as well as other characteristics, such as authoritarianism and asceticism. GE settlements in Judea and Samaria are distinct concentrations of intensified religiosity exhibiting these characteristics; as communities of the pure and elect activist-believers, they constitute "virtuous societies." In the Israeli case, as in other cases of religious radicalism, the pattern thus obtained is *ultra-traditional*. At the same time, and not without some connection to this pattern, fundamentalism is clearly also *revolutionary-traditional:* while fundamentalism originates in tradition and avows to uphold and reinforce it, it also clearly transcends that very tradition and may eventually challenge its hold on believers, while employing it as a tool for radically changing the environment. Yet fundamentalism is also *neo-traditional,* since intensification of religious commitment is a conscious process, a choice from a range of options offered by the modern religious menu. GE fundamentalism provides an explicit ideology which justifies such selection and anchors each of its components in an integral and consistent whole.

Furthermore, these two features of Jewish fundamentalist religiosity—conscious selection and ideological backing—are now becoming the province of nearly all members of the religious-political community. There is diffusion of the activist-believer's ability to explain the significance of his extremism to himself and to others. Unlike other cases of religiosity, even extreme ones, this explanatory ability is no longer restricted to the group's leaders or to a small core of ideologues. Any rank-and-file fundamentalist is capable of and interested in providing a well-substantiated and coherent presentation of his movement's views. The fundamentalist's rationale for his extremism, which often appears well rehearsed, generally extends beyond the confines of parroting slogans and attests to a certain religious sophistication.

This very extremism, its attendant awareness, and especially its underlying rationalization, distinguish fundamentalists from those who apparently constitute the majority of the religious public. The latter comprise persons who are religious out of inertia or convention, such as the petite bourgeoisie who practice a kind of Jewish ritualism or traditionalism not necessarily accompanied by any particular reflection, intention, or pretension. GE subscribes a basic maxim of religious extremism (also held by the haredim): *Da'at Torah* (the position mandated by stringent interpretation of halakha, or the pronouncements of Torah sages) and *Da'at Ba'aleibatim* (literally, the views of householders, that is, the mores of laymen engrossed in pursuing their livelihoods and well-being) contradict one another.[75] However, unlike the Jewish-Zionist fundamentalists of GE, most ultra-Orthodox do not or cannot serve as apologists for their extremist way of life. This is especially true of those who are not religious functionaries and have no public responsibilities, e.g., haredi women, who are neither well-versed in the Torah nor skilled as spokespersons for their own group. This is not true, however, of women in the movement. At every available opportunity, female members of GE are ready to provide both a religious and a political account of the movement's positions. The same is true of the children of Torah-centered settlers, whose exposure to systematic indoctrination and to the media renders each of them a professional propagandist.

Mystical Messianism and Ritualism

To the element of systematic and nearly totalistic ideologization of religious extremism is added the complementary element of zeal. Various indications betray a strong religious experience underlying the course of fundamentalist eruption and fervor in conforming to both the Orthodox norms and the religious-political norms idiosyncratic to the radicals. For example, GE cadres at prayer display a familiar set of mannerisms which are the behavioral expression of *kavvanah* (literally, "intention," the kabbalistic term for the intensive spiritual concentration accompanying fulfillment of a religious precept, which aims at fostering comprehension of its deep significance, enabling one to embody its original rationale, its internal essence). Kavvanah embodies the mystical-theurgic assumption that the spiritual effort behind a ritual act can uplift man closer to the godhead, enabling him to arouse it and assist it in rectifying the cosmos. These mannerisms include closed eyes, a pained expression, powerful swaying, wailing, etc. The activist-believers often manifest such gestures at their daily prayers, especially during periods of high political—and ipso facto religious—tension. Moreover, they perceive their scuffles with officials and clashes with policemen, in attempts to prevent the evacuation of illegal settlements, as the fulfillment of a commandment accompanied by particularly intense kavvanah.

In this context, GE leaders recall one of the esoteric trends identified with a radical fringe of the Hasidic movement in Eastern Europe during the eighteenth and nineteenth centuries: especially far-reaching believers selected one of the 613 Torah precepts as an object in which they invested most of their devotion. Concentration of powerful religiosity on a specific ritual commandment was manifested in its ostensibly exaggerated, and at times even eccentric, fulfillment, extending far beyond required behavior according to the norms mapped out in canon law and in actual practice. Activist-believers in Israel—notably Yehuda Etzion, a leader of the underground in the Territories—liken themselves to those Hasidim. Just as some Jews were especially zealous about *tefillin* (phylacteries), wearing them not only during morning prayers but all day, or *tzitzit* (ritual fringes), wearing them to bed as well, the Torah-centered settlers are most zealous about the commandment to conquer and settle the Land of Israel.

Opponents of GE, especially among the Orthodox, criticize the movement for devoting itself to the commandment of conquering and settling the land at the expense of fulfilling other precepts. The liberal-Orthodox claim that settlement zeal leads to neglect of precepts concerning human dignity and public responsibility, whereas the ultra-Orthodox claim that the zeal displayed by GE would be better applied toward commandments concerning modesty, exclusive study of Torah, etc. Jewish radicalism is indeed meticulous about fulfilling all precepts; however, it ranks them according to their perceived importance. GE is prepared to recognize that under certain circumstances, the fulfillment of a particular precept may contradict the fulfillment of another, whereupon there is no choice but to prefer one over the other. To rationalize its religious-political orientation, the movement cites several holy books which declare that "the commandment to settle the land is considered tantamount to all other commandments."

According to a popular conception, shared by GE, Judaism is based on three foundations, namely the Torah of Israel, the People of Israel, and the Land of Israel. Haredim and even many secular Jews agree that GE accords too much weight to the land component; the former accusers claim that it supplants emphasis on Torah, whereas the latter claim that it takes precedence over the people. The activist-believers are well versed in responding to such accusations. First, they stress, love of the Land of Israel obviously incorporates love of the people and the Torah within it. In fact, the very act of separating the three Jewish foundations from one another is perceived as the root of all evil. Their unity is the main thrust of GE's message. GE adherents then proceed to a counterattack, decrying the haredim for focusing on Torah at the expense of the people and the land and denouncing the secular for concentrating on the people and the land at the expense of the Torah. The Jewish radicals complement this response with the contention that in various historical situations, one of the three foundations may emerge as more critical than the other two. And in our generation, the land obviously merits premier status. This observation has a negative side, as international circumstances have transformed the land into an urgent element on which physical survival depends. However, there is a positive side as well: in each generation the heart of the cosmos has been situated in a different Jewish sphere, toward which Israelis should aspire and thereby achieve the objective of Jewish wholeness. According to this mystical-messianic doctrine, there is a key, whose location is variable, which constitutes a major means of approaching and placating the godhead. At present, the linchpin of religious fulfillment is the land. At one time the critical medium for serving the Creator was yeshiva study; today it is settlement.

The ritualistic concentration on specific components of Judaism is curiously related to the belief in reincarnation which has accompanied the kabbalistic heritage. Believers maintain that in their current incarnation, they are obligated to compensate for laxity in observance of precepts in their previous life. One returns to this earth to rectify what he neglected in his previous incarnation, thereby rehabilitating the roots of his soul and contributing toward global reformation. Tradition tells of one who was not punctilious in observing the laws pertaining to the *sukkah* (booth) during the week of the Sukkot (Tabernacles) holiday and was consequently fated to attend to the details of sukkah laws all year round. Rabbi Haim Vital, a successor to the Lurianic Kabbalah (sixteenth century), declared that he had been a murderer in his previous life. Consequently in his later more renowned life, he became a vegetarian and was careful not even to tread on an ant. Because he was a scholar of halakha in his previous incarnation, he subsequently returned to earth as a kabbalist. GE is the successor to this Hasidic outlook; however, Jewish-Zionist radicalism transfers the kabbalistic principle from the individual plane to the collective one. This continuation cum revolution has its roots in Rabbi Kook's thought. Israeli fundamentalists claim that they apply this principle when they declare that it behooves them—as the avant-garde of the current Jewish incarnation—to become more extreme in those aspects of religion that were abandoned by the Orthodox in past generations. The resulting deficit in a particular aspect of Judaism demands redoubled efforts to close the gap. Obviously they refer to the national and political dimension of religion, whose ritual essence is the commandment to settle the land. According to them, the fulfillment of this precept is of paramount importance in the endeavor to redeem and be redeemed.

Even within GE, however, certain reservations and challenges have been expressed at times regarding the exclusive focus on this specific issue. Several members of the movement asked why is it that such a rich and ambitious conception which ought to advance on a broad and substantial front, instead limits itself to an isolated and ostensibly minor issue, namely settlement of the Land of Israel, which by assuming an all-inclusive and near-exclusive character, has gradually rendered the radical doctrine narrow and one-dimensional. The idea of annexing Judea and Samaria becomes the medium of religious performance, which is supposed to exhaust the gist of the whole of Jewish religiosity. Some of the fundamentalists have detected the irony of this pendulum effect: the farther you go toward one extreme, the greater the inclination toward its diametric opposite. On the one hand, one isolated precept is inflated to grand status; the commandment attached to settlement takes over and replaces all other commandments, to become the very accomplishment of the newly defined Judaism. And on the other hand, the value on which redemption of the Jewish people and the entire universe depends is inadvertently reduced to the status of just another precept.

Ironically the result is a kind of ultra-Orthodox quality, measured according to the punctiliousness of petty behavior. Instead of opening Judaism to encompass the entire people of Israel, it closes it in by applying one more restriction differentiating the religious from the secular. One Torah-centered settler suspects that the Israeli fundamentalist movement, which strove to combine all Jews and Zionists into a unified, dynamic body, will eventually be transformed into a kind of *kloiz* (Yiddish for small room, the label applied to congregations closed within themselves, the Hasidic equivalent of a cloister), which "makes a big deal" of yet another ritualistic item.

In a sense it is only natural for Judea and Samaria to have become the axis of the new religion, radical-Zionist Judaism, as its conquest/liberation (1967)—along with the establishment of the state (1948)—constitutes the primary and perhaps the sole element of the classic messianic vision which was indeed fully realized. Moreover, Jewish radicalism puts all its trust in territory, partly because this issue was believed to be the common denominator between the religious and the secular. Judea and Samaria is perceived as both a religious and a political lever for recruiting Israelis from various camps—under the Jewish-Zionist banner—to the fundamentalist doctrine and code of behavior. However, the integrity of the Land of Israel, intended as a symbol and means of achieving Jewish harmony which transcends the distinction between sacred and profane, has become instead another bone of contention between them. Nevertheless, fundamentalists in Israel persist in anchoring the entire Jewish and Zionist world in the issue of the whole Land of Israel. Thus, they become more distant from the Orthodox as well as from the secular Zionists.

Other cases of religious fundamentalism are similarly characterized by the selection of several specific elements—often those which have immediate political implications—from a vast and varied religious reservoir as a focal point for divine worship and religious activism. Fundamentalism typically tends toward contraction of everything religious to one focal point of super intensity. Sometimes it is the assassination of the iniquitous prince, and sometimes the annexation of territory.

Conspicuous Pietism and Martyrdom

Obviously fundamentalism seeks to emphasize its chosen religiopolitical foci, which concentrate the radical message and therefore deserve promotion. GE is aware of the value of public relations and excels in use of the mass media. The movement's campaigns receive extensive press coverage, and numerous forums are available for expression of its views. The Israeli public is extensively exposed to scenes of settlers ascending the hills of Judea and Samaria. Television viewers can recite GE slogans by heart and are almost intimately acquainted with the movement's spokesmen and activists, settlements, and institutions. The activism of the fundamentalists possesses a somewhat exhibitionistic dimension. A less predictable phenomenon is the pretense and pomp that GE members often express in aspects of their religiosity otherwise free of radical significance. Apparently they enjoy parading not only their political initiatives but also their ritualistic lives, often in a demonstrative and essentially spiteful manner. Practices which are habitual among regular religious people are performed by fundamentalists with a high level of awareness and some measure of presumptuousness. Furthermore, routine Orthodox rites may also be exploited as an expression of protest or provocation. For example, group members wear prayer shawls and long beards, identified traditionally with the ultra-Orthodox, as part of a distinctive ensemble combined with jeans or military fatigues.

The skullcaps GE members wear are also meant to express confidence and pride in their distinctive cause. Until about twenty years ago, Israeli nationals tended to conceal their religiosity and were even embarrassed by it. During this peak period of the secular, modern Zionist ethos, religion was the object of ridicule and even a certain suppression. Many of the Orthodox sought integration into general Israeli social, economic, and political circles and either removed the traditional head covering altogether, replaced it with neutral headwear, or reduced the size of their skullcaps and moved them to the side where they could barely be seen. The significant rise in self-esteem—or perhaps even vanity—among the Israeli Orthodox which accompanied the rise of GE may be measured according to the gradual increase in the skullcap's diameter and its assumption of increasingly blatant colors and forms over the past fifteen years.

Today, the younger generations of the national-religious population—over half of all religious Jews in Israel, more than 10 percent of the population—proudly wear a new variety of head covering: the knitted skullcap.[76] One speaks of "knitted skullcap culture." For more than a decade, it was wholly identified with GE. During the mid-1970s, the knitted skullcap was considered glamorous, as reflected in songs, political cartoons, and pictures. Wearing the knitted skullcap was then an unequivocal sign of identification with the cause of settlement in Judea and Samaria, so much so that the few knitted skullcap wearers who were not among the movement's supporters found it necessary to explain and justify themselves; those who wanted to display their reservations openly simply exchanged their knitted skullcaps for another variety (now that differences of opinion have emerged even within the national-religious camp, there is even some subdifferentiation among the various types of knitted skullcaps). In any event, it is difficult to separate the rise of GE from the rise of the knitted skullcap as an almost snobbish emblem of a new Zionist Judaism.

On the internal front as well, Jewish-Zionist fundamentalism was meticulous and blatant in exhibiting its piety, both in its campaigns and in ritual routine. The movement developed a "conspicuous devotion" also implemented by the wives of the Torah-centered settlers. There is a kind of hierarchy of devotion, asceticism, and tribulation, in which women are ranked according to the number of rabbinic decisions they seek regarding household, education, and employment, or the number of winters they have spent with their infants in a leaky tent on a mountaintop in Judea and Samaria. The extent of their puritanism and austerity is measured with precision: the greater the length of their sleeves and the smaller the area of their kitchens, the closer they are to the religious ideal. The activist-believers also ascribe great importance to the number of children they bear, despite the physical and security problems affecting the settlements and the material shortage resulting from the breadwinners' devotion to Torah study. Family size has become an index of piety. GE families compete not only with one another but also, as a group, with the haredim to demonstrate "who's really more Jewish," and with the secular, whom they wish to show "who's contributing more to the Zionist effort" (many families have ten or more children; Rabbi Levinger has eleven).

GE also boasts an incipient martyrology. Among GE wives and their husbands, there is a tendency toward mortification—a suffering at the altar of God, measured in terms of sacrifice for Torah and for settlement of the Land of Israel. Sometimes it borders on a new variation of the classic motif of martyrdom. Over the years there developed a near-saintly caste: a closed circle of the victims of Jewish Zionist radicalism, i.e., Torah-centered settlers who were killed or wounded in acts of Palestinian aggression of a nationalistic or religious nature, and their orphans and widows.

Just as the cadres of GE appear to compete with each other regarding the number of nights they spent in police detention following an illegal demonstration, or the severity of the blows they received from soldiers during evacuation from an illegal settlement, so too do they assess a person's worth according to the number of hours per day he spends studying Torah or the time he devotes to prayers. The Jewish radicals spend more time at prayer than the average Orthodox Jew. It is commonly believed that the amount of time devoted to performance of a ritual precept attests to one's seriousness toward its fulfillment. Prayers recited during GE's political activity take an especially long time. Under operative circumstances, the activist-believers' standard rites are also augmented by a somewhat theatrical dimension. In general their services are somewhat ostentatious (both the three regular, but nonetheless elaborated, weekday services and the more complex Sabbath and Holiday rites, as well as blessings and prayers of thanksgiving which accompany extraordinary events and routine activities, ranging from inter-city traveling to eating or relieving oneself).

The ethos of the movement, which resembles Hasidism in many ways, tends to relate prayer to *dvekut*—the Jewish concept closest to *unio-mystica*—which obviously involves great emotion.[77] The GE ritual has a markedly ecstatic dimension. In all cases, fundamentalism embodies various qualities called "enthusiasm" in the history of religions, which accord faith and ritual "heat" and vitality.[78] This enthusiasm nourishes movement activism, which in turn arouses religious faith and ritual practice. In this sense fundamentalism is a passionate phenomenon which manifests a kind of religious revivalism through the medium of political action.[79]

Religion is Politics

The activist surge, clearly invested with numerous drives that are not strictly religious but born of social and political frustration, exhibits such high levels of religious energy that existing religious structures cannot contain them, at which point they erupt and overflow, threatening civil order. Less acknowledged is the fact that the explosion carries seeds of subversion that threaten the existing religious order itself. Fundamentalist activism constitutes a challenge both to the sociopolitical and to the religious status quo in part because it is not merely a function of intensified religiosity. Political activity is the realization of religion; it is nourished by the religious experience but also creates and intensifies it. Jewish radicals manifest as much zeal in politics as they do in fulfillment of divine precepts; after all, political involvement is a precept, even a pivotal one.[80] Fundamentalism condemns politics for not being religious and condemns religion for not being political. The movement criticizes not only the secular state, but also the religious establishment, including "progressive" Orthodoxy and various reformist trends, for laxity in fulfilling religious precepts and for stressing universal human aspects at the expense of political and national ones. Radical Jews also blame ultra-Orthodoxy for limiting itself to study and ritual aspects of religion and for abandoning the application of precepts in general social spheres, particularly those concerning political matters.

Augmenting religion with politics (and not vice versa) is the message of the activist-believers. We are thus not considering a case of "religious politics"—politics charged with holiness because it contributes to the interests of the religious sector and religious institutions—but rather "political religion," whose sanctity is inherent and unconditional from the outset. Jewish-Zionist fundamentalism considers politics as a mode of religious expression even more than it employs "religion as a mode of political expression."[81] As such, the phenomenon is exceptional in the political world and even more so in the religious world.[82] Fundamentalists might agree with the axiom recorded in Khomeini's will: "Politics is religion." GE says: "Religion is politics," and adds: "Politics is the most perfect and exalted type of religion." It denies politics apart from religion any measure of autonomy in an authentic society.

In the sphere of politics, then, as in ritual worship, GE attempts to operate according to the rules of Torah and halakha. However, GE also attempts to conduct the former sphere according to mystical and messianic rules more than in any other individual or public sphere. As in other cases of religious radicalism, politics is intended to fulfill the will of God and to glorify His name on earth. In the Israeli case, politics is presented explicitly as divine worship in the full sense of the term.

The religious value of Jewish-Zionist politics is derived from its simultaneous function as a reflection of the totality of holiness and as a tool for its achievement by introducing the sacred without exception into all aspects of the profane. According to the activist-believers, this trend leads to the consummation of redemption, toward communion with God. Politics is thus a messianic and mystical medium. The logic behind the theological system deployed with politics at its center is kabbalistic in nature. The more practical politics is, the more it is considered and described as "spiritual" and "internal." The GE campaigns most outstanding in their tactical sophistication and logistic complexity were recorded in the annals of the movement as those with an especially lofty religious quality. Accordingly, the attempt to uncover the regularities of actual politics, and especially to manipulate them, amounts to the discovery and handling of the concealed holiness—the most sacrosanct of all. Involvement in politics, which is considered tantamount to engaging in the secrets of Creation, can lead to genuine revelation, as divinity is inherent in history, in the praxis of the secular, so much so that some GE leaders have confided: "Before we sink into the gutter of politics, we should purify ourselves in the *mikve* (ritual bath), as it is like delving into the secrets of the Torah."[83] This analogy has another aspect: devotion to politics to the point of inebriation is like diving recklessly into the mysteries of divinity and the universe to the point of total self-nullification: both are very dangerous and demand caution from the outset.

In the conception of GE, the politics which moves the world is that which sanctifies it in its entirety; the world's inherent holiness renders it entirely political. "The politics of Israel" is a sui generis category distinguished by its essentially religious nature, which accords it a supreme morality. Politics is indeed a noble virtue, a Jewish-Zionist quality. At the same time, GE's politics are well integrated into the local and regional political system. However, the "fantastic" features of this sacred politics, which render it somewhat indifferent to the conventional rules of the political game, enhance the perception of the movement's ruthlessness and accord it an advantageous position in the game of power politics.

Consider, for example, the Jewish-Zionist fundamentalist stand with regard to peace with Israel's Arab neighbors. The partner, whether Egyptian or Palestinian, does not matter at all from GE's point of view. The claims of the other side are considered irrelevant and its rights are in principle unrecognized, regardless of their content. Decision making should not consider the other side, since affairs between Israel and the Gentiles are of no account, only those between Israel and itself. Peace is exclusively a Jewish matter. Middle East politics in general are only a secondary concern. Peace is something between the nation and its God, between Israel, the Torah, and faith—not a complex web of diplomatic or strategic relations between communities and states but rather a spiritual orientation toward the sacred. Once this fundamental principle is acknowledged, everything else will fall into place of itself.

In its objections to the peace accords with Egypt, GE developed a series of rather powerful claims at the geopolitical level through which it sought to persuade the public and the authorities. The movement used all possible legal means—and did not hesitate to employ illegal ones—in the struggle which brought Israel to the brink of conflict with the United States and renewed hostilities with Egypt, and to the brink of what then appeared to be civil war, all because peace was perceived as sabotaging the security, honor, and morality of Israel. On a deeper level, it was not considered a "true" peace, a "Jewish" peace, a "divine" peace. The activist-believers recall the etymological affinity between the words *shalom* (peace) and *shlemut* (wholeness, perfection, something which is undivided, free of defects). According to GE, peace subsumes both territorial and religious integrity; all three are in fact identical. Genuine peace is the whole Land of Israel and complete Judaism. The Israeli fundamentalists were not prepared to compromise on anything less.

A similar mystical-messianic conception guided GE's political schemes in the power maneuvers for control of the administration, political parties, the army, and public opinion in Israel, dictating decisions and parliamentary and extraparliamentary acts concerning the fate of the Territories. Even specific conjunctions are linked with cosmic processes in a kind of kabbalistic mechanics. Rabbi Levinger combines a sharp intuition for realpolitik with an esoteric approach in his somewhat sarcastic assessment of events in the Territories. During the early days of efforts to establish a permanent Jewish presence in Palestinian Hebron, which then seemed to have no chance of success, he sat on the ground in the town marketplace, then closed for the evening. After midnight prayers and a Torah lesson, by the light of a kerosene lantern, he lectured the young cadres about the dynamics which combine the terrestrial world with the celestial one. This was a kind of briefing and encouragement before they stole past the army patrols and climbed up ladders over the barbed wire fences into the building targeted for settlement. He concluded: "Peres [then Israel's Defense Minister] bows down before Jaabari [then Arab Mayor of Hebron]. Jaabari bows down before Rabbi Moshe [Levinger] and Rabbi Moshe bows down before the Creator—who will help us settle in the heart of this area."

Restoring Biblical Justice and Rebuilding the Temple

Fundamentalist "sacred" politics turns on formulas selectively retrieved from a mythical-historical ensemble canonized in a sacred text, regarded as an authentic revelation of religion. This authoritative source is interpreted, often by a charismatic personality, as binding the faithful in all its minutiae. Thus, it offers a prescription for the social and religious conduct of the faithful and guides their relations with the surrounding world. In other words, this view posits the relevance and practicality of an ancient code; it avers the applicability of the events, morals, hierological rationale, and rules of the past not only to ritual but to the political agenda in the here and now.

GE provides numerous examples of this religiopolitical archaism. One source of inspiration and authorization for the drive to institute Israeli sovereignty in the Territories is the biblical narrative concerning God's promise to the Patriarchs and its realization by the Israelites who returned from Egyptian exile to settle in Canaan. The basis for this claim can be found in the various versions of the commandment to conquer and settle the land and in a selective medley of its subsequent commentaries dating from Mishnaic sources at the end of the Ancient Era, through Nahmanides of the Middle Ages and up to rabbinic authorities of the early modern era.Thus ancient religious norms, values, and religious reasoning join in a specific program which provides motivation and a blueprint for present-day action. Fundamentalism identifies and develops the ideological nucleus latent in the religious heritage and transforms it into a total and exclusive vision. GE sums up its goal as follows: "To elevate the Torah to a level at which it will no longer be an article of religion, manifested solely through synagogue services and study, but rather function as a platform for actual praxis of farmers and soldiers."

This leads to another characteristic of fundamentalist politics: the aspiration to establish a new-old society. First, the change considered here is not just oriented to the individual, not purely reformist in nature, and not postponed to the End of Days.

There must be a rapid, profound, and comprehensive transformation of the collectivity, which will bring about the ultimate state. Second, the patterns for a radically reconstructed society are taken from an idealized version of the glorious Beginning of Days, projected on the longed-for End of Days. Judaism's arsenal possesses a vast repertoire of valid, ready-made models on which GE could easily draw for inspiration and legitimacy when necessary. Letters, diaries, and other intimate records kept by activist-believers indicate that during their service in the IDF, for example, they likened themselves to the warriors of King David conquering Jerusalem. On other occasions, they identified with the troops of the Maccabees and felt as if the battle cry "Whoso is on the Lord's side, let him come unto me" was spontaneously emanating from their lips. It is only natural that Jewish-Zionist fundamentalism would derive the patterns of its ideal society from the classic object of nostalgic yearnings and utopian longing—the Israelite golden age, characterized by a great Judaism which possessed proto-Zionist dimensions, especially that of settlement in an independent and whole Land of Israel. The inevitable ideal of the biblical kingdom of the House of David is generally augmented by elements of the Hasmonean kingdom of the Second Temple Period. The amalgamation of these two pinnacles of Jewish history comprises imagery of national pride, political sovereignty, administrative efficacy, heroics and military might, material abundance, and, of course, extensive borders, along with vast religious creativity and a full and active religious life. The apex and symbol of all the fundamentalist desires is the worship of God in the Holy Temple, standing intact on its original site. This, of course, is the epitome of the messianic ideal in Israel.

The rebuilding of the Temple (destroyed first by the Babylonians in 586 B.C.E. and then by the Romans in 70 C.E.) is perceived by the activist-believers as the desired culmination of their movement's endeavors. Political activism, which commenced with the settlement of Judea and Samaria, is eventually supposed to lead to this objective. The same is true of the parallel path of activism in the cultic domain. Besides expressing hope for the rebuilding of the Temple in their regular daily prayers and contributing to the realization of these yearnings through Torah study and fulfillment of conventional precepts—like all Orthodox Jews—the Jewish radicals follow a path which is both ancient and revolutionary, one certainly considered deviant in the Orthodox world. They have taken steps to facilitate and accelerate the building of the Temple and to prepare for divine worship therein, according to the standards stipulated in Holy Writ with regard to the details of the rites. This is yet another messianic trend whose particulars are halakhic in nature. In the meantime, dedication to the Holy Temple in Jerusalem is concentrated in a protected and well-supported niche in the warm bosom of GE. Alongside its political obsession, the movement leaves some room for ceremonial, less aggressive, and more exotic initiatives.

Some activist-believers devote all their time and energies to specialization in those parts of the Torah which pertain to Temple worship—such as ritual purity and sacrifice—and are preparing themselves to serve as priests. Others exploit various opportunities to deceive the police and the *Waqf* (Moslem Religious Trust) and penetrate the well-guarded Temple Mount area, pray there, and wave the Israeli flag. During Passover of 1989, they planned to smuggle parts of the altar inside, assemble them, and offer a sacrifice to God. There are also those who encircle the Temple Mount during the Jewish Festivals, carrying Torah scrolls and binoculars, attempting to capture details of the remnants and to determine the precise location of that room which could be entered only by the High Priest and only once a year (there is a fear that others might violate this awesome prohibition and accidentally trespass on its site). At night there are people who clandestinely dig deeply beneath the Temple Mount, struggling to reach the foundations of the ancient structure. Movement folklore tells of a much-admired figure among the Torah-centered settlers, who piled cedar beams behind his house in Judea and Samaria. Convinced that they were remnants of the destroyed Temple, he had purchased them at considerable cost and set them aside for its imminent reconstruction.

At the periphery of the GE hard core are institutions specializing in various aspects of fulfilling this messianic dream. Workshops weave cloth for the priestly raiments, as stipulated in the Pentateuch, using no needles to produce the golden fringe, miter, etc. A research institute is studying the technical aspects of Temple worship and is directing the manufacture of sacred vessels, such as the censer. Several settler-rabbis close to the Jewish-Zionist fundamentalist leadership have recently invested their best efforts and funds in locating a "red heifer." So far, the road toward redemption of the Temple is blocked by a rabbinic injunction forbidding Jews from entering the destroyed Temple complex, lest they violate the site because of the "impurity of the dead" by which all contemporary Jews are contaminated. According to halakha, only the ashes of the cremated red heifer, mixed with special water, can purify the Israelites and prepare them for ascending the Mount. But such heifers are rare indeed; in fact their meticulous specifications render them virtually unobtainable. The heifer must be completely red, including its horns and nose, without even one hair of a different color. Furthermore, it must never have carried any burden whatsoever; no one may even lean on it for a moment. For this messianic project, they recruited rabbis, livestock farmers, and scientists, who are cooperating in a sophisticated genetic engineering project to produce a creature which, according to tradition, has had only nine predecessors since the dawn of history. Here, fundamentalism and high technology go hand in hand.

The Holy Temple branch of Jewish radicalism includes eccentric figures who are essentially detached from the activism for which the movement is famous. However, several leaders of this cultic trend are also among the most extreme of GE's political agitators. The two methods of activity—esoteric ritual and operative militancy—are considered complementary. They were combined in the actions of the Jewish terrorist underground in the Territories uncovered in 1984. Such cult-like projects may be found in the partial overlap between GE and other religiopolitical circles, generally in the extreme right wing. The overlap is generally personal and ideological but not necessarily organizational. Specifically, several of the Temple-oriented personalities are close to the Kach movement of Rabbi Kahane, while their status in GE is anything but marginal.

Torahcracy

The ancient model is used by religiopolitical radicals to map the future with regard to both ritual matters and actual social affairs. The GE vision, for example, includes not only the restoration of all details of biblical worship in toto but also institution of the Bible as the standard for conduct of public systems normally regulated by the state. Activist-believers in Israel even fantasize about an economic system based on the Pentateuch, observing the sabbatical year and the Jubilee, institutions which functioned two or three millennia ago or even earlier. In this fundamentalist doctrine and others, activist-believers stress that restoration of such institutions fulfills a religious obligation and will automatically cure the nation's moral decadence and solve social problems. Nevertheless, GE does not express any specific or binding views concerning the overall social aspects of the ideal kingdom; its explicit declarations are limited to a narrow and essentially political front.

The sphere of economics remains relatively untouched by the fundamentalists;[84] in general they concentrate more powerful and specific efforts on the legal and constitutional spheres, in which they seek to institute the ancient system of law and justice. The Jewish radicals seek to reconstruct the relevant Torah system, embodied in the Sanhedrin (the communal court comprising the era's seventy greatest sages). From the outset, GE has been troubled by Israel's legal system, basically inherited from the Ottomans and the British, and as Rabbi Kook the Younger stated: "they would even take from the Hottentots, but not from the Jews." Activist-believers recently commenced activity in this sphere, studying biblical and mishnaic law and professionally examining the possibilities of its application. A special institute was established, which publishes a journal whose purpose is "to promote the full application of ancient Hebrew law in the modern national state," recognizing that the issue of law is "the very heart of the problem of religion and state in Israel." Significantly, the journal, whose staff includes professors and university students, is called *Takdim* (precedent). The motto inscribed on its masthead serves as a greeting for this circle of Jewish radicals: "Toward revival of the nation and its law."

The typical point of departure of its articles is the current situation, in which Jewish law is applied within one specific sphere of the modern Israeli judicial system, namely, the laws of matrimony. The very existence of this isolated, narrow "nature preserve" underscores what is missing in the system as a whole and the severity of the situation. At present, such jurisdiction, which concerns personal status, is delegated to the rabbinic (or Shari'a) courts. The Jewish radicals hint that when Jewish law is applied to all aspects of society and state, these Orthodox institutions will become insufficient. The leading project on this front is the "Proposed Torah Constitution for the State of Israel," whose opening statement declares: "The State of Israel is a Torahcratic republic." Recently, its author, Yoel Lerner, has been linked with the initiative to establish the "State of Judea," which is supposed to arise in Judea and Samaria as a substitute for the sovereignty of the State of Israel if the latter decides to withdraw from the Territories. Lerner, an academician and a man of letters, has already served time in prison for his involvement in attempts to blow up the mosques on the Temple Mount.

The spiritual father of the initiative to revive the archaic law is Shabtai Ben-Dov, the paragon adopted by Yehuda Etzion, an ideologue of the Jewish underground in the Territories. Since his release from prison, Etzion has devoted himself to the editing and publishing of the thick volumes examining legal issues in light of biblical precedents. According to his view, the conclusions of this research are an inseparable part of the convictions which once guided him and his comrades along the path which commenced with "abbreviating" the legs of Palestinian mayors in the West Bank and sought to continue by "trimming" the mosques on the Haram al-Sharif (Temple Mount). Etzion's Israeli fundamentalist friends differ from him in the extent of their willingness to declare their objectives openly, but not so much in the essence of their content. Even if they sometimes hedge, hesitate, and tone down their pronouncements, the activist-believers ultimately admit that GE aspires toward a halakhic state.

In its politics, fundamentalism seeks to bring its religious message to all society and even to impose it if necessary. GE is prepared to render salvation obligatory for society. Not only do the activist-believers seek to save their souls, they also yearn to bring about the salvation of the world. In this context, fundamentalism is more of a movement than a sect: although in practice it constitutes a negligible minority which meticulously defends its own boundaries, it generally thinks in terms of transforming great masses and entire collectivities. The religiopolitical radicals' ambition is essentially inclusive in principle, its pretensions directed outside the circle of those already committed. The fundamentalist mission is universal, but not in the sense which limits itself to the assertion that fulfillment of all religious obligations by members of the select group and that group's consequently outstanding religiosity can substitute for enforcing the law for others or serving as a tool for redeeming the masses. Even if the movement withdraws from its surroundings and becomes sect-like at a certain stage, this situation is not idealized but is rather apologetically presented as force of circumstance, a tactical measure, a temporary setback, a closure designated for reorganization in preparation for a renewed breakthrough. One may assume that fundamentalism is tackling the classic dilemma of social movements, which are torn between centrifugal and centripetal tendencies. GE leaders held extensive discussions concerning the question of whether to continue the struggle on the external front or to withdraw temporarily for "reinforcement from within" and wait until "the people are ready" to accept the message. Today they tend to vacillate between these positions.

Furthermore, in its quest for social change, fundamentalism does not restrict itself to the option of proselytizing alone, although it does not disdain missionary work carried on parallel to its main efforts. One may perhaps perceive fundamentalism as commencing from the point at which religious radicals conclude that propaganda is insufficient for achievement of their objectives and sense that transition to an actual movement operative phase is inevitable.[85] Jewish-Zionist fundamentalism does invest certain efforts in what it calls "converting the Jews to Judaism," i.e., *teshuva*—returning the secular Israelis to Torah and divine precepts. Actually, GE's success on this front has been limited; however, according to GE, return to Judaism is inadvertently accomplished anyway via Zionist commitment and not necessarily through adoption of Orthodox norms. Missionary work is certainly not a significant or distinguishing aspect of fundamentalism in Israel or elsewhere. Recent achievements in recruiting Israelis to religion have been attained by Orthodox camps which are not at all interested in nationalism, the state and political activism. If there is any crossing of borders from Zionism toward Judaism, the main beneficiary is that haredi brand of religion which is not fundamentalist according to the definitions proposed herein.[86]

Sacred Militant Activism

GE essentially constitutes a chain of sporadic operations: units of ecstatic activity focusing on a defined political or settlement objective, built on total recruitment and short-range but absolute dedication, vanishing as suddenly as they spring up. GE then hibernates until the next operation (generally scheduled for yeshiva and school vacations during Jewish holiday weeks). These are the famous GE campaigns, charismatic pulses of a sort which gave the movement its rhythm. They are the peaks of religious intensification or revitalization and simultaneously the pinnacles of operative efficacy. This combination has ensured their political impact. GE's achievements are derived directly from these campaigns, the milestones of movement progress, in which the activist-believers discover and hone their organizational talents and in which their mystical messianic experience is concentrated. A GE campaign is a kind of fundamentalist spasm.

The surge of GE activism reveals ceremonial as well as political logic. The campaigns are festivals of divine worship. These events have an almost magical content: through them activist-believers can participate in the messianic dynamics, in a cosmic process. Redemption is indeed fundamentally immanent and deterministic, but man still retains some influence thereupon. GE stresses that "awakening from above" is largely contingent on "awakening from below." Some activist-believers indicate the movement's ability and obligation to "accelerate" and "facilitate" messianic progress; others express GE's objectives in terms of "synchronization," a mechanical expression used by activist-believers which calls for adapting political activism to the "secret rhythm of the universe."

This idiosyncratic conception of a kind of sacred mechanics contributes to the activism of the Jewish-Zionist fundamentalists. The messianic status of the universe is measured in concrete, specific terms, enhancing the tendency to act religiously and politically. The appointment of a particular cabinet minister or army officer can advance or delay redemption; consequently it is incumbent on Israelis to influence such decisions, say the activist-believers. So tangible is this redemption that one can "grasp it and impel it forward." It has actual physical dimensions, such as direction, velocity, and volume. During a settlement operation implemented in defiance of government and army orders and against the opposition of local Arabs, GE leader Hanan Porat suddenly left his companions, pulled up a few poles marking the area, and began running wildly toward the nearby hills. He drove the poles into the earth there to expand the area of the future settlement and then, as though possessed, pulled them up again and drove them into the hillside even farther away. When he returned to the original place, panting and puffing, he exclaimed: "We just extended the area of redemption." The others cheered: "He stole another piece of redemption."

In a way, were it not for the militant activism factor, we would find it difficult to differentiate between fundamentalism and establishment religion; after all the fundamentalists often strive for goals shared by conventionally observant religious people, at least de jure. Most Orthodox Jews hope for messianic fulfillment, as expressed both in their daily prayers and in their responses to a direct question on the issue. As such, at least in theory, or perhaps only as lip service, they also support the establishment of a political structure whose constitution and source of authority are derived from the Torah. How to bring about its practical implementation and what one is willing to contribute to achieve this end—these are different matters entirely.

Does this imply that fundamentalists may be distinguished only for their consistency in drawing conclusions, and especially for their readiness for self-sacrifice in realizing them? Is GE explained by the extent to which they "take their religion seriously?" More often than not, the activist-believers themselves would respond to this question in the affirmative. Actually, this does appear to be at least partially true. We are aware that various extremist phenomena—and not only religious ones—constitute no more than a demand for uncompromising realization of a legitimate, accepted ideology and an attempt to meet all its demands, even if they proved difficult for the public to fulfill and were therefore relaxed if not defiled over the years. Actually the influence of extremists appears to draw largely on the public's a priori recognition of their ideology, on the one hand, and a realization that its commitment to that ideology is somewhat dubious, on the other. This engenders feelings of guilt and admiration toward the extremists, feelings subject to manipulation. Consider, for example, the closing of ranks among all shades of Israeli Orthodox in line with the small ultra-Orthodox faction. Even when GE was at the peak of its public prestige and self-confidence, it barely challenged the status of the haredim as representatives of the highest moral standards within religious Jewry. GE criticizes the haredim for their non-Zionism and pretends to represent a more authentic Judaism, yet it can hardly ignore their religious authority.

The ability to maintain a thoroughly consistent extremist Jewish identity is contingent on the possibility of sustaining a social system which is only partial—and some would add parasitic. A sectarian framework is required to ensure long-term religious extremism: a life of full purity and total consistency demands a closed and isolated world. But this in turn can only exist within a broader, stronger world which tolerates the radical social system and satisfies the security and material needs which the system itself cannot supply. Such is the story of the haredi community—which never knew a better period than the present—situated in pockets within pluralistic urban concentrations in affluent welfare states. In New York City or in Jerusalem, there is always someone—a Gentile or nonreligious Jew—to remove the trash, drive the buses, supply electricity, and provide protection from thieves, even on the Sabbath. In contrast, fundamentalism in its GE manifestation demands breaking down sectarian enclaves of religion in favor of full integration and total operation of society and state according to its own principles. Such Jewish radicalism, like its Islamic counterpart, demands that the Torah not only withstand the test of internal consistency, as is accomplished through traditional yeshiva study, but also the test of applicability in the external environment. Jewish-Zionist fundamentalism aspires to project ultra-Orthodoxy, which is so far valid only under ghetto or monastic conditions, onto the broader expanses of Jewish life.

Gush Emunim: Appraisal and Conclusion

Zealotry, according to one definition, means the doubling and redoubling of efforts precisely when the objective disappears beyond the horizon.[87] How will GE react if new circumstances force an agreement entailing Israeli withdrawal from all or part of the Territories? An apocalyptic scenario is now developing both within and outside the movement.[88] The precedent set by the 1982 evacuation of Yamit tells us little about the future, if only because the West Bank is more important than Sinai militarily, historically, and religiously. Israeli children have been born and raised, and homes have been built in the Territories. Generally speaking, activist-believers' material, political, and emotional investments in the Territories vastly exceed those invested in Sinai. Will the Jewish radicals fold their tents quietly, if unwillingly, after they have exhausted all possibilities allowed within the rules of the democratic game, or will they turn to underground organization and armed resistance? GE's confrontation with the challenge has a religious aspect which is no simpler than the political one: What will happen to the movement's messianic faith, which is based on a correlation between cosmic events and geopolitical circumstances measured in square miles?

The Intifada has brought about substantial change in Israel and the surrounding region. It has opened a new perspective towards the Territories and ipso facto toward GE. Naturally their respective destinies are closely intertwined. GE's distress intensified with the increase in worldwide recognition of the legitimacy of a Palestinian state in the Territories, as elements of Palestinian sovereignty gradually became institutionalized reality, and as Israel payed a higher and higher price in its attempt to halt processes which, in turn, seemed increasingly inevitable. During the mid-1970s the movement was at its peak, perceived by itself and others as a serious threat not only to the emerging Palestinian entity but also to the existing Jewish and Zionist entities. But during the first two years of the Intifada the movement seemed to sink to an unprecedented low.

GE's frustration was exacerbated as its sense of siege by local Arabs was accompanied by discomfort with its status as an isolated, sparse minority in Israeli society, virtual outcasts among Israel's Jews. The Torah-centered settlers facing the masked Palestinian stone throwers no longer enjoyed the popular solidarity and government backing to which they had become accustomed. GE felt despised by much of the public, abandoned by many of its former supporters, and betrayed by the authorities. GE's confidence was undermined regarding the movement's hold on Judea and Samaria and on Jewish consciences alike. Consequently GE split into camps; the ideological and tactical disputes between them evolved into an organizational struggle. The echoes of this internal disharmony have resounded far beyond the boundaries of GE and have reached the general public in Israel, which follows the details of GE upheaval in the mass media. Roughly speaking, one may distinguish between an extreme camp and a relatively moderate one. Their relations are characterized by denunciation and ostracism of one another. The former refuses to budge from GE's original stance. Basing itself on messianic-mystic theology, it will brook no compromise with the other side, not even Israelis, let alone Arabs. The latter faction displays varying degrees of readiness for dialogue, re-evaluation, and even occasional initial hints of the possibility of concession. The zealous camp is now losing its once nearly total hegemony. The group comprises the hard core of GE, which conceived the movement, molded its character, and determined its moves.

From the earliest stages of its history the movement also included a variety of other elements. In general they assimilated and accepted the word of the true believers out of support and admiration or submission. Even if they ultimately contributed some input to routine administrative or cultural aspects of the settlement world, they found it difficult to acquire a status of moral authority. Only recently did they consolidate into a real internal opposition offering a viable alternative to the movement. GE loses its uniqueness and common denominator as formerly peripheral factors increase in prominence and influence at the expense of the Kookist core. The religious and political character of the original GE components, which seemed to have been overwhelmed and swept away in the fervor of movement enthusiasm, are suddenly exposed anew. Thus, even if the movement's radicalism has not declined, its "Jewish radicalism" has certainly decreased. Generally speaking, GE's singularity vis-à-vis both the Jewish and the Zionist world has weakened.

Many researchers were so captivated by the fundamentalist revival that we may have underestimated the perseverance of modern secularity and its institutions, from the nation-state to television entertainment, and belittled the power of its complementary side—"conventional" religion, especially Orthodoxy. In the Israeli case at least, it now appears possible that traditional Judaism—if not traditional Zionism—may overcome the new strain of Jewish-Zionist fundamentalism.

From the outset, GE avowed that the test of its success is the possibility of its voluntary disbanding. The movement preferred not to phrase its objective in terms of attaining power but rather as achieving a situation in which the authorities, and with them the entire nation, voluntarily follow the path charted by GE. At that juncture, according to early GE claims, the activist-believers will hand the torch to the heads of government and will return to devote themselves to what they always perceived as their ultimate objective, Torah study. There were chapters in GE history when the movement felt it was at the threshold of actually witnessing the moment when it could afford to leave the arena. One such occasion was the May 1977 election upheaval, which brought the Likud to power and appeared to entail the institution of an assertive nationalism. This was enhanced by the renaissance of a distinctly Jewish style, saturated with formulas such as "with God's help," "sanctification of the [holy] name," etc. This "winning combination" was obviously accompanied by the new cabinet's commitment to the concept of the Whole Land of Israel. GE's euphoria reached its peak when Menachem Begin, having just assumed his new position as prime minister, went to the home of Rabbi Kook to receive his blessing. Several days later, he made a pilgrimage to a settlement in the heart of Judea and Samaria. Standing between Rabbi Levinger and Ariel Sharon, wearing a skullcap and holding a Torah scroll, Begin announced that there would be many more settlements. Needless to say, the radical Jews were soon disillusioned. In November of that year, on the arrival of President Sadat in Jerusalem, the movement's situation began to deteriorate. As cries of peace echoed throughout Israel, GE felt itself locked in the bear hug of the new Jewish nationalism, which had passed it on the right to negotiate with the Arabs for withdrawal from part of the whole Land of Israel. This was not the outcome for which GE had prayed and worked so hard. The movement's achievements bore the seeds of its defeat. Moreover, the activist-believers realized that there was no genuine religious content in the national resurgence prevailing in Israel. After intoxicating itself with the Jewish component of the Likud's Zionism, and even exploiting it for its own purposes, GE's frustration grew as it began to suspect that this element comprised only outward mannerisms.

It is only recently that GE members have come to understand the tricky character of its success, as a great settlement momentum has developed. Tens of thousands of Israelis have settled in Judea and Samaria, consolidating their hold in the Territories with massive national budget allocations and the political and administrative support provided by senior cabinet ministers, an efficient lobby of about two dozen Knesset members, and sophisticated systems for public relations, security, etc. Nevertheless, the sparse network of small Jewish enclaves never reached critical mass.[89] Moreover, the State systematically avoided officially declaring the annexation of the Territories. Was GE's cup half empty or half full? Less than one quarter of the adult settlers in the Territories have views similar to those of GE, while others are totally indifferent to religiopolitical radicalism, if not repelled by it. Many of them had some hawkish inclinations initially or at least developed them subsequently. A decisive majority of Israelis living in the Territories were motivated by the opportunity for improving their quality of life at a relatively low cost. The movement's recruitment potential was undoubtedly exhausted and its upper boundaries revealed. From the outset GE declared that it aspired toward a situation in which settlement in the Territories would be "normal" and "popular," representing the various sectors and broad strata of the population and of course supported by the establishment.

As the unanticipated wave of immigration from the Soviet Union began in 1990, GE experienced something akin to an awakening. For many years, the movement had claimed that mass immigration was not a dream but a reasonable possibility. By leading to the Judaization and consequent annexation of the Territories, the immigration would be the solution to Israel's problems. Accordingly, GE embarked on a systematic and enthusiastic campaign to encourage the immigrants to settle in Judea and Samaria and to welcome them at settlements. However, the realities of 1990—the meager percentage (0.5 percent) of immigrants moving to Judea and Samaria and the international opposition the issue arouses—were a source of bitter disappointment to the

Jewish radicals. Some GE watchers believed that this development even more than the Intifada was sealing the fate of the Whole Land of Israel campaign.

Thus the balance sheet of GE's achievements is somewhat ambiguous, lending itself to various readings, even diametrically opposed interpretations, depending upon one's point of view and upon the moment in history. This is primarily true with regard to Israel's hold on the Territories. To this day, more than twenty years after their conquest, their status is still the subject of debate: Will they be returned to Arab sovereignty or remain under Israeli control? Which option is more desirable or more reasonable when considering the chances of success versus the risks and the price to be paid? The fact that the question is still open can be considered either as utter failure or impressive success for GE. Perhaps it would be more correct to say that in the meantime, there is no firm decision, but rather an apparent admixture of the two, as both GE and its rivals tend to admit.

Jewish radicalism in Israel has not succeeded in seizing the reins of government. However, the telling fact about GE political involvement is the massive investment of effort and resources by the Israeli authorities in their war against GE, in which they also yielded and compromised to a considerable extent. Beyond purely strategic or parliamentary matters, the movement's influence spread among a variety of strata and permeated deeper layers of society and the state. Many Israelis were immersed in a lively debate concerning GE, whether in popular settings or in forums of the intelligentsia. For about a decade, the movement represented either the promise of a breath of life for both Judaism and Zionism, or a demon haunting them. Either way, GE has recently ceased fulfilling either of these parallel functions in Israel.

Even when GE was at its peak, when supporters and opponents alike admitted that the movement was carrying the majority, it was still a minority group, as evidenced in cases enabling relatively accurate proportional estimates. At the one time that positions which many ascribed to "Israeli zealotry" were tested by the electorate—when voters were offered a clear and viable alternative—the positions were rejected. The nation and its delegates displayed mass support for the peace agreement with Egypt, even though it entailed withdrawal. Tehiya, the party which stood for maximalist expansion and also included representatives of maximalist religion, was then identified with the GE cause, but received only 2.3 percent of the vote. No one need be reminded that the government of Begin, Shamir, and Sharon executed the Camp David Accords to the last detail, despite provocations and a desperate attempt by GE to sabotage the agreement.

One can argue, of course, that Sinai was relinquished only to reinforce Israel's hold on the West Bank. But it is hard to ignore the fact that GE deeply believed that the peace agreement was a catastrophe from a Zionist point of view and a sin from the Jewish perspective, and that it sincerely maintained that the withdrawal was spiritual and physical suicide. Yet the number of Jewish-Zionist radicals mobilized for an emergency campaign against the governments of Israel, Egypt, and the United States, who bitterly opposed the evacuation of Yamit, was no greater than two thousand. Nevertheless, GE is living proof that under certain circumstances, a sectarian group of a few hundred activist-believers is capable of galvanizing and activating an entire society.

Inherent Tensions

Since numbers alone do not reveal the full extent of GE's power, we must add perspective by recalling the sectors active in the Israeli system which impinge on the movement. They resemble the movement in some important respects but not in others. One may present them as a reserve for potential GE recruitment or as potential members of a coalition with GE. First, we should realize that only 15 percent of Israel's Jewish population of 3.5 million is defined as religious. Among them, sectors of prominent size and status harbor grave misgivings about GE. The movement drew considerable support from a less intensively religious category, generally called "traditional," numbering more than a quarter of the population. Some researchers identify fundamentalism in Israel with the hawkish political conception represented by the Likud and factions to the right of it. This category comprises approximately half the Jews in Israel. Arrayed against this self-proclaimed national camp is a body of more or less equal size comprising the liberal center and dovish left. Most of the elite cadres of Israeli society are in that group. They also fill the ranks of movements like Peace Now, which since its establishment has consistently opposed GE. Peace Now managed to attract four hundred thousand Israeli citizens to its rally; GE attracted a maximum of one hundred thousand. The dovish camp is almost entirely composed of secular Jews. Its rivalry with GE thus has both a political and a religious level. At the same time, the political camp close to GE includes both religious and secular Jews. Publicly GE downplays the differences between them, emphasizing their common Jewish-Zionist characteristics. In practice, however, it faced the problems of relations between the camp's two components. GE's attempt to establish mixed settlements for religious and nonreligious Jews ended in a fiasco. Furthermore, GE's pretensions notwithstanding, no secular Jew has ever succeeded in penetrating the movement's inner circle of decision makers and moral authorities.

According to GE, the concept of *klal Israel*—the wholeness or integrity of the Jewish People—is no less lofty than the wholeness or integrity of the Land of Israel, with the latter largely serving the former. Cooperation between the movement and its non-observant allies is sanctified, yet in practice it was always ad hoc—short-lived and specific in content.[90] Moreover, most joint undertakings of religious and secular Israelis in the movement have failed. The violent scandal and schism in the Tehiya Party is one noteworthy example.

One key question for GE with both practical and ideational implications concerns the extent to which believers should form coalitions with nonbelievers. GE members know full well how difficult and fateful that decision is for the movement's future. Among the activist-believers, no one doubts the sanctity of the alliance itself or its contribution to the goal of a greater Israel. Nevertheless, they are aware that consensus with secular Israelis concerning general principles, such as the need for a "renewal of Zionist spirit" or "keeping the Jewish spark alive," is vastly different from an agreement regarding smoking or watching television on the Sabbath in a public dining room. This represents a basic dilemma for Israeli fundamentalism.

The basic internal contradiction characterizing GE is undoubtedly the one between loyalty to the laws of the State and loyalty to the laws of the Torah. This is evident despite movement propaganda, which denies or ignores it, and despite movement theology's negation of it in principle. Another major source of tension is extremely touchy, and its symptoms are consequently rare and faint, especially those extracted from GE publications disseminated beyond the reticent circles of activist-believers: Behind the facade of Kookist dialectic discourse lies a deep awareness of the potentially explosive contradiction between devotion to the Whole Land of Israel and subjection to halakha. Activist-believers tremble at the prospect of having to choose between them in what they themselves call a moment of truth. Pushed to the wall, they allude to the probability of choosing the path of Torah if it clearly reveals itself as contradictory to the path of land and state. In that scenario, they will have to dissociate themselves entirely from their secular partners, even though the latter are equally committed to ultranationalist goals.

The movement has always enjoyed considerable success in facing the difficult test of containing this tension. It maintained its affinity for the world of the pork eaters dedicated to settling the Whole Land of Israel and at the same time preserved its affiliation with the world of talmudic scholars who call for withdrawal in order not to provoke the nations of the world and not to act brazenly before God. GE's ultimate fate will, however, depend on which principles will serve as the crux of self-definition. Is the most portentous dividing line the one between non-believing Israelis and God-fearing ones or the one between the advocates and opponents of settlements in the Territories (although the former dichotomy is carefully downplayed, while the flames of the latter are constantly fanned)? The recent reappearance of Orthodox bodies favoring territorial compromise and dialogue with the Palestinians (e.g., Netivot Shalom and Meimad) remind us to observe developments not only between religious and secular Israelis in the hawkish camp but also those between hawks and doves in the religious camp. In the final analysis, the essential dilemma of Jewish-Zionist fundamentalism may partially reflect a mystery surrounding Israeli society in general: Which is its continental divide, the one separating hawks from doves or the one separating religious from secular Jews?

Israeli Fundamentalism and Modern Secularity

GE's several thousand activist-believers today represent the limits of the movement's religious recruitment rather than its political capability. The movement has been less successful in conversion than in mobilization. Religio-political radicalism remains a small-scale phenomenon, isolated both politically and religiously. Virtually no secular Jews were absorbed into Jewish-Zionist fundamentalism—not even those who agreed with its Zionist approach. Eventually they were left behind along with the vast majority of religious Jews: the former were apparently repelled by the traditional halakhic foundation of GE's religiosity, whereas the latter were deterred by its messianic-mystical basis. In view of the importance which GE ascribes to the incorporation of secular Jews and its early euphoria over what then appeared to be outstanding progress on that front, it is easy to explain the movement's disappointment in the face of realities which have become more pronounced over time. Most of GE's secular allies did not maintain their loyalty past the initial phase of excitement or beyond a particular campaign; the few who remained did not attract more activists from their own ranks (usually they were figures of relatively high stature but were nonetheless marginal; some were even rather eccentric). The harnessing of secular Israelis to political and operational activism was never conceived as more than a phase, and means, on the road to returning those Jews to the religious fold. The goal of the movement's expansive activism is "the mountain peaks to the east of the old border, and consequently the mind and hearts of citizens to the west of them," as a GE leader confessed in a rare, revealing moment of truth.

Buttressing this dual ambition is a bold interpretation of Judaism which surpasses the religious-secular dichotomy. These categories are considered overly narrow concepts, inappropriate for the Era of Redemption, which has already begun. This will soon be appreciated as the hidden saintliness of the Zionists (who "only think they are secular" and are "mistakenly regarded as such by others") comes to light. Once they are conscious of their true nature, they will speedily begin to observe Torah rules. Until then, in contrast to the myth prevailing in Israel regarding the return to Judaism, GE cannot point to many more than a dozen "penitent Jews" in its membership.

Behind GE's inability to break the numerical barrier and expand the ranks of activists and believers alike lies the movement's withdrawal from its efforts to erase the line differentiating religious Israelis from secular Israelis and to expand the definition of Judaism. Beyond a defined period and an essentially sectarian framework, GE did not succeed in preserving the new national religion which it developed as a perfection of and alternative to traditional religion. The bold adventure of breaking through the boundaries of Orthodoxy appears to lack both staying power and attractiveness to a broader public. After taking significant independent and innovative strides forward, Jewish-Zionist fundamentalism tends to return to the warm and safe bosom of Orthodoxy. The built-in constraint of religiopolitical radicalism in Israel is reflected in the unlikelihood of its obtaining political control and in its decreasing chances of controlling the rabbinate. If there is any Judaization of Israelis, it is not of the revolutionary type which GE proposed but rather a quasi-classical Judaization involving a certain detachment from Zionism. Consequently while GE's national political status has been undermined, its religious legitimacy and confidence have suffered a mighty blow. Paradoxically, the recent trend of an increase in the power of Orthodox and even ultra-orthodox Judaism in Israel at the expense of secular and national Judaism (as evidenced in the results of the Knesset elections of November 1988) is a reflection and component of the decline of radical Judaism à la GE.

The drop in secular society's status is commonly linked to the rise of fundamentalism. The prevailing model recalls a balance scale: the descent of one side entails the ascent of the other. Sometimes the crisis of secularity is indeed the negative definition of religious revival and expansion, and vice versa. This situation has also obtained in the history of relations between traditional Judaism and modern Zionism. As long as secular Jews were on the rising end of the scale, religion was in distress. But in the last generation, a new situation has emerged, perceived by the secular culture itself, and obviously by the opposing religious world, as a crisis of secularity, with both ideological and sociopolitical reflections. The crisis clearly concerned the decline in the secular majority's self-confidence, which is both a precondition for and a result of religious pretensions and a virtually universal concomitant of religious resurgence. A sense of failure and confusion in the secular Zionist realm was the inevitable companion of GE's efflorescence.

This description, however, can only be attributed to the advanced stages, when the formative experience of religiopolitical radicalism was completed and its symbolic system developed and accepted. Only then did the radicals pounce on the secular public, exploiting its demoralized state. This was also true with regard to GE: the movement filled the vacuum left in Israel by the modern national ideological and leadership crises. The situation did not last long, however. Once the movement exhausted its revolutionary potential, it required additional new forces, which could be supplied by the very secular political Zionism which the movement ostensibly opposed in the name of religious Judaism. From the outset, it was Zionism, still in the ascendant and radiating self-confidence, which served as the basis for the awakening of this Jewish radicalism. The religious revival is rooted in the rise of its competitor—modern secular nationalism.

Fundamentalism is generally presented as a response to the crises of modernity rather than as a reaction to modernity itself. It is commonly claimed that religiopolitical radicalism fills the void, the dimensions of which are as vast as the illusions once generated by modernity. Yet the disappointment caused by the forces of the new Western civilization—technology on the one hand and nationalism and socialism or liberalism on the other—determined the timing and circumstances of the outbreak of religious militance, and perhaps also the extent of its success, but not its essence and its sources. Fundamentalism is substantively connected with the achievements of the forces of modernity. Jewish-Zionist fundamentalism should likewise be understood as relating to what was once convincingly perceived as modernity at the peak of its successes and promises.

Several of the outstanding religious schools of thought which were later adopted by the activist-believers in various countries, and ex post facto universally viewed as the gospel of fundamentalism, were originally written in a preceding era as secular modernity burst forth and flourished, to be admired and celebrated by the people. The case of Jewish-Zionist fundamentalism supplies a powerful illustration of this phenomenon. Rabbi Kook wrote the most significant elements of his doctrine primarily during the first third of the twentieth century. He was impressed by the end of World War I, self-determination for many nations, Wilson's Fourteen Points, the Balfour Declaration (1917) which promised a national home for the Jews, and the momentum of pioneer immigration to Palestine and the building of its Jewish community. His words were suffused with the optimism which characterized his circle at the time, and it is reasonable to assume that this optimistic outlook even influenced his messianic vision, in which Israel is seen as already undergoing a process of redemption. His view of the achievements of the time—in science, art, philosophy, and world politics—was so positive that today his successors find it difficulty to explain (they apply apologetic scholastic acrobatics, for example, to prove that he even foresaw the Holocaust). Moreover, Rabbi Kook advanced his doctrine in Palestine, when the Jewish national enterprise was under a modernist-secularist hegemony and manifested overwhelming creativity and achievements. The first disciples of Rabbi Kook, headed by his son, developed and cultivated his doctrine after the establishment of the State of Israel, during Ben-Gurion's statism, when the banner of secular modernity was waved proudly once again, and Zionism was universally accepted as triumphing in the battle for Judaism. Only the second generation of disciples has witnessed the emergence of cracks in the modern secular national dream—and the rise of the successors of the Kookist doctrine to inherit the declining Zionism.

The spiritual father of GE developed a doctrine which is deeply religious yet simultaneously entirely national and modern. Rabbi Kook's greatness can be measured in terms of his success in containing the national experience and the modern experience within the framework of religion, thus enriching both sides. His achievement is perhaps more complex and ambitious than that of Reform Judaism, for he modernized religion and "nationalized" it and even rendered modern nationalism a key issue for religion. Yet he did not divorce religion from its old symbols and traditional norms; on the contrary, he gave them a considerable reinforcement.

Fundamentalism thrives in the modern world not only because of the many frustrations that accompany modernity, or because modernity is not yet pervasive in contemporary society.[91] There remain protected niches here and there that provide fertile soil for the growth of traditionalism. Yet contemporary religious revivalism also flourishes by drinking directly from the fruitful springs of modernity. Advanced technologies and even advanced political patterns are not the only features which radical religion borrows from modernity. Rather, modernity actually nurtures religious experiences and thought. One consequence of such nurturing is fundamentalism. Activist-believers have internalized modern content, including secular values and norms. Their immersion and investment in modern national political life has created their intensified religiosity, a genuine and original religiosity. Thus, the point of departure for comprehending GE and similar radical movements is their obsession with modernity. At least in the Israeli case, they are actually consumed with jealousy of secularism itself. The combination of fascination with modern secular nationalism and politics and an authentic religious need and bold religious creativity is an important power behind the militancy under study here. Jewish radicalism draws its inspiration from secular Zionism. Ironically, the religiopolitical revival derives not only its political foundations but also its religious foundations from modern nationalism. Even its messianism is not derived directly from its old heritage but rather through the mediation of Zionism. It was Zionism which extricated the idea and impetus of redemption from the grasp of Orthodoxy. Thus, after hundreds of years of emasculation, messianism attained vitality and centrality. Indeed, Zionism may be perceived as grounded in several central religious principles which it secularized. Zionists rediscovered the Bible and reintroduced the Land of Israel to collective consciousness. GE then arose and confiscated all those assets from modern nationalism and restored them to religion.

Current Trends and Future Possibilities

Zionism is not only the foundation of the national experience of the activist-believers but also a source and focus of their religious experience. Consequently as modern national Judaism's crisis persists, its partner and rival, revolutionary religious Judaism, declines as well, whereupon traditional religious Judaism, the genuine adversary of GE, arises once again. Jewish-Zionist fundamentalism nourished the tension between Judaism and Zionism and was in turn maintained by it. Recently this tension—the challenge facing Israeli radicalism—has attenuated somewhat. Perhaps we are witnessing a certain normalization of the State of Israel, to the dismay of GE.

Two parallel and apparently unrelated trends appear to have developed in Israel over the past few years. On the background of the trend which characterized the previous generation—from 1967 to the mid-1980s—the novelty lies in their mutual independence rather than in their existence *per se*. One trend is the rise in radical nationalism, which has virtually nothing to do with religion, and the other is the rise in radical religion, which has almost nothing in common with nationalism. Most of the recently successful ultrapatriots—such as Rafael Eitan and Rehavam Zeevi of the Zomet and Moledet parties—are bareheaded. Moreover, most of the recently successful ultraorthodox—such as those of Agudat Israel or Shas—are doves. A somewhat complementary process is taking place within GE: the combination of religiosity and nationalism, once the secret of the movement's success, is now splitting into its component elements. The current crisis in GE is embodied by the movement's withdrawal from "Zionist religion" and a return to the more familiar notion of "religious Zionism," in which Zionism and religiosity are mutually autonomous. In other words, GE has inclined in a direction opposite the one which originally set it apart, returning from political religion back to religious politics. In terms of my definition, GE is thus becoming less fundamentalist.

This does not mean that the movement is necessarily becoming less militant or less effective in its influence on geohistorical realities, although there are some signs of this trend as well. Moreover, GE is in no way becoming less political or less religious. However, its politics, from the moment that it stands on its own, is becoming more or less conventional. The same is true of its religiosity, which, lacking its former political component, becomes conventional as well. In lieu of the revolutionary combination of religion and politics, whose premise was mystical and messianic, GE is gradually re-embracing the Orthodoxy of the old school. Consequently observers find it somewhat difficult to discern signs of the Kookism which was once the hallmark of GE, whose messianic elements were so attractive and potent in their day. Today it has been overshadowed by the two variations of normative Judaism: the haredi and the liberal.

During the heyday of Israeli fundamentalism, the movement's two components—the Jewish and the Zionist—maintained a mutual affinity in a delicate balance. The religious factor pulled in a centripetal direction and the national component in a centrifugal one, keeping the movement in orbit until its decline. Once the cement combining the two internal poles became weakened and the opposing forces increased in strength, the revolutionary nucleus split apart. Some elements sank into the Torah world and others were assimilated into the political one. Each side developed autonomous dynamics: religion without active Zionist impulses (Torah scholars returning from movement activism to the confines of the yeshiva, for example) and "net" Zionism (movement cadres leaving for activity in the Knesset within the framework of fundamentally secular parties, such as Tehiya). Between these two options, there is still the old religious Zionism, from which the camp originated and to which most of its varying factions have returned.

There were a few GE true believers who refused to forego the intoxicating freedom they had enjoyed briefly within a limited sphere of what they experienced as true redemption. Devoting themselves totally to messianism, they became even more radical than they had been previously. Naturally they began to gravitate in an underground direction. It gradually dawned on them that the movement's original and fundamentally religious mission remained unfulfilled. This was underscored by failures, such as the withdrawal from Sinai, and perhaps even more by political and organizational successes, such as the proliferation of settlements. Consequently the radical element in GE has become introverted. The Jewish-Zionist fundamentalist movement has turned inward and shrunk to the size of what can better be defined as a sect.

One may perhaps speculate that an Israeli withdrawal from Judea and Samaria forced on GE by the authorities and public opinion would actually relieve the movement of its distress. I have claimed elsewhere that the problem of religious Judaism originates in the partial fulfillment of the messianic vision epitomized by national political revival in the Land of Israel.[92] Apparently, official and effective annexation of the Territories would yield only short-lived happiness and only partial fulfillment for activist-believers, who would soon realize that their old problems were not solved but rather actually intensified. For example, which law would be imposed in the redeemed territories? Could they institute halakhic law in the sacred realms falling under their control? The existing rabbinic codex, as it is, makes it impossible to maintain a sovereign national entity which fulfills all contemporary social and political functions. Would powers emerge from within Orthodoxy to enable emendation and radical change of normative religious law? GE's experience has shown us that ultimately the Torah takes precedence over redemption.

GE's total success in realizing its original objectives would not solve the problems affecting the faithful living in both the religious world and the modern secular one. They would not find true redemption in the integrity of the Land of Israel, nor even in the rebuilding of the Temple, but rather in the integrity of the religious experience—in overcoming the frustrating compartmentalization which characterizes life in two worlds.

And if Israel does withdraw from the territories, where would Jewish radical energies then be directed? Perhaps they will be diverted from the Arabs and aimed directly against secular Israelis. In the meantime, it appears that the original religious political foundation responsible for the GE revivalist and activist thrust has not been entirely extinguished. It is merely becoming subterranean, as it was in its premovement past. There is no guarantee, however, that this fundamentalist spark will not ignite, causing Jewish-Zionist militancy to erupt anew.

Notes

The essay is dedicated to the memory of Professors Yosef Ben-David and Jacob Talmon. I thank my teachers and colleagues for their helpful comments on earlier drafts of various parts of this study: I. Cohen, M. Cook, J. Gager, A. Hamori, B. Lewis and A. Udovitch at Princeton University and V. Azaria, E. Ben-Ari, H. Goldberg, Z. Gurevitch, J. Katz, J. Liebes, M. Lissak, B. Shamir, P. Sheldon and E. Sivan at the Hebrew University of Jerusalem.

1. This essay draws on extensive fieldwork, including participant observation and analysis of a rich collection of confidential records and about forty in-depth interviews with nearly all GE's leadership and a sample of its cadres and review of published sources. The list of references does not include primary or secondary sources in Hebrew, except in isolated cases. I preferred referring to material accessible to the American reader even if better, original alternatives were available. All non-referenced citations in this study are derived from my field notes. Cf. G. McCall and J. Simmons, *Issues in Participant Observation* (Reading, Mass.: Addison-Wesley, 1969); C. Geertz, "From the Native's Point of View," *Bulletin of the American Academy of Arts and Sciences* 28 (1974).

2. Cf. GE's *Yesh* Program, written by Hanan Porat and published more than a year before the Likud assumed power (*Yesh*, the Hebrew acronym for Judea and Samaria, is also a word which expresses tangibility, an existing fact). Appended to the program was a map of the projected infrastructure in the Territories. In its margins was a list of planned settlements, with attendant details. In early 1976, this fantasy comprised fifty-nine points, i.e., half the number of actual settlements which were eventually established at those very sites and with the same names. Within five years of the program's publication, more than a billion dollars in public funds were invested in its realization.

3. This figure does not include Jews living in East Jerusalem, although it does include about five urban concentrations, most of which are close to the Green Line. The total constitutes about 1.5 percent of the population of Israel (excluding the Arabs of the Territories). Until 1967, there was not one Jewish settler in the Territories. By 1972, there were about 1,500 (primarily in Sinai). At the time of the Likud's rise to power (1977), the number had risen to 3,000. There were 15,000–20,000 Jews in the Territories in 1981 and 45,000–50,000 in 1985. Cf. Publications of the Council of Jewish Settlements; *Statistical Abstract of Israel,* no. 40 (Jerusalem: Central Bureau of Statistics, 1989); M. Benvenisti, *The West Bank Data Project Report* (Boulder, Colo.: Westview, 1988).

4. Concerning the Underground, cf. R. Ledeen, "The Temple Mount Plot," *The New Republic,* 18 June 1984; Y. Yishai, "The Jewish Terror Organization," *Conflict* 6, no. 4 (1986); E. Sprinzak, "From Messianic Pioneering to Vigilante Terrorism," *Journal of Strategic Studies* (December 1987); D. Rapoport, "Why Does Messianism Produce Terror," *Comparative Politics* (January 1988). Especially revealing is the story of the Underground written by one of its members: H. Segal, *Dear Brothers* (Jerusalem: Keter, 1987).

5. Cf. the testimony of the accused Underground members at their trial. *Records of the Jerusalem District Court,* commencing 17 June 1984.

6. Cf. Rabbi Zvi Yehuda Kook, "Psalm XIX to the State of Israel," in A. Ben-Ami, *Everything: The Book of the Whole Land of Israel* (Tel Aviv: Friedman, 1977) (Hebrew). This is a kind of song of praise to the State, accompanied by reproach and programmatic guidelines.

7. This is a typical career path in GE: After the consolidation of the Jewish hold in Hebron, the most outstanding members of the pioneer group continued to move from one settlement front to another. Several of them eventually settled in the Golan Heights (also conquered, from the Syrians, in 1967), from which they were summoned to lead the

movement's campaigns. Among the most prominent were "Akaleh" Ganiram and "Bentz" Heineman, followers of Levinger and later members of the Jewish Underground, who were sentenced to seven and four years imprisonment, respectively.

8. Actually, the Whole Land of Israel Movement initiated the protest and started the hunger strike. GE activists subsequently joined them and assumed leadership as they increased in number and enthusiasm.

9. Cf. G. Aran, "From Religious Zionism to Zionist Religion," reprinted in C. Goldscheider and J. Neusner, eds., *The Social Foundations of Judaism* (Englewood Cliffs, N.J.: Prentice-Hall, 1990).

10. G. Aran, "A Mystic-Messianic Interpretation of Modern Israeli History," in J. Frankel, ed., *Studies in Contemporary Jewry IV* (New York: Oxford University Press, 1988).

11. For example: *Lights, Lights of Holiness* (3 vols.); *Lights of Revival, Lights of Penitence;* and *Lights of Israel.* A translated anthology of selected writings of Rabbi Kook appeared in B. Bokser, trans. and ed., *The Classics of Western Spirituality: A. I. Kook* (New York: Paulist Press, 1978). For a concise presentation of the main principles of Rabbi Kook's religious-national thought, cf. A. Hertzberg, *The Zionist Idea* (New York: Harper and Row, 1966), chap. 7; S. Avineri, *The Making of Modern Zionism* (New York: Basic Books, 1981), chap. 16.

12. Concerning Jewish messianism, cf. G. Scholem, "Toward an Understanding of the Messianic Idea in Judaism," in G. Scholem, *The Messianic Idea in Judaism* (New York: Schocken, 1971); Z. Werblowsky, "Messianism," in A. Cohen and P. Mendes-Fluhr, eds., *Contemporary Jewish Religious Thought* (New York: 1987); E. Schweid, "Jewish Messianism: Metamorphosis of an Idea," *Jerusalem Quarterly* 36 (1985).

13. On the social history and political sociology of Israel, cf. D. Horowitz and M. Lissak, *Troubles in Utopia: The Overburdened Polity of Israel* (New York: State University of New York Press, 1989), esp. chaps. 3 and 6.

14. The Whole Land of Israel Movement preceded GE in raising the issue of a Greater Israel and placing it on the public agenda. Immediately after the Six-Day War, it called for settlement of the West Bank, Golan Heights, and Sinai and demanded the immediate extension of Israeli sovereignty over these areas. The sole English-language study of the movement is somewhat limited: R. Isaac, *Israel Divided: Ideological Politics in the Jewish State* (Baltimore: Johns Hopkins University Press, 1976), esp. chap. 3.

15. There are three recognized school systems in Israeli education—State (nonreligious), State/Religious, and Independent (haredi). In recent years, a fourth, unofficial system has emerged which is gaining increasing prominence and influence, called Haredi-National. The guiding force behind it is comprised of rabbis and graduates of the Merkaz Harav yeshiva in Jerusalem.

16. Cf. the original study, which constitutes the basis for the theory: L. Festinger et al., *When Prophecy Fails* (Minneapolis: University of Minnesota Press, 1956). For a clear summary and demonstration of this social-psychological principle, cf. E. Aronson, *The Social Animal* (New York: Freeman, 1988), chap. 4.

17. G. Scholem, *Sabbatai Sevi: The Mystical Messiah* (Princeton: Princeton University Press, 1973).

18. J. Heineman, "The Messiah of Ephraim," *Harvard Theological Review* 68 (1975); J. Klausner, *The Messianic Idea in Israel* (New York: 1955), part 3, chap. 9. For English language translation of various intertestamental texts relating to traditions involving Messiahs ben Joseph and ben David, cf. Raphael Petai, *The Messiah Texts* (Detroit: Wayne State University Press, 1979), esp. chap. 17.

19. This is a free translation of the Hebrew idiom. I borrowed the concept from Emmanuel Sivan, who thus translates a parallel Farsi expression appearing in connection with the Shi'ite revolution in Iran. Cf. E. Sivan and M. Friedman, eds., *Religious Radicalism and Politics in the Middle East* (Albany, N.Y.: State University of New York Press, 1990), introduction.

20. Keshet is the first settlement estab-

lished by GE (after the Yom Kippur War). However, it was not recorded as the pioneer movement settlement because it was not initiated by GE but was set up in response to requests by non-religious settlers in the area, belonging to the *Kibbutz Meuhad* movement. Furthermore, it was situated in the Golan Heights, a Jewish settlement region which enjoyed virtually total backing in Israel (and was later officially annexed to the state). At the outset, Keshet was unique for its mix of religious and non-religious settlers; the brief harmony between them was considered as heralding a new era. In time, however, only the religious ones remained. Keshet is perceived as a Merkaz Harav settlement more than as a GE settlement proper. Nevertheless, it has integrated into the northern Kookist settlement complex which supplies particularly radical cadres to the movement. Their proportion among the convicted Jewish Underground members is especially striking.

21. GE inherited the pattern of settlement by elite groups, inspired by a sense of national mission, from a hundred-year-old Zionist tradition in which conquest of the Land of Israel served not only as the main tool for the promotion of political interests, but also as a medium through which a new man and new society were to be forged. GE often presents itself as the heir to the now defunct classic Zionist movement. But critics point out that the movement does not bear a universal-humanistic message and certainly has no socialistic-revolutionary aspirations. A geographer who specializes in the settlement of Judea and Samaria calls the GE-type community settlement a "rurban settlement." Cf. D. Newman, "Defining the Rurban Settlement," *Urban Geography* 10, no. 3 (1989). Cf. also D. Newman, "Ideological and Political Influences on Israeli Rurban Colonization: The West Bank and Galilee Mountain," *Canadian Geographer* 27 (1984). Concerning the dispersal of movement settlements in Judea and Samaria, cf. D. Newman, *Jewish Settlement in the West Bank* (Durham, N.C.: Center for Mid-Eastern and Islamic Studies, 1982).

22. Examples: Rabbi H. Druckman, Rabbi E. Waldman, Hanan Porat, Gershon Shafat: members of the GE executive and members of Knesset; Beni Katzover and Uri Elizur: heads of the settlement enterprise in Judea and Samaria who were accorded realistic places on the Tehiya and NRP Knesset lists, etc.

23. P. Demant, "Ploughshares into Swords" (Ph.D. diss., University of Amsterdam, 1988) indicates that GE's success was dependent on the cooperation of both politicians and civil servants at middle and upper levels (e.g., directors-general of Jewish Agency Departments, the O. C. Central Command, and the Military Governors of Nablus and Ramallah).

24. Activist-believers stress that the movement's name is the Movement to Stop Withdrawal in Sinai (and not from Sinai). Cf. G. Aran, *The Land of Israel: Between Politics and Religion* (Jerusalem: Jerusalem Institute for Israel Studies, 1985) (Hebrew). Cf. also G. Aran, "The Price of Peace: The Removal of the Israeli Settlements in Sinai," *Journal of Applied Behavioral Sciences* (special issue) 23, no. 1 (1987).

25. D. Weisburd, *Jewish Settler Violence: Deviance and Social Reaction* (Philadelphia: University of Pennsylvania Press, 1989). Also cf. D. Weisburd and B. Vinitzky, "Vigilantism as Rational Social Control: The Case of Gush Emunim," *Political Anthropology* 4 (1984).

26. From the beginning of the Intifada to this writing, about twenty-five Palestinians were killed by Jewish settlers (out of a total of about 640 casualties, most of whom were injured by the security forces). It should be noted that in only one or two of these cases was the investigation file closed and an Israeli citizen brought to trial. (See report of the humanitarian organization Betzelem [established by the Ratz political faction], Jerusalem. The IDF spokesman's estimate is slightly lower.)

27. The current Ashkenazi chief rabbi, Avraham Shapiro, issued a statement in reaction to the controversy set off by Rabbi Yitzhak Ginzburg, head of the Joseph's Tomb Yeshiva in Nablus. Rabbi Ginzburg had made comments at the trial of seven

of his students for the murder of an Arab girl during a violent rampage through the West Bank village of Kifl Hares, to the effect that Arab blood before the law was by nature unequal to Jewish blood, and therefore Arabs who kill Jews should be punished, but Jews who kill Arabs should go free. Rabbi Shapiro condemned this view, and in so doing was virtually alone among the Israeli rabbinate.

28. The importance of changing names in the process of conquering territory is well known. Assimilation of the name "Judea and Samaria" in normal and official language, as well as in jargon, attests to GE's political and cultural achievements. In January 1990, the American press reported that in the official Middle East maps of the United States, published by the State Department and the CIA, the term "West Bank" was recently replaced with "Judea and Samaria." The maps also indicated the cease-fire lines between Israel and Jordan, whereas previously the disputed territories were marked as belonging to Jordan.

29. The theory of irreversibility in the process of de facto annexation of the Territories to Israel is identified with Meron Benvenisti, a scholar and public figure who specializes in intercommunity conflicts and heads an institute for documentation and social, economic and demographic research of the Territories. Cf. *Pilot Study Report of the West Bank Data Base Project*, October 1983.

30. At the inception of the Intifada, GE itself predicted a decline of about 10 percent in the number of settlers in Judea and Samaria. However, by the end of the Intifada's second year, GE prided itself on a rise of nearly 20 percent. With the attenuation of a direct threat to the settlers' physical security and the continuing political deadlock regarding the future of the Territories, the movement's self-confidence has now been restored somewhat; it foresees an increment of about ten thousand Jews in Judea and Samaria in the coming year.

31. The popular books on GE are dragged into a debate with the movement. See Z. Raanan, *Gush Emunim* (Tel Aviv: Sifriyat Poalim, 1980) (Hebrew); D. Rubinstein, *On the Lord's Side: Gush Emunim* (Tel Aviv: Kibbutz Meuhad, 1982) (Hebrew); A. Rubinstein, *From Herzl to Gush Emunim and Back* (New York: Schocken, 1984). There are numerous academic studies accessible to the public, some of which were written in English. Cf. K. Avruch, "Traditionalizing Israeli Nationalism: The Development of Gush Emunim," *Political Anthropology* 1, no. 1 (1975); J. O'Dea, "Gush Emunim, Roots and Ambiguities," *Forum* 2, no. 25 (1976); L. Weissbrod, "Gush Emunim Ideology," *Middle Eastern Studies* 18, no. 3 (1982); M. Aronoff, "Gush Emunim: The Institutionalization of a Charismatic Religious-Political Revitalization Movement in Israel," *Political Anthropology* 3, no. 4 (1984); G. Goldberg and E. Ben-Zadok, "Gush Emunim in the West Bank," *Middle Eastern Studies* 22, no. 1 (1986); E. Don-Yehiya, "Jewish Messianism, Religious Zionism, and Israeli Politics: Gush Emunim," *Middle Eastern Studies* 23, no. 2 (1987). For an anthology of articles on various aspects of GE, see D. Newman, ed., *The Impact of Gush Emunim* (Beckenham, Kent: Croom Helm, 1985). Finally, see also I. Lustick, *For the Land and the Lord* (New York: Council on Foreign Relations, 1988). This is the first book about GE intended for the American public, eloquently written by an authoritative scholar, it should have some influence in academic circles, on public opinion and even among decision-makers. Unfortunately, an abundance of disconcerting mistakes and conceptual shortcomings mars the book.

32. I differ both with those who tend to blur the distinction between GE and the political camps which sometimes joined a coalition with it, and with those who identify GE with the culture of the young national-religious population in general. Cf. E. Sprinzak, "Gush Emunim: The Iceberg Model of Political Extremism," *Jerusalem Quarterly* 21 (1981). For comments on this study, cf. K. Avruch, "The Iceberg Model of Extremism Reconsidered," *Middle East Review* 21, no. 1 (1989).

33. The Intifada shed light on the dis-

tinctiveness of GE. At times, the movement's hard core suited and attracted this periphery, and at other times parted from it and followed an autonomous path. Recently, in the religious kibbutz movement, Bnei Akiva and—to a certain extent—the NRP and even many of the Hesder yeshivas, the trend is entirely different from that of GE.

34. Cf. E. Shils, "Center and Periphery," in E. Shils, *Center and Periphery: Essays in Macrosociology*(Chicago: University of Chicago Press, 1975).

35. Cf. D. Horowitz and M. Lissak, *The Origins of Israeli Polity* (Chicago: University of Chicago Press, 1975).

36. 2 Sam. 10:12.

37. Judea and Samaria—also referred to in this essay as the Territories—is a region east of the (Green) line demarcating the 1948–49 armistice boundaries, up to the Jordan River.

38. This is an amalgam of several such proclamations.

39. The original is *yehareg u'val ya'avor* ([better to] be killed and not transgress). In a comprehensive survey conducted among GE settlers, interviewees were asked to respond to the following statement: "It is forbidden under any condition to withdraw from Judea and Samaria, as the above dictum is applicable." Seventy-five percent of the respondents agreed, with over 50 percent indicating "strong agreement." See Weisburd, *Jewish Settler Violence*, chap. 6.

40. Cf. Gen. 13:14–15; Num. 33:52–56; Deut. 7:1–2; and Josh. 1:1–4.

41. As conceived by M. Weber in *The Sociology of Religion* (Boston: Beacon, 1964).

42. Field research notes.

43. The PLO Command was said to have condemned Levinger to death and to have transmitted instructions to the Territories to carry this sentence out.

44. During his trial, Levinger eventually changed his testimony and admitted having committing the act. He was found guilty of homicide due to negligence and received a relatively light prison sentence, causing an uproar in Israeli public opinion. As the left complained of overly favorable treatment for Jews, Hebron settlers held a solidarity rally, accompanying Levinger to the prison gates with a convoy of flag-decked vehicles.

45. Cf. B. Kimmerling, "Between the Primordial and Civil Definitions of the Israeli Collective Identity," in E. Cohen et al., eds., *Comparative Social Dynamics* (Boulder, Colo.: Westview, 1985).

46. Knowledgeable discussions of the movement's political dimension have not been complemented by equally skillful treatments of the movement's religious nature. Moreover, some scholars have reduced the phenomenon to its political aspects, leading to absurd conclusions. It is difficult to overstate GE's political importance, yet Ian Lustick, for example, in *For the Land and the Lord,* states that the movement "has emerged as the single greatest obstacle to Arab-Israeli peace." Jews in Israel must indeed contend with an intramural and formidable "Jewish problem" of their own (just as Arabs must contend with an intramural "Arab problem"). But Israel's "Arab problem" has a palpable existence apart from the mystical-messianic conspiratorial schemes. The explanation for Israel's dilemma cannot be exhausted by fundamentalism alone. The tendency of presenting the religiosity of the radical movements as "rhetoric" or as a mere "veil" concealing "genuine" political content is exemplified in J. Aviad, "The Messianism of Gush Emunim," *Studies in Contemporary Jewry*, forthcoming. Aviad concludes that "GE is [an] ultranationalist [phenomenon] thinly cloaked in messianic language."

47. Cf. M. Hill, *The Religious Order: A Study of Virtuoso Religion* (London: Heinemann, 1973).

48. A comprehensive survey of GE settlers indicated that religious attitudes primarily constitute the basis of the movement's establishment and its activism. For example, 60 percent of the respondents stated that halakhic precepts represented their predominant settlement motivation, while only 14 percent claimed that they were motivated by self-interest (e.g., a desire to improve quality of life). Similarly, it was found that religious attitudes are far more influential than

Zionist views regarding support of "serious anti-Government violence." Furthermore, a significant link was found between a messianic outlook and the sanctioning of vigilante action towards local Arabs. Cf. Weisburd, *Jewish Settler Violence,* chaps. 3 and 6.

49. Compare not only other cases of fundamentalism but also the conventional variety of return to religion, which is exemplified by unchallenged acceptance of the traditional boundaries of religion. Cf. J. Aviad, *Return to Judaism* (Chicago: University of Chicago Press, 1983).

50. We may undoubtedly explain GE's successes in social and psychological terms which are totally unrelated to religion. Consider, for example, the recruitment of the periphery from the national-religious sector in Israel. The attractiveness of the movement's campaigns in Judea and Samaria was enhanced by their provision of outdoor public recreation for the entire family during holiday vacations, serving a public whose leisure-time alternatives (e.g. cinema) were generally limited. Thus, activities in the Territories simultaneously constituted religious fulfillment and a mass picnic. Moreover, the catharsis was not entirely spiritual but also somewhat sexual; GE campaigns enabled orthodox young men and women to spend time together, in contrast to the usual separation of the sexes, especially at school. These activities were thus popular and charged with tension: the campaigns even became a vibrant market for matchmaking (the ranks of GE include many married couples who met during activity as individuals and continued their movement commitment as families).

One may also explain the flourishing of GE in terms of closing youth culture gaps. Up to the 1960s, orthodox youth had enjoyed little success in penetrating the circles of "blood, sweat and sex"—the experiences which shape the new Israeli, as realized within elitist systems imbued with national mission, i.e., the army, the kibbutz and socialist youth movements. Secular Zionists enjoyed all the glory. Recently, however, as they sought alternative patterns of fulfillment, the "pioneer arena" became vacant and the religious—long deprived of formative Israeli experiences—could finally rush in and make up for all they had missed. Consequently, some see GE as an anachronism, not because of its religious tendencies but because of its patriotic enthusiasm, which appears to be one generation too late.

51. It is commonly assumed that involvement in public affairs and existing political frameworks leads to a gradual, imperceptible moderation of religiosity. In this context, it is interesting to recall the Israeli public's response to the strengthening of the three haredi parties in the last Knesset elections (1988): the shock and anxiety marking initial reactions among the secular were replaced with hope that contact with the authorities and with various sectors of Israeli society, along with assumption of legislative and administrative responsibility, would bring the haredim closer to the Zionist camp and foster commitment to the state, leading them to soften if not abandon their original radical religious stands.

52. Haredim oppose GE because of its political nature (and Zionism) in general and its hawkishness in particular. The former tend to dissociate themselves from involvement in state affairs, yet when they do express their views nonetheless regarding political matters in dispute, they are generally pragmatic, conciliatory and even dovish, claiming that this is the Jewish way (Lubavitcher Hasidim diverge on this matter). They contend that an assertive foreign and security policy is not only not binding and not only dangerous to the survival of the Jewish collectivity because it represents a kind of "provocation of the nations of the world," but also even non-Jewish in nature, as it relies on power rather than spirit.

53. For example, cf. D. Apter, "Political Religions in New Nations," in C. Geertz, ed., *Old Societies, New States* (New York: Free Press, 1963); R. Bellah, "Civil Religion in America," *Daedalus* 96 (1967).

54. D. Vital, *The Origins of Zionism* (London: Oxford University Press, 1975). Also, cf. E. Don-Yehiya, "Jewish Orthodoxy, Zionism, and the State of Israel," *Jerusalem Quarterly* 31 (1984).

55. E. Sprinzak, *Every Man Whatsoever is Right in His Own Eyes* (Tel Aviv: Sifriyat Poalim, 1986) (Hebrew), esp. chap. 8, presents GE as another chapter in the extensive tradition of "illegalism" in Israel.

56. Concerning Israel as a Jewish state, cf. C. Liebman and E. Don-Yehiya, *Civil Religion in Israel* (Berkeley: University of California Press, 1983).

57. On the "theology of paradox," cf. G. Aran, "Redemption as a Catastrophe: The Gospel of Gush Emunim," in Sivan and Friedman, *Religious Radicalism*.

58. J. Katz, "The Messianic Component in Modern Jewish Nationalism," *Commentary* (April 1987).

59. This includes several intensive years of sermons and frontal lessons, as well as further clarification in intimate study circles, with regular close contact with rabbis who explain, guide, and serve as models for emulation.

60. These refer to personal contacts, which in the well-illustrated case of Islamic fundamentalism, included schools or prisons. See L. Zurcher and D. Snow, "Social Movements," in M. Rosenberg and R. Turner, eds., *Social Psychology* (New York: Basic Books, 1981), pp. 454–58.

61. Cf. C. Geertz, "Religion as a Cultural System" and "Ritual and Social Change," in W. Lessa and E. Vogt, eds., *Reader in Comparative Religion: An Anthropological Approach* (New York: Harper and Row, 1972).

62. Not only do researchers "buy" the activist-believers' myth concerning the strong covenant binding secular and religious Jews in GE, but their conceptualization coincides with the believers' mystical-messianic theology. Lustick's book, for example, represents precisely what GE hopes to achieve in reality: the inclusion of secularity in the sacred domain. Individuals who never uttered a blessing, who never followed a halakhic decision, are presented here as an integral and central part of a religious trend—and only because they advocate the expulsion of Arab stone throwers from Nablus and oppose the ban on Jewish residency there.

63. Lustick, *For the Land and the Lord*, states that "the beliefs and political behavior of secular ultra-nationalist Jews require that they also be included in the fundamentalist [category, as] their absolute commitment to the achievements of maximalist Zionist ambitions reflect their sense of political action, as determined by uncompromisable, transcendentally valid imperatives." One could thus infer that A. D. Gordon and Y. Tabenkin, leaders of the Socialist "Second Aliyah," are fundamentalists. A greater folly is to apply that judgment to a peasant and professional soldier like Raphael Eitan, to a local version of Dr. Strangelove like Yuval Ne'eman, to a quixotic fighter against ossified bureaucracy like Ezra Zohar, and to other secular Israelis described as fundamentalist. There are many among them who contemptuously dismiss all slogans, dogmas and abstractions, let alone transcendental values. For many of these "leading fundamentalists," their ideology begins and ends with an impulsive expression of bitter criticism against the corruption of the long-lived Mapai. For others, their support of GE emanates from a guilty conscience and from a kind of "vicarious fulfillment," in other words, admiration for the "idealists" who, in an era of egotism and crisis in values, are ready to sacrifice themselves for the common good and in the name of cherished values, whose interpretation does not interest the aforementioned secular Israelis in the least. There are secular Israelis, chiefly *moshavniks* and *kibbutzniks* of the famous *Ein Vered* circle, whose motives for supporting GE are strictly practical and down to earth. Theirs is a security-oriented position, and they are regarded as no-nonsense pragmatists. Those in their midst who have developed a more systematic and complete worldview take pride in waving the banner of realpolitik. They are utter strangers to the world of religion. Privately, their attitude toward religion is tinged with sarcasm. Usually they emphasize the specificity of the basis for their support of GE and apologetically add that for the sake of Israel's physical survival, they are willing to conclude a pact with the devil. Many began to distance themselves from the movement as soon as they saw signs that it was undermining the

image and strength of the Israel Defense Forces. There are some secular Israelis who, in the course of their relationship with GE, espouse a superficial and generally diffuse and nostalgic concept of Judaism. Sentimental outpourings about one's grandfather in a shtetl of Eastern Europe or in a Jewish quarter of Yemen and stirring references to the heroic exploits of King David and Bar-Kochba—in the style of Geula Cohen, an MK close to GE's leadership—are familiar tendencies among the movement's friends, naively construed as evidence of religious repentance. Yet these same people continue to desecrate the Sabbath and ignore Jewish dietary laws. In Judaism, the ultimate test of religious commitment is not in one's emotional or philosophical attitude but rather one's adherence to halakhic behavioral norms. The fundamentalist Jews themselves take great pains to remind their secular friends who join them at settlements, rallies, and meetings with heads of state that the mark of committed Jews is the observance of the Torah and its commandments. Incidentally, not one of these allies of GE is a settler in Judea and Samaria.

64. Cf. G. Scholem, "Three Types of Jewish Piety," *Ariel Quarterly Review* 32 (1973).

65. Ariel "Arik" Sharon's "camp" is comprised of party followers in hawkish factions of the Likud and other nationalist parties. Kach under Rabbi Kahane is a quasi-legal extreme right wing group, usually characterized by openly racist appeals.

66. See Weisburd, *Jewish Settler Violence,* chap. 3, for the demographic characteristics of GE settlers as contrasted with those of the general Jewish population of Israel (see table 5.1).

67. Elsewhere, I refer to them as Kookists. G. Aran, "The Origins and Culture of GE: A Messianic Movement in Modern Israel" (Ph.D. diss., Hebrew University of Jerusalem, 1987), chaps. 4–6. Since I first coined this expression (and also used it in conversations with GE people, aware of its possible pejorative associations), it has caught on among the intelligentsia and even among the believers themselves.

68. This concept was originally developed in the context of subcultures of youth, criminals, the lower classes, and bohemians. Cf. T. Roszak, *The Making of a Counter-Culture* (New York: Doubleday, 1969); L. Miller and J. Skipper, "Sounds of Protest: Jazz and Militant Avant-Garde," in M. Lefton et al., eds., *Approaches to Deviance* (New York: Appleton, 1968). Orientalists have already applied the concept to the case of Sunni fundamentalist groups in Arab countries. For example, cf. E. Sivan, *Radical Islam* (New Haven: Yale University Press, 1985).

69. In a similarly critical vein, opponents of GE tend to describe the activist-believers as "neo-Sabbataists." Many scholars imply a kinship between GE and the notorious seventeenth-century Sabbatianism, a Jewish messianic movement that took hold in both the elite and lower echelons of the Jewish people in its various localities and sociopolitical circumstances. But the patently few similarities overshadow essential differences. For example, the cataclysm resulting from the doctrine and person of Shabbetai Zevi was of a blatantly antinomial character, and that has left its traumatic imprint on the Jewish religion to this day. In contrast, the eruption of GE is of a hypernomial character. Thus, we are dealing with an unusual case of a redemptionist movement which, defying public expectations and defamation, takes great care to observe the Torah and its commandments.

70. On this spectrum, cf. for example H. Lazarus-Yafeh, "Contemporary Fundamentalism: Judaism, Christianity, Islam," *Jerusalem Quarterly* 47 (1988).

71. Cf., for example, S. Baharuddin, "A Revival in the Study of Islam in Malaysia," *Man* 18 (1983), cited in L. Caplan, ed., *Studies in Religious Fundamentalism* (Albany, N.Y.: State University of New York Press, 1987), p. 2.

72. On the Zealots, cf. R. Horsley and J. Hanson, *Bandits, Prophets, and Messiahs: Popular Movements at the Time of Jesus* (New York: Harper and Row, 1985). The equation of contemporary Jewish fundamentalism and diverse zealots from the Second Commonwealth is facile, tempting, and even

buttressed by the movement's rhetoric—in which GE is compared to the glorious Hasmoneans who heroically rededicated the Temple and restored Jewish independence—and by the rhetoric of its enemies, who liken GE to the Sicarii accused of destroying the Temple and the last vestiges of Jewish independence. Inadvertently thousands of years are erased. For example, forgotten is the fact that the militants of yore lived in a world that did not entertain even the possibility of secularity, in which the idea of Jewish secularity would not have entered the wildest of imaginations.

73. Cf. C. Liebman, "Extremism as a Religious Norm," *Journal for the Scientific Study of Religion* 22, no. 1 (1987).

74. T. Luckmann, *The Invisible Religion* (New York: Macmillan, 1967); P. Berger "Religious Institutions," in N. Smelser, ed., *Sociology* (New York: Wiley, 1967), pp. 369–79.

75. Compare: J. Liebes, "The Haredim and the Ancient Judean Desert Cult," *Jerusalem Studies in Jewish Thought* 3 (1972) (Hebrew).

76. The size of the religious Jewish sector in Israel is debated by both politicians and researchers. The various estimates range between 10 percent and 25 percent, depending on the criteria: some are more stringent (for example, a male who dons phylacteries daily is considered religious) and some less so (for example, a religious person is anyone who defines himself as religiously observant and who is rather cautious about eating only kosher food).

77. Cf. M. Idel, *Kabbalah: New Perspectives* (New Haven: Yale University Press, 1988), esp. chaps. 3, 4, and 5.

78. R. Knox, *Enthusiasm* (Oxford: Clarendon Press, 1950).

79. Cf. W. McLoughlin, *Modern Revivalism* (New York: Ronald Press, 1959).

80. The religio-politics of GE recalls historical models such as the Puritan-type activism of the Revolution of the Saints (Cf. M. Walzer, *The Revolution of the Saints* [Cambridge: Harvard University Press, 1970]), which stands out for its bureaucratic-like discipline, and the Anabaptist-type activism of the previous historical era, whose outburst of energies were not particularly restrained or calculated. Cf. Norman Cohn, *The Pursuit of the Millennium* (New York: Oxford University Press, 1970).

81. For this formulation of the prevailing approach, see E. Mortimer, *Faith and Power: The Politics of Islam* (New York: Vintage, 1982).

82. Cf. G. Kepel, *The Prophet and the Pharaoh* (London: Al Saqi Books, 1985).

83. This is a paraphrase of the Sabbatian principle, originating in the Lurian Kabbalah, according to which one must dive into the depths of the *klipot* (outer shell, i.e., evil) to save the good and sacred "sparks." See G. Scholem, *Major Trends in Jewish Mysticism* (New York: Schocken, 1971), chaps. 7, 8.

84. Success in coping with contemporary economic problems is considered by researchers as a critical test of the fundamentalists' ability to live up to their ideals. Students of religious-political extremism seek to determine if the current regime in Iran can indeed tackle modern economic constraints using tools provided by traditional religion while conforming to its prerevolutionary pretensions. Cf. S. Bakhash, *The Reign of the Ayatollahs* (New York: Basic Books, 1986), especially chap. 7; cf. also his review essay: "Islam and Power Politics," *The New York Review of Books*, 21 July 1988.

85. Compare GE's dilemma in this matter with the parallel case of radical Sunni groups who find themselves in dialectical tension between *haraka* and *da'wa*. See G. Kepel, *The Prophet and the Pharaoh*, conclusion.

86. Note that the extent of return to Judaism in Israel is much less than people tend to believe. Over the past forty years, only a few thousand secular Israelis have changed their life-style drastically, opting for regular, meticulous observance of the commandments and yeshiva study. Cf. S. Meislish, *Return and Repentance* (Tel Aviv: Massada, 1984), chap. 1 (Hebrew).

87. Attributed to the philosopher George Santayana.

88. M. Feige, "Gush Emunim Facing the Possibility of Evacuation of the Territories: A Strategy for Constructing a Traumatic Scenario," in Y. Dror, ed., *Israel Facing Trauma* (Jerusalem: Davis Institute, forthcoming).

89. In 1982, when fulfillment of the terms of the peace treaty with Egypt were concluded, there were seventy settlements in Judea and Samaria. However, only eight of the twenty most important GE settlements had more than one hundred residents each and at least five had populations of less than fifty persons each (including children).

90. The Ein Vered circle, the crowning achievement of GE's pact with Labor settlements, numbered only a few score individuals. After several meetings over a period of less than a year, they split up; only a few still maintain positive, and regular connection with the movement.

91. Wilson, for example, claims that the success of the "new religious movements, in fact confirms the assumption regarding secularization of the Western world, indicating that religion has become inconsequential for modern society. Cf. P. Hammond, ed., *The Sacred in a Secular Age: Toward Revision in the Scientific Study of Religion* (Berkeley: University of California Press, 1985).

92. Cf. G. Aran, "Redemption as a Catastrophe," in Sivan and Friedman, eds., *Religious Radicalism.*

Select Bibliography

Aran, Gideon. "The Beginnings of the Road from Religious Zionism to Zionist Religion," *Studies in Contemporary Jewry,* II, 1986, Indiana University Press. Reprinted in Goldscheider, C. and Neusner, J., eds. *The Social Foundations of Judaism.* Englewood Cliffs, N.J.: Prentice Hall, 1990.

———. "Redemption as Catastrophe: The Gospel of Paradox," in E. Sivan and M. Friedman, eds. *Religious Radicalism and Politics in the Middle East.* Albany, N.Y.: State University of New York Press, 1990.

Arnoff, Myron J. "Gush Emunim: The Institutionalization of a Charismatic, Messianic, Religious-Political Revitalization Movement in Israel." In Aronoff, Myron J. ed. *Political Anthropology* 3, no. 4 (1984).

Avineri, Shlomo. *The Making of Modern Zionism.* N.Y.: Basic Books, 1981.

Avruch, K. "Traditionalizing Israeli Nationalism: The Development of Gush Emunim." *Political Anthropology* 1, no. 1 (1975).

Be'er, H. *Time of Trimming.* Tel Aviv: Am Oved, 1987 (Hebrew).

Bokser, B. ed. and trans. *A. I. Kook.* New York: Paulist Press, 1978.

Cohen, Arthur., and Paul Mendes-Fluhr, eds. *Contemporary Jewish Religious Thought.* New York: 1987.

Don-Yehiya, E. "Jewish Messianism, Religious Zionism, and Israeli Politics: Gush Emunim." *Middle Eastern Studies* 23, no. 2 (1987).

Horowitz, Dan and Lissak, Moshe. *Troubles in Utopia.* N.Y.: State University of New York Press, 1989.

Idel, M. *Kabbalah: New Perspectives.* New Haven: Yale University Press, 1988.

Isaac, R. *Israel Divided: Ideological Politics in the Jewish State.* Baltimore: Johns Hopkins University Press, 1976.

Katz, Jacob. "Orthodoxy in Historical Perspective. *Studies in Contemporary Jewry,* II, 1986, Indiana University Press.

Kohn, M. *Who's Afraid of Gush Emunim?* Jerusalem: Jerusalem Post Press, 1978.

Liebman, Charles S. and Eliezer Don-Yehiya, *Civil Religion in Israel: Traditional Judaism and Political Culture in the Jewish State.* Berkeley: University of California Press, 1983.

———. *Religion and Politics in Israel.* Bloomington: Indiana University Press, 1984.

Newman, David. ed. *The Impact of Gush Emunim: Politics and Settlement in the West*

Bank. New York: St. Martin's Press, 1985.

O'Dea, J. "Gush Emunim: Roots and Ambiguities." *Forum* 2, no. 25 (1976).

Oz, A. *In the Land of Israel*. New York: Harcourt Brace Jovanovich, 1983.

Petai, Raphael. *The Messiah Texts*. Detroit: Wayne State University Press, 1979.

Raanan, Z. *Gush Emunim*. Tel Aviv: Sifriyat Poalim, 1980 (Hebrew).

Rubenstein, A. *From Herzl to Gush Emunim and Back*. New York: Schocken, 1984.

Rubenstein, D. *On the Lord's Side: Gush Emunim*.Tel Aviv: Kibbutz Meuhad, 1982 (Hebrew).

Sharot, S. *Messianism, Mysticism, and Magic*. Chapel Hill: University of North Carolina Press, 1981.

Scholem, Gershom. *The Messianic Idea in Judaism*. New York: Schocken, 1971.

———. *Sabbatai Sevi: The Mystical Messiah*. Princeton, Princeton University Press, 1973.

Sivan, Emmanuel, and M. Friedman, eds. *Religious Radicalism and Politics in the Middle East*. New York: SUNY Press, 1990.

Sprinzak, E. "Gush Emunim: The Iceberg Model of Political Extremism." *Jerusalem Quarterly* 21 (1981).

———. "The Emergence of the Israeli Radical Right." *Comparative Politics* 21, no. 2 (1989).

Vital, D. *The Origins of Zionism*. London: Oxford University Press, 1975.

Weisburd, D. *Jewish Settler Violence: Deviance and Social Reaction*. Philadelphia: University of Pennsylvania Press, 1989.

CHAPTER 6

Fundamentalism in the Sunni Arab World: Egypt and the Sudan

John O. Voll

On 6 October 1981, soldiers jumped from trucks in a military parade in Cairo, Egypt, and shot President Anwar Sadat as he stood in the reviewing stand. The killers were identified as Islamic fundamentalists, members of a group called Jihad, who hoped to spark a Muslim revolution in Egypt by their action. At the same time, in cities and provincial towns, other Egyptians, also identified as Islamic fundamentalists, were engaged in running medical clinics for the poor, special help classes for students in overcrowded universities, and a variety of other social welfare activities. The revolution which was desired by the killers of Sadat did not take place, but the more broadly based Islamic fundamentalist resurgence in Egyptian society continued to gain momentum throughout the 1980s.

For many people, the bloodstained reviewing stand seemed to be the symbol of Islamic fundamentalism in Egypt. During the preceding decade, there had been a series of incidents which reached a climax with the murder of Sadat. When the leader of the killers shouted, "I have killed Pharoah, and I do not fear death," he expressed the emotions of militant fundamentalists in Egypt. Jihad was one of a number of small, militant groups that had emerged during the 1970s. While they disagreed on specifics of program and method, they agreed on the need for the Islamization of Egyptian society.

Leaders of Jihad believed that armed struggle against a wicked government was a requirement of their faith. For such militants, Sadat had become the modern Pharoah, who in Islamic tradition is the prime example of the evil ruler. When Khalid al-Islambuli, a member of Jihad, was placed in charge of a transport vehicle to be used in the 6 October parade, he decided to act. The assassination did spark a revolt in the city of Asyut, but most of the country remained quiet, and suspected members of Muslim militant organizations were arrested. Al-Islambuli and four others were executed in April 1982.

Although there were other demonstrations and terrorist acts attributed to militant groups throughout the 1980s, none of them rivaled the significance of Sadat's death. The failure of the militant fundamentalist groups to ignite a popular Islamic revolution in the years following the murder of Sadat did not, however, signal the end of the Islamic resurgence. To the contrary, the dynamism of the spirit of Islamization is reflected in the growing numbers of people involved in social and political activism of a non-militant style. While membership in the militant groups was always small, millions of Egyptians were involved in many of the activities associated with the Islamic resurgence. In a provincial city like Minya, for example, with a population of around 200,000, there are possibly forty voluntary benevolent societies, many associated with mosques, engaged in a wide range of social services.[1]

Some of the most visible Islamic institutions in the resurgence are the medical clinics. Fundamentalist Muslims have been active in establishing health care facilities to meet the diverse needs of the Egyptian populace. One of the largest is the clinic in the Mustafa Mahmud Mosque in Cairo, which treats more than 250,000 people each year.[2] The medical service clinics are among the most widely used facilities of the fundamentalist Muslim Brotherhood organization, and they are found in more than twenty-thousand non-governmental mosques.[3]

If one looks simply at the militants in groups like Jihad, the numbers involved are small. However, if one looks at those who are actively involved in some way in the Islamic resurgence, then the number of people is in the millions and, in some respects, represents the majority of the society. In addition to the twenty thousand non-governmental mosques, there are more than six thousand private schools founded and sustained by Islamic groups. Thousands pray weekly in the mosques of the revivalist preachers in Cairo and other cities and millions listen to the popular fundamentalist television preachers such as Shaykh Muhammad Sha'rawi and Shaykh 'Abd al-Hamid Kishk. In the other Arab societies of the Middle East as well, the participants in this broad Islamic revolution come from all sectors of society. Furthermore, it is clear that the Islamic resurgence is not primarily the accomplishment of those with little experience with, or knowledge of, the modern West. Indeed, those who constitute the hard core of this broad-based Islamic revolution have had the greatest exposure to modern technologies, educational systems, political processes, cultural values, and lifestyles.[4]

This hard core in Egypt nonetheless recognizes important affinities between their experiences and those of millions of their fellow Egyptians. Youth who are attracted to the militant groups "would normally be considered ideal or model young Egyptians"[5] who share with all advocates of fundamentalism a commitment to transform Egyptian society into an authentic Islamic society. The advocates may and indeed do differ in terms of occupation, level of education, place of origin, and economic status, but they find a powerful basis for unity in a dissatisfaction with the contemporary character of Arab society common to them all.

The contrast between Khalid al-Islambuli and the doctor in the Mustafa Mahmud Mosque clinic thus raises important questions for consideration. Which figure better represents the reality of Egyptian fundamentalism? Beyond the Egyptian context, how may we speak of Islamic fundamentalism in the Sunni Arab world? Who are the Muslim fundamentalists? Why have they adopted a fundamentalist stance in their societies and what are their goals? Are they a significant force in the shaping of their societies? What has been their role in the recent historical development of those societies?

Defining Islamic Fundamentalism

The wide diversity of individuals and groups associated with Islamic fundamentalism indicates that it is not a monolithic movement and renders a simple definition difficult. In addition, some contemporary Muslim thinkers and non-Muslim scholars have reservations about using the term because of its original application to a Western Christian movement. Nonetheless, there is widespread recognition of the reality to which the term refers, and many observers and participants find it useful to have a term which can refer to the complex cluster of movements, events, and people who are involved in the reaffirmation of the fundamentals of the Islamic faith and mission in the final decades of the twentieth century. "Islamic fundamentalism," then, will here denote the reaffirmation of foundational principles and the effort to reshape society in terms of those reaffirmed fundamentals. This involves, in the words of Muslims who have described Islamic fundamentalism, the effort "to call Muslims back to the path of Islam," "an assertive surge of Islamic feeling" which pervades the Islamic world, and "the reliance on Islamic fundamental principles to meet the needs and challenges of contemporary times."[6]

The nature of Islamic faith itself, however, demands further explanations of the nature of Islamic fundamentalism. All Muslims affirm the truth of the revelation in the Qur'an and they have an obligation to implement the fundamentals of that truth in their lives and societies. However, those commonly referred to today as "fundamentalists" adopt an identifiable approach to this common obligation, an approach marked by an exclusivist and literalist interpretation of the fundamentals of Islam and by a rigorist pursuit of sociomoral reconstruction. Islamic fundamentalism is, in other words, a distinctive mode of response to major social and cultural change introduced either by exogenous or indigenous forces and perceived as threatening to dilute or dissolve the clear lines of Islamic identity, or to overwhelm that identity in a synthesis of many different elements.

Eighteenth-Century Antecedents

Because Islamic revivalists are today reacting to, and interacting with, a complex and unprecedented set of social, political, and cultural circumstances associated with the term "modernity," contemporary Islamic fundamentalism assumes a distinctive shape set apart from previous renewals and reform attempts. However, today's fundamentalists consciously draw upon, and see themselves in a type of continuity with, premodern reformers such as Ahmad Ibn Hanbal (d. 855) and Ahmad Ibn Taymiyya (d. 1328).[7] From the example of those figures fundamentalists derive an attitude marked by an unwillingness to compromise with an imperfectly Islamic status quo. Further, they tend to reject the incorporation of non-Muslim practices into Islamic life and place a strong emphasis on the *comprehensive* and *universal* nature of the message of God as presented in the Qur'an. The historical foundations for this fundamentalism in the modern Arab world lie, however, in the eighteenth century. At that time, major movements of renewal developed within the framework of premodern, precolonial historical conditions; accordingly, the major impetus for the initial emergence of a sustained fundamentalism was found not in organized opposition to Western expansion but instead in an indigenous movement of reform.

By the eighteenth century (the twelfth century of the Islamic era), a belt of interactive Muslim societies stretched across the Eastern Hemisphere from the Atlantic to the Pacific. The Islamic world had expanded through the efforts of merchants, teachers, saints, and soldiers, and the century was an era of consolidation. However, the attempts to create and maintain the large-scale political structures and social organizations that had developed in earlier centuries proved only partly successful, and reformers began to call for a socio-moral reconstruction of society on the foundations of Islam.

The decline of institutional effectiveness was most visible in the political life of the three great Islamic empires of the preceding centuries. In South Asia, the Mogul Empire, founded by the Mongol warrior Babar, had gained control over India in the sixteenth century. Achievements in the arts, architecture, poetry, and painting enhanced the reputation of the empire as a center of culture and refinement. A nominally Islamic government ruled over the ethnic and religious diversity of the subcontinent. Babar's grandson, Akbar the Great (d. 1605), responded to the situation by developing a court religion that sought to blend elements of Islam, Hinduism, Buddhism, and Christianity. By the advent of the rule of Alamgir (d. 1707), however, a reaction against this type of synthesis and the growing divisions within Mogul domains resulted in efforts to Islamize state and society along fundamentalist lines. The intellectual foundations provided by Shah Wali Allah for this reformism are an important part of the modern Islamic heritage in South Asia.[8]

The second great core Islamic empire was the Safavid Empire in Iran. Beginning as an activist mystic Brotherhood, the Safavids conquered Iran at the beginning of the sixteenth century and established Shi'ite Islam as the official religion of the state. The beautiful mosques and palaces of Isfahan, the Safavid capital, reflect the power and refinement of the state at its peak. In the early eighteenth century, however, the dynasty fell prey to military adventurers and foreign invaders.

Much of the Arab world in the eighteenth century was, however, under the control of the third great core Islamic empire, the Ottoman Empire. From its origins as a small Islamic warrior state in the eastern Mediterranean, the Ottoman Empire had grown into a major world power by the sixteenth century. Its capital was the old Eastern Roman capital, Constantinople, which the Ottomans had conquered in 1453. Ottoman rule extended across North Africa and throughout most of the Balkan peninsula and included most of the Arabic-speaking world. However, by the eighteenth century, the central institutions of the empire had become less effective. The sultans became more isolated from actual command and administration by the development of the palace-harem institutions, and the military, perhaps relying on its past greatness, was unwilling to accept some of the new technologies. As a result, territories in Europe were lost, and in the Arab world, the empire fragmented as local governors became virtually independent in a number of regions.

Arabic-speaking Sunni Muslims in the Middle East responded to the political fragmentation and decline in various ways, one of which was the formation of Islamic movements of renewal in Cairo, the smaller cities of Yemen, and the holy sanctuary cities of Mecca and Medina in the Arabian peninsula. In Yemen and south Arabia, for example, scholars from China, Southeast Asia, Africa, and India assembled in the schools of prominent local scholars such as the members of the Mizjaji, Ahdal, and Aydarus families. Cairo was a crossroads for pilgrims and scholars from North and sub-Saharan Africa, while the holy cities of Mecca and Medina attracted travelers from throughout the Islamic world. Revivalist thought was born, nurtured, and disseminated in these cosmopolitan centers.

One of several revivalist movements that formed at the time was the Wahhabi movement, established on the Arabian peninsula by Muhammad Ibn ʿAbd al-Wahhab (1703–92), a peripatetic scholar born in central Arabia, in the Nejd region. The dominant school of Sunni legal interpretation in the region was the Hanbali, in the tradition of the early medieval fundamentalist, Ahmad Ibn Hanbal. However, the religious life of local tribes and townspeople had become involved with non-Islamic practices, including the worship of the tombs of Muslim saints, magic, and divination. Despite the Hanbali reputation for strictness, the Muslim learned establishment tended to tolerate the superstitions of the masses rather than cause social tension and conflict.

As part of his education, Muhammad Ibn ʿAbd al-Wahhab traveled to a variety of places, including Mecca and Medina, and studied with scholars from India as well as local Hanbali teachers. His travels inspired in him a sense of mission, and upon his return home, he began a teaching career dedicated to the task of reconstructing society along rigorous sociomoral lines. He initially settled in his birthplace, the town of al-Uyaynah, but his preaching and active fundamentalist opposition to local popular religious practices like pilgrimages to special natural sites and a cult of saints created tensions which undermined the compromising local religious establishment. In addition, his demands for reform implied an attack on the ruling prince. He was forced to leave and found refuge in the town of al-Darʿiyyah (near present-day Riyadh), ruled by Muhammad Ibn Saʿūd. The revivalist teacher converted the prince, and their alliance created the foundations for a new state.

In principle, the teachings of Muhammad Ibn ʿAbd al-Wahhab challenged all of the compromises which had held Muslim society in Arabia together: the new message challenged the social order in which popular cults were tolerated by the Muslim teachers, and it confronted rulers who tolerated a non-Islamic society for the sake of internal tranquility. The Saudi state created by Ibn Saʿūd and Ibn ʿAbd al-Wahhab expanded rapidly by conquest and conversion throughout the eighteenth century, with the teachings of Ibn 'Abd al-Wahhab providing the ideological and legitimizing basis for the state. The major themes of his teachings reflect the concerns of Sunni Muslim fundamentalists in any era, although the Wahhabi presentation was notably uncompromising and provided a final, premodern articulation of those themes in a way which could be used by later, modern thinkers.[9]

The basic teaching of Ibn 'Abd al-Wahhab was *tawhid,* or the transcendent unity of God. Characteristically, Ibn 'Abd al-Wahhab presented this bedrock principle of Islamic monotheism—the witness that "There is no deity but the One God"—in such a way as to disallow even any appearance of compromise.[10] The attack on popular cultic practices and the visitation of tombs of saints posed a challenge to the elite rulers and teachers of the day. Ibn 'Abd al-Wahhab's goal was to ensure that society be permeated by this principle, that the transcendence of God be acknowledged by a people living in strict accord with the prescriptions of the Qur'an, under a political system designed to promote and protect such a lifestyle. Thus the teaching of tawhid in this form was more than a statement of monotheistic faith: it was a quid pro quo of social and political legitimacy.[11]

The Wahhabi mission, then, was first to perfect the faith and practice of the individual believer, and Ibn 'Abd al-Wahhab's interpretation of tawhid provided the conceptual foundation for the program. Popular devotional practices were to be those required or recommended in the Qur'an and the Sunna. All other practices were considered a form of polytheism. This approach reflects the tension which exists to this day between the common themes of all Islamic societies and the particularities of each locale. In the tension, the fundamentalist response has embraced the cosmopolitan and universalist pole of the spectrum of Islamic faith and practice. In this sense, Islamic fundamentalism builds upon and heightens the believer's sense of belonging to a broader global community of the faithful *(ummah)*.

Ibn 'Abd al-Wahhab also attacked the religio-intellectual establishment of his time. He opposed the blind acceptance of authority in religious matters and criticized the *ulama* (learned men) who had taken the medieval systems of Islam as the final word and had thus eliminated any role for the independent rethinking of the religious tradition.[12] Islamic fundamentalists have, like Ibn 'Abd al-Wahhab, advocated *ijtihad,* the use of informed independent judgment in interpreting and applying the basic sources of Islam, rather than simply adhering to the inherited interpretations of the great medieval scholars. The rationale for rejecting the authority of the medieval thinkers is that they accepted or allowed innovations which went beyond the prescriptions of the Qur'an. Ibn 'Abd al-Wahhab argued that if something was not found in the Qur'an, it was an innovation, and if it was found in the Qur'an, the later teaching was either redundant or was simply a gloss that was not authoritative. The positive dimension of ijtihad is that it requires study of the Qur'an itself rather than relying solely on later handbooks.

However, the Qur'an is not viewed in isolation by Muslims but is seen in the context of the traditions about the Prophet Muhammad *(hadith)*. The traditions reveal how he lived under the inspiration of revelation and recount the experience of Muhammad and his immediate followers as they worked to create the divinely-described community. Thus the Qur'an and this added authoritative source, the Sunna of the Prophet, have provided the fundamentals for the revivalists of all eras. Advocating a return to the fundamentals of both the Qur'an and the Sunna means, then, "advocating allegiance not to the Qur'an as pure idea, but to the Qur'an as implemented."[13]

The responsibility for defining the specifics of the application of the Qur'an and the Sunna to a particular situation remains with the individual exercising ijtihad. Like other practitioners of ijtihad, Ibn 'Abd al-Wahhab did not depart radically from the main lines of interpretations over the centuries. However, if the initial teacher is a persuasive and effective leader, a tradition of interpretation capable of gathering its own momentum could emerge. Ibn 'Abd al-Wahhab has, for example, remained a preeminent authority for his descendants, but the practice of ijtihad by another teacher remains possible within the Wahhabi tradition and is in fact characteristic of most modern Sunni fundamentalist movements.

The vision of creating a society in which the Qur'an is implemented means that Ibn 'Abd al-Wahhab's mission would inevitably entail political consequences. It was the local rulers who forced him to leave the town where he began teaching, and it was another local ruler, Ibn Sa'ūd, who provided necessary support. The political system created by the Wahhabis did not place the inspirational teacher in a position of political rule. Instead, the Wahhabi state was based on the close cooperation of a learned teacher *(shaykh)* and an able commander *(emir)*. The combination reflected a long-standing perception of the proper relations between the institutions of the scholars and those of the commanders. Such a system of institutionalization reflected a reduced emphasis on charismatic leadership among Sunni fundamentalists and was also an important aspect of the great Sunni sultanates of the medieval era.[14]

"Wahhabism" is thus a term used today to indicate the type of reformism elucidated in Ibn 'Abd al-Wahhab's opposition to popular religious superstitions and innovations, his insistence on informed independent judgment over against the rote reliance on medieval authorities, and his call for the Islamization of society and the creation of a political order which gives appropriate recognition of Islam. Wahhabism represents an important type of fundamentalism that continues to operate within the modern world but was not initiated as a result of conflict with the modernized West. The Wahhabis succeeded in establishing a state which, while imperfect, has nonetheless been recognized by many in the Islamic world as consonant with the fundamentalist mission to create an Islamic society. It is the most enduring experiment within the broader mission and as such has provided a standard against which other movements and states could be measured.

The actual historical experience of the Saudi state and the Wahhabi community of course included failures as well as successes. However, as a concrete fundamentalist effort it has been an important example for others and has provided a basic repertoire of concepts and ideas from which modern fundamentalists draw. Saudi influence is felt today in the development of fundamentalist movements throughout the Islamic world, not only by dint of ideological inspiration but also by the financial support for the export of Wahhabism made possible by the sale of Saudi petroleum products.[15]

Nineteenth-Century Antecedents

The nineteenth century presented social and economic conditions strikingly different from those of past eras of Islamic history. The Industrial Revolution, introduced to the Arab world via the intrusion of Western European powers after 1800, brought with it a demand for raw materials, imported foodstuffs, and stable markets for European goods and capital. The encroachment of the West had an immediate economic impact, first manifested in changed trading patterns brought on by the introduction of the steamship and the expansion of the railroads in the Middle East and in Islamic North Africa. These dramatic improvements in transportation opened new markets and led to a massive infusion of Western capital, the corresponding introduction of the rudiments of a Western-style financial system, and most important, an influx of European immigrants engaged in pursuits ranging from agriculture to banking to government administration, all under the nominal aegis of local powers such as the Ottoman rulers in Egypt. The cash economy in turn fueled the growth of agriculture under the control of native landlords employing local peasants. Cotton, tobacco, silk, opium, wine, dried fruits, and cereals were among the export crops in regions in which land was plenteous and labor cheap. Conversely, as export agriculture expanded, the traditional merchant class declined. Given the prior stagnation of Middle East and North African economies and the lack of strong mediating economic or political institutions capable of regulating the Western influence, the rapid distortion of traditional economic patterns quickly led to economic dependence on the West and eventually to the assertion of direct Western colonial control of the Islamic world. In the Arab world, the French came to control Algeria in 1830, Tunisia in 1881, Morocco in 1911, and Syria and Lebanon after World War I. The British occupied Egypt in 1882, conquered the Sudan by 1898, and took control of modern Iraq, Jordan, and the Palestine mandate following World War I. Even the small states in the Persian Gulf, South Arabia, and Libya were under some form of European control by World War I.

The social dislocation which ensued was traumatic and widespread. By the late nineteenth century, for example, the sequestering of large tracts of land for corporate agricultural purposes created a landless peasant class. Traditional urban elites were also displaced; for example, the ulama gradually relinquished their hegemony over legal and educational matters to a new class of Western-influenced bureaucrats.[16]

Muslim fundamentalists in the nineteenth century continued to advocate a more strict adherence to the Qur'an and the Sunna, but also struggled to resist what was increasingly identified as foreign rule. This is clear in the case of those fundamentalists in the Arab world who resisted European expansion, although some also came to oppose non-Arab Muslim rulers as well. However, the major and most visible reform efforts in the Islamic world at this time were no longer primarily based on restoring past glory or reaffirming Islamic fundamentals. Instead, the major focus of Islamic political and intellectual activity was devoted to large-scale efforts to utilize the new technologies coming from Europe and to adapt European political and administrative ideas to the structures of Middle Eastern societies. Thus, Muslim fundamentalists were most active in the more peripheral or frontier areas in which the processes of adaptation had not yet taken root.

While several nineteenth-century movements provide models for today's fundamentalist activists, perhaps the most evocative is the case of Muhammad Ahmad, the Sudanese leader who proclaimed his mission as Mahdi and drove the Ottoman-Egyptian forces out of his country in the 1880s. His mission was to create a more purely Islamic society by eliminating the innovations introduced by outsiders, even though they called themselves Muslims. The Sudanese Mahdi rejected the corrupt practices of the Turko-Egyptian rulers and fought the British, but he did not reject modern military technology. Although he is frequently described as an opponent of foreign rule and an enemy of Western intrusions into the Islamic world, he also opposed certain local religious customs, engaged in ijtihad, and in other ways recalled the example of Ibn ʿAbd al-Wahhab. Although he envisioned his mission in messianic terms, he stands well within the heritage of Sunni fundamentalism.[17]

Although the Mahdi himself died in 1885, he created a state which lasted until British and Egyptian forces conquered the Sudan in 1898. The Mahdist movement remained an important force in Sudanese society throughout the twentieth century. In the 1940s, the Mahdist movement became the basis for one of the major Sudanese political parties, and a great grandson of the Mahdi, Sadiq al-Mahdi, served as prime minister of the independent Sudan in the 1960s and again in the 1980s. The political dynamism of the Mahdist movement, in both the nineteenth and twentieth centuries, has provided Muslim intellectuals throughout the Islamic world with an example of effective Islamic political activism.[18]

In this case as in others in North Africa, the struggle to free a local community from exogenous forces took precedence over the specific teaching or ideals of the leader. In the twentieth century, memories of the fundamentalist leaders were maintained, or revived, in the context of a growing national identity and of efforts to establish nation-states.[19] Thus the state created by the Mahdi came to be seen, not as a functioning fundamentalist Islamic state, but as the first independent Sudanese state in the modern era. Because the first priority for nineteenth-century Muslims was the defense of an imperfect Islamic society from non-Muslim rule (rather than the sociomoral reconstruction of an imperfectly Islamic society), the trend toward nationalism influenced fundamentalists and underscored the necessity of strengthening the political dimension of the fundamentalist programs. Fundamentalist emphasis began to shift from the reform of devotional practices to the establishment and defense of national and communal identity. For example, Ibn Taymiyya came to be cited less for his writings on the problems of popular devotional practices and more for his analysis of the issues raised by the occupation of Muslim lands by non-Muslims during the Crusades and the Mongol invasions. This analysis included an elaboration of the concept of holy war.[20] This description of the increased importance of the political solution is not to deny the enduring motivational force of Islam: throughout the modern era, it has been observed, the real dynamism of mass movements, even those led by secular leaders, has been generated by devotion to the faith.[21]

However, at the beginning of the twentieth century Islamic revivalism did not appeal to the majority of the educated Arabic-speaking people in urban centers such as Cairo and Damascus. They were occupied by the task of modernizing society and looked to Western forms of nationalism, secularism, and technology for models in this endeavor. Islamic revivalism was viewed as rigid and irrelevant to the process of modernization.[22] The fundamentalist movements in the Arab world at the time were restricted to central Arabia and to rural areas of Islamic Africa, to those Muslims who had not yet had significant contact with Western technology or Western systems of education.[23] Yet the fundamentalists who would arise in the urban centers of the twentieth century did have at hand a repertoire of symbols and concepts developed by revivalist leaders of the Sunni past.

The Twentieth-Century Experience: Egypt

During the twentieth century, movements of nationalism succeeded in obtaining independence. Independence was achieved sometimes by negotiation, as in the Sudan and Tunisia in 1956, or only after long struggle, as was the case in the Algerian war for independence in the 1950s. However, by the 1970s the challenge of creating effective independent state structures, developing modern economies, and coping with the strains of modernization provided an important part of the context for the reassertion of Islamic fundamentalism. As the first country in the Arabic-speaking world and one of the earliest in the Islamic world as a whole to undertake a major program of Westernizing reforms, Egypt represents, if not the typical case of Sunni Arab engagement with twentieth-century modernity, at least a historically influential one, and it is to Egypt that we now turn.

It is generally agreed that Napoleon's invasion of the Ottoman province of Egypt in 1798 marked the beginning of the modern era in the Arab world. The Ottoman sultan installed a military commander by the name of Muhammad 'Ali (d. 1849) as governor of Egypt after the withdrawal of the French. Muhammad 'Ali began a program of rapid modernization of the Egyptian military, government, and economy using Western European advisers and models. Muhammad 'Ali and his successors in the nineteenth century created the foundations for Egyptian modernization by establishing educational institutions on the Western model designed to transform the mode of life and thought in Egypt. Thus began a rapid shift away from traditional Qur'anic schools to schools specializing in the sciences and Western languages. Inherent in this shift was the displacement of the previous emphasis on Islamic ethics in favor of the secularist and nationalistic outlook of the West. The shift was in keeping with the policies pursued by Muhammad 'Ali and his successors; for although they were not anti-Islamic, the rulers had as their goal the creation of Western-style, modern societies, and they paid little attention to explicitly Islamic issues.

In the new situation, the ulama and the leaders of popular Islamic organizations came under more direct government control. They were increasingly subordinated to the new political power groups created by the reforms of the nineteenth century. There are indications that the peasants who did not benefit directly from the reform programs engaged in a variety of protest movements. Because the urban ulama and large popular Islamic organizations were increasingly under government supervision, they provided little leadership for the creation of a viable opposition. When the rural revolts did assume an Islamic character, leadership came from the traditional ulama associated with the local shrines and tombs. However, modern Islamic fundamentalism in Egypt did not arise out of the protests of the rural peasants and the traditional ulama. Neither of those groups was in a position to draw upon the fundamentalist repertoire of symbols and concepts effectively in the modern context.[24] The roots of modern fundamentalism in Egypt lie instead in the responses of urban, educated youth to the unmistakable intellectual and moral crises created by the rapid introduction of Western ideas and technology.

By the final third of the nineteenth century, a new group of intellectuals attempted to bridge the gap between the traditional masses and the modern groups favored by Muhammad ʿAli and his successors by creating an effective synthesis of modern and Islamic concepts. The hope of this new intellectual movement was the creation of an alternative acceptable to both the secularist Westernizers and the more conservative traditionalists. The major figures in the movement were Jamal al-Din al-Afghani (1838–97) and Muhammad ʿAbduh (1849–1905); the alternative that they developed has come to be called "Islamic modernism." Their careers and ideas illustrate the main themes in the movement.[25]

The Islamic modernism of al-Afghani and ʿAbduh began with a call for a major reform of Islamic teaching and practice. Al-Afghani argued that the ulama had discredited the search for scientific truth and warned that "those who forbid science and knowledge in the belief that they are safeguarding the Islamic religion are really the enemies of that religion."[26] Al-Afghani advocated a synthesis of Islam and modern science on the premise that there is no incompatibility between science, knowledge, and the foundations of the Islamic faith. ʿAbduh also criticized the Muslim thinkers of his day and worked to reform the major Islamic educational institution in Egypt, al-Azhar. He stressed the importance of reason in religious thought and contended that Islam is "not a creed which scared away reason. For reason is the pioneer of authentic belief."[27] The thinking of ʿAbduh and al-Afghani provided the basis for Islamic modernism, the effort to combine a modern, Western-style scientific rationalism with an Islamic faith. The Islamic modernists rejected the complex formulations of the traditional ulama and the medieval interpretations and called for a return to the example of the pious ancestors *(salaf),* the companions of the Prophet. In fact, Islamic modernism as defined by ʿAbduh came to be called the "Salafiyyah."

Islamic fundamentalism and the Islamic modernism articulated by al-Afghani and ʿAbduh could be considered intellectual twins in that both movements formed in response to the same set of ills and offered surprisingly similar diagnoses (if not prescriptions). The modernists also embraced ijtihad, rejected the "superstitions" of popular religion and the stagnant thinking of the ulama, and renewed the discussion of the concept of tawhid. There was also an emphasis on the need for independence from foreign control, especially in the teachings of al-Afghani. However, Islamic modernism did not share with fundamentalism a repudiation of the Western ethos and Western ways, and it aimed at creating a synthesis of Islam and the modern West rather than a purified society constructed primarily along Islamic lines. In short, the modernist stance was more conceptually and practically open than the exclusivist style of Islamic fundamentalism.

Despite these differences, Islamic modernism provided fundamentalism with a sophisticated modern vocabulary for the defense of Islam. Later fundamentalists, for example, appropriated the modernist articulation of the proper relationship between Islam and science, including the claim that Western science is indebted to Islam, from which it has borrowed heavily. Similarly, while Muslim fundamentalists have emphasized the relevance of Islam for all aspects of life, it was the modernists who provided the special articulation of this theme in modern terms, by identifying and then rejecting the Western distinctions between church and state, material and spirit, secular and religious. The focus on secularism and materialism as problems at the core of the modern experience of the West is yet another aspect of the heritage of the early Muslim modernists appropriated by later fundamentalists.

The fundamentalist potential in Islamic modernism was developed by one of 'Abduh's principle students, Rashid Rida (1865–1935), who assumed the role of leading spokesperson for the Salafiyyah after 'Abduh's death in 1905. Rida became increasingly mistrustful of the rationalist tendencies in the thinking of other modernists. He was concerned by the secularist aspects of the thought of Egyptian liberals who considered themselves followers of 'Abduh. One student of 'Abduh, Osman Amin (1865–1908), for example, had written a book calling for the liberation of women from traditional Muslim restrictions. Another, Ahmad Lufti al-Sayyid (1872–1963), became a leading exponent of a European-style Egyptian nationalism. In the face of these developments, Rashid Rida moved toward a more fundamentalist articulation of Islam.

The Beginnings of Modern Fundamentalism, 1905–28

Frequently discussions of modern fundamentalism in Egypt commence with the establishment of the Muslim Brotherhood in 1928. Yet the first quarter of the twentieth century witnessed the formation of an elite class with a distinctive political orientation, along with new patterns of protest among the lower classes. Both developments would contribute to the milieu of the nascent fundamentalists.

Egypt in 1905 was still legally a part of the Ottoman Empire but had been effectively separated from direct Ottoman control since the beginning of the nineteenth century. Muhammad 'Ali, the Westernizing reformer, had established effective autonomy for himself and his successors. After the British occupied Egypt in 1882, the local representative of Great Britain was the de facto ruler of Egypt, although both the legal ties to the Ottoman Empire and the dynasty of Muhammad 'Ali's family were maintained. The situation was altered by World War I, when the British declared Egypt to be a protectorate, separating it from the Ottoman Empire, with which they were at war. This raised the issue of the status of Egypt at the end of the war.

Britain would not allow a delegation *(wafd)* of Egyptians to act independently at the Peace Conference, and forced into exile the Egyptian who had become identified with the idea of sending the delegation, Sa'd Zaghloul. The result was a series of nationalist demonstrations in 1919 organized in the name of the Wafd, which soon became the name of the political party organized by Zaghloul and his followers. The nationalist demonstrations grew into a major revolt that spread to all parts of the country. The British crushed the revolt but were unable to resolve the basic political issues by negotiations. In 1922 they unilaterally declared Egypt to be an independent monarchy under the rule of King Fu'ād, a descendant of Muhammad 'Ali. The British maintained their military control over the country, and the Wafd under Zaghloul emerged as a mass nationalist political party.

These events inspired both the secular elites and the masses to dedicate themselves to ridding Egypt of foreign rulers. The image of the independent Western nation-state ruled by elected parliaments, enhanced by the common perception that such a system had enabled the British and French to colonize large portions of the underdeveloped world, had captured the attention of Western-educated groups throughout the world. Although the majority of Egyptians may not have supported, or even understood, the details, liberal nationalism was the political model preferred by the articulate political elite in Egypt. In this view, a person could reject British domination of Egypt, but this did not mean that one rejected having a Western parliamentary model as the goal for an independent Egypt. Furthermore, this vision commended itself to the Islamic modernist as an effective combination of Western principles and Muslim independence, even though liberal nationalism was implicitly and sometimes explicitly secularist in tone.

The key element in the appeal of liberal nationalism was its call for Egyptian independence. The first priority was the removal of the British army of occupation. In this context, people who advocated alternatives which seemed to divert attention from the main goal, including those who proposed the re-establishment of the Islamic caliphate, received little support in Egypt in the 1920s. The simple, concrete demand for British withdrawal supplied the Wafd Party with a political cause which virtually every Egyptian could understand and support. By the end of World War I, "nationalism and its demands, not the problems of Islamic reform, had become the central social force in both Egypt and the Fertile Crescent."[28] Although nationalism was not necessarily antithetical to Islamic reform, in Egypt during the 1920s it provided a different agenda from those of both Islamic modernism and Islamic fundamentalism. While fundamentalism and nationalism might possibly be complementary, there was a tendency for a tension to develop in the Egyptian context between the advocates of the two approaches. Intense support of secular nationalism was found among the Western-educated elite, but it would be inaccurate to report that the masses had abandoned Islamic aspirations. However, in the 1920s the majority of the population did seem to accept the articulation of those aspirations through the vocabulary of nationalism and Western liberalism rather than demanding a more strictly Islamic articulation: as long as the critical issue was the elimination of foreign control, Zaghloul and the Wafd spoke for most Egyptians.[29]

In fact, in the period from after the death of ʿAbduh to the end of the 1920s, conditions were not favorable for the establishment a formally organized fundamentalist mass movement. The withdrawal of the British army was not the only issue of concern. In the countryside, villagers felt the influence of non-Egyptian moneylenders and merchants, and urban workers often blamed poor working conditions on foreign owners of the large economic enterprises. Although the peasants, who revolted in 1919, may have had different specific goals in mind from those of the educated urban professionals, both found the vocabulary of nationalism more useful and apt than that of an explicitly Islamic reformism. Furthermore, whereas Western imperialism was resented, the strength and effectiveness of Western methods was not.

The Wafd Party, led by Saʿd Zaghloul, was the beneficiary of such sentiments. A former student of al-Afghani, Zaghloul had abandoned the program of Islamic reform in favor of Egyptian nationalism, and from the end of World War I until the late 1920s, the Wafd Party seemed poised to win the battle for true Egyptian independence. Rationalist Islamic modernists enjoyed little support at the time. In 1925, for example, ʿAli ʿAbd al-Raziq (1888–1966) published a book which held that the medieval Muslim form of government was not specifically defined by the Qur'an but was a product of particular historical circumstances. In the following year, Taha Husayn published a study of pre-Islamic poetry which cast doubts upon the traditional methods of interpreting basic Muslim texts. These were not intellectuals who were rejecting Islam. Instead, they were reinterpreting basic elements of the Islamic tradition in the spirit of ʿAbduh. Both were forced to withdraw their books, were subjected to judicial harassment, and had their careers affected by the opposition to their efforts. The core of the attack came from conservative ulama and political enemies of liberalism. Liberal modernists were not strong enough to defend them, and the secular nationalists were not interested in defending them, even though the ideas of Husayn and ʿAbd al-Raziq provided support for some secularist positions.[30]

The fundamentalist strand of ʿAbduh's heritage was also relatively weak in the 1920s. Rashid Rida continued to publish *Al-Manar,* the journal of the Salafiyyah, but he was increasingly marginal to the main events of the day. In a period when mass political organizations were being established, he remained without a formal organization to present his views. At a time when there was an increasing emphasis upon Egyptian identity, the fact that Rida was Syrian in origin reduced his effective influence on Egyptian politics. In broad terms, his overt mistrust of nationalism in its more secular and liberal forms meant that he was out of the mainstream of Egyptian thought and sentiment. Later Egyptian fundamentalists respected his works but nonetheless described him simply as the "archivist" and "historian" of early reformism rather than as a major actor.[31]

The attraction of Western-style nationalism and the corresponding lack of interest in Islamic reformism in Egypt during the first three decades of the twentieth century was also heightened by the lessons offered by contemporary world events. The Japanese victory in the Russo-Japanese War in 1905 provided an example of the rapid and effective modernization of a non-European state. Similarly, following the war, Mustafa Kemal (later Atatürk), the most secular and nationalist of the postwar leaders in the Islamic world, won a resounding victory in Turkey's war for independence. "Borrowing" from the West seemed to be an effective policy, and the results in Turkey and Japan seemed difficult to refute; and fundamentalists who tried to counter the secularist tone of emerging Egyptian nationalists could be accused of dividing the country in a time of crisis.

The few proponents of fundamentalism did not help their cause by presenting it, as Rashid Rida did, in a highly intellectualized form which had little to offer to the majority of Egyptians. Their diatribes seemed irrelevant. While fundamentalists preached against the "superstitions" of the peasants, nationalism presented itself as a vehicle by which to revolt against the wealthy landlords and foreign creditors. Moreover, the most visible representatives of fundamentalism were not particularly compelling as leaders. While Zaghloul had emerged as a charismatic figure capable of voicing the concerns of the nation, most advocates of a return to Islam confined their advocacy to discussion groups and classrooms.

It was not until the end of the 1920s that these conditions began to change significantly.

The Establishment of the Muslim Brotherhood, 1928–54

Zaghloul, by far the most effective advocate for nationalism and rule by a parliamentary majority, died in 1927. Soon after his death many Egyptians began to lose confidence that the political system and institutions would be able to realize his vision. Zaghloul was succeeded in the leadership of the Wafd Party by Mustafa Nahhas, a less inspiring leader, and the party seemed reduced to a political interest group rather than a platform for national self-expression. The evolution of the Egyptian political scene accelerated these developments. Egypt had become legally independent with the unilateral declaration of the British in 1922. In theory Egypt was a constitutional monarchy with multiparty politics and an elected parliament. In practice Egypt was a country with a certain amount of political autonomy for local affairs but dominated in all major issues by the British, whose military occupation of the country continued. King Fu'ād exercised control over administrative structures, enjoyed the power of patronage, and by means of police powers could determine the results of parliamentary elections. The Wafd Party thus competed for influence with both the British and the king. Through its massive popular support, the Wafd could influence politics through its ability to organize major demonstrations. In any unrigged election, the Wafd could win a majority of the parliamentary seats, and from time to time, for policy reasons, the British and the king would calm popular unrest by permitting a Wafd election victory. This climate of political manipulation and open struggle for political patronage was not conducive to the pursuit of the greater interests of Egypt in any sustained or systematic fashion.

The "loss of hope" thus began with a general disappointment with Egyptian political leadership, but it was soon reinforced in the 1930s by the global economic crisis of the Great Depression.[32] Subsequently new movements emerged which broke with the secularist nationalism and liberalism of the emerging political and intellectual establishments. In this context the more rationalist strand of Islamic modernism became widely accepted by the elite; however, its acceptance was challenged by a new and more activist form of Islamic fundamentalism which strove to articulate the aspirations of the uprooted masses.

The heart of the new fundamentalism was the Muslim Brotherhood, formed by Hasan al-Banna (1906–49) in 1928. Al-Banna was born in a small town about ninety miles from Cairo.[33] His father was a local Islamic teacher and al-Banna received a traditional Islamic education in his early years. Al-Banna then went to a primary school, a Primary Teachers' Training School, and completed his education at Dar al-Ulum in Cairo. Although Dar al-Ulum attempted to provide a combination of a modern education and familiarity with the more traditional Islamic disciplines, al-Banna's was not the formal Islamic education required of the ulama. He prepared instead to become a teacher in the modern school system of Egypt.

During his school years al-Banna joined or organized a number of groups dedicated to improving the moral life of the students and helping people to live more strictly in accord with Islam. In addition, from the age of twelve he attended instruction and devotion sessions of the Hasafiyyah Tariqah, a Sufi Brotherhood which had been organized in the late nineteenth century. Al-Banna studied the life and writings of Hasanayn al-Hasafi (1848–1910) and was impressed by al-Hasafi's strict adherence to the fundamentals of Islam. In al-Banna's description, al-Hasafi "always opposed innovations that had crept into the Sufistic system of prayer and supplication." He admired al-Hasafi because "he brought tremendous change in the society by wiping out numerous un-Islamic practices from it."[34] Al-Banna himself believed that mysticism "played a very important role in the propagation of Islam," but the later mixing with non-Islamic ideas "had rendered it ineffective."[35] As was the case with other fundamentalists, al-Banna did not oppose mysticism, but he did repudiate the cultic customs that had been incorporated into the devotional exercises of many of the Brotherhoods. Indeed, the spirit of strict devotion of the Hasafiyyah appealed to al-Banna, and he adopted the reformist Sufi spirit as part of his life-style.

Al-Banna studied in Cairo in the mid-1920s and then, in 1927, was given his first appointment in the state school system and went to Ismailia in the Suez Canal zone. His exposure to the life-style of these cities convinced him that Egyptian culture had lost its Islamic moorings. For him, Egypt presented the picture of a society in the midst of moral crisis: "Just after the First World War and during my stay in Cairo, the wave of atheism and lewdness engulfed Egypt. It started the devastation of religion and morality on the pretext of individual and intellectual freedom. Nothing could stop this storm."[36] It seemed to al-Banna that the West was engaged in a new crusade to destroy Islam by means of social corruption and unbelief. Europeans had "imported their half-naked women into these regions, together with their liquors, their theaters, their dance halls, their amusements, their stories, their newspapers, their novels, their whims, their silly games, and their vices." Most troubling, they had "founded schools and scientific and cultural institutes in the very heart of the Islamic domain, which cast doubt and heresy into the souls of its sons and taught them how to demean themselves, disparage their religion and their fatherland, divest themselves of their traditions and beliefs, and to regard as sacred anything Western." For al-Banna this sociocultural campaign "was more dangerous than the political and military campaigns by far."[37]

Al-Banna thus came to perceive his life's mission as the countering of the corruption of Islamic society. The religiomoral leadership disappointed him by their passivity in the face of the situation. For example, a prominent Islamic scholar whose writings he respected, Shaykh Yusuf al-Dajwi, advised him that "in such circumstances it is enough for a man to take care of himself and to steer himself clear in this age of gross materialism and godlessness."[38] Encounters like these led al-Banna to believe that existing groups, even those concerned by the moral corruption of the times, were not effective in meeting the challenge. On the basis of the reception to his informal lectures and speeches in coffeehouses in Cairo and Ismailia, al-Banna determined early in 1928 that the time had come to organize formally, and with six of his associates he established al-Ikhwan al-Muslimun (the Muslim Brothers).

Initially the Brotherhood concentrated on educational and devotional programs, calling people to a life proper to Islamic faith and practice. The movement spread rapidly in villages and towns near Ismailia and then in the Nile delta area, in Cairo, and beyond. By 1934, when al-Banna moved to Cairo, the Brotherhood had established schools for girls as well as boys, trade schools, and home textile industries in fifty towns. In keeping with Hasan al-Banna's reaffirmation of the teaching that Islam is a comprehensive way of life, the Brotherhood grounded its teaching in a wide network of social service institutions that provided direct assistance to displaced rural migrants newly arrived in urban areas. Such concrete, practical assistance was not available from either the more traditional associations like the Sufi Brotherhoods or the government agencies. The Muslim Brotherhood was perceived as making the effort to meet widespread human needs and grew rapidly in the 1930s.

The Muslim Brotherhood had a distinctive character in that it was Islamic in its goals and concepts but not directly associated with older Islamic institutions or structures. It did not reject them so much as go beyond them. Although al-Banna had a close association with a Sufi order, the action orientation of the Brotherhood "was very different from the passive retreatism of the Orders."[39] In its organization, however, the Brotherhood made use of techniques that reflected the *tariqah* traditions of the Sufi Brotherhood. New members swore an oath in a process similar to admission to a tariqah, and members were expected to perform regular devotional exercises similar to those required by an order. Al-Banna listed prayer and *dhikr* (the Sufi-style remembrance of God) as the first of the duties in the Qur'anic reformation of society and prescribed a daily recitation of a selection from the Qur'an. However, the Brotherhood went beyond the tariqah-style organization in providing social welfare services and in its political activism. Similarly, although the Brotherhood sometimes worked through mosques and later established its own mosques, it was not simply a mosque organization. In addition, while al-Banna consulted and worked with ulama, the learned traditionalist scholars did not contribute significantly to the organization. The Brotherhood was composed instead of devout non-ulama who studied their faith and advocated putting it directly into practice.

The formal organization of the Muslim Brotherhood evolved over time.[40] It began simply with a small core of people who undertook tasks as the need arose. However, as the movement grew, certain structures were established to meet organizational needs. At the core of the Muslim Brotherhood was, first, the general guide who served as supreme authority of the group but was required from the outset to be in active mutual consultation with General Guidance Council which developed in place of the older inner core of original members. By the mid-1930s, the membership of this Guidance Council was elected by the third major part of the organizational structure, the Consultative Assembly. The Assembly met annually, its membership taken from the regional branches of the Brotherhood. The regional organizations duplicated the national, with the final level of organization being the small group at the local level, the "battalions" or "families" within which the regular members worked.

In addition to the regular structure, there was a variety of other special-function organizations associated with the Brotherhood. These included the groups active in publications and various social welfare activities. In addition, during World War II, under pressure from militants within the group and increasing government pressures on the organization, a "special section" or "secret apparatus" was created. The secret apparatus became the group most active in defending the movement against the police and was responsible for those activities of violent opposition in which some Muslim Brothers engaged during and after World War II.

The broader issue of the appropriateness or necessity of the use of force in accomplishing the mission of the Brotherhood also began to be debated by the late 1930s. A small group left the Brotherhood and formed the Shabab Muhammad when al-Banna rejected reform by violent methods. A debate commenced among fundamentalists which continues to the present in Egypt regarding whether or not it is obligatory to engage in holy war to purify society. Although the issue was theologically significant, the defections in the 1930s and 1940s "did not seriously retard the Society's [i.e., the Brotherhood's] advance in numbers and influence."[41]

The Muslim Brotherhood was similar in organization to a revolutionary political party on the Leninist model or an activist labor union. In an often-quoted statement, al-Banna defined the movement as "a Salafiyya message, a Sunni way, a Sufi truth, a political organization, an athletic group, a cultural-educational union, an economic company, and a social idea."[42] In another context, al-Banna emphasized the importance of the mission rather than the organization when he told the brothers, "you are not a benevolent organization, nor a political party, nor a local association with strictly limited aims. Rather, you are a new spirit making its way into the heart of this nation and revivifying it through the Qur'an."[43]

The Brotherhood rapidly became a rival of the Wafd Party as a mass organization in Egypt, although it never formally became a political party. During the 1930s it continued its role as a social and religious support group advocating the transformation of Egyptian society based on a return to Islam—a message of increasing political significance as Egyptians became discouraged with the Wafd and the other representatives of the political elite. The political impact of the Brotherhood was felt directly through its organization of, or participation in, mass demonstrations. During World War II the increasingly visible corruption of the Wafd and the pressure of the British occupation under wartime conditions gave the Brotherhood opportunities to show its strength through popular protests. In addition, the growing competition helped to strengthen the role of the "secret Apparatus" which had been created by militants within the Brotherhood because of the need to defend members from government pressures and to take the initiative in the battle for control of the streets during demonstrations.

Al-Banna was jailed briefly in 1941 for his role in organizing a mass meeting condemning the British, and animosities between the Brotherhood and the government deepened during the years of the Second World War. The situation in Egypt after the war bordered on the chaotic, with the king (now King Farouk), the British, the Wafd Party, and the Brotherhood all competing for popular influence. The political turmoil reached a violent climax in 1948 when a member of the Brotherhood murdered the Egyptian prime minister. In the following year, Hasan al-Banna was murdered, probably in retaliation, and the Brotherhood was officially suppressed. Egypt was heading toward revolution.

Although these events plunged the organization into disarray in the early 1950s, core members nonetheless formed an alliance with young officers of the Egyptian military who had begun to plan for the overthrow of the government. This group, the Free Officers, led by Gamal Abdel Nasser, took control of Egypt in 1952. In the period of consolidation and definition of the revolution from 1952 to 1954, the Brotherhood and the new Revolutionary Command Council worked together. However, when Nasser emerged as the leading figure in the new political system, an attempt was made by some in the Brotherhood to kill him in 1954. This provided the occasion for the execution and imprisonment of many of the Brotherhood. For a time the movement was crushed, ending twenty-five years of prominence on the Egyptian scene.

As powerful as the Brotherhood was, it nonetheless represented a minority voice within Egyptian society. Following World War II it reached a peak of influence, with one-half million people actively involved and another one-half million supporters and sympathizers. Nonetheless, the power elite of the time was committed to a vision of Egypt as a modern and Westernized society. The period represents the ascendancy of the rationalist Islamic modernist tradition, personified in the experience of Taha Husayn (1889–1973). Rejected and harassed for his writings in the 1920s, he became the dominant intellectual and literary critic of the 1940s and beyond. He was minister of education from 1950 to 1952 and, following the Revolution, continued to be a major force in the cultural life of the Egyptian elite. Taha Husayn believed that "Europe is the modern world" and that "independent Egypt must become a part of Europe, for that is the only way to become a part of the modern world."[44]

That was the challenge for the fundamentalists, who had yet to counter effectively the positive vision of Europe. In that era the fundamentalists ultimately lost the battle for the soul of Egypt, for the masses were mobilized by young military officers who promised, not a return to Islam, but a more effective program of progress and modernization. Nasser was himself more representative of the liberal tradition of Zaghloul than of the revivalist tradition of the Sudanese Mahdi or Jamal al-Din al-Afghani. Fundamentalism was not persuasive to Sunni Arabs caught up in a general enthusiasm for Western civilization. The message of the Brotherhood appealed instead to those, still in the minority, who were concerned or alarmed about the impact of the West on Egypt. This group was characterized not so much by a shared class and status as by the degree of social dislocation and disruption visited upon its members by the social transformations of the twentieth century. An observer who met regularly with Brotherhood groups early in the 1950s characterized the membership of the organization as including people from rural and urban lower class backgrounds, but in tone and spirit the "membership largely represented an emergent and self-conscious Muslim middle class."[45] The emergence of the Muslim Brotherhood, then, could be seen as "an effort to reinstitutionalize religious life for those whose commitment to the tradition and religion is still great, but who at the same time are already effectively touched by the forces of Westernization."[46]

Teachings and Message

The message of the Brotherhood in its first era was basically the message of al-Banna. In continuity with earlier fundamentalist missions, it stressed the comprehensive and inclusive nature of the Islam based on tawhid and the need for a transformation of all of society through a program based on the fundamentals of Islam, rather than a blind traditionalism or uncritical borrowing. Indeed, the core organizational activity of the early Brotherhood was the direct study of the fundamental sources of Islam, the Qur'an and the Sunna of the Prophet. Brotherhood leaders recognized that traditional teachers might be helpful, but they were not final authorities. One was freed from any obligation to accept the word of the medieval scholars, for the "greatest fear of the Muslim Brotherhood is that Eastern Islamic peoples may let themselves be swept along by the current of blind traditionalism."[47] In practical terms, this meant that a basic "principle of action" was the exercise of informed independent judgment, ijtihad, in order to guide "the endeavor of present-day Muslims to meet the needs of the community."[48] Al-Banna's fundamentalist emphasis on the doctrine of the unity of God (tawhid) carried with it implications for actual life in human society. More than an important tenet in a creed, "the oneness of God" served as the foundation for a program in which Islam is the proper point of reference for all aspects of life. If there is only one sovereign for humanity, it is not possible to separate religion from politics. Thus the essential message of the Brotherhood held that "the rules of Islam and its teachings are comprehensive . . . and Islam as a general faith regulates all matters of life for every race and community, in every age and time."[49]

Accompanying the message of sociomoral reconstruction was a detailed critique of the religious teachers and devotional practices of Muslims. Like Muhammad Ibn 'Abd al-Wahhab before him, al-Banna and the Brotherhood presented strong criticisms of the ulama of the day. Although al-Banna had friendly relations with some teachers and students at al-Azhar, he was strongly critical of the institution for not actively defending the cause of Islam. The ulama in general were seen as a party to the decline and corruption of the Muslim community. Al-Azhar in particular and the ulama in general were repudiated as the authentic voice of Islam. It is in this context that the nature of the Muslim Brotherhood as a nontraditional style and non-ulama or lay organization takes on special significance. Although the Brotherhood itself was not very successful in organizing activities in the rural areas, it also rejected many of the popular devotional practices of the countryside. Veneration of holy men, the use of talismans, and respect for special natural sites were all viewed as innovations which compromised the soundness of the faith.

In the villages, the processes of modernization sometimes made fundamentalist teachings attractive. Where social change undermined local customs, the resulting vacuum could open the way for a more fundamentalist approach. For example, in Kanuba, a village of Nubians was displaced in the 1930s by the flooding of their village after the extension of the Aswan Dam. The local saint cults and particularist devotional practices were disrupted by the move, and traditional Nubian popular religion found itself in crisis. The trend in Kanuba was not, however, uniformly toward secularism but toward Islamization.[50] It is difficult, however, to determine the degree of support for the Muslim Brotherhood at the village level, for the mere existence of a branch does not necessarily imply that significant numbers of peasants were involved, and until 1936, fewer than one hundred such rural branches even existed. Instead, the growth in membership in the Muslim Brotherhood up to 1954 was concentrated in the urban areas and provincial towns. Much of the contact with rural peasants occurred through the provision of medical or educational services by the Brotherhood cadre.[51]

This examination of the rural presence of the Brotherhood suggests that in addition to drawing upon themes available in the Sunni Arab fundamentalist past, al-Banna developed his own distinctive features of the fundamentalist program. Indeed, al-Banna's teachings mark a departure from a form of fundamentalism which has itself become somewhat conservative and traditional in mid- and late-twentieth-century Saudi Arabia. Modern fundamentalism is not simply a single, monolithic movement but takes many forms, reflecting the diversity of conditions within which it develops. Because fundamentalism is a response to a perceived crisis, the programs of specific fundamentalist movements are in some measure conditioned by the specific ideas and practices of "the enemy." Thus, in 1936 al-Banna issued a statement of policy touching upon some fifty issues across a spectrum of Egyptian concerns. Only a few of these addressed the special needs of the villages (the improvement of local mosque schools, the upgrading of sanitation and water purification systems), while most focused on the problems of the cities and provincial towns. The primarily urban character of the Brotherhood was also reflected in the 1951 decision to subsume under the department of labor affairs all activities on behalf of the rural peasantry.[52]

The fundamentalism that emerged in Egypt between the two world wars thus reflected the leadership's interpretation of the spirit and conditions of the times. In this sense, the Brotherhood of al-Banna was a counterforce to the emergent liberal nationalism in Egypt—in contrast to the fundamentalism of the twentieth-century Wahhabis who acted to preserve an established fundamentalist order in Saudi Arabia. It was also different from the fundamentalism that was to emerge later in opposition to the "radical" Arab Socialism of Nasser.

In short, each expression of fundamentalism, as a response to a particular perceived ideological and sociomoral threat, assumed its own life by appropriating its own unique configuration of fundamentalist options from the Sunni Arab revivalist past. This is another way of stating the fact that both the self-understanding and the sociomoral agenda of fundamentalism is of necessity shaped, at least in part, by the opposition at a particular time in a particular place. Thus the fundamentalism of the liberal era identified closely with the reform tradition of al-Afghani, ʿAbduh, and Rashid Rida and so endeavored to demonstrate the viability of Islam in the modern world.[53] This gave the message a strongly apologetic cast, similar in tone to the Islamic modernist school as a whole, and tended to obscure the more direct message of affirmation of the fundamental and not specifically modern authenticity of Islam.

Influenced to a degree by the liberal tone of the times, the Brotherhood did not advocate a revolutionary political program. As a result of the activities of the secret apparatus during and immediately following World War II and the murder of the Egyptian prime minister, al-Nuqrashi Pasha, in 1948 by a member of the Brotherhood, the organization gained a reputation for violence. However, it did not advocate the overthrow of the state by violent means, and the violent acts were often retaliatory and targeted at specific individuals. As late as 1945, in fact, Hasan al-Banna stood for election to parliament and maintained that the transformation of society was to come primarily from the transformation of the individuals within society. Although he believed that the power to reform was inextricably linked to the power to rule, al-Banna insisted that the Muslim Brotherhood was committed to broad-based social reform, not to the direct exercise of political power.[54]

Conclusion

Hasan al-Banna and the Muslim Brotherhood created and developed an urban-based fundamentalism for the Sunni Arab world which emerged as the alternative to the conservative fundamentalism of the Wahhabis. While Rida and other fundamentalist ideologues commended the efforts of ʿAbd al-ʿAziz Ibn Saʿūd to foster an Islamic state in the Arabian peninsula, Wahhabism was ill-suited to the needs of an Egyptian population facing the opportunities and the challenges of modernization on a Western model.

Muslim Brotherhoods also developed in other regions of the Sunni Arab world, such as Syria and the Sudan. The movement in Syria was created by Mustafa al-Sibaʿi

(1915–64),[55] who had lived in Egypt in the 1930s and worked with the Brotherhood there. He became a close associate of al-Banna while at the same time studying at al-Azhar and receiving the appropriate training for one of the ulama. As a student he was active in anti-imperialist demonstrations and spent time in jail in both Egypt and Syria. His treatment in a French prison during World War II permanently damaged his health.

The Syrian Brotherhood, like the Egyptian group, was active in educational and social welfare programs. Siba'i worked to develop Syrian education programs which would combine understanding of Islam and modern issues. The Syrian Brotherhood was active in politics but did not advocate revolution. Siba'i himself participated in party and parliamentary politics in the 1940s and 1950s when it was legally possible for him to do so.

In his teachings, Siba'i made a more conscious effort to present the economic implications of the Islamic message than al-Banna. He developed the concept of what he termed "Islamic Socialism" as the basis for the economic dimensions of a truly Islamic society. In this conceptualization, Siba'i did not support large-scale nationalization and opposed the concept of class conflict, while he affirmed the lawful character of private property and constructive competition.[56]

The Syrian Brotherhood clashed with the emerging political power in Syria of military officers who took control of the government and also with the Ba'th Party, the major force in Syria in the development of Arab Socialism. The organization was suppressed in the 1950s and endured persecution during the period of Egyptian and Syrian political unification under Nasser's leadership from 1958 to 1961. As was the case in Egypt, the era of non-revolutionary participation within a liberal parliamentary political system ended with the rise of Arab Socialist leaders in the 1950s.

In the Sudan the Muslim Brotherhood movement emerged in the late 1940s as a merger of local Islamic groups with leaders influenced by the Egyptian Brotherhood. Islamic reformist and revivalist groups had developed among the Western-educated Sudanese in the 1930s, but they were little more than intellectual discussion groups at that time. However, the groups became more visible in the era of nationalist politics following World War II. The British, who still controlled the Sudan in the years immediately following World War II, began to allow more direct action by Sudanese political parties. This made public advocacy of the Islamic revival less dangerous than it had been previously.

In 1954 leaders of local Islamist groups and students returning from Egypt combined to form the Sudanese Muslim Brotherhood. The Sudanese group had no formal organizational ties with the Egyptian Brotherhood, but there were many shared interests. Egyptian publications were widely read by Sudanese Brothers, and the group in the Sudan demonstrated to support the Egyptian Brotherhood in their opposition to negotiations which compromised on the issue of British withdrawal from Egypt. In addition, the Sudanese organization shared the Egyptian opposition to the emergence of Nasserite Arab Socialism. During the 1940s and 1950s the Sudanese Brotherhood appealed primarily to students and young educated professionals and did not organize significant social programs outside of the campuses. In this formative era, the Brotherhood in the Sudan was a small group of intellectuals who were beginning to think through the implications of the Islamic message for the Sudan.

A distinctive challenge in the Sudan lay in the fact that the major political organizations were also identified with Islam. The two major political parties which dominated the newly created parliament in the early 1950s were the Ummah Party, created by a son of the Sudanese Mahdi as the political wing of the Ansar movement, and the National Unionist Party, which was supported by Sayyid 'Ali al-Mirghani, the leader of the largest tariqah in the Sudan. The Sudanese Brotherhood thus had to compete to prove its Islamic legitimacy in a way that was not necessary in Egypt, and to do so without the natural advantages provided by the tribal bases of support enjoyed by both the Ansar and the Khatmiyyah in their home regions.

As did their counterparts in Egypt, the Sudanese branch of the Brotherhood responded to the concerns of the era of liberal nationalism. It was active in opposing imperial control of Islamic countries and sought reform rather than revolution, preferring to work within a system of parliamentary politics. The lay organizational model was perhaps the most significant contribution of the Egyptian Muslim Brotherhood to its counterpart in the Sudan, for in providing an alternative to both the traditional popular organizations (such as the Sufi orders) and the modern associations (such as trade unions and political parties), the new model served well as "a protest movement couched in a traditional Islamic idiom that expresses the ethos of a people."[57]

The era of liberal Egyptian nationalism came to an end with the victory of Nasser in the struggle for control of Egypt in the 1950s. This victory also signaled the end of al-Banna's fundamentalism, which can be said to have died in the jails of Nasser's Egypt. The organization created by al-Banna was outlawed, but survived underground, and thus entered a new era in the 1950s.

Egyptian Fundamentalism in the Age of Nasser

The victory of Nasser and his revolutionary leadership in Egypt changed the situation within which fundamentalism would develop in Egypt. The period from 1954 until 1967 was for all practical purposes, the "Age of Nasser." The rapid growth of Nasser's stature from a young unknown officer in the Egyptian Army to the symbol of resurgent Arab nationalism and then of Arab socialism pre-empted any other potential mass movement in Egypt.

Under Nasser, the basic debate and discourse took place within the framework of a more radical and socialist set of concepts than had been provided by liberal nationalism. The new regime in Egypt was able to create a widespread sympathy and mass support for its goals. Nasser was able, with this support, to bring an end to the organizations of liberal nationalism such as the Wafd Party. He was also able to reduce the effective action of both the Egyptian radical left and the Muslim fundamentalists. Jailed or threatened with persecution after 1954, the leaders of the Brotherhood had little opportunity to present their case to the people. A second round of suppression and executions in the mid-1960s only exacerbated this situation.

In response, Egyptian fundamentalism became an underground movement, with much of its activity within the prisons of Nasser's Egypt. In this context, fundamentalism itself became radicalized.

The evolution of Muslim fundamentalism in Egypt in this period is epitomized in the life and career of Sayyid Qutb (1906–66). In his student days Qutb was influenced by the ideals of liberal nationalism and became a supporter of the Wafd Party. He had contact with the major rationalist modernists of the 1920s and 1930s. In his early career, Qutb was a secularist author and critic, but by the early 1950s, his perspective shifted "from that of a secularist *adib* [literary intellectual] . . . to that of an Islamic *da'iyah* [missionary or summoner]."[58]

This shift mirrored Qutb's increasing disaffection with the West, deepened by his perceptions of political developments in Egypt and the broader Arab world. During World War II, British control of Egypt had been exercised openly in ways that publicly humiliated Egyptian leaders. Qutb also came to believe that Great Britain and the United States were promoting Jewish emigration to Palestine as a way of attacking Islam. Coupled in his mind with these offensive behaviors was Qutb's examination of the French suppression of nationalist movements in Syria, Morocco, Tunisia, and Algeria. The accumulating evidence convinced him that the goal of the Western states was to conquer and destroy Islam.[59]

Increasingly aware of the social problems in Egyptian society in the postwar era, Qutb felt that the "Western solution" only made things worse, while the widespread adoption of secularist attitudes threatened to strip Muslims of their one indisputable indigenous prize, their religious faith. "There is a ridiculous servility to the European fashion of divorcing religion from life," he wrote, "a separation necessitated by the nature of their religion, but not by the nature of Islam."[60] Possessed of the conviction that Islam provides the comprehensive remedy to the problems of social injustice and political oppression, he moved toward the position of the Muslim Brotherhood of the late 1940s, although he was still not directly affiliated with the organization.

Qutb's negative view of Western civilization was reinforced by his experiences during a two-year visit to the United States, in order to study educational administration. He found Americans to be materialistic and lacking in spiritual values and was disturbed by the popular and media support in the United States for the nascent state of Israel. After his return to Egypt, he wrote that in the United States, "any objectives other than the immediate utilitarian ones are by-passed and any human element other than ego is not recognized. Where the whole life is dominated by such materialism, there is no scope for laws beyond provisions for labor and production. The result is class struggle which becomes inevitable and visibly evident."[61]

Of course Qutb was not the only Egyptian intellectual of the younger generation to be disenchanted with liberal nationalism and secular rationalist thought and to be radicalized by the failure of the westernizing liberals in Egypt. However, in contrast to most of the intellectuals of the time, he did not embrace the radical modernism of Nasser's Arab Socialism as a solution. Instead, he appropriated the historical message of Islamic fundamentalism and adapted it to the circumstances present in Nasser's Egypt. Moreover, he attempted this adaptation at a critical time in the life of the Muslim Brotherhood. The murder of Hasan al-Banna had come at a time, in the late 1940s, when the Egyptian political system was disintegrating and the call for reform was replaced by demands for revolution. It was hardly a propitious moment for the Brotherhood to lose their most visible leader. Al-Banna's successor as general guide, Hasan al-Hudaybi, had not been in the original core group and did not have significant intellectual influence. The task of Brotherhood intellectuals initially was to interpret the heritage of al-Banna, who had not left many publications.

Soon, however, the revolution of 1952 and the suppression of the Brotherhood in 1954 created a major ideological crisis for the organization. Until this time, the Brotherhood had focused its polemics against Britain and the role of the king in Egyptian politics. Now, however, an Egyptian and Muslim government (of the Free Officers) had put them through the "great ordeal" of 1954—a different situation altogether, and one that left them wanting for theoretical tools capable of analyzing this new regime in terms of the categories of Islam.

Sayyid Qutb thus played a major role in the history of fundamentalism in Egypt in providing the intellectual framework by which to analyze Nasser's regime. It was not as a secular literary critic, or even as a pre-revolutionary writer inclined toward a more vigorous affirmation of Islam, that he performed this role. It was instead in the prisons of Nasser's Egypt that Qutb developed the concepts and perspectives which made an effective fundamentalist critique of Nasser possible. With this achievement, Qutb became influential outside of Egypt as well, since Muslims in many areas faced newly successful nationalist governments which posed challenges and threats similar to those posed by Nasser.

The radical fundamentalism of Qutb challenged the ideology of the Nasser regime on almost every key issue. Indeed, Qutb's final book, *Ma'alim fi al-tariq (Milestones)*, provided the basis for the charges brought in the Egyptian courts against members of the Brotherhood in the trials of the mid-1960s, for it presented unambiguously the radical fundamentalist indictment of Muslim society of the 1960s and proposed immediate and direct steps toward the establishment of an authentically Islamic society.

Nasser's popularity rested on his position as the great hero of Arab nationalism and the creator of the most prominent form of Arab socialism. Nasserism held that liberation from foreign rule should be accompanied by the Arab repudiation of domestic exploiters as well. The most complete articulation of Nasserism is presented in the National Charter of 1962.[62] The public visibility of non-Nasserite Muslim positions was therefore limited. Even in Saudi Arabia, where leaders were insulated by the prestige of the Wahhabi tradition, there was concern over the impact of the spread of Nasserism. A prominent prince of the Saudi royal family announced his support for Nasser's ideas, and the Saudi government itself announced reforms in 1962 in partial response to the rhetoric of nationalism and social reform associated with Nasserism. In Egypt, Nasser successfully co-opted most of the Muslim establishment. He nationalized al-Azhar University in 1961, expanded the curriculum, extended government controls over the faculty, and increased the number of scholarships for foreign students at al-Azhar as a means of exporting his principles. And in general, leaders of the Egyptian ulama proclaimed the compatibility of Arab socialism and Islam, presenting Nasserism as a form of Islamic socialism.

The Brotherhood's ability to stem the tide of Nasserism seemed severely limited. However, the special attention given by Nasser to the trial and execution of Qutb and others in the mid-1960s indicates that he regarded the Brotherhood as a serious threat. This was especially true in ideological terms, and Qutb's ideas represented the major force in this challenge.

Qutb's ideas have been summarized by the Egyptian historian Abdel Azim Ramadan, who notes that Qutb "considered belief in God's divinity, and performing the rites of prayer inadequate as long as a man owed worship to other than God, and rested sovereignty on man. He branded all Islamic societies unbelieving."[63] Ramadan notes that Qutb believed that for the necessary Islamic revival to take place, "a vanguard must resolve to set it in motion and to proceed in the abyss of *jahiliyya* [unbelief] reigning all over the world. . . . The forming of this vanguard begins with an individual who believes in the faith coming from God to mankind; and in him begins the existence of the Islamic society."[64] All of this will involve real struggle and conflict, because unbelieving people will not surrender easily. There is an obligation to fight for the cause of true Islamic revival which all Muslims share.

This was a direct challenge to the fundamental principles of Nasserism and was recognized as such by the government. The report in 1965 by the Legislative Committee regarding the Brotherhood charged them with the denial of Arab nationalism, defense of class divisions, and rejection of patriotic morality. In making these charges, they quote *Milestones* directly.[65]

The major conceptual contribution of Qutb was to provide an intellectual and theoretical foundation for the concrete rejection of Nasserism and the other Western-based radical ideologies of his day. One could no longer simply attack the state as being a foreign puppet. Nasser was the first authentically Egyptian ruler of the country for millennia. Egyptians had gotten what they wanted: a successful nationalist committed to social transformation. Qutb explained why true Muslims could not accept this.

Qutb's historical analysis of the basis for rejecting nationalism and socialism opened the way for a broader conceptual basis of criticism. The enemies of the Prophet Muhammad were the people of belligerent and stubborn ignorance. It is this concept that is developed by Sayyid Qutb and becomes a key principle in his analysis. Before Qutb, the word jahiliyya simply refered to the period before the time of the Prophet Muhammad or to those people at the time of Muhammad who did not know about him. However, Qutb used the term inclusively, extending it to all who rebelled willfully against God's rule. In this sense, "jahiliyya . . . takes the form of claiming the right to create values, to legislate rules of collective behavior, and to choose any way of life that rests with men, without regard to what God has prescribed."[66] Jahiliyya is rebellion against God and results in oppression and the exploitation of humanity. In Qutb's analysis nationalism imparted sovereignty to the Arab nation rather than to God. The duty of the true Muslim was to combat this satanic form of unbelief.

The South Asian Muslim revivalist, Maulana Abul-Ala Maududi, has also appropriated the concept of jahiliyya in analyzing modern society. However, Qutb brought the idea to a "more literal, militant conclusion."[67] From the very early days of the Muslim community, for example, people had argued about the legitimacy of identifying self-described Muslims as unbelievers and inflicting some punishment upon them. *Takfir* is the act of identifying someone as an unbeliever *(kafir)*. Many Muslims felt that this judgment was for God alone, while others felt that it was their obligation in order to preserve the faithful community. The early Kharijite community, a group of anarchistic purists who separated from both Shi'ism and Sunnism, engaged in takfir during the first civil war in the Islamic community, and fundamentalists have since been labeled as Kharijites because of their strong criticisms of fellow Muslims. Takfir is implied in Qutb's usage of jahiliyya and made explicit in many of his evaluations of his contemporaries.

Furthermore, Qutb lifted the term *hijrah* from its original context in the flight of Muhammad and his followers from Mecca to Medina and used it to describe a general stage in the development of any Muslim society: hijrah is the act of devout Muslims living in a society which is at the stage of jahiliyya. The devout are to withdraw from that society in order to create a core of activists who can transform society into an authentic Islamic society. In this view, Islam and jahiliyya cannot coexist, and the prevailing social order must be overturned.[68]

In Qutb's hands, the themes of Islamic fundamentalism were woven into a dramatic liberation theology demanding an unremitting commitment rather than offering a choice. In discussions in the era of liberal nationalism, one could speak "the Islamic alternative." Many committed Muslims still speak in those terms. Even the more dramatic affirmations of contemporary Islam as presented by Muammar Qaddafi of Libya speak of Qaddafi's approach as the Third Universal Theory. In Qutb's later writings, however, there is little willingness to recognize anything beneficial in the West and a similar lack of desire to create a synthesis or a bridge to the West. In Qutb, the inclusive vision of the Islamic modernism of 'Abduh virtually disappeared.

Qutb himself had undergone a development in this regard. The ideology he once had offered as a guideline hardened into dogma by 1965. The varieties of possibilities for Islamic reform were narrowed to one cast in absolute terms, requiring the complete allegiance of the believers.[69] The duty of a Muslim was to obey the divine imperative. Here was a formal Islamic rationale for a modern revolution.

Underground Fundamentalism

The organizational expressions of the emerging ideologies were curtailed by the ruthlessness of Nasser's suppression of the old Muslim Brotherhood, whose leaders were in prison or in exile. The possibilities of recruiting new members were very limited in that situation. There was, however, a small, faithful core of fundamentalists drawn from those who had been members of the Brotherhood and some new recruits from among the same social groups that were first attracted to the organization. Contacts with the jailed leaders al-Hudaybi and Qutb continued, with female members of the Brotherhood apparently playing an important role. Zaynab al-Ghazali, for example, had been head of the Muslim Women's Association, and by the late 1940s she had worked closely with the Brotherhood. After the suppression of the Brotherhood in 1954, she had maintained contact with Hudaybi and other leaders and her home became a study center for members of the Brotherhood. In 1962, she met with the sisters of Sayyid Qutb, and her groups began to use sections from *Milestones* as a basis for their studies. At this time, Qutb was writing this book in prison, and his sisters would smuggle portions out from time to time.[70]

The spirit of the time, and the structure of authority, is reflected in Zaynab al-Ghazali's discussion of their aims in that era. "We decided—with instructions from the Imam Sayyid Qutb and with the permission of al-Hudaybi—to continue the period of instruction and creation and preparation and planting the faith in tawhid."[71] Al-Ghazali concludes this section of her autobiographical account with the observation: "What is it to us if some generations come to an end and other generations come? The important thing is that the preparations continue. The important thing is for us to keep working until our generation is finished and then we pass the banner which raises "There is no god but the One God and Muhammad is the Messenger of God' to the noble sons who come after us."[72]

In this way, a small, dedicated cadre was maintained, and the thinking of the group was refined. The group around Zaynab al-Ghazali had ties with other similar groups based on the remnants of the old Brotherhood organization. By 1964 the groups had recreated a small and still weak structure which had little impact. The release of Sayyid Qutb and others from prison in that year helped to increase the activity. However, this was soon brought to an end by the government. In 1965 Nasser's police arrested or detained hundreds of people on charges of conspiracy to overthrow the government. This time even those who simply were engaged in educational work, like Zaynab al-Ghazali, were jailed. Qutb and other leaders were executed, and the prisons became the theater of operations for what was left of the fundamentalist organizations.

In the period between 1965 and the release of most of the religiopolitical prisoners by Anwar al-Sadat in 1971, the main strands of fundamentalist ideology crystalized. One group followed the older leadership of the Brotherhood, who continued to emphasize a nonrevolutionary strategy. In prison al-Hudaybi wrote a book called *Missionaries, Not Judges (Du'ah la Qudah)*, published in 1969, in which he opposed the radical tendencies articulated in *Milestones* although he did not directly attack Qutb. For al-Hudaybi and the other old-guard Brotherhood leaders, the problem was that Egyptians needed to be educated and called to the faith, not that Egyptians had ceased to be Muslims. Al-Hudaybi rejected the practice of takfir, thereby rejecting the rationale for active revolution.

Al-Hudaybi's position was not accepted by many of the younger militants in the prisons. The comprehensive efficiency of Nasser's police had brought into the jails hundreds of young people who were suspected of favoring an Islamic program. Students who had simply distributed a few pamphlets on a campus found themselves in jail along with experienced militants. The prisons became a new kind of educational center, in which the new recruits studied Qutb and Maududi and became persuaded that the society which produced the torturers and the prison camps was indeed worthy of being labeled jahiliyya—an unbelieving, anti-Islamic society. The debates among the prisoners in the period between 1965 and 1971 laid the ideological foundations for the different groups which emerged during the 1970s. The critical issues were, first, whether and under what conditions takfir was permissible, and second, whether all of Egyptian society, or only the state itself, should be identified as jahiliyya. These were hardly abstract debates, for they eventuated in a variety of concrete fundamentalist programs in the era of the "Islamic Resurgence."

The Era of Nasser: The Sudanese Case

As might have been expected in the heyday of Nasserism, Islamic fundamentalism was weak and barely visible virtually everywhere in the Sunni Arab world. The dominant ideals of the day were defined in terms of nationalism and socialism. In Syria, for example, the appeal of Arab Socialist ideologies and the effective suppression of the Brotherhood meant that fundamentalist organizations had little support.

The Sudan was one of the few places in the Arab world in the era of Nasser where a fundamentalist group maintained positive visibility. During the 1950s nationalism and socialism were not active rivals of Islam in the Sudan, for nationalism had an Islamic character, since it had been developed and articulated by northern Muslim Sudanese. Furthermore, the largest political parties at the time of independence in 1956 drew their support from the major Muslim organizations in the Sudan. While this meant that the particular concerns of the small Sudanese Muslim Brotherhood were often overshadowed, advocates of Muslim programs were not jailed. The Brotherhood continued to participate in the political system along with the other major parties. When a conservative military group took control of the country in a 1958 coup, the Brotherhood joined the illegal democratic opposition with the other outlawed parties and participated in the revolution of 1964 which ousted the military regime. Thus, in 1965, while Sayyid Qutb was on trial in Egypt, Dr. Hasan Turabi, the leader of the Brotherhood in the Sudan, was emerging as a major leader of the parliamentary opposition. The party supported by the Brotherhood, the Islamic Charter Front, did win seats in parliament and advocated an Islamic constitution for the Sudan.

The conflict between the Sudanese Brotherhood and an Arab socialist challenge occurred in the 1970s. In 1969, the second parliamentary political system was overthrown by another military group, this time made up of younger officers who were more prone to radicalism. The leader of this group was Ja'far al-Numayri, who admired Nasser and in the early years of his rule attempted to bring Arab Socialism to the Sudan. In the early 1970s he attempted to create a single mass political organization, the Sudanese Socialist Union, which was modeled after the Arab Socialist Union of Nasser.

In the early years of his rule, Numayri attempted to destroy the power of the older political organizations. He was able to suppress a Mahdist revolt in 1970 and destroyed the Sudanese Communist Party after Communist officers attempted a coup in 1971. However, Numayri did not have the nationalist and personal appeal of Nasser, and the parties that he faced continued to have considerable popular support, in contrast to the Wafd and other parties in Egypt in the 1950s. As a result, Numayri's efforts to mobilize popular support seemed more artificial than Nasser's, and the end result was that Numayri faced effective opposition from the civilian political organizations throughout the 1970s.

The Sudanese Muslim Brotherhood was part of the continuing opposition. They cooperated closely with the Mahdist Ummah Party and the National Unionist Party (NUP), which had Khatmiyyah support. In particular, Hasan Turabi, the Brotherhood leader, worked closely with the leader of the Mahdists, Sadiq al-Mahdi. The opposition coalition mounted a number of efforts to overthrow Numayri, reaching a climax in 1976 when a major coup attempt failed. The 1976 experience showed that Numayri did not have the power or influence to destroy the opposition, but it also showed that the old parties did not have the strength by themselves to defeat Numayri. (When Numayri was finally overthrown in 1985, the revolution involved support from unions and professional associations as well as the older parties and was accomplished through a military coup in support of those groups.)

During the 1970s, the Sudanese Brotherhood continued to support the ideal of a parliamentary political system. Islamization was to be a gradual process of conversion of society through the transformation of the lives of individuals. The Brotherhood did not seek to withdraw from society but rather cooperated with other organizations within society. In this the Brotherhood of Turabi was in sharp contrast to the Egyptian Brotherhood as inspired by Qutb.

By 1977, the conflict between Numayri and the older political parties appeared to have reached a stalemate. After a series of meetings and negotiations, Numayri announced, in 1977–78, a series of actions as a part of a "national reconciliation." Hasan Turabi and Sadiq al-Mahdi were the two major opposition figures who became reconciled with the Numayri regime. Turabi became the attorney-general of the Sudan and Numayri appointed him as the chair of a committee to examine Sudanese law to begin the process of bringing it into conformity with Islamic law. The careful deliberations of the committee under Turabi's leadership reflected the gradualist approach of the Sudanese Brotherhood.

The Brotherhood was the only older political group that became clearly active in the Numayri regime. The Mahdists and the Khatmiyyah made some compromises with Numayri, but neither group formally participated in the government in the same way that members of the Brotherhood did. As Numayri became more autocratic in the late 1970s, the older political groups again began to pull away from Numayri, who had never taken the step of legalizing the old parties.

The development of fundamentalism in the Sudan during the 1970s thus is different from the experience in Egypt. While there was conflict between the chief articulator of Arab Socialism and the Sudanese Brotherhood, in the end Numayri and the

Brotherhood cooperated in a way that Nasser and the Egyptian Brotherhood never did. Numayri never had the independent appeal of Nasser and thus by the late 1970s needed the added support that could be gained by reconciliation with at least one major Islamic organization. By the late 1970s Arab Socialism was losing its appeal, and the day of the resurgence of Islam had come.

The Resurgence of Islam

The new, radical form of fundamentalism generated from the prisons of Nasser's Egypt awaited a moment when the appeals of Arab Socialism would wane. The moment came suddenly in 1967 when Israel defeated the leading Arab Socialist states in the Six Day War. The time from the defeat in 1967 until Nasser's death in 1970 marks the beginning of a major reorientation of perspectives within the Sunni Arab world and a radical reassessment of Arab Socialism as it had developed during the 1960s. One interpretation of the defeat held that it was God's punishment on a people who had abandoned the straight path of Islam. In fact, the secularism of the era of Nasser was giving way to a heightened sense of religious awareness among Christians and Muslims.

The new mood was clearly expressed in the reactions to visions of the Virgin Mary reported at a small Coptic Christian Church in Zeitoun, near Cairo, beginning in April 1968. Reports of the sightings brought thousands of Muslims and Christians to Zeitoun, and the gathering took on symbolic significance as a representation of the increased religious sensitivities of all Egyptians. An observer at the time noted that for "most Egyptians the apparition is connected to the Six-Day War of June 1967, in which Egypt suffered a military defeat that left the country in despair. Specifically, the Virgin had come to the Egyptians to restore faith in God and give hope and moral support to the defeated, perhaps even to lead the Egyptians to victory."[73] Significantly, the crowds at Zeitoun included sizable numbers of middle-class workers and well-educated semiprofessionals disillusioned by the 1967 defeat and by continued uncertainty within the country.

This return to religion on the part of a significant proportion of the Egyptian population indicates that the Islamic resurgence of the 1970s was not solely or simply the creation of the small groups of militants spawned in Nasser's jails. They were instead able to draw upon a deeper and more widespread disaffection with modern secularist approaches to life. The evolution of the political system reflected this disaffection as well, and the political reaction against Nasserism was even more prominent than a fundamentalist or "return-to-religion" critique. As a result of the conditions created by the 1967 War, Nasser was forced to retreat from his earlier activist leadership of the Arab world. He was constrained to accept financial support from those in the Arab world who had most opposed his Arab Socialism, especially Saudi Arabia. Unable to bear the cost of the continuing War of Attrition with Israel, he accepted the peace initiative of the U.S. Secretary of State William Rogers in 1970. Nasser also began the process of modifying the vast bureaucratic structure of state socialism which dominated the Egyptian economy.[74]

Fundamentalism in the Era of Sadat

Upon his death in 1970, Nasser was succeeded by Anwar as-Sadat. Sadat had been personally loyal to Nasser but was not among those in the leadership group clearly identified with ideological Nasserism. In the struggle for prominence within the group, Sadat downplayed the socialism advocated by his rivals and encouraged anti-socialist elements in Egypt, especially students who were susceptible to the claims of resurgent Islamic fundamentalism. Banned by Nasser from public meetings, the nascent fundamentalists welcomed Sadat's lifting of the ban and aroused expectations that the rise of this self-styled "Believing President" boded well for their cause. Sadat's decision to release Islamic militants from prison in 1971 served to nurture those expectations. Other acts also opened the way for greater public visibility of fundamentalist Islam. The new constitution promulgated in 1971, for example, asserted that the principles of Islamic law would now be "a principal source of legislation." At the same time, fundamentalists were allowed more freedom in presenting their views publicly. The media, under government control, increased the amount of programming devoted to religious subjects, much of it catering to fundamentalist positions. Although formally outlawed, the Muslim Brotherhood published *al-Da'wa* and *al-Itisam,* popular magazines which were recognized as organs of the group.

In short, Sadat adopted what he thought to be a politically pragmatic attitude toward the revivalists. Although he was not a fundamentalist, he seemed convinced that the encouragement of fundamentalist Islamic expressions would ultimately strengthen his political position across the board. His political strategy aimed at the removal of leftists and hard-line Nasserites—a goal shared by the members of the Muslim Brotherhood. The tacit alliance with the Islamic opposition in Egypt, including the Brotherhood, won Sadat the political strength with which to liberalize and privatize the Egyptian economy, reform the constitution toward a greater protection of human rights and the legalization of some opposition parties, and in the larger historical picture, nudge Egypt ever closer to a democratic polity. However, his Islamic base was alienated by certain of his policies, not the least of which was his move toward reconciliation with Israel in the wake of Egyptian euphoria over the perceived military victory over Israel in 1973.[75] The decline in Egypt's economic fortunes in the late 1970s reinforced the Islamic opposition in its increasing mistrust of Sadat and his retinue, and in January and May 1977 large-scale food riots exposed the instability of the regime.[76] His assassination at the hands of the forces he had unleashed occurred a decade after the promulgation of the new constitution. During this decade, Islamic fundamentalism expanded beyond its core advocates—the militants in the prisons of Nasser—to become one of the major forces in Egyptian politics.

The 1970s was not a time of a simple return to "Islam-in-general." There are many ways in which the Islamic message can be expressed, but the resurgence in the 1970s adopted a fundamentalist mode. Islamic modernism had played an important role in the development of Muslim Brotherhood ideology in the days of Hasan al-Banna. However, Islamic modernism tended to be identified with the attempts to borrow from the West and with the liberal nationalist and Nasserite ideologies. 'Abduh's perspective was the "theological orthodoxy" of the 1950s and 1960s. The chief representatives of this orthodoxy were now seen as compromising with westernizing secularism and as having become the "ulama of the authorities," a phrase which was to become a pejorative description by the 1980s.[77] Similarly, although there continued to be active participation by some Egyptians in Sufi Brotherhoods, the tariqahs were not the basic organization for the resurgence either. Instead, the resurgence most frequently took the form of a reaffirmation of a relatively literalist interpretation of the basic sources of Islam with an effort to avoid incorporating non-Islamic elements—in short, a fundamentalist form. Visible Islamic affirmation took place at four broad and overlapping levels.

The first level was that of the state itself. Sadat consciously identified himself and his efforts more clearly with Islam than was the case with Nasser. However, although Sadat made possible a greater freedom of expression for fundamentalists, his own state policy reflected, if anything, a greater orientation toward Islamic modernism.[78] Sadat, for example, identified the Shari'a as "a source" rather than "the source" of legislation in the constitutional debates of 1971, and his position on personal status law involved a definition of women's rights which was more modernist than fundamentalist. Through increasing state control over religious institutions, Sadat attempted to maintain the Islamic legitimacy of his state without creating an effective Islamic basis for opposition to it. However, as organized fundamentalist groups assumed a stronger role in articulating opposition to Sadat's policies throughout the 1970s, his initial support for them waned. Nonetheless, Islamic approaches had become a vital part of the political dialogue by the end of the decade. In response, Sadat did not attempt to remove Islam from the forefront of the political scene; rather, he developed and promoted a nonfundamentalist alternative which could become a kind of "civil religion" for the state, with the "Believing President" at its center.

By 1981 Sadat was moving in two major directions with regard to Islam. On the one hand, he worked actively to strengthen the Islamic image of the state. On the other hand, he began an active suppression of fundamentalist opposition groups. During the summer and autumn of 1981 he ordered the arrest and detention of thousands of people as a part of this effort. He was killed in the midst of this ongoing operation. The organizer of the assassination, Khalid al-Islambuli, acted because his brother had been arrested in this suppression.

Sadat had reaffirmed Islam as the religion of the state and the political establishment; however, it was the Islam of the modern technocratic elite, more congenial to the perspectives of Islamic modernism than to revivalism. Fundamentalist opposition to Sadat's state thus carried overtones of opposition to Islamic modernism.

A second level of Islamic affirmation in Egypt during the Sadat era was tied to a more general outpouring of renewed religious sentiment among Egyptians—the sentiments reflected in the excitement caused by the vision of the Virgin Mary at Zeitoun. Among Muslims the general revival of religious sentiment was visible in the newly crowded mosques during Friday noon prayer. Many women began to adopt Islamic dress, making use of the veil and more modest or conservative clothing. Increasing numbers of books on explicitly Islamic subjects were published, purchased, and read, while Muslim preachers and interpreters became the new media stars.

The tone and conceptualization of this level of the resurgence was fundamentalist but not socially radical. On one end of the spectrum was the immensely popular writer, Mustafa Mahmud, who achieved celebrity as a Marxist sympathizer and then, after finding Islam again, became the author of many books demonstrating the superiority of Islam to all other ideologies and the constructive relationship between Islam and modern science. His medical clinic (he started his career as a physician) is now a showplace for "the quiet Islamic revolution," and his popularity is a reflection of the influence of the "electronic mosque" and the media in the religious revival.[79] In his writings the influence of Islamic modernism is still quite visible.

Other major figures in the popular resurgence were less open to modernist ideas and more explicitly fundamentalist in their approach. Shaykh Muhammad Mutawalli al-Sha'rawi became one of the most popular preachers of the 1970s. He was educated at al-Azhar and served as minister of religious affairs (1976–78) in Sadat's cabinet. However, his fame and popularity rest on his television shows and his writings. He affirmed the specifics of the Islamic message and advocated the creation of an Islamic state, but his methods were the methods of persuasion and conversion. He stated that the "implementation of Islam starts in your heart. If everyone of us were to implement Islam in his heart and his doings—the rulers, who do not (yet) rule according to Islam—would be toppled by themselves."[80] Sha'rawi represented a middle position in the return to religion of the 1970s, in that he was not known for major new interpretations but instead affirmed a relatively strict adherence to the Islamic heritage which mirrored the religiosity of "millions of moderately educated Egyptians."[81]

Another very popular preacher, Shaykh 'Abd al-Hamid Kishk, embodied the activist, fundamentalist end of the spectrum. Kishk became blind as a child but was blessed with a remarkable memory and succeeded in gaining a degree from al-Azhar. He started a career as a preacher in 1964 in the 'Ayn al-Hayat Mosque in Cairo but was arrested during the suppression of the Muslim Brotherhood during the mid-1960s. His prison experiences deepened his opposition to the political and intellectual establishments.[82] During the 1970s he became a very popular preacher who attracted large crowds to 'Ayn al-Hayat Mosque and sold thousands of cassettes of sermons and lectures. He became an active and articulate opponent of Sadat's peace initiative with Israel and a strong critic of modernist orthodoxy and the materialist public morality of many in the political and intellectual elite. For most of the 1970s, Kishk was part of the permitted opposition, but he was imprisoned again in Sadat's last major wave of arrests. Kishk was released in 1982 and resumed his role as one of the most popular preachers of Mubarak's Egypt, although he continues to face occasional restrictions by the government.

Kishk's popularity indicated that the general return to religion was not simply a renewal of personal devotion. The resurgence involved a broader awareness of the social and political dimensions of faith and envisioned the believer as an active player in the dynamics of public life. Kishk's sermons were presented in the clear language of the people rather than the complex jargon of modernist secular ideologies, and his popularity signaled the entry of broad segments of the population into the political process, an event which shattered the assumptions of the cosmopolitan rulers and intellectuals. Political discourse was now resonant with local idioms and religious sensibilities leading to a political and social climate in which "all ideological constructions seemed thin and contrived."[83]

A third level of visible Islamic reaffirmation during the era of Sadat was the publicly permitted Islamic opposition. In addition to the popular expressions of the Islamic revival, smaller groups were actively dedicated to the propagation of fundamentalist Islam through non-revolutionary means. The core of the effort was what survived of the formal Muslim Brotherhood organization. While the Muslim Brotherhood was formally an illegal organization, Sadat allowed it to engage in many activities as if it were legal. It published magazines, organized a variety of social welfare services, and established independent mosques and schools. The leadership of the continuing group was the surviving Old Guard of the older organization. They represented those fundamentalist advocates who were willing to accept some compromise with the Sadat regime in return for some freedom of action (although Sadat never extended legal recognition to the organization). Emerging from prison in the early 1970s, the old guard presented a reformist rather than a revolutionary alternative. Hudaybi, the general guide, had set the tone in his rejection of Qutb's willingness to engage in the act of identifying people as unbelievers (takfir). The reconstituted Brotherhood (aptly labeled the "neo-Muslim Brotherhood" by the French scholar Gilles Kepel) opposed Zionism and Israel, the Christian and Western "Crusade" against Islam, communism, and secularism.[84] The group did not, however, advocate a radical program of social transformation. Its approach was gradualist, although on many occasions during the 1970s, the neo-Brotherhood was the most outspoken public group in its criticism of Sadat.

The neo-Brotherhood has not created a new ideological framework for its efforts. It remains tied to the intellectual legacy of Hasan al-Banna and, with some reservations, of Sayyid Qutb. When General Guide Hudaybi died in 1973, leadership passed to 'Umar al-Talmasani (who did not actually take the title of general guide until later), who was the leading figure in the publication of *al-Da'wa* (The call), the Brotherhood magazine. The major shift represented by the neo-Brotherhood was its commitment to nonviolent tactics. While the neo-Brotherhood continued to be committed to the goal of establishing a truly Islamic socio-political order, it pursued that goal without recourse to violence, by influencing the Muslim masses and seeking a hearing among the "Muslim" rulers.[85]

The social mission of this level of Islamic affirmation was often a matter of individual initiatives. Some members of the Brotherhood who lived outside of Egypt during the Nasser years, for example, had become quite wealthy. When they returned to Egypt during the 1970s they provided resources for Islamic economic enterprises like interest-free banks. Others provided support for the social welfare and educational institutions identified with the neo-Brotherhood. Governmental agencies were often inefficient and expensive and the Brotherhood came to be seen as providing a viable Islamic alternative to the Sadat state and its vision of society.

The fourth level of Islamic affirmation in the 1970s was the most controversial. On the extremes of the groups working to create a truly Islamic society were small groups who with varying ideological justifications advocated militant activism and violence in achieving that goal. Most Egyptians did not approve of the methods of the extremists. However, in the context of a reorientation of government policy away from radical socialism and of a major social reaffirmation of Islam, many Egyptians had sympathy for the fringe groups. Most of the groups in the 1970s had some initial tie to the old Muslim Brotherhood tradition but had already begun to break away from the old guard leadership in the last days of Nasser. The young militants, educated in Nasser's prisons, were strongly influenced by the most militant aspects of the thought of Sayyid Qutb. They did not represent a single unified movement but were instead a shifting and interacting collection of individuals and groups about whom little was known until some dramatic event would bring them to the attention of the police and the media.

The most public, and least violent, of the more militant groups are the "Islamic societies" *(jama'at islamiyyah)* which developed among students on the university campuses and, in the early 1970s, shared with Sadat an interest in eliminating the leftist—socialist domination of the campuses. The Jama'at hoped to create a truly Islamic society by first transforming university life, and they did prove useful in the overcrowded universities. They organized tutorials, assisted students in acquiring textbooks, and soon came to dominate all student organizations. They demanded gender-segregated seating in classes and special separate facilities for women. As they gained strength, the more extreme elements in the Jama'at began to engage in intimidation and violence to achieve their goal of "purified" university campuses. The showing of "unapproved" films, concerts, and various performances were disrupted by militants, and unveiled female students were sometimes assaulted. Oriented to action rather than to the elaboration of theory, the members of the Jama'at also became involved in Muslim-Christian conflicts in some of the provincial towns with large Coptic populations. An ideologue of the group, 'Isam al-Din al-'Aryan, adopted a rationale for militance based on Qutb's teachings.[86]

Thus the Jama'at were a special target in the government suppression of fundamentalist groups in 1980–81. Muslim-Christian riots in the al-Zawiyyah al-Hamrah district of Cairo in June 1981 provided a rationale for the crushing of the known Jama'at organizations. Despite Sadat's statement that only the ringleaders were arrested, and that the young people involved deserved another chance, the Jama'at groups were effectively suppressed at that time and did not reemerge as an effective force in the years following the murder of Sadat. People from the Jama'at tended either to move to the more militant groups, like al-Jihad, or to become a part of the revived Muslim Brotherhood of the 1980s.

Two different traditions of militancy had developed in the experience of Nasser's prisons. One was a politically revolutionary tradition, exemplified in both the Islamic Liberation Organization (sometimes called the "Military Academy Group") and in Jihad, which held that most Egyptians were devout Muslims and victims of an unbelieving state. Accordingly, these groups advocated programs designed to destabilize and ultimately to overthrow the government and replace it with a truly Islamic one.

The other tradition rejected all of society as unbelieving and held that all institutions in society were godless and beyond reform. These groups advocated withdrawal from society and the formation of a new, alternative, believing society which would eventually supplant the old, unbelieving one. The leading advocate of the separatist sectarian position was Shukri Mustafa, whose organization was the Society of Muslims (known as al-Takfir w'al-hijra by the media and the Egyptian authorities). Mustafa had been an agriculture student at the state university in Asyut when he was arrested in 1965 for distributing religious pamphlets as a member of the Muslim Brotherhood. Following his release from prison in Sadat's 1971 amnesty, he separated from the Brotherhood, completed his studies at Asyut, and began a preaching mission in which his newfound radicalism found a voice.

The activist themes of Qutb, no less than the historic traditions of Islamic fundamentalism, echoed in Mustafa's message. Egyptian society was irredeemable and represented as a whole the modern jahiliyya.[87] Only a small "society of Muslims" who would be separate from the unbelieving society could create the nucleus for the new truly Islamic society of the future. The medieval Muslim authorities must be rejected in favor of examination of the Qur'an and the Sunna of the Prophet as the only basis for authentic Islamic action. Mustafa advocated independent judgment (ijtihad), stressed the sole sovereignty of God (tawhid), and asserted the right to accuse others of unbelief (takfir).

In the early 1970s, his Society of Muslims lived an isolated life. Recruited largely from young, educated Egyptians of rural or lower-middle-class backgrounds, the members may have numbered as many as two thousand by the middle of the decade. The membership was watched by Egyptian security, but they did not seem to pose a threat to the state. In time, however, the society reserved the term "Muslim" only for its members, and labeled as kafir (infidel) anyone who did not accept the judgment that Egyptian society was jahiliyya. Marriage and family relations were sanctioned only within the confines of the group, and family members outside of the group were to be forgotten. Prayer and Islamic ritual were to take place only under the guidance of the group's prayer leaders who at times, the evidence suggests, released members from certain traditional obligations including Friday prayer and the hajj (pilgrimage to Mecca). Branches were established in Kuwait, Jordan, and Syria, and there is evidence of Libyan support as well.[88]

As the Egyptian government became more active in controlling the extremist movements after some incidents in 1974–75, including an attack in 1974 on a military school by another group, the Party of Islamic Liberation, Shukri Mustafa and his followers became involved in a series of events which led to the suppression of the group. The government Ministry of Waqf (Islamic trusts) issued a pamphlet charging the group with major errors of belief. In 1977 the group kidnapped the government religious official deemed responsible for the pamphlet and killed him when their demands for the release of imprisoned group members were not met. In retaliation, the Egyptian security forces arrested over six hundred members of the society and executed its leaders, Mustafa among them. Following the destruction of Shukri Mustafa's organization, the separatist, sectarian impulse seems to have receded among the younger militants. The lesson drawn from the experience of the Society of Muslims seems to have been that the jahiliyya society would not allow separation. Survival would have to involve more direct opposition. In this way, the experience of this group may have encouraged the development of jihad organizations.

The jihad tradition of militant fundamentalism started from somewhat different premises than those of Shukri Mustafa. The jihad tradition believed that the basic task was to overthrow the government of jahiliyya, accordingly it pursued a political revolutionary program. The first such group to gain significant attention was the Islamic Liberation Organization (sometimes refered to as the Military Academy Group). Salih Siriyya, a Palestinian who had been a member of the Muslim Brotherhood in Jordan and active in various revolutionary organizations before he came to Egypt in 1971, formed the militant organization after contact with the Egyptian Brotherhood. He and his followers worked for the creation of a society in which Qur'anic values and regulations would be strictly observed. Specific programs were not spelled out in detail in the early stage. The major goal was to establish an Islamic government. The perspective was defined by one of the leaders in an interview: "We believe that the Egyptians are basically the most religious of all Islamic peoples . . . all that the religious Egyptians need is a sincere Muslim leadership."[89]

Within the organization there was some debate over tactics and timing, but in 1974 the group decided to act. They raided the Military Academy in Heliopolis, apparently in the hope of acquiring arms to enable them to attack the Arab Socialist Union building, in which Sadat was scheduled to deliver a major address. The raid on the Academy was, however, intercepted by the Egyptian police, participants were jailed, and Sirriya was executed. However, the revolutionary tradition of militant fundamentalism did not die with Sirriya. Some of his followers and other activists created a number of smaller groups which created a network of common cause, with strong regional groups in Asyut and Minya as well as in Cairo. It was this loose network of groups which came to be known as the organization, al-Jihad.[90]

The basic ideological position of al-Jihad was presented in a booklet by Muhammad 'Abd al-Salam Faraj, *al-Faridah al-Gha'iba (The Forgotten Duty)*.[91] In this work, Faraj presents a critique of all of the fundamentalist strategies and argues that they all have failed and in fact are not appropriately Islamic. He argues, for example, that the strategy of withdrawal from society is an odd idea which results "from having forsaken the only true and religiously allowed road towards establishing an Islamic state," namely, fighting the jihad of God.[92] With this, he clearly rejects the ideas of Shukri Mustafa. Faraj provides similarly succinct rejections of the strategies of the Jama'at, the Muslim Brotherhood, and populist preachers like Kishk and Sha'rawi. Holy combat to overthrow the unbelieving state is the basic message and mission of al-Jihad. The focus of Faraj's thought is on the question of power rather than on a broader analysis of the nature of jahiliyya and Islamic societies. In this he advances the tradition of political revolutionary fundamentalism which concentrates on defeating the government rather than transforming society.

It was in this tradition that Khalid al-Islambuli acted in assassinating Sadat. Faraj and others believed that once Pharoah was killed, the faithful Egyptians would rise in holy war against the unbelieving state. Instead, even though there was a revolt in

Asyut, which was put down by the army only after hundreds were killed or wounded, the country as a whole did not rise up in revolt. Control of the state passed smoothly from Sadat to the Egyptian vice president, Hosni Mubarak. Mubarak released many of those who had been imprisoned by Sadat, but he ordered the arrests of those suspected of working with al-Jihad.

The era of Sadat witnessed the resurgence of Islam in Egypt. However, this was not a simple or monolithic phenomenon. At one level, the state itself made a significant effort to adopt an Islamic identity through constitutional revision, legal reform, and public acts of piety by its leaders. At the same time there was a mass return to religion which manifested itself in visible changes in the personal life of many Egyptians and in the popularity of preachers and writers like Mustafa Mahmud, Shaykh Sha'rawi, and Shaykh Khishk. Beyond these large-scale activities, there were organizations of fundamentalist Islam with a variety of different approaches, ranging from the nonviolent strategies of the neo-Muslim Brotherhood to small militant groups like al-Jihad, which ultimately brought an end to the era of Sadat by killing him.

The Era of Mubarak

After the charismatic leadership of Nasser and the flamboyance of Sadat, it has seemed to many that the administration of Hosni Mubarak "has been marked by overcautiousness in policy-making and a marked lack of dash in style."[93] During the 1980s Egypt survived without a major upset, and although it faced great problems, Mubarak's steady, quiet leadership maintained a remarkable degree of apparent stability during the decade. The Egyptian state under Mubarak continued the attempt to control and direct the development of the Islamic movement and to identify itself in significant ways as the primary Islamic institution of society. However, Mubarak's methods were significantly different from those of Sadat. Mubarak continued to suppress forcefully any group that was involved in violence or direct threats to the state, but his actions tended to be focused and narrow. Instead of the sweeping arrests of large numbers of people that characterized the last months of Sadat's rule, Mubarak tended to arrest only specific groups at any given time. Thus, at the same time that those suspected in connection to al-Jihad were being arrested in the months following the killing of Sadat, Mubarak released most of those who had been detained by Sadat earlier in 1981. Even those arrested following the killing of Sadat, for example, were explicitly connected either to the actual murder plot or to specific actions of revolt, like those that took place in Asyut. Similarly, although thousands were involved in police riots in 1986, and the minister of the interior suggested that fundamentalists might have provoked the unrest,[94] there was no national suppression of fundamentalist militants.

The strong but narrow policy of suppression was combined with a policy of openness and dialogue with Islamic opponents of the government. Even in dealing with the militants, there were efforts to establish dialogue in order to persuade them to adopt nonviolent methods of opposition. Efforts early in 1989 provide an example of this policy in operation. There had been clashes between government security forces and Islamic militants. In December 1988, police had arrested more than sixty activists in the Shubra area of Cairo for obstructing regular community social activities, and others were arrested in the ʿAyn Shams area of Cairo after a government security agent had been killed there. Later in the month, police and the ʿAyn Shams activists had a gun battle in which three activists were killed.[95] The government announced that it would hold dialogues with the young fundamentalists in prison in order to provide them with an opportunity to express their views and receive guidance from prominent Muslim teachers. Since major Muslim scholars rejected the idea of holding such conversations in jails, forty young members of fundamentalist groups were released and had discussions with ulama.[96]

The government expended most of its energies, however in working with the larger, nonviolent groups. Whereas Sadat had lumped his religiously motivated opponents together, Mubarak and his advisers "have learned to distinguish between the handful of underground revolutionary groups that are sworn to destroy the regime and the wide assortment of mainstream religious organizations that are pursuing various visions of an Islamic state through peaceful and legitimate means."[97] Opportunities have been provided for most groups to feel that they can participate in national deliberations. The Muslim Brotherhood, for example, has yet to be recognized as a legal organization but has nonetheless been allowed to participate in party coalitions and during the 1980s has built up an increasingly influential position in the National Assembly.

The government's own Islamic identification has changed from the days of Sadat. Sadat attempted to create a government position that was a clear Islamic alternative to the more fundamentalist groups, but this was not successful. In contrast, the Mubarak government has come to realize that the Islamic movement is an indigenous phenomenon with a considerable history, and it is not necessarily or inevitably a subversive force in Egyptian society.[98]

In this context, the government position reflects the moderate fundamentalism of the 1970s "return to religion." Officials are willing to discuss and consider the gradual implementation of Islamic law in Egypt, although activist fundamentalists do not seem appeased in the absence of substantial commitments. Similarly, Mubarak has allowed the restriction of some activities of the Coptic Christian minority in terms of public worship and liberties in dress as a part of his cooperation with the fundamentalists in the National Assembly, but at the same time, he has delayed or stopped some specific Islamic-oriented legislation in recognition of Coptic objections. For example, his family planning program was actively opposed by fundamentalists but reflects the more modernist positions that were a part of Sadat's governmental policies. In these ways, the government position has become a reflection of the broader and relatively moderate mainstream of the Islamic revival, balancing the stronger fundamentalism of the activists against the more pragmatic needs of the state and society and against the generally nonviolent mood of Egyptian Islamic life.

The second level of Islamic affirmation, the popular return to religion that had begun early in the 1970s, continues today, inspired by many of the same personalities;

Mustafa Mahmud and Shaykhs Sha'rawi and Kishk, for example, continue to have huge followings in the media and to reflect the variety possible in the mass resurgence. The relative openness of Mubarak's policies toward fundamentalism is symbolized by the fact that Shaykh Kishk, banned from radio or television under Sadat, has become something of a media star in the Mubarak era without significantly nuancing his message.

By the 1980s the return to religion had also attracted significant numbers even of the old leftist and secular intellectual elite. Advocates of political Islam now include major figures in secularist and Marxist analysis, such as Hasan Hanafi, a philosopher who is now developing a conceptual synthesis of Islamic and leftist ideas, former Marxists such as Anouar Abdel-Malek, Muhammad Amara, and Adil Husayn, and the famous advocate of a secular state in the years following World War II, Khalid Muhammad Khalid.[99] It seems clear that in the current atmosphere "liberal secularists . . . no longer represent the predominant intellectual trend in Egypt."[100]

With the involvement of a broader range of intellectuals and professionals in the reaffirmation of the Islamic tradition, the resurgence of Islam reached the stage where it was no longer a new phase of religious life. By the end of the 1980s the resurgence stage might be said to have passed and the normalization of the affirmation of Islam in public and private life was reached. The religious fervor of the crowds who went to Zeitoun to see the vision of the Virgin was born of special despair and hope. The adoption of the veil by young women in secularist families was a controversial action in the 1970s. However, by the late 1980s the Islamization of daily life had become part of the normal social processes lending a unique and new character to the popular affirmation of Islam in the Mubarak era.

The organized and publicly permitted Islamic opposition had been a third level of visible Islamic affirmation during the Sadat era, and it continued with even increased significance in the 1980s. The neo-Muslim Brotherhood assumed an increasingly important and visible role in Egyptian politics and society. It was more active in the professional and student associations, and by careful alliances with legal political parties became the largest single opposition group in the Egyptian parliament. The Brotherhood joined with the New Wafd Party in the national elections of 1984, and the coalition won 65 out of 450 seats, to become the largest opposition group. Brotherhood members held 7 of the 65 seats. In the national elections of 1987, the Brotherhood joined with the Socialist Labor Party and the Liberal Party to create the Islamic Alliance, which became the largest opposition group in Parliament, with 60 seats. This time the Brotherhood held 38 of those seats. From its role as a nonviolent advocate in the arena of public opinion, the Brotherhood has emerged as an organized and influential participant in the political system. The years of building public confidence that Brotherhood participation in politics would not mean revolution and the more Islamic orientation of the general public opened the way for this new role. The years of experience in publishing and careful political management under Sadat and then under Mubarak provided a leadership group for the Brotherhood which was able to take advantage of the opportunities of the 1980s.

The Brotherhood's political participation is characterized by a strategy of moderation, gradualism, and constitutionalism, as articulated in the program for Alliance candidates in the elections for the Consultative Council.[101] There is a strong affirmation that "Islamic law must be implemented in the educational, media, political, economic, and social fields," and that "Islam is a state religion and comprehensive ideology and system." The charge is made that the "main reason for the economic, social, and political problems plaguing the nation is the absence of the good values cherished by the true Islamic religion," but neither state nor society is identified as unbelieving. The program advocated is one of constitutional review, elections, and reforms. The Alliance stresses national unity and attempts to include all Egyptians. In its 1989 program it asserted that "Islam is the religion of the overwhelming majority of Egyptians. Islam is a state and a civilization owned by all those who contributed to it. Thus, the brother Copts in particular and the people of the book in general have the same rights and obligations as Muslims." This was a reaffirmation of the Alliance's position in the 1987 elections in which the Alliance placed several Copts on its lists of candidates.[102]

With its greater political activism, the nonviolent mainstream of Islamic fundamentalism has begun to attract a broader group of people. In different formats and contexts, new groups are emerging which can in some ways be seen as the effective Islamization of the Egyptian political scene. This mainstream establishment includes some of the more militant figures of the 1970s. For example, 'Isam al-Din al-'Aryan, the important Jama'at ideologue and activist of the 1970s, became in the 1980s a prominent medical doctor and one of the important members of the Islamic group in parliament.[103]

The new dynamics are also reflected in the emergence of activist groups which engage in demonstrations that often result in violence. The groups are an intermediate type between the nonviolent mainstream and the small conspiratorial militants in the jihad tradition. They are often organized around a prominent Islamic teacher and are tied to their local community through their mosques and other social organizations. Many of the major incidents involving what the Egyptian security forces call the "extremists" involve these groups. The incidents in al-Fayyum in the spring of 1989 involved this type of group. People protesting the performance of a play in the city came into conflict with security police. The conflict involved a large community group which had significant local support. The activity was centered around Shaykh 'Umar 'Abd al-Rahman, one of the ulama with close personal ties to members of al-Jihad. He had been put on trial along with the killers of Sadat but was acquitted because the court found that although he legitimized violence against an apostate ruler, he was not directly associated with the extremist violent organizations.[104] Shaykh 'Umar's positions are confrontational, but he does not formally advocate violence. In an interview after a violent confrontation between security forces and local activists in another city, he affirmed that "the Qur'anic and prophetic teachings must be explained to people in a gentle and amiable manner. We must invite people to the way of God with wisdom and good preaching."[105] He also charged that al-Azhar leaders had provided neither proper counsel for the government nor appropriate direction to the youth of the country.

The first such shaykh-centered opposition group to gain national and international attention in the Mubarak era was based in al-Nur Mosque in Cairo and led by Shaykh Hafiz Salamah, a distinguished preacher who had come to Cairo from Suez. In 1985 he led a popular effort to have Islamic law implemented immediately in Egypt. He first organized a conference of Islamist scholars and then announced a peaceful procession which would march to the presidential residence carrying Qur'ans. This came at the time that the National Assembly had voted to implement Islamic law "gradually and scientifically," rather than immediately. The government brought large numbers of security forces to the al-Nur Mosque area, and the government banned the proposed parade. When the government also attempted to replace Shaykh Salamah as head of al-Nur Mosque, his supporters and Salamah defied the government order. Salamah and his chief followers were quickly arrested and he was accused of instigating the people against the authorities and jailed. Shaykh Salamah, like Shaykh 'Umar, does not openly advocate violence. When accused of inciting the 1985 riots, he responded: "We are peaceful people. We are not the ones carrying weapons. We're carrying the Qur'an."[106]

The activist community shaykhs are not presenting radically new interpretations of the faith. They are instead advocating a strict adherence to the rules and regulations which are familiar to most of the population. In this way the Islamic agenda is reenforced in the political scene. The shaykhs reflect an important transition in the public respectability of fundamentalist activism. "The 'extremist' stance of university students who were easily accused of being rash, inexperienced, and lacking in adequate religious learning is now being overtaken by well-established sheikhs whose religiosity cannot be challenged."[107]

The fourth level of Islamic affirmation, that of the small militant group, also took advantage of the general religious reawakening and the willingness of the populace to welcome Islamic solutions. At least some branches of al-Jihad, for example, made active efforts to mobilize communities. One of the most publicized instances of this in the late 1980s involved al-Jihad's operations in the 'Ayn Shams section of Cairo, a working-class area in which there is also a large university. The community was at the time experiencing economic difficulties resulting from inflation and unemployment, and attracted a substantial number of student Islamic activists. During 1987 and early 1988, members of al-Jihad established a center in Adam Mosque in 'Ayn Shams. They implemented and staffed a number of social welfare, educational, and medical services and also helped to organize demonstrations against higher food prices in the community. Characteristically, they wedded these social relief efforts to the dissemination of a fundamentalist ethos by encouraging local residents to adopt fundamentalist-style clothing and to eliminate practices contrary to Islam (such as the social mixing of men and women). In the final months of the year, police entered Adam Mosque to expel the activists, and street fighting ensued in the next weeks.[108]

Security forces and Egyptians opposed to the fundamentalists speak of such groups as gaining control of communities and harassing them and keeping control through violence and intimidation. Shaykh 'Umar 'Abd al-Rahman rejected such accusations and criticized the Shaykh of al-Azhar for condemning the 'Ayn Shams group without going to the area. "If he had gone there, he would have heard very good things instead of the evil things he read: he would have heard that the Islamic group reconciles people, treats patients in its clinics, resolves people's problems, and helps the oppressed and confronts the oppressor until the right of the oppressed is recovered."[109]

It is this willingness to confront the authorities directly, and violently if necessary, that characterizes the groups that maintain the jihad tradition in the Mubarak era. There is relatively little certain knowledge about the groups. No single group is dominant; there seem to be regional clusters of groups rather than a national network. However, most seem to have some ties with the old organization of al-Jihad and exhibit similarities in organizational style and ideology. Estimates of the numbers involved vary greatly. Both the sympathizers and the security police tend to give inflated estimates. In terms of the general order of magnitude, an Egyptian newspaper noted that some foreign embassy reports estimated that the Islamic groups taken together included about seventy thousand members, with one in four associated on some occasion with acts of violence.[110]

Whatever the actual numbers are, the militant organizations have become recognizable players on the Egyptian stage. Mubarak's policy of active and focused suppression of the groups did prevent any one group from amassing predominant wealth, resources, and influence, but the policy was not able to eliminate the destabilizing disruptions of the violent groups. In 1985 the government's abiding fear of a broad-based uprising incited by Islamic activists was revealed in the swift action taken against Shaykh Salamah; one Egyptian commentator on the national mood described Egypt as "a gas-filled room waiting for a spark."[111]

The worldview of the militant groups is reflected in the views of 'Ali Muhammad 'Ali, the leader of the al-Jihad organization in Minya and the preacher in the mosque identified with the group.[112] 'Ali emphasized the supportive social programs of his organization. "We believe that all Muslims are one body and the believers support each other," he has said. The society has a special committee "to help the wealthy people calculate their almsgivings" for the poor. In the broader political sense, the activities "aim to instill a religious duty ordained by God, which is to call for God, lift the suffering and injustice done to the oppressed, and build the Muslim individual." 'Ali believes that Egypt's basic need is for "people who call for God and contribute to saving the nation from its spiritual crises, because the corruption in which we live is due to the nation's departure from its religion." The group became involved in violent actions, he explained, because it had been attacked by the security forces who prevented prayer services and "pursued all of us without any apparent cause." The group became involved in bombing Christian churches in Minya because "church activities are becoming increasingly provocative." His group has chosen Christians as a target for attack on the basis that "they cannot live a comfortable life while I am impoverished."

No new ideological expression of the jihad tradition has emerged in the 1980s.

Instead, the fundamentalists pursue the example of Qutb and Faraj in the somewhat different political and cultural context of the Mubarak regime. The broader Islamization of politics and daily life means that jihad-type organizations are likely to be active within a community context rather than on an isolated fringe. The ultimate effect of their more visible community presence on their own sensibilities remains uncertain: there is historical evidence, as we have seen, that such participation may serve to moderate the groups; however, many of the groups have yet to renounce militancy and violence as strategies in their opposition to the imperfect Islamization attendant upon the Mubarak regime. It may be said without qualification, however, that the resurgence of Islam which began under Sadat has moved the current government to engage the fundamentalist presence in a more sustained and serious fashion than had thus far been the case in the twentieth century, and that Egyptian political and social life has been Islamized to a greater degree as a result of the interactions of fundamentalists and society as a whole.

Sunni Fundamentalism in the Era of Resurgence: The Sudan

The Sudan is the one country in the Arab world where a formal effort was made in the 1980s to initiate the formal implementation of the Shari'a. One remarkable feature of the attempt is that it was made by the same kind of leadership that in Egypt (and Syria) has resisted such efforts. Both Egypt and the Sudan, for all of the 1970s and much of the 1980s, were led by people who were military in background and initially Arab Socialist in perspective. Sadat, Mubarak, and Numayri (the Sudanese leader) all began as followers of Nasser and were strongly influenced by his example.

The Egyptian military rulers have resisted formal and full implementation of the Shari'a. While Sadat tried to be the "Believing President," the Islamic program that he advocated was modernist in interpretation and gradualist in method. While Mubarak has been more open to working with fundamentalists, he has remained a gradualist in approach. However, in the Sudan, it was the military ruler and former Arab Socialist Ja'far Numayri who began a program of strict implementation of Islamic law in 1983. Although the Sudanese Muslim Brotherhood was involved in the effort, it was not the prime agent, and the program was not in specifics the one advocated by the Sudanese Brothers.

The Muslim Brotherhood in the Sudan had been a regular participant in parliamentary politics. As a result, its political fortunes were similar to those of the other civilian political organizations, the largest of which were based on the large Muslim popular organizations of the Ansar and the Khatmiyyah Tariqah. When politics in the Sudan were civilian and parliamentary, the Brotherhood had an open public role. It was one of a number of civilian interest groups competing in the political arena. In contrast, during most of the times of military rule, the Brotherhood was part of the illegal opposition working in cooperation with the other civilian political groups.

The situation changed significantly in the later years of the Numayri era. The Brotherhood leader, Hasan Turabi, agreed in 1978 to participate in a national reconciliation. This was part of a reorientation of the Numayri regime. Numayri had gone through a radical socialist phase and a more pragmatic phase. However, by the late 1970s, Numayri began to adopt an explicitly Islamic orientation for his policies. In this effort, he welcomed reconciliation with Turabi and named Turabi to the cabinet as attorney general. In addition, Numayri charged Turabi with leading a committee which would study Sudanese laws and bring them into conformity with Islamic law.

In practical terms, the shift reflected Numayri's belief that the adoption of a fundamentalist-like program would serve to build a broader base of support among northern Muslim Sudanese. And given the general Sudanese return to religion similar to that in Egypt (in which Numayri himself may have shared), it was indeed a practical policy. In the late 1970s, however, the Islamization of government policy was gradualist. Numayri published a book at the time called *Why the Islamic Path? (al-Nahj al-Islami limadha?)* in which the Islamic faith is identified in rather general terms and gives some emphasis to the Islamic path as a path of Sudanese national unity.[113] At that time Numayri's turn to an Islamic orientation was similar in many ways to the religious policies of Sadat, in that Numayri was consciously identifying his state and program as Islamic but was not formally and explicitly implementing traditional Islamic law.

The Sudanese Brotherhood was able to work successfully within the context of the gradualist approach. Turabi was a former dean of the University of Khartoum Law School, and his approach to Islamization was scholarly and intellectually thorough. The Brotherhood's strategy was to revive the faith and Islamize the practice of individuals, who would in turn gradually Islamize society. The Brotherhood became the strongest group among the students in the Sudan and enjoyed substantial influence among government officials.

Numayri became impatient with the gradualist approach by 1983 and wanted to move more rapidly and directly. His own personality was very different from that of Turabi, and in the fall of 1983 he instituted a program of Islamization whose methods reflected his own more activist and military approach. In September he and his staff began to promulgate a series of specific codes of law which demanded immediate implementation of Islamic law, often without any consideration for the particular conditions of the Sudan at the time.[114]

Although the general goals of the Islamization of law and state were shared by both Numayri and Turabi, leaders of the Brotherhood had reservations about some of the specifics of Numayri's program, which came to be called the "September Laws." They were not a systematic or thorough program of legal Islamization but instead a collection of Islamic ordinances rapidly drawn together by his legal advisers from a variety of sources. Numayri's ordinances were recognizably Islamic in that they included the most visible traditional rules—prohibition of alcohol, interest-free financing, amputation as a punishment for theft. However, changes in the judicial system in order to obtain "instant justice" were open to criticism even on traditional Islamic procedural grounds.[115]

Turabi and other Brotherhood leaders did not participate directly in the formulation of the Shari'a implementation decrees. Turabi had in fact been transferred from his posts dealing with legal matters to a position of presidential adviser on foreign affairs and thus was separated from the process of the actual formulation and promulgation of the decrees. Despite this, the Brotherhood initially gave its support to the Islamization program.

Other Muslim groups within the Sudan tended to oppose the September Laws as not being correctly Islamic. Sadiq al-Mahdi, the leader of the Mahdist political party, publicly condemned the decrees and was jailed. Although the Mahdists had consistently supported the ideal of an Islamically identified state, Sadiq had long advocated a major rethinking of traditionally accepted Muslim legal thought and viewed Numayri's program as reactionary and rigid.[116] Muhammad ʿUthman al-Mirghani, the leader of the largest politically active Sufi order, the Khatmiyyah Tariqah, quietly criticized the laws.

The most comprehensive critique came from Mahmud Muhammad Taha, the leader of a small reformist group called the Republican Brotherhood. Since the end of World War II, "Ustaz Mahmud" had been preaching about the need for an Islamic renaissance based on a major re-examination of the foundations of Islam. By the early 1980s he had gathered a small organization of dedicated followers. Although his power was limited, his radical critique of traditional Islamic law and his call for the creation of a whole new Islamic legal structure had attracted attention even outside of the Sudan.[117] Ustaz Mahmud's strong criticism of Numayri's laws led to his trial and execution in January 1985.

The debate in the Sudan reflects the acknowledgement by ideological activists on all parts of the spectrum of the need for an examination of the foundational sources of communal identity and the importance of validating their conclusions by an appeal to those sources. Few would identify, for example, the Republican Brothers as fundamentalists in the usual sense of the term, but the core of the movement's position is a careful analysis of the revelations recorded in the Qur'an. As presented by a leading intellectual in the group, Abdullahi Ahmed An-Naʿim, the Republican Brotherhood's position distinguishes between the revelations received by the Prophet Muhammad in Mecca and the later ones received in Medina. "The Medina message is not the fundamental, universal, eternal message of Islam. That founding message is from Mecca." The importance of the appeal to the foundational message, even in this more radical reinterpretation, can be seen in An-Naʿim's conclusion that "we [the Republican Brothers] are the *super-fundamentalists*."[118]

Secularists also vigorously opposed the September Laws. Although they were weak in the northern Sudan, especially after the suppression of the Sudanese Communist Party by Numayri, the secularist position was strongly advocated by the emerging Sudan People's Liberation Movement (SPLM), a primarily southern group which led the fighting against the Khartoum government that had been renewed in the southern provinces in the early 1980s. By 1985, the SPLM was contesting government control of areas in southern Sudan. Active opposition to Numayri began to swell in the north, as well as the cost of the civil war, and government mismanagement and corruption increased the deterioration of the economy. By 1985, Numayri had suppressed the Muslim Brotherhood, even though it had not publicly expressed its reservations about specifics of his program.[119]

Yet Numayri's reaction to his critics did not address the basic issues of national unity and economic crisis, and a Transitional Military Council, a group of high-ranking officers, expelled him in April 1985 and held elections the following year to restore parliamentary government. Sadiq al-Mahdi regained the post of prime minister but presided over a shifting coalition of parties that was unable to come to terms with the SPLM and end the civil war. On 30 June 1989, Sudan endured another military coup.[120]

Although the Muslim Brotherhood privately rejected the particulars of the September Laws, it had initially supported Numayri on the grounds that the implementation of the laws committed the Sudanese state to an Islamic identity, and that it would be very difficult to reverse that identification once it had been established. This assumption seems to be born out in the post-Numayri era of civilian politics. Even though Sadiq al-Mahdi had been jailed for his criticism of the program and had pledged during the election campaign of 1986 that he would eliminate the September Laws, he was unable to fully or formally abrogate them during his term as prime minister from 1986 to 1989.

The Islamization program thus became one of the major issues of Sudanese national politics in the 1980s. The non-Muslim Sudanese, comprising about one-third of the population, strongly opposed the program, and its implementation gave added impetus to the civil war; the secularization of the state became the leading demand of SPLM. There was at the same time a strong base of support among northern Muslim Sudanese for some form of official recognition of Islam. All of the major parties were based in a significant way on an Islamic identification, and the largest single group in the Sudan, the Ansar, had the heritage of having been the creators themselves of a fundamentalist state. In addition, many Muslim Sudanese had also experienced the more general return to religion that was taking place throughout the Islamic world. Many who were not affiliated directly with the more traditional organizations felt a reaffirmed adherence to Islam. These factors enhanced the growing persuasiveness and visibility of the Brotherhood. All of this provided a strong basis of support for continuing some form of Islamic identification for the Sudanese state.

In this context, many of the politicians in the era of civilian politics in the 1980s were unwilling to support moves that would give the appearance of de-Islamizing the state. That was Sadiq al-Mahdi's dilemma as prime minister, since the issue was not simply whether or not to repeal the September Laws. He was able to suspend application of many elements. In the context of the civil war and the demands of the SPLM for a secular state, the major issue of debate became whether or not the state should be Islamically identified at all. Given northern political realities, most politicians had no choice when the issue was stated in those terms. In a choice between some form of an Islamic state or a secular state, most Muslim Sudanese would chose the Islamic state and reject a secular state.

The Sudanese Brotherhood was a significant political force in the situation. It could appear to be the strict Islamic conscience in the north without having to engage in violent opposition to the government of al-Mahdi. It was supported by the northern Islamic revival. In the elections of 1986, the National Islamic Front (NIF), the

Brotherhood's political party, received almost 20 percent of the total vote in the northern provinces. While this still was not as much as either of the two older parties received, it was significantly more than the Brotherhood had received in earlier elections. The results reflected the success of the Brotherhood in expanding its base of support beyond the students and younger educated professionals.

In turn the military government established in the summer of 1989 by Omar Hassan Ahmed Bashir has been identified ideologically with the NIF or the Muslim Brotherhood—an identification that bodes ill for the possibility of reconciliation with the SPLM. The prospect is that thousands will continue to die as a result of famine and the ongoing war. After a cease-fire in September 1989, talks between representatives from the Bashir regime and the SPLM broke down over the issue of Islamic law and the SPLM call for "nonsectarian political parties" and for the convening of a national constitutional conference (excluding Islamic political parties like the NIF). Fighting resumed in many regions early in 1990, even as Bashir faced a large foreign debt, a deteriorating infrastructure, and growing anarchy in the countryside.[121]

In the Sudan, then, the Islamic resurgence has occurred at a number of levels, with some contrasts to the Egyptian experience. The state has been more clearly associated with a fundamentalist-style identification. The military group that took power in the Sudan in the summer of 1989 gave every indication during its first few months of rule of continuing that association. Many felt that the new government of Ahmad al-Bashir represented the coming to power of the Brotherhood-inspired element of the Sudanese military. In any case, in his first months as ruler, al-Bashir did little to lessen the formal Islamic identity of the Sudanese state.

At the level of Islamization of daily life, there has also been an intensification. However, in contrast to Egypt, this has not been accompanied by the emergence of highly visible and popular preachers like Shaykhs Kishk and Sha'rawi. It is possible that the continuing vitality of the more traditional organizations like the Ansar and the Khatmiyyah has inhibited the emergence of nonorganization religious media stars.

The third level, that of organized nonviolent fundamentalism, has been very successful in the Sudan. Under Numayri and during the parliamentary period in 1964–69 and 1985–89, the Brotherhood was legally recognized and was becoming an increasingly significant political force. It has also shown an increasing ability to cope with the conditions of military rule, as its experience in the last years of Numayri showed. During the first student organization elections at the University of Khartoum after the 1989 military takeover, fundamentalists won all of the seats in the Student Council. Brotherhood influence in the Bashir regime represented an important continuation of this development at the beginning of the 1990s.

The success of the Brotherhood appears to have provided the channel for the expression of activist fundamentalist views, with the result that there has been virtually no organized activity of the Jihad type in the Sudan. It is in the absence of the fourth level of fundamentalism that the Sudanese experience is in greatest contrast to Egypt. Instead, the militant, violent revolutionary group is that which advocates a secular state and the de-Islamization of society.

The experiences of Egypt and the Sudan in the era of the Islamic resurgence demonstrate that the particular patterns of interaction of the different levels of Islamic affirmation are of significance in determining the overall impact of the Islamic movement on society. The sheer physical power of the modern state to suppress opposition assures that it has the ability to affect the development of fundamentalism and, under certain conditions, to curtail its effectiveness. However, a policy of suppression without nuance is less effective and perhaps even counterproductive in areas in which a generalized popular return to religion has forged a broad base of sympathy for even the most militant of fundamentalists. In addition, in instances in which nonviolent expressions of fundamentalism have been allowed to become a visible and credible part of the political system, the appeal of the violent marginal groups has been reduced.

At the beginning of the 1990s, Islamic fundamentalism in the Sunni Arab world remained a significant force. It was no longer a novelty, challenging the modernist or radical socialist establishment. Instead, the processes of Islamization had become in societies like Egypt part of the normal operations of the political system, as well as a visible shaper of social institutions and daily life.

The strategies and specific programs of Islamizing states, of popular preachers, and of the various groups are of course shaped by the particular conditions of time and place. However, the underlying themes and aims have remained predictably consistent with the historic traditions of fundamentalism in Islam. There remains an emphasis on the comprehensive and universal nature of the Islamic message, based on a strict interpretation of God's Oneness, which allows for no independent sovereignty outside of God. In this way, at least in the ideal, religion and politics are not separate realms, and economics is as much a matter of Islam as is theology. This message of tawhid is in both the premodern and modern fundamentalist view to be understood not by simply accepting the interpretations handed down by generations of past teachers. Instead, it is to be understood by a return to the fundamental sources of Islam, the Qur'an and the Sunna of the Prophet, as they are directly interpreted by the exercise of ijtihad. The reliance on ijtihad ensured that the Islamic resurgence of the 1970s and 1980s reflected the continuing dynamism of the Islamic tradition in interaction with political, social, and economic developments.

Notes

1. Patrick D. Gaffney, "The Local Preacher and Islamic Resurgence in Upper Egypt," in Richard T. Antoun and Mary Elaine Hegland, eds., *Religious Resurgence* (Syracuse: Syracuse University Press, 1987), pp. 46–47.

2. Robin Wright, "'Quiet' Revolution: Islamic Movement's New Phase," *Christian Science Monitor,* 6 November 1987, pp.18–19.

3. Saad Eddin Ibrahim, "Egypt's Islamic Activism in the 1980s," *Third World Quarterly* 10, no. 2 (1988): 642–43.

4. For an analytical description of the backgrounds of the members of al-Jihad, see Gilles Kepel, *Muslim Extremism in Egypt: The Prophet and the Pharoah,* trans. Jon Rothschild (Berkeley: University of California Press, 1985), pp. 214–22. See also the comments on the occupations of members

of al-Jihad in R. Hrair Dekmejian, *Islam in Revolution* (Syracuse: Syracuse University Press, 1985), p. 106.

5. Saad Eddin Ibrahim, "Anatomy of Egypt's Militant Islamic Groups: Methodological Note and Preliminary Findings," *International Journal of Middle East Studies* 12, no. 4 (1980): 440. See also Ibrahim, "Egypt's Islamic Activism," p. 652.

6. Karm B. Akhtar and Ahmad H. Sakr, *Islamic Fundamentalism* (Cedar Rapids, Iowa: Igram Press, 1982), p. 61, and citing Ismail R. al-Faruqi (p. 123) and M. Cherif Bassiouni (p. 136).

7. In the great synthesis of Hellenism, Middle Eastern culture, and Islamic monotheism that created medieval Islamic civilization of the ninth and tenth centuries, the "People of the Traditions" and followers of Ahmad ibn Hanbal, author of the Hanbali legal code, insisted that belief and practice must be based on the fundamentals as found in the Traditions of the Prophet Muhammad. Similarly, in the later medieval period, the development of an inclusivist mystic theology, as seen in the works of Muhyi al-Din Ibn Arabi (d. 1240), elicited an exclusivist, fundamentalistic response in the teachings of Ahmad Ibn Taymiyya (d. 1328). See Fazlur Rahman, "Revival and Reform in Islam, " in P. M. Holt, Ann K. S. Lambton, and Bernard Lewis, eds., *The Cambridge History of Islam* (Cambridge: Cambridge University Press, 1970) 2: 632–56; and John O. Voll, "Renewal and Reform in Islamic History: Tajdid and Islah," in John L. Esposito, ed., *Voices of Resurgent Islam* (New York: Oxford University Press, 1983), pp. 32–47.

8. John Obert Voll, *Islam, Continuity, and Change in the Modern World* (Boulder, Colo.: Westview, 1982), pp. 64–67.

9. Descriptions of Muhammad Ibn 'Abd al-Wahhab's teachings can be found in Fazlur Rahman, *Islam,* 2d ed. (Chicago: University of Chicago Press, 1979), pp. 196–201; and Ayman Al-Yassini, *Religion and State in the Kingdom of Saudi Arabia* (Boulder, Colo.: Westview, 1985), pp. 26–32.

10. See Muhammad Ibn 'Abd al-Wahhab, *Kitab al-Tawhid,* printed by Maktabah al-Ma'arif (al-Riyadh: n. d.).

11. This dual concern for the broader social order and for the personal faith and practice of individual believers is characteristic of most fundamentalist Muslim teachers. It is a reminder that the mosque-clinics and schools of Egyptian fundamentalists are as important a part of their mission, as they conceive it, as the transformation of the state and society as a whole. Indeed, many contemporary fundamentalists view the individual level as the starting point for the Islamic transformation of society. See, for example, Abul A'la Mawdudi, *The Process of Islamic Revolution* (Lahore: Islamic Publications, 1977).

12. Rahman, *Islam,* p. 197.

13. Wilfred Cantwell Smith, *Islam in Modern History* (Princeton: Princeton University Press, 1957), p. 43.

14. Ibn Taymiyya, the medieval fundamentalist scholar, had such a vision, and Ibn 'Abd al-Wahhab was firmly in this tradition. See Al-Yassini, *Religion and State,* p. 30.

15. William Ochsenwald, "Saudi Arabia," in Shireen T. Hunter, ed., *The Politics of Islamic Revivalism* (Bloomington: Indiana University Press, 1988), p. 109, and the sources cited there.

16. Charles Issawi, *An Economic History of the Middle East and North Africa* (London: Methuen and Co., 1982).

17. John Voll, "The Sudanese Mahdi: Frontier Fundamentalist," *International Journal of Middle East Studies* 10 (1979): 145–66.

18. Cf., for example, the discussions of the political role of Sudanese Mahdism in Gabriel Warburg, "Islam and State in Numayri's Sudan," in J. D. Y. Peel and C. C. Stewart, eds., *"Popular Islam" South of the Sahara* (Manchester: Manchester University Press, 1985), pp. 400–13.

19. For example, the Sanusi movement in Libya became the foundation for a political elite in a newly independent state rather than the basis for a revived network of social and educational centers.

20. Cf., for example, the analysis of the

role of Ibn Taymiyyah's ideas in contemporary Muslim radical thought in Emmanuel Sivan, *Radical Islam* (New Haven: Yale University Press, 1985), pp. 94–104.

21. Cf., for example, the comments by H. A. R. Gibb in *Modern Trends in Islam* (Chicago: University of Chicago Press, 1947), pp. 119–21.

22. Cf. Hisham Sharabi, *Arab Intellectuals and the West: The Formative Years 1875–1914* (Baltimore: Johns Hopkins Press, 1970), pp. 129–31.

23. Voll, *Islam, Continuity, and Change,* pp. 145–47.

24. Gabriel Baer, "Islamic Political Activity in Modern Egyptian History: A Comparative Analysis," in Gabriel R. Warburg and Uri M. Kupferschmidt, eds., *Islam, Nationalism, and Radicalism in Egypt and the Sudan* (New York: Praeger, 1983), p. 38.

25. Al-Afghani traveled widely in the Islamic world and Europe and had already gained a reputation as a strong advocate for Islamic reform when he came to Egypt in 1871. During his stay there of eight years, he attracted a number of students, especially from the great Islamic university of Al-Azhar, including his most famous associate, Muhammad 'Abduh. Later, in political exile in Paris after 1884, he was joined by 'Abduh, and they published a journal and worked further on the articulation of the Islamic modernist position. 'Abduh's subsequent career, after he returned to Egypt in 1888, as the Grand Mufti, or leading official interpreter of Islamic law, and as an educational reformer, brought him to the forefront of the movement to create the synthesis of Islam and modern Western ideas. A helpful introduction to the situation and the people involved can be found in John L. Esposito, *Islam, The Straight Path* (New York: Oxford University Press, 1988), pp. 127–36. Short selections illustrating the ideas of al-Afghani and 'Abduh can be found in John J. Donohue and John L. Esposito, eds., *Islam in Transition* (New York: Oxford University Press, 1982), pp. 16–28.

26. "Lecture on Teaching and Learning," in Nikki Keddie, ed., *An Islamic Response to Imperialism: Political and Religious Writings of Sayyid Jamal ad-Din 'al-Afghani* (Berkeley: University of California Press, 1968), p. 107.

27. Muhammad Abduh, *The Theology of Unity,* trans. Ishaq Musa'ad and Kenneth Cragg (London: George Allen and Unwin, 1966), p. 145.

28. Sharabi, *Arab Intellectuals,* p. 132.

29. Cf. the discussion in Christina Phelps Harris, *Nationalism and Revolution in Egypt* (The Hague: Mouton, 1964), pp. 89–101.

30. Albert Hourani, *Arabic Thought in the Liberal Age, 1798–1939* (London: Oxford University Press, 1962), chaps. 7 and 12.

31. Richard P. Mitchell, *The Society of the Muslim Brothers* (London: Oxford University Press, 1969), p. 321.

32. Afaf Lutfi al-Sayyid Marsot, *A Short History of Modern Egypt* (Cambridge: Cambridge University Press, 1985), p. 88.

33. Both Mitchell, *Society of Muslim Brothers,* and Ishak Musa Husaini, *The Moslem Brethren* (Beirut: Khayat's, 1956) draw upon al-Banna's autobiography, "Mudhakkarat Hasan al-Banna," translated as *Memoirs of Hasan Al-Banna Shaheed,* trans. M. N. Shaikh (Karachi: International Islamic Publishers, 1981).

34. *Memoirs of Hasan,* pp. 68–69.

35. Ibid., p. 76.

36. Ibid., p. 109.

37. Hasan al-Banna, *Five Tracts of Hasan Al-Banna (1906–1949),* trans. Charles Wendell (Berkeley: University of California Press, 1978), p. 28–29.

38. *Memoirs of Hasan,* pp. 112–13.

39. Michael Gilsenan, *Saint and Sufi in Modern Egypt* (Oxford: Clarendon Press, 1973).

40. The most complete discussion of the organization of the Brotherhood in the period up to 1954 is found in Mitchell, *Society of Muslim Brothers,* part 2.

41. Mitchell, *Society of Muslim Brothers,* p. 19.

42. Mitchell, *Society of Muslim Brothers,* p. 14; Husaini, *Moslem Brethren,* p. 41.

43. Hasan al-Banna, *Five Tracts,* p. 36.

44. Hourani, *Arabic Thought,* p. 329.

45. Mitchell, *Society of Muslim Brothers,* p. 330.

46. Ibid, p. 331.

47. Hassan al-Banna, *Five Tracts,* p. 88.

48. Mitchell, *Society of Muslim Brothers,* p. 239.

49. Muhammad Abdallah al-Samman, *Hassan al-Banna, al-Rijal wa al-Fikrah* (Cairo: Dar al-I'tisam, 1977), p. 62. For a general discussion on this point, cf. Esposito, *Islam, Straight Path,* pp. 155–56.

50. Hussein M. Fahim, "Change in Religion in a Resettled Nubian Community, Upper Egypt," *International Journal of Middle East Studies* 4 (1973):174.

51. Uri M. Kupferschmidt, "The Muslim Brothers and the Egyptian Village," *The Journal of the Israel Oriental Society* 10, no. 1 (1982): 157–70.

52. Ibid. In the late 1940s the Brotherhood did begin to consider the problem of land reform and rural inequalities.

53. Mitchell, *Society of Muslim Brothers,* p. 234.

54. Ibid., p. 308.

55. A short biography of al-Siba'i can be found in Umar F. Abd-Allah, *The Islamic Struggle In Syria* (Berkeley: Mizan Press, 1983), pp. 96–101.

56. A selection of his writings on Arab socialism can be found in Kemal Karpat, *Political and Social Thought in the Contemporary Middle East*, rev. ed. (New York: Praeger, 1982), pp. 104–8.

57. Afaf Lutfi al-Sayyid Marsot, "Muslim Brotherhood," in Mircea Eliade, ed., *The Encyclopedia of Religion* (New York: Macmillan, 1987), 10: 218.

58. Adnan Ayyub Musallam, "The Formative Stages of Sayyid Qutb's Intellectual Career and his Emergence as an Islamic Da'iyah, 1906–1952" (Ph.D. diss., University of Michigan, 1983), p. 250. Other helpful sources on Sayyid Qutb are Yvonne Haddad, "Sayyid Qutb: Idealogue of Islamic Revival," in Esposito, *Voices of Resurgent Islam,* pp. 67–98; Gilles Kepel, *Muslim Extremism,* chap. 2; and biographical introductions to translations of some of his works, such as S. Badrul Hasan, "Syed Qutb Shaheed: A Brief Life Sketch," in Syed Qutb Shaheed, *Milestones,* trans. by S. Badrul Hasan (Karachi: International Islamic Publishers, 1981), pp. 1–43.

59. Musallam, "Formative Stages," pp. 161–65.

60. Quoted in Donohue and Esposito, *Islam in Transition,* p. 125.

61. Sayyed Qutb, *Islam and Universal Peace* (Indianapolis, Ind.: American Trust Publications, 1977), p. 45.

62. See Abdel Moghny Said, *Arab Socialism* (New York: Barnes and Noble, 1972), pp. 89–133.

63. Abdel Azim Ramadan, "Fundamentalism in Contemporary Egypt: The Muslim Brotherhood and the Islamic Fundamentalist Groups," paper prepared for the American Academy of Arts and Sciences Fundamentalism Project, p. 23.

64. Ibid, p. 19.

65. "Report by the Legislative Committee of the U.A.R. National Assembly on the Republican Law Regarding the Moslem Brotherhood," in *Arab Political Documents 1965* (Beirut: American University of Beirut), Document No. 183.

66. Sayed Qutb, *Milestones,* in the edition published by Unity Publishing in Cedar Rapids, Iowa, with no date or translator given, p. 11.

67. John L. Esposito, *Islam and Politics* (Syracuse: Syracuse University Press, 1984), p. 134.

68. Haddad, in Esposito, *Voices of Resurgent Islam,* p. 89.

69. Ibid., p. 78. See also Yvonne Y. Haddad, "The Quranic Justification for an Islamic Revolution: The View of Sayyid Qutb," *The Middle East Journal* 37, no. 1 (1983):14–29.

70. These activities are described in Zaynab al–Ghazali, *Ayyam min Hayyati* (Cairo: Dar al-Sharug, 1400/1980), pp. 30–38.

71. Ibid., p. 37.

72. Ibid., p. 38.

73. Cynthia Nelson, "The Virgin of Zeitun," *Worldview* 16, no. 9 (1973): 8.

74. An analysis of changes in Nasser's policies following the 1967 war can be found in Fuad Ajami, *The Arab Predicament* (Cambridge: Cambridge University Press, 1981), especially chap. 2.

75. Editors' note: At the time of the cease-fire, the Syrian front had collapsed, leaving the Israelis in control of the Golan Heights. The Egyptian Third Army was surrounded in the Sinai. Nonetheless, the 1973 war was portrayed as a great victory for Egypt, in large part because the Arab forces had crossed the Suez Canal and broken the Bar Lev line of defense in the process. It is important to note that this interpretation of the war as resulting in a resounding Arab victory was advanced by Jewish radicals as well. See chap. 5. On the Egyptian perspective of the war, see Ismail Fahmy, *Negotiating Peace in the Middle East* (Cairo: American University in Cairo Press, 1983), chap. 2.

76. Saad Eddin Ibrahim, "An Islamic Alternative in Egypt: The Muslim Brotherhood and Sadat," *Arab Studies Quarterly* 4, nos. 1 and 2 (1982): 75–93; Hassan Hanafi, "The Relevance of the Islamic Alternative in Egypt," *Arab Studies Quarterly* 4, nos. 1 and 2 (1982): 54–74.

77. Cf. the dialogues with young Muslims in the 1980s, the efforts of some of the popular preachers to emphasize that they are not "ulama of the authorities." An example is from *al-Sha'b,* 3 January 1989, reported speeches by Shaykh Muhammad al-Sha'rawi and Shaykh Muhammad al-Ghazali. Foreign Broadcast Information Service, FBIS-NES-89-013 (23 January 1989).

78. Cf. the discussions in Bruce M. Borthwick, "Religion and Politics in Israel and Egypt," *The Middle East Journal* 33, no. 2 (1979): 146–63; and R. Stephen Humphreys, "Islam and Political Values in Saudi Arabia, Egypt and Syria," *The Middle East Journal* 33, no. 1 (1979): 1–19.

79. Wright, "'Quiet' Revolution," p. 18. Cf. Bruce Borthwick, "Egypt's Electronic Mosque," *Christian Science Monitor,* 25 September 1981. This experience is described in his autobiographical account, Mustafa Mahmoud, *Rahlati Min al-Shakk ila Al-Iman* (Tunis: Maktabah al-Jadid, 1989).

80. Quoted in Hava Lazarus-Yafeh, "Muhammad Mutawalli al-Sha'Rawi—A Portrait of a Contemporary 'Alim in Egypt," in Warburg and Kupferschmidt, *Islam Nationalism,* pp. 290–91.

81. Ibid., pp. 293–94. A good example of his position is his short introduction to Islam, Muhammad Mutawalli al-Sha'rawi, *Al-Islam: 'aqidah wa minhaj* (Tunis: Dar Bu Salamah, 1983).

82. For background on Kishk, see Kepel, *Muslim Extremism,* chap. 6, and Johannes J. G. Jansen, *The Neglected Duty* (New York: Macmillan, 1986), chap. 4.

83. Ajami, *Arab Predicament,* p. 187.

84. Kepel, *Muslim Extremism,* p. 107. Kepel provides a helpful description and analysis of the basic themes of neo-Muslim Brotherhood propaganda in chap. 4.

85. Saad Eddin Ibrahim, "An Islamic Alternative in Egypt," p. 81. Also cf. Ibrahim, "Egypt's Islamic Activism," pp. 644–46.

86. Kepel, *Muslim Extremism,* p. 155.

87. Ibrahim, "Anatomy," pp. 429ff., and Kepel, *Muslim Extremism,* chap. 3.

88. Ibid. Also cf. H. N. Ansari, "The Islamic Militants in Egyptian Politics," *International Journal of Middle East Studies* 16 (1984): 123–44.

89. Ibrahim, "Anatomy," p. 431.

90. Ibrahim, "Egypt's Islamic Activism," p. 650.

91. Translated in Jansen, *Neglected Duty.*

92. Ibid., p. 188.

93. Paul Jabber, "Egypt's Crisis, America's Dilemma," *Foreign Affairs* 64, no. 5 (1986): 968.

94. *The New York Times,* 3 March 1986, 5 March 1986.

95. Cf. the description of these events in "Chronology," *The Middle East Journal* 43, no. 2 (1989): 266.

96. *Middle East News Agency Report*, 3 March 1989. FBIS-NES-89-041 (3 March 1989).

97. Robert Bianchi, "Islam and Democracy in Egypt," *Current History* 88, no. 535 (1989): 93.

98. Ibid, p. 94.

99. Cf. the discussion in Alexander Flores, "Egypt: A New Secularism?" *Middle East Report* 18, no. 153 (1988): 27–28.

100. Nancy E. Gallagher, "Islam v. Secularism in Cairo: An Account of the Dar al-Hikma Debate," *Middle Eastern Studies* 25, no. 2 (1989): 214.

101. The text of this program appeared in *al-Ahrar,* 22 May 1989, with a translation in FBIS-NES-89-102. The quotations are from this translation.

102. Ibrahim, "Egypt's Islamic Activism," p. 647.

103. James Pittaway, "Egypt: A Benign Brotherhood?" *The Atlantic* 263, no. 1 (1989): 25, 32.

104. A. Chris Eccel, "'Alim and Mujahid in Egypt: Orthodoxy Versus Subculture, or Division of Labor?" *The Muslim World* 78, nos. 3 and 4 (1988): 205.

105. Interview in *al-Ahrar,* 16 January 1989. FBIS-NES-89-014 (24 January 1989).

106. *New York Times,* 15 June 1985.

107. "Islamisation momentum continues," *Arabia* 4, no. 48 (1985): 37.

108. A helpful summary of these events is found in George D. Moffett, III, "Waging War on Islamic Extremists," *Christian Science Monitor,* 17 March 1989.

109. Interview with 'Umar 'Abd al-Rahman in *al-Ahrar.* FBIS-NES-89-014 (24 January 1989).

110. *al-Wafd,* 16 January 1989. FBIS-NEA-89-012 (19 January 1989).

111. Abdelwahab el Affendi, "Egypt's fuse burns short," *Arabia* 5, no. 51 (1985): 16.

112. Interview with Hasan 'Abd al-Basit, published in *al-Watan* (Kuwait), 9 February 1989. FBIS-NE5-89-030 (15 February 1989). The quotations are taken from this translation.

113. Ja'far Muhammad Numayri, *al-Nahj al-Islami limadha* (Cairo: al-Maktab al-Masri al-Hadith, 1978). For part of the discussion of national unity, cf. chap. 6.

114. Most of this account of the Islamization program is based on interviews with Sudanese officials, including Hasan Turabi and Nayal Abu Qurun and Awad al-Jeed (Numayri's administrative assistants in the Islamization program) in August 1984.

115. The actual operations of institutions of the Numayri Islamization program are now beginning to be studied in some detail. One valuable study of this type is Ibrahim M. Zein, "Religion, Legality, and the State: 1983 Sudanese Penal Code" (Ph.D. diss., Temple University, 1989).

116. For an introduction to Sadiq al-Mahdi's ideas about the nature of an Islamic state, cf. al-Sadiq al-Mahdi, "Islam, Society and Change," in Esposito, *Voices of Resurgent Islam,* pp. 230–40.

117. His basic teachings are found in Mahmoud Mohamed Taha, *The Second Message Of Islam,* trans. Abdullahi Ahmed an-Na'im (Syracuse: Syracuse University Press, 1987).

118. Abdullahi Ahmed An-Na'im, "The Reformation of Islam," *New Perspectives Quarterly* (Fall 1987), p. 51. For a more complete presentation of his views, see Abdullahi Ahmed an-Na'im, *Toward an Islamic Reformation* (Syracuse: Syracuse University Press, 1990).

119. Cf. John O. Voll, "Political Crisis in Sudan," *Current History* 89, no. 546 (1990): 153–54.

120. Ibid.

121. Ibid., p. 179.

Select Bibliography

Abd-Allah, Umar F. *The Islamic Struggle In Syria*. Berkeley: Mizan Press, 1983.

Abdhuh, Muhammad. *The Theology of Unity*. Trans. Ishaq Musa'ad and Kenneth Cragg. London: George Allen and Unwin, 1966.

Ajami, Fouad. *The Arab Predicament*. Cambridge: Cambridge University Press, 1981.

Akhtar, Karm B., and Ahmad H. Sakr. *Islamic Fundamentalism*. Cedar Rapids, Iowa: Igram Press, 1982.

Antoun, Richard T., and Mary Elaine Hegland, eds. *Religious Resurgence*. Syracuse: Syracuse University Press, 1987.

al-Banna Shaheed, Hasan. M. N. Shaikh, trans. *Memoirs of Hasan Al-Banna Shaheed*. Karachi: International Islamic Publishers, 1981.

Berger, Morroe. *Islam in Egypt Today*. London: Cambridge University Press, 1970.

Dekmejian, R. Hrair. *Islam in Revolution*. Syracuse: Syracuse University Press, 1985.

Donohue, John J., and John L. Esposito, eds. *Islam in Transition*. New York: Oxford University Press, 1982.

Enayat, Hamid. *Modern Islamic Political Thought*. Austin: University of Texas Press, 1982.

Esposito, John L. *Islam and Politics*. Syracuse: Syracuse University Press, 1984.

———. *Islam, The Straight Path*. New York: Oxford University Press, 1988.

Esposito, John L., ed. *Voices of Resurgent Islam*. New York: Oxford University Press, 1983.

Gibb, H. A. R. *Modern Trends in Islam*. Chicago: University of Chicago Press, 1947.

Gilsenan, Michael. *Saint and Sufi in Modern Egypt*. Oxford: Clarendon Press, 1973.

Harris, Christina Phelps. *Nationalism and Revolution in Egypt*. The Hague: Mouton, 1964.

Hourani, Albert. *Arabic Thought in the Liberal Age, 1798–1939*. London: Oxford University Press, 1962.

Husaini, Ishak Musa. *The Moslem Brethren*. Beirut: Khayat's, 1956.

Issawi, Charles. *An Economic History of the Middle East and North Africa*. London: Methuen, 1982.

Jansen, Johannes J. G. *The Neglected Duty*. New York: Macmillan, 1986.

Keddie, Nikki, ed. *An Islamic Response to Imperialism: Political and Religious Writings of Sayyid Jamal ad-Din 'al-Afghani*. Berkeley: University of California Press, 1968.

Karpat Kemal. *Political and Social Thought in the Contemporary Middle East*. Rev. ed. New York: Praeger Press, 1982.

Kepel, Gilles. *Muslim Extremism in Egypt: The Prophet and the Pharoah*. Trans. Jon Rothschild. Berkeley: University of California Press, 1985.

Marsot, Afaf Lutfi al-Sayyid. *A Short History of Modern Egypt*. Cambridge: Cambridge University Press, 1985.

Mawdudi, Abul A'la. *The Process of Islamic Revolution*. Lahore: Islamic Publications, 1977.

Mitchell, Richard P. *The Society of the Muslim Brothers*. London: Oxford University Press, 1969.

Peel, J. D. Y., and C. C. Stewart, eds. *"Popular Islam" South of the Sahara*. Manchester: Manchester University Press, 1985.

Qutb, Sayyed. *Islam and Universal Peace*. Indianapolis, Ind.: American Trust Publications, 1977.

Sharabi, Hisham. *Arab Intellectuals and the West: The Formative Years 1875–1914*. Baltimore: Johns Hopkins Press, 1970.

Sivan, Emmanuel. *Radical Islam: Medieval Theology and Modern Politics*. New Haven: Yale University Press, 1985.

Smith, Charles D. *Islam and the Search for Social Order in Modern Egypt*. Albany: State University of New York Press, 1983.

Smith, Wilfred Cantwell. *Islam in Modern History*. Princeton: Princeton University Press, 1957.

Taha, Mahmoud Mohamed. *The Second Message Of Islam*. Trans. Abdullahi Ahmed An-Na'im. Syracuse: Syracuse University Press, 1987.

Voll, John O. "The Sudanese Mahdi: Frontier Fundamentalist." *International Journal of Middle East Studies* 10 (1979): 145–66.

———. *Islam, Continuity, and Change in the Modern World*. Boulder, Colo.: Westview, 1982.

———. *The Political Impact of Islam in the Sudan*. Washington D.C.: Department of State, 1984.

Warburg, Gabriel R., and Uri M. Kupferschmidt, eds. *Islam, Nationalism, and Radicalism in Egypt and the Sudan*. New York: Praeger, 1983.

Wendell, Charles., trans. *Five Tracts of Hasan Al-Banna 1906–1949*. Berkeley: University of California Press, 1978.

al-Yassini, Ayman. *Religion and State in the Kingdom of Saudi Arabia*. Boulder, Colo.: Westview, 1985.

CHAPTER
7

Activist Shi'ism in Iran, Iraq, and Lebanon

Abdulaziz A. Sachedina

"There were three idol breakers, Abraham, Muhammad,
and Ruh Allah Khomeini."

I heard this slogan and its variants hundreds of times in the street demonstrations in Tehran and other cities of Iran in 1978–79. The slogan captured the aspirations of the Shi'ite Muslim masses in Iran that ushered in the Islamic revolutionary movement under the leadership of the Ayatollah Khomeini. The Islamic revolution marked the beginning of an innovative idea in Shi'ite Islam, namely, the creation of an Islamic government in the modern nation-state of Iran under the religious leadership of its learned scholar, the ayatollah.[1] To the Shi'ite masses, the notion of a legitimate religious authority assuming political power corresponded to their historical affirmation of the theological leadership of the Prophet Muhammad's male descendants as divinely guided Imams (temporal-religious leaders). They believed that there had been twelve such Imams, the last of whom had disappeared in the tenth century C.E., to return at some future date as the Mahdi, the messianic deliverer. The Shi'ite creed had consistently depicted the ultimate divine victory as a time when the last Imam would return to establish an Islamic government and create the rule of justice and equity on earth. However, no human being could know the day or hour of that victory. During the extended period of waiting, Shi'ism developed and drew upon an identity rooted in a sense of a communal suffering and passion in anticipation of that day when God would send the Imam to deliver the community from tyrannical absolutist political power. In the meantime, pending the return of this messianic Imam at the End of Time, they had acknowledged the religious leadership of their scholars, who continued to guide the community in their mundane as well as spiritual affairs.

On 1 February 1979, Ayatollah Khomeini returned from a fifteen-year exile to institute a "rule of justice and equity" in Iran.[2] The welcome that he received among the Shi'ites reflected their heightened sense of expectation, sparked by the prophecy of one of the Shi'ite Imams, heard repeatedly in Iran at the time, that "A man will rise from Qum [as a precursor to the Mahdi] and he will summon people to the right path. People will rally to him like pieces of iron [to a magnet], not to be shaken by strong winds, free and relying on God." The suffering-and-passion motifs developed in Shiʿism served for Khomeini as a ready-made source of inspiration in the successful mass mobilization of the Shiʿites in their struggle against the "unjust" rule of the "Pharaoh" of Iran, the Shah Reza Pahlavi. In place of the shah's regime he proposed to erect an alternative in keeping with the cherished messianic vision of Shiʿism: an Islamic government guided both by the leadership of the ayatollah and by the expectation of the return of the last Imam. In my conversations with various persons of different social strata at the time of Khomeini's ascendancy, I discovered that, despite widespread enthusiasm for this vision of Iranian society, almost no one, whether religious or secular in orientation, had a clear understanding of the nature or goals of "Islamic government" in the absence of the legitimately and theologically acknowledged last Imam of the Shiʿites.

The question to be posed in examining the recent Shiʿite revolution in Iran turns on this insight: given the continued absence of the Imam and of specific prescriptions for "Islamic government," how, then, did the Ayatollah Khomeini succeed in "activating" politically quietist Shiʿites? How, in other words, did he succeed in transforming the suffering-and-passion motif, an element of Shiʿite identity that had previously generated political quietism and withdrawal, into an activist ideology of rebellion and confrontation in the context of the modern age?

On 9 April 1980, Ayatollah Muhammad Baqir al-Sadr, a renowned Shiʿite religious scholar and leader of the Shiʿite struggle for political justice in Iraq, was executed by Saddam Hussein, the ruler of Iraq. When I visited Iraq during the summer of that year, it was evident that the victory of the Islamic revolution in Iran had at that time a receptive audience of Iraqi Shiʿites, especially among the leading Shiʿite scholars in the holy city of Najaf whom I interviewed. The Shiʿites of Iraq comprised the largest religious community in the country, and constitute a majority of the total population. The determination of the "downtrodden" Shiʿites of Iraq to press ahead with their demands for sociopolitical justice was evident in spite of Saddam's policy of ruthlessly suppressing any such Shiʿite-inspired threat to his own regime.

The execution of Baqir Sadr, often termed the "Khomeini of Iraq," was prompted by his numerous writings and speeches, widely circulated in the Islamic world, which encouraged the Arab Shiʿites of Iraq to demand their political rights. Like Khomeini, Baqir Sadr appealed to the latent radicalism of Shiʿite theology, with its emphasis on suffering and martyrdom as elements of the divine plan. This emphasis, with its glorification of the role of the underdog, appealed to adherents moving in the direction of activism to enhance their social position in Iraq. The Iraqi regime's fear of this inchoate activism was also revealed in its decision to execute Muhammad Baqir Sadr's sister, Bint al-Huda, who had collaborated with her brother in carrying on his struggle among the Iraqi Shiʿite women. Again, the question arises: how did Muhammad Baqir Sadr overcome the traditional restraints of Shiʿism which had required the Shiʿites to maintain the purity of their faith by shunning politics?

On 31 August 1978, Imam Musa al-Sadr, the leader of the Lebanese Shiʿites, was seen for the last time in a hotel in Tripoli, Libya. Musa Sadr had come to Lebanon in

1959 as a trusted representative of an Iraqi Ayatollah in Najaf and thereafter emerged as the leader of the Lebanese Shi'ites, who up to that point had made accommodation with their world of alien domination. Musa Sadr changed the subdued attitude of the Shi'ite community within a few years of his arrival. The heightened sociopolitical awareness among the Lebanese Shi'ites was underscored after his disappearance in Libya, when his mantle was inherited by another religious scholar, Sayyid Muhammad Husayn Fadl Allah, at present the reputed spiritual leader of the Hizbullah (the "Party of God"). Like other contemporary Shi'ite leaders, Fadl Allah (b. 1934) was educated in Najaf, where he lived until the 1960s while keeping in close touch with the Shi'ites of Lebanon by visiting them from time to time. After his permanent return to Lebanon in the mid-1960s, he dedicated himself, through his numerous writings and lectures, to the nurturing of activist Shi'ism. From the pattern of political quietism and submission prior to the 1970s, the Shi'ites of Lebanon emerged as a major political force in Lebanese affairs in the 1980s. What prompted a radicalized Shi'ism at this time in Lebanon?

In order to answer the questions that these developments in the Shi'ite Muslim world raise, we must consider "the historical development in Islam within the hegemony of the West during the past century and a half" which has given rise to the religious fundamentalism among Muslims in the modern age.[3] Religious fundamentalism among Muslims stems from the acute awareness of a conflict between "the religion which God has appointed and the historical development of the world which He controls."[4] To correct the spiritual crisis caused by this awareness, Islamic fundamentalism has endeavored to strike a balance between the divine promise of earthly success to the Muslims and their contemporary situation by moving in two directions: first, by introducing reforms to prevent further internal deterioration of Islamic religious life; and second, by protesting and resisting alien domination in any form over the Islamic character of Muslim societies.

The first direction—the requirement of internal reform—has been dominated by the repeated call to return to the original teachings of Islam in the Qur'an and the Prophet's paradigmatic life (the Sunna), in variant degree and form. The proponents of this form of Islamic response to the perceived corruption and heedlessness among contemporary Muslims firmly believe that the earthly power and success of the first generation of Muslims were due to their strict adherence to the pure faith, to the fundamentals of Islam. Consequently, if the Muslims want to regain their early position of power and prestige, they must fashion their practice, including their government, on the ideals prescribed by the Qur'an and by the pristine community. In a sense their religious fundamentalism is puritanical. It has a considerable following among numerous sectors of Muslim brotherhoods throughout the Islamic world.

The second direction—the requirement of resistance to alien intrusion—has been far more challenging in that it has meant providing an Islamic alternative to the consciously imported or externally imposed sociopolitical systems during the past century and a half. Because of the importation of modernized legal codes and social norms, the proponents of this form of Islamic response to the threat of the alienation of the Muslim peoples from the Islamic way of life have also had to fall back on the fundamentals of original Islam. However, their return to the Islamic fundamentals is based on the acceptance of the linear notion of development of an Islamic society. As such, their retrieval of relevant teachings that would enable them to build an Islamic system adaptable to the modern circumstances is selective. In other words, their fundamentalism can be designated as an activist type of reaction involving creative interpretation of religious ideas and symbols to render them applicable to contemporary Muslim history.

In answering the questions raised above in connection with Shiʿite activism in Iran, Iraq, and Lebanon, we will encounter both of these directions of Islamic fundamentalism, adopted in varying degrees of emphasis by the Shiʿite leaders responding to the perceived deterioration of Islam in the modern age.

At the outset it is important to state the difficulty faced by a Muslim Islamicist, who has actually witnessed the phenomenon of religious fundamentalism in the areas under consideration and whose primary interest is in conveying the actual practice in the Islamic world, in interpreting information pertaining to the dynamics of this practice so it will be intelligible and manageable to persons living and working in another culture. Ironically, at the present time, neither prejudice nor a lack of information stands in the way of understanding the phenomenon of Islamic fundamentalism; rather, the problem is that the considerable information we have has not advanced or refined our discernment of the *religious experience* of modern-day Muslims. In other words, what demands further clarification in Islamic fundamentalism relates to the essential nature of the Islamic religious experience. Most of the scholars on Islamic fundamentalism, because of a methodological insistence on neutrality and impersonality, have either denied its existence or have treated it casually. However, a central thesis of this essay is that the core of Islamic fundamentalism is the religious idealism that promises its adherents that once the Islamic norm is applied, it will effect dramatic change and vanquish the manifold sociopolitical and moral problems afflicting the Muslim peoples. In other words, it is Islamic religious experience, above all else, which guides believers in reasserting the relevancy and applicability of the normative pattern of pristine Islamic revelation to the task of creating the ethical order on earth. The self-confidence which arises from religious conviction inspires the believer to embark on the venture of reducing or eliminating altogether the existing gap between the ideal and the real. Thus our understanding of Islamic fundamentalism will have to be concerned with the innermost aspect of the ways in which Islam, as an eternal divine blueprint for ordering human life, provides its adherents with both revelatory and rational guidance as they experiment with ways of fulfilling the divine command in history.

Islamic civilization is founded on a unique understanding of creation and revelation which has been decisive in the shaping of Islamic identity. This difference in understanding can be studied in the Muslim comprehension of a salient feature of their history since Islam was proclaimed as a religion in seventh-century Arabia. The early history of Islam was marked by "centuries of temporal as well as spiritual achievement, an age of conquest and brilliance. . . . Muslim achievement was seen as intrinsic to their faith."[5] This faith maintained that the divine purpose is reflected in the cosmic order and in divine guidance for individual and collective conduct. Humanity is constantly faced with a fundamental moral choice of conducting itself so as to conform to the divine norm and be prosperous or face perilous doom as a consequence of rejecting that norm. Accordingly, human beings, as an inseparable part of the divinely originated cosmos, should aim at implementing God's normative will as expressed in the Islamic religious-moral law, the Shari'a. In this sense secularism, which in the context of modern Western civilization signifies a movement away from God, will inherently remain alien to Islam's theocentric emphasis.[6] Commentary on the most important goal of Islamic fundamentalism (i.e., the creation of a social order based on Islamic norms of society) must recognize this subtle yet substantial distinction between the worldviews of Islam and modern secularism, lest it be reduced to descriptive data "without soul."[7]

Islamic fundamentalism is rooted in the widespread Muslim belief that the centuries of temporal and spiritual achievement in the past were the result of the religious experience of the Muslim community. This understanding of religious history orients and guides the sociopolitical behavior of the Muslims at the present time, in part because religious leaders and increasingly the masses perceive that the imported Western models for creating social institutions and a social ethic have failed to respond to their aspirations.

Of course Islam as a religious phenomenon is not severed from the mundane stage of human political, social, and economic endeavor; on the contrary, Islamic faith becomes a self-propelling and self-reinforcing inducement to the establishment of a just order, the advent of which is to be heralded by the success of these endeavors. Accordingly, the religious culture of Islamic fundamentalism is seen as playing a meaningful, even irreplaceable, role in nurturing new social, political, and cultural attitudes and in building new social and political institutions capable of responding to the demands of modernity. With this relationship between religious culture and sociopolitical contexts in mind, the present study of Shi'ite activism as an objective illustration of religious fundamentalism in Islam will undertake to sketch the religious history of the Shi'ites in the context of the sociopolitical vicissitudes of the community in Iran, Iraq, and Lebanon in the last century and a half in order to answer the central question: why now?

The Vitality of Religious Experience in Islam

Islamic religious experience originates in a worldview shaped by revelatory monotheism that emphasizes individual and collective life as a reflection of God's purposeful creation to further the establishment of ethical order on earth. Accordingly, this religious experience has always involved attempts to comprehend and submit to God's revelation and to institute the just and good society. More importantly, this religious experience has created an ongoing tension between the exigencies of a timeless and immutable revelationary norm and its applicability for the Muslim community on earth. This tension has furthermore caused the Muslim community to perpetually reevaluate the extent of its responsibility to the divine norm and, in the face of repeated failure, has caused Muslims to reform themselves to conform to its objective realization in history. The impact of the hegemony of the West, while not irrelevant, is secondary in importance to this fundamental burden of the religious experience of the Muslim. The religious concern of a Muslim today is how to live as a Muslim in a world dominated by forces that fail to see the challenge of his faith.[8] The challenge of living as a Muslim in the modern age requires one to attend to the rehabilitation of the earthly success of early Islam, which was accomplished in a time when Muslims were in control of their own destiny without intrusion from colonial powers; when Muslims were themselves but still were successful and excelled in the world, reputedly because of their obedience to God's commands.[9]

The attempt to meet this ongoing religious challenge, complicated as it has been by the existence of injustice in the Muslim polity, gave rise in history to two distinct and in some ways even contradictory attitudes, namely, quietism and activism. Both of these attitudes had sanction in the revelational authority of the Qur'an and the Prophetic practice, the Sunna. However, the exponents of a quietist posture were often supporters of authoritarian politics and offered unquestioning and immediate obedience to almost any Muslim authority which publicly accepted the responsibility of upholding the Shariʿa. Gradually, as the development of the political history of Islam bears out, the quietist and authoritarian stance became associated with the majority Sunni Muslims. Sunni religious leaders (the ulama) had a major role to play in shaping the quietist posture toward rulers: in many cases, they acted as the legitimizers of the de facto Sunni power and encouraged Muslim peoples to accept and obey the de facto Sunni authority. On the other hand, the exponents of an activist posture supported radical politics and taught that there was no obligation of obedience to corrupt and wicked rulers; indeed they insisted that the duty of "commanding the good and forbidding the evil" in the Qur'an necessitated the removal of an unjust authority from power. In the early centuries, the activist and radical stance became an attribute of Shiʿite Islam.[10] However, following numerous unsuccessful attempts by the Shiʿite leaders at different times in their history to overthrow the ruling power (even when that power was Shiʿite), Shiʿites adopted the quietist attitude rather than the activist one. There is sufficient historical precedent to argue that the quietist attitude was at times adopted as a strategy for survival rather than as principle in itself. In the face of unfavorable circumstances it became imperative to protect Shiʿite life from destruction. Moreover, such quietist passivity was justified as a religiously sanctioned strategy *(taqiyya)* to allow for time to regroup and reorganize for future activism.

These realities render difficult the task of charting precisely the ebb and flow of Shiʿite activism, for given the proper sociopolitical conditions, the activist mentality may be seen as merely dormant or latent within Shiʿite quietism. As this essay argues, recent Shiʿite activism has, as in the past, emerged after a period of relative quietism in large part because of the central role played by Shiʿite religious leaders and their radical teachings in response to specific sociopolitical conditions. In other words, Shiʿite activism is in an important sense a function of the religious leaders' discernment of both the "signs of the times" and of the possibilities for action present within the historical tradition.

As a minority group living under adverse conditions, Shiʿites had by the end of the third century of their existence following the death of the Prophet in 632 C.E. developed a religious-legal intellectual mechanism for resolving pressing problems encountered by the believers in crisis situations. This intellectual development, initially prompted by practical problems encountered by the Shiʿites in dealing with political vicissitudes, followed a dialectical pattern, incorporating positions that at one time seemed untenable but that through further interpretation of theological-political doctrines in the context of sociopolitical exigencies were declared valid.

Thus, for instance, one of the major problems facing the Shiʿites as a minority living under Sunni domination in ninth-tenth century Arabia, Iraq, central Iran, or Khurasan (today the southern Soviet Union) was whether a member of the community could enter the service of an "unjust" (meaning Sunni) authority and accept an official administrative position in its government. As it turned out, the Shiʿites had penetrated the Sunni administration even before a solution to satisfy a Shiʿite believer's conscience was sought. Accordingly, the resolution that it was permissible for a Shiʿite to accept an official position and remuneration for service rendered to an unjust administration as long as that "benefited the brethren in faith" (i.e., other Shiʿites) was given in the form of a religious justification for engaging in something that was earlier deemed to be prohibited and even harmful to one's faith. Such intense Shiʿite preoccupation with preserving the original purport of Islamic revelation was necessary, it was argued, given the absence of the divinely designated Imam to lead Shiʿite affairs on a day-to-day basis.

The Shiʿites believed that the Prophet had designated their first Imam ʿAlī (d. 660) to succeed him as the head of the Muslim community. However, he was passed over for succession three times in a row by the caliphs Abū Bakr (d. 634), ʿUmar (d. 646), and ʿUthman (d. 656), who were recognized as such by the Sunni Muslims. Finally, almost a quarter-century after the Prophet's death, the caliphate was assumed by ʿAlī in 656. But ʿAlī's leadership was marred by political turmoil in the Muslim polity, and after a brief and contested rule, ʿAlī was murdered, and his son and designated successor, Hasan, became the caliph. Hasan's caliphate lasted for less than six months; then circumstances forced him to abdicate in favor of Muʿawiya, a member of the Umayyad clan whose enmity to the Hashimite clan of the Prophet dated back to pre-Islamic days in the seventh century C.E.

However, Hasan continued to be acknowledged by the Shiʿites as their second Imam. Against the backdrop of the political undoing of the Shiʿite leadership in the early history of Islam, the Shiʿite creed did not require the Imam to be invested with political authority in order to be accepted as the leader. The position of Imam was transmitted from one legitimate Imam to his successor through the process of special designation, which according to Shiʿite belief, also guaranteed authoritative transmission of the knowledge about Islamic revelation through these rightful and infallible Imams. Following Hasan, his brother Husayn became the third Imam of the Shiʿites. Both Hasan and Husayn held a special status in Muslim popular piety because they were the grandsons of the Prophet through his daughter Fatima. The popular veneration of the Prophet's family *(ahl al-bayt)* was common among Muslims in general.

However, in Shiʿism, the Prophet's family was regarded as the bearer of authentic Islam. Accordingly, all the Imams of the community had to be the descendants of ʿAlī and Fatima. The Shiʿites held that there were altogether twelve such Imams, including ʿAlī and his two sons, Hasan and Husayn. The twelfth Imam, the Mahdi, according to Shiʿite belief, is the last and the living Imam who disappeared in the year 874. His return as the messianic restorer of Islam is awaited by the Shiʿites.

The disappearance of the twelfth Imam is designated as the doctrine of "occultation." The period of occultation is divided into two forms: the "Short Occultation" and the "Complete Occultation." According to this division, during the Short Occultation, which lasted for some seventy years (874–941), the last Imam had appointed some of his prominent followers as his "special deputies" to carry on the function of guiding the community in its religious and social affairs. However, during the Complete Occultation (941–present), the learned jurists (the *faqih* or *mujtahid,* as they are also known) among the Shiʿites were believed to have been appointed by the twelfth Imam as his "general deputies" to guide the believers pending his return.[11] In other words, the learned Shiʿites were to assume the role of functional imams.

Undoubtedly the role of the functional imam was bound to become very influential and efficient in the community. Additionally, the community, whose single justification to be organized as the Shiʿa ("partisan" or "supporter") was its unquestionable loyalty to the Imam, did not find it religiously problematic to include in that loyalty the tangible, functional imam, the Shiʿite jurist. Evidently this sense of faithfulness on the part of the Shiʿites toward their religious leaders made feasible the emergence of Ayatollah-like leadership in Shiʿism.

Modernization and the Reaction of Shiʿite Religious Leadership

One of the ironies in the history of modernization in the Islamic world lies in the fact of its introduction from outside by the Western colonizing powers and by westernizing elites within the Muslim community. Modernization, along with the reaction of the religious leaders in the Islamic world to its failure to arrest the sociopolitical and moral breakdown of Muslim life, thus cannot be fully appreciated without taking into consideration the way modernization was introduced by "modernizing dictators" who failed to establish appropriate mediating institutions by which the indigenous populations might have developed the attitudes and techniques required to deal with the demands of modernity.[12] When the aggressive Western nations began, in the second half of the nineteenth century, to dictate the direction of Muslim polities, the complacency of the Muslim governments seemed almost to welcome the modernizing policies of the westernizers among the Muslims. To these westernizers, the obvious course of action under those circumstances involved replacing the weaker sociopolitical system of Muslim societies with the stronger Western model. Their solution—westernizing as a means either for the Muslim polity to hold its own in relation to the hegemonistic Western states, or simply as a means to attain power in the new order—served to extend and deepen Muslim dependence on the West.

Nevertheless, the Muslim westernizers failed to recognize that *westernization* was problematic without the attitudes and spirit which had imbued *modernization* in the West, including a "sense of innovation, of enterprise, of spontaneity" without which "the copier must always be several crucial steps behind."[13] In other words, modernization could not be adopted merely by westernizing externally. Muslim societies had to find their own resources from which to build their new social order. The Muslim westernizers were slow to recognize this and instead hastened to shed their weaker Islamic heritage in favor of the stronger Western heritage. Because this policy rendered them dependent upon an alien cultural and political world, it robbed them of the sense of unassailable identity necessary for them to be able to shape the world on their own terms.

This fateful policy led to disastrous consequences, at least in the eyes of the Shi'ite opponents of the westernizers within their ranks. One such consequence was the importation not only of Western technology but also of its accomplice, the Western secular worldview, which in the wake of the Enlightenment and its scientific and social advances, called into question the saving power in religion. Hence, modernization through westernization in the Islamic setting implied nothing less than the displacement of the view that the Qur'an and the Sunna could provide a framework for prescribing appropriate social institutions and social ethics in the technical age. More important, this approach to modernization had adverse implications for the cultural and the political future of the Muslim nations and threatened to leave Muslims "culturally homeless" in their own nations.[14]

Nonetheless, Muslim leaders, both religious and the modernizers and westernizers, whether in Iran or in other parts of the Islamic world in the nineteenth century, were confronted by almost constant foreign intervention. The traditional ruling elite and the existing military and administrative institutions were no longer capable of resisting or checking this intervention that destabilized the Muslim public order. In the face of the Western encroachment and the inability of the Islamic heritage to check the loss of independence because of internal decay of the Muslim societies, there was a unanimous call for change through reform and adaptation to deal with the political and social decline that had shaken the confidence of Muslims. In this way, the Muslim ordeal with modernization through westernization began with the need to respond effectively to the deeply felt attacks on the Muslim community by Western interference and even outright colonization of their homelands.

At any rate, the development of such a response was complicated by the fact that westernization had been accepted as a necessary tool to combat political decline, and this acceptance led in fact to an inability to control the wholesale and indiscriminate importation of Western ideas. In fact, for the Muslim modernizers, westernization was the only way of dealing with the political predicament caused by Western powers. Islamic universalism came to be regarded as internally incapable of arousing a Western type of nationalistic attitude deemed necessary, ironically, to free a Muslim land from foreign intervention. However, the adaptation of Western ideas not only served to eliminate the historical Muslim ambivalence toward the European concept of nation-state and to foster the national solidarity needed for success in implementing modernization; it also became the model for restructuring institutions dealing with the modern nation-state and the infrastructure to sustain public welfare.[15]

Nevertheless, an active reaction to Western domination, in some cases amounting to a militant anti-Western Muslim modernism, coincided with the despotism of the Qajar monarchs (1796–1925) in Iran and developed in response to their overt alliances with foreign powers for personal gain. Whereas the Shiʿite populace in Iran submitted to Qajar absolutism, the religious leaders, in alliance with their followers in the bazaar, attempted to carve a greater political role for themselves as the defenders of Islam "against the encroachment of infidels."[16]

In the nineteenth century, the interests of the Qajar shahs were served by the traditional and hierarchical organization of Persian society, in which arbitrary monarchical power was exercised through an elaborate system of formal alliances with various factions. Leading members of the village or tribal groups loyal to the Qajars were favored, for example, over their local and regional rivals, while urban leaders and neighborhood trade and bazaar merchants were pitted against each other. By appointing members of the Qajar tribe to the most important posts in the state and provincial bureaucracies, by imposing arbitrary taxes on dissenting factions, and by strengthening local alliance relationships, the shahs secured absolute control over the military and government administration. However, the resulting rivalries, including that between "the men of the sword" (administrators and military officials) and "the men of the pen" (the intellectual class, who played a increasingly prominent role in affairs of state) led to a contentious political climate that made possible British and Russian intervention in the nineteenth and twentieth centuries.

The "men of religion," the ulama, also enjoyed great influence in society through their performance of public services (e.g., they administered local justice, solemnized marriages, presided over funerals, and acted as guardians for orphans and widows). Consequently, they too developed an independent patronage network in Iran, centered largely in the bazaar, but with lines of influence throughout the urban slums and to a lesser degree in the rural areas. By virtue of their religious learning and their representation of the masses before the government, the ulama were also popularly regarded as representatives of the Hidden Imam. The Qajars realized that they could harness the prestige enjoyed by the ulama to their advantage. Accordingly, the shahs treated the ulama with a show of respect even as they attempted to reduce the influence of those among them who were potential leaders of popular discontent.[17]

The mid-nineteenth century witnessed a subtle but important increase of European influence. Iran established an institute of higher learning on Western lines, even as the Europeanization of urban life in the Qajar capital of Tehran became widespread. However, although increasing numbers of Iranian students were coming in direct contact with the Western lifestyle by pursuing an education in Europe, Iranian society in general remained unaffected by the new admiration of the West and retained its loyalty to Islamic cultural tradition. However, the somewhat superficial westernization of urban life upset traditional alliances, and the ulama found it necessary to defend the religion of Islam itself against the subversive influence of foreigners and foreign-educated Iranian youth.[18] In the eyes of some prominent ulama, the Qajar rulers had failed to uphold their principal duty of defending the boundaries of an Islamic polity from the incursions of non-Muslims. One explanation for this lapse that gained currency among the masses held that the elite segments of the society—Qajar family members, educated bureaucrats, and the wealthier families—had abandoned or compromised Islam in their eagerness to acquire the reputed wealth to be gained, presumably, by accepting Western domination and by mimicking the West. Subsequently a twentieth-century Iranian intellectual, Jalal Al-e Ahmad, denounced the situation as "Westoxication."[19]

As the nineteenth century entered its final quarter, some of the ulama became dissatisfied with the governmental policy of pursuing foreign money, which led to further foreign domination of the Muslim lands. Consequently they organized to oppose the tobacco monopoly granted to a British company in 1891.[20] The ulama saw the monopoly as a threat of foreign, infidel intervention in Muslim society.[21] The chief mujtahid, Mirza Hasan Shirazi, residing in Iraq at the time, issued a judicial decision *(fatwa)* prohibiting the smoking of tobacco until the monopoly was withdrawn. The decision by the mujtahid was obeyed throughout the Qajar realm. The success of the prohibition was achieved through the collaboration of intellectual, commercial, and religious groups: the religious class, operating in a traditional society in which actions contrary to religious authority were, and still are, regarded as a serious matter, were bound to play a leading role in political reform, but they did not do so in isolation.

The abolition of the tobacco concession was in large part facilitated by the emergence of a type of Qajar diplomacy, itself conditioned by the internal policy of "divide and rule" as a measure to keep the dynasty in control, which sought to draw contending foreign powers into Iran in order to pit them against each other and so maintain a rough balance of power and a maximum amount of freedom for the indigenous ruling power. In the case of the tobacco monopoly, Russia and Britain each took advantage of the Qajar concessions within the larger context of their rivalry for dominion over Iranian affairs.[22] The ulama and their supporters interpreted the Qajar concessions as an outright capitulation of Muslim territorial integrity to the foreign powers and hence regarded the powers, without any distinction, as an undivided, utterly hostile Western presence. (This perception of the foreign interference in Muslim affairs would be enshrined in the foreign policy of the Islamic Republic of the 1980s as expressed in the words of Khomeini's famous dictum: "Neither East nor West.")

That the Shi'ite ulama were able, in stark contrast to their Sunni counterparts, to assume a leading public role in opposition to the regime during the 1891–92 protests over the tobacco monopoly can best be understood in terms of the Shi'ite recognition of the more centralized religious leadership of the learned jurist. During the Qajar period, this recognition made it possible for a prominent mujtahid to assume the most authoritative religious office in Shi'ism, namely, that of *marja' al-taqlid* (source of imitation [for religious practice]). By virtue of a sound faith, knowledge, and character, marja' al-taqlid are entrusted with the rational interpretation *(ijtihad)* of the sources of Islamic law, the Qur'an and the Sunna, in the light of the requirements of modern life. When the Shi'ites acknowledge someone as the marja' al-taqlid, the latter's rulings in any matter become binding on them. Moreover, the wealthy in the community send their religious offerings to the marja. This practice assured the independence of the Shi'ite religious authority, who resided in Iraq to escape royal pressure. This unique feature in the Shi'ite religious institution allowed Mirza Hasan Shirazi, the acknowledged marja' al-taqlid in 1891, to command obedience to his decree prohibiting the smoking of tobacco. However, as pointed out earlier, the religious decree could not have by itself achieved the social mobilization of all the elements in the society. The alliance between the religious and the modernizing secular sections of the society, on the one hand, and the cooperation of the commercial sector with the ulama, on the other, was of great consequence in turning the concession into a national movement.

The Constitutional Revolution in the first decade of the twentieth century provided a second occasion for alliances between the ulama and different and at times disparate, and secular, factions within a society absorbing the impact of modernization. However, the Revolution (1906–11) also resulted in the dissolution of the ulama-secular coalition which had proven so effective in 1892. The initial demands of the coalition for reforms in the legal and governmental systems through constitutionalism represented "the first direct encounter in modern Iran between traditional Islamic culture and the West"[23] and generated an intense debate between different factions belonging to a spectrum of ideologies.

The last decade of the nineteenth century and the early years of the twentieth century was a time of heightened popular resentment against the Qajar family. And although the shah Muzaffaruddin made certain attempts at domestic reform in 1900, concessions granted to Europeans and Russians to pay for his extravagant travels in Europe led to foreign interference in the internal affairs of Iran. Moreover, the shah disregarded the warnings of religious leaders to abide by the Shari'a and thus was perceived to be abandoning the delicate relationship with the ulama that served as the basis for religiopolitical consensus. Popular resentment led in turn to demands for reforms in political procedures in order to effectively limit the autocratic power of the ruler through the promulgation of a constitution, and to guarantee active participation of the new political elite in the elected consultative assembly.[24] There was support for the establishment of a "chamber of justice" with the authority to address sociopolitical grievances.

Thus the opening of the first representative assembly *(majlis)* in 1906 was in large measure a victory of Iranian intellectuals seeking political redress by the various means of a constitution, a national assembly empowered to set limits on royal finances and to regulate administrative practices, a code of laws, and in the place of the shah and his governors, regular courts to administer them. The intellectuals were able to muster the support of the religious leaders and their popular constituencies. Moreover, their familiarity with European constitutionalism earned them the leading role in providing the general direction and in making specific demands such as the one for a chamber of justice. The Shiʿite jurists provided the necessary religious legitimation for these demands and reminded the shah of the temporary nature of his rule in the absence of the Imam of the Age, the only authentic ruler of the Muslim community.

However, not all the jurists in Iran were supporters of political reforms and liberalization. Some prominent jurists regarded the modernization of political institutions as un-Islamic and were accordingly royalists, even when they believed in the necessity of legal restraints on the monarchical authority. Consequently they encouraged counter-revolutionary associations to oppose the liberal democratic ones that had sprung up throughout Iran. Undoubtedly, besides their misgivings about the overall advantages of modernization through westernization, the opponents of political liberalization regarded the reforms undertaken by the Constitutionalists, especially in the areas affecting judiciary and financial administration, as a challenge to their traditional authority.[25]

In 1907 the opposition to the Constitutionalist reforms was led by a prominent jurist, Shaykh Fadlullah Nuri, who formed a political association to demand that all parliamentary legislation (which he regarded as an innovation of a sort in the Islamic context) be subject to ratification of a committee of leading members of the Shiʿite religious leadership to ensure its religious validity. Nuri's proposal, which was passed and made part of the constitution, marked the tumultuous relationship between the secularly conceived legislative assembly and the religiously derived legal doctrine that regarded the divine law, the Shariʿa, as the perfect and sufficient norm for sociopolitical organization at any time. Moreover, it created a political rift between the modernizers and the religious leadership that would continue to the present time and would adversely affect much of what the Constitutional Revolution had accomplished in the area of political liberalization.

However, because the constitutional movement had embraced a vast group of people from every social quarter, it also generated varying expectations. Each element in the governing elite—the educated westernized intelligentsia, commercial leaders, and the Shiʿite jurists—had its own agenda in supporting the creation of modern institutions to bolster the aims of the Constitutional Revolution. Whereas the westernizing intelligentsia and the commercial leaders had little or no interest in pursuing any Islamic goals in providing the means to satisfy the demands of the people, the Shiʿite jurists saw the revolution as an opportunity to implement the Shariʿa, the divine blueprint for a just order, in all its aspects throughout Iran.[26]

The Constitutional Revolution thus failed to unite the disparate and at times conflicting intellectual elements to create a uniform ideology and carry out its program of action (which was, according to the jurists, that of implementing the Shariʿa, and according to the modernizing intellectuals, that of establishing a constitutional system of government and modernization of the state apparatus). A conflict between traditionally educated jurists and the modernizers with a modern secular education seems in retrospect inevitable. Through their traditional juridical training in the theoretical basis of the Shariʿa, which prepared them to inferentially deduce fresh judicial decisions under changed circumstances, the jurists found the application of Islamic norms in the modern age both relevant and feasible. On the other hand, the modernizers, under the influence of European secular ideologies, recognized immediately the tension between the concept of a state based on Western-influenced institutions and the traditional Muslim ambivalence to a political life founded on such an exalted sense of nation. Accordingly they deemed it impossible for the traditional Islamic norm to provide democratic structure and thus facilitate public participation in government in a modern nation-state. Consequently the religious leaders and their modern-educated partners in the constitutional movement disagreed on the implementation of the Islamic norms in the changed environment.

With subsequent sessions of the majlis came unprecedented and ever more complex laws for electors which had the practical effect of continually reducing the religious component of the chamber. It soon became clear that the traditional ulama and the westernizing Muslims simply had little in common beyond their opposition to the regime. The westernizers sought in European models the ideal constitution, while the ulama-merchant coalition sought to protect religious prerogatives and the traditional bazaar economy. The atomization of the constitutionalist movement, first into modernizing and traditionalist camps and then within each camp, accelerated as primordial loyalties and radical ideologies splintered the antiroyalist forces. However, the coup de grace was delivered to the constitutionalist forces, ironically enough, by the West.

The 1907 Anglo-Russian entente divided Iran into three spheres of influence, comprising a Russian-dominated north, a small neutral zone, and a British-controlled south. In June 1908, with the treaty as justification, the Russians instigated a successful coup and backed by troops in Tabriz, quickly assumed control of much of the country. They were kept from Tehran itself only by the concerted action of an alliance of northern revolutionaries and Bakhtiyar tribesman. In 1911, however, Russian forces found a pretext to march on Tehran, causing the collapse of the majlis and the dissolution of the modernist-ulama alliance.

This disagreement between the secularly educated Muslim modernizers and the religious leaders had wider ramifications in the future role of Islam and its interpreters. The jurists became suspicious of the religious sincerity of the liberal modernizers and their imported Western ideas about modernization. Moreover, the ultimate defeat of the constitutional regime in 1911–12 and the restoration of the traditional ruling class through the intervention of the foreign powers of Great Britain and Russia, who saw control of Iran during the First World War as essential to their military strategy against the Germans and Ottomans, left very little opportunity for the jurists to test their refined juridical methodology in deducing laws and to demonstrate its feasibility in sociopolitical relations in the modern situation. Furthermore, the position of the most prominent among the Shiʿite jurists, who were regarded as functional imams and thus as models for the believers, became increasingly confined to strictly religious matters, a development which forced their withdrawal from a sociopolitical setting which now required a new type of expertise. The establishment of institutes of technology and higher learning on the Western model, dedicated to training the new bureaucrats of the modern governmental and administrative systems, weakened and finally undermined the monopoly of the Shiʿite jurists as shapers of their followers' worldview.

Hence, modernization through westernization left the religious leadership isolated from the public domain and from public discourse. In light of this precedent, the revolution of 1978–79 is all the more striking in that both the leadership and the general body of the Shiʿa had for the balance of the twentieth century been conditioned to accept that doctrinally as well as functionally, Shiʿite jurists could not assume political leadership, *especially* in the modern context.

Following the deposition of the last Qajar ruler in 1925 and prior to the revolution of 1978–79, Iran was ruled by Reza Khan and his son Muhammadreza, who assumed the crown under the dynastic name of the Pahlavi. Reza Shah was at first cautious in his dealings with the ulama, whom he had assured of his intention to fulfill Islamic law and to forego any type of radical reforms like those introduced in the neighboring Turkish republic with the secularist policies of Kemal Atatürk. However, Reza Shah pursued a despotic program of modernization that included the suppression of all opposition. Between 1925 and 1941 the program was undertaken with a careful eye on conservative and religious sensibilities. Educational reform included the institution of a public elementary school system and a uniform school curriculum during the years 1925–30 and the establishment of Iran's first modern university in 1935. Coupled with the development of industry and other economic enterprises, the reforms reinforced the decline in the influence of the ulama and their traditional allies in political and social life.

By the late 1930s, the consolidation of royal autocracy allowed for a more direct attack on the religious establishment. The conflict was intensified by a series of direct attacks on the centers of ulama power in Iran. Attempts were made to control the Shiʿite mourning rites commemorating the martyrdom of Imam Husayn; mosques were opened to tourists; exit visas for the annual hajj pilgrimage to Mecca became a state prerogative; the veil was outlawed and women were ordered to dress in western-style clothing; and statues of the shah (suspicious of idolatry, the ulama had prohibited the representation of human figures) began to appear everywhere. The leading ulama within Iran were left with minimal jurisdiction in the public order to challenge the shah's policy of modernization, which continued to restrict the public role of Islam.

With World War II came the end to Reza Shah's development program and his rule. In the wake of the German attack on Russia in 1941 and Germany's intention to use Iran as a base against Russia, the British and the Russians demanded free transit and military assurances from Reza Shah, who refused to comply. As a result, Iran was occupied in the north by the Russians and in the south by the British. In September 1941 the allies pressured the shah to abdicate, and his young son Muhammadreza was put on the throne.

The young shah assumed the crown under politically unstable conditions created by the occupation. These conditions were a major factor in the growth of oppositional organizations and economic and social disruptions. From 1943 to 1945 political activity increased and political groups emerged under diverse ideologies, from the conservative, religious party on the right, supported by the ulama and their allies in the bazaar, landlords, and tribes, to the leftist Tudeh, with its communist and socialist program. Between the two was a nationalist group led by Mohammed Mosaddeq, whose opposition to foreign intervention in Iranian affairs was well-known.

The conflicting currents of ulama politics came most clearly to the surface in the Mosaddeq interregnum. Whereas leading members of the religious class remained withdrawn from political involvement, some politically activist ulama adopted a radical stance by organizing small but enthusiastic anti-Western groups to combat the antireligious attitude perpetrated by the regime. One such group was the *Fida'iyan-i Islam* under the Ayatollah Kashani, made up of a small number of young zealots who assassinated persons they regarded as enemies of Islam. The Fida'iyan, like other small groups under the leadership of the activist ulama, were a religious nationalist group and as such had supported Mosaddeq's anti-British policies during the nationalization of the oil industry, a move designed to ease the economic and social crisis that faced Iran in the late 1940s and early 1950s. However, some senior ulama, including Ayatollahs Bihbahani and Burujirdi, suspicious of the secularist tendencies in Mosaddeq's nationalist movement, were in favor of a constitutional monarchy. Thus, by the time of the overthrow of the nationalist Mosaddeq regime in 1953 by an American- and British-supported coup, the ulama from both quietist and activist camps were united in their support of the coup, which returned the shah to power. The shah returned with a vengeance and took repressive measures to deal with his opposition, whether religious or otherwise.[27]

After World War II, Iran experienced massive economic transformations with significant political consequences, including the social and cultural dislocation of particular groups. Throughout this experience the government was engaged in implementing a program of development and modernization through the building of a high-capital, high-technology economy. This process virtually destroyed the traditional social fabric of Iranian society, creating as a consequence political difficulties of varying intensity. The shah's modernization policy "completed the destruction of important sectors of the rural and bazaar economies and it forced large numbers of people out of ancestral homes and villages into the urban labor market and into new patterns of life. Moreover, much of the social and cultural impact of the shah's program was erratic and inconsistent."[28] The program notably failed to extend opportunities for active participation in the political process to a new generation of modern, educated Iranians; it also tended to alienate the new generation from their comprehensive cultural roots through educational and cultural policies which diluted the Iranian religious identity by overemphasizing its pre-Islamic component. In the eyes of many who would come to oppose the regime, the forced modernization, bereft of opportunities for the political development of potential citizens, was to proceed at any cost and through ruthless measures adopted by a despotic authority.[29]

The economic and political conditions under the shah in the 1960s and 1970s created circumstances ripe for the emergence of a new type of leadership in Iran, though not necessarily a religious one. There is evidence to support the argument that the development policies pursued by the shah's absolutist system were bound to create an oppositional unifying leader who would attempt to reinspire confidence in the traditional Iranian culture as capable of producing an alternative to modernization programs that had threatened the traditional and religious security of the ordinary people and, more dramatically, had led to the human misery attendant upon profound social and economic dislocation. Certainly it is clear that the conditions under the shah were the sine qua non for the emergence of political activism among the previously quiescent Shi'ites of Iran.

The Shi'ite religious leadership seized upon this potential for activism in the growing disillusionment with the rapid modernization and the social consequences of Western "cultural colonization."[30] Moreover, the religious leadership was fully aware of the direct or indirect attempts at undermining their influence and appropriating their traditional perquisites. However, because of their self-imposed aloofness from the complex sociopolitical developments of the period and their lack of intellectual preparation to respond effectively to the developments, the leaders were ill-equipped, in dealing with modern ideologies, to engage in a critical analysis of the factors contributing both to the social dislocations and to the weakening of tradition. In addition, modernization had the effect of alienating many members of the Muslim community from their religious leaders. Because the potential of Shi'ite religious culture for political activism rested upon the interpretations of the social, economic, cultural, and political conditions pronounced by the marja' al-taqlid, it is probably correct to suggest that, by weakening the influence of the religious leaders, the shah's government in the 1960s sought to undermine the practical religious culture and the sense of moral responsibility toward these conditions.

The de-emphasis of the Islamic element in the restructuring of a modern Iranian society was directed more particularly toward the educated class and the younger generation in the high schools and universities. Development programs that as a matter of policy ignored Islam as an important factor in orienting Iranian society to modernity were hardly concerned about the erosion of traditional moral and religious values that increasingly affected the educated class. The marja' al-taqlid and other leading members of the religious class found it most difficult to reach the young and the educated, disoriented as they were, the religious leaders believed, by the corrupt, narrowly materialistic lifestyle associated with Western prosperity.

Educated Muslim youth, frustrated in the 1960s and the early 1970s with the failure of imported Western ideologies and institutions to satisfy their sociopolitical aspirations, began to exert pressure on their religious leaders to reinterpret Islamic revelation and apply it to their situation. However, any attempt to shape responses to meet the needs and demands of the people in the contemporary setting inevitably involved revising, or even abandoning, traditional (and socially outmoded) religious prescriptions, especially in the area of interpersonal relationships, that were often conditioned by an outdated sociopolitical perspective. For example, traditional Islamic sources are almost silent on the public role of a Muslim woman, because their ideal involvement in traditional Muslim society was always conceived of in terms of their domestic pursuits. With the introduction of compulsory education for girls and the opportunities that became available to the modern educated Muslim women outside their homes, religious leaders were expected to provide necessary religious sanction for their extradomestic exposure.

Such an attempt to shape a response to modern living was perceived as requiring "rethinking" and "reapplying" of independent reasoning (ijtihad). In the past, application of personal independent reasoning by the Shi'ite jurists had made it possible to maintain a smooth interaction between the demands of the original teachings of Islam and the new contingencies underlying the social, political, and economic conditions of the time. In the context of the rapid pace of social and political change in the affairs of the Shi'ite community during the modernization program of the shah, the religious leaders were not yet willing to venture innovative decisions to ease the burden of the Muslim conscience as it struggled to find an answer to the vital question: is Islam capable of providing direction to a modern life?

In the absence of the twelfth Imam, the functional imam (i.e., the marja' al-taqlid), was seen as legitimately invested with the discretionary authority to make binding decisions for the public interest of the Shi'ite community; he alone could undertake to rethink the relevancy of Islamic norms to modern life. As far as the political order was concerned, the assumption of the Hidden Imam's constitutional authority by anyone, including a well-qualified Shi'ite jurist, would depend on a juridical reinterpretation of the doctrine that the ideal ruler was the Imam in occultation. Accommodation with changed circumstances within the context of existing political arrangement had precedents in the long history of Shi'ism. The historical precedents would guide them to infer solutions in modern times.

Historical Roots of Contemporary Shi'ite Activism

If Islamic fundamentalism in the modern setting signifies the "reassertion of the relevancy and applicability of the given norm, with the intent to enhance its effective application,"[31] then Shi'ism offers the modern world a rare glimpse of the dynamics of a religious ideology that embodies postulates about active divine intervention in human history and claims that its program will establish the best social order of which human beings are capable.

As a religious ideology Shi'ism functions within a specific sociopolitical order which it constantly evaluates and calls upon its adherents either to defend and preserve or to overthrow and transform. Moreover, it operates within a specific cultural setting whose most powerful symbols it utilizes in order to articulate its subtle and even complex ideas in the general language of the people. Accordingly, Shi'ite religious ideology is both a critical assessment of human society and a program of action, whether leading to a quietist authoritarianism or an activist radicalism, as the situation may require, to realize God's will on earth to the fullest extent possible.

From this ideological perspective, Shi'ite movements, at different times in history, have reflected the intent of Islamic revelation to the construction of a new society and polity. The obvious question that arises in the minds of pious Muslims when they experience injustice, whether personally or collectively, is: do Muslims have an obligation to take arms to oppose and expunge tyranny and corruption within the community? The response to the question of perceived injustices has depended upon the current sociopolitical circumstances and has been conditioned by the precedents set by the Shi'ite Imams whose reactions to similar situations remain a precedent for their followers.

Shi'ite theologians and jurists have treated the major question of armed revolt against an unjust government by examining whether such an action is justifiable without the leadership of a divinely appointed Imam, or whether any individual qualified Shi'ite can undertake to fight the tyranny and corruption of his time if it has reached an intolerable level. Historically the guidance of Shi'ite jurists, whether leading to radical political action or otherwise, turned on their interpretation of the two basic doctrines intrinsic to an authoritative perspective or worldview that organizes the mundane existence of Shi'ite Muslims. These two doctrines are the justice *(al-'adl)* of God and the leadership *(al-imama)* of the righteous individuals. In the highly politicized world of Islam there have been numerous ideas and conceptions about God's purpose on earth and leadership of human society. Territorial expansion in the name of Islam and the process of supervising the conquests and administering the affairs of the conquered peoples not only demanded strong and astute leadership, it also required the creation of a system that would provide stability and prosperity. Undergirding this social, political, and economic activity in the early centuries was the promise of Islamic revelation that only through obedience to God will believers accomplish the creation of a just and equitable public order embodying the will of God. The promise was buttressed by the certainty that God is just and truthful. Divine justice demanded that God do what was best for humanity, and divine truthfulness generated the faith that God's promise would be fulfilled if humanity kept its covenant of working toward a truly godly life.

The proof that God is just and truthful was provided by His creating the rational faculty in human beings and sending revelation through the prophets to guide it toward the creation of an ethical world order. The indispensable connection between divine guidance and the creation of an ethical world order provided an ideological mandate for the interdependency between the religious and the political in Islam. It also pointed to some sort of divine intervention being necessary in the creation of a just society. Consequently, the focal point of the Islamic belief system envisions the Prophet and his properly designated successors as representing God on earth—the God who invested authority in them in order for them to rule over humankind rightly. In other words, the linkage between the divine investiture and the creation of an Islamic world order became a salient feature of Islamic ideological discourse almost from the beginning. Accordingly, the basic religious focus on the creation of just order and leadership, which can create and maintain it, orients the worldview of the Muslims in general and of the Shi'ite Muslims in particular.

However, the essential connection between the religious and the political became an underlying source of crises in the Muslim community. The first major crisis in the political history of Shi'ite Islam occurred with the death of the Prophet (632 C.E.). At this time the first Imam of the Shi'ites, 'Alī, according to Shi'ism, was denied his legitimate claim to succession as the head of the Muslim community, their caliph. This was regarded as usurpation of the rights of 'Alī. The circumstances demanded that Muslims explain the situation that seemed to point toward the breach of divine promise. The desperation felt by the pious observers of the political scene is discernible in the subsequent insistence upon a qualified leader who would assume political power to further the divine plan and to enable God's religion to succeed.

The crisis prepared the ground for the emergence of the early *Shīʿa* (partisans) of ʿAlī as a distinct group in the Muslim community who refused to acknowledge the legitimacy of the three caliphs, Abū Bakr, ʿUmar, and ʿUthman, who had preceded ʿAlī in the Medinan caliphate (632–56). However, these caliphs, including ʿAlī, are regarded by the Sunni as the ideal Muslim rulers who, because of their personal character, deserved the position of leadership in the community.[32] The differences in the Muslim community over the question of rightful successor to the Prophet marked the permanent rift between the two factions that would gradually develop into two distinct schools of thought in Islam, namely, Sunnism, the majority, and Shiʿism, the minority faction. Sunnism and Shiʿism, even when they have shared common beliefs in the matters of fundamentals of Islam, have differed substantially in their conceptualization of early religious history. Whereas Sunnism has regarded this religious history as the period of the great earthly success of Islam to which later generations of Muslims should aspire to return, Shiʿism has downplayed the period as a deviation from the true Islamic position. The ideal period in Shiʿism hence is to come in the future when the last messianic Imam, the Mahdi, will establish a rule of justice.

The period that followed this first crisis in Shiʿite history witnessed discontent among all Muslims. Some were moved by profound religious conviction and deep moral purpose to seek activist political steps to confront injustices. The activist solution to seek redress for wrongs committed by those in authority was by no means limited to the Shiʿites only; rather, dissatisfaction and dissension were widespread among all people, a situation which led to the murder of the third caliph ʿUthman in 656. He was regarded by the rebelling Muslims as both personally corrupt and politically unjust.[33]

The period, moreover, generated much discussion and deliberations regarding the duty of obedience to an unjust ruler who caused disobedience to God. The most important questions that were raised in this connection and that had implications for the political stance adopted by some activist groups, including the Shiʿites was, what were the limitations over the power of a Muslim authority in the state that ideally existed as a divinely approved necessity to promote justice and equity? And what were justifiable courses of action that the community could take if the authority in power became unjust, thereby making the state evil?

Responses to these questions could not ignore the Qur'anic imperative that calls for "commanding the good and forbidding the evil," which in fact was the underlying principle in the permission for undertaking *jihad* (the struggle, up to and including armed struggle, to realize God's will for humanity). Jihad, as such, becomes a divinely sanctioned instrument to procure the divine will on earth. However, jihad in the sense of "holy war" is less evident in the Qur'an. The Qur'an justifies defensive warfare on moral grounds, namely, to fight injustices and persecution in society. A legitimate Muslim ruler is obligated to undertake defensive jihad to protect the lives and property of the Muslim community. Thus it became firmly established in early Shiʿite theology that every pious Muslim was to oppose any nominally Muslim authority regarded as corrupt and degenerate, as long as such opposition did not endanger the believers' lives.

By the time of the second crisis, the end of manifest leadership of the Imams through the occultation of the twelfth and last Imam Muhammad al-Mahdi (941), the notion of a revolution to overthrow unjust authority favored by the radical element in the Shiʿite community had taken on an apocalyptic cast: the revolution would come in a future time of fulfillment. This belief in the future coming of the Mahdi, the restorer of pristine Islam, is shared by all Muslims, Sunnis and Shiʿites alike (although the term "Mahdi" has become associated more with its Shiʿite connotations). However, in Shiʿism, belief in messianism has served a complex, seemingly paradoxical function. It has been the guiding doctrine behind both an activist political posture, calling upon believers to remain alert and prepared at all times to launch the revolution with the Mahdi who might appear at any time, and behind a quietist waiting for God's decree, in almost fatalistic resignation, in the matter of the return of this Imam at the End of Time.[34] In both cases the main problem was to determine the right course of action at a given time in a given social and political setting. The adoption of the activist or quietist solution depended upon the interpretation of conflicting traditions attributed to the Shiʿite Imams about the circumstances that justified radical action. Resolution of the contradiction in these traditions in turn was contingent upon the agreement about, and acknowledgement of, the existence of an authority who could undertake to make the Imam's will known to the community. Without such a learned authority among the Shiʿites, it was practically impossible to acquire reliable knowledge about whether a government had indeed become evil, and whether a radical solution was an appropriate form of struggle against it.

In Shiʿism, authentic religious knowledge was regarded as part of the divine guidance that was available to the community even though the Imams were not invested with political authority and were living under the political power exercised by the de facto governments. With the termination of the theological Imamate in the tenth century, when the last Imam went into occultation, the Shiʿites were faced with the issue of the continuation of this guidance. The Imam's authority (notwithstanding his lack of political power, he still had the right to demand obedience from his followers) had been located in his ability to interpret divine revelation infallibly. The Imam's interpretation and elaboration of the revelation formed, in fact, part of the religious obligations binding on believers. Moreover, the interpretation was regarded as the right guidance needed by the people at all times. In the absence of the twelfth Imam during the occultation, the Shiʿites sought that guidance in the authority that could assume the decisive responsibility of guiding the community to the will of God under critical circumstances.

Following the occultation, the Shiʿites believe that the authority was assumed by the deputies of the Hidden Imam, who were believed to have been directly appointed by him. During the Short Occultation for some seventy years following 874, four prominent members of the Shiʿite community became the functional imams. The year

941 marked the beginning of the Complete Occultation which extends to the present time. During the Complete Occultation the duty of guiding the community was undertaken by the qualified Shiʿite jurists who, according to Shiʿite belief, became the leaders of the community through a general designation of the Hidden Imam.

This development consolidated the authority of Shiʿite jurists by initiating an unprecedented relationship between believers and their religious scholars. This sense of devotion to the religious leaders as the representatives of the Imam made possible, after 941, the exercise of powerfully influential religious leadership in the Shiʿite community, pending the return of the messianic Hidden Imam.

The Leadership of the Jurist and its Legitimation in Shiʿite Political Jurisprudence

The question of religious leadership has always received greater attention in Shiʿism than in Sunnism. This is reflected in the debate among the Shiʿites regarding the theological propriety of the religious scholars (the mujtahid or faqih) assuming the leadership of the Shiʿite community as the specifically designated deputies of the Hidden Imam. However important the question of the continuation of divine guidance might have been for the Shiʿites to survive under the de facto governments of their times, it was not for just anyone to undertake the responsibility of guiding the community. In accordance with the Shiʿite expectations of their religious leadership, the position of a jurist as a deputy of the Imam certainly needed authorization from the Imam himself, a sort of deputization that could guarantee the availability of reliable guidance. But in view of the prolonged occultation of the Imam and the absence of special designation during this period, no realization of this prerequisite was possible. The issue of the proper designation of leadership was discussed, and exegetically resolved, in the works of Shiʿite political jurisprudence. Therein the lack of specific designations by the Imam led to an important distinction between "power" (which could exact or enforce obedience) and "authority" (which reserved the right to demand obedience, depending on legal-rational circumstances), a situation that had existed even during the lifetime of the Imams. Under those concrete historical circumstances (the lack of actual power) Shiʿite jurists argued that both the investiture of authority and the assumption of political power were necessary for the creation of the rule of justice.

However, delegation of the Imam's authority to a jurist who could assume both the authority and the power of the Imam without specific deputization was deemed dangerous by the jurists themselves. As historical events unfolded, and as Shiʿite peoples were subjected to one seemingly arbitrary, autocratic rule after another, the jurists grew increasingly wary of the exercise of absolute authority without divine protection in the form of the infallibility that the Shiʿite Imam enjoyed as a successor of the Prophet, and taught that government by anyone besides the Imam was evil and those engaged in it inevitably corrupted. This attitude toward contemporary governments can be discerned in the works of Shiʿite jurisprudence in which those jurists took it upon themselves to produce a coherent response to the problem and the nature of delegation of the Imam's authority to a Shiʿite jurist and to assert the Twelver Shiʿite doctrine that the infallible Imam was the only Just Ruler *(al-sultan al-ʿadil)*. Pending the establishment of the ideal rule of the Hidden Imam, the possibility of an absolute claim to political power *(saltana)* and authority *(wilaya)* resembling that of the Imam himself was ruled out. Nevertheless, the rational and revelational need to exercise authority in order to manage the affairs of the community was recognized and legalized.

During the Occultation the establishment of the Twelver Shiʿite dynasties like those of the Buyids (945–1055), the Safavids (1501–1786) who converted Iran to Shiʿism, the Zands (1750–94), the Qajars (1794–1925) and the Pahlavis (1925–79) did not alter the basic doctrine of the Twelver Shiʿite leadership, that is, the doctrine of the theological Imamate. According to this doctrine, the twelfth Imam was the only legitimate ruler of the Muslim community, and he would return at the End of Time to establish the Islamic public order. Nonetheless, the indefinite absence of the Imam allowed the jurists to develop a profile of a just Shiʿite figure of authority, however temporary and fallible, who could in the interim follow the Qur'anic mandate of creating a public order that would "enjoin the good and forbid the evil."

It is important to bear in mind that Shiʿite jurists were individually responding at specific times to specific political situations created by the establishment of Shiʿite temporal power in their works on jurisprudence. Their works included judicial opinions about the reigning political power, whether Sunni rulers or the professing Twelver Shiʿite dynasties. Thus there was a lack of any definite organization or strict uniformity of response among them. The Shiʿite jurists in the classical age (ninth–twelfth centuries), although often living under some sort of state protection (especially under the Shiʿite dynasty of the Buyids), continued to be private individuals as they are today. Although less willing than their Sunni counterparts to relax the limits of Islamic authority or to encourage obedience to unjust and tyrannical governments, Shiʿite jurists were themselves engaged in rationalization of, and accommodation to, their historical circumstances. These responses to the existing political order reflect the tensions within the Shiʿite political jurisprudence created not only by the occultation of the Imam but also by intellectual interaction between Shiʿite and Sunni scholars. The occultation of the Imam and the minority status of the Shiʿites made it possible, and in some instances necessary, for them to be quite pragmatic and realistic in their contacts with contemporary de facto governments and in the formulation of their judicial opinions about them, more so if the de facto rulers happened to be professing Shiʿites. Accordingly, each work of jurisprudence is copiously documented by quotations from the fundamental sources of Islamic religious practice, the Qur'an and the Sunna, as well as the critical evaluation of the opinions of precedent-setting jurists. Meticulous examination of past legal decisions and the rational and traditional proofs produced to support them reveal that these decisions were never simply theological abstractions but, to the contrary, were made in intimate dialogue with specific situations in the Muslim polity at the time.

In order to trace the development of the jurist's authority that culminated in the powerful position of an Ayatollah in the 1970s and 1980s, it is necessary to proceed chronologically, from period to period of Shi'ite jurisprudence. It is convenient to divide the responses of Shi'ite jurists in regard to the nature of deputyship and the extent of its authority into four historical periods when major judicial decisions with implications for the contemporary Shi'ite leadership were inferentially deduced.[35]

The first was the Buyid era (945–1055), the time of a decentralized Iranian dynasty that controlled such centers as Baghdad in Iraq and both Shiraz and Kirman in Iran. This was the first instance of a Twelver Shi'ite dynasty coming to power. However, the Buyids did not lay any claim to religious authority. In fact, they allowed the Sunni caliph to remain as the head of the Muslim community. Consequently, the Buyid assumption of temporal power did not affect the basic Shi'ite doctrine regarding the constitutional leadership of the twelfth Imam. Nevertheless, according to the juridical formulations at this time, a number of obligatory religious acts had implications for the Imam's constitutional authority. Islamic law required that either the Imam or his specifically designated deputy should be present to undertake or convene the religious duties with political implications. Thus, for instance, in the case of waging offensive jihad against nonbelievers, Shi'ite law required that only the Imam as the head of the Islamic polity could initiate the war against the nonbelievers, or he could appoint his deputy to undertake it on his behalf. Evidently in the absence of the Imam or his special deputy during the Occultation, the question of offensive jihad was ruled as suspended until the Imam reappeared as the messianic restorer of pristine Islam.

While the question of engaging in offensive jihad had little relevance for the Shi'ites living as a minority in the Islamic world in the tenth century, there were other obligations in the Islamic law, such as the duty of preservation of social order, collection of religiously ordained taxes, and administration of justice, which had relevance for the existence of the Shi'ite community under changing sociopolitical circumstances. The performance of these sociopolitically relevant obligations could not be postponed indefinitely, and the juridical works produced during the Buyid period advocate and support the major development of that period, namely, the assumption of leadership of the Shi'ite community by their qualified jurists. This assumption of leadership was in turn (and necessarily) seen as a logical extension of the leadership of the Imam as the dependable guide of the Shi'ites.

The Shi'ite jurists became the custodians of the Shi'ite creed, including the theory of the spiritual and temporal authority of the Imam. The establishment of a Twelver Shi'ite temporal authority of the Buyids during the occultation of the Imam, although an innovation of a sort, had absolutely no impact on the central doctrine of Shi'ism, namely, the Imamate. Accordingly, no attempts were made to explain this development in political jurisprudence as a political development. The juridical decisions made at this time disclosed the conviction of Shi'ite jurists that the continuation of the socioreligious structure of the community did not depend upon the temporal authority of the Shi'ite dynasty; rather it depended upon the consolidation of the institution of the Imam's deputyship. In almost all the cases in which religious acts with political implications were required, the jurists deemed it permissible for the

Twelver Shi'ite jurists to substitute for the Imam or his specifically designated deputy. For the jurists of the first period, deputyship was a sort of trust on behalf of the Hidden Imam. As a trustee of the Imam among his followers, a Shi'ite jurist could assume all those functions that the Imam as a political head of the community was entitled to undertake himself or would have delegated to someone qualified to represent him. Thus, the Shi'ite jurists were authorized to undertake functions with political implications as functional imams, in the general interest of the Shi'ites.[36]

The second period of Shi'ite political jurisprudence (twelfth–fourteenth centuries) witnessed political turmoil in the central Islamic lands (the modern-day Middle East) following the breakdown of the Sunni political authority and the destruction of the Baghdad-based Abbasid caliphate by the Mongols in the thirteenth century. This unfavorable situation in the Sunni world, in addition to the earlier downfall of the Shi'ite Buyid dynasty under which the Shi'ites had enjoyed relative peace and security, convinced the Shi'ite jurists that the existence of a just Shi'ite political authority (other than that of the Imam) willing to consider the implementation of the Islamic laws was not only expedient but necessary. The reason was that the existence of such an authority would fulfill the Qur'anic obligation of "enjoining the good and forbidding the evil." The fulfillment of this obligation would also provide religious grounds to apply the phrase *al-sultan al-'adil* (the just ruler) to any Shi'ite authority committed to the promulgation of the Islamic laws. In other words, the Islamic public order under a just ruler was an end in itself only inasmuch as the community required it for "drawing close to obedience to God and away from disobedience."[37]

Among the administrative institutions that had grown up in the Islamic empire, administration of justice became one of the most important in preserving the popular sense of justice. Consequently, at times when the central power of Muslim rulers had disintegrated, the prestige and influence of the Muslim judge as the upholder of that popular sense of justice in general became immeasurable. In Shi'ism the administration of justice became the most fundamental aspect of the growing political power of the jurists, who, in their well-established position as the deputies of the Imam by this time and hence competent administrators of justice in the juridical writings, were regarded as the protectors of the people against the unjust behavior of those in power. In addition, the expectations of the Shi'ite community required the jurists to undertake the wider role of functional imam (beyond their already acknowledged role as the interpreters of the Islamic revelation), in their capacity as the "general" deputy of the Hidden Imam. During this period the new role of the functional imam was carefully explored in detail in jurisprudence under the rubric of the "Guardianship of the Jurist" *(wilayat al-faqih)*.

The third period in the development of Shi'ite political jurisprudence was the Safavid era (1501–1786). During this time the first Shi'ite state was established in Iran under the Safavids. The successful conversion of their domains to Shi'ism afforded natural legitimacy to the Safavid rulers. Thus the jurists had little difficulty in validating the Shi'ite temporal authority by interpreting the rational necessity for the management of the affairs of the community by the ruler of the age *(sultan al-zaman)*. Meanwhile, the most significant argument justifying the authority of the jurist as the "guardian" of the community turned on the desirability of implementing fully the Shariʿa before the messianic return of the twelfth Imam. The jurist, according to this argument, had to be asked by the ruler to undertake the responsibility of the execution of the divine norm. The comprehensive authority of the jurist as the functional imam had the same validity, in this line of reasoning, as the power of a ruler in whom authority was invested in the Muslim public order. Moreover, just as the investiture of authority was a precondition to assuming any official political function in Islamic public order, so the investiture of comprehensive authority in Shiʿite political jurisprudence was regarded as necessary to carry out the obligation of enjoining the good and forbidding the evil. This latter obligation, as noted earlier, was the main religious justification for the existence of any government during the occultation. However, as the opinions of the leading jurists of this period indicate, the assumption of the political authority by the ulama was contingent upon their investiture by the ruler.

The fourth period of Shiʿite political jurisprudence began with the establishment of the Shiʿite dynasty of the Qajar in Iran in the late eighteenth century. The role of Shiʿite religious leadership received fuller elaboration during the nineteenth and early twentieth century, until it reached its logical conclusion in 1980 in the constitutionalization of the "Guardianship of the Jurist" in the modern nation-state of Iran. During this fourth period, the position of the jurist as the guardian of the community became institutionalized and centralized through the process of an obligatory religious requirement for all Shiʿites to accept the authority of a mujtahid in the position of marjaʿ al-taqlid. It is significant that with the weakening and discrediting of the Shiʿite temporal authority, the jurist was seen as an alternative head of the Shiʿite public order who could fulfill the function of the just ruler. In popular Shiʿite belief at the time, the marjaʿ al-taqlid was the deputy of the twelfth Imam authorized to assume the duty of guiding the community during the occultation. Moreover, in the perception of the Shiʿite masses, the learned, pious jurist had a more legitimate claim than did the monarch to exercise the comprehensive authority in the name of the Hidden Imam pending his return. The jurist in the position of marjaʿ al-taqlid, then, came to enjoy the popular confidence to function as the guardian of the Shiʿite community.

However, to generate the loyalty of the Shiʿa, the marjaʿ al-taqlid had to demonstrate objectively that he possessed "sound belief," "sound knowledge," and "sound character."[38] He demonstrated sound belief and sound knowledge through his learning, his publications on religious subjects, and the training of disciples. His sound character was established by his piety, which qualified him to become the leader of daily congregational worship and to receive religiously ordained taxes for distribution among the needy.

As depicted above, the Qajar and post-Qajar eras coincided with the introduction of modernization, that is, a modern system of administration, modern education, and modern values. The modernization of traditional institutions in Shiʿite society, however gradual and at times mismanaged, created tensions in the sociopolitical life of the community and undermined the effectiveness of traditional Shiʿite leadership. Additionally, during the reign of the shah the Shiʿites exerted enormous pressure on their religious leaders to resolve the tensions created by changed expectations under the forces of modernization. The leaders' response to this pressure was the retrieval, assertion, and final development of the doctrine of the "Guardianship of the Jurist" *(wilayat al-faqih)*, a concept the relevance of which now outstripped academic concerns, for it offered the theological sanction by which to legally consolidate the position of a Shi'ite jurist as the executor of the affairs of the Shi'ites in a Shi'ite state in modern times. The consolidation of a jurist's position was sought by raising the fundamental question taken up by many Shi'ite jurists since the founding of Shi'ite dynasties: If a temporal ruler can assume and exercise the discretionary authority of the twelfth Imam in a Shi'ite state, then is not a well-qualified jurist, who has exercised most of this authority as a de facto functional imam during the occultation, a more fitting candidate for this position?

The response to this question regarding the candidacy of the Shi'ite jurist as a legitimate head of a Shi'ite state to administer the affairs of the community in modern times was undertaken by prominent jurists such as Ayatollah Khomeini of Iran and Ayatollah Muhammad Baqir Sadr of Iraq. They offered their own nuanced interpretation of the Guardianship of the Jurist in the modern context.

Shi'ite Ideology in the Modern Age

In analyzing Shi'ite activism as a manifestation of contemporary Islamic fundamentalism I have thus far discussed the theological-political and juridical sources of the modern upheavals in the Shi'ite world precisely in order to underscore the importance of the ideas which constituted Khomeini's Shi'ite ideology. However, it is unrealistic to think that the Shi'ite public has responded primarily, if at all, to the purely intellectual basis of Shi'ite juridical leadership in their collective decision to become supporters of the temporal authority of the marja' al-taqlid. Nor did ordinary believers automatically recognize sound belief, knowledge, and character in the jurist whom they acclaimed as their religious authority and, in the events of 1978–79, their revolutionary leader. What made the Shi'ites responsive to their religious leaders, especially to Khomeini and Baqir Sadr, relates in large measure to a threefold religious experience which shapes their political attitudes and inspires their willingness to strive to preserve their religious identity in the context of the larger Muslim community. Khomeini and Baqir Sadr, among other Shi'ite religious leaders, well understood this dynamic, and so availed themselves of these three religious experiences in order to mobilize the Shi'ite community for the sociopolitical causes they desired to pursue.

The threefold experiences, in approximate chronological order, were martyrdom *(shahada)*, occultation *(ghayba)*, and precautionary dissimulation *(taqiyya)*.

Martyrdom (Shahada) *in Shi'ite Religious Experience*

Martyrdom has been sustained as a religious ordeal in Shi'ite political history by the conviction that God is just and commands human society to pursue justice in accord with the guidance provided by divine revelation to the Prophet. When the Shi'ite

Imam, following the death of the Prophet, was denied his right to assume the temporal authority invested in him by divine designation, as the Shiʿites believed, direct political action was regarded as justified to establish the rule of justice—to replace a usurpatory rule by a just and legitimate one. The ensuing struggle to install a legitimate political authority resulted in the murder of several Shiʿite leaders. In the light of this conviction, the violent deaths were interpreted by succeeding generations as martyrdom suffered in order to defeat the forces of oppression and falsehood.

The most powerful symbol of this religious experience has without question been the third Imam of the Shiʿites, Husayn b. ʿAlī (d. 680), the grandson of the Prophet, whose martyrdom is annually commemorated with solemnity throughout the Shiʿite world. Imam Husayn provides Shiʿa history with its pathos. Husayn's journey to Kerbala in southern Iraq in 680 was undertaken in response to the political circumstances created by the ascension of Umayyad ruler, Yazid, as a caliph of the Muslims in Damascus, Syria. In Kerbala, on the tenth of Muharram, the day of ʿAshura, Husayn and his family and friends were mercilessly killed by the Umayyad troops. The Shiʿites have preserved this moment in their religious history as a tragic event reminding humanity of the sullied nature of power and the way the righteous ones suffer in the world. For the greater part of Shiʿite history, the memory of the tragedy of Kerbala has been tempered by the tradition of political quietism among the Shiʿa minority; however, there were times when the episode was interpreted by the religious leaders in such a way as to encourage activism to counter injustice in society.

The importance attached to the commemoration of Imam Husayn's martyrdom has provided the Shiʿite community with a rare paradigm that is traced with remarkable enthusiasm by lay believers. In modern times, the commemoration went beyond its basic purpose of recounting the tragedy that befell the family of the Prophet. It provided a platform that was used to communicate Shiʿite teachings to the populace, which had little or no academic preparation to utilize written sources on the subject. It was also in such gatherings that prominent Shiʿite jurists lectured or engaged in debate with other Islamic schools of thought, thus demonstrating their leadership abilities to the community. Indeed, these important gatherings have served as the principal platform of communication with the Shiʿite public, among whom politically adroit marjaʿ al-taqlid such as Khomeini and Baqir Sadr found their main support.

In fact in the case of the Lebanese Shiʿites from the 1970s onward, it is remarkable that this religious institution has been the primary medium through which socio-politico-religious ideas have been disseminated by their leaders, including Imam Musa Sadr and Shaykh Fadl Allah. But with the increasing literacy of Lebanon's Shiʿites, Fadl Allah's publications, in particular *Islam and the Logic of Force,* have been influential as well. Recognizing the low level of religious education among the Lebanese Shiʿites, these leaders used the commemorative gatherings as a forum by which to awaken their followers to the injustices of the sociopolitical realities of modern Lebanon. Imam Husayn's act of self-sacrifice became a model in the struggle to improve the standing and increase the influence of the Shiʿite population in the country.[39]

With the increase of political awareness among the Shiʿites came a demand for some detailed information on religious topics that were touched upon in the commemorative gatherings in the 1960s and 1970s. Subsequently the mourning gatherings were utilized to disseminate religious literature which among other things included information on both quietist and activist postures of Shi'ite ideology, depending upon the sociopolitical climate at the time. Unlike the theological and juridical corpus produced by the jurist-theologians for themselves, this religious literature was written in the language of the people and in response to their religious and social questions. This widely read or read aloud (in rural gatherings where the literacy rate still continues to be low) literature recounted the miracles of not only the Imams but also their deputies, those who held the prestigious position of marja' al-taqlid. The spread of this devotional literature was instrumental in legitimating the Shi'ite jurists, at least in the eyes of the Shi'ites, as legitimate guardians of the community pending the return of the twelfth Imam. Certainly the stories about learned and pious jurists were disseminated with the purpose of strengthening the belief of the Shi'ites in the tenet that even during the absence of the Imam, divine guidance had been continuously available to the community through these pious eminent scholars, the marja' al-taqlid, and their erudite representatives among the Shi'ites like Imam Musa Sadr and Shaykh Fadl Allah. These pious gatherings took place in the special buildings constructed for that purpose and known as *husayniyya*, or they were simply convened in a mosque.

The husayniyya or the mosque served, then, as a crucial center for public religious education and in the 1970s and 1980s were important indicators of political and social awareness among the believers. Representatives of the leading marja' al-taqlid lectured in these centers and gave the gatherings either an activist or a quietist tone. They were in most cases students in the *madrasa* (centers for learning Islamic theology and jurisprudence) of that marja' al-taqlid whose stance on religious and political matters they represented among the Shi'ites. They made the marja' al-taqlid's religio-political position known among his followers, who through the formal process of declaring that they abided by his rulings had accepted his authority in matters pertaining to the faith. In addition, these deputies of the marja' al-taqlid functioned as the collectors of the religiously ordained taxes. The administration of the religious taxes paid by the Shi'ite community to their religious leaders became the most significant source of their independence and the independence of their institutions of religious learning, the madrasa, from any sort of government control. Indirectly this independence from the government increased their power and prestige as the trustworthy protectors of the Shi'ites against the perceived oppression and tyranny of government officials.

The religious experience of martyrdom in Shi'ism thus provided Shi'ite leaders with a formidable channel for mobilizing the Shi'ite populace. The intense glorification of martyrdom in Shi'ite religious experience, with its appeal to human suffering causing sorrow and lamentation at times of defeat, as well as the human sense of justice demonstrating political choice and courage at times of revolution, created and nurtured religious institutions like the commemorative gatherings, the husayniyya, and the mass-educating preachers in the context of the sociopolitical circumstances of the community. These in turn directly contributed to the acknowledgment and confirmation of the leadership of the Shi'ite jurists as the guardian of the community pending the final revolution of the twelfth Imam.

Occultation (Ghayba) *in Shi'ite Religious Experience*

The second religious experience, namely, occultation (the removal of the Twelfth Imam from the temporal sphere), signified the postponement of the establishment of just Islamic order pending the return of the messianic Imam. Moreover, it reflected and helped to explain the failure of the Shi'ite revolts provoked by atrocities of the ruling house in the centuries before Shi'ite political power became consolidated in Iran under the Safavids in the sixteenth century. Such revolts, endemic among Shi'ites after Kerbala, tended to be of comparatively small scale and in the central Islamic heartlands of Iran and Iraq tended to be efficiently suppressed. In essence it was extremely difficult under conditions of ghayba to mobilize significant sectors of Shi'ite society to political action, for such action was often seen as futile in the face of overwhelming state power and in the absence of incontrovertible evidence that the ensuing struggle was legitimized by divine will and to be marked by the fulfillment of Shi'ite messianic expectations. Thus those revolts that succeeded in establishing independent dynasties including the Fatimid Isma'ili Shi'ites, who founded a ruling dynasty in Egypt (909–1171), and the Zaydi Shi'ites, who ruled in Yemen until the 1962 coup, tended to be restricted to the frontiers of Islamic society. However, neither the Fatimids nor the Zaydis maintained the belief in ghayba as the Twelver Shi'ites did. Conversely, as the success of the Buyids and the Safavids demonstrates, Twelver Shi'ite dynasties could be and were established in periods of political weakness or disorder through external imposition, that is, through the successful conquest of outside, invariably tribal, forces. In all these cases, it should be noted, the intense revolutionary fervor that brought these movements to power tended to dissipate once the reins of government were firmly in hand.

Religiously speaking, the doctrine of occultation connoted some sort of divine intervention in saving the life of the Imam, the only awaited Just Ruler, by moving him from the realm of visible to invisible existence, and conveyed the idea that the situation was, at least before the Safavid era, beyond the control of those who proposed to overthrow the tyrannical rulers in order to establish the Islamic rule of justice. Furthermore, belief in the occultation of the Imam and his eventual return as the Mahdi of the Muslim community at a favorable time helped the Shi'ites to persevere under difficult circumstances and to hope for some degree of reform pending the Imam's messianic return. Such expectation necessarily implied postponement of the establishment of the thoroughly just Islamic order pending the reappearance of the last Imam, who alone could be invested with valid political authority.

As with the religious experience of martyrdom, the belief in the occultation of the twelfth Imam led, given a particular religious leader and particular sociopolitical circumstances, to the promotion of both the activist and the quietist attitudes. On the one hand, the doctrine raised questions about the pretext for any Shi'ite leader to venture to create a thoroughly Islamic public order during the absence of the twelfth Imam; on the other hand, it demanded that the entire Shi'ite community provide the means for its religious, social, and political survival pending the final return of the Imam. The attitude of resignation that can properly be derived from this religious experience has been adopted by a number of leading marja' al-taqlid today, for whom, it appears, the establishment of an Islamic social order without divine intervention through the return of the infallible Imam is impossible. It is for this reason that they have slighted any political involvement in the contemporary demand for sociopolitical justice. Moreover, they have regarded public involvement of any other marja' al-taqlid in assuming the political authority, even within a limited national boundary of a modern state, as theologically and juridically problematic. The problem, as they see it, is in its implications for the universalistic authority of the Imam as the sole Just Ruler whose political authority cannot be delegated to any Shi'ite, however qualified he may be.

On the other hand, the attitude of responsibility for the survival of the community generated by the religious experience of occultation convinced marja' al-taqlid such as the Ayatollahs Khomeini and Muhammad Baqir Sadr to argue for an activist interpretation of occultation. Thus they called for the active involvement of the religious leadership as theologically legitimate and juridically incumbent and articulated a religious and moral obligation of Shi'ites to support their marja' al-taqlid in the struggle against the unjust sociopolitical system.[40] By this interpretation, activist religious leaders delegated the Imam's political as well as juridical authority to a qualified marja' al-taqlid, who in his capacity as the trustee responsible for supervising the affairs of the Shi'ites during the Occultation would be willing to shoulder the obligation of "enjoining the good and forbidding the evil." In the eyes of both Khomeini and Baqir Sadr and of those who followed them in Iraq, Iran, and Lebanon, the "Guardianship of the Jurist" became almost an absolute, religiously sanctioned political institution. As an absolute type, this institution was empowered to make all necessary binding decisions that cover the broad range of moral, legal and religious matters in a modern state.[41]

Precautionary Dissimulation (Taqiyya) *in Shi'ite Religions Experience*

The open call for the redress of injustices committed against the Shi'ites in Iran, Iraq, and Lebanon in the 1970s and 1980s to some extent minimized the preponderance of the third religious experience, namely, precautionary dissimulation *(taqiyya)*, which in the past had been a predominant consideration in determining the political direction of the Shi'ite community. Historically, this practice of shielding the true intent of the faithful community from unbelievers and outsiders characterized the political attitude of all the Imams and their followers subsequent to the martyrdom of the third Imam Husayn. The Shi'ite leaders encouraged taqiyya and even declared it to be a duty incumbent upon their followers, so as to avoid pressing for the establishment of the Shi'ite rule and the overthrow of the illegitimate caliphate. In a sense, taqiyya signified the will of the Shi'ite community to continue to strive for the realization of the ideal Islamic polity, if not by launching the revolution contingent upon the appearance of the messiah and his consolidation as the leader of the community, then at least by preparing the way for such an insurrection in the future. In the meantime, the Shi'ites had to avoid expressing their true opinions publicly about the shortcomings evident in the various de facto Muslim governments, regardless of whether they were Shi'ite or Sunni, in such a way as to cause contention and enmity. Consequently the practice of taqiyya was determined by the conditions of the Shi'ites as a minority group living under adverse settings; here again, the religious leadership determined the appropriate time for the community to abandon quietist passivity and engage in activism.

Shi'ite activism in recent years, as in the earlier times, has been the result of its leadership appropriating the stance symbolized by the religious experience of martyrdom. Such an experience, as interpreted by the leaders in the 1970s, regards martyrdom a new revolution in itself, violent death suffered in order to uphold justice against oppression. Thus, in his major work on the justification of resorting to force in Islam,[42] Shaykh Muhammad Husayn Fadl Allah, the leader of the Hizbullah (the Party of God) in Lebanon, regards the notion of quietist passivity in Shi'ism as rooted in an erroneous understanding of the theologico-political doctrine of precautionary dissimulation.[43] In order for Lebanese Shi'ites to seek redress for their oppressive sociopolitical condition, Shaykh Fadl Allah has consistently encouraged them to actively pursue the establishment of social justice as provided in the Shari'a. Moreover, he contends that the Islamic revelation places that responsibility on them at all times without limiting its relevance or applicability to a particular place.

The transformation of traditional Shi'ism in the 1960s from a politically quietist, taqiyya-oriented stance to an activist preparation for revolution was deepened by the reinterpretation of the role of religion and the custodians of religion, the ulama, in modern society by a modernly educated intellectual, Dr. 'Alī Shari'ati (d. 1977). There is sufficient evidence to show that Shi'ite activism under the leadership of the ulama, as maintained by Ayatollah Khomeini in his lectures in Iraq in the later part of the 1960s, was elicited by Shari'ati's criticism of the ulama's role in modern society. The 1960s in Iran were the decisive years for bringing the religious scholars in tune with modernity. Several leading scholars of Shi'ite jurisprudence, including Murtada Mutahhari (d. 1979), one of the intellectual leaders of the Iranian Islamic Revolution of 1978–79, made pertinent suggestions about reforming the most important institution of the religious leadership during the occultation, namely, the marja' al-taqlid establishment.[44] But Shari'ati took it upon himself to confront the religious leaders, who were satisfied with their traditional submissive interpretation of the Shi'ite religious experience and had abdicated their social and political responsibilities. He challenged them to plumb the activist potential of Shi'ism and provide the Shi'ite community with much-needed ideological leadership in modern times.

In his position as a teacher at the University of Mashhad, Iran, Shari'ati was in close contact with the Iranian youth exposed to the shah's modernization program. Aware of the predicament of the majority of the rural, industrious, educated youth, he proposed a form of Shi'ism which took into consideration the personal, social and political bonds inherent in the concept of Islam as a total way of life. As the title of his seminal work, *Islamology,* suggests, Shari'ati analyzed the interaction between the underlying values of Islam and society—the very embodiment of the cultural life of the community that continued to nurture the youth. In his discussion of Shi'ite history, Shari'ati depicted original Shi'ism of Imam 'Alī as dedicated to egalitarianism, preeminently concerned with social justice, and most of all as unabashedly revolutionary. Shari'ati denounced the official Shi'ism of the Safavid court (and by implication, of the Pahlavi court) for all the later accretions and the aloofness of the prominent members of the religious leadership. The manipulation of Shi'ism and the religious leadership by the rulers had led, he charged, to the distortion of the original Shi'ism of the Imams 'Alī and Husayn, and more devastating, to the quietist authoritarian politics which had plagued so much of traditional Shi'ism.[45]

Accordingly, Shari'ati introduced a crucial distinction between the original Shi'ite spirit and its later political and social incarnations under Shi'ite temporal authority. This move served in his scheme to portray authentic Shi'ism as a socially and politically binding ideology, open to reinterpretation in the light of modern contingencies. To become politically effective within the Shi'ite community, however, such a reinterpretation had to be undertaken by an enlightened religious scholar, a mujtahid, who would engage in a sort of jihad to make it compatible with the aims of original Islam, namely, the creation of a just and progressive social order. The ordinary Muslim, though not a mujtahid in the technical sense of the term and not required to think as one, is nevertheless, capable—and indeed must exercise the capacity—of making up his own mind about whose interpretation of Islam to follow.

Shari'ati's appeal to reappropriate "original Shi'ism" gained a sizable following among the educated, the urban, the politically aware, and those seeking an Iranian clarification of a true Muslim-Iranian identity that might be in harmony with modernity. It also had an impact on the young activist preachers, who were the followers of the prominent jurists and who without acknowledging it were using Shari'ati's equation of true Shi'ism with a radical revolutionary Islam as a vehicle for instituting divine justice on earth.[46] For Shari'ati, the religious history of Shi'ism, interpreted through the lens of the martyrdom of Imam Husayn, suggested the authentic Islamic response to the unbearable sociopolitical conditions. The martyrdom of Husayn was not simply a tale of sorrow and lamentation; it was a militant assertion of the Islamic sense of justice.

Shari'ati's main consideration in his lectures was to provide a constructive critique of the ritualized character of Iranian religious life, which had the affect of reducing the Shi'ite population to passivity and acquiescence in the face of oppression. His forceful discourses about the potentially activist aspects of Shi'ite Islam were intended to forestall the sociopolitical indifference among the religious leaders, and he sought to appropriate religious ritual in the service of the activist cause. Thus, Shari'ati reformulated the themes of martyrdom so as to awaken the spirit of sacrifice for the ideal of justice and provided the impetus to transform the ritual of commemorative gatherings to mourn the tragedy of Kerbala to the popular social and educational institution of the husayniyya. In this modern version of husayniyya, he introduced the symbol of Imam Husayn's struggle against the Umayyads as a model for the struggle of Iranian Muslims to transform their own oppressive circumstances into a just social order. Accordingly, Shariʿati rejected "the logic of taqiyya" as involving compromise, passive endurance, or "a non-dangerous approach to the struggle."[47]

Shariʿati was not alone in his critique, and his challenge to the ulama was repeated by a number of politically activist members of the religious class in Iran and Iraq. In his Najaf lectures on the Guardianship of the Jurist, Ayatollah Khomeini had criticized his colleagues for their lack of social and political vision which betrayed the dignity and true mission of their class.[48] Similarly, Ayatollah Muhammad Baqir Sadr, Iraq's most renowned Shiʿite jurist, called upon the religious leaders of the Iraqi Shiʿites and their young students at the seminaries in Najaf, Iraq, to mobilize in order to roll back the sociocultural dislocations among Shiʿite youth caused by unchecked modernization and legitimated by secular communist and Baʿthist ideology.

In the 1970s it became apparent that secularly educated Iranian intellectuals, who had been prepared to assume the Iranian leadership, were alienated from the majority of the groups that formed the traditional alliances in Iran and thus could not muster the popular support necessary to guide the future of that nation.[49] Technocrats, bureaucrats, and other government officials on the prosperous side of the Iranian economic divide were targets of envy and bitter criticism for their perceived abandonment of the traditional values, which continued to orient the everyday life of the majority of the Iranian population. This popular perception and the rift it caused between the intelligentsia and the citizenry created an opportunity for the religious leadership to encourage religious activity in general and to synthesize traditional and modern ideologies and devices for social influence. Key to the success of the Iranian religious leadership in mobilizing the populace was the identification of the Iranian nation exclusively with the spirit, practices, and history of Shiʿite Islam.[50]

In their accommodation with modernity and in their efforts to provide a viable Islamic alternative ideology in a modern nation-state, jurists such as Khomeini and Sadr had to make meaningful choices of their own, which included accepting some elements of modern secular political culture like nationalism and even popular political participation—an anomaly to the traditional conceptualization of political authority. By the mid-1970s, Khomeini had provided the Iranians an innovative, but authentically traditional, alternative to the "colonizing culture" of the West. This alternative eliminated the compromise of retaining the constitutional monarchy of the 1906 revolution. Instead, the Islamic revolution of 1978–79 called for the establishment of an Islamic government based on justice and freedom (in the sense of freedom from sinful license) for all, as interpreted by the leading jurist.[51]

The concept of the "Islamic Government," which was never worked out in any systematic detail by Khomeini, was ambiguous enough to unite all segments of Iranian society predisposed to political activism and opposed to the repressive rule of the Shah. In the absence of an elitist institutional base that could have provided the new political leadership and steered Iranian society smoothly into the era of mass politics, Khomeini's politico-religious leadership was acknowledged, invariably, even by those who did not necessarily believe in the relevance of Islamic norms in the modern age.[52]

More significantly, Khomeini's call to resist an unjust government found supporters among the leftists and Islamic socialists who saw in Khomeini, and in Shari'ati, revolutionary pawns that could be manipulated to their advantage.

Thus, Khomeini's politico-religious "guardianship" of the Islamic state, granted legitimacy in part through its commitment to promulgate the Shari'a, managed to convince many quietist religious leaders of various standings in the hierarchy of Islamic learning to actively participate in the different roles demanded by a modern Islamic public order. Furthermore, Khomeini managed to bridge differences not only between disparate secular and religious ideologies (by emphasizing his opposition to Western imperialism and cultural colonization) but also between a religious ideology and the apparently secularized process of modernization in the service of justice and human welfare (through the promulgation of the divine will in the Shari'a). As events in the decade after the revolution proved, however, Khomeini's mere occupation of the position of Guardianship in the Islamic state did not guarantee that Iran would develop as the perfect model of an Islamic government for all Muslims in search of their Islamic identity and political destiny in the modern age.

The Search for Identity in Iraq and Lebanon

A brief review of the quite different political and social contexts for the Shi'ites of Iraq and Lebanon may serve to illustrate the point that the shape and direction of Shi'ite activism is determined not only by the interpretations of a charismatic leader elevated to a position of supreme authority but also by the particular sociopolitical circumstances in which the Shi'ite masses find themselves at a given time and place. Indeed, what was presented to the Iranian Shi'ites as an Islamic alternative could not be offered to the Shi'ites of Iraq and Lebanon living under quite different political systems. At the same time, the manner in which the religious leadership attained a prominence based on the threefold religious experiences of the Shi'ites, namely, martyrdom, occultation, and precautionary dissimulation, applies to all three regions under consideration and provides a basis for comparison of the Shi'ites' varying responses to oppression.

There was, then, a substantial difference in the way the Shi'ite religious leaders under the secularly oriented and largely Sunni-dominated government of Iraq could make the particular Shi'ite religious experiences with political implications relevant and applicable to the circumstances of their followers there. Moreover, to the Shi'ites of Iraq, Khomeini's Islamic Republic under the all-comprehensive Guardianship of the Jurist had a limited appeal, for the Sunnis of Iraq could neither comprehend nor participate in this exclusivist and particularist vision of Islamic public order based on Shi'ite religious experiences. Furthermore, the religious requirement to accept the authority of a leading Shi'ite jurist as a marja' al-taqlid and to abide by his rulings in matters pertaining to religious practice in its present form was peculiar to Twelver Shi'ism only. Accordingly, the Shi'ite paradigm of the religiopolitical leadership under the leading scholar presented by Ayatollah Khomeini and endorsed by the Ayatollah Muhammad Baqir Sadr, both in form and content proved unable to win the support of the Sunnis of Iraq.

Instead the Arab Shi'ites of Iraq drew upon particular moments in their own historical experience in developing an activist posture in the 1970s and 1980s. To provide the necessary context for understanding contemporary Arab Shi'ite activism it is necessary to begin with the 1920s, when, under the Hashemite monarchy, created by the English in 1921, profound political changes were introduced in Iraq. The Hashemite monarchy promoted Arab nationalism, an attitude designed to generate a new sense of loyalty to the nation in order to displace the old divisive sectarian and tribal loyalties. Although the force of the nascent Arab nationalist movement eroded the traditional patterns of the body politic in Iraq, it also made possible for the first time the integration of the Shi'ites and the Sunnis as a national community. To understand this complex process, it is necessary to briefly examine the nature of the traditional patterns.

First it must be understood that a sense of national community had been essentially alien to an Iraqi polity characterized by extremes of localism, sectarianism, and tribalism. These conditions may be traced in the first place to geography: communication between mountain and plain, desert and marsh, city and city, before the late nineteenth century was virtually impossible. Further reinforcing the harsh nature of Iraqi geography was the essentially decentralized nature of government control. For these reasons, the first concerted efforts to unify and centralize national administration would not be undertaken until the late Ottoman period (1831–1914). Moreover, the Ottoman effort could not have been undertaken without the rapid technological advances introduced into Iraq in the late nineteenth century.[53]

However, below the elite level these efforts did little to alter the primarily tribal-local outlook of the average Iraqi. So strong was the sense of division that within cities, people lived within segregated city quarters *(mahallas),* divided one from another by religious sect and ethnicity. Even within quarters, streets were subdivided into residence patterns based roughly on work or craft associations, and then again into extended-family units. Linkages binding one quarter to another were minimal and, as such, were much less conducive to generating so abstract a concept as metropolitan identity, and still less national consciousness. So complete was the isolation that, for instance, when the people of the Shi'ite shrine city of Najaf rose successfully against the Turks in 1915, the four quarters of the city, organized on tribal lines, established independent and autonomous city-states and would remain as such until the British occupation of 1917.[54]

Conversely, even while the primarily local-tribal outlook of Iraqis remained impervious to change, the impact of Ottoman centralization, followed as it was by the experience of British colonialism and rapid socio-economic and technological change, dissolved the traditional social and political bonds cementing tribal-local relationships. In the countryside, tribal leaders were becoming increasingly alienated from the tribal members through the increasing adoption of a cash economy, which in practice linked tribal elites to governing elites and resulted in the land laws of 1858 and 1932.

These laws favored the gathering of vast tracts of tribal land into the sole possession of tribal chiefs, leading further to large-scale cash real estate speculation by urban elites who dealt exclusively with the tribal chiefs, thus strengthening the new alliance of urban and rural leaders. By the 1920s and 1930s, this alliance, including top government officials and military officers, was able, when the need arose, to put aside their own intense personal rivalries to pursue their own interests on the national level, that is, to grant themselves such boons as tax exemptions and to guarantee a virtual monopoly of state offices. Meanwhile, the Shi'ites, whose own elites were rapidly advancing as traders, and a few of whom were favored by royal policy as civil servants in the nascent bureaucracy, found their further advance blocked by the monopolistic character of the new coalition. They were nevertheless being integrated into the emerging Iraqi state. These two decades would mark the high point of Shi'ite identification with their Sunni counterparts in the context of the Iraqi state.

The rise of nationalism in the 1920s failed to fill the vacuum left by the breakdown of local-tribal ties, as it tended to be absorbed into traditional Sunni-Shi'ite symbols. Nationalism did forge some ties between Shi'ite and Sunni elites, but the rise of cities and the new forms of social organization as a result of the modernization process essentially doomed tribal cohesion, and the alienation of tribal leaders from their tribesmen was symptomatic of a greater malaise. Rapid modernization invariably favored the cities at the expense of the tribes, resulting first in the breakdown of the great tribal confederations and then in the dissolution of the tribes themselves. The breakdown was reflected in rapid migration. Baghdad, for example, quadrupled in size between 1922 and 1957. But significantly, when the migrants arrived in the cities, they tended to group together and isolate themselves through private compacts aimed at continuing tribal custom. The influx, however, could not but speed the breakdown of traditional urban relationships, themselves undergoing a process of dissolution not dissimilar to that experienced by the tribes.[55]

The Hashemite monarchy administered the civil service in such a way as to allow some opportunities for promising young Shi'ites, and for its own stability thus provided means to accommodate the rising national consciousness during the period from the 1920s to the 1958 revolution. However, while these modernizing and centralizing forces could and did speed the breakdown of traditional localistic ties, they proved largely unable to unify their highly segmented populace within the context of a modern nation-state. This process resulted ultimately in conditions of feuding, economic struggle, and near anarchy in the countryside, and urban tensions that promised to result in confrontations of great violence at the slightest pretext, as the urban risings of 1948, 1952, and 1956 indicated. Thus, historic moments of Iraqi national accord tended to be short-lived and were invariably directed at a clear foreign foe, in this case the British.

In the period between 1921 and 1939, the monarchy succeeded for a time in integrating diverse elements into the Iraqi body politic, as it expanded Iraq's educational program based on the common Arab history and language and the common ethnic origin of the majority of Iraqis. This two-decade process served to cultivate the new national feeling among the educated Shi'ites and Sunnis. The educational policy also assisted, as it had in Iran, in the spread of modern ideas drawn from Western modes of thought. The increasing number of the new educated middle class from both the Shi'ite and Sunni affiliations became the carriers of the increased sense of patriotism and even the pan-Arab ideal.[56]

However, Shi'ite loyalty to Iraqi nationalism always remained in question. Because of the common religious ties to Iran, in addition to the presence of marja' al-taqlid sometimes commonly recognized by both the Iraqi and Iranian Shi'ites, the Sunni Iraqi politicians suspected the Iraqi Shi'ites of divided loyalties.[57] From the British perspective, these signs of factionalism in Iraqi nationalism were hardly ominous. In pursuing their colonial policy of balance of power, the British (and later the British-backed monarchy) favored, and even encouraged, Shi'ite advancement in the economic sphere in the southern and central parts of Iraq to create a sort of power parity between them and the dominant Sunnis. By the 1940s, the royal policy of integration of the Shi'ites in the Iraqi body politic and the diffusion of the new national sentiment through modern education effected noticeable changes in the social as well as political situation of the Shi'ites, perhaps the most significant of which was the stratification of Shi'ite society. Finding that their generally low standard of education limited their access to state offices, the Shi'ites turned their energies toward commerce, and a portion of the community acquired significant wealth. However, many Shi'ites in Iraq did not share in this new prosperity, and "if in 1958 the richest of the rich were often Shi'ites, so were also predominantly the poorest of the poor."[58]

Indicative of this rise in the fortunes of a portion of the Shi'ite community were the growing number of intermarriages between the wealthy Shi'ites and Sunnis, as well as Shi'ite political achievements in the wake of commercial success. Whereas before 1947 not a single Shi'ite was raised to the premiership, in the period between 1947 and 1958, four Shi'ites were appointed to that office. At the same time, the new wealth only served to exacerbate the chronically chaotic social conditions among the poorest Muslims, both Sunni and Shi'ite. As revenues from oil exports flooded into the coffers of the elites during the post-World War II boom, an unprecedented wave of inflation eroded the economic status of the urban poor, increasing the price of food almost beyond the reach of the mass of the urban population and increasing the overall cost of living. Thus while the average wage of unskilled laborers rose about 400 percent between 1939 and 1948, the price of food had risen 805 percent.[59] Although not as severe, this same pattern of decline affected the middle class, teachers, clerks, civil servants, writers, and journalists, as well. As the majority of Iraqis tied to the urban-based money economy suffered a decline in economic position, the elite coalition of aristocrats, privileged government officials, top military officers, and tribal chiefs, both Sunni and Shi'ite, grew increasingly wealthy. The resentment this engendered contributed to the conditions leading to the popular rebellion of 1948, and with it the rise of revolutionary ideologies.

By the 1950s, communist ideas of social justice evoked powerful passion among the Iraqis in general, leading to the political movements which disturbed the last years of the monarchy. The rulers in Baghdad, regarded as insensitive to the needs of their subjects, had done little to eradicate poverty and to generate a sense of loyalty among the poor to the existing institutions. To the poor, whether Sunnis or Shi'ites, the government came to be regarded as an object of distrust and hatred. Moreover, "the Sunni character of the government, which rendered it a usurpation in the eyes of the Shi'ite majority, turned popular enmity into an act of faith."[60]

Thus Shi'ism provided recruits for the protest movements of the 1940s and 1950s and found itself in a sort of alliance with Communism which, insofar as it bred opposition to the existing authority which was perceived as tyrannical, found resonances in the oppositional spirit of Shi'ism. For example, Najaf, the holy city of the Shi'ites and "the seat of oppressive wealth and dire poverty,"[61] became the staging ground for a number of significant communist uprisings. This Shi'ite city was and remains today both a center for religious reaction and protest and a breeding ground for revolutionary ideas. Many of the militant communists in the 1950s were the sons or relatives of men in the lower ranks of the ulama who had suffered a decline in prestige and prosperity because of the new and remote economic and political forces transforming the shape of Iraqi commerce and industry.[62] The communist uprisings of the 1950s thus coincided with the declining role of the Shi'ite ulama, whose appeal to the common people to abide by the commands of religion had no effect on either the communists or the nationalists, influenced as they were by modern secular ideologies.

As in Iran, modern secular ideologies, whether in the form of nationalism or Communism, or as disseminated in the methods and content of modern education, had become popular at the expense of traditional patterns of Islamic religion. And although the introduction of the modern sense of loyalty to the nation did not displace the emotional ties and the structural organization of traditional Iraqi social patterns, especially in the rural areas, it did serve to undermine the role of traditional education in the Islamic seminaries and thus the authority of the religious leadership. The historical independence of the Shi'ite religious leaders from government control, thanks to their independent financial resources, was also compromised in the wake of reforms that were introduced by the government in the management of the revenues from religious endowments and related sources. The ulama became dependent on the merchants in the bazaar to fund and execute their religious projects. Consequently the Shi'ite religious institutions had to remain sensitive to the traditionalist outlook of the bazaar before they could offer solutions to the pressing problems of modernity. The fear that the bazaar could withhold financial contributions if it found their traditionalism threatened by innovative religious prescriptions rendered the ulama incapable of providing critical religious guidance in encountering the influences of secular ideologies.[63] Indeed in the 1950s and 1960s, Islamic education and the leadership it had nurtured in the past in Iraq was enfeebled considerably. Increasing numbers of young students of religion were dissatisfied with and abandoned the isolated life in the religious seminaries to pursue modern education and to acquaint themselves with modern thinking in the universities. Meanwhile, in spite of the economic prominence of a greater number of Shi'ites, the vast majority remained economically underprivileged in Iraq, even as the influence of religious leaders dwindled. The Shi'ites suffered the hardships attendant upon their lot as the "poorest of the poor": squalid and unsafe living conditions, crowding, and lack of access to health care institutions and schools.

In the early 1970s, however, a new generation of activist and militant Shi'ite organizations and leaders emerged in response to this situation. Their initial raison d'être was the development and implementation of programs by which the social and economic deprivations could be eased.[64] The rise of these groups followed a period in which Ayatollah Muhammad Baqir Sadr promulgated his activist interpretation of the Shi'ite ideals of justice and equity among the ulama and among the masses gathered at ritual commemorations of past Shi'ite struggles against oppression such as 'Ashura. Baqir Sadr and his disciples were intent in the early 1970s on interpreting the sacred past in such a way as to mobilize the Shi'ite masses to form and join socially and politically activist Shi'ite organizations such as *al-da'wa al-islamiyya* (The Islamic Call) and *al-Mujahidin* (The Islamic Fighters).[65]

Modernization through westernization, which in Iraq was perceived by the poorer Shi'ites as the wholesale, uncritical adaptation of secular Western ideas and economic practices, had ramifications for religious life similar to those experienced in Iran. Leading Shi'ite ulama were of course painfully aware of the critical situation in the 1950s and 1960s when secular communist ideas were infiltrating the displaced lower classes in strongholds of Shi'ite Islam such as the holy cities of Najaf and Kerbala, and religious practices were being abandoned by graduates of modern schools and colleges. Most of the prominent ulama in Iraq, however, remained bound to the traditional restraints of Shi'ism which had required them to maintain their probity by shunning politics. And given their constrained political situation at the time, they adopted a posture of aloofness, complained about the decline of religious practices among their followers, but had neither the will nor the intellectual or political preparation to guide them in crafting a supple response for their (erstwhile) followers among the poor.

When Shi'ite activist leaders attempted to reverse this tradition of aloofness by providing concrete guidance and a blueprint for political action, they faced two fundamental problems in the Ba'thist Iraq of the 1970s. First, they had to contend with the ever-present fear that they would be regarded as the agents of the Shi'ite Iranian regime employed to subvert the Iraqi administration and would consequently be subjected to the fate of a number of prominent religious personages executed under that pretext. Second, and less dramatic but equally difficult, was the exercise of their role as the custodians of Shi'ite ideology over against the rival Sunni Islamic vision (considered the majoritarian position). Because these ideologies differed radically on the precise question of the proper response to an unjust government, and because even the criteria for identifying an unjust government were significantly different, Shi'ite religious leaders faced an uphill battle in mobilizing their own followers for specific political action, not to speak of the entire Iraqi Islamic community. Any political solution designed to forge a unified Islamic front would have to proceed from a series of accommodations and doctrinal compromises on both sides.

Nonetheless, the existence of several explicitly activist Shi'ite organizations attested to the appeal of the notion of an Islamic revival among the Iraqi Shi'ites. The most important of these, *al-da'wa al-islamiyya* (The Islamic Call), illustrates both the difficulty of analyzing the Shi'ite movement in Iraq with any precision and the extremely precarious situation of any oppositional political or religious organization under the

Ba'thist regime. The Da'wa was founded in Najaf, probably in the early 1960s, possibly influenced either by Ayatollah Khomeini's residence in that city, or, conversely, by the shah's regime in Iran as an anti-Ba'thist policy instrument (in the world of Middle East politics, the two contentions are not necessarily exclusive). The organization clearly appealed to the younger and junior ranks of the religious class of Najaf, Kerbala, and Kazimayn. The precise program of the organization is difficult to determine, although it is clear that the triumph of the Iranian revolution had great resonance in the Da'wa ranks. Thus, in 1979, in response to the Ayatollah Khomeini's call to action on the eve of 'Ashura demonstrations, there was a discernible wave of Shi'ite unrest in Iraq, which was quickly and ruthlessly suppressed.[66] Under these circumstances, some prominent ulama in Najaf and Kerbala, including the senior marja' al-taqlid, Ayatollah Abu'l-Qasim al-Khu'i, refused political involvement of any sort.[67]

The campaign of repression against the Shi'ites reached its height in 1980 with the hanging of Sadr. His execution came despite the fact that no evidence appeared linking him directly to any particular oppositional group in Iraq; the regime seemed convinced nonetheless of his critical role as the guiding genius behind the activist Shi'ite cells. What is certain is that his open support for the Iranian revolution was seen by the Ba'thist as a dangerous instigation of the Iraqi Shi'ites.

The risk of death had not prevented Sadr from formulating an Islamic alternative to the "godless communism" of the Ba'thists. In this venture he was unique (and virtually alone) among the Najaf ulama, the majority of whom had very little training in modern secular thought. When Sadr embraced openly Khomeini's principle that religion and politics in Islam are inseparable and that therefore the religious leadership should assume political responsibility, he was criticized by leading conservative ulama of Najaf. Defying this criticism, Sadr recognized that given the political reality of Iraq in the 1970s, the only forum through which the Shi'ites might voice their political grievances against the oppressive measures adopted by the Ba'thist regime was the annual 'Ashura martyrdom commemorative gatherings in Najaf and Kerbala. At these gatherings Sadr proclaimed that the only religious authority that could guarantee justice in Iraq was the Shi'ite marja' al-taqlid—a seeming endorsement of the temporal and religious Guardianship of the Jurist as it was being interpreted in Iran.

The Iraqi regime at this time was in a rule-or-die situation. By publicly voicing this activist message Sadr had emerged as the most dangerous force against the Ba'thist regime by the late 1970s as it became clear to the regime that the Shi'ites had begun to look to him for political leadership. It was in this climate that Sadr and his sister, Bint al-Huda, who had collaborated with her brother in activating the Shi'ite women in Najaf, were executed in 1980.

Along with the repression of any manifestation of dissent among the Shi'ite, however, the regime also pursued a strategy of appeasing Shi'ite unrest. On the rhetorical level it mounted a campaign to portray Saddam Hussein as an "Islamic" leader and to depict the militantly secular Ba'th Party as not incompatible with religion. This campaign culminated in 1979 with Saddam's analysis of Islamic history, in which the perception of Shi'ite dispossession and historical injustice was for the first time in a millennium endorsed by a Sunni head of state. Muʿawiya, the Umayyad caliph whose rebellion had dispossessed ʿAlī of the caliphate, was explicitly denounced, ʿAlī was praised, and most remarkable, the revolt of Imam Husayn was held up as a model that the Iraqi president was proud to follow.[68] With the campaign of rhetorical Islamization, the regime began in 1979 to invest large sums of money in the Shiʿite areas, revitalizing the shrines at Kerbala and Najaf, upgrading Shiʿite mosques, schools, neighborhoods, and economic infrastructures to win the Shiʿites over. This sum is reported to have exceeded 24.4 million dinars on religious institutions in 1979 alone,[69] and the program continues to this day.

The message to Iraqi Shiʿites is both clear and historically resonant: cooperation is rewarded economically, if not politically, while its opposite is ruthlessly and efficiently suppressed. This may in large part explain the reticence of Iraqi Shiʿites to respond to the Iranian call. But there is another factor, immeasurable but, below the elite ulama level deeply rooted. It is put best by one of the anonymous Iraqi Shiʿites speaking to Hanna Batatu in 1981: "In their heart of hearts, Iraq's Shiʿites like things of their own soil."[70]

This attitude, common to Iraq and Lebanon no less than to Iran itself, may help to illustrate the powerful barriers to concerted action which have to date hampered the forging of effective transnational ties on a religious or confessional basis. For what the above quotation refers to is not an allegiance to Iraq as a nation-state but to deeper primordial ties of family and clan, language and culture, which underlie the very self-perception of an Iraqi Shiʿite.

In Lebanon the Shiʿites were faced with a somewhat different situation from that of their brethren in either Iran or Iraq. As the largest of the seventeen religious sects officially recognized in Lebanon, the Lebanese Shiʿites attracted international attention in the wake of the tragic death of 241 U. S. marines near Beirut airport in 1983. While it is true that these and other events of the 1980s with dramatic implications for the American and other Western interests in Lebanon raised widespread concern about Shiʿite activism as a manifestation of Islamic fundamentalism, this radicalization of the Shiʿites should be considered the culmination of a process of politicization initiated by Imam Musa Sadr. Musa Sadr came to Lebanon as the representative of the marjaʿ al-taqlid, Ayatollah Muhsin al-Hakim (d. 1970) of Iraq. Like Sadr in Iraq and Khomeini in Iran, this religious leader made it his chief cause to activate the politically quiescent Shiʿites of Lebanon. And like Sadr and Khomeini, he offered his followers an innovative ideology comprising a potent combination of traditional values and modern concepts.

The Lebanese political structure was based on the national pact of 1943, which had vested the most important political office of the country in the then-largest of the religious sects, the Maronite Christians. In the late 1950s, the Shiʿites began to migrate from their villages in the south in large numbers to settle in the southern suburbs of Beirut. The main purposes of this migration seem to have been the quest for better economic and social opportunities and the promise of modern education at government schools or at the newly established national university. The migrant Shiʿites from the south, uprooted from their villages, belonged to the underprivileged in Lebanese society, a condition that made them prone to radicalization.

The arrival of Musa Sadr in 1959 as a trusted deputy of an Iraqi marja' al-taqlid, Ayatollah Hakim, ushered in a new era in the history of Lebanese Shi'ites. Musa Sadr had received his training in religious sciences in Qum, Iran, during the crucial years of the awakening of the religious leaders to the realities of modern challenges to Islam and to Muslim societies. He set out to organize the Shi'ite community as a formidable, independent political force in Lebanon. With the change of demographic balance in Lebanon in favor of the Muslims, the Muslim community was beginning to demand a restructuring of the political institutions that would reflect the new situation. However, the Muslim demand initially took only the Sunni interests into consideration, because, like other sects—the Maronites, the Druze, the Greek Orthodox, and others—the Sunnis had an established and officially recognized institutional structure under the leadership of the Grand Mufti of the Lebanese republic. The Shi'ites lacked such an institutional body to represent their interests. In 1969, however, following massive Israeli bombing raids on southern Lebanon, Musa Sadr's efforts led to the establishment of the first such organization in Lebanese Shi'ite history, the Higher Shi'a Council.

Before this official recognition of the Shi'ite community as an independent voice in Lebanese affairs, the Shi'ites had most closely resembled their brethren in Iraq—a sizable presence underrepresented in the body politic. The Sunni-Shi'a relationship in Lebanon had remained tense for most of the history of the republic. With their courts and schools and philanthropic associations in Beirut, the Sunnis were able to exert greater influence in the political life of that city, whereas the Shi'ites, through the calculated policies of the Sunni leaders in Beirut, remained on the periphery of political life. Thus, the Shi'a Council, a democratically elected organization entrusted with some responsibility for the distribution of relief funds to Shi'ites, was conceived primarily as a forum for Shi'ite "new men" (newly wealthy and influential Shi'ites) who were effectively blocked from political power or social influence by traditional Lebanese Shi'ite leaders. The council provided the Shi'ites with a concrete expression of their identity as a distinctive people—an identity which they had lacked and which Musa Sadr offered them without rejecting the particularism of Shi'ite history. Not surprisingly, he was criticized by the politically quiescent Shi'ite ulama of Lebanon, who themselves had failed to raise objections to the exclusion of Shi'ites from the deliberations of the sects and had failed to provide their followers with adequate guidance in adopting strategies to preserve their identity in the modern age.[71] Musa Sadr responded to their criticism by citing these failures and by faulting the Shi'ite feudal families for having done little to remedy the social injustices and governmental neglect suffered by their communities in the south.

Known as "Imam" to his large number of supporters, Musa Sadr soon became the symbol of the new politically aware Shi'ite presence in the multireligious society of Lebanon. Of central importance in understanding Musa Sadr's meteoric rise is the fact that the Shi'ite tradition of submission and political indifference encouraged by some of their quiescent religious leaders had contributed significantly to the political marginalization of the Shiʿite masses. Musa Sadr recognized this and strove to reinterpret the tradition by drawing upon selected moments in the Shiʿite past, elevating them to a position of prominence infused with political meaning, and claiming that political activism was now not only necessary in order to preserve Shiʿite identity in Lebanon but, equally important, was in keeping with authentic Shiʿism. In this Musa Sadr's charismatic leadership approximated, in tone and content, that of Khomeini and Baqir Sadr; and it is this type of leadership that has been associated with the term "fundamentalist."

As did Khomeini and Baqir Sadr, he too appropriated ritually and symbolically the historic threefold religious experience of the Shiʿites (martyrdom, occultation, and precautionary dissimulation) in his successful efforts to organize a mass movement, originally conceived as nonviolent, to campaign for social justice. Shiʿism here, as in the case of Iran and Iraq, provided the imam's followers with religiously expressive categories; instead, however, of interpreting the sufferings of the Imam Husayn in Kerbala as a warrant for political quietism and submission, Musa Sadr presented the event as an identity-shaping episode of political choice and courage. Furthermore, during the crisis of national and personal identity in the 1970s, Musa Sadr's activist interpretation highlighted the experience of martyrdom in the quest for justice as the fundamental core of Shiʿite religious identity. Under oppressive circumstances, Musa Sadr taught, martyrdom suffered for the lofty ideals of a just and equitable public order on earth became plausible, and if the occasion demanded, desirable through violent revolution.[72]

This aspect of the Shiʿite movement of Imam Musa Sadr came to fore when his nonsectarian "Movement of the Deprived" of the 1960s developed into a military movement known by its acronym, AMAL (*afwaj al-muqawwama al-lubnaniyya,* meaning "Battalions of Lebanese Resistance"). AMAL acknowledged Imam Musa Sadr as its spiritual guide, although he held no official position in it. AMAL was thus uniquely placed to unite the different classes of Shiʿite "new men," businessmen and professionals, with the aspirations of the poorest of Shiʿite society through its community development programs and to spearhead a Shiʿite movement that would effectively respond to the political scene in modern Lebanon.[73]

In the late 1960s another political factor was added to the already tense atmosphere of the Lebanese political scene. Following the Cairo Agreement of 1969, Lebanon, as an expression of its identity as an Arab nation, was to allow the PLO to establish bases there. The Shiʿites lived through further painful days in Jabal ʿAmil and in the suburbs of West Beirut where they bore the brunt of Israeli reprisals against the Palestinians. As Muslims and Arabs, the Shiʿites had supported the Palestinian demand to be allowed to return to their former homeland. However, that support had not involved their active participation in the Israeli-Palestinian hostilities launched by the Palestinians from the villages in the south. Nevertheless, the Shiʿites suffered heavy casualties for the moral support they lent to the Palestinian cause, thereby intensifying the bitterness they felt toward the PLO forces in the south.

The Sunni-Shiʿite demand for the restructuring of the political institutions to reflect the Muslim majority in the 1970s set in motion the civil war that has plagued that nation with sectarian animosity almost unknown in modern times. The civil war which ensued has deepened ancient sectarian wounds and fragmented the state to such an extent that today many voices are heard calling for the breakup of the state into the strongholds of different religious communities. The Shiʿites were themselves caught up in the bid for power between the Christians and Druze in the early stages of the civil war and suffered heavy casualties fighting in an ideologically left-wing coalition formed by the Druze leader Kamal Jumblatt to challenge the Maronite ascendancy. As a result of their participation in this coalition, during the civil war years the Shiʿites were evicted from east Beirut by the Maronite militias, and their shantytowns of Maslakh and Qarantina were destroyed in another attack in 1976. Following this destruction, Shiʿite settlements in other places in and around east Beirut were forcefully evacuated and looted by the militia, leaving thousands of Shiʿites homeless, while thousands more Shiʿites in the south were uprooted by the intensifying struggle between the PLO and Israel. These circumstances served only to further radicalize the Shiʿites.

In 1976 yet another political element was added to the existing oppressive situation in the south. The Israeli-backed rebel Lebanese army of Major Saad Haddad terrorized the entire border region to deter the Shiʿites from aiding the Palestinians.[74]

Finally, in that decade, during the 1978 Israeli invasion of the south, when Shiʿite villages and homes were destroyed completely, hundreds of thousands of these homeless villagers sought refuge in and around Beirut. The relations between the Shiʿites and the PLO worsened under these conditions. All the radical elements necessary for the Shiʿite refugees to explode in retaliatory violence seemed to be in place, including the desperate hope that such violent operations would at least earn the attention of the international community and thus publicize the injustices committed against the Shiʿites. The role of Imam Musa Sadr at this juncture is not clear and remains a matter of speculation—he had encouraged his followers to pursue, as far as possible, nonviolent methods of demanding justice, but as we have seen, he also saw violent revolution as a last resort—for he disappeared in Libya later that year. As it happened, the "explosion" did not occur until 1982, in the violent Shiʿite reaction to the Israeli invasion and the U. S. intervention in Lebanon.

However, the evidence indicates that with the disappearance of Musa Sadr in Libya in 1978, the Shiʿites lost any remaining confidence in the Arabs, especially the so-called socialist block among them.

Given the emphasis of this essay on the role of religious leadership in guiding the course of modern activist movements in Shiʿism, it is worth comparing the period after the disappearance of Musa Sadr in the 1980s with numerous historical revolutionary movements in the larger Shiʿite community in the era after the occultation of the twelfth Imam. In both the historical and the contemporary postdisappearance situations, the Shiʿite faithful abandoned previous attitudes of political quiescence and in the face of circumstances of economic and political deprivation, split into factions at least in part over varying interpretations of the anticipated messianic Imam's final restoration of justice. In both cases, this splintering produced a range of moderate and extremist interpretations of the final restoration, represented by various religious leaders claiming to be knowledgeable regarding the aims of the messianic Imam and by various organizations, each with its own unique program for hastening the moment of final vindication. In contemporary Lebanon this pattern emerged after the disappearance of Imam Musa Sadr, when AMAL experienced similar factionalization and radicalization upon including a political dimension in its predominantly social and military program.

The younger generation in AMAL was, after 1978, attracted to the sense of religious identity generated by an activist interpretation of Shiʿite ideals under the radical-traditional leadership of Shaykh Muhammad Husayn Fadl Allah, to whom a measure of Musa Sadr's influence and power had passed. Fadl Allah, often described as the spiritual leader of the Party of God, the Hizbullah, was trained in Najaf. After his permanent return to Lebanon in the mid-1960s, he dedicated himself to the cause of the elaboration, through his regular sermons and numerous writings, of an activist Shiʿite religious identity. However, the extent of Fadl Allah's influence and authority were felt only after Musa Sadr's disappearance in 1979.

Nabih Berri, an American-educated lawyer and secularist in outlook, eventually took over AMAL after Imam Sadr and developed his peaceful formula to redress the Shiʿite grievances, but he came under constant pressure and criticisms from both the Islamic AMAL, a splinter group headed by Husayn Musawi, and the Hizbullah under Shaykh Fadl Allah.

The ability of these radicalized Shiʿite movements to sustain themselves over the course of time and, more important, throughout a series of community-threatening traumas, was demonstrated in the events that followed the Israeli invasion of 1982 and the U. S. intervention in 1983 and 1984 in Lebanon. The Western policies have been interpreted by these groups as overtly hostile to their identity, indeed, to their survival. As is well known, the religious leaders of these radical groups have repeatedly pointed to the American opposition to Khomeini's rule in Iran; to the American support of Iraq and by extension of Iraq's treatment of the Shiʿites, and to the American support of the Israelis and Christians against Muslim interests. In this way the "successors" to Imam Musa Sadr have not allowed the revolutionary fervor to subside: the presence and threat of the enemy is the warrant for Shiʿite activism. Shaykh Fadl Allah has, to the time of this writing, continued to make symbolic use of bloody episodes in Shiʿite history in his widely attended lectures and circulated writings. His polemic against the West evokes Shiʿite feelings about the "arrogant silence" of the Western powers toward the suffering of the oppressed in the Third World.[75]

It is important to underscore the fact that although Fadl Allah has attempted to emulate Khomeini's role in Iran, which he sees as providing a viable public order in which the Shiʿites would find their appropriate social and political place and identity, he is pragmatic enough to realize that the multi-religious political structure in Lebanon could not be modeled after Islamic Republic of Iran with a qualified Shiʿite jurist as the head of the government. Interestingly, the Shiʿite religious leaders of Lebanon, perhaps because of the absence of a local marjaʿ al-taqlid, find their voices to be in unison with the Sunni leaders when speaking about the rule of the Shariʿa rather than that of the guardian of the Shariʿa (as embodied in Khomeini's concept of the Guardianship of the Jurist). Furthermore, the Shi'ite leaders of Lebanon are fully aware that they and their followers share the Arab identity and the burden of Arab destiny, with Israel and the West as active players in their present and ongoing crisis.

Hence, however devoted to and influenced by the political activism of their coreligionists in Iran they might be, the Lebanese Shi'ites are faced with problems peculiar to them, in which Shi'ism functions as a reformist ideology that calls upon its adherents to transform an unjust social order. As long as the imbalances in the social and political institutions persist in Lebanon, one might expect the Shi'ite struggle to rectify the situation to continue.

However, the subject matter covered in the preachings of the religious leaders has changed significantly. As Fadl Allah has pointed out in the preface of his book, *Islam and the Logic of Force,* to speak about force *(quwwa)* in the context of modern Shi'ism is no longer an abstract idea philosophically related to the attribute of Almighty God. Force and its legitimate use is a subject that touches the very survival of the believers in the world beyond their faith. The reinterpreted traditional teachings of politically quiescent Shi'ism by Khomeini, Muhammad Baqir Sadr, Musa Sadr, and Fadl Allah have consequently provided modern Shi'ite preachers with renewed confidence in leading their followers to come to terms with the real and often merciless world in which they find themselves. In that world, they contend, there lies a warrant for resort to violent means to pursue the traditional aim of preserving Shi'ite religious practice and identity.[76]

Concluding Remarks

Shi'ite activism in Iran, Iraq, and Lebanon in the 1970s and 1980s was a form of religious fundamentalism stemming from the acute awareness among Muslims in general, and the Shi'ites in particular, of the discrepancy between the divine promise of success and the historical development of the world which the divine controls. In order to address this discrepancy, a task they believe is mandated by Islamic revelation, Shi'ites have endeavored to strike a balance between the divine promise of the earthly success to the Muslims and their contemporary situation by moving in two directions: first, by introducing reforms in the religious institutions to prevent further deterioration of Islamic religious life in the modern age; and second, by protesting and resisting alien interference, whether direct or indirect, over the Islamic character of their societies.

In both these directions particular sociopolitical conditions were taken into account by the religious leaders who were involved in directing the internal reform as well as resisting domination by exogenous forces. Shi'ite history provided relevant precedents for the ulama to extrapolate in order to impart necessary guidance to the believers at a given time. The process of extrapolation in the terms of the precedents took into account various sociopolitical factors that were important to the strategy that was ultimately adopted by the ulama as the appropriate course of action. In the pre-modern period, the tendency among the ulama was to shun politics and public life for the preservation of the pure faith. But, as the Shi'ite world began to be dominated by alien, exogenous forces of colonialism and its attendant westernization, the ulama retrieved from their historical repertoire of sociopolitical responses a radical activism. In addition to the imperialism of the colonizing powers, the ulama felt the danger of secular ideologies in the form of communism, socialism, and nationalism seducing Muslim leaders educated on Western models, who in the later part of nineteenth century and throughout the twentieth century were engaged in moving the Muslim countries toward modernization through westernization. However, modernization, as it proceeded within this time frame, proved unable to eradicate the social and political ills suffered by the Muslims. This failure was due in some measure to the inability of Muslim modernizers to establish adequate political institutions capable of easing the transition to a technologically based society and generating a positive attitude toward the government and its development programs.

By the second half of the twentieth century, the support lent to the dictatorial and at times oppressive governments by the Western nations convinced many ulama and the educated Shiʿites of Iran, Iraq, and Lebanon that modern secular ideologies imported from the West or the East were not only inadequate for providing them with solutions to their identity crisis; they were also incapable of correcting the sociopolitical injustices endured by the downtrodden in those countries. The 1960s were the decisive years in bringing the Shiʿite ulama out of their self-imposed aloofness and in exposing them to modernity. Those years prepared them to supply the Shiʿites with an Islamic alternative: the potentially activist Shiʿism of the Imams ʿAlī and Husayn. This activist Shiʿism, often termed "fundamentalism," contrary to the traditionally quiescent and submissive interpretation of the events surrounding Imam Husayn's martyrdom, sought to encourage the Shiʿites to become politically assertive and successful in the modern world without sacrificing their identity as Shiʿite Muslims. Activist Shiʿism has, moreover, provided the Shiʿites with renewed confidence in encountering the modern world with its new subtle forms of colonization. Whether Ayatollah Khomeini's Islamic alternative will emerge as the only viable solution to the multifarious problems faced by the Muslim societies in these last years of the twentieth century will depend on the ability of the ulama and their followers to restore the earthly success of Islam in the coming years.

Notes

1. Literally, the word means "the sign of God." It is a title that is given to the most learned Shiʿite jurist, the *mujtahid*.

2. The phrase appears in Shiʿite writings to indicate the function of the messianic Imam, the Mahdi, in Shiʿism. That the return of the Ayatollah Khomeini in 1979 was viewed as a prelude to the final restoration by the Mahdi in Iran is evident from the popular expectation of the establishment of justice by their religious leader.

3. Fazlur Rahman, "Roots of Islamic Neo-Fundamentalism," in Philip H. Stoddard, ed., *Change in the Muslim World* (Syracuse: Syracuse University Press, 1981), p. 23.

4. Wilfred Cantwell Smith, *Islam in Modern History* (Princeton: Princeton University Press, 1977), p. 41.

5. Ibid., pp. 28–29. Smith contrasts this characteristic of Islam with the history of early Christianity which "was launched upon a world already organized." Moreover, whereas Islam's efforts were directed to build on earth the kind of social order that the divine purpose required, Christianity, as the religion of a persecuted minority, was concerned with nurturing an individual who by inner resources would be able to stand against the course of history. Consequently, Christians, unlike Muslims, have not regarded their earthly success as an achievement of or for their faith.

6. C. A. O. van Nieuwenhuijze, "Secularization or Essentialism? Fertile Ambiguities in Contemporary Middle Eastern Civilization," in *Le Cuisier et le philosophe: Hommage a Maxime Rodinson: Etudes d'ethnographie historique du Proche-Orient,* assembled by J. P. Digard (Paris: Maisonneuve et Larose, 1982), pp. 285–86.

7. The phrase is borrowed from Eustace A. Haydon, "Twenty Five Years of History of Religions," *The Journal of Religion* 6 (1926): 32.

8. Fazlur Rahman, *Islam* (Chicago: University of Chicago Press, 1979), epilogue to 2d ed., pp. 255–65.

9. Smith, *Islam in Modern History,* pp. 38–39.

10. Bernard Lewis, *The Political Language of Islam* (Chicago: University of Chicago Press, 1988), chap. 5, pp. 91ff.

11. *Ulama* (plural of *'alim*), *mujtahid,* and *faqih* mean the expert on Islamic jurisprudence. However, a *mujtahid* is a jurist who applies *ijtihad* (independent reasoning) to deduce a judicial decision in Islamic law.

12. The phrase has been quoted by Shireen K. Hunter in her introduction to *The Politics of Islamic Revivalism: Diversity and Unity,* Shireen T. Hunter, ed. (Bloomington: Indiana University Press, 1988), p. xiii.

13. M. G. S. Hodgson, *The Venture of Islam: Conscience and History in a World Civilization* (Chicago: University of Chicago Press, 1974), vol. 3, p. 246.

14. Ibid., pp. 241ff. Hodgson uses the phrase to describe the situation of the Egyptians under Lord Cromer (1883–1907), the representative of a classic modern Western attitude to those peoples who had not participated from within in the modern transmutation.

15. James P. Piscatori, *Islam in the World of Nation-States* (Cambridge: Cambridge University Press, 1986), in the chapter entitled, "The Theory and Practice of Territorial Pluralism," pp. 40–75, has shown with much evidence that the practice of Muslims over the centuries shows an overwhelming acceptance of the reality of territorial pluralism and is firmly on the side of the state. This practice has received a sort of legitimation through a "consensus of action," despite the views of some Muslim thinkers who have maintained the "universal and all-embracing" nature of the Islamic polity.

16. Ann K. S. Lambton, *Qajar Persia: Eleven Studies* (Austin: University of Texas Press, 1987), pp. 212.

17. Ibid., pp. 218–19.

18. Ibid., p. 212; Hodgson, *Venture,* pp. 306–7.

19. The Persian title of the book: *Gharbzadagi,* has been translated variously by different translators of the work in English. See, for instance, *Weststuckness,* published by Mazda Publishers in 1982.

20. In 1872, Baron Julius de Reuter, a British subject, purchased from Naser al-Din Shah (1848–96) a major portion of Iran's economic potential, as well as its very infrastructure. For some £40,000 and 60% of customs revenue, de Reuter obtained exclusive control of the state bank, most mineral wealth, communications, including the construction of railways and canal traffic, telegraph lines, and factories, in addition to custom farming. It was too much for even Great Britain, and after protests from Russia and Great Britain, combined with outrage throughout all strata of Iranian society, the concession was withdrawn. The shah nonetheless managed to parcel out almost all elements of the Reuter Concession to various foreign governments and businessmen. In the internal protests against the Reuter Concession, ulama were prominent, but by no means were they to take the sort of leadership role which they would assume almost twenty years later in

the Tobacco Revolt. For further details, cf. Ervand Abrahamian, *Iran between Two Revolutions* (Princeton: Princeton University Press, 1982), p. 55; and Nikki Keddie, *Roots of Revolution: An Interpretive History of Modern Iran* (New Haven: Yale University Press, 1981), pp. 58–60.

21. Lambton, *Qajar Persia,* pp. 195–276.

22. The rivalry continued under the Pahlavis until World War II, when the United States would supplant Russia as the anti-British foil. In an ironic twist in the early 1970s, the Russian presence returned on occasion to counteract the influence of American power.

23. Hamid Enayat, *Modern Islamic Political Thought* (Austin: University of Texas Press, 1982), p. 166.

24. Richard Cottam, "The Iranian Revolution," in Nikki Keddie and Juan R. Cole, eds., *Shi'ism and Social Protest* (New Haven: Yale University Press, 1986), pp. 60ff., has dealt with this aspect in his thesis developed to demonstrate that the Khomeini phenomenon is a product of the "alteration of natural change patterns in Iran by the interference of external powers."

25. Said Amir Arjomand, *The Turban for the Crown: The Islamic Revolution in Iran* (New York: Oxford University Press, 1988), pp. 48ff.

26. In the light of the tyranny of the Shi'ite rulers of Iran and oppression suffered by the people at the hands of government, prominent Shi'ite jurists provided necessary guidance in legitimizing the development of modern political institutions, especially the consultative assembly with the responsibility of legislating for the modern state under the guidance of the leading ulama. But for some other jurists, as pointed out earlier, such a legitimation of a modern legislature was an innovation and in direct conflict with the purposes and function of the theological and juridical authority of the Imam. See Abdulhadi Hairi, *Shi'ites and Constitutionalism in Iran* (Leiden, 1977), for a discussion on the problems of legitimizing constitutionalism, the dispute among the jurists, and the question of legitimacy (especially chap. 6). The existence of a modern legislature and its power to legislate in an Islamic state are by no means resolved even now. This has led to the notion of the absolute authority of the jurist, who, according to the ruling of Khomeini in February 1988, can exercise his delegated authority to resolve the problem of legislation on the subjects on which the traditional Shari'a has nothing to say.

27. Keddie, *Roots of Revolution,* pp. 142–45.

28. Leonard Binder, "Iran: Crises of Political Development," *Revolution in Iran, Middle East Review-Special Studies,* no. 1 (1980): 29.

29. Ibid.

30. The phrase is employed by Nikki R. Keddie, in "Islamic Revival as Third Worldism," in *Le Cuisier et le philosophie,* pp. 275–81, in her discussion about the social classes to whom "third worldism" appeals. Islamic revivalism is also, in her opinion, a form of "third worldism" that appeals to the militantly oriented classes who have a lower place on the socio-economic ladder.

31. van Nieuwenhuijze, "Secularization," p. 288.

32. I have discussed this development in great detail in my study, *The Just Ruler in Shi'ite Islam: The Comprehensive Authority of the Jurist in Imamite Jurisprudence* (New York: Oxford University Press, 1988). The following discussion is derived from this study.

33. For a detailed account of this early predicament in Islamic history, cf. S. H. M. Jafri, *The Origins and Early Development of Shi'a Islam* (London: Longman Group Ltd., 1981).

34. I have dealt with the idea of the messianic Imam in Shi'ism in *Islamic Messianism: The Idea of Mahdi in Twelver Shi'ism* (Albany: State University of New York Press, 1981).

35. There is certainly some overlapping between these four periods, particularly when, as I have demonstrated in *Just Ruler,* introduction, pp. 3–57, some eminent scholars who dealt with the question of juridical authority were witness to two periods. It is also possible to identify the four periods with the four regions of the Shi'ite jurisprudence, namely, Baghdad, Hilla, Isfahan, and Tehran-Qum-Mashhad. How-

ever, for the purpose of this chapter, I found it expedient to treat the chronological aspect of the development in political jurisprudence. The juridical authority evolved chronologically as the period of occultation became prolonged and the political history of the Shi'ites took a different turn in Iran.

36. Sachedina, *Just Ruler,* pp. 113–17.

37. This is the meaning of "divine grace" *(lutf)* in Islamic theology where the means of procuring the divine purpose for humanity are discussed. According to this doctrine, it is necessary that God appoint prophets and the Imams to create the ideal public order on earth. Cf. Sachedina, *Islamic Messianism,* pp.122–32.

38. "Sound belief" *(iman sahih)* implied upholding the Imamate of the twelve Imams; "sound knowledge" *('ilm sahih)* connoted learning acquired from the Imams; and "sound character" *('adala)* was the moral probity required of all those individuals who served in an official capacity as the leaders of congregational prayers, judges, witnesses, and so on.

39. For an adequate account of the Shi'ites of Lebanon, cf. Helena Cobban, "The Growth of Shi'ite power in Lebanon and Its Implications for the Future," in Keddie and Cole, *Shi'ism and Social Protest,* pp. 137–55; and, Augustus Richard Norton, "Shi'ism and Social Protest in Lebanon," *Shi'ism and Social Protest,* pp. 156–78. Also cf. Marius Deeb, "Shia Movements in Lebanon: Their Formation, Ideology, Social Basis, and Links with Iran and Syria," *Third World Quarterly* 10, no. 2 (1988): 683–98; Robin Wright, "Lebanon," in Hunter, *The Politics of Islamic Revivalism,* pp. 57–70. All these studies are mainly concerned with analyzing the political turmoil in Lebanon and the emerging role of the Lebanese Shi'ites from an insignificant, socially backward group to one of the most important factions in the shaping of the political future of that war-torn country.

40. An account of sociopolitical conditions under which the jurists like Muhammad Baqir Sadr's activist interpretation of Shi'ite ideology in the context of the unjust treatment of the Shi'ites of Iraq by the Ba'thist government gave rise to the Shi'ite protest movements is given by Hanna Batatu, "Shi'ite Organizations in Iraq: Al-Da'wa al-Islamiyyah and al-Mujahidin," in Keddie and Cole, *Shi'ism and Social Protest,* pp. 179–200. A detailed analysis of Sadr's socioreligious thought in the contemporary Shi'ite intellectual-religious milieu of Najaf, Iraq, that molded Shi'ite militancy in Iraq has been provided by Chibli Mallat, "Religious Militancy in Contemporary Iraq: Muhammad Baqer as-Sadr and the Sunni-Shi'a paradigm," *Third World Quarterly* 10, no. 2 (1988): 699–729. See also his article "Iraq," in Hunter, *The Politics of Islamic Revivalism,* pp. 71–87.

41. Before the judicial opinion of Ayatollah Khomeini in February 1988, in which he ruled in favor of the absolute authority of the Shi'ite jurist who is invested with the *wilayat al-faqih* (The Guardianship of the Jurist) in the public interest of the nation, Muhammad Baqir Sadr, in his lecture on the legality of the Iranian constitution, had argued for such an absolute authority for the well-qualified jurist, who, in the interest of the community, could even postpone those forms of worship that were in conflict with the public interest. Cf. the text of his lecture in *al-Islam yaqudu al-hayat* (Tehran: Wizarat al-Irshad al-Islami, 1403/1983), pp. 3–19. For Khumayni's judicial opinion and its political implications and its various interpretations among the leading government officials, cf. Hamid Algar, "Recent Developments in the Concept of *Wilayat al-faqih,*" in the forthcoming collection of papers presented at the conference on *Wilayat al-faqih* in London in June 1988. For the text, and analytical and critical commentary on the events that preceded and followed this important decision by Khumayni to facilitate the government in resolving numerous outstanding issues connected with the legislature and other administrative organs of Iranian government, cf. *Tafsil va tahlil-i vilayat-i mutlaqa-yi faqih* (Tehran: Nihzat-i Azadi-yi Iran, 1367/1988).

42. The work is entitled *al-Islam wa mantiq al-quwwa* (Islam and the logic of force) (Beirut: Dar al-Islamiyya, 1979). It was published for the first time in 1978 at the

critical moment in the political history of Lebanese Shi'ites when Imam Musa Sadr disappeared in Libya and Israel invaded south Lebanon. Iran was going through the demonstrations that culminated in the overthrow of the shah. Both these episodes led the Shi'ite leaders to adopt a radical political response.

43. In his *Khutuwat 'ala tariq al-islam* (Beirut, 1982), pp. 266ff. Fadl Allah defines the scope of *taqiyya* in the juridical injunction, critically evaluating the traditions justifying a submissive attitude.

44. These suggestions are part of the collection of essays by prominent teachers and professors of Shi'ite studies in Qum and Tehran in 1963 entitled *Bahthi dar bara-yi marja'iyyat va ruhaniyyat* (Discussion on the religious and spiritual authority [of the *marja' al-taqlid*]) (Tehran, 1341/1964).

45. Ali Shari'ati, *Tashayyu' ' alavi va tashayyu' safavi* (Shi'ism of Imam 'Alī and Shi'ism of the Safavids) (Tehran, 1971/1350).

46. I have drawn material in this section from my article: "Ali Shari'ati: The Ideologue of the Iranian Revolution," in John L. Esposito, ed., *Voices of Resurgent Islam* (New York: Oxford University Press, 1983). There are numerous studies dedicated to the role of Shari'ati in the revival of Islam in Iran. However, no one has considered Shari'ati's proposed program for Iranian youth in the light of his conviction that only a committed Muslim intelligentsia who could come to grips with the society's inner contradictions and totally commit themselves to remedy the sociocultural malaise and resulting identity crisis would be effective in communicating the sociological fact of Islam to modern youth. It is thus not surprising to see that the religious leadership of the Islamic Republic of Iran, after a period of discrediting Shari'ati's interpretation of Islam and its role in the mobilization of Iranian Muslim youth for the revolution, have rehabilitated him as a truly Muslim intellectual whose writings continue to exercise immeasurable influence among Muslims with modern educations.

47. See Shari'ati's speech on the occasion of the 'Ashura commemoration in the *husayniyya* in Mehdi Abedi and Gary Legenhausen, eds., *Jihad and Shahadat: Struggle and Martyrdom in Islam*(Houston: The Institute of Research and Islamic Studies, 1986), pp.163–67.

48. Ruhullah Khumayni, *Hukumat-i islami* (Islamic government) (Najaf, 1971), pp. 24–25.

49. Arjomand, *Turban,* in his chapter, "The Revolution of February," pp. 103ff. describes how the shah's propagation of alien culture accompanied by the massive influx of foreign civil and military technology and the morale that goes with them created the new middle class, the class that could have assumed the nation's political leadership by virtue of its educational and economic resources, but did not do so.

50. In December 1978, at the peak of the revolution, following the pronouncements of some leading ulama on the intrinsic relationship between Iran and Shi'ism, the shah, in his last effort to avert his impending downfall, appealed to the Iranians by showing the exclusive relationship of the Iranian nation to Shi'ite Islam and by declaring his commitment to preserve this "sacred" relationship. Moreover, he appealed to the ulama to support him in preserving "the only Shi'ite nation on earth." The shah's speech was given much publicity in the Iranian newspapers and received much attention in foreign broadcasts. I was in Mashhad at the time, and the BBC sought my assistance as a translator when it interviewed Ayatollah Shirazi and asked him to comment on the conciliatory tone of the shah as the "protector of the only Shi'ite nation."

51. Binder, "Iran: Crisis of Political Development," pp. 18–40, has treated the political development in the sixties and seventies leading to the revolution.

52. Arjomand, *Turban,* provides a detailed sociological analysis of the political events that led to the power of the Shi'ite jurists.

53. Hanna Batatu, *The Old Social Classes and the Revolutionary Movements of Iraq* (Princeton: Princeton University Press, 1978), pp. 22ff.

54. Ibid., p. 19.

55. Ibid., p. 35–36.

56. Ibid., p. 23–24.

57. Phoebe Marr, *The Modern History of Iraq* (Boulder, Colo.: Westview Press, 1985) treats the question of divided loyalties of the Shi'ites in Iraq and uses the migration of the Shi'ite religious leaders to Iran to avoid arrest by British in 1923 as an example that confirmed the suspicions of the Iraqi politicians, without duly emphasizing the intellectual, cultural, and religious relationship that existed historically between the Shi'ite leaders of Iran and Iraq. While these migrations of the Shi'ites were understandably interpreted by Iraqi Sunni politicians as a breach of loyalty, the Shi'ite ulama on both sides of the border between Iran and Iraq regarded it as a religiously expected reaction under unfavorable circumstances.

58. Batatu, *Old Social Classes,* p. 47.

59. Ibid., p. 472.

60. Ibid., p. 466.

61. Ibid., p. 752.

62. Ibid., p. 1000.

63. See Murtada Mutahhari, "Ijtihad dar islam," in *Bahthi dar bara-yi marja'iyyat va ruhaniyyat,* pp. 25–68.

64. Chibli Mallat, "Iraq," p. 74.

65. Ibid., pp. 76–77. Cf. Batatu, "Shi'ite Organizations," p. 200.

66. Batatu, "Shi'ite Organizations," pp. 179–200.

67. In the summer of 1980, when I met with Ayatollah Khu'i in Najaf, he explained the reason for his quietist approach by pointing out that the Ba'thist government was waiting for any excuse to bring the Shi'ite center of learning in Najaf to an end by expelling or imprisoning the students and getting rid of the prominent ulama. This was the summer following the execution of the Ayatollah Muhammad Baqir al-Sadr.

68. Ofra Bengio, "Shi'is and Politics in Ba'thist Iraq," *Middle Eastern Studies* 21, no. 1 (1988): 6.

69. Batatu, "Shi'i Organizations," p. 196.

70. Ibid., p. 199.

71. Fouad Ajami, *The Vanished Imam: Musa al-Sadr and the Shia of Lebanon* (Ithaca: Cornell University Press, 1986), pp. 115–17.

72. Musa Sadr's interpretation of the 'Ashura events has been reported in numerous Beirut newspapers such as *al-Nahar, al-Hayat,* and so on, that covered his speeches on that occasion.

73. Ibid., p. 117.

74. Cobban, "Growth of Shi'i Power," pp. 145–46.

75. Following the tradition established by Musa Sadr, in a lecture delivered on the occasion of 'Ashura celebrations in 1977, Fadl Allah explained the political message of the martyrdom of the Imam Husayn and called upon the Shi'ites of Lebanon to defend their rights. Cf. *Afaq islamiyya wa mawadi' ukhra* (Beirut, 1980).

76. It should also finally be pointed out that Shi'ite activism in both Iraq and Lebanon is not so much the result of frustration with the failure of foreign ideologies and value systems as it is the "realization," through modern education and mass information, of the ways in which these foreign systems and their engineers have failed to respond to the issue of social justice in an era marked by a perhaps exaggerated sense of political, social, and economic expectations.

Select Bibliography

Ajami, Fouad. *The Vanished Imam: Musa al-Sadr and the Shia of Lebanon.* Ithaca: Cornell University Press, 1986.

Arjomand, Said Amir. *The Shadow of God and the Hidden Imam.* Chicago: University of Chicago Press, 1984.

———. *The Turban for the Crown: The Islamic Revolution in Iran.* New York: Oxford University Press, 1988.

Batatu, Hanna. *The Old Social Classes and the Revolutionary Movements of Iraq.* Princeton: Princeton University Press, 1978.

Dekmejian, R. Hrair. *Islam in Revolution: Fundamentalism in the Arab World.* Syracuse: Syracuse University Press, 1985.

Enayat, Hamid. *Modern Islamic Political Thought.* Austin: University of Texas Press, 1982.

Hairi, Abdul-hadi. *Shi'ism and Constitutionalism in Iran*. Leiden: n.p., 1977.

Hodgson, M. G. S. *The Venture of Islam: Conscience and History in a World Civilization*. 3 vols. Chicago: University of Chicago Press, 1974.

Hunter, Shireen T., ed. *The Politics of Islamic Revivalism: Diversity and Unity*. Bloomington: Indiana University Press, 1988.

Jafri, S. H. M. *The Origins and Early Development of Shi'a Islam*. London: Longman, 1981.

Keddie, Nikki R. *Roots of Revolution: An Interpretive History of Modern Iran*. New Haven: Yale University Press, 1981.

Keddie, Nikki R., ed. *Religion and Politics in Iran: Shi'ism from Quietism to Revolution*. New Haven: Yale University Press, 1983.

Keddie, Nikki R., and Juan R. Cole, eds. *Shi'ism and Social Protest*. New Haven: Yale University Press, 1986.

Lambton, Ann K. S. *Qajar Persia: Eleven Studies*. Austin: University of Texas Press, 1987.

Lewis, Bernard. *The Political Language of Islam*. Chicago: The University of Chicago Press, 1988.

Marr, Phoebe. *The Modern History of Iraq*. Boulder, Colo.: Westview, 1985.

Momen, Moojan. *An Introduction to Shi'i Islam: The History and Doctrines of Twelver Shi'ism*. New Haven: Yale University Press, 1985.

Moosa, Matti. *Extremist Shiites: The Ghulat Sects*. Syracuse: Syracuse University Press, 1988.

Mottahedeh, Roy. *The Mantle of the Prophet: Religion and Politics in Iran*. New York: Pantheon Books, 1985.

Piscatori, James P. *Islam in a World of Nation-States*. Cambridge: Cambridge University Press, 1986.

Rahman, Fazlur. *Islam*. Chicago: University of Chicago Press, 1979.

Sachedina, Abdulaziz A. *Islamic Messianism: The Idea of Mahdi in Twelver Shi'ism*. Albany: State University of New York Press, 1981.

———. *The Just Ruler in Shi'ite Islam: The Comprehensive Authority of the Jurist in Imamite Jurisprudence*. New York: Oxford University Press, 1988.

Smith, Wilfred Cantwell. *Islam in Modern History*. Princeton: Princeton University Press, 1977.

Stoddard, Philip H., ed. *Change in the Muslim World*. Syracuse: Syracuse University Press, 1981.

Watt, W. Montgomery. *Islamic Fundamentalism and Modernity*. New York: Routledge, 1988.

CHAPTER
8

Islamic Fundamentalism in South Asia: The Jamaat-i-Islami and the Tablighi Jamaat of South Asia

Mumtaz Ahmad

In November 1989, the Jamaat-i-Islami Pakistan held a three-day national conference in the historic city of Lahore. It was an event that the Jamaat-i-Islami workers had been waiting for since 1963, the year when its last national conference had been held in the same city. The 1989 conference was attended by more than one hundred thousand Jamaat workers and supporters from various parts of Pakistan. Punjabis, Sindhis, Baluch, Pathans, and Muhajirs (Urdu-speaking refugees from India who had immigrated to Pakistan at the time of partition in 1947) mingled together and presented a rare scene of Islamic unity, especially at a time when two major cities of southern Pakistan were under twenty-four-hour curfews to quell violence between warring Sindhis and Muhajirs. While the majority of the participants were clad in traditional Pakistani dress—*shalwar kameez*—Western attire was also quite common. The meeting ground was full of banners proclaiming the inevitable victory of the Muslim freedom fighters in Palestine, Afghanistan, and Kashmir. The list of foreign guests attending the conference read like a *Who's Who* of international Islamic political movements: Dr. Muhammad Siyam of the Islamic resistance movement of Palestine, Hamas; Rashid-al-Ghannoushi of the Islamic Tendency Society of Tunis; Mustafa Mashoor of the Muslim Brotherhood of Egypt; Maulana Abul Kalam of the Jamaat-i-Islami, Bangladesh; Mohammad Yasir of the Hizb-i-Islami of Afghanistan; Mahmud Nahna of the Islamic Movement of Algeria; Dr. Fazal Noor of the Parti Islam Se-Malaysia; Shaikh Issa bin Khalifa of Jamiyat-al-Islah of Bahrain; and Necmettin Erbakan of the Rafah party of Turkey. Surveying the huge crowd of devotees from an elevated platform, Jamaat-i-Islami president, Qazi Hussain Ahmad, began his inaugural address with the words:

> We are gathered here to reaffirm our pledge to Almighty Allah that we will make Pakistan a truly Islamic state, a state where Shari'a will reign supreme, a state based on justice for the people and accountability of the rulers, a state which will be a model of Islam-in-power for the rest of the Muslim world.[1]

Simultaneously, at a distance of less than thirty miles from Lahore, another massive crowd—ten times larger than that of the Jamaat-i-Islami—had also gathered in the name of Islam. This was the international conference of the Tablighi Jamaat, an annual event that attracts about a million Muslims from various parts of the world, most of whom are plain folk, dressed in traditional attire; almost none of them can be described as Islamic VIPs. While the Jamaat-i-Islami conference in Lahore made full use of such modern technological devices as video cameras, closed-circuit TVs, fax machines, and IBM computers, the Tablighi Jamaat conference in the small railroad station town of Raiwind looked like a traditional communal gathering. There were no press reporters and no TV cameras. In tent after tent, people were either praying or reciting the Qur'an or listening to each other's testimonies of faith and spiritual reawakening. There was no mention of Kashmir, Afghanistan, or Palestine. Concluding his farewell instructions to the Tabligh workers, Maulana Inamul Hasan, the emir (president) of the Tablighi Jamaat, earnestly exhorted:

> Go and take the eternal message of Islam to the four corners of the globe. Remind your brethren of their religious duties; remind them of the day of Judgement; and call them to the remembrance of Almighty Allah, to submission to His Will, and obedience to Prophet Muhammad (peace be upon him).[2]

The Jamaat-i-Islami and the Tablighi Jamaat, the two most important Islamic movements of South Asian subcontinent in the twentieth century, also represent two fundamentally different approaches to Islamic revivalism. While the Jamaat-i-Islami's main emphasis is on the resacralization of political life and the establishment of an Islamic state with the Qur'an and Sunna (the way of the Prophet) as its constitution and the Shari'a as its basic law, the Tabligh movement, on the other hand, focuses its activities on the moral and spiritual uplift of individual believers, asking them to fulfill their religious obligations irrespective of whether there is an Islamic state or not. However, in view of their literalist interpretation of the Qur'an and the traditions of the Prophet, as well as their common hostility toward Islamic liberalism, both of these movements can be described as fundamentalist movements. Both claim that they are working for the revival of pristine Islam. Both are regarded as equally legitimate Islamic responses to the challenges of modernity and are thus mainstream rather than fringe movements. Both of them enjoy enormous support in certain important sectors of Indian, Pakistani, and Bangladeshi societies, and their influence has reached far beyond the country of their origin.

Apart from these similarities, there are important differences in their ideologies, organizations, and methods of *da'wa* (call). While the Tablighi Jamaat is a grass-roots movement with followers from all sections of society, the Jamaat-i-Islami's support base consists mainly of educated, lower-middle-class Muslims from both the traditional and modern sectors of society. The Jamaat-i-Islami's emphasis on the Islamization of politics and state has tended to transform the movement into a modern cadre-type political party, while the Tablighi Jamaat's program of strengthening the spiritual moorings of individual believers has helped it retain its character as a daʿwa movement. The Jamaat-i-Islami is a highly structured, hierarchically organized, bureaucratic-type organization that has established a clear line of authority and a huge network of functional departments and nationwide branches; the Tablighi Jamaat, on the other hand, is a free-floating religious movement with minimal dependence on hierarchy, leadership positions, and decision-making procedures. Although both are primarily lay movements with minimal participation by the ulama, the Tablighi Jamaat is definitely closer to traditional forms of Islam than is the Jamaat-i-Islami, which in its own self-perception represents a synthesis of tradition and modernity.

In the following pages, I will attempt to highlight the salient features of the ideologies, organizations, and methods of these two Islamic movements. I will also discuss their positions on various social, economic, and political issues that confront Muslims of South Asia and will assess the consequences of these positions for the religiopolitical situation of the South Asian subcontinent.

The Jamaat-i-Islami

Religious revival in the postcolonial era is not limited to newly independent Muslim countries. The Buddhist upsurge in Sri Lanka, the Hindu revival in India, and the recent Sikh reassertion in Indian Punjab are no less important than the activities of Islamic fundamentalist parties. From this perspective, Islamic fundamentalist revivalism in Muslim countries might be understood as a search for identity and reassertion of tradition in transitional societies.

What might be of interest in the context of Muslim societies, however, is the emergence of disciplined, organized, and mass-based fundamentalist political groups that aim at restructuring the affairs of the state and reorganizing social relations on Islamic principles.[3] These groups aspire to reestablish an idealized Islamic system as first introduced and implemented under the leadership of the Prophet Muhammad. The Muslim Brotherhood in the Arab countries, Jamaat-i-Islami in Pakistan, India, and Bangladesh, Dar-ul-Islam in Indonesia, Islamic National Front in Sudan, Islamic Tendency Society in Tunis, Parti Islam Se-Malaysia in Malaysia, and the Rafah party in Turkey represent an interesting and important phenomenon in their respective countries. These organizations have played an important role in determining and shaping the nature of political debates and events and have occupied center stage during several critical periods in the history of their nations.

By the beginning of the nineteenth century, most Islamic countries were being ruled or effectively controlled by European powers. This loss of political control had been preceded by a steady decline in the intellectual and material capabilities of these societies. Colonial rule challenged Islamic societies at two levels. First, it subjugated them politically and thus shook the Muslims' self-confidence as a people who had dominated the world politically for centuries. Second, it challenged these societies in the realm of ideas by emphasizing the role of scientific and rational discourse as against the revealed word.[4]

In the specific case of South Asia, what further compounded the political and psychological dilemma of the Muslims was the fact that, despite their seven-hundred-year rule in India, they still constituted a minority. The loss of political power to the British was a devastating blow to their historically grounded sense of cultural and political superiority. Equally unsettling psychologically was the realization that their Hindu compatriots were advancing far ahead of them as a result of their readiness to acquire Western education and use new occupational opportunities offered by the British. The early phase of the British ascendancy also witnessed a new and vigorous wave of Hindu religious revival and a rearticulation of Hindu national identity rooted in the period before the Muslim conquest of India. Pressured by the British, who considered them the main instigators of the mutiny of 1857, and fearful of the Hindus who had surpassed them in economic and educational pursuits, the Muslims faced choices with monumental consequences at the time when the East India Company formally handed over the reigns of power in India to the British Crown.

The first and seemingly instinctive reaction of the Muslims to the challenge of the West was to withdraw from the mainstream of contemporary developments and to seek comfort in Islam's past glory. They sought to reassert the cultural traditions derived from their religion and "clung tenaciously . . . to the memory of a brilliant civilization which, in their eyes, was irreplaceable by anything the West had to offer."[5] The main concern of most orthodox theologians and the great theological seminaries such as the Deoband was to safeguard and preserve the normative and institutional structures of tradition from the increasingly aggressive onslaught of Western ideas and institutions. In order to achieve this objective, the ulama established a network of *madrasas* (traditional Islamic educational institutions) throughout the Indian subcontinent, in which they sought to preserve the purity of tradition. Soon the Deoband school became a center for the reassertion of Sunni orthodoxy and a focus of conservative opposition to modern Western thought and institutions.

While the majority withdrew, a small group was greatly impressed by the intellectual prowess and material achievements of the conquering West and either grudgingly or gladly decided to adapt to the ways of the conqueror. Sir Sayyid Ahmad Khan (1817–98), the great Muslim reformer of the Indian subcontinent, epitomized this modernist reaction. He sought to bring the Muslim community out of medievalism into the new age of scientific and rational discourse. His efforts to persuade his people to learn modern scientific methods, acquire new technological skills, and embody the spirit of liberalism and progress prevalent in late-nineteenth-century Europe culminated in the establishment of such progressive institutions as the Scientific Society (1863), Mohammedan Anglo-Oriental College (1876), later known as Aligarh Muslim University, and the All-India Muslim Educational Conference (1886). The main thrust of Sir Sayyid's educational and political activities was, first, to convince his fellow Muslims that their very survival as a community demanded that their religio-intellectual outlook be broadened to acquire new ideas from the West in the same spirit that had been the hallmark of Islamic society in its earlier centuries, and second, to impress upon the Muslims that a modus vivendi with the British rule was both possible and desirable for their material progress.

This first phase of Islamic modernism was followed by a period of apologetics. The apologists were no doubt impressed with the new Western ways; nevertheless, in their search for self-identity, they were led to interpret their past on the basis of newly acquired values. Sayyid Amir Ali (d. 1928), the author of *The Spirit of Islam* (1891), represented this important phase in the history of the intellectual thought of modern Islam. Deeply influenced by the English liberal thought of the late nineteenth century, he presented Islamic history and Islamic ideas, especially with regard to the role of reason, in terms that were understandable and attractive to the new generation of English-educated Muslims. Amir Ali sought to demolish the Western and Christian notions of their intellectual and religious superiority over Islam and defended his faith with the help of the intellectual apparatus he had acquired through English education. He challenged Western critics of Islam on such questions as the role and status of women in Islam, the institution of slavery, the treatment of non-Muslims under Islam, and the conflict between revelation and reason. Amir Ali's main concerns were to restore self-confidence to the new generation of educated Muslims concerning their own faith, history, culture, and civilization and to demonstrate the essential compatibility between Islam and Western liberal values.

A third stage of anticolonial upsurge followed, bringing hitherto dormant social forces into action. The answer to the challenge of the West was neither in withdrawing into the shells of tradition nor in embracing the adversary but in aggressive self-assertion. This was the promise of the fundamentalist Muslims: self-assertive Islamic nationalism and simplicity of argument in the hope of recapturing the pristine purity and political glory of Islam. The fundamentalist Muslims were indigenous and traditional, yet not identified with the decline of Muslim societies in the past, as were the ulama and the nobility. They were sufficiently knowledgeable about Western ideas to be able to confront the West, yet not so immersed in them that they would be estranged from their own heritage. Thus they appeared to be the defenders of Islam against the inroads of foreign political and intellectual domination. Maulana Abul Ala Maududi (1903–79), the founder of the Jamaat-i-Islami, is the most definitive representative of this trend in modern Islam.

Islamic modernists also tried to play the role of defender of Islam, but the mass appeal enjoyed by fundamentalists escaped them. Indeed, the modernist writings were addressed primarily to Westerners and those Muslims who had acquired Western education; the fundamentalists, on the other hand, targeted the Muslim masses. The former were mostly academic and scholastic, the latter inspirational and devotional.[6] With the expansion of education, the development of a vernacular press, the opening of new occupational opportunities, and the emergence of new social groups by the middle of the twentieth century, secular and modernist thinkers found themselves surpassed by fundamentalists, at least in terms of the ability to articulate and respond intellectually to popular concerns.

Indeed the popularity of fundamentalist ideology *as a reaction against secular modernism* increased in the postindependence period. The failure of both liberal and socialist paths to development, as pursued by Kemal Atatürk of Turkey, Reza Shah Pahlavi of Iran, Ayub Khan of Pakistan, Gamal Abdel Nasser of Egypt, and Sukarno of Indonesia, further strengthened the appeal of fundamentalists. The fundamentalists in Pakistan and elsewhere in the Muslim world adopted Western ideas of organization, made full use of modern publishing technology, and accepted the Western premise of instrumental, if not substantive, rationality. They were thus able to communicate with the large number of young people who had or were obtaining Western education. Their strategy was not that of adaptation to the West but of equality with and independence from the West, without jeopardizing the prospects of using the technological benefits the West had to offer. They wanted socioeconomic changes in their societies and in their pursuit of a share in political power were driven to radicalism. This further increased their attraction to the newly mobilized social groups feeling deprived and/or being victimized by the adverse consequences of modernization. Fundamentalist organizations became popular because they offered an authentic Islamic cultural identity during a period of Muslim identity crisis, and they effectively articulated in Islamic idioms the socioeconomic and political concerns of social strata that fared poorly in the newly emerging world of modernity.

The Jamaat-i-Islami as a Fundamentalist Organization

The Jamaat-i-Islami became the prime representative of the phenomenon known as Islamic fundamentalist revivalism in modern times. One of the best organized and disciplined religiopolitical organizations of South Asia, it has served as a model for many Islamic political movements in the Muslim world and as a valuable source of intellectual inspiration and moral support for the nascent Islamic political and da'wa groups in many countries of Asia, Africa, and the Western world. Its contribution toward redirecting the ideological orientation of the Afghan resistance to the Soviet occupation from a nationalist to an Islamic one has been enormous. The Jamaat-i-Islami has repeatedly been in the forefront of resurgent Islam as a movement of Pan-Islamic scope and significance.

Before I proceed to give an outline of the history of the Jamaat-i-Islami and discuss its ideology, organization, and activities and policies in the South Asian context, it is important that I identify those aspects of its religious ideas that bind the Jamaat with other Islamic fundamentalist political movements, such as the Muslim Brotherhood of the Middle East. These could be considered core ideas of contemporary Islamic fundamentalism.

First, the Jamaat-i-Islami seeks to restore the original teachings of the Qur'an and Sunna and to re-create the socioreligious system established under the direct guidance of the Prophet and his first four successors—"the rightly guided caliphs."

Second, at least in theory it tends to reject the later developments in Islamic theology, law, and philosophy as well as the institutional structures of historical Muslim societies that evolved during the period of empires. In actual practice, however, like most of the other fundamentalist groups, it does not deny outright the legitimacy of historical Islam insofar as the legal-religious structures of Islamic orthodoxy are concerned.

Third, unlike the conservative ulama, who, for all practical purposes, maintain that the gates of *ijtihad* (independent legal judgment) have long been closed, the Jamaat-i-Islami upholds the right to ijtihad and fresh thinking on matters not directly covered in the teachings of the Qur'an and the Sunna. But, unlike Islamic modernists, who would like to institutionalize the exercise of ijtihad in the popularly elected assemblies, the Jamaat restricts this right only to those who are well versed in both the classical sciences of Islam and in modern disciplines. Again, in actual practice the extent to which the fundamentalists of the Jamaat do exercise the right to ijtihad has been rather limited. In many cases, especially those involving a consensus among the orthodox imams of legal schools, they have tended to be one with the conservative ulama. The only areas in which the Jamaat leaders have shown readiness to accept fresh thinking are in the implementation of the socioeconomic and political teachings of traditional Islam: political parties, parliaments, elections, etc. However, if we look at the major issues with which the Jamaat-i-Islami and other fundamentalist movements have concerned themselves in modern times and at their opposition to the liberal-modernist trends in Islam, we see very little difference between them and the conservative ulama. Besides their demand for the establishment of an Islamic state and the introduction of an Islamic constitution—the two demands that have become their trademark—the other main questions on which the fundamentalists have taken a rigid and uncompromising position include abolition of bank interest, introduction of the *zakat* system (obligatory alms tax for charitable purposes), introduction of Islamic penal and family laws, enforcement of a strict sociomoral code in sex roles, prohibition of birth control as a state-funded program, and suppression of heretical groups. None of these issues distinguishes them from conservative Islam.

Fourth, fundamentalists do differ from the conservative ulama in their concept of Islam as a *deen,* which they interpret as a "way of life." The Jamaat-i-Islami criticizes the conservative ulama for reducing Islam to the five pillars—profession of faith, prayer, fasting, almsgiving, and pilgrimage. The Jamaat views Islam as a complete system and a comprehensive way of life which covers the entire spectrum of human activity, be it individual, social, economic, or political. For them, Islam means the total commitment and subordination of all aspects of human life to the will of God.

Fifth, as a revitalized formalism, the Jamaat-i-Islami seeks to replace the folk and popular practices of Sufi Islam with the approved rituals of orthodox Islam. In line with Islamic modernism, fundamentalists militate against the fatalistic quietism of the mystic fraternities. They present Islam as a dynamic and activist political ideology which must acquire state power in order to implement its social, economic, and political agenda.

This brings us to one of the most important defining characteristics of the Jamaat-i-Islami and other Islamic fundamentalist movements: *unlike the conservative ulama and the modernists, the fundamentalist movements are primarily political rather than religio-intellectual movements.* While both the ulama and the modernists seek influence in public policy-making structures, the fundamentalists aspire to *capture* political power and establish an Islamic state on the prophetic model. They are not content to act as pressure groups, as are the ulama and the modernists. They want political power because they believe that Islam cannot be implemented without the power of the state.

Finally, as lay scholars of Islam, leaders of the fundamentalist movements are not theologians but social thinkers and political activists. They are less interested in doctrinal, philosophical, and theological controversies associated with classical and medieval Islamic thinkers. The main thrust of their intellectual efforts is the articulation of the socioeconomic and political aspects of Islam. Out of his more than 120 publications, for example, the Jamaat-i-Islami's founder, Maulana Maududi, has only one title on a purely theological issue. In passages of his celebrated six-volume commentary on the Qur'an, *Tafhim al Qur'an,* Maududi explicates and interprets the verses of the Qur'an that have political and legal implications. His entire commentary on the Qur'an reads like an Islamic legal-political text, clarifying for the modern reader "how Islam furnishes man with definite guidance in the fields of constitutional, social, civil, criminal, commercial and international law."[7]

Maududi and the History of the Jamaat-i-Islami

The history of the Jamaat-i-Islami is integrally linked with the life and works of its founder, Maulana Sayyid Abul Ala Maududi (1903–79). Maududi is regarded as one of the most important thinkers of twentieth-century Islam and has become a symbol of the Islamic renaissance in our time. A systematic thinker and a prolific writer, Maududi was also a dynamic orator, a seasoned politician, an astute and indefatigable organization builder, and a charismatic leader who launched one of the most effective and well-organized Islamic movements of the twentieth century. His abiding faith in Islam and the consistency and perseverance with which he sought to make Islam supreme in the social and political life of the Umma have few parallels among his contemporaries. His influence on contemporary Islam is so pervasive that whether one agrees with him or not, no modern Muslim discourse on the social, economic, and political teachings of Islam can avoid using the terms first coined by him. Maududi gave a new language—a political language—to Islamic discourse. Terms and phrases first used by Maududi, such as "the Islamic system of life," "Islamic movement," "Islamic ideology," "Islamic politics," "the Islamic constitution," "the economic system of Islam," and "the political system of Islam," have now become common parlance for Muslim writers and political activists everywhere.

Above all, Maududi was an Islamic scholar; his fame and influence rest primarily on his writings. He had a lucid style in Urdu prose and brought to his works an amazing breadth of scholarship. Equally at home in several of the Islamic sciences, he was familiar with the issues in modern social science disciplines. He authored works of *tafsir* (exegesis of the Qur'an) and Hadith (Traditions of Prophet Muhammad), and wrote on Islamic law and political theory, Islamic economic and social relations, Islamic philosophy and culture, and above all, on Islam as an ideological alternative to both Western liberalism and Soviet Marxism. His books have been translated into all the major languages of the world and are widely read in most Muslim countries.

Born in 1903 in Hyderabad Deccan (India), Maududi received his early education at home. His father, a product of both religious and modern English education, practiced law in the British courts. At the time when Maududi was born, his father had given up his law practice, finding it not in accord with his religious beliefs. Because of his hostility toward modern English education, he did not send his son to the English schools. Instead, he took his son's education into his own hands and employed tutors to teach him the Qur'an, Hadith, Urdu, Arabic, and Persian. Maududi was not trained as an *'alim* (religious scholar) in a traditional madrasa. In fact, he detested the traditional system of madrasa education and described it as dead weight of an archaic tradition. His growth as a student of Islam was the result of his own efforts. By the time he was sixteen, Maududi had, through self-study, acquired enough knowledge of Arabic, Persian, and English to be able to read scholarly writings in these languages.

Maududi's public career began in 1920 when, at the age of seventeen, he became the editor of an Urdu weekly magazine, *Madina*. The next year he was offered the editorship of a daily newspaper, *Taj*. Later he edited the daily *Jamiyat*, Delhi, the most outspoken anti-British Muslim newspaper. He left the *Jamiyat* when the newspaper and the party behind it, the Jamiyat Ulama-i-Hind, became closely allied with the views of the Indian National Congress. Maududi's most outstanding work of this period was his study of the laws of war and peace in Islam, *Al-Jihad fil Islam*. This highly acclaimed work on Islamic and comparative international law and on the concept and operational procedures of jihad in Islam established Maududi's credentials as an original Islamic thinker and as a competent defender of Islam against its European and Hindu critics. What was most striking about the book was its "arrestingly confident tone about Islam."[8] There was no apologizing for Islam and no effort to show that Islamic laws of war and peace were in harmony with the respectable ideas of the time.[9] The book attracted the attention of Muhammad Iqbal, who invited Maududi to come to Lahore and help him in the codification of Islamic jurisprudence.

In 1933 he took up the editorship of the monthly *Tarjuman-al-Qur'an* (exegesis of the Qur'an), a responsibility that he continued to shoulder until his death in 1979. *Tarjuman-al-Qur'an* soon became the most important forum for Maududi to disseminate his ideas on Islam and the prevailing political situation in British India. He focused his attention on an exposition of the basic demands and principles of Islam as an ideology and a way of life and later concentrated on the issues arising out of the conflict between Islam and modern Western thought. In these pages he also argued at length that Islam was superior in all respects to such contemporary socioeconomic and political ideologies as capitalism, socialism, and nationalism. During the following phase of his scholarly career Maududi developed critiques of the religiopolitical movements then operating in India (the Khilafat Movement, the Khaksar Movement, the All India National Congress, Jamiyat 'Ulama-i-Hind, and the All India Muslim League) and devoted himself to the task of defining the ideological parameters of an alternative movement based on Islamic universalism.

The core concept on which Maududi sought to build the new movement was *iqamat-i-deen* (literally, "the establishment of religion")—the total subordination of the institutions of civil society and the state to the authority of divine law as revealed in the Qur'an and practiced by the Prophet. For Maududi, it is not enough to practice Islam in one's personal life; faith must manifest itself in social, economic, and political spheres as well. The way of life that emerges with the willing acceptance of Allah's sovereignty and His guidance is *al-Deen*. This means that *al-Deen* is not a set of rituals; it encompasses all areas of human life, "from the sanctuary of man's heart to the arena of socio-political relations; from the mosque to the parliament, from the home to the school and the economy; from art, architecture and science to law, state and international relations."[10]

During this formative phase of his religio-intellectual career, Maududi was influenced by the writings of Shibli Noamani, Abul Kalam Azad, and Muhammad Iqbal.[11] Shibli attracted him with a fresh Islamic theology that entailed a revolt against the traditional system of madrasa education. Maududi also admired Shibli both for the modernism of his early career and the fundamentalism of his later writings. The rationalistic and logical approach that marked the literary style of Shibli later became the main strength in Maududi's own writings. Although Maududi was deeply influenced by Abul Kalam Azad's power of persuasion and dialectical reasoning, he had no use for Azad's romanticism and effusiveness. It was Iqbal, however, who remained Maududi's ideal throughout his life. In Iqbal he found a Muslim scholar well versed in both the Islamic sciences and Western thought, a passionate protagonist of Islamic renaissance. Maududi's brief stint as a journalist with Mohammad Ali Jauhar of the Khilafat Movement was also quite an instructive experience for him. He was very much impressed with the dynamism and mass support of the Khilafat movement but was also able to see that the movement had failed because of the lack of organization and programmatic focus.[12]

With this background, Maududi decided to proceed with his work on two levels: first, the rearticulation in a systematic manner of the intellectual neofundamentalism that had already made its mark on the Indo-Islamic scene, and second, the transformation of this neofundamentalist ideology into an organized political force. In the process of formulating his ideas on Islamic ideology, Maududi was greatly impressed by the then-emerging ideologies of communism and fascism. However, what impressed Maududi was not the ideals of the communists and fascists but their methods and organizational strategies. His frequent references in his writings to the ideological purity, organizational discipline, and ascetic character of the communist and fascist movements seem quite consistent with the way he later proceeded to organize his own party. Maududi came to the conclusion that the best way to transform a society was to create a small, informed, dedicated, and highly disciplined group which would work to assume social and political leadership. What he wanted to achieve at that point was the organization of a *Saleh Jamaat* (a righteous group), or a "holy minority," that would one day capture political power and establish the Islamic system in its entirety.

In August 1941, Maududi founded the Jamaat-i-Islami to give institutional shape to his ideas on the reconstruction of Muslim society based on Islamic principles and to prepare and train a cadre of Islamic workers who could act as a vanguard of an Islamic revolutionary movement. The seventy-five people who responded to his call to join him in the founding of the new movement came from all walks of life. Although the majority of them were lay, educated Muslims who had some exposure to modern English education, some prominent ulama, including Maulana Manzoor Noamani, Maulana Abul Hasan Ali Nadvi, Maulana Amin Ahsan Islahi, and Maulana Muhammad Jaafar Phalwari also offered their services. (Within a few years, however, not finding the environment of the Jamaat-i-Islami congenial to their temperament, all of these ulama left the Jamaat).

The Jamaat-i-Islami set as its objective "the establishment of the Islamic way *(al-Deen)* so as to achieve God's pleasure and seek salvation in the Hereafter." In order to achieve this objective, the Jamaat set out the following five programs for itself:

1. To construct human thought in the light of the ideals, values, and principles derived from divine guidance
2. To "reform and purify" individual members of society so as to enable them to develop a truly Islamic personality
3. To organize these individuals under the leadership of the Jamaat and to prepare and train them to invite humanity to the path of Islam
4. To take all possible steps to reform and reconstruct the society and all of its institutions in accordance with the teachings of Islam
5. To bring about a revolution in the political leadership of society, reorganize political and socioeconomic life on Islamic lines, and finally, establish an Islamic state

As is obvious from this program, the Jamaat had no intention of directly participating in the political life of Muslim India at that time. In the initial phase, it sought to concentrate its activities on the Islamic training of its members and the strengthening of its organizational base. But this was precisely the time when the demand for Pakistan had been gaining considerable momentum under the leadership of the Quaid-i-Azam Mohammad Ali Jinnah. The demand for a separate homeland, based on the ideology of Muslim nationalism as propounded by the emerging Muslim educated middle classes and bourgeoisie, soon captured the imagination of Muslim masses throughout the subcontinent. Although the Jamaat-i-Islami did not actively oppose the Pakistan movement, as did most of the ulama, who sided with the Indian National Congress and launched a vigorous campaign against the Muslim League, it nevertheless expressed serious reservations about the Islamic character of the movement. Maududi's main criticism was that Islam, a universalist ideology, cannot be used as the ideological underpinning of a nation-state. For him, Muslim nationalism, which formed the basis of the demand for Pakistan, was no less abominable than Hindu or German nationalism. Maududi was also critical of the lack of Islamic character in the leadership of the Muslim League and believed that such secular-minded and westernized leadership was not capable of establishing an Islamic state in Pakistan. Maududi was, however, equally critical of the ulama of the Deoband school, who supported the All India National Congress and espoused the cause of territorial nationalism and secular democracy. Nevertheless, the political stigma created by the Jamaat-i-Islami's indifferent attitude to the creation of Pakistan has been a persistent source of embarrassment for the Jamaat in independent Pakistan. Various regimes and political rivals have used this to discredit the Jamaat and to delegitimize its participation in national politics.

The period between the founding of the Jamaat-i-Islami and the creation of Pakistan—that is, from August 1941 to August 1947—was devoted to organization building and consolidation. Maududi trained newly recruited Jamaat members so that they would be able to bring about the "required ideological change" when the struggle entered a new phase after independence. This was also a period of great intellectual productivity for Maududi. He published a series of studies on the economic system of Islam with special reference to such issues as interest, banking, insurance, land tenure, capitalism, and socialism. He also wrote on issues arising from the conflict between Islam and modern Western intellectual thought. During this period Maududi began his magnum opus, *Tafhim-al-Qur'an* (Toward Understanding the Qur'an), in which the Qur'an was presented as a guidebook, or manifesto, of a universal ideological movement intimately bound up with the prophetic career and mission of the Prophet Muhammad. This Urdu translation and exegesis of the Qur'an remains the finest expression of Maududi's clarity of thought, depth of scholarship, and elegance of literary style. *Tafhim-al-Qur'an* has run into several reprints and has been the most widely read commentary of the Qur'an in the Urdu language.[13]

The Jamaat-i-Islami in Action, 1948–88

Maududi would have preferred to stay away from active politics for a few more years to concentrate on writing, leadership training, and organization building, but the partition of India and the establishment of Pakistan forced him to change his plans. With the emergence of two independent states of India and Pakistan in 1947, the Jamaat-i-Islami had to be split into two separate organizations. At the time of partition, the Jamaat members totaled 625, of which 240 stayed in India and organized themselves as a separate entity.[14] Maududi moved to Lahore, the city of Muhammad Iqbal, where he started his work in the new state with 385 members, more than half of whom were refugees from India. While the Jamaat-i-Islami India, under the leadership of Maulana Abul Lais Islahi, an Islamic scholar in his own right and a close confidant of Maududi, now focused its activities on the propagation of Islam and the purely religious concerns of the Indian Muslim community, the Jamaat-i-Islami Pakistan, under Maududi's leadership, began its new work by mounting a massive campaign for the creation of a truly Islamic state in Pakistan. Given the hostile relations between India and Pakistan since their very inception, the Indian and Pakistani Jamaats have had minimal "official" contacts with each other despite their ideological affinities and common origins in the ideas of Maududi. In fact, as will be shown later, their political programs took two different paths in the context of new political realities in India and Pakistan.

"Hamara Mutalaba: Islami Dastur!" (We Want an Islamic Constitution)

When Pakistan came into being, the main question faced by the country's rulers concerned its relationship with Islam. With the exception of a few secularists, the majority of the political leadership of the new nation agreed that Pakistan's constitution and government should reflect the teachings and traditions of Islam. The problem, however, was how to relate Islam to the needs of a modern state. The definition of an Islamic state formulated by the ulama and the fundamentalists, which included the application of the Shari'a and the overarching authority of the religious scholars to pronounce judgments on the Islamic character of all legislation, was not acceptable to the modernists. The Jamaat-i-Islami insisted that the laws and practices in force in the country that were in conflict with the Qur'an and Sunna should be repealed or amended forthwith in conformity with Islamic law. In marked contrast were the views held by the Western-educated, Western-oriented politicians, civil servants, judges, and military officers. Although they did not seem to have abandoned the concept of Islam as embracing all spheres of life, they nonetheless allowed it to be overwhelmed by the intellectual approaches produced by Western secular education, which assumed the separation of state and religion. While the Jamaat-i-Islami defined and formulated the goal of the newly born state in terms of Islamic revivalism, very few politicians and administrators saw the goal as anything other than social and economic development. The only thing they could promise the Jamaat-i-Islami was that they would try to create conditions favorable for the realization of Islamic ideals. They would not, however, commit themselves to the actual legislation of these ideals as public policies.

In the context of these religiopolitical debates and differences, the Jamaat-i-Islami launched a massive publicity and public contact campaign in 1948 to seek popular support for its demand for an Islamic constitution. Although the ulama took part, Maududi and his Jamaat played the central role in the demand for an Islamic constitution for Pakistan. *"Hamara Mutalaba: Islami Dastur"* (We want an Islamic constitution) became a popular slogan throughout the country. Maududi demanded that the Constituent Assembly make an unequivocal declaration affirming the "supreme sovereignty of God" and the supremacy of the Shari'a as the basic law of Pakistan.[15] The existing anti-Islamic laws should be abrogated, and the state, in exercising its powers, should have no authority to transgress the limits imposed by Islam.

The Jamaat-i-Islami found a ready and receptive audience for its demand among the refugees from India, who were led to contrast their "wretched present" with a "glorious future" to be ushered in by the establishment of an Islamic state in Pakistan.[16] In the process, the Jamaat emerged as the sole spokesman for Islam and the Islamic state. Through his speeches and writings on Islam, politics, and the state, Maududi crafted an appeal to the educated classes. The Jamaat also made concerted efforts to reach the masses by sending preachers, spreading its literature, and organizing processions, rallies, conferences, and seminars throughout the country in order to press its demand to make Pakistan an Islamic state. There was no other group in Pakistan at the time so unified, disciplined, and certain of what it wanted.[17] The government soon found itself inundated with demands for an Islamic state and Islamic constitution, and the Jamaat appeared to be winning the support of a large number of educated people in the urban areas. The country appeared to be swept with enthusiasm for an Islamic order, and the Western-educated, modernist groups who were in control of the government began to fear this new force. As a result of these apprehensions, the government jailed Maududi under the Public Safety Act, using some of offhand remarks of his on the war in Kashmir as a pretext.

Undaunted, the Jamaat-i-Islami continued to agitate for an Islamic state. When Maududi was released after about eighteen months of detention without trial, he was more powerful and popular than before. The organization had grown to cover a large part of the country; there were branches, study circles, and reading rooms in every city and town of both West and East Pakistan. It had also organized an extensive program of relief work, mobile medical clinics dispensing free medical care, and an elaborate program of publications of books, pamphlets, and periodicals. In the major cities, a network of cell structures was created, each holding weekly workers' meetings, where issues of Islamic ideology and policies and strategies of the Jamaat were discussed.

The Jamaat-i-Islami scored its first major victory in March 1949, when the Constituent Assembly of Pakistan passed the Objectives Resolution incorporating "the main principles on which the constitution of Pakistan is to be based." The resolution accepted the Jamaat's position that "sovereignty over the entire universe belongs to God Almighty alone, and the authority which He has delegated to the State of Pakistan through its people for being exercised within the limits prescribed by Him is a sacred trust." The resolution also promised that "the Muslims shall be enabled to order their lives in the individual and collective spheres in accord with the teachings and requirements of Islam." But the resolution also accommodated the modernists' position by stating that "the principles of democracy, freedom, equality, tolerance and social justice, as enunciated by Islam shall be fully observed." The Jamaat interpreted the Objectives Resolution as a document that had laid the foundation for an Islamic state as a "theo-democracy" in order to transform the entire spectrum of collective life in accordance with the teachings of the Qur'an and Sunna. The acknowledgement of God's sovereignty was seen as an acceptance of the Shari'a as the law of the land.

After the passage of the Objectives Resolution, the Jamaat focused its activities on educating public opinion and impressing upon the policy makers the need for, and modalities of, a truly Islamic constitution for the state. Strong public pressure mobilized by the concerted campaign of the Jamaat under Maududi forced the law makers seriously to consider fulfilling the promises they had made in the Objectives Resolution. Maududi and his colleagues toured the length and breadth of the country, addressing public meetings, contacting lawmakers, and motivating their own workers to intensify their efforts to make Pakistan a truly Islamic state. Maududi produced some of his finest writings on Islamic political theory, Islamic law and constitution, and Islamic judicial and legal structures during this period. He presented a comprehensive scheme for an Islamic political system, elaborating on such issues as the functions and duties of an Islamic state; Islam and democracy; Islam and elections, parliament, political parties, and civil rights; rights of non-Muslims in an Islamic state; and the election and powers of the head of the state. Maududi was able to produce this enormous amount of scholarly writings at a time when he was involved in the most hectic political activities, such as public campaigning for an Islamic political order and restructuring the Jamaat-i-Islami's organization to meet the challenges of its new role as a political party, not to mention serving periodic jail terms. The Jamaat's campaign during this period had two aims: to clarify the concept and modalities of an Islamic state and prepare the ground for the framing of an Islamic constitution; and to train a new generation of religiopolitical leaders from among the workers and supporters of the Jamaat who could shoulder the responsibilities of an Islamically oriented administration, judiciary, media, and educational system.

At a time when the Jamaat-i-Islami wanted to focus all its attention on the issue of an Islamic constitution, it was drawn into the anti-Ahmadiya movement launched by the ulama in 1953. This movement subsequently degenerated into widespread and violent anti-Ahmadiya riots. The ulama demanded that the government declare the Ahmadis—a heretical sect founded by Mirza Ghulam Ahmad (d. 1908), who claimed to be a prophet and the promised Messiah—to be outside the pale of Islam. The Jamaat wholeheartedly endorsed this demand but was reluctant to launch a popular movement on the issue, fearing that this would sidetrack the fundamental issue of writing an Islamic constitution. Maududi published a book on the Ahmadiya question, arguing that since the sect had denied one of the fundamental beliefs of Islam, the finality of the prophethood of Muhammad, it was no longer a part of the Muslim Umma and thus deserved to be declared non-Muslim. However, Maududi disassociated himself and his party from the mob violence against the Ahmadis and asked the government to resolve the issue peacefully. The government nevertheless considered Maududi's book provocative. Martial law was imposed in Lahore and Maududi and a few other ulama were arrested on the charge of inciting people to violence. A military court tried and sentenced Maududi to death. In view of the popular indignation over the severity of the punishment, however, the sentence was later commuted by the government to life imprisonment.[18] Maududi had served about three years of his term when the courts declared his detention illegal and ordered his release.

"Tajaddud Band Karo!" (Stop the Innovations!)

The first permanent constitution of Pakistan, approved in 1956, was mainly a collection of modern secular laws for the administration of a Westminister-type parliamentary democracy with broad Islamic ideology as its guiding but nonbinding factor. Surprisingly, the Jamaat-i-Islami greeted the 1956 constitution with praise and accepted it with only minor suggestions for amendments. The constitution stated that no law should be enacted that was repugnant to the injunctions of Islam, and that existing laws should be brought into conformity with such injunctions. However, contrary to what the Jamaat had been demanding, the constitution made the parliament responsible for deciding whether any law was repugnant to Islam. Maududi was nevertheless satisfied that most of his demands had been met in the constitution, which he characterized as both Islamic and democratic. He also believed that the new constitutional framework reflected a national consensus and therefore deserved a fair chance to succeed.

The Jamaat-i-Islami was therefore greatly disappointed when General Mohammad Ayub Khan abrogated the 1956 constitution and imposed martial law on the country in October 1958. The Jamaat had gained considerable popularity in the process of its campaign for the Islamic constitution—as was evident from its spectacular success in the Karachi Municipal Corporation elections in early 1958—and was looking forward with great expectations to the scheduled national elections in 1959. The abrogation of the 1956 constitution meant that the decade-long campaign of the Jamaat for the Islamic constitution had been in vain.

The ten-year rule of Ayub Khan, however, raised a new set of issues for the Jamaat. During the years of martial law, the Jamaat, along with other political parties, remained outlawed. But unlike other political parties, the Jamaat continued to operate under the cover of religious, educational, and social welfare activities and was thus able to keep its organizational network, leadership, and cadre of workers intact. When political activities were resumed in 1962, the Jamaat-i-Islami was the first among the political parties to come back into political field with full vigor and a long list of criticisms of the government.

Ayub Khan's coming to power was seen by the Jamaat-i-Islami as a major ideological reversal for the country. Unlike the Jamaat, which maintained that Pakistan had been created to implement Islamic principles, Ayub Khan had a different interpretation of why Pakistan had come into being: "one of the major demands of independence was the elevation of national character, progress of the country and prosperity of the masses."[19] He therefore wanted to build a "modern, progressive, united and strong Pakistan."[20] Economic development, national integration, and political stability were the three pillars on which Ayub Khan planned to build the edifice of Islamic Pakistan in order to meet the requirements of modern times. "We must go forward, keep pace with the modern scientific world; we cannot be backward by thousands of years," he declared. To implement his ideas, Ayub Khan undertook a massive program of modernization and institutional reorganization of the state, economy, and religion. He presented Islam as a progressive, liberal, and forward-looking religion. In the religious sector, his two most important measures were (1) to provide for the reform of Muslim Family Laws restricting polygamy, regulating divorce procedures, and improving maintenance provisions for women, and (2) for government takeover of major religious *auqaf* (endowments) from their hereditary custodians, who were associated with traditional landowning interests. Ayub Khan also established educational and research institutions in order to promote a liberal, rational and innovative approach to the interpretation of Islamic teachings.

The Jamaat-i-Islami charged that Ayub Khan's government had acted un-Islamically and had undermined the Islamic basis of Pakistan by introducing a Westernized version of Islam, had frustrated the prospects for democracy in the country by introducing an authoritarian type of constitution, and had formed a corrupt administration, unjust and devoid of moral legitimacy.

In retrospect, the most serious challenge to the Ayub regime from religious groups came from the Jamaat-i-Islami. With the exception of the seventeen-day temporary cease-fire during the September 1965 Indo-Pakistan war, the guns of the Jamaat continued to bombard Ayub Khan's government throughout his reign of power. It was the Jamaat Secretary General, Mian Tufail Mohammad, who took the initiative in March 1961 of organizing the ulama in Lahore to oppose the Muslim Family Laws Ordinance. Mian Tufail was also the first religious leader who was arrested by the martial law authorities. And during the four years of martial law when political parties were banned, the Jamaat-i-Islami continued to operate as "a religious organization." With its publicity resources, worker's loyalty, nationwide organizational network consisting of hundreds of branches, and its solidly entrenched "nonpolitical" subsidiary organizations of students, laborers, and professionals, the Jamaat was able to launch an effective challenge to the legitimacy of the regime even during this period. However, during the years of martial law, the Jamaat chose not to confront the regime head-on, except on the issue of the Family Laws in 1961. Instead, it launched indirect but possibly more effective counter-ideological warfare against the modernist ideas being propounded by the government-controlled research centers. Professor Khurshid Ahmad, a prominent Jamaat-i-Islami intellectual, brought out two special issues of his monthly magazine *Chiragh-i-Rah,* one entitled "Ideology of Pakistan" and the other entitled "Islamic Law." These two volumes became the most frequently quoted works on the ideological basis of Pakistani statehood and the efficacy of the Islamic legal system at the time and provided the ideological opponents of the government with powerful intellectual weapons. At the same time, Maududi's works *Islam and Birth Control, Parda* (Veil), *Sud* (Interest), *Family Relations in Islam, Islamic Law and Constitution,* and *Sunnat ki A'ini Hassiyat* (The constitutional status of the Sunna) were reprinted in the thousands and were made widely available through the Jamaat's extensive marketing and distribution network. In 1963, the Jamaat established its own research institute, the Islamic Research Academy, in Karachi to counterbalance the effects of the modernist interpretations of Islam propounded by the Central Institute of Islamic Research, which was then under the leadership of Professor Fazlur Rahman.

The Jamaat-i-Islami intensified its political-religious opposition to Ayub Khan after the withdrawal of martial law and the restoration of political activities. Maududi undertook a tour of all major cities of the country and attacked Ayub Khan's religious and political policies in the strongest of terms at mass meetings. In October 1963, the Jamaat held its national convention of workers in Lahore. The convention was marred by government-sponsored violence in which one Jamaat worker was killed. The publicity posters announcing the Lahore Convention described the political system established by President Ayub Khan as *"Yeh Holnak Khala!"* (This dreadful void!).

The government's reaction was equally swift and severe. In January 1964, the provincial governments of East and West Pakistan through two separate orders declared the Jamaat-i-Islami to be an illegal organization, locked its offices throughout the country, and confiscated its records and assets.[21] Simultaneously all members of its central executive council were arrested under the Maintenance of Public Order Ordinance. However, the Supreme Court declared null and void the official ban on the Jamaat in September 1964, just a few months before the proposed presidential election in January 1965. This allowed the Jamaat to resume its oppositional activities and join the Combined Opposition Parties (COP) in their support of the candidacy of Miss Fatima Jinnah for the presidency of Pakistan.

The main thrust of the Jamaat's Islamic critique of the Ayub regime could be summed up in its popular slogan during the 1960s: *"Tajaddud Band Karo!"* (Stop the innovations!). It blasted the regime for its "general secular orientation," its "deliberate disregard of Islamic norms and way of life," its clear violation of traditional Muslim personal law, its policy of promoting family planning and birth control, which in the Jamaat's view was intended to encourage sexual permissiveness and licentiousness, and above all its vigorous campaign to "modernize" Islam and to legitimize the Western way of life by "distorting Islamic teachings."[22] The opposition of the Jamaat to Ayub was so strong that it was ready to reverse the position taken earlier by Maududi, that women were not allowed to hold public offices in an Islamic state. In October 1964, the Central Executive of the Jamaat passed a resolution declaring that "in the present unusual situation the candidature of a woman for head of the state is not against the Shari'at."[23] Although Maududi's support for Miss Jinnah's presidential bid was consistent with his political goals, it presented "something of a difficulty for him to reconcile his new political associations and his advocacy of a woman candidate with his Islamic principles."[24]

"Soshalizm Kufr Hai!" (Socialism Is Disbelief!)

The last days of the Ayub regime witnessed an urban-based revolutionary upheaval over such issues as wages, prices, and the economic dominance of twenty-two families. Despite the fact that the Jamaat-i-Islami was an important part of the coalition that had spearheaded the anti-Ayub movement, religious issues remained peripheral. The main thrust of the popular movement against Ayub was for socioeconomic justice, political participation, and regional autonomy. In East Pakistan, Sheikh Mujibur Rahman's demand for complete autonomy and in West Pakistan, Zulfikar Ali Bhutto's new socialist manifesto had changed the nature of political debate in such a fundamental way that the religious issues came to be seen as irrelevant—or trivial at best—by the emerging political forces. The political initiative had passed from the centrist and religious groups to the regionalists in East Pakistan and to secularists and socialists in West Pakistan.

This realization led the Jamaat-i-Islami to take a pro-status quo political stance during the later part of anti-Ayub agitation. The alarming prospects of the rise of secular, socialist, and regionalist political forces had in fact left the Jamaat with no option but to support the existing power structures, which at least paid lip service to Islam.

The new political scenario fully crystalized after General Yahya Khan took over as the Chief martial law administrator in March 1969, and presented major challenges to the Jamaat-i-Islami. Bhutto challenged the centrality of Islam as the organizing principle of socioeconomic relations in a Muslim society and presented an alternative ideology based on atheistic socialism. The Jamaat saw in Bhutto a man who had nothing but contempt for traditional forms of religiousness and orthodox religious practices. Furthermore, Bhutto's economic program, which promised nationalization of all major productive sectors of the economy and sweeping land reforms, violated the sanctity of private property, which according to the Jamaat, constituted as one of the basic economic principles of Islam. In addition, the socialist rhetoric of Bhutto was seen as an attempt to undermine the Islamic basis of Pakistani statehood.

Mujib's emphasis on Bengali ethnic identity and his demand for the cultural, political, and economic autonomy of East Pakistan was equally disquieting for the Jamaat-i-Islami. The Jamaat had seen East Pakistan as a test case to demonstrate the efficacy of ideological bonds in a situation in which the differences in ethnicity, language, ecology, demography, and culture were relatively acute. Therefore the rise of Bengali nationalist forces and separatist elements in East Pakistan was not only a threat to the integrity of Pakistan but was also likely to be interpreted as an evidence of the failure of Islam as a basis for political unity.

Under these circumstances, the Jamaat-i-Islami joined the forces of the status quo in order to save the country from both dismemberment and socialism. The Jamaat justified its collaboration with the military regime of General Yahya by declaring that it could not be expected to stand aside and watch while the country disintegrated and its ideology was subverted. Perhaps to compensate for its nonparticipation in the creation of Pakistan, the Jamaat now joined the rulers in Islamabad in emphasizing the integral relationship between Islam and Pakistani nationalism. It is no coincidence, therefore, that General Yahya Khan's call to the people on the occasion of the birthday of the Prophet "to come forward and defend the ideology of Pakistan by word or deed" was followed, a week later, by Shawkat-i-Islam (Glory of Islam) Day, organized by the Jamaat-i-Islami. There were processions attended by thousands of the Jamaat workers and sympathizers in all major cities and towns of East and West Pakistan, with slogans such as "Soshalizm kufr hai" (Socialism is disbelief) and *"Muslim millet ek ho"* (Let the Muslim people remain united).[25] Earlier the Jamaat had joined a faction of the ulama in Karachi in sponsoring a *fatwa* (a religious decree), later signed by 113 ulama of all schools of thought, denouncing Bhutto's socialism as *kufr* (disbelief).

In fact, the Jamaat-i-Islami's campaign against socialism during 1968–70 became the most important event in its recent history. The Jamaat was convinced that the Pakistan People's Party (PPP) was a front organization of Marxists who were planning to stage a communist coup in the wake of the violent mass movement against Ayub Khan. If successful, such a move would frustrate the Jamaat's thirty years of efforts for Islam, democracy, and political power.[26] Hence, in close collaboration with the business community of Karachi, the Jamaat launched a vigorous campaign against the atheistic ideology of socialism. In its struggle against socialism and Bhutto, it formed a coalition with other right-wing and centrist political parties. The workers and supporters of the Jamaat's students and the labor wings engaged themselves in violent confrontation with their left-wing counterparts in Karachi, Lahore, Rawalpindi, and

Peshawar. The Yahya Khan period thus witnessed the transformation of the Jamaat's students' wing, the Islami Jamiat-i-Talaba (IJT), from a peaceful da'wa organization into a militant force, even willing to meet violence with violence.

In the midst of the violent conflicts between Islam and socialism in West Pakistan and between Islam and Bengali nationalism in East Pakistan, General Yahya Khan announced elections for December 1970. The Jamaat-i-Islami chose to contest them in order to counter the onslaught of both socialism and separatism. During the election campaign, this strategy appeared to be quite effective, and most observers expected that the Jamaat would win a substantial number of seats in the national legislature.

Although the elections were fair, the expectations were misplaced. The Jamaat, which appeared to be a formidable force throughout the campaign, turned out to be a complete disaster. Out of a total of three hundred National Assembly seats, it was able to win only four, two from Karachi and one each from Punjab and the North-West Frontier Province (NWFP). This was "the greatest political set-back the Jamaat had received ever since its inception."[27] It was as if "the prophecy had failed." For twenty years the Jamaat had been calling for democratic elections on the assumption that given a free choice, the overwhelming majority of the people of Pakistan would vote for Islam. And now that a fair election had been held, their expectations of twenty years were shattered.

This highly disappointing experience of December 1970 elections had important consequences for the future political thinking and strategy of the Jamaat-i-Islami. First, the Jamaat decided to pay more attention to the practical bread-and-butter issues—of food, housing, employment, and the like—which it had neglected in the past in its general enthusiasm for an Islamic constitution. Second, the election defeat diminished the Jamaat's already feeble belief in democracy. Third, it led the Jamaat to plan a new political strategy based on street power rather than the number of seats in parliament. This subsequently became its most effective weapon against Bhutto during the *Khatmi-e-Nabuwwat* (finality of Prophethood) and *Nizam-e-Mustafa* (System of the Prophet Muhammad) movements. The popular manifestation of Islamic resurgence at the street level during the mid-1970s owes much to this new strategic thinking of the Jamaat and other religiopolitical groups. Finally, the disappointing results of the 1970 elections also psychologically prepared the leadership of the Jamaat to seek influence and power through nondemocratic means, including collaboration with the military regimes. The facility and ease with which the Jamaat joined hands with the martial law regime of General Zia-ul-Haq in 1977 can be explained by their disenchantment with the democratic process which they had experienced in 1970.

The first instance of the partnership between the Jamaat-i-Islami and the military came about in March 1971, when the martial law regime of General Yahya Khan decided to take a decisive military action against the separatist forces of Sheikh Mujib's Awami League in East Pakistan. In pursuit of its firm belief that the defense of the territorial integrity of the Pakistani state was a religious obligation, the Jamaat collaborated with the military government throughout the East Pakistan crisis. Its workers and its followers among students organized themselves in the paramilitary unit of

Al-Badr and fought side by side with regular Pakistan army troops against the Mukti Bahini rebels and the Indian forces.

The battle of East Pakistan having been lost, the Jamaat continued its jihad against Bhutto and his socialist program under the leadership of Mian Tufail Mohammad, who was elected as the new emir of the Jamaat after Maududi resigned from the position for reasons of health. Surprisingly, simultaneous with its defeat in the national elections, the Jamaat's student wing swept the student union elections throughout the major campuses in Pakistan. This restored the Jamaat's self-confidence in its efficacy as a major political force in the country. In 1972 it went on to test its political strength on the issue of the recognition of the newly independent state of Bangladesh and was able to force Prime Minister Bhutto not to extend recognition to the new state unless Pakistani prisoners of war were repatriated.

Although the Jamaat had only four members in the national parliament, their role in the writing of the new constitution in 1973 was critical. Under the leadership of Professor Abdul Ghafoor Ahmad, the Jamaat's member of the National Assembly from Karachi who later led the joint opposition movement against Bhutto in 1977, the Jamaat's representatives in the parliament lobbied vigorously for the inclusion of Islamic provisions in the proposed constitution. Veterans of twenty-five years of struggle for an Islamic constitution, the Jamaat leaders were better prepared for and well qualified in the art of constitutional negotiations. In the end, despite the Pakistan People's Party's overwhelming majority in the parliament and its insistence on incorporating its socialist manifesto in constitutional provisions, the 1973 constitution turned out to be "the most Islamic constitution in the history of Pakistan." Islam was declared the state religion for the first time. All important Islamic provisions of the 1956 constitutions were retained. The constitution stated that both the president and the prime minister of Pakistan had to be Muslims. Above all, the Objectives Resolution was also retained as a preamble to the new constitution.

The cooperation and the truce between the Bhutto government and the Jamaat-i-Islami on the issue of constitution proved to be short-lived. An incident at the Rabwa (Punjab) railway station involving a scuffle between the students of the Islami Jamiat-i-Talaba (IJT), the Jamaat's students' wing, and some members of the Ahmadiya community—also known as Qadiyanis—sparked another nationwide movement demanding that the sect be declared non-Muslim. Unlike the 1953 anti-Ahmadiya movement, in which the Jamaat-i-Islami was involved as a reluctant partner, the 1974 Khatam-e-Nabuwwat movement saw the Jamaat in the forefront. It is a testimony to the great organizational capability of the Jamaat and the IJT that only one day after the incident on 29 May 1974, major protest meetings were staged in Lahore, Bahawalpur, Sargodha, Faisalabad, and Islamabad. The IJT organized the anti-Ahmadiya movement methodically. It divided the Punjab province—the center of the movement—into ten sectors and assigned its prominent leaders to take charge of the agitation by touring all major cities and towns of their respective sectors. Young student leaders of the IJT from different campuses toured throughout the Punjab and in seven days addressed 150 public meetings, led 27 processions, and raised the emotional pitch of the people to such an extent that by 27 June the entire law and order machinery of the government in Punjab was in a shambles. The extent of the role and the street power of the IJT can be seen from the fact that during this anti-Ahmadiya agitation, its leaders addressed 8,777 public meetings and led 47 processions.[28] Soon the government was forced to concede; through a constitutional amendment, Bhutto declared the Ahmadis to be outside the pale of Islam.

The Khatam-e-Nabuwwat movement, like the struggle for an Islamic constitution in the 1950s, demonstrated the political power of the IJT and its ability to destabilize even a populist regime such as that of Zulfikar Ali Bhutto. It provided an opportunity to the Jamaat, through the IJT, to penetrate the mosques and the madrasas which were traditionally the monopoly of the ulama. The Jamaat made full use of this new avenue of public contact: all major meetings were held in mosques and most processions were started after the Friday congregational prayers. According to reports filed by IJT workers, for example, in only one day in June, anti-Ahmadiya and anti-government meetings were held in 876 mosques in 43 cities of Punjab, and the number in the audience was estimated to be 1,100,000.[29] This linkage with the mosque and the madrasa helped the Jamaat-i-Islami repair its relations with the ulama, which had been strained in the past because of Maududi's devastating critique of their archaic system of education and their role in pre-independence politics. Indeed, the Khatam-e-Nabuwwat movement turned out to be a rehearsal for the ultimate showdown with Bhutto in 1977.

The Jamaat used the period between 1974 and 1977 to strengthen its cells and chapters in labor unions, teachers' associations, and other professional organizations and institutions, including the civil service and the military. Through such movements as the Enforcement of the Shari'a campaign in 1975, the Jamaat also renewed its efforts toward mass contact and recruitment of new associates and workers. During the Enforcement of the Shari'a movement, for example, the Jamaat workers individually contacted six hundred thousand people in Punjab, Sind, NWFP, and Baluchistan, as a result of which one hundred thousand people signed up as Jamaat supporters.[30] A similar exercise was repeated in 1976, during which, in Karachi alone, the Jamaat workers contacted about two hundred thousand people and obtained pledges from about forty-one thousand to join the Jamaat as associates.[31] During this period, the Jamaat also consolidated its organizational outreach in the Gulf states of the Middle East, Europe, and North America, where many of its workers had moved for jobs. The remittances in hard currency from its expatriate workers and supporters in the Middle East and the Western world have become a major source of Jamaat's income since the 1970s.

The final showdown between Bhutto and the Jamaat-i-Islami came during the March 1977 elections. The religiopolitical opposition against Bhutto consolidated under the leadership of the Jamaat and its associates among the ulama, and formed a grand right-wing alliance to demand the enforcement of Nizam-e-Mustafa and the dislodging of Bhutto and all that he stood for. Just four months before the scheduled elections, the IJT had firmly established itself as a potent and major political force, not only on the streets but also on the campuses. In November 1976 student union elections at the University of Karachi, the IJT won a complete and sweeping victory. Earlier the IJT had won elections in twenty-four out of twenty-eight colleges and professional schools of Karachi. In another twelve colleges, the IJT panels had won all seats unopposed, and the University of the Punjab was already under the IJT control.[32] Thus, when the Pakistan National Alliance (PNA)—the coalition of nine parties opposed to Bhutto—launched the Nizam-e-Mustafa movement in March 1977, the IJT was already strategically placed to play an important role in mobilizing the students and using other resources of educational institutions against Bhutto. There is no doubt that without the organizational skills of the Jamaat-i-Islami and the mobilizing capabilities of the IJT, the PNA movement against Bhutto would not have picked up the momentum it did in its earlier phase. Although madrasa students belonging to other religiopolitical parties also played an important part during this mass movement, they were relatively inexperienced in the arena of political agitation, street demonstrations, barricade building, strikes, and processions. IJT, on the other hand, had a twenty-year history of religiopolitical struggle on the campuses as well as in the conference halls and streets. The Jamiat cadres were also well trained in the art of confrontation with the police and other security forces.

During the 1977 elections and the postelections agitation, Islamic issues came to be politicized so much that Bhutto was forced to give in to the pressure built up by the Jamaat and other religious groups. He introduced several Islamic measures which later became the basis for further Islamization by General Zia-ul-Haq. One can therefore argue that the Islamization program of Zia was in fact a continuation of the momentum built up for Islam by the Jamaat-i-Islami in the form of political mobilization and by Bhutto to seek Islamic legitimacy for his faltering regime.

Cometh the Hour? The Jamaat and Zia's Islamization

> At last, Almighty Allah rid the nation of the rule of socialist despotism [of Zulfikar Ali Bhutto] and the reins of Government fell to the hands of General Zia-ul-Haq on 5th July 1977, who has declared more than once that he would introduce the Islamic Order in Pakistan and would hold fair elections. We are all looking anxiously to the fulfillment of these hopes of the people and for the inauguration of a truly Islamic era in the life of this country.[33]

This announcement, which was issued from the headquarters of the Jamaat-i-Islami in September 1977—just two months after the military coup that brought General Zia into power—is indicative of the high hopes with which the Jamaat greeted the martial-law regime. The earlier rulers had paid only lip service to Islam and did nothing to incorporate the teachings of the Qur'an and Sunna into public policies. General Zia, on the other hand, promised that the establishment of a social order based on Nizam-e-Mustafa would be the cornerstone of his policies. He was therefore hailed as a welcome change by the Jamaat leaders, who extended their fullest cooperation to Zia's military regime and even joined his civilian cabinet for about a year—the only time in the history of the Jamaat when it was associated with the power of the state. General Zia was a good, honest, practicing Muslim, the Jamaat leaders reasoned to themselves, who wanted to enforce the Shariʿa and therefore deserved their whole-hearted support and cooperation.

In retrospect, however, the decision of the Jamaat-i-Islami to support the military regime was not an easy one. All along, the Jamaat had campaigned for both Islam *and* democracy. The PNA movement that dislodged Bhutto was also based on the twin slogans of Islam and the restoration of a truly democratic order in the country. In the case of Zia, however, the Jamaat was faced with the dilemma of choosing between Islam *or* democracy. Here was a military dictator who had overthrown an elected government and had thus violated the fundamental norm of an Islamic political system that people have "the right to elect their rulers by the exercise of their free will and to replace them in a similar manner."[34] But the dictator also promised to build an Islamic socioeconomic and political order in the country. Within a few months of coming into power, Zia had already instituted several Islamic reforms. His speeches and exhortations seemed to come right from the pages of Maududi's books. With Maududi in retirement and failing health and Mian Tufail Mohammad at the helm of affairs, the Jamaat-i-Islami chose Islam over democracy and decided to support Zia's military regime, with the twin objectives of helping it to get rid of Bhutto and of implementing the Shariʿa. Unlike Maududi, whose definition of Islamization gave equal emphasis to both the substantive and procedural aspects of the process, Mian Tufail Mohammad, the new emir of the Jamaat, focused solely on the enforcement of the Shariʿa. Too much time should not be wasted in discussing the political means to achieve this objective: the people of Pakistan wanted an Islamic system, whether it was introduced by an unelected ruler or an elected parliament. "It is the duty of every Muslim to strive for the establishment of the Islamic system and it is immaterial whether he is a politician, a religious ʿalim, or a military officer."[35] Although based on the formulations of the classical Muslim political theorists, the view that whoever enforces Shariʿa—whether he is an hereditary monarch, a military officer, a mullah, or a politician—can claim Islamic legitimacy was nonetheless contrary to what Maududi and the Jamaat had advocated in the past.

The Jamaat's acceptance of Zia's military regime and his Islamization program can also be understood with reference to the Jamaat's views on the process of Islamization. Despite his emphasis on the Islamic *tarbiya* (training) of a dedicated corps of workers and his recognition of the importance of reforming institutions of the civil society, Maududi saw the process of Islamization as essentially a transfer of state power from the secular-minded (corrupt) elite to the *saleheen* (pious Muslims), who by appropriating authoritative positions in the various institutions of the state, would create conditions conducive to the establishment of the complete deen. In one of his earlier works, Maududi described the state as a train and said that in order to change the direction of the train the only thing needed was to remove the present driver and replace him with a new driver.[36] Although Maududi's views on Islamic history became more critical and discriminating in his later writings and showed keen awareness of the socioeconomic and political factors that had determined the policies of various Islamic regimes in the past, most other intellectuals of the Jamaat continued to view major religious developments in Islamic history as reflecting the relative degrees of piety and corruption of various rulers. Thus, the starting point and most important point in the process of Islamization in their view was the capturing of political power by men of piety. The state should be ruled by men of the superior virtue as enunciated by Islam; these virtuous men would then set an example for the rest of the people. General Zia thus represented and embodied the classic formulation of Islamic polity: a good and pious Muslim who was committed to the enforcement of the Shari'a in consultation with the ulama and the Jamaat-i-Islami. True to the medieval Muslim political tradition, no questions were asked about the mode of his coming into power or the methods he chose for Islamizing the society. Much of this formulation was not consistent with what Maududi had advocated in his writings on the Islamic state, but the Jamaat, under its new leadership, had its own pragmatic reasons to support Zia. Mian Tufail Mohamaad and the majority of the members of the Jamaat's central executive committee from Punjab went along with the decision to support Zia's Islamization and his government wholeheartedly. The Karachi leadership of the Jamaat viewed the Jamaat's collaboration with the military in instrumental rather than affective terms; that is, without committing themselves to affirming or rejecting Zia's claim of sincerity, they accepted his Islamic rhetoric at face value and tried to use it to promote Islamization. This was also the view of Professor Khurshid Ahmad, the Jamaat leader who became a close confidant of Zia and played an important role in the introduction of Islamic economic reforms. These leaders maintained that the basic objective they wished to achieve through this collaboration was the introduction of certain important Islamic measures in education, law, and the economy, and the establishment of a network of Islamic institutions within the state apparatus—measures for which, they claimed, there was already a broad consensus in the society. However, the negative motivation of "the Bhutto factor" was also an important consideration that aligned the Jamaat with the military. Both the Jamaat and the military shared the fear of the return of Bhutto until he was hanged in April 1979. They also feared the ghost of Bhutto after his hanging.

Thus the Jamaat joined the martial law government in August 1978, with four cabinet ministers holding the portfolios of information and broadcasting, water and power, national production (incorporating all public sector enterprises), and economic planning and development. Notwithstanding their initial enthusiasm, the actual experience of the Jamaat cabinet ministers within the corridors of power proved to be highly disappointing.[37] With the exception of Khurshid Ahmad, who spearheaded the academic and legislative battles for the introduction of the Zakat system and interest-free banking in his capacity as a minister for economic planning and development, the other three cabinet ministers of the Jamaat proved totally ineffective in the face of opposition by the entrenched bureaucrats and senior generals. Not a single policy initiative by the Jamaat ministers was allowed to pass through the bureaucratic hurdles.

While the Jamaat's cabinet ministers remained ineffective in their own ministries and departments, their influence in the formulation of the Islamization policies of the military regime was not insignificant. The Jamaat succeeded, for example, in having two of its supporters appointed as members of the Council of Islamic Ideology (CII), a constitutional body entrusted with the task of advising the government on the Islamization of laws. Another Jamaat leader was nominated as a judge of the Federal Shari'at Court, an appellate bench with the power to review cases for their conformity with Islamic laws. The Jamaat nominees on the CII played an important role in formulating recommendations that culminated in the package of Islamic penal and economic reforms announced by Zia on 10 February 1979. The package included the introduction of the *Hudood* (penal code), providing Islamic punishments for drinking alcohol, theft, adultery, and false accusations concerning sexual offenses. Another ordinance introduced the Zakat and *'Ushr* fund and procedures for its collection, management, and distribution among the poor and the needy.

The penal laws were introduced while the Jamaat was still a part of the martial law government. It is therefore fair to assume that these measures had the tacit, if not the wholehearted, support of the Jamaat leadership. In fact, Mian Tufail Mohammad later complained that the laws were not being enforced effectively, since no one had been stoned to death for adultery and no hands had been cut off for stealing. Yet Maududi himself did not approve of the introduction of Islamic penal laws by the martial law government. His argument was that "mere introduction of Islamic laws does not shape a country into a truly Islamic one"[38] In a brief note he published a few months before his death in September 1979, Maududi wrote:

> The introduction of the criminal laws of Islamic Shari'a does not pose any serious problem. But who would execute the implementation of these laws? To be sure, the onus for the execution of these laws would ultimately rest with the same police that is notorious for the abuse of justice, for providing shelter to the criminals and perpetrating atrocities on the innocent. . . . More than this, the most vital question is: would it serve the purpose of Islam if the courts award punishments to those who are found guilty of committing theft and robbery, while retaining the same economic structure that promotes theft and brigandage, the same law enforcing agencies that provide protection to the offenders? Again, would it be in keeping with the spirit of Islam to punish a person who commits adultery, while the factors contributing to this crime are allowed to remain unchecked? . . . What is rather imperative is the implementation of the entire scheme of life which Islam has prescribed for us. . . . The socio-economic and political order remaining the same as we inherited from the past, the implementation of Islamic laws alone cannot yield the positive result Islam really aims at. . . . For, merely by dint of this announcement [of Islamic laws] you cannot kindle the hearts of people with the light of faith, enlighten their minds with the teachings of Islam, and mould their habits and manners corresponding to the virtues of Islam.[39]

One month after the execution of Zulfikar Ali Bhutto, the Jamaat cabinet members resigned from the government, in disagreement with the indefinite postponement of general elections scheduled for November 1979. From 1979 to 1984, the Jamaat remained in an uneasy opposition to the policies of the martial law administration. It criticized the government for slowing down on Islamization and for not holding elections and lifting the martial law but refused to join the Movement for the Restoration of Democracy (MRD)—a coalition of opposition political parties—to oppose Zia directly.[40] In the meantime, the Jamaat and Zia had found another common cause that further strengthened their relations: both were intensely committed to the jihad in Afghanistan against the country's Marxist revolution and Soviet occupation.

The leadership of the Jamaat were painfully aware of the obvious contradictions in their policies of both opposing the martial law administration and supporting General Zia. Mian Tufail Mohammad attempted to resolve this contradiction by contending that while Zia was a "sincere Muslim," the civil administration was responsible for frustrating his Islamic policies.[41] There was thus an urgent need, Mian Tufail argued, to support the Islamic thinking that Zia represented and to help him build a support base outside the military and civil service so that he could implement his Islamic reforms.

A large majority of the Jamaat workers, as well as its constituency, endorsed this strategy, which culminated in the party's support for Zia to continue as president for five more years in a national referendum held in December 1985. The Jamaat had agreed to support President Zia, because in a meeting with Mian Tufail, the president had promised to make the Shari'a the supreme law of the land, to restore the 1973 Constitution, and to lift martial law without delay.[42]

Although the Jamaat-i-Islami had provided consistent support to Zia, and Mian Tufail Mohammad and Khurshid Ahmad had developed a good personal rapport with him, its relationship with the oligarchy of the military establishment and the higher civil service remained uneasy at best. After instituting his nominated Majlis-i-Shoora (Advisory Council) in 1984, Zia also became estranged from the Jamaat. There were many factors that contributed to the estrangement between the former allies. From the very beginning, the martial law government was ambivalent about the growing political power of the Jamaat's students' wing, the IJT. During 1977–82, the government seemed to have encouraged the IJT activities on campuses in order to counter the influence of the pro-Bhutto People's Students Federation. During this period, the IJT enjoyed almost complete veto power in most of Pakistan's twenty universities in matters of student's admissions and faculty appointments and promotions.[43] By 1982, however, things were seen by the ruling establishment in a different perspective. First, Bhutto had already been executed and the threat of a possible PPP-led, youth-dominated antigovernment agitation had passed, thanks to the IJT control over the campuses. Second, with the war in Afghanistan and the newly formed United States–Pakistan relations, the Zia regime no longer considered itself an isolated pariah junta; it had now gained self-confidence and had become confident in its staying power. Third, Zia had found new allies from among the nonpolitical ulama who were equally, if not more, qualified to confer Islamic legitimacy on his regime. He was thus no longer dependent on the Jamaat-i-Islami for Islamic support. Fourth, the growth of an independent, street-based political force such as the IJT with a nationwide organizational network, even though it was supporting the regime at the time, was seen as a potential challenge to the authority of the military regime. Finally, Zia wanted to weaken the national political parties before the scheduled non-party national elections in order to encourage the victory of independent candidates who could constitute his support base in the new parliament.

Meanwhile, the Jamaat-i-Islami's political strength was based largely on its students' wing. Thus, when in February 1984, the government banned all student unions and organizations in the country, it was obvious that the main target of this martial law order was IJT, which had emerged as the strongest student organization in the student union polls held earlier in the year. The objective was to hit at the very base of the Jamaat's political power. The IJT tried to defy the ban—apparently against the advice of its parent organization, which by that time had become too much involved in the Afghanistan war and had thus become subject to blackmail by the regime. There were clashes between the police and the IJT workers both on and off campus. More than two hundred IJT activists were expelled from colleges and universities.[44] There were also reports of severe torture of the IJT workers while they were in police detention. The Jamaat-i-Islami, however, took a low-key position on the issue, and given the "broader understanding" with the regime, especially on the Jihad in Afghanistan, did not confront the regime. As expected, the ban on the activities of the IJT affected the performance of the Jamaat in the February 1985 elections. It was only able to win seven seats in the house of two hundred members.

Another major source of the Jamaat's political influence and power was the city of Karachi, with its population of seven million and its considerable political clout. The Jamaat had earlier won, with a comfortable majority, the elections for the Karachi Municipal Corporation and had succeeded in having one of its members elected as the mayor. In 1986 Zia had the provincial government of Sind quash the elected government of the city and dislodge the Jamaat from the city administration in order to promote the ethnically based Muhajir Quami Movement (MQM). Earlier, the government had disbanded several labor unions in the state-run enterprises where Jamaat's labor wing, the National Labor Federation, had won elections. The ban on the activities of the Jamaat-led labor unions in the Pakistan Railways, Pakistan International Airlines, and the Pakistan Steel Mills—the three largest employers in the public sector—was a great setback for the Jamaat's political influence among the urban white-collar workers.

Given these developments, it is not surprising that the relationship between Zia and the Jamaat-i-Islami that began in 1977 with great expectations and enthusiasm ended in equally intense ill will and antipathy by the time Zia's reign came to an end. The bitterness on the part of the Jamaat was caused not only because of what it considered Zia's betrayal of its trust but also because for the first time in the history of Pakistan, the state had taken the Islamic initiative from the Jamaat's hands. In June 1988, two months before Zia's death in a plane crash, the new emir of the Jamaat-i-Islami, Qazi Hussain Ahmad, vowed to launch a massive popular movement against the government and announced that his party had reached an understanding with Ms. Benazir Bhutto's People's Party "for jointly tackling" the regime. As for Zia, who had earlier been described by Mian Tufail as a "sincere Muslim," Qazi Hussain Ahmad had this to say: "A man who dissolves a government on charges of corruption and forms a new government with the same faces cannot be regarded as a true Muslim. . . . This is sheer hypocrisy."[45]

Jamaat-i-Islami in Politics: An Assessment

Looking at the history and activities of the Jamaat-i-Islami during the past four decades, one is struck by the overwhelming importance that the Jamaat gives to political struggle. From its demand for the introduction of an Islamic constitution to its struggle against Islamic modernism, secularism, socialism, and ethnic separatism, it has kept aloft the banner of the Islamic way of life through the primacy of political action. The political struggle of the Jamaat has been based on the assumption that Islamic change in society will occur only when political power is transferred into the hands of a party of God-conscious, Islamic activists, who by taking over the state, will establish the necessary conditions for reforming society. Thus, according to the Jamaat, society is reformed as a consequence of the change in the nature and direction of political power. The transformation of the Jamaat from a religious revivalist movement to a political party deeply involved in the national political process had important consequences for both the ideology and organization of the Jamaat. As a result of its active participation in political life, the Jamaat, like other political parties, had to make compromises and sometimes revise its positions on several issues to accommodate political exigencies. It has over the years changed its views on such crucial issues as the Islamic character of the electoral process, the authority of the popularly elected parliament to legislate on Islamic religious doctrines and practices, restrictions on private property, and the Islamic legitimacy of a woman becoming the head of an Islamic government. In each case, the Jamaat leadership has used "reasons of politics" to explain its ideological shift and to justify the reinterpretation of a traditional Islamic doctrine.

One of the characteristics of "political religion" is that although it retains religion as the basis of legitimacy, its religious content tends to become increasingly instrumental. The Jamaat-i-Islami, in its role as a religiopolitical movement of opposition, protest, and change, has been no exception. The prime example of this trend is a recent publication by a Jamaat leader in which the system of proportional representation has been prescribed as an important norm of Islamic polity, obviously because proportional representation suits the Jamaat in the election process.

And unlike the ulama, the Jamaat-i-Islami, as a political party, has not used the mosques and madrasas as the main centers of its activities. Instead the centers of its activities have been the elected assemblies, trade unions, campuses, professional organizations, publishing houses, seminars, conferences, think tanks, and survey research institutions. The use of these modern forums of political activities, and of physical and socio-organizational technologies has also tended to dilute the purely religious content of the Jamaat's ideology over the years. One can argue, therefore, that the fundamentalist movements, by adopting political techniques, organizational technologies, and institutional forms (such as bureaucratic organizations, elections, political propaganda methods, etc.) from the very Western sources they purport to be repudiating, may inadvertently be acting as agents of change in their societies. They may in fact be subjecting the very traditions they wish to preserve to significant intellectual and theological reformulation. It is possible, therefore, that the revivalist-fundamentalist phenomenon may over the long run become an important phase in the ideological reorientation of Islam. Some may even detect elements of what Eli Kedouri saw in Jamal-ud-Din-al-Afghani (1839–96)—a "hidden secularism."

Furthermore, the Jamaat's increasingly active involvement in politics and the processes of institutionalization and routinization of its charisma have gone hand in hand. During the past three decades of its mainstream political activities, the Jamaat lost most of the sectlike characteristics with which it had emerged in the 1940s. During the 1960s and 1970s, it built alliances with religiopolitical groups of all schools of Islamic thought, and even cooperated in joint political actions with the secular and left-wing political parties.

The most significant developments, however, have taken place in the Jamaat's organization. Since the 1970s, when the Jamaat decided to build the huge complex of its headquarters in a suburb of Lahore called Mansoora, the officials of the Jamaat in the central secretariat have more or less become bureaucrats with fixed salaries, fringe benefits, allowances, specialized roles, and a substantial number of subordinate employees. This transformation of a charismatic group into a huge bureaucratic organization with centralized authority and hundreds of branches throughout the country linked with the headquarters through the hierarchy of tehsil, district, and zonal organizations—and now through computer networks, telex, and fax machines—was a natural outcome of the expansion of the Jamaat-i-Islami activities and its influence during the 1960s and 1970s. It was during this period that the Jamaat entered the arena of electoral politics with full vigor and established a whole network of subsidiary and affiliated organizations consisting of its supporters among the students, teachers, workers and farmers, women, doctors, lawyers, the ulama, journalists and writers, and other professional and occupational groups. This expansion naturally gave rise to a huge number of full-time salaried workers within the Jamaat organization. Today a substantial portion of its budget goes to the maintenance of its organization and the huge bureaucracy that runs the organization.

Not all members of the Jamaat-i-Islami are happy with these developments. There are many who do not like the full-time and exclusive involvement of the Jamaat in politics. They want their party to pay more attention to da'wa work and to the moral and spiritual development of its own workers. In fact, the first and the only internal dissension that the Jamaat has experienced since its establishment in 1941 took place precisely on this issue in the mid-1950s when several of its prominent ulama members left the Jamaat, complaining that it had become "too much of a political party" and had ceased to function as a religious revivalist movement. Since then, the involvement of the Jamaat in Pakistan's national politics as well as in developments in the rest of the Islamic world has become even greater. The party old guard are worried that "some workers have developed an attachment to this world and have adopted a careerist attitude towards Islamic work."[46]

They also point out that the social welfare and educational programs of the Jamaat that were its hallmark in the 1950s have been neglected as a result of the emphasis on electoral politics. The Jamaat once operated the largest network of mobile clinics outside the public sector, which dispensed free medical care to the poor neighborhoods in all the major cities of the country. It had also set up model Islamic schools and colleges in various cities where Islamic subjects were taught along with modern disciplines. In 1972, Mr. Bhutto nationalized these schools and colleges along with other privately owned educational institutions. The emergency relief work of the Jamaat, however, has remained intact and has provided remarkably efficient assistance to the people during floods, earthquakes, and other crises.

The Worldview and the Ideology of the Jamaat

One of the most important contributions of Maududi in twentieth-century Islam has been his presentation of Islam as a system of life, a complete code of conduct that governs all aspects of human existence. Maududi insists that in order to be viable, Islam must be obeyed and implemented in its entirety. Since it is a system of life, the elements constituting Islam cannot be separated from one another. A person cannot be a true Muslim if he fulfills Islamic obligations in his personal life but neglects Islamic teachings in his political and economic behavior.[47] Maududi writes: "The final purpose of all the blessed Apostle of God was to set up the rule of God so that they could implement the entire system of life in the manner ordained by God. They were not prepared to allow the unbelievers to retain the keys of power. . . . That is why all prophets tried to bring about political revolutions."[48]

The task of a Muslim, according to Maududi, is "to try to make the whole of Islam supreme over the whole of life." It is not enough to give "an Islamic color to one or a few aspects of life. . . . The all-encompassing supremacy of Islam alone can give us an opportunity to fully enjoy the spiritual, moral, and material benefits that are the natural and inevitable results of working according to the guidance of the Lord."[49]

The idea that Islam encompasses the whole spectrum of life and that there is no separation of religion and state in Islam is of course not original with Maududi. His real contribution was "to offer a set of clear and well-argued definitions of key Islamic concepts within a coherently conceived framework" and then build a systematic theory of Islamic society and the Islamic state on the basis of these concepts.[50] Through a systematic treatment of such key Islamic terms as Allah, *rab* (lord), *malik* (master), *'ibada* (worship), *deen* (way of life), and *shahdah* (to bear witness), Maududi demonstrated a rational and logical interdependence of Islamic morality, law, and political theory.[51] The key Qur'anic concept that Maududi has used to advance his idea of Islam as a complete system and a way of life is *deen*. Throughout his commentary on the Qur'an, Maududi keeps coming back to this holistic and primarily political meaning of the word *deen*. At one point, translating the word *deen* as "law," Maududi writes: "This use of the word categorically refutes the view of those who believe that a prophet's message is principally aimed at ensuring worship of the one God, adherence to a set of beliefs, and observance of a few rituals. This also refutes the views of those who think that deen has nothing to do with cultural, political, economic, legal, judicial, and other matters pertaining to this world."[52]

Another key concept of the Qur'an which in fact constitutes the very raison d'être of the Jamaat-i-Islami, is *iqama-al-deen* (establishment of the deen). It is this concept that provides the doctrinal and theological justification for the politico-ideological struggle of the Jamaat in Pakistan.[53] But how to enforce al-deen? How to establish a society based on the Islamic principles of *taqwa* (God-consciousness), brotherhood, equality, fairness, and justice—in short, a society based on Shari'a? Maududi's answer is that we cannot achieve the ultimate objectives of Islam unless we establish an Islamic state. An Islamic state does not come about by a miracle. Such a state or government will only come about when there is a movement based on the ideology, worldview, and standards of morality and character of Islam. The movement should consist of leaders and workers who are ready to mold their entire lives in accordance with the standards set by Islam. Then they should preach these ideas and virtues to the larger society and establish a new system of education and training which is capable of preparing a whole new generation along Islamic lines. This system of education would produce Muslim administrators, Muslim managers, Muslim scientists, Muslim philosophers, Muslim economists, Muslim bankers and jurists—in short, people who are experts in all areas of human activity and are also true and practicing Muslims. This Muslim intelligentsia will act as the vanguard of the movement for the reconstruction of modern thought, and will formulate a "complete blueprint of practical solutions" for contemporary socioeconomic problems in accordance with Islamic principles. These Muslim intellectuals would also establish their "intellectual leadership and superiority" over the God-denying ideologies and leaders of the world.

With this intellectual apparatus, the movement would then engage in a struggle against the prevailing secular ideologies and power structures. During the struggle, the leaders and workers of the Islamic movement would face intense opposition from the existing power structures and would suffer numerous hardships. They should remain steadfast, loyal, and sincere in their commitment to their goal of establishing an Islamic government and should give a practical example of the Islamic way of life through their words and deeds. It is only through their exemplary behavior that the "good-natured elements" of society will be attracted to them. With their sheer moral force and dedicated work, the Islamic workers would be able to bring about a "revolutionary change" in the "mental makeup" of the people at large and the society would then "feel a need for Islamic government." When the majority of the people have thus developed a "longing" for an Islamic government, the prevailing system of government would find it impossible to sustain itself.[54]

Maududi describes this process as "natural, evolutionary, and peaceful." An Islamic revolution can be successfully launched only when a sociopolitical movement based on Qur'anic principles and the prophetic model is first able to change the entire intellectual, moral, psychological, and cultural bases of social life.[55] Thus, while Maududi's goals are revolutionary, his methods to achieve these goals are evolutionary. His frequent use of the term "revolution" for total Islamic change should not be confused with the methods and processes of change associated with some violence-prone revolutionary movements of modern times. In fact, Maududi was at times critical of the revolutionary techniques that engender hatred and use violence.[56]

The main mission of the Islamic state is, in the words of the Qur'an, "to command what is amicable and forbid what is indecent" (3:110). Such a state uses all its resources to ensure that the intent of the Shari'a is fulfilled and conditions are created to promote Islamic principles of economic justice, social harmony, and political equality. An Islamic state would, therefore, not be merely a law-and-order and revenue-collecting agency; it would be an interventionist state in the fullest sense of the word. Its overarching moral mission would make it incumbent that it regulate and oversee all aspects of its citizens' lives.

Although Maududi's concept of an Islamic state remained all-encompassing in that the state governed all aspects of life, he also emphasized that the methods of governance of the state should not be authoritarian. First, the heads of the state and the government would be elected for a fixed term through free elections based on the universal adult franchise. Similarly, members of the *shoora* (parliament) would also be elected by the people. Second, the Islamic state would be based on the principle of the distribution of power, that is, with distinct jurisdictions of the three wings of the state: executive, judiciary, and legislature. The Islamic state would ensure the functioning of an independent judiciary and no one, including the head of state, would be above the law. Hence, Maududi insists repeatedly that the Islamic state is not a theocratic state, since it does not recognize the right of any religious person or group to rule in the name of God. Maududi describes the Islamic state as a "nomocracy" (government of the law) and at one place as "theodemocracy," a government appointed and elected by the free will of the people but conforming in its policies to the Islamic principles as contained in the Qur'an and Sunna.

In his earlier formulations, Maududi had given more powers to the executive branch of the government than to the elected parliament. In his later writings, however, Maududi's definition of the governmental structure of an Islamic state was no different from a Westminister-type parliamentary democracy: universal adult franchise, periodic elections, guaranteed human rights and civil liberties, an independent judiciary and the rule of law, and multiple political parties. Maududi also became more concerned with problems of procedural justice, which could partly be explained by his own experience of periodic jail terms, "preventive detention," and censoring of his writings and speeches by various regimes in Pakistan. The experience of his ideological counterparts—the Muslim Brotherhood—in the Middle East also inspired his aim of building a "sound and unadulterated democratic system."

Economic Policies and Programs of the Jamaat

The Jamaat-i-Islami resents its characterization as a right-wing movement. According to the Jamaat, the term "rightist" is used for supporters of capitalism and feudalism and for those who wish to retain and defend the status quo. The Jamaat describes itself as a party of "the middle road," which is equally opposed to the excesses of both Western capitalism and Soviet Marxism. Islam, according to Maududi, envisages a free economy in which individual initiative and economic freedom of the people are safeguarded by recognizing their right to private property. Also, by making a clear distinction between *halal* (permissible) and *haram* (forbidden) methods of earning and spending, Islam restrains people from earning money in prohibited ways. Islam also ensures that wealth does not concentrate in only a few hands, and that it circulates and reaches the weaker sections of society. The Jamaat, in its election manifesto of

1970, promised to abolish all kinds of monopolies of the means of production so that permanent privileged classes may not come into being.[57] The Jamaat emphasizes equality of opportunity as a basic principle of its economic philosophy and maintains that those who excel in entrepreneurship must be rewarded and should be allowed to pursue their economic goals and make as much progress as they wish, provided they do so through lawful means.

As for the class distinctions and social imbalances in society, the proper solution, according to the Jamaat, does not lie in the nationalization of the means of production or similar methods of state controls and regulations but in the implementation of such Islamic economic injunctions as the introduction of zakat and the abolition of *riba* (interest). According to the Jamaat, the natural classes created by God are present in every society, but their constituent groups keep moving from one class to another in a natural process. However, if class distinctions have been created and perpetuated as a result of monopolies, unjust laws, and corrupt state apparatus, then the distinctions must be removed through state policies in order to ensure free and unhindered social and economic mobility. In addition, Islam guarantees that there is no hostility between the well-to-do classes and the weaker classes produced by the laws of nature and that the well-to-do classes help the weaker sections to stand on their own feet. The institutional mechanism through which Islam achieves this is the zakat, which obligates the faithful to share their wealth with the poorer sections of the community. The Jamaat also believes that it is the duty of an Islamic state to provide its citizens with the basic necessities of life, such as food, clothing, dwelling, education, and medical aid.[58]

Initially the Jamaat-i-Islami did not approve of any restrictions on private property, either industrial or agricultural. Only in the late 1960s did the Jamaat show a new concern for issues of socioeconomic justice and endorse a ceiling on maximum land holdings. This was obviously in response to Mr. Bhutto's vigorous campaign on a similar platform and his characterization of the Jamaat as a reactionary party that served the interests of landlords and industrialists. In response to Mr. Bhutto's election platform and to the perceived socialist threat, the Jamaat came out with a socioeconomic program that was quite revolutionary as compared with its earlier position.

Organizational Structure and Support Base

The Jamaat-i-Islami is headed by an emir (president), who is elected for five years by its members. He is assisted and counseled by a *Majlis-i-Shoora* (Consultative council), which is also elected by the members. All provincial, divisional, district, and local heads of the Jamaat are similarly elected. In its internal structure, therefore, the Jamaat is among the most democratic political organizations in Pakistan.

One of the most important aspects of the Jamaat-i-Islami's organizational structure has been its three-level hierarchy of membership. Full membership *(rukn)* is restricted to an elect few who have fully submitted themselves to the discipline of the Jamaat. On 30 June 1989, there were 6,044 such members of the Jamaat in Pakistan.[59] Full membership is awarded only after a lengthy indoctrination and a vigorous training program, during which an individual must prove to the Jamaat authorities that he has adequately internalized the ideas of Maulana Maududi, has gained sufficient knowledge of Islamic doctrines and practices as interpreted by Maududi, and has undergone, as it were, a conversion experience. The emphasis on exclusiveness means that members can be expelled for contravening doctrinal, moral, or organizational norms. Exclusivity of membership privileges also means that the Jamaat conceives itself as an elect group, possessing special insights into the real meaning and purpose of Islam which the traditional ulama have missed.

The second tier in the hierarchy is workers *(karkun)* or associate members. These people, who aspire to become full members of the organization some day, constitute the backbone of the Jamaat. The workers do not vote in the elections of the emirs or members of the Consultative Council but they have considerable input in the day-to-day working of the Jamaat at local levels. In 1989, there were 16,364 workers in the Jamaat in Pakistan.[60] The third tier consists of supporters *(muttafiq)* who form the majority in the Jamaat. These are the people who agree with the ideology and program of the Jamaat, support the Jamaat in elections and other activities, and contribute funds, but are not yet ready to subject themselves to the strict discipline of the Jamaat's organization. There were 389,000 registered supporters of the Jamaat in Pakistan in 1989.[61] It is estimated that there are about 150,000 to 200,000 people who agree with the Jamaat's program and occasionally participate in its activities but have not signed the supporters' pledge for various reasons.

The Jamaat-i-Islami justifies selectiveness in its full membership by maintaining that it is not a political party in the usual sense of the word; it is rather an ideological movement and as such must insist on the ideological purity and organizational loyalty of its members. It wants the participation only of those who are ideologically committed and are ready to devote themselves to its program of action. Its membership must therefore consist of an ideological cadre that is capable of providing intellectual, moral, religious, and political leadership to the Jamaat's associates and supporters, on the one hand, and to society at large, on the other. There have been several attempts from within the Jamaat to relax the requirements for full membership in order to broaden the support base of the organization, but the Jamaat's puritans have always resisted any change in the exclusive character of its membership. Critics have argued that this restrictive system of membership has been a major factor in the Jamaat's failure to win electoral support in proportion to its organizational strength and political influence. The leaders insist, however, that the present system of membership has ensured an unusually high level of commitment and a deep sense of brotherhood among the Jamaat members. These qualities can only be retained if membership is based on strict screening.

There has been a steady growth in the number of the Jamaat's local chapters and organizational units consisting of associate members. The most spectacular growth has been in the number of the reading rooms and libraries organized by the Jamaat throughout the country: their number rose from 586 in 1978 to 2,269 in 1983 and 3,801 in 1989. Like the Christian Science Reading Rooms in the United States, the Jamaat-i-Islami-sponsored reading rooms and libraries only carry a select number of approved books, mostly written by the founder of the Jamaat. Another area of notice-

TABLE 8.1
JAMAAT MEMBERS OF VARIOUS CATEGORIES AND ORGANIZATIONAL UNITS, 1978–89

	1978	1983	1989
Full members	3,497	4,430	6,044
Workers	10,800	12,426	16,364
Supporters	376,289	—	389,000
Local Chapters	441	529	619
Circles of associates	1,177	2,858	3,095
Women's units	215	317	554
Reading rooms & libraries	586	2,269	3,801
Women members	—	160	321

Sources: Weekly *Takbeer* (Karachi), 23 November 1989, p. 22, for 1983 and 1989 data as reported by the secretary general of the Jamaat in his report presented at the November 1989 conference in Lahore; and *Jamaat-i-Islami Pakistan: An Introduction* (Lahore: Jamaat-i-Islami, 1978) for 1978 data.

able growth has been the women's membership, which has doubled since 1983. In this regard, the contribution of the Islami Jamiat-i-Talabat, the female student wing of the Jamaat, has been quite significant since the early 1980s.

It should also be noted here that the Jamaat has a considerable following in the civil service and the military, but because of government restrictions, it does not register its supporters from the bureaucracy and the armed forces in its records. However, some civilian employees of the government have been organized in professional organizations that have links with the Jamaat. Thus, the Jamaat-i-Islami-sponsored trade unions, labor and student organizations; professional associations of doctors, engineers, teachers, accountants, journalists, and writers have their own separate membership, which is not included in the records of the parent organization.

Among the Jamaat-sponsored organizations, the most important is the Islami Jamiat-i-Talaba (IJT), its student wing. Much of the political strength of the Jamaat-i-Islami, especially its ability to mobilize the masses to confront the government, depends on the IJT. Since the 1960s, the IJT has been the most effectively organized arm of the Jamaat and has served as an assured and fertile base for the recruitment, socialization, and training of new members and supporters for the parent organization. Some prominent leaders of the Jamaat today are former IJT workers.

Through the efforts of the IJT the Jamaat has been able to successfully penetrate and control the educational institutions of the country and organize the urban youth, who constitute one of its most important constituencies, under the umbrella of Islamic ideology. The IJT has also helped the Jamaat to impose ideological censorship on educational institutions, neutralize the influence of secular, left-wing, and liberal-minded teachers, and intimidate political opponents. It has also helped the Jamaat to launch agitational movements, whose tactics included forced closing of educational institutions, street processions, violent protests, demonstrations, and strikes. In short the IJT has helped the Jamaat build an image of an invincible political force in the country.

The IJT was established as a separate organization on 23 December 1947 in Lahore by a group of 25 students sympathetic to the Jamaat-i-Islami.[62] The constitution adopted by the IJT was a carbon copy of the constitution of the Jamaat. It even retained the three-tiered membership structure from the Jamaat. Since then, the IJT has developed into the largest, best-organized, and most successful student movement not only in Pakistan but in the entire Muslim world. It has offices and branches in almost all cities and towns of the country. Like its parent organization, the IJT restricts the privilege of full membership to a select few. In 1987, it had 550 full members, 2,000 associate members, and close to 240,000 sympathizers and supporters.[63] Its organizational reach is even more extensive than that of its parent organization. It has more than 620 branches, which are called local chapters, and units throughout the country. In addition, campus units, of which there are estimated to be about 600, are organized separately.[64] In Karachi alone, the IJT has 30 residential units, 35 college units, 40 school units, and 5 madrasa units—a total of 110 organizational units. It operates more than 1,400 libraries and reading rooms in the country and conducts tuition-free coaching classes for students in all major cities.[65] This enormous organizational power has ensured the IJT its success in student union elections in colleges and universities throughout the country over the past two decades. No mass-based political agitation can be successfully launched in the urban centers without the participation of the IJT. During his five-year rule, neither Prime Minister Bhutto nor any of his cabinet ministers could visit any major campus in the country because of the IJT's complete control over the educational institutions.

The IJT also tried to penetrate the madrasas in the 1960s but could not make any headway in view of strong opposition from the ulama. The Jamaat later decided to organize a separate association of the madrasa students, Jamiat Talaba-i-Arabiya (Society of Arabic students), which played an active role in the anti-Ahmadiya agitatiion of 1974, the anti-Bhutto movement of 1977, and later in the Afghan jihad. Since the mid-1970s, the Jamaat has devoted its attention and resources to establishing its own madrasas in order to establish a permanent foothold in the traditional religious sector. The number of Jamaat-sponsored madrasas has increased considerably since 1980, when the Jamaat embarked upon a massive program of establishing religious educational institutions for the 3.5 million Afghan refugees in Pakistan. At present, the number of Jamaat-administered madrasas, mostly located in the NWFP and Baluchistan, is estimated to be 820.

Leadership

Like most of its counterparts in other Muslim countries, the Jamaat-i-Islami is not a party of ulama. An overwhelming majority of the Jamaat leaders and members are educated laymen and are not trained as religious clergy. The number of ulama (those with formal training from a traditional madrasa) has always been very small in the Jamaat. Maududi was a self-taught scholar of Islam with no formal madrasa education; accordingly, many of the ulama refuse to acknowledge Maududi's views on religious issues as authentic.[66] His successors, Mian Tufail Mohammad and Qazi Hussain

Ahmad, attended modern secular schools and obtained graduate degrees in science. Mian Tufail joined the Jamaat as a full-time worker immediatedly after his graduation, while Qazi Hussain Ahmad became a successful businessman in the pharmaceutical industry before becoming first secretary general and later emir of the Jamaat. Mian Tufail was elected emir on the basis of his life-long service to the Jamaat and his loyalty to Maududi. Qazi Hussain Ahmad impressed the members of the Jamaat with his political skills and his ability to motivate the Jamaat workers at a time when the ambivalence of the Jamaat toward Zia's regime had created considerable confusion among the rank and file of the party.

The majority of those who are in leadership positions in the Jamaat come either from the modern professions or from the business sector. A 1975 survey of the leadership of the Jamaat at the district and provincial levels and in the central consultative committee found that, besides those who were full-time workers, the majority of the Jamaat leaders (52 percent) were independent businessmen, mostly in small-scale manufacturing or in the retail trade. Professionals (lawyers, doctors, accountants, etc.) accounted for 28 percent, and educators 12 percent. The remaining 8 percent were ulama, landlords, and traditional medical practitioners.[67] In the 1983 survey, the number of professionals with degrees from modern secular schools rose to 32 percent, and the number of independent businessmen rose to 57 percent.[68] A similar pattern can be seen in the candidates of the Jamat-i-Islami in national elections. Of the 106 candidates the Jamaat-i-Islami nominated for the national and provincial assemblies during the 1970 elections, 37 percent were independent businessmen, 25 percent professionals, 10 percent full-time Jamaat workers, 8 percent landlords, 7 percent ulama, 5 percent educators, 4 percent student leaders, 3 percent *pirs* (those associated with religious shrines), and 1 percent retired army officers. During the 1985 nonparty elections, the share of independent businessmen and professionals among the Jamaat's candidates rose to 44 percent and 31 percent, respectively, while the number of ulama and pirs decreased to 4 percent.[69]

Since the death of Maulana Abdul Aziz, Maulana Moinuddin, and other widely acclaimed traditional Islamic scholars, the leadership of the Jamaat-i-Islami has been placed almost entirely in the hands of modern educated laymen, none of whom is known as a scholar of traditional Islamic sciences. Table 8.2 gives the educational and occupational background of the top fifteen leaders of the Jamaat-i-Islami Pakistan today.

Another important change that has taken place in the leadership structure of the Jamaat since the 1970s is that both the intellectual and political leadership of the Jamaat and the IJT has passed from the Urdu-speaking refugees to the "sons of the soil." Thus the locus of power and influence within the Jamaat has shifted from Karachi to Lahore.

The degree of integration and harmony between the leadership, on the one hand, and the general body of members, associate members, and supporters, on the other, is unique to the Jamaat. Unlike other political organizations, the Jamaat has never had a serious problem of dissent. As guardians of a moral community that is dedicated to the task of building an ideal social order, the leaders of the Jamaat have never had

TABLE 8.2
EDUCATIONAL AND OCCUPATIONAL BACKGROUND OF THE JAMAAT-I-ISLAMI LEADERS, 1990

Name	Position in the Jamaat	Education	Occupation
Qazi Hussain Ahmad	Emir (president)	M.S., University of Peshawar	Businessman
Khurshid Ahmad	Vice-president	M.A. (economics) Leicestor (U.K.)	Former university professor
Ahdul Ghafoor Ahmad	Vice-president	M.A. (commerce) University of Allahabad	Former college professor; Corporate Consultant
Khurram Murad	Vice-president	M.S. (civil engineering) University of Minnesota	Consulting Engineer
Jan Mohammad Abbasi	Vice-president	Madrasa graduate	Former teacher in a Madrasa
Rahmat Ilahi	Vice-president	M.A. (political science) Karachi University	Former government employee
Aslam Saleemi	Secretary-general	LL.B. Punjab University	Former attorney
Hafiz Mohammad Idris	Assistant secretary-general	M.A. (humanities) Punjab University	Full-time Jamaat worker
Liaqat Baluch	Assistant secretary-general	M.A. (journalism) Punjab University	Businessman
Fateh Mohammad	Emir, Punjab Province	M.A. (humanities) Punjab University	Former college professor
Munawar Hasan	Emir, Karachi Jamaat	M.A. (sociology) Karachi University	Research
Asad Gilani	Emir, Lahore Jamaat	M.A. (humanities) Karachi University	Writer, journalist
Mahmud Azam Faruqi	Member, executive committee	M.A. (finance) Karachi University	Corporate executive, publisher
Naeem Siddiqui	Member, executive committee		Writer, journalist
Fazel Ilahi Qurashi	Secretary, Baluchistan Jamaat	M.S. (food technology) Sind University	Food technology

their legitimacy questioned. Hence, both "exit" (quitting the organization) and "voice" (expressing dissatisfaction), in Hirchman's sense, have been rare. To be sure, the ideology of the Jamaat plays an important part in ensuring the total commitment and loyalty of the members. *Ata't-i-Nazm* (obedience to the leadership of the Jamaat) is cultivated as a religious virtue and sustained through a concrete set of organizational norms and arrangements. It is a testimony to the high level of commitment to, and confidence in, the leadership that a single call of the emir mobilizes the whole Jamaat and its affiliated organizations for whatever Islamic cause is at stake.

Although the religious experience of conversion of the first generation of leaders is considered unique and has acquired the mystique of folklore in the Jamaat, the second generation of leaders is also endowed with its own legends of heroic struggles for Islam and democratic political change in the country. Qazi Hussain Ahmad and Seyyed Munawar Hasan represent the new generation of leadership. While most of the Jamaat leaders of the first generation had their conversion experience in their adult lives, the majority of the current leaders became committed to their Islamic mission while they were still teenagers.

The Social Bases of Jamaat's Support

The question of the social bases of support of the Jamaat-i-Islami has not been adequately addressed in the literature. Professor Leonard Binder, in his 1964 collection *The Ideological Revolution in the Middle East,* briefly addressed this question and provided interesting insights into the class base of the leaders and the followers of contemporary Islamic fundamentalist movements in Pakistan, Egypt, Indonesia, and Iran. He found that Jamaat-i-Islami members were drawn from the lower middle class and that its supporters were students and bazaar merchants.[70] Although he offered important suggestions concerning the sociopsychological characteristics of the "small core of adherents" of the fundamentalist movements, he warned against drawing the conclusion that "all persons filling the description will join a fundamentalist group."[71] With this proviso, I will attempt to identify the social, religious, educational, and occupational backgrounds of the social groups which provide the nucleus of the Jamaat-i-Islami Pakistan.

It is not the lower classes—the landless peasants, the urban proletariat, the uprooted migrants from the rural areas struggling for two square meals in the slums of the big urban centers—who join the religious revivalist movement such as the Jamaat-i-Islami; rather it is the lower sections of the new middle classes and traditional petty bourgeoisie who form the backbone of such movements. The latter groups are psychologically alienated, socially declining, relatively well-off economically, but insecure and politically ineffective. They are reacting against social deprivation at the hands of the upper social classes and government bureaucrats, on the one hand, and against the increasing militancy of the lower classes, on the other. This amalgamation provides the main strength of the urban and small town-based semirevolutionary struggle for an ideal Islamic social order based on justice and equity. The countryside remains almost completely indifferent toward this movement; whatever support for Islami Nizam comes from the rural sector is essentially from the better-off, middle-range landowners, and to some extent from former servicemen. The landless peasants and big landlords, in both rural Sind and rural Punjab, remain totally unconcerned about Islamic revivalism.

The lower-middle strata, both traditional and modern, are thus the main loci of the social unrest which acts as a propellent for the revivalist upsurge. While demanding the revival of traditional Islamic moral-social institutions, they are primarily protesting the processes of enslavement by big business and oppressive bureaucratic structures. One must, however, note an important ideological and policy ambivalence here; that is, they are against neither capitalism nor the state per se. In line with the socioeconomic program of the Jamaat-i-Islami, they seek reform, improvement, and "purification" of institutions in order to facilitate their own entry into them.

It may, however, be argued that the overall material conditions of the traditional petty bourgeoisie and the lower echelons of the new middle class (schoolteachers, clerks, lower-level professionals) have improved considerably since the 1960s. Opportunities for overseas employment as unskilled or semi-skilled laborers have further improved the economic conditions of these strata in recent years. What matters most to these groups, however, is their sense of political impotency. It was only during the Ayub Khan period when, through the system of Basic Democracy, a section of this stratum was provided with an opportunity to participate in local-level politics, particularly in small towns. The Bhutto period was both economically and politically a period of disenfranchisement for this stratum. Bhutto's policies favored the upper classes and his rhetoric supported the lower classes, the urban proletariat and the rural peasants. In a way, the intermediate strata were in fact sidetracked into a marginal position. Even in the traditional social stratification pattern, the petty bourgeoisie never had an autonomous power base and were usually uncomfortably situated in the social hierarchy dominated by landlords, courtiers, and state functionaries. In the emerging modern social stratification system, their political powerlessness, social isolation, status inconsistency, and economic struggle against big business, big government, and relatively well organized and articulate labor has become more pronounced. For the last thirty years, as governmental policies favored the big industrial and commercial bourgeoisie on the one hand, and the opposition's rhetoric championed the cause of the underprivileged and downtrodden urban proletariat and rural peasants on the other, the problems and dilemmas of the petty bourgeoisie's class and status situations never figured prominently in the policies and manifestos of any political party.

The Bhutto period, during which the material and ideal interests of the traditional petty bourgeoisie merged with the ideology of the Jamaat-i-Islami, was especially disturbing for the petty bourgeoisie. Distributive trade was completely politicized. The sale of essential commodities was licensed to the People's Party workers. Another major economic blow to the petty bourgeoisie was the nationalization of small-scale rice husking, cotton ginning, and flour mills. Moreover, the credit facilities of the nationalized banking sector were directed to the import-export business, agriculture, and state enterprises rather than to the small-scale sector.[72] By monopolizing the production and distribution sectors and by appropriating a major portion of institutional credit resources, big business threatened the very existence of the petty bourgeoisie. Similarly, the trade unions tended to encroach upon their meager and insecure profits, and the local and national bureacracies appropriated a considerable proportion of their profits in the form of taxes and bribes (in exchange for their minor violations of business laws).

For these reasons the lower-middle strata of society constitutes the backbone of Islamic fundamentalist-conservative politics in Pakistan. This is manifest in their membership in the Jamaat-i-Islami and other religious political parties, their voting behavior, involvement in community religious activities, financial support of mosques and madrasas, and participation in religiopolitical rallies and meetings. Finding themselves unable to compete technologically or organizationally with the modern, bureaucratized business and industrial sectors and fearing the radicalized lower classes of the society, they seek protection under an umbrella ideology of Islamic fundamentalism, whose economic program tends to maintain a balance between ruthlessly competitive capitalism and property-destroying socialism.

In addition to the traditional petty bourgeoisie, the students, the majority of whom are drawn from lower-middle-class backgrounds, and the mass of elementary, middle, and secondary schoolteachers, clerks, and paraprofessionals in the government and private sectors, are another significant assortment of groups which are attracted to the fundamentalist movement in Pakistan.

It is not uncommon in Pakistan, with its chronic problem of unemployment at all levels, for people to continue acquiring higher degrees in order to be able to compete successfully with others in the job market. The proliferation of degrees, mostly in general studies and humanities, has created a situation in which people with B.A.'s and M.A.'s and law degrees are doing jobs which require only simple mathematics and a minimum level of reading and writing capability. This group of people, mainly from the town-based or urban lower-middle classes, whose sole purpose in acquiring degrees was to enter into the most prized positions in the civil service or to seek admission into professional schools, ultimately are forced to settle down in the lower level clerical jobs in the government or private business or to become schoolteachers. Ironically, the government's response to the situation—opening new colleges and universities and liberalizing admission criteria to ease the pressure, at least temporarily, from the job market—serves only to encourage students to acquire more degrees. Yet a growing number of young graduates are poorly trained for the available jobs and are unable to get satisfying employment. This situation is also typical for students in small towns and medium-sized cities. The level of frustration and the feeling in these people of having been let down by the system is tremendous.

In many cases, young men from the lower echelons of the middle strata were unable to compete because of a lack of proficiency in the English language, a lack of proper social etiquette or demeanor associated with the Westernized upper middle classes, and above all, a lack of adequate social and political connections. In seeking to extend to lower-middle-class youth opportunities for upward social mobility which so far have been generally limited to the upper-middle-class urban population, fundamentalist social ideology offers a normative solution to this phenomenon of status frustration born of structural contradictions. Rather than demolish the existing system of social rewards, the fundamentalist program seeks to make the system more open, honest, and fair. Thus, the relationship between fundamentalist Islam and the dominant semi-capitalist structures of society is not necessarily antagonistic; the principal conflict between them is focused on the proper mode of entry into the dominant structures and their relative openness. Whatever conflict appears to exist can be viewed as a result of the mutual perceptions of the actors involved—a false consciousness—rather than as originating at the level of structural relationships.

A section of the new middle classes consisting mainly of post-partition refugees from northern India constitutes another important support base for the fundamentalists. The majority of the theoreticians and intellectuals of the Jamaat-i-Islami (and of the Tablighi Jamaat) come from this class. Their major concentration is found in urban Sind, especially in Karachi, Hyderabad, Sukkur, and Nawabshah—the cities which consistently voted for the Jamaat-i-Islami and the Jamiyat Ulama-e-Pakistan until the middle of 1980s, when the Muhajir Quami Movement (MQM), a political party representing the interests of the Urdu-speaking refugees, emerged as an important rival to the Jamaat. In Karachi, considered the media center of Pakistan, the refugee intelligentsia have exercised a complete hold over such professions as journalism, radio and television broadcasting, publishing, education, business management, the scientific and technical professions, and until recently, federal, provincial, and local government jobs.

Their receptive affinity with the religious and political ideology of the Jamaat-i-Islami is integrally related not only to the question of the preservation of north Indian Muslim culture, including the Urdu language, but also to their very survival in the wake of increasingly assertive ethnic-regional identities and distinctions between the "sons of the soil" and the "outsiders." As refugees from pre-partition India who left their ancestors' homes for the sake of Pakistan and adopted this new country as their new home, they view an Islamic Pakistan as the only raison d'être for their continued survival and the only justification for their being there in the first place. To them, a secular Pakistan would be indistinguishable from the India they consciously rejected when they migrated to Pakistan. A Pakistan which is characterized as consisting of distinct regional subcultures with distinct ethnic nationalities—as some ethnically oriented political groups in Pakistan characterize it—would be a Pakistan of Punjabis, Sindis, Baluch, and Pathans with no place for the refugees. Hence, during the first three decades of independent Pakistan, they continued to support the Jamaat-i-Islami, whose political program showed concern for a strong central government, rejection of the idea of regional autonomy—both political and cultural—and identification of Pakistan with Islam and the Urdu language.

Unlike other, rural-based and feudal class-dominated political parties, the Jamaat-i-Islami had no regional exclusiveness. Led primarily by Urdu-speaking people from the middle and lower classes, it was already predisposed to the ideological and material concerns of the refugee population. It is no wonder, then, that the middle-class refugee constituencies in Karachi have consistently returned the Jamaat-i-Islami candidates to the national parliament since the 1970s. The loss of this constituency to the MQM was a great setback for the Jamaat in the Zia era.

This analysis of the relationship between the socioeconomic conditions of certain social classes and the ideology of Islamic neofundamentalism as articulated by the Jamaat-i-Islami is not, however, meant to suggest that the ideology by itself had no independent influence on the people and events. The point emphasized above is that ideas are not impersonal agents; they work through specific social classes. One can argue that it is through the mediatory role of the Islamic neofundamentalist ideology that the social experiences of certain individuals and groups within the contemporary social structure of Pakistani society come to be articulated in political action. However, Islamic neofundamentalism not only provided a coherent ideology which articulated their life experiences and gave them a vision of an alternative social order based on the Islamic principles of justice, equality, and brotherhood, but it also created a pool of highly dedicated workers, publicists, and leaders to realize this vision in a moral community of the Jamaat-i-Islami.

The Jamaat-i-Islami as a Reformist Movement

Some observers who consider fundamentalism synonymous with radicalism have branded the Jamaat-i-Islami a "radical" or "militant" movement. The Jamaat-i-Islami, however, is a reformist party which has used constitutional and legal methods to achieve its Islamic goals. Despite some degree of militancy in its rhetoric, it has been accommodationist in its ideological orientation and evolutionist in its methodology of change. It does not approve of the violent methods adopted by some of its ideological kin in the Middle East and advocates a policy of peaceful transition from the existing state to an Islamic one. According to Khurshid Ahmad, a prominent theoretician of the Jamaat, Islamically oriented social change does not involve any "friction and disequilibria": it is a "planned and co-ordinated movement from one state of equilibrium to a higher one, or from a state of disequilibrium towards equilibrium." As such, he believes, the Islamic movement will work for a change that is "balanced and gradual and evolutionary."[73]

Maududi eschewed violence and was a great believer in the ultimate triumph of Islamic forces through democratic elections. He denounced the violence that had crept into the politics of Pakistan and disapproved of the militant and violent tactics of the IJT during the Islam vs. Socialism strife of the late 1960s. He hoped that if the Islamic movement continued to educate people and strive patiently, it would one day succeed in bringing righteous men to power.[74] Change of political leadership through agitational politics, coups d'état, and assassinations is in this view not only unjustifiable in Islamic terms but also detrimental to the prospects for a permanent and lasting Islamic change. Maududi emphasized that both the ends and the means must be "clean and commendable" in order that a healthy, peaceful, and harmonious Islamic order can take shape.[75]

This "soft" approach of the Jamaat-i-Islami toward the Islamization of society and the state can also be explained with reference to Pakistan's political culture. Although Pakistan has experienced periodic military coups and prolonged martial law, the normative appeal of the British legacy of constitutional democracy and the rule of law, including an independent judiciary, political parties, and a free press, has not diminished. The Jamaat-i-Islami not only operates in the context of a political culture that considers democracy its ideal but also accepts this ideal as Islamic. Even during the military regimes, political parties of all persuasions continued to operate, albeit under some restrictions, and take advantage of the freedoms available to them under the constitution. Thus, when the Jamaat-i-Islami was banned by Ayub Khan in 1964, the Supreme Court of Pakistan came to the party's rescue and declared the government's action to be illegal. Although different Pakistani regimes have been against both the right- and left-wing radical groups, they have never been as repressive and vindictive as were the regimes of the shah in Iran and of Nasser in Egypt. One can argue that it is usually the repressive policies of governments and the total absence of freedom to pursue normal political activities that tend to drive religious and other political groups to radicalism and violent methods of change.

Moreover, unlike the Takfir wal-Hijrah group of Egypt and the Saudi dissidents who seized control of the Kaaba in 1979, the Pakistani Islamic movement does not exist on the fringe; rather, it is very much in the mainstream of Islamic religious thought and hence does not suffer from the rejection complex which often drives minority-based, sect-like peripheral movements to adopt violent means.

Finally, the social-class base of the Jamaat inhibits radical tendencies. The rank and file consist of sections of the new middle classes and the traditional petty bourgeoisie. Both of these classes take reformist and nonradical approaches to the solution of their problems and want to work through the system and not against it.[76]

Jamaat-i-Islami Bangladesh

Although the Jamaat-i-Islami received only 6 percent of the total vote in the 1970 elections in East Pakistan, it was fighting against an unprecedented popular movement for regional autonomy led by the Awami League party of Sheikh Mujibur Rahman. During the 1971 civil war, the Jamaat was the only political party in East Pakistan that openly collaborated with the central government and, with arms and weapons supplied by the Pakistan army, organized the Al-Badr paramilitary unit to fight for a united Pakistan. Al-Badr, which consisted mainly of the Jamaat's student wing, Islami Chatro Shango (Bengali for the IJT), fought pitched battles against the secessionist Mukti Bahini guerrillas and the invading Indian troops. Hundreds of Jamaat workers died for Islamic Pakistan, fighting against their co-ethnics in what was soon to become the independent state of Bangladesh.

Because of the close collaboration with the central government of Pakistan, the Jamaat-i-Islami and its supporters were branded as traitors by the ruling Awami League party after Bangladesh became independent. Many of the Jamaat leaders and activists were taken as prisoners of war by the Indian troops and were sent to various prisoners' camps in India. Some had to escape to Pakistan—through Burma or India—in order to avoid being captured by the Mukti Bahini. Many of them went underground.

Against this background the revival and increasing popularity of the Jamaat-i-Islami in post-independence Bangladesh can be considered a remarkable accomplishment. Since the Jamaat was declared an illegal organization in Bangladesh because of its pro-Pakistan leanings and could not operate under its own name, it worked out another strategy to stage a comeback. It began organizing local-level Islamic youth circles, mosque councils, and religiously based cultural, social welfare and educational associations immediately after the emergence of the new nation. By the end of 1972, the Jamaat was able to set up 120 such local-level units, which held regular weekly meetings and provided institutional resources to the Jamaat workers. The main aim of its activities at this phase was to regroup its scattered forces, to relink Bengali Muslims with their Islamic heritage, and to educate the people against the secular nationalism which had been incorporated in the constitution as the ideology of the new state.

Only after Sheikh Mujib was assassinated in a military coup and General Ziaur Rahman took power was the Jamaat-i-Islami formally revived under its own name. The general disillusionment with the Awami League's post-independence performance and the resurgence of anti-India feelings further added to the appeal of the Jamaat. The Jamaat scored its first victory when Ziaur Rahman, through a constitutional amendment, deleted the article that mentioned secularism as one of the fundamental principles of state policy and replaced it with the phrase "absolute trust and faith in Almighty Allah."[77] The new openness under Zia allowed the Jamaat to revive its organizational units in colleges and universities as well. By 1978–79, its student wing, now renamed Islami Chatro Shibir (ICS), was able to successfully challenge the combined opposition of the Awami League and the communists. The ICS won impressive victories in the student union elections in Rajshahi, Chittagong, and Dhaka universities, where only five years earlier even a suspicion that someone was connected with the Jamaat-i-Islami was enough for him to be subjected to a lynch mob. Today the Jamaat has its own daily newspaper, *Sangram,* its own publishing establishment, and a well-staffed Islamic research institute. It has also organized separate wings for laborers, youth, women, and professionals.

The most important arm of the Jamaat-i-Islami Bangladesh, as for its sister organization in Pakistan, remains its student wing, the ICS. The ICS has branches in more than 60 percent of the high schools in all twenty-one districts of Bangladesh. Since 1980, it has consistently won more that 55 percent of the student union elections in colleges and universities. "One of strongest students fronts in the universities of Dhaka, Rajshahi and Jahangirnagar," its influence is "steadily increasing not only among traditional elements but also among the modern educated young men."[78] Its activities are primarily focused on religious and cultural programs with a view to "reawaken the Islamic consciousness" among Muslim Bengali youth and to counter the influence of Bengali nationalists, socialists, and secularists. In the late 1980s its parent organization, the Jamaat-i-Islami, resumed its political activities with full vigor. Table 8.3 details the Jamaat's progress during this period. The political agenda of the Jamaat in 1990 included: (a) the forming of alliances with other like-minded political groups for the restoration of democracy; (b) resistance to Indian hegemony; (c) the strengthening of relations with Islamic countries, especially with Pakistan; and (d) the active involvement of Bangladesh in Muslim world affairs. The Jamaat's persistent

TABLE 8.3
Jamaat-i-Islami Bangladesh: Members and Organizational Units, 1989

Full members	5,000
Workers	50,000
Registered supporters	500,000
Unregistered supporters	2,000,000
District branches	68
Subdistrict branches	460
Union Council branches	3,000
Local branches	5,000
Jamaat-operated schools	500
Jamaat-operated hospitals	200

Source: *Tarjuman-ul-Qur'am* (Lahore), May 1990, pp. 213–14.

opposition to selling natural gas to India and its insistence that Bangladesh should take a tough stand on the Farakka Dam issue with India are significant given the background of the 1971 Indo-Pakistan war and the secession of Bangladesh.

Since 1987, the Jamaat-i-Islami has once again been subjected to persecution by the government of H. M. Ershad and to violence by the remnants of the Mukti Bahini. This renewed harassment of the Jamaat began soon after the student union elections of 1987, in which the Jamaat's ICS unexpectedly won important victories in many colleges and universities of Bangladesh, defeating the secular nationalist forces of the Awami League. Since then forty leaders and workers of the Jamaat and the ICS have been assassinated by the Mukti Bahini.[79] Because of its leading role in the Islamic Democratic League Alliance—a coalition of Islamic groups opposed to the military regime of General Ershad—the Jamaat became a target of attack by the government as well. On 12 November 1988, for example, President Ershad, addressing a meeting of freedom fighters, declared his determination to "eliminate" the Jamaat-i-Islami. "Those who opposed the liberation war in 1971 and killed the freedom fighters have now joined politics with their heads high," he said. "Will you remain silent? Will you sit idle? It is high time these enemies of liberation are eliminated. They have no place in this country."[80] Within a couple of weeks of this open call to violence against the Jamaat-i-Islami, two of its student workers and two district level leaders were assassinated.[81]

The catastrophic events of 1971 did not leave the Jamaat-i-Islami unscathed. Almost all of its Urdu-speaking leaders had to leave East Pakistan when it became Bangladesh. Some of its prominent intellectuals and leaders left Bangladesh for the Middle East. Maulana Abdul Rahim, the president of the Jamaat-i-Islami East Pakistan at the time of Pakistan's dismemberment, left the main body of the Jamaat after the war and organized his own nonpolitical Jamaat-i-Islami to pursue "purely religious" goals and preach the "original revivalist mission" of Maududi. Although the new organization did not last long, it took the Bangladeshi Jamaat leaders four years to heal the wounds of the split. Mr. Ghulam Azam, a former professor of political science and a close confidant of Maududi during the united Pakistan era, was elected president of the Jamaat to preserve the integral ideological links between the four sister organizations—Jamaat-i-Islami Pakistan, Bangladesh, India, and Kashmir.

Jamaat-i-Islami India

At the time of partition in 1947, the Jamaat-i-Islami India was organized as a separate organization under the leadership of Maulana Abul Lais Islahi, who continued to lead the Jamaat until 1990. Since the Jamaat was not very active in pre-partition politics and was not associated with the Muslim League's demand for Pakistan, it did not encounter any difficulty in its da'wa work in post-independence India. Initially the Jamaat focused its attention on programs of social welfare, educational development, and the religious reawakening of the Muslim community and stayed away from political activities. Given the fact that India was a secular state and the Muslims constituted only 11 percent of the total population, the Jamaat had no option but to abandon the goal of establishing an Islamic state in India—a goal that became the primary concern of its sister organization in Islamic Pakistan. However, the Indian Jamaat soon became preoccupied with the preservation of the three most vital identity symbols of the Indo-Islamic community: Muslim Family Laws, the Urdu language, and the Muslim University of Aligarh. Coupled with its extensive publishing and Islamic religious educational programs, it was primarily through its struggle to save the Muslim Family Laws and the Urdu language that the Jamaat sought to assert a distinctive Muslim identity in a secular constitutional framework and a communally defined sociopolitical context.

Since the 1950s, the Jamaat-i-Islami has operated at three distinct levels. First, within the Muslim community (estimated at 120 million) the Jamaat's emphasis has been on Islamization—"purifying" the beliefs and practices of coreligionists in order to bring them closer to the teachings of Islamic orthodoxy as enunciated in the Qur'an and Sunna of the Prophet. Here there has been little difference between the Jamaat-i-Islami and the Tablighi Jamaat. Second, with respect to the rest of Indian society, the activities of the Jamaat have centered on the reassertion of Muslim religious rights and identity. It has also been active in "fighting the menace of communalism" in cooperation with other Muslim and interfaith organizations. The Jamaat believes that it is only through participation in the national political process that the problems faced by the Muslims and the discrimination to which they are subjected can receive national attention and form part of national agenda. It was on the basis of this policy that in the 1960s the Jamaat joined the All India Muslim Majlis-i-Mushawarat (All India Muslim Consultative Committee), a coalition of various Muslim political parties and religioeducational organizations. The emphasis of the Jamaat in this respect has been on promoting "national unity and harmony" on the basis of shared religious values and "within the parameters of a multi-racial, multi-lingual, and multicultural Indian society."[82] According to Maulana Sirajul Hasan, the secretary general of the Indian Jamaat, the moral uplift of Indian society is a joint responsibility of all religious communities of India. Hence, the Jamaat, in its outreach activities among followers of other religions, emphasizes those moral values that are common in all religions and that promote mutual harmony and understanding.[83] The Jamaat believes that Islamic missionary work has little chance of success in "an atmosphere charged with communal frenzy and moral corruption." Unless the tensions are defused and the misgivings allayed, there is not much likelihood of "the Islamic message being understood in the right spirit."[84]

Third, with respect to its international relations, the Jamaat has campaigned for better Indo-Pakistan relations and has lobbied the Indian government to support the cause of the Palestinians and the Afghan resistance. On the question of Afghanistan, for example, the Jamaat-i-Islami India organized more than three hundred rallies and protest marches during 1980–85 against the Soviet occupation of a fellow Muslim nation. Interestingly, while the Jamaat-i-Islami Pakistan has opposed India's participation in the activities of the Organization of Islamic Conference (OIC)—an organization of Muslim heads of states—the Indian Jamaat has been a consistent supporter of its government's efforts to seek OIC membership. Obviously both

Jamaat-i-Islami India and Pakistan are defending in this case what they perceive to be the best interests of the Indian and Pakistani Muslims, respectively.

At the level of ideas and political strategy too, the Indian Islamic scene offers an interesting example of how a religiopolitical movement tends to articulate its ideology in two different political contexts. When the Jamaat-i-Islami became formally organized into two separate entities at the time of partition, the Pakistani Jamaat launched a campaign for the establishment of an Islamic state as the most important means for creating the order envisaged by Islam, while the Indian Jamaat, operating in a secular constitutional framework, deleted all references to the goal of establishing an Islamic state from its program of action.[85] The raison d'être of the Jamaat-i-Islami Pakistan is that Islam does not admit any separation between religious and public affairs. Hence, the Islamic state is not a matter of choice but a fundamental obligation of Islam. This state, which is based on the political sovereignty of God, is to be governed by people of clear Islamic vision, commitment, and character.[86] Jamaat-i-Islami of India, on the other hand, had no alternative but to give up the idea of an Islamic state. It was, however, able to find a plausible justification for its revisionist ideology in the original critique of its founder of the creation of Pakistan. Maududi had argued that the geographical delimitation of the Islamic umma in the territorial confines of Pakistan would obstruct the growth and spread of Islam as a universal message. The Indian Jamaat has thus successfully avoided the question of establishing an Islamic state as it was articulated in its original constitution of 1941 by emphasizing the concept of the worldwide Islamic umma of which the Indian Muslims are an integral part. Furthermore, according to the Two Nation theory of the Muslim League, the Muslims who chose to remain in India should still be considered members of the same Muslim nation which had established a separate homeland for itself, namely, Pakistan. The Jamaat-i-Islami India has sought to resolve this anomaly by disassociating the concept of Muslim nation from the nation-state of Pakistan, and instead relating it to the concept of universal *ummah Islamiyya*. This is not only a politically safe conceptualization but is also intended to provide Indian Muslims with an enormous psychological sense of security and strength in their immediate context of their numerical and political weakness.

It is on the issue of secularism, however, that the two sister organizations are sharply divided. While the Jamaat in Pakistan denounces secularism and the secular state as "an evil force," the Jamaat in India is equally vigorous in defending secularism as a "blessing" and as a "guarantee for a safe future for Islam" in India.[87] Although both wings of the Jamaat agree that religion and secularism are incompatible, the Indian Jamaat makes a distinction between secularism as an atheistic ideology and "secularism as a state policy which implies that there should be no discrimination or partiality on the basis of religious belief."[88] According to the Jamaat of India, there is nothing wrong with the latter formulation of secularism. In fact, the Jamaat has categorically stated that "in the present circumstances it wants the secular form of government to continue."[89] But the Jamaat is also quite candid in stating that its approval of secularism as a state policy is based on "utilitarian expediency" and should not be construed as its endorsement of "the deeper philosophical connotations" of secularism that are essentially Western in origin "and carry a spirit and a history which are totally foreign to our temper and need."[90] As Mushir-ul-Haq has noted, the Jamaat seems to believe that "the state must remain secular but the Muslims should be saved from secularism."[91]

Jamaat-i-Islami Kashmir

Because of the disputed nature of the state of Jammu and Kashmir, the Jamaat-i-Islami leadership decided to organize two separate Jamaats on the two sides of the cease-fire line, i.e., the Jamaat-i-Islami Jammu and Kashmir on the Indian side and the Jamaat-i-Islami Azad Kashmir on the Pakistani side. The Azad Kashmir Jamaat has operated mostly as an adjunct to the Pakistani Jamaat and has pursued policies and programs of action decided in Lahore. The Jamaat-i-Islami in the Indian-held Kashmir, however, has emerged as a totally independent movement of Kashmiri Muslims whose interests do not usually coincide with those of the Indian Muslim community. While Muslims in India are scatttered and do not form a majority in any of the Indian states, Kashmir is a Muslim majority region with a history of struggle for freedom and self-determination. The Jamaat, like most other Muslim political and religious organizations, has refused to acknowledge the legality of Kashmir's accession to India and has consistently demanded that the future of Kashmir should be decided through a plebiscite, as stipulated in the United Nations resolutions of 1949, 1951, and 1957.

During the first three decades of its existence, the Kashmiri Jamaat operated mainly as a religious revivalist movement and did not actively participate in state politics. Although it publically rejected the political status quo in Kashmir and demanded the right of self-determination for Kashmir's Muslims,[92] it did not join other organizations which were fighting for Kashmir's accession to Pakistan. During this period, the Jamaat leadership in Kashmir believed that the Islamically inspired mobilization of Kashmiri Muslims would ultimately culminate in the establishment of an Islamic state, either as an independent entity or as a unit federated with Pakistan.[93] It was only after the Iranian revolution in 1979 that the Jamaat-i-Islami Kashmir came into the forefront of the political struggle for "the liberation of Kashmir" and for "Islamic revolution." In August 1980, the leader of the student wing of the Jamaat in Kashmir publically called upon Kashmiri youth to work for "an Iranian-type Islamic revolution in Kashmir in order to achieve independence" from India.[94] This call was issued a few days before a proposed international conference to discuss the relevance of the Iranian revolutionary experience for the Kashmiri Muslims. The Indian government reacted swiftly and banned the conference. Foreign guests, including an Iranian official delegation, were sent back from the Srinagar airport. The public protest that followed resulted in the arrest of hundreds of Jamaat workers and youth leaders. Again in 1982, Mrs. Indira Gandhi's government sent the army to curb the Jamaat-sponsored popular movement. More than three hundred Jamaat workers, including its entire top leadership, were arrested under the National Security Act.[95] In 1984, Sayyid Ali Geelani, a prominent leader of the Jamaat, was charged with "conspiracy to annul Kashmir's accession to India through using Islamic religious institutions for this purpose."[96] In October of that year, the Srinagar police arrested seventy-one youth workers of the Jamaat on the charge that they had been distributing pamphlets asking people "to follow the glorious example of Imam Khomeini and bring about an Iranian-type Islamic revolution."[97]

Given the peculiar situation in Kashmir, it is not surprising that among the various wings of the Jamaat-i-Islami in South Asia, it is only the Kashmiri Jamaat that has been heavily influenced by the experience of the Iranian revolution and the Afghan jihad. It is possible that the Jamaat in Kashmir may be using Iranian-style revolutionary rhetoric in order to terrify the Indian authorities and to express widespread anti-India feelings among the Kashmiri Muslims.[98] Whatever the reason, the increasingly assertive political role and the militancy of the Jamaat in Kashmir will have important consequences for the future of both the state of Jammu and Kashmir—as is evident from the violent events of January–February 1990—and the Jamaat itself. The Jamaat is in the forefront of the current upsurge of the freedom movement in Kashmir. Hizb-ul-Jihad, the clandestine guerrilla organization that is challenging the Indian army throughout the valley of Kashmir, consists mainly of the youth wing of the Jamaat.

Conclusion

Islamic neofundamentalism is a modern phenomenon that emerged on the intellectual and sociopolitical scene of the Islamic world during the interwar period and assumed worldwide significance in the post–World War II era. It is inspired by the belief that Islam, as a complete way of life encompassing both religion and politics, is capable of offering a viable alternative to the prevalent secular ideologies of capitalism and socialism and that it is destined to play an important role in the remaking of the contemporary world. Islamic neofundamentalism thus has two distinctive but complementary dimensions: politico-ideological and cultural-religious.[99] At the politico-ideological level, Islamic neofundamentalism is engaged in a war against foreign political domination and economic exploitation and also against cultural influences and ideological intrusions of both Western liberalism and Soviet Marxism. At the cultural-religious level, Islamic neofundamentalism expresses itself in the assertion of a distinctive Islamic cultural identity and recovery of faith based on pristine Islamic beliefs, norms, and practices.

The emergence, growth, ideology, and organization of the Jamaat-i-Islami of the South Asian subcontinent is a prime example of the neofundamentalist trend in contemporary Islam. As we have seen, its program has clustered around four major points: (1) to elucidate the teachings of Islam with reference to the contemporary social, economic, and political situation facing Muslim societies; (2) to create an organization of highly dedicated, disciplined, and righteous people to form an inner core of Islamic revival; (3) to initiate at the level of civil society changes that are conducive to the total transformation of society; and (4) to establish an Islamic state which would implement the Shariʿa and would direct all affairs of the society, economy, and polity in accordance with the Islamic scheme of things. Thus, unlike the Tablighi Jamaat, which focuses its activities on reforming the individual, the Jamaat-i-Islami perceives Islamization as a process of the purification of self, society, and state, a process by which Muslims would consciously accept Islam as their only guide in their daily lives and the state would submit to the sovereignty of Allah.

The Jamaat-i-Islami began its work as a religious revivalist movement in 1941 in India. After independence, it split into two separate organizations, the Jamaat-i-Islami India and the Jamaat-i-Islami Pakistan. While the Indian Jamaat continued to operate as a religious revivalist movement, the Pakistani Jamaat was gradually transformed into a political party as a result of its politico-ideological struggle to make Pakistan into a truly Islamic state. During the past forty-three years, it has fought for an Islamic constitution, Shariʿa, democracy, and a united Pakistan. In the process of its active participation in politics, the Jamaat in Pakistan has shown considerable flexibility and has revised its positions on certain important religiopolitical issues. At a more popular level, its energies have been expended on efforts to "reform the education system on Islamic lines; purify the public media from obscenity, vulgarity and sexual permissiveness; ban the literature based on atheistic ideologies; and abolish the system of coeducation."[100] Since the 1970s, there have been two major pillars of the Jamaat's religiopolitical strategy: (1) increasing its influence in politically and socially salient loci of decision making, and (2) building coalitions with like-minded socioeconomic and political groups and organizations with a view to molding them into more suitable vehicles for achieving Islamic sociopolitical transformation. Taken together, these two strategies represent the Jamaat's efforts to build an Islamic base at the level of civil society and at the same time to seek changes in the state institutions. Although the politics of consensus building has won the Jamaat many new allies and has helped bring it into the mainstream, it has also tended to dilute its distinct revolutionary identity in the process.

The political and economic ideology of the Jamaat remains largely corporatist in its vision of the relationship between civil society and state. The producer should not charge more than a just price for his goods; the laborer should be paid fair wages for his services and should be well treated. Producers and consumers, industrialists and wage laborers, landlords and peasants should fulfill their mutual obligations and thus reap mutual benefits through cooperative efforts and harmonious relations. Their relationships should be governed by Islamic ethical considerations rather than by class conflict. Unlike Sayyid Qutb of Egypt and Ali Shariati of Iran, who emphasized egalitarianism as the basic norm of an Islamic social structure, Maududi's view of an Islamic society is dominated by notions of cohesion, harmony and solidarity.

At the social-structural level, the main thrust of the struggle of the Jamaat-i-Islami has been to shift the locus of power from the traditional oligarchy to middle sectors. Simultaneously, it has provided ways of absorbing the newly mobilized social groups into the prevailing structures and has helped channel certain benefits to them without much real transfer of wealth and power. The Jamaat has thus helped the political system—although without great success in the case of Muhajirs—to accommodate new contenders of power.

Surprisingly, the Jamaat-i-Islami has not been very successful in converting its enormous organizational strength and widespread political influence into electoral support. From 1970 to 1988, four national elections were held in Pakistan. The Jamaat participated in all of them but failed to obtain more than ten seats in any contest, although its share of popular votes was a little higher. The Jamaat's lack of electoral success is due in part to the fact that it has not paid sufficient attention to the rural areas where 70 percent of Pakistan's population lives. Being an urban-based movement of a literate population, its electoral appeal remains extremely narrow. Furthermore, it is the folk and popular form of Islam that dominates the rural areas of Pakistan, and not fundamentalist Islam with its emphasis on strict observance of Shariʿa. Neither is the Jamaat-i-Islami the only champion of Islam in Pakistan's politics; rival religiopolitical organizations such as Jamiat Ulam-i-Islam and Jamiat Ulama-i-Pakistan, the political parties of the traditional ulama, have equal, if not greater, claims on the religiously inclined voters. These two parties of the ulama have in fact challenged the Islamic religious credentials of the Jamaat more vehemently than the secular parties. The sectarian division of the Pakistani Muslim community has also been an important factor in limiting the electoral support of the Jamaat. The Shiʿites, who constitute about 10 percent of Pakistan's population, have generally preferred secular political parties over the Jamaat. Finally, the Jamaat has not paid sufficient attention to the bread-and-butter issues and has thus failed to relate its program for the Islamization of society and economy to the day-to-day problems of the masses.[101] Despite its narrow electoral base, however, the Jamaat's ability to influence policy, especially on Islamic religious issues, and to destabilize any regime in Pakistan remain indisputable.

The rise of Islamic neofundamentalism is often described as as a reaction against the kind of modernizing policies pursued by the secular-minded political elite of Muslim societies in the recent past. The Jamaat-i-Islami, however, makes a distinction between Westernization and modernization. It defines modernization in terms of those processes and institutional innovations that are necessary for the socioeconomic and technological development of society. It does not believe, however, that these developments must necessarily be accompanied by the marginalization of religion and by secularization, by the breakdown of the family and laxity in sexual morality, or for that matter, by the primacy of human reason over God's revelation. In other words, the Jamaat does not consider the sociocultural components of modernization—which it describes as "Westernization"—an integral part of the package needed to achieve the technological and economic development of Muslim societies.

The present leadership of the Jamaat-i-Islami has no clear views on modernity except that Muslim societies must strive toward the development of an autonomous science and technology of their own. None of the Jamaat-i-Islami intellectuals—or for that matter intellectuals of Islamic movements in other Muslim countries—has tried to articulate the issues of modernity beyond its instrumental aspects. It is not surprising, therefore, that when the debate on modernity is extended beyond science, technology, and development to include such issues as pluralism, democracy, tolerance of differing views, and freedom of thought and conscience, their attitude is at best ambivalent. However, given the socioeconomic situation in which the majority of Jamaat members and its support groups find themselves, one can argue that the basic thrust of the Jamaat's struggle is not simple social protest (opposing, for example, having a Pakistani women's field hockey team play in the Asian games)—as the popular stereotype of the Jamaat would suggest—but "reappropriating" the processes of modernization, that is, directing the processses of social change into channels that are easily accessible to its clientele, thereby ensuring their well-being, both materially and morally. Thus, the struggle of the Jamaat-i-Islami members is not merely a reaction against social dislocation which results from processes of socioeconomic change; it is more than anything else an attempt to find a secure place in the new social arrangements. Their selective retrieval of the Islamic past is intended to gain a firm foothold in the present.

The Tablighi Jamaat

The Tablighi Jamaat of the Indo-Pakistan subcontinent constitutes one of the very few grass roots Islamic movements in the contemporary Muslim world. In 1926 the Jamaat began da'wa work in the limited confines of Mewat near Delhi and consisted of a few dozen disciples of Maulana Mohammad Ilyas (1885–1944). Today the movement claims to have influenced millions throughout the Muslim world and the West. Its 1988 annual conference in Raiwind near Lahore, Pakistan, was attended by more than one million Muslims from over ninety countries of the world. The Raiwind International Conference of the Tablighi Jamaat has now become the second-largest congregation of the Muslim World after the hajj. The 1988 Tablighi Jamaat convention in Chicago, Illinois, attracted more than six thousand Muslims, probably the largest gathering of Muslims ever in North America.

Despite its enormous significance as a mass-based da'wa movement that has influenced Asian, African, and Arab Muslims alike, the Tablighi Jamaat has received scant attention in the literature on modern Islamic movements.[102] The available literature on Tablighi Jamaat is mostly in Urdu and consists mainly of inspirational works by its leaders and devotional writings by followers and admirers.[103] No attempt has been made so far to understand the dynamics of its ideology, methods, and impact either in its own terms or with reference to the work of other Islamic movements operating in the same sociopolitical space. This section is thus an attempt to fill a gap in the available literature on contemporary Islamic movements. It discusses the specific circumstances of Tablighi Jamaat's origin in Muslim India of the 1920s, its growth in the Indo-Pakistan subcontinent and beyond in subsequent years, the nature, content, and methodology of its da'wa, and the religiopolitical consequences of its ideological orientation, especially with reference to the conflict between Islam and secularism in Muslim South Asia.

The two decades preceding World War II witnessed the emergence of a number of Muslim socioreligious and political movements in the Indo-Pakistan subcontinent. It was a period of considerable stress and uncertainty, yet pregnant with expectations in the wake of major political and constitutional changes during the declining days of the British raj. The Muslim League, although not yet a major political force to reckon with, was engaged in a relentless struggle, under the leadership of the Qaid-i-Azam, Mohammad Ali Jinnah, to establish its credentials as the only representative of the Indian Muslim community in political affairs. The Khilafat movement, which began in 1920 to protest the liquidation of the Ottoman Empire by the Allied powers under the Treaty of Sèvres, had stirred up the Pan-Islamic sentiments of Indian Muslims to an unprecedented magnitude. Although the movement could not save the Ottoman caliphate from the European powers' machinations and the Arabs' revolt, the vigor and energy generated by the mobilization of Indian Muslims in the name of Pan-Islamism found other channels in the subcontinent. The Khilafat movement helped restore the self-confidence of the Muslims and assert their separate identity. It also taught them how to use modern organizational and publicity techniques for religiopolitical mobilization. The training in organization building, mass-contact, the utilization of the printing press, religiopolitical mobilization, and articulation of shared Islamic symbols helped the aspiring Muslim religious and political leadership to create and serve an all-India Muslim religiopolitical constituency. The beneficiary of the Khilafat movement was not only Mr. Jinnah, the founder of Pakistan; Maulana Maududi, Allama Inayatullah Mashraqi (the founder of the militant Khaksar movement), and Maulana Ilyas (the founder of the Tablighi Jamaat) also benefited from the emotionally charged religious environment of Indian Islam in the late 1920s. The emergence of these new movements unleashed religious and political forces that had the combined effect of directing the Muslim position on a parallel course vis-a-vis Hindus and dividing the two religious communities—a division which ultimately culminated in the creation of the Muslim state of Pakistan.

These developments were also facilitated by the emergence of right-wing Hindu revivalist movements, especially the *shuddhi* (purification) and *sangathan* (consolidation) movements that were founded to reclaim those fallen-away Hindus who had converted to Islam in the past. The special target of the proselytizing movements were the so-called borderline Muslims who had retained many of the customs and religious practices from their Hindu past. The Tabligh movement of Maulana Ilyas, a Muslim missionary response to the militant Hindu efforts of shuddhi and sangathan, should be seen in this proximate context. The essential thrust of the movement was to "purify" the borderline Muslims from their Hindu accretions and to educate them about their beliefs and rituals so that they would not become an easy prey to the Hindu proselytizers. Its aim was thus to bring about a reawakening of faith and a reaffirmation of the religiocultural identity of Muslims. The Tabligh movement, however, did not try to convert non-Muslims to Islam; its exclusive focus remained on making Muslims better and purer Muslims.[104] Its message to the Muslims was simple: *Ae Musalmano Musalman bano* (Oh, you Muslims, be good Muslims.)

The Tablighi Jamaat originated in Mewat, a Gangetic plateau in northern India, inhabited by Muslim peasants who had been converted to Islam long ago but had retained much of their Hindu past.[105] Their birth, marriage, and death rituals and their social customs were based on Hindu culture and had very little to do with orthodox Islam. Many of these Muslims even kept their old Hindu names. Their marriage, divorce, and inheritance practices were governed by local customs rather than by the Shari'a. Their religious life consisted mainly of the celebration of rites of passage, the veneration of saints, and a host of magical and superstitious rites and customs associated with both Muslim and Hindu religious occasions and personalities. Most of them could not correctly recite the shahadah and did not know how to say their daily ritual prayers. Very few villages in Mewat had mosques or religious schools. Their contacts with the mainstream religiocultural centers of Muslim India were minimal.[106]

Maulana Mohammad Ilyas, an Islamic religious scholar in the tradition of the orthodox Deoband Seminary, became aware of the situation in Mewat through his disciples in the area. His initial efforts toward the Islamization of Mewat were essentially in the Deoband tradition, namely, establishing a network of small scale madrasas in order to promote the Qur'anic education among the local population.[107] However, he soon became disillusioned with the madrasa approach to Islamization.

Through his experience with more than one hundred madrasas he had established in Mewat,[108] Maulana Ilyas concluded that these institutions were not adequately equipped to produce Muslim preachers who would be willing to go from door to door and remind people of their Islamic obligations. These institutions remained peripheral to mainstream Mewat society and attracted only a very small number of local students. It was because of his dissatisfaction with the madrasas that Maulana Ilyas resigned from a prestigious teaching position at Mazaharul Uloom Seminary in Saharanpur (Uttar Pradesh) and came to Basti Nizamuddin in the old quarter of Delhi to begin his missionary work. The Tabligh movement was formally launched from this place in 1926.[109] Basti Nizamuddin later became the movement's international headquarters.

The new movement, which later assumed the name of Tablighi Jamaat, met with dramatic success in a relatively short period of time. As a result, many Muslims joined Maulana Ilyas to preach the message of Islam in every town and village of Mewat. The rapid success of his efforts can be seen from the fact that the first Tabilighi conference held in November 1941 in Mewat was attended by twenty-five thousand people. Many of them had walked ten to fifty miles in order to attend the conference.

Maulana Ilyas was neither a charismatic leader like Maulana Mohammad Ali Jauhar of the Khilafat movement nor an outstanding religious scholar like Abul Kalam Azad of the Jamiyat Ulama-i-Hindi, the party of the nationalist ulama. He was not even an effective public speaker like Sayyid Ataullah Shah Bukhari of the Ahrar movement. In fact, he had a stammer and on occasion found it extremely difficult to express himself. Unlike Maududi, Maulana Ilyas did not author a single book in his life. Physically frail and intellectually unassuming, Maulana Ilyas nevertheless had the zeal of a dedicated missionary. His passion to reach out to the Muslim masses and touch them with the message of the Qur'an and Sunna knew no bounds. Like a true missionary, he was persistent, untiring, and wholeheartedly devoted to his cause. During one of his many tours of Mewat, a peasant upon whom he was impressing the importance of leading a religious life struck him. The Maulana, already physically frail, collapsed. When he regained consciousness, he embraced his assailant and said: "You have done your job. Now would you let me do my job and listen to me for a while." As one of his colleagues put it, "Maulana Ilyas, though a mere skeleton, can work wonders when he takes up anything." His eagerness and indomitable determination to reach every Muslim and remind him of his obligations as a believer took precedence over everything else. His passionate concern for the spiritual welfare of his fellow Muslims caused him great anguish. On his deathbed Maulana Ilyas greeted a friend by telling him: "People out there are burning in the fire of ignorance and you are wasting your time here inquiring after my health!" He wanted every Muslim to be on his feet and preaching the message of Islam to others. He exhorted his friends and followers to dedicate their whole lives to this purpose. Once, when no one responded to his call to volunteer for a missionary trip to Kanpur (U.P.), Maulana Ilyas asked one of his friends in the audience what prevented him from going to Kanpur. His friend was suffering from a serious ailment and told Maulana Ilyas that he was almost dying and could not travel. The Maulana said: "If you are dying already, you had better die in Kanpur."[110]

The method adopted by Maulana Ilyas was to organize mobile units of at least ten persons and send them to various villages. These tablighi units, or *jamaats* (groups), would visit a village and invite the local people to assemble in the mosque, if there was one, or at any other meeting place, and would present their message in the form of the following six demands.[111]

1. Recite and know the meaning of the shahadah ("There is no God but Allah and Muhammad is His Prophet"). The idea is not only to teach the Muslims the correct wording and meanings of the shahadah but also to make them realize its implications for their daily behavior. A Muslim who becomes fully conscious of the real import of shahadah will develop complete faith in God and will submit to the commands of the Almighty in everything he does in this world.
2. Say *salaat* (obligatory ritual prayer) correctly and in accordance with its prescribed rituals. Salaat, one of the five pillars of Islam enjoined on all Muslims, is offered five times a day. A Muslim should not only say his daily prayers regularly and earnestly, he should also be mindful of their significance as an act of submission to the will of God.
3. Learn the basic teachings of Islam and to do *dhikr* (ritual remembrance of Allah). Dhikr is intended to inculcate a habit of ceaselessly remembering Allah and to create God-consciousness so that submission to the will of Allah becomes an instinctive impulse.
4. Pay respect to and be polite to fellow Muslims. This is not only a religious obligation but is also a basic prerequisite for effective da'wa work. Good manners, modest demeanor, and soft speech will win more converts than elocution and rhetorical skills. The idea of *ikram-i-Muslim* (respect for

Muslims) is also to recognize and respect the rights of others—the rights of elders, neighbors, the poor, etc.—and the rights of those with whom one may have differences.

5. Take time from worldly pursuits and regularly tour areas away from home in the form of groups *(jamaats)* in order to preach Islam to others. This constitutes the most important and innovative aspect of the Jamaat's approach to daʿwa work. People are usually asked to volunteer for a *chilla* (forty days of daʿwa work), which is the maximum time for the stint of outdoor missionary activity a new member is encouraged to undertake. As Maulana Ilyas put it: "The main advantage of this method is to encourage people to come out of a worldly and static environment in order to enter a new, purer and dynamic one where there is much to foster the growth of religious consciousness. Besides, travel and emigration involve hardship, sacrifice and self-abnegation for the sake of God's cause, and thus entitle one to divine succour."[112]
6. Inculcate honesty and sincerity of purpose in such endeavors. The tasks are to be performed only for the sake of Allah and for serving His cause and not for any worldly gains. It is only the purity of motive and intention that can guarantee the success of one's missionary endeavors.

Hundreds and thousands of groups were organized and sent to almost every village and town in Mewat. As a result of these efforts a majority of the Muslims in Mewat became what might be called "practicing Muslims." Illiterate Mewatis who could not even correctly recite shahadah became teachers and *muballighs* (preachers). The most important impact of the Tabligh movement in Mewat was the Islamization of the social customs. As a result of the efforts of the Jamaat, the Hindu and syncretistic elements of the traditional Mewati culture were replaced by orthodox Islamic practices. Mosques were built and madrasas opened in every corner of Mewat. There was an ambience of religious revival visible everywhere in the area. The program was thus a great success, and by the time Maulana Mohammad Ilyas, who had now become a legend, died in 1944, the Tablighi Jamaat had already extended its activities across the Mewat borders and was penetrating other parts of India as well. Everywhere they went, the Jamaat missionaries not only taught Muslims the basic teachings and injunctions of Islam but also exhorted them to discard non-Islamic sociocultural practices. The process of Islamization generated by the Tabligh movement thus became an important vehicle for the reassertion of Islamic orthodoxy. This in turn strengthened the consciousness of a distinct Muslim identity, the basis of the Two Nation theory and of Pakistan.

After the death of Maulana Ilyas, the Jamaat was led by his son, Maulana Mohammad Yusuf (1917–65), during whose tenure it spread in the entire Indo-Pakistan subcontinent and its missions visited the countries of Southeast Asia, the Middle East, Africa, Europe, and North America.[113] Since then the movement has grown enormously in terms of its numerical strength, though no formal membership counting or registration has ever been undertaken.

Unlike the ulama-led Islamic groups which maintain that in order to be able to preach the message of Islam to others one must be an ʿalim and a model practicing Muslim, the Tablighi Jamaat believes that the daʿwa work itself is a mechanism of reform. The fact that a Muslim falls short of the highest standards of Islamic scholarship or religious and ethical conduct is no reason for him not to preach the message of Islam to others. The Qur'an and Hadith do not require that Muslims must become fully practicing believers before inviting others to Islam.[114] Daʿwa is one of those commandments of God that are "absolute requirements." Muslims therefore cannot postpone the fulfillment of this obligation for any reason or pretext whatsoever.[115]

The secret of Jamaat's success lies in its direct, simple, and personal appeal as well as the limited religious demands which it makes on Muslims. The core of its methodology is to isolate individuals from their familial, occupational, and geographical environment for a period of time, form them into a microcommunity or a group, and as a result of the group's inner dynamics and exclusive internal network processes, organize a system of religious learning and other devotional activities. The assumption underlying this methodology is that people learn by doing and that the very act of their association with, and involvement in, an Islamic group, even if it is only for a short period, will transform their personalities and mold their characters in accordance with the teachings and requirements of Islam. Since the group will not be preoccupied with worldly pursuits, it will devote itself entirely to the learning and preaching of Islam. As a matter of fact, the daily schedule of the group is so tightly arranged that most of the time members remain busy either saying prayers and dhikr or reading the Qur'an and other religious literature and contacting people for purposes of tabligh.

Another important reason for the successful appeal of the Tablighi Jamaat is to be found in its communal structure, a normative system of intense personal relationships among the members that is based on shared religious experiences. Maintaining frequent contacts, traveling together to far-off places for missionary purposes, and listening to each other's testimonies of faith and religious reawakening is a spiritually and socially rewarding experience. The members receive moral-psychological support from each other even as they spread the faith. For many recent migrants from the rural areas to the urban centers in Pakistan, the Jamaat is not only a community of worship and a source of spiritual nourishment but a badly needed substitute for the extended family left behind.

As with the eighteenth-century English evangelical Nonconformists, the primary instrument of the Tablighi Jamaat workers is itinerancy. Itinerant preaching has been the hallmark of the Jamaat and also the most important factor in its growth. This fervent and seemingly unsophisticated approach is ideally suited to attracting semi-educated people from small towns and cities. One need not be a scholar of Islamic theology or a professional orator in order to preach the simple message of the Jamaat to others. A few missionary trips in the company of a senior Jamaat worker are enough to teach most people how to deliver the formulaic speech or to read from a prescribed text. The Jamaat has thus become an important religious training ground for aspiring laymen among the small-town shopkeepers, schoolteachers, government clerks, artisans, and para-professionals in the private sector. The heavy reliance on lay preachers and lay initiative in itinerancy has produced a dynamism of its own and has helped expand the movement throughout the subcontinent and beyond.

The da'wa methodology of the Jamaat by its very nature is predisposed to expansion rather than consolidation or organization building and has mitigated against the usual processes of institutionalization and bureaucratization which so characterize the Jamaat-i-Islami. After the more than sixty years of its existence the Tablighi Jamaat remains a free-floating and informal association with no full-time workers, no elaborate office records, no division of labor, and no institutional network of functional departments and branches. This is despite the fact that its work has expanded to more than one hundred countries. There is an emir, who is elected for life by the elders of the Jamaat, and a shoora (consultative body) which advises the emir. However, there are no formal decision-making procedures. In fact, decisions are sometimes made on the basis of dreams and *basharat* (inspirations).[116] Thus, the Jamaat has been successful in maintaining the spirit of informality and spontaneity that gave birth to the movement in the 1920s. However, in the absence of a formal, bureaucratic organization, the strict discipline of the routine of missionary activities required of the faithful gives the Tablighi Jamaat its strength and vitality. What is lacking in formal organization is amply compensated for by religious discipline.

In some other respects, however, the Jamaat has gradually become a closed system. There has been no change in the da'wa methods first introduced by Maulana Ilyas more than sixty years ago.[117] Furthermore, the Tablighi Jamaat workers and followers are discouraged from reading any books other than those written by Maulana Mohammad Zakriya and Maulana Manzoor Noamani, the two scholars whose works are prescribed as texts for all Tablighi workers. A Tablighi worker reads very little outside the prescribed Tablighi curriculum, which consists of seven essays. These essays by Zakriya have been compiled in a single volume entitled *Tablighi Nisab* (Tablighi curriculum) and are now required reading for every Tablighi worker.[118] The essays deal with life stories of the companions of the Prophet and the virtues of prayer, dhikr, charity, hajj, and salutation *(darood)* to the Prophet and the Qur'an. Written in a simple and lucid Urdu and based mostly on inspirational but historically suspect traditions, *Tablighi Nisab* is probably the only book that the majority of the Tablighi workers would consider worth reading. The seven essays constitute the basic source material for the formulaic speech delivered by the Tabligh missionaries before the assemblies throughout the world. "Tablighi work is not a book," says Maulana Manzoor Noamani, "it is action." The disdain for *kitabi 'ilm* (book knowledge) is shared by most Tablighi leaders and workers, and they remain deeply suspicious of scholarship, especially the Islamic religious scholarship that gained popularity as a result of the intellectual efforts of Muslim reformers and modernists with their emphasis on rational explanations of Islamic religious beliefs and practices. The Jamaat believes that people will become good Muslims not by reading books but by receiving the message through personal contacts and by active participation in da'wa work. The anti-intellectual approach of the Tabligh movement stands in sharp contrast to the approach of the Jamaat-i-Islami, whose daʿwa work is based almost entirely on books and pamphlets.

As a true heir to the Deoband tradition, the Tabligh movement is thoroughly orthodox. Although it is not as militant as the Wahabi school of the Ahl-i-Hadith, its rejection of popular forms of religion such as veneration of saints, visiting shrines, and observing the rituals associated with popular Sufism, is categorical. From this perspective, the Jamaat can be considered to be the continuation of the reformist-fundamentalist tradition of Shah Waliyullah of Delhi (1703–62) with its approval of purified Sufism combined with the rigid observance of the Sunna. One can argue, therefore, that the phenomenon known in the history of Indian Islam as "the revival of the orthodoxy" finds its latest expression in the program and activities of the Tablighi Jamaat. The Tabligh workers are extremely rigid in following the orthodox rituals and do not approve of what they consider the "modernist" and lax attitudes of the Jamaat-i-Islami. Unlike their counterparts in the Jamaat-i-Islami, the Tabligh workers emphasize both the form and the spirit of the religious practices. Their insistence on conformity to Shariʿa is uncompromising. They strongly believe in the seclusion of women and regard any secular education of girls as unnecessary and un-Islamic. They are also very particular about preserving all outward forms of Islamic culture and following the Sunna of the Prophet to the letter. Most of them, for example, keep the beard to its proper Shariʿa length, wear their trousers above their ankles, and cover their heads.[119]

Notwithstanding its conservative orientation and rigid adherence to the orthodoxy, the Tablighi Jammat does not look unfavorably at modern secular education. As a matter of fact, many of the young Tabligh Jamaat followers in India, Pakistan, and Malaysia are graduates of modern educational institutions, including professional schools. Because of their implicit acceptance of the separation of what is religious and what is secular, the Tabligh workers do not believe that their pursuit of secular education will in any way affect their religious beliefs and practices. The two realms remain distinctly separate and compartmentalized.

The exclusive focus of attention of the Tablighi Jamaat is the individual. In the belief that an individual can sustain his moral character even in the context of a hostile social environment, the Jamaat does not seem to have concerned itself with issues of social significance including the reform of political and social institutions. The Jamaat insists that a political formulation of the basic Islamic beliefs and concepts undermines the authentic religious core of Islamic values and robs them of their spiritual significance. Emphasis on Islam as a political ideology threatens the integrity of the traditional meanings attributed to the basic concepts of Islam. It is not that the Tablighi Jamaat does not regard the issue of reforming society and its institutions as important; it is that it wants to achieve this goal through the education and reform of individuals. The Tablighi Jamaat maintains that nations and social systems do not have an independent, separate existence; they exist only by virtue of the individuals who form them. Therefore if a nation or a society is to be changed, the reform effort must begin with the individual and not at the level of political structures.

In fact, the Tablighi Jamaat detests politics and does not involve itself in any issues of sociopolitical significance. It has always taken a neutral or rather indifferent stance about the most deeply divisive sociopolitical issues. Even in controversies relating to the sociopolitical role of Islam in Pakistan and the future of Muslim minority in India, the Jamaat has remained apparently unconcerned. Of course, this stance was helpful to the Jamaat in at least one respect: while other Islamic parties were facing opposition by secular forces and being harassed by various regimes for their Islamic activities, there was little opposition to the Tablighi Jamaat. As a matter of fact, the Ayub Khan regime in Pakistan in the 1960s issued secret memos to government officials ordering them to desist from participating in the Jamaat-i-Islami activities or lose their jobs, and even spied on those who were found reading Maududi's commentary on the Qur'an. At the same time, the Tablighi Jamaat received encouragement from official circles. Instructions were issued to the State Bank of Pakistan to grant liberally the foreign exchange requested by the Tablighi groups bound for foreign countries. Similarly, while the Jamaat-i-Islami public meetings were disrupted and even fired upon by the security forces, the government went so far as to schedule special trains from major cities of Pakistan to convey people to the Tablighi Jamaat's annual conferences in Raiwind. A former official of the Ayub Khan government confirms that the decision to patronize the activities of Tablighi Jamaat was taken at the cabinet level on direct instructions from the president in order to "neutralize the influence of the Jamaat-i-Islami and other politically activist ulama groups."[120]

A similar situation also prevailed in India, where the secular government of Mrs. Indira Gandhi looked favorably at the activities of the Tablighi Jamaat. It is said that workers of the Tablighi Jamaat could obtain exit visas and foreign exchange with no problems during the 1975–77 emergency, while there were severe restrictions on foreign travel by the Jamaat-i-Islami activists.[121]

The critics of Tablighi Jamaat, especially those associated with the Jamaat-i-Islami, ask who has gained as a result of the political apathy and neutrality of the Tablighi Jamaat—Islam or secularism? Taking an indifferent and neutral stance during a decisive conflict between Islam and anti-Islamic forces, these critics point out, deprived the Islamic forces of the potential reinforcement that could have come from the large contingents of the Tablighi Jamaat, and as a consequence helped the cause of the anti-Islamic forces. "It was surprising, and rather painful," as one Jamaat-i-Islami leader put it, "to see the Tablighi Jamaat completely indifferent during the conflicts on such crucial issues as the introduction of an Islamic constitution in Pakistan in the early fifties, Islam versus socialism during 1969–71, the communal riots in India in the 1970s and 1980s, the Khatam-e-Nabuwwat movement (against the Ahamdiya) of 1974, and the Nizam-e-Mustafa movement of 1977."[122]

The Tablighi Jamaat leaders defend their position by saying that it is only by eschewing political debates and conflicts that the Jamaat has been able to focus its attention on influencing the faithful and reawakening their spiritual consciousness, which is the core of religion. The apolitical program of the Jamaat has helped it to operate freely and without official hindrance, thus enabling it to reach a large number of government officials and to educate them about Islamic beliefs, ethics, and practices.

It has also spared the Jamaat from the vicissitudes of the conflicting ideological orientations of the various political regimes in Pakistan. Political neutrality is thus considered as an asset to da'wa work. Jamaat leaders point to the Islamic political groups who, "inspired by a purely political interpretation of Islam," raise the slogans of Islamic revolution against their respective governments and thus invite the wrath of the rulers and create conditions of government hostility against Islam. If Islamic groups would refrain from their "erroneous politicking" and instead preach the message of Islam in nonpolitical terms and in a peaceful manner, they would serve the cause of Islam much more effectively.[123]

The Tablighi Jamaat leaders also believe that true religious faith can be maintained only in freedom from politics. Politics for them is a realm infested with corruption. A senior Tablighi worker from Pakistan summed up the Jamaat's attitude toward politics thus: "In order to be successful in politics, one has to tell lies, to cheat and deceive others. One has to indulge in double-dealing and dishonesty. Those who are engaged in politics, whether they call themselves Islamic or secular, are always ready to compromise on their principles and values in the name of pragmatism, political strategy, tactics, or whatever. The truth is that one cannot remain in politics for long without compromising on the moral values that are so dear to Islam."[124]

While Islamists in Iran, Pakistan, and Egypt consider the acquisition of political power and the establishment of an Islamic state a basic prerequisite for creating a truly Islamic society, the Tablighi Jamaat believes that political power does not in itself ensure the effective organization of an Islamic social order. It insists that political change must be preceded by, and consistently augmented with, the moral transformation of individuals and society.[125] Maulana Wahiduddin Khan argues that Muslims have been called upon by the Qur'an and the Prophet to organize themselves for religious purposes. An Islamic social organization is thus essentially a religiously based organization and is not necessarily an Islamic state. The task of organizing Muslims for religious purposes such as regular attendance at prayers, collection and distribution of zakat, and the systematic propagation of Islam need not depend on the establishment of an Islamic government or a state; these are obligations that have to be undertaken by individual Muslims. Muslims may form local-level religious organizations and appoint community leaders to supervise the observance of religious duties, but the aims of such organizations will be fulfilled only if they are carried out without the coercive and external power of the state. "A social order," Wahiduddin maintains, "to be truly Islamic, must evince itself in a spontaneous system of organization, such as we see in a mosque."[126] Thus, the socioreligious order of Islam is not contingent upon the acquisition of political power; on the contrary, if the socioreligious organization of Islam has not developed voluntarily and has been imposed upon the people by the coercive apparatus of the state, it will have no religious value whatsoever.[127]

Arguing against the Jamaat-i-Islami position, which maintains that the establishment of an Islamic political order is a religious obligation, Wahiduddin asserts that Islamic principles enunciated in the Qur'an are of two categories: objectives and duties. Objectives include those imperatives which have to be followed and observed despite the circumstances. Duties, on the other hand, are to be discharged only when one has the requisite wherewithal. Being grateful to God, for example, is an objective to be followed irrespective of circumstantial contingencies. It is a requirement inherent in an Islamic scheme and spirit of life. Charity, on the other hand, is a duty which must be discharged only when a person has sufficient wealth. A less fortunate member of the community is not expected to strive to make money at all costs simply in order to be able to implement divine commandments with regard to charity and alms-giving.[128] It is obvious therefore that while "on all occasions and in all circumstances, we must be thankful to God," the commandments regarding money "will be applicable to us only when God has already granted it" to us.[129]

In Wahiduddin's view political power and government can be categorized as "matters of duties rather than as objectives" to be achieved at all costs. That is, if Muslims enjoy position of power, it becomes their duty to exercise that power in accordance with the teachings of the Qur'an and Hadith. Political power is thus "a gift of God bestowed by Him at His own discretion when and where He wills."[130] Once blessed with political power, Muslims must rule according to God's commandments. Yet Wahiduddin notes that the verbal forms used in the Qur'an on the wielding of political power are conditional. The policy implication of this formulation for the Indian Muslims is obvious: since Muslims in India are neither in possession of political power nor in a position to achieve it in the foreseeable future, those portions of the Qur'anic teachings that deal with government, state, and politics do not apply to them and will remain suspended. Moreover, simply to be able to fulfill their duties as rulers, Muslims are not required to wage a struggle to achieve political power, just as a poor man is not expected to make money at all costs in order to be able to pay the almstax.

Even on the issue of communal riots, an almost everyday affair in the Indian context, the Tablighi Jamaat has refrained from joining other Islamic organizations. It disapproves of even lodging complaints and protesting the frequent anti-Muslim actions of the local law enforcement authorities: the very act of complaining against police behavior or protesting against the majority community is contrary to the way of the Prophet. Muslims should refrain from reacting to these provocations; instead, they should "pray for the guidance of those who offer provocations" and leave the matter to God.[131] The Prophet's companions, Maulana Wahiduddin reminds his fellow Indian Muslims, "never marched in processions, burned homes, destroyed property or even shouted slogans in the streets against non-Muslims."[132] What Indian Muslims need is the preservation and strengthening of their religiocultural identity. For this they do not need to launch one demand movement after another. Their religiocultural identity will be saved by the strength generated from within themselves. Thus the only solution to the problems faced by Indian Muslims is to look inward to their own weaknesses, rectify the moral lapses in their personal behavior, and realize their potential as bearers of the universal message of Islam. They should raise themselves above the petty concerns of "material injustices and should not entertain any bitterness, envy or anger against the majority community."[133] It is only through nurturing moral qualities that Muslims will be able to build "a protective barrier" against all kinds of conspiracies and plots.[134] (Wahiduddin applies this logic to the Palestinian problem as well. Despite all the efforts, wars, petrodollars, and human sacrifice Muslims have not succeeded in freeing the holy land because "Muslims have not performed the most important of all the tasks set for them by God: they have not communicated the divine message to all nations of the world. . . . The Palestinian question, as well as other problems affecting the Muslim community, can be resolved only if the realization comes to the Muslims that they must once again take up their duty," i.e., to present themselves to others as "God's witness on earth.")[135] All else, including international conflicts, become secondary and peripheral to this duty. In fact these conflicts become obstacles in the way of Islamic da'wa. Muslims are therefore asked to unilaterally put all their worldly conflicts with other nations aside and concentrate on spreading the message of Islam in a peaceful and friendly manner. Only in an atmosphere of peace between Muslims and other nations will non-Muslims be favorably disposed to the Islamic message and give it serious thought.[136] Hence, the Tablighi Jamaat leaders strongly disapprove of the way politically oriented Islamists present Islam as a rival to contemporary secular political and economic ideologies such as capitalism and socialism. Referring to often-repeated statements by Islamic political groups that the world of today is in need of a "new order," Maulana Wahiduddin remarks that "the world has got all the order it needs." Rather, it is "food for soul" and "spiritual nourishment" which mankind requires.[137]

During its formative phase, the Tablighi Jamaat did not exhibit the intense antipathy to politics that became its trademark in the postpartition period. Although Maulana Ilyas kept himself completely aloof from politics and focused his program of action exclusively on making Muslims aware of their religious obligations, he never criticized Islamic groups actively engaged in politics. On the contrary, he maintained extremely cordial relations with Maulana Husain Ahmad Madni and other ulama of the Deoband school whose political organization, Jamiyat Ulama-i-Hind, an aggressively anti-British and pro-Indian National Congress group, was active in Indian politics. Maulana Ilyas had equally warm relations with the pro-Pakistan faction of the Deoband school led by Maulana Ashraf Ali Thanvi. However, he refused to take a position on the issue of a united India vs. a separate Muslim state of Pakistan, for the obvious reasons that this would distract his movement from its main religious tasks and would also create dissension within its ranks. Maulana Ilyas was of the view that the Tabligh movement and politically oriented Islamic groups, although operating in two different spheres, were complementing each other's work. Hence there should be no competition and rivalry between them.

The change from an apolitical to an explicitly antipolitical stance of the Tablighi Jamaat came about as a result of three developments: the traumatic experience of the partition of India which lead to death and misery for millions, the post-partition Indian situation in which Muslim politics came to be seen as a lingering remnant of Muslim separatism, and the increasing popularity of the politically oriented Jamaat-i-Islami in Pakistan among the refugees from India, especially during its vigorous and popular campaign for an Islamic constitution in the 1950s. This was also the period when the Tabligh movement was sending exploratory missions to Southeast Asia,

England, and the United States. It was believed that a rearticulation of the movement's policy explicitly rejecting the legitimacy of political action as a means of achieving Islamic goals would facilitate its work in those countries and would help alleviate the apprehensions of the host governments about its activities.

Harry Hiller has argued that fundamentalists tend to renounce politics because either they do not regard political change as a valued end or they believe that political change is not attainable because of the lack of power or other necessary resources.[138] The Tablighi Jamaat has abstained from participating in politics, arguing that Islamic political change is not attainable in a Hindu-majority state. But the Jammat also justifies its repudiation of politics on the ground that compared to much more important religious concerns, political involvement is a low-level activity and hence not worthy of the time, efforts, and energy of an Islamic movement. In contrast to the Tablighi Jamaat's view of politics as a morally inferior activity, the Jamaat-i-Islami regards politics as a form of *'ibada* (worship) if pursued for the cause of Islam.

Although the Tablighi Jamaat has attempted to isolate itself from social and political issues and to confine itself to moral reform and the religious uplift of the individual, it must be remembered that individuals do not live in a vacuum. As Daniel Levine has argued, the connection between individual choices and social consequences must not be overlooked.[139] Individual choices aggregate into social choices and thus have political consequences. "For religion and for politics, whether the original choice is neutrality or activism, the result is equally political."[140] From this perspective, even the most profoundly spiritual goals of believers will have political consequences.[141]

Thus one can argue that the Jamaat's apolitical stance has had important political consequences. In India, for example, its view of religion as a personal and private affair of the individual was conducive to the acceptance of secularism among Indian Muslims. The Jammat has flourished in the secular political system of India and has lent support and legitimacy to secularism through its doctrines. In Pakistan, Bangladesh, and to a certain extent, Malaysia, it has depoliticized a large number of religiously inclined people by casting them as itinerant preachers. As Seymour Lipset has argued, fundamentalist religion "drains off" energies that would probably have otherwise been channeled into political action.[142] In the case of the Tablighi Jamaat, the directing of religious energies into nonpolitical outlets tended to impair severely the efforts of religiopolitical groups, such as the Jamaat-i-Islami, to expand their recruitment and support base. Furthermore, the Tablighi Jamaat's nonpolitical approach to the Islamization of society has posed a serious challenge to the Islamic legitimacy of the politicized alternative offered by the Jamaat-i-Islami and other religiopolitical parties.

The Tablighi Jamaat has also not been completely free from political controversies and doctrinal debates with political consequences. For example, the fatwa issued by its leaders, especially Maulana Mohammad Zakriya, against Maududi and his Jamaat-i-Islami has been a major source of hostility between the two Islamic movements since the 1950s. Furthermore, the Tablighi Jamaat leaders consider the Jamaat-i-Islami's approach to religion as to be politically motivated and devoid of any spiritual content.

They accuse Maududi of interpreting Islam as a worldly ideology which is concerned only with the mundane affairs of politics and the state. In contrast, the Jamaat-i-Islami, whose ideology is based on the concept of Islam as a "complete way of life," considers the Tablighi Jamaat to be a "pocket edition" of Islam and accuses it of making an un-Islamic distinction between religion and politics. The political neutrality of the Tabligh workers is interpreted by the Jamaat-i-Islami as their willingness not only to operate within the existing socioeconomic and political conditions but by their aquiescence, to help perpetuate and strengthen, if not legitimize, them. Besides these doctrinal differences, the hostility between the two major Islamic movements can also be explained by the fact that their recruitment base and constituency of support are approximately the same. The Tablighi Jamaat tends to recruit its itinerant workers from the same social groups which also constitute the main targets of the Jamaat-i-Islami's ideological appeal.

The Brelvi ulama and their political organization, the Jamiyat 'Ulama-i-Pakistan, consider the Tablighi Jamaat their main adversary in the rural areas and small towns of India and Pakistan. The puritanical and reformist zeal of Tablighi workers is regarded as a great threat to the popular and folk-oriented Islam of the Brelvi school. The Brelvi ulama have therefore written extensively against the Tablighi Jamaat, describing it as a popular version of the Wahabi ideas of the Deoband school. Tablighi Jamaat assemblies are completely banned in the mosques controlled by the Brelvi ulama and their followers.

Many of the prominent Deobandi ulama and the leaders of their political party, the Jamiyat Ulama-i-Islam, have been closely associated with the Tabligh movement. Their close relations are based on both doctrinal affinity and institutional affiliations between the Deoband school and the Saharanpur school—the later being the intellectual center of the Tabligh movement. As a result of the close relationship, the Tablighi Jamaat workers have consistently voted for the Jamiyat Ulama-i-Islam candidates in Pakistani elections and have thus contributed significantly to the successful showing of the Jamiyat in the North-West Frontier Province and Baluchistan.

Recently the Tablighi Jamaat and some of its leaders were also mired in a controversy with the Shi'ite ulama on the question of the Islamicity of the Iranian revolution. As with most political issues, the Tablighi Jamaat has not taken any official position on the Islamic revolution of Iran. However, two of its most prominent spiritual guides and ardent supporters have published devastating critiques of the Iranian revolution, saying that it has nothing to do with Islam.[143] They accused Imam Khomeini of being an "archsectarian Shia" out to sow the seeds of dissension within the umma and destroy the solidarity of the Islamic world. They declared Imam Khomeini to be outside the pale of Islam.[144] They describe the philosophy of the Iranian revolution as an "unmitigated hatred" which has no relationship to Islamic principles. Maulana Wahiduddin Khan also characterizes the Iranian revolution as a triumph of hatred and accuses the Iranian religiopolitical leadership of driving the world away from Islam by their "macabre witlessness" and vengeful policies that could only come from "sick minds."[145]

Conclusion

The Tablighi Jamaat has been one of the most influential religious movements in twentieth-century Islam. It has reached millions of Muslims in South Asia, Southeast Asia, Africa, the Middle East, Europe, and North America. The apolitical stance of the movement has helped it to penetrate and operate without hindrance in Muslim and non-Muslim societies where politically activist Islamic groups face severe restrictions. It has truly become an international Islamic movement.

With specific reference to South Asia, one can argue that besides depoliticizing an important segment of the religiously inclined population, the major impact of the activities of the Tablighi Jamaat has been the rapid religious mobilization of a large number of Muslims in the subcontinent. Gathering approximately a million people for a three-day conference in a small town of Punjab, Pakistan, every year is an achievement such that few other movements can boast of. This large-scale religious mobilization has profound consequences for the religious situation of the subcontinent. First of all, a large number of previously quiescent and inert Muslims have been motivated to come forward and actively participate in the propagation of Islam. Second, the Jamaat has created a nucleus of trained religious personnel around which a large population can be mobilized and trained for Islamic da'wa. Third, the da'wa methodology and approach of the Tablighi Jamaat has not only tended to blur the distinction between the ulama and lay preachers but has also effectively challenged the monopoly of the ulama on Islamic missionary work.[146] Fourth, and possibly more important from the point of view of the long-term prospects of religious establishments in South Asian Islam, the Jamaat has relinked the Muslim masses with Islamic religious institutions. As a result, it has helped reassert the authority of orthodoxy and brought it closer to the common people.

Since the beginning of Muslim rule in India, the ulama had remained permanently allied to an elite north Indian Muslim culture; hence, the orthodox forms of Islam had not penetrated deeply into the daily lives of the Muslim masses, who continued to cherish the customs and practices they had inherited from their Hindu past. Since the nineteenth-century Mujahideen movement of Sayyid Ahmad Shaheed (1786–1831) and the Faraidhi movement of Haji Shariatullah, the Tabligh movement is the most important attempt to bridge the gap between orthodox Islam and the popular, syncretic religious practices that are prevalent among the Muslim masses. However, the Jamaat's emphasis on the devotional and pietistic aspect of religion differs considerably from orthodoxy's single-minded concern with doctrinal hairsplitting, legalism, and institutional forms of religion. The Tabligh movement can thus be characterized as what Jaroslav Pelikan has called, in another context, "the affectional transposition of doctrine."

Notes

1. *Takbeer* (Karachi), 23 November 1989.

2. *Mashriq* (Lahore), 6 November 1989.

3. Ijaz Shafi Gilani, "Fundamentalist Political Groups in Muslim Countries" (1975), p. 4.

4. Ibid.

5. Stephen Hay and I. H. Qureshi, eds., *Sources of Indian Tradition,* vol. 2 (New York: Columbia University Press, 1958), p. 187.

6. Gilani, "Fundamentalist Groups," pp. 4–5.

7. Mustansir Mir, "Some Features of Mawdudi's Tafhim al-Qur'an," *American Journal of Islamic Social Sciences* 2, no. 2 (1985): 244.

8. Khurshid Ahmad and Zafar Ishaq Ansari, *Islamic Perspectives* (Leicester: Islamic Foundation, 1979), p. ix.

9. Ibid.

10. *An Introduction to the Jamaat-i-Islami Pakistan* (Lahore: Jamaat-i-Islami, 1978), p. 5.

11. Gilani, "Fundamentalist Groups," p. 15.

12. Ibid.

13. Several English translations of *Tafhim-al-Qur'an* are available. The latest and most competent English rendering is Zafar Ishaq Ansari, *Towards Understanding the Qur'an* (Leicester: Islamic Foundation, 1988).

14. *Introduction to the Jamaat-i-Islami Pakistan,* pp. 3–4.

15. Leonard Binder, *Religion and Politics in Pakistan* (Berkeley: University of California Press, 1962), p. 103.

16. Ibid, p. 99.

17. Gilani, "Fundamentalist Groups," p. 16.

18. Binder, *Religion and Politics,* pp. 302–3.

19. Mohammad Ayub Khan, *Speeches and Statements,* vol. 4 (Karachi: Government of Pakistan, Department of Films and Publications, 1964), p. 78.

20. Quoted in Edgar A. Schuler and Kathryn R. Schuler, *Public Opinion and Constitution Making in Pakistan 1958–1962* (East Lansing: Michigan State University Press, 1967), p. 119.

21. Karl von Vorys, *Political Development in Pakistan* (Princeton: Princeton University Press, 1967), pp. 259–60.

22. See the speech of Maulana Maududi in November 1964 in Karachi, published in a pamphlet, *Ayub Khan Ka Daur-e-Hakumat* (Ayub Khan's rule) (Karachi: Jamaat-i-Islami, 1964), pp. 2–14.

23. *Pakistan Observer,* 3 October 1964, quoted in Karl von Vorys, *Political Development,* p. 175.

24. Gilani, "Fundamentalist Groups," p. 18. The Jamaat-i-Islami once again returned to its original position in 1989 when it opposed Prime Minister Benazir Bhutto because, among other things, "Islam does not approve of a woman as the head of an Islamic government or state."

25. *Morning News,* 1 June 1970.

26. Gilani, "Fundamentalist Groups," p. 18.

27. Ibid, p. 19.

28. Raja Shafqat Hayat, "The Role of Students in National Politics," (M.A. thesis, Punjab University, 1979), pp. 67–69; see also the weekly *Lail-o-Nihar,* August 1974, pp. 11–17, and September 1974, pp. 15–21; and the weekly *Asia,* June 1974, pp. 21–28.

29. *Hamqadam* (1980): 10.

30. Data collected from *Jasarat* (Karachi), various issues from 15 to 25 November 1975.

31. *In Pakistan* (New York) 9, no. 6 (September 1976).

32. *Jasarat,* 28 March 1976.

33. *Introduction to Jamaat-e-Islami Pakistan,* p. 10.

34. Maulana Maududi's speech in Lahore in 1978, published later in *Arabia: The Islamic World Review* (March 1984): 76.

35. *Zindagi,* 19–25 January 1979.

36. Abul Ala Maududi, *Khutbat* (Sermons) (Lahore: Islamic Publications, 1957).

37. Javed Ansari, "Jamaat-i-Islami and the Politics of Pakistan," *Arabia: The Islamic World Review* (December 1985): 64.

38. Abul Ala Maududi, "How to Establish Islamic Order in the Country?" reprinted in *The Universal Message* (May 1983): 9.

39. Ibid., pp. 9–10.

40. A Jamaat-i-Islami leader told me in an interview in 1983, "We oppose General Zia with our tongues but support him with our hearts."

41. Javed Ansari, "Jamaat-i-Islami," p. 64.

42. Ibid.

43. Trevor Fishlock, "Fundamentalists put universities in peril," *London Times*, 6 September 1982.

44. *Arabia: The Islamic World Review* (April 1984): 27.

45. *Jasarat* , 19 June 1988.

46. Javed Ansari, "Jamaat-i-Islami," p. 64.

47. Mir, "Some Features," p. 243.

48. Abul Ala Maududi, *Come Let Us Change This World!* (Washington, D.C.: 1972), p. 102–3.

49. Ibid, pp. 104–5.

50. Mir, "Some Features," p. 241.

51. Hamid Enayat, *Modern Islamic Political Thought,* p. 102.

52. Abul Ala Maududi, *Tafhim-al-Qur'an,* vol. 2., p. 422, quoted in Mir, "Some Features," p. 242.

53. The word *iqama* used in the Qur'an, according to Maududi, means not only that we should simply preach the religion—as the Tablighi Jamaat does—but that we must "act upon it, promote it and actually enforce it" so that "the entire administration of the state could be run under its supervision." (Mir, "Some Features," pp. 242–43).

54. Abul Ala Maududi, "Islamic Government," reprinted in *Asia,* 20 September 1981, p. 9.

55. Ibid.

56. Ahmad and Ansari, *Islamic Perspectives,* p. 280.

57. *Jamaat-i-Islami Key Mâashi Program ka ek Ijmali Khaka* (An outline of the Jamaat-i-Islami's economic program) (Karachi: Jamaat-i-Islami, 1969), p. 5.

58. In a booklet written more than forty years ago, Maududi defined the nature of the economic problem of man as follows: "In order to sustain and advance civilization, how to arrange economic distribution so as to keep all men supplied with necessities and to see that every individual is provided with the opportunities adequate to the development of his personality."Abdul Ala Maududi, *Economic Problem of Man and Its Islamic Solution* (Reprint, Lahore: Islamic Publications, 1960), p. 12.

59. These figures were given by the secretary general of the Jamat-i-Islami in the report which he presented at the conference of the Jamaat held in Lahore in November 1989; see *Takbeer,* 23 November 1989, p. 22.

60. Ibid.

61. Ibid.

62. Most of these twenty-five founding members of the IJT later rose to positions of political and intellectual leadership in the Jamaat-i-Islami.

63. *Annual Report* (Lahore: Islami Jamiat-e-Talaba Pakistan, 1988), pp. 4–10.

64. Ibid. p. 5–8; see also *Pakistan,* January 1984, pp. 26–30.

65. *Islami Jamiat-e-Talaba Pakistan: Panoramic View* (Karachi: Islami Jamiat-e-Talaba, 1981), pp. 13–14.

66. A Deobandi *'alim,* in an anti-Maududi speech, once raised two critical questions: "From which *madrasa* did he (Maududi) graduate? Who was his teacher?"

67. Author's survey, September 1975.

68. Author's survey, March 1983.

69. Data compiled from the list of the Jamaat candidates for February 1985 elections.

70. Leonard Binder, *The Ideological Revolution in the Middle East* (New York: Wiley, 1964), p. 43.

71. Ibid., p. 45.

72. For a perceptive analysis of the economic policies of Zulfikar Ali Bhutto, see Shahid Javed Burki, *Pakistan under Bhutto* (New York: St. Martin's, 1980). Also, see Khalid B. Sayeed, *Pakistan: Direction of Political Change* (New York: Praeger Publishers, 1980).

73. Khurshid Ahmad, "Economic Development in an Islamic Framework," in Khurshid Ahmad, ed., *Studies in Islamic Economics* (Leicester: Islamic Foundation, 1980), p. 177.

74. Ahmad and Ansari, *Islamic Perspectives,* pp. 378–80.

75. Ibid, p. 381.

76. A detailed discussion on the issue of Islamic radicalism in Pakistan can be found in my chapter, "Pakistan," in Shireen T. Hunter, ed., *The Politics of Islamic Revivalism* (Bloomington: Indiana University Press, 1988), pp. 230–46.

77. *The Bangladesh Observer*, 23 April 1977.

78. Emajuddin Ahmed, "Current Trends of Islam in Bangladesh," *Economic and Political Weekly,* 18 June 1983, p. 117.

79. *The Message International,* January–March 1989, p. 4.

80. *The Bangladesh Observer,* 13 November 1988, p. 1.

81. *The Message International,* January–March 1989, p. 5.

82. *Radiance,* 3–9 November 1985, p. 14.

83. Ibid.

84. "Jamaat Campaigns for Harmony in Karnataka," *Arabia: The Islamic World Review* (May 1984): 87.

85. For my analysis in this section, I have drawn on my previous work, in particular, my "Islamic Revival in Pakistan," in James W. Bjørkman, ed., *Fundamentalism, Revivalists, and Violence in South Asia* (Riverdale, Md.: Riverdale, 1988), pp. 88–106.

86. Ahmad and Ansari, *Islamic Perspective,* pp. 378–81.

87. Speech by Maulana Abul Lais Islahi, emir Jamaat-i-Islami India at the Muslim Students Association Convention, Indianapolis, Indiana, on 31 August 1983.

88. *Introducing The Jamaat-e-Islami Hind* (Delhi: Jamaat-e-Islami, 1971), pp. 31–32.

89. Ibid., p. 32.

90. Ibid., p. 32.

91. Mushirul Haq, *Islam in Secular India* (Simla: Indian Institute of Advanced Study, 1972), p. 12.

92. *Ayeena,* 15 August 1984, p. 6; and *Aftab,* 4 December 1984, p. 7.

93. Interview with Mr. Ghulam Nabi Fai, executive director, Kashmiri-American Council, 12 December 1986.

94. *Arabia: The Islamic World Review* (January 1985): 13.

95. Ibid (August 1984): 23.

96. *Srinagar Times,* 14 August 1984; *Aftab,* 1 February 1984.

97. *Roshni,* 20 October 1984.

98. Ghulam Nabi Khayal, "Valley of Unrest," *Illustrated Weekly of India,* 20 October 1985.

99. Abdul Rahman Momin, "Islamic Fundamentalism," (1988), p. 6.

100. This is a direct quote from Maulana Fateh Mohammad, emir of the Punjab Jamaat, as reported in *Jang,* 17 July 1982, p. 1.

101. An example of this tendency can be seen in the campaign speeches of Mian Tufail Mohammad during the 1970 elections. Mian Tufail, who ran for election for the National Assembly from an urban constituency of Lahore with acute problems of sewage and waste disposal, continued to deliver lengthy discourses on the evils of dialectical materialism and the merits of the Islamic philosophy of history to his mostly illiterate constituents. Needless to say, his opponent, who promised to get more trucks for waste disposal, was elected.

102. The recent interest in the Islamic resurgence in the West has produced numerous books and journal articles on the

contemporary Islamic movements. None of these, however, discusses the significance, role, and impact of the Tablighi Jamaat.

103. For example, Mohammad Ayub Qadri, *Tablighi Jamaat ka tarikhi ja'iza* (Karachi: Maktaba-e-Muaviya, 1971); Wahiduddin Khan, *Maulana Mohammad Ilyas aur un ki deeni tahreek* (Lahore: Maktaba-e-Zakriya, n.d.); Mohammad Sani Hasni, *Savaneh Hazrat Maulana Mohammad Yusuf, Amir Tablighi Jamaat Pak-o-Hind* (Lahore: Nasharan-e-Qur'an, n.d.) Mohammad Shahid Saharanpuri, *Akaabar key khatut* (Lahore: Maktaba-e-Zakriya, n.d.); Maulana Mohammad Ilyas, *Hazrat Sheikh aur un ki apbeeti* (Lahore: Maktaba-e-Zakriya, n.d.): Maulana Manzoor Ahmad Noamani, *Da'wat-e-Tabligh* (Lahore: Maktaba-e-Zakriya, n.d.); Rashid-ul-Qadri, *Tablighi Jamaat* (Jamshedpur, India, A.H. 1379); Rashid-ul-Qadri, *Tablighi Kam* (Delhi: Anjuman Taraqqi Urdu, 1967); and Abul Hassan Ali Nadvi, *Hazrat Maulana Mohammad llyas aur unki deeni d 'awat* (Karachi: 1965).

104. I. S. Marwa, "Tabligh Movement Among the Meos of Mewat," in M. S. A. Roa, ed., *Social Movements in India,* vol. 2 (New Delhi: Manohar, 1979), pp. 96–97.

105. See Maulvi Abdul Shakoor, *Tarikh-e-Mewat* (Delhi: 1919) for a detailed discussion on the socioreligious situation of Mewat at the turn of the century.

106. Manzoor-ul-Haq Siddiqu, *Maathur-al-Ajdad* (Lahore: Maktaba-e-Salafiya, 1964), pp. 97–108; Maulvi Abdul Baqi Sehvani, *Akhbar Qila' Rai Seen* (Lucknow, 1924), p. 33. See also Nadvi, *Hazrat,* pp. 76–78.

107. Khan, *Maulana Mohammad Ilyas,* p. 7; Hasni, *Savaneh Hazrat,* pp. 138–39.

108. Saharanpuri, *Akabar ke khatutu,* p. 158.

109. Hasni, *Savaneh Hazrat,* p. 140.

110. Wahiduddin Khan, *Tabligh Movement* (New Delhi: Islamic Center, 1986), pp. 10–11, 14–16.

111. Qadri, *Tablighi Jamaat,* pp. 92–93; Hasni, *Savaneh Hazrat,* pp. 142–43.

112. Quoted in Khan, *Tabligh Movement,* p. 26.

113. For the contribution of Maulana Mohammad Yusuf toward the da'wa work of the Jamaat, see Hasni, *Savaneh Hazrat.*

114. Wahiduddin Khan, "Reflections," *Al-Risala,* February 1987, p. 26.

115. Ibid.

116. Tabish Mahdi, *Tablighi Jamaat Apne Bani Key Malfuzat Key A'iney Mein* (Deoband, India: Maktaba Al-Iman, 1985), p. 10.

117. The Jamaat leaders maintain that its da'wa methodology is based on the Sunna (practice) of the Prophet; hence, there can be no change in it.

118. Maulana Mohammad Zakriya, *Tablighi Nisab* (Lahore: Madni, n.d.).

119. The rigorous manner in which such forms of practice are observed by the Tablighi Jamaat are not always seen by other Muslims as doing "something for Islam." For example, in an obviously unsympathetic observation of a Jamaat "religious gathering" in Canada, Iqbal Yunus Khan writes: "Just north of Toronto, we had the *Ijtima* of Tablighi Jamaat. In the three-day camp, between four to five thousand Muslims participated. Muslims who get easily impressed by statistics in the Western press should read the following with interest. According to one expert, the total length of beards in this three-day camp was about 20,000 inches; the combined length of turbans was 50,000 inches, and the total length of robes was estimated at about 80,000 inches." In "Tablighi Jamaat's Show," *New Trend,* Kingsville, Maryland, July 1986.

120. Author's interviews with former officials of the Ministry of Law and Parliamentary Affairs, government of Pakistan, Islamabad, September 1979.

121. Author's interviews with officials of the Consultative Committee of Indian Muslims (CCIM), Chicago, June 1981.

122. Author's interview with the Jamaat-i-Islami leaders, Lahore, March 1986.

123. Author's interview with Tablighi Jamaat leaders from India and Pakistan, Washington, D.C., September 1989.

124. Author's interview with a Tablighi

Jamaat delegation from Pakistan in Washington, D.C., September 1989.

125. Maulana Manzoor Noamani, Maulana Abul Hasan Ali Nadvi, and Maulana Wahiduddin are all former members of the Jamaat-i-Islami. Both Maulana Noamani, who is currently the editor of a religious magazine, *Al-Furqan* (Delhi), and Maulana Nadvi, who is at present director of a prominent seminary, Nadvat-ul-Ulama, in Uttar Pradesh, India, left the Jamaat-i-Islami soon after its founding in 1941. Maulana Wahiduddin, currently the director of the Islamic Center, Delhi, resigned from a prominent position in the Jamaat-i-Islami of India in the 1960s. All three of them accused Maulana Maududi and the Jamaat-i-Islami of being overly concerned with temporal power and politics and of neglecting the basic purpose of Islamic da'wa, which is to bring people closer to God and to raise their religious consciousness.

126. *Al-Risala,* January 1988, p. 17.

127. Ibid., p. 1826.

128. *Al-Risala,* July 1987, p. 8.

129. Ibid.

130. Ibid.

131. *Al-Risala,* January 1987, p. 2; February 1987, p. 3.

132. *Al-Risala,* January 1987, p. 2.

133. *Al-Risala,* January 1988, p. 24.

134. *Al-Risala,* March 1988, p. 13.

135. *Al-Risala,* September 1988, p. 9.

136. *Al-Risala,* March 1987, pp. 16–17.

137. *Al-Risala,* July 1987, pp. 20–21.

138. Harry H. Hiller, "Religious Fundamentalism and Political Change," in *Changement social et religion* (Paris: C. I. S. R., 1975), p. 389.

139. Daniel H. Levine, *Religion and Politics in Latin America* (Princeton: Princeton University Press, 1981), p. 27.

140. Ibid.

141. Peter Worsley, *The Trumpet Shall Sound: A Study of Cargo Cults in Melanesia,* 2d ed. (New York: Shocken Books, 1968), pp. xxvi–xxvii.

142. Seymour Martin Lipset, *Political Man: The Social Bases of Politics* (Baltimore: Johns Hopkins University Press, 1981), p. 100.

143. Mohammad Manzoor Noamani, *Khomeini aur Inqilab-i-lran* (Delhi: Maktaba Al-Furqan, 1986).

144. Ibid. pp. 6–17, 85–96.

145. *Al-Risala,* April 1988, p. 13.

146. The Jamaat-i-Islami in its formative phase has been much more radical in challenging the monopoly of the ulama on Islamic da'wa. Maulana Maududi's devastating critique of the intellectual impoverishment, political ineptness, and moral inadequacy of the ulama, remains unsurpassed even by Islamic modernists.

Select Bibliography

Ahmad, Khurshid, and Zafar Ishaq Ansari. *Islamic Perspectives.* Leicester: Islamic Foundation, 1979.

———. "Economic Development in an Islamic Framework." In Khurshid Ahmad, ed., *Studies in Islamic Economics.* Leicester: Islamic Foundation, 1980.

Ahmad, Mumtaz. "Islamic Revival in Pakistan." In James W. Bjørkman, ed., *Fundamentalism, Revivalists, and Violence in South Asia.* Riverdale, Md.: Riverdale, 1988.

Binder, Leonard. *Religion and Politics in Pakistan.* Berkeley: University of California Press, 1962.

Gilani, Ijaz Shafi. "Fundamentalist Political Groups in Muslim Countries." Unpublished paper. 1975.

Haq, Mushirul. *Islam in Secular India.* Simla: Indian Institute of Advanced Study, 1972.

Hay, Stephen, and I. H. Qureshi, eds. *Sources of Indian Tradition,* vol. 2. New York: Columbia University Press, 1958.

Hayat, Raja Shafqat. "The Role of Students in National Politics." M.A. thesis, Punjab University, 1979.

Khan, Mohammad Ayub. *Speeches and Statements,* vol. 4. Karachi: Government of Pakistan, Department of Films and Publications, 1964.

Khan, Wahiduddin. *Tabligh Movement*. New Delhi: Islamic Center, 1986.

Marwa, I. S. "Tabligh Movement Among the Meos of Mewat." In M. S. A. Roa, ed., *Social Movements in India,* vol. 2. New Delhi: Manohar, 1979.

Mawdudi, Abul Ala. "How to Establish Islamic Order in the Country?" Reprinted in *The Universal Message*. Karachi, May 1983.

———. *Come Let Us Change This World!* Washington, D.C.: n. p., 1972.

Mir, Mustansir. "Some Features of Mawdudi's Tafhim al-Qur'an." *American Journal of Islamic Social Sciences* 2 (2) 1985.

Schuler, Edgar A., and Kathryn R. Schuler. *Public Opinion and Constitution Making in Pakistan 1958–1962*. East Lansing: Michigan State University Press, 1967.

Vorys, Karl von. *Political Development in Pakistan*. Princeton: Princeton University Press, 1967.

Worsley, Peter. *The Trumpet Shall Sound: A Study of Cargo Cults in Melanesia.* 2d ed. New York: Shocken Books, 1968.

CHAPTER
9

Organized Hinduisms: From Vedic Truth to Hindu Nation

Daniel Gold

Prologue

The town of Ayodhya in the eastern Gangetic plain is known to pious Hindus as the birthplace of King Ram, the human incarnation of Lord Vishnu and the prime exemplar of orthodox Hindu virtues. Home to ascetics and visited by devotees from all over India, Ayodhya has nevertheless managed to escape the chaotic excitement and hucksterism that comes with the worst excesses of the pilgrim trade. To the jaded researcher of traditional Hindu life, it can seem an unusually peaceful place, with visitors and residents calmly following their customary pursuits in the shops and temples throughout the town. Only once during my several sojourns there in 1980 and 1981 was an attempt made to draw me into a charged religious situation—and this by no traditional pilgrim's guide.

Ram was born, they say, on a hill inside the town, which the Hindus refer to as "Ram's birthplace." But this same hill is also the site of a mosque said to have been established by Babur, the first Mogul emperor of India, during a sojourn to Ayodhya in 1528.[1] To Muslims, then, the site is known as *Bābrī masjid,* "Babur's mosque." In 1949, two years after India became independent as a Hindu-majority but officially secular state, an image of Ram appeared in the building at the site—by the agency of god, say pious Hindus; by the agency of Hindu activists, say cynical Muslims. Following the clashes between Hindus and Muslims that ensued, the building was closed and the district magistrate was ordered to remove the image. This, however, he refused to do, citing concerns about renewed communal violence. But the magistrate's refusal to act had further consequences. Because Hindus expect their images to receive regular worship, they have been permitted to enter the building once a year on the anniversary of the image's appearance; a program of devotional singing, moreover, has been instituted in front of the building. The issue of Ram's birthplace/Babur's mosque has since prompted several Hindu and Muslim groups to initiate litigation, but no suit seems likely ever to reach satisfactory resolution.[2]

The case has become a cause more important for religious activists from outside the area than for the local population. Eventually large sectors of the Hindu public would be roused with a highly effective image depicting Ram in jail.[3] During the time of my visit, both sides were maintaining a presence at the site. Approaching a booth well stocked with literature presenting the Hindu point of view, I was assured by a fiery-eyed young man that the present building had originally been an important temple; Babur had then wrongfully turned it into a mosque to commemorate his victory over the Hindus. Besides, my interlocutor reasoned, there was only one birthplace of Ram, and it was in the sacred Hindu soil of Ayodhya. Even if Babur had built the mosque himself, he was just a marauder from outside. The young man looked down and murmured: If the Muslims want someplace special to worship, let them go to Pakistan. Then he continued with more energy, didn't I want to sign my name on their list and give a financial offering to their cause?

This was not the traditional Hinduism of temple priests and ritual but an organized defense of perceived Hindu rights, and it was encountering similarly organized Muslim forces. Relations between the two sides were tense, but they were not yet murderous. They were, however, to become so. In 1986, as the result of a legal petition, a local court allowed the building to open for Hindu worship. While not making a final ruling on the case, the judge saw no legal reason for the building to be closed; moreover, he had been assured by the Ayodhya police that opening the building would lead to no violence in the area. Instead, violent rioting soon broke out in six other towns scattered through the north Indian plains. Shops were burned and a bomb set off; at least twenty people died.[4]

By 1989, the confrontation at Babur's mosque had turned into a major political issue. At a convention of Hindu activists held that February, a decision was made to build a new temple at the site. The project was conceived as an event that would involve Hindus across the nation and from all strata of society. Small donations were sought from common people, and bricks for the temple's construction were consecrated in villages all over north India to be carried to the site. Vigorous organizational efforts in the summer and autumn led to increased unrest, with riots flaring up between Hindus and Muslims throughout the northern regions.[5] Tensions heightened in November, when both the laying of the temple's foundation stone and the Indian general elections were scheduled to take place. Although Rajiv Gandhi's government had been trying to mediate the escalating dispute, its attempts were unsuccessful and managed to alienate both Hindu and Muslim activists, contributing to Gandhi's defeat at the polls.[6] In the north, where reverberations from the temple dispute were most severe, Gandhi's party lost most of its seats in parliament, and an unexpectedly large number of them passed to candidates from the Hindu right. Through skillful organization, legal ploys, and political maneuvering, Hindu activists had, for the moment, gained unprecedented influence on the national government.

The Arya Samaj and RSS as Movements of Organized Hinduism

With their petitions, provocative placards, and populist militancy, the defenders of Ram's birthplace offer a version of Hinduism that diverges greatly from the ritual and devotion of most of the pious Hindus who come to pray in the temples of Ayodhya. Yet this politicized, activist Hinduism, although taken up only by a minority, has considerable precedent. Movements of organized Hinduism arose in British India from the first two decades of the nineteenth century, alongside parallel movements of Muslims and Sikhs. As movements of collective solidarity, all these groups recognized a number of collective competitors, with whom they interacted and from whom they learned. The Indian groups then, as now, faced off against one another—both beyond their broad religious communities and within them. All, moreover, also confronted Christian missionaries, whom they understood to be in league with the British colonial power. This perceived threat from the West was in its origins more pressing than the challenge of other Indian groups and in its results more revolutionary. For in reacting to threats understood as modern and Western, all the Indian groups end up having to adapt Western organizational models.

In the Hindu case especially, the adaptation of Western models entails some drastic transformations of the structures of traditional religion. The importance of caste membership may be outweighed by that of committee membership. Where once people found religious authority in their family priest or a lineage of gurus, they may now find it in a formalized organizational hierarchy. Together with these structural innovations, moreover, come changes in ideas about Hindu community itself: questions arise about both its external boundaries and the traditional socioreligious divisions within it. Indeed, many think that even if it has to entail drastic reforms in tradition, a new socioreligious order among Hindus is nevertheless necessary, crucial for the vitality, if not the very survival, of Hinduism in the modern world. To effect these internal reforms within and to ward off external threats, Hindus must organize. If fundamentalist religion implies a resolute religious reaction to forces of modernity, then fundamentalist Hinduism is necessarily organized Hinduism.

Arising in various regions and catering to different constituencies, movements of organized Hinduism have sometimes cooperated with one another and just as often not. Nevertheless, the major politically active groups reveal a line of development traceable from the last quarter of the nineteenth century. To present a sense of the direction of organized Hindu reaction, I will deal with two groups: the Arya Samaj, vital at the beginning of the period, and the Rashtriya Svayamsevak Sangh, commonly abbreviated RSS, still very important today. The Arya Samaj was in its origins a nineteenth-century movement of religious reform that served in part as an organ of Hindu nationalism during the political tensions of the early twentieth century. This was the era when the RSS emerged, the creation of an individual political activist with a vision of Hindu cultural renewal through personal discipline. Phenomenologically, the Arya Samaj and the RSS present contrasting assertions of Hindu identity in a secular, pluralistic world: the first grounded in specifically religious reforms of doctrine and practice, the second in cultural and national loyalties. Historically, they reveal a development from a narrowly based sectarian organization to a movement reaching out to encompass a wider segment of the Hindu population.

Established in Bombay in 1875, the Arya Samaj found its greatest strength among the educated classes of the Punjab and the north Indian plains. From the end of the nineteenth century through the first decades of twentieth, its growth was steady and robust: from 39,952 in 1891, to 243,000 in 1911, to 990,233 in 1931, the last year in which the Indian census counted its members separately. By Indian independence in 1947 total membership in the Arya Samaj worldwide has been estimated at more than one and a half million.[7] Although the Arya Samaj is known to Hindus of north India through its network of schools and colleges, it has not been a significant presence in the south, where it has intervened at times during specific crises but has never had a vital membership base.

In Hindu India the term *Arya* carries complex connotations. It refers first of all to the early Indo-Aryans who settled in the subcontinent in the second millennium B.C.E., bringing with them the early Vedic scriptures still revered by all Hindus. In modern Hindi, the term also means "cultured" or "refined," a meaning highlighted by important leaders of the RSS as well as the Arya Samaj.[8] Thus the Arya Samaj, literally, the "Society of Aryas," suggests an association of cultured Hindus following the pristine tradition of the ancient Vedas. For as educated reformers, members of the Arya Samaj adhere to what they perceive to be the core tradition of Vedic texts and dismiss much of later Hindu tradition as degenerate practice that is best forgotten. In its attempts to build directly on the Vedic corpus—the earliest of Hindu scriptures—the Arya Samaj presents one of the closest parallels to Western fundamentalism of all the Indian groups. And like most Western fundamentalists, members of the Arya Samaj usually see themselves as belonging to a specific movement within a world religious community: a definite religious group with its own leaders, guiding texts, and sacraments.

Prominent members of the RSS, by contrast, often describe their group publicly not as a religious institution within Hinduism but as a Hindu cultural organization—a characterization that seems most apt when culture is understood in its most broadly inclusive sense, informing religious, economic, and political life. The vast majority of members of the RSS remain conventional Hindus by most people's standards, putting faith in the accumulated wisdom of tradition and following most (but not all) traditional practices. They may say they have joined the RSS to "build character," as a favorite RSS expression goes—both their own character and that of the nation. The full name of the RSS—which translates as the "National Union of Volunteers"—thus reflects an ethos of patriotic service.

Its top leadership long dominated by Maharashtrian Brahmans, the RSS continues to maintain its national headquarters in Nagpur, Maharashtra, where western India meets the cultural north. From there the movement has spread deep into the Hindi-speaking northern heartland, where it is particularly vital among the urban middle classes. In recent years, the RSS has also become a visible presence in some areas of the south, particularly Kerala. Although its active membership has fluctuated since Indian independence, it grew rapidly through the eighties: from estimates of about 200,000 on the eve of independence in 1947, to 1,000,000 in 1979, to 1,800,000 in 1989.[9] With a disciplined core of workers, a widespread following, and a network of affiliated organizations, the RSS works both publicly and behind the scenes to promote a vision of Hindu cultural ideals that is often at odds with the policies of the secular Indian state. Thus, at the initial confrontation between Hindus and Muslims at Ayodhya in 1949, the district magistrate who resolutely refused orders to remove Ram's image and so consolidated Hindu gains was known as an RSS supporter; he was, however, eventually forced into early retirement, his activist role being unacceptable to the ruling powers.[10]

Socioreligious Contexts

From the point of view of the secular nationalists who have governed independent India, then, the aims sometimes espoused by the Arya Samaj and usually articulated by the RSS can appear intolerably rooted in communalism—a concept of group self-interest that normally has negative connotations in the mainstream Indian press.[11] There the term is used in reference to struggles for local power among regional Hindu caste groups as well as to rivalries between members of India's broad religious divisions. The former struggles seem to have been long endemic to traditional India, but the latter conflicts entail an idea of religiously defined community originally shaped by British colonial policy.

Hindus—with their many castes and subcastes living in various distinctive regions of the subcontinent—have historically been aware of themselves, not as a single religious group, but as many discrete communities living together in various states of domination, cooperation, and distanced alienation. The advent of Islam, Christianity, and a distinct Sikh identity complicated matters, but the Hindu perspective of separate communities could still contain these large traditions in all their varieties. With the establishment of British colonial rule in the nineteenth century, however, the perspectives of the native Indian communities on both themselves and one another began to change.

In all the Indian communities, traditional elites had to come to terms with the idea of a new dominant class as well as the reality of a new social and economic order. To many Indian thinkers, the ease with which their people had been brought to submission by much smaller numbers of Europeans meant that there were serious problems in the contemporary state of Indian society. Reform movements emerged that looked to models from both the contemporary West and different idealized Indian pasts. At the same time, the British regime created fresh cadres of clerks and administrators at middle ranks and higher. New, city-based Indian elites emerged—both bureaucratic and commercial. Although these were never as exalted as the British overlords, they were often wealthier and more powerful than the descendants of the old landed gentry. Crucial to advancement within the new elites was a knowledge of Western ways, for which an English education was usually seen as a valued prerequisite. But an education alone was not enough to secure a good administrative appointment, many of the best of which were reserved for Europeans. The competition for positions at all levels was strong, and its terms were defined by the British.

The form of competition that developed in urban India by the end of the nineteenth century emerged from a Western model that was adapted to the exigencies of the colonial situation. Certainly the spirit of competition between relative equals that was imported by the British from capitalist, increasingly democratic Europe was essentially alien to the traditional Hindu ethos, which features hierarchy and synergy among separate communities. Although the communities that made up the traditional Hindu socioreligious hierarchy were often able to compete over their relative positions within it, they joined in the assumption that the hierarchy itself should be the basis for an organic whole, whose elements would naturally cooperate. The British recognized the composite nature of traditional Indian society but distinguished larger communities that, from their point of view at least, were indeed relative equals. Thus, the leaders of the religiously neutral colonial government formally defined the major socioreligious components of their realm in terms of the broad traditions that they understood as religious from their Western perspective: Hindu, Muslim, and Sikh.

British administrators then used these broad communal divisions as a basis for governing their realms. From early encounters with particular segments of wide-ranging communities, the British were liable to form stereotypes of the communities as wholes (e.g., Hindus appeared docile but were cunning; Muslims were warlike and could be fanatical). They then tried to favor groups that seemed loyal to them and keep a balance among the rest, while trying to employ the perceived nature of each to their own best advantage. Thus, in the administration, a tacit system of quotas took communal membership as an important criterion for military and civilian employment: Sikhs, for example, typed as both loyal and martial, were given preferential treatment in the army. In the communities themselves, leaders by the turn of the century found that the government would listen to them if they could show that their voice was somehow collective, representative of a larger whole. For the colonial rulers, then, the Western idea of a religious community as something broad and homogeneous was a factor in apportioning limited resources and making political decisions.[12]

This new idea of religious community was further inculcated among the Indian elite by both the general example of the British and some of their particular administrative policies. European Christians—dispersed all over India—certainly did not display complex socioreligious distinctions among themselves of the sort recognized by caste Hindus. Meanwhile, Christian missionaries effectively preached a religion that was egalitarian in spirit if not always in colonial practice, and it was their concept of religion that became the one taught in Western curricula. When taken to Indian religious traditions by liberal, Western-educated teachers, moreover, this concept was often colored by an Orientalist vision of a glorious past that students could take as a simplified, uniform model of what their religion should be. Of more practical import were two instruments of British policy. The decennial census, introduced in 1871, formally defined Indians according to religion and made them aware of the relative sizes and rates of growth of their communities. Separate electorates, introduced with the expansion of democratic institutions in 1909, assured representation by members of all religions. Based on the census data, a certain number of constituencies were reserved for the Muslims of each province; similar arrangements were made for Christians in Madras and Sikhs in the Punjab. The political power of separate religious communities was thus made explicit, and its potential became cast in clearly quantified terms.

It eventually became evident to the new elites that the adoption of Western-style religious institutions alongside social and political ones would be necessary for success in the colonial order, and Western-educated members of all communities began organizing themselves along broader religious lines. For the Hindus especially, this meant delineating a broad-based communal identity beyond caste that had not been emphasized strongly before. Movements of organized Hinduism thus give expression to problems of pluralism long familiar to India, but which have become transformed and exacerbated in modern contexts of colonialism, nationhood, and democracy. For at the same time that Hindus organized against British political and cultural imperialism, organized groups of educated Hindus, Muslims, and Sikhs competed against each other for a privileged position in colonial society. With the British gone it is the tensions between these large religious communities that have become most visible.

Historical Continuities

Although always found predominantly among literate city dwellers, organized Hinduism as it has developed has become increasingly less elite and more compatible with the fabric of everyday Hindu life. As a movement of Hindu reform, the Arya Samaj had a precursor in the Brahmo Samaj, which emerged among the Calcutta aristocracy in the middle of the nineteenth century to offer a religion that appeared compatible with Western rational thought.[13] A radical departure from orthodox Hinduism, the Brahmo Samaj nevertheless offered culturally alienated Bengalis renewed access to their own traditions. With the Arya Samaj, organized Hinduism became solidly established among the upper-middle classes—bourgeois professionals and tradespeople. Although offering its members a distinct religious identity, it was compatible enough with common practice that most did not have to break family ties. The RSS, finally, has its greatest strength among lower-middle-class clerks and shop owners, who see their RSS activities as an enrichment and enhancement of conventional Hindu life.

As religious movements, versions of organized Hinduism have been sharply informed by the visions of their founders. But these lived during different moments of a widespread religious, cultural, and political reaction against non-Hindu influence. Moreover, they drew on the traditions of distinct Indian cultural areas and found initial success within different social and regional populations.

Swami Dayananda Sarasvati, the founder of the Arya Samaj, was born in 1824 to well-to-do parents from rural Gujarat, on the west coast of India. Although Dayananda has never revealed his family name, he did state that his family was Brahman, from the hereditary priestly class.[14] Even as a boy, he tells us, he had begun to question the validity of his ritual heritage, and in his autobiography Dayananda relates an incident from his youth to illustrate the point. His family—devotees of Shiva—took the deity's annual festival seriously, celebrating it with the traditional fasts and vigils. When he was fourteen, Dayananda went with his father and other devotees to participate in an all-night vigil in Shiva's temple. But Dayananda was the only one who managed to stay awake that night, and, alone in his vigil, saw a mouse come out from its hole, climb all over the image of Shiva, and even eat up the food offered by the devotees. Troubled by what seemed to him to be a casual desecration of the deity, he woke up his father. He felt it was impossible, he said, "to reconcile the idea of an omnipotent, living god with this idol which allows the mice to run over his body and thus suffers his image to be polluted without the slightest protest."[15] The iconoclastic, rational religious sensibilities that Dayananda experienced then would continue to underlie his message as religious teacher until the end of his days.

When he was twenty-one, Dayananda left home to lead the life of a holy man—a general socioreligious option for Hindus of all castes and backgrounds. A year later, in 1847, he was able to convince a member of an old and revered religious lineage to give him formal vows of renunciation, which entitled him to be addressed by the honorific "Swami."[16] For thirteen years Dayananda wandered about India as holy men do, until he finally met a preceptor whose somewhat idiosyncratic teachings he developed into a rational doctrine. According to Dayananda, the gods and goddesses of developed Hinduism were just figments of the human imagination; the true divinity was the invisible one known to the seers of old, who adored it in the Vedic hymns and worshiped it through pristine ritual whose secret Dayananda thought he had rediscovered. After three years with his teacher, Dayananda wandered around India again, now preaching his distinctive message, but without particular success. During a stay in Calcutta in 1873 he became acquainted with the person and work of Keshub Chandra Sen, an extraordinary leader of the Brahmo Samaj.[17] From this encounter Dayananda learned that the urban educated classes might be more receptive to his message than the rural population with whom he had been working. He was thus led to follow some practical advice from Keshub: the Gujarati-speaking, Sanskrit-educated Swami would cease preaching in Sanskrit to traditional pandits and instead start to convey his message in Hindi, a widely understood vernacular.[18] Two more years of itinerant preaching took the Swami back to western India, his native area, where his organization would first take shape.[19]

Although the Arya Samaj was established in Bombay by a Swami from Gujarat, it did not begin to flourish until Swami Dayananda visited the Punjab two years later in 1877. This was no accident. The northwesternmost area of the Indian subcontinent, the Punjab is geographically the bridge to the Islamic world, with a large population of Muslims and later of Sikhs. Hindus have long been aware of themselves as one of many communities—often a minority—in the Punjab, which has been and still is a place of marked communal tensions.

Moreover, educated Punjabi Hindus would have been familiar with the idea of a reform organization from contacts with imported Bengali Brahmos. The Punjab was one of the last areas of India to be annexed into the British administration, which had already developed a trained professional class in Calcutta that was ready to serve throughout the subcontinent. The Brahmos appeared in Punjab as urbane, well-placed outsiders. The model of a new socioreligious organization was there to be seen, but the Brahmo Samaj remained essentially cosmopolitan, Bengali religion. In this context the Arya Samaj emerged as a nativist reform movement, with a more distinctly Hindu identity grounded in a specific vision of the fundamentals of Vedic tradition.

By the first decade of the twentieth century, some Punjabi members of the Arya Samaj became seriously engaged in political action. Their increased activism was due in large part to the socioeconomic effects of British colonial policy, which had begun to take their toll. With the supply of potential government functionaries far outstripping the demand, large numbers of educated young men, now disdainful of menial employment, grew alienated from both their own traditions and the British regime. And those who had the coveted salaried jobs were squeezed by the decade's high rate of inflation, which particularly affected lower-level clerks.[20] Meanwhile, the decennial census had since its inception shown a decreasing percentage of Hindus in the Punjab population. The official loss of Hindu numbers was due in part to conversion and increased reproductive rates among other groups, but it also derived from conventions in counting that themselves became issues of sectarian dispute: Sikh groups had successfully objected to the practice of counting Sikhs as Hindus that was followed in the first census in 1861, and now Muslims were objecting to the inclusion of outcastes in the Hindu population.[21] Hindus became anxious: certainly they had reason to fear for their community's political strength—and, some thought, even for its very survival.

In 1909, prominent Punjabi leaders of the Arya Samaj were instrumental in founding the first politically oriented Hindu communal group: the Punjab Provincial Hindu Sabha (council).[22] This group was reorganized into the Sarvadeshik (panregional) Hindu Sabha in 1915, and in 1921 was renamed the All-India Hindu Mahasabha (great council)—under which title it would become one of the best known institutions of Hindu reaction. Through the twenties and thirties the Hindu Mahasabha would continue to find influential leaders among Aryas;[23] at the same time it actively nurtured the early growth of the RSS, which some of its leaders then saw as a potential youth wing.[24] Through the Hindu Mahasabha, then, the Arya Samaj and the RSS find a line of historical continuity as Hindu communal movements.

By the early twenties—the decade during which the Hindu Mahasabha became vital and the RSS was founded—outbreaks of violence between Hindus and Muslims were sweeping across the nation. To face the communal challenge, some said, Hindus should not only organize but also adopt military virtues. To this end a number of Maharashtrian leaders looked to the cultural traditions of their own native region. In its seventeenth-century glory, Maharashtra was a land of Hindu warriors, offering a new surge of Hindu military power that contributed to the collapse of the Mogul empire. Geographically the southernmost of the Indo-Aryan speaking areas of northern India, Maharashtra in its caste structure also culturally resembles the Dravidian south, with relatively few occupational castes mediating between Brahmans at the top of the hierarchy and the bulk of peasant, farming groups below. Although the great military heroes of the seventeenth and eighteenth centuries came largely from peasant castes, many of their councillors were Brahmans, who often served as de facto rulers, amassed great power, and sometimes even ventured into battle. Entering into business pursuits too in ways not typical in Northern regions, Brahmans in Maharashtra had reason to be proud of their temporal power as well as their traditional sacred learning.[25] From the Maharashtrian Brahman community would come V. D. Savarkar, an early revolutionary and leading intellectual on the Hindu right who served as president of the Hindu Mahasabha from 1937 to 1942, and K. B. Hedgewar, the founder of the RSS.

In both education and outlook the founder of the RSS presents a sharp contrast to that of the Arya Samaj. Hedgewar received an English-language education and trained to be a physician. During his medical instruction in Calcutta he became involved in revolutionary activities, which he continued on his return to Maharashtra in 1916—even serving a year in prison.[26] But Hedgewar eventually grew dissatisfied with the nationalist stance and nonviolent methods espoused by Gandhi's Congress Party. When rioting between Hindus and Muslims came to Nagpur in 1923, Hedgewar became active in forming the local unit of the Hindu Mahasabha, whose confrontational tactics against Muslims and British aroused great popular Hindu support. Hindus could be strong, he saw, when they came together and acted cohesively as a community. Although Hedgewar's thought was strongly influenced by Savarkar's ideas, he resisted the increasingly politicized direction in which Savarkar would take the Hindu Mahasabha. For by the 1930s the Mahasabha had developed into an organization actively advocating communal interests in the political arena—a Hindu counterpart to the Muslim League in opposition to the secular nationalism of the Congress. Like Swami Dayananda, Hedgewar had a more inward vision. What the Hindus needed, according to Hedgewar, was not a political party of their own but communal discipline and revitalization.

As communal organizations that were nurtured during the period of nationalist struggle, both the Arya Samaj and the RSS suffered traumas at India's independence in 1947. The Aryas of India lost their main center at Lahore, which was included in West Pakistan. Thousands of well-to-do Punjabi Aryas became refugees. When shortly after independence Gandhi was assassinated by a Maharashtrian Brahman extremist, suspicion immediately fell on the RSS. The organization was officially banned for a year and a half, and its head at the time, M. S. Golwalkar, was arrested and detained for six months. Although the assassin had previously been a member of the RSS and at the time was editor of a pro-Hindu Mahasabha newspaper, no evidence could be found that he was acting under orders from the leadership of either group, who some suspected of trying to take over the government.[27] Nevertheless, the connection between the RSS, Maharashtrian Hindu extremism, and the assassination of Gandhi remains alive in the minds of many Indians.

Although the RSS was seriously shaken by the ban, it soon recovered its numbers and over the next decade reestablished itself and developed in new directions. The ban had led to the arrest of volunteers all over the country, and many of those who had joined in the heat of communal tensions in the forties were frightened away. Of the approximately two hundred thousand active members in February 1948, when the ban was imposed, only a core of about one hundred thousand remained in the

RSS when it was lifted in July of the following year.[28] The reconstruction of the RSS entailed some new orientations. A number of the middle-level activists, left to their own devices when top RSS leadership was imprisoned during the ban, began to chafe under the reimposition of conservative reins. New subsidiary associations were organized as channels for their energy and initiative: a student association, a labor union, a political party.[29] The period of reconsolidation—from the fifties to the early sixties—was framed by foreign crises unleashing patriotic sentiment on which RSS leaders were able to capitalize. The year-long conflict with Pakistan over Kashmir beginning two months after partition in August 1947 was followed in early 1950 by a mass exodus of Hindus from Pakistani East Bengal—whose resettlement gave the RSS a chance to demonstrate its value as a public-spirited organization.[30] The Sino-Indian war of 1962 finally unleashed enough nationalistic fervor to let the government allow the RSS to march in the next January's Republic Day parade, conferring on it an official legitimacy it had never had before.[31]

Through the sixties and early seventies the network of RSS organizations begun in the fifties expanded, but the RSS itself—still not quite respectable in the eyes of many—continued to keep a low profile. Then in 1975, Indira Gandhi, faced with an imminent threat to her rule, enacted sweeping emergency laws. The RSS was again banned, but this time it paradoxically gained increased visibility and new stature. With important RSS volunteers now imprisoned alongside other political and communal activists of all sorts, the organization could appear as an element of the popular opposition. Waxing in strength through the eighties, by the end of the decade it appeared as an increasingly open and aggressive actor in Indian political life.

For the Arya Samaj, by contrast, the damage suffered through the permanent loss of important Punjabi centers at partition could not be restored. During the fifties and sixties, much of the Aryas' energy was devoted to rebuilding their wealth and institutions,[32] while the world around them was changing. In its heyday at the beginning of the century, the Arya Samaj had combined a concern for active social reform essential to success in the colonial milieu with an emphasis on religious revival and communal identity. By the time it reestablished itself, many of the social causes for which it had worked either seemed less pressing or were taken over by other organizations. While continuing to maintain its educational institutions and provide a routinized personal religion for old Arya stalwarts and their families, the Samaj has directed its newer surges of vitality more exclusively toward sectarian revival and Hindu communalist ends. In the late twentieth century, then, radical Aryas join forces with militant members of the RSS—who both see themselves as fulfilling the vision of the fundamentals laid down by their movements' founders.

Creating Hindu Identities: Fundamentals, Ideologies, Communities

In locating authoritative grounds for the new Hindu communities they envisioned, both Dayananda and Hedgewar looked to past Hindu tradition. Their heritage presented them with a wide range of choices of what are thought of as religious fundamentals: scriptural canons, codes of law, and philosophical doctrines. Yet in their diversity, none was as practically crucial to cumulative tradition as their correlates seized on by Western fundamentalists, none concrete enough to bear alone the weight of a religious movement. This contrast in the role of fundamentals in tradition stems in good part from the very *abundance* of scriptures, laws, and philosophies in Hinduism. It becomes very difficult to single out any one specific item of tradition as basic. Religious specialists in Hinduism have tended to treat them all with a creative nonchalance, choosing and interpreting them freely to fit the needs of particular situations.

This diffuse nature of the Hindu heritage was a fact understood by both Dayananda and Hedgewar. Both recognized Hinduism as an evolving religiocultural tradition that encompasses many dimensions of life. But they also made their own judgments: of the many different elements emphasized at times during Hinduism's long evolution, some were more valuable than others. Each then looked back to what he saw as the most glorious Hindu epoch and tried to codify a framework for Hindu community that would reunite Hindus around the values foregrounded there.

Dayananda turned to the era of the Vedas—the ancient period of scriptural compilation that scholars usually locate at the end of the second millennium B.C.E., but which Dayananda understood to be much earlier. Since it was the eternal truths embodied in the Vedas themselves that made this era so great, a revitalization of the modern Hindu community should be rooted in a revitalization of the Vedic texts. Thus, crucial to the foundations of the Arya Samaj is the idea of a definite scriptural canon, a very ancient canon that deserves to be taken to a visibly modern world.

Hedgewar, by contrast, looked not to Vedic scripture but to the legends of Shivaji, the seventeenth-century Maharashtrian hero who led a successful revolt against the Mogul empire. The son of a military officer of peasant origins, Shivaji was able to mount a successful challenge to Aurangzeb, the last of the great Moguls and the sternly orthodox heir to five hundred years of Islamic political dominance in the subcontinent. Shivaji's success is usually understood by nationalist writers to derive from both spiritual and practical virtues: on the one hand, martial valor and support for Brahmanical institutions; on the other, worldly wisdom and an organizational talent that gave him the ability to forge an effective fighting force out of soldiers from diverse peasant castes.[33] Loyalty, discipline, reverence for one's heritage, and skill in effectively rousing ordinary people: these were the virtues Hedgewar admired. Around quasi-military ideals and a philosophy of Hindu Nation, then, he attempted to shape an organization that would have broad popular support.

Fundamentals and their Implications

Vedic Authority in the Arya Samaj

In highlighting Vedic authority, Swami Dayananda certainly looks to a widely acknowledged basis of Hindu traditions. Indeed, a recognition of Vedic authority is one of the very few convictions that the many diverse people who think of themselves as Hindus share.[34] However, the idea of Vedic authority known to traditional Hindus is much more diffuse and abstract than the idea of a closed biblical canon known to the

West. Christians, for example, variously interpret a revealed text to which most people have access and of which they can make some literal sense. For Hindus, by contrast, a reverence for scriptural authority can often mean simply that they think that what they do somehow comes from the Vedas, texts which in their antiquity are very rarely used or understood anymore. The complex rituals at which these texts were used long ago ceased to be vital, and the old Vedic hymns no longer have much referential meaning for most Hindus. They exist now primarily as words of power incorporated in newer rites. The ancient scriptures that continue to have referential meaning are the Upanishads, speculative works appended to the end of the ritual texts and also taken as revealed—Veda in an extended sense. Speaking with no one voice, and highly abstract as well, the Upanishads are capable of generating any number of philosophical meanings. Thus, Hindu tradition has acknowledged all sorts of ritual as coming from the Vedas and almost any imaginable type of religious philosophy as grounded in the Upanishads.

To provide some foundation for his Hindu revival, Dayananda wanted to move from scriptural authority to scriptural canon. Moreover, he put particular emphasis on the old Vedic hymns themselves, giving a lesser role to the more easily accessible Upanishads. In this he differed from his precursors in organized Hinduism, the leaders of the Brahmo Samaj.

The Brahmo Samaj, "the Society of Brahma," emerged in the 1830s within the highest strata of Hindu society in Calcutta, then the seat of British power in India. Its founder, Rammohan Roy, was influenced by Christian Unitarian thought and saw in the Upanishads a kindred rational truth at the root of Hinduism. Through the Brahmo Samaj, Bengalis attracted by Western ways who had been converting to Christianity could break with some of the more onerous practices of their tradition and still find a religious source in pristine Hindu monism. Yet as the sole fixture of tradition, Upanishadic thought—diverse, speculative, and subject to wide-ranging interpretation—did not provide the Brahmo Samaj with much stability. Very soon it split into a number of rival groups, with radical social reformers abandoning social conservatives proud of traditional Hindu ways, and fervent followers of a charismatic leader breaking with sober men of affairs.

Clearly, whatever their virtues for Calcutta folk trying to come to terms with the West, the Upanishads alone did not have the substance for the type of widespread Hindu revival Dayananda had in mind. More than a flexible vehicle for philosophical speculation, the Vedas as propounded by Dayananda were rooted in a firm theistic vision and offered a modicum of ritual practice. Gaining exposure to organized Hinduism from the Brahmo Samaj and learning from its leaders, Dayananda would nevertheless break with them over the issue of Vedic authority.[35] For the Swami had previously had an encounter with a religious teacher he had respected much more than the Brahmo leaders, one who had already shaped his basic ideas about the Vedas and their glorious era.

After a stormy break with his family and years of wandering around north India, Swami Dayananda eventually met a guru, Swami Virjananda, then eighty-one years old. Blind and cantankerous, "with acute stomach trouble,"[36] Swami Virjananda was a renowned Sanskrit scholar with his own ideas about Hindu tradition that he continued to propagate actively through the final years of his life.[37] Virjananda took very seriously the Hindu precept that the cataclysmic war described in the epic Mahabharata marked the beginning of the age of Kali, the current dark age of mankind. Any work written after the age of the Mahabharata—traditionally understood to have been about five thousand years ago—was thus hopelessly corrupt. According to Virjananda, then, the scriptures commonly revered by Hindus could be divided into two classes: those composed before the legendary war, which were *ārṣ*, (of the rishis), the old Vedic seers, and those composed after it which were *anārṣ*, (not of the rishis). The first works were worth preserving and reviving; the second were unfortunate error and had led people astray.

From his guru Swami Dayananda not only learned Sanskrit but also accepted this fundamental bifurcation of Hindu tradition. But while Virjananda, old and blind, made written entreaties to government officials and princes to propagate his doctrine,[38] his younger disciple Dayananda would find his mission in preaching that doctrine vigorously to a wide constituency. It was, in fact, a radical teaching. Encouraging people to observe only those parts of the cumulative Hindu tradition that were "of the rishis" meant exhorting them to discard other large portions of it, including the ceremonial worship of images that was central to the religious lives of most Hindus. Thus, in Dayananda's most basic work, *Satyārth Prakāś,* "The Light of Truth," the Swami gives a long list of traditional Hindu writings that should *not* be read, "condemned by the author in his scheme of studies."[39]

Although Dayananda parted from his guru with the idea that only the genuine core of Hindu tradition was valid, it took him several years to arrive at a clear concept of just what this meant. Crucial to his understanding of the Vedic foundations of Hinduism were three ways of thinking about religion current in the intellectually progressive circles of nineteenth-century India. Of these, the most directly influenced by Western models was Dayananda's understanding of a highly specific scriptural canon—an idea with little precedent in Hindu thought. He developed this concept in accordance with two intellectual strains that do have roots in Indian tradition, but which could appear particularly enlightened in the nineteenth century: a rational theism congruent with beliefs found in Western Protestantism, and a scientific literal-mindedness.

Dayananda seems to have come to his doctrine of the Vedas after his experience with the Brahmo thinkers. Drawn from an elite class exposed to the Persian high cultural legacy of the Moguls as well as to the new Western ideas of the British, the Brahmos had long been struggling with the idea of revelation proposed by Islam and Christianity, "religions of the book." Where most of these had reached conciliatory—if sometimes eclectic—conclusions, agreeing that all the great scriptures held revelation, Dayananda outdid even the most Hinduizing of the Brahmo thinkers. The revelation of the ancient Hindus was not only the highest ever received by humankind, but it also contained all knowledge, a claim not made in such assertive terms even by Western scripturalists.

Although traditional Hindus sometimes speak of the Vedas as containing all knowledge, it can be reasonably assumed that they do not usually mean this in any specific way but more abstractly to imply that the Vedas contain the essence of all knowledge, or the seeds of it. Dayananda, however, took this traditional dictum in a very rational, literalist sense. Thus, Dayananda understood the Vedic sacrifices to have an intelligible basis that could be comprehended in terms of a materialist science: when butter and other substances are consumed in the Vedic fire, they "purify the air, rain, and water [and] thereby promote happiness on this earth."[40] Since the knowledge of the Vedas is of general applicability, all references to kings and battles are in fact political or military directives. Moreover, since the Vedas are of universal scope, all specific geographical and botanical references are explained away.[41] "All the knowledge that is extant in the world originated in Aryavarta."[42]

Thus ancient Aryavarta—the Swami's term for India between the Himalayas and the Vindhyas—was truly a wondrous place. It was "called the Golden Land as it produces gold and precious stones." Its kings ruled over all the earth and taught the wisdom of the country to all. Through their great knowledge, the ancient Indians were able to produce the extraordinary weapons of war described in the epics. There were iron balls filled with substances that catch fire when exposed to the sun or air; there were also defenses for these weapons: a kind of smoke bomb that turned into rain to extinguish the fire. After the great war described in the Mahabharata, however, all this knowledge was lost. Ignorant priestcraft swept through the land.[43] The Swami's mission was to restore Aryavarta to its ancient glory.

Aware of himself as the propagator of unconventional doctrines and institutions, Dayananda several times during his career would affirm codified outlines of ritual and belief that could serve as a foundation for a new Hindu community. The elements of the reformed ritual traditions were described in a work called *Saṃskār Vidhi,* in which Dayananda presented the sixteen traditional life-cycle rites—called *saṃskāras*—in a simple form that he thought was authentic and suitable for performance by his contemporaries.[44] The marriage rite in particular was to be less elaborate and expensive, pointing to a problem that still remains in contemporary Hindu life. For those who wanted them, Dayananda also offered a simplification and revival of the old Vedic celebratory rites. Prescribing options in personal religion rather than practice necessary for community membership, these strictly ritual enunciations of Dayananda did not prove controversial in tradition. The doctrinal ones, however, did.

The doctrinal points affirmed by Dayananda were of two types: those that were presented as tenets to be held by all Aryas and those in which he believed personally himself. Of the first, the most definitive is a list of ten rules prepared by a committee of Lahore Aryas and approved by Dayananda in 1877.[45] The first three of these assert that God the creator is the source of all knowledge and that the Vedas are the books of all knowledge, which all Aryas should read. The rest are fairly conventional moral injunctions. Catholic in their outlook, these ten rules aim to open up the Arya Samaj widely to all Hindus. In a tract published at the end of *Satyārth Prakāś,* however, Dayananda himself lists fifty-two articles of belief that are more restrictive. These defined his scriptural canon more precisely, gave a more complete delineation of his theistic doctrines of creation, and offered rational redefinitions of many traditional Hindu terms.[46]

The combination of the Swami's catholicity of general approach and explicit specificity of personal views in fact proved to be destabilizing to Arya Samaj tradition. What most Aryas shared was a conviction that Hinduism needed reform to be able to fare successfully in the modern world; but they differed about how drastic that reform should be and what should be its primary direction: personal, political, or social. Doctrinally this meant that they could argue about whether it was enough for good Aryas to follow the ten rules and go about their business of social reform or political agitation, or whether they should respect more carefully the Swami's personal beliefs and pious example. The potential for disagreement over which tenets were truly fundamental to tradition thus added impetus to already latent divisions, and within a decade after Dayananda's death, the Arya Samaj suffered a major split.

RSS and the Ideology of Hindu Nation

The RSS finds its intellectual foundations for a new Hindu community not in codified doctrines that might provide reasons for discord but in a few basic nationalistic concepts more ideologically attractive than analytically precise. In this treatment of ideational foundations the RSS appears closer to the intellectual moorings of Hindu tradition than does the Arya Samaj. For the beliefs that Hindus have traditionally held in common have not been neatly formulated creeds but broad ideological understandings: ideas about hierarchy, pollution, and transmigration with obvious relevance to the socioreligious order. Within this general ideational context, great latitude was given to particular doctrines, which multiplied in the philosophical schools of classical India.

The role of these doctrines in defining Hindu identity was limited. Although scholastic philosophers could be totally convinced of the rightness of their own particular views, they generally condemned other views as simply inadequate, not heretical. Those were lesser truths, for the more simple-minded, who might one day see the light—if not in this birth, then in another. One could believe just about anything and still be considered a good Hindu. In building on nationalistic concepts adapted from Western political thought instead of codified scriptures and doctrines inspired by Western religious models, the RSS has found a way to harness the cohesive powers of Hindu tradition.

Savarkar's Ideology. Keshavrao Baliram Hedgewar, the founder of the RSS, was an organizer, not an intellectual. His achievement lay in conceiving and nurturing a cohesive, disciplined, and loyal body of workers who would have a broad influence on many areas of Hindu national life. Unlike Dayananda, he neither wrote prolifically nor enunciated new doctrines himself. Like others on the Hindu right, he was deeply impressed by the early writings of V. D. Savarkar known as *Veer*, the national "hero," a brilliant radical whose active revolutionary career was cut short in 1910 through his imprisonment by the British. In prison Savarkar managed to compose *Hindutva,* a short book that when smuggled out of prison in 1923 was to give some concrete shape to nascent ideas of Hindu community.[47]

Two catch phrases are highlighted in Savarkar's work: Hindu Nation *(hindū rāṣṭra)* and Hindu-ness *(hindutva)*. The idea of Hindu Nation stands in contrast to the idea of a composite, territorially defined political entity that developed among the secular nationalists and would be enshrined in the Indian constitution. The modern Western idea of nation, according to Savarkar, does not do justice to the ancient glory of the Hindu people, the indigenous and numerically dominant population of the subcontinent. The people whose culture grew up and developed in greater India—from the Himalayas to the southern seas, by some accounts from Iran to Singapore—this, for Savarkar, was the Hindu Nation.[48] The subcontinent is their motherland, and Hinduness is the quality of their national culture.

One of the characteristics of Hinduness is that it has nurtured many religions. Indeed, in addition to the religion of orthodox Brahmans, it has given birth to the religions of Jains, Sikhs, and Indian Buddhists—who are thus all in this sense Hindu. Savarkar's idea of Hinduness, then, explicitly distinguishes the Hindu Nation from the orthodox Hindu religion that acknowledges the authority of the Vedas. At the same time it distinguishes followers of Indic religions from those of non-Indic religions. For Savarkar, the Muslims and Christians in India are foreign elements in the Indian subcontinent, which rightfully belongs to Hindus. Hindus should actively reject any alien dominance: they have done so in the past and should renew their struggle valiantly whenever necessary.

Savarkar thus tried to inspire Hindus through historical writings, identifying the alien element differently according to the major threats he saw on the horizon at the times he wrote. Before he went to prison he wrote a highly provocative history of the 1857 uprising of the Indians against the British.[49] In this early work Hindus and Muslims fight together against European tyranny. In 1925, as communal tensions mounted between Hindus and Muslims, he wrote a book subtitled "A Review of the Hindu Empire of Maharashtra," which focuses on the development of the empire after the death of its great founder, Shivaji.[50] Although Savarkar explains to his "Muhammadan countrymen" that the blunt words to be used against the Mogul rulers are necessary and justifiable,[51] the Moguls here serve primarily as a testing ground for Hindu glory. Savarkar's final work, an interpretive history of India first published in 1963, portrayed the Muslims as the most important in a long string of foreign invaders against whom the Hindus had been successful.[52] With the section on the Muslims comprising about two-thirds of the whole, the history of India finally appears here, as it does in the eyes of many Hindu communalists, to be an incessant string of confrontations between the two communities.

Symbol and Ritual in the RSS. To this vision of the embattled Hindu Nation the RSS gives symbolic and corporate form, drawing on concepts deeply rooted in Hindu religious tradition. Imagery of the Divine Mother was taken both to the Hindu Nation itself and to the land which it inhabited.[53] The latter had in the past been desecrated by foreigners and would be "raped" by partition. The former was a "living

God" who should be served through selfless, active devotion.[54] The RSS would then offer itself as a field for heroic service to the nation. A strong RSS would foster a strong Hindu Nation.

The corporate body of the RSS is in fact strengthened by regular group life. The daily neighborhood meetings with which the movement began in the mid-twenties continue to play a vital role, instilling discipline and personal loyalties in individual members. The expansion of the movement in the thirties led to the institution of larger group meetings, which today include a cycle of six RSS festivals. Revealing the power of symbolic expression in the RSS, these festivals usually coincide with those of traditional Hindu festivals but reinterpret them in a nationalistic vein. The most elaborate observance of the RSS cycle, for example—drawing disciples from all over a geographic area—is Dashehra, an autumn celebration. Commemorating the victory of Lord Ram, the embodiment of Hindu virtue, over his demon enemy, Dashehra, is observed all over north India through elaborate folk enactments: Ram's praises are given melodramatic recital; an effigy of the demon is burned. The RSS celebration, by contrast, takes a distinct martial tone, with the demonstration of military exercises and the worship of weapons associated with Shivaji. Shivaji's coronation day itself then becomes the occasion for a festival of "Hindu Victory." The most solemn festival of the year is the traditional day of guru worship. During this festival monetary offerings are presented and worship is offered to the saffron-orange RSS banner. The banner itself is recognized as the guru, the image of the divine that RSS members are encouraged to worship. Thus, although pictures of Hindu heroes—including Hedgewar and his successor, Golwalkar—flank the banner, it is to the organization itself that primary loyalty is pledged.[55]

Since the development of ritual tradition in the RSS builds on familiar customs, it appears less obviously radical than that of the Arya Samaj, but it is in many ways more revolutionary. The reformed rituals of Dayananda remained novel versions of the individual rites long performed by traditional Hindus. They might make a statement of socioreligious protest and mark group membership, but they did not seem to have an obviously different psychological effect from the rituals they replaced. The ritual festivals of the RSS, by contrast, seem designed actively to affect its members' psyches. As a long-standing member recognizes, they "signify the attempt to awaken a national consciousness,"[56] instilling Hindu identity and forging ties within the group. Indeed, the character-building exercises of the RSS are themselves spoken of as *Saṃskārs*—the life-cycle rites thought by pious Hindus to inform personality and recodified by Swami Dayananda for Aryas in *Saṃskār Vidhi*. While Swami Dayananda attempted to present the traditional rites in their pristine simplicity, the RSS gives them a radically new meaning.

Hindu Unity: Establishing the Bounds, Attenuating Divisions

In order for Hindus to reclaim the glory of their homeland, they had somehow to unite. The Hindu drive toward strength through unity is sometimes referred to as *saṃgaṭhan*, which became an important rallying cry within Hindu nationalist circles of the 1920s.[57] In the face of both the diffuse external bounds of the Hindu community and its marked internal divisions, Hindu *saṃgaṭhan* has proven very difficult to accomplish. Activist groups that attempted to organize Hindus faced problems on two fronts. First, they had to know just who to organize: to define the limits of their group. This entailed arriving at a concept of a broad Hindu community and an understanding of their own relationship to it. Second, they had to overcome the importance of traditional Hindu caste divisions, which remain crucial to the self-understandings of most Hindus. The problem of self-definition, largely conceptual, was addressed with ingenuity. The problem of caste, however, rooted in centuries of tradition and sentiment, has not yet been successfully resolved.

Definitions: The Large Community and the Small

The most succinct definition of the concept "Hindu" on the religious right was formulated by Savarkar in *Hindutva*. Translating a Sanskrit verse of his own composition, he declared that "a Hindu means a person who regards this land of Bharatvarsha from the Indus to the Seas, as his Fatherland as well as his Holyland."[58] A nationalist definition of the "cultural Hindu," this statement is at the same time geographical (referring to "Bharatvarsha," i.e., India), genealogical (referring to a "Fatherland"), and religious (referring to a "Holyland"). It is meant to include all Indian followers of Indic religions, encompassing Sikhs, Jains, and South Asian Buddhists, as well as orthodox Hindus. But by requiring recognition of India as *both* fatherland *and* holy land, it excludes (1) East Asian Buddhists and Western devotees of Indian religions, for whom India is not a fatherland[59] and, more pointedly, (2) Indian Muslims and Christians, for whom India is not a holy land. From the viewpoint of Hindu cultural nationalism, Savarkar's formulation effectively isolates the perceived other.

Both explicitly and implicitly, the notion of the cultural, national Hindu articulated in Savarkar's definition corresponded to a concept that was vital to Hindu fundamentalists of all persuasions. Bhai Parmanand, an Arya activist and leader of the Hindu Mahasabha, espoused the definition in print soon after it was published in 1923, fourteen years before Savarkar himself ascended to the Mahasabha's presidency.[60] And although officially endorsed by neither the RSS nor the Arya Samaj, the definition encapsulates important attitudes found in both movements. For the RSS, the idea of Hinduism as a national culture explains the logic of its calling itself a Hindu cultural organization while in fact promoting the culture of the Hindu Nation. Moreover, when the inclusive dimensions of the concept are emphasized, the idea of the cultural Hindu lets the RSS keep its own explicit criteria for membership hazy, which can help it counter accusations of narrow communalism: cannot any Indian whose first loyalty is to his national culture be considered a cultural Hindu?[61] In most cases Aryas too have been ready to see themselves as Hindus in Savarkar's broad national sense—but sometimes only in that sense.

The attitude of the Arya Samaj toward the larger Hindu community has always been ambivalent. On the one hand, Aryas see themselves as the true followers of the Vedic dharma and thus practitioners of the aspect of Hindu tradition professed by most orthodox Hindus to be most essential. On the other hand, they reject in principle the majority of the practices that are in fact most crucial for ordinary Hindu life.

Depending on the circumstances, either of these attitudes could be paramount for both the larger Arya community and particular Arya individuals.

Driven by the tide of historical events and the internal development of tradition, the general stance of the Aryas has undergone some broad oscillations. As late nineteenth-century reformers, the Aryas began with a radical break from established Hinduism, but as they reached out to work within the larger Hindu community, they increasingly identified with it, particularly during the communalist conflicts of the twenties and thirties. Then after they lost many of their important Punjabi centers with the creation of Pakistan in 1947, the Aryas had to focus on reestablishing their separate institutional and religious identity. Secure again by the beginning of the seventies, they have increasingly appeared as champions of the Hindu side when communal tensions arise.

On an individual level, the ambivalence of the Aryas toward the larger Hindu community is presented by the diverse writings of Lala Lajpat Rai, an Arya active in both communal causes and the independence movement. Maintaining the distinction between religion and culture seen in Savarkar's formulation, Lajpat Rai seems to have transferred his allegiance from his Arya religion to his Hindu national culture as his involvement with the saṃgaṭhan movement increased in the twenties. In 1914, when he was forty-nine and already a well-known figure, he was still able to put a positive slant on the ambivalent Arya attitude toward Hinduism. Clarifying his position to an Arya youth group, he asserted that the Arya Samaj "has a double mission."[62] On the one hand, it is a world religion with a truth for all humanity: it "believes that the Vedic religion affords the best solution to the world's difficulties" (1:188) and "it preaches . . . to mankind in general without distinction of creed, colour or climate" (1:187). On the other hand, it has a special obligation to the Hindus, "the people who have from times immemorial believed in the teachings of the Vedas. . . . In this sense the mission of the Arya Samaj is national" (1:188). By 1919, Lajpat Rai was expressing strong concerns for communal Hindu unity. Writing in a public newspaper, like a good Arya he still considered the Vedas to be ideally definitive for Hindus but for the sake of unity was ready to expand the scope of the Hindu community: for those "who cannot accept the authority of the Vedas" it is enough if they "maintain the distinguishing features of Hindu culture in their thought and life."[63] By 1924 his enthusiasm for the Arya Samaj had clearly diminished. Now writing as a strong proponent of the saṃgaṭhan movement, Lajpat Rai expressed both detachment from and disgust with the Samaj: at one time he "was an active member of the Arya Samaj" which "signally failed to realize [the goal of saṃgaṭhan] as it went on developing its sectarian proclivities. . . . In the case of Sangathan, the Arya Samaj and the Sanatan Dharam Sabha [an orthodox Hindu group] will not allow it to flourish and succeed."[64] For Lajpat Rai at that time, the Arya Samaj, as a potentially universal but doctrinally exclusive religion, seemed less attractive than the Hindu unity he saw as practically necessary for Indian independence.

In independent India, Aryas have found themselves members of a movement whose vital glory has passed, its sectarian dimensions appearing less dangerous than they had to Lajpat Rai, but perhaps less attractive, too. By the time the Aryas had reestablished themselves at the end of the sixties, many could find congenial the Hindu Nationalist sentiments expressed in a long series of writings by Balraj Madhok, a politician of Arya background who was also a member of the RSS: India, says Madhok, is not merely a congery "of castes and communities with no element of cohesion"; like Savarkar, he understands it instead to have a defining national character, and adopting the latter's term declares that "it is the Hinduness of a man that makes him a national of India."[65] But despite the Hindu Nationalist ideals that many Aryas share with Savarkar and RSS volunteers, practical reasons can lead them to use the distinction between community and religion to assert their own particularity as members of a universal religion. Indeed, they might even use the distinction to invoke the government protections for minority religions that Hindu Nationalists do *not* generally favor. Article 30 of the Indian constitution provides protections against government interference in schools run by religious minorities—protections that are not granted to other schools.[66] Aryas, with their many educational institutions, can understandably want to have themselves classed as a distinct religious minority for these governmental purposes. Thus, in a book published in 1983 in the midst of ongoing legal proceedings on the matter, D. Vable, a contemporary Arya, describes Hinduism as the traditional Puranic religion that the Aryas do *not* follow. Citing Savarkar's definition (pp. 53–54), he asserts that the Aryas constitute a distinct religion, even though they are still Hindus by community (p. 62).

The idea, then, of a broad-based Hindu community—rooted in the national culture of the subcontinent and incorporating in spirit all Indic religions—seems to be a concept on which Hindu fundamentalists of many different persuasions can draw for their own diverse ends. All, moreover, agree that one of the major problems facing this community are its entrenched internal divisions, products of the complex institution of caste.

The Intransigency of Caste

Caste institutions have proved so intransigent to Hindu reformers and nationalists because they are so basic to Hindu tradition. Being a good Hindu does not depend very much on what individuals think or what scriptures they revere, but it does depend on what they do, and proper interaction with both human and divine beings is governed in good part by concerns of caste. Individuals are born into groups understood to be distinct by nature, and each group has its role in the economy of the universe. It was precisely through its divisions, well-ordered and well-defined, that Hindu society recognized itself as an organic whole. Yet this society, so coherent in its own terms, could not easily present itself as a cohesive force against outside communal interests. Deeply ingrained concepts of organic completeness were thus at odds with twentieth-century political imperatives of Hindu unity. Paradoxically, what may in fact be the most fundamental aspect of traditional Hindu society runs counter to one of the modern fundamentalists' most explicit goals.

The Arya Samaj: Purification without Assimilation. The solutions to caste divisions proposed by the Aryas were dramatic. In *Satyārth Prakāś,* Swami Dayananda put forward a revolutionary program to reform caste institutions. Like many Hindu reformers, he saw some value in the old Hindu division of society into four hierarchical orders: the ideals of priests, warriors, merchants, and servants, according to Dayananda, did indeed represent a natural order in society. But like other reformers, Swami Dayananda also thought that one's status in this hierarchy should not be determined by birth. The problem they all faced, then, was how to know who fits naturally into which caste. Dayananda's approach, although divorced from the affectional realities of his aspiring middle-class constituents, nevertheless reflected the competitive, egalitarian spirit that they learned from their colonial milieu. Dayananda proposed that young people, after completing their education, take comprehensive competitive examinations to determine their rank. "By adopting this system all will advance," argued Dayananda. "The higher classes will be in constant fear of their children being degraded [and] . . . the same fear will also make the children acquire knowledge and culture."[67] The motivations for education among the classes he addressed, Dayananda recognized, were the desire for socioeconomic status and the fear of its loss. Adapting the rational spirit of the age, he would harness natural self-interest to the creation of the ideal Aryan society.

Aryas after Dayananda attempted to ameliorate the worst aspects of caste society through ritual means. Ancient rites of purification revived by Aryas in the 1880s to reclaim Indians lost to Islam or Christianity were later used to purify the status of low-caste Hindu groups. Mass ceremonies were performed on large groups of outcastes and aboriginals. Beginning in the Punjab in 1900, by the second decade of the twentieth century these mass purification rituals spread into Kashmir and the Gangetic plain.[68] The rituals were simple, often comprising a bath, shaving the head, and initiation into simple ritual formulas. Nevertheless, their grandiose scale could make them seem impressive to those who witnessed them. Arya Samaj preachers were thus often successful when they exhorted villagers to accept the efficacy of the rites and receive the newly purified as people whose touch no longer polluted. Accordingly, the ceremony might be concluded with a caste Hindu taking food from the hand of a former untouchable, or with a newly purified person drawing water from the village well. Neither of these acts would have been tolerated before.[69]

These two strategies of caste reform, however, had little lasting effect in integrating Hindu society. Despite the efforts of a few utopian radicals, Swami Dayananda's program of examinations was never put into practice. And while mass purification rites were sometimes exciting events, they had little practical value in bringing Hindus of different castes together. For the traditional villagers among whom the newly purified would still live, the Aryas' rites were powerful enough to cleanse only the higher of the ritually impure castes, not those who actually did dirty work like tanning and scavenging. Moreover, when successful, a group conversion meant only that a marginally untouchable caste came to be seen as marginally touchable; there was still no reason for high-caste village Hindus to have much to do with them. For the educated urban Aryas who might want consciously to integrate the newly purified, there were genuine social obstacles: they simply had little in common with the former outcastes, who were mostly rural and illiterate. Ritual purification proved no quick path to social integration.

Recognizing the failure of the Samaj to transform caste structures even within its own ranks, idealistic Aryas have twice attempted radical reform. In 1895 a small group of radicals formed the Arya Bhratri Sabha. Since fear of censure from caste fellows (collectively known as *bhrātri* in Sanskrit) was one of the principal reasons why most Aryas would not put reformist ideals into practice, these radicals would form a caste of their own. They would practice the rites codified by Dayananda in *Saṃskar Vidhi* and interdine and intermarry with one another regardless of birth caste. The plan, however, was never realized, in part because the members could not agree over the matter of vegetarianism—the problem of what to eat, not with whom.[70] In 1922, a new group was formed along different lines: the Jat Pat Todak Mandal, the "Circle to Destroy Caste Differences." This was a society that would work to undermine caste distinctions throughout the Hindu community, publishing pamphlets, holding conferences, and sponsoring intercaste dinners and marriages. Although it was begun as part of the Arya Samaj, it extended its membership to all who would pledge to work against distinctions in their personal practice, preferably through the very radical step of intercaste marriages. Indeed, in promoting their society's goals, members went so far as to deny the classical theory of four ideal social orders that even Dayananda retained in revised form: too many Aryas were using the theory as a pretext for continuing traditional caste practices. Recognizing the enormity of its task, the Jat Pat Todak Mandal was able to take pride in its very modest successes, but it did not succeed in visibly altering the Arya Samaj, let alone the greater Hindu world.[71]

Thus, for most Aryas, Swami Dayananda's radical ideas about caste led to few radical reforms. For the majority, there were only two practical results. First, born Brahmans had no monopoly on ritual functions in the Arya Samaj, although Brahmans, being educated, often did serve as ritual specialists. Second, orthodox restrictions on intermarriage and interdining among members of Arya Samaj families might be relaxed somewhat—as they might among members of many Hindu sectarian groups—but radical departures would risk the opprobrium of caste elders, a risk that only the most principled would take.

In their reconciliation to most traditional Hindu caste restrictions, the Arya Samaj majority is able to invoke the example of the mature Dayananda. Whatever he might have believed in principle, the Swami during his later years avoided actions that would alienate him from orthodox Hindus. He wanted to be a leaven in Hindu society, he would say, not an outcaste from it.[72] The leaders of the RSS seem to have understood these lessons experienced by the Arya Samaj and its founder. Instead of suggesting radical alternative models that were difficult to attain, they are content to transform caste society slowly from within.

RSS: Attenuation and Equalization. The Hindu Nation envisioned by the RSS would live in the subcontinent as an ordered organic whole. This vision is in many ways consistent with traditional views of caste hierarchy, where different castes serve complementary functions; but as is often the case in moderate Hindu reform, the RSS ideal of caste is revised to emphasize all functions as *equal* in the sense of being necessary for the social organism.[73] The RSS preaches against caste pride but does not try actively to abolish caste institutions at large. M. S. Golwalkar, the second head of the RSS, affirmed that the Sangh "simply does not recognize" untouchability.[74] At summer training camps people say they don't know and don't care what the caste of their fellows is. Work is assigned regardless of birth caste.[75]

Yet however sincere in-group feelings of solidarity and disregard for ritual pollution may be, to outsiders the RSS can easily appear to represent forces of caste privilege. If, as Golwalkar asserts,[76] working actively to address past social injustices can promote caste separatism, with oppressed groups singling themselves out for privileges, failure to do so in fact upholds the status quo. Like American conservatives against quotas, Golwalkar stresses the need for individual discipline "for building up a homogeneous unified . . . people."[77] At the same time, in Maharashtra and Madras traditional frictions between a Brahman elite and a large non-Brahman peasant population have influenced the actual caste composition of the RSS: in those regions, a preponderance of Brahmans in *any* organization may lead non-Brahmans to shun it, which has caused the RSS branches there to evolve as largely Brahman groups perceived as serving Brahman interests.[78] Moreover, since many of the RSS's senior elder statesmen have come from the Maharashtrian Brahman community in which it first emerged, the RSS is sometimes seen at the national level too as an instrument of a Brahman elite. In its current north Indian strongholds, however, the RSS is not predominantly Brahman. RSS supporters there come mainly from middle castes of clerks and shopkeepers; upwardly mobile members of lower castes join too, although they remain poorly represented in leadership positions.[79] Perhaps more marked in the profile of the usual volunteer than any type of caste is that he belongs to a middle to lower-middle economic *class*.

Although neither the Arya Samaj nor the RSS has radically altered traditional caste customs, they may have been able to alter caste attitudes, some more, some less, conscious. With the daring public innovations of the Arya Samaj, powerful symbolic meaning could be conveyed to Hindus at large. Swami Dayananda, in declaring the Vedas to be fundamental to the strength of the Hindu community, opened up the sacred scriptures to all castes. He taught that all Hindus should be allowed to hear and study the Vedas, no longer just the well-born; whatever caste they remained, all Hindus, in this very basic religious sense, would become equal. Moreover, well-publicized mass "purifications" of low-caste groups suggest the possibility that the status of a particular caste need not be static, but can be improved—a principle developed in practice by modern caste associations. The group dynamics of the RSS, by contrast, can powerfully affect the caste consciousness of those within its own ranks, who in fact often come from the groups that most need their caste consciousness transformed. Distinctions of caste within the group seem less important as loyalties strengthen over long periods of time. Discussing the value of regular group meetings, an RSS enthusiast asserted that if a volunteer "believes in the distinctions of caste, mixing with different people broadens his outlook and he rises above [these] petty distinctions."[80]

Certainly RSS members like to believe this is the case. Balasaheb Deoras, the third and current RSS head, tells a story to illustrate how the formal integration of RSS programs can lead even a fastidious high-caste Hindu at least temporarily to abandon ritual restrictions and thus to question their validity. Thus, the subtle wisdom of RSS institutions is said to have brought the young Bachharaj Vyas, a notable conservative politician from an orthodox Brahman family, to rethink Brahmanical restrictions on intercommensality. Bachharaj, it seems, was so orthodox that he wouldn't even eat at Deoras's house, let alone at the common mess at training camps; Deoras took the problem to Dr. Hedgewar, the RSS founder, who "did not quote any rule . . . to prevent Shri Bachharaj from attending the camp. He was certain that the desired reformation would definitely take place in him. . . . He told me 'Let him come to the camp. We shall give him the utensils and the rations, let him cook his own food.' This went on for the first year. Next year, Shri Bachharaj himself said to [Hedgewar] 'I shall take meals with the rest'!"[81] Thus, more important than rational argument in changing peoples' attitudes toward caste is participation in RSS activities: "Without consciously discussing equality, egalitarianism becomes a part of the ethos of the volunteers."[82]

Organization: Hierarchies and Egalitarianisms

The organizational patterns of the two groups were shaped in good part by the role they recognized for themselves in the larger Hindu community. The Arya Samaj was created and remained a *samāj,* a "society," in the sense of a voluntary organization, a group of individuals joined in a common cause. Swami Dayananda did not intend to establish a new sect with himself as guru but instead tried to set up local groups of responsible people who were to work cooperatively to foster Vedic ideals. Authority was diffused both spatially, scattered among local *samājes,* and functionally, invested in committees that could not always agree. Thus, although Swami Dayananda provided an inspiring example for generations of Aryas, he was guarded in the direct guidance he gave to those of his own time. One of the most conspicuous characteristics of the RSS, by contrast, has always been its strong hierarchical organization, with an apex in charismatic leaders who have by and large maintained practical control. Like its vision of the ideal Indian society, the RSS would consistently appear as a coherent, organic body, with a recognized head guiding firm limbs. Through disciplined action on themselves and others, members of the RSS would strengthen the Hindu Nation.

The Network of Arya Samaj Associations

While the RSS appears to have adapted some ideas of Western military discipline, the Arya Samaj seems to have learned much from the British about the administration of charitable institutions. In the more than one hundred years of its existence, the Arya Samaj has developed an extensive but loose amalgamation of associations that have allowed individual groups and their leaders to pursue their own particular ends: educational, social, political, and religious. The local groups of urban Punjabis with whom the Arya Samaj emerged in the last quarter of the nineteenth century had by the century's end inaugurated a lasting network of educational establishments. During the first two decades of the twentieth century, Aryas would further attempt to strengthen the Hindu community in the colonial environment by diversifying their socioreligious directions. Now spread throughout north India and venturing on missions abroad, they initiated associations, large and small, with aims ranging from social reform among all Hindus to aggressive sectarian missionizing. The general deterioration of relationships between Hindus and Muslims in the twenties and thirties led to increasing militancy among Aryas too, as they brought their organizational resources and initiative to the Hindu communal cause. Although the partition of India in 1947 seriously diminished the scope of Arya institutions, it did not diminish the communal spirit and religious fervor of many individual Aryas. While maintaining the educational establishment they have inherited, Aryas in the last decades of the twentieth century have given new vitality to those of their institutions that propagate Arya sectarian teachings and promote broader Hindu identity.

The complexity of organization that would develop in the Arya Samaj could not have been foreseen by Swami Dayananda. Before his death in 1883, he had set up the Paropkarini Sabha, a "Benevolent Society"—a body of twenty-three respected individuals that would be his legal heir.[83] The Paropkarini Sabha was entrusted with the Swami's wealth—including his presses and publications—and charged with continuing his religious legacy in three ways: "disseminat[ing] the Vedas . . . and . . . promoting . . . [their] teachings"; "organizing a body of teachers and lecturers to work in India and other countries"; and "protecting . . . the orphans and destitutes of India."[84] But this appointive committee did not inherit the Swami's charisma. Indeed, containing a large minority of non-Arya members—many named during the latter part of the Swami's life, when he was interested in propagating his message among Hindus at large—the Paropkarini Sabha was nowhere given formal authority over the many local Arya Samaj "societies." With no mechanism in place for coordinating their activities, the local groups were initially left free unto themselves. Eventually Pratinidhi Sabhas, "representative councils," were organized—along provincial lines beginning in the Punjab in 1886 and on a nationwide basis in 1909.[85] By 1940, the provincial councils together could count more than two thousand affiliated local units.[86] In addition to coordinating the activities of the local samājes and the various charitable institutions attached to them, the councils also launched some larger socioreligious organizations of their own. The activist religious legacy entrusted by Dayananda to a single appointed committee was thus vigorously implemented through groups that were often locally based and beholden to little central authority. Impressive in scope but loose in its internal organization, this network of Arya Samaj institutions found its greatest coherence during times of crisis.

The first major coordinated effort among the local samājes of the Punjab, sparked by the crisis of Dayananda's death, turned out to be a resounding success: in the Swami's memory, a college was to be built at Lahore. Proposed publicly with great initial enthusiasm in the year that the Swami died, the institution eventually opened on a small scale three years later, in 1886, after a long fund-raising campaign.[87] Flourishing as the "Dayanand Anglo-Vedic" college, it was the first, and long the most important, of a broad complex of schools and colleges throughout north India that bear that name.[88] As the name implies, these institutions were to provide instruction in Indological subjects as well as Western ones. Generally well regarded, they have provided the Aryas with an important link to the larger Hindu community, from which most of the students eventually came.

Becoming entrenched in the Indian education system, the DAV schools (as they are commonly abbreviated) ultimately differed little from many institutions covering the standard government curriculum. This was not what many in the Samaj had intended, and within a few years of the original college's founding a significant faction of activists objected to the direction that they saw the college taking. That direction, they correctly understood, was due to the dominant role in the college of moderate worldly nationalists who, they felt, had abandoned the radical truths of Swami Dayananda's religious ideas. In 1893 a formal split occurred between the two groups in Lahore, with the moderates holding their annual meeting at the college and the radicals holding theirs at the Arya Mandir, the "temple" in the city.[89] By 1902, the radicals were able to open a school of their own that gave more emphasis to traditional learning—the *gurukul* at Kangri, outside Hardwar. The split eventually extended far beyond Lahore to create two broad groups with parallel organizations, still referred to as college and gurukul Aryas.

The first of the Arya institutions to develop, the educational establishments were also the most widespread and enduring. Of these, the network of DAV institutions had the widest scope, from their first years receiving many of their students from non-Arya Brahman and Hindu mercantile communities.[90] Within a decade of its founding, the college at Lahore inspired local groups throughout the Punjab to found elementary, middle, and high schools with similar orientations. These frequently sought association with the DAV managing committee at Lahore, which by 1910 found it necessary to establish formal rules for their affiliation.[91] The movement soon spread throughout north India, with many schools being run by local samājes and provincial committees. The 1941 Arya Directory listed 179 schools and 10 colleges in India and Burma, with outposts as far south as Sholapur, Maharashtra, and Hyderabad state.[92] At the same time, the gurukul at Kangri became the nucleus for an alternative educational network catering to a more narrowly Arya constituency. Inspired by the ideal of the ancient forest hermitage, the original gurukul was a boarding institution established at an isolated site, where students experienced a daily routine of early rising, physical exercises, and morning and evening prayers. Although much attention was given to Sanskrit, academic work still included Western as well as Indian subjects.[93] The ascetic regimen and practical Indian education of the gurukul had enough appeal to Hindus of idealistic vision to lead to the founding of similar institutions in less isolated locations of the Punjab and Gangetic plain. In 1911 an important gurukul was founded at Vrindavan,[94] and by 1941 the number of gurukul institutions at all levels totaled 33.[95] Parallel to the original DAV and gurukul organizations, exclusively for boys, there developed separate networks of girls' schools. The first of these, started by members of the radical party in 1896 in Jullundur, Punjab, by 1934 had spawned more than 100 other establishments, large and small, throughout north India.[96] Clearly, educational institutions that would somehow bring together Vedic knowledge and worldly wisdom played a vital and continuing role in the Aryas' activist program.

Additional Arya institutions arose to address specific socio-religious problems. Some of these problems, like the plight of Hindu widows, had earlier been identified by Hindu reformers; others were newly tackled by Aryas themselves. In both cases, the strength and wide spread of Arya organization aided the effectiveness of the Aryas' work. Thus, in a new Arya initiative to raise the status of low castes, at least twelve associations were dedicated to "the uplift of the oppressed" between 1903 and 1930.[97] Toward the cause of Hindu unity, these associations proceeded to purify untouchables ritually, inculcate Sanskritic customs among them, and increase their literacy.[98] During the twenties, as communal tensions grew, the mass purification techniques pioneered by the Aryas were increasingly adopted by more traditional Hindus for the "reconversion" of Muslims. The twenties and thirties thus saw the development of several large "purification associations," in which Aryas and non-Aryas worked in differing degrees of exclusivity and cooperation.[99]

In 1927, at a large Arya Samaj conference specifically called out of concerns about the continuing communal violence,[100] the Arya Vir Dal was organized. Its name translating as the "Troop of Arya Heroes," the Arya Vir Dal introduced an overtly militant element into the complex of Samaj associations. The Arya hero was enjoined to cultivate the virtues of the *kṣatṛiya*—the traditional Hindu warrior—which included fearlessness, a good physique, and, explicitly, proficiency in the use of weapons.[101] His foremost duty was to protect the culture and rights of his nation,[102] which in practice could mean participation in some of the more overt political exercises of the Aryas that began with the Hyderabad demonstrations of 1938–39.[103] Like the RSS, with which it sometimes found itself in competition,[104] the Arya Vir Dal was one of a number of organizations cultivating Hindu strength through military ideals that developed during the height of the saṃgaṭhan movement in the twenties.[105] Linked to the larger Arya network, it was particularly active in Arya causes. Although even during its heyday its numbers were not large—with about four hundred members listed in the Punjab in 1931 and five hundred in the United Provinces[106]—it has endured, an established Arya institution ready for revitalization in the communal tensions of late-twentieth-century India.

At the same time that the Arya Samaj was active during the first decades of the century as one of a number of Hindu communal organizations in India, it was alone among major organization in serving the Hindu diaspora. From the 1830s, Hindus had emigrated to other parts of the British empire, first as indentured laborers, later as traders. By the time of the first Arya missionary work abroad at the turn of the century, Hindus could be found living in isolated pockets of Africa, the Caribbean, and the Pacific. In 1902 a Bengali soldier, before leaving Mauritius with his regiment, left copies of *Satyārth Prakāś* and *Saṃskār Vidhi* with some local Hindu reformers—an incident remembered as the launching of the oldest Arya community abroad.[107] Later, in 1904 and 1905, prominent Arya leaders would visit Kenya and South Africa. By the twenties, the Aryas were established in Fiji, and by the thirties in the Caribbean and the Guyanas.

The Arya missions to Indian communities abroad were remarkably successful. Maintaining a Hindu identity, but growing distant from Hindu ways, these communities were often eager for the religious fundamentals and community organization that the Aryas offered them. Indeed, as visible minorities, these Hindus existed in circumstances akin to those in the Punjab, where the Arya Samaj first emerged in strength. Moreover, they often included large percentages of low, laboring castes like those served by Arya associations for the "uplift of the oppressed" in India, castes that could similarly benefit from the techniques to promote community solidarity and education cultivated by the Aryas. By the twenties and thirties, local samājes abroad were organizing along regional lines and affiliating as provincial bodies with the central committee in India, which thus grew to have an international scope. Serving important educational and cultural roles in their home areas, branches of the Arya Samaj outside India have more often than not continued to thrive with their local Hindu communities, although they often also suffered internal rifts as serious as those of Aryas in India. And while the Indian Aryas suffered serious institutional ruptures when India was partitioned in 1947, those abroad have been able to maintain vital institutional continuities. In South Africa, Mauritius, and Fiji, among other countries, schools, publications, and youth organizations have continued to expand and flourish through the fifties and sixties and still do today.[108] Thus, when the Arya Samaj celebrated its centennial anniversary in Delhi in 1975, members of the international branches were among the most enthusiastic participants.

The Expanding RSS Core

While the expansion of the Arya Samaj was spurred by individual initiative at the local level, that of the RSS has been guided by a central leadership and has consequently been more measured and coherent. For the first six or seven years after founding the RSS in 1925, Hedgewar apparently made little effort to recruit volunteers outside his home district of Nagpur. But he trained these diligently, by all accounts practicing himself what he preached. Although by 1932 there were probably no more than five hundred volunteers, these would be able to serve as the disciplined core of the wider RSS organization.[109] In that year Hedgewar decided to expand: first in Maharashstra, in north India five years later, and into the south at the end of the decade. By 1940, the RSS would claim one hundred thousand volunteers.[110] The forties provided fertile conditions for RSS growth. With much of the Congress leadership in jail for the duration of World War II, and with communalist Muslims increasingly vocal about the creation of Pakistan, the RSS provided a ready focus for pro-Hindu loyalties. Before its banning in 1948, membership has been reckoned at figures ranging between a core of two hundred thousand to a much larger circle of five million, depending on what range of sympathizers, youthful associate members, registered members, and active participants are counted.[111]

Throughout its growth, the RSS has continued to appear as a cohesive movement. Although there were some large-scale personnel changes during the reorganization of the RSS in the early fifties,[112] on the whole it has been free of major public rifts of the sort experienced by the Aryas from the early stages of their movement. Early disaffected leaders unable to resolve differences behind the scenes have simply dropped away.[113] Harnessing the enthusiasms and frustrations of the Hindu middle classes, the RSS manages successfully to combine modern populist ideals with some traditional Hindu patterns of spiritual hierarchy.

While authority in the RSS has regularly emanated out from the center, the vital strength of the organization has always stemmed up from the bottom: from what are called *śākhās*, "branches." The number of these in 1989 was estimated at about twenty-five thousand in more than eighteen thousand cities and villages across India.[114] The śākhās are neighborhood organizations of Hindu men and boys, divided according to age groups. Observers in both the early fifties and the late seventies report that the majority of participants at śākhā appear under 25,[115] and particular attention has been paid to the youth organization, which consists of boys aged twelve to fifteen. Ideally, the volunteers meet once a day for an hour of games, training in Indian martial arts, and maybe some songs and a lecture, finishing with a prayer to the motherland.[116] Weekly and monthly śākhās are also held for members who cannot come regularly in the morning or evening.[117]

The ethos of the śākhā has changed little since the days of Hedgewar's neighborhood groups of the twenties. The activities at śākhā are referred to as *sādhana,* a term commonly employed for a personal religious practice like worship or meditation, and are understood to shape the volunteers' character. In practice, most of the games involve cooperation as a team, and some seem specifically chosen to demonstrate the power of organization and solidarity. In one game, for example, called "nine into one," nine volunteers try to lift another up from the ground using one finger each.[118] For those who stay with śākhā, it can offer a lasting sense of being part of a larger whole. "Those who attend śākhā are one," a volunteer writes, "and the remaining are divided by caste and class."[119] Realized amid symbols of Hindu nationalism, moreover, the sense of community engendered at śākhā can be extended to both the larger RSS body and the Hindu Nation itself.[120] Only after a period of regular śākhā attendance is the oath administered that accompanies full membership in the RSS.[121] A solemn pledge, it invokes both god and the ancestors and is supposed to be binding for life.[122]

The formal leadership hierarchy of the RSS begins at the sub-śākhā level. Group leaders are responsible for age-graded troops of volunteers of about twenty or less, who usually live in a particular locality. As moral exemplars for those in their charge, group leaders are expected to provide models of service and enthusiasm.[123] They may even personally make a daily round early in the morning to wake up the volunteers in their area to come to śākhā—this daily round having become a recognized duty dignified by the title "collecting the people."[124] At the same time, the group leaders maintain links to the larger communities in their areas, inviting people to the regular cycle of RSS celebrations as well as to the special functions it sponsors. A separate individual, known as an instructor, is responsible for program in the individual groups: games, exercises, and discussion. At the śākhā level there are two corresponding offices: the secretary, the nominal head; and the chief instructor, who wields much of the practical authority.[125] Beyond the śākhā leaders are city chairmen—often prominent persons with little experience in RSS but who give it prestige—state chairmen, and a national headquarters in Maharashtra.[126]

Complementing the formal hierarchy is a network of professional organizers,[127] who provide the RSS with much of its coherence and dynamism. Of these, there may be "a few thousands spread over the country."[128] The institution of organizers in the RSS is modeled after that of renunciates in Hindu society: dedicated to a higher goal, organizers are supposed to abandon family ties and material wealth.[129] Generally young, unmarried men in their twenties, the organizers wear Indian-style dress and are expected to lead a fairly ascetic existence. Although the calling of the organizer, like that of the renunciate, is theoretically for life, many expect to return to family life after some years of service. Organizers officially serve without salary, but they get they what they need to live and function effectively, which often includes a motor scooter for getting around the city.[130]

The organizers provide much of the circulation within the larger RSS body. In touch with one another during deliberations at city, state, and national levels, they also meet two or three times a month with group leaders and instructors at sub-śākhā levels. At these meetings they discuss RSS policy on specific social and political problems, as well as practical matters of attendance, program, and administration.[131] Organizers also participate in the many social and political associations that the RSS supports, providing some coherence in a broad network of Hindu nationalist affairs. In all of their activities the organizers maintain a low profile, paying deference to the official officeholders, while in fact often wielding considerable influence.[132] Keeping in the background, they implement policy throughout the RSS and provide much of the practical leadership.[133]

At all levels, the quality of leaders is highly valued. Local leaders can inspire deep personal loyalty. Even a disaffected RSS member recalls the "demonic energy for work" of his chief instructor: "Not a little of my attachment to the RSS was the result of my deep attachment to him."[134] The ranks of middle-level organizers are carefully chosen from among the many young men selected for leadership potential and trained in camps that meet for several weeks during the year. Top leaders, finally, have been seen as spiritually gifted individuals whose judgment should be trusted. They in turn adopt an Indian ascetic style, working hard and living fairly modestly. Although they do not encourage democratic ideals, they have been legendarily accessible to disciples: even while bedridden during his final illness, we are told, Dr. Hedgewar regularly took tea with those who came to call.[135]

Membership and Leadership: Some Contrasts

The activities of the RSS and the Arya Samaj have made consistently different demands on their members. Many RSS volunteers have been initially attracted by the activities held during śākhā: games, stories, and the opportunity to attend camps.[136] Since these activities themselves are seen to build character, importance is given to regularity of attendance. Attrition remains high, and sustained absence may result in a home visit from a group leader. Value has thus been given to qualities that enhance the interpersonal dynamics of the group: loyalty, energy, and good social skills. Group life has obviously been less crucial, however, in shaping the character of Aryas. The virtues of the early Arya reformers included courage in conviction and daring to break with convention. These gave them the initiative to start new projects in the larger Hindu world, but also an independence of spirit that could make cooperation among themselves difficult. The decades around the turn of the century, when Arya institutional accomplishments were at their most vital, also resounded with dissension among individuals.[137] Indeed, one internal critic of the period attributed the Aryas' lack of progress in effecting major socioreligious reform in the larger Hindu world to the lack of community among ordinary members: "Beyond *namaste* [a polite greeting] and meeting together for an hour or so on Sundays there is hardly any living connection between us."[138] Today, too, Aryas are likely to display both the virtues and shortcomings of an independent spirit. If their social causes now seem less radical, many remain active Aryas because they are attracted to Dayananda's radical religious teaching. Although some may find comfort in formal gatherings and informal company with one another, as voluntary members of an unorthodox, missionizing religious group Aryas are still often strong individuals, outspoken in a minority view.[139] The different virtues cultivated in members of the Arya Samaj and RSS find their complement in different styles of leadership. In the RSS, the several levels of hierarchy continue to encourage the social skills of the company man. In addition to energy and initiative, a professional organizer has to know how to "get along with others."[140] Arya spokesmen, however steadfast in their doctrines, have long been known for their abrasiveness to those outside. H. D. Griswold, a turn-of-the-century missionary and Orientalist who had himself been held up to polemic in an Arya newspaper, notes "the violence displayed [by Aryas] in controversy, especially when the Dayanandi method of interpreting the Vedas is criticized."[141] Within Arya circles, moreover, separate institutional bases with their own memberships have given local leaders the freedom *not* to cooperate with one another. The biggest difference between leadership ideals in the two groups, however, may be at the highest ranks, where both have adapted models of the traditional Hindu guru.

Swami Dayananda, although unconventional in his ideas, was nevertheless an ordained *sannyāsī,* formally a renunciate who was liable to be revered as a traditional guru. While he clearly did want to be heeded as a teacher, he discouraged the worshipful adulation of his person—an attitude toward the guru frequently taken by Hindu devotees. This seems to have suited the majority of sober citizens with whom Dayananda worked during his life. They were attracted to his general message of Hindu national revival and reform, not to all the visionary specifics of his "Vedic" program. For these people, the basis of the college Arya constituency, Dayananda after his death remained an inspiration, not a model. For the more radical Aryas who started the gurukul, the Swami's specific doctrines and personal practices grew more crucial.[142] Like followers of a traditional Indian sect, they began to see the master as an extraordinary being whose every word and deed had meaning. The difference between these understandings of Dayananda as teacher seem to have been more pronounced at the turn of the century than they are today, as the two groups have converged in both practical attitudes and religious perceptions. For the radicals, Dayananda has become more distant, for the moderates, more ideal. Citizens and educators, most Aryas today understand themselves to profess a reforming message first enunciated by a lofty figure of the past.[143]

A converse of this situation is seen in the way the role of the traditional guru is adapted in the RSS. Here the top leaders have always been lay people and as such were able to serve as role models for ordinary volunteers. At the same time, they have been revered by most members as gurus, in the sense of wise men who should be obeyed. The first two RSS heads in particular struck imposing figures and were consistently, like gurus, referred to by honorifics: Dr. Hedgewar (1925–40), a large, mustachioed man, was called Doctorji; Golwalkar (1940–73), long-haired like an ascetic, was called Guruji. Like traditional gurus, the heads of the RSS have served for life and have in fact appointed their own successors. With no bitter succession struggles, the top post in the RSS has remained sacrosanct. Whatever rivalries go on within the upper RSS echelons, ordinary volunteers have a leader they can trust.

As Hindu religious institutions, the Arya Samaj and the RSS both differ structurally from traditional Hindu sectarian lineages, which still continue to find an echo in the salvational movements found around many popular Indian gurus. What are usually referred to as the Hindu sects are continuations of the legacy of a spiritual seer who has attracted a group of disciples. Perhaps there is an initial universalizing burst at the beginning of lineages, when they want to admit everyone. But when sects last, they usually find a place as a group in the Hindu caste hierarchy and are careful of their purity. Group identity is preserved through particularistic rituals and scriptures that are taken to be the legacy of the guru. Hindu religious tradition in this way becomes highly fissiparous.

The Hindu fundamentalist movements have sought consciously to preserve the universalistic moment normal at the formative stages of Hindu sect formation, attenuating and collapsing distinctions among diverse groups. Around a charismatic holy man, this universalistic moment ideally features spontaneous enthusiasm, but its preservation in a fundamentalist movement demands an emphasis on formal organizational structures that can be a basis for social change. In many ways, the idea of the guru as a manifestation of the divine has served as a key fundamental in the creation of new Hindu sectarian traditions: the guru's word and presence are what in fact command ultimate authority. Nevertheless, the guru alone is rarely able to sustain lasting social innovation. The Arya Samaj, born in an early phase of modern Hindu interaction with the West, brought ideas of traditional gurus and Western bureaucracy into an uneasy and unstable amalgamation. The RSS, a later movement, revises traditional ideas of guruhood and weds it to a larger leadership organization that has acquired a sanctity of its own. This has given the RSS the potential to be both more socially effective than the Arya Samaj and politically more dangerous.

The Movements as Social Phenomena: Organizing and Opposing

Certainly the RSS is often perceived as dangerous by some people outside it. Although many Hindus approve of its character- and nation-building activities, more are suspicious of it, remembering its association with the assassination of Gandhi.

Liberals may see it as a fascist organization that wants to take over the country and demote all non-Hindus to second-class citizens at best. Many Muslims understandably hate it.[144] About the Arya Samaj today, opinions are less pronounced and generally more benevolent. This has not, however, always been the case. By the turn of the century, Aryas in the Punjab had managed to incite a reaction among Sikhs (see chap. 10), and by the 1920s had become involved in violent confrontations with Muslims. Aryas were then visibly at the forefront of communal agitation, and as the drive toward Indian independence continued in a fitful progression through the first half of the twentieth century, Hindus and Muslims of many persuasions joined forces and split into bitterly opposing camps with unhappy regularity.[145]

Relations with Non-Hindus

Aryas: Penetration by Purification

North Indian Hindus had been on the defensive since the end of the nineteenth century. As the decennial census introduced by the British made the different communities aware of themselves in terms of their simple numerical strength, the Hindus seemed to be losing ground. Without drastic action, it appeared, the decline could be irreversible. Christianity, Sikhism, and Islam were all proselytizing religions, with active mechanisms for conversion; Hinduism was not. As things stood, the traffic in conversion was one-way, and those lost to Hinduism were gone forever. To meet this challenge, the Aryas revived an ancient rite of purification that readmitted to proper caste status Hindus who had been defiled by association with impure outsiders. Purification rituals, as we have seen, were eventually taken to low-caste Hindus to keep them within the Hindu fold. First, however, the rituals had been performed on non-Hindu Indians, beginning with individuals and later in groups. The initial group work was among castes recently converted to Sikhism or Islam, or less visibly, to Christianity.

Although it was among low-caste Hindus that purification in fact had its greatest success—leading to the difficult problem of their assimilation into caste society—it was the conversion of non-Hindus that led to the greatest conflict. Attempts at proselytization elicited protest from organized groups in other communities. The first reaction was from the Sikhs. In 1900 a group of Rahtias, recognized as low-caste members of the Sikh community, underwent purification at the hands of the Aryas. Sikh leaders had tried to intervene, but could not in fact promise the Rahtias the improvement in ritual status they desired. The purification rites themselves then enraged Sikh spectators, whose sensibilities were particularly violated when the converts—who had previously remained unshorn in Sikh fashion—had their heads ritually shaved.[146] The incident led to protest meetings by educated Sikhs and fueled already simmering controversies on the problem of Sikh separatism: in what ways were Punjabi Sikhs radically different from Punjabi Hindus?[147] Conversion of Muslims in the midst of the communal conflicts of the twenties, however, led to widespread violence.

In 1923, Swami Shraddhananda, a dynamic Arya leader and long-standing head of the gurukul at Kangri, founded the Bharatiya Hindu Shuddhi Sabha, the "Indian

Hindu Purification Council."[148] This committee would coordinate the purification efforts of Arya and more orthodox Hindu groups. Their immediate goal was to reclaim to Hinduism the Malkana Rajputs, a group of recognized high-caste origin that had become Islamized over the centuries. Muslim proselytizing groups organized in response, competing in converts, cash, and acerbity of argument.[149] Contributing to the tension were incendiary pamphlets produced by both sides. Muslim and Hindu communalists employed their verbal skills in ways that seemed intentionally designed to infuriate each other.

The tone of the debate had already been set by Swami Dayananda. In *Satyārth Prakāś,* Dayananda presents an apology for Hinduism against other religions, treating the latter very specifically. Buddhism and Jainism were really just offshoots of Hinduism. Trinitarianism in Christianity was the same kind of anthropomorphic confusion found in traditional Hindu image worship. The sharpest treatment is saved for the last chapter, on Islam, where traditional images of heaven are mocked and no quarter is given to the prophet. Later Aryas followed suit, with sarcastic tracts like *Rangīlā Rasūl,* "The Merry Prophet," which gave particular references to Muhammad's sexual exploits. Muslims responded in kind, with bitter treatments of Arya practices.[150] Things had to come to a head, and in 1926 Swami Shraddhananda was murdered by an Indian Muslim posing as a prospective convert.

In the decades since Indian independence, Aryas have continued to make converts from non-Hindu groups, although changes in their approach make the process generally less controversial now than then. The exterior and ritual nature of the process of mass conversion in its heyday was noted by Christian observers, who decried the lack of spiritual preparation and inner conviction that is supposed to accompany genuine conversion to Christianity.[151] Much like the social role of conversion in Indian Islam, purification was instead a formal rite of allegiance to, and acceptance by, a traditional religious community. Thus, when the Muslim Mappila community of Kerala rose against the British in 1921, they reacted against the Hindus they saw to be in league with the oppressors by forcing them to swear allegiance to the prophet and wear a Muslim-style hat; these forced converts, however, could be reconverted by ritually consuming the products of the cow and wearing Hindu dress.[152] Today, the rite is more often performed for individuals—and at a higher cost in evident sincerity, moral uprightness, and time for preparation.

No longer a mass ritual performed largely for north Indian villagers, contemporary Arya purification has become a sedate ceremony occasionally enacted for personally motivated members of the urban middle classes all over India. At a rite performed in 1970 for an Indian Catholic in Bangalore, south India, the Arya preacher stressed the inner meanings of purification—"the purity of the heart": "Above all, remember the threefold purity and pray: Let God purify my speech, my actions, my whole life."[153] But despite the present emphasis on purification's inward aspects, conversion is still often undertaken largely out of social concerns, particularly, as in this case, for marriage with a Hindu.[154] And especially to cover such cases, the Arya Samaj has extended the practical meaning of purification from a resanctification of Indians of other religions, who were by birthright Hindu, to the outright "conversion" of Europeans.

RSS: Religion, Culture, and Assimilation

The Aryas' confrontations with the Muslims in British India straightforwardly employed the religious tools developed by Dayananda: formal ritual process together with rational, if literal-minded and sarcastic, argument. The approach of the RSS toward minorities is more subtle—some would say insidious—giving a new turn to Savarkar's distinction between Hindu religion and Hindu national culture. Since religion is a personal matter, RSS members may say, all individuals should be able to have whatever religion suits them: Christianity, Islam, Hinduism, whatever. Nevertheless, Muslims and Christians should not remain culturally apart from the body of the nation. They should instead become fully integrated into the national culture, which is in fact Hindu.

This development of Savarkar's teachings has taken a few decades to work out, and has not always worn such a benign face—which indeed sometimes does seem to be a façade. In *Hindutva,* Savarkar clearly identified Muslims and Christians as the "other." Their alien presence in the subcontinent was understood to be a problem for the Hindu Nation, but no suggestions were offered about how this problem was to be resolved. Over his career, however, M. S. Golwalkar, the second head of the RSS, has presented some solutions of more and less drastic sorts. Writing before and after Indian Independence, his ideas show a clear continuity in substance but differ radically in tone and expression.

The solution offered by Golwalkar in *We* (1939) falls short of a "final solution" of the sort that was simultaneously being proposed in Germany, but not by much: "There are only two courses open to the foreign elements, either to merge themselves in the national race and adopt its culture, or to live . . . [in] the country at the sweet will of the national race . . . the foreign races . . . must lose their separate existence . . . or may stay in the country, wholly subordinated to the Hindu Nation, claiming nothing, deserving no privileges, far less any preferential treatment—not even citizen's rights."[155] Indeed, Golwarkar was impressed by the example of European Fascism: "Germany shocked the world by her purging the country of the semitic Races—the Jews. Race pride at its highest has been manifested here. Germany has also shown how well-nigh impossible it is for Races and cultures, having differences going to the root, to be assimilated into one united whole, a good lesson for us in Hindusthan to learn and profit by."[156]

Writing before the full horror of Nazi persecution would become known, Golwarkar did not later flaunt this aspect of his intellectual lineage, and the RSS has tried to suppress it. *We,* Golwalkar's only deliberate composition, is no longer in print—despite the repeated publication of haphazard collections of Golwalkar's interviews and addresses of the fifties and sixties.[157] In those later works, Golwalkar's tone toward non-Hindus in India is more paternalistic. The only realistic option he seems to be able to see in independent India is: "the merging of non-Hindus into the main [i.e., Hindu] national stream. . . . They should experience the same "sense of belonging" as the Hindus do to this country, its people, its culture. . . . If, after fulfilling all these anybody says that he studied the Koran or the Bible and that that way of worship strikes a sympathetic chord in his heart, he is welcome to follow it."[158]

When religion really is separated from culture, "Hinduness" can tolerate even more religions than the Indic ones Savarkar originally had in mind. Thus, Golwalkar can speak of "Hindu Muslims,"[159] presumably Hindu by culture and Muslim by religion. This expression, moreover, does seem to reflect a partial truth, particularly in respect to popular Indian Islam on the ground, which is itself often decried by orthodox Muslims as corrupt and "Indianized." Yet Golwalkar's tolerance remains limited, not extending beyond a narrow sphere of personal piety. A Muslim "has a choice in a portion of his individual life. For the rest he must be one with the national current."[160]

Merged in "the national current," members of minority groups should not seek special treatment. Although the idea that all should be absolutely equal under the law may strike Western democrats as just, its practice within the corporate pluralism of India can also be seen to retain power in the hands of high-caste Hindus and to discriminate against particular groups. Traditionally oppressed Hindu castes would get no special compensatory evaluation of civil service and university entrance examinations. Muslims, for whom traditional law is an integral part of their religion, would not be able to obey it in their own interpersonal relationships—an issue that exploded in the eighties with the case of Shah Bano, an elderly Muslim woman whose traditional Islamic divorce settlement was challenged in Indian civil court.[161] For most Muslims, then, restricting religious identity to a narrow sphere of personal piety, as Golwalkar would do, is not enough; being religiously Muslim in India is also likely to demand acting socially and culturally Muslim.

Many RSS members, one suspects, realize this. Is not their Hindu religion intimately bound up with their culture and society? A good part of the socioeconomic dynamics behind this largely middle-class, high- and middle-caste movement seems to derive from the accurate perception that separate minority groups will *not* easily merge away, and that present political arrangements do offer them special, apparently advantageous, treatment. Class interests come together with religiocultural vision. Like the fascist youth groups of the thirties with which it bears a more than passing resemblance, the RSS wants the majority group to *rule*.

Roles in Hindu Society

RSS: the Attractive Nucleus

Members of the RSS would realize their vision of a Hindu Nation by serving as an active nucleus for it. The character-building exercises practiced in its wide network of śākhās would instill Hindu cultural values on a wide scale, while its dedicated core of organizers would spread out to work energetically in many directions. The RSS itself tries to maintain a lofty status as a religiocultural organization and still have an active influence on national life by maintaining unofficial links with particular labor unions, student groups, and other organizations. It maintains these links in large part by supplying the institutions it favors with its trained, professional organizers. The organizers, working temporarily in different places, will readily admit that their primary loyalty is to the RSS, but they are also quick to add that the RSS does not dictate policy to them.[162]

All the groups supported by the RSS say they have a particular Indian approach to their activity. The labor movement, for example—echoing ideas of natural aptitudes found in idealizations of the caste system—says that work should be tailored to the needs of each individual. Workers with similar aptitudes should be grouped together into occupational families, with the families themselves determining working conditions. Ideals like this do not obviously support the interests of industrial barons or the landed aristocracy, and there is in fact a strong element of populism running through RSS ideas and programs, which tend to favor the small farmer and entrepreneur. Neither communism nor capitalism is right for India, which must find its own way along the lines of the Hindu organic model of society. And whatever individual RSS members might have in mind for minorities, the reformed Hindu social ideals they advocate also run counter to Western fascisms. The latter generally imply a monolithic nation under a powerful leader, not the nation composed of individual communities in organic cooperation envisioned by Hindu reformers from Dayananda on. Alongside a strident communal stance, then, runs a nativist economic progressivism and Hindu egalitarianism.[163]

Accordingly, the Jana Sangh, the erstwhile political affiliate of the RSS, cultivated a program that was reactionary more in a communal than an economic sense. As early as 1954, its working committee advocated labor-oriented approaches in both industrial and agricultural sectors: for factory workers, profit sharing and participation in management; for farmers, the absolute abolition of landlordism, in most cases without compensation. The same year, the committee proposed a maximum ratio of one to twenty for incomes in the country—a figure repeated RSS writings. All this did not please the party's conservative, pro-business wing, who finally bolted, claiming that the party had been taken over completely by the RSS.[164] Taking the "common man's approach to political problems,"[165] Jana Sangh workers were able to advocate the party's well-known pro-Hindi stance by arguing that an English education is not only un-Indian but also elitist and expensive.[166]

The experience of building a solid core for an egalitarian Hindu Nation may be psychologically reinforced through the bonding experience at śākhā, which seems to be one of the RSS's lasting attractions. Long-time RSS members idealize the sense of community cultivated in śākhā "inter-personal relationships develop over the years into unbreakable friendships . . . the personal relations developed in the śākhās are the perennial source of power in reserve" for the Sangh.[167] Although the majority of active participants in śākhā are between eighteen and twenty-five years of age, children can come as early as six or seven,[168] so for some, ties to the group can take root very early.

The bonding experience offered by the RSS is one between males. Women are not permitted membership in the organization, although they have a separate, much smaller group, joined informally to the RSS by family links. In Hedgewar's judgment, the admission of women into the Sangh would not be appropriate; and the mixing of the sexes—particularly in the situation of physical contact at śākhā—would in fact run counter to Hindu norms.[169]

Indeed, part of the reason for the wide spread of the RSS is that it offers a vital, moderately egalitarian vision of Hindu life without radically departing from conventional Hindu beliefs and practices. It does not try to argue against tradition but instead tries to play to sentiments, traditional and otherwise. "Rational arguments separate people from us," volunteers have been told at training camp: volunteers should instead appeal to people's hearts and "attract society with a sweet tongue."[170] Thus, RSS workers are known for their polite and conciliatory manner. The polish of the RSS workers and the openness of the organization to all Hindus has made it attractive to members of lower castes, for whom it may boost social status.

Arya Samaj at the Forefront

The strategy of the Aryas for shaping Hindu society presents a sharp contrast to that of the RSS volunteers. The Arya Samaj appears not as a cohesive, broad-based nucleus of a nation but as an exceptional vanguard of national reform. In this role it can even affirm its separateness from traditional Hinduism, feeling the need to keep its own particular base firm in order to change the greater whole. Moreover, whatever its stance toward the Hindu community, the Arya Samaj relates to the public not through sweet words and affective ties but through argument—both rational and dogmatic—and educational institutions.

Although upwardly mobile Hindus have long sent their children to Arya Samaj schools, many have been uncomfortable with Arya Samaj belief and practice. To traditional Hindus, the Aryas' reforming ways seemed unorthodox at best, if not blasphemous and polluting: Vedic sacrifices might be a fine thing now and then, but not at the cost of disdainfully dismissing image worship; and the idea of eating with newly converted untouchables was beyond what many could bear. Yet some of the Aryas' reforms became accepted by the larger community. Early on, setting trends found in modern urban society, the Aryas gave full membership to women: how could society advance if the men adopted new attitudes and the women carried on the old customs in the home? The Aryas pioneered the practice of Hindu conversion; orthodox Hindu groups followed their lead—particularly after the forced conversion of Hindus to Islam by the Mappilas in 1921, which made even the most orthodox see the necessity for the practice.

Because of their religious differences, the Aryas sometimes found it hard to work with other Hindu communal groups. Why should a devout Arya help purify people from the defilement of Islam just so they could take up false Hindu image worship? Orthodox Hindus, to be sure, had corresponding qualms.[171] Outspoken, educated, and willing to be innovative, Aryas have found themselves more on the forefront of communal affairs than in the middle of them.

Political Roles: Agitation or Representation?

Although the communal agitation to which both the Arya Samaj and RSS have lent support frequently aim to influence specific government policies, they do not in themselves represent sustained attempts to share in political power. Nevertheless, many members of both groups, wanting to create an ideal Hindu order in the subcontinent, have been attracted to direct political action, through legal or illegal activities during the British Raj or through the electoral process in independent India. The organizations themselves, however, have remained ambivalent. In the Arya Samaj the ambivalence about politics has been due to conflicts at the religious root of tradition: what was the real import of Dayananda's message? In the RSS the ambivalence seems more pragmatic, hinging on the most effective role for the organization in the practical circumstances it faced. Although through most of the 1980s both groups seemed to find active agitation in Hindu communalist causes a more productive use of their energies than direct participation in electoral politics, by the end of the decade these two dimensions of activism had combined into a surprisingly powerful political force.

Arya Agitation in British India

The message of Swami Dayananda—essentially one of religious revival and reform—was liable to two major political interpretations. The golden age of the Vedas, according to the Swami, was one in which Indian kings had subdued the world;[172] thus, if the glory of that age were to be renewed, the inheritors of the Veda would again certainly rule in their own homeland. On this much most Aryas could agree. They differed, however, on whether they understood Vedic religious renewal or Hindu political rule to be the most appropriate immediate goal. At the initial split in the movement at the end of the nineteenth century, the gurukula Aryas generally opted for the first choice, seeking to build a bastion of Vedic community away from the world. Some prominent college Aryas, on the other hand, became active in nationalist politics, cooperating with other Indians against British rule.

The attitude of the British to the two groups thus differed. They were most concerned about the college Aryas—established people with an influence on urban youth that might be tapped for political ends. Moreover, one of the college Aryas, Lala Lajpat Rai, had become a major nationalist leader who in 1907 would be sent into exile. But the gurukul party, too, could seem suspicious. Wasn't the gurukula itself supposed to produce preachers of the Arya message for the larger Hindu community? Who knows what the teachings on self-reliance and Vedic glory of these well-trained zealots might forbode?[173] British power still reigned mightily in India during the first decade of the twentieth century, and as government suspicions against the Aryas increased following the deportation of Lala Lajpat Rai, both groups hastily issued proclamations affirming their nonpolitical roles.[174]

The Aryas still continued in communal causes, however, which toward the end of British rule found overt political expression. In the winter of 1938–39 the Aryas, together with the Hindu Mahasabha, began to organize mass demonstrations in the large south Indian state of Hyderabad, which was ruled by a wealthy Muslim monarch known as the Nizam. Out of sheer bigotry, claimed the Aryas, the Nizam and his government were violating the rights of his Hindu subjects. In July 1939, after eight thousand Hindus had been jailed, the government announced political reforms, and the Aryas could headily claim victory.[175] The success of this broadly communal initiative later encouraged the Aryas to take political actions toward their own sectarian goals. In 1943, Muslim leaders who objected to the portrayal of Islam in the last chapter of *Satyārth Prakāś* were pressing for its ban in Sind—a Muslim-majority area in present-day Pakistan. The Arya Samaj responded with threats of mass action. Over the next few years the government wavered, declared a ban it did not enforce, and tried to reach accommodations with the Aryas. But the Aryas stood firm and enlisted the support of other Hindu groups. Finally, in 1947, protesters were called in from other provinces to join in mass demonstrations.[176] Thus, sixty years after Dayananda's death, the book expressing his vision of a renascent nation grounded in Vedic truth would provide a rallying point for Hindus able to foresee an independent India.

This movement toward renewed popularization of fundamentalist politics, which the RSS would continue to foster, seems consistent with the larger lines of development of fundamentalism in Hinduism as it moves its center of gravity from higher to lower socioeconomic strata, becoming increasingly more indigenous. The fundamentalist impetus takes hold among Hindus as the Aryas become impressed with a new idea of religion: aggressive, nationalistic, and advocating social change. Its focal symbol, the Vedas, had wide authority among Hindus but was associated with a Brahmanic elite and practically divorced from most peoples' experience, pointing to a golden age in a very distant past. Moreover, despite eventual orthodox acceptance of several Arya innovations, the immediate result of the radical programs espoused—if not practiced—by most Aryas was often divisive within the Hindu community, leading to doctrinal quarrels and the threat of social ostracism. With the RSS, the symbols are drawn from a more immediate past and have a more effective emotional impact. Avoiding divisive religious issues and keeping social reforms low-key, it penetrates a broader socioreligious sphere. From a principal self-identification as an embattled, aggressive sectarian minority, Hindu fundamentalists began to see themselves more defiantly as righteous representatives of a threatened majority. Forging themselves into a disciplined corporate body, they would mobilize the Hindu Nation.

The RSS and Party Politics

Although the RSS can easily appear as a potent political force, it has consistently stayed officially aloof from electoral politics. This was particularly true in its early days, before the RSS had developed its network of affiliated organizations. Indeed, a possible overt political role for the RSS became a point of tension between Hedgewar and Savarkar, who sought the active support of the RSS for the Hindu Mahasabha when he led it during the late thirties and early forties. Even though the two were ideological allies, Hedgewar refused in principle to align the RSS formally with any political party. This stance led Savarkar to make a pointed comment on the ineffectiveness of the RSS: "The epitaph on a Sangha Svayamsevak [RSS volunteer] will be: 'He was born; he joined RSS; he died.'"[177] RSS leaders, of course, see it differently. Perhaps they would prefer to play the role of institutional guru to the nation, keeping their own sanctity as an institution pure and unstained by the tough and sometimes dirty business that electoral politics in India often entails.[178] Of the many tales of the military hero Shivaji narrated at śākhā, one of the favorites, they say, is the story of Shivaji offering his rule to his own guru Ramdas—with the emphasis on the figure of the guru himself.[179]

Thus, whether or not the RSS itself should be considered a political organization depends in good part on one's definition of politics. By its own narrow definition of fielding candidates in elections, the RSS is clearly not a political group. But with its wide network of affiliates, it does obviously try to influence national life. A well-disciplined organization working behind the scenes, the RSS is open to widespread suspicions. To its supporters, frequent, and sometimes ill-founded, accusations against the RSS can make it appear as a "whipping boy for all."[180] Formal ties to the RSS may then prove to be an embarrassment for contemporary politicians, certainly a more problematic association than the Arya roots of some early nationalist leaders. While membership in the Arya Samaj could be viewed by most Hindus as an idiosyncrasy—a personal belief that did not bind them to any policy—membership in the RSS may be taken as allegiance to another, quasi-political authority.

Moreover, despite its claims to be nonpolitical, the RSS has counted among its affiliates two political parties: the Bharatiya Jana Sangh, usually referred to simply as the Jana Sangh; and its de facto successor, the Bharatiya Janata Party, commonly abbreviated as the BJP. The names of both groups have much the same meaning, variants of "The Indian People's Party." Founded in 1951 with the support of the RSS leadership, the Jana Sangh began as the political vehicle of S. P. Mukerji, a nationally known member of parliament from the Hindu Mahasabha who disagreed with its policies on restricting membership to Hindus.[181] Through the Indian general elections of 1952, 1957, and 1962, the Jana Sangh established a political base, but was nowhere a significant force against Nehru's Congress. By the elections of 1967, however, the political situation had changed: Nehru had died, the economy was in recession, and there was visible dissension within the ruling party.[182] The Congress under the newly installed Indira Gandhi was returned to power by only a small majority. Many of the Congress losses in fact proved to be gains for the Jana Sangh—now the second party after Congress in total number of votes cast and state assembly seats.[183] In the 1971 elections, called by Indira Gandhi after she had established her authority, the Jana Sangh saw its strength erode, but then became an important partner in the Janata coalition that displaced her regime in 1977. The BJP emerged in early 1980 with the disintegration of that coalition, but did not become a viable political force until the elections of 1989.

As it did with its other affiliated groups, the RSS supported these political parties in good part by lending them its professional organizers. A dedicated core of like-minded people who value cooperation is a precious asset to any organization, not least in the fractious world of Indian politics. Indeed, to other elements of the Janata Coalition of the late 1970s, the cohesiveness of the Jana Sangh group could appear as a threat, prompting a public call for all Janata members to renounce RSS affiliation—an issue that figured in the government's collapse.[184] But it was not so much the formal RSS link that gave coherence to the Jana Sangh and BJP cadres as it was their organizational skills and their common political goals. While changing according to practical circumstances, these goals have usually included a strong defense, entailing a nuclear arsenal,[185] Indian control of industry,[186] and as we have heard from Golwalkar, the removal of preferential quotas for depressed castes as a step toward ending "casteism" in general.[187]

Although the political objectives espoused by the Jana Sangh and the BJP are consistent with an RSS perspective, they are not articulated in the rhetoric of Hindu culture found in the works of Golwalkar. Instead they are put forward with slogans highlighting Indian national development and distinctive Indian ways of life—"Self-Reliance,"[188] "Indianization,"[189] and an "Integral Humanism" taken "in direct contrast with with the compartmentalized thinking of the West."[190] Indeed—unlike the Hindu Mahasabha, a political party explicitly of and for Hindus—the Jana Sangh and BJP have aimed for a national scope and emphasize that they admit non-Hindus, occasionally fielding Muslim and Christian candidates.[191] Moreover, some leaders of these parties have emerged as prominent national figures. L. K. Advani and A. B. Vajpayee have both risen from RSS organizers, to ministers in the Janata coalition government, to president of the BJP: Vajpayee from 1980 to 1985; Advani from 1986 into the 1990s. Moreover, Vajpayee, as Janata foreign minister, maintained a nonsectarian national stature, visiting Pakistan, eating with Muslims, and giving addresses in cultured Urdu.[192] Thus, during times when there is a modicum of discontent with the government in power, the Jana Sangh and the BJP have been able to appear as significant parties of opposition.

Despite the continuities in the leadership of the Jana Sangh and the BJP, the two parties have cultivated differences in political image. The Jana Sangh had developed its strength within much the same circumscribed constituency in which the RSS expanded in the fifties and sixties: middle-class Hindus of the Hindi-speaking north Indian plains.[193] The symbols of the party came clearly out of Hindu tradition. Its banner, like that of the RSS, was saffron—a color associated with Hindu asceticism; its emblem was the Hindu prayer lamp. With the creation of the Janata Party in 1977, the Jana Sangh lost its formal identity. When the the old Jana Sangh leaders established a new political party after the Janata's collapse, they attempted to preserve something of the broader base of support they had known when in power. Forming the Bharatiya (Indian) Janata Party, they now presented themselves as the true inheritors of the Janata coalition and a genuine national alternative to the Congress. Several delegates not affiliated with the old Jana Sangh were on the party's first working committee, and a Muslim, Sikhandar Bakht, was one of its general secretaries. To the saffron of the Jana Sangh's banner, that of the BJP added green, a color associated with Islam, and which, together with saffron and white, is featured in the Indian flag. The symbol of the new party, the lotus, had connotations that were more Indian than distinctly Hindu. "Gandhian Socialism" replaced "Integral Humanism" as the party's articulated first principle, although at its first plenary session BJP president Vajpayee was careful to explain away inconsistencies between the two ideological positions.[194]

Certainly, marrying the organizational power of the Jana Sangh's RSS workers with the political breadth of the Janata's following was a creative idea, but it did not soon bear substantial fruit. In the early 1980s the BJP enjoyed a few initial successes, but then it suffered a disillusioning string of electoral losses. The new party did not in fact prove particularly attractive to the general Indian public, who had recently opted in overwhelming numbers for Indira Gandhi's proven, authoritative style. Nor did it broadly inspire RSS activists, still wounded by their experience of electoral alliances. Moreover, after the 1984 assassination of Mrs. Gandhi in the cause of Sikh independence, her son Rajiv represented a fresh ray of hope, and support for the Congress seemed a realistic strategy for achieving the national unity valued on the Hindu right. The BJP thus lost much of its potential clientele.[195]

Disenchanted with the political process, RSS organizers turned their attention to Hindu revival. The mid-eighties saw the dramatic expansion of the RSS's religiously oriented affiliate, the Vishva Hindu Parishad, the "World Hindu Society." The incident sparking the emergence of the VHP, as it is known, is familiar from the early part of the century: the conversion in 1981 of a small group of low-caste Hindus in Minakshipuram, south India, to Islam. The incident has, moreover, evoked responses similar to the Arya Samaj's early social programs: extending services to low castes to keep them in the fold and promoting Hindu unity. But the latter effort has entailed offering rallying points more visible and all-encompassing than those earlier held out by the Aryas. Elaborate "unity processions" across the country featured a portrait of Mother India in the form of a goddess and large urns containing water from the holy river Ganges.[196] And the VHP became active in the agitation at Ayodhya: a celebration of Ram's birthday it organized at Ayodhya in April 1986 brought together large numbers of devotees and religious dignitaries to plan strategies for the liberation of Ram's birthplace.[197]

By 1989 the VHP was very effectively promoting the building of a new temple at Ram's birthplace as a force for Hindu unity both across regions and within castes. In villages all over north India the VHP organized ceremonies called *Rām Śilā Pūjā:* "the worship of Ram's foundation stones," which in this case are ordinary bricks. Like icons of Vishnu's incarnations that are put in cradles and carried to the river to be bathed on particular holidays, these bricks are also put in cradles and worshiped with flowers and incense, together with a picture of Ram. But as one informant explained, while most Vaishnava icons are not taken into low-caste neighborhoods, these were carried throughout the village, thus symbolically equalizing castes in the Hindu community; after their worship, the bricks were taken to district headquarters, regional headquarters, and thence to Ayodhya. Through careful and widespread organization, then, the VHP has been able to involve a diverse Hindu population in its cause.

Whatever the value of such VHP work for promoting feelings of Hindu unity, it also added to the communal tension that by the late 1980s had helped transform the Indian political climate. Contributing to the growing politics of communalism was a growing dearth of political charisma in the central government. Almost inevitably, Rajiv Gandhi did not live up to people's high expectations of him. Widely referred to as "Mr. Clean" when he came into office in 1984, within two years he began to fall from public grace, becoming perceived as jealous of power and, by the end of decade, subject to corruption. And as Hindu Nationalist ideals became attractive to a broader Indian public, the BJP grew closer to its RSS roots. In 1986, the party presidency was assumed by L. K. Advani, who was more outspoken than his predecessor in his ties to the RSS, which was then seeking greater respectability and more widespread support.[198] Thus, toward the Sikhs both the RSS and the BJP continued to pursue policies that, compared to those of other Hindu-oriented groups, can appear conciliatory.[199] Unlike Punjabi Aryas, who are likely to view Sikhs as both economic rivals and doctrinal opponents, the RSS and its political affiliates have taken them as an integral element of a broadly conceived "Hindu nation." For many members of both groups, then, accommodating a Sikh-oriented Punjab within the Indian union is in principal preferable to alienating Sikh separatists. Advani has thus repeatedly referred to the help that BJP workers rendered to Sikhs during the 1984 Delhi riots following Mrs. Gandhi's assassination—and what it has at times cost them in terms of the electoral support of more extremist Hindu elements.[200] By the elections of 1989, however, a broadened BJP base together with growing communal sentiment and dissatisfaction with Rajiv Gandhi's Congress led to surprisingly large BJP gains. From two seats in the previous parliament, the BJP's representation rose to as many as eighty-eight.[201] The party was able to draw support not only from Hindu communalists confronting their Muslim counterparts but also from Delhi Sikhs who saw the Congress government as their principal foe. As a crucial ally of a minority government, the BJP had overnight turned into a significant political force.

The Persistence of Colonial Experience: Organized Hinduism and Mob Violence Today

Although contemporary Hindu fundamentalism has found growing political expression, the actual political imperatives behind it seem less pressing now than in the colonial situation within which it emerged. Certainly Hindu fundamentalism can no longer be seen simply as a religious response to social and economic problems deriving from foreign rule. Why, then, does it continue to flourish in modern India, an increasingly growing force in cultural as well as political life? What socioreligious continuities span the pre- and post-independence periods to perpetuate fundamentalist religion among Hindus? Indeed, if the Indian subcontinent provides an apt illustration of the impact of colonialism in the rise of fundamentalist movements, their persistence there may also reveal some broader dimensions of the colonial situation. On the one hand, the experience of *feeling* colonized—whatever the actual historical circumstances—can lead to religious sentiments that may be an element in fundamentalist movements as transcivilizational religious phenomena. On the other hand, an important historical residue of Western colonialism—at least in India—is the urban bureaucratic environment in which fundamentalism there flourishes. Even though the large urban areas established by the British are now largely under Hindu control, they still provide little scope for practicing traditional Hinduism. How then do the new masters react?

Feeling Colonized as a Religious Sensibility

In many ways, the nationalistically oriented, socially reformist Hindu movements treated as fundamentalist here seem polar opposites to the doctrinally conservative, traditionalist movements characteristic of Western Protestant fundamentalism. Among the most striking of the attributes they both *do* have in common, however, are those that underscore collective religious identity: group self-assertiveness, defiance, and proclivities to sporadic violence. These sensibilities of active self-righteousness are just the sort of human qualities that are likely to arise within a situation of political and cultural domination. Historically manifest in the Indian situation, this situation is also evident experientially in the West. Western fundamentalisms too derive in part from a feeling that one's world is being colonized, taken over by an alien power that is secular and perhaps demonic. In both cases, righteous religious actors must stand firm to regain their own. More than do many other religious movements, then, fundamentalists define themselves against a powerful other: the *We* of Golwarkar's notorious RSS treatise necessarily implies a "they." For Hindu fundamentalists the "theys" have always been many but after independence have increasingly included a secular government favoring religious pluralism. As among their Western counterparts, temporal power is understood to be in the hands of others, but is not thought to be so rightfully. In both Hindu India and Protestant America, the fundamentalist group is likely to see itself as the genuine representative of the majority, fighting for the majority's true interests. The paradox for both is that within their own larger traditions they are in fact distinct minorities, attempting to shape the majority to their own ideals.

The Paradox of the Defensive Majority

In Hindu tradition, the diverging loyalties brought together in this paradox of the minority as the majority is illustrated in the current state of the Arya Samaj. Before Indian independence, the Aryas maintained a full spectrum of organizations through which they could practically promote their various visions of the ideal Indian society. Whatever their different senses were of themselves as Aryas in a Hindu environment—and these were many and ambivalent—activist Aryas could find a channel for their energies. What was left of this network after Independence were largely educational establishments catering to mainstream Hindus. Through combining Western learning and Indian values, the DAV schools still attempt to inculcate Arya goals in a general way, but they do not provide much scope for activist visionaries. These then move to two opposite extremes: on the one hand, missionizing on behalf of the Arya sectarian minority; on the other hand, organizing for Hindu-majority communalism. Thus, some are fervent proselytizers of the Arya way, attempting to propagate Dayananda's iconoclastic Vedic ideals within the Hindu community and the world at large. Others are equally fervent Hindu communalists, likely to espouse the right of Hindus to worship at Ram's birthplace despite the condemnation of traditional ritual in *Satyārth Prakāś*. And many Arya activists no doubt comprehend both sectarian and communalist sensibilities, showing different sides in different situations.

Fundamentalisms in other South Asian traditions show us more clearly the other side of the paradox: that of the majority as the minority.[202] Although appearing as minorities in the subcontinent as a whole, Buddhists, Sikhs, and Muslims do have areas in which they constitute majorities: Buddhists in Sri Lanka, Sikhs in modern Indian Punjab, and Muslims in British west Punjab, now Pakistan. And it is precisely in their majority areas that fundamentalist versions of these minority South Asian religions have emerged. Variously seeing their religiocultural identity—as well as their economic well-being—threatened by Hindus with a vast nearby population base, they challenge their governments to action: to a more overtly Islamic cultural stance in Pakistan, to the establishment of the Punjab as a Sikh political entity, to the curtailment of perceived advantages given to Hindus by the secular government of Sri Lanka. Hindu fundamentalists in India, feeling their position in their own country to be eroded by government concessions to minority groups, seek similar goals of religiocultural authority and political power. Feeling threatened by hostile forces outside their own larger traditions, and sometimes even within them, fundamentalists anywhere can see themselves as righteous representatives of a majority who must act like an embattled minority. In standing firm as the majority on the defensive, fundamentalists usually develop two resources: new weapons, which they will readily adapt from their enemies, and some vivid emblems of their own.

Learning to Use Contemporary Weapons

One of the greatest enemies perceived by fundamentalists among both Hindus and Christians has been Western secular culture: pluralist, bureaucratic, and technical. Yet in experiencing its impact, fundamentalists have also assimilated much of it and recognize important sources of its strength. These they have not hesitated to use for their own ends, adapting not only the technologies and institutions of the secular West but also its symbols. Indeed, the ways that fundamentalist movements are shaped by the contemporary forces they confront are perhaps what most mark them as modern phenomena: whatever experience of colonization that fundamentalists suffer, it is largely of the late-industrial, Western variety.

Just as fundamentalisms have been selective in the elements they retrieve from their own traditions, they have also been selective in those they adapt from the secular culture they oppose. Nevertheless, science—as a symbol of that culture's power—is something that is difficult to ignore, particularly for groups that highlight fundamentals of *doctrine*. These usually must either flatly deny the authority of science or assimilate it with apparent strain: through creationist theology, say, or the Aryas' evocation of the ancient Indian science of the Vedas. Other symbols of Western power have seemed more important to the RSS, with its martial, nondoctrinal stance. The organized drills of the RSS recall Western military practice, and as Ashis Nandy ironically notes, the khaki shorts donned by volunteers during their drills are modeled on the uniform of the British Indian police: to build the Hindu Nation, they would mimic British lackeys.[203] The practical dimensions of secular culture adapted by fundamentalists vary greatly among groups. Certainly, Protestant televangelists have made dramatic use of contemporary communications technology, often in loosely structured family-oriented organizations. Aryas, also with a doctrinal message to propagate, in the first decades of the twentieth century used imported print technology enthusiastically in newspapers and tracts. The RSS, however, historically keeping a low profile, has until very recently eschewed media technology, combining a disciplined organization with a direct, interpersonal approach to recruitment.[204] More central to all Hindu fundamentalisms are new organizational structures adapted from Western models. It was through being organized in more effective, integral ways, activist leaders thought, that Hindus could build their own characters, restructure their larger community, and make changes in the world.

Religious Fundamentals as Emblems of Embattled Tribes

Although new forms of organization have been a necessary attribute of fundamentalist groups among Hindus, they have not in themselves been a distinguishing attribute. The Brahmo Samaj, the best-known precursor to the Aryas as an organized Hindu group, is not a fundamentalist movement but one of reform. Other late nineteenth- and twentieth-century groups—most notably the Ramakrishna mission—have looked to Western organizational models as they attempt social work within India and propagate an inward spirituality to non-Hindus abroad.[205] The stances of these groups toward the colonialists' religion was more open and generous than those of either the Arya Samaj or the RSS. Since they understood the ultimate truths they professed to be at the root of all religious traditions, they did not present their own objects of faith in a highly proprietary way: the Brahmos' Upanishads taught a monism similar to the Unitarians'; Ramakrishna, although first of all a devotee of the Hindu mother goddess, had experienced all the traditions of Hinduism, and Islam and Christianity too. The defensive stance of the Arya Samaj and RSS, by contrast, has led them to present the religious bases of their movements in defiant opposition to those of other groups. In doing this they not only delineate these bases more sharply as fundamentals but also identify with them more aggressively and particularistically. Thus, if for Ramakrishna, the mother goddess was a divine being who took many forms and was available to all, in the RSS, mother symbolism was used to refer to the holy Indian subcontinent, which was for those born into the Hindu Nation. Similarly, in the Arya Samaj, the Vedas were a sign of the temporal as well as spiritual supremacy of the ancient Aryans, which should now be revived. As fundamentals, these religious standards heralded by the RSS and Aryas thus serve as concentrated emblems of religious identity.

The South Asian context, then, can present a curiously Durkheimian perspective on religious fundamentals: they appear as totems of the group, symbols of collective identity.[206] In order to defend their larger communities in the modern world, most fundamentalists have thought it necessary to disrupt the patterns of smaller socioreligious loyalties traditional in Indian life; the religious fundamentals they offer then provide new foci for allegiance. With cries of "Aryavarta for the Aryans" and "Hindu Nation," Hindus over the years have faced similarly embattled communities in the subcontinent, their configurations varying according to cultural region and political circumstance. In the eighties, the ancient Indian Christian community in the southern state of Kerala has joined the confrontation, alongside Muslims and Sikhs in other parts of India.[207] Indeed, the dramatic growth of the RSS in Kerala in the late twentieth century—rising to three thousand śākhās in 1989—recalls that of the Arya Samaj in the Punjab a century earlier.[208] In neither case did Hindus appear as a large majority, and in both they faced two other substantial communities that were organizing as well: in the Punjab, Muslims, and Sikhs; in Kerala, Muslims and Christians. Now, as then, Hindu fundamentalism finds strength when Hindus see their community facing genuine competition.

Historically, the attitudes of Hindu fundamentalists toward Sikhs, Muslims, and Christians have differed. Only in the Punjab have Sikhs formed a community substantial enough to compete with Hindus, and the turn of the century saw confrontations between Sikhs and Punjabi Aryas embroiled in doctrinal conflicts and local politics. But the dominant tone of Hindu cultural nationalists toward Sikhs throughout the century has tended to be conciliatory and inclusive. Savarkar, with reason, saw Sikhs as a Hindu reformist tradition, which can thus constitute a rightful part in the Hindu Nation, whatever the Sikhs' sense of themselves as a religious community. And during the traumatic division of the subcontinent into Hindu- and Muslim-majority states in 1947, Sikhs and Hindus found themselves clearly on the same side of the fence. Certainly the claim of Hindu fundamentalists that Sikhs are essentially Hindu has inflamed their Sikh counterparts, who are proud of their own religious identity.[209] But it also means that the rise of Hindu fundamentalist animosity against Sikhs in the 1980s derived not from a sense of a deep-rooted social and cultural divide but from the accurate perception that some radical Sikhs were violently attempting political secession, threatening the geographic integrity of the Hindu Nation, together with Hindu lives. The cultural gap has always been wider between Hindus and Muslims, who have consistently appeared to Hindu fundamentalists as an alien presence on the subcontinent, a population apart from the Hindu Nation. Communal tensions between Hindus and Muslims increased through the twenties and thirties, peaked at partition in 1947, and have simmered at different degrees of intensity ever since. In Hindus' confrontations with both Sikhs and Muslims, violence committed on all sides has left wounds that are difficult to heal. Nevertheless, even though the political situation of the eighties has highlighted organized Hindu response to Sikh separatism, the continuing presence of Muslims in India is likely to appear as a more genuine problem to Hindu Nationalists—and may indeed prove to be one that is more lasting.[210]

The attitudes of Hindu fundamentalists toward the Christians of India have differed markedly from their attitudes toward Muslims and Sikhs. Outside Kerala, Christian communities had not presented the same sort of economic and political competition as the other two groups. In north India, Christians have appeared largely either as members of the ruling elite or as recent low-caste converts. Although for early Aryas the low-caste converts seemed to threaten Hindu numerical strength, they did not directly challenge their middle-class social or economic status. Christianity itself—as the religion of the ignorant, if powerful, West—was an object of diatribe by Dayananda, but Aryas through the first two decades of the twentieth century were guarded in their dealings with the Christian colonial power, trying to allay suspicions of sedition. As the independence movement gathered momentum through the twenties and thirties, it lead to a widespread politicization of Hinduism and increasingly attracted the attention of fundamentalist Hindus. When independence finally came, Hindu cultural nationalists could feel feel triumphant over the Western power. Yet together with their victory came defeat: the partition of the subcontinent was felt as a severe loss, and one for which Muslim communal pressure was to blame. Perhaps at least in the new Indian state the Hindus would finally be able to prevail!

The New Colonialists?

Postcolonial Hindu fundamentalism can thus appear as a new colonialism of the victors. In representing an emergence of Indic group consciousness in new forms shaped by the colonial experience, it can easily lead to a tyranny of the majority. For it keeps the Western idea of religious community as an ideally homogeneous group, but abandons the ideas of equality among communities and protections for minorities introduced with the secular British administration: a flourishing, united Hindu Nation should need no legal protection for any special group. Even in independent India's present imperfect political situation, many fundamentalists think, shouldn't the Hindus as an 82 percent majority be allowed to benefit collectively from the policies of the state? In the words of a VHP official and former state director-general of police "We feel that what we are doing is for the good of the country. After all, what is good for 82 percent of the country is good for the rest of the country, isn't it?"[211] Since this statement refers to the VHP agitation for the restoration of Ram's birthplace—a patently sectarian goal—its faulty logic should be easily apparent to Indian Muslims.

Moreover, although the the spirit of competitiveness between communities introduced by the colonial experience may remain, Hindus have less reason now to feel economically threatened by minorities. This is particularly so with respect to the Muslims: although many individual Muslims flourish in modern India, as a group they lag behind Hindus in education and, relative to their population, are underrepresented in government jobs.[212] Indeed, the total number of Muslim communal institutions is less than the combined total of the VHP and Arya Samaj alone.[213] Less obviously a response to cultural threats from Western imperialism or to competing communal rivals of equal strength, the resurgence of fundamentalism today may be nurtured by more specifically religious factors.

Urban Religion, Collective Identity, and Violence

As characteristically modern forms of Indian religion, fundamentalist groups are marked by their urban, middle-class members—people with an experience of imported bureaucracy, if not always an English education. But fundamentalism is not the only new religious phenomenon that has emerged in Indian cities. Gurus, yogic centers, and devotional movements all also flourish—all, moreover, appearing as adaptations of Hindu tradition to an urban environment. Certainly it can be difficult to live the full ritual life of traditional Hinduism while carrying on business in a contemporary city; at the same time, the effectiveness and value of such a life with its distant metaphysical orientation can easily be questioned by a modern, scientifically inclined consciousness. The new phenomena offer alternative ways of being religious that are more practicable in an urban environment. Devotional movements give intense, temporary experiences in which caste distinctions can lose significance. Gurus and yogic centers present the same type of unorthodox inward religion in Indian cities as they do in Western ones.[214] As religious traditions, Hindu fundamentalisms offer another alternative, one demanding no devotional enthusiasm or yogic inwardness. Hindu fundamentalisms appeal instead to what may be urban Hindus' lowest common religious denominator: a Hindu identity. If personal religion entails among other things the identification of the individual with some larger whole, then the Hindu Nation may appear as a whole more immediately visible and attainable than the ritual cosmos of traditional Hinduism. For some urban Hindus, fundamentalist groups may offer the most viable personal religion available.

Potentially attractive to many, Hindu fundamentalist groups flourished through the eighties. Between 1979 and 1989, membership in the RSS had grown by 80 percent,[215] and smaller groups with names like "The Great Hindu Assembly," "National Defense Committee," and "The Forum for Hindu Awakening" have become increasingly visible, engaging in activities of local and national scale.[216] Many of these groups maintaining links with the RSS-affiliated VHP, have formed around particular leaders, flourish in different areas, and may devote themselves to their own projects. Especially active in the Ayodhya controversy, for example, is the Bajrang Dal, the "Troops of Hanuman"—the strong monkey deity worshiped as Ram's faithful servant, a traditional patron of wrestlers. The national leader of the Bajrang Dal has declared that the group is "committed to the cause of the temple."And in July of 1989 the Bajrang Dal youth pledged to lay down their lives for this cause.[217] The recent popularity of militant Hindu groups has altered the character of older organizations, not only encouraging militant strands in the Arya Samaj, but substantially transforming the Maharashtrian based Shiv Sena, the "Army of Siva." Founded in 1966, the Shiv Sena began as a Maharashtrian nativist political party protesting the professional rise of (typically Hindu) south Indians in the Maharashtrian metropolis of Bombay.[218] But with the rise of pan-Hindu nationalism in the 1980s, the charismatic founder and longtime leader of the Shiv Sena, journalist Bal Thackeray, has broadened the group's allegiances and extended its geographical scope. The Shiv Sena has now become a conspicuous vehicle of Hindu militancy throughout north India, and Thackeray himself has been referred to as a "symbol of Hindu chauvinism and revivalism."[219] Retaining its political base in Maharashtra, the Shiv Sena was well positioned to participate in the renewed politicization of the Hindu right at the end of the decade. In the 1989 polls it formed an electoral alliance in Maharashtra with the BJP and participated in the latter's unexpected success. Certainly a positive Hindu identity can bring a healthy pride: as Yadvrao Joshi—joint general secretary of the RSS—notes, "Hindus are no longer shy of calling themselves Hindus."[220] The RSS accordingly became more open about its activities in the late 1980s, acknowledging a dominant hand in some of its affiliated organizations.[221] With the celebration of the birth centenary of its founder in 1989, it has sought public respectability, giving wide distribution to leaflets that describe its social projects across the nation.[222] But the new openness of the RSS about its own and Hindu identity can also lead to a more frank assertiveness in its tone. In a 1989 interview, K. C. Sudarshan, an important RSS ideologue, presents a position on minorities in a Hindu state that in fact does not differ substantially from Golwalkar's pronouncements of the fifties and sixties but is couched in considerably less guarded terms: "It should have been made clear at the start that they were free only to worship differently, but they have to kowtow on other issues. If they want to stay citizens of this country, the minorities must give up all their special privileges." Although "peaceful co-existence" with Muslims is an ideal, according to Sudarshan, it should not come "by appeasement." He recognizes moreover, that it is fruitless to give rational religious justifications for communal issues like the conflict at Ayodhya. The temple there, he says, "is a symbol. . . . Will the court decide . . . that Ram was born there? Beliefs and traditions cannot be logical. The dispute has been created. We will worry no more about any disorder." If there is bloodshed, "this is nothing. There will be more. We are not scared."[223]

When leaders of organized Hinduism recognize the irrational forces with which they deal and even anticipate bloody reverberations from them, it seems difficult to absolve them from any responsibility for outbreaks of communal violence. Certainly the links between larger organized groups and individual violent acts at times appear only indirect. Nevertheless, such indirect links are frequently presumed and justifiably or not have been used to warrant government action. In a letter written in 1948, Sardar Patel, then home minister, rationalized the continued banning of the RSS to Golwalkar, its leader at the time. The virulent opposition of RSS volunteers to the governing Congress party, he said: "created a kind of unrest in the people. All their speeches were full of communal poison. It was not necessary to spread poison in order to enthuse the Hindus and organize for their protection. As a final result of the poison, the country had to suffer the sacrifice of the invaluable life of Gandhiji."[224]

More direct relationships between organized Hinduism and mob violence become apparent when communalist leaders authorize demonstrations in already tense situations, as they have historically done.[225] Following the opening of Ram's birthplace to Hindu worship in 1986, for example, the triumphant VHP started to lead six ceremonial processions of images to Ayodhya. Rioting erupted when the procession halted for the night at a small town of mixed population through which a vanload of Muslims going to hear one of their own leaders also passed.[226] Even if we generously assume that leaders on both sides would have liked to avoid violent confrontations, they were also no doubt aware of the risks, and like K. C. Sudarshan could not "worry . . . about any disorder" when asserting their communal identities.

As a religious phenomenon, communalism in all its manifestations derives strength from the irrational forces of religious identity, which are magnified in India through individuals' traditional awareness of themselves as members of larger groups. Organized Hinduism, in attempting to consolidate and give power to a larger Hindu group, tries to channel these forces and control them. Its leaders, however, know that they cannot always exert full control, and—one fears—may sometimes judge it to be to their strategic advantage to let these forces run amok.

The religious forces at work in forging together the Hindu Nation thus differ substantially from those of traditional Hinduism. The Hinduism of ritual and law displays an extreme preoccupation with the play of cosmic order on earth, a concern for following codes of behavior deemed divinely ordained and morally proper. Building the Hindu Nation, by contrast, demands staunch identification with the group, an evocation of group loyalty and assertiveness that need not inherently respect traditional codes—thus belying the professed broad aims of the Hindu demonstrators at Ayodhya. The demonstrators talk about the restoration of Ram Rajya: the legendary rule of Ram, where a perfect monarch upheld Hindu law on earth. But while Hindu fundamentalists espouse Hindu virtues, the religious force behind much of what they do presses first of all for Hindu rule.

Notes

I wish to acknowledge the generous help offered by Scott Appleby, Gerald Barrier, Wendy Doniger, Kenneth Jones, and Jack E. Llewellyn, who all offered detailed comments on an earlier draft of this manuscript. Professors Jones and Llewellyn in addition very generously shared with me the results of their specialized research.

1. Sushil Srivastava, "The Ayodhya Controversy: A Third Dimension," *Probe India* (January 1988), p. 32; the story of the temple is also given in Peter van der Veer, *Gods on Earth: The Management of Religious Experience and Identity in a North Indian Pilgrimage Centre,* London School of Economics Monographs on Social Anthropology, no. 59, ed. Michael Sallnow (London and Atlantic Highlands, N.J.: Athlone Press, 1988), pp. 19–21.

2. See Ainslie T. Embree, "Religion and Politics," in Marshall M. Bouton, ed., *India Briefing, 1987* (Boulder Colo.: Westview, 1987), p. 62; for the history of Hindu-Muslim relationships in Ayodhya, see van der Veer, *Gods on Earth,* pp. 37–43.

3. Inderjit Badhwar, Prabhu Chawla, and Farzand Ahmed, "Hindus: Militant Revivalism," *India Today,* 11 May 1986, p. 78.

4. Ajay Kumar, S. Premi, and Ghulam Nabi Khayal, "The Muslims: Anger and Hurt," *India Today,* 15 March 1986, pp. 41–42.

5. Inderjit Badhwar, et al., "Communalism: Dangerous Dimensions," *India Today,* 31 October 1989, pp. 14–22.

6. See Uli Schmetzer, "Temple Dispute Doomed Gandhi," *Chicago Tribune,* 3 December 1989.

7. Kenneth W. Jones, "The Arya Samaj in British India, 1875–1947," in Robert D. Baird, ed., *Religion in Modern India* (New Delhi: Manohar, 1981), pp. 36–39.

8. The founder of the Arya Samaj treats the term Arya in two of his fifty-two tenets of personal belief: the word Arya means virtuous man . . . (tenet 29); this country is called Aryavarta because it has been the abode of Aryas from the dawn of creation . . . (tenet 30) (Swami Dayananda Saraswati, *Autobiography,* K. C. Yadav, ed. [Delhi: Manohar, 1976], p. 61). Emphasizing the amalgamation of Dravidian and Aryan peoples in a single Hindu India, M. S. Golwalkar, an important RSS leader, says: "In Bharat [India] the word Arya has always been a measure of culture, and not the name of a race." Madhavrao Sadashiv Golwalkar, *Spotlights: Guruji Answers* (Bangalore: Sahtiya Sindhu, 1974), p. 14.

9. Membership figures of the RSS are not public information. The 1947 number is an estimate of those who regularly engaged in daily RSS activities given by J. A. Curran, Jr., *Militant Hinduism in Indian Politics: A Study of the R.S.S.* (New York: Institute of Pacific Relations, 1951), p. 43. The figures for 1979 and 1989 are plausible estimates of those who attend daily meetings, given in a popular Indian newsmagazine: Pankaj Pachauri, "RSS: Open Offensive," *India Today,* 30 June 1989, p. 41.

10. Peter van der Veer, "'God must be Liberated!': A Hindu Liberation Movement in Ayodhya," *Modern Asian Studies* 21 (1987): 290.

11. For an inclusive discussion of the meaning of communalism in India, see Bipan Chandra, *Communalism in Modern India* (Delhi: Vikas, 1984), chap. 1.

12. Insightful analyses of the colonial situation are given by Surjit Mansingh, "The

Political Uses of Religious Identity in South Asia," in *Fundamentalism, Revivalists, and Violence in South Asia,* James Warner Bjørkman, ed. (Riverdale, Md.: Riverdale, 1988), pp. 177–79; and by G. R. Thursby, *Hindu-Muslim Relations in British India: A Study of Controversy, Conflict, and Communal Movements in Northern India 1923–1928* (Leiden: E. J. Brill, 1975), pp. 173–80.

13. The most complete source on the Brahmo Samaj is David Kopf, *The Brahmo Samaj and the Shaping of the Modern Indian Mind* (Princeton: Princeton University Press, 1979).

14. Dayananda, *Autobiography,* p. 11.

15. Ibid., p. 15.

16. Swami literally means "master." Through his initiation, Dayananda can trace a spiritual lineage back to the great philosopher and reformer Shankarach arya. See his *Autobiography,* p. 26 and J. T. F. Jordens, *Dayananda Sarasvati: His Life and Ideas* (Delhi: Oxford University Press, 1978), pp. 20–21.

17. Dayananda, *Autobiography,* p. 75.

18. Lala Lajpat Rai, *The Arya Samaj: An Account of its Origin, Doctrines, and Activities, with a Biographical Sketch of the Founder* (London: Longmans, Green and Co., 1915), p. 51.

19. While traveling in his home region of Gujarat, Dayananda started two societies in Rajkot and Ahmedabad under the name of the Arya Samaj, both of which quickly disintegrated: see Kenneth W. Jones, *Arya Dharm: Hindu Consciousness in Nineteenth-Century Punjab* (Berkeley and Los Angeles: University of California Press, 1976), p. 35; and James Reid Graham, "The Arya Samaj as a Reformation in Hinduism with Special Reference to Caste," (Ph. D. diss., Yale University, 1943), pp. 155–60. In his *Autobiography,* p. 51, Dayananda states that he established the Arya Samaj in Bombay.

20. Valentine Chirol, *Indian Unrest* (London: Macmillan, 1910), p. 2.

21. Jones, *Arya Dharm,* pp. 305–6.

22. Indra Prakash, *Hindu Mahasabha: Its Contribution to India's Politics* (New Delhi: Akhil Bharat Hindu Mahasabaha, 1966), p. 11.

23. Three prominent Aryas are found in the annual list of Mahasabha presidents given in Indra Prakash, *Hindu Mahasabha,* pp. 183–84. Of these, Swami Shraddhananda (1922) and Lala Lajpat Rai (1925) were well-known leaders active in many causes who were not closely identified with the Sabha for long periods of time; Bhai Parmananda, however, president in 1933, remained active and would be influential in guiding the Sabha toward its militant communalist direction in the thirties (Jones, "Arya Samaj in British India," pp. 461–65). On the development of the Hindu Mahasabha, see Kenneth W. Jones, "Politicized Hinduism: The Ideology and Program of the Hindu Mahasabha," in Robert D. Baird, ed., *Religion in Modern India* (New Delhi: Manohar, 1981), pp. 447–80; and Richard Gordon, "Hindu Mahasabha and the Indian National Congress, 1915–1926," *Modern Asian Studies* 9 (1975): 145–203.

24. Walter K. Andersen and Shridhar D. Damle, *The Brotherhood in Saffron: The Rashtriya Swayamsevak Sangh and Hindu Revivalism,* Westview Special Studies on South and Southeast Asia (Boulder, Colo.: Westview, 1987), pp. 39–40. Most of my material on the RSS comes from this excellently researched volume.

25. On Maharashtrian Brahmans and their role in modern India, see D. D. Karve, ed., *The New Brahmans: Five Maharashtrian Families* (Berkeley and Los Angeles: University of California Press, 1963).

26. From August 1921 to July 1922, Hedgewar served time in prison for defying a ban on political meetings. Andersen and Damle, *Brotherhood in Saffron,* p. 32.

27. Andersen and Damle, *Brotherhood in Saffron,* pp. 50–53. For a detailed journalistic account of the assassination plot, see Manohar Malgonkar, *The Men Who Killed Gandhi* (Delhi: Macmillan, 1978).

28. Curran, *Militant Hinduism,* p. 43.

29. Andersen and Damle, *Brotherhood in Saffron,* pp. 110–14.

30. Ibid., p. 111.

31. Ibid., p. 114.

32. Jones, *Arya Samaj in British India,* p. 51.

33. Cf., for example, Vinayak Damodar Savarkar, "Hindu Pad-Padashahi or a Review of The Hindu Empire of Maharashtra," *Hindu Rashtra Darshan,* Samagra Savarkar Wangmaya, vol. 6 (Poona: Maharashtra Pranthik Hindusabha, 1965), pp. 99–108, 256–68.

34. On the the authority of the Vedas as definitive for Hinduism, see Brian K. Smith, "Exorcising the Transcendent: Strategies for Defining Hinduism and Religion," *History of Religions* 27 (1987): 32–55.

35. Lala Lajpat Rai, *Arya Samaj,* pp. 103–5.

36. Dayananda, *Autobiography,* p. 43.

37. See Jordens, *Dayananda Sarasvati,* pp. 35–39.

38. Ibid., p. 37.

39. Swami Dayananda Saraswati, *Light of Truth or an English Translation of the Satyārth Prakāś,* trans. Dr. Chiranjiva Bharadwaja (New Delhi: Sarvadeshik Arya Pratinidhi Sabha, 1975), p. 733.

40. Ibid., p. 343.

41. Jordens, *Dayananda Sarasvati,* p. 271.

42. Dayananda, *Satyārth Prakāś,* p. 332.

43. This is described at length in chapter 11 of Dayananda, *Satyārth Prakāś.*

44. An English translation is available: Swami Dayananda Saraswati, *The Sanskar Vidhi (The Procedure of Sacraments),* trans. Acharya Vaidyanath Shastri (New Delhi: Sarvadeshik Arya Pratinidhi Sabha, 1976).

45. See Jordens, *Dayananda Sarasvati,* p. 175.

46. Thus, for example, point 20: "I hold that *devas* [the traditional Hindu term for "gods"] are those men who are wise and learned; *asuras* ["demons"] are those who are ignorant." Dayananda's tract on his personal beliefs, called "Swamantavyamantavya," has also been published as the last chapter of his fragmentary *Autobiography* (citation from p. 60).

47. Vinayak Damodar Savarkar, *Hindutva* (Bombay: Veer Savarkar Prakashan, 1969), pp. vi–vii. On Savarkar's influence on Hedgewar, see Narayan Hari Palkar, *Dr. Hedgewar* (Prayag: Dr. Surendra Mital, 1962 [2019 v.s.]), pp. 139–40; in Hindi.

48. Madhavrao Sadashiv Golwalkar, *Bunch of Thoughts* (Bangalore: Vikrama Prakashan, 1966), p. 83.

49. Vinayak Damodar Savarkar, *A Guide to Indian Revolutionary Movement,* Samagra Savarkar Wangmaya, vol. 5 (Poona: Maharashtra Pranthik Hindusabha, 1964).

50. "Hindu Pad-Padashahi," in *Samagra Savarkar Wangmaya,* vol. 6.

51. Ibid. pp. 95–96.

52. Vinayak Damodar Savarkar, *Six Glorious Epochs of Indian History* (New Delhi: Rajdhani Granthagar, 1971).

53. Golwalkar, *Bunch of Thoughts,* pp. 79–88.

54. Ibid., pp. 24–25; 91–92.

55. Andersen and Damle, *Brotherhood in Saffron,* pp. 92–94.

56. Dina Nath Mishra, *RSS: Myth and Reality*, trans. D. P. Pandey (New Delhi: Vikas, 1980), p. 61.

57. Thursby, *Hindu-Muslim Relations*, pp. 158–72.

58. Savarkar, *Hindutva,* p. 1.

59. The exception here is foreign wives of Hindu men, who traditionally become incorporated into their husbands' patriliny.

60. Thursby, *Hindu-Muslim Relations,* p. 168.

61. At the same time, the participation of Muslims in RSS activities (but not, perhaps, as duly recognized *members*) is noted by propagandists of the movement: Mishra, *RSS: Myth and Reality,* p. 182; K. R. Malkani, *The RSS Story* (New Delhi: Impex India, 1980), p. 99.

62. Lajpat Rai, *Writings and Speeches,* Vijaya Chandra Joshi, ed. (Delhi and Jullundur: University Publishers, 1966), vol. 1, pp. 187.

63. Lajpat Rai, "On Hindu Nationalism," *Punjabee,* 23 October 1919, pp. 3–4. Thanks to Ken Jones for this source.

64. Lajpat Rai, *Writings and Speeches,* vol. 2, pp. 208–10.

65. Balrāj Madhok, *Indian Nationalism* (New Delhi: Bharati Sahitya Sadan, 1969), pp. 93, 95; this 1969 edition is the second revision of a work that was originally written in 1946 and revised again in 1955; see also Madhok's *Rationale of Hindu State* (Delhi: Indian Book Gallery, 1982). Madhok was born in an Arya Samaj family (Bal Raj Madhok, *R.S.S. and Politics* [New Delhi: Hindu World Publications, 1986], p. 23) and has taught at DAV colleges in Ambala (ibid., p. 45) and Srinagar (Manga Ram Varshney, *Jana Sangh, R.S.S., and Balraj Madhok* [Aligarh: Manga Ram Varshney, n.d.], p. 3). J. F. Seunarine refers to him as an "active Arya Samajist" (*Reconversion to Hinduism through Shuddhi* [Madras: Christian Literature Society, 1977], p. 69). At the same time, Madhok has been an energetic RSS organizer, having come to the group as a college student in 1938 (Madhok, *R.S.S. and Politics,* p. 23). His autobiographical reflections show the attraction of the RSS for some people of Arya backgrounds in the late thirties and forties—not only in his own case, but in that of others too (ibid., pp. 23–25, 47). Madhok is best known as a rightist politician, a cofounder and past president of the Jana Sangh, an RSS-affiliated party. He broke with both for political reasons in 1972 (see Andersen and Damle, *Brotherhood in Saffron,* pp. 186–87).

66. D. Vable, *The Arya Samaj: Hindu Without Hinduism* (Delhi: Vikas, 1983), p. 197. Thanks to Jack Llewellyn for pointing out the context of Vable's remarks.

67. Dayananda, *Satyārth Prakāś,* p. 103.

68. Graham, "Arya Samaj," pp. 493–500.

69. Ibid, pp. 499–504.

70. On the Arya Bhratri Sabha, see ibid., 475–87, and Jones, *Arya Dharm,* pp. 204–5.

71. On the Jat Pat Todak Mandal, see Graham, *Arya Samaj,* pp. 538–44.

72. Jordens, *Dayananda Sarasvati,* pp. 204, 285.

73. For Gandhi's version of this revision of caste, see Joan V. Bondurant, *Conquest of Violence: The Gandhian Philosophy of Conflict,* rev. ed. (Berkeley and Los Angeles: University of California Press, 1971), pp. 167–72.

74. Golwalkar, *Spotlights,* p. 183.

75. Andersen and Damle, *Brotherhood in Saffron,* p. 95.

76. Golwalkar, *Spotlights,* pp. 183–84.

77. Ibid., p.183.

78. See Curran, *Militant Hinduism,* p. 48.

79. See Andersen and Damle, *Brotherhood in Saffron,* p. 105.

80. Mishra, *RSS: Myth and Reality,* p. 56. On caste associations, see Lloyd I. Rudolph and Susanne Hoeber Rudolph, *The Modernity of Tradition: Political Development in India* (Chicago and London: University of Chicago Press, 1967), pp. 29–36.

81. Quoted in Malkani, *RSS Story,* p. 170.

82. Mishra, *RSS: Myth and Reality,* p. 53; Mishra writes the Hindi *swayamsevaka* for volunteers.

83. Graham, "Arya Samaj," pp. 221–23.

84. Dayananda, *Autobiography,* p. 92; a translation of the full will is given as appendix 4, pp. 90–95.

85. Jones, "Arya Samaj in British India," pp. 32, 37.

86. From the Arya Directory of 1941, cited in ibid., p. 39.

87. Graham, "Arya Samaj," p. 395; on the origins of the Arya college, see Jones, *Arya Dharm,* pp. 67–93.

88. In Hindi words of Sanskritic origin, final short *a*'s are usually not pronounced and frequently not written in Anglicized form: thus the conventional spelling of the Swami's name in the college's title.

89. Graham, "Arya Samaj," p. 406.

90. Jones, *Arya Dharm,* p. 225.

91. Ibid., pp. 228–29.

92. Jones, "Arya Samaj in British India," p. 39.

93. Radhey Shyam Pareek, *Contribution of Arya Samaj in the Making of Modern India 1875–1947,* Arya Samaj Foundation Centenary Publications (New Delhi: Sarvadeshik Arya Pratinidhi Sabha, 1973), pp. 200–201. On the early history of the gurukul at Kangri, see J. T. F. Jordens, *Swami Shraddhananda: His Life and Causes* (Delhi: Ox-

ford University Press, 1981), pp. 66–102; for a study of the continuing gurukul movement, see Saraswati S. Pandit, *A Critical Study of the Contribution of the Arya Samaj to Indian Education,* Arya Samaj Foundation Centenary Publications (Delhi: Sarvadeshik Arya Pratinidhi Sabha, 1974).

94. Pareek, *Contribution,* p. 204.

95. Jones, "Arya Samaj in British India," p. 39.

96. Pareek, *Contribution,* p. 206.

97. Ibid., p. 138.

98. Ibid., pp. 138–46.

99. Ibid., pp. 155–64.

100. Jones, "Arya Samaj in British India," p. 44.

101. Pareek, *Contribution,* p. 325.

102. Ibid., p. 326.

103. Jones, "Arya Samaj in British India," p. 45. On the Hyderabad demonstrations, see the section below on political roles.

104. Jones, "Arya Samaj in British India," p. 54, fn. 56.

105. On these early Hindu paramilitary organizations, see Thursby, *Hindu-Muslim Relations,* pp. 168–69.

106. Pareek, *Contribution,* p. 326.

107. Pandit Nardev Vedalankar and Manohar Somera, *Arya Samaj and Indians Abroad,* Arya Samaj Centenary Publications (Delhi: Sarvadeshik Arya Pratinidhi Sabha, 1975), pp. 35, 103. This book, sponsored by the South African Samaj for the Aryas' centenary celebrations, surveys the history of the Aryas abroad; for a concise overview see Jones, "Arya Samaj in British India," p. 38.

108. Vedalankar and Somera, *Arya Samaj and Indians Abroad,* pp. 76–77 (on South Africa); 113–20 (on Mauritius); 126–27 (on Fiji).

109. Curran, *Militant Hinduism,* pp. 12–13.

110. Ibid., p. 13.

111. Ibid., p. 43.

112. Andersen and Damle, *Brotherhood in Saffron,* pp. 110–11.

113. Cf. ibid., p. 37.

114. Pankaj Pachauri, "RSS: Open Offensive," *India Today,* 30 June 1989, p. 40.

115. Curran, *Militant Hinduism,* p. 50; Andersen and Damle, *Brotherhood in Saffron,* p. 104.

116. Ibid., pp. 89–91.

117. Ibid., p. 84.

118. Mishra, *RSS: Myth and Reality,* p. 54.

119. This is a fragment from a volunteer's diary of lecture notes kept during an RSS training camp: Andersen and Damle, *Brotherhood in Saffron,* p. 96.

120. See discussion in ibid., p. 84.

121. Ibid., p. 98; Curran, *Militant Hinduism,* p. 49. Andersen and Damle's data of the seventies and eighties suggest more stringent requirements for taking the oath than Curran's data of the early fifties.

122. Changes were introduced into the pledge after independence and the temporary ban on the RSS. The original pledge reads: "In the name of God and my ancestors, I hereby become a member of the Rashtriya Swayamsevak Sangha in order to free Hindu Rashtra by safeguarding holy Hindu Dharma [religion], Hindu Sanskriti [culture] and Hindu Samaj [society]. I shall do Sangha work selflessly and dutifully and to the best of my ability all my life. BHARAT MATA KI JAI [Victory to Mother India!]." The changes introduced reflect, first, the realization of political independence—the volunteer pledges to become a member "for the all-round progress of Bharatavarsha [India] by strengthening the holy Hindu Dharma," and second, a slight weakening in the terms of allegiance: the volunteer pledges to "do Sangha work with all [his] heart to he best of [his] ability." (Malkani, *RSS Story,* p. 200).

123. Andersen and Damle, *Brotherhood in Saffron,* p. 85.

124. Mishra, *RSS: Myth and Reality,* pp. 55–56.

125. The Hindi terms used for these four local offices are, in order treated: *gatanāyak, śikṣak, kāryavāḥ,* and *mukhya śikṣak.*

126. Andersen and Damle, *Brotherhood in Saffron,* p. 86; Curran, *Militant Hinduism,* p. 461.

127. *Pracārak* in Hindi.

128. Mishra, *RSS: Myth and Reality,* p. 64; the author writes in 1980.

129. Curran, *Militant Hinduism,* p. 55.

130. Andersen and Damle, *Brotherhood in Saffron,* p. 88.

131. Ibid., p. 84.

132. Ibid., p. 87.

133. Curran, *Militant Hinduism,* p. 55.

134. Andersen and Damle, *Brotherhood in Saffron,* p. 86.

135. Narayan Hari Palkar, *Dr. Hedgewar: Charitra* (Prayag, India: Dr. Surendranath Mital, 2019 Vikram era [1962 C.E.]), pp. 423–24 (in Hindi).

136. Andersen and Damle, *Brotherhood in Saffron,* p. 85.

137. See Graham, "Arya Samaj," pp. 403–12; and Jordens's description in *Swami Shraddhananda.*

138. *Arya Patrika,* 16 January 1897, p. 6; quoted in Graham, "Arya Samaj, " p. 477.

139. Thanks to Jack Llewellyn for sharing some impressions gained from field research among contemporary Aryas.

140. Andersen and Damle, *Brotherhood in Saffron,* p. 87.

141. H. D. Griswold, "The Problem of the Arya Samaj," *Indian Evangelical Review,* 1 January 1892, reprinted in Lahore as a separate tract, p. 6; see also Graham, "Arya Samaj," pp. 401–3.

142. Graham states that the spiritual status of Dayananda was "the basic point at issue between the two parties" ("Arya Samaj," p. 405).

143. On problems of understanding the guru in modern Indian traditions, see Daniel Gold, *The Lord as Guru: Hindi Sants in North Indian Tradition* (New York: Oxford University Press, 1987), chap. 6.

144. See the discussion in Curran, *Militant Hinduism,* p. 5.

145. Kenneth W. Jones, "Socio-Religious Movements in British India," *The New Cambridge History of India* 3:1 (Cambridge: Cambridge University Press, 1989), p. 184, notes the cyclical oscillation between communal violence and enthusiasm for secular nationalism, which peaked in 1905–7, 1919–22, 1930–34, and 1942.

146. Jones, *Arya Dharm,* pp. 207–9.

147. See chap. 10.

148. Shraddhanda and his times are treated in Jordens's excellent biography, *Swami Shraddhananda.*

149. Thursby, *Hindu-Muslim Relations,* pp. 146–58.

150. Ibid., pp. 36–72.

151. Graham, "Arya Samaj," pp. 514–15.

152. Ibid, pp. 509–11; on the Mappilas, see Stephen Frederic Dale, *Islamic Society on the South Asian Frontier: The Mappilas of Malabar 1498-1922* (Oxford: Clarendon Press, 1980).

153. See J. F. Seunarine, *Reconversion to Hinduism through Shuddhi* (Madras: Christian Literature Society, 1977), p. 99.

154. A full description of the case referred to is given in ibid., pp. 41–57.

155. M. S. Golwalkar, *We or Our Nationhood Defined* (Nagpur: Bharat, 1939), pp. 47–48.

156. Ibid., p. 35; Italy is glorified, too: "Look at Italy, the old Roman Race consciousness of conquering the whole territory round the Mediterranean Sea, so long dormant, has roused itself, and shaped the Racial-National aspirations accordingly," p. 32.

157. M. S. Golwalkar, *Bunch of Thoughts,* and *Spotlights.*

158. Golwalkar, *Spotlights,* p. 48.

159. Ibid., p. 51.

160. Ibid., p. 48.

161. The case, which began in 1978, was eventually heard by the Supreme Court of India. In 1985, Chief Justice Chandrachud, a Hindu, cited the Qur'an in support of the civil law and explicitly suggested that it was time for all Indians to live under one civil code. Given the modesty of the traditional settlement, the Justice's ruling was lauded by many liberals and feminists as well as by the Hindu right. Muslims of all classes, how-

ever, were outraged at both the audacity of the justice and the abrogation of their tradition. The next year Rajiv Gandhi's government countered the ruling through legislation. The Shah Bano case has caused enough controversy in India to lead to the publication of two collections of documents related to it: Asghar Ali Engineer, ed., *The Shah Bano Controversy* (Hyderabad: Orient Longmans, 1987), and Janak Raj Jai, ed., *Shah Bano* (New Delhi: Rajiv Publications, 1986); both include copies of Justice Chandrachud's judgment and the ensuing Muslim Women's Bill. The case is also treated briefly in Embree, "Religion and Politics," pp. 58–60. On the problems caused in secular India by different, communally based codes of personal law—which treat substantial matters of inheritance as well as of marriage—see Robert D. Baird, "Uniform Civil Code and the Secularization of Law," in Baird, ed., *Religion in Modern India* (New Delhi: Manohar, 1981), pp. 417–55.

162. Andersen and Damle, *Brotherhood in Saffron,* p. 87.

163. See the discussion in ibid., p. 83, 129–30.

164. Ibid., pp. 81, 103.

165. Statement made by Atal Bihari Vajpayee, then Jana Sangh president, in the *Statesman,* Calcutta, 3 September 1969; quoted in ibid., p. 103. For the continuation of these policies in the current RSS political affiliate, see L. K. Advani, *Bharatiya Janata Party: Presidential Address* (New Delhi: Bharatiya Janata Party, 1986), p. 16: "The party stands for political as well as economic democracy, so that the benefits of economic development go to the smallest man. The party believes that for this deconcentration of economic power presently concentrated in the hands of the state or of big business is necessary. Primacy for agriculture and importance to the small-scale sector in industry are commitments that flow from this."

166. Andersen and Damle, *Brotherhood in Saffron,* p. 81.

167. Mishra, *RSS: Myth and Reality,* p. 54.

168. Andersen and Damle, *Brotherhood in Saffron,* p. 84; Curran, *Militant Hinduism,* p. 50.

169. The women's organization, called the Rashtra Sevika Samiti, was started in 1936 by Lakshmi Bai Kelkar, mother of an RSS volunteer. See Andersen and Damle, *Brotherhood in Saffron,* pp. 38–39.

170. Ibid., p. 96.

171. Thursby, *Hindu-Muslim Relations,* pp. 152–53.

172. Dayananda, *Satyārth Prakāś,* pp. 329–30.

173. Chirol, *Indian Unrest,* pp. 115–16.

174. Jones, *Arya Dharm,* pp. 274–6; 299–301.

175. Jones, "Arya Samaj in British India," pp. 47–49.

176. Ibid., pp. 50–52.

177. Malkani, *RSS Story,* p. 115.

178. For remarks to this effect by RSS leaders in the early eighties, see Andersen and Damle, *Brotherhood in Saffron,* p. 227.

179. The analogy of Ramdas and Shivaji as an ideal model of the relationship of the RSS to the government is used in Malkani, *RSS Story,* p. 120.

180. L. K. Advani, current president of the Bharatiya Janata Party, quoted in Barbara Crosette, "A Militant Hindu Leader Gets King-Maker's Role," *New York Times,* 28 November 1989.

181. Andersen and Damle, *Brotherhood in Saffron,* pp. 126–27. On the history of the Jana Sangh in the 1960s, see Craig Baxter, *The Jana Sangh: A Biography of an Indian Political Party* (Philadelphia: University of Pennsylvania Press, 1969).

182. Ibid., p. 263.

183. The Jana Sangh was the third party in the number of seats in the national parliament; ibid., p. 289.

184. The so-called "dual-membership controversy"; see Andersen and Damle, *Brotherhood in Saffron,* pp. 216–22.

185. Cf. Andersen and Damle, *Brotherhood in Saffron,* p. 235.

186. L. K. Advani, *Bharatiya Janata Party: Presidential Address* (New Delhi:

Bharatiya Janata Party, 9 May 1986, pp. 13–14.

187. Cf. Balraj Madhok M. P., *Indianization? (What, Why, and How)*, (Delhi: S. Chand, 1970), pp. 68–69. Madhok, president of the Jana Sangh during its 1967 electoral successes, was a leader of its more reactionary wing and has broken with the present BJP leadership.

188. The reference is to Indian control of industry: L. K. Advani, *Bharatiya Janata Party: Presidential Address* (1986), p. 13.

189. "Indianization—by which we mean the subordination of all narrow loyalties like those of religion, case, region, language or dogma to the overriding loyalty to the nation"; from the resolution of the Bharatiya Jana Sangh passed at the plenary session at Patna on 30 December 1969; given as appendix 2 of Madhok, *Indianization?*, pp. 101–3.

190. D. B. Thengadi, "Integral Humanist," in Sudhakar Raje, ed., *Pt. Deendayal Upadhyaya: A Profile* (New Delhi: Deendayal Research Institute, 1972), p. 47. The term "integral humanism" was coined by Deendayal Upadhyaya, longtime head of the Jana Sangh. See also Andersen and Damle, *Brotherhood in Saffron*, pp. 175–76.

191. On Muslims and Christians in the Jana Sangh in the 1960s, see Baxter, *Jana Sangh*, p. 311.

192. Des Raj Goyal, *Rashtriya Swayamsewak Sangh* (New Delhi: Radha Krishna Prakashan, 1979), p. 174.

193. The Jana Sangh had, however, little strength in Maharashtra, where its populist credentials were belied by the preponderance of old-guard RSS Brahmans. These, moreover, were often unenthusiastic political workers, more interested in conventional RSS goals of self-cultivation. See Andersen and Damle, *Brotherhood in Saffron*, pp. 165–68.

194. Ibid., pp. 227–28. The first plenary session of the BJP was held in Bombay in December 1980.

195. Ibid., pp. 231–34.

196. Ibid., p. 135; and "Ekatmata Yatra: Setting National Vision Right" in H. V. Seshadri, *Hindu Renaissance Under Way* (Bangalore: Jagarana Prakashana, 1984), pp. 179–94.

197. Badhwar, Chawla, and Ahmed, "Hindus: Militant Revivalism."

198. Andersen and Damle, *Brotherhood in Saffron*, p. 236.

199. As early as 1960, Golwalkar advocated some of the Sikh-sponsored Punjabi-language policies; and during the late 1960s, the Jana Sangh actively cooperated with the Akali Dal, a Sikh party, in Punjab state government. See ibid., pp. 169, 232, and Baxter, *Jana Sangh*, p. 293.

200. Crossette, "Militant Hindu Leader," and Advani, *Bharatiya Janata Party: Presidential Address* (1986), p. 7: "The BJP strongly condemned the killing of innocent Sikhs, and our units actively exerted to give them shelter and relief. In purely electoral terms this cost us dearly. But we have no regrets on this score."

201. Prabhu Chawla, "Crisis, Conflict, Change," *India Today, International Edition*, 15 January 1990, pp.18–25.

202. The phrase "a majority with a minority complex" was first used by S. J. Tambiah about the Sinhalese in *Ethnic Fratricide and the Dismantling of Democracy* (Chicago: University of Chicago Press, 1986), p. 92.

203. Although the insight is Ashis Nandy's, I am not sure where I read (or heard) it. In any event, his *The Intimate Enemy: Loss and Recovery of Self under Colonialism* (Delhi: Oxford University Press, 1983) provides valuable insights into such phenomena.

204. Mishra, *RSS: Myth and Reality*, p. 56.

205. On the Ramakrishna movement see George M. Williams, "The Ramakrishna Movement: A Study in Religious Change," in Baird, *Religion in Modern India*, pp. 55–79.

206. The classic study is, of course, Emile Durkheim, *The Elementary Forms of the Religious Life*, trans. Joseph Ward Swain (New York: Free Press, 1965).

207. According to tradition, the Christian Church in Kerala, which clearly predates European settlement, was started by

the apostle Thomas in A.D. 52. On the basic patterns of communalism in Kerala, see P. M. Mammen, *Communalism vs Communism: A Study of the Socio-religious Communities and Political Parties in Kerala, 1892–1970* (Calcutta: Minerva Associates, 1981).

208. Ramesh Menon and Guha Prasad, "The South: Spreading Saffron," *India Today,* 30 June 1989, pp. 42–43.

209. See Madhu Limaye, "Sikhs: An Alien People?" in Abida Samiuddin, ed., *The Punjab Crisis: Challenge and Response* (Delhi: Mittal Publications, 1985), pp. 551–52.

210. See Embree's judgment in "Religion and Politics."

211. Ajay Kumar, S. Premi, and Ghulam Nabi Khayal, "The Muslims: Anger and Hurt," *India Today,* 15 March 1986, p. 43.

212. Inderjit Badhwar, "Social Status: Questions of Parity," *India Today,* 15 March 1986, pp. 42–43.

213. Badhwar et al., "Militant Revivalism," p. 85.

214. Lawrence A. Babb, *Redemptive Encounters: Three Modern Styles in the Hindu Tradition,* Comparative Studies in Religion and Society, no 1, ed. Mark Juergensmeyer (Berkeley, Los Angeles, London: University of California Press, 1986) presents some other forms of modern Hinduism. The roles these have played in the West are discussed in Daniel Gold, *Comprehending the Guru: Towards a Grammar of Religious Perception,* American Academy of Religions Academy Series 57, ed. Carl Raschke (Atlanta: Scholars Press, 1988), pp. 105–123.

215. Pachauri, "RSS: Open Offensive," p. 41.

216. Badhwar et al., "Militant Revivalism," p. 85; Madhok, *R.S.S. and Politics,* p. 88. These names translate, respectively, *Virāt Hindū Sammelan, Raṣṭrīya Surakṣā Samiti,* and *Hindū Jāgaraṇ Manc.*

217. Badhwar et al., "Communalism: Dangerous Dimensions," p. 17.

218. On the role of the *Shiv Sena* as a Maharashtrian nativist group, see Mary Fainsod Katzenstein, *Ethnicity and Equality: The Shiv Sena Party and Preferential Policies in Bombay* (Ithaca: Cornell University Press, 1979).

219. Badhwar et al., "Communalism: Dangerous Dimensions," p. 21.

220. Badhwar et al., "Militant Revivalism," p. 80.

221. Pachauri, "RSS: Open Offensive," p. 40.

222. Ibid., p. 43.

223. Pankaj Pachauri, "K. C. Sudarshan: 'There Will Be Bloodshed'," *India Today,* 30 June 1989, p. 41.

224. Letter dated 11 September 1948, cited from Madhav Sadashiv Golwalkar, *Justice on Trial: A Collection of Historic Letters between Sri Guruji and the Government (1948–49),* 5th ed. (Bangalore: Prakashan Vibhag, Rashtriya Swayamsevak Sangh, Karnatak, 1969), p. 27.

225. See Thursby, *Hindu-Muslim Relations.*

226. Kumar, Premi, and Khayal, "The Muslims: Anger and Hurt," p. 42.

Select Bibliography

Andersen, Walter K., and Shridhar D. Damle. *The Brotherhood in Saffron: The Rashtriya Swayamsevak Sangh and Hindu Revivalism.* Westview Special Studies on South and Southeast Asia. Boulder Colo.: Westview, 1987.

Babb, Lawrence A. *Redemptive Encounters: Three Modern Styles in the Hindu Tradition.* Comparative Studies in Religion and Society, no. 1, Mark Juergensmeyer, ed. Berkeley, Los Angeles, London: University of California Press, 1986.

Baird, Robert D., ed. *Religion in Modern India.* New Delhi: Manohar, 1981.

Baxter, Craig. *The Jana Sangh: A Biography of an Indian Political Party.* Philadelphia: University of Pennsylvania Press, 1969.

Bipan, Chandra. *Communalism in Modern India*. Delhi: Vikas, 1984.

Bjørkman, James Warner, ed. *Fundamentalism, Revivalists, and Violence in South Asia.* Riverdale, Md.: Riverdale, 1988.

Bondurant, Joan V. *Conquest of Violence: The Gandhian Philosophy of Conflict*. Rev. ed. Berkeley and Los Angeles: University of California Press, 1971.

Chirol, Valentine. *Indian Unrest*. London: Macmillan, 1910.

Curran, J. A., Jr. *Militant Hinduism in Indian Politics: A Study of the R.S.S.* New York: Institute of Pacific Relations, 1951.

Dale, Stephen Frederic. *Islamic Society on the South Asian Frontier: The Mappilas of Malabar 1498–1922*. Oxford: Clarendon Press, 1980.

Farquhar, J. N. *Modern Religious Movements in India*. New York: Macmillan, 1987.

Gold, Daniel. *The Lord as Guru: Hindi Sants in North Indian Tradition*. New York: Oxford University Press, 1987.

Golwalkar, M. S. *We or Our Nationhood Defined*. Nagpur: Bharat, 1939.

———. *Bunch of Thoughts*. Bangalore: Vikrama Prakashan, 1966.

———. *Justice on Trial: A Collection of Historic Letters between Sri Guruji and the Government 1948–49)*. 5th ed. Bangalore: Prakashan Vibhag, Rashtriya Swayamsevak Sangh, Karnatak, 1969.

———. *Spotlights: Guruji Answers*. Bangalore: Sahtiya Sindhu, 1974.

Jones, Kenneth W. *Arya Dharm: Hindu Consciousness in Nineteenth-Century Punjab*. Berkeley and Los Angeles: University of California Press, 1976.

———. *Socio-Religious Movements in British India*. The New Cambridge History of India. Cambridge: Cambridge University Press, 1989.

Jordens, J. T. F. *Dayananda Sarasvati: His Life and Ideas*. Delhi: Oxford University Press, 1978.

———. *Swami Shraddhananda: His Life and Causes*. Delhi: Oxford University Press, 1981.

Karve, D. D., ed. *The New Brahmans: Five Maharashtrian Families*. Berkeley and Los Angeles: University of California Press, 1963.

Katzenstein, Mary Fainsod. *Ethnicity and Equality: The Shiv Sena Pary and Preferential Policies in Bombay*. Ithaca and London: Cornell University Press, 1979.

Kopf, David. *The Brahmo Samaj and the Shaping of the Modern Indian Mind*. Princeton: Princeton University Press, 1979.

Madhok, Balraj. *Indianization? (What, Why, and How)*. Delhi: S. Chand, 1970.

Malgonkar, Manohar. *The Men Who Killed Gandhi*. Delhi: Macmillan, 1978.

Malkani, K. R. *The RSS Story*. New Delhi: Impex India, 1980.

Mammen, P. M. *Communalism vs. Communism: A Study of the Socio-religious Communities and Political Parties in Kerala, 1892–1970*. Calcutta: Minerva Associates, 1981.

Pandit, Saraswati S. *A Critical Study of the Contribution of the Arya Samaj to Indian Education*. Arya Samaj Foundation Centenary Publications. Delhi: Sarvadeshik Arya Pratinidhi Sabha, 1974.

Pareek, Radhey Shyam. *Contribution of Arya Samaj in the Making of Modern India 1875–1947*. Arya Samaj Foundation Centenary Publications. New Delhi: Sarvadeshik Arya Pratinidhi Sabha, 1973.

Prakash, Indra. *Hindu Mahasabha: Its Contribution to India's Politics*. New Delhi: Akhil Bharat Hindu Mahasabaha, 1966.

Rai, Lala Lajpat. *The Arya Samaj: An Account of its Origin, Doctrines, and Activities, with a Biographical Sketch of the Founder*.London: Longmans, Green, 1915.

Rudolph, Lloyd I., and Susanne Hoeber Rudolph. *The Modernity of Tradition: Political Development in India*. Chicago: University of Chicago Press, 1967.

Samiuddin, Abida., ed. *The Punjab Crisis: Challenge and Response*. Delhi: Mittal, 1985.

Saraswati, Swami Dayananda. *Light of Truth or an English Translation of the Satyārth Prakaś*. Trans. Dr. Chiranjiva Bharadwaja.

New Delhi: Sarvadeshik Arya Pratinidhi Sabha, 1975.

———. *The Sanskar Vidhi (The Procedure of Sacraments)*. Trans. Acharya Vaidyanath Shastri. New Delhi: Sarvadeshik Arya Pratinidhi Sabha, 1976.

Savarkar, Vinayak Damodar. *A Guide to Indian Revolutionary Movement*. Samagra Savarkar Wangmaya, vol. 5. Poona: Maharashtra Pranthik Hindusabha, 1964.

———. *Six Glorious Epochs of Indian History*. New Delhi: Rajdhani Granthagar, 1971.

Seunarine, J. F. *Reconversion to Hinduism through Shuddhi*. Madras: Christian Literature Society, 1977.

Smith, Brian K. "Exorcising the Transcendent: Strategies for Defining Hinduism and Religion." *History of Religions* 27 (1987).

Thursby, G. R. *Hindu-Muslim Relations in British India: A Study of Controversy, Conflict, and Communal Movements in Northern India 1923–1928*. Leiden: E. J. Brill, 1975.

Vable, D. *The Arya Samaj: Hindu Without Hinduism*. Delhi: Vikas, 1983.

Vedalankar, Pandit Nardev, and Manohar Somera. *Arya Samaj and Indians Abroad*. Arya Samaj Centenary Publications. Delhi: Sarvadeshik Arya Pratinidhi Sabha, 1975.

CHAPTER

10

The Double-edged Sword: Fundamentalism and the Sikh Religious Tradition

T. N. Madan

Learn the religion of the age, brothers, from the perfect guru.
Adi Granth, M3, Gauri 3

We are always affected, in hope and fear, by what is nearest to us, and hence approach, under its influence, the testimony of the past. Hence it is constantly necessary to inhibit the overhasty assimilation of the past to our own expectations of meaning. Only then will we be able to listen to the past in a way that enables it to make its own meaning heard.
Hans-Georg Gadamer, *Truth and Method*

Fundamentalists or Defenders of Faith?

Alone among the countries of South Asia, India is a secular state by constitutional proclamation.[1] A secular state in the context of India's major indigenous religious traditions—Buddhism, Jainism, Hinduism, and Sikhism—does not mean that a constitutional wall separates the state from the church here as it does, for instance, in the United States, for none of these religions is associated with an institutional structure comparable to the Christian Church.[2] The Sikh *gurdwārā* (temple) is sometimes loosely compared to the church, but such a comparison does not withstand close scrutiny. Also secularism does not mean in India that religion is privatized: such an idea is alien to the indigenous religious traditions, which are holistic in character and do not recognize such dualistic categories as sacred versus profane, religious versus secular, or public versus private.

In India a secular state means simply, perhaps naively, that the state (or government) shall not discriminate between one citizen and another on the basis of religion, and that it shall create conditions in which everyone will be free to pursue his cultural and religious life according to his own lights. Articles 25 to 28 of the Constitution of India, forming part of the "Fundamental Rights," guarantee "freedom of conscience and free profession, practice and propagation of religion" (art. 25), "freedom to manage religious affairs" (art. 26), "freedom as to payment of taxes for promotion of any particular religion" (art. 27), and "freedom as to attendance at religious instruction or religious worship in certain educational institutions" (art. 28).

The freedom to hold any religious beliefs and engage in related religious practices has, however, given rise to one of the most agonizing dilemmas of the Indian polity: how to cope with the demand of some religious communities, notably the Sikhs, for the recognition of their "right" to repudiate the separation of religion and politics in the conduct of their own community life.[3] There is an apparent contradiction here: while religious identities are sought to be neutralized at the national or federal level, it is demanded that such an identity should be allowed to become the basis of the political structure at the regional or state level because politics should not be separated from religion. If a religion does not allow autonomy to politics, can the state forge an identity as powerful as the one offered to a people via their religious community? The assumption has been that it can and it should do so. The main means to this end have been identified as the promotion of civic ties and class interests to take the place of the primordial bonds of race, language, and religion. It is, however, by now widely recognized that "political modernization" and "economic development" are Western notions and do not have easy passage in non-Western settings. This conflict of world-views and desired futures provides the setting for one of the most tragic events in the forty-two-year history of independent India.

Given the self-proclaimed secular character of the Indian state, it might well appear both puzzling and shocking that in June 1984 the government of India should have ordered units of its regular army (including Hindu, Sikh, and Muslim servicemen), under a chain of command consisting at the top of three generals (two Sikhs and a Hindu),[4] to storm the precincts of the holiest of Sikh shrines, the Golden Temple at Amritsar, to clear it of elements which the government considered to be in unlawful possession of it. The military action, code-named Operation Blue Star, resulted in extensive damage to the buildings in the complex and the killing of over a thousand people, including pilgrims. It shocked Sikhs everywhere and saddened millions of Indians.[5]

A few words about the character and historical importance of the Golden Temple (so called because of the gold plate cover of its dome) will be helpful at this point. Since the Sikh religion is, unlike Hinduism, against idolatry in principle, a Sikh place of worship, called *gurdwārā* (gateway to the guru or preceptor), is a place for congregational listening to readings from the Sikh holy book, called the Adi Granth or the Granth Sahib, and for saying prayers. The only true object of veneration is the Granth Sahib itself. The temple was built with the help of common people by Guru Arjan (1563–1606), the fifth of the ten Sikh gurus. Located in the middle of the sacred tank *(sarovar)* of Amritsar, constructed earlier, it was named Harmandir, the temple of god. Its construction was begun in 1588 and its unusual architectural style, marked by a doorway on each of the four sides, stressed that the new faith was open to everybody. According to tradition, the guru said: "My faith is for the people of all castes and creeds from which ever direction they come and to which ever direction they bow."[6]

Arjan's son, Guru Hargobind (1595–1644), built a second temple (ca. 1606) facing the original shrine and outside the sacred tank; it was called the Akal Takht, "the throne of the immortal god." Here, "instead of chanting hymns of peace, the congregation heard ballads extolling feats of heroism, and, instead of listening to religious discourses, discussed plans of military conquests."[7] Besides the tank and the two temples, the sacred complex includes the walkway *(parikramā)* to enable pilgrims to circumambulate the Harmandir Sahib as an act of piety.

In its present form, the Golden Temple dates back to the early nineteenth century, having been rebuilt by Maharaja Ranjit Singh after suffering damage at the hands of Muslim invaders. Today, while the temple houses the Granth Sahib, the Akal Takht is the home of traditional weapons associated with the sixth and tenth gurus. Rituals and ceremonies link the two temples to constitute one "sacred complex." The rituals, called *maryādā* (tradition), consist mainly of daily veneration of the Granth Sahib, including readings from it. Apart from daily worshipers and occasional pilgrims who visit the Golden Temple for religious devotions, many Sikh functionaries concerned with its maintenance and other laymen are allowed by a legally constituted managerial body, called the Shiromani Gurdwara Prabandhak Committee (SGPC), to stay in the buildings that constitute the outer rectangle of the sacred complex. In June 1984 such "residents" included armed Sikhs who formed part of a statewide militant movement for the assertion of the political and economic rights and religious prerogatives of the Sikhs, which, they maintained, were in danger.

Their leader was a charismatic Sikh preacher, Jarnail Singh Bhindranwale (b. 1947), who, fearing arrest by the government, had actually taken sanctuary in the Akal Takht late in 1983 and had fortified it. Both his residence inside the temple and its fortification were unprecedented. Bhindranwale and his associates carried on their persons not only the traditional Sikh sword, as a part of their religious obligation, but also modern firearms. They were trained in the use of the latter by a former Sikh general of the Indian army who had been dismissed from service by the government on charges of corruption.

In the judgment of the government, largely shared by the public (including many Sikhs), Bhindranwale was a fundamentalist. In contemporary political discourse in India, a "fundamentalist" is a person who resorts to selective retrieval, picking out from his religious tradition certain elements of high symbolic significance with a view to mobilizing his coreligionists for action. The goals of such action are usually a mixture of religious objectives (pursuit and propagation of the traditional way of life and of the Truth as stated by the proponents) and the politico-economic interests of one's own community as against those of similarly defined other communities. The government, too, is opposed if it comes in the way. Fundamentalists are seen by their critics as closely associated with, or as being themselves, political "extremists" (those who press communal or regional demands against the state so hard as to constitute a threat to political stability) and in certain situations with "terrorists" (those who use different forms of terror, including murder, to further political ends). In Punjab, Bhindranwale had himself been charged twice with complicity in political murders but had not been prosecuted. The fundamentalist is very much a creature of his situation rather than a pure traditionalist, and fundamentalism is not pristine orthodoxy. Orthodoxy would in fact discourage fundamentalism: if the teachings of the gurus are our guide, they advocate catholicity and not narrowness of the mind.

The situation in Punjab just before Operation Blue Star is summed up thus by Murray Leaf, an American anthropologist : "There does not seem to be any doubt that Bhindranwale was the main organizer of a terrorist campaign that was responsible for the murder of several hundred innocent Hindus and that in publicly wearing arms and defiantly proclaiming his willingness to use them he was making himself a target for retribution. Moreover, by setting up his headquarters in the Golden Temple he was in effect daring the authorities to violate the temple in order to capture him. Neither the people of Punjab nor the precepts of the Sikh religion condone murder."[8] When the Indian army finally mounted an assault on the temple complex on 5 June 1984—a siege had begun two days earlier—Bhindranwale was killed, along with many associates.

If Bhindranwale and his associates were fundamentalists and terrorists in the judgment of the government and their critics, what were they in their own estimation? There is no doubt that they considered themselves true Sikhs *(gursikh)*, defenders of the "basic teachings" of the Sikh gurus *(gurbānī)* and of the economic interests of the Sikh community *(qaum)*. It is noteworthy that Bhindranwale was referred to and addressed as "Sant" by his followers. This usage is of considerable significance in Sikh cultural and political history.

Traditionally, *sant* means a seeker of truth and salvation who devotes himself individually as well as in the company of fellow seekers to acts of piety, notably the remembrance of god through the repetition of his name *(nāmsimran)* and the singing of hymns *(kīrtan)*. The hymns sung are usually from the Granth Sahib. The original usage of around the fifteenth century was gradually transformed so that by the nineteenth century it became the designation of religious teachers who gave spiritual discourses and provided scriptural commentary and exegesis. This is the current usage too, though it must be added that since India's independence, some *sant*s (notably Sant Fateh Singh and Sant Harchand Singh Longowal) have become actively involved in politics.[9] The preachers in some cases have been associated with a seminary-like institution, significantly known as the *ṭaksāl* (mint) where pupils receive rigorous religious instruction in the traditional style. Bhindranwale was a product of, and since 1977 head of, the Bhindranwale or Damdama ṭaksāl[10] but had no more than about five years of modern primary school education. He gained considerable prominence in 1978 and the following years as a result of his involvement in Punjab politics.

What happened in Punjab in 1978 is important to our attempt to understand the character of contemporary Sikh fundamentalism. At that time the state was governed by a coalition government formed by two religion-based political parties, the Sikh Akali Dal and the Hindu Jana Sangh (the latter had merged into the larger professedly secular Janata Party). This was a curiously opportunistic alliance between political rivals with the sole aim of being in office. Allegedly under the pressure of its Jana Sangh members, the coalition government gave permission to the Nirankari sect to hold their annual convention in the city of Amritsar, the home of the Golden Temple. The Nirankaris believe in a living guru, so repudiating the ruling of Gobind, the tenth Sikh preceptor, that after his death the Granth Sahib would be the spiritual guru, and temporal authority would vest in the community. The Nirankaris have also made additions to the Sikh holy book. This is, from the orthodox point of view, apostasy, for the tenth guru had also announced the closure of the canon (*gurbānī,* or the spoken word of the guru) and had refrained from including any of his own numerous compositions in it. Besides these two very serious lapses, not all Nirankaris strictly follow currently prevalent Sikh injunctions about personal appearance. In the eyes of the orthodox and orthoprax Sikhs, these unforgivable sins of commission and omission make the Nirankaris obnoxious foes of the true faith.

To prevent the convention, which attracts thousands of people from far and wide, Bhindranwale marched from the Golden Temple to the site of the meeting at the head of a procession, shouting anti-Nirankari slogans, and vowed not to allow the convention to take place. The processionists mutilated a shopkeeper on the way and finally made an unsuccessful attempt on the life of the head of the Nirankari sect. In the violence that ensued, swords and firearms were used freely by both sides: three Nirankaris and a dozen Sikhs lost their lives. Both sides complained of lack of protection by the police, the Sikhs perhaps with greater justification than the Nirankaris. Bhindranwale, who was a relatively unknown preacher till then, became suddenly famous as a fundamentalist and soon afterwards became embroiled in party politics.[11]

Bhindranwale's close association with Amrik Singh, son of the previous head of the Damdama seminary, whom he considered his ritual brother, turned out to be immensely useful. Amrik Singh was the leader of the All-India Sikh Students Federation. In that capacity he had mounted an offensive against the influence of the communist parties among Sikh students and achieved considerable success. Although his father had nominated Bhindranwale rather than him as his successor, he remained close to Bhindranwale, placing the institutional resources and networks of the Federation at the latter's disposal. Amrik Singh was an educated youth and his followers included diverse elements, ranging from idealists to extremists. Between 1980 and 1984, the Federation was the backbone of Bhindranwale's movement. Amrik Singh died with him in Operation Blue Star.

Bhindranwale's call to the faithful was to return to the fundamental or true teachings of Sikhism, adhere to the codes of conduct, and find through them the good, moral, life. It will be worthwhile at this point to clarify briefly the nature of the Sikh canon or scripture (as a source of basic teachings) and of the codes of conduct which define the outward signs of Sikh identity. In his speeches Bhindranwale laid more stress on the latter than on the former, talking little of theological or cosmological ideas as such and more about behavioral matters and politico-economic issues. Commentary on such ideas, it may be noted, would have been a major concern of his in his earlier role as sant, i.e., Sikh preacher, speaking to largely rural audiences. The change of substance did not, however, alter the style. There was a rustic simplicity about his utterances which gave them immense appeal. "You cannot have courage without reading gurbānī (the sayings of the gurus, i.e., the scripture). Only the bānī-reader can suffer torture and be capable of feats of strength."[12] The derivation of behavior (feats of strength) from the reading of scripture in fact reduces scripture to behavior. I have been told by many educated Sikhs that the refrain of Bhindranwale's speeches was *Tusī changē Sikh bano* (You should become good Sikhs): "Who would object to that?" ask my informants. The proof of one's religiousness is thus seen to lie in practice. The priority of the canon is, however, unquestionable in principle.

To take the nature of the scripture first. Guru Nanak (1469–1539), the first Sikh preceptor, repudiated the authority of the written word, whether that of the Brahman's Veda or the Muslim's Qur'an. The emphasis was on "interiority," on listening to the "holy word" *(śabad)* with the inner ear rather than reading it or listening to it with the external ear. The idea of a holy book came later: it was the third guru, Amar Das, who had a two-volume hymnal compiled consisting of the devotional poems of the first two gurus, earlier medieval religious poets, and himself. According to Sikh tradition, an enlarged edition was prepared by the fifth guru, Arjan. It would seem that his "enemies . . . were circulating spurious works bearing the name of Nanak in order to seduce Sikhs from their loyalty to the legitimate succession. In order to combat this threat to his authority Guru Arjan decided to prepare an authorized text bearing his own imprimatur."[13] This was done in 1603–4, and the holy book was placed in the Golden Temple.

In the next hundred years, the main interest seemed to lie in who had the possession of the Granth Sahib. Thus, the sixth guru, Hargobind, removed it from the Golden Temple and kept it in his own home. The tenth guru, Gobind, had new copies made, according to tradition, relying upon his memory. He did something more important: he announced the closure of the canon and invested the holy book with personhood, declaring it to be the guru after his death. It thus became Sri Guru Granth Sahib, the auspicious and revered guru: "I abolish from now on the succession of persons through heredity or selection. The God's Word as enshrined in the Adi Granth (Original Book) will be the eternal and the spiritual Guru, and the secular Guru will be the Panth, or the whole community of the Khalsa."[14]

It was another 175 years or so before the scriptural guru acquired its present position of supreme authority. The context in which this happened was the emergence of Sikh fundamentalism in the late nineteenth century. A definitive text of the holy book, being the recension believed to have been prepared by the tenth guru and containing the compositions of the first five and the ninth gurus, was finalized as recently as 1962. The uncertainty about its precise contents has not, however, stood in the way of the deepest reverence for the Granth Sahib. We have here a historic example of the supremacy of symbol over substance.

Turning to behavioral matters, on which Bhindranwale laid the greater stress, the beginnings of a code of conduct may be traced to the unusual happening of 13 April (some say it was on 30 March) 1699, when the tenth guru, Gobind, instituted the order of baptized Sikhs, namely, the Khalsa (the purified or the chosen), who were to call themselves Singh (lion) in the manner of Hindu Kshatriyas (the warrior caste), and who were required to wear the five *k*'s—*keś* (unshorn hair), *kanghā* (comb), *kaḍā* (steel bracelet), *kacchā* (knee-length drawers such as were worn by soldiers), and *kirpān* (sword). The significance of these symbols has been given various interpretations.[15] Other restrictions, notably on smoking and sexual intercourse with Muslim women, were also established.

But the principal emphasis seems to have been on being unshorn. When asked by what marks his Sikhs were to be recognized, Guru Gobind is said to have replied: "My Sikhs shall be in their natural form, that is, without the loss of their hair or foreskin, in opposition to the ordinances of the Hindus and the Muhammadans."[16] The concern was with physical identity and to that extent was political rather than directly with spiritual matters. Khushwant Singh puts it thus: "The Guru wanted to raise a body of men who would not be able to deny their faith when questioned, but whose external appearance would invite persecution and breed courage to resist it."[17]

Although the core of a code of conduct is fairly clear, the details are far from clear. As a Sikh historian puts it: "The Rahitnamas (Sikh codes of conduct) were all written by the Sikhs after the demise of the last Guru and do not tally with one another, except in some basics. That is why the Gurdwara act of 1925 defined the Sikh as 'one who believes in the Ten Sikh Gurus and the Guru Granth Sahib and has no other religion'. . . . Up to now, in spite of several attempts by Sikh intellectuals, the SGPC has not been able to issue a certified code of Sikh conduct, as there was great difference of opinion among the participants themselves. When we talk, therefore, of Sikh fundamentalism, we do a great disservice to this great, catholic, all inclusive faith."[18]

And yet Bhindranwale did have a clear concept of who was a good Sikh and who his enemies were. In his numerous speeches between 1978 and 1984, he identified three principal foes of Sikhism. These were, first, the apostates *(patit)* or, in his own words, "Those who profess Sikhism but do not behave as Sikhs."[19] The emphasis on behavior, on orthopraxis rather than orthodoxy, is noteworthy. Not only are Nirankaris and other heretical sects the target of attack, but also those Sikhs who have modernized or secularized their life-style. Bhindranwale demanded strict adherence to the codes of conduct which had evolved during the eighteenth and nineteenth centuries and promised political and economic rewards and not merely spiritual good in return for it. The emphasis on behavior goes well with material gain.

Here is a typical exhortation : "We shall only rule if we become Khalsa [pure or true Sikhs] . . . i.e. keep unshorn hair and take *amrit* ['nectar,' baptismal holy water]. Being the sons of Sikhs you are trimming your beards. We ourselves are ruining Sikhism. . . . The communists[20] have started telling boys at school and students that they are not slaves and therefore they need not follow this [Bhindranwale's] movement. . . . I will tell you how we are slaves: We have a minority complex. But don't consider yourselves a minority. We are not losers. A loser is a man whose Father is weak. . . . Our Father says, 'When I make my single Sikh fight against 125,000 enemies only then do I deserve to be called Gobind [the reference is to the tenth guru].' What a great promise that was!"[21]

Similarly, he mocked his audiences: "You people cut your beards, do you think you resemble the image of Guru Gobind Singh? And if you don't and He was your Father then what does that make you? I hesitate to say what you should be called [bastards]."[22] A third example of Bhindranwale's rhetoric regarding the Sikh way of life should perhaps suffice here: "Young men: with folded hands, I beseech you. . . . Until we enter our home, until we have swords on us, shorts on our bodies, Guru's word on our tongues, and the double-edged sword in our hands, we shall get beatings. It is now up to you to decide . . . the decision is in your hands."[23]

Bhindranwale repeatedly drew pointed attention to the traditional symbols of Sikh identity (notably the beard, the sword and the shorts—all three indicative of the fighting spirit) and added new ones of a similar kind, the motor-cycle and the revolver. Here is another typical harangue: "For every village you should keep one motorcycle, three young baptized Sikhs and three revolvers. These are not meant for killing innocent people. For a Sikh to have arms and kill an innocent person is a serious sin. But Khalsaji [O, baptized Sikh], to have arms and not to get your legitimate rights is an even bigger sin."[24]

Not only did the fallen Sikhs have to be brought back to the true path—by exhortation, persuasion, ridicule, and if necessary, the threat of violence—the enemies from without also had to be faced with full might. What his opponents saw as the practice of terrorism, he himself considered the call to heroic action. Who were these external enemies?

First, those Hindus who denied Sikhs a separate socioreligious identity, and second, the central and state governments which gave protection to apostates and other "enemies" of the Sikhs and denied the latter the opportunity to put their religious beliefs into practice. The religious beliefs that were singled out by Bhindranwale above all others were, first, the inseparability of religion and the state or politics, tracing this teaching to the sixth guru, Hargobind, and, second, the indivisible or corporate character of the Sikh community, deriving it from the praxis of the tenth guru, Gobind. More than any other gurus, including the first, it was these two and certain elements of their teachings which Bhindranwale recalled selectively to emphasize militancy as righteous action. The fundamentals or basic teachings of Sikhism were thus given an intentionally specific, if not narrow, definition.

Speaking of the external foes, Bhindranwale said: "They are perpetrating atrocities on us, exterminating our youth, burning our Holy Book, and insulting our turbans. When this is so you don't need to file a writ or a suit. There is no need to get a licence for arms. Neither Guru Hargobind took a licence from Jehangir nor Guru Gobind sought one from Aurangzeb."[25] Similarly, "the Hindus are trying to enslave us, atrocities against the Sikhs are increasing day by day under the Hindu imperialist rulers of New Delhi: the Sikhs have never been so humiliated, not even during the reign of Mogul emperors and British colonialists. How can the Sikhs tolerate injustice?" And so "it should be clear to all Sikhs . . . that we are slaves and want liberation at any cost. To achieve this end, arm yourself and prepare for a war."[26] In one of his last messages to his followers he said: "Peaceful means—*śānti mai*—these words cannot be found together in any part of the Sikh scriptures, in the history of the Gurus, nor in the history of the Sikhs."[27] The *words* as formulated by Bhindranwale may indeed be absent; but he surely went against the *spirit* of gurbānī.

In interpreting the basic teachings of the Sikh religious tradition in such militant terms, Bhindranwale was making a careful and calculated choice. Like any other tradition, the Sikh cultural tradition has its "pasts," not a single past, and selective retrieval is possible: indeed this would seem to be essential to all fundamentalist movements. A careful student of the scriptures and religious history of the Sikhs has observed: "Although neither in Nanak's *Japjī* (recited by all practising Sikhs as their morning prayer) nor in Arjan's *Sukhamaṇi* (psalm of peace) is there a hint that war is a just expression of Sikh power and a righteous means of accomplishing Sikhism's mission, the martial mood was nevertheless in the making—to be seen as the guruship itself continued. Not one of the first five gurus ever handled arms—in general there was no occasion for it. Arjan himself had declared 'the divine Guru is Peace.' Guru Nanak had previously said, as the legend has it: 'Take up arms that will harm no one; let your coat of mail be understanding; convert your enemies into friends; fight with valor, but with no weapon but the word of God.'[28] When the occasion arose for it, the last guru, Gobind, is believed to have written to Aurangzeb (in a famous epistle in Persian verse called the *Zafarnāmā*) that when all else fails, it is but righteous to lift the sword in one's hand and fight.[29] Militancy is advocated but only as the last resort.

It is noteworthy that while those Sikhs who today take very seriously the task of religious revival turn to the militant strand in their tradition, their critics who accuse them of being fundamentalists are at great pains to argue that there is an alternative tradition which is older and ethically superior. These critics, whether Hindus or Sikhs, would all go along with fundamentalism if it were to mean the pacifism, piety, and interreligious understanding of the earlier gurus. While they agree that the struggle between good and evil is a recurrent phenomenon in human history and has been recognized as such by all ten gurus, violent action is not an essential element of the Sikh religious tradition. Bhindranwale too employed the rhetoric of good versus evil, but he interpreted it through the lens of militancy.

Exclusive Sikh Identity

The issue of a return to the fundamentals or true teachings acquired great salience for the Sikhs in the second half of the nineteenth century. The Sikh-dominated state which Ranjit Singh (1780–1839) had established at the end of the eighteenth century collapsed in 1846, within seven years of his death, and Punjab came under British occupation. Large numbers of Sikhs from among those who had taken to following the codes of conduct in the years of Ranjit Singh's rule reverted to their earlier easier ways. This process was apparently highly noticeable, for the British governor general, who visited Punjab in 1849, observed that the Sikhs were gradually relapsing into Hinduism. Four years later (in 1853), the secretary to the government, Richard Temple, wrote: "The Sikh faith and ecclesiastical polity are rapidly going where the Sikh political ascendancy has already gone. . . . The Sikhs of Nanak, a comparatively small body of peaceful habit and old family, will perhaps cling to the faith of [their] fathers, but the Sikhs of Gobind . . . who are more specially styled the Singhs or Lion, and who embraced the faith as being the religion of warfare and conquest, no longer regard the Khalsa now that the prestige has departed from it. These men joined in thousands, and they now depart in equal numbers. They rejoin the ranks of Hinduism."[30]

Half a century later the situation seemed no better. Max Arthur Macauliffe, a British civil servant devoted to the cause of the Sikhs, who authored a monumental six-volume work on Sikh religion, wrote: "Truly wonderful are the strength and vitality of Hinduism. It is like the boa constrictor of the Indian forest . . . Hinduism has embraced Sikhism in its folds; the still comparatively young religion is making a vigorous struggle for life, but its ultimate destruction is, it is apprehended, inevitable without State support."[31] Macauliffe had first used this rather dramatic imagery to describe the Hindu-Sikh relationship about forty years earlier.[32] Obviously he chose to ignore two major developments of the previous fifty years when he repeated this judgment. He played down, first, the very support of the state (i.e., the British government of India) to the Sikhs, which he strongly advocated, and second, the emergence of sectarian and socioreligious reform movements among them, seeking a return to the basic teachings and a purification of Sikh prayer and practice. State patronage and the birth of fundamentalism reinforced the concern for an exclusive Sikh socioreligious identity.

The British were at first wary of recruiting Sikhs into the army and debarred veterans of the old Sikh army, but gradually they were allowed entry. This was done at least partly in recognition of the support the Sikhs had given to the British during the 1857 Mutiny, of which the symbolic figurehead was the Mogul "emperor." The Moguls were the traditional foes of the Sikhs: the fifth guru had been tortured to death and the ninth beheaded on the orders of Jehangir and Aurangzeb, respectively; the tenth guru had spent a good part of his life in militant defiance of the latter. What is more significant is that the British encouraged baptized Sikhs to adhere to their code of conduct and once they were recruited disallowed the abandonment of the conventional marks of Sikh identity.[33] Building upon the tradition emanating from the sixth and tenth gurus, the British helped in shaping the notion of the Sikhs as a martial race and indeed as a distinct and separate nation.[34] The Singh or "Lion" identity of the baptized Sikhs thus gained ground.

Apart from recruitment to the army, collection of revenue and other civil matters brought the administration into daily contact with the Sikhs. The bureaucracy tended to be friendly toward the Jat Sikhs, the demographic core of the community, enabling them to maintain their prominent position in the countryside. Besides, many favours and honors, including land grants *(jāgīr)*, were bestowed upon loyal Sikhs. The propagation of the Sikh religion received official support, and the government sponsored two English translations of the Granth Sahib. The first, by Ernest Trumpp (in the 1870s), turned out disastrously from the intended point of view: he maintained that the gurus had not intended to found a new religion and spoke disparagingly of the "contents and style" of their hymns.[35] The second was by Max Arthur Macauliffe at the turn of the century.[36] Macauliffe was untiring in his efforts in the cause of the religion of the Sikhs and in his patronage of them.

State support, however, is by itself never sufficient to galvanize people. Despondency over the reversal of worldly fortunes understandably leads to spiritual soul-searching. Two major sectarian movements emerged in Punjab in the 1850s and

1860s with the avowed purpose of purifying the Sikh way of life and returning to the fundamentals. These were the Nirankari and Namdhari movements, but they had very limited influence among the masses. Moreover, and ironically, while they began as purificatory or fundamentalist movements, they ended up being heretical, the Nirankaris reinstating a living guru and the Namdharis predicting the rebirth of the tenth guru.[37]

More significant than these sectarian movements was the emergence of, first, social reform organizations called Singh Sabhas in the 1870s and second, Hindu-Sikh estrangement in the following decades. In addition to the weakness of the Sikh body politic, the activities of the Christian missions, the proselytization by a new Hindu organization known as Arya Samaj, and the rationalism that came with the introduction of scientific ideas into everyday life also contributed to the weakening of the Sikh community.[38]

In such a setting a combination of religious and secular concerns was a precondition for the success of any movement or organization. Thus the first Singh Sabha founded at Amritsar in 1873 had as its main objective efforts "to arouse the love of religion among the Sikhs," followed by efforts "to propagate the true Sikh religion everywhere" and to bring out "the greatness and truth of the Sikh religion." The distinctiveness of Sikhism from Hinduism was not, however, a major concern. In fact, some of the leaders of this rather elitist Sabha were quite willing to see themselves and the Sikhs generally as reformists among Hindus. They came to be known as *sanātan,* or traditional Sikhs. Friendly Hindus agreed, saying that the Sikhs were a Hindu sect. To achieve its goals, the Sabha envisaged educational, literary, journalistic, and social activities. It laid emphasis upon the learning of Punjabi in Gurmukhi script, but also upon interreligious tolerance, and resolved not to come into conflict with the government.[39] Loyalty to British rulers was maintained throughout the quarter century that the Sabhas were active. The British recognized this: in 1890 the viceroy, Lord Lansdowne had declared that the government was sympathetic to the Singh Sabha movement.[40]

A second Singh Sabha came up at Lahore in 1879. Its lower-caste and middle-class leadership emphasized the need for reform, which included a call for simplification and purification of social customs and, as a prerequisite to these aims, "an assertion of Sikh separateness."[41] Expectedly, the two Sabhas were embroiled in conflict over issues of doctrine and authority and made efforts to mobilize support for their respective positions among urban and, in the course of time, rural Sikhs. But this conflict was not wholly destructive: "The Singh Sabhas built schools and a college, opened orphanages, established archives and historical societies and produced a flood of polemical and scholarly literature on Sikh tradition."[42] They also cooperated with each other in facing up to the upsurge of Hindu communalism represented by the Arya Samaj. By the close of the century there were over a hundred Sabhas all over Punjab, together contributing to the tide of Sikh separatism.

On a superficial view, the Singh Sabha movement "remained true to the orthodox tradition of 'no guru save the *granth*' . . . [and] met the challenges of modern times with modern weapons,"[43] most notably modern education in combination with religious instruction. A more balanced judgment would be that the Sabhas played a "complex role and instead of asserting a lost orthodoxy, put together elements from diverse and often conflicting traditions so as to enhance the distinct nature of the religion. This resulted in a new and different Sikh identity, complete with ideology and practices commonly associated with Sikhism today."[44]

The foregoing does not take away anything from the fact that as a result of the efforts of the Sabhas, the Granth Sahib began to be freely available in printed editions and acquired a new salience. *Granthīs*, that is, people who could read the multilingual granth, also gained in social visibility—a process of which we encounter certain unintended consequences today in the post-Bhindranwale period.

When the first Singh Sabha opted for interreligious tolerance, it had not reckoned with the emergence of the revivalist Hindu Arya Samaj which was brought to Punjab in 1877.[45] Although many Sikhs reacted to it positively in the beginning, welcoming its anti-ritualistic, anti-idolatrous, and social egalitarian emphases, it soon became apparent that not only did the Arya Samajists not hold the Sikh religion and its gurus in high esteem, they also denied the autonomy of the Sikhs as a sociocultural community. The crucial development in this context was the purificatory *(śuddhi)* movement launched by the Arya Samaj. It was at first aimed at preventing the conversion of Hindus to Islam and Christianity. Later the objective became bolder and envisaged purification and reconversion. It was during this phase that Arya Samajist Hindus, who split among themselves into militant and moderate factions, came to be seen as enemies by the Sikhs. Samajist polemics often became disrespectful of the gurus and insulting toward the Sikhs, and the latter were dismissed as lacking true knowledge. "In 1900 the Arya Samaj purified a group of outcaste Rahtia Sikhs and as part of the ceremony shaved their heads and beards, transforming them into pure caste Hindus."[46] The importance of unshorn hair for Khalsa Sikh identity has been mentioned above. Inevitably, the Singh Sabhas retaliated and attempted to win latitudinarian *(sahajdhārī)* Sikhs and Hindu admirers of the faith into the fold of the baptized *(amritdhārī)* and the unshorn *(keśdhārī)*.

This breach between Hindus and Sikhs found manifold expression, including pamphleteering and legal battles, and has never been healed. Puzzlement and incomprehension of one another's intentions and actions were the dominant emotions, but hostility and hatred were not altogether absent . Each side resorted to the reconstruction of history in a partisan spirit, presenting Sikhism as a *new* religion, or as *reformed* or *debased* Hinduism. There were two fundamentalisms here, each seeking supremacy over the other. While Hindu publicists wrote pamphlets under the title of *Sikh Hindū haiṅ* (the Sikhs are Hindus), a scholarly Sikh of high position, Kahan Singh, published a pamphlet entitled *Ham Hindū nahīṅ* (We are not Hindus)[47] which became very influential.

A careful Sikh scholar, Harjot S. Oberoi, has recently drawn attention to the radical character of Kahan Singh's tract,which, he points out rightly, brought four centuries of Sikh tradition to an end. Prior to the Singh Sabha movement, Sikhs and Hindus not only lived together in Punjab but also shared a common cultural life, with common symbols and common cognitive and affective orientations. Moreover, most

Sikhs identified themselves variously in terms of village, cult, lineage, or caste, depending upon the context, and did not project a single Sikh identity. No single source of authority within the Sikh tradition was recognized, and thus several competing definitions of who was a Sikh were possible. This, Oberoi points out, was in conformity with the general social situation in India, where religious identities are usually defined regionally and even locally.[48]

The sociological approach helps us to appreciate better the role of the new social and cultural elites which constituted the leadership of the Singh Sabha movement. These elites cut across the primordial ties which had long provided the bases for identity definition. Perceptively, they focused on pluralism as the target of their attack. From then onwards Sikhs, in Oberoi's words, "were required to speak and dream through one language," and this was the language of cultural elites. A Sikh Great Tradition was being invented, and those Sikhs who did not fall in line were sidelined and even excluded from the emergent mainstream. "The older forms of Sikhism were displaced forever and replaced by a series of inventions: the demarcation of Sikh sacred space by clearing holy shrines of Hindu icons and idols, the cultivation of Punjabi as the sacred language of the Sikhs, the foundation of cultural bodies exclusively for Sikh youth, the insertion of the anniversaries of the Sikh Gurus into the ritual and sacred calender and most important of all, the introduction of new life-cycle rituals."[49]

To meet the challenges of the times (not merely the Hindu challenge but also that of new opportunities), the Singh Sabhas, which were brought together under the umbrella of a new body called the Chief Khalsa Diwan in 1902, opted for the Khalsa subtradition as *the* Sikh tradition. The Khalsa, or the community of the pure, baptized Sikhs, was instituted by the tenth guru, Gobind. He had not, however, prescribed more than a minimum code of conduct and had not excluded from the Sikh fold those who were reluctant or slow to conform. In other words, in the name of conforming to the Great Tradition, a tradition was being slowly constructed from selected old elements and newly invented ones. Thus it was the Chief Khalsa Diwan which, though accommodating in its overall approach, was instrumental in having Hindu idols removed from the Golden Temple in 1905, and a special marriage ritual enacted as law (the Anand Marriage Act) four years later.[50] It is clear that in the manner in which it came to be established late in the nineteenth century and early in the twentieth, Sikh fundamentalism had its character fixed not as a return to fundamentals—an original doctrine—but as a bending of traditional elements to contemporary uses. This is what is happening today. We have, however, some more ground to cover before we return to the present situation.

Gurdwara Agitation

In the drive to establish an exclusive Sikh identity and make some fundamentals of belief and behavior its basis, the Singh Sabhas and subsequently the Chief Khalsa Diwan had their eyes on the gurdwārās, particularly the Golden Temple, as very visible means of mobilizing the community.[51] In utilizing this powerful symbol, they had to reckon with two impediments: the government, which was becoming increasingly suspicious, and the hereditary temple custodians (*mahants*) and priests (*pujārīs*), who were openly hostile. The government had handled the Sikhs with caution, combining patronage with control. Pro-British groups and important individuals were the recipients of this patronage. In return they were expected to help in keeping volatile elements under control. This was perhaps best exemplified by the fact that the government never allowed the management of the Golden Temple to go completely out of its hands. It thus stood behind the mahants, who were almost invariably unbaptized Sikhs (though claiming affiliation with the Udasi sect founded by one of the sons of the first guru) or plain Hindus. They kept alive idolatry and a great deal of Brahmanical ritual in the temples and were considered venal by the fundamentalists. The managers of the Golden Temple were particularly disliked, not only for their Hindu origin and ways but also for their loyalty to the British.[52]

The support of the temple custodians and priests was one of the many miscalculations of the British in Punjab. It led to what has been called the third Sikh war, but it was a war with a difference.[53] It is here necessary to cut one's way through a great deal of detail and focus on the issue of the promotion of the purity or fundamentals of faith within the community. The first critical event was very visible and dramatic. It happened in 1914. The construction of the new imperial capital had commenced in south Delhi, and in the clearing operations for the construction of the viceregal lodge, the government demolished a boundary wall of the gurdwārā at Rikabganj with the concurrence of the custodian. The opportunity to cry sacrilege and challenge both the guilty parties had been offered on a platter, as it were. The situation was prevented from escalating into open conflict by the outbreak of the war in Europe. The agitation was resumed in 1918, and the government yielded: the wall was rebuilt and the displacement of the custodian by a committee, which had meanwhile occurred, was recognized. Radical Sikhs felt emboldened to ask for community control of all their gurdwārās. This actually happened at a few places.

The situation took a decisive turn late in 1920. First, in October there was a congregation of Sikhs at Jallianwala Bagh, in Amritsar, where a very significant decision was taken, that is, to administer holy baptismal water to Sikh converts from among the so-called Hindu untouchable castes and then lead them for prayers into the nearby Golden Temple. The custodian-priests resisted the proposed entry, pronouncing it an act of desecration. The Granth Sahib was consulted, using the traditional method of interpreting the first verse on a particular page. The verdict went in favor of the congregation and against the priests. The choice of the venue of the gathering too had been significant. It was here that a British general had, the previous year, ordered the machine-gunning of a peaceful crowd, mostly Sikhs, on a festival day, killing 309 and injuring one thousand. He was later honored by the custodian of the Golden Temple!

Then, in November, a proclamation from the Akal Takht, the seat of temporal authority, set up a committee for the community management of all Sikh shrines. It was called Shiromani Gurdwara Prabandhak Committee (SGPC). Almost simultaneously, in January 1921, the Akali Dal (band of immortals) was set up for the forceable eviction of the custodians wherever necessary. Both institutions were envisaged as instruments of the Sikh community for the furtherance of a purified way of religious and social life, without idolatrous priests and in repudiation of ritualism and caste distinctions. Such indeed had been the fundamental teachings of the gurus. Fundamentalism at this time was primarily religious, but it was soon to become political.

In the following year, the Akalis came into conflict with the custodians, first at Tarn Taran and then at Nankana Sahib, the birthplace of the first guru. The custodian at the latter gurdwārā and his mercenaries resisted with savage force a band of 150 Sikhs who sought entry into the temple, resulting in the death of over 130 of them. (According to some accounts there were no survivors.) Mahatma Gandhi commended the nonviolent approach of these Sikhs and called their self-sacrifice exemplary. He also invited the Sikhs to see their struggle to cleanse their gurdwārās as inseparable from the cleansing of the "bigger gurdwārā," i.e., India. This was the typical Gandhian view of the inseparability of religion and politics. The SGPC leadership accepted this advice and formally associated themselves with the national movement. Fundamentalism and nationalism thus became allies.

Alarmed by these developments, the government made one last bid to keep control of the Golden Temple by appointing a custodian, thus preventing its take-over by the SGPC. The keys of the treasury became the symbol of a new agitation which was completely peaceful: thousands of Akalis courted arrest and refused to cooperate with the government. Both weapons were taken from the Gandhian armory. The government had to yield once again, and the keys were handed over to the SGPC. Its president received a telegram from Gandhi: "First battle for India's freedom won. Congratulations!!"

More was to follow in 1922. Conflict between the Akalis and one more government-backed custodian, this time at Guru-ka-Bagh, resulted from the latter's refusal to allow Sikhs to use firewood cut from temple land. For several months unarmed protestors marched to the gurdwārā, only to be beaten there by government forces or to be arrested and whipped in jails. They remained nonviolent, however, and won countrywide admiration for their fortitude. Eventually, the government yielded once again. By the end of January 1923, about one hundred gurdwārās were under the control of the SGPC. It is noteworthy that the backbone of these peaceful agitations, involving much hardship and suffering for the protectors, was the Sikh peasantry. It was not a peasant movement, however.

By 1924, another Akali agitation against the British was mounted, this time for the restoration of his authority to the deposed Sikh ruler of the state of Nabha. The espousal of a purely political cause resulted in a split among the radicalized Sikhs and the domination of the SGPC by the Akali Dal. Already disturbed by the pressure tactics that had emerged as a characteristic feature of Akali movements and concerned about the communalization of Punjab politics, with Hindu or Sikh concerns overriding common or national interests, Gandhi called for the abandonment of the movement, saying it had nothing to do with religion, which was what the SGPC should be concerned with. This has been seen by many Sikhs as a volte-face by Gandhi. They ask, was it not Gandhi who first asked the Sikhs to link their gurdwārā reform movement to larger political issues? One can argue both ways, but this is not the place for it.[54]

The gurdwārā battle was finally waged on the floor of the Punjab Legislative Council with the support of non-Sikh (Hindu and Muslim) nationalist leaders and won. The Gurdwara Reform Act of 1925 placed the control of all Sikh shrines of Punjab in the hands of SGPC. Statutory restraints (*see* section 108[3] of the Act) were placed upon the participation of the SGPC in politics. These were to be, however, honored more in the breach than in compliance. From then on, the Akali Dal (as political party) and the SGPC (as custodian of the shrines), though by definition concerned with two different areas of activity, were in practice to work in tandem. In fact the political party established complete control over the religious body, reversing the Gandhian hierarchy of values encompassing interests.

Sikh Separatism

Fundamentalism among the Sikhs came to serve two ends in the twenties: first, the establishment of the control of the community over the gurdwārās, and second, the maintenance of the boundary that distinguished Khalsa Sikhs from Hindus. The definition of the boundary became increasingly political, but politics itself did not emerge as an autonomous domain, the encompassing national movement for independence notwithstanding. Instead of religion providing the value premises of politics, as Gandhi had envisaged and advocated, religion came to be used to further political ends. This happened at the national level no less than at the regional level. To use a perceptive observation of Louis Dumont,[55] made in another context, religion was thus reduced from being "the essence and guide of life in all spheres" to "a sign of distinction" between politically organized communities. In this sense religious fundamentalism is really antireligious. If this appears to be an overly reductionist view of the Akali position (and for that matter of the Arya Samaj position too), it should be made clear that we are not here concerned with ideology in the abstract but rather with how it is used and bent in real-life situations.

During the two decades between the passing of the Gurdwara Reform Act in 1925 and the independence of the subcontinent in 1947, Sikh public life became polarized between fundamentalists (Akali Dal), who retained control of the SGPC, and secularists (Congress and the Communist Party), who dominated politics. Each party sought legitimacy by invoking its own reconstruction of the Sikh religious tradition, its own strategy of remembering and forgetting. It is significant that each side emphasized the secular character of the tradition, but while this meant for Akalis the religious legitimacy of worldly (political and economic) interests, and therefore the inseparability of religion and politics, for the Congress and the Communist Party it meant the separation of religion and politics. Reconstructions of tradition in such circumstances are naturally *partial* in both senses of the term: they are *selective* and they are *partisan*. This does not, however, mean that such reconstruction is illegitimate. The issue is not to press rhetorically for legitimacy, contrasting "living" movements with "dead" traditions: it is rather recognizing that the selection is presented as the Truth, single and whole.

The Akali Dal, with membership which is exclusively Sikh, has inevitably been led to political separatism which has depended upon fundamentalism for its hoped-for success. To hold one's religious beliefs and pursue religious practices without any hindrance, it is argued, one needs the protection of the state: the demand for a state where the Sikhs will rule is therefore considered a religious demand. In fact, those Sikhs who say their daily prayers include the words *rāj karegā khālsā* (the community of baptized Sikhs will rule) in the last prayer: they even seek to attribute this slogan without evidence to the tenth guru.[56]

Although the Akali movement of the 1920s was directed against the government and was brought close to the national movement by Gandhi, it nevertheless acted as a pressure group on behalf of the Sikhs. But gradually, as the Muslim demand for a separate state where Muslim cultural, religious, and economic interests could be safeguarded gathered momentum, the Akali Dal too began to stress increasingly the religious and political autonomy of the Sikhs. The case for political autonomy was more difficult to establish, since both the Muslims and the Hindus, each community by itself, outnumbered the Sikhs. The Akali Dal therefore put forward in 1943 the demand for an independent Punjabi state so constituted that the Sikhs, comprising 20 percent of the population, would hold the balance between the Hindus and the Muslims (40 percent each). A year later (in 1944), the Akali Dal leader Tara Singh put forward the demand for a separate Sikh state.

This demand was given explicit formulation in a 1946 resolution of the Akali Dal: "Whereas the Sikhs being attached to the Punjab by intimate bonds of holy shrines, property and language, traditions and history claim it as their homeland and holy land . . . and whereas the entity of the Sikhs is being threatened on account of the persistent demand of Pakistan by the Muslims on the one hand and of danger of absorption by the Hindus on the other . . . the Akali Dal demands for the preservation and protection of the religious, cultural, and economic and political rights of the Sikh nation, the creation of a Sikh state."[57] Although the demand was not conceded by the British, it has never really died down, notwithstanding a great many changes in its formulation.

Loyalty to a common religion, namely, Sikhism, has not generally been stressed explicitly as the sole or real basis for regional autonomy or for an independent Sikh state. Such political aspirations, whether limited or separatist, have usually been expressed through a rhetoric about the preservation of cultural identity based on the Punjabi language written in the Gurmukhi script. The insistence on Gurmukhi has been of crucial importance, because Punjabi is as much the language of the Hindus of Punjab (and of the Muslims across the international frontier in Pakistan's Punjab province) as it is of the Sikhs. But the argument has not been entirely convincing: although the Sikh Holy Book is written in Gurmukhi, there is no evidence of the use of the script among the Sikhs for secular purposes having been widespread or until recently of any general ability among them to read it. More to the point therefore has been the demand for the protection of the economic interests of the Sikhs against those of Hindu landowners and traders. Thus, religion, culture, and economic interests have in turn, or in various combinations, been emphasized as the key element or elements in the demand for autonomy or independence.

The face is the same, but the masks worn over it have been various. Thus, the Akali Dal leader Tara Singh said in 1955: "The cover of a Punjabi-speaking state slogan serves my purpose well since it does not offend against nationalism."[58] The fear of loss of identity remains crucial. To quote Tara Singh again: "the Sikhs are Hindus and I feel they are so. But I do not say so, as in that case the Hindus would absorb the Sikhs."[59] The language argument finally won and a Punjabi state was carved out of the Indian half of the original Punjab in 1966. This was the second partition of Punjab, the first having taken place in 1947 at the time of the creation of Pakistan. It is important to note that the shift in emphasis from religion to language coincided with the displacement of Tara Singh, a schoolteacher by profession, from a position of dominance in the Akali Dal by Fateh Singh, a sant (religious teacher). It would be fair, and not from a fundamentalist point of view alone, to regard the sant's strategy of separating religion from language as chicanery. Punjabi, written in Gurmukhi script developed by the second guru, is the sacred language of the Sikhs, being the mother tongue of the gurus and one of the vernaculars in the Granth Sahib. It symbolizes the availability of revelation *(śruti)* through the speech of ordinary people no less than it represents the right of nationalities to self-determination.[60]

The Punjabi state was of course not a Sikh state. It could not be, for despite the redrawing of boundaries, Sikhs in the new state could not account for more than 54 percent of the population as against the 44 percent of the Hindus. In fact when elections were held in the reorganized state, the secularist Congress succeeded in electing more Sikh legislators than the Akali Dal, and the latter had to seek the support of the right-wing Hindu party, Jana Sangh, and the Communists to form a coalition government. Such a coalition was bound to be short-lived.

The Akalis now turned to grievances on the economic front and launched a series of mass agitations against the central government during the 1970s and 1980s. The new manifesto was an Akali Dal resolution adopted in 1973 at Anandpur Sahib, a place associated closely in Sikh tradition with the last two gurus. It was here that the tenth guru proclaimed the formation of the Khalsa. The text of the resolution has been a matter of controversy. The central issues are, however, quite explicit: they include the assertion that Sikhs need "a congenial environment and a political set-up" for the preservation of their religion and culture, and they need more resources and administrative freedom for their socio-economic development.[61]

Based on the Anandpur Sahib resolution, several sets of demands were put forward after 1980, when the Congress returned to power in the state of Punjab and in New Delhi. The situation escalated into a confrontation with the state and central governments despite divisions among the Akalis. In 1981 the demand for an independent Sikh state, to be called Khalistan, was first voiced at an educational conference and then, significantly, on a festival day (Holi) at Anandpur Sahib by extremist (Dal Khalsa) and militant (Nihang) elements. Various Akali factions dissociated themselves from this demand, but as the pressures built, they came together and announced in

1982 the beginning of a battle for righteousness (or a righteous battle, *dharma yuddha*). Seeking to contain the movement, the Congress had earlier (1978–80) pushed Bhindranwale into politics, hoping that his religious influence among the Sikh masses would be greater than that of the Akalis. And so it was, but he turned against his promoters, that is, Congress politicians, in 1980 and outdid the Akalis in the vehemence and violence of his own campaign for the acceptance of the demands, religious as well as economic. Early in 1984 Bhindranwale broke with the Akalis: he had by then entrenched himself inside the Akal Takht and become a phenomenon in his own right.

Several scholars have maintained that Bhindranwale used the language of religion to give utterance to genuine and widespread economic grievances of the Sikhs of both rural and urban areas. It is argued that had the central government been responsive and taken adequate steps to remove the causes of discontent, the secular bases of Sikh identity would have been strengthened. The government's indifference and ineptitude opened the way for Bhindranwale to present the issue of center-state relations in a religious framework—as discriminatory treatment of a religious minority by the government and as a threat to cultural identity. It was therefore a matter of general concern to the entire Sikh community. Needless to say, the religious idiom proved to be the most effective for general mobilization of support.[62]

It is not our intention here to deny that the Punjab economy had run into a development crisis by the 1980s, arising from the tapering off of the gains of the Green Revolution and their unequal distribution, intersectoral imbalance, rising unemployment, etc. Applauded at home and abroad for its success in increasing agricultural productivity as well as production (with the use of high-yielding varieties of seeds and other inputs), Punjab ironically remains trapped in agriculture: half of its domestic product comes from this source and supports almost 60 percent of the labor force. The state has lagged behind in industrial development, and this has become a major grievance. People complain that the surplus generated by the Punjabi agriculturist is drained off and used as investment elsewhere in the country. Further, it is argued that the rich have become richer in Punjab and the poor, poorer. Thus, while relatively larger farmers (with holdings of 20 acres and more) are making good profits, small farmers (with holdings of less than five acres) are actually net losers.[63] The overall picture then, is that while compared to other states, Punjab is a success story in the field of economic growth, within the state itself there are complaints that there is not adequate and balanced development and equitable distribution. The central government and a succession of state governments are blamed for this state of affairs.

Some social scientists have rightly argued that one of the routes that leads to communalism or fundamentalism runs via economic discontent, which is of course a subjective feeling, although it may be based on objective facts.[64] Nor is it our concern to apportion blame between the government and Sikh politicians. More important for the present discussion is to emphasize that, contrary to what is sometimes suggested, Akali demands have at no stage been purely secular: they could not be, because Akalis of all shades of opinion consider the inseparability of religion and politics the first article of their faith. The economic situation will therefore not by itself help us to understand the character of the present expressions of Sikh fundamentalism. For this we have to turn to the past also and examine the uses that have been made of it.

The Two Swords

The foregoing discussion brings us to Bhindranwale and the contemporary manifestations of Sikh fundamentalism. And Bhindranwale takes us back to the sixth and tenth gurus: to Guru Hargobind's doctrine of temporal power-spiritual authority *(mīrī-pīrī)* and Guru Gobind's practice of righteous war *(dharma yuddha)*. The Sikhs will wage battle for their rights, Bhindranwale said, and they will do so from the Akal Takht, for the temple is also the fort. This is not politics, he maintained, but religion, the true teaching. And in our words, this is fundamentalism.

Now, what did the sixth guru, the builder of the Akal Takht, teach and do? We are here dealing with tradition and not with history in the formal sense. And the tradition was well recorded by Macauliffe. According to him, when Hargobind (1595–1644) succeeded his father as the guru, he refused to wear the traditional *selī* (a woolen cord worn as a necklace or twisted round the head by the former gurus) and the turban, saying: "My *selī* shall be a sword-belt, and I shall wear my turban with a royal aigrette."[65] Tradition has it that the Sikh elder who was requested to invest the guru with his raiment put the sword on Hargobind's right side, which is the wrong side for it, but the guru would not let him remove it. He asked for a second sword and then explained: "I wear two swords as emblems of spiritual and temporal authority."[66] Of his subsequent actions cast in the warrior mold, the building of the Akal Takht is perhaps the most notable. Two sovereignties, the spiritual and the temporal, were clearly underlined in these actions. While some interpreters, such as the Sikh historian Gopal Singh,[67] point out that the two swords and the two temples point to collaterality and separation, the fundamentalists emphasize that they symbolize the inseparability of religion and politics.

Whatever is the interpretation, there can be no denying that Guru Hargobind made a radical departure from past practice, and those close to the guru, including his mother and the Sikh elder involved in the installation ceremony, remonstrated with him for it, but he persisted in his resolve. The first guru's teaching that a true Sikh's only weapon should be the holy word had thus been set aside. Some Sikh scholars acknowledge the enormous change in the political environment between the first guru's time and the sixth guru's but maintain that there is no break in the teaching, only adaptation to changed circumstances; they say that gurbānī is continuous. On the theological plane, this may be a valid argument—every guru, it would seem, considered himself one with Nanak—but in terms of social and political history it is questionable.

The process of transformation found full expression in the teachings and doings of the tenth (and last) personal guru, Gobind (1666–1708). He merged the divinity and the sword: the former came to called "pure steel" (*sarbloh,* whole iron). The train of thought is as follows: "God subdues enemies, so does the sword; therefore the sword is God, and God is the sword."[68] It was to emphasize the need for armed action and bravery to fight Muslim oppression that Guru Gobind instituted the custom of baptism by sweetened water stirred with a double-edged dagger *(khāṇḍā)*. The dagger with a sword on either side of it has since acquired the status of the supreme symbol *(niśān sāḥib)* of the Sikh faith: it is usually shown on a flag with the phrase *ik oṃkār* (the supreme is one and indivisible) also painted or sewn on it. The baptized Sikhs, the guru is said to have declared, would be transformed from jackals into lions and would obtain political power (kingdom) in this world and spiritual bliss hereafter.[69]

Now Bhindranwale held that in the situation in which the Sikhs found themselves in the 1980s, the true and basic teaching for them was what the sixth and tenth gurus had taught and done. When the government and the so-called moderate Sikhs protested the fortification of the Akal Takht and its occupation by armed Sikhs, calling these actions desecration, Bhindranwale was supported by many Sikhs, who said that he was actually safeguarding the sanctity of the temple, which was likely to be violated by the government sending police or the army into the complex.

That is what ultimately happened during Operation Blue Star, in which Bhindranwale lost his life. The storming of the temple complex turned out to be a severe blow to the Sikh psyche, a wound which has still not healed. It has given new and unprecedented power to the managers *(jathedārs)* and scripture readers *(granthīs)* of the gurdwārās in the political affairs of the Sikh community. It has led to the revival of several Sikh institutions of critical importance, notably the *sarbat k͟hālsā* (a general gathering of Sikhs called by the jathedār of the Akal Takht) convened for ascertaining the collective will of the community of believers, which would then be deemed to be the guru's decision *(gurmattā)* according to the teaching of the tenth guru, and would result in "orders" *(hukamnāmā)* to various individuals or groups. The manner in which these gatherings have been convened and their frequency have, however, violated the relevant conventions. Similarly, the declaration of particular Sikhs as *tank͟hāhiyā* (those who have sold their faith), and in some cases their subsequent rehabilitation, have been done in a far from prescribed or serious manner.

Thus, on 26 January 1986, a *sarbat khālsā,* which had not been convened properly was held within the precincts of the Golden Temple under the auspices of two organizations associated with Bhindranwale, namely, the Damdama ṭaksāl and the All-India Sikh Students Federation, to give the call for the resumption of the struggle for the leadership of the Sikh community.[70] Besides, the intruders performed two symbolic acts of great visibility to give expression to their defiance of the state. First, they burnt the national flag from the balcony of the Akal Takht and hoisted a Khalistan flag atop the temple. Second, five Sikh priests, representing, according to tradition, the Sikh community, inaugurated the demolition of the Akal Takht. This shrine had been extensively damaged during Operation Blue Star and had been subsequently repaired quickly at the initiative of the government of India, but with much-publicized public participation *(kār sevā),* another Sikh tradition associated with the building of gurdwārās. This symbolic support had been made possible by the cooperation of a leader of the militant Nihang Sikhs who had stood aloof from Bhindranwale. Now, in 1986, it was the head of the Damdama ṭaksāl who led the demolition so that the temple could be reconstructed by true, and not tank͟hāhiyā, Sikhs.

A rapid flow of events during the following year included the proclamation of Khalistan, or the autonomous Sikh state, at the temple complex on 29 April, followed the next day by an unsuccessful attempt by the civil police to clear the area of the intruders. Chief Minister Barnala's decision to send the police into the temple complex split the ruling Akali Dal. In February 1987, five so-called high priests, under the leadership of the custodian of Akal Takht, excommunicated Barnala, charging him with religious misconduct, and dissolved all competing Akali political parties *(dal)*, replacing them by a unified Akali Dal, of which Bhindranwale's father was made the figurehead. In a bizarre turn of events a few months later, the custodian of Akal Takht, finding himself unable to control the extremists, withdrew from the scene. This was an unprecedented act and highlighted the emergence of several centers of Sikh fundamentalism. These are Akali politicians, "high priests," and extremist-terrorist elements. The religious basis of Akali politics goes back to its beginnings in the early 1920s. Akali politicians are the original fundamentalists and have a large following, but they have been rendered ineffective by internecine factionalism.

A recent split resulted from the accord which Sant Harchand Singh Longowal signed with Prime Minister Rajiv Gandhi in 1985 to bring satisfaction to the Sikhs and peace to Punjab. Surjit Singh Barnala became chief minister following the elections held under the accord later that year, but his Akali Dal (faction) was opposed by the Akali Dal led by Prakash Singh Badal, a former chief minister, who was against the terms of the Gandhi-Longowal accord. There have been further splits since then, and Barnala has lost some of his supporters. The rampant factionalism has diminished the political weight of the Akali politicians generally, opening the way for other fundamentalist groups.[71]

Sikh fundamentalism today grows around the custodians *(jathedārs)* of three major temples of Amritsar (Akal Takht), Anandpur (Sri Keshgarh Sahib), and Bhatinda (Damdama Sahib), and the granthīs of Harmandir Sahib and Akal Takht. The Sikh tradition recognizes five *takhts* (thrones), i.e., seats of temporal authority. These include, besides the first three temples just mentioned, the shrines at Patna (Bihar) and Nanded (Maharashtra). The jathedārs of Patna and Nanded, being located outside Punjab, have been excluded from consultation by the other three jathedārs.[72] But since five Sikhs are needed to represent the will and authority of the community, the granthīs of the two Amritsar shrines have been roped in. It is these five personages who are today generally but quite erroneously referred to as the Sikh "high priests." Although Sikh temple rituals are a departure from the teachings of the early gurus, they are quite simple and not dependent upon ritual specialists. It is therefore, a misnomer to refer to gurdwārā custodians and scripture readers as "high priests." They have nevertheless acquired political clout and follow Bhindranwale's strategies of mobilization: they articulate the grievances of Sikhs against the government, caution the faithful about the poison of heresy and secularization, and warn them about the ever-present danger of absorption into Hindu society. The call to return to fundamentals arouses hope in some and guilt in others.

Drawing attention to the threefold teaching of the first guru—piety, labor, and sharing of the fruits of labor—the fundamentalists ask if this is what prevails today. Now Punjab has made great strides on the economic front and is one of the main areas where the Green Revolution has been a great success story. But income disparities and poverty also persist. Punjab is often humorously referred to as "chicken-and-whiskey land," pointing to both the rise of prosperity and the decline of piety. In an atmosphere surcharged with religiosity, it is not difficult to arouse guilt among people, identify enemies in compensatory reaction, and then mobilize the followers of the faith for political action, which is articulated in a religious idiom.

Such religious rhetoric is, however, explicitly interwoven with politics. Political parties, extremist groups, and others seek to gain control of the SGPC and have their own nominees appointed as jathedārs and granthīs. Alternatively, the SGPC is bypassed and efforts are made to have the positions filled through other means. The appointees are then expected to make political pronouncements and give directions to political parties or the general public along lines previously laid down. The terrorists and the government too are trying to make use of these so-called high priests, who have thus emerged as the core group of fundamentalists among the Sikhs today.

It would be a mistake, however, to consider the jathedārs and granthīs simply as usurpers. When the tenth guru declared closure of the lineage of personal gurus, his intention was to do away with intermediaries between the One True Guru (God) and the community of believers. As already stated, the Granth Sahib was proclaimed the spiritual guru and temporal authority was vested in the community. Given the length and linguistic diversity of the holy book, it may be read and chanted (which it is meant to be) properly only by those who have been trained, the granthīs and the *ragīs*. Ironically, the granthīs have emerged as intermediaries through their special reading ability, and so have the jathedārs through their responsibility for organizational matters connected with the gurdwārās, including the daily routine *(mān-maryādā)* connected with the veneration and reading of the Granth Sahib. Traditionally these functionaries have not been highly educated people or conversant with economic matters or political issues. Their roles and responsibilities, like those of the sant preachers, have been not only specific but also limited. In today's situation they are called upon to pronounce on the very matters which lie beyond their ken. They thus become tools in the hands of others, who, needless to say, are far removed from the religious life as usually understood.

The others are the extremists and terrorists who have stalked the plains of Punjab for well over half a decade and killed thousands, not only Hindus but also Sikhs, sparing neither women nor children. They have links with established organizations such as the All India Sikh Students Federation, and they are organized on their own under such names as the Khalistan Commando Force, fighting for the establishment of an independent Sikh state, or the Bhindranwale Tigers, swearing allegiance to the dead leader's goals. While these groups project themselves as the vengeance squads who seek to eliminate the foes of the faith and as the vanguard that spearheads the march into Khalistan, numerous Sikhs deny them the right even to call themselves the followers of the gurus, because of their terrorist activities. And they are engaged in an ongoing bloody battle with the security forces.

In short, what we encounter among the Sikhs today is a multiplicity of fundamentalist groups. They bear a family resemblance to one another inasmuch as they claim to speak in the name of the gurus and seek to pull all true Sikhs together and set them apart from non-Sikhs. Fundamentalism is like the double-edged dagger, a sacred symbol of the Sikh religious tradition. While it claims to remove with one edge the dross that has come to sully Sikhism, it simultaneously succeeds in cutting with the other edge the bonds of brotherhood among the Sikhs themselves and between them and the Hindus. Whether the first guru, Nanak, wanted to build a bridge between Hinduism and Islam—a mediating or a synthesizing religious faith—or promulgate a new religion is a matter of scholarly argument. Even those who say that Nanak's aim was the building of a third way acknowledge that neither he nor the successor gurus allowed the use of violence except in self-protection and as a last resort. Those who maintain that the historical significance of Sikhism lay in its potential as a peacemaker regret that the exclusivism of militant Sikh fundamentalism divides rather than binds, wounds rather than heals.

Characteristics of Sikh Fundamentalism

To conclude, I will first try to highlight and elaborate some of the major points that have emerged from the foregoing discussion in the hope that they will be of comparative interest. I will then close with a few observations about the future of Sikh fundamentalism.

Fundamentalism in the broad sense of insistence on certain basic beliefs and practices is perhaps an essential component of all religious traditions. What is specific to a particular fundamentalist movement is, I think, more significant for understanding it than what it shares with others. Fundamentalism as a forceful affirmation of religious faith and cultural identity, combined with a militant pursuit of secular interests, is associated in the Sikh cultural tradition with the tenth guru. Sikh fundamentalism is not therefore a recent phenomenon. However, its expressions, shaped by changing historical circumstances, have been varied. The situation in the wake of the decline of Ranjit Singh's kingdom and the rise of Hindu fundamentalism in the late nineteenth century was quite different from that faced by Guru Gobind Singh two hundred years earlier. The current manifestations of Sikh fundamentalism have several characteristics in common with the earlier ones, but they also have distinctive features. In what follows I concentrate on Sikh fundamentalism today.

Sikh fundamentalism is a reactive phenomenon, a defense mechanism. Its apparent confidence hides many doubts, and its aggressiveness is a cover for fear and anxiety, fear of the threatening "Other," seen as people and processes: nonconformists, secularists, and Hindus; heresy, modernization, cultural disintegration, and political domination. Of course not all Sikhs experience these fears and anxieties about cultural identity, but the fundamentalists (in their own eyes, true Sikhs) would want everybody to. I would stress that any attempt to explain religious fundamentalism in terms of states of mind alone amounts to reductionism and is therefore just as fallacious as economic determinism. Complex phenomena, needless to say, have multiple causes.

While mono-causal explanations of fundamentalism must be rejected, the claim of fundamentalists to be in possession of the Truth should be noted if we are to understand what motivates them and how they mobilize and hold their following. This does not mean that we recognize their claim as valid. In relation to their followers, however, fundamentalists do not allow the legitimacy of dissent and multiple opinions or individual judgments: a single judgment representing the collective will must prevail. This is considered axiomatic. It follows that Sikhs must have political power in order to enforce conformity. In the words of Khushwant Singh, "in the Sikh state the Sikhs would not only be free of Hindus and Hindu influences, but the Sikh youth would also be persuaded (if necessary, compelled) to continue observing the forms and symbols of the faith."[73] This implies that if Sikhs are not rulers, they must be rebels; but when they establish the "just order" and become rulers, they cannot be rebels against themselves. In short, fundamentalism is totalitarian.

As a response to circumstances that are believed to be adverse, Sikh fundamentalism is marked not so much by deep theological concerns or intellectual vigor as by religious fervor and political passion. Modern scholars generally serve it; they do not lead or guide it. Thus, scholastic efforts have been made to argue that although the Sikh scripture contains many words and phrases (such as *śabad, śunya, śiva, śakti*) which are also found in the Hindu and Buddhist religious traditions, they do not mean in Sikhism what they mean in the other religions.[74] Similarly, the roots of Sikhism in the sant tradition of socioreligious reform[75] are played down, but this is not easy, for the Granth Sahib itself bears witness to them. The first guru certainly made his choices regarding theological, cosmological, social, and other matters, but he made them out of the traditions with which he was most familiar, Hinduism and Islam, in that order. According to Grewal,[76] "it was a rich and lively religious atmosphere. And it was this atmosphere that Guru Nanak breathed." But such scholarly disputations are of only limited interest to the fundamentalists or their lay followers, who emphasize action. It may be noted here that, with some exceptions, scriptural exegesis has not been a major concern of Sikh intellectuals. Inside the gurdwārās scripture is read, chanted, and venerated (very much as idols are in a Hindu temple); there are no discourses on it.

Understandably, therefore, it is not so much to the canon or scripture that Sikh fundamentalists turn for authority as to the tradition about what particular gurus or martyrs did. Sikh fundamentalism is orthoprax rather than orthodox. The emphasis is upon action and the expected fruits of action, and these fruits are this-worldly—economic and political. Piety or conformity to codes of behavior is seen as valuable in instrumental terms. For the orthodox, who do not think of belief and practice in dualistic terms, piety is its own reward. If action is motivated by the desired fruits, it is propelled by its situational logic. In today's situation, it is the tradition of violent action, characterized as righteous, and retribution for any attack on Sikh honor, that are emphasized. Joyce Pettigrew[77] has shown how deeply rooted these values are, though not in scripture but in the cultural tradition of the Jats, who account for the great majority of the Sikh community. The assassination of Mrs. Indira Gandhi, prime minister at the time of Operation Blue Star, by her own Sikh bodyguards, and of General Vaidya, then the chief of the Indian army, are notable acts of revenge which the fundamentalists consider honorable, for they consider these two persons responsible for the attack on the Golden Temple complex. The same is true of the assassination of the Sikh (Akali) leader Sant Harchand Singh Longowal, within weeks of his having entered into an accord with prime minister Rajiv Gandhi in July 1985, which the pro-Bhindranwale Sikhs considered a betrayal of the cause of the community. Betrayal by anybody is bad, but by a leader it is particularly grievous.

Sikh fundamentalism depends upon charismatic leaders who are seen in the image of the sixth and tenth gurus as saint-soldiers *(sant-sipāhī)*. Such a leader must be willing not only to kill but also to die for the cause. Thus Bhindranwale said, using the words of Guru Gobind: "when the struggle reaches the decisive phase may I die fighting in its midst."[78] And he did, achieving for himself the halo of a martyr among his followers. There has been official confirmation that Bhindranwale's men inside the Akal Takht, many of whom were apparently hardly virtuous persons, fought with uncommon bravery to the last man. They also inflicted heavy casualties on the troops. How important the role of a charismatic leader is has been borne out by the relative ease with which the Punjab armed police were able to flush out in May 1988 (Operation Black Thunder) the terrorists who had reoccupied the Golden Temple complex in 1986. But as Bhindranwale's case so well illustrates, charisma needs material and institutional resources for its magic to work. He had the support of the institutional apparatus of the All India Sikh Students Federation; besides, well-to-do Sikhs in India and abroad (UK, USA, Canada) provided him and his supporters with money to buy arms and for other activities.

The strategy of the fundamentalist leader, as is well borne out by Bhindranwale's speeches and actions, is characterized by a selective appropriation of the tradition in a manner which is simultaneously revivalist and futurist. The notion of a Sikh state perhaps took shape in the tenth guru's time, or soon after, but the hope has not been realized. Guru Gobind's avenger, Banda Bahadur, conquered territory but hardly established a state.[79] Maharaja Ranjit Singh's kingdom (1799–1839) was multireligious. Fundamentalism today nourishes the hope of a Sikh state and points to destiny: the Khalsa will rule! Fundamentalism is explicitly soteriological.

The revivalist-futurist vision is not, however, unproblematic. On the one hand, the Sikh religious tradition is presented as a perennial philosophy; on the other, sensitivity to contextual variation is stressed. While the Sikh way of life is said to be unaffected by space-time *(deś-kāl)* differences, Sikhs try to establish a territorial state of the true (baptized or Khalsa) Sikhs (Khalistan). As Pettigrew has pointed out, "Temporal power was vested in the Panth, but precisely what this meant was difficult to ascertain, since Panth was the religious community of all Sikhs and not the localized community."[80] Similarly, Gopal Singh asks: "if the Sikh must combine [religion and politics], what about others who must live in their realm?"[81] In other words, the fundamentalist strategy for political autonomy depends more upon emotive appeal than rational argument or—a much harder task—willingness and capacity to confront contradictions within the Sikh tradition.

Contradictions also mark the present expressions of Sikh fundamentalism. This is most obvious in the attitudes to science and technology. In principle, the modern secular and rational weltanschauung is opposed to any religious worldview, and since technology is the applied aspect of science, this too should be suspect. But the Sikh fundamentalists' interest in general issues—the principles of things—is overshadowed by their pragmatic concerns. The Sikh is a doer, typically a farmer, a carpenter, or a soldier—all three well-known and much admired images. While voicing their concern about the erosion of traditional belief and practice by modern life-styles, they have not hesitated to use science and technology in the limited context of their own needs. One of the demands written into the Anandpur Sahib resolution is for the installation of a radio transmitter at the Golden Temple for readings from the Granth Sahib and the singing of hymns to be broadcast. Bhindranwale allowed his speeches to be recorded and sold on cassette tapes. His exhortations to Sikh youth included appeals for motorcycles and firearms. To this day the most effective mode of killing used by terrorists is shooting by the second passenger on a motorbike. A highly respected retired police officer, K. F. Rustamji, has observed: "For a number of years, the dominant image in the minds of people of India will be that of a young Sikh spraying a group of people with an automatic, and killing women and children mercilessly. And along with it may appear the thought that few Sikhs condemn them."[82] The image of the nonviolent Sikh protestor of the 1920s, who had won the admiration of Gandhi, has been replaced by that of the killer. This goes hand-in-hand with the displacement of the brave Sikh (the Singh or "Lion") by the Sikh as victim which was a recurrent theme of Bhindranwale's speeches.

The valorization of violence as righteous killing has resulted in Sikh fundamentalism becoming inextricably involved with terrorism, for the Akali politicians and the temple functionaries have not only not clearly distanced themselves from the terrorists but have often collaborated with them. That most terrorists have little interest in religion or piety seems to have dawned on many Sikhs, particularly after the indisputable desecration of the Golden Temple in May 1988, when a group of terrorists occupied it for several days during which they performed polluting bodily functions of evacuation within it. Details about captured terrorists reveal that many of them are simply criminals or desperate jobless youth, generally of rural origin.

Disillusionment among people in general with regard to the alleged idealism of terrorist fundamentalists, combined with more efficient police operations under the overall direction of a tough chief (who is himself a Sikh), has given rise to the hope that terrorism in Punjab may be contained. The SGPC also has shown signs of wanting to assert its authority: in October 1988 it announced a ban on the carrying of weapons into the Golden Temple and on residence there. When a demand to this effect was made in May 1988 following Operation Black Thunder, Sikh fundamentalists, including former ministers of the state, reacted negatively, calling it interference in religious matters and against the basic teachings of Sikhism.

Economic compulsions also reinforce the need for peace and stability. It is noteworthy that despite the unsettled law and order situation, agricultural production in Punjab continues to soar. Sikh farmers must sell their surplus grain to the government and in the market. Because of the size of the surplus, local consumption is not the answer. In fact, during 1987–88, a year of drought, about 55 percent of the paddy produced, and 43 percent of the wheat, were procured by the government. In a normal year the percentages would be much higher. There are also market sales. While one may therefore be optimistic about a decline in terrorist activities, there is little to indicate a downturn in Sikh fundamentalism. The politicians and the priests keep it alive. An acute and sober Sikh intellectual, Amrik Singh, observes rather helplessly: "fundamentalism is a fact of life. . . . The only safe statement that one can therefore make in regard to the next decade or two is that fundamentalism (whatever the term may include or exclude) will continue to be a force and shape the thinking of a substantial number of people, particularly in the younger age group."[83]

Writing over twenty years ago, Khushwant Singh observed pithily, "there is no such thing as a clean-shaven Sikh."[84] The mid-sixties were marked by the last and successful phase in the agitation for a Punjabi-speaking state. Fundamentalism was present then too, but it was not the kind of overwhelming sociopolitical phenomenon it has become since then. It follows that the above observation by Khushwant Singh, which many Sikhs themselves would have then characterized as a specimen of the author's engaging style, would today find almost universal support among Sikhs. In the same author's words, "the sense of belonging to the Sikh community requires both the belief in the teachings of the Adi Granth [Granth Sahib] and the observance of the Khalsa tradition initiated by Guru Gobind Singh."[85]

Sikh fundamentalism today, as in the late nineteenth century, feeds and is fed by Hindu militancy. While in the earlier period the militancy was linked to the religious revivalism advocated by the Arya Samaj, today it is associated with the Bharatiya Janata Party and some militant Hindu groups and is predominantly political. The agitation for a Punjabi-speaking state during the fifties and sixties divided the two communities badly. While the Hindus complained that language was being used as a cover for religion, the Sikhs complained that the Hindus had become so hostile that they did not hesitate even to disown their mother tongue, Punjabi.[86] There is considerable truth in both charges. The continued killing of Hindus and moderate Sikhs, including widely respected granthīs, by terrorists occasionally generates incidents outside Punjab (as in the far-off town of Bidar in the state of Karnataka, a thousand or more miles away, where half a dozen Sikh students were killed by Hindu militants in September 1989) and keeps communal tension alive. The ability of Muslim fundamentalists to impose their will on the government (there are six Muslims to every Sikh in India, and they have many areas of population concentration as opposed to one in the case of Sikhs) is an additional factor in the present uneasy political situation in India.[87]

Sikh fundamentalism draws sustenance from the deep sense of injury which almost every Sikh feels on account of Operation Blue Star and the massacre of over 2,700 Sikhs in Delhi and elsewhere in the wake of Mrs. Gandhi's assassination.[88] The government's failure to punish any of the killers does not exactly soothe the wounded Sikh psyche. The suspension of a democratically elected government in Punjab in 1987 because of its alleged inability to control terrorism and the complete disarray into which Akali politics has fallen, riven by factionalism, will make a satisfactory political solution difficult in the near future. But elections will have to be held sooner rather than later—this is a constitutional requirement—and the main issues will be the preservation of Sikh religiocultural identity and the protection of their politico-economic interests on the Akali side, and the fight against fundamentalism and terrorism on the other. The fate of Sant Longowal will deter moderate Sikhs from asserting their views on these issues.

Sikh fundamentalism is unlikely to show any signs of abatement in the foreseeable future. And as long as the relationship between religion and the state is defined in diametrically opposite ways in the Indian Constitution and by Sikh (and other) fundamentalists, the scope for reconciliation is limited. The government's efforts to neutralize the appeal of militant fundamentalism will obviously be based on removing real as well as imagined economic grievances and on dividing Sikh political opinion. In the latter task, it might even seek to use some fundamentalists, despite the way things turned out in the case of Bhindranwale. In fact Bhindranwale's nephew is believed to have had government support when he made a bid in 1988 to become the custodian of the Akal Takht, but it did not work. Obviously, these are short-term, and usually short-sighted, stratagems.

What is needed today is far-sighted vision. This calls for true statesmanship. It also calls for some honest and clearheaded rethinking of such fundamental issues as the relations between religion, state, and society. The ideology of secularism borrowed from the West, where it has its roots in Christianity as much as in the Enlightenment, has been found wanting in India in significant ways. The search for a context-sensitive approach is imperative.[89] The task ahead is daunting, but may no longer be evaded.

Notes

I am deeply and happily indebted to Professors R. Scott Appleby, N. Gerald Barrier, M. S. Dhami, Mark Juergensmeyer, and J. P. S. Uberoi for their close and critical reading of the first draft of this paper and for many excellent suggestions. I would also like to thank all those colleagues who heard me present this paper at our conference in Chicago in November 1988 and gave me encouragement.

1. The Preamble to the Constitution refers to India as "a sovereign socialist secular democratic republic." It is noteworthy that the words "socialist" and "secular" were added to it only in 1976 by the forty-second amendment.

2. Hindus account for 83 percent of the population of India (1981 census). Muslims come next with 11.35 percent, followed by Christians with 2.43 percent, Sikhs with 1.96 percent, Buddhists with 0.71 percent, and Jains with 0.48 percent.

3. Tradition-oriented or orthodox Muslims also adhere to the same position, though with one qualification. While they reject the separation of religion and the state in principle, they accept it as an arrangement for Muslims living in a non-Islamic state.

4. It should be stressed that the composition of these units and of the chain of command happened to be as described here: no special efforts were made for them to be so composed.

5. Among India's religious minorities, Muslims and Sikhs have been politically the most active. Muslim separatism developed in

less than a hundred years into a very powerful force in the Indian subcontinent and was mainly responsible for the partition in 1947 and the creation of Pakistan. However, there are today more Muslims in India (75,512,439, or 11.35 percent of the total population of India, according to the 1981 official census) than in any other country except Indonesia and Bangladesh.

By comparison, there may not seem to be many Sikhs—they number 13,078,146 (1.96 percent)—but they have much greater social visibility and political weight than numbers alone would lead one to expect. Actually there are more Christians in India than Sikhs, but neither they nor the smaller religious minorities—Buddhists, Jains, Zoroastrians (0.42 percent)—stand out as prominently as the Sikhs. For one thing, Sikhs, with their characteristic unshaven beards, unshorn hair, and carefully tied turbans, are readily distinguishable from other Indians. Also, in the minds of most Indians, Sikhs are associated with excellence in farming, trading, soldiering, and mechanical skills. They are a geographically mobile people and although concentrated in Punjab (about 80 percent), are found in all parts of the country, mostly in urban areas. Many Sikhs have traveled abroad in search of job opportunities and there are sizable Sikh communities in such far-flung countries as Australia, Afghanistan, Britain, Canada, and the United States. It is estimated that in North America alone there are about 150,000 to 250,000 Sikhs. In all, the number of Sikhs living outside India is estimated to be well over a million, perhaps 1.5 million.

Finally, a few words about the social composition of the Sikh community. One of the first principles on which the Sikh community was founded was the rejection of caste, but Sikhs retain a memory of caste origins, and their daily social conduct is influenced in significant ways by caste traditions and stereotypes. Thus, Sikhs of the Jat caste, who account for 50 to 60 percent of all Sikhs, do not look kindly upon menial work and favor agriculture, their traditional occupation. The first Sikhs came from clean upper castes, as indeed did the ten gurus, who were all Khattris. Conversions from among Hindu "scheduled" (low) castes occurred around the beginning of the twentieth century in large numbers. Today these converts are estimated to account for 12 percent of the Sikh population. The intermediate artisan castes are also present; Zail Singh, president of India at the time of Operation Blue Star, comes from the Ramgharia (carpenter) caste. Intercaste marriage is still uncommon and occupational specialization common. Politically Sikhs are a divided people and have supported not only the Akali (exclusively Sikh) parties but also notably the Congress and the Communist parties. Cf. Rajiv Kapur, *Sikh Separatism: The Politics of Faith* (London: Allen and Unwin Kapur, 1986); Joseph T. O'Connell, et al., eds., *Sikh History and Religion in the Twentieth Century* (Toronto: University of Toronto Press, 1988).

6. Gopal Singh, *A History of the Sikh People* (New Delhi: World Book Centre, 1988), p. 177. According to Sikh tradition, unsupported by historical evidence, the foundation stone of the Golden Temple was laid by a Muslim Sufi, Mian Mir. It bears testimony to the traditional Sikh approach to religious differences that such a story should be believed.

7. Khushwant Singh, *A History of the Sikhs,* vol. 1 (Princeton: Princeton University Press, 1963), p. 63.

8. Murray J. Leaf, "The Punjab Crisis," *Asian Survey* 25, no. 5 (1985): 494. Cf. Patwant Singh, "The Sikhs and the Challenge of the Eighties," in O'Connell, *Sikh History,* p. 415: "Jarnail Singh Bhindranwale did what no Sikh had done in the past: he placed the supreme emblem of Sikhism in the direct line of fire."

9. Cf. W. H. McLeod, "The Meaning of Sant in Sikh Usage," in Karine Schomer and W. H. McLeod, eds., *The Sants: Studies in a Devotional Tradition of India*(Delhi: Motilal Banarasidass, 1987), pp. 256–61; and Kapur, *Sikh Separatism.*

10. Jarnail Singh Bhindranwale derived his last name from the place-name Bhindranwala; it means 'belonging to Bhindranwala.'

11. Cf. Mark Tully and Satish Jacob, *Am-*

ritsar: Mrs. Gandhi's Last Battle (New Delhi: Rupa, 1985).

12. Cf. Joyce Pettigrew "In Search of a New Kingdom of Lahore," *Pacific Affairs* 60, no. 1 (1987): 5.

13. W. H. McLeod, *The Evolution of the Sikh Community* (Oxford: Clarendon Press, 1976), p. 60.

14. Gopal Singh, *The Religion of the Sikhs* (New Delhi: Allied, 1987), p. 27.

15. Cf., for example, Khushwant Singh, *The Sikhs* (London: Allen and Unwin, 1953); Khushwant Singh, *History of the Sikhs,* vol. 1; Gopal Singh, *Religion of the Sikhs;* J. P. S. Uberoi, "The Five Symbols of Sikhism," in Fauja Singh, et al., *Sikhism* (Patiala: Punjabi University).

16. Max Arthur Macauliffe, *The Sikh Religion,* vol. 5 (Oxford: Clarendon Press, 1909), p. 99.

17. Khushwant Singh, *Sikhs.*

18. Gopal Singh, *Religion of the Sikhs,* p. 191.

19. Cf. Joyce Pettigrew, "In Search of a New Kingdom of Lahore," p. 15.

20. Marxism as a politico-economic ideology has attracted many Punjabis, including, rather paradoxically, Sikh intellectuals and politicians, who have not been without a following among the Sikh masses.

21. Cf. Pettigrew, "In Search of a New Kingdom of Lahore," p. 15.

22. Ibid.

23. Cf. Mark Juergensmeyer, "The Logic of Religious Violence: The Case of the Punjab," *Contributions to Indian Sociology* 22 (1) (1988): 70.

24. Cf. Tully and Jacob, *Amritsar,* p. 114. Cf. another version of the same quotation by Juergensmeyer, "Logic," p. 86: "It is a sin for a Sikh to keep weapons, to hurt an innocent person, to rob anyone's home, to dishonor anyone or to oppress anyone. But there is no greater sin for a Sikh than keeping weapons and not using them to protect his faith."

25. Cf. Joyce Pettigrew, "Take Not Arms Against the Sovereign," *South Asia Research* 4, no. 2 (1984):113. Jehangir (r. 1605–27) and his grandson Aurangzeb (r. 1658–1707) are counted among the great Mogul emperors of India.

26. Cf. Kapur, *Sikh Separatism,* p. 227.

27. Quoted in Pettigrew, "In Search of a New Kingdom of Lahore," p. 4.

28. John Clark Archer, *The Sikhs in Relation to Hindus, Muslims, Christians, and Ahmadiyas* (Princeton: Princeton University Press, 1946), p. 170.

29. See Khushwant Singh, *History of the Sikhs,* vol. 1, p. 78.

30. Cf. Kapur, *Sikh Separatism,* p. 8.

31. Macauliffe, *Sikh Religion,* vol. 1, p. lvii.

32. Personal communication from N. Gerald Barrier, November 1988.

33. Cf. Kapur, *Sikh Separatism,* pp. 11, 24.

34. For a corroborative statement by an early observer, D. Petrie, see Surendra Chopra, "Ethnicity, Revivalism and Politics in Punjab," in Paul Wallace and Surendra Chopra, eds., *Political Dynamics and Crisis in Punjab* (Amritsar: Guru Nanak Dev University, 1988), p. 474.

35. Cf. Kapur, *Sikh Separatism,* p. 19.

36. Cf. Macauliffe, *Sikh Religion,* and Gerald N. Barrier, "The Sikhs and Punjab Politics 1882–1922," in Wallace and Chopra, *Political Dynamism,* pp. 507–8.

37. Cf. Khushwant Singh, *History of the Sikhs,* vol. 2, (Princeton: Princeton University Press, 1966), pp. 123–35; Gopal Singh, *History of the Sikh People,* pp. 602–25.

38. Khushwant Singh, *History of the Sikhs,* vol. 2, p. 137.

39. Cf. N. Gerald Barrier, *The Sikhs and their Literature* (Delhi: Manohar, 1970), pp. xxiv–xxv.

40. Cf. Gopal Singh, *History of the Sikh People,* p. 625.

41. N. Gerald Barrier, "Sikh Politics in British Punjab prior to the Gurdwara Reform Movement," in O'Connell, *Sikh History,* p. 171; also cf. Barrier, " Sikhs and Punjab Politics."

42. Barrier, "Sikhs and Punjab Politics."

43. Khushwant Singh, *History of the Sikhs,* vol. 2, p. 122.

44. N. Gerald Barrier, "The Singh Sabhas and the Evolution of Modern Sikhism, 1875–1925" (Typescript, n.d.), p. 2.

45. Cf. Kenneth W. Jones, *Arya Dharm: Hindu Consciousness in Nineteenth Century Punjab* (New Delhi : Manohar, 1976); and Daniel Gold's paper (chap. 9) in this volume.

46. Kenneth W. Jones, "Communalism in the Punjab," *The Journal of Asian Studies* 28, no. 1 (1968): 50.

47. Cf. Khushwant Singh, *History of the Sikhs,* vol. 2, p. 147.

48. Cf. Harjot S. Oberoi, "From Ritual to Counter-Ritual: Rethinking the Hindu-Sikh Question, 1884–1915," in O'Connell, *Sikh History,* pp. 136–40.

49. Ibid., p. 149.

50. Cf. Gopal Singh, *History of the Sikh People,* pp. 603–4. The short and simple anand marriage ceremony, which may be performed in a gurdwārā or at home and does not require any priests, was devised by a son of the founder of the Nirankari sect.

51. The main sources for this section are: Richard G. Fox, *Lions of the Punjab: Culture in the Making* (Berkeley: University of California Press, 1985); Gopal Singh, *History of the Sikh People;* Khushwant Singh, *History of the Sikhs,* vol. 2; Mohinder Singh, *The Akali Movement* (Delhi: Macmillan, 1978).

52. Cf. Fox, *Lions of the Punjab,* p. 158.

53. Ibid., pp. 79, 228. The expression "the third Sikh war" was used by Sardul Singh Caveeshar, a participant. The two earlier wars, which were wars in the usual sense of the word, were fought by the Sikhs against the Muslims and the British.

54. Cf. Partha N. Mukherji, "Gandhi, Akalis, and Non-Violence," *Man and Development* 6, no. 3 (1984): 58–77.

55. Louis Dumont, *Religion, Politics, and History in India* (Paris: Mouton, 1970), p. 91.

56. Cf. Khushwant Singh, *History of the Sikhs,* vol. 1, p. 90, n 29.

57. Cf. Baldev Raj Nayar, *Minority Politics in the Punjab* (Princeton: Princeton University Press, 1966), p. 89.

58. Ibid., p. 37.

59. Ibid., p. 72.

60. I owe this formulation to J. P. S. Uberoi.

61. Cf. Kapur, *Sikh Separatism,* 218ff.; also see Gopal Singh, *History of the Sikh People,* pp. 789–801, for details.

62. Cf. Joyce Pettigrew, "Take Not Arms," p. 113; and Pettigrew, "In Search of a New Kingdom of Lahore," p. 20.

63. Cf. Sucha Singh Gill, "Contradictions in the Punjab Model of Growth and Search for an Alternative," *Economic and Political Weekly,* 23 (1988): 436–37.

64. Ibid., pp. 436–50. According to many observers, the emergence of fundamentalism and extremist politics as a result of economic hardship is particularly regrettable because it is alien to the Sikh way of thinking. Professor M. S. Dhami, political scientist (formerly of Guru Nanak Dev University, Amritsar) writes (in a personal communication of 11 September 1989): "Peasantry, especially small peasants, who comprise about 90 percent of the Punjab peasantry, have been one of the pillars of secularist forces in Punjab. They were recruiting ground for diverse Marxist/Communist groups. It is true that when peasantry is under the pressure of adverse economic forces, they do produce in critical times 'bandits' about whom Hobsbawm has written. Their ideology may be colored by their religious traditions, as in rural Punjab, under specific circumstances. Some of the terrorist groups are versions of the old bandit groups. But to resort to extremism and fundamentalism does not amount to ideological commitment. It is more a symptom of social and political decay . . . Today an additional factor is state terrorism."

65. Macauliffe, *Sikh Religion,* vol. 4, p. 2.

66. Ibid., p. 4.

67. Gopal Singh, *History of the Sikh People,* p. 830.

68. Macauliffe, *Sikh Religion,* vol. 5, p. 83.

69. Ibid., p. 93.

70. The main sources for this account of the events from 1984 onwards are the newspaper *Times of India* and the newsmagazine *India Today*. These are not cited in the text to avoid unnecessary accumulation of references. Short accounts may be seen in Mohinder Singh "Akali Struggle: Past and Present," in O'Connell, *Sikh History;* Patwant Singh, "Sikhs and the Challenge of the Eighties," Wallace and Chopra, *Political Dynamics*.

71. The general parliamentary elections of November 1989 saw the emergence of one more Akali party. It took shape around the personality of Simranjit Singh Mann, a former police officer who had been under detention since 1984 in connection with Indira Gandhi's assassination. Although still in prison at the time, not only was he himself elected (with a massive majority), all the nominees of Akali Dal (Mann), who included the father and widow of Indira Gandhi's assassin, were also elected. The Akali parties led by Surjit Singh Barnala and Prakash Singh Badal, both former chief ministers, drew a blank.

72. The history of the gurdwārās and the takhts and the manner in which they have been made a part of Sikh consciousness is an important subject. Of the five takhts, three, that is, those at Anandpur, Patna, and Nanded, are deeply interwoven with the biography of the tenth guru. Guru Gobind himself never visited the Akal Takht or Harmandir Sahib: in fact none of the last four gurus did so. The events of the last one hundred years have seen changes in the importance of the various temples. The process of redefinition of sacred places is not confined to the shrines but is comprehensive and includes the land of Punjab itself. Thus Oberoi perceptively observes: "Surprisingly, despite [many] historical linkages with the Punjab, for most of the Sikhs' history, territory has not played a key role in their self-definition. It was only in the 1940s . . . when the cold truth dawned that the Punjab may after all be divided, that the Sikhs with a tragic desperation began to visualize the Punjab as their homeland. . . . It is the intersection of history and geography, discourse and space, territoriality and metacommentaries, that has transformed the Punjab into Khalistan." Cf. Harjot S. Oberoi, "From Punjab to 'Khalistan': Territoriality and Metacommentary," *Pacific Affairs* 60, no. 1 (1987): 27–28.

73. Khushwant Singh, *Sikhs,* pp. 84ff.

74. Cf. Trilochan Singh, "Theological Concepts of Sikhism," in Fauja Singh et al., eds., *Sikhism* (Patiala: Punjabi University, 1969).

75. Cf. Schomer and McLeod, *Sants*.

76. J. S. Grewal, *Guru Nanak in History* (Chandigarh: Punjab University, 1979), p. 140.

77. Joyce Pettigrew, *Robber Noblemen: A Study of the Political System of the Sikh Jats* (London: Routledge and Kegan Paul, 1987).

78. Cf. Juergensmeyer, "Logic," p. 65.

79. Cf. Khushwant Singh, *History of the Sikhs,* vol. 2, pp. 101ff.

80. Pettigrew, "In Search of a New Kingdom of Lahore," pp. 6ff.

81. Gopal Singh, *History of the Sikh People,* p. 833.

82. K. F. Rustamji, "Why Terrorism Has Seized Punjab,"*The Telegraph* (Calcutta), 5 June 1988, p. 8. K. F. Pustamji is himself a member of the minuscule Parsi community.

83. Amrik Singh, "Sikhs at the Turn of the New Century," in O'Connell, *Sikh History,* p. 440. The appeal of fundamentalism among the young and the emigre is a subject of much interest. I have talked with many such persons and seen several statements by them. An obviously enthusiastic Sikh youth, born and brought up in England, objected to any reference to Guru Nanak's Hindu origin and argued that any Sikh who identifies himself by caste is a hypocrite and anti-Sikh. Such a fundamentalist attitude is of course empirically unsound and sociologically naive. If all Sikhs who acknowledge caste origins were to be excommunicated, there would be hardly any followers of the faith left to live by it.

84. Khushwant Singh, *History of the Sikhs,* vol. 2, p. 303.

85. Ibid.

86. Kapur, *Sikh Separatism,* pp. 211–19.

87. Before any Islamic country had done so, the government of India banned on 5 October 1988 Salman Rushdie's novel *The Satanic Verses* on the request of some Muslim politicians who, though they had not themselves read the book, but had only read reviews of it, warned that disturbances would break out if it was made freely available.

88. Patwant Singh, "Sikhs and the Challenge of the Eighties."

89. Cf. T. N. Madan, "The Historical Significance of Secularism in India," in S. C. Dube and V. N. Basilov, eds., *Secularization in Multi-Religious Societies* (New Delhi: Concept, 1983); T. N. Madan, "Secularization and the Sikh Religious Tradition," *Social Compass* 33 (1986): 257–73; T. N. Madan, "Secularism in Its Place," *The Journal of Asian Studies* 46, no. 4 (1987): 747–60; T. N. Madan, "Religion in India," *Daedalus* 118, no. 4 (Fall 1989): 115–46.

Select Bibliography

Archer, John Clark. *The Sikhs in Relation to Hindus, Muslims, Christians, and Ahmadiyas.* Princeton: Princeton University Press, 1946.

Barrier, N. Gerald. *The Sikhs and Their Literature.* Delhi: Manohar, 1970.

Coward, Harold, ed. *Modern Indian Responses to Religious Pluralism.* Albany: State University of New York Press, 1987.

Dietrich, Angela. "The Khalsa Resurrected: Sikh Fundamentalism in the Punjab." In Lionel Caplan, ed., *Studies in Religious Fundamentalism.* Albany: State University of New York Press, 1987.

Dumont, Louis. *Religion, Politics, and History in India.* Paris: Mouton, 1970.

Jones, Kenneth W. *Arya Dharm: Hindu Consciousness in Nineteenth Century Punjab.* New Delhi: Manohar, 1976.

Juergensmeyer, Mark, and N. Gerald Barrier, eds. *Sikh Studies: Comparative Perspectives on a Changing Tradition.* Berkeley: Graduate Theological Union Press, 1979.

Kapur, Rajiv. *Sikh Separatism: The Politics of Faith.* London: Allen and Unwin Kapur, 1986.

Macauliffe, Max Arthur. *The Sikh Religion.* 6 vols. Oxford: Clarendon Press, 1909.

Madan, T. N. "Secularization and the Sikh Religious Tradition." *Social Compass* 33, (1986).

McLeod, W. H. *The Evolution of the Sikh Community.* Oxford: Clarendon Press, 1976.

Nayar, Baldev Raj. *Minority Politics in the Punjab.* Princeton: Princeton University Press, 1966.

O'Connell, Joseph T., et al., eds. *Sikh History and Religion in the Twentieth Century.* Toronto: University of Toronto, 1988.

Pettigrew, Joyce. *Robber Noblemen: A Study of the Political System of the Sikh Jats.* London: Routledge and Kegan Paul, 1987.

Schomer, Karine, and W. H. McLeod, eds. *The Sants: Studies in a Devotional Tradition of India.* Delhi: Motilal Banarasidass, 1987.

Singh, Fauja, et al. *Sikhism.* Patalia: Punjabi University, 1969.

Singh, Gopal. *The Religion of the Sikhs.* New Delhi: Allied, 1987.

———. *A History of the Sikh People.* New Delhi: World Book Centre, 1988.

Singh, Khushwant. *The Sikhs.* London: Allen and Unwin, 1953.

———. *A History of the Sikhs.* 2 vols. Princeton: Princeton University Press, 1963–66.

Singh, Mohinder. *The Akali Movement.* Delhi: Macmillan, 1978.

Sinha, N. K. *The Rise of Sikh Power.* Calcutta: A Mukherjee, 1960.

Tully, Mark, and Satish Jacob. *Amritsar: Mrs. Gandhi's Last Battle.* New Delhi: Rupa, 1985.

Wallace, Paul, and Surendra Chopra, eds. *Political Dynamics and Crisis in Punjab.* Amritsar: Guru Nanak Dev University, 1988.

CHAPTER
11

Fundamentalistic Movements in Theravada Buddhism

Donald K. Swearer

Today we are more likely to think of religious fundamentalism in relationship to Islam and Christianity than to Buddhism. After all, these "religions of the Book" share three major elements associated with religious fundamentalism: a commitment to the authority of scripture, a concern for orthodox belief, and a history of involvement with the state. These elements seem to contrast sharply with Buddhism. Indeed, Prince Siddhattha (the Buddha [Sanskrit Siddhartha]) renounced life as a householder to found a monastic community and taught a Noble Eightfold Path which emphasized right practice rather than right belief. Furthermore, the contemporary Buddhist monk in his forest hermitage seems far removed, behaviorally as well as geographically, from the religious-political lobbyist of the Moral Majority of the United States or the Shi'ite Muslim revolutionary of Iran.

Despite an element of truth in such a characterization, Buddhism has been concerned throughout its history with authoritative scripture and orthodox belief and has contributed as much as any religious tradition to the definition of particular cultural, social, and political identities. It is perhaps not surprising, furthermore, that the contemporary forces which have influenced the rise of religious fundamentalisms in the West and the Middle East have exerted a similar impact on the cultures of South, Southeast and East Asia. Accordingly, it seems appropriate to focus the interpretative lens of religious fundamentalism on such matters as the relationship between religion and nationalism in Japan, the Vietnamese Buddhist protest against the Diem regime in the 1960s, or the late-nineteenth- and early-twentieth-century Buddhist revival in Burma. This essay, however, proposes to examine specific aspects of Theravada Buddhism in Sri Lanka and Thailand from the perspective of religious fundamentalism.

The Theravada Tradition

Theravada Buddhism is one of the three great streams or subtraditions of Buddhism which developed in India after the death of Buddha (544 B.C.E.) through the first centuries C.E. The other two are known as Mahayana (the Great Vehicle) and Vajrayana (the Diamond Vehicle). Theravada has its earliest roots in the sectarian traditions of the Hinayana or so-called Small Vehicle of Buddhism, and claims historical precedence over Mahayana and Vajrayana. Doctrinally the Theravadins have emphasized the historicity of the Buddha as the Great Teacher of the path to enlightenment. The core of this path is the overcoming of suffering and the habituating bondage of our worldly actions through endless lives by means of an individual practice of mediation leading to a state of moral purity, mental equanimity, and profound insight into the ever-changing and impermanent nature of reality.

The later Mahayana and Vajrayana schools of Buddhism developed more highly complex philosophical understandings of the nature of the Buddha and the meaning of salvation. Furthermore, although a variety of folk and popular beliefs and practices were absorbed into the Hinayana-based traditions of which Theravada is an expression, the Mahayana and Vajrayana sects became more broadly syncretic and eclectic. This eclecticism stemmed in part from currents of devotional pietism which transformed the Buddha from a teacher of a self-striving path to enlightenment into a salvation-granting deity and broadened the concept of the morally perfect being *(bodhisattva)* into saviors the likes of Kuan Yin in Chinese Buddhism and the ever-popular Jizo in Japan. The eclecticism of Mahayana and Vajrayana, however, also developed out of the encounter between these Indian forms of Buddhism and the religious and cultural traditions they absorbed as they spread out of northern India into Tibet, Nepal, Mongolia, China, Korea, and Japan from the second through the seventh centuries C.E. Thus, for example, Zen Buddhism in Japan owes an immense debt to Chinese Taoism and Confucianism as well as to the Japanese folk tradition we call Shinto.[1]

The traditions of Theravada thought and practice were gradually compiled from the sixth to the third centuries B.C.E. During the reign of the Indian monarch, Asoka (c. 268–233 B.C.E.), traditional Buddhism flourished and the canonical texts were systematized and scrutinized by Pali commentators, a practice culminating in the work of the great Buddhaghosa (fifth century C.E.).[2] There followed a "medieval age," during which Theravada was carried to mainland Southeast Asia from Sri Lanka and over the course of five centuries absorbed indigenous and vernacular traditions of thought and practice. Modern Theravada, a Buddhism of revival and reformation, was fashioned from these historical roots but within the context of the Westernization and modernization incumbent upon an age of European colonialism which reached its apogee during the late nineteenth and early twentieth centuries.[3]

The Theravada tradition thus has a long history in Sri Lanka and Southeast Asia. The major Theravada chronicles trace the mythic roots of the tradition in these areas to miraculous visits by the Buddha himself; however, they link the historical origins of Theravada Buddhism in Sri Lanka and the Southeast Asian mainland to missioners sent by King Asoka of India in the third century B.C.E. Although Theravada Buddhism may have become the "central value system"[4] of Sri Lanka with the formal establishment of kingship during the reign of Tissa (250–210 B.C.E.),[5] a similar claim cannot be made for mainland Southeast Asia until several hundred years later when the Mon and then the Burmese, Khmer, and Thai appropriations of Theravada helped to consolidate their states ideologically.

The core worldview of Southeast Asian Theravada Buddhism shares much in common with other religious traditions which developed in India during the so-called axial age period of world history (sixth century B.C.E.). Basic to many of these axial age worldviews is a distinction between the mundane world of ordinary sense experience and a transmundane reality or state of being perceived or attained through extraordinary means such as mystical knowledge or divine grace.[6] Classical Theravada Buddhism characterizes this distinction specifically as *mundane* (Pali *lokiya*) and *transmundane* (Pali *lokuttara*). The mundane realm of experience is described as one of suffering (Pali *taṇhā*) rooted in blind attachment to sense desires and, consequently, a distorted understanding of the true nature of things. Theravadins argue that wrong desires compel us to seek an everlasting worldly happiness when, in fact, nothing in the realm of ordinary sense experience offers permanent satisfaction and fulfillment.

Buddhaghosa's account of the life of the Buddha reflects this worldview. According to the legend, the Buddha was born as Prince Siddhattha, son of the Gotama family that ruled the Sakyas of northern India (now southern Nepal). Protected by his status from life's inevitable sorrow, he happened upon four unusual and thought-provoking scenes while riding one day through his pleasure gardens: an old man, a person who was sick and diseased, a corpse, and finally a mendicant truth seeker. This "Legend of the Four Sights" poses a fundamental question about the nature of life: Does existence promise more than old age, suffering, and death? In a quest for an answer, the prince renounced his privileged life and spent six years in the forests of northern India studying with the great teachers of his day and engaging in various forms of asceticism. With his discovery of a higher truth, Siddhattha became the "Buddha" (Enlightened One). Nirvana (Pali *nibbāna*) is the term for the Buddha's enlightenment experience: it tells us little about *what* the Buddha discovered but clearly indicates that enlightenment emerges from the conquest of the desires and ambitions which bind us to continuous rounds of worldly existences (Pali *saṁsāra*). The Buddha and those who immediately followed him (Pali *bhikkhu* [monk]) embody for the monastic orders of Sri Lanka, Burma, Thailand, Laos, and Cambodia the ideal of nonattachment to worldly goals.

Theravada Buddhism, however, has always been much more than Nirvana-seeking monks meditating in forests or teaching in monastery schools in villages and towns. From its origin the religion also served to define moral virtue and the social-ethical ideals of generosity, compassion, nonviolence, righteousness, and wisdom narrated in the tales of moral exemplars such as the legendary Prince Vessantara, whose generous spirit led to extremes of self-sacrifice, or the noble Asoka, who governed his Indian kingdom with justice and righteousness. Prohibitions against killing, theft, dishonesty, and other immoral acts that developed from these sacred narratives were eventually codified and set within a typically Indian cosmology, depicting heavenly realms of reward for the virtuous and damnation for the unjust. The moral calculus of reward and punishment was determined by *karma* (Pali *kamma),* an inexorable law of cause and effect. To this worldly life of karmic bondage and infinite rounds of rebirth was juxtaposed the way of the Buddha and the saints (Pali *arahants*)—a way of life in critical tension with the existing social order, an ethos not unlike the one enjoined in the biblical admonition to be "in the world but not of it."

Like the other great historical religions, institutional Theravada Buddhism has also been closely intertwined with the cultural, social, economic, and political orders in which it has developed. Monasteries acquired substantial landholdings bequeathed by royalty and the wealthy; Buddhist institutions reflected and sometimes legitimated social status, class, and caste hierarchies; and the classical Theravada worldview adjusted to various systems of belief and practice, in particular the indigenous animisms of Sri Lanka, Burma, Thailand, Laos, and Cambodia.[7] These adjustments often threated to reduce the Theravada tradition to a magical and protective system for the material well-being of its practitioners and the empowerment of its political rulers.[8] Nonetheless the compromises occurred within the possibilities of the Theravada cosmology described above: a universe of mundane illusion and transmundane reality, a cyclical view of time, the exemplary role of the Buddha and the saints, and the religiously based righteousness of rulers within a morally just universe. The Buddha may have become allied with the protective deities of the Burmese and Thai or with the Brahmanical gods of the classical Indian Vedas, but he still embodied the way of truth and the moral and natural law—the *dharma* (Pali *dhamma*). The glory of the saints may have taken on a magical and peculiarly Thai, Burmese, or Cambodian character, but such assimilation did not attenuate the fundamental belief in the supramundane power of those who adhered rigorously to the Buddha's Eightfold Path of moral virtue, mental discipline, and higher wisdom.

Nonetheless, the Buddhisms of Sri Lanka, Burma, Thailand, Laos, and Cambodia are hardly interchangeable, given ancient cultural variations reflecting various ethnic traditions and differing levels of assimilation of Indian and Chinese influence. Furthermore, while Theravada Buddhism has been characterized by a relatively consistent normative tradition of doctrine and practice from its classical definition to the present, it has obviously evolved and changed significantly over the twenty-five hundred years of its existence. As suggested above, however, the changes from its inception through its medieval period were more in the nature of eclectic adjustments and syntheses between the classical-traditional system and the various cultural contexts in which Theravada developed.

The modern period, however, presented a decisive challenge to the traditional Theravada worldview and its institutional forms. It threatened a revolutionary transformation of all systems of human organization—political, social, economic, intellectual, religious and psychological—and thereby necessitated a reinterpretation of basic beliefs and values by those who sought to maintain the validity of the Theravada tradition.[9] For some the encounter with modernity led to the rejection of Buddhism and/or the adoption of elements of beliefs and values from non-Buddhist systems such as Christianity, Western humanism, or Marxism; for others, it meant a defensive, and sometimes militant, reassertion of traditional beliefs and values; and for still others, it resulted in a radical sectarian or millenarian vision of the establishment of a new Buddhist golden age.[10]

From the late nineteenth century to the present, then, Buddhist apologists such as Anagarika Dharmapala in Sri Lanka, U Chan Htoon in Burma, and Bhikkhu Buddhadasa in Thailand have fashioned new interpretations of the traditional Theravada worldview. These new interpretations share a tendency to demythologize the heaven and hell of karmic reward and punishment and to emphasize the impermanent and interdependent nature of existence, the moral and spiritual value of nonattachment and equanimity, and the centrality of the practice of meditation for the attainment of spiritual fulfillment in the present. In some cases, political leaders such as Kings Mongkut and Chulalongkorn in Thailand (1851–1910) contributed to the modernization of both Buddhist doctrine and Buddhist monastic institutions. Asian academics with American or European Ph. D.'s have interpreted Buddhist doctrine through the lenses of the Western disciplines of philosophy, psychology, and religion, and in doing so have created an intellectually sophisticated Theravada apologetic aimed at their own educated elites and a comparable Western audience. For example, in the 1960s, K. N. Jayatilleke, chair of the department of philosophy at the University of Peradeniya (Sri Lanka) produced noteworthy interpretations of Buddhist epistemology, and his former students have made singular contributions to Buddhist psychology, ethics, and Buddhology.

With the decline in the social role (and hence prestige) of the Buddhist monk as a result of colonial policy in Sri Lanka and Burma and with the increasingly dominant role of government and private organizations in the areas of educational and social services in Thailand, Buddhist reform has often been spearheaded by the laity rather than by monks. For example, in Sri Lanka, a teacher, A. T. Ariyaratna, has revitalized the role of Buddhism in addressing the problems of village development through the creation of the Sarvodaya Sharamadana Movement; in Thailand, Sulak Sivaraksa, publisher, lecturer, and noted lay Buddhist social critic, has cofounded that country's most influential human and civil rights organizations, including the Coordinating Group for Religion in Society (1976).

The early decades of the twentieth century also witnessed a revival of the practice of meditation in Theravada countries, especially among the laity. In this regard U Ba Khin and Mahasi Sayadaw of Burma have developed large followings not only in that country but elsewhere in Asia and in the West, as have Acharn Cha and Acharn Mahabua, who carry on the tradition of the famed Acharn Man Bhuridatta (1871–1949) in northeastern Thailand.[11] Although meditation has been at the heart of the Theravada tradition since its inception, it has, unlike the relatively time- and culture-bound mythologies of traditional Theravada, adapted well to the varied cultural and historical contexts of the twentieth century. Indeed, Buddhist meditation practitioners have joined social reformers at the forefront of the revitalization of the Theravada tradition in Sri Lanka, Burma, and Thailand since the beginning of the twentieth century.[12]

Another striking aspect of Theravada Buddhism in the modern period has been its contribution to nationalist movements. In Sri Lanka and Burma, Buddhism stirred anti-British sentiment by providing "the only universally acceptable symbol to represent an accumulation of grievances, economic, social and psychological, which were as yet, for the most part, inarticulate and incapable of direct political exploitation."[13] From 1918 to 1930, the nationalist cause was led primarily by the General Council of Burmese Associations and by politically active monks such as U Ottama and U Wisara. In Sri Lanka (Ceylon) from 1864 to 1873 nationalist sentiment was fanned by debates between Buddhist monks and Christian missionaries in the southern part of the island. These debates attracted the attention of the American theosophist Colonel Henry Steele Olcott, who journeyed to Ceylon to support the Buddhist cause.[14]

The modern histories of Sri Lanka and Thailand differ in several respects. Sri Lanka was colonized by the Portuguese, later the Dutch, and finally by the British, who claimed control over the island in 1819 with the defeat of the last of the Kandyan kings. Thailand was never formally colonized by a Western power, partly as a result of the astute political leadership of Kings Mongkut (Rama IV) and Chulalongkorn (Rama V), who ruled the country from 1851 to 1910, but also because Thailand served as a convenient buffer between British interests in India and Burma and the French in Indochina.

Despite these differences, however, neither Sri Lanka nor Thailand has escaped the social dislocations and cultural disorientation attendant upon the processes of modernization and Westernization. Responses to these processes have varied within the traditional Buddhist cultures of the two countries and have been discussed and categorized with considerable insight by Robert Bellah, among others.[15] In this essay I propose to examine contemporary Theravada Buddhism from the analytical perspective of "fundamentalism," which shares some commonalties with patterns of "traditionalism," "neotraditionalism," and "nationalism"—interpretative categories that, as Bellah recognized, are not mutually exclusive but are nonetheless helpful in organizing and distinguishing among the plethora of phenomena that characterize the dynamic and changing nature of religion in modern Asia. The category, fundamentalism, functions in a similar manner in that it delineates characteristics of modern Theravada Buddhism in Sri Lanka and Thailand associated with certain religious movements as distinct from others, especially in terms of their appropriation of the historical religious tradition and the implications of this appropriation for the definition of national and communal identity.[16] The fundamentalist dimension of modern Theravada Buddhism shaped, and was shaped by, the various developments described above: the revival of meditation, the activist role of the laity, the development of a new apologetic, and the renewal or reassertion of a religiously grounded communal identity. The fundamentalist impulse in this interaction between the religious tradition and modernity assumed, moreover, a uniquely aggressive, critical, negative, and absolutist character. The fundamentalist response to modernity contrasts decidedly with, in Bellah's term, reformist accommodations to various modern trends and developments, especially with regard to the synthesis between traditional and modern worldviews. We turn first to Buddhist fundamentalism in Sri Lanka, especially as an ingredient in the tensions between the Sinhalese and the Tamils.

The contemporary conflict between segments of the Sinhalese Buddhist and Tamil Hindu populations in Sri Lanka has many causes, among them the ethnic, linguistic, and religious differences between the Tamils and the Sinhalese; the colonial policies of the British in the nineteenth and twentieth centuries that created an educated, elite class who felt alienated from their British rulers; the rise of Sinhalese nationalism in the first half of the twentieth century culminating in the election victory of the Sri Lanka Freedom Party and of S. W. R. D. Bandaranaike as Prime Minister in 1956 on a pro-Sinhalese, pro-Buddhist platform; the economic policies of the Sri Lankan government over the past few decades which have accelerated the breakdown of traditional values and forms of social identification and have widened the gulf between the rich and the poor; and the political radicalization of unemployed or underemployed youth with little vested interest in the maintenance of the status quo. Because fundamentalist religious sentiment has been a prominent factor in the Tamil-Sinhalese conflict in Sri Lanka, this case merits examination in terms of the relationship between nationalism and fundamentalist movements in modern Theravada Buddhism. In the following discussion I shall focus on the Sinhalese Buddhist side of religious extremism in Sri Lanka rather than on Hindu-Tamil fundamentalism and shall describe the major features of fundamentalist Sinhalese Buddhist nationalism within its contemporary context. In examining this case with an eye toward developing a definition of fundamentalism in this context, I shall focus on the reinterpretation of Buddhist doctrine by Anagarika Dharmapala (a reinterpretation labeled "Protestant Buddhism" by such students of Sri Lankan culture and religion as Gananath Obeyesekere and George D. Bond); the marriage of that "modern" Buddhist worldview with the Buddhist nationalism of the 1950s; and the violent, confrontational expression of these trends in the 1980s.

Fundamentalism and Nationalism in Sri Lanka

I was in Colombo on 26 July 1983 when the usual announcement of Air Lanka, the country's only airline, put out its blurb, "Visit Sri Lanka: A Taste of Paradise." This advertisement, with pictures of the brand new hotels with expanses of beach and ocean and tables overflowing with lobster and tropical fruit, routinely appears on national television, except that on this occasion the advertisement was not quite in good taste: the paradise isle was in flames, the houses and business establishments of the minority Tamil community were being systematically burnt and looted by well-organized mobs belonging largely to the . . . proletariat of the cities and small towns of Sri Lanka. The brutality was unbelievable: homes and shops were burnt, cars were doused with gasoline and lit, sometimes, with the occupant inside: some people were hacked to death, others burnt alive. Thirty-five political prisoners were killed by irate regulars in the country's maximum security prison. The next day seventeen more were slaughtered in the same manner. There was a total breakdown of law and order in the nation that had been praised by foreign governments as the model of stability, the apogee of free enterprise. A few days and the illusion was shattered: the house of cards had crumbled.[17]

So everyone scrounges for explanations. A political paroxysm, says one diplomat . . . A socioeconomic crisis, says an economist with an economic bent . . . A plot by the Indian government (the darkest theory) to divide the country . . . The Sinhalese fear that Tamil extremists in the south Indian state of Tamil Nadu have linked up with Sri Lankan Tamils to take over the whole island as a paradise for Tamils everywhere, a new kind of Israel. Tamils fear that extremist Sinhalese have decided to run *them* out to preserve a Sinhalese homeland for themselves and their Buddhist priests.[18]

Ethnic fratricide between the Tamils and Sinhalese in Sri Lanka has been an unavoidable fact of life during the past seven years. Sri Lanka today has a population of fifteen million, approximately 75 percent of whom are Sinhalese and 25 percent Tamil. Most Sinhalese are Buddhists, while Tamils are either Hindu (18 percent) or Muslim (7 percent). The Sinhalese claim a north Indian origin and speak an Indo-European language; Tamils derive from south India and speak a Dravidian language. Sinhalese assert historical precedence over the Tamils on the island, tracing their ancestry to a mythological hero by the name of Vijaya, the grandson of a union between a lion *(singha)* and a north Indian princess.[19] Hence, the term "Sinhalese" translates as the "lion race." Sinhalese "lionization" of their own traditions exclusive of Tamil influence distorts the political and cultural history of Sri Lanka and also ignores the many mutual interactions and influences that have characterized relations between the two ethnic groups through the centuries. Nevertheless, Sinhalese Buddhist identity in Sri Lanka has been fashioned, at least in part, over against the Tamil-Hindu minority.

Prior to the widespread reports from Sri Lanka in 1983 of violent strife between the two dominant ethnic and linguistic groups, the Sinhalese and the Tamils, relatively few Americans were even aware of this tropical island a few miles off the southern tip of India, referred to as the "Pearl of the Orient" because of its configuration and its beauty. Although the last Sinhalese king of the Kandyan dynasty was captured by the British in 1819, foreign intervention in the island began much earlier. The Portuguese occupied the island's coastal areas in the early sixteenth century and were succeeded by the Dutch, who ruled from 1656 to 1796 through military governors representing the Dutch East India Company. In 1948 Ceylon became independent after nearly 450 years of European presence and colonial rule, and established a parliamentary form of government headed by a prime minister. In 1972 the island became the Republic of Sri Lanka, indicating the country's complete independence from Great Britain and a neutralist posture in international politics.

The three centuries of Dutch and British rule and economic exploitation disrupted the island's traditional way of life by challenging the ancient cultural synthesis fostered through the royal and religious institutions, particularly the Buddhist monastery. The extensive remains of the ancient capital cities of Anuradhapura and Polonnaruva stand as monuments to the glorious achievements of the precolonial classical period from the third through the fifteenth centuries C.E. They also bear physical testimony to Peter Berger's claim that classical religious traditions bestow on social institutions an ultimately valid cosmological status and an overpowering stability by depicting them as manifestations of the underlying structure of the universe.[20] Although this sense of cosmic status, of an enduring place in an essentially interrelated and harmonious universe, was guaranteed in the Buddhist past by the righteous (dhammic) reign of the king, it remains a persistent appeal of modern fundamentalistic movements.

Buddhism has also permeated the practical and material aspects of Sinhalese life. Until the colonial period, for example, the Buddhist monastic order *(sangha)* was the recipient of royal land grants and other forms of patronage, making it one of the country's major landlords. Caste hierarchy, furthermore, became a part of Buddhist sectarian divisions in the eighteenth century as a consequence of King Sri Vijaya Rajasimha's efforts to revitalize Buddhism.[21] Buddhist monks were a part of the fabric of Sinhalese society, whether resident in monastic headquarters in Kandy or located in small monasteries throughout the island where they functioned as teachers, ritual practitioners, and moral exemplars. Thus, whether we look to the cosmology of Theravada Buddhism, which grounded Sinhalese social and political realities in the enduring structures of the universe, or to the pervasive presence of monks in the daily lives of townspeople and peasants, or to the economic and social power of monasteries as landowners and maintainers of caste hierarchy, Buddhism was a basic ingredient of Sinhalese social, political, and economic identity from the time of the first Sinhalese kings to the British defeat of the Kandyan Sinhalese in 1819.

The Emergence of Fundamentalistic Buddhist Nationalism

Although the fundamentalistic and militant character of contemporary Sinhalese Buddhist nationalism has been shaped by recent political, economic, and social events, it was forged in the fires of the early-twentieth-century Buddhist nationalist movement identified in particular with the Anagarika Dharmapala, and was tempered by the emergence of a charismatic Buddhist political leader in the 1950s, S. W. R. D. Bandaranaike.

Throughout the nineteenth century, British colonial policy served to undermine the traditional place of Buddhism among the majority Sinhalese population. Among other measures, the British privileged Christian converts in government civil service and administrative positions and established educational and economic systems which had the effect of eroding the prestige of the monk as teacher and weakening the traditional ties between monk and laity. Upwardly mobile Sinhalese Buddhists found it possible and desirable to adopt an ambiguous attitude toward Sinhalese culture and the Buddhist tradition.

By the end of the century, a reaction to this deterioration of Sinhalese Buddhism had set in, led by a group of well-educated, articulate monks and laity supported by sympathizers from the West, in particular, Colonel Olcott. With his assistance, the Buddhist revival movement worked for and obtained a number of concessions from the government, including passage of a bill returning temple land management to the Sangha, approval to open Buddhist schools and appoint Buddhist marriage registrars, and recognition of Vesak (the full-moon day of the lunar month of *Visākhā* on which the Buddha is reputed to have been born, gained enlightenment, and died) as a national holiday. The major propagandist of the revival was Don David Hevavitarana (1864–1933), also known as the Anagarika Dharmapala (The Homeless Guardian of the Dharma).[22] Dharmapala belonged to a group of low-country newly elite families who had become ardent supporters of Buddhism. In 1891 he founded the Mahabodhi Society of Colombo, a major arm of the Buddhist revival not only in Sri Lanka but in other Theravada countries as well. The same year he founded the *Mahabodhi Society Journal* in Calcutta, where he lived for most of the rest of his life. In part through his association with the theosophical movement, Dharmapala gained an international reputation bolstered by charismatic speeches he delivered at the World Parliament of Religions in Chicago in 1893 that won for him an admiring audience in America, England, and Europe.

Through these various activities Dharmapala formulated a simplified, moralistic Buddhist ideology aimed at restoring Sinhalese national pride. The pointedly rationalist exposition of this ideology appealed to a new class of educated Sinhalese civil servants, bureaucrats, businessmen, and professionals, as did Dharmapala's efforts to demythologize Buddhism and to rid it of syncretistic elements such as the worship of the Hindu deities and the magical practices of village monks. His achievement was essentially a reinterpretation and transformation of the Buddhist spiritual ideals and core teachings—epitomized in the Four Noble Truths and the Eightfold Noble Path—into a program designed to mobilize both monk and layperson for the task of personal and social moral reconstruction. Influenced to a significant degree by the moralistic ethos of the Victorian missionary Protestantism which characterized the teaching in Christian schools in Sri Lanka during his lifetime, Dharmapala fashioned what some have termed a "Protestant Buddhism," which condemned alcohol, horse racing, and gambling and promoted in its adherents an ascetic lifestyle, orderliness, cleanliness, and the performance of duty.[23]

Dharmapala's message was also imbued with a nationalistic rhetoric which rooted Sinhalese pride in Ceylon's Buddhist heritage. This marriage of a chauvinistic nationalist ideology with a moralistic, simplified Buddhist worldview divested the historic tradition of its richly textured myths and legends, its deities and magical adepts, and its moral and spiritual inclusiveness. It also formed the basis of fundamentalist Buddhist movements of a later period.[24]

Nonetheless, Dharmapala was a propagandist rather than a philosopher, a crusader inclined to retrieve a handful of fundamental teachings from the Pali canon as the basis of a morally correct, mundane Sinhalese-Buddhist lifestyle. In this delimitation of Theravada sources, the traditional emphasis on the pursuit of a transmundane reality, a transcendental wisdom, was lost. Dharmapala's ideology also tended to ignore the more complex philosophical distinctions elaborated in the centuries-old Theravada scholastic tradition (i.e., the Pali *Abhidhamma*). Furthermore, unlike such contemporary reformers as Bhikkhu Buddhadasa in Thailand, Dharmapala's apologetic proposed no new or profound reformulations of the rich whole of Buddhist doctrine; rather, it concentrated on a few tenets extracted from the whole and reworked in dialogue with his own reading of the times. Similarly, Dharmapala's nationalistic rhetoric appealed only very selectively to the great Sinhalese Buddhist chronicles such as the *Mahāvaṁsa,* and overlooked their variety of substance and subtlety of meaning. From these chronicles he drew particularly upon the accounts of prototypical Buddhist heroes such as King Dutthagamani, 161–137 B.C.E. who wrested control from the Tamil king ruling in Anuradhapura and thus became the model, in Dharmapala's eyes, of the exemplary Buddhist-nationalist leader.

In agreement with other Sinhalese elites, Dharmapala disapproved of folk Buddhist traditions. However, he broke with Olcott and the Buddhist Theosophical Society ostensibly because of their rejection of Buddhist pilgrimage and of the Kandy Asala Perahera celebration honoring the Buddha's tooth relic. While Dharmapala had little patience with Buddhist folk traditions in general, in his eyes the major Buddhist pilgrimages and festivals served to reinforce a sense of Buddhist cultural, social, and national identity, and he therefore favored a selective appropriation of them.

Like other Theravada revivalists in Burma and Thailand, Dharmapala's life and teachings reflected an ambivalent attitude toward the West, especially Great Britain. Although he attacked Western imperialist culture for undermining Sinhalese identity and admonished audiences to lead a strict moral life by first rejecting the corrupting influence of Christianity, his moral rhetoric was shaped in part by that of the zealous Christian missionaries he had encountered in India and in Sri Lanka. Though asserted over against the "immoral" lifestyle of the Western Christian world, his synthesis of nationalistic pride and Buddhist moralism often approximated the tone of a temperance crusader: "My message to the young men of Sri Lanka is . . . Believe not the alien who is giving you arrack whisky, toddy, sausages, who makes you buy his goods at clearance sales . . . Enter into the realm of our King Dutugemunu in spirit and try to identify yourself with the thoughts of the great king who rescued Buddhism and our nationalism from oblivion."[25]

Dharmapala initiated a process of "identity affirmation" in Ceylon, especially among the village intelligentsia: schoolteachers, monks, ayurvedic physicians, various types of government officials, and village leaders who attended his rallies.[26] Believing themselves to be excluded from the privileged colonial forms of education, legal institutions, and government bureaucracy, this coalition of lay and monastic Sinhalese Buddhist supporters drawn from the middle class responded to an ideology crafted with their situation in mind. These villagers harbored high aspirations as a result of their education in Sinhalese schools but had under British rule been cut off from access to the sources of political and economic power to which the Anglo-Sinhalese and the Anglicized elite had at least partial access. This middle-class group was thus "betwixt and between," able to identify neither with the Anglicized Sinhalese ruling population of Colombo nor with the traditional Buddhist ethos of rural Sri Lanka. Accordingly, Dharmapala fashioned a new identity that was first of all oppositional in nature: Buddhist in opposition to non-Buddhist Sinhalese and Sinhalese in opposition to non-Sinhalese.[27] His method was to shame his audience for aping Western ways and then point to the path of redemption through the restoration of Sri Lanka's Buddhist past. In Dharmapala's view, the country's essential identity was Sinhalese-Buddhist; Tamils and Muslims were exploiters and Christians were condemned as low-caste meat eaters.[28] The rhetoric and ideology inspired by Dharmapala would attract a similar configuration of supporters to form the political basis of the S. L. F. P. victory a generation later in 1956.

Dharmapala's message, moreover, reached beyond the shores of Sri Lanka. The battle for identity was not simply personal, social, or even national in scope; it was a cosmic confrontation between good and evil, being and nonbeing: "Young Buddhists of Asia! The time is come for you to prepare yourself to enter the battlefield of truth, love and service. . . . Let the people of these countries know the Four Noble Truths, the Noble Eightfold Path, the seven Principles of Enlightenment and the Twelve Bases of the Law of Causality. Arise, awake, unite and join the Army of Holiness and Peace and defeat the hosts of Evil."[29]

Dharmapala embodied a restoration of traditional Sinhalese-Buddhist identity in his person and career as well as in his teaching. As an "Anagarika" he wore a distinctive white robe which differentiated him from both the ordinary layman and the monk. Although he took a vow of celibacy, his way of life as an Anagarika was less restricted in other ways than that of the Buddhist monk. He assumed an intermediate position not only between monk and layperson but between tradition and modernity as well. He exemplified, on the one hand, the values of self-control and nonattachment at the core of the ideal Buddhist identity by his semi-ascetic, Anagarika lifestyle; furthermore, he promoted this identity by urging certain symbolic practices such as the adoption of Sinhalese or Buddhist personal names and surnames and of native dress. Yet on the other hand Dharmapala chartered a modern Buddhism appropriate for an educated and increasingly urbanized population which took the form of an absolutistic, moralistic, and nationalistic ideology ostensibly Buddhist but in fact an innovative departure from the religious system of classical Sinhalese Buddhism.

Though other movements, such as the Young Men's Buddhist Association (YMBA) of Colombo (1891) and the All Ceylon Congress (1919), led by reformers such as D. B. Jayatilleke, contributed to the Buddhist revival in Sri Lanka, none of them defined Sinhalese Buddhism as Ceylon's true heritage in the exclusivist terms of Dharmapala. None embraced his moral dualism, at odds with the classical Buddhist worldview. The Buddhist fundamentalist worldview, in short, is absolutistic and one-dimensional rather than relativistic and multidimensional.[30] Western Christians were the prime target during the opening decades of the twentieth century, much as Tamil Hindus have been during the closing decades.

Dharmapala died in 1933. Four years later, in 1937, S. W. R. D. Bandaranaike, hailing from a wealthy, elite family that had broken with its Anglicized past and identified with Buddhist revivalism, formed a conservative political group known as the Sinhala Maha Sabha, which represented the interests of rural Sinhalese Buddhists, the same middle-class group who had responded to Dharmapala's apologetic. In 1945,

Dudley S. Senanayake gathered under the banner of the United National Party (UNP) the political leaders who had fought for independence. An upper-class Anglicized elite, educated in English schools, thus assumed political power from the colonial government and ruled Ceylon for the next decade. While many of the UNP leaders, including Senanayake, had been active in Buddhist lay organizations, the party sought to maintain a delicate balance among the various ethnic, linguistic, and religious groups on the island. In 1946 Bandaranaike and the Sinhala Maha Sabha merged with the UNP but broke away again in 1951 to form the opposition Sri Lanka Freedom Party (SLFP).

By 1956, a combination of labor troubles, fluctuations in the world market prices of Sri Lanka's main exports (tea, rubber, and coconuts), pressure from a middle class which had been excluded from political power, and the rhetoric of nationalistic Sinhalese Buddhism swept Bandaranaike and the SLFP into power. This event was a watershed in the development of Sinhalese Buddhist fundamentalism. Bandaranaike was elected prime minister on a pro-Buddhist, pro-Sinhalese ticket. He astutely recognized that the political, social, and religious vision of large segments of the Sinhalese Buddhist population had not been realized by the policies of the liberal, Westernized UNP politicians who had endorsed a pluralistic, secular state. The SLFP gained mass support on a platform which appealed to the chauvinistic interests of the Sinhalese majority, Sinhalese as the national language, Buddhism as the state religion.

A rise in Sinhalese Buddhist nationalism, coupled with the politicization of the Sangha, contributed to Bandaranaike's election. The nationalist sentiments to which he appealed had been deepened first by the publication in 1953 of the Report of the Buddhist Commission of Inquiry denouncing the treatment of Buddhism at the hands of the British and later, in 1956–57, by the celebration throughout Theravada Buddhist Asia of the 2500th anniversary of the birth of the Buddha (Buddha Jayanti), which had also become a means of keeping alive the bitter memory of the British suppression of Buddhism on the island. The Jayanti celebrated the nationalist myth which wed the faith to the land and to the race and held that the Sinhalese nation "had come into being with the blessing of the Buddha as a 'chosen race' with a divine mission to fulfill, and now stands on the threshold of a new era leading to its 'great destiny.'"[31] The celebration of the Jayanti, following upon the inquiry report, was used by the SLFP to promote an ethos of fundamentalistic Sinhalese Buddhism invigorated by millennial expectations. Bandaranaike and the SLFP were depicted successfully as the harbingers of the imminent age of renewed Buddhist glory.

The politicization of the Sangha was represented by the formation of the United Monks' Front (Eksat Bhiksu Peramuna), which campaigned actively and aggressively on behalf of the Sri Lanka Freedom Party. While opinions varied in both the monastic and lay communities regarding the appropriateness of the political involvement of monks, the most definitive monastic statement (1946) supporting clerical involvement echoed Dharmapala's rhetoric:

> In ancient days, according to the records of history, the welfare of the nation and the welfare of the religion were regarded as synonymous terms by the laity

> as well as by the Sangha. The divorce of religion from the nation was an idea introduced into the minds of the Sinhalese by invaders from the West who belonged to an alien faith. It was a convenient instrument of astute policy to enable them to keep the people in subjugation in order to rule the people as they pleased.
>
> It was in their own interests and not for the welfare of the people that these foreign invaders attempted to create a gulf between the bhikkhus and the laity—a policy which they implemented with diplomatic cunning. We should not follow their example and should not attempt to withdraw bhikkhus from society. Such conduct would assuredly be a deplorable act of injustice, committed against our nation, our country, our religion.[32]

The United Monks' Front, heir to this sentiment, admonished monks to be at the polling booths in the election of 1956 to tell people how to vote in order to elect a government that would "work for the country, religion and its culture," and to be ready to sacrifice their lives to restore a Buddhist Ceylon.[33] In turn Bandaranaike promised to support Sinhalese Buddhism: "I . . . ask for the vast majority of Buddhists in this country, whose religion has been linked with their lives for two thousand years and is one which has suffered more than any other religion under foreign rule, certain just things we can expect to be done by the Government of this country."[34]

After his election Bandaranaike pursued three measures designed to restore Ceylon's Buddhist heritage. First, he established a Ministry of Cultural Affairs to rehabilitate Buddhism through measures such as the restoration of Buddhist shrines, a new translation of the Buddhist canon *(tipiṭaka)* into Sinhalese, and the compilation of a Buddhist Encyclopedia. Second, he announced a plan for a Buddhist Religious *(sāsana)* Commission to investigate the possibilities of mutually beneficial liasions with monastic courts, monastery landholders, and other Buddhist institutions. Third, he elevated the two monastic colleges (*pirivenas*) to university status.[35] Perhaps because these initiatives were fundamentalistic (and modernistic) rather than simply traditional, they met with mixed success at best. The proposed Buddhist Religious Commission encountered resistance from the conservative monks of the Siyam sect who were wary of the strong identification with the state, and lay Buddhists objected to the elevation of the monastic colleges on the grounds that monks should not study a secular curriculum with lay students, especially women.

Bandaranaike's policy of "restoring Buddhism to its rightful place," however, foundered on his two major platform issues: Sinhalese as the national language and Buddhism as the state religion. These issues in particular fanned the flames of Sinhalese Buddhist nationalism. Bandaranaike's government passed a bill making Sinhalese the sole official language, but political realities forced the prime minister to negotiate with the Tamils, who wanted their language as a parallel national language. The United Monks' Front staged massive demonstrations opposing any compromise on Sinhalese as the sole national language. In the face of that pressure, Bandaranaike finally gave in to their demands and refused to compromise with the Tamils, who flooded the streets of Colombo in a protest action that came to be known as the language riots of 1957. The riots involved thousands of protesters and government forces and led to an unprecedented communalistic bloodletting.

Bandaranaike was the political heir of Anagarika Dharmapala's fundamentalistic, Sinhalese Buddhist nationalism that had effectively mobilized large segments of the Buddhist Sangha and the laity to work for the restoration of the glories of Ceylon's Buddhist past. From the perspective of my emphasis on the close connection between Theravada fundamentalism and the search for identity, the process of "identity affirmation" initiated by Dharmapala assumed a political form in 1956 that was to accelerate the militant, chauvinistic, and absolutistic nature of Sinhalese Buddhist nationalism. Bandaranaike himself was to be one of the first victims of the fundamentalistic ideology. On 25 September 1959, he was assassinated in a plot instigated by Mapitigama Buddharakkhita, a secretary of the United Monks' Front, whose anger at Bandaranaike's failure in the aftermath of the riots to bring about the promised Buddhist millennium, resulted in an act of violence that tragically foreshadowed the future of fundamentalistic Sinhalese Buddhism.

The Context of Contemporary Militant Buddhist Nationalism

The contemporary retrieval of the rhetoric of Dharmapala and the ideology of Bandaranaike has occurred on the heels of recent economic, political, and social disruptions that have created an environment in which the traditional identification of Theravada Buddhism and Sinhalese nationalism has once again become fundamentalistic, militant, and tragically violent. During the last two decades, Sri Lanka has become increasingly authoritarian and politically divided socially and economically. Three major dislocations have encouraged this ethos: (l) an unevenness of economic development and pauperization of the lower income groups; (2) factional competition with the ruling UNP (United National Party), combined with an advance toward total power which has left no space for countervailing opposition groups as checks and balances; (3) an increasing populism and chauvinism among the urban masses at large who were attracted to an ideology of a politicized Buddhism and a dangerously simplified racism.[36]

Sri Lanka's *economic development* over the past quarter of a century has created a social environment throughout many parts of the country which has destroyed the homogeneous kin-based nature of village life and has produced a variety of groups competing for scarce resources, with the spillover from increasingly large and heterogeneous villages moving into market towns and in particular into the capital city of Colombo.[37] In addition, new towns were created in conjunction with government-sponsored irrigation schemes, such as the Mahaweli Project, in the north central and southern dry zones. Rather than colonizing these areas with local villagers, the settlers were outsiders, often chosen by MPs from among their party supporters.[38] Finally, traditional villages were infiltrated by merchants and entrepreneurs from Colombo and market towns. In short, in the decades since independence there has been a dramatic disruption of the traditional social environment in Sri Lanka. In addition, economic competition among merchants in the new environments was often between Sinhalese, Tamils, and Muslims. Observers have concluded that practically all civil disturbances, such as post-election riots (endemic after the 1960s) and race riots, have occurred primarily in these colonization schemes, in the relatively traditionless market towns, and in Colombo.[39]

In addition to these economic and social changes, there has been an *authoritarian drift in government* since 1977 and an increasing cycle of provocation and repression after the 1982 election.[40] The UNP party of Mr. J. R. Jayawardena (often referred to as "JR") was elected in 1977 and held a five-sixths majority in the British-style parliament. JR instituted two major policies, one economic and the other political. Economically, he moved away from the socialist policies of the SFLP led by Mrs. S. W. R. D. Bandaranaike, who succeeded her husband in 1960. Sirimavo Bandaranaike had continued the economic programs begun by her husband, such as the nationalization of the up-country tea plantations, and supported the cult of S. W. R. D. Bandaranaike as a national hero and martyr for the Sinhalese Buddhist nation.

In contrast, JR adopted an open economy with a free trade zone north of Colombo. Along with the development programs referred to above, this liberal capitalist market-oriented policy contributed to a significant increase in a poverty-level class and greater economic disparity between wealthy capitalists and the rural poor.[41] Politically, JR used his five-sixths majority to create a Gaullist-type system. He amended the constitution, making himself president and giving himself the authority to fill vacancies in parliament. In the October 1982 presidential election, JR was voted into office with a 52 percent plurality, but he then canceled the general election on the grounds that the police had uncovered an anarchist plot to assassinate him and several government and military leaders. Jayawaradena then reshuffled his own party's parliamentary membership, a move which muffled criticism from within the UNP, and further increased his power by reinterpreting article 35 of the constitution as providing him immunity from judicial proceedings. He was reported as saying, "The country needs one strong individual who fears not the Judiciary, the Legislature nor the Party, but only the general public to develop it, and I have the power to do anything for six years."[42]

The authoritarian drift in government was also buttressed by the ideology of fundamentalist Buddhist nationalism. When Jayawaradena came to power in 1977, he promised to introduce a *dharmishta* Society, a state of righteousness and justice based on Buddhist principles. An attack on JR was then tantamount to an attack on those very principles.[43]

Whether the authoritarian character of Sri Lanka's government will gradually ameliorate depends on a variety of political, economic, and social factors. In the country's 15 February 1989 parliamentary elections, 60 percent of the 9.4 million eligible voters braved one of the most violent elections in Sri Lanka's history to give the UNP party 125 out of 225 contested seats.[44] Ranasinghe Premadasa, a former MP and one of the UNP's political bosses who had been supported by the JSS, was elected president. In his first cabinet he retained the posts of defense, policy planning, and the portfolio of Buddhist affairs. Violence in the country was greatly reduced with the virtual destruction of the JVP leadership in the south and the departure of the Indian peacekeeping force (IPKF), which had arrived in Sri Lanka in July 1987. In addition, there was a fragile accommodation between the UNP and the Tamil Liberation Tigers, who had consolidated their power among the Tamils in the north and the east; an economic turnaround with a renewed injection of tourist dollars into the country; and the reopening of the universities, which had been closed for two years.

Growing stability, however, was used by President Premadasa to further consolidate his power. In April 1990 he reconstituted his cabinet and reappointed his former prime minister (Dingirir Banda Wijetunge) instead of making it a "rotating prime ministership." Contrary to the advice of the World Bank and the IMF, Premadasa vastly increased the number of ministers in the cabinet and made no changes in the direct control the presidential secretariat exercises over ministeries. In 1990, at this writing, all ministrial secretaries were determined by President Premadasa, and all key appointments to corporations and statuatory boards are cleared by him.[45]

Accompanying the authoritarian drift in government has been the *institutionalization of violence* that occurred after the massive UNP victory in 1977. This accompanied the emergence of several political bosses who effectively bought a following from among the new proletariat and who commanded their absolute loyalty. Particularly noteworthy was the National Workers Organization's (the Jatika Sevaka Sangamaya or JSS) support of its president, Cyril Matthew, who became the Minister of Industries, and of Ranasinghe Premadasa. Cyril Matthew effectively molded the JSS into an organization which controlled government offices and corporations and intimidated high officials. In these efforts the JSS appropriated the twentieth-century fundamentalist identification of Sinhalese identity with Buddhism and the accompanying Sinhalese-Buddhist political ideology. In this way, the identity of an economically marginal group of people has been given a new reality and meaning.[46]

The festering problem of *Tamil-Sinhalese animosity* is the final element leading to the paroxysm of ethnic violence which swept Sri Lanka in July 1983.[47] Until the rise of powerful South Indian states in the fifth century, there is little evidence of ethnic conflict on the island. These Hindu states were to invade Sri Lanka from time to time, however, eventually establishing an independent Tamil kingdom in the thirteenth century based largely on the Jaffna peninsula. From the thirteenth to the seventeenth centuries, only infrequent conflict between the Tamils in the north and the Sinhalese to the south punctuated an otherwise cooperative and mutually tolerant relationship.[48] The colonial period, however, changed that situation. Under the British, the Tamil population increased with the importation of plantation workers from south India, and a split gradually developed between the low-country, Westernized Sinhalese and the Kandyan Sinhalese who were more attached to traditional values. Generally speaking, the colonial administration unified the country at the national administrative level but not on local and regional levels. In this situation, minority ethnic and religious groups possessed no institutional framework by which to organize themselves, even in the areas where they formed a majority.[49]

In the latter part of the nineteenth century a stronger sense of ethnic identity emerged among the Sinhalese and Tamils, partly as a reaction against the proselytizing activities of Christian missionaries. Ethnic feelings were also promoted by issues of proportional representation in the government after the introduction of universal suffrage in 1931 and the question of language preference in education and government. Fragile alliances between Sinhalese and Tamil ruling elites struck at the time of independence in 1948 were soon to fall apart. Conflicts centered around four basic issues: language and employment, regional autonomy, settlement of Sinhalese on lands claimed to be the traditional homelands of the Tamils, and access to higher education.[50]

As we have seen, S. W. R. D. Bandaranike's Sinhalese-Buddhist ticket of 1956 exacerbated the tensions by pursuing policies favoring the Sinhalese over against the Tamils in terms of political appointments, education, and most divisive of all, national language preference. The language riots of 1957 foreshadowed the ethnic violence and race riots which became the dominant fact of Sri Lankan life with the emergence of a political-ethnic-religious extremism embodied both by radical Tamil separatists (Tamil Eelam, the Tamil United Liberation Front), and an equally militant and extremist Sinhalese group, the JVP (Janata Vimukti Peramuna, the National Liberation Front). The Liberation Tigers of the Tamil Eelam (LTTE) coalesced in the Jaffna region in 1981 and 1982 as the radical wing of the Tamil separatist movement and demanded a separate Tamil homeland located in the north and northeastern portions of the country. The Sinhalese JVP emerged largely as a response to the LTTE, though it claims to be a revived version of the 1971 Marxist JVP movement that sought to overthrow Srimavo Bandaranaike. Membership in the JVP is young—between 18 and 26—and the most active supporters are unemployed villagers in the central and southern provinces. While they sometimes use Marxist terminology, they are apt to evoke the glories of Sri Lanka's Buddhist past rather than a utopian socialistic future.[51]

Buddhist nationalist rhetoric has resounded amid the violent conflicts of the past decade. For example, the immediate cause of the July 1983 riots in Colombo, in which hundreds of Tamil Hindus were killed and thousands relocated in refugee camps, was the ambush of an army truck and the murder and mutilation of thirteen soldiers in the Jaffna district by a group of Liberation Tigers of the Tamil Eelam. The massive retaliation by the government as well as private citizens was accompanied and legitimated by the rhetoric and ethos of fundamentalistic Sinhalese Buddhist nationalism.

There have been, of course, other more moderate and reformist voices within the spectrum of contemporary Buddhism in Sri Lanka. Some have sought to renew Buddhist spiritual idealism through the practice of meditation; others are attempting to inform efforts for social and economic renewal with Buddhist ethical teachings; still others have openly despaired at what they see as a chauvinistic and violent aberration of the ideal of a just, peaceful, and open-minded Buddhist state.

An important negative influence on Tamil-Sinhalese relations from July 1987 until March 1990 was the Indo-Lankan Accord and the occupation of the northern and eastern provinces by a forty-five-thousand-member Indian Peacekeeping Force (IPKF) to combat the secessionist Liberation Tigers.[52] The presence of the IPKF created a wave of distrust directed not only at India but also at the ruling UNP party, even though Premadasa had called for the withdrawal of Indian troops as early as 1 June 1989 in a speech at a Buddhist temple. Indian occupation in the north and east thwarted the political aims of the LTTE in that region and contributed to an increase in anarchy and terrorism among Sinhalese in the south, a good deal of which was sponsored by the JVP. Provincial elections were held in 1988 despite significant intimidation and some bloodshed, with the consequence that the Tamil-dominated northern and eastern provinces were joined for local administrative purposes, and a fragile national unity has been maintained.[53]

During the two and a half years the IPKF troops were in Sri Lanka, the JVP attacked the Indian presence with the same kind of vitriolic rhetoric Dharmapala had marshaled against the British and the Tamils. They declared a boycott of Indian goods and businesses and Indian buses and used the IPKF as their principal excuse to try to overthrow the government by terrorism. They penetrated the armed forces, police, state and private workplaces, and student bodies at both secondary and university levels. Although they commanded only about eight thousand active supporters, the JVP tactics of violence brought the south to its knees on several occasions, forced hundreds of schools and all of the universities to close, and even brought Colombo to a standstill on 12 September 1988.[54] Opposition to the Indo-Lankan Accord was strong among other segments of the population as well, however, especially among younger Buddhist monks in rural areas. A group known as the Sri Lanka National Sangha Council denounced the accord and urged the government to resign.

The violence spawned by the JVP had little support among the general populace, however. Therefore even moderate and liberal Buddhists were not overtly critical of the government's repressive and violent destruction of the JVP leadership. At this writing it appears that the policy has succeeded in eliminating the top leaders. Furthermore, with the withdrawal of the last of the IPKF in March 1990, the raison d'être of the essentially leaderless JVP has been effectively undermined. It remains to be seen, however, whether the violence that has plagued Sri Lanka for the past seven years can be stopped.

With the withdrawal of the IPFK in the northern and eastern provinces, the more moderate Tamil groups supported by the Sri Lankan and Indian governments—the Tamil United Liberation Front (TULF) and the Eelam People's Revolutionary Liberation Front (EPRLF)—have been badly outflanked by the LTTE and its political wing, the People's Front of Liberation Tigers (PELT). The upcoming provincial council elections will be a test of how well the Sri Lankan government and the LTTE will be able to manage their future relations. In the guarded opinion of one observer, "The future of the surf-washed picturesque island continues to hang like a question mark. The ethnic trouble in the island may be under wraps at the moment, but the peace-loving Sri Lankan is apprehensive that the powder-keg will explode at any time."[55]

The violent nature of the Sinhalese-Tamil conflict has many facets. The Tamil and Sinhalese radical extremists represented by the LTTE and JVP have taken countless innocent lives. But the conflict cannot be reduced to two relatively small groups of political extremists, nor can it be seen solely as the reflection of the social dislocations brought about by the government development schemes, the political hooliganism of the past decade, or the increase in unemployed youth. A major component in the violence has also been a cultural ethos of militant Sinhalese Buddhist nationalism which in turn has been a consequence of a fundamentalist rereading of the Theravada Buddhist worldview. This reinterpretation of the tradition was a response to the dramatically disruptive effect of Westernization and modernization. It was a reassertion of Sri Lanka's Buddhist heritage as a mode of affirmation of identity. But the apologetic polemic became in effect a secularized civil religion expressed in a rhetoric of protest rather than in the richly textured myths, legends, and tales of moral exemplars available in the classic texts and traditions of Theravada Buddhism.

Buddhist Fundamentalism: The Transformation of Myth

The ideology of fundamentalistic Sinhalese Buddhist nationalism of the type enunciated by the Anagarika Dharmapala and promoted politically by S. W. R. D. Bandaranike makes a distinctive use of texts, in particular, the Theravada chronicles. The *Mahāvaṁsa* portrays Sri Lanka as an island of dhamma *(dhammadīpa)* sanctified by the Buddha himself; as a kingdom founded by a north Indian prince and as ruled by just and righteous kings who defended the Buddhist religion *(Buddhasāsana)* against evil forces, particularly the Tamils. From the mythic past of chronicle history, two culture heroes stand out: Vijaya, who gives the Sinhalese a unique north Indian ethnic, cultural, and linguistic identity; and Dutthagamani, who became the sovereign ruler of Sri Lanka in 161 B.C.E. after a fifteen-year war against Elara, a Tamil king from Cola who had conquered the northern part of the island. Devanampiyatissa, a friend of King Asoka who opened the gates of Anuradhapura to Mahinda and Sanghamitta and planted the first bo tree on the island, and Parakkamabahu I, whose missionaries were responsible for the spread of the Mahavihara tradition to much of Southeast Asia, are overshadowed by Vijaya and Dutthagamani in the ideology of modern Sinhalese Buddhist nationalism. This is because these two heroes are more centrally connected to Sinhalese identity both in terms of the original settlement of the Sinhalese on the island, and their early conquest of Tamil usurpers.[56]

Because the Pali chronicles root Sinhalese identity in Buddhism, that is, in a transcendent source immune to erosion—the chronicles have taken on heightened significance in contexts in which Sinhalese identity has been threatened—whether by the Tamils in 161 B.C.E., by the colonizing West in the nineteenth century, or by the Indian troops sent to maintain peace between the Sinhalese and the Tamils. In the rhetoric of the Anagarika Dharmapala, the description of Sri Lanka (Ceylon) as an island of dhamma (truth, righteousness [Sanskrit dharma]) became a rallying cry for Sinhalese self-esteem and provided the irreducible basis for a new ethic and way of life. Similarly, the 1954 Report of the Buddhist Committee of Inquiry commissioned by the All-Ceylon Buddhist Congress issued its own patriotic call which prepared the way for Bandaranaike's election two years later: "Without doubt [Buddhism is] the highest form of patriotism—the only patriotism worthy of the name, worth fighting for or dying for. And some of the finest men and women who have ever lived have fought for it and died for it, and so long as tyranny and injustice exist in the world, it will continue to command the religious fervor and self-sacrifice of such men and women."[57]

This absolutist and exclusivist view of history promoted by Dharmapala, the Buddhist Committee of Inquiry, the All Ceylon Buddhist Congress, and Bandaranaike alike recalls Ortega y Gasset's notion of the "worship of culture."[58] What are the specific features which render this approach fundamentalist? What insight does "fundamentalism" as an analytical perspective provide into the meaning of Sinhalese Buddhist nationalism as it has developed from the late nineteenth century to the present?

Focusing on Sinhalese Buddhist nationalism through the lens of fundamentalism heightens the contrast between the modern reductionist Buddhism of the Anagarika Dharmapala and others with the cosmological and ethical richness of the classical Theravada Buddhist symbol system. Furthermore, it focuses our inquiry on the question of identity—personal, communal, national—which is the most potent and explosive aspect of the revival of fundamentalist religion throughout the world today. In short, in its most basic meaning, modern fundamentalism is an assertion of identity—personal, communal, and, ultimately, national—in the face of the threat of its loss. The threat to identity may come from many quarters—in the Sri Lankan case, British Christendom or Tamil Hindus. The fundamentalistic response to the threat is couched in terms of a rhetoric of persecution aimed to produce a sense of unity against a common enemy. This sense of being over against becomes a necessary ingredient to the restoration of identity.[59]

In religious fundamentalism, identity is understood as *ontological,* as rooted in the very nature of being and the cosmos and thus beyond the reach of human temporal and spatial considerations and the relativizing force of history. In their own lives, those who adopt this view of the cosmos and of human affairs seek to bring their world into objective harmony with the cosmic order depicted in myth and legend. To encompass and control the disorder about them, they may engage in acts of violence that are, in Mark Juergensmeyer's words, "justified and therefore exonerated because they are part of a religious scenario: they are the ritualized playing out of the cosmic drama of good and evil."[60]

Indeed, the rhetoric of the Buddhist fundamentalists profiled above was based upon a cosmological dualism in which the Sinhalese are aligned with the forces of good, and outsiders—the Tamils, the British, the Indian troops—represent the forces of evil. This moral-cosmological dualism informing the ideology of fundamentalism is, moreover, imbedded in a simplified worldview held with absolute certitude by its proponents. Such reformulations of a classic religious tradition as the Buddhism of Dharmapala, which represented a fundamental shift from the complex symbol system of the traditional Sinhalese Theravada synthesis, have their counterparts in Sri Lanka among the Tamil Hindus as well. The Hindu equivalent of Dharmapala is Armugam Navalar, who spearheaded a Tamil Hindu revival movement.[61] In Dharmapala's case the reinterpretation affirmed the ascetic and abstract values of a rigid doctrinal Buddhism which was in some ways a creation of Western students of Buddhism, in particular, Henry Steele Olcott. It is interesting to note the similarities between the rather puritanical morality of Olcott's "Buddhist Catechism" and Dharmapala's "Daily Code of the Laity."[62] From this pastiche Dharmapala created a worldview and a way of being in the world for socioeconomic classes that had practically no historical parallel in the Theravada past, a bourgeoisie and proletariat that had emerged in the colonial and postcolonial periods.[63] By the Bandaranaike era, Dharmapala's fundamentalist Buddhism had created a context in which "Buddhism had become the effective political and civil religion of the state."[64]

I wish to highlight in this analysis the one-dimensional or univocal nature of modern fundamentalistic Buddhistic nationalism, for I take this characteristic to be typical of fundamentalisms everywhere, not just in Sri Lanka, or for that matter, Buddhist Asia. Dharmapala's ideology lacked the philosophical complexity, narrative variety, and ritual vitality of Sri Lanka's Buddhist inheritance. By "homogenizing" the tradition and reducing it to a simplified core teaching and a moralistic program of right living and Sinhalese-Buddhist nationalist identity, he ignored the polar dynamic between the transmundane and the mundane, a distinction basic not only to traditional Theravada Buddhism but to the other great historical religions as well. This "vertical" dimension of belief seems to be transformed by the fundamentalisms of the 1980's into a variety of political, economic, and social movements legitimated in terms of an idealized religious past but which evade the transcendental ground from which all political, economic, and social systems are judged to be inadequate. Obeyesekere, for example, contends that a careful reading of the chronicles and later commentaries reveals a multiplicity of views with regard to Dutthagamani's destruction of the Tamils; indeed, in the *Mahāvaṁsa*'s account, the aftermath of the king's action is a of conscience," not merely an assertion of the righteousness of the Sinhalese Buddhist cause.[65] In the classical tradition, Buddhist values informed the traditional Sinhalese culture through the retelling of moral legends and fables and through various kinds of ritual enactments of the legends. In Buddhist fundamentalism, the subtleties and nuanced variations are lost, and with them the ethical parameters that call into question particular courses of action, point to the moral ambiguities of life, and uphold lofty moral and spiritual ideals. Obeyeskere recalls:

> In the villages of my childhood people recited the story of King Vessantara, in popular and poignant verse, as part of the funeral wake; nowadays in these same villages gambling sessions are organized by local entrepreneurs during the wake since the police do not raid a house where a death has taken place. The generation of my nephews and nieces studying in Sri Lanka's modern schools, where Buddhism is taught as a school subject, is largely unaware of the tradition of stories that nurtured the Buddhist conscience and the forms of life in which they were embedded.[66]

The absolutism of fundamentalism stems from this basic transformation of the religious worldview. The narrowly ideological nature of fundamentalism means that it is not religious in the classical sense of that term but rather a variant of a secular faith couched in religious language and elevating traditional religious symbols stripped of their symbolic power to evoke a multiplicity of meanings. Indeed, the claim of astute interpreters of Sinhalese religion and culture that Dharmapala's "intellectualist" view of Buddhism was derived from Westerners such as Olcott, who were fundamentally agnostic and used Buddhism as a foil against Christianity, supports my assertion that fundamentalism divests the religious worldview of its richly textured multivocality.

This character of modern religious fundamentalism has an analogue in the nature of the relationship between fundamentalistic movements and nationalism, or more specifically, the transformation of Sinhalese Buddhism into a "civil religion." It is precisely at this point, as an expression of and reaction to a crisis of identity, that fundamentalism reveals itself as an assertion, or reassertion, of cultural, social, and personal identity in which religion, violence, and the quest for ultimate order are inextricably interrelated. Thus, the primary "fundamentalism" extracted from the sacred source texts of Sri Lanka (the myths and legends) is properly speaking more reflective of, and at the service of, the nationalist rather than the Buddhist worldview, although the two are inseparable in the rhetoric of the charismatic fundamentalist leaders. In other words, the specifically Buddhist character of the myths and legends is subservient to the personal and social identity both threatened and affirmed in the texts. Cultural identity in effect becomes a "religious fetish, an idol, a thing which has self-contained magical properties," rather than a transcendent and transforming moral and spiritual ideal in terms of which all systems and institutions are judged as limited or only a partial embodiment.[67] Religions thus harnessed to nationalism are often regarded as more pure and orthodox than the traditional forms they seek to supplant; in turn, nationalism readily takes on the character of a fervid, absolutistic revival of religion. In the case of Sri Lanka, as elsewhere, the search for national identity is prior and conditions the fundamentalism of the religion(s) incorporated into nationalism.[68]

The worldview of the foundational myths of the Sinhalese are encompassing and consequently hierarchic. In the cosmology of Sinhalese Buddhist nationalism, non-Sinhalese Buddhists are maintained in hierarchic subordination to Sinhalese Buddhists. The integrity of the state therefore is dependent on its capacity to maintain by the exercise of its power the hierarchical interrelation of all those it encloses.[69] In terms congenial to Buddhism: when the *Buddhadhamma* (the truth represented by the Buddha's teaching) is opposed, chaos results, the hierarchic social order is compromised, the principle of encompassment is attacked, and demonic forces are unleashed.[70] When these myths and legends are contextualized politically and given a narrow, particularistic meaning by Dharmapala, Bandaranaike, contemporary spokespersons for a militant Sinhalese Buddhist nationalism, and the JVP, then the variety of possible interpretations of the myths or moral arguments contained in the commentaries, are subverted. Consequently they assume a totalitarian, highly ideological form, redundant in meaning. In this the basic dialectic of the myths is lost; the "other," the demonic, is no longer merely encompassed but is destroyed. In this way the dynamic polarities of the classical myths become an oppositional moral and cosmic dualism, a battle between the forces of *dhamma* (truth) and *adhamma* (untruth) with the potential for mindless, destructive violence. This point is illustrated by the following recent conversation with a prominent Sinhalese Buddhist monk:

> The *bhikkhu*'s [monk's] main concerns . . . are with the current state of Sri Lankan society. "We live in a time of *dukkha* [suffering]," he explained. As he elaborated this point it became clear that he was more than simply restating the first of the Four Noble Truths. In the bhikkhu's mind the concept of dukkha has a definite social significance. "We live in an adhammic world," he stated, and gave examples of immorality to buttress the point: gambling, slaughtering animals for meat, and drinking arrak—the locally produced alcohol. . . .
>
> It was not just morality that he wanted the state to uphold: it was the very notion of a Sinhalese Buddhist nation. He used the phrase "Sinhalese Buddhist" as if it demarcated a particular kind of society. . . . "And see how tiny, how fragile Sinhalese Buddhist society is. We are only a tear drop, a grain of sand, in an enormous sea." As he continued, he lowered his voice and his eyes blazed: "And it is in danger of being forever dashed away."[71]

Both Sinhalese Buddhist monks and laity would agree that Buddhist culture has given Sri Lanka its identity over the years and that the protection of Buddhist values and Sinhalese identity is central to the state. The more radical members of the JVP envision a Marxist political order; the more moderate ones, along with less radical low-country monks, prefer a parliamentary democracy. Neither group, however, would deny that a Buddhist nation has the legitimate right to take life to protect its authentic identity.[72]

Will Sri Lanka be able to resolve the ethnic violence between the Sinhalese and the Tamils? The solution to this problem will not come about merely through the restitution of a relatively just electoral process, the creation of a social and economic environment sufficiently stable to restore the prosperous tourist trade, the opening of the universities, or simply the creation of more jobs. These measures must be accompanied by the self-conscious rebuilding of a transformed cultural identity no longer at the mercy of the fundamentalistic ideology of a militant, chauvinistic Buddhism, but rather one which weaves a new web of meaning from the richly textured past. A contemporary Sinhalese Buddhist anthropologist has voiced the hope that the Buddhism of the Sinhalese scholar and his middle-class counterpart will be able to rise above an intellectualist, demystified Buddhism that in the hands of Dharmapala, Bandaranaike, J. R, and to a certain extent, the JVP, has bolstered an ideology of an exclusivist Sinhalese-Buddhist state. Shorn of these contemporary influences, Buddhism may well continue to shape Sinhalese conscience toward the building of a truly universal and inclusive Buddhist state of righteousness, justice, and peace envisioned by many non-fundamentalistic Buddhists.[73]

Fundamentalism, Sectarianism, and Religious Revitalization in Thailand

The relationship between fundamentalism and nationalism may also be explored from the perspective of religious sectarianism and revitalization in the case of two new religious movements in Thailand—Dhammakaya and Santi Asoka—which have gained national attention because of spectacular growth in one case, political prominence in another, and sectarian challenges to mainstream Thai Buddhism in both instances. Dhammakaya may be seen as a fundamentalistic expression of the civil religion tradition founded by King Rama VI and Santi Asoka as a fundamentalist transformation of the "forest monk" tradition within Theravada Buddhism.[74]

The Ethos of Dhammakaya and Santi Asoka

Visakha Puja is the holiday which memorializes the birth, enlightenment, and death of the Buddha. Today the largest Visakha Puja celebration in Thailand takes place at Wat Dhammakaya, a new religious center at Prathum Thani, forty-five minutes by car from Bangkok. The roads to the *wat* (the Thai term for centers of monastic and lay religious practice) are jammed with upwards of sixty thousand pilgrims from every region of the country—buses from Chiang Mai, Korat, and Chonburi, Benz limos from Bangkok, and local rice farmers on bicycles. Early in the morning, many of the faithful line the main entrance road to present food donations to hundreds of barefoot, identically dressed, saffron-robed monks. The laity, too, appear to be almost uniformed—men and women, children and adults dressed alike in white. The white uniform is said to bring special merit: it promotes orderliness and quiet, creates an ethos conducive to religious practice, encourages polite behavior toward others, and stills one's mind.[75]

Gradually the crowds move up the central walkway lined with the *dhammacakka* (Buddhist flag) and the tricolor national flag to a white marbled temple gleaming in the bright morning sunlight. Its simplicity contrasts with the elaborate architectural design of the traditional Thai temple, just as the orderly lines of the devotees seem at odds with the milling crowds at the average Buddhist temple compound on a festival day. On their way into the temple many pause before a large framed picture of an elderly monk, paying respects to and seeking the blessing of Phra Mongkhon Thepmuni, the deceased abbot of Wat Pak Nam, the spiritual leader of Wat Dhammakaya and teacher of the *wat*'s two leading monks, Thammachayo and Thattachiwo.

The temple interior contrasts even more sharply with the traditional Thai Buddhist meeting hall. A solitary spotlighted Buddha image commands the viewer's attention. No money trees, secondary figures, altar decorations, flags, or even grandfather clocks distract from the central, modern image—an image lacking in any distinctively Thai characteristics. The carpeted room projects a sense of order and stability. Other meeting halls on the compound convey a similar feeling of power, orderliness, and cleanliness. Rows of monks and lay people meditate in the halls during the day; the celebration culminates in a presentation of new robes to the Dhammakaya monks (Thai *thawai pha ba*) led by a high government official, an event "instructive in merit and dispensing happiness."[76] The day ends with a group photo, hundreds of saffron-robed monks and thousands of pilgrims uniformly dressed in white—military and civil servants, teachers and students, businessmen and housewives, young, middle-aged, and elderly, row upon row surrounding the temple.

4 September 1985. The Santi Asoka center at Nakorn Pathom. When the People of Asoka (Thai *chao asok*) started building the center about three years earlier on twenty-five acres outside of the city, local residents suspected that the group harbored communists and shot at them. But the People of Asoka persisted and today there are nineteen monks, seven female novices (Thai *sikkhāmāt*) and about seventy lay families living together as simply as possible as a self-sufficient community. Everyone is a vegetarian and encouraged to eat only one meal a day, a kind of communal potluck at 11 A.M. The only people who are allowed to become monks or sikkhāmāt are those who have completed a five-year apprenticeship, adhering to a vegetarian diet, eating only one meal a day, following the eight precepts. The people at the center weave their own cloth, mill their own rice by hand, and are building their own water system. No one has personal possessions. All food, cloth, and other essentials are available from the community storehouse—a modest but neat and attractive building. Simplicity and naturalness are encouraged. No electricity is allowed, although solar cells are. Lay people wear blue village shirts and loose peasant trousers. Most are barefoot. The quarters of the monks and sikkhāmāt are extremely small and simple, and the houses of the families are not much larger. All the lay people living at the center must accept the basic principles of the community and attempt to live by them. The goal is to grow from seventy to two hundred families.

The regimen is demanding. All are up at 3:00 A.M. to study Buddhism as a group. At 5:00 A.M. food is prepared for those who commute to work in Bangkok. Full-time residents work on community buildings, tend the vegetable and herb gardens, or work in the rice fields. Several members pointed out that everyone is expected to work in the fields, especially those who had previously done only desk work. Despite the demands of hard work, the People of Asoka seem proud to be there and are committed to the ideals of the movement. A young woman, an economist with the Ministry of Industry, spoke of how happy she was living at the Santi Asoka center. She was unquestioning in her acceptance of the rules of the community and the views of the controversial founder of Santi Asoka, Phra Bodhiraksa.[77]

These movements have emerged from the Buddhism that has been a part of Thai culture, society, and politics since the establishment of the princely states in Sukhothai, Ayutthaya, and Chiang Mai (in the area now known as northern Thailand) in the twelfth and thirteenth centuries by peoples migrating there from the Yunnan region of China. The early monarchial states and their attendant institutional and legal traditions were informed by both Hindu and Buddhist ideals and left a legacy to be appropriated in the development of the modern Thai nation-state, a process that began upon the destruction of Ayutthaya in 1767 at the hands of the Burmese. Under the leadership of Taksin, an Ayutthayan provincial governor, the Thais retaliated, defeating the Burmese in battle and establishing a new capital city first at Thonburi and then at Bangkok on the banks of the Chao Phraya River. Taksin was deposed by the man who was to become Rama I (1782–1809), the first monarch of a dynasty that has ruled continuously to the present day.

Rama I appealed to the traditions of the classical Ayutthayan state, including a new edition of the fourteenth-century cosmological treatise, the *Trai Phum Phra Ruang* (The Three Worlds According to King Ruang), which had been at the core of the Siamese Buddhist system of belief.[78] The king endorsed a rationalized and partially demythologized presentation of the classical Theravada cosmology. This presentation gained full ascendancy several decades later in the courts of Rama IV (King Mongkut) and Rama V (King Chulalongkorn).[79]

In 1851, Mongkut took the throne after living as a monk for over twenty-five years. During his monastic tenure he had become critical of various traditional rites and of the laxity of monastic discipline as practiced by the Mahanikaya monks of Thailand. As a consequence, he founded a new order, the Thammayut (Adhering to the Buddha's Truth), with a separate ordination tradition and distinctive interpretation of the monastic discipline. At the same time, influenced partially by correspondence with Sinhalese monks who were defending their faith against Christian missionaries and by discussions with Catholic and Protestant missionaries in Thailand, Mongkut began to complement the cosmology and mythologies of the *Trai Phum Phra Ruang* with naturalistic explanations of the universe. Many of Mongkut's ideas for religious reform were realized during the reign of his successor, King Chulalongkorn, who appointed his half-brother, Vajiranana (1860–1921), as the head of the Thammayut order and the supreme patriarch of the Thai Buddhist Sangha. Vajiranana's scholarly erudition was matched by his administrative skills, and he guided the development of a new monastic curriculum and a restructuring of monastic education.

The reformed Buddhism of Mongkut, Chulalongkorn, and Vajiranana represented a "shift from viewing the world in cosmological terms to viewing it psychologically, and . . . from practice centered on communal rituals to practice centered on self-cultivation."[80] These developments occurred at the time when Thailand, although never under direct colonial rule, was nonetheless greatly influenced by nineteenth-century Western colonial commercial, political, legal, and educational traditions in Southeast Asia. These changes in the nature of monastic education and the contemporizing of the Thai Buddhist worldview mirrored other reforms instituted by Chulalongkorn in Thai bureaucracy, provincial administration, the military, the judiciary, and the fiscal system. He also instituted social reforms that undermined the old hierarchical system of status and rank and led to the eventual abolition of slavery. The modernization of the political bureaucracy and legal and educational systems continued under Chulalongkorn's son, King Vajiravudh (1910–25).[81] Vajiravudh blended the concepts of "nation," "religion," and "king" into a governing ideology for modern Thailand and advocated a "civil" religion in Thailand, in which "nation" seemed to supersede "religion" (Buddhism). This notion of a civil religion was reinforced under the military regimes of Phibul Songgram (1938) and Field Marshal Sarit Thanarat (1957). Sarit in particular exploited the civil religion tradition as a way of legitimating his 1957 coup d'état and of promoting national integration through the creation of the national Dhammacarika mission to the hilltribes and the national Dhammadhuta programs in rural development.

Such programs featured the Buddhist Sangha as an arm of government national integration schemes. The National Sangha Act of 1962, for example, promulgated a highly centralized Sangha with increased potential as a pawn of the government for the promotion of the goals of a secular nation-state.[82] Coupled with the post-World War II rise of a secular ethos of Thailand, especially in urban areas, the promotion of Buddhism as a civil religion provided the conditions under which fundamentalist sectarian trends emerged as an oppositional response within the Thai religious spectrum.

Today, Thailand is a country of over fifty million people, roughly the size of Texas, governed by a constitutional monarchy with an elected parliament. An otherwise open political and economic system is kept in check by a strong and omnipresent military. With its rice-rich alluvial central plains, extensive northern forests, southern tin deposits and rubber plantations, and abundant varieties of fruit, Thailand has been an economically prosperous, politically stable country, especially when compared to its troubled neighbors—Burma, Cambodia, and Laos. Thai Buddhism continues to contribute to this stability, but the pervasive and dramatic changes Thailand has experienced during the past generation have called into question the traditional assumption that to be a Thai is to be a Buddhist.

The push toward national integration has served to undermine regional and local identities often rooted in religious traditions. The changes accompanying this form of political modernization have included rapid industrialization and urbanization, dramatic increases in landless, wage-dependent peasants, the expansion of higher learning throughout the country with an emphasis on the acquisition of technical skills, and the development of a nouveau riche commercial class accompanied by a new classism based primarily on wealth and economic power. In addition, there has been a rapid despoliation of the environment through the cutting of Thailand's northern forests and an extensive overuse of chemical fertilizers and pesticides.

Economic growth since 1985 has led to skyrocketing land values in many parts of the country, prompting peasants to sell their land and speculators to accumulate fortunes. Industrialization has been so rapid that, of the 10.46 percent growth rate in 1989, less than half (4.01 percent) has been in the agricultural sector, with a dramatic decline to 1.98 percent predicted for 1990.[83] Higher inflation rates, accompanied by lower agricultural prices, are predicted over the next few years. Increasing urbanization has displaced traditional village-based forms of social identification and has contributed to the increase in urban blight created by largely unchecked development. Perhaps one of the most pervasive challenges to traditional Thai culture has been the impact of tourism, which has become one of Thailand's major industries. The most notorious aspect of tourism has been prostitution. It is conservatively estimated that over 10 percent of all women between the ages of fourteen and twenty-four are prostitutes, and that women of this age group are nearly absent in whole villages of certain northern provinces.[84]

The traditional symbol of Thai identity, loyalty to "the religion"*(sāsāna)* is being eroded by these changes, as is loyalty to the king. These two institutions still constitute the basic cement of Thai cultural identity, but visible cracks have begun to appear in the foundation. Buddhist reformers from various points along the spectrum of Thai religion are attempting to fill in some of the cracks. While Dhammakaya and Santi Asoka represent fundamentalistic reactions, there are other responses. Liberal lay reformers like human rights activist and publisher Sulak Sivaraksa and innovative monastic interpreters such as Bhikkhu Buddhadasa constitute another important group and provide a marked contrast to Dhammakaya and Santi Asoka.[85] Dhammakaya represents a mainstream fundamentalistic revivalism with strong nationalistic overtones, a movement which can be seen as a particular transformation of Thai civil religion. In contrast, Santi Asoka may be seen as a form of sectarian fundamentalistic revivalism on the periphery of the sociocultural mainstream. As a consequence, Santi Asoka is more communalistic and less nationalistic in nature. Like other fundamentalist movements, Dhammakaya and Santi Asoka speak to a time of religious and cultural confusion, decline abetted by rampant modernization and secularization.[86] They are one type of response to the stress of cultural and religious disruption, value disorientation, and social anomie brought on by the economic, social, and cultural disruptions referred to above.[87]

Dhammakaya

Wat Dhammakaya[88] was officially registered with the Thai government in 1978; in 1980, its ordination hall was consecrated. In nine years it has become the fastest-growing religious group in Thailand, with activities focused at its national religious center near Bangkok. Although formally a member of the ancient *mahānikāya* tradition of Thai Theravada Buddhism, Dhammakaya has established itself as a distinctive, aggressively evangelistic movement dedicated to the renewal of a Thai Buddhism perceived as stultified by hierarchy and ceremonial ritual and weakened by a steady loss of young, able leaders.

The Dhammakaya movement is characterized by a strong leadership centralized in its two cofounders, the current abbot and the assistant abbot. It boasts an impressive religious center at Pathum Thani that has become a national focus for major Buddhist celebrations and regularly attracts several thousand devotees on Sundays, and a network of lay centers connected to provincial monasteries in some fifty provinces. Furthermore, the movement controls Buddhist Student Associations in over thirty post secondary institutions and commands a broad-based middle-class constituency augmented by notable support from the royal family and important military and government figures. The uncomplicated, moralistic ideology promulgated at its own centers and throughout the Thai educational system is coupled with a practical, simple method of personal religious practice promoted at intensive, prolonged training sessions. These various programs and constituencies are served by a technically sophisticated and highly developed publications and media network.

Dhammakaya As National Religious Center

Wat Dhammakaya was founded by Chaiyaboon Sitthiphon and Phadet Phongasawad who, as students at Kasetsart University in Bangkok, studied with a lay meditation teacher in the lineage of the late Phra Monkhon Thepmuni (Luang Pho Sot), Abbot of Wat Paknam Phasi Charoen in Thonburi. Both young men completed their university training; Chaiyaboon took a Ph.D. in economics and Phadet went to Australia for further studies. In 1969 they were ordained as monks at Wat Paknam, Chaiyaboon assuming the monastic name of Thammachayo (Pali *Dhammajayo*) and Phadet the name of Thattachiwo (Pali *Dattajīvo*). Thammachayo pledged himself to work for a worldwide renewal of Buddhism, beginning in Thailand.

The growth of the Dhammakaya movement has been spectacular. Its center at Pathum Thani begun on less than a hundred acres and has expanded tenfold (one thousand acres). Building growth has kept pace with land acquisition. Informal estimates place the broader range of Dhammakaya adherents in excess of one million. Regular Sunday meetings attract well over five thousand, and special events between fifty thousand to sixty thousand people.

Dhammakaya commands national attention. The abbot and assistant abbot are frequently heard on television and radio and appear at Dhammakaya meetings throughout the country; Dhammakaya Foundation publications are widely distributed. Its success has come not only from an aggressive and skillful manipulation of modern technology and the media but also through the development of a movement providing a practical alternative to a conventional Thai Buddhism which, they believe, is hindered by a hierarchical structure and a preoccupation with religious ritual. Further, Dhammakaya has succeeded in symbolizing in a compelling, contemporary manner the ancient identification of Buddhism with the state. In short, at the deepest level the movement addresses issues of personal, communal-religious, and national identity.

The Pathum Thani center holds both symbolic and practical significance for the Dhammakaya movement. In his detailed study of the relationship between Buddhism and polity in Thailand, S. J. Tambiah argued that the classical Thai kingdom of Ayutthaya (1350–1767) was structured around "a galactic polity"; that is, "[a] polity composed of a grouping around a center. At the core is the royal domain . . . with the capital city of Ayutthaya; this core region is surrounded by certain principalities or provinces ruled by princes or appointed governors."[89] The symbolic focus of the capital city was a royal *wat*, a religious center containing a Buddha relic enshrined in a reliquary mound. The capital city in effect was not only located at the center of political power and authority but at the axial center of the universe. Despite the survival of the Cakri Dynasty established in the late eighteenth century, the old notion of galactic polity has essentially disappeared. Politically it was undermined by the gradual development of a bureaucratically organized modern nation-state from the middle of the nineteenth century and by the dissolution of the absolute monarchy in 1932.

By fashioning a distinctive movement within the Mahanikaya tradition, organized around a single national center, Dhammakaya proposes in effect to recreate the old galactic polity model and thereby to restore a vivid and dynamic past to a fragmented Thai society and a political environment continually beset by corruption and factionalism, in which the symbolic power of the monarchy is waning and the practical power of religion is virtually nonexistent.[90] Departing from the practice of traditional Thai monastic centers (Thai *wat*), Dhammakaya actively recruits members and buses them to the thousand-acre headquarters near Bangkok for activities ranging from the celebration of major Buddhist holy days to the practice of meditation. It has been particularly aggressive in recruiting members from secondary schools and institutions of higher learning and has also been successful in building support among the military, government officials, and members of the royal family. Hence, its constituency comes from a wide range of youth, college-educated young adults, and leaders in the economic and political sectors. Thus, while Dhammakaya is not formally disassociated from the structure of Thai Buddhism, it represents a particular sectarian movement within it, with its unique forms of ordination, propagation of doctrine, practice, and leadership.

The movement's decision not to build other Dhammakaya wats throughout Thailand protects it from the charge of creating a new sectarian tradition. Regionally and locally, however, the movement has built and opened centers for lay meditation in over two-thirds of Thailand's provinces[91] and has made extensive use of the national network of schools at all levels, in particular, in post-secondary institutions. The Dhammakaya-sponsored "religious emphasis week" (*Thāng Kāw Nā,* The Way Forward) I attended in September of 1985, for example, was held on the campus of Chiang Mai University. Nearly two hundred volunteers from six universities throughout the country assisted in administering the book stalls, organizing *dhamma* examinations for schoolchildren, running audiovisual events, and supervising dramatic productions put on by elementary school groups from Chiang Mai and outlying districts.

Dhammakaya and the Renewal of Thai Buddhism as a Religious Institution

Within the context of a modern nation-state which has increasingly fragmented traditional forms of social and cultural identification, Dhammakaya has sought to create a visible focus for a new sense of national, religious, and personal identity—a sense of unity no longer effectively engendered by the tripartite symbol of "nation, religion, and king" coined by King Rama VI in the 1920's and represented by the three colors of the Thai national flag.

The singular importance of the Dhammakaya movement is especially evident at major festival and ceremonial occasions. Throughout the year, activities at Dhammakaya are attended by hundreds of thousands of the faithful. At three major holiday gatherings in particular—Visakha Puja, Makha Puja, and Thod Kathin—attendance exceeds fifty thousand, thus providing an actual experiential enactment of unity, identity, and purpose for a significant number of Thais. Visakha Puja (May) memorializes the birth, enlightenment, and death of the Buddha; Makha Puja (July) celebrates a miraculous assembling of 1,250 *arahants* (enlightened beings) at Veluvana monastery and the promulgation of the monastic rules or *paṭimokkha;* Thod Kathin (October) marks the end of the period of monastic retreat from mid-July to mid-October during the height of the monsoon rains. Let us examine how Visakha Puja is utilized by the Dhammakaya movement as means of renewing a sense of Thai Buddhist identity.

Visakha Puja celebrations at Dhammakaya feature a communal ritual central to the monastic-religious life of the movement: lifetime ordination. In traditional Thai Buddhist practice, only a small percentage of ordinands make the monkhood a lifetime vocation. The customary practice of temporary ordination, most often for a rain's retreat or a three-month period, traditionally symbolized the male passage into adulthood. Indeed, conventional wisdom held that until a young man was ordained, he was "unripe" and not a good marriage prospect. At the climax of the Dhammakaya's Visakha Puja celebration, however, a large contingent of young men make a lifetime commitment to the Buddhist Sangha. In the words of one ordinand, the ceremony holds a strong moral appeal and suggests a critique of the customary Thai Buddhist practice of temporary ordination:

> To give one's life as an offering to the Buddha is to be ordained for a lifetime in order that one may truly practice dhamma . . . It is a difficult thing to do, especially for the young men of today. It takes a great deal of courage, willingness to sacrifice, endurance, and an abundance of wisdom . . . It is difficult to find individuals of such matchless value. Before being ordained at Wat Dhammakaya one must train here for five years, observing the eight precepts the entire time. Those who sponsor ordinations must also dedicate themselves to a serious practice of the dhamma for this is an exceedingly meritorious and auspicious act.[92]

As the above quotation suggests, the Dhammakaya movement seeks to promote not only a renewed sense of unity but a seriousness of religious practice for both monk and laity. In addition to lifetime ordinations, the movement has developed a special category of temporary ordinations labeled "dhamma-heirs" (Thai *thammathāiyāt*). Although it might be argued that the movement had to compromise on its practice of lifetime ordinations in order to promote interest in the movement at this level, Dhammakaya literature describes *thammathāiyāt* ordination as an outgrowth of its summer training programs of two to four weeks which were begun in 1972. By 1979, a new option was made available to the dhamma-heir trainees. After one month they could be chosen to be ordained at one of Bangkok's most famous royal monasteries, Wat Benchamabophit (the Marble Temple), and then complete a second month at Wat Dhammakaya under a monk's discipline before leaving the order and returning to high school or university. The success of the program is indicated by the numbers, which grew from sixty in the first class to nearly one thousand in 1985.[93]

The Dhammakaya movement's practical emphasis on training in meditation and also in moral discipline is evidenced in its literature as well as many of its activities, especially its annual workshops (*Thāng Kāw Nā,* The Way Forward) conducted at schools in various parts of the country. Dhamma-heir practice is rigorous. Its major elements are strict observance of the eight precepts, living under the shade of an umbrella protected only by a mosquito net as practiced by *thudong* monks, listening to dhamma talks, and practicing meditation.[94] The movement's application of the term *thudong* (Pali *dhutaṅga*) to the lifestyle of the young men observing the dhamma-heir training regimen is instructive. The dhutaṅga discipline originally referred to an ascetic lifestyle which distinguished an eremitic practice from the more conventional communal forms of monastic life.[95] While the regimen of the thammathāiyāt monk is certainly more rigorous than that of most monks observing temporary ordination, the term *thudong* is symbolic rather than descriptive of the dhamma-heir trainee's lifestyle and functions to enhance the perceived value and significance of temporary ordination as practiced in the Dhammakaya movement.

The central features of the movement emphasize the qualities of unity, simplicity, and purity. Wat Dhammakaya at Pathum Thani stands at the center of a *Buddhacakka,* a sacred realm uniting all Thai Buddhists. It is at same time a *patipati-dhamma,* a place to practice the dhamma more authentically and seriously than it can be practiced in most ordinary Buddhist centers. The exemplary role is that of the monk who is ordained, not out of social convention, but for life. Yet the monk and the layperson walk the same path toward an enriched and more meaningful life. Even laypersons in the Dhammakaya movement have a special dress as a sign not only of the seriousness of their intent but also as an expression of the unity of all members of the movement where, as the Dhammakaya members put it, "the monastery is really the monastery, where monks are truly monks, and where people realize their fullest humanity." Thus Wat Dhammakaya renews a sense of Thailand as a moral community and of Thai Buddhism as the religious community at the heart of the Thai nation.

Praxis and Personal Identity

Wat Dhammakaya stands in the lineage of Wat Pak Nam Phasi Charoen in Thonburi, an old religious center and one of the 150 or so designated royal monasteries throughout the country, made famous in the contemporary period by its recently deceased abbot, the late Phra Mongkhon Thepmuni (Luang Pho Sot). The fame of Phra Mongkhon stems from his unique method of meditation which involves a visualization technique not unlike that associated with certain yogic or tantric forms of meditation. It is a relatively simple type of meditation practice, is reputed to produce extraordinary effects associated with *samatha* trance-producing forms of Buddhist meditation, and is easily taught to large groups of people. This form of meditation practice is the linchpin of the movement. It is included in all of the Wat Dhammakaya meetings, is described in most of its publications, and is the movement's most typical characteristic.

Meditation in the Dhammakaya movement plays several important roles. By providing for all members a common religious experience that has been held in highest esteem from the earliest days of the tradition, it has a practical, unifying effect. In that meditation has become a recognized part of lay religious life in contemporary Sri Lanka, Burma, and Thailand,[96] the Dhammakaya movement is capitalizing on an increasingly popular form of Buddhist practice that purports to make the quintessential experiences of the Buddhist life available to everyone. As a ground for a common Buddhist identity, the ecstatic value of meditation is celebrated in Dhammakaya books such as *Phuthathanaphāp* (The Power of the Buddha), which recounts miraculous visions and other types of paranormal events. The Dhammakaya movement associates meditation practice with the dhamma-heir training sessions, in particular through the use of the term *thudong*. This association adds an important symbolic dimension to the place of meditation in the movement. The thudong lifestyle on the well-groomed

Dhammakaya compound is a far cry from living in the mountainous jungles of northern Thailand, but the appropriation of the term helps to legitimate Dhammakaya's religious practices and also serves to emphasize the sense of specialness derived from the experience of being a dhamma-heir. In short, meditation, thudong, and dhammaheirship serve to engender a "liminal" ethos, a shared personal experience and feelings of uniqueness, authenticity, and authority which bond the movement together. The authoritarian ethos of the movement may be rooted as much in the personal, experiential basis of the central practice of the Dhammakaya movement as in its highly centralized organization.[97]

The following account provides a more detailed picture of the specific form of the Dhammakaya meditation technique:

> In a relaxed, well-controlled voice . . . the Abbot advises devotees, "lay all worldly cares and concerns to one side, assume the proper pose as comfortably as possible, close the eyes, and relax from all tension. There is to be no talking or whispering. All are to meditate at once. Now try to imagine at the center of your body, two inches above the level of the navel, this clear crystal ball, clear and pure, of fresh, transparent purity. Visualize it at the center of your gravity. If you cannot see the crystal, try a small Buddha image. If you cannot visualize the image, then simply focus concentration at the center of your being, as you silently repeat the mantra, *Samma arahang, samma arahang, samma arahang.*"
>
> Those who follow his directions frequently experience a giddy falling sensation. The meditation masters take this as evidence that the mind is descending to what they call the "seventh position of the mind." Also called the bodily center, it is that same point two inches above the level of the navel on which the meditator was directed to focus. The instructors urge that the falling sensation be allowed to continue until the mind falls to the center, where it will at last be capable of receiving a clear vision of the *pathommak,* a glowing crystal within the body that replaces the imagined one with which the meditation sitting began. The pathommak is said to be a vision of great beauty and clarity, producing a great coursing of joy, peace and strength when it appears.
>
> Continued concentration on the pathommak, which can be done sitting, walking, or even while teaching or performing daily duties, will allow one to proceed through a series of sheaths and images, culminating finally in a vision of the Dhammakaya itself. This Dhammakaya is said to have revealed its name directly to Luang Pho Sot when he first encountered it. . . . [He claimed] . . . that the vision of the Dhammakaya was . . . an encounter with the Buddha's eternal essence. . . . Continued meditation on the Dhammakaya, said the Luang Pho, would enable one to attain Nirvana.[98]

The parallel between Wat Dhammakaya's unique method of meditation and its self-conscious construction of Pathum Thani as a Buddhacakka, or Buddha realm, serves to reenforce the interpretation of Wat Dhammakaya as a fundamentalistic movement which addresses the problematic of a threatened personal, communal, and national identity. Circumambulating the main image hall with thousands of adherents holding candles and incense, silently chanting the three refuges, or sitting under a thudong umbrella while visualizing a glowing crystal together with 150 other dhamma-heir trainees are different ways of experiencing the same reality—the Buddha realm or the body of dhamma *(dhammakaya)*, or in less philosophical terms, one's deepest identity as a Thai Buddhist.

Ideology, Organization and Mission of Wat Dhammakaya

One might argue that Wat Dhammakaya's emphasis on practice—whether it be participation in major celebrations, participating in dhamma-heir training sessions, or meditating—does not require a supporting ideology; indeed the movement has not yet developed a nuanced philosophical analysis of the world based on a wide range of Buddhist texts or even a sophisticated apologetic. Instead, its basic teachings are relatively simple and primarily ethical in nature. The Dhammakaya literature does not engage in debates about the nature of the Buddha or the meaning of kamma. Rather, it tends to highlight personal testimonials or, as in the case of the Dhammakaya publication *Mongkhon Chīwit,* advocates a personal moral code or a path of moral and spiritual development.

The Dhammakaya movement, moreover, is not fully consistent with the reform Buddhism associated with Mongkut's founding of the Thammayut order in the mid-nineteenth century and the further development of the tradition under Chulalongkorn and Vajiranana. This order advocated a stricter form of monastic discipline[99] and a reinterpretation of the traditional Buddhist worldview which de-emphasized (or rejected) the classical Buddhist cosmologies of multiple heavens and hells, legends, and the historicity of the Buddha's miracles.[100] Reform Buddhism also bore a concern for canonical orthodoxy rooted in the study of Pali and the canonical texts of Theravada Buddhism.[101] While this reformist mindset had been characteristic of the educated urban elites in particular, by the 1970s it had permeated into rural areas.[102]

The Dhammakaya movement's worldview demythologizes the traditional cosmological structure of classical Thai Buddhism,[103] but it lacks the erudition of the earlier reform tradition. The Dhammakaya worldview is also highly simplistic relative to the sophisticated and sometimes controversial interpretations of various brilliant contemporary reformers—monastic intellectuals such as Buddhadasa Bhikkhu or scholars such as Phra Depvedi (Prayutto).[104] The movement, furthermore, is certainly not "scripturalist" in the sense of the Thammayut reform of King Mongkut.[105] The monastic leaders in the Dhammakaya movement are students neither of Pali nor of the Pali scriptures and its commentaries, nor are they educators in any substantial sense. Yet Dhammakaya is "scripturalist" in the sense that it has reinterpreted for popular use the *Maṅgala Sutta,* a text hallowed by traditions of Theravada thought and practice and associated with the name of the spiritual founder of the movement, Phra Monkhon (Pali *maṅgala*) Thepmuni. In short, the movement does not reflect the intellectual richness of late nineteenth- and early-twentieth-century reformist Thai Buddhism.

In its focus on moral and ethical concerns, the Dhammakaya movement seems primarily concerned with conservative issues of personal morality. Sulak Sivaraksa, the liberal social critic, addresses what he considers to be systemic illnesses in Thai society and in so doing creatively applies traditional Theravada concepts to persistent and pervasive social, economic, and political problems.[106] By way of contrast, Dhammakaya's personalistic view of the world is espoused in authoritarian language with a clear and simple message: there is a correct way of religious practice, a correct way of acting, and that is the Dhammakaya way. There is, in other words, little ambiguity in the Dhammakaya worldview, and it is a worldview to be adopted by every Buddhist.

At the moment, the most widely used instructional text in the movement is a book entitled *Mongkhon Chīwit* (The Auspicious Life). Officially its publication was sponsored by the Buddhist Student Associations at nine post-secondary educational institutions, including Thailand's two most distinguished universities, Chulalongkorn and Thammasat. *Mongkhon Chīwit* borrows its title from a famous Pali text, the *Maṅgala Sutta,* chanted on auspicious occasions as part of the *paritta* or "protection," suttas (Sanskrit, sutras) central to Theravada merit-making rituals. The title evokes the name of Phra Mongkhon Thepmuni, the spiritual father of the movement, and while the text reflects the ethical orientation of the *Maṅgala Sutta,* it reads like an ethics primer similar to the Ministry of Education's *sīla* (ethics) curriculum. A translation of part of the introduction of the *Mongkhon Chīwit* indicates its place in the movement.

> In Thailand Buddhism is the national religion. More than 90 percent of our people are Buddhists, but their knowledge of Buddhism for the most part was learned while they were in school and is at the most elementary level. It reflects very little serious study and reflection. Most people do not understand the dhamma at any depth, having merely memorized a few passages to repeat parrotlike on an examination. They are unable to integrate the dhamma into their daily lives. . . . Because of this situation groups of undergraduates with the support of their professors and others who recognized the importance of the practice of the dhamma joined together to form Buddhist associations in various institutions to be centers for the study, correct understanding, and propagation of the teachings of Buddhism.
>
> As part of their activities and consistent with their purpose, the Buddhist associations of these institutions of higher education then joined together for dhamma-heir training during the summer months at Wat Dhammakaya to enable students to deepen their understanding of the dhamma through rigorous and disciplined study *(pariyatti)* and practice *(paṭipatti)*. This involved meditation practice, listening to lectures on the dhamma, and in particular, the study of the *Maṅgala Sutta*.
>
> The Buddha taught the thirty-eight levels of dhamma practice in the *Maṅgala Sutta* for the progress and happiness of the world. They are simple enough to read but difficult to put into practice. . . . Those who truly put into practice the steps of the *Maṅgala Sutta* will improve their lives whether they be layperson or monk. Indeed, following them leads to the very highest level of Buddhism.[107]

Mongkhon Chīwit reflects the central features of the Dhammakaya movement: a simple, ethical message or ideology which bypasses both the mythic-cosmological and the more complex philosophical aspects of the Theravada Buddhist tradition; a simplified text necessitated by the general lack of knowledge of the Buddhist population of Thailand, but which is associated with the most distinctive mode of training of the Dhammakaya movement; and a comprehensive teaching applicable to layperson and monk, conducive both to moral well-being and the highest spiritual attainment.

The introduction to *Mongkhon Chīwit* contends that these are times of confusion and protest, times in which young people do not know who to believe or who to follow, times when "anyone who has a following can become a teacher."[108] The introduction then goes on to reject this kind of relativism, a view which claims that anything can be valuable or auspicious (*mongkhon*), and the corollary that there is really nothing enduring and certain. The Buddha's teaching is an essential truth, eternally valuable and auspicious, which when followed will lead to certain consequences. It cannot be explained away or challenged. What the thirty-eight teachings of the *Mongkhon Chīwit* provide, contends the author, is a standard and guide for life in an age of relativism, competing voices, and confusion.[109] The list of thirty-eight precepts is perceived as an accelerated course in moral and spiritual training, beginning with general ethical admonitions, advancing to specific ethical precepts and moral virtues, and concluding with a spiritual condition associated with the monastic life. The *Mongkhon Chīwit* thus affirms on an ideological level the sense of unity and identity, expressed by the Pathum Thani center as the Buddhacakka, and the meditation practice at the core of dhamma-heir training, expressed as the realization of the dhammakaya.[110]

Although *Monkhon Chīwit* is specifically targeted to a youthful audience, the two sermons I heard by Thatthchiwo, the assistant abbot of Wat Dhammakaya, were not dissimilar either in style or content from the text. He began an evening talk at the Chiang Mai University meeting, attended by about two hundred adults and students, with a reference to Sri Mangala Acariya, the Thai author of the famed Pali commentary on the *Maṅgala Sutta,* claiming that his remarks would be an amplification of that text in an effort to make it relevant to everyday life. Thattachiwo is obviously an adept public speaker, but what began as a somewhat informal engagement with his audience soon evolved into a formal, conventional, and authoritatively delivered sermon. The monk spoke of the "valuable life" in terms of a hierarchy of authority—the Buddha, monks, parents, teachers, in that order. He stressed the importance of the right kind of role models, cautioning, on the one hand, that outward appearances can be deceiving: "A handsome or beautiful person on the outside can, after all, be bad on the inside." He urged his audience to look for a true pandit (*paṇḍita,* a teacher, a wise man, or a scholar). Being a paṇḍita does not depend on academic degrees, he contended, but knowing the difference between right and wrong, good and evil. A person who is disciplined, who speaks the truth, and who leads people to the good is a paṇḍita and should be honored in heart, word, and deed.[111]

The Dhammakaya movement has launched an aggressive campaign to revitalize Thai Buddhism and eventually to establish Dhammakaya centers in other parts of the world. In September of 1985 I interviewed a former medical doctor and graduate from Chulalongkorn University who hoped to establish a Dhammakaya center in Japan. Currently a Dhammakaya monk is studying in England with plans to establish a center there, and the Thai wat outside of Philadelphia represents the Dhammakaya teachings and practice. Interviews and the movement's literature verify that Wat Dhammakaya projects an international image based in Thailand but with the hope of revitalizing Buddhism around the world.

Wat Dhammakaya is formally a monastery within the *mahānikāya* tradition of Thai Buddhism and is thereby under the authority of the Supreme Sangha Council *(mahātherasamakhom)*. As we have seen from the preceding description, however, it has established a de facto sect of its own with only one national *wat,* allied meditation centers in over two-thirds of the provinces in the country, a network of programs conducted in post-secondary schools, and an international vision. It is, in other words, a large, efficiently run, and well-financed organization. According to Dr. Prawes Wasi, Wat Dhammakaya has a monthly budget of approximately $600,000: "Wat Dhammakaya is organized like an army which requires a large budget and a strict obedience to command."[112]

Unlike the conventional Thai monastic order, the monks of the Dhammakaya movement are university educated. In the Sangha at large, monks who have attained positions of leadership at the provincial and regional levels have been educated through the monastic system. They have had varying degrees of training in Pali and traditional subjects of Buddhist studies but a very limited secular education. By way of contrast, the great majority of monks in the Dhammakaya movement have dedicated their lives to the monastic life after post-secondary education. This means that Dhammakaya monks are much better educated in secular subjects but lack background in Pali and traditional Buddhist studies.

The two most important leaders of the movement are the abbot, Phra Thammachayo, and the assistant abbot, Phra Thattachiwo. Both are powerful speakers, compelling personalities, and radiate charisma. One trainee described Thammachayo as follows:

> His carriage was magnificent, his complexion clear, clean, and radiantly glowing beneath the yellow robe. The attractiveness of his appearance . . . caused me to be filled with such joy that tears flowed without my realizing it. That picture will surely remain firmly in my heart and and mind as long as I live. Immediately I thought of a *thammathāiyāt* student who had told me how startled he had been when first laying eyes on Luang Po Thammachayo. He had wondered, "So this is the Luang Po? Could he really be human? Why does his skin shine so?" And now I had seen it with my own eyes. Truly it was a thing of great merit for me.[113]

Similar hyperbolic testimony is found in Takkasarano Bhikkhu's account of his journey to a new life as a Wat Dhammakaya monk.[114] Both Thammachayo and Thattachiwo provide an exemplary focus of belief and practice for their fellow monks and for lay people as well. Within the Thai context, they embody the power or charisma of the man of merit, "a visual presentation capable of being communicated in the mere act of sitting or walking."[115]

The Dhammakaya movement assumes a fundamentalistic cast in that its proposed revitalization of Thai Buddhism is based on a blueprint for society tied to its particular religious worldview. The immediate religious context is the relatively moribund state of Thai Buddhism,[116] weakened internally by a lack of strong, dynamic leadership, hampered by concerns of hierarchy and status, preoccupied with performances of ritual and ceremony, its distinctive voice stifled by the government. The traditional roles of the Buddhist monk have in many cases been assumed by public and private agencies, particularly in the field of education.[117]

In response to this weakening of Buddhism, Dhammakaya has reduced the earlier reforms in monastic education, Sangha organization, and Buddhist ritual into a simplified religious practice and moralistic ideology under a highly organized, authoritative, and authoritarian religious structure dominated by two charismatic leaders. Emphasizing uniformity of both thought and practice (including the dress worn to religious events), the movement promotes a distinctive sense of Thai Buddhist identity associated with the attainment of this-worldly goals, success and well-being, experienced vividly by members who participate in major celebrations at Wat Dhammakaya and in the practice of the Dhammakaya form of meditation.

The Dhammakaya movement thus appears fundamentalistic on the basis of its selective retrieval of the past; its programs for religious renewal, conceived by an aggressive and charismatic leadership; its propagandistic, simplistic, and moralistic ideology and emphasis on experience over reason; its centralization of organization and activities; its inspiration in an explicit and implicit criticism of the Thai monastic order; and its political alliances with government figures and policies designed to enforce a nationalistic ethos inseparable from this ideological Buddhism.

Dhammakaya has openly advocated the institutionalization and cultural spread of Buddhist civil religion by political and, sometimes, hard-sell means and has supported government efforts to promote national unity through Buddhist mission programs to the hill tribes and development programs in the northeast.[118] The movement has also been associated with the controversial right-wing monk, Phra Kitthivuddho, the founder of a semi-independent, militant movement centered at Cittabhavana College on Thailand's eastern coast.[119] In the politically volatile mid-1970s, Kitthivuddho actively supported the Village Scouts Movement, a group designed by the government to promote national unity during a time of fractious national debate. Moreover, as a supporter of the militant, reactionary political group known as the "Red Guards," he helped to organize against student and labor activists and authored a pamphlet outlining a Buddhist justification for killing communists (being "less than human," communists were not included in the prohibition against killing sentient beings).[120] Dhammakaya also endorses the civil religion values of the *Phan Din Thamma, Phan Din Thong* (Land of dhamma, land of gold) program created by the government in 1986. As the name implies it signifies national unity, economic prosperity (land of gold), and Buddhism (land of dhamma).

Wat Dhammakaya, however, is more than a group encouraged by the political power structure to promote loyalty to the central government. Its broad-based popular support stems from an astute packaging of a fundamentalistic form of Thai Buddhism that offers a way of embracing a secularized modern lifestyle while retaining the communal identity once offered by traditional Buddhism—all the while maintaining that it is "authentic" or "true" Buddhism, in contrast to its competitors. Indeed, Wat Dhammakaya has been compared to fundamentalistic born-again Christianity because of its skillful use of the media, its lavish productions at its Pathum Thani headquarters, and its emphasis on ecstatic meditative experience as the binding force of communal identity.[121]

Wat Dhammakaya has been criticized for its strong support from political and military elites, offered, presumably, because the movement has gained a sufficient standing to lend religious legitimacy to political, economic, and social status. General Arthit Kamlengek, for example, the commander in chief of the army from 1982 to 1985, was featured prominently in Wat Dhammakaya publications for his support of the movement. The movement has also been attacked for its excessive affluence (spiritual consumerism), its aggressive methods of fund-raising, and its promotion of a method of meditation which has traditionally been suspect within the Theravada tradition.

Thus, although Dhammakaya has been the fastest-growing religious movement in Thailand today, with upwards of a million adherents, critics contend that the movement has peaked, because it has compromised its spiritual ideals with business and economic interests.[122]

Santi Asoka

The Santi Asoka movement, or People of Asoka (Thai *Chao Asok*), may strike the casual observer as the mirror opposite of Wat Dhammakaya. Its centers in Bangkok, Nakorn Pathom, Sisaket, and Nakorn Sawan are simple, austere places, devoid of the comfortable affluence of Dhammakaya. Its Visakha Puja and Makha Puja celebrations on the outskirts of Bangkok attract between five and ten thousand devotees instead of the fifty or sixty thousand pilgrims who journey to Pathum Thani. While Dhammakaya has remained a monastery in good standing with the Mahanikaya tradition, Santi Asoka declared itself independent of the national Sangha hierarchy. In fact, the Santi Asoka monks were recently defrocked by the government. Although the governor of Bangkok has been an active member of Santi Asoka, high-ranking government and military officials and royalty are notably absent from their larger gatherings. Indeed, its support comes largely from a middle-class constituency.

Santi Asoka also differs from Wat Dhammakaya in the extreme degree with which it attacks conventional social ills such as prostitution and violence and in its advocacy of an extraordinarily high standard of personal discipline and moral virtue (e.g., vegetarianism and the rejection not only of alcohol but also of stimulants such as coffee and tea). While Dhammakaya's ideology is moralistic, its moral code is more in line with conventional Thai behavior. Santi Asoka has also gone much further in rejecting both contemporary Thai religious practice and social mores than has Wat Dhammakaya. While Dhammakaya has developed its own distinctive religious ethos, represented by a trademark image of the Buddha, Santi Asoka has altogether banned images of the Buddha from its assembly halls. Since one of the crucial features of most popular Buddhist ceremonies is a specially consecrated Buddha image, its elimination signifies a radical transformation of the meaning of Buddhist rituals. In essence, the Santi Asoka movement rejects what its considers to be the magical, superstitious, superficial, and meaningless aspects of ritual. Thus, the People of Asoka do not believe in the efficacy of Buddha images or amulets, and Santi Asoka monks do not offer holy water to the laity. The Asoka movement strives to strip away the "chaff" and return to the "fundamentals" or essence of Buddhism, a moral and religious transformation which does not rely upon, and rejects as superfluous, the usual magical and merit-making rituals.

Despite these differences, however, Santi Asoka and Dhammakaya both represent resurgent forms of fundamentalistic religion. Each movement has replaced the ethos of conventional Thai Buddhism with its own, associated with a particular center; each has developed a distinctive ideology and religious practice; each is led by strong, charismatic figures; each has gained national prominence within the past decade; and each has strong supporters and equally strong detractors. In particular, they both appear as efforts to create a new moral and religious environment designed to restore the integrity of national, community, and personal identity over against non-Buddhist and morally corrupted Buddhist influences.

Moreover, unlike Dhammakaya, which has fashioned a fundamentalistic ethos for the Thai Buddhist mainstream, the Santi Asoka movement has designed a sectarian fundamentalism for the few. While both movements reflect modern Thai reformism's ethical orientation, Santi Asoka is more radical in its criticism of Thai society and in the details of its own vision of what constitutes a truly religiomoral community. The Dhammakaya movement can be characterized as a fundamentalist extension of the Thai Buddhist nationalism fashioned in the 1920s and 1930s, while Santi Asoka is rather a transformation of the "forest monk" revival from the same period, as represented by the Acharn Man tradition and more particularly by Bhikkhu Buddhadasa's center, Wat Suan Mok, in southern Thailand.[123] From its early days the Buddhist tradition has been associated with renunciation of the householder life and the pursuit of monastic training in centers removed from towns and cities. In the Theravada tradition a distinction emerged between "town" monasteries, in which the principal activity was study and teaching, and "forest" monasteries, where monks pursued the practice of meditation. Although forest monks have had a somewhat ambiguous position in the Theravada tradition, in ideal terms the forest monk tradition has been perceived as being closer to the monastic environment of early Buddhism and therefore more authentic. It is not surprising, therefore, that Theravada revival movements in the late nineteenth and early twentieth centuries included forest monk groups in Sri Lanka, Burma, and Thailand.[124]

Phra Bodhiraksa, Charismatic Founder of Santi Asoka

Phra Bodhiraksa was born on 5 June 1934 in Sisaket, northeastern Thailand, as Monkol Rakpong; he later changed his name to Rak Rakpong. He lived with his uncle in Nongkai and Sakonnakorn, finishing his primary schooling in Ubonrajathani and senior high in Bangkok before pursuing further studies in the fine arts.[125] As a youth, Rak had to work at odd jobs to support himself, primarily as a food and charcoal vendor. As a student in Bangkok he sold newspapers, but he also liked music and composed songs. This led him to a professional life in music and entertainment, and he eventually achieved success as a movie producer, TV host, and songwriter. He was able to live a comfortable life, owning his own home and automobile, buying expensive clothes, and enjoying life with a generally affluent group of friends. However, at age thirty-six, at the peak of his career, he made an abrupt change in lifestyle. He gave his house and most of his belongings to family and friends, dressed in short pants and a white T-shirt, and walked barefoot. Finally he resigned from his job, feeling that he was then "free from any form."[126]

Several striking elements emerge from Bodhiraksa's discussion of this conversion. Although it did not come about all at once, there was a decisive, revelatory experience: "At two o'clock in the morning of Tuesday 27 January 1970 (2513 B.E. [Buddhist Era]) I woke up and walked from my bedroom into the bathroom to relieve myself. Suddenly a brilliant flash occurred within me—a brightness, openness, and detachment which could not be explained in human terms. I knew only that my life opened before me and that the whole world seemed to be revealed. I knew at that moment that I had no more doubts."[127]

Bodhiraksa's conversion gave him an authority derived from experience rather than from books. When someone asked him why he became a monk, he replied, "I was ordained a monk because I have attained the dhamma, and I have continued to answer the question in this way."[128] Bodhiraksa believed that he had experienced the truth of the Buddha's teaching, a belief by which he justifies his unique interpretations of Buddhist scriptures. Bodhiraksa's revelatory experience prior to being ordained a monk also led him to a conception of the true monk or true religious person as an *ariya,* or worthy disciple of the Buddha, which in the most profound sense transcends the distinction between monk and layperson. He said of himself, "I have practiced dhamma since I was a layman. I was a real monk when I was a layman even though I wasn't ordained."[129] Being an ariya, he contends, puts one in a privileged position from which to criticize the religious practice of others. Beyond that, however, attainment of the highest level of dhamma gives such persons a responsibility to speak out strongly on behalf of the truth. Bodhiraksa believes that those who have gained the ariyadhamma should act on the basis of their own knowledge and experience, and that contemporary Thai Buddhism is like a "blank religion" because this kind of testimony is prohibited by the Thai Sangha hierarchy.[130]

> I am a person who talks straight, strong, loud, and openly. I want people to wake up, to understand and thereby to reap the benefit of my teaching. Such a strong approach doesn't just hit one person, but a thousand. I'm not a babysitter who rocks the cradle and lulls people to sleep![131]

> I have to attack guilty people because they're guilty. I have a duty to correct, and to transmit the truth of the Buddha. I will plant righteousness until I die

or run out of energy. . . . I attack evil because most monks don't have the courage to do so. . . . When I speak the truth I take risks, risks arising from the defilements of laymen and monks.[132]

I have in myself a splendid virtue, like having ten precious jewels. The problem with the world today is that they can't recognize a jewel. When I show people jewels it disturbs them. I try to reveal the truth gradually, i.e., *sīla, samādhi, paññā* [virtue, concentration, wisdom] but people don't understand. I have been trying gradually to reveal the truth, and to assure people that I am an *ariya sotāpanna* [stream enterer] and *ariya sakadāgāmin* [once returner]. Unfortunately, people think I am boasting and criticize me.[133]

Shortly after Bodhiraksa had his experience of ariyadhamma, he was permitted by the abbot of a noted Thammayut monastery in Bangkok, Wat Asokaram, to build a simple cottage within the monastery compound. Later, on 7 November 1970, he was ordained a Thammayut monk. From the beginning, his monastic career was marked with controversy. Rather than spending time performing traditional monastic chants, he preferred to engage in lively talks about the dhamma. Although some of the senior monks objected to his critical, acerbic style, he gained a following at Wat Asokaram and at Wat Mahadhatu, a major mahānikāya monastery. Referring to his followers as the "Asoka group," he established a center outside of Nakorn Pathom which he called Asoka's Land (Thai Dan Asok) where lay people and monks, both Thammayut and Mahanikaya, could practice the dhamma together. His Thammayut preceptor strongly objected to Bodhiraksa's project and demanded that he resign his Thammayut membership by turning in his official monastic identification card (Thai *bai suthi*). Bodhiraksa's solution to this problem was to be reordained in the Mahanikaya order in 1973. Dan Asok continued to be a bone of contention at the national Sangha level, however. The Supreme Sangha Council ordered Bodhiraksa to tear down the cottages at Dan Asok and to cease his activities there and ordered the monks of the Asoka group to wear the traditional saffron monastic robe rather than the dark brown color they had adopted. Bodhiraksa and his followers refused and on 6 August 1975 decided to cut all ties to the national sangha orders.[134] From that time the People of Asok have been an independent Buddhist sect, or as some might characterize them, an independent utopian community within the Thai body politic.[135]

Santi Asoka As Communitas

Santi Asoka's most distinctive feature is the creation and development of centers of both lay and monastic residence and religious practice. The movement's reputation is based on its adherence to a strict moral code characterized in particular by vegetarianism. It has also developed an ideology to justify or rationalize the creation of the "communitas" centers and their lifestyles.[136]

Several organizations fall under the rubric of Santi Asoka. Three *phutasathans* (Buddha centers) were founded in 1976 (Santi Asoka in Bangkok, Sri Asok in Srisaket, and Sali Asok in Nakorn Sawan), and one in 1980 (Pathom Asok in Nakorn Pathom). In addition, there is the Dhammasanti Foundation (1977), which handles the hundreds of Santi Asok publications; the K'ngtap Tham Mūnniti (Dhamma Army Foundation), of which General Chamlong Srimuang, the current governor of Bangkok, has been the president; and the Samakhom Pupatibat Tham (Dhamma Practitioner Association), with over ten thousand members (founded in 1984). While this number is probably an accurate assessment of the hard-core membership of Santi Asoka, estimates of peripheral members of the movement range up to one hundred thousand.[137] Santi Asoka is quite small in comparison to Wat Dhammakaya, but given the dedication of its members, its numbers are certainly not inconsequential. Recent government repression of Santi Asoka monks has inhibited the growth of the movement, however.

Bodhiraksa is exceptionally outspoken in his social criticism. This critical stance toward Thai society and the mainstream Buddhist establishment is an element in the movement's sense of liminal identity. Santi Asoka literature details the ills which it believes pervade Thai society, particularly its materialistic hedonism. It has launched a vociferous attack on the use of alcohol, drugs, and cigarettes as part of the general pursuit of sensual pleasure and indulgence. The traditional five precepts or training rules *(sikkhā)* at the foundation of Theravada ethics aim at the restraint of self-gratifying behavior, e.g., drunkenness, theft, and adultery, destructive to the social good. In practice, however, the Thai moral ethos has been characterized by a relativistic and nonjudgmental stance toward violations of this code. In contrast, Santi Asoka's uncompromising stand against drinking, smoking, gambling, prostitution, and the dissemination of a hedonistic ethos via cinema and television represents an assertion of ideal Buddhist moral values in a social environment the movement judges to be immoral.

In response to what they perceive as the milieu of excess and materialism passively accepted by their fellow Buddhists, the adherents of Santi Asoka have developed an ethical system which is considerably more exacting than one based on a mere repetition of traditional Buddhist moral values. Furthermore, the moral criticisms made by the People of Asoka extend beyond standards of personal and social behavior. The espousal of vegetarianism is defended on the grounds of precedent in early Buddhist practice, as a means of addressing the problems of malnutrition in keeping with a strong sense of non-killing or nonviolence *(ahiṁsā)*. The title of a Santi Asoka pamphlet on vegetarianism is entitled, "Vegetarianism: Eliminating Meat Consumption Reduces Vice *(pāpa)* and Builds Virtue *(puñña)*." The picture on the cover shows Sujata offering rice gruel to the Buddha on the day of his enlightenment, not only suggesting that the Buddha was a vegetarian but making a connection between vegetarianism and enlightenment. The following quotation from the pamphlet will provide an example of the style of Santi Asoka's argumentation:

> Where has all the food gone? Thailand considers itself to be a major agricultural power because it exports grain, a claim only one in six countries can make. Every year it exports hundreds of thousands of tons of grain. But, despite our apparent agricultural prosperity, a recent study of the Food Research Institute of Mahidol University reports that more than 66,000 children under six years

> of age died of malnutrition, and that another 420,000 people in the country are undernourished. . . . We know that raising meat is one of the principal causes of food shortages in various parts of the world. . . . Meat consumption not only exploits animals, it exploits people as well—especially the weak—with disastrous consequences.[138]

Santi Asoka also attacks violence and exploitation in films, television, and the media in general, and even criticizes violence in competitive sports, in particular the viciousness in Thai boxing. The movement advocates a simple, noncompetitive lifestyle, depicted as a counterforce and a challenge to Thailand's consumerism and appropriation of Western capitalistic materialism.

Those the People of Asoka consider enemies include the Thai monastic order, which they criticize for abrogating its role of moral and religious leadership in Thai society and conventional Thai Buddhist practice, which they chide for its superficiality. The movement's publications continually make a moral distinction between "outer covering" and "inner core," or appearance and essence.[139] Everyone, monk and layperson alike, should strive to realize the highest moral and spiritual ideals taught by the Buddha. In this sense no essential distinction exists between monk and laity.

> A true monk is the good person, one who has realized his or her highest moral potential. In other words, it is a religious person in the deepest or truest sense. Being a monk doesn't depend on having a shaved head, wearing yellow robes, or whether one has gone through an ordination ceremony. A monk is one who has fully realized the five virtues *(sīla)* and who has overcome the fires of attachment. . . . A person who has been ordained a monk is not morally pure unless he has fully developed the five virtues. Just to become a monk without this kind of attainment is like play-acting. It's not for real. The real monk, the real stream enterer *(sotapanna)* is one who has attained the essence or core of the five *sīla*.One doesn't have to be ordained for that. . . . This is what it means to be an *ariya* [i.e., one who is truly worthy], a disciple of the Buddha.[140]

One important consequence of Santi Asoka's critical view of the model of Thai society promoted by the monastic order is the elimination of social distinctions (between monk and layperson, for example), status distinctions, and gender distinctions. The Asoka community reflects this leveling, even though it has developed its own hierarchy, which depends on a distinctive moral or disciplinary calculus. Male and female lay practitioners may follow either five or eight precepts, a typical distinction within Thai Buddhism. Female monks or *sikkhāmāt* follow the ten-precept pattern of the male novice, and the monk who has received full ordination subscribes to the usual 227 *patimokkha* rules. These distinctions are standard in Theravada practice. What distinguishes Wat Santi Asoka, however, is the self-conscious sense of moral progress indicated by moving up the ladder of training rules. In particular, prior to ordination the candidate may have to observe a probationary period of one to two years.[141] While such distinctions in the Asoka community are calculated according to training rules or levels of moral and spiritual seriousness and attainment, the community remains, in contrast to the conventional Thai social order, a single moral "communitas" of male and female monks and laypersons.

The community at Nakorn Pathom mentioned at the beginning of this section may reflect the founder's vision of a "primitive" Buddhist community, or a Buddhist *sangha* in an ideal sense, but its historical precedent is obscure, and it is certainly at odds with the usual Thai Buddhist view. In conventional Buddhist practice there are no female nuns;[142] there are definite distinctions between monk and laity and, for the most part, we find an unself-conscious cultural acceptance of Buddhism as the religion of one's birth and culture. By setting an example for monk and layperson alike to follow, the People of Asoka intend to repudiate this "superficial" sense of what it means to be a Thai Buddhist and to pose a constant and vigorous challenge to all Buddhists to follow their faith with the utmost moral earnestness rather than with the complacency of simple custom. To be a Buddhist in this sense means to live a unique lifestyle, different from both conventional Thai social and monastic life.

Thus Santi Asoka not only rejects traditional Thai Buddhism but also attempts to transform the tradition into its own ethical model. An excellent example of this transformation is Phra Bodhiraksa's reinterpretation of the ceremony for the consecration of Buddha amulets *(pluk saek phra)*. In the Santi Asoka movement, the ceremony involves gathering a group of lay disciples and monks together for an intensive training session and has nothing to do with the conventional magical, protective properties associated with wearing an amulet. During the retreat, everyone is required to follow a strict set of rules governing all aspects of personal behavior and group interaction. Unlike Dhammakaya, which aims to restore the traditional ideals of Thai Buddhist identity, Santi Asoka deems this impossible without a prior radical transformation of Thai belief and practice. The movement's detractors fear that this is equivalent to the virtual abandonment of the historical tradition.

Santi Asoka and Politics

In contrast to the Dhammakaya movement, Santi Asoka chose a role as a religious, social, and cultural critic on the periphery of the mainstream that would appear to make it apolitical in any practical sense. A politically significant aspect of Santi Asoka's development, however, has been the involvement of Chamlong Srimuang, a retired army major general and currently the governor of Bangkok. He provides the movement with a direct political influence that it otherwise might not have had, even though the People of Asoka have criticized corruption in all levels of Thai society, including politics.

Chamlong's rise to power reflects three recent developments in Thai politics: a growing desire, especially among the urban middle class, for a "clean" political leader; the hope of a small but significant number of politically oriented people for a party promising meaningful participation in politics; and the electoral legitimation of former military leaders on their way to higher office, especially that of prime minister.[143] Chamlong symbolizes not only the prospect of clean politics in Thailand's capital city but also a restoration of a primitive Buddhist communitas and the recovery of a Thai personal, social, and national identity unbesmirched by corruption and party politics. This communitas is represented by the Santi Asoka communities themselves.

Chamlong was elected by a two-to-one margin in 1985, running on a "clean government" program as a candidate of his newly launched Phalang Dhamma (Moral Force) Party. In the Bangkok election for governor and city assembly held on 7 January 1990, Chamlong was overwhelmingly re-elected despite a campaign to discredit his personal integrity as well as a strong attack on his political competence. Of the 3,201,188 eligible voters, 1,147,576, or 35.85 percent turned out to vote. Chamlong won 703,671 votes, compared to 283,777 for the Prachakorn Thai party candidate and a modest 86,676 votes for the candidate fielded by the Democrat and Muang Chon parties.[144] Compared to his 49 percent victory in 1985, Chamlong won reelection by a 66 percent margin. Perhaps even more striking is the fact that in 1985 the Phalang Dhamma Party won only nine seats in the city assembly, while in 1989 it took fifty out of fifty-seven.[145]

Political analysts have pointed to several possible reasons for Chamlong's resounding victory. In the months prior to the election, a battle between Chamlong and the interior minister Pramarn Adiriksar, who wields a great deal of power over the policies of the Bangkok city government, abetted the voter's view of Chamlong as an independent man of the people. During the same period, charges of widespread corruption in the government of Prime Minister Chatchai Choonhavan served to heighten the public perception of Chamlong as "Mr. Clean," and to discredit his opponents, all of whom are associated with national political parties.[146] Finally, even though prior to the January 1990 election the Santi Asoka movement had come under public attack, the governor's simple, religiously grounded lifestyle appealed to Bangkok voters, many of whom find themselves excluded from, or on the periphery of, Thailand's booming economy. Like Bodhiraksa, Chamlong is a strong, outspoken, charismatic leader whose ascetic, Buddhist lifestyle has attracted a core of followers and earned him the respect of a growing number of voters.[147] The media have made Chamlong's private life his public persona by fostering a mystique around his lifestyle (a vegetarian, he lives in an old garment factory with little furniture and sleeps on a mat; he and his wife observe the eight Buddhist precepts, including abstinence from alcohol and sex). His physical trademark is the wearing of a traditional collarless, dark-blue peasant work shirt *(mohom):* "I try to wear a mohom everywhere, almost everyday because it warns me that our country is not rich. I think that wearing a shirt like this (he points to my shirt and tie) is more beautiful than wearing a mohom. So, I have to control myself to overcome my desire."[148] The mohom symbolizes Chomlong's unpretentious lifestyle, his identification with the common people, and his ascetic-religious orientation. In his autobiography, *Chīwit Chamlong (Chamlong's life),* published on 1 January 1990, Chamlong portrays himself as a man without personal ambition who has been willing to assume a role of political leadership out of necessity:

> I got something I had never wanted in 1985; I was elected governor. I took it because I thought it was necessary and it was my responsibility. Many strongly believe that I'm ambitious and want to be bigger than I am now. Whatever I

do seems to be promoting myself. . . . No one will believe that if I had the freedom to make my own choice, I would want to retreat to being "Chamlong" living in a 7×12 hut enjoying nature and practising Dhamma to curb my worldly desires. I have no future.[149]

As a Santi Asoka member, Chamlong's vegetarian diet symbolizes personal discipline, sincerity, and integrity. Unlike Bodhiraksa, however, Chamlong does not allow his vegetarianism and other personal moral disciplines to serve as a barrier to outsiders. His success as a politician has been won with a ready smile and a gentle sense of humor. Wearing a peasant shirt and sandals, he recently entertained an audience of four hundred listeners with a forty-five-minute talk that included such comments as: "Last year, I won the 400 meter race at the National Stadium. I'm not 35, I'm 53. Why did I win? . . . Because I eat soybeans everyday. When I was in Egypt I climbed to the top of the pyramids. I don't eat meat, I eat only one meal a day. . . . But my meat-eating Egyptian guides were afraid to follow me because they might not have made it back down . . . . Call me an advertisement for soybeans!"[150]

The ideology of the Phalang Dhamma Party reflects the ideals of the Santi Asoka movement—a concern for moral purity aimed at cleaning up the political system and a quasi-puritanical regimen for the development of moral character. The Santi Asoka literature makes *sīla* (ethics) the basis of its ideology. The core of the religious life is a moral transformation. Phra Bodhiraksa spells out this position in detail in many of his writings, in particular, *Den Drong Khaw Sū Kān Pen Phra Ariya* (Becoming an Ariya), an uncompromising and sarcastic piece of social criticism grafted onto an identification of the highest Buddhist ideals with the five Asoka precepts or training rules.[151]

The Santi Asoka philosophy aims at cleansing individual character, but it also addresses the ills of Thai social, political, and economic life more rigorously than the Dhammakaya movement. This ideological bent is reflected in the movement's literature. In an essay entitled *Quamrak Sipmiti* (Ten kinds of love), for example, Bodhiraksa contends that the highest kind of love is the knowledge attained by the Buddha and Bodhisattvas. This love is beyond any attachment and has the power to transform the world.[152] Translated into political terms, this means that candidates who run on the Phalang Dhamma platform must agree to accept only "legitimate" support, cannot buy votes, and cannot fight for cabinet positions.

In sum, the Santi Asoka movement proposes a radical moral critique of Thai society, offers an exemplary utopian communitas as a model of the ideal Buddhist community, and has spawned a political party which seeks to restore moral integrity to the nation. The key to its ideology is its emphasis on the moral exemplar. Practically speaking, this ideal is embodied particularly by Bodhiraksa and Chamlong but also by the lifestyle of the People of Asoka.

The future of the Phalang Dhamma party is uncertain. Despite its recent victory in Bangkok, it has not emerged as a national party.[153] Furthermore, in his first four years in office, Chamlong was unable to solve the city's horrendous traffic and pollution problems. Although the party has taken steps to dissociate itself from any formal relationship with the Santi Asoka movement, various critics argue that Chamlong's "half-monk, half-man" image runs counter to the national political environment and the country's tolerant, relativistic moral ethos. Even those sympathetic with Chamlong's moral idealism fear that his fundamentalist worldview would result in rigid, authoritarian policies should he gain a position of more unrestricted political power. It has been alleged, for example, that Chamlong was involved in the anti-student movement in the turbulent year of 1976, and that he stage-managed rallies against student activists accused by ultra-rightists of being communists.[154]

The Santi Asoka movement has been widely criticized, and Phra Bodhiraksa especially, on the grounds that Santi Asoka monks are "unlawful" because the movement has declared itself independent of the national sangha organization which regulates monastic life in the country, and thus the People of Asoka espouse practices contrary to the Buddhist *vinaya* (disciplinary rules). Further, the detractors claim, Bodhiraksa's interpretations of the Pali canon are subjective, unorthodox, and ignorant, and his claims to have attained supranormal states and to base his interpretations on these realizations is a form of behavior specifically rejected by the monks' disciplinary rules in the Pali canon. Bodhiraksa has thus seriously exacerbated divisions within the Thai Buddhist sangha by his constant extremist rhetorical attacks on people and institutions outside Santi Asoka that do not embrace its moral ethos.[155]

The activities of Phra Bodhiraksa and the Santi Asoka movement have prompted a series of responses on the part of both the ecclesiastical hierarchy and the government. On 2 September 1988, the Ministry of Education instructed Santi Asoka to join the national sangha organization, to constitute itself as a wat under the regulations of the National Ecclesiastical Act of 1962, and to refrain from its excessive criticism of the Thai sangha.[156] A meeting of 151 ecclesiastical governors on 22 November 1988 passed a resolution to instruct the Supreme Sangha Council to defrock Bodhiraksa. At a 6 May 1989 national sangha meeting of ten thousand monks, seven charges were read against Phra Bodhiraksa, of which the most serious were that he had broken the National Ecclesiastical Law of 1962 by ordaining eighty monks on his own authority, and that he had transgressed the vinaya prohibition against claiming supernormal attainment, such an infraction being punishable by expulsion from the monkhood. Three days later a government decree requiring Bodhiraksa to defrock was delivered by the secretary of the Ministry of Education to Santi Asoka headquarters. Failing to comply with the order, Bodhiraksa was arrested on 16 June. Because the government feared demonstrations against the arrest of Bodhiraksa sympathizers, radio and television coverage was banned. Two days later he was freed on bail with the prospect of an eventual court hearing and a maximum penalty of six months in jail for contravening the 1962 National Ecclesiastical Act.[157]

Bodhiraksa refused to respect the formula for defrocking from the monastic order, but he did agree to exchange his brown monastic robes for a set of white robes associated in Thailand with Brahman priests and unordained "homeless" religious practitioners *(anagarika)*. He was also allowed to retain the name, Bodhiraksa. In August, the eighty monks ordained by Bodhiraksa were likewise required to "defrock" in a similar manner. Today they can be seen wearing white robes over their brown monastic garb and are now referred to as "the Bodhiraksa group."

Bodhiraksa's case is currently still in the courts with no prospects for a quick resolution. Informed monks and laity hold the view that Bodhiraksa will not be punished, but at the same time, will not be allowed to reordain.[158] Santi Asoka publications still appear in bookstores, and activities continue at the Santi Asoka centers. It appears that neither the government nor mainstream Thai Buddhism will allow the sect to continue as a separate religious body outside of the authority of the Department of Religious Affairs and the discipline of the national sangha organization. Santi Asoka may well survive as a lay movement within Thai Buddhism, continuing to offer its particular brand of fundamentalistic thought and practice as an alternative the Thai Buddhist mainstream.

Bodhiraksa's born-again Buddhism distills several of the ingredients of the fundamentalistic dimension of religion in the postmodern period—that is, in an age in which the solutions of modernity seem to have failed, and the Thai people are searching for a synthesis of the traditional and the modern. The Santi Asoka movement is both a product of, and a reaction against, a secular, materialistic culture encroaching upon a traditional way of life. Consequently, Bodhiraksa's movement represents both a radical rejection of a culture, including its mainstream religious institutions, and a one-dimensional utopian remedy to the ills of Thai society. Bodhiraksa and his followers reject much of traditional Thai Buddhism, even though they seem to lack an in-depth knowledge of the language, literature, and history of that tradition. As a result, Santi Asoka harbors a dualistic and absolutistic worldview that lacks both the subtleties of the traditional Theravada cosmology and the transcendental *(lokuttara)* grounding which relativizes all sociopolitical views. In historical terms, Santi Asoka capitalizes on a characteristic dimension of Theravada Buddhism—the forest monk tradition—but unlike the efforts of either Acharn Man or Bhikkhu Buddhadasa, the movement transforms that irenic tradition through a militant rhetoric of persecution designed to set stark boundaries between insiders and outsiders.

Conclusion: Theravada Buddhist Fundamentalism

Fundamentalisms in Sri Lanka and mainland Southeast Asia have arisen from the collapse and transformation of classical religious and cultural syntheses following upon the colonial period and the introduction of Western values, technology, education, and economic and political systems. Seen from this perspective, fundamentalisms are "modern" in the sense that they are part of the dynamic of the disintegration of traditional, self-contained societies associated with the processes of modernization.[159] Theravada "fundamentalism" might be even characterized as postmodern in that it seems to be a direct consequence of, and formed in reaction to, the adjustments traditional Theravada Buddhism made to the challenge of modernity in the late nineteenth and early twentieth centuries. By critically appropriating elements of modernity alongside transformed traditional elements, fundamentalists have created an innovative and popular synthesis of religion and culture designed to preserve Thai Buddhist identity over against conventional Thai Buddhism and a morally compromised secular society.

Indeed, fundamentalistic movements in Theravada Buddhist societies involve a quest for and assertion of identity (national, communal, individual), not merely in a social-psychological sense but at the deepest level of one's (or a culture's) being or personhood. Furthermore, the fundamentalist search for identity assumes the character of a "return to roots"—to an original situation perceived as a primordial and ideal condition of unity, certainty, and purity—but transformed and adapted in line with a critical posture toward, or rejection of, the contemporary status quo, as well as specific aspects of the historical tradition. The rhetoric of the leaders of the movements profiled above depicts unfettered postcolonial modernity as a "fall" from an earlier cultural and communal integrity and thus as characterized by disunity and chaos, ambiguity and uncertainty, impurity and spiritual laxity.

Fundamentalistic movements in this region are, moreover, frequently led by strong, often militantly aggressive, charismatic leaders whose followers, whether at the center or periphery of the cultural and sociopolitical mainstream, perceive themselves to be variously threatened as individuals, communally, or as a nation. The ideologies embraced by such movements tend to rest upon simplistic, dualistic, and absolutistic worldviews. Often exclusivistic (although often evangelistic), the movements reject competing groups whether from within the same tradition or from other traditions, as morally evil, spiritually confused, and/or intellectually misguided.

Possessed of an almost obsessive sense of their unique role or destiny, these movements may be quasi-messianic or explicitly millenarian in nature. Those described above share anti-rationalist, anti-intellectual, and even anti-ritualist tendencies; they tend to stress the value of direct experience coupled with plain and simple religious practice; and while they may embrace modern education for reasons of economic and social advancement, they suspect it of being morally, religiously, and culturally compromised.

In conclusion, the fundamentalist solution to the postmodern quest for identity is open to the criticism that it not only lacks the depth of its classical predecessors but, despite its religious rhetoric, more closely approximates a secular rather than a strictly religious solution—a *civil* religion—to problems that intertwine political, cultural, and social, but also spiritual and moral, aspects of communal life.

Notes

1. Because of the greater familiarity of certain Mahayana-Sanskrit terms in the West, I have chosen to use ***karma, dharma, bodhisattva,*** and ***nirvāṇa,*** rather than their Pali equivalents ***(kamma bodhisatta, nibbaña).*** The reader should bear in mind, however, that in Sri Lanka and Thailand, the Pali terms are in more general use.

2. Richard Gombrich sees a remarkable consistency in the ideology of Sinhalese

Theravada Buddhism from Buddhaghosa to the present, as does Michael Carrithers. Richard Gombrich, *Precept and Practice: Traditional Buddhism in the Rural Highlands of Ceylon* (Oxford: Oxford University Press, 1971); and Michael Carrithers, *The Forest Monks of Sri Lanka: An Anthropological and Historical Study* (Delhi: Oxford University Press, 1983).

3. I have adopted this periodization from S. J. Tambiah, "The Persistence and Transformation of Tradition in Southeast Asia with Special Reference to Thailand," *Daedalus* 103, (1): 55–84; Heinz Bechert, "Sangha, State, Society, 'Nation': Persistence of Traditions in 'Post-Traditional' Buddhist Societies," *Daedalus* 102, (1): 85–95; and George D. Bond, *The Buddhist Revival in Sri Lanka: Religious Tradiition, Reinterpretation, and Response* (Columbia: University of South Carolina Press, 1988). Michael Ames spells out the differences between "modernization" and "westernization" in "Westernization and Modernization: The Case of Sinhalese Buddhism," *Social Compass* 40, 1–2: 19–41.

4. Terminology borrowed from Edward Shils, "Center and Periphery," in *The Logic of Personal Knowledge: Essays Presented to Michael Polanyi* (London: Kegan Paul, 1961).

5. Cf. Kitsiri Malalgoda, *Buddhism in Sinhalese Society 1750–1900: A Study of Religious Revival and Change* (Berleley: University of California Press, 1976), chap. 1.

6. Cf. S. N. Eisenstadt, ed., *The Origins and Diversity of Axial Age Civilizations* (Albany: State University of New York Press, 1986).

7. In this essay I have chosen to use Burma and Cambodia designations rather than Myanmar and Kampuchea.

8. In a much-debated analysis of Burmese Buddhism, Melford E. Spiro divides its ideological system into four components: Nibbanic, Kammatic, Apotropaic or magical, and Esoteric or chiliastic. Cf. Spiro, *Buddhism and Society: A Great Tradition and Its Burmese Vicissitudes* (London: George Allen and Unwin, 1971).

9. See Manfred Halpern, "The Revolution of Modernization in National and International Society," in Carl J. Friedrich, ed., *Revolution: Nomos VII* (New York: Atherton Press, 1966), p. 179.

10. See Charles F. Keyes, "Millennialism, Theravada Buddhism, and Thai Society," *Journal of Asian Studies* 38, no. 2 (1977): 282–302; and E. Michael Mendelson, "A Messianic Buddhist Association in Upper Burma," *Bulletin of the School of Oriental and African Studies* 24: 560–80.

11. Acharn Man and the forest monk tradition in Thailand has been studied by S. J. Tambiah; see *The Buddhist Saints of the Forest and the Cults of Amulets* (Cambridge: Cambridge University Press, 1984).

12. See George D. Bond, *A New Gradual Path: Aspects of the Lay Buddhist Revival in Sri Lanka* (Columbia: University of South Carolina Press, 1989), chaps. 4 and 5 for an extensive treatment of the *vipassana bhavana* meditation movement in Sri Lanka.

13. John F. Cady, *A History of Modern Burma* (Ithaca: Cornell University Press, 1958), p. 190.

14. The contribution of Westerners, especially the British, to the revival of Theravada Buddhism in Sri Lanka and Burma was considerable at several levels. One was scholarly. The Pali Text Society, founded by Mr. and Mrs. T. W. Rhys Davids, began an interest in the critical study of Theravada texts and their translation into English and other European languages. Another was apologetic. Christmas Humphreys and the London Buddhist Society contributed to the reinterpretation of Buddhist doctrine, not only in British-dominated areas but in Thailand as well. That country's most noted philosopher-monk, Bhikkhu Buddhadasa, has acknowledged being influenced by articles in *The Middle Way,* the publication of the London Buddhist Society.

15. From a purely descriptive point of view, developments attendant to modernization are so varied they defy any easy characterization. Nonetheless, it has been suggested that in general terms, modernization can be analyzed as creating a more "rational" understanding of the meaning of the world and of human existence, or an increased capacity for rational goal setting.

This means a move away from the culturally specific, mythologized cosmology of classical and medieval Theravada Buddhism to an understanding of the world based on more general, and hence rationalized, principles. For a discussion of the terms "traditional" and "post-traditional," see *Daedalus* 102, no. 1 (1973), on "Post-traditional Societies." For an analysis of the uses of tradition for political legitimation, see Bardwell L. Smith, ed., *Religion and Legitimation of Power in Thailand, Laos, and Burma* (Chambersburg, Pa.: Anima Books, 1978). Robert N. Bellah described the responses to modernization by traditional Asian religions in terms of the following descriptive categories: (1) conversion to Christianity in which Christian institutions, especially schools, were an important catalyst for change; (2) traditionalism—a critical, often violent, attack on the modernization brought by Westerners, and an attempt to return to the status quo ante; (3) reformism—a reinterpretation of a religious tradition to show its compatibility with modernization; (4) neotraditionalism—an unstable middle ground between traditionalism and reformism which seeks to maintain traditional orientations as basic, but utilizes modern science, technology, and education as auxiliary. Bellah added three "secular" ideological responses: liberalism, nationalism, and socialism. Cf. Robert N. Bellah, "Epilogue: Religion and Progress in Modern Asia," in R. N. Bellah, ed., *Religion and Progress in Modern Asia* (New York: Free Press, 1965), pp. 203–15.

16. "The dilemma of modernity is that religious institutions and their memberships . . . are confronted with . . . the question of identity, in an age where the tension between sacred and secular is shattered or unperceived, or where the sacred is allowed [only] one room in a mansion seen [essentially] as secular." Bardwell L. Smith, "Sinhalese Buddhism and the Dilemmas of Reinterpretation," in *The Two Wheels of Dhamma: Essays on the Theravada Tradition in India and Ceylon* (Chambersburg, Pa.: American Academy of Religion, 1972), p. 84.

17. Gananath Obeyesekere, "Political Violence and the Future of Democracy in Sri Lanka," *Internationalses Asienforum* 15, no. 1 and 2 (1984): 39.

18. C. S. Manegold, "Trouble in Paradise: The Endless War That Is Destroying Sri Lanka," *Philadelphia Inquirer Magazine,* 7 August 1988, p. 38.

19. The Vijaya myth has been interpreted by various students of Sri Lankan culture. See Bruce Kapferer, *Legends of People: Myths of State* (Washington. D.C.: Smithsonian Institution Press, 1988), pp. 50–57. My own interpretation of religious fundamentalism and nationalism in Sri Lanka utilizes Kapferer's study and the work of Professor Gananath Obeyesekere, Princeton University, who has been provided helpful advice and bibliographic suggestions.

20. Peter Berger, *The Sacred Canopy: Elements of a Sociological Theory of Religion* (New York: Doubleday, 1967), pp. 29ff; referred to by Bardwell L. Smith in "Kingship, the Sangha, and the Process of Legitimation in Anuradhapura Ceylon: An Interpretative Essay," in Smith, *Religion and Legitimation of Power in Sri Lanka* (Chambersburg, Pa.: Anima Books, 1978), p. 76.

21. The Siyam sect, founded in 1753, became the monastic fraternity of the highest caste (the Goyigama) located in the Kandy area, while non-Goyigama elites in the low country founded the Amarapura and Ramanna sects. Richard Gombrich analyzes these and other aspects of the classical Buddhist tradition in *Theravada Buddhism: A Social History from Ancient Benares to Modern Colombo* (London: Routledge & Kegan Paul, 1988), chap. 6. For more extensive discussions, see R. A. L. H. Gunawardana, *Robe and Plough: Monasticism and Economic Interest in Early Medieval Sri Lanka,* AAS Monograph no. 35 (Tucson: University of Arizona Press, 1979); and Malalgoda, *Buddhism in Sinhalese Society,* especially pt. 1.

22. B. G. Gokhale contends that Dharmapala played three roles in the Buddhist revival in Sri Lanka: Sinhalese patriot and modernizer, restorer of ancient Buddhist sites in India and Sri Lanka, and spokesperson for Buddhism throughout Asia and the West. Gokhale refers to Dharmapala as a

"propagandist" who worked to show the superiority of Buddhism to other religions. B. G. Gokhale, "Anagarika Dharmapala: Toward Modernity through Tradition in Ceylon," in Bardwell L. Smith, *Tradition and Change in Theravada Buddhism,* Contributions to Asian Studies, vol. 4 (Leiden: E. J. Brill, 1973), pp. 35–37. Also see Gombrich, *Theravada Buddhism*; and Malalgoda, *Buddhism in Sinhalese Society*. Gombrich refers to Dharmapala as, "the most important figure in the modern history of Buddhism." (p. 188). Also see B. H. Farmer, "The Social Basis of Nationalism in Ceylon," *Journal of Asian Studies* 24, no. 3 (May 1965): 433.

23. See Bond, *Buddhist Revival,* pp. 57–60.

24. For a discussion of the Anagarika Dharmapala and the notion of "Protestant Buddhism," see Gombrich, *Theravada Buddhism,* chap. 7; Malalgoda, *Buddhism in Sinhalese Society,* pt. 2; Gananath Obeyesekere, "Personal Identity and Cultural Crisis: The Case of Anagarika Dharmapala of Sri Lanka," in Frank E. Reynolds and Donald Capps, eds., *The Biographical Process* (Paris: Mouton, 1971), pp. 221–52, and also his "Social and Ethical Transformation in Modern Theravada Buddhism," manuscript.

25. Anagarika Dharmapala, *Return to Righteousness,* Ananda Gurgue, ed. (Colombo: Government Press, 1965), p. 510.

26. Gananath Obeyeskere, "Social and Ethical Transformation in Theravada Buddhism," pp. 25–27. I am indebted to Obeyeskere's central category of "identity" for my analysis of modern Buddhist fundamentalism, although I use the term in more of a philosophical (i.e., ontological or the very nature of being) sense than he does. Obeyeskere's psychologically oriented theoretical approach resembles Anthony Wallace's work, to which I refer in my analysis of fundamentalist sectarianism in Thailand, although Obeyeskere utilizes self-esteem rather than stress reduction as the basis of his analysis.

27. Ibid., p. 29.

28. Anagarika Dharmapala, *Return to Righteousness,* pp. 659f.

29. Anagarika Dharmapala, *Return to Righteousness,*pp. 659–66.

30. To be sure, hierarchies abound in the traditional Buddhist cosmology, morally defined as states of reward and punishment by the casual law of *kamma* (Sanskrit karma), but the heavens and hells of traditional Buddhism populated by their divine, demonic, and human beings are dynamically interrelated; there are no absolute distinctions among them. Similarly, in traditional Theravada, the mundane and transmundane, *saṁsāra* (samsara) and *nibbāna* (nirvana), are but two sides of the same coin. See Heinz Bechert, "S. W. R. D. Bandaranaike and the Legitimation of Power through Buddhist Ideals," in Smith, *Buddhism and the Legitimation of Power in Sri Lanka,* pp. 202ff.

31. Quoted in Donald E. Smith, ed., *South Asian Politics and Religion* (Princeton: Princeton University Press), p. 458.

32. Walpola Rahula, *The Heritage of the Bhikkhu* (New York: Grove Press, 1974), p. 133. Quoted in Bechert, "S. W. R. D. Bandaranaike and the Legitimation of Power Through Buddhist Ideals," p. 206.

33. Quoted in Bechert, "S. W. R. D. Bandaranaike and the Legitimation of Power through Buddhist Ideals," p. 205. Bechert's work is the most extensive analysis of this period. See also his *Buddhismus Staat und Gesellschaft in den Landern des Theravada-Buddhismus,* vol. 1 (Frankfurt: A. Metzner, 1966).

34. S. W. R. D. Bandaranaike, *Towards a New Era: Selected Speeches of S.W. R. D. Bandaranaike,* ed. G. E. P. de Silva Wickramaratne (Colombo: Department of Information, 1961), p. 693.

35. Bond, *Buddhist Revival,* pp. 91–92. See also Rahula, *Heritage of the Bhikkhu,* pp. 104–5.

36. I have taken these "dislocations" from S. J. Tambiah, *Sri Lanka: Ethnic Fratricide and the Dismantling of Democracy* (Chicago: University of Chicago Press, 1986), p. 34. Tambiah identifies the politicized Buddhism as "millenarian." My interpretation of the current militant, fundamentalistic chauvinism of Sinhalese Buddhism sees it not as millenarian but as a consistent outgrowth of trends emerging from the early nationalist

period which have been catalyzed by recent political and economic policies.

37. Gananath Obeyesekere, "The Origins and Institutionalization of Political Violence," James Manor, ed., *Sri Lanka in Change and Crisis* (New York: St. Martin's Press, 1984), p. 159. Obeyesekere and Tambiah essentially agree in their analysis of the socio-economic conditions behind the ethnic violence in Sri Lanka.

38. Ibid.

39. Ibid. S. W. R. de A Samarasinghe of the University of Peradeniya provides an extensive analysis of the economic aspects of the ethnic conflict in Sri Lanka, with recommendations for the future, in an unpublished paper, "Ethnic Conflict and Economic Development in Sri Lanka."

40. See Eric Meyer, "Seeking the Roots of the Tragedy," in James Manor, ed., *Sri Lanka in Change and Social Crisis* (New York: St. Martin's Press, 1984), p. 145.

41. Tambiah, *Sri Lanka,* p. 37.

42. *The Island,* February 1983. Quoted in Gananath Obeyesekere, "Political Violence and the Future of Democracy in Sri Lanka," p. 52.

43. Elizabeth Nissan, "Some Thoughts on Sinhalese Justifications for the Violence," in Manor, *Sri Lanka in Change,* p. 181.

44. "A Decisive Mandate," in *Asia Week,* 3 March 1989, p. 20.

45. "Premadasa Firmly in Political Saddle," *Indian Express,* 1 April 1990, p. 12.

46. Gananath Obeyesekere, "Origins and Institutionalization of Political Violence," p. 161.

47. For example, see the thorough discussion by Kumari Jayawardena, "Ethnic Consciousness in Sri Lanka: Continuity and Change," in Committee for Rational Development, *Sri Lanka: The Ethnic Conflict Committee for Rational Development* (New Delhi: Navrang, 1984), p. 115–74. Michael Roberts of the University of Adelaide has also written extensively on this subject: "Ethnic Conflict in Sri Lanka and Sinhalese Perspectives: Barriers to Accommodation," *Modern Asian Studies* 12, no. 3 (1978): 353–76, and "Problems of Collective Identity in a Multi-Ethnic Society: Sectional Nationalism vs. Ceylonese Nationalism, 1900–1940," in Michael Roberts, ed., *Collective Identities: Nationalities and Protest in Modern Sri Lanka* (Colombo: Marga Institute, 1979).

48. C. R. de Silva, "The Sinhalese-Tamil Rift in Sri Lanka," in A. J. Wilson and Dennis Dalton, eds., *The States of South Asia* (Honolulu: University of Hawaii Press, 1982), p. 156.

49. Ibid., p. 157.

50. Ibid., p. 163.

51. The JVP emerged out of the 1971 insurrection composed of educated, underemployed, radicalized, and almost exclusively Sinhalese Buddhist youth. It has tended to be Marxist in orientation, while exploiting Buddhism as one of the bases of Sinhalese identity. During the Indian's army's occupation, the JVP became the most violent and disruptive force on the island.

52. Cf. Bruce Matthews, "Sri Lanka in 1988: Seeds of the Accord," *Asian Survey* 29, no. 2 (1989): 229–35.

53. Ibid., p. 231.

54. Ibid., p. 233.

55. Ramesh Menon, "Return of the Tigers," *India Today,* 15 April 1990, p. 123. For a concise discussion of the IPFK, the JVP, and Tamil politics in 1989, see Shelton U. Kodikara, "The Continuing Crisis in Sri Lanka," *Asian Survey* 29, no. 7 (July 1989): 716–24. It now appears that the Premadasa government is using the same tactics against the LTTE that it successfully used to eliminate the leadership of the JVP.

56. Discussions of the *dhammadīpa* concept and the mythic heroes of the Sinhalese chronicles abound. See Regina T. Clifford, "The Dhammadipa Tradition of Sri Lanka: Three Models within the Sinhalese Chronicles," and Alice Greenwald, "The Relic on the Spear: Historiography and the Saga of Dutthagamani," in Bardwell L. Smith, ed., *Legitimation and Power in Sri Lanka.* Gananath Obeyesekere has written a moving appraisal of Dutthagamani entitled *A Meditation on Conscience,* Social Scientists' Association of Sri Lanka Occasional Paper no. 1 (Colombo, 1988).

57. Quoted by Mark Jurgensmeyer in "Patterns in Modern Militant Religious Nationalism: The Case of Sri Lanka," in D. C. Vejayavardhana, *The Revolt in the Temple* (Colombo: Sinha Publications, 1953), p. 9.

58. Bruce Matthews, "The Sri Lankan Buddhist Philosophy of History and Its Relationship to the National Question," *Ethnic Studies Report* 3, no. 2 (July 1985): 81–86.

59. See Bond, *Buddhist Revival,* pp. 106–7.

60. Mark Jurgensmeyer, "Patterns in Modern Militant Nationalism," pp. 9–10.

61. Obeyesekere, "Political Violence and the Future of Democracy in Sri Lanka," p. 42.

62. Cf. Bond, *Buddhist Revival,* pp. 48–59.

63. Ibid.

64. Ibid., pp. 42–43.

65. Cf. Obeyesekere, *Meditation on Conscience.*

66. Ibid., p. 37.

67. Bruce Kapferer, *Legends of People, Myths of State* (Washington, D.C.: Smithsonian Institution Press, 1988), p. 2.

68. Kapferer, *Legends,* p. 5.

69. Ibid., p. 7.

70. Ibid., p. 12.

71. Mark Jurgensmeyer, "Patterns in Modern, Militant Religious Nationalism: The Case of Sri Lanka," (1988), pp. 5–6.

72. Ibid., pp. 17–18.

73. See Obeyesekere, *Meditation on Conscience,* pp. 50–51.

74. The most extensive treatment in English to date of the Dhammakaya and Santi Asoka movements is Peter A. Jackson, *Buddhism, Legitimation, and Conflict: The Political Functions of Urban Thai Buddhism* (Singapore: Institute of Southeast Asian Studies, 1989), chaps. 7 and 8. Jackson's sociopolitical analysis aims to show how various new religious movements reflect the conflicting political interests of competing groups in Thai society. In contrast, my aim is to analyze Dhammakaya and Santi Asoka as means of furthering our understanding of specific dimensions or aspects of Theravada Buddhist fundamentalism, e.g., chauvinistic nationalism, aggressive sectarianism, moralistic piety, and a reductionistic worldview. I see these characteristics as "dimensions" of Theravada fundamentalist movements in order to envisage them not only in their singularity but as interconnected parts of a whole. (I take a similar analytical approach in my study of Wat Haripunjaya in Lamphun, Thailand. Cf. Donald K. Swearer, *Wat Haripuñjaya. A Study of the Royal Temple of the Buddha's Relic, Lamphun, Thailand,* AAR Monograph no. 10 [Missoula, Mont.: Scholars Press, 1978]). Although fundamentalist movements in Theravada Buddhism are unique to particular times and places, they also share certain common features with other fundamentalist movements in other religious traditions and cultures.

75. *Phuthabucha. Visakhaburana* (Buddhapuja. Restoration of Visakha) (Bangkok: Dhammakaya Foundation, 1984/2527 B.E.), p. 9. Transliteration of Thai names and terms is modified from the Library of Congress system. Pali terms, however, are often retained in their Pali form, e.g., Dhammakaya rather than Thammakai.

76. Ibid., p. 19.

77. Several of my informants conjectured that some members of Pathom Asoka may have been part of the student group that "went into the jungle" after the 1976 crackdown on student dissent at Thammasat University in Bangkok. I am indebted to Susan Miller for details in this description.

78. Craig J. Reynolds, "Buddhist Cosmography in Thai History, with Special Reference to Nineteenth-Century Culture Change," *Journal of Asian Studies* 35, no. 2 (1976): 203.

79. David K. Wyatt, "The 'Subtle Revolution' of King Rama I of Siam," in David K. Wyatt and Alexander Woodside, eds., *Moral Order and the Question of Change: Essays on Southeast Asia* (New Haven: Yale University Southeast Asia Studies, 1982), p. 40.

80. Charles F. Keyes, "Buddhist Politics and Their Revolutionary Origins in Thai-

land," *International Political Science Review* 10, no. 2 (1989): 126.

81. The nature of modernization in Thailand has been much debated among historians and political scientists. It has been argued, for example, that the 1932 revolution was merely a transfer of power and authority from the monarch and royal family to a new group of elites dominated by the military, and that the changes in the past thirty years have been primarily in the economic rather than the political sphere of life. See Somboon Suksamran, *Political Buddhism in Southeast Asia* (New York: St. Martin's Press, 1976), chap. 3.

82. See Charles F. Keyes, "Buddhism and National Integration in Thailand," *Journal of Asian Studies* 30, no. 3 (1971): 551–67. See also Frank E. Reynolds, "Civil Religion and National Community in Thailand," *Journal of Asian Studies* 36, no. 2 (1977): 267–82.

83. "Into the 1990s: Can the Rollercoaster Ride Continue?" *The Nation,* 5 January 1989, p. 13.

84. Pamela S. DaGrossa, "Kamphaeng Din: A Study of Prostitution in the All-Thai Brothels of Chiang Mai City," *Crossroads* 4, no. 2 (1989): 1–7.

85. See Bhikkhu Buddhadasa, *Me and Mine: Selected Essays of Bhikkhu Buddhadasa,* Donald K. Swearer, ed. (Albany: State University of New York Press, 1989), for an introduction to Bhikkhu Buddhadasa; also Peter A. Jackson, *Buddhadasa—A Buddhist Thinker for the Modern World* (Bangkok: Siam Society, 1988). See Seri Phongphit, *Religion in a Changing Society* (Hong Kong: Arena Press, 1988), for a study of several new Buddhist centers and movements. He puts these movements in the following context: "The process of modernization has had a significant impact on Thai society. It is not enough to consider only the economic phenomenon since the whole change is rooted in the structure of society itself. The philosophy of education is related to the economic and political set up. In theory, some Buddhist principles may be quoted, yet the essence is a pragmatism which corresponds to a capitalist society.

"The young generation is growing up in a confusing environment. Teenagers and children form today the majority of Thai population and they are, thus, the biggest target groups for consumerism. The mass media contribute only minimally to the real education of this young generation who, it seems, are put in a one-way traffic society."

86. See Berger, *The Sacred Canopy,* for a discussion of the impact of secularization on the shape of religious systems.

87. A. F. C. Wallace's psychologically oriented interpretation of revitalization movements emphasizes their emergence as a response to personal and cultural stress. See Wallace, "Revitalization Movements," *American Anthropologist* 58 (1956): 264–81; also Wallace, *Religion: An Anthropological View* (New York: Random House, 1966), pp. 27ff.

88. I am indebted to the recent unpublished papers of Edwin Zehner, "Phutthabucha Makhaprathip at Wat Thammakai," and Grant Olson, "Sangha Reform in Thailand: Limitation, Liberation and the Middle Path" (M. A. thesis, Department of Religion, University of Hawaii, 1983). Both have completed extensive fieldwork in Thailand as part of their Ph.D dissertation research at Cornell University. My description of the Dhammakaya movement utilizes several of the organization's publications in Thai, a visit to Wat Dhammakaya at Prathum Thani in September 1985, participation in a Wat Dhammakaya "evangelistic week" at Chiang Mai University in August 1985, attendance at a Wat Dhammakaya sponsored sabbath service at Wat Sampakhoi, Chiang Mai, the same month, and interviews with Dhammakaya monks and various lay supporters on these occasions.

89. S. J. Tambiah, *World Conqueror and World Renouncer : A Study of Buddhism and Polity in Thailand Against a Historical Background* (Cambridge: Cambridge University Press, 1976), p. 133.

90. The national Thai government has essentially negated the political power of the Buddhist monastic order at the national level. The government's control is exercised through law but also by appealing to the strongly held view that "monks should not

be involved in politics." There have been exceptions to this rule, especially during the "experiment with democracy" period (1973–1976). See, for example, Charles F. Keyes, "Political Crisis and Militant Buddhism in Contemporary Thailand," in Bardwell L. Smith, *Buddhism and Legitimation of Power in Thailand, Laos, and Burma* (Chambersburg, Pa.: Anima Books, 1978), and Frank Reynolds's discussion of the events of 1973 in terms of the rubric of "civil religion" in the same volume: "Legitimation and Rebellion: Thailand's Civil Religion and the Student Uprising of October, 1973."

91. Critics have objected to the location of some of these centers and have also pointed out that some of the land given to the movement has come from national forest preserves.

92. *Wat Phrathammakai . . . Suthudongsathān . . . Thammauthayān Khong Chāw Phut* (Wat Dhammakaya . . . A place to advance the practice of meditation . . . A Dhammapark for all Buddhists)(Bangkok: Dhammakaya Foundation, 1984), p. 32. Translation mine.

93. *Thammathaiyāt, Quamwāngmai Khong Khon Thai Thang Chāt* (Heirs of the *dhamma,* The new hope of the Thai nation), vol. 4 (Bangkok: Dhammakaya Foundation, 1985), p. 26.

94. The daily schedule of the dhammaheir training program is as follows: rise, meditation, morning Chanting Service, morning walking exercise, breakfast and personal time, meditation, lunch and personal time, *dhamma* lecture, meditation, rest, refreshment (rain water), evening chanting service, meditation, discussion, prepare for bed.

95. The *Visuddhimagga* describes thirteen *dhutaṅga,* or ascetic practices, e.g., wearing patched-together robes, sleeping in a sitting position, living in the forest.

96. See Bond, *The Buddhist Revival in Sri Lanka,* chaps. 4 and 5; and Winston L. King, *A Thousand Lives Away* (Cambridge: Harvard University Press, 1964), chap. 6, for discussions of lay meditation movements in Sri Lanka and Burma.

97. The term "liminal" is taken from Victor Turner, *The Ritual Process* (Chicago: Aldine, 1969). Liminal experiences engendering a sense of group identity seem to be one of the general characteristics of fundamentalistic groups and movements. Liminality chracterizes both Dhammkaya and Santi Asoka, especially the latter.

98. Edwin Zehner, "Phuttabucha," pp. 22–23. I should add that Zehner's main argument throughout his paper is that the Dhammakaya movement exploits major celebrations like Makha Puja and traditional meditation practices as modes of legitimation. While I do not disagree with this particular analysis, I think that other and possibly deeper meanings are uncovered by interpreting the same kind of data using my characterization of Wat Dhammakaya as a fundamentalist movement.

99. See S. J. Tambiah, *World Conqueror,* pp. 157ff.

100. Ibid, p. 212.

101. Cf. Walter Vella, *Siam under Rama III, 1824–1851,* AAS Monograph no. 4 (New York: J. J. Augustia, 1957), p. 39.

102. One noted American anthropologist observed at the time that middle-class elements in the northeastern Thai village in which he worked "espoused a worldview more like that of reform Buddhism than that of the traditional cosmologically structured worldview still shared by most villagers." Charles F. Keyes, "Ethnography and Anthropological Interpretation in the Study of Thailand," in Eliezer B. Ayal, ed., *The Study of Thailand* (Athens, Ohio: Ohio University Center for International Studies, 1978), p. 36.

103. See Frank Reynolds and Mani Reynolds, *The Three Worlds of King Ruang* (Berkeley: Asian Humanities Press, 1988), for a translation and analysis of the classical Thai Buddhist cosmological treatise.

104. Buddhadasa is arguably one of the most brilliant reinterpreters of Theravada Buddhism in the contemporary period and stands as a kind of modern counterpoint to Theravada fundamentalism. He could be analyzed under Robert Bellah's "reformism" rubric.

105. Mongkut's scripturalism was partly a consequence of his extensive study of Pali and the Pali scriptures, a training which also characterized the work of Prince Vajiranana, who, in addition to his extensive scholarship, is looked upon as the architect of Thailand's educational reform. See David K. Wyatt, *The Politics of Reform in Thailand: Education in the Reign of King Chulalongkorn* (New Haven: Yale University Press, 1969), pp. 325–28, 233–55.

106. See Sulak Sivaraksa, *A Buddhist Vision for Renewing Society* (Bangkok: Tienwan, Ltd., 1986); idem, *A Socially Engaged Buddhism* (Bangkok: Thai Inter-Religious Commission for Development, 1988).

107. *Mongkhon Chīwit* (Bangkok: Dhammakaya Foundation, 1982), pp. 3–4; my translation. This book went through seven printings between 1982 and 1984. At least 100,000 volumes have been distributed.

108. Ibid., p. 12.

109. Ibid., pp. 17–19.

110. Ibid, pp. 21–27. Each of these mongkhon precepts is laid out in a simplistic, catechistic style. For example the discussion of the first mongkhon is divided into the following sections: What is a bad person? (Answer: One who is resentful, who holds the wrong opinions, follows the wrong customs and who does not know the difference between right and wrong). What are the characteristics of a bad person? (Answer: One who likes to think, speak, and act in evil ways). What are the consequences of being an evil person? (Answer: Defaming yourself and your family, not having anyone's respect, etc.). How to recognize a bad person? (Answer: Bad people like to lead others into wrongdoing, for example, skipping school, gambling, etc.). What does it mean to associate with a bad person? (Answer: To be around bad people where you work, etc.). What are the consequences of being around bad people? (Answer: To allow yourself to be drawn into evil ways, etc.). How should one behave every day? (Answer: Try to prevent yourself from doing even the slightest thing you consider wrong, like waking up late; practice the precepts, etc.). What are the values of not associating with evil people? (Answer: To be able to give yourself wholeheartedly to doing the good, to be firm and steadfast, etc.).

111. Fieldnotes, 26 August 1985.

112. Praves Wasi, *Suan Mōk, Thammakai, Santi Asok (Suan Mōkkha, Dhammakāya, Santi Asoka)* (Bangkok: *Folk Doctor Publishers* (1987/2530), p. 34.

113. Zehner, "Phuttabucha," pp. 19–20.

114. Takkasarano Bhikkhu, *Kgn Cha Koet Mai Nai Phēt Samana* (In anticipation of becoming a monk) (Pathum Thani: Wat Dhammakaya, 1985/2528), p. 24.

115. Zehner, "Phuttabucha," p. 21.

116. Niels Mulder offers the following critical analysis of the Thai monkhood: "The Thai monkhood is highly hierarchical, highly stratified, and the opinion of the 'elders' cannot easily be circumvented. While there are a few mildly progressive members in the governing bodies of the monkhood, and while progressiveness is not even uncommon among the staff of the Buddhist universities, the atmosphere of the hierarchy tends to be stultifying, formal, and even non-religious in the sense that it concentrates only on the performance of the right ceremony at the right time and not on bringing life and relevance to the essence of the Buddha Dhamma in contemporary society. The respect for hierarchy and tradition that once characterized Thai society as a whole is still fully alive in the institution of Thai monkhood so much even that the monkhood may well be judged to the most old-fashioned of all Thai institutions; it lacks leadership, vision, purpose and inspiration beyond the guardianship of ceremonies and tradition. In that atmosphere there is little room for bright young people who want to perform or reform." Niels Mulder, *Everyday Life in Thailand: An Interpretation* (Bangkok: Duang Kamol, 1979), pp. 136–37.

117. Phra Maha Prayudha Payutto, "Problems, Status, and Duties of the Sangha in Modern Society," *Visākhā Pūjā* 2511, pp. 58–72.

118. Cf. Charles F. Keyes, "Buddhism and National Integration in Thailand," *Journal of Asian Studies* 30, no. 3 (1971): 551–67.

119. Charles F. Keyes, "Political Crisis and Militant Buddhism in Contemporary Thailand," in Smith, *Religion and Legitimation of Power in Thailand, Laos, and Burma,* pp. 147–64. Keyes also includes Kittivuddho in his sketch of alternative Buddhist visions of the Thai sociopolitical order, in "Buddhist Politics and Their Revolutionary Origins in Thailand."

120. Ibid., pp. 147–64. See also Donald K. Swearer, "The Monk as Prophet and Priest," in *The Countries of South Asia: Boundaries, Extensions, and Interrelations* (Philadelphia: Department of South Asian Studies, University of Pennsylvania, 1988), pp. 72–90.

121. See Paisal Sricharatchanya and Ian Buruma, "Praise the Buddha and Pass the Baht," *Far Eastern Economic Review* (18 June 1987), pp. 53–55.

122. Perhaps a mainstream fundamentalist movement like Dhammakaya, with shallow roots in a tradition already ravaged by modernism, which flowered in an age dominated by economic pursuits, will be like that of the fundamentalist televangelists in the United States. In Robert Bellah's terms, such neotraditionalist movements lack a "creative tension" with their environment. This creative tension results from a transcendent perspective which the Dhammakaya movement seems to have lost by obviating the fundamental Theravada tension between the mundane and the transmundane. I borrow the term "creative tension" from Bellah, "Epilogue."

123. It should be noted, however, that Santi Asoka criticizes forest monks for their "selfish" lack of social concern.

124. These include the Pannanada lineage within the Ramanna Nikaya in Sri Lanka, the Sagaing forest monks in Burma, and the Acharn Man tradition in Thailand. The forest monk tradition in the modern period has been examined in several recent studies of Theravada Buddhism. See Carrithers, *Forest Monks of Sri Lanka,* Tambiah, *Buddhist Saints,* and Michael Mendelson, *Sangha and State in Burma: A Study of Monastic Sectarianism and Leadership,* John P. Ferguson, ed. (Ithaca: Cornell University Press, 1975). Michael Carrithers interprets the modern ascetic monk tradition in Sri Lanka as a "fundamentalistic reform" (p. 142). I would argue the necessity of differentiating among various of the forest monk revivals. Some of these movements are appropriately characterized as fundamentalistic; others are not. I make such a differentiation between Wat Suan Mok and Wat Santi Asoka.

125. Prawes Wasi, *Suan Mōk, Thammakai, Santiasok* (*Suan Mōkkha, Dhammakāya, Santi Asoka*) (Bangkok: Folk Doctors Publishers, 1987/2530).

126. Phra Bodhiraksa, *Sacca Haeng Chīvit* (My life story) (Bangkok: Dhammasanti Foundation, 1982/2525), p. 180. I am grateful to Tavivat Puntarigvivat for translation of sections of Bodhiraksa's autobiography and for discussions about Wat Dhammakaya and Wat Santi Asoka.

127. Ibid. p. 186.

128. Ibid., p. 192.

129. Ibid.

130. Ibid., pp. 214–16.

131. Ibid. Paraphrased from p. 213.

132. Ibid. Paraphrased from p. 233.

133. Ibid. p. 237.

134. Prawes Wasi, *Suan Mōk,* p. 68.

135. Even though there are obvious utopian aspects to the Santi Asoka movement, to my knowledge it does not share the millennial characteristics of some earlier movements in northern and northeastern Thailand and in Burma. In some of these movements the charismatic leader identified himself as the future Buddha Metteya. See Keyes, "Millennialism, Theravada Buddhism and Thai Society," and Mendelson, "A Messianic Buddhist Association." In other words, I see more connection between Suan Mok and Santi Asoka than between the latter and millenarian movements in Theravada Buddhism. For useful comparative discussions, see Prawes Wasi, *Suan Mōk;* and Jackson, *Buddhism, Legitimation,* pp. 164–66.

136. I borrow the term "communitas" from Turner, *The Ritual Process.* Communi-

tas "emerges recognizably in the liminal period, is of society as an unstructured or rudimentarily structured and relatively undifferentiated comitatus." Communitas is differentiated from common modalities of living. It emphasizes the essentiality of the generic human bond (pp. 96–97).

137. Interviews in Chiang Mai, 1986.

138. *Āhān Mangsavirat, Ngod Wen Nu'a Sat Tat Bāp Dai Pun,* n.d. My translation.

139. For example, see Phra Bodhiraksa, *Phutaplu'ak* (The Externals of Buddhism) (Bangkok: Dhammasanti Foundation, 1985/2528).

140. Ibid., pp. 31–32. My translation. Some observers suggest that even if Santi Asoka does not survive as a separate Buddhist sect, it may continue as a distinctive ascetic communitas of lay religious life and practice. It would continue to offer the same kind of sectarian, fundamentalistic alternative to mainstream Thai Buddhism.

141. Olson, "Sangha Reform in Thailand," p. 66.

142. There is a status of ordained women in Thai Buddhism referred to as *mae chī,* but for the most part the women do not command broad public respect. There are, however, some exceptions to this rule. In 1977 I met a renowned *mae chī* from southern Thailand who had been invited to live and meditate in a cave outside of Mae Hong Son in northwestern Thailand. It should also be pointed out that in the past few years there have been efforts to restore a Theravada female monastic line. The major force behind the International Buddhist Women's Activities organization is Professor Chatsumarn Kabilsing of Tammasat University, whose mother was instrumental in establishing Wat Songdharmakalyani, a monastery for female monks in Thailand. For comparisons between the female "renouncers" of Burma and Thailand, see Ingrid Jordt, "Bhikkhuni, Thilashin, Mae-Chii . . . " *Crossroads* 4, no. 1 (Fall 1988): 31–39.

143. I am indebted for this analysis to my former student, Erik Guyot, a fellow with the Institute of Current World Affairs, who has been assigned to Bangkok to study the role of U.S security assistance to the Philippines and Thailand. My comments on General Chamlong are informed by Mr. Guyot's newsletter of 6 May 1988.

144. *The Nation,* 8 January 1990.

145. On 14 January 1990, the Phalang Dharma Party won 184 out of 220 Bangkok District seats.

146. See "A Rock in a Political Storm," *Asia Week* 16, no. 3 (19 January 1990): 18, 23.

147. Guyot newsletter, 6 May 1988, p. 2.

148. Ibid.

149. Saowarop Panyacheewin, "Chamlong's Life, Work, and Thoughts in His Own Words," *The Bangkok Post,* 11 January 1990.

150. Guyot newsletter, 6 May 1988, p. 1.

151. From the first printing of this book in 1974 to its sixth printing in 1985, 45,000 copies had been distributed. Typical of the Santi Asok ideology, it develops a kind of moral hierarchy, with the highest level represented by those people who have strived for and achieved the "essence" of Buddhism, and the lowest represented by those who do not even recognize the most superficial aspects of the religion.

152. Phra Bodhiraksa, *Quamrak Sipmiti* (Ten dimensions of love) (Bangkok: Dhammasanti Foundation, 1972/2518), pp. 148–49.

153. It is speculated that the Palang Dhamma Party will use the issue of corruption to make its move into the national political arena. Cf. *Siam Rath,* 6–12 May 1990), pp. 6–8.

154. "Controversial Chamlong Supporter Passes Away," *The Nation,* 13 January 1990.

155. The most extensive and thoughtful criticism of Phra Bodhiraksa is Phra Depvedi, *Karanī Santiasok* (The case of Santi Asoka) (Bangkok: Buddhadhamma Foundation, 1988/2531). Depvedi is one of the most highly regarded scholars in the Thai monastic order, so his criticisms have been taken very seriously. The *Siam Rath,* Thailand's most distinguished newspaper, later published an interview with Phra Bodhiraksa in response to Phra Depvedi's book.

156. Bunruam Theimcan, *Khadi Santi Asōka* (The case of Santi Asoka) (Bangkok: Saeng Dao, 1989).

157. Rodney Tasker, "Troublesome Priests," *Far Eastern Economic Review* (6 July 1989), p. 13; "Thai Cliffhanger: Case of the Puritanical Buddhist," *The New York Times,* 12 July 1989.

158. Dr. Grant A. Olson, Northern Illinois University, attended the court hearings in December 1989 and is writing an article about the Bodhiraksa case.

159. S. N. Eisenstadt, "Post-Traditional Societies and the Continuity and Reconstruction of Tradition," *Daedalus,* 102, no. 1 (Winter 1973): 2.

Select Bibliography

Bandaranaike, S. W. R. D. *Towards a New Era: Selected Speeches of S.W. R. D. Bandaranaike.* Ed. G. E. P. de Silva Wickramaratne. Colombo: Department of Information, 1961.

Bechert, Heinz. "Buddhism and Mass Politics in Burma and Ceylon." In Donald Eugene Smith, ed. *Religion and Political Modernization.* New Haven: Yale University Press, 1974.

Bellah, R. N., ed. *Religion and Progress in Modern Asia.* New York: Free Press, 1965.

Berger, Peter C. *The Sacred Canopy.* New York: Doubleday, 1967.

Bond, George D. *The Buddhist Revival in Sri Lanka: Religious Tradition, Reinterpretation, and Response.* Columbia: University of South Carolina Press, 1988.

Buddhadasa, Bhikkhu, *Me and Mine. Selected Essays of Bhikkhu Buddhadasa.* In Donald K. Swearer, ed. Albany: State University of New York Press, 1989.

Cady, John F. *A History of Modern Burma.* Ithaca: Cornell University Press, 1958.

Carrithers, Michael. *The Forest Monks of Sri Lanka: An Anthropological and Historical Study.* Delhi: Oxford University Press, 1983.

Dharmapala, Anagarika. *Return to Righteousness.* Ed. Ananda Gurgue. Colombo: Government Press, 1965.

Eisenstadt, S. N., ed. *The Origins and Diversity of Axial Age Civilizations.* Albany: State University of New York Press, 1986.

Friedrich, Carl J., ed. *Revolution: Nomos VII.* New York: Atherton Press, 1966.

Gombrich, Richard. *Precept and Practice: Traditional Buddhism in the Rural Highlands of Ceylon.* Oxford: Oxford University Press, 1971.

———. *Theravada Buddhism: A Social History from Ancient Benares to Modern Colombo.* London: Routledge & Kegan Paul, 1988.

Gunawardana, R. A. L. H. *Robe and Plough: Monasticism and Economic Interest in Early Medieval Sri Lanka.* AAS Monograph no. 35. Tucson: University of Arizona Press, 1979.

Kapferer, Bruce. *Legends of People, Myths of State.* Washington D.C.: Smithsonian Institution Press, 1988.

Keyes, Charles F. *Thailand: Buddhist Kingdom as Modern Nation-State.* Boulder: Westview Press, 1987.

King, Winston L. *A Thousand Lives Away.* Cambridge: Harvard University Press, 1964.

Malalgoda, Kitsiri. *Buddhism in Sinhalese Society 1750–1900: A Study of Religious Revival and Change.* Berkeley: University of California Press, 1976.

Manor, James, ed. *Sri Lanka in Change and Crisis.* New York: St. Martin's Press, 1984.

Mendelson, Michael. *Sangha and State in Burma: A Study of Monastic Sectarianism and Leadership.* John P. Ferguson, ed. Ithaca: Cornell University Press, 1975.

Mulder, Niels. *Everyday Life in Thailand: An Interpretation.* Bangkok: Duang Kamol, 1979.

Phongphit, Seri. *Religion in a Changing Society.* Hong Kong: Arena Press, 1988.

Rahula, Walpola. *The Heritage of the Bhikkhu.* New York: Grove Press, 1974.

Reynolds, Frank E., and Donald Capps, eds.

The Biographical Process. Paris: Mouton, 1971.

Reynolds, Frank, and Mani Reynolds. *The Three Worlds of King Ruang.* Berkeley: Asian Humanities Press, 1988.

Roberts, Michael, ed. *Collective Identities: Nationalities and Protest in Modern Sri Lanka.* Colombo: Marga Institute, 1979.

Sivaraksa, Sulak. *A Buddhist Vision for Renewing Society.* Bangkok: Tienwan, 1986.

———. *A Socially Engaged Buddhism.* Bangkok: Thai Inter-Religious Commission for Development, 1988.

Smith, Bardwell L., ed. *The Two Wheels of Dhamma: Essays on the Theravada Tradition in India and Ceylon.*Chambersburg, Pa.: American Academy of Religion, 1972.

———. *Tradition and Change in Theravada Buddhism.* Contributions to Asian Studies, vol. 4. Leiden: E. J. Brill, 1973.

Smith, Bardwell L., ed. *Religion and Legitimation of Power in Thailand, Laos, and Burma.* Chambersburg, Pa.: Anima Books, 1978.

———. *Religion and Legitimation of Power in Sri Lanka.* Chambersburg, Pa.: Anima Books, 1978.

Smith, Donald Eugene, ed. *Religion and Political Modernization.* New Haven: Yale University Press, 1974.

Spiro, Melford E. *Buddhism and Society: A Great Tradition and Its Burmese Vicissitudes.* London: George Allen & Unwin, 1971.

Suksamran, Somboon. *Political Buddhism in Southeast Asia.* New York: St. Martin's Press, 1976.

Swearer, Donald K. *Wat Haripunjaya: A Study of the Royal Temple of the Buddha's Relic, Lamphun, Thailand.* AAR Monograph, no. 10. Missoula, Mont.: Scholars Press, 1978.

———. *Buddhism and Society in Southeast Asia.* Chambersburg, Pa.: Anima Books, 1981.

Tambiah, S. J. *World Conqueror and World Renouncer: A Study of Buddhism and Polity in Thailand Against a Historical Background.* Cambridge: Cambridge University Press, 1976.

———. *The Buddhist Saints of the Forest and the Cults of Amulets.* Cambridge: Cambridge University Press, 1984.

———. *Sri Lanka: Ethnic Fratricide and the Dismantling of Democracy.* Chicago: University of Chicago Press, 1986.

Turner, Victor W. *The Ritual Process.* Chicago: Aldine, 1969.

Vejayavardhana, D. C. *The Revolt in the Temple.* Colombo: Sinha Publications, 1953.

Von der Mehden, Fred R. *Religion and Modernization in Southeast Asia.* Syracuse: Syracuse University Press, 1986.

Wyatt, David K. *The Politics of Reform in Thailand: Education in the Reign of King Chulalongkorn.* New Haven: Yale University Press, 1969.

Wyatt, David K. and Alexander Woodside, eds. *Moral Order and the Question of Change: Essays on Southeast Asia.* New Haven: Yale University Southeast Asia Studies, 1982.

CHAPTER
12

Islamic Resurgence in Malaysia and Indonesia

Manning Nash

In a scene that would become familiar to millions of television viewers around the world, a long-standing Islamic insurgency movement, bowing to the constitutional government's superior military power, agrees to lay down its arms following the capture and execution of its charismatic leader. In a fifteen-year armed struggle, more than forty thousand people had lost their lives.[1] Yet, despite the scale of the movement, few in the West would hear of it, for the scene of this action was not Tehran, Cairo, or Jerusalem, but the island of Java, the political hub of the Indonesian archipelago. The year was 1962, long before the term *Islamic fundamentalism* became prominent in the vocabulary of journalists and academics.

The movement called itself Dar'ul Islam, or House of Islam, a frequent and by now widely recognized metaphor for a fully Islamic state. The founder of this particular House of Islam, one Sekarmadji Maridjan Kartosoewirjo (1905–62), proved to be a transitional figure. Born in east Java, he had attained a high level of Dutch education but at the same time came under the close tutelage of prominent leaders among the traditional Islamic teachers of his day. Devout, articulate, keen in absorbing broader learning, and credited with mystical powers of an animistic sort, such as the ability to suddenly vanish,[2] Kartosoewirjo used his unique blend of talents and beliefs to launch an anticolonial Islamic movement in central Java. At first he taught that leading a completely Islamic way of life could provide a communal means of withdrawal from the colonial order. For him the *hijra* was the Islamic exodus. But later, after the war years, when competition ensued for setting the terms of Indonesia's nationhood, his Dar'ul Islam became a full scale armed rebellion. Hijra was transformed into *jihad*.

Even during Kartosoewirjo's time, Islamic insurgency was by no means a new phenomenon in Indonesia. In the past century religious revolt had often been the most overt expression of indigenous resistance to colonial rule. One Indonesian authority even declared such outbreaks to be "endemic occurrences" in nineteenth-century Sumatra and Java; they took place in thirty of the thirty-six years from 1840 to 1875.[3] Usually they were quite localized; always they were forcefully suppressed.

The memories of these uprisings were kept alive by the people, if not by Western chroniclers. Traditional religious education is carried out in a highly personalized idiom, in the *pesantren* and *pondok* scholastic traditions of Indonesia and Malaysia, respectively. In this idiom, disciples and teachers assume a lifelong commitment to each other. Established lines or pedigrees of religious authority pertain to each school and its leading gurus. These lines are traced as *silsilah* (genealogies) that link each renowned disciple to his respective guru in a succession of knowledge that by convention goes all the way back to the prophet Muhammad. Given such strong institutional motivation for preserving the names and reputations of leading religious figures, it seems quite unlikely that the larger events of religious revolt, or of charismatic careers ending in fatal confrontations with the authorities, would be allowed to fade as nothing from the collective memory of the devout. Every new movement, whether militant or pacific, has to consider the prior cases with which it is certain to be compared.

The most important difference between Kartosoewirjo and his many predecessors was neither in his doctrine of hijra nor in his final militancy. Rather it was in the fact that his turn from teaching to arms happened to coincide with a watershed in the twentieth-century history of Southeast Asia. In the wake of the Japanese surrender, the face of the enemy abruptly changed. Dar'ul Islam no longer faced a foreign oppressor but found itself fighting against the forces of secular nationalism. Its ultimate crushing defeat at the hands of the Indonesian army was for Islamic revivalists a rueful harbinger of the new order.

In the years since these events Indonesia, which rightly claims a larger Muslim population than any other nation, and Malyasia, which officially honors Islam as its national religion, have together firmly, if not forcefully, rejected the tradition that Kartosoewirjo attempted to establish. Yet that tradition has a curious way of returning to haunt the national psyches and the politics of these two ethnically diverse, rapidly modernizing, and fundamentally secular states. An underlying tension exists regarding the degree to which either of these two secular states can ever fully satisfy the often-changing expectations of the Islamic populace. Yet in part because of contrasting colonial legacies, the Indonesian and Malaysian governments respond differently to each new wave of Islamic revivalism that breaks upon their respective shores. This essay will explore the ramifications of these differences for the "local" manifestation of a worldwide Islamic resurgence that has affected both societies, as well as their mutual neighbor, Singapore, over the last twenty years.

In Malaysia, the new religious current is popularly known as the *dakwah,* or "evangelist," movement. There the movement appears to be much more conspicuous and more influential culturally than its counterparts in Indonesia. Indeed in Malaysia, and to a lesser degree in Singapore, dakwah is a phenomenon widely noticed and discussed in the media and repeatedly researched by outside scholars.

This general accent on difference should not obscure the fact that there are frequent and influential contacts between the Muslims of Indonesia, Malaysia, and Singapore, most of whom share a common language and culture.[4] And the dynamics of this broad Islamic movement in Southeast Asia have changed as modern technology has linked what had hitherto been an isolated and distant outpost of Islam with the Arab and Persian centers of Islamic belief and practice.[5] Official Malaysian membership in a number of international Islamic organizations such as the World Assembly of Muslim Youths and the Islamic Call Society, as well as the membership of private Malaysian citizens in a number of such international organizations, has further bound that country to the worldwide Islamic *ummah* (community of believers).[6] In Indonesia these bonds are even more striking in that substantial numbers of graduates of the eighty-two Islamic religious faculties in the fourteen Islamic state universities journey abroad for further religious education. Cairo's Al-Azhar University is the most notable destination.[7] These personal contacts are bolstered by the television, the radio, and the printed word.

There is a visible turning toward Islam among large segments of the population in both countries. This is reflected most strikingly in Malaysia, with the emergence of local imitations of Middle Eastern dress, increased attendance at Friday prayer services, and increasingly vocal criticism of foreign (Western) ways. It is to such criticism that Indonesian leaders exhibit great sensitivity, thus accounting for the more circumspect form of the Indonesian revival. This renewal of Islamic fervor moved one longtime observer to remark, concerning Malaysia in particular, that "the younger generation of *abangan* [nominal Muslims] are becoming *santri* [devout Muslims]."[8]

Introduction to Dakwah: The Kelantan Group

At the edge of the second-largest settlement in the state of Kelantan in northeast Malaysia, a dakwah group, one of many such groupings, came into being in the early 1970s, at the same time that other movements and settlements dedicated to some form of dakwah arose elsewhere in the Malaysian peninsula. The movement as a whole involved more than thirty thousand followers in and around Kuala Lumpur and in the predominantly Malay states of Kelantan, Trengganu, Kedah, Perlis, and Parak. The term *dakwah,* from the Arabic root *da'a,* "to call," generally refers to the proselytizing that is incumbent upon every Muslim. This call to Islam may take various forms, from setting a good example for others to the waging of jihad (any form of spiritual "struggle," up to and including holy war). The appeal need not be addressed exclusively to non-Muslims but may also be directed at lax members of the Islamic community, inviting them back to a more strict observance of the faith. In fact, the main thrust of the dakwah movement has been in this direction, that is, aimed at those already born and raised as Muslims.

By 1982 the dakwah settlement in Kelantan had over a hundred members including families with children. Although they have no name for their movement other than dakwah, their community life expresses their joint search for a fully Islamic way of life—a *din* (totality) that calls for conduct that is life-enriching in the present moment and will lead eventually to salvation. This notion of din—of "Islam as a complete way of life"—is the most constant refrain in the entire dakwah movement. But its implications vary. Not all participants in dakwah, or *orang berdakwah* (people who do dakwah), live in special dakwah settlements like the one under consideration here. They may simply attend religious discussion groups and become stricter in prayer and other ritual observances. Certainly they will begin to study Islam more intensively than they had done before engaging in dakwah. But whatever approach is taken, the attempt to make Islam a complete way of life always carries with it the important proviso that all non-Islamic behavior becomes either redundant or defiling or both.

The community approach adopted by the group in Kelantan offers the possibility of shutting out what is deemed non-Islamic so that full concentration can be given to the ideal path ahead. Although relying solely on the authoritative sources of Islam to light that path, these followers of dakwah discover in daily life opportunities for implementing religious norms. Thus group ideology is neither fixed nor frozen: the movement looks backward, lives in the present, and has future aspirations. Though critical of the current state of affairs, the group holds out some hope of better things to come. Their need to construct Islam as they go, knowing that there is great diversity of practice in the Muslim community around them, makes even this highly concentrated approach to the din a rather fluid process. There is an exploratory dimension here that is not usually associated with fundamentalism.

The Kelantan group shuns publicity and has no formal organization. People hear of it by word of mouth or when some of its members speak at *kampong* meetings (a kampong is a Malaysian village or city neighborhood) or at local mosques, always by invitation. Part of this low profile is of course designed to avoid the prying eyes of the police and to escape being labeled as a subversive or socially undesirable. In Malaysia the government still has wide emergency powers and is not reluctant to use them when it perceives a threat to "national security," which is often equated with the political hegemony and interests of the ruling National Alliance.

Although without formal leadership or outside affiliation, this dakwah community has two central figures. One, a former *uztaz* (religious teacher), is the administrative head, attending to the mundane details of a sizable group of people who live in the world while rejecting much of it. The other pivotal figure is a guru-type leader. In Malaysian society there is an old and honorable role for the *tok guru* as a religious teacher, charismatic preacher, or head of a pondok (a traditional school focusing on religious training). The guru leader of the dakwah group possesses all the best credentials of an intellectual and a religious figure, including an extensive knowledge of Arabic, the Qur'an, the Hadith, and much of Western philosophy. He has taught in the University of Malaya and has written books and articles. He leads discussions, gives religious sermons, and often acts as imam in the daily prayers at the mosque adjacent to one of the dakwah settlements.

One might pose the analogy of the layers of an onion in describing the composition of the group. These two central individuals have around them a core of followers who have been committed to the movement since the group migrated from Kuala Lumpur to Kelantan in 1971 and took up residence in this particular kampong in 1972. These "hard-core" members are considered more knowledgeable and adept in the way of Islam as compared with the next ring of adherents, who have not been involved for as long a time. Clinging tentatively to the outer layer of the onion are the interested and curious new followers, some of whom will stay, some of whom will float in and out, and some of whom will disappear from dakwah altogether.

Dakwah is basically a youth movement, urban based, and intellectually oriented. The "elder" of the group is now in his mid-forties, and the members are younger as one moves from the core to the periphery. Unlike the major Muslim political party in Kelantan, dakwah did not start as a mass movement among peasants and their religious literati and is neither the voice of the pious peasant nor the vehicle for the traditional ulama. The dakwah adherents are instead young men with middle-class or professional backgrounds.[9] A significant proportion of the younger members are or were university students. Many from this background respond readily to the dakwah group's discontent with the modern, urban, pluralistic, and secular world. They describe this milieu as sensual, corrupt, and neurotic, and thus ephemeral and trivial.

The modern Malay world evokes contempt and merits rejection not only because of what it is, but also because it stands in the way of the true end of life: serving Allah through the teachings of his Prophet. Dakwah members are, accordingly, stridently opposed to a number of other strong trends in Malyasian popular culture and the arts. A frequent target for condemnation and boycott is the pop music scene and its many local stars, especially the Muslim entertainers. It is seen as a great dakwah triumph, whatever the loss to entertainment, should one of these local favorites finally see the light and "convert" to dakwah.[10] Pursuing the way of dakwah ensures eternal rewards to the convert and at the same time makes daily life meaningful, vibrant, and even joyous.

Discontent with contemporary society is also fueled by the impatience and dissatisfaction of the youth who desire rapid social change and hold the present Malaysian political order in contempt. In contrast to the focus on an eventual salvation among the older adherents at the core of the group, the younger followers are more impatient with the status quo and more willing to call for radical and openly rebellious resistance.

The ideology of the dakwah community is partly a reaction against modern Western values, as these are understood in Malaysia, and partly an affirmation of pristine Islam. The affirmation is expressed chiefly by trying to reconstruct the *salaf,* the practice and belief of Muhammad and his immediate followers. However, this conception of "basic" or "pure" Islam has not been developed in isolation. The guru and some of his disciples read the international literature of Islam in the journals devoted to it. They try to keep up with the academic essays, books, tracts, and newspapers that make up a burgeoning Islamic apologetic literature in a multiplicity of languages and philosophical traditions. For Islam these are perilous and exciting times, and to be part of dakwah links one with currents of thought and activity that appear from this corner of the world to be shaping the agenda of world history.

These ideological commitments have cultural and symbolic implications for both behavior and belief. The dakwah must emulate in Malaysia what the pious ancestors of the salaf lived and believed. The first and most striking aspect of the dakwah is the dress of the people involved. Males wear turbans, a long, loose shirt, trousers sometimes tight at the ankles, and in colder weather a long coat over the shirt. Women are covered to the wrists and ankles and in public wear a form of *chador* or semi-veil. This distinctive attire underlines the separateness of the dakwah from the surrounding world, while challenging a vain and self-indulgent style of dress. It has symbolic values for the wearers. The turban is thought to be a crown, referring to man as the apex of creation, since the turban was the last thing Allah took from Adam. The whole body covering of women separates man from animals, who know neither modesty nor shame. The women's clothes minimize body outlines and hence reduce the temptation of lust and sexual overstimulation of men. In the houses of strict dakwah followers, furniture is absent. Neither chairs, tables, nor beds are used. Woven mats and pillows are the furnishings of the ordinary house. These minimal furnishings, people in the dakwah believe, are quite sufficient and safeguard against decadence and an inordinate desire for the luxurious. This abstemiousness deadens the concern for material things and creature comforts which, members are told, distract men from the truer, deeper concerns of Islam.

The division of labor in the community is along the lines of age and sex, and within those categories all work is seen as socially equal and valuable. Women perform the domestic tasks and are supposed to confine their activities to kitchen, children, and husband. In fact, dakwah women are in strict purdah (isolation). Males must do the shopping and local errands in the market and in the town. These segregated and limited tasks for males and females are almost a complete inversion of the usual gender roles in Kelantan, which is famous for the active female traders in its busy local markets. This difference serves as a real and symbolic barrier between the dakwah people and the environing community of Kelantanese Muslims.

In the sphere of economics, the dakwah members usually do not hold jobs and certainly do not have careers. They try to have minimal and independent ways of earning a livelihood. They maintain small businesses or stalls to earn enough to meet their modest needs for food, clothing, and shelter. Some of them bake cakes and bread and sell these locally, others run a small catsup-bottling factory, still others deliver tea and sundries to be resold. These petty, discontinuous forms of trade provide the economic basis for dakwah life. Contributions come from sympathizers, but these are not large and cannot be depended upon to sustain the dakwah community. The economic activity of the followers of dakwah is in keeping with their idea that materialism is the great enemy of spiritualism—that "things" debauch the soul, and possessions lead to concern with the unessential.

Although there are in Kelantan a variety of schools, including those sponsored by the secular government, modified religious institutions, and a pondok, children of dakwah families do not attend any of these for fear of mixing with worldly and irreligious people who would provide bad examples. The adherents of dakwah contend that the subjects taught in the national schools are of little or no use in the pursuit of salvation. Even the education in the religious schools is superfluous. The curriculum in those institutions culminates in certificates which qualify the graduate to teach Islam, but the people of dakwah do not highly value official Islamic teaching. So the children are kept at home, where they learn the fundamentals of Islamic monotheism, law, history, Arabic, and writing—all that is needed to follow the path laid down by the Prophet Muhammad. Although these same fundamentals are in fact taught in the official religious schools, dakwah purists still object to the latter's reduction of Islam from a complete way of life to a mere subject of study alongside others.

Other forms of modern knowledge are equally derided, especially the medicine of doctors and hospitals. Most of the ills of mankind, the dakwah people hold, are the self-inflicted consequences of abusing the perfect human body that Allah created. Improper diet (eating *haram,* forbidden food), gluttony (eating more than needed to sustain health), the use of forbidden stimulants and drugs, and the excessive pandering to sensual appetites (especially sexual appetites) are at the root of most sickness. If the way of the pious ancestors were followed, people would be less prone to illness, and there would be little need for doctors, medicine, or hospitals.

This puritanical, abstemious style of life has the double-edged consequence of setting the dakwah apart from the culture around it and enforcing a moral discipline that makes daily life into something of a devotional experience. In the eyes of the dakwah followers, their everyday routine is both a rebuke to the behavior of the less conscientious and an example for the less conscientious to follow. They are proud of their hard and moral life and continually insist that it brings them real joy, something they did not have when they lived outside of the movement.

The lifestyle in a dakwah community rests on a complex religious interpretation of authoritative sources and requires continuous study and growth in both knowledge and consciousness. All the characteristic beliefs and behavior of the group are based on some passage in the Qur'an, or on some aspect of the Hadith and Sunna. Everything must be rooted in scripture, in the word or intent of Allah as anchored in Qur'an and Hadith, and as synthesized in the commentaries beginning with the massive compilations of al-Ghazali (1058–1111 C.E.). Although much time and energy are devoted to the study and explication of sacred and authoritative texts, the level of learned discourse depends on the kinds of questions asked. The same question may be asked over and over again, with slight variations, and the same answer given.

In the most direct and simplest terms, tradition is what the dakwah teaches, interprets, and tries to apply to daily life. Those involved in this group's interpretation of Islamic tradition want to transcend the physical world (the *elam shada,* the *Zahir*) for the spiritual world *(al-ghaib, or batin)*. They want to follow the timeless, universal, and unchanging laws of Allah as laid out in Islam. Now they seek to build a fortress against the world so that desire can be dampened and thought and energy be directed toward Allah and his prescribed way of life which is the road to salvation. Eventually they hope to receive the great gift of grace (*baraka*) and be among the elect on the day of final judgment. Life is defined as a hierarchy of obedience and submission. It is a chain from Allah to religious teachers, to parents and elders down to children. For them the value of the dakwah life-style is that it trains one in submission and obedience—it is the true embodiment of Islam as a complete way of life both outwardly and inwardly. Authentic, true, and faithful Islam can be practiced only with the proper *niat* (heartfelt intention), but niat can only be nourished in a proper dakwah setting, because the larger world, with its mundane concerns, corrupts people so that their lives are either trivial or immoral or both. So they believe.

The Historical Background of Malaysian Dakwah

Part of a movement that is international in scope, the Kelantan group is but one small leaf on the tree of dakwah. That the community stands out as different even in Kelantan, where the heritage of religious training in pondok schools runs very deep, is a clear sign that the entire dakwah movement has been viewed as something of a novelty in Malaysia. With a history of religiously based political opposition to the dominant ruling authority in Malaysia, Kelantan has exhibited characteristics conducive to the rise of dakwah. Yet Kelantan is not self-contained. Nor is this particular group a home-grown example of Kelantanese piety. Rather, it has its origin in the Malaysian capital, Kuala Lumpur, a city that could hardly ever compete with Kelantan for the honor of being known as Malaysia's "Qur'an belt." So it may be said that this leaf on the tree of dakwah is not an isolated phenomenon; to the contrary, it is a local expression of a new style of religiosity present among a very highly educated new generation of Malays.

The new style of religiosity and its sociopolitical implications has been the concern of national leaders and social analysts since the dakwah movement first began to blossom in the early 1970s. No simple answers can be given. But a review of Malaysia's history and some of the ongoing tensions in Malaysian society will offer some clues. Now some twenty years into the movement, it is clear that the Islamic consciousness of the Muslim population has been raised significantly. In 1971 when Malays would tell a foreign visitor about Malay customs they would say, *"Kita orang Melayu"* ("We Malay people"). Now they say, *"Kita orang Islam"* ("We Muslim people"). Conversion to Islam in Malaysia was once described as *masuk Melayu* (entering Malay ways). Now it is termed *masuk Islam* (entering Islam). The difference is clearly due to the ripple effect upon the entire Malay community of a movement that has not only increased the religious accent on ethnic identity but has also made the individual's social credibility dependent on the validation of religious authority. There has in turn been a competition for such religious authority.

This pervasive competition for religious authority, for a way of "constructing the orthodox" in differing social contexts, is a reminder that the dakwah movement was both born in and partakes of religious diversity. The guru of the dakwah group profiled above enjoyed sufficient religious authority to be invited to give Friday sermons at nearby mosques, yet the group he led refused to send its own children to any outside "official" religious schools. As a recent study of contemporary Islam in Singapore shows, Malay religiosity is constantly being pulled between a "subsidiary awareness" of religious diversity and a more general acceptance of the notion of Islam as embodying certain universal truths.[11] These truths about Allah, Muhammad, and the Qur'an are themselves subject to interpretation. Thus while all Malays regard themselves and are regarded by others as Muslims from birth, they do not all practice their faith in the very same way. Moreover, they are aware of the heightened diversity of a society that includes Muslims who are not Malays (for example, Indian and Pakistani Muslims, or Chinese converts to Islam). This subsidiary awareness of diversity among Muslims is in tension with the deeply held conviction that Islam is uniformly true everywhere. Because such uniformity is not realized in the daily life of the society, a pressing and ongoing need exists for an active construction of "orthodoxy" on the part of individual believers or groups of believers who seek to establish their religious authority—and thereby, in many present-day Malaysian social contexts, their social credibility as well. In short, orthodoxy, whether conceived in a fundamentalist or a traditionalist mode, is the third term situated between actual diversity and an ever elusive and vaguely conceived uniformity. Dakwah is in many ways the open pursuit of this orthodoxy as a means of acting on one's convictions that "Islamic truth" really holds in the face of one's experience of diversity. The significant question is why at a particular time this pursuit of the orthodox should become so charged and urgent as to require a special label, namely, dakwah.

That orthodoxy must always be constructed and thus imposed through competition for religious authority gives the multiple orthodoxies promulgated by the various Malaysian dakwah groups their somewhat fluid quality. Indeed, the social competition for religious authority among Malay Muslims occurs openly and unhindered, and dakwah groups typically imbue their intense commitment with a spirit of openness and exploration. Thus "tolerance" is actually a strategy within this competition, and it is not uncommon to hear accusations of *kafir-mengafir* (calling each other heathens) voiced by rival Islamic leaders and organizations.

A similar deepening of Islamic and ethnic consciousness affected the Malay world in the first decades of this century. A dispute arose between a reformist group known as the Kaum Muda (the Young Party) and a traditionalist group known as the Kaum Tua (the Old Party).[12] Though confined to intellectual circles, unlike the present-day dakwah movement, the Kaum Muda movement drew on a similar dynamism and manifested the ability to win over young Malays who were receiving modern secular forms of education. Significantly, it represented the first strong identification in modern times of Malay Muslims with the wider international world of Islam.

The Kaum Muda reformers had two goals. First, they advocated modernization, including the reform of education on a secular model. Second, they endorsed a religious program that would sound quite fundamentalist today: a return to the Qur'an and the Hadith and, perhaps more revolutionary in a Sunni context, a return to the conscious practice of *ijtihad* (independent interpretation) of these fundamental sources.[13] They challenged the Malay sultans and their traditional religious bureaucracies, both of which had been given renewed authority in cultural and religious affairs by the British colonial administration. In response, the Kaum Tua defended an integral view of Malay culture and Islam, a position that, subject to shifting interpretations, remains quite relevant today. Indeed, the equation of Malay identity with Islamic identity is one of the few axioms in the cultural logic of Malaysian ethnic pluralism.

Though lacking the mass appeal of today's dakwah movement, the Kaum Muda movement was able to produce and sustain for decades a polarization in Malay discourse about Islamic consciousness and conduct. A contemporary observer of the Malay world of the 1940s described the situation as consisting of three parties: the Kaum Muda, the Kaum Tua and the Orang Mudaz, who "waver between the two."[14] This legacy of contentiousness appears again in the competition for religious authority that pervades Malay social encounters today.

There was, however, a significant difference between the old and the new reformers. While the Kaum Muda accepted a measure of Westernization as a result of modernization, the present-day revivalists, already more Westernized, denounce this connection. Westernization for them is corrupting and un-Islamic. And modernization, even if it can be separated from Westernization, is to be approached with great caution if it is to be reconciled with Islam as a complete way of life. (The current dakwah groups differ in their assessments of the possibility for such reconciliation.) This radical devaluing of Western cultural influences widened the religious generation gap on the eve of the birth of the contemporary dakwah among Malay students.

The riots of 13 May 1969 between Malays and Chinese in Kuala Lumpur set the stage for the birth of the movement. The events precipating the riots form the background to the cauldron of ethnicities that is modern Malaysia. A sense of the pivotal nature of the riots in the everyday understanding of Malay society can be gathered from an observation made in 1971, when they were still a fairly fresh memory. Older and middle-aged Malays of that time described themselves as having lived through four *masas* (ages or periods): the *masa orang putch* (European colonialism), the *masa Jepun* (Japanese occupation), *Merdeka* (Independence), and *Tigabelas Mei* (13 May). In other words, the changes in social expectations brought on by the riots and the subsequent government measures to prevent future clashes were experienced as being equal in magnitude to the rise of European colonialism, the Japanese takeover of Malaya, or the founding of an independent Malaysian nation-state.[15]

In the wake of the riots there would be new guarantees that Malays would retain political control of the nation, and promises of a New Economic Policy (NEP) featuring strong affirmative action measures aimed at raising Malay educational and economic levels to a parity with those of the Chinese population. There would also be a general effort to eradicate (later revised to "lessen") poverty among all citizens of Malaysia, whether Malay or non-Malay. (The NEP was to run for twenty years, after which, in 1990, the time of this writing, its accomplishments would be reviewed and a decision made on its continued implementation or on a suspension or revision of its main provisions.) Ironic as it may seem now, at the time the NEP was formulated to address the nation's ills of poverty and ethnic conflict, none of its authors could have anticipated that over the twenty-year course of its implementation the government would spend much of its energy in reaction to an Islamic resurgence led by the very first beneficiaries of the new plans as put forth. The rise and viability of dakwah came as a surprise to the government.

Dakwah was not an altogether welcome surprise at that. Religion had simply not figured in the pragmatic calculations designed to stimulate economic progress. Such calculations presumed a level of political stability, and for the sake of political stability there would have to be a containment of ethnic tensions. Dakwah entered as a wild card in national planning. Would it be easily politicized? Was it simply a new ground for ethnic polarization? Both the government and Malaysia's non-Muslim minorities were put on the defensive by the movement. Malays themselves became somewhat polarized by it. The government's post–13 May promise of *muhibbah* (goodwill) to all was drowned out by dakwah, the call to return to the faith, and by its own policies which were now so strongly biased toward Malays.

The historical and social context of the 13 May riots is therefore crucial to an understanding of the appeal and prominence of dakwah. Since independence in 1957, the ethnic breakdown of Malaysia's population, which now numbers close to fifteen million, has remained fairly constant, with 50 percent Malay, 37 percent Chinese, and 11 percent Indian (peninsular figures).[16] With most of the Chinese and many of the Indians concentrated in the larger towns and cities of Malaysia's west coast states, there are many sizable local districts in which these "minorities" actually outnumber the Malays. It has been impossible to govern without the active involvement and consent of each of the groups. Still, each of the groups has a different historical and economic relation to the development of the nation, and so their respective roles, politically, economically, and even culturally, are negotiated apart from the consideration of sheer numbers alone.

This divided mix is of course a heritage of colonialism. For a century, from 1820 to 1920, there was a period of free immigration into parts of British Malaysia. In the building of the British Empire three "mother races" were involved—the British, the Chinese, and the Indians. Indians came as plantation laborers, minor clerks, railway workers, money lenders, and traders. The Chinese came as laborers, tin miners, vegetable farmers, and itinerant merchants. During this century of the growth of Western enterprise, the Malay population was largely indifferent to the influx of immigrants and hardly involved in modern economic activities. The Malays were sultans and nobles, paddy farmers, fisherman, artisans, or civil servants. The three major groups did not compete economically, did not mingle socially, and in the colonial situation, did not contest for political power.

In legal terms, the Malays under the British were considered to be the host population, and so while sovereignty rested with the British colonial administration, political legitimacy, as expressed through existing political and legal custom, remained vested in the sultans and their courts. The Chinese were considered sojourners, come for economic reasons, who would move on when their economic ends were met. The Chinese were mysterious (to the British, Malays, and Indians), with languages difficult to speak and more difficult yet to read. They were organized in a form of indirect rule under "Capitans China," responsible for local order and labor discipline. Islam in Malaya did not need to, nor did it, take a position on the Chinese, except as possible converts to a not very dynamic or evangelical Malay Islam.[17]

Plantation Indians, mainly Tamils, were organized in the workers lines on the plantations under British managers and overseers. Hospitals, schools, and temples grew up in the closed world of Tamil culture structured on the plantation division of labor, where whole families engaged in economic activity. It was unclear if the majority of Indians expected to return to the subcontinent, but many did. The question of identification with Malaya, a mere administrative entity from a Tamil point of view, never arose. Hinduism, in its manifold South Indian modes, lived at ease with Islam, and the Malays abided the temple-centered worship of the Tamils.[18]

After the 1920s there was a sizable increase in both Chinese and Indian populations. The first stirrings of Malay nationalism date from this time, as do the stronger reactions of the Kaum Tua conservative Malay Muslims to what were recognized as the foreign influences upon Malays of the Kaum Muda.[19] These cleavages were further deepened by forms of Malay proto-nationalism of a purely secular and radical (for the era) sort that arose among the tiny segment of Malay graduates of the British-created vernacular (Malay) school system. This movement was aimed as much against the traditional Malay elites who comprised the Islamic Kaum Muda-Kaum Tua controversy as it was against the British. And like the Islamic elites, they too failed to establish a mass following and as a result had little impact. A third strand of emergent national consciousness coalesced in the late 1930s among the sons of the traditional Malay elite: the princely and titled families. Graduates of the exclusive Malay College Kuala Kangsar, and comfortably ensconced in the colonial civil service, this loosely organized group found greater popular resonance, if no greater immediate results, with a conservative set of demands centering around a vague interest in protecting Malay interest from "outside threats" (immigration was clearly the threat that concerned them).[20]

The era from the Japanese occupation (1941–45) and World War II to independence in 1957 was marked by shifts in relations among the Malays, Chinese, and Tamils. In this period it became clearer that most of the Chinese were not going to return to an unstable war-torn mainland China. Furthermore, there was a significant number of Malaya-born Chinese who had no longings for a land they had never known. The Chinese had diversified to fill most of the openings in the economy for commercial middlemen. Some became very rich *Towkays*, as the local capitalists were called, while others remained in the urban proletariat. Because of the postwar insurrection called "the Emergency" (1948–60), involving Chinese identified with communism, almost all of the Chinese had become urban, having moved or having been moved from the countryside for security and military reasons. They also began to demand citizenship and participation in the political processes of Malaya. These demands were most effectively articulated on the national level by the Malayan (later Malaysian) Chinese Association (MCA), founded in 1949 in Kuala Lumpur and controlled largely by the heads of the powerful Chinese business community.[21]

This growth of Chinese political consciousness was inevitably to run into the rising tide of Malay nationalism, which by this time had also taken organizational form in the creation of several ethnically based political parties. The two most prominent of these were the United Malay National Organization (UMNO), founded in 1946, and the Malayan National Party (MNP), founded in 1945. The Malay parties were all quite steadfast in resisting Chinese encroachments into political domains which they regarded as their own rightful heritage as passed down through the Malay rulers.

Under the British, Malays and Indians did not have to deal directly with each other politically, but immediately prior to and following independence, they did. From the outset this has been a process of Malays negotiating with non-Malays over those things which will no longer be negotiable, such as the status of the Malay rulers, the special rights of Malays, the importance of the Malay language, and the official status of Islam. The idea of a fully equal citizenship for non-Malays did not and still does not merit acceptance.

Thus the question of "Who or what is a Malay?" is foundational to the Malaysian nation. And history's legacy is somewhat complicated when it comes to answering this central question of identity. The constitution designated birth, language, custom, and religion as the criteria of Malayness. The Malay political parties have generally worked within this framework but are differentiated by which of the multiply indexed criteria of Malayness each champions. For UMNO, it has been race, language, and custom, especially those customs and arts that had for so long flourished as a way of demonstrating loyalty to the Malay rulers. But for UMNO's main rival, the former MNP, it has been Islam, race, and language. Indeed, the MNP has twice reconstituted and renamed itself so as to declare its evolving commitment to Islam as the first priority in Malay politics. Thus in 1951 it became the Pan-Malayan Islamic Party (PMIP),[22] and then again in 1973, with an eye to embarrassing its rival, UMNO, for having only an English-language name, it became Partai Al-Islam Se-Malaysia (the Islamic Party of Malaysia), better known as PAS.

In trying to unite Muslims, and in particular to unite Malays as Muslims, the PMIP/PAS began both as reformist, in that it agitated for a return to the Qur'an and the Hadith, and as traditionalist, in that it allowed some scope for the rulings of Muslim teachers through the operation of ijtihad. Made up of Malays (it excluded Indian Muslims from its hierarchy), it attempted early on to avoid the old division between the Kaum Muda and the Kaum Tua.[23] Though having its strongest support in states like Kedah, Kelantan, and Trengganu, where the traditional forms of Islamic education and sultan's religious councils are the strongest, PMIP/PAS's potential challenge to UMNO has always injected into Malaysian national politics the question of which ethnic Malay party best speaks for the Malays. Is it the more conspicuously Islamic one? Or the one more broadly and emphatically oriented to Malay sovereignty? At the national level it has been the latter, UMNO, which has most often won out. But it has done so primarily through a successful coalition with the two leading non-Malay ethnically based parties, the MCA and the MIC (the Malaysian Indian Congress). And each of these key partners in what was known for over a decade as the Alliance coalition has always had to contend with its own set of co-ethnic rivals and internal divisions.

The collapse of this delicate balance of power precipitated the communal riots of May 1969. From 1957 to 1969 the Alliance of communal parties controlled the national government and most of the state governments. Competing interests among ethnic groups were quietly negotiated among like-minded leaders of the Alliance's constituent ethnic parties. An "understanding" existed to the effect that the Malays, by virtue of their numerical superiority and indigenous status, were to enjoy primacy in independent Malaysia. This would be expressed by Malays holding, through a victorious UMNO, the top political offices; by special consideration for Malays in the civil service and educational sectors and in the licensing of businesses; by the symbolic recognition of Islam as intrinsic to the state; and most critically, by the recognition that a gradual implementation of Malay as the language of government and education was inevitable.[24] There remained for non-Malays a substantial opportunity for business growth, vernacular primary schools, some civil service and educational opportunities, an equitable judiciary system based on secular English law, and freedom of religion.

By May 1969 these understandings and compromises worked out among Malaysia's various founding fathers were beginning to wear thin. After a very divisive campaign in which the primary issue centered on the increasing concentration of power and influence in the hands of ethnic Malays, the Alliance coalition was handed a significant defeat, losing twenty-three seats in the lower house of parliament, and with them, a ruling majority. The Alliance collapsed amid bitter recriminations, leaving as winners an unlikely group of small parties, including the PMIP/PAS, the Democratic Action Party, which appealed to younger Chinese, and several leftist parties. This opposition victory was the catalyst for two weeks of bloody rioting. As opposition supporters took to the streets to celebrate their victory, fighting broke out, apparently the result of racial epithets hurled at Malays by opposition supporters. Though most of the fighting remained confined to Kuala Lumpur, with only a few sporadic incidents in other areas, hundreds of people, mostly Chinese and Indians, were killed. The government declared a state of emergency and formed the National Operations Council (NOC) under the leadership of Deputy Prime Minister Tun Abdul Razak, which effectively governed the country until the restoration of parliamentary rule on 20 February 1971.

This rupture had a traumatic impact that is hard to imagine. The possibility of open civil war loomed large in Malaysia. In the writings about the events of May 1969, the religious idiom of the end of the world is frequently invoked. The danger was clear, even though the future was not.

The primary legacies of the interim period of NOC rule were the further strengthening of the special status of the Malays, a reconfirmation of Malay as the national language, the dissolving of any political groups opposing Malay special status, the promulgation of a national ideology or creed *(Rukun Negara),* and the launching of the New Economic Policy (NEP) in the Second Malaysia Plan (1971–75).[25] Yet it became clear that electoral politics in Malaysia could never be used to erode the special position of the Malays, and massive new efforts began to integrate Malays fully into the higher levels of the modern economy. The effort at symbolic renewal in the creation of a national creed had a much less lasting impact. In fact the Rukun Negara faded from national consciousness about as quickly as it rolled off the tongues of the thousands of Malaysia's schoolchildren who were required to memorize it.

With order restored and the Malays assured of a preeminent place in the political, if not the economic, life of the nation, politics resumed with the replacement in 1972 of the old Alliance coalition with a new and broader one under the banner of Barisan

Nasional (the National Front). UMNO was again the senior partner, and the original allies, the MCA and the MIC, stayed in. But in addition, and after some careful maneuvering, two former opponents, the Democratic Action Party (DAP) and the PMIP/PAS, were also brought in. This new combination scored a major success at its first opportunity in the 1974 elections, winning 130 out of 154 parliamentary seats and 344 out of 392 state assembly seats.[26] It has since continued to dominate through a succession of three different prime ministers, much internal wrangling within its constituent parties, the withdrawal in 1977 of PAS, an economic recession, growing discontent among non-Malays regarding the provisions of the NEP, and the rise of dakwah.

The Rise of Malaysian Dakwah

The transition period that began before the riots and lasted until Malaysia's return to parliamentary democracy in 1972 was a time of student activism. But this was a broadly social and nationalistic activism, not yet an Islamic activism. Anwar Ibrahim, then president of the University of Malaya Malay Language Society, later became founder and president of Angkatan Belia Islam Malaysia (ABIM, the Muslim Youth Movement of Malaysia), the dakwah movement's foremost organization. In a 1987 interview he recalled the beginnings of dakwah: "It was an explosive time. There were lots of issues . . . Malay poverty, language, corruption. And after May 13, you just got hooked on immediately. It was all a question of the survival of the ummah, of the Malay race. Previously we had been thinking about all these problems outside Islam, when actually we could have solved them through Islam."[27]

It is quite likely that the reference to "the ummah" is an anachronism introduced by virtue of hindsight. For the idealism of the students in the days following the riots was devoted to "the cause of the Malay people" and to a general concern for social justice—a concern articulated prior to a conscious Islamic formulation thereof. Apart from their strong Malay nationalism, the stated goals of the students were those of many other sincere young people seeking to improve conditions for the underprivileged. Gradually, however, over a period of about three years, this concern for social justice came to expressed in an Islamic idiom: "the underprivileged" became the ummah, and the "solutions" followed Islamic prescriptions.

The experience of the riots obviously radicalized the students and others who participated in it. But why did it also eventually Islamicize them? That is more difficult to grasp. Did Malay nationalism, having reached this militant boiling point and feeling threatened, simply rally around Islam? Did the young men interpret their role in the riots as participation in jihad? Perhaps. Did this interpretation then move them to study the Qur'an and Hadith more seriously in subsequent years? That seems less likely. Curiously, many participants or witnesses to the events of those tragic nights described their violent intensity with the Malay term *mengamuk* (running amok), rather than as jihad. And mengamuk enjoys a type of legitimacy in the Malay world. It can refer either to an unprovoked violent rampage or to intense and suicidal bravery in defense of a proper Malay ruler or lord. Given that the riots followed by only three days the first serious threat to the Malay political establishment after twelve years of independent rule, the description of the event as mengamuk may in fact be appropriate.

The Islamization of the participants likely came after the fact. In the Malayan context, this shift among the students under a period of political and social crisis may have been very similar to the shift reported above for the old Malayan National Party before independence. For it was during the nationalist struggles and dissatisfactions of that time that an important offshoot of the MNP found its Malayness in Islam. Then as the re-formed PMIP/PAS it went on to erode the UMNO's popular identification with both Islam and the Malay language.

The initial motivation behind dakwah two decades later—service to the cause of Malay social justice—and the subsequent (re)discovery of Islamic principles duplicated the earlier process. But the outcomes have been different, and in some ways incompatible, since the respective repertoires of concepts from which to construct and supply Islamic principles were very different in the two periods. The PMIP/PAS leaders consisted of ulama and ustazes whose lives had been devoted to the study and teaching of Islam. From their standpoint, the students of the next generation seemed eager but shallow. But the students in turn were smug and condescending in their attitudes toward these religious leaders, for they considered the traditional Islam of rural Malays to be rife with Indic and superstitious accretions.

The key point is that in its inception the dakwah movement went through a transition that had political origins quite parallel to those of PMIP/PAS. Later student generations recruited into dakwah groups and activities would often lose touch with the original political motivations. Some would focus more on individual religiosity; others would articulate their goals in the revivalist idiom of an immediate call for an Islamic state, rather than in terms of the founders' more inclusive call for "social justice."

But if the students returned from the riots of 1969 to their campuses not yet fully committed to a specifically *Islamic* resurgence, events on the international Islamic front, coupled with the tight controls placed on their more overt political activities at home, were soon to push them in that direction.

First among the events on the international scene that led to the sudden emergence of the dakwah movement was the oil boom of the early 1970s and the rise in power of the oil producing states over the industrial West. This was interpreted as a part of Allah's grace, a special dispensation. Some Arab money from the oil revenues even came to Malaysia to assist in the spread and strengthening of Islam via such international Islamic organizations as the Mecca-based World Muslim League. When oil was discovered offshore in Malaysia, this was understood as a sure sign of Allah's bounty to followers of the last Prophet: Allah had blessed Islamic peoples with oil to enable them to compete with others who received different gifts. Folk wisdom about the divine distribution of of good things in this world holds that the West received science and technology; the Jews (or modern Israelis), intelligence, acumen, and solidarity; the Chinese, diligence and business sense. The Malays had received Islam and now oil to further its spread and hasten the establishment of a just society leading to the promised Day of Judgment.

A second, later international event which at least momentarily increased the prestige of dakwah was the Islamic revolution in Iran under the aegis of the charismatic Khomeini. It was noted in Malaysia that Khomeini, like Muhammad, rose to political and worldly power on faith alone. Once such interpretations gained credence, world-historical events took on a dramatic religious significance in the minds of some Malaysians, and the dakwah movement seemed part of a larger divine drama.

In Malaysia itself other events influenced the early phase of the movement. Important among these was the imposition in 1971 of the Universities Act and the even tougher Universities and University Colleges Act of 1975, which prohibited student membership in political parties and greatly restricted student rights to hold independent public meetings, rallies, or demonstrations. Religious meetings, on the other hand, seemed not to fall under these curbs. So it was almost certain that existing Malay/Muslim student activism would be further, if at first somewhat quietly, channeled into overtly religious forms.[28]

Equally important to the birth and then sudden spread of dakwah was the fact that Anwar Ibrahim and the student leaders around him in the University of Malaya Malay Language Society clearly possessed exceptional organizational abilities enhanced by personal charisma. They succeeded in winning the leadership of several other important campus and national student organizations, including the coveted leadership of the University of Malaya Student Union.[29] In addition, they effectively involved many students in service projects for the poor in Malaysia's rural villages. In this way they tried to instill in upwardly mobile, degree-bound new students a continuing concern for the masses of poorer Malays who were yet to receive any real benefits from the country's supposed development. In one case they even turned their egalitarian ideals to organizational advantage when they declared a moratorium on the rather harsh "ragging" or initiation tradition at the University of Malaya. They instead provided alternative orientation programs for incoming students, thereby winning many grateful new recruits to their cause.

Some academics also lent support to the movement. Syed Naguib al-Atlas, the dean of Arts at the university, acted as a kind of mentor to Anwar. At the same time Inradudin Abdul Rahim, from the Institute of Technology in Bandung, Java, was teaching at the University of Technology, Malaysia. He brought ideas from the Indonesian Islamic renewal to Malaysia. And many Malaysian students made trips to Indonesia to learn more about a vibrant Islam from the pious (santri) teachers there.[30]

Then, in a tactical move, Anwar and al-Atlas founded the Muslim Youth Movement of Malaysia (ABIM) in 1971 as a permanent organization outside the university through which the first generation of dakwah leaders could continue their organizational activities well past graduation. With Anwar as its president from 1972 to 1982, ABIM opened many new chapters throughout Malaysia, even while continuing its special services for, and recruitment efforts among, the new generations of students who would pour onto the major campuses throughout the 1970s and 1980s. The group's leaders estimate that membership grew from nine thousand in 1972 to thirty-five thousand by 1980. Of current members, it is estimated that 90 percent are between fifteen and forty years of age, with about 11 percent female. Women in ABIM have a separate women's section.

The early success of ABIM must, of course, be seen in light of the mood of that time. The Malay college and university students of the immediate post–riot years believed themselves to be a generation of destiny as the first of their people to inherit an independent nation and to have the doors of modern opportunity open for them. For them there was promise and privilege, but also there was peril: the peril of competitive exams upon which their new mobility was to be launched; the peril of the unknown, new standard of the NEP; the perils of competitive encounters with alien people—Chinese, Indians, and Europeans—and finally the peril of an unknown future for the Malay people in their own land and for the Malaysian nation as then constituted.

These young people had their own private worries in their hearts and the public burdens of their people on their shoulders. Their desire to serve justice and their families was strong within them. As individuals, most were timid, but they were prone to idealism, and as their peer group leaders began to act on this idealism, charismatic leaders emerged. At first equality, Malay nationalism, and economic development were the bywords for their idealism. Vocation outreach programs in the Malaysian countryside were the hallmark of their early activism. Their concern for disadvantaged rural Malays was the touchstone for their often critical stance vis-à-vis the dominant Malay political party, UMNO, and its leaders. The government was expected to do more to improve the lot of the poorer Malays. The idealistic students of the time were willing to support official programs aimed at economic development, and would even volunteer to help with some programs, but still expected much more. They also began to question the political motivations and the secular rationale behind the actions and policies of UMNO leaders. Coupled with the inability of populist socialism to serve as an alternative in Malaysia, this discontent with governmental policies prompted a sharp turn to religion—to a confirmation of individual faith and to the expression of that faith through an activism associated with the wider world of Islam—as the best way to meet the leadership needs of the Malay people and their nation.[31]

In the 1970s, when the government opened up university education to Malays as part of its efforts to "level up" that segment of the Malaysian population, dakwah gained momentum from three sources. First, there was a large increase in students from rural and peasant backgrounds recruited to the urban universities. This first contact with the modern, pluralistic urban milieu left many of the newcomers disoriented and vulnerable to the appeals of what seemed on first contact to be a traditional group. Second, there was also a great flood of students, some with government support, going overseas to study. Far from home, confronted by an alien and sometimes threatening environment, Malaysian Muslim students have often found some consolation in the company of Muslims from other nations. In this context they have also been exposed to the ideas of Islamic revivalism which have become popular with their foreign coreligionists.[32] Third, Malaysian dakwah was spread among Malay students abroad, especially in the British universities of Brighton and Sussex. There a Pakistani, Javed Ansari, formed an organization called Suara Islam that was the first to denounce the Alliance ruling coalition in Malaysia as "un-Islamic." Thus dakwah entered politics, not as an effective party, but as a rebuke to the dominant parties.

The choice of the term *dakwah* was appropriate in that the major activity of the students was to recruit other students in a very personalized each-one-teach-one sort of way. The mutual urging to greater Islamic consciousness or religious commitment that characterized the early campus cell groups and networks soon took on the outward manifestation of Arabic-style clothing—mini prayer shawls for women, turbans and long shirts for men. This visible sign of religious reawakening led to the women in the movement being called "the dakwah girls"[33] (Malay *orang berdakwah,* "the people who preach"). This choice of label has by now taken on a life of its own but may still be regarded as revealing. It suggests that the Malaysian Islamic resurgence has labeled itself after its most immediate religious experience, namely, the act of renewing or strengthening one's own personal faith by the reinforcing act of converting someone else. The each-one-teach-one interpersonal locus of the young Muslims' search for a deeper faith is the immediate context in which the weakness of faith within oneself is repeatedly overcome by actively convincing another of the need for faith. Dakwah—calling the other to faith—is the most fundamental act of Islamic fundamentalism in Malaysia.

Despite differences in ideology, all dakwah movements are similar in organizational structure. The basic unit is a cell-like body called the usrah. The usrah is made up of about ten students of a single sex. This is a discussion and a mutual support group that develops an esprit de corps and deep camaraderie. Here the sense of mission and purpose is honed. As members pray together, talk together, and socialize almost exclusively within the usrah, it becomes the sole focus of the person's life. Involvement with the usrah separates the student from those not sharing the same depth of commitment to the dakwah. This cell also is a recruiting station for new adherents.

By the mid-1980s the usrah had effectively become a separate part of student subculture in general. They seem to form effortlessly whether closely tied to a single larger group or not. Indeed, some usrah are independent of any larger organizations, and their members sample the varieties of Islamic educational, service, and prayer programs available regardless of sponsorship. With the usrah as a home base, dakwah in the universities has recently become more diffuse and a bit less restrictive.

What has the rise of dakwah meant to the Malaysian state and society? Dakwah's impact to date must be analyzed first in light of the movement's origins in the post-1969 cultural struggle to forge a distinctively Malaysian national identity that would not be compromised by ethnic or racial or religious tensions. As one force in that struggle, dakwah attained a measure of visibility and influence by offering coherent (if perhaps partial) alternative ways of coping with a harshly competitive socioeconomic environment suffused with ambiguous and conflicting worldviews. In that sense dakwah is a protest ideology: it protests the shortcomings of a venal secular world concerned with pragmatics, power, and material things and offers a vision of an exalted moral life as a remedy. Malaysia is a nation in which ethnic identity is a pressing issue, in which socioeconomic disparities among communal groups demand both explanation and remediation, in which Western, secular, and modern ideas and life styles challenge older Malay, religious, and traditional ways. In such contexts, dakwah's appeal to the young is partially explained by the power of a religious language of transcendence and absolutism in the face of a challenging, ambiguous, and modernizing national state beset by growing disillusion with the ruling elites and disaffection with government and its policies. Dakwah also provides a footing for Malay identity among Malay students who must compete in the Malaysian educational system against their Chinese and Indian peers who have by now so mastered textbook Malay as to have erased the used of the Malay language as a marker and shield for Malay identity. The success of the national language policy has in this way disrobed Malay ethnic identity, forcing it to be reclothed (both literally and figuratively) in Islam.

The Impact of Malaysian Dakwah

As the first generation of dakwah has matured and entered all spheres of Malaysian society, the movement's cultural impact has been considerable. Its political role in relation to the politics of ethnicity in Malaysia is also considerable—if ridden with paradox.

All Malay states as well as the federal government in Malaysia have official bodies to promote and further Islam. But the dakwah groups so attractive to the young have been more spontaneous.[34] Studies of the student population at the University of Malaya show that 60 to 70 percent of the Malays are involved with dakwah in various degrees. Among the "colonies" of Malay students sent abroad, similar figures are likely. The dress of the female university students mentioned above is a visible and sensitive indicator of the depth and kind of dakwah support. The minimally committed wear the mini-*telekung;* the middle range of commitment is exhibited by wearing the *hijab,* covering the body to the wrists and ankles, as well as the head and chest veil; and the fullest degree of attachment is this costume, but all in black, and called *purdah*. Biographical accounts indicate similar gradations as individuals move through personal dakwah careers. Some start with actual resentment of the holier-than-thou attitude of the groups that seek their participation but then later move all the way up to wearing the hijab. The range is dynamic.

Reflecting this range of commitment and self-understanding is the variety of forms of dakwah organizations that have appeared in Malaysia since the early 1970s—a variety that may be seen in microcosm at the University of Malaya to this day. In addition to the ABIM, dakwah is represented there by Darul Arqam, by the Jama'at-i Tabligh, and by the most recent of these groups, the Islamic Republic. Of these,

ABIM has been the strongest organization but is being challenged currently by the more militant Islamic Republic.

From the beginning, young people were attracted to ABIM because other more directly political organizations had been suppressed. Even those with genuine religious motivations for joining generally do not have a strong religious educational background, and so ABIM has had to develop religious programs. Thus, one of the prominent achievements of ABIM is a series of independent schools established in urban centers in western Malaysia that, like the educational institutions attached to other religious and dakwah groups in Malaysia, offers a course of studies combining secular and religious educational patterns. ABIM has also supported an attempt to develop cooperative economic schemes to encourage greater economic independence for Malays.

ABIM is the least chauvinistic of the dakwah organizations in Malaysia, but there is still significant pro-Malay and anti-Chinese sentiment within the organization. On the issue of making Malaysia into an Islamic state, ABIM has been cautious. While calling for an extension of Islamic law, the focus of the party is on outlawing public displays of immorality (such as prostitution) rather than on a full-fledged reorganization of the state. There has been some cooperation in the past between ABIM and PAS, though this relationship has not been without its problems. The rural and older constituency of the PAS, which includes conservative ulama, has often been at odds with the young urban revivalists of ABIM.

In a dramatic move that would epitomize the ambivalence of ABIM's relations with PAS, its very personification and leader, Anwar Ibrahim, not only chose to resign as head of ABIM to run for public office but he then ran as an UMNO and not as a PAS candidate. This move not only confounded some old supporters; it also blurred the distinction between fundamentalists and accomodationists in the spectrum of Malaysian politics. Indeed UMNO's successful co-option of Anwar was a very important turning point in the politics of the movement. Of course Anwar has moved up in UMNO, with much to gain on his own side of the bargain. Working within the system, he has remained his own man, still pursuing many of ABIM's original goals. As for ABIM itself, its prestige has eroded somewhat without Anwar. But it remains a very effective organization. Its somewhat moderate stance seems in keeping with the times, as Malaysia enters the 1990 NEP revision process. While consistently supporting a strengthening of Islamic identity among the Muslims of Malaysia, ABIM has long recognized that Malaysia as a nation will remain multi-ethnic and multireligious.

The Darul Arqam maintains a commune just outside of Kuala Lumpur led by Ustaz Ashari and dedicated to practicing an Islamic way of life. In many ways this group resembles the dakwah group in Kelantan, except that the Darul Arqam commune strives for even greater self-sufficiency through its own schools and workshops that make handicrafts for sale. Everybody in the group wears distinct white Islamic clothing. The commune school has been notably successful, with the majority of students coming from outside the commune. Many of the students live together in a pondok-type environment. Known for its distinctive Malay chauvinism and anti-

Chinese animus, the Darul Arqam focuses its energies primarily on economic activities. The group seeks to develop enterprises run in a manner consistent with Islamic principles and independent of Chinese and foreign control. In the beginning, Darul Arqam consistently refused any involvement with the government in its economic activities. Since 1978 it has compromised somewhat, by purchasing from government marketing agencies, for example, but it still refuses any direct financial aid. Darul Arqam also operates a clinic in which Western therapies are combined with other approaches. One of the prominent activities of the clinic has been the rehabilitation of drug addicts, no small undertaking in a nation in which even possession of relatively small quantities of illegal drugs warrants the death penalty. There apparently has been a move in recent years in the leadership of the Darul Arqam community to a more mystical and even syncretic Islam, which has alienated some of the faithful.[35]

The Jama'at-i Tabligh, an offspring of an Indian Muslim organization in Delhi, is the most philosophically inclined (see chapter 8). Of the three main dakwah organizations in Malaysia, the Tabligh is the least structured. It relies entirely on the work of volunteer missionaries. Tabligh is an exclusively male organization, although certain modes of dress and behavior are of course expected of the women and households of members of that group. A retreat is obligatory for members for one day a week, three days a month, forty days a year, or four months in a lifetime. Members are encouraged to go to the organization's headquarters in Delhi for longer retreats. Though missionaries claim to use persuasion rather than coercion, there have been reports of aggressive street preaching which leans toward the latter. Originally Tabligh was strongly identified with immigrant Muslims from South Asia, but in recent decades the movement has successfully reached out to Malays as well. Tabligh has been more successful than ABIM or Darul Arqam in the rural community, if only because its non-controversial character has not alienated village ulama. But the bulk of Tabligh's support comes from the same source as the other main dakwah organizations, that is, urban, well-educated youth. Tabligh today deliberately maintains a low social profile and publishes no literature, making it difficult to determine with any certainty its views on specific issues. In fact members seem to hold varying views on some controversial questions.[36]

The most recent offshoot of dakwah is a revolutionary student group known as The Islamic Republic. Apparently galvanized by the example of the Islamic revolution in Iran, this organization calls for activism in support of the establishment of an Islamic state. Such a state would necessarily be imposed upon the ethnically and religiously diverse population of Malaysia. Closely allied with PAS, the Islamic opposition party, the Islamic Republic wrested control of the Islamic Student Society (PMIUM—Persatuan Mahassiwa Islam Universiti Malaya), the most influential student organization for Islamic and dakwah activities, from the ABIM in 1983 and has brought a more militant tone to that organization.[37]

Meanwhile, Malay students abroad are organized in dakwah groups praying together, wearing emblems of Islamic dress, and monitoring the behavior of Malays on the foreign campuses. They greet new arrivals, induct them into the dakwah group, police their conduct, and isolate those who do not commit to dakwah or scoff at it. At American universities with large Malay student bodies, the dakwah group is indeed an intimidating force for the young scholar away from home in a strange culture with a range of permissiveness unknown in Malaysia.[38]

Whether or not these various expressions of dakwah become a coordinated mass movement of enduring political importance with a lasting impact on the life of Malaysia depends on how they interact with UMNO, the chief secular arm of the Malay community, and with PAS. Of some moment is the role that dakwah will play in estrangement or reconciliation between the major communal groups in Malaysia, the Malays, Chinese, and Indians. A crucial factor in this calculus is the stance of the government. Suppression from the capital could push the dakwah groups toward hostility and intolerance on political and communal questions. Yet recent events such as the departure of Anwar from ABIM, the subsequent exodus of some leaders from ABIM to UMNO and PAS, and an Islamization program announced by the government, suggest that dakwah is instead riding the crest of a wave.

The PAS has for some time attempted to mobilize a population in Islamic terms without fully adopting a program of Islamic fundamentalism. The PAS opposes the UMNO, the organization of town-based, salaried, and commercial Malays who made the political pact that was the Alliance. This pact, the PAS maintained, locked people like themselves into the lower strata of the economy, bereft of political power and without dignity in a land owned by strangers and run by Muslims whose cooperation with nonbelievers brought their orthodoxy under suspicion. With appeals to *bangsa* (Malay race or ethnicity), *agama* (a society modeled more closely on the tenets of a pure Islam), and *tanah ayer* (ownership of the land and natural resources by Malays only), the PAS has articulated real economic, class, and cultural grievances. Up to the present these appeals have been made by the local literati—the imams, uztazes, pondok leaders, and the pious. But such a movement cannot stand still. It must make compromises with the national elite or move on to greater and more forceful opposition. Poised for a time between remaining a national opposition party with an Islamic program or gravitating toward more fundamentalist demands, PAS seems now headed in the latter direction.

Meanwhile, the UMNO is engaged in an internecine battle which will determine the character of that party and perhaps the future shape of national politics. To the date of this writing, 1990, a fundamentalist version of Islam has not come to dominate the body politic in Malaysia. Were dakwah to become a major political force in the PAS, which is now within the realm of probability, then the victory of fundamentalism would be more likely. With the unstable mix of religion, ethnicity, politics, and economics in Malaysia, such an event is possible.

Whatever the outcome is of these internecine struggles within and between the political parties of Malaysia, there can be no question that the dakwah movement has already had a substantial impact on Malaysian political culture, and that the ultimate response of that political power structure to the challenge posed by the dakwah movement will determine the fate of Malaysian democracy. One indication that compromise and accommodation are likely stems from the fact that the main dakwah organizations are not apocalyptic in orientation. They are basically concerned with the here and now and promote social policies informed by a desire for social justice and correct behavior (as they understand them) rather than thaumaturgical or millenarian crusading.

Although there has not been a single, united government response to dakwah, it is possible to say that there has been a general feeling of apprehension about the negative impact the movement could have on Malay unity, as well as on the UMNO itself. In this situation, because of the very popularity of dakwah, the government attempts to deflate the movement but cannot allow itself to appear to openly oppose it. Consistent with this policy, the government has established dakwah organizations of its own. In 1974, the Religious Council for the Federal District (Majlis Ugama Islam) was created. It has attempted various initiatives to counter or to supplant dakwah. Since 1969, the Islamic Educational Centre has occasionally been involved in similar projects. Ironically, the programs of the Centre sometimes have served to sensitize rural areas to religious issues, thus opening the door for more effective dakwah preaching. In the 1970s, the Dakwah Foundation was created specifically for training in the Muslim faith along the lines of dakwah. Through its journal *Dakwah* the group airs varying views but in a blend which tends to support the government's policies toward Islam.

The government has also instituted a number of small but visible changes which are at least symbolically important. For example, there are now prayer rooms in all government offices and army barracks. The government is concerned that it not be identified as standing in the way of individuals who wish to be observant. Although most government employees are not encouraged to wear full Islamic dress because it might give an image of backwardness to outsiders, religious content has none the less steadily increased in the mass media, which is dependent upon the government for approval of programming and licences.[39]

While generally pursuing an accommodationist policy, the Malaysian government has also taken some steps toward limiting the activities of the various dakwah groups. Government officials occasionally denounce the "extremism" of "certain groups" as antithetical to true Islam. The groups in question are often not named, which allows the government to crank out general warnings without directly alienating specific groups. There was in the mid-1980s some suspicion that civil service employees involved in dakwah would be subject to purge. Local officials look for technicalities to block speeches by dakwah leaders, fearing the growing power of dakwah at the expense of their own influence. The most effective government counter to dakwah, however, has been neither dire warnings nor minor harassment, but the creation of the Islamic Welfare and Missionary Association (Pertubuhan Kebajikan Islam Malaysia, or PERKIM). In its missionary activities, PERKIM has been directed mostly at the Chinese community. Since the mid-1970s, and in response to dakwah, PERKIM has become more aggressive in its missionary initiatives. For example, it now frequently publishes a statistical update of the number of people converted.

PERKIM represents a relatively safe channel for the energies unleashed by the dakwah movement. Missionary activity, among the Chinese or among the *orang asli* (aboriginal tribal peoples) holds little substantive risk for the government. So long as missionary activities are conducted on the rhetorical level, convincing by example and rational persuasion only, there will probably be little overall negative impact on the delicate fabric of Malaysian communal relations. Further, the channeling of dakwah energies into PERKIM may have some impact on the dramatic rise of revival movements in the other ethnic communities in Malaysia. Among the Chinese, for example, there have arisen in recent years millenarian-type syncretic groups, various charismatic Christian groups, and a return to a "purer" Theravada Buddhism. Among Indians, there has been a resurgence of interest in a more intellectualized form of the Hindu faith.[40]

The Role of Islamic Resurgence in Malaysia: A Comparison with Indonesia

The scale of Indonesia compared to Malaysia makes for some basic divergences despite the long shared history and culture of the two. Indonesia is made up of more than 13,600 islands containing in excess of 120 million people spread over three thousand miles of equatorial water with a diversity of languages, cultures, and religions. It dwarfs its Malaysian neighbor, which makes comparison difficult. Nonetheless, the contrasts are fruitful for an understanding of the vicissitudes of Islam in Southeast Asia.

Islam came to Southeast Asia through Indian Ocean trade from India, from Gujerat via Cambay, Aden, and Sumatra, and then to Malacca on the peninsula. This probable route of the diffusion of Islam meant that Sufi and Persian elements were already part of the Islamic heritage transmitted beginning in the twelfth century. The temple architecture from the Dieng plateau to the monumental Borobodur give mute testimony to the power of the Hindu-Buddhist states that awaited the Islamic merchants as they approached Indonesia. On Sumatra, for example, Islam was absorbed and transformed by an existing Hindu-Buddhist political and cultural elite. Thus, when Paramesvara fled Indonesian Sumatra for Malaysian Malacca and became in 1414 a Muslim ruler with the title of Iskander Shah, he was retreating to a much less complex political and cultural environment. Malaysia was a harbor center oriented to maritime trade and ruled by a riverine chieftain who controlled a small bureaucracy and minor nobility. This kingdom was not developed culturally, a fact reflected in the absence, then and now, of a strong Hindu-Buddhist heritage in the religious outlook of Malaysians.

However, in Indonesia, especially on the island of Java, the island where over half the population of Indonesia lives, a syncretic religion developed, dominated by Islam but including elements of the formerly regnant Hindu-Buddhist synthesis with local animistic practices. In 1619, the Dutch East India Company established its first outpost in the islands on Batavia, and a new force came to preeminence not only in the political life of Indonesia but also in its overseas trade. Driven inland by the Dutch, Muslim merchants established a system of local markets, which led to the spread of Islam to the hinterland.[41]

In Indonesia, then, Islam was, and has remained, a force for cultural diversification rather than homogenization: the religion took on different forms in different segments of Indonesian society and remains marked by a peculiarly Indonesian syncretism. Aside from the Christians and pagans, who make up only 6 percent of the population, most people in Indonesia today consider themselves Muslims. But this includes an Islam dominated by Indic religiosity among the privileged classes in Java; an Islam suffused with local folk religious motifs among the peasants, the abangan; and an Islam which aspires to orthodoxy, the santri.[42] To further complicate matters, a strong Sufi element has enabled Javanese santri Islam to accomodate many elements of a less orthodox folk practice.[43] Thus there is a continual interaction between normative piety and Sufism within santri itself.

During the nineteenth century this Indonesian melding of Islam with pre-Islamic religious practices led to a rift between the syncretic abangan Muslims and the (purportedly) purist santri. A major catalyst for the santri movement to purify Indonesian Islam was the technological advances that made the hajj to Mecca less arduous and led to a significant increase in the number of Indonesian hajjis from the turn of the century. In the Arabian peninsula Indonesian pilgrims encountered an Islam substantially different from that of their homeland and became acquainted with reformist ideas such as those of the Egyptian modernist Muhammad Abdu. Many of the returned pilgrims in Indonesia set themselves up as *kiyayis* (the Indonesian Muslim religious elite, similar to the ulama in other Islamic nations). Some pesantren students carried the pilgrims' ideas about reforming Islam throughout Indonesia. The dissemination of santri ideas was further facilitated by itinerant Muslim traders and a network of hostels associated with mosques which gave shelter to these peddlers. This renewed santri movement was not only opposed to the Indic syncretism but also came to be a focus of resistance to the Dutch colonial government.[44]

According to a recent study of the pesantren tradition, these tensions of the early and middle parts of the nineteenth century produced a fairly cautious reaction on the part of most kiyayi. They feared strong repression should their actions be deemed too political or disruptive. Also they saw their links with Mecca jeopardized by Dutch power to restrict travel. In effect many kiyayi were walking a thin line between resistance to colonial power and their desire simply to preserve the religious heritage that had been bequeathed to them and which they felt truly obligated to preserve and pass on.[45] Thus, through deliberate caution, much of Java's Islam became rather inward-looking, and the santri combination of Sufism for some and normative piety for others, with a blend of the two for the many, amounted to a kind of passive fundamentalism. Years of study in a pesantren would give one an appreciation of two basic essentials of Islamic life: closeness as well as obedience to Allah. The mystical elements in this system of dialectically blended fundamentals of faith actually make it difficult even to draw a sharp line between santri Muslims and many in the abangan stream. After the beginning of the twentieth century, some lines could be more clearly drawn as Indonesians directly influenced by modern reform movements from the Middle East began to launch campaigns such as the Muhammadiyah movement, aimed at purifying the faith in Indonesia and the greater Malay world. A distinction then emerged between *santri moderen* (modern santri) and *santri kolot* (traditional, old-style santri).

I mention these distinctions to emphasize the immense and complex diversity of Indonesian Islam. In general, however, it can be said that santri, whether modern or kolot, do stand out among other Indonesian Muslims, particularly in Java, as cultivating a distinctive orthodoxy. Meanwhile, the group that has been variously labeled as abangan, syncretist, or even "casual" Muslims has felt less charged to define themselves vis-à-vis orthodoxy. While no reliable estimates exist as to the current relative numbers of adherents of each position in Indonesia, or for that matter on Java alone, abangan Muslims even today are probably a majority of the population. This is significant in comparison with Malaysia, which has no counterpart of the abangan Muslims of Indonesia. Even the many Javanese who entered Malaysia early in the twentieth century seemed to adopt a santri orientation. Likewise, the Sumatran entrants into the Malay states have a reputation for orthodoxy. The ordinary believer in Malyasia may mix a few pre- or non-Islamic elements with his Sunni Islam, but in no way does this approach the amalgam that is abangan. The santri (observing) Muslim in Indonesia is much closer in terms of belief and religious practice to the ordinary Malaysian Muslim. In short, though diversity is present in both communities, the spectrum of Islamic diversity is represented more fully in Indonesia.[46]

Accordingly, when fundamentalism emerges in Indonesia, it competes with a more differentiated Islam. It also must contend with powerful and prestigious groups who are just barely Islamic or perhaps not Islamic at all. This social and cultural contrast between the two states underlies the seeming anomaly that, while 80 percent of Indonesia is Muslim (on the census count), with only about 45 percent counted as Muslims in Malaysia, Islam is the official religion in Malaysia, and not in Indonesia.

Indonesian Islam and Politics

The social and political organization of Islam is also different in Indonesia and Malaysia. Islam has a religious and cultural bureau, or ministry, at the national level in both places, but in Malaysia the effectiveness of such a centralized institution is diluted by a strong and jealously guarded state organization in each of the nine states ruled by sultans. From colonial times the administration of Islam and Malay custom has been the last bastion of Malay royal authority. The sultan of each state actively controls a religious council and legal organization which in the everyday lives of the people effectively supersedes the influence of the federal government (which in any case has been loath to become too heavily entangled in religious issues). Indonesia, on the other hand, is more effectively centralized. So, while Indonesia's ummah may be more diversified, it is nonetheless far less divided from an administrative point of view.

There are parallels in religious education between Indonesia and Malaysia but their recognizably similar institutions have played historically different roles. In the Malaysian countryside, Islam is taught in madrasas, religious schools not quite at the level of a seminary (the newer Islamic colleges and University of the 1980s might well be called seminaries), and through pondoks. Each of these teacher-led boarding schools has a tok guru as its head and chief pedant. The subjects taught are only those considered "Islamic," such as monotheism, law, Arabic, Qur'an, and Hadith. There are no exams, no fixed number of years to attend, no degrees awarded, and no fees charged. Students maintain themselves or live off the charity of family, neighbors, or other patrons. The tok guru also receives gifts from students and others who may attend Friday congregations and listen to his sermons after prayer. The tok guru may be a product of pondok education, although it is entirely possible that he was educated in such prestigious centers of Islamic learning as Mecca or al-Azhar in Egypt. Some of the tok gurus have international reputations and draw students from foreign lands. The students, once they leave the pondok, may found smaller schools, become village teachers of Qur'an reading and reciting, or simply live more pious lives.

In Indonesia, rural organization also centers around teachers and pesantren. The santri Muslim is also oriented to an Islam based on school and text. Religious teachers and their santri followers can, under the proper circumstances, become politically active, as they have from time to time in recent Indonesian history. Santris often oppose the practitioners of what they consider to be an impure and corrupt Islam, and the "godless," which often included local members of the communist party (when it was legal). The towns and cities of Indonesia are likely to be strong centers of santri or orthodox Islam and have prestigious schools and teachers, although foreign training at the reputed international centers in Mecca, Egypt, and India carries a special cachet.

Education in Indonesia is, however, not simply santri in character rather than abangan, as it would first appear on the surface. Thus secular subjects are taught in most conservative of Islamic institutions, while Arabic and classical Islam are taught in the purely secular schools, with only the hours devoted to each subject in practice differentiating the two. Further, it is not unusual for adults and university students to attend a "modern" (secular) school in the day and attend classes in a madrasa in the evening. Such is the demand for Islamic education that two distinct streams of Islamic higher education have developed. An innovative state-supported experiment in modernizing Islamic studies in Indonesia began in 1960 called the IAIN (Institut Agama Islam Negeri, or State Institute of Islam). Patterned after the faculties of Cairo's al-Azhar (Shari'a education, teacher training and Islamic humanities), the two pilot institutions in Jakarta and Jogjakarta seek to produce scholars and leaders who will lead Indonesian Islam into the mainstream of the global ummah. Parallel to these are the numerous traditional pesantrens. The trend toward homogenization of santri and abangan Muslims depends on a scenario in which the traditional pesantren schools will produce a top layer of graduates who will be accepted into an expanded state system of IAINs.[47]

However, Islamic political parties and Islamic teachers' movements in Indonesia have only sporadically and fitfully appealed to the peasants and have appealed even less to the urban proletariat. In general, they have been the bearers of a distinctly modernist form of orthodoxy which, under the heading of Islamic modernism, has been associated with such scholars as Abdu and Rida. By contrast, their Malaysian counterparts have been the carriers and exponents of traditional Islam. The very different roles of the kiyayi of Indonesia and the tok guru of Malaysia are an indication of this contrast.

Modern and traditional orthodoxy have fought doctrinal battles in both countries. The interpretation of Islam has been contested by factions of ulama and other Muslim intellectuals. Though the intensity of these disputes are decades in the past, they still echo in disputes about the role of Islam in contemporary life and in the urge to organize politically in defense of traditional Islam. In Malaysia's battle between Kaum Tua and Kaum Muda, the latter was tied to the school, the text, and urban intellectuals, while the former lived among the rural peasantry and in some of the pondok and traditional literati circles. In Indonesia the pressures attendant upon the criticism of the prevailing religious syncretism eventually led to a split mentioned above within the ranks of the santri themselves. In contemporary Indonesia, particularly on Java, pious Muslims identify themselves either as moderen or kolot. The kolot have a totalistic view of religion in which all acts take on a religious significance, while the moderen draw a rather clear boundary between the religious and the secular and tend to limit the secular sphere. The kolot are more willing to allow some non-Islamic rites a minor place in their religion, while moderen work to completely expunge non-Islamic elements from their practice in favor of a purified Islam. The kolot emphasize religious experience, while the moderen focus on religious behavior.[48] Finally, the moderen are prone to turn to the original sources of Islam, the Qur'an and Hadith, in attempting to meet the challenges of the modern world, while rejecting the more confining ways of legal precedent. In kolot Islam, practices are justified by custom and the scholastic precedents provided by traditional Islamic texts. This may be explained by the fact that kolot leaders tend to be kiyayis who find precedents in Islamic writings to justify some Javanese customs. Their followers accept the position of the leaders on these matters, as the kolot tend to be older, rural, and relatively uneducated, while the moderen are young, urban, and more educated.

The most important institutional expression of moderen Islam in Indonesia has been the Muhammadiyya. First established in 1912, the Muhammadiyyah has dedicated itself to education and other social service activities. By scrupulously avoiding politics, this organization managed to escape repression from both Dutch colonial officials and later the government of the Republic of Indonesia. Though primarily a missionary movement, the Muhammadiyya has supported educational and social programs. It has a dynamic women's branch 'Aisjijah, and its former political affiliate, Masyumi, now defunct, was once the most powerful party in Indonesia. A widespread and powerful organization, the Muhammadiyya boasted six million members throughout Indonesia by 1970. Today it is undoubtedly "the most prominent non-governmental educational and social welfare institution in the country."[49]

Perceived pressure from moderen groups in 1926 led kolot Muslims to band together to form Nahdatul Ulama, "the Reviver of the Ulama." As the name itself indicates, the Nahdatul Ulama (NU) represented the interests of the conservative, rural Islamic elite, the ulama or kiyayi. The ideological impetus for the formation of the NU may be traced to the widespread kiyayi fear that the moderen had rejected the ultimate authority of all of the existing schools of Shari'a, and with this rejection had fatally undermined the recourse to ijtihad, which was fully in the hands of the kiyayi. Indeed, ijtihad was the basis for the kiyayi's traditional authority and influence in Indonesian society.[50]

The differences between moderen and kolot Muslims were ameliorated to a certain extent during the period of the Japanese occupation of Indonesia from 1942 to 1945. In 1943 for their convenience the Japanese consolidated the various Muslim organizations into one entity, Masyumi. Through Masyumi, the Japanese used the network of Muslim organizations throughout the islands to disseminate propaganda in favor of their Greater East Asia Co-Prosperity Sphere. But when it came to writing a constitution for Indonesian independence, the Japanese tended to support secular nationalists such as Sukarno. In attempting to develop an ideology that encompassed nationalists of all kinds from Muslims to Marxists, Sukarno promulgated the Panca Sila (the Five Principles) on 1 June 1945. "In the preamble to the Constitution these are set out as belief in the one Supreme God; a just and civilized humanity; the unity of Indonesia; democracy led by the wisdom of unanimity arising from deliberations among representatives of the people, and social justice for the whole people of Indonesia."[51]

At the time of the writing of the constitution, there was some disagreement about what the nature of the Indonesian state should be. A number of the Muslim members of the committee set up by the Japanese to write the constitution believed that Indonesia should formally declare itself an Islamic state. Eventually a compromise was reached that the preamble would provide for belief in one God "with the obligation for adherents of Islam to practice Islamic law."[52] In Bahasa Indonesia, this formula translates into seven words, which became a rallying cry for both those who found in the reference little more than a rhetorical bow toward the cherished ideal of an Islamic state and those who interpreted the phrase to be a dagger pointed at the heart of Indonesian pluralism. Even some prominent religious Muslims feared that, armed with this phrase, Muslims would be bound by law to support the Shari'a, as interpreted, of course, by the kiyayi, thus threatening moderen interests.[53] In the interest of Indonesian unity, Sukarno urged that the seven words, along with a provision that the Indonesian president be born an Indonesian and a Muslim (Sukarno met both criteria), be retained in the final document. While this motion carried the day, Sukarno and his vice-president made no reference to Islam in the 17 August 1945 declaration of independence. A short time later, Sukarno convened a preparatory committee which recommended that the seven words be omitted completely from the constitution so that the document would not spell out any official relationship between the nation of Indonesia and Islam or Islamic law. Although the nationalists were not able finally to wrest control from the Dutch until 1949, the constitution of 1945 was to become the basis of the state for most of the history of the Republic of Indonesia. Consistent with the Panca Sila, Indonesia is a state which recognizes the existence of God, but which remains nonetheless officially secular.[54]

Even among less-radical Muslims there was no consensus as to the direction that Indonesia should take. The Muslim groups that had been forcibly coalesced into Masyumi by the Japanese during the occupation found that they could not pull together. In 1948 the moderen Partai Sarekat Islam Indonesia (PSII) withdrew from the governing coalition, and in 1950, the kolot Nahdatul Ulama also broke away. Masyumi then fell under the control of modernist Muslims associated with the Muhammadiyya and proved less willing than conservative groups to accommodate itself to the reign of President Sukarno. In 1960 Masyumi was outlawed, after being implicated in CIA-backed plots against Sukarno.

As the dawning of Malaysian independence was burdened by the dark clouds of a protracted communist insurgency, so Indonesia's independence was bloodied by a protracted series of militant Islamic insurgencies. The constitution of 1945 left many Muslims disconcerted with the new secularism of Indonesia. It is in this context that the aforementioned rebellion lead by Kartosoewirjo (1948–62) in central Java, and others carried out in South Sulawesi (1952) and Aceh (1953), should be understood. In reaction against the secular republican model of Sukarno and his allies, Kartosoewirjo and Dar'ul Islam fought for Negara Islam Indonesia, an Indonesian Islamic state to be governed completely by Muslim law. Still, there were modern provisions in the Constitution and Penal Code of Negara Islam Indonesia: the state was to be a republic; the legislative power was to be exercised by an elected parliament; the head of state would be called the imam, but he would be elected by the parliament and would have no power to legislate independent of the parliament; there would be equality before law of all citizens, and freedom of worship, speech, and assembly. On the other hand, the proposed Islamic constitution would hold some discriminatory articles, including a provision for punishing apostasy and backsliding by Muslims, different criminal penalties for Muslims and non-Muslims, and a requirement that all civilian and military officeholders be both orthodox and pious Muslims.[55] This latter provision clearly barred Sukarno, hardly noted for his piety, from holding office, and it was on the constitutional issue that the dispute between the two forces, the Islamic and the secular, would be centered.

Immediately after the war with Japan, in the fluid situation of Indonesia's fledgling nationalism and efforts at mobilization under various banners, Kartosoewirjo repeatedly proclaimed the founding of the Islamic state, but then threw his support to the Republic declared by Sukarno on 17 August 1945.[56] However, during a series of Dutch "police actions" in the late 1940s which aimed at regaining colonial control of the country, Kartosoewirjo seized the opportunity to form an army and, on 7 August 1949, declared himself the Imam of the Islamic state of Indonesia. With the nationalist army in full retreat from central to west Java, Kartosoewirjo's army harried Sukarno's forces, inflicting great casualties, but was unable to inflict a decisive defeat on the nationalists because of the loyalty of the population of west Java.[57] This failure was the effective death knell for the Dar'ul Islam, although Kartosoewirjo's slowly disintegrating force fought on through the 1950s. The leader's own capture and execution in 1962 brought about the surrender of a force which by then had all but dissolved into a terrorist band.

The government's victory was due to a shrewd combination of policies. Government officials negotiated with the insurrectionists and offered amnesty to those who would surrender, providing Dar'ul Islam soldiers with an alternative besides victory or death. The Indonesian army also eventually developed more effective tactics to combat the guerilla warfare of the insurgents. In 1960 the Masyumi Party was outlawed by Sukarno, and the military was free to move against the insurgents without fear of complaint by the country's Muslim political party.[58]

Close study of the supporters of the Dar'ul Islam and their social and religious backgrounds does not show them to be significantly different from other Indonesians who opposed and fought that movement. It appears that Islam has supplied a panoply of symbols for heterogenous groups. Leadership used these symbols to legitimatize its position and to ignite political or military action en masse. Islam provided organizational media for reinforcing interpersonal loyalties and adherence to traditional authority. These traditional attachments and loyalties became involved, in the Dar'ul Islam, in an emerging political configuration—an involvement reinforced by the invocation of the Islamic theory of political organization against the alien, Western notion of a republican state. That Dar'ul Islam did not drift toward a more fundamentalist stance and political format was primarily because of military defeat rather than religious or ideological shifts in commitment.

The Sumatra and Sulawesi uprisings served as the last gasp of widespread Islamic radical violence in Indonesia. In 1952, in south Sulawesi, an army officer named Kahar Muzakkar proclaimed himself commander of the Fourth Division of the Islamic Army of Indonesia. His Islamic rebellion lasted until 1965. More successful was the 1953 Sumatran action, in which Daud Beureu'eh proclaimed Aceh a part of the Islamic State of Indonesia headed by Kartosoewirjo. Eventually Daud Beureu'eh came to a negotiated settlement with the central government, gaining special status for Aceh in 1962.

As Malaysia, once free of its communist insurgency, was to experience the pivotal event of violence erupting at its center in the 1969 riots, so too, and with even deeper repercussions, Indonesia sustained a shock to its body politic subsequent to its eradication of the Islamic threat. Perhaps the most crucial event in modern Indonesian history, which established indelibly the might of the military over against insurgents of any ideological persuasion, was the attempted communist coup of 30 September 1965 which led to the fall of Sukarno. Until 1965, President Sukarno had for two decades served as the personification of Indonesia's aspirations, first standing for independence from Dutch colonial control, then for liberation from Japanese military occupation during the war years, then for resistance against the abortive attempts of the Dutch to reassert control of the archipelago. Sukarno enjoyed widespread support at all levels of society and was widely credited as the author of the Panca Sila ideology. His stature rose with the world spotlight brought by the 1955 Bandung Conference, which formally founded the so-called Non-Aligned movement. Indonesia emerged as a prize in the Cold War contest for the allegiance of Third World states, a contest conducted through open diplomatic channels, as well as through covert intelligence operations of the United States, the Soviet Union, and the People's Republic of China. CIA-backed revolts in the decade following the Bandung Conference attempted to destabilize the country. Similarly, the Chinese influenced the Indonesian communist party and are suspected of utilizing the large Chinese minority of Java to destabilize the government.[59]

By 1965, the year the United States introduced massive ground forces into Vietnam, Sukarno's rhetoric had become increasingly strident and anti-American. This rhetorical campaign was backed by an increasingly close relationship between Sukarno, the Chinese-supported Indonesian Communist Party headed by Dipa Nusantara Aidit, and Beijing's ambassador to Indonesia, Yao Chung-ming.

On the evening of 30 September 1965, a group of communist officers, centered in units of the Indonesian Air Force, joined by specially trained shock troops drawn from the Communist Youth League, set out from Halim airbase on the outskirts of Jakarta armed with lists of noncommunist generals targeted for assassination. Despite some initial successes, a group of senior generals survived the initial onslaught, regrouped their forces, and struck back at communists, suspected party sympathizers, and an unknown number of bystanders. The coup was crushed, as was the communist party. Yet Sukarno's popularity was such that he remained in the presidency, albeit as a figurehead for the generals, for another two years. On 20 February 1967, Sukarno formally resigned, ceding control of the government to General Suharto, a heretofore little known forty-five-year-old senior army commander. Suharto moved to consolidate his power under the structure of a one-party state, which he came to relax gradually throughout the 1970s. At this writing, Suharto remains in power.[60]

The trauma of the year-long spasm of violence which the attempted coup unleashed cannot be understated. The actual death toll throughout the archipelago may never be ascertained with any certainty, but estimates range in the hundreds of thousands. Many leaders of the coup remain in prison to this day. Whatever the proximate causes of the violence, against this background it is not difficult to understand the relative quiescence of the Islamic parties in the last two decades.

Order was eventually restored by General Suharto, and there was a return to limited democracy. In an effort to stabilize the political situation, Suharto banned all parties based on religion in 1973. The four Islamic parties which held seats in the national parliament were amalgamated into the Partai Persatuan Pembangunan (the PPP, or the United Development Party). (The last general election in which the Muslim parties campaigned independently was in 1971. At that time all four parties were only able to win 94 seats out of more than 350 in the parliament.)[61] Thus, while ignoring the substantial cleavages dividing the Muslim parties, indeed while removing any mention of Islam from the new party's name, the PPP was allowed to compete with the ruling Golkar Party and the even more incongruous PDI (Indonesian Democratic Party) coalition, also created by government dictate in 1973.[62]

Thus, following upon the bloodbath of 1965, a tightly controlled political system emerged, directed largely by the army. The leaders of this system have not used religious or Islamic symbolism to justify their regime but have rather relied on the nationalist ideology formed under Sukarno and widely disseminated since then by all the national agencies of communication, including the school system. Political life is contained in the Golkar Party, a functional coalition which operated until recently as a one-party system. Now there are elections at the local levels, but the military is in control, though problems of succession to Suharto loom on the horizon.

The common theme running through the vicissitudes of Islam in Indonesia seems to be a strong central government. If and when fundamentalistic Islamic movements seemed threatening, the army suppressed them. The military was able to do this in part because it was seen as the heir of the nationalist revolution with its powerful symbolic armory, and because the mass of the population, given the diversity of Islam in the islands, was not supportive of fundamentalism, nor was it appalled when it was suppressed.

Contrast with Malaysia

Indonesia's open reliance on the military for stability contrasts with Malaysia, where the central government is a coalition among ethnic groups and there is no strong symbolic system among the Malay majority that competes with Islam. Further, the army does not have the legitimacy, enjoyed by its Indonesian counterpart, that comes from revolutionary and independence victories. After the 13 May 1969 affair in Kuala Lumpur, the central government, the elite, and the military had no alternative in Malaysia other than to renegotiate the compact of 1952 along the lines of a movement toward greater Malay privileges and consequent openings to a more militant Islam.

The open system of Malaysia is thus more vulnerable to fundamentalism in the political arena than is the highly controlled government in Indonesia. Yet the major axis of contrast is not the relative openness of the two political systems, important as that may be for the short run. Identity problems, along ethnic lines, are an important source of political and cultural tension in Malaysia for which few effective solutions have been proposed. Furthermore, the ethnic and cultural differences in Malaysia tend to follow the cleavages of religions, making for major fault lines in the social system.

Most of the minority peoples of Indonesia do not aspire to national state status; rather, they appear content to be one of the diverse building blocks of the nation. The "unity in diversity" slogan on the official seal of the government seems grounded in social fact. It appears to have been subjectively internalized by a significant majority of Indonesians. There have been exceptions to this pattern. Cultural integrity is sought by the minority peoples and is sometimes threatened by the dominance of the Javanese or other large and localized groups, such as the Batak on Sumatra. It is also true that ethnic group membership may be used as the basis for organizing political or economic opposition in those areas, but nowhere in Indonesia does the coincidence of ethnicity, culture, and religion aspire to shape the national entity to a fundamentalist vision.

The fact that the Indonesian military fought a war of independence and on many occasions has defended the nation against "extremists" gives it a national position and legitimacy that the Malaysian military does not have. And the different meanings and structural positions of ethnicity in the two nations also makes it easier for Indonesia to exert secular authority and not abide open religious challenge. The secular authority of the central government is, however, partly ideologically based, and that basis has a religious component, though not an Islamic component as such. Indonesia's Panca Sila ideology is capable of various interpretations, but it clearly gives no warrant for a theocracy, nor does it favor an Islamic view of the state or of society. The first pillar, belief in one supreme God, is in accord with the major theological premise of Islam, but it also accords with other book religions and can even accommodate tribal pantheons if they have a "high god" concept. This cuts some ground from under Islamic fundamentalists and at the same time gives a religious tinge to the national government. An extensive literature has not grown up about the significance of this or any of the other principles of the Panca Sila. Rather, they seem to mean what the government of the last quarter century says they mean. The central government and the military have been quick to move against fundamentalists and communists in the name of defense of the constitutional principles on which the nation was founded. In the 1980s the Suharto government pressured all groups to accept the Panca Sila as their sole ideological basis. Victories came in 1984 when both the PPP and the NU (which continued as a religious organization, though not a political party after it was forced to join PPP) accepted the government's demand.

A similar willingness to live within these rules is echoed in the slogan used by the Himpunan Mahasisiva Islam (the Association of Islamic Students), an influential organization of students and young reform-oriented intellectuals. They say "Islam yes, partai-partai Islam, no" ("Islam yes, Islamic political parties, no"). In defending their stance, they claim that political interests would taint the renewal of faith and make it easily subject to manipulation.[63]

Another key tool of government control of religion in Indonesia is the Ministry of Religion. Although the overwhelming majority of Indonesians consider themselves Muslim, Islam is not the state religion. The Ministry of Religion includes sections for Protestants, Catholics, and "Other Religions," but is dominated by santri Muslims, who make up almost all of the ministry's staff. The ministry is divided into the Bureau of Religious Administration (responsible for the activities of local mosques), the Bureau of Religious Education (which oversees religious education in religious and secular schools), the Bureau of Religious Propaganda (which distributes some religious literature), and the Bureau of Religious Justice (which oversees the functioning of Muslims jurists, active in areas of personal law, where parties to a dispute may voluntarily have recourse to Islamic law rather than to the secular legal system).

The government's control of Islamic movements is particularly important given that Indonesians seem to have become more religiously active in recent years. After a decrease in the 1950s and 1960s, a large number of the faithful made the hajj again in the 1980s. Mosque attendance and Ramadan observance are up. Women are more likely now to wear conservative Islamic dress than in past decades. People are more concerned that the food they consume be halal. Despite the government's attempt to suppress Muslim opposition, Islam is becoming an increasingly important part of the identity of many citizens of Indonesia.[64]

And though the Suharto administration has been relatively successful in stifling public opposition from Islamic groups, there is some evidence of discontent on the grass-roots level. For example, in recent years, the *ceremah,* a religious sermon with political implications, whether printed or on audiocassette tape, has become a primary vehicle for expressing protest. The ceremah has also been a locus of protest in Malaysia. The ulama have long involved themselves in politics by preaching for and against local candidates. Lately this has taken an extreme turn, with the ulama denouncing their political opponents as *kafirs* or infidels. There is even some concern that the ceremah are the occasion for the propagation of particularist, even heretical, interpretations of Islam. In Indonesia, lacking the comparatively open political environment of Malaysia, these groups tend to be small and are forced to be somewhat circumspect. Nonetheless, one of the primary foci of opposition to the Suharto regime has come from isolated mosques and prayer groups. Recently associations and individuals from these groups have been tried for sedition on Java, Sumatra, and reportedly even on some of the outer islands.[65]

Compared to Indonesia, Malaysia has weaker ideological resources with which to stem the tide of Islamic fundamentalism. The nationalist movement was less successful in forging a Malaysian identity. Indonesian identity is a social and cultural fact, while the Malaysian is a citizen category made up of Malays, Chinese, Indians, and others. The coining of the category of *Bumiputra* (son of the soil), a term for Malays which emphasizes their connection with the land of Malaysia rather than the religion of Islam, has proven to be a political maneuver with little impact. It represents a further attempt in an unending series of attempts to define who a Malay is. Such an effort to consolidate the national identity is not required in Indonesia—that identity already exists.

One ambiguous comparison between Malaysia and Indonesia is in their particular relations with the wider Islamic world and with the so-called Third World in general. Malaysia is often called "neocolonial," a label which is clearly meant to stigmatize it, for reasons that are unclear. Successive Malaysian governments, however, have proven sensitive to Indonesian barbs on this point. Seeking to lay this point to rest before the United Nations Security Council in 1964, Dr. Dato Ismail bin Dato Abdul Rahman, Minister of Home Affairs and Justice, contrasted Sukarno's Chinese-inspired theories of permanent revolution with Malaysia's own ideas of revolution in terms of peaceful economic development: "The Malaysian revolution is not a romantic revolution, it is a very real revolution, a very dynamic revolution which has brought our people the goods of life, which has built new roads and bridges and schools and hospitals. . . . It is not a revolution of words, it is a revolution of sweat and effort and organization. It is a revolution to meet the rising expectations of our people, not to divert their rising frustrations . . . because we choose to act and not coin facile abbreviations or grandiose slogans, let no one misread the tempo and temper of our revolution."[66]

The Mahathir administration seems determined to place Malaysia on the international stage in a very different light from its former "neocolonial" image. Against the empty rhetoric of the past, Mahathir has championed many causes of the Third World and Islam. He also initiated, and in 1990 hosted on Malaysian soil, the first meeting of an organization of Southern Hemisphere and developing countries, now called the Group of Seventeen, G-17, which aims at counterbalancing the dominant influence of the seven leading industrial nations, the so-called G-7. In this we hear an echo of the 1955 Bandung Conference.

As host of the 1955 Bandung Conference, Indonesia was one of the founders of the Third World movement. As we have seen, the Indonesian perception of the nonaligned movement and the Third World in general as both a source of international identity and as a special mission led to an increasing radicalization of Indonesian policy. This radicalization complicated Indonesia's relations with the outside world and aborted the development of relations with the newly independent state of Malaysia. Thus when on 15 September 1963, Malaya became the united state of Malaysia, taking with it North Borneo, claimed by Indonesia, Jakarta withheld recognition. On 21 September, Indonesia broke off economic relations (losing in the process a trade surplus of $189 million). The situation quickly deteriorated, with the Indonesian embassy burned to the ground in Kuala Lampur and the British embassy in Jakarta suffering the same fate.[67] An intermittent three-year war began in 1963, called a "confrontasi" by both parties, in which British military forces played a considerable role in holding the Indonesian army in check, especially in Borneo.[68] And when on 30 December 1963, Malaysia, despite the conflict with Indonesia, was seated on the UN Security Council, Indonesia abruptly withdrew from the organization and all its specialized agencies.[69]

Since the fall of Sukarno, Indonesia has been moving in a consistently pro-Western direction, and it has not expanded or deepened its ties to the Islamic world. Its major connection with the Third World has been as a member of OPEC, and that may be viewed as a nonideological involvement in a cartel for economic advantage.

Rhetoric about internal development in recent years in Malaysia has not been accompanied by a fundamental restructuring of an economy closely tied to the world capitalist markets. Unlike Indonesia, Malaysia is engaged in redefining its place in the wider world of Islam. The very size, scope, and cultural accomplishments of Indonesia, in comparison with Malaysia, make it less imperative for the former to seek roots in Islam or to claim outside sources of cultural stature. In terms of culture, Malaysians have often viewed themselves as the "little brother" of Indonesia. Recent efforts to consolidate a Malay culture related to that of Indonesia have resulted only in a common spelling system in which colonially imposed differences in orthography are erased.

In spite of the considerable differences between the manifestations of Islamic activism in Indonesia and those of Malaysia—variations traced to differences in demography, geography, history, and religious practices and outlooks—there exists in the view of some observers an organic connection between the two nations which allows for a great deal of interaction between the Muslims of Indonesia and Malaysia. They do, after all, share a common language, albeit with great dialectal differences, and some authors are popular in both countries. Further, they share common roots in Hindu, Buddhist, and animistic traditions, despite the differences which have over time developed in this area.

Radical activities, violent activities, or conspiracies designed to undermine the state have been rare but significant in Malaysia. The most noteworthy events in this category were attacks on Hindu temples by South Indian Muslims in 1978 and a 1980 incident involving an attack on a rural police station by a group of white-robed men led by one Mohamad Nasir. Nasir, a charismatic leader, claimed that the reign of Muhammad was over and proclaimed a jihad to establish an Islamic state. In the ensuing struggle, twenty-six policemen and civilians, as well as eight attackers, were killed. Another incident in 1985 resulted in the deaths of an "extremist Muslim leader" and eighteen others.[70]

Neither has Indonesia completely suppressed or extinguished Islamic fundamentalism, much less its occasional radical expressions. Any state where the scriptural religions have a hold on a sizable population can never fully expunge fundamentalist tendencies. What is crucial from the point of view of the cultural and social systems is the relative power and salience of the fundamentalist worldview and its location in organized social and political groupings. In the relatively open political system of Malaysia, fundamentalism seems but a goad which forces Malay political parties to take increasingly pro-Islamic public positions. In Indonesia, with its tighter central control over the political process, the relative strength of Islamic parties and of fundamentalist tendencies among those parties is much more difficult to assess. In the 1955 Indonesian elections (by all accounts an honest and open procedure), for example, Masyumi finished second to Sukarno's nationalist party. Masyumi then included all the Islamic groups, and had voiced opposition to the leftist government, so its popularity was based only partially on Islamic grounds and not on a platform for implementing a fundamentalist program in state and society. Masyumi is currently banned, however, and as in Malaysia, the current leadership of the Islamic movement has fallen to Islamic intellectuals in the university and among the ulama. From the current periodical literature, such as the magazine *Tempo,* which is widely circulated among Indonesia's intelligentsia, the two leaders appear to be Abdurrahman Wahid of the Nahdatul Ulama and Nurcholish Madjid, a leading Islamic intellectual. Both these individuals reject a fundamentalist Islamic state and appear to exemplify the dilemmas of fundamentalist Islam in Indonesia, which is (1) weighted toward the abangan stream; (2) not in a position to challenge the modern ulama's dominance; (3) without social or doctrinal unity; (4) exclusivist in its inability to find allies; and (5) laboring under the suspicion that it secretly yearns for an Islamic state.[71] Of course, the ulama and Islamic intellectuals speak and write under the vigilant eye of the central government and the military and are therefore constrained as to public utterance and action, making it difficult to verify if their repudiation of an Islamic state is authentic or merely strategic.

That there is discontent below the apparently placid surface of Indonesian life is evidenced by the Tanjung Priok riots in 1984. There, in the old port section of Jakarta, the military put down a demonstration by Muslim students. In an apparent overreaction, more than one hundred were killed. The force brought to bear indicates the deep-seated official fear of militants and Islamic fundamentalists. Students and youth, in both Indonesia and Malaysia, are in the forefront of Islamic movements. If these young people could win middle-class backing, a major upheaval could result (as it has in similar situations in other parts of the Islamic world). But for the moment, it appears that the "enemies" of the regime (defined as fundamentalists and communists) are not a serious threat. Indonesia is still groping toward a more open political system, but this effort seems to be leading to a symbolic and ideological idiom constructed between the polar claims of the clerics and the would-be revolutionaries.

Conclusion: Fundamentalism and the Contradictions of Malaysian Society

Scholars of Malaysia's dakwah movement have pointed to a series of social and ideological contradictions in Malaysian life that have made the movement a compelling alternative for the young. The comparison with Indonesia, which seems better able to live up to its own national motto of unity in diversity, gives added weight to such an interpretation. Though both countries share the initial contradiction of being Islamic nations yet secular states, other contradictions and tensions present in Malaysia compound matters and make the option of reinforcing Islamic identity through a turn to fundamentalism all the more attractive. Most of these tensions are carefully documented in the recent monographic literature on the region, as well as in more popular accounts of the Malaysian scene.[72]

As we have seen, the dakwah movement in Malaysia emerged and developed in the context of the secular nature of the Malaysian state, the highly diffuse nature of Islamic authority in Malaysia, the ambiguity arising from the intimate connection of Islam with Malayness, the increasing social stratification within the Malay community itself, and the problematic nature of Islamic orthodoxies in the face of diversity.[73]

For many Muslims the fact that Malaysia is a secular state, with Islam as its official religion but with tolerance for other forms of belief and worship as a constitutional imperative, is an oxymoron. It does not comfort the *lebai* (the pious) that other societies with Muslim majority populations have similar problems and ambiguities about Islam and the state. It is small consolation that the relationship of *vatan* (the modern state), *kaum* (fellow tribesmen or the Arabs), and the ummah has posed a persisting set of conundrums for all Islamic theorists. The very fact of a secular Malaysian government is seen by the pious to contradict the Qur'anic mandate for a genuinely Islamic state.

The tension between Islam and secular government in Malaysia is exacerbated by the organization of religious life. This is the second set of contradictions which has contributed to dakwah. There is a Malaysian national religious organization at the ministry level, but each of the Malay states under a sultan (in all nine of the thirteen in Malaysia) has its own Majlis Agama, religious bureau and keeper of Malay custom. So there are nine courts of muftis and nine systems of courts of *kadis* (Islamic judges) whose rulings are not always consistent. All of this fracturing of traditional religious authority, as well as the inherent ambiguity in such a state of affairs, seems intolerable to the committed Muslim. Hence the present confusion is rejected in favor of a future built on centralized, and thus strong and enduring, Islamic foundations.

The third tension is involved with ethnicity, religion, and citizenship. These may be summed up under the rubric of "identity," if identity is seen as a social process. Identity in Malaysia must be understood as continually in the making, arising from the flow of group interaction and historical events. It is not simply a reassertion of some quasi-mystical primordial features and sentiments. A Malaysian need not be a Muslim; a Muslim need not be either a Malay or a Malaysian citizen. Just what is a Malay/Muslim? And where do Malay/Muslims fit in the international world of Muslims, most of whom are not Malay? Fundamentalists in the Malay context, then, are seeking an identity that is more than a shifting social process. Thus, they often seek refuge in a concept of an absolutist Islam, which is perceived as transcendent and thus as stable and immune to erosion as they once hoped "Malayness" was.

The fourth tension which prompted dakwah, hardly articulated before the 1970s, results from the growing class distinctions within the ethnic Malay bloc itself. With economic development have come increasing occupational, status, and class differences among Malays, as well as growing competition across ethnic lines. The once-simple tripartite division of Malays into aristocrats, peasants, and town civil servants has been complicated by the emergence of a commercial middle class, numerous professionals, and an urban proletariat in the new factories and assembly plants of Malaysia. The strain is heaviest on the new middle class. This group has been formed by recent economic expansion and is distinct from the older middle class of bureaucrats, officials, and professionals. Many of the new middle class find the urban lifestyle, with its more ambiguous and flexible norms, trying and shallow. The need for Western sophistication is a continual abrasive reminder of recent rustic roots. The constant demand for interethnic tolerance is threatening to personal identity and to core cultural values. For these people, dakwah is often a fitting and welcome bastion of relief and retreat.

And we have also seen that, as a special movement and as a defined ideology in Malaysia, dakwah arose from the turmoil of the 1969 riots and from the examples of Iranian fundamentalism and recently translated books of the Egyptian Islamic resurgence. As such, dakwah, like many nativistic and fundamentalist movements, arises from crises. In this case the crisis centers on a new urban middle class in tension with Western modernism in a multi-ethnic society of open and competitive politics.

The fifth contradiction that has manifest itself in the dakwah movement is one inherent in the raising of religious consciousness. Orthodoxies multiply and rewakened faith seems as confused and uncertain as it is dogmatic. This is because orthodoxy is always being constructed as a third term between the believer's awareness of diversity and the vaguely held notion of Islam as a uniform truth. Given the previous contradictions, this leads to a social competition even in daily life over religious authority.

At this historical moment, Islamic fundamentalism in the form of dakwah is one of the responses to these recurrent strains.[74] For some of the actors, these tensions come as spurs to conversion to dakwah, though other modes of diagnosing the current malaise are available which lead to alternative therapies. As a response to these circumstances, dakwah can be described in part as a social movement with a religiously oriented ideology and symbol system. This movement attempts to solve social and personal conflicts and to create a world where the solutions will contribute to a just society and a life filled with purpose and satisfaction, leading ultimately to salvation. The current generation of Malays, particularly those recently involved with secular higher education, feel they have a special burden and destiny upon them. They fervently believe that their activities and beliefs will determine the shape and future of Malay identity, the Islamic religion, and national integration in Malaysia.

Fundamentalism (and revolutionary socialism) are still possibilities not only in Malaysia but also in Indonesia, in part because of the shared Southeast Asian cultural view of the meaning of social change. In both countries, change has been viewed as redemptive—as restoring past glories, reasserting frayed identities, and reopening a future of bright and shining promise. For programs of social change, a strong sense of moral righteousness has been a necessary ingredient, and arguments centering on political utility have not been sufficient. Pragmatic politics has almost no hold on the national imagination in either nation. Incremental change is not valued unless it is seen as contributing to the larger ends of social and cultural redemption in an effort leading to religious or secular salvation, peace, abundance, and dignity. This view of politics as a struggle for the meaning of life, not as the art of the possible, permeates the ethos of Malays in Malaysia as well as both the santri and the abangan elites of Java.[75]

Some themes sounded by dakwah members in Malaysia and Masyumi members in Indonesia seem to echo those voiced by the al-Ikhwan (Muslim Brotherhood) in Egypt, the Jamaat-i-Islami in Pakistan, and even among the seminary students at Qum in Iran before the Khomeini takeover. The Islamic resurgence in Malaysia, as it does throughout the world, relies heavily on anti-Western and anti-modern themes. Youthful radicalism and Islamic affirmation are as intertwined in Malaysia as they are elsewhere in the Islamic world. To the members of the dakwah groups in Malaysia, the West is seen primarily as the threatening "other," personified variously by the United States and Western Europe—a chaotic power, lacking in discipline, in morality, and indeed in simple human decency. Thus, for most dakwah organizations, the West remains the principle enemy, an aggressor who through its educational systems and its mastery of science has been successful in implanting atheism, materialism, and moral decadence in the heart of Malaysian Islam.

Seen in these terms, anti-modern attacks have to do with the loss of meaning in modern societies. The absence of transcendent goals in contemporary life are decried, while activity in the modern world is characterized as merely instrumental, an endless chain of means leading to a hedonistic excess of consumption. The Islamic resurgence in Malaysia does not, however, reject Western science but seeks instead to put it in the service of wisdom, which is usually couched in Islamic terms. As in other Islamic fundamentalist movements throughout the world, the perceived corruption in Western society is often contrasted in Malaysian dakwah circles to an idealized past, or more precisely, to a pristine traditional state which was disrupted by the invasion of hostile, outside forces.

For the fundamental and thoroughgoing social change which the revivalists call for, young people—with the energy, and the willingness to take the risks of great change and only a minimal stake in the prevailing social order—serve both as the movement's target audience and its greatest hope for the future. This radical restructuring of society which, it is fervently hoped, will be carried out by the youth of Malaysia is thoroughly rooted in the teachings of Islam. Islam is the one indigenous glory not tied to the West, and the themes handed down from the glorious history of the Islamic past are the cultural content of all forms of Islamic resurgence.

It is important to note that the particular form which Islamic revivalism may take will vary in accordance with particular local circumstances due to differing conditions concerning ethnic pluralism, communal politics, and wealth and occupational divisions among the chief population segments. Between Malaysia and neighboring Indonesia, as we have seen, considerable differences exist among the forms of Islamic revivalism that have emerged in recent years. These profound differences exist despite the geographic and linguistic proximity of the countries, and may in general be accounted for by such factors as the variance in social structures and different historical circumstances. The Indonesians' unhappy colonial experience under the Dutch was considerably different than the relatively enlightened rule of the British in neighboring Malaysia, for example, leaving the Malaysian state at a considerable advantage in organizing modern governmental and educational structures at independence. As we observed, however, this advantage has also led to a political and social milieu perhaps more conducive to the rise of Islamic fundamentalism than in Indonesia.

While respecting the national and regional variations in the forms of the Islamic revival, one may identify eight social and cultural features held in common by dakwah groups and by the new groups they have generated. These features combine to give an ostensive definition of fundamentalism in Southeast Asia:

1. Fundamentalist groups base their arguments on a literalist reading of scripture. The Qur'an, Hadith, and Shari'a are presented, without much theological debate or subtlety of interpretation, as the reliable and unwavering font of normative belief and behavior;
2. An idealized past, a golden age of purity, is reconstructed from this literalist reading of the Qur'an and the Sunna and presented as attainable in the future. This glorified past and glorious future is described in contrast to the cultural and religious degradation of the present moment.

3. Though the past serves as a model, what fundamentalists seek is not simply to turn back the clock but to create an ideal society based on Islamic tenets in the context of contemporary reality. The emphasis in fundamentalist movements therefore is on change here and now, with the reformed society as a short-range goal, leading to salvation in the long run.
4. Fundamentalists organize themselves into a network or cadre movement, with a leader and a cell-like structure. The fervor of the group is focused both on spreading its ideology to others and on monitoring the behavior of its own individual followers.
5. The group tends to be actively opposed to the modern West, with hedonism and materialism seen as the vehicles of secularism and self-indulgence. However, the fundamentalist movement is neither anti-technological nor anti-scientific.
6. The group combines antimodernism with defense of an ethnic identity. It seeks to see rapid change toward greater social and cultural equality for the oppressed ethnic group. Hence it attracts young people made uncomfortable by recent social mobility—both spatial mobility from rural to urban areas, and status or class mobility from lower to middle class and from peasant or laborer to salariat (salaried professional) or proletariat status.
7. The continued social existence of the fundamentalist movement depends on a charismatic leader who is capable of mobilizing masses for political action in the event of a protracted social and cultural crisis of a magnitude beyond the capacity of existing authoritative institutions to manage.
8. Finally, fundamentalism carries with it an inherent theodicy by which everything that is wrong—that produces unjust suffering—can be meaningfully explained as having come about because of departures from the true faith.

At varying levels of social incidence, these features seem to exist in societies with substantial Muslim populations recently freed of the colonial yoke in which a literati confronts a modernizing, secular elite in a situation in which national and ethnic identities are fragile or are in the process of self-definition because of intense cultural and political pressures.

Islam is in this context a reservoir for cultural and social turbulence, for it provides an idiom, a set of symbols, and a body of ideas for a critique of a world that falls short of the idealized state of the founder and his immediate followers. It harkens back to a golden age and looks forward to a future which will replicate that age. The faint drumbeats of a return to purity in a corrupt world can swell to a deafening cacophony in times of social and cultural crisis.[76]

The revival of the sacred polity in the form of Islamic fundamentalism in much of the Islamic world is a twentieth-century phenomenon, built out of the tensions and dilemmas of new nations with old societies facing challenges from the industrial, modern West. These pressures fall most heavily on the young, the newly mobile, the recently urbanized, and those in new occupations. Islam provides a ready lexicon of protest and of promise, and in the proper conditions of crisis, has and will continue to figure prominently in the political and cultural life of these two nations. As long as social change is viewed as redemptive, Islam remains a contender for the role of redeemer, and the fundamentalist version of Islam an auspicious vehicle for salvation.

Notes

I am deeply indebted to Professor Robert McKinley for his many contributions to this essay.

1. Karl D. Jackson, *Traditional Authority, Islam, and Rebellion: A Study of Indonesian Political Behavior* (Berkeley: University of California Press, 1980), p. 15.

2. Ibid, p. 23.

3. Sartono Kartodirdjo, "The Peasants' Revolt of Banten in 1888: The Religious Revival," in Ahmad Ibrahim, Sharon Siddique, and Yasmin Hussain, eds., *Readings on Islam in Southeast Asia* (Singapore: Institute of Southeast Asian Studies, 1985), p. 103. Originally published as *The Peasants' Revolt of Banten 1888*. Verhandelingen van het Koninklijh Instituut voor Taal-Landen Volkenkunde, Luden, The Netherlands. (Gravenhage: Martinus Nyhoff, 1966).

4. With regard to interaction between Muslims in these three countries and those in nearby Thailand and the Philippines, the influence upon religious trends in Malaysia and Indonesia seems less pronounced. A solidarity is felt, but the cultural admiration is less marked.

5. Malaysians making the hajj (pilgrimage) to Mecca increased from a mere 9, 511 in 1979 to 24,749 in 1984. Indonesian hajjis in the same period, possibly as a result of economic factors, actually declined from a 1980 high of 74,741 to a still substantial 1984 figure of 40, 928. Cf. James Piscatori, "Asian Islam: International Linkages and Their Impact on International Relations," in John L. Esposito, ed., *Islam in Asia: Religion, Politics, and Society* (New York: Oxford University Press, 1987), p. 251.

6. Fred R. von der Mehden, "Malaysia and Indonesia," in Shireen T. Hunter, ed., *The Politics of Islamic Revivalism: Diversity and Unity* (Bloomington: Indiana University Press, 1988), pp. 253–54.

7. Fred R. von der Mehden, "Malaysia: Islam and Multiethnic Polities," in Esposito, *Islam In Asia,* p. 204.

8. von der Mehden, "Malaysia and Indonesia," p. 260, ff. 20. The quotation cited appeared in the *Christian Science Monitor,* 2 January 1986. Although von der Mehden's comment does capture the notable rise in Islamic consciousness, it is important to point out that the terms *abangan* and *santri* as he employs them derive from Clifford Geertz's attempt to identify ideal types of religiosity among Javanese town dwellers. Several Indonesian writers have objected that neither term, as Geertz defines them, corresponds closely to any native category. A further objection is that in setting up his ideal types, Geertz made mutually exclusive categories out of attitudes and activities that often overlap and in the final analysis are very context determined. Cf. Clifford Geertz, *The Religion of Java* (New York: Free Press of Glencoe, 1960). Also see Harsja W Bachtiar, "The Religion of Java: A Commentary," in Ibrahim, et al., *Islam in Southeast Asia*; and Mitsuo Nakamura, *The Crescent Arises over the Banyan Tree: A Study of the Muhammadiya Movement in a Central Javanese Town* (Yogyakarta: Gajah Mada University Press, 1983).

9. I use "men" advisedly because all of the decisions to join were made by men, some of whom were heads of families. The families followed, sometimes reluctantly.

10. Cf. the case of popular Malay singer, Rahimah Rahim, who voluntarily ended her singing career at age thirty-four shortly after completing the pilgrimage to Mecca. Reported in *The Malay Mail,* 26 April 1990.

11. Mariam Mohamed Ali, "Uniformity and Diversity Among Muslims in Singapore," (Master's thesis, National University of Singapore, 1989) pp. 3–6.

12. Cf. C. Kessler, "Malaysia: Islamic Re-

vivalism and Political Disaffection in a Divided Society," *Southeast Asia Chronicle* 75 (October, 1980).

13. The actual degree to which ijtihad was practiced is the subject of some scholarly debate. Cf. James L. Peacock, *Muslim Puritans: Reformist Psychology in Southeast Asian Islam* (Berkeley: University of California Press, 1978), p. 18.

14. William R. Roff, *The Origins of Malay Nationalism* (New Haven: Yale University Press, 1967), pp. 56–90.

15. Robert McKinley, "Zaman das Masa, 'Eras and Periods' : Religious Evolution and the Permanence of Epistemological Ages in Malay Culture," in Alton Becker and Aram Yengoyan, eds., *The Imagination of Reality: Essays on Southeast Asian Coherence Systems* (Norwood, N.J.: Ablex, 1979), pp. 303–324.

16. The author's fieldwork and hence the major focus of this article is on peninsular Malaysia. The contemporary nation of Malaysia is made up of the peninsula (West Malaysia) and Sabah and Sarawak (East Malaysia), but the discussion here centers on the former.

17. Kay kim Khoo, "Chinese Economic Activities in Malaya: A Historical Perspective," in Manning Nash, ed., *Economic Performance in Malaysia: The Insider's View* (New York: Professor's World Peace Academy, 1988), pp. 170–223.

18. R. K. Jain, *South Indians on the Plantation Frontier in Malaysia* (New Haven: Yale University Press, 1970).

19. Judith Nagata, *The Reflowering of Malaysian Islam: Modern Religious Radicals and Their Roots* (Vancouver: University of British Columbia Press, 1984), p. 31.

20. Clive S. Kessler, *Islam and Politics in a Malay State: Kelantan 1838–1969* (Ithaca: Cornell University Press, 1978), p. 25.

21. Diane K. Mauzy, *Barison Nasional: Coalition Government in Malaysia* (Kuala Lumpur: Marican & Sons, 1983), p. 9.

22. Roff, *Origins of Malay Nationalism,* p. 15.

23. Peacock, *Muslim Puritans,* p. 178.

24. Mauzy, *Barisan Nasional,* p. 22.

25. The *Rukun Negara* set forward five principles: Belief in God (although stopping far short of endorsing a specifically Islamic emphasis), loyalty to the king and the nation, morality (in the most general sense), obedience to the law, and observing the national Constitution. Cf. *Area Handbook Series Malaysia: A Country Study* (Washington, D.C.: United States Government, 1984), pp. 60–62.

26. Mauzy, *Barison Nasional,* p. 112.

27. Quoted in Zainah Anwar, *Islamic Revivalism in Malaysia: Dakwah among the Students* (Selanya, Malaysia: Pelanduk Publications, 1987), p. 11. Anwar Ibrahim is presently Malaysia's minister of education in the Mahatir administration.

28. Ibid., p. 13.

29. Ibid., pp.14–17.

30. Indonesia has long held a place of cultural preeminence in the minds of Malay students and intellectuals. Indonesia has a literature, a culture, and a version of Islam which is the heritage of Indonesia Raya, the great and glorious Malay empires of which contemporary Malaysia was once a part.

31. Robert McKinley, private letter of 18 November 1988, based on journal notes and interviews with Malay students from 1970 to 1972, and again in 1982.

32. Judith Nagata, *Reflowering of Malaysian Islam,* p. 57.

33. The distinctive female garb has always been the movement's most conspicuous sign. That the active participation of women in the dakwah movement has done little to alter their traditional status or the way their male colleagues regard them can be seen by the jokes and ridicule which they attracted.

34. Nagata, *Reflowering of Malaysian Islam,* p. 81.

35. Ibid., pp. 104–15.

36. Ibid., pp. 116–22.

37. Zainah Anwar, *Islamic Revivalism.*

38. Ibid.

39. Nagata, *Reflowering of Malaysian Islam,* pp. 158– 62.

40. Ibid., pp. 124–26.

41. Deliar Noer, "Masjumi: Its Organization, Ideology and Political Role in Indonesia" (Masters thesis, Cornell University, 1960).

42. Clifford Geertz, *Islam Observed: Religious Development in Morocco and Indonesia* (Chicago: University of Chicago Press, 1968), pp. 12–13, 66.

43. Mark Woodward, *Islam in Java* (Tucson: University of Arizona Press, 1989).

44. Ibid., p. 68. Between 1820 and 1880 there were at least four santri revolts against the Dutch and their Hinduized fellow travelers.

45. Zamakhsyari Dhofier, *Tradisi Pesantren: Studi tentang Pandangan Hidup Kyai (The Pesantren tradition: A study of the Kiyayis' view of life)* (Jakarta: Penerbit LP3ES, Lembaya Penelitain, Pendidikan, dan Penerangan Ekonomi dan Social [Publisher, Board of Safety, Education, Information, Economy, and Society], 1982) pp.12–15.

46. Today this is visible in that most Malaysian and Singaporean Malay women no longer allow themselves the *sarong kabaya* (the tight-fitting traditional shirt and blouse) as a clothing option, whereas most Indonesian women still do.

47. Fazlur Rahman, *Islam and Modernity* (Chicago: University of Chicago Press, 1982), pp. 126–27.

48. Ibid. For example, the santri moderen condemn all arts but the recitation of the Qur'an. In practice, this tends to put them outside of the rich Javanese heritage of music, dance, *wayang* (puppet theater), and the like. The kolot, conversely, maintain several traditional arts, involving music, dancing, singing, and the martial arts.

49. Sarekat Islam (the Islamic Foundation), the first truly modern Muslim political grouping, which diffused from Egypt, served as the major political outlet for moderen Muslims in Indonesia until the coalition crisis of 1950.

50. From the point of view of many traditionalist Indonesians, the moderen were also upsetting the system of traditional checks and balances which allowed for gradual social change without the danger of intense social dislocations. After Indonesia became independent, NU formally entered elections as a political party in the 1950s and 1960s. Since then it has continued to voice the concerns of the kijaji as a religious organization. Cf. Anthony H. Johns, "Indonesia: Islam and Cultural Pluralism," in Esposito, *Islam In Asia,* p. 207.

51. Ibid., p. 203.

52. Jackson, *Traditional Authority, Islam, and Rebellion,* p. 9.

53. Johns, "Indonesia: Islam and Cultural Pluralism," p. 210.

54. Ibid., p. 211.

55. Jackson, *Traditional Authority, Islam, and Rebellion,* pp. 1–5.

56. Ibid., p. 9.

57. Johns, "Indonesia: Islam and Cultural Pluralism," pp. 211–212.

58. Jackson, *Traditional Authority, Islam, and Rebellion,*p. 18.

59. There are a number of sources for the activities of the CIA in Indonesia at this time. Perhaps the most balanced is John Ranelagh, *The Agency: The Rise and Decline of the CIA* (New York: Simon & Schuster, 1987), pp. 332–35, 468n. Cf. also A. M. Halperin, *Policies Toward China: Views From Six Continents* (New York: McGraw-Hill, 1965), pp. 262–302; and Winberg Chai, *The Foreign Relations of the People's Republic of China* (New York: Capricorn Books, 1972), pp. 272–77. Chai translates the treaty on dual nationality concluded between the PRC and Indonesia in 1955 which was designed to regulate the PRC's relations with the Indonesian Chinese population. Ladislav Bittman, a former officer of Czech intelligence, relates details of his involvement in the "Operation Palmer," in Ladislav Bittman, *The Deception Game: Czechoslovak Intelligence in Soviet Political Warfare* (Syracuse: Syracuse University Research Corporation, 1972), pp. 106–22.

60. Cf. John Hughes, *Indonesian Upheaval* (New York: David McKay, 1967), pp. 3–17; and Hal Kosut, ed., *Indonesia: The Sukarno Years* (New York: Facts on File, 1967).

61. Nahdatul Ulama captured fifty-eight seats. Partai Sarekat Islam Indonesia won

twenty-four. Partai Muslimin Indonesia, which had the support of many former members of the banned Masyumi, was only able to grab ten spots. The remaining two positions of the ninety-four for Muslim parties went to a small traditionalist party, Partai Tarbia Islam.

62. The PDI coalition included the Catholic Party, the Protestant Party, and the remnants of the old Indonesian Nationalist Party. This reorganization had the virtue of allowing the Muslim and Christian parties to contest elections, whether open or not freely conducted, while conforming with the constitutional primacy of Panca Sila's nonsectarian requirement.

63. Victor Tanja, *Hinipunan Maliasiswa Islam* (Jakarta: Bright Hope Press, 1982.)

64. Johns, "Indonesia: Islam and Cultural Pluralism," pp. 221–24.

65. In Malaysia, these politicoreligious conflicts culminated in a violent clash between police and the followers of the charismatic preacher, Ibrahim Mahmud in Malaysia in 1985. Having established a rural school in the Kedah area, two hundred local police seeking to arrest Mahmud were met by villagers prepared to resist, resulting in the deaths of Ibrahim, some fourteen villagers and four policemen, and resulting as well in a number of arrests. Reported in von der Mehden, "Malaysia and Indonesia," pp. 252–53.

66. A. G. Mezerik, ed., "Malaysia-Indonesia Conflict," *International Review Service* 11, no. 86 (1965): 8.

67. Ibid., pp. 36–37.

68. For the basic facts of this conflict, see Kosut, *Indonesia,* pp. 84–107. For a brief but fascinating view of this conflict from Sukarno's point of view, see Sukarno and Cindy Adams, *Sukarno: An Autobiography* (Indianapolis: Bobbs-Merrill, 1965), pp. 300–4, 306–7.

69. Mezerick, "Malaysia-Indonesia Conflict," pp. 54–55.

70. Ibid., p. 249.

71. Zainah Anwar, *Islamic Revivalism in Malaysia: Dakwah among the Students* (Selanya, Malaysia: Pelanduk Publications, 1987).

72. Cf., for example, C. Kessler, "Malaysia: Islamic Revivalism and Political Disaffection in a Divided Society," *Southeast Asia Chronicle* 75 (October 1980); and V. S. Naipaul, *Among the Believers: An Islamic Journey* (New York: Vintage Books, 1981).

73. M. L., Lyon, "The Dakwah Movement in Malaysia," *Review of Indonesian and Malayan Affairs* 13, no. 2 (December 1979): 34–45.

74. Cf. Manning Nash, "Fundamentalist Islam: Reservoir for Turbulence," *Journal of Asian and African Studies* 19 (1984): 73–79.

75. Benedict Anderson, *Imagined Communities: Reflections on the Origin and Spread of Nationalism* (London: Versor, 1983).

76. Manning Nash, "Fundamentalist Islam."

Select Bibliography

Abdurrahman, Wahid. "The Islamic Masses in the Life of State and Nation." *Prisma* 35 (1985).

Abu Bakar, Mohamad. "Islamic Revivalism and the Political Process in Malaysia." *Asian Survey* 21 (1981).

Ackerman, Susan E., and Raymond L. M. Lee. *Heaven in Transition: Non-Muslim Religious Innovation and Ethnic Identity in Malaysia.* Honolulu: University of Hawaii Press, 1988.

Anand, Sudhir. *Inequality and Poverty in Malaysia: Measurement and Decomposition.* New York: Oxford University Press, 1983.

Anderson, Benedict. *Imagined Communities: Reflections on the Origin and Spread of Nationalism.* London: Versor, 1983.

Anwar, Rosihan. "Islam and Politics in Indonesia." In *Man, State, and Society in Contemporary Southeast Asia.* Robert O. Tilman, ed. New York: Praeger, 1969.

Anwar, Zainah. *Islamic Revivalism in Malaysia: Dakwah among the Students.* Selanya,

Malaysia: Pelanduk Publications, 1987.

Benda, Harry J. "South-East Asian Islam in the Twentieth Century." In *The Cambridge History of Islam.* P. M. Holt, et al., eds., vol. 2. Cambridge: Cambridge University Press, 1970.

Boland, B. J. *The Struggle of Islam in Modern Indonesia.* The Hague: Martinus Nijhoff, 1978.

Bonner, Raymond. "A Reporter at Large: The New Order." *New Yorker*, 6 June 1988 and 13 June 1988.

Dessouki, Ali E. Hillal, ed. *Islamic Resurgence in the Arab World.* New York: Praeger, 1982.

Esposito, John L., ed. *Islam and Development: Religion and Sociopolitical Change.* Syracuse: Syracuse University Press, 1980.

———. *Islam in Asia: Religion, Politics, and Society.* New York: Oxford University Press, 1987.

Ewing, Katherine P., ed. *Shari'at and Ambiguity in South Asian Islam.* Berkeley: University of California Press, 1988.

Funston, John. *Malay Politics in Malaysia: A Study of UMNO and PAS.* Singapore: Heinamann, 1980.

Funston, N. J. *Malay Politics in Malaysia: A Study of the United Malays National Organization and Party Islam.* Kuala Lumpur: Heineman Educational Books, 1980.

Geertz, Clifford. *The Religion of Java.* Chicago: University of Chicago Press, 1960.

———. *Islam Observed: Religious Development in Morocco and Indonesia.* Chicago: University of Chicago Press, 1968.

———. "Modernization in a Muslim Society: The Indonesian Case." In Robert O. Tilman, ed., *Man, State, and Society in Contemporary Southeast Asia.* New York: Praeger, 1969.

Hassan, M. K. *Muslim Intellectual Reponses to "New Order" Modernization in Indonesia.* Kuala Lumpur: Dewan Bahasa dan Pustaka Kementerian Palajaran Malaysia, 1980.

Holt, P. M., et al., eds. *The Cambridge History of Islam.* Cambridge: Cambridge University Press, 1970.

Hughes, John. *Indonesian Upheaval.*New York: David McKay, 1967.

Humphreys, R. Stephen "The Contemporary Resurgence in the Context of Modern Islam." In Ali E. Hillal Dessouki, ed., *Islamic Resurgence in the Arab World.* New York: Praeger, 1982.

Jackson, Karl D. *Traditional Authority, Islam, and Rebellion: A Study of Indonesian Political Behavior.* Berkeley: University of California Press, 1980.

Jain, R. K. *South Indians on the Plantation Frontier in Malaysia.* New Haven: Yale University Press, 1970.

Jay, Robert R. "History and Personal Experience: Religious and Political Conflict in Java." In Robert F. Spencer, ed., *Religion and Change in Contemporary Asia.* Minneapolis: University of Minnesota Press, 1971.

Johns, Anthony H. "Indonesia: Islam and Cultural Pluralism." In John L. Esposito, ed., *Islam in Asia: Religion, Politics, and Society.* New York: Oxford University Press, 1987.

Kessler, Clive S. *Islam and Politics in a Malay State: Kelantan 1838–1969.* Ithaca: Cornell University Press, 1978.

Khoo, Kay kim. "Chinese Economic Activities in Malaya: A Historical Perspective." In Manning Nash, ed., *Economic Performance in Malaysia: The Insider's View.* New York: Professor's World Peace Academy, 1988.

Kosut, Hal, ed. *Indonesia: The Sukarno Years.* New York: Facts on File, 1967.

Lyon, M. L. "The Dakwah Movement in Malaysia." *Review of Indonesian and Malayan Affairs* 13, no. 2 (1979).

Mauzy, Diane K. *Barison Nasional: Coalition Government in Malaysia.* Kuala Lumpur: Marican & Sons, 1983.

Mezerik, A. G., ed. "Malaysia-Indonesia Conflict." *International Review Service* 11 (86).

Milne, R. S., and D. K. Mauzy. *Malaysia: Tradition, Modernity, and Islam.* Boulder, Colo.: Westview, 1986.

Muzaffar, Chandra. *Islamic Resurgence in*

Malaysia. Petaling Jaya, Malaysia: Penerbil Fajar Bakti, 1987.

Nagata, Judith. *The Reflowering of Malaysian Islam: Modern Religious Radicals and Their Roots*. Vancouver: University of British Columbia Press, 1984.

Naipaul, V. S., *Among the Believers: An Islamic Journey*. New York: Vintage Books, 1981.

Nash, Manning. "Fundamentalist Islam: Reservoir for Turbulence." *Journal of Asian and African Studies*19 (1984).

Rauf, M. A. *A Brief History of Islam with Special Reference to Malaya*. Kuala Lumpur: Oxford University Press, 1964.

Roff, William R. *The Origins of Malay Nationalism*. New Haven: Yale University Press, 1967.

———. "Islam Obscured? Some Reflections on Studies of Islam and Society in Southeast Asia." *Archipel* 29 (1985).

Smith, Donald Eugene, ed. *Religion and Political Modernization*. New Haven: Yale University Press, 1974.

Spencer, Robert F., ed. *Religion and Change in Contemporary Asia*. Minneapolis: University of Minnesota Press, 1971.

Stowasser, Barbara Freyer, ed. *The Islamic Impulse*. Center for Contemporary Arab Studies. London: Croom Helm, 1987.

Sukarno and Cindy Adams. *Sukarno: An Autobiography*. Indianapolis: Bobbs-Merrill, 1965.

Tilman, Robert O., ed. *Man, State, and Society in Contemporary Southeast Asia*. New York: Praeger, 1969.

von der Mehden, Fred R. *Religion and Nationalism in Southeast Asia: Burma, Indonesia, the Philippines*. Madison: University of Wisconsin Press, 1968.

———. "Islamic Resurgence in Malaysia." In John L. Esposito, ed., *Islam and Development: Religion and Sociopolitical Change*. Syracuse: Syracuse University Press, 1980.

———. "Malaysia and Indonesia." In Shireen T. Hunter, ed., *The Politics of Islamic Revivalism: Diversity and Unity*. Bloomington: Indiana University Press, 1988.

Wertheim, W. F. *Indonesian Society in Transition: A Study of Social Change*. 2d rev. ed. The Hague: W. van Hoeve, 1969.

CHAPTER
13

The Search for Roots In Industrial East Asia: The Case of the Confucian Revival

Tu Wei-ming

The sociologist Peter Berger relates his personal encounter with Asian folk religion in a fascinating anecdote:

> I was in Singapore, on a tour of a part of the city in the company of an anthropologist, when we came upon a spirit temple. We went in and talked to the medium, a young man who, as I recall, was an electrician by occupation. He conducted seances in the living room of his home and he gladly explained things to us. The center of the room was occupied by a bookshelf with several shelves, on which were arranged plaster-of-paris statuettes of different divinities and supernatural beings. On the top self, in the middle, was the statuette of Kuan Yi[n], the Chinese Goddess of Mercy. All the other figures were placed hierarchically in relation to her. What impressed me was the manner in which the medium spoke about them. He would say something like this: "This fellow over here has been very bad. He is not good for anything and we have just demoted him, putting him down from the third to the fourth shelf. If he doesn't improve his performance, he will be thrown out completely. But this one has been very helpful to the community, so we have placed him very close to the Goddess." And so on. What struck me was that this man was speaking about supernatural beings in very much the same way, and indeed in the same tone of voice, that a corporation executive might speak about his staff. The little pantheon in the living room, then, could be seen as a sort of metaphysical table of organization.[1]

This encounter suggested to Berger that Asian spiritual orientation is this-worldly, pragmatic, and eclectic. Similar examples may be easily found in Japan, Korea, Hong Kong, and Taiwan. The eclectic blending of Shintoist and Buddhist symbols in Japan, of Christian and Confucian practices in South Korea, and of the precepts of the Three

Teachings (Confucian, Buddhist, and Taoist) in Hong Kong and Singapore is characteristic of East Asian religiosity. The pervasive and deliberate mixing of symbols, practices, and precepts in New Religions such as the Tenri in Japan, the Unification Church in South Korea, and the I-kuan-tao in Taiwan clearly indicates that the eclectic tendency remains strong in contemporary East Asia.

Two salient ideas underlie this particular East Asian religious tendency: (1) a pragmatic demand for concrete material consequences, and (2) the hope that genuine quests for human well-being are at least compatible and often mutually beneficial. Historically these two ideas have featured prominently in the popular religions of the Sinitic world.

The first idea, rooted in the thesis of the "mutual responsiveness between Heaven and humanity,"[2] assumes that ghosts *(gui)*, spirits *(shen)*, and gods *(kami)* are an integral part of the human world: their ontological status is inseparable from their performance in everyday human interaction. The seemingly outrageous practice in imperial China of the magistrate punishing the earth god for not providing proper rain for the county by burning his sacred altar is an example of this idea in practice. However, such an act was never frivolous, because it could and should lead to grave consequences for the magistrate, his family, and the community at large. Often it was out of desperation that such a dramatic measure was taken; only after they had exhausted all human means to alleviate the situation would they question the responsibility of the gods as a last resort. Even then, solemn rituals of atonement were performed to underscore the fact that the political leadership had to bear the main burden for the people's suffering. What Berger observed was a secularized and vulgarized practice in which the seemingly arbitrary manipulation of the temple manager is actually predicated on the principle of correspondence and mutuality in a complex symbolic universe. One wonders if the manager did not make earnest supplication with proper offerings regularly in order to keep the gods content as a precondition for their efficaciousness.

The second idea was derived from the commonsense belief that since human beings are fated to be particular persons, the paths toward salvation must be diverse indeed. This belief discourages missionary exclusiveness and allows religious traditions to coexist in an inclusive vision of human flourishing. Thus the standard proselytizing rhetoric in East Asia is accommodating: "My way can accommodate yours and more," rather than "Mine is the most authentic!" The perceived distinction between the "great vehicle" and "small vehicle" in East Asian Buddhism, for example, is that the bodhisattva, inspired by true compassion, is more accommodating, while the small-minded person is confined only to the salvation of a single individual. It is not unusual for a Taoist shrine in Singapore to honor Buddha, for a Buddhist master in Hong Kong to advocate Taoist teachings, for a Shinto priest in Kyoto to lecture on a Confucian classic, for a Christian church in Seoul to practice Confucian ancestral veneration, or for a predominantly Lamaist sect in Taipei to embrace the doctrine of the unity of the Three Teachings. Indeed, there are numerous Shinto-Buddhists in Japan, Buddho-Taoists in Taiwan, and Confucian Christians in South Korea. If the this-worldly, pragmatic, and eclectic temple manager of Berger's story is indicative of

East Asian spiritual orientation, "fundamentalism," as either theory or practice, seems not to fit the East Asian order of things.

Yet the fundamentalist problematic characteristic of Christian, Jewish, and Islamic societies is obviously relevant to contemporary East Asia. Strategically it may be more fruitful to explore distinctive fundamentalist movements in East Asia, such as Christian evangelism in South Korea and Shinto ultranationalism in Japan.[3] If we focus on the Confucian revival, however, it may become clear that the "search for roots," which has been identified as fundamentalistic in nature, proceeds from a critique of modernity that presents a threat to, rather than a confirmation of, values held by the Western academy: tolerance, reasonableness, flexibility, open-mindedness, dialogue, and pluralism. Yet the examination of fundamentalist-like attitudes, if it is to reflect these very values, may not simply proceed as a psychopathological study of radical "otherness."

Perspective

The significance of encountering the Confucian phenomenon is twofold. It helps us to understand a dimension of the fundamentalist quest, namely, the search for roots as a perennial human concern. Arguably such a concern is far from being simply a psychopathological response to the challenge of modernity as a result of inability to deal with dynamic change in society and pluralistic complexity in culture. Rather, it may signify a wholesome attitude toward the modernizing process as, among other things, an unprecedented threat to the survival of the human species. Furthermore, the fundamentalist pattern as a conceptual lens enables us better to understand some of the distinctive features of East Asian spirituality, especially those aspects which have been informed by the Confucian discourse.

Confucianism, commonly regarded as a form of social ethics and a way of life, is one of the longest-continuing spiritual traditions in human history, and was celebrated as such by an international scholarly conference in commemoration of Confucius's 2540th birthday held in Beijing in 1989 and jointly sponsored by the Confucius Foundation in the People's Republic of China and the UNESCO. Although minor disagreement does occur about the exact date of Confucius' birth in 551 B.C.E., 28 September has been officially declared The Teacher's Day in Taiwan.[4] Confucius has been honored in East Asian history as a sage who by personal self-cultivation became an exemplar of humanity. As the Confucian *Analects* amply demonstrates, Confucius's greatness as "a teacher for myriad generations" lies in his unadorned human qualities.

However, despite the centrality of Confucius himself in the Confucian tradition, and perhaps precisely because his life was perceived as ordinary, Confucianism has not developed from a myth or cult of "the founder" to the extent that other major traditions such as Christianity and Buddhism have. To be sure, Confucius has often been characterized as the founder of Confucianism, but he was self-identified and publicly acknowledged as a great transmitter of a scholarly tradition that was not available to the West until the dissemination of Jesuit translations in the seventeenth century.

Actually, "Confucianism," strictly speaking, is a misnomer, for it has no East Asian equivalent; moreover, when translated literally into Chinese, Japanese, or Korean, it is likely to be misleading. The Chinese term for Confucianism is "scholarly tradition" *(rujia)*.[5]

Understood as a dynamic process rather than a static structure, the Confucian tradition originated centuries before the time of Confucius. The scholarly tradition that he and his disciples inherited and enlarged was one of several currents of thought contending for supremacy during the period of the Warring States (fifth to third century B.C.E.). By the first century it had become the most powerful intellectual persuasion in China proper. However, although the Confucian tradition has often been characterized as synonymous to Chinese culture, it has gone through a few noticeable phases in the Chinese historical landscape, not all of them marked by growth and prosperity. In fact, the period from the third to the ninth century witnessed the introduction, domestication, and development of Buddhism in a Buddhist age in China. Although Confucian classics, rituals, and ethics continued to flourish in the political culture of the Tang empire (618–907), Confucianism as a form of spiritual cultivation did not inspire the most original minds in thought and religion. The revival of Confucian humanism, widely known as Neo-Confucianism in the West, in the eleventh century enabled the Confucian stream to flow beyond the Chinese borders to become, in Shimada Kenji's term, a manifestation of East Asian spirituality. Indeed, Confucian culture informed by Neo-Confucian ideas has been a dominant intellectual discourse in East Asian education both for the elite and the populace, for formal and informal social organizations and bureaucracy both at the central and local levels. Prior to the impact of the modern West—specifically China since the thirteenth century, the Chosŏn dynasty in Korea since the fifteenth century, and Tokugawa Japan since the seventeenth century—East Asia had been seasoned in Confucian culture.

Unlike other major world religions, Confucianism is strictly speaking neither an organized religion nor a founder's religion. Actually, whether or not Confucianism is even a religion remains a controversial issue among scholars of comparative religion. It should be noted, however, that while Confucian teaching is focused on the lived experience of the mundane human condition, it involves a powerful spiritual dimension which enables it to address profound religious issues such as the ultimate concern, the path of salvation, faith, and transcendence. As a form of life, not unlike Hinduism in its diversity, Confucianism is noted for its wisdom books (for example, the Five Classics and the Four Books), political institutions (such as the court rituals and the examination system), social organizations (such as community compacts and local schools), family ethics (notably, ancestral veneration and respect for parents), and single-minded attention to self-cultivation. The Confucian concern for personal well-being, family harmony, social solidarity, political stability, and universal peace has become a defining characteristic of the East Asian view of the good life. Its preference for group orientation, collaborative effort, mutual support, and communicative rationality has greatly influenced the East Asian work ethic: "a positive attitude to the affairs of this world, a sustained lifestyle of discipline and self-cultivation, respect for authority, frugality, and overriding concern for stable family life."[6]

However, as inclusive humanism, Confucian ethics seeks to integrate not only the human community but the individual, communal, natural, and transcendent in an organismic whole. Since the highest Confucian ideal of self-realization is the "unity of humanity and Heaven" *(tianren heyi),* Confucian humanism seeks to transcend anthropocentrism as well as egoism, nepotism, parochialism, ethnocentrism, and chauvinistic nationalism. While the Confucian tradition, intent on transforming the secular world into a sacred domain, fully recognizes that the self, family, community, nature, and world in the human condition are intractable realities of life, its primary purpose is individual and communal self-realization with a view toward Heaven. Understandably the Confucian project for human flourishing is predicated on the faith in the malleability and improvability of the human condition through self-effort rather than a commitment to the legitimacy of the status quo. Max Weber's characterization of the Confucian life orientation as "adjustment to the world"[7] is therefore misleading. The Confucian insistence that as human beings we are embedded in the temporality of this earth is singularly relevant to the search for roots as an inseparable dimension of global consciousness.

The recognition that primordial conditions of human existence such as ethnicity, mother tongue, ancestral home, gender, class, and religion are lived realities of modern industrial societies compels us to reexamine the modernizing process, especially the notion of modernization as the triumph of instrumental rationality which, in Weber's view, tends to undermine cultural diversity and traditional patterns of social solidarity.[8] It is intriguing that the search for cultural roots is so pervasive worldwide despite universalizing tendencies occasioned by industrialization, urbanization, bureaucratization, the development of science and technology, and the spread of mass communication. The assumption that modernity entails the passing of traditional society is no longer tenable in light of this dialectical interaction between global consciousness and local awareness.

East Asia has been perhaps the most volatile economic and political region since the Second World War and is a remarkable example of the coexistence, if not the blending, of tradition and modernity (and by implication, of East and West). It is fascinating to observe that seemingly outmoded traditional motifs not only endure but flourish in metropolitan East Asia. Unfortunately, the conceptual apparatuses employed by cultural comparativists tend to give the mistaken impression that East Asian societies tolerate contradictions, learn to adapt to incongruous lifestyles, or fail to move beyond eclecticism. The apparent lack of powerful fundamentalist movements in East Asia which take an exclusive dogmatic position on ultimate truth gives the mistaken impression that commitment to religious ideas and affiliation with religious institutions means less in East Asia than in the West or the Middle East.

However, the interpretation that East Asian people under the influence of Confucian humanism often take an uncommitted, eclectic attitude toward religious matters confuses open-mindedness with perfunctoriness. The acceptance of religious pluralism, an ideal consistent with the Confucian golden rule—"Do not do unto others what you would not want others to do unto you"—is perhaps the single most important reason that by and large, East Asians consciously refuse to subscribe to an exclusive dogmatic position on ultimate truth.[9] This of course does not imply that one should remain aloof from, or make light of, commitment to a particular religious faith. The characterization of the Chinese literatus as Confucian in office and Taoist out of office, of a typical Japanese as Shintoist in youth, Confucian in adulthood, and Buddhist in old age, or of a Korean woman as Confucian by obligation but shamanistic at heart has a measure of truth. Yet the proverbial wisdom in these sayings should not obscure the intellectual clarity and emotional intensity of East Asian religious life. The Confucian commitment to the sanctity of the earth and the sacredness of human institutions—families, schools, societies, and states—signifies a distinctive feature of East Asian spirituality.

Approach

Prior to the arrival of the modern West in the nineteenth century, East Asia had already developed a complex modern civilization of its own. Confucian ethics, which provided a universal code of conduct for the political and cultural elite in China, Korea, and Japan, was the lingua franca of the civilized world of East Asia. Western superiority in the military technology of gunboats, cannons, and firearms generated fear and resentment rather than admiration among those seasoned in Confucian discourse. Although the Confucian heritage is not monolithic and the modernizing paths taken by the three "Confucian states" diverged, the encroachment of the West, as represented by soldiers, merchants, and evangelical preachers, did provoke a highly consistent Confucian response. A focused investigation of this Confucian response to the Western impact is vitally important for understanding the psychocultural dynamics of present-day East Asia. Such an approach challenges our conceptualization of fundamentalism in a global context.

To make such an inquiry theoretically sound and practically workable, the goal of this essay is neither to find in East Asia the functional equivalents of fundamentalist movements characterized by evangelistic Christianity in North America and revivalist Islam in the Middle East nor to establish a unique East Asian case as an alternative to its Christian and Islamic counterparts. Indeed, my main purpose is not to label the Confucian revival "fundamentalist" but to begin to bring the conceptual resources derived from thick descriptions of fundamentalist phenomena in North America and the Middle East to bear on other parts of the world. By underscoring salient features of the Confucian revival, I wish to show that, though bearing a "family resemblance" to familiar forms of fundamentalism, they have been motivated by significantly different concerns. Confucians in the twentieth century have been compelled by a sense of urgency to establish a humanistic common creed and common ground in our increasingly pluralistic global village; their concentration on the question of cultural identity as a universal category is a concrete manifestation of this ethical and religious concern. Their concerted effort to revive the spiritual tradition of the past by searching for cultural roots has made them critical of the modernizing process, especially such attendant phenomena such the vulgarization of culture, the fragmentation of society, the parochialization of the public sphere, and the glorification of wealth and power. The vast majority of Confucians are also committed to the realization of modern Western values such as science, democracy and economic development in their own countries. But unlike the Westernizers, they believe that traditional resources, if properly mobilized, can enhance the modernizing process.

Thus this essay will necessarily examine the "Confucian hypothesis," which holds that psychocultural dynamics informed by the Confucian ethic may have engendered economic productivity in industrial East Asia. An underlying assumption of this hypothesis is that the modern transformation of Confucian humanism is an integral part of East Asian modernization.[10] The Confucian revival thus raises issues familiar to scholars of fundamentalism, even as its motivation, justification, and interpretation suggest that its overall spiritual orientation is significantly different from that in Christianity, Islam, or Buddhism. Furthermore, East Asian Confucian revivals in the twentieth century are frequently led by sophisticated intellectuals and are often supported by the central government. While these revivals may on the surface have little to do with mass movements, secret societies, and subversive organizations, they signify a general psychocultural pattern in East Asia in its response to the impact of the West.

History

East Asia has undergone convulsive changes in the last hundred and fifty years. Whether or not we accept the thesis that Western imperialism superimposed from the outside has been the main cause of changing East Asia into a restless landscape, China, Korea, and Japan—the Confucian culture area—have responded to the Western impact in a manner unprecedented in their own history and unique in the world. The sense of crisis is laden with cultural and ethnic implications and has been heightened by national elites through the printed media.[11]

This sense of crisis reflects the historical fact that prior to the arrival of the West, China, Korea, and Japan had already developed their own highly integrated political and social systems. The interaction among East Asian states and the dynamics generated within in the economic and cultural arenas enabled East Asia to cultivate a form of life comparable to that of the modern West in cultural sophistication, if not in economic power and military might. Although the story of East Asian modernization is intertwined with the uninvited participation of Europeans and Americans, the East Asian quest for cultural identity informed by the Confucian heritage remains a basic motif.

This is understandable, because Confucian culture dominated East Asian education both for the elite and the general public prior to the impact of the West.[12] And if we consider a more generalized culture pattern rather than the specific Confucian heritage defined in terms of Neo-Confucian thought, East Asia as a closely knit international community can be traced back to the seventh century. Informed by the same written script and the same kind of political ideology, the culture of East Asia had already been profoundly influenced by Confucian values in the Tang dynasty (618–

906). Thus, in the age of Mahayana Buddhism (roughly from the fifth to the tenth century), the written languages and bureaucratic institutions in East Asia bore a distinctly Confucian imprint. In this sense the intellectual elites in China, Korea, and Japan, divergent as they were in social background, participated in Confucian discourse for centuries.[13]

In recent times there has been a radical restructuring of the East Asian value systems as a result of attempts to deal with the impact of the West and its challenge to the continued viability of traditional structures of meaning. The story of the modern transformation of East Asian civilization in response to the challenge of the West is too complex to be told here even in summary. Suffice it simply to note that as a consequence of Westernization by default and also by deliberate choice, the presence of the Enlightenment mentality informed by Western values since the French Revolution is by far the most conspicuous element in the cultural heritage of the modern East Asian intellectual elite. For decades the rhetoric of democracy and science has been most influential in East Asian intellectual communities. By contrast, the Confucian values that have for centuries defined the moral fabric of the East Asian form of life, such as filial piety and loyalty, are often relegated to the background as outmoded, if they are not condemned by articulate Westernizers as detrimental to the cultivation of the modern spirit. This of course does not mean that East Asian intellectuals have become carriers of liberal democratic ideas, but the deep penetration of the perceived Western values in the psychocultural construct of the East Asian intelligentsia, with its far-reaching implications for traditional patterns of thought, must be recognized as a primary datum for assessing the complexity of the symbolic universes in East Asian societies. In other words, for more than a century, generations of East Asian intellectuals have taken the task of learning from the West as their major, if not ultimate, concern.

The preoccupation with the superior Western methods of management in economy, polity, and society compels East Asian cultural elites to abandon their traditional roots as a sacrifice necessary for surviving in the social Darwinism game.[14] The modern West has loomed so large in the East Asian consciousness that what happens in England, France, Germany, and more recently, the United States may turn out to be more important than domestic affairs. Currently there are more than two hundred full-time Japanese journalists of the print media, fluent in English, residing in the United States to meet the insatiable public demand for knowing what is going on "there," as contrasted to no more than sixty, mostly part-time and "illiterate," American correspondents in Tokyo.[15] A well-educated Japanese, Chinese, or Korean in industrial East Asia may have a much better sense of current Western ideas than of his or her own cultural roots. The very fact that the interpreters of modern East Asia raised the question of the "fate" of Confucianism in the twentieth century indicates the poignancy with which the issue of whether or not the Confucian tradition will survive must be addressed.[16] While it is beyond dispute that Buddhism will continue to be vibrant and that Christianity will flourish in the East Asian spiritual landscape, the question of the authentic possibility of a "third epoch" of Confucian humanism remains open.[17]

Nevertheless the Confucian discourse has endured. Historians have shown that the first phase of Westernization in all three East Asian countries displayed remarkable similarities. China's repeated failure to launch its self-strengthening movements since the 1860s and Korea's inability to translate ideas of "practical learning" into comprehensive political reform in the 1880s have been sharply contrasted with the success of the Meiji restoration in Japan in 1868. However, the Confucian belief in the generative power of the state and the efficacy of people's moral indignation has provided strong motivation for national reintegration in all these efforts. The underlying grammar of action suggests that a leadership of the central government comprising the intellectual elite must assume full responsibility for the well-being of the country. The primacy of the political order and the commitment to the nation as a civilization-state have never been questioned. As a result, the quest for political independence as a precondition for national survival is taken for granted.[18]

However, although East Asia, with the notable exception of Hong Kong, has never been fully colonized by the West, and the impact of imperialism does not seem to have significantly impeded indigenous economic growth, the invasion of the "western wind" is the single most important event in modern East Asian history. China's fall from the Middle Kingdom to the "sick man of the East" in two generations; Korea's inability to chart an independent course and its tragic annexation by the Japanese in 1910; the collapse of the tributary system which served as an East Asian international order of diplomacy and trade based on an elaborate ritual of bilateral relationships between China and her neighbors; and the rise of Japan as a full-fledged imperialist power—each of these developments occurred against the background of the emergence of a new international order "fashioned by the Faustian spirit of the West and justified by the Social Darwinian dictum of the survival of the fittest."[19]

The willing, if tacit, "acceptance of the United States and the industrialized Western countries as the innovators, executors, and judges"[20] of the newly constituted rules of the game of international politics by East Asia for the last hundred years may have blinded us to the awareness that the process by which they were coerced to play a different game has been painfully difficult. One of the terms most frequently used to depict China's collective psychology in modern history textbooks is *chi* (humiliation). A comparable term for depicting the Korean sense of the communal modern experience is *hahn* (remorse, regret, and bitterness). Both terms have deep roots in the psychocultural universe defined by the Confucian discourse. The case of Japan requires a more elaborate explanation, but the word *nin* (patience and endurance), a cherished Confucian virtue, presents itself as a fitting symbol for depicting the modern Japanese mentality.

Japan's Departure from Asia

It is often observed that Japan's success since the Meiji Restoration in transforming herself into a development state was mainly the result of her ability to transcend her Confucian roots and undermine her feudal past. A clear indication of Japan's willingness to do so was the highly provocative pronouncement by the foremost Japanese Westernizer, Fukuzawa Yukiji (1835–1901), when he urged his nation "to leave Asia" as a strategy for survival.[21] The perceptiveness of the Meiji leaders in sizing up the desperate situation and realizing that the rules of the game were irreversibly changed and that a new language of wealth and power was in the offing may partly be reflective of Japan's cultural flexibility in borrowing and discarding foreign ideologies. But the case is complicated by the same kind of convulsive changes that the Japanese intelligentsia experienced in accepting the Western form of life as the wave of the future. The Japanese may not have the counterpart of either the Chinese chi or the Korean hahn in their modern vocabulary, but their sense of crisis at confronting the West, combined with a profound fear of annihilation and a powerful feeling of destiny, made them equally, if not more, vulnerable to humiliation, remorse, frustration, resentment, and bitterness. Yet under the leadership of the Meiji oligarchy, the communal psychic response of the Japanese intellectual to the unprecedented crisis was characterized by a fierce determination to endure hardship in order to confront violence with disciplined patience, namely the careful cultivation of the art of nin.

The East Asian intellectuals may have accepted the Western rules of the game, but in the light of their own shared discourse, they saw that the new international order was "brutally exploitative, unjust, and unstable." The indignant tone with which the foremost prewar Japanese thinker and the founder of the Kyoto School, Nishida Kitarō, expressed his doubt is illustrative. The tendency of Europeans to consider their cultural archetype the most advanced in the sense that other races, if they progress, will necessarily be like Europeans, is in Nishida's view a parochialism unjustifiable in comparative culture studies.[22]

It is not entirely clear whether Fukuzawa, a well-seasoned Confucian literatus, fully appreciated the Western ideas that he advocated as intrinsic to human flourishing, but he was acutely aware of their instrumental value for national survival. For example, individualism could help to unleash the creative energy of the people for national reconstruction. Obviously Japan's wholesale Westernization was at best a mixed blessing. It was as much a strategic move for achieving tangible political and social goals as a drastic rearrangement of the value system. The ideological explosiveness on the political scene around the turn of the century is a case in point. Japan may not have encountered a watershed event, like the March First in Korea or the May Fourth in China (both occurred in 1919), that defined a new intellectual agenda for the whole nation, but the profound sense of alienation that resulted from a series of failures to transform polity and society according to Western norms may help explain the rise of ultranationalism and the triumph of militarism prior to the Second World War.[23]

Japan's success in transforming herself into a Western-style imperialist power engaging in aggression against her neighbors did not prevent her from continuously participating in the Confucian discourse, if only to justify her determined competitiveness. Since the Meiji restoration, the Japanese ruling minority, namely, the Meiji oligarchy, with the active involvement of the military and civilian elite and the willing participation of the general populace, engaged in a concerted effort to transform itself from a feudal monarchy into a modern state in search of wealth and power. With telling effectiveness, the Meiji oligarchy was most impressive in mobilizing the whole country and bringing all of her indigenous symbolic resources to bear on the national goal of "catching up" with England, France, and Germany. The critical role that Confucian values played in formulating seminal ideas such as "the Imperial Way" *(kōdō)* "the samurai way" *(bushidō),* "the Japanese soul" (Yamato Damashii), "the Oriental spirit" (Tōyō-keisei), or "the national essence" *(kokutai)* is widely acknowledged in East Asian interpretive literature.[24] Indeed, the ethic underlying what is often referred to as "Shinto nationalism" in English is Confucian in character: loyalty to the state, filial piety, purity of mind, selflessness, dedication, sacrifice, and so forth. Framed in the psychology of nin, these symbols, as indigenous responses to the crisis of survival, take on a new meaning vis-à-vis the West: Even though the violence you have brought upon us is totally unjustified, through patient watchfulness and measured self-strengthening, we will endure the hardship and our way will eventually prevail. As the Meiji Educational Rescript clearly instructs, the moral fabric of Japanese society is to be woven with Confucian values long part of the Japanese "habits of the heart": group orientation and communal participation rather than self-interest, privacy, and individualism.

The rise of ultranationalism in the 1930s, partly due to Japan's failure to put liberal ideas and practice into a constitutional democracy, further enhanced the politicization of Confucian ethics as both ideological justification and psychocultural motivation for the national goal of self-strengthening, also known among historians as the Showa restoration, a revitalization of indigenous consciousness as a more authentic way of confronting the Western challenge than the model of deliberate Westernization offered by the Meiji restoration. The combination of a profound fear of annihilation as a nation and race, a keen awareness that the rules of the game in the international arena had been dictated by the West, and a strong faith in the eventual triumph of the Japanese spirit empowered the leadership to assign itself a sense of mission: we shall overcome not only for ourselves but for East Asia as a whole.

The rhetoric of the Greater East Asian Co-Prosperity Sphere was more than political propaganda formulated in bad faith. The recurring theme that Japan was engaged in a gallant struggle against Western domination as a vanguard on behalf of East Asian brotherhood had a great deal of persuasive power in prewar Japan. It was for a while successfully instilled in the Japanese mind as a noble cause, even though it was repeatedly used to justify the megalomaniac adventurism of the Japanese military establishment. Although Sakuma Shōzan's (1811–64) balanced dictum, "Eastern ethics and Western science" *(Tōyō no dōtoku, Seiyō no gakugei)* is perhaps a more enduring legacy,[25] the Pan-Asianism bluntly expounded in Okama Shumei's (1886–1957) *Way of Japan and the Japanese* seems to have been more consequential in formulating national policy in the prewar era:

> The words "East-West struggle," however, simply state a concept and it does not follow from this that a united Asia will be pitted against a united Europe. Actually there will be one country acting as champion of Asia and one country acting as the champion of Europe, and it is these who must fight in order that

> a new world may be realized. It is my belief that Heaven has decided on Japan as its choice for the champion of the East. Has not this been the purpose of our three thousand long years of preparation? It must be said that this is a truly grand and magnificent mission. We must develop a strong spirit of morality in order to carry out this solemn mission, and realize that spirit in the life of the individual and the nation.[26]

The "history textbook" incident in 1986, seen in this light, suggests that in the Japanese educational leadership, the thought that Japan's role in World War II can be morally justified lingers on.[27] Despite strong criticism from Japanese liberals as well as from governments in mainland China, Taiwan, and South Korea, the repeated attempts on the part of the Japanese educational authorities to rewrite, if not to whitewash, the history of Japanese military atrocities in Asia demonstrate this powerful need to rectify her own history as a collective memory. The Confucian demand for the "rectification of names" may appear to be in conflict with the Japanese insistence on *honne* (true intention) and *tatemae* (principle) but the demands for correspondence between word and deed has become so routinized in the ritual and rhetoric of the Japanese self-understanding that any deviation from the norm causes apprehension. The need for the Japanese political leadership to protect the emperor, particularly the symbol of emperorship, from any incrimination accounted for the reluctance of Emperor Hirohito to make any explicit statement of guilt concerning the Second World War. It is therefore significant in the East Asian cultural context that South Korea insisted on, and the new emperor acquiesced in, a formal verbal "apology" as a precondition for face-to-face communication between the heads of state.[28]

However, despite irritation and tension, Japan and her former victims (mainland China, South Korea, Taiwan, Hong Kong, and Singapore) are more than willing to "rectify" the past through ritual and symbolic expiation. Despite pervasive anti-Japanese feelings throughout East Asia, deliberate attempts on the part of the governments and cultural elites to make a distinction between Japanese militarism as a heinous aberration and the basically peace-loving nature of the Japanese people seem to have worked well in providing a solid basis for establishing amicable diplomatic and trade relationships with Japan. The absence of guilt, if not "humiliation, remorse, regret, and bitterness," in Japan with regard to her military atrocities against Asian peoples during the Second World War and the much longer Sino-Japanese War (1937–45) is in sharp contrast to the collective guilt experienced by the German people, not to mention the political leaders, who accepted the verdict that they are all implicated in the brutality of the Holocaust. The 1988 summer visit of Prime Minister Nakasone to the Shinto shrine, symbolizing ultranationalism, since it was the most sacred place for the Japanese imperial army, evoked bitter memories of the past, but the official protests from China and Korea were mild and caused no more than slight embarrassment. The memories of the past still persist, but they are sufficiently neutralized to allow the prospects of the future to dictate the present course of action.

The irony of history is manifest here: the United States and her colleagues, having definitively destroyed the Japanese dream of conquering East Asia by force in the

Second World War, helped to make Japan's idea of the co-prosperity sphere an economic reality in industrial East Asia in the last four decades. Japan has been identified as a junior partner of the United States in geopolitical terms for some time. During the cold war era, Japan was an integral part of the American Pacific defense against Soviet, Chinese, Korean, and Vietnamese communism. Her crowning success as a major power in international trade in recent years more than qualifies her as a full member of the economic summit. Since she is the only non-Western country to attain that coveted position, Japan is often perceived to be part of Western Europe and North America. Occasionally her leaders unabashedly characterize Japan as European and Western rather than Asian and Eastern. For example, as recently as 1983, Prime Minister Nakasone, on the occasion of the economic summit, proudly announced that Japan is a "Western" nation.[29] Yet, as Fukuzawa's proposal to leave Asia has been realized, the question of Japan's Asian roots begins to loom large, especially in light of her strong desire to harmonize relationships with her Asian neighbors, notably the People's Republic of China and the Republic of Korea.

A case in point: the Japanese educational authorities, under Korean and Chinese pressure as well as under fire from Japan's own liberal intellectuals, decided not to revise its own history in a way that may be perceived as covering up atrocities committed by Japanese soldiers against the civilian population in East Asia. Such a decision indicated concern about Japan's public image among neighboring countries and fear that that particular chapter in Japan's past may hamper the effort to formulate a more pacific self-understanding. Japan's great success in playing the social Darwinism game may have fulfilled Fukuzawa's wish to depart from Asia, but it also complicated the new mission to return home as a true leader of the Pacific Rim.

The fervor of *Nihonjinron* (On being Japanese), a kind of communal obsession of the Japanese cultural scene, has also raised fundamental questions about Japanese cultural identity.[30] What is the Japanese soul made of? Can Japan continue to adapt to influences from the outside without ever asking what the inner core of her culture is? Are the Japanese so open-minded that no matter what they become, they are always in tune with the basic rhythm of their native form of life? Is their native form of life so flexible that it can accommodate any alien impact without losing its internal coherence? Although there are no easy answers to these questions, the deep emotional and intellectual concern for defining and redefining "Japaneseness" clearly shows that the search for roots is a timely subject in present-day Japan. Despite the open-mindedness, flexibility, accommodation, and other remarkable qualities of the Japanese mind which have enabled it to benefit brilliantly from Confucianism, Buddhism, and modern Western values to enrich its own cultural resources, the perennial challenge of rootedness has been a salient feature in Japanese intellectual discourse for some time.

On the surface, Japanese nativism is a particular province of Shintoism. Surely the *basso ostinado* (the background beat or most enduring, if submerged, theme) of the Japanese mentality, which in recent years has occupied the attention of such intellectual luminaries as Maruyama Masao, is informed by ethnic purity, common myths, and a shared aesthetic vision and is thus Shintoistic.[31] As an animistic worldview, it reveres spiritual forces *(kami)* in nature and celebrates life and vitality in the human community. It gives a unique texture to Japanese life. It is difficult to imagine being Japanese without this Shintoist flavor, and Shintoism, unlike the variety of cultural forms assumed by Buddhism, Christianity, or Islam, can only be Japanese.

Shintoism is Japanese, but to characterize Japaneseness merely in Shintoist terms is misleading. The expression *Shinto* (the Way of the Spirit) was coined recently in Japanese history. The term *Neo-Shintoism* is sometimes used to designate the self-conscious Shintoist revival of the nativistic scholars of the nineteenth century. In fact the Japanese nativistic consciousness as articulated through Shintoist symbolism was mediated by a language laden with Confucian, Taoist, and Buddhist overtones. Historically, the corporate intellectual awareness that helped transform Shintoism from a folk tradition into a cultural movement of the educated elite, as in the case of Motoori Norinaga's (1730–1801) "national learning" *(kokugaku)* was occasioned by the scholarly, often philological, endeavor to retrieve spiritual meanings from ancient Chinese as well as Japanese classical literature.[32]

It is commonly assumed that the *kokugakusha* (the scholars of "national learning"), intent on freeing the Japanese classics, notably *Kojiki* (Records of Ancient Masters) and *Nihongi* (Chronicles of Japan), from misleading Chinese-style interpretations, were definitely anti-Confucian. But the matter is complicated by the fact that the language that they concientiously used, which entails a moral universe, was inextricably intertwined with Confucian ethics. The relationship between *kogaku* (ancient learning) and *kokugaku* demonstrates that the Confucian-Shinto mixture, a combination of moral idealism and impassioned mystic animism, gives Japanese nativism a fascinating and intriguing contour.[33] "Shinto nationalism" as, for example, manifested in the national ideology and personal art of the bushidō, is so richly textured in ancient learning that, paradoxically, the archaism embedded in Japanese nativism requires sophisticated knowledge of Confucian classics for full appreciation.

Nevertheless, to the Japanese it is superfluous to disinter archaic myths to justify Japan's uniqueness. The attempt of Hirata Atsutane (1776–1843) to characterize Japan as the "land of gods" may have little persuasive power in present-day metropolitan Tokyo, but the native Japanese sense of *our* land as sacred, *we* as the descendents of a divine source, and *we-ness* versus *they-ness* remains strong as a reflection of the Japanese national consciousness as a distinctive people and culture *(kokumin-shugi)*.[34] The "three sacred treasures"—the mirror, the jewel, and the sword—may have lost much of their magic power in a modern commercial economy replete with luxury goods, but the shamanistic charm they symbolize is still a presence in Japanese society.[35] The narcissistic tone of the "I-novel" (the *watakushi shōsetsu,* an extraordinary phenomenon in modern Japanese literature in which the author speaks in an intensely autobiographic voice for the sake of self-expression)[36] and the Japanese preoccupation with cleanliness, fleeting moments of beauty, elegant style of gift-giving, and enchanting decorative arts, may not fully reflect the Japanese nativistic mentality, but the vitality of the popular way of the samurai as a form of personal cultivation and an attitude of life is manifestly rooted in the Confucian moral idealism and the Shintoist mythic animism mentioned above. The Tokugawa warrior, seasoned in the "way of the kami" and the Confucian ethic of *giri-ninjō* (rightness principle and human feelings), may resemble the late medieval knight who combined a sort of Faustian drive with Christian ethics. However, the concept of *bushidō* (the way of the warrior) which evolved into a cult of loyalty for national salvation was significantly different from any patriotic sentiments prior to the nineteenth century. The Japanese motion pictures glorifying the *seishinshugi* (spiritualism) of the warriors in the late 1930s and early 1940s vividly show that the Showa restoration was a Confucian revival in the form of Shinto nationalism.[37]

The resurgence of such ultranationalistic militarism today is unlikely. The establishment of a constitutional democracy, the development of a vibrant economy, and the emergence of an affluent middle class, partly as the result of American tutelage during the occupation after the Second World War, all militate against such a possibility. Yet the unique Japanese sense of ethnic, cultural, and national identity will be greatly enhanced as the nation assumes a more active role in shaping the geopolitical context abroad. The general American perception that Japan, since 1984 the largest creditor country, has not allocated an adequate percentage of her GNP for military defense, has not spent enough on foreign aid, and has not assumed sufficient responsibility for international affairs is at variance with what the Japanese leadership undoubtedly remembers as the explicit American intention during the tutelary occupation: a junior partner under the protection of the American economy without her own military buildup.

I am not suggesting that the Japanese leadership is in any sense bound by a historical covenant. The Japanese have acted in their own self-interest and have developed independent courses of action with their own national interest in mind. The "Tanaka Shock" in 1972, when Japan went far beyond the American initiatives in China by establishing diplomatic relations with the People's Republic and recognizing it as the sole legal government of China as a response to the Nixon-Kissinger overture to Beijing which had caught the Japanese by surprise, clearly illustrates that Tokyo has been self-consciously pursuing an independent diplomatic posture for almost two decades. Nevertheless, whether or not it is a calculated risk, Japan's decision to maintain a low military profile while vigorously pursuing an ever-expanding economic base is completely consistent with her sense of fair play.

Japan's stunning performance in the social Darwinism game is justifiably characterized as an "economic miracle." She has captured virtually all the major prizes (for example, shipbuilding, steel, automobiles, and electronics) in the manufacturing sector among industrialized nations. Her financial strength in recent years has been so robust that her presence in banking, real estate, and multinational corporations is not only felt but feared throughout North America. Japan's economic success notwithstanding, the Japanese sense of their "life world," informed by their awareness of the intractable realities, is far from being optimistic. The incongruity between what they are perceived to be and what they realistically think they are merits serious investigation.

Isolation, exclusivity, and solidarity, terms frequently used by Japanese scholars to define their national mentality, seem easily understandable in reference to geographic location, ethnic composition, and historical continuity.[38] The Japanese are not known as settlers or assimilators. As a rule, they may go abroad to establish permanent settlements in Brazil, Hawaii, and California, but they do not allow foreigners *(gaijin)* to become fully assimilated. Paradoxically, geographic isolation and ethnic exclusivity have not only helped the Japanese to develop a sense of solidarity and inner identity but have compelled them to become remarkably open to external influences and adaptable to changing global conditions.

This is not to suggest that Japanese have achieved a delicate balance between foreignness and nativism without conflict and tension. On the contrary, the Japanese sense of insecurity and uncertainty is so intense that by and large, the political leadership, the cultural elite, and the general populace in Japan all regard the status quo as vulnerable and precarious. The yearning for a simpler life, the condemnation of the meaningless quest for wealth and power, strong attachments to vanishing values, and a horrifying vision of an uncertain future are common motifs in modern Japanese literature. The themes of death, separation, loss, hopelessness, and futility are explored with telling effectiveness and human sensitivity by the leading Japanese writers. Mishima Yukio's last novel, *The Sea of Fertility*, employs the name of a "sea" on the moon, mainly for ironic effect, to depict the sterility of contemporary Japanese culture. His dramatic suicide in 1970 was replete with samurai ritualism. Whether it signifies a crisis of meaning in general or was the lonely cry of a disillusioned ultranationalist, Mishima's death symbolizes the explosive tension between modernization as secularization and tradition as the embodiment of nativist spirituality.

More recently the upsurge of teenagers' consumerism, not to mention the spectacular purchasing power of the unmarried full-time female workers, has prompted a widespread discussion of the "new human race" *(shinjinrui)*, specifically the new generation of Japanese youth. Presumably these youth will so fundamentally restructure and thoroughly undermine the moral foundation of Japanese society that the whole discussion of "being Japanese" will soon become irrelevant. Yet the fear that young Japanese are self-indulgent and that the Japanese way of life is being threatened by negative foreign influences has been a consistent theme of modern Japanese intellectuals and cultural leaders. It is significant that one of the fastest-growing and politically influential new religions in postwar Japan is the Sōka Gakkai (Value-creating association).[39] Despite its own political troubles, Sōka Gakkai's rationale for entering into the political arena is to "purify the world through the propaganda of teachings of the Nichiren Sho Denomination."[40]

Japan is at an ideological crossroads. Having left Asia to join the competitive game of the imperial West for more than a hundred years, she is on her way home to lead the Pacific Rim into the twenty-first century. But she has not learned to justify her role as an economic giant in terms of attendant values such as self-interest, maximization of profit, human rights, and individual liberties. The moral tone of her political rhetoric clearly shows that loyalty, duty, self-sacrifice, dedication, and the well-being of the people are still highly charged operative principles in society. With the passing of the Shōwa era (1926–89), deep-rooted sentiments concerning not only the symbolism of the emperor but also the nature of the Japanese state have been aroused. The choice of the reign title for the new emperor, Heisei (peace completing), conveys the collective self-image of Japan both as a nation in the family of nations and as the land of the rising sun.[41] "Peace completing" is obviously meant to be a continuation of "brilliant harmony," the literal meaning of Shōwa.[42]

What is unstated, however, is the indelible memory that the era of "brilliant peace" was in part brutal militarism fired by ultranationalism. The reluctance of the Japanese intellectual community to offer a balanced assessment of the role of Emperor Hirohito implies that the "harmony-peace" *(wa-hei)* linking the two imperial reigns is only a surface manifestation of Japan's difficult passage to modernity. The unprecedented intervention of Emperor Hirohito may have convinced the Japanese government to surrender on 14 August 1945, but the centrality of the emperorship which served as the expression of Japanese "national essence" is undeniable. The only condition that the Japanese cabinet insisted on in their proposal to President Truman for surrender on 12 August was the retention of the imperial system.[43]

The "Imperial Rescript on Education" (1890), which was read regularly as a well-established ritual in prewar Japan remains to this date a source of inspiration for Japanese moral education. It begins with the exhortation: "Our Imperial Ancestors have founded our Empire on a basis broad and everlasting and have deeply and firmly implanted virtue. Our subjects, ever united in loyalty and filial piety, have from generation to generation illustrated the beauty thereof. This is the glory of the fundamental character of Our Empire, and herein also lies the source of our education."[44] The Rescript ends with a fundamentalistic claim that its teachings are "bequeathed by Our Imperial Ancestors, to be observed alike by Their Descendants and subjects," and that it is "infallible for all ages and true in all places."[45] In the main body of the Rescript, the basic Confucian virtues—filial piety, brotherly affection, conjugal harmony, trust in friends, modesty, benevolence, learning, and self-cultivation—are combined with a sort of civil religion for the modern citizen: "advance the public good and promote common interests, always respect the Constitution and observe the laws; should any emergency arise, offer yourselves courageously to the State; and thus guard and maintain the prosperity of Our Imperial Throne, coeval with heaven and earth."[46] The former Minister of Education Nagai Michio notes that this four-hundred-word Confucian statement, which took about ten years to compose, served as a sort of "backbone of Japan until defeat" and is still vitally important to Japanese moral education.[47]

The revival of Confucian ethics in postwar Japan has been evident in a variety of ways: in the continuous vitality of privately organized societies of Confucian studies; in government-sponsored programs to promote moral education; in the reanimation of the samurai spirit and a return to Eastern spirituality; in the development of a distinctive Japanese style of management; and in the discussion of "national essence" and the quest for cultural identity.[48]

Perhaps the most significant attempts at renewing Confucian discourse in present-day Japan are the work of a core of influential individuals, among them Okada Takehiko. An internationally renowned authority on Confucian thought, he realized the scholarly endeavor of his teacher, Kusumoto, by transforming Confucian studies from an academic pursuit into a way of living. His self-conscious identification with Yamazaki Ansai (1618–82), who is thought to have domesticated Confucian learning into a distinct Japanese form of spirituality, has encouraged several generations of his students to continue the line of transmission. Through tutorials, public lectures, and extensive publication projects, he has breathed vitality into Confucian, especially Neo-Confucian, ideas.

Although his intellectual influence is limited and his mission to make Confucian studies a true "learning of the body and mind" is often ignored by mainline Sinologists, his concerted effort to make Kyushu University a center of Confucian learning and Fukuoka a home for scholarly excellence in Confucian studies is recognized and supported by scholars throughout East Asia. Intent on broadening his social responsibility, since his retirement in 1974, he has been increasingly involved in training Japanese business executives and government officials in the Confucian ideal. Particularly noteworthy is Professor Okada's insistence that the centrality of Confucian learning is self-cultivation as a precondition for public service. His method of "quiet-sitting," a spiritual discipline designed to enhance self-understanding without diluting social engagement, is highly acclaimed as a unique Confucian contribution to the art of living in modern industrial society.[49]

In Professor Okada's case, the Confucian revival in Japan is predicated on a critical self-awareness, a realization that spiritual resources in the Confucian tradition are particularly relevant to the quest for personal integrity in an increasingly fragmented modern society. Specifically, the Confucian assertion that we are embedded in the human condition and therefore must take for granted the sanctity of the earth enables us to be fully committed to the world defined in "secular" spheres of interest so that we can actively participate in politics as concerned citizens. Furthermore, the Confucian belief that although we are embedded in the human condition and therefore "in the world," we are not "of the world" empowers us to be sufficiently detached from the body politic defined in terms of existing power relationships so that we can critically reflect upon the functions of realpolitik without identifying ourselves with the status quo. The traditional Confucian distinction between political loyalty and moral rectitude thus assumes a new shade of meaning: as loyal citizens we regard the affairs of the world as our personal affairs, but as reflective educators we have a duty to take a critical stance against the corruptible tendencies of the political arena.

Strictly speaking, Professor Okada has never been involved in contemporary Japanese politics; his cultural enterprise is apolitical. His own works on Song-Ming as well as Tokugawa Confucian thought and his massive anthologies of primary sources and interpretive literature in Confucian studies are primarily academic accomplishments. Even his direct involvement in training business executives to become culturally sophisticated and socially responsible is nonpolitical. However, as a self-conscious transmitter of the Confucian way and as an exemplary teacher of the Confucian form of life, Professor Okada is a powerful critic of the contemporary Japanese intellectual scene. His cultural analysis, intent on reorienting the postwar Japanese obsession with commercialism to a style of human flourishing which takes the Confucian idea of self-cultivation as its ultimate concern, is not merely a romantic yearning for a simpler life or an angry reaction to the complexity of the modernizing process but a reasoned argument for enhancing the meaning of human existence in all its spiritual dimensions. The questions he raises include the moral responsibility of public servants, politics not merely as statecraft but also as moral education, family as an ethicoreligious institution, authorities as standards of inspiration rather than as patterns of domination, the proper function of business in the social network, and the task of self-realization as a communal act and as a public good. Professor Okada's role as a cultural transmitter, as an exemplary teacher, and as a social activist is laden with profound political implications. His Confucian revival may not be as well known as the creative appropriation in the Kyoto School, but it has generated enough dynamism to keep the Confucian mode of questioning alive.[50]

The pattern of cultural influence represented in the work of Okada exemplifies the dynamics of the Confucian tradition in Japan. The incipient Confucian revival has not yet received much attention from either the liberal-minded or the socialist intellectuals. But, given Japan's evident attempt to reconstruct its sense of rootedness with a view toward a wholesome return to East Asia, the potential for fruitful interaction between Confucian humanism and liberal-democratic ideas on the one hand and socialist (including Marxist) concerns on the other is great.

South Korea's Sense of Mission

Although Japan has galvanized the "Four Dragons" (South Korea, Taiwan, Hong Kong, and Singapore) to perform superbly in economic development, South Korea among the newly industrialized countries has the greatest potential to compete effectively with Japan in the international arena. However, although the normalization of the relationship with Japan plays a pivotal role in Korea's economic development, Korean-Japanese bilateral international politics is an extremely delicate matter. Among the minority groups in Japan, the six hundred thousand Korean expatriates are the loudest protesters against racial discrimination. This strains the diplomatic and trade relations between the two countries. Moreover, the bitter memory of Japanese colonialism (1910–45) and earlier devastating invasions makes the Japanese aggression an important factor in the pervasive collective psychology of hahn in Korean culture.[51]

The matter is further complicated by the increasing awareness among Korean intellectuals, based on solid scholarship as well as self-serving political propaganda, that Japan was for centuries under the influence of Korean civilization. Although the claim that the Japanese imperial household and the Japanese language may have originated in Korea seems far-fetched, archaeological evidence has identified several significant points of convergence between Korea and Japan. For example, much of what is known as distinctively Japanese, including the Creation Myth, may be shown to belong to a symbolic universe characterized by a sort of Korean-Manchu mentality in Northeast Asia. To be sure, the relationship between Shintoism and Korean shamanism is still a controversial subject and, contrary to the assertion of some Korean scholars, the importation of Neo-Confucian ideas to Japan was occassioned by Zen monks in the late thirteenth century. But it is a historical fact that the Hideyoshi's

Korean expeditions (1592 and 1597) enabled the Korean interpretation of Neo-Confucianism, notably that of Yi Toegye, to exert a shaping influence on Japanese thought. Whether or not competition with Japan is an important motivating force in Korea's search for her own roots, the Koreans' concerted effort to engage themselves in reanimating the old as a way of defining their own cultural identity anew is noteworthy.

For almost thirty years, from the time when General Park Chung-hee seized power in 1961 to form a military government until the outbreak of student demonstrations and labor union activities in recent months, the Korean political leadership, intent on wholesale modernization at any cost, managed to secure the reluctant support of the intelligentsia and the tacit acceptance of the populace in a drastic restructuring of polity and society for the sake of economic development. Traditional institutions and values have been, and continue to be, relevant to Korea's modernization. Centralized planning through the delicate art of negotiation, social stability, family cohesiveness, widespread educational opportunity, the work ethic, frugality—each trait has significantly contributed to Korea's economic boom.[52]

However, for decades the intellectual community, dedicated to the task of modernizing the nation (i.e., promoting rapid economic growth), turned its back on the indigenous traditions as if they were dispensable trappings of the past. The passing of traditional society was heralded as a necessary condition for achieving modernity. Westernization—or more appropriately, Americanization—was accepted by a whole generation of Korean intellectual leaders as synonymous with modernization. It should be mentioned, however, that the first president of the Republic of Korea, Syngman Rhee, became a staunch anti-American for nationalist reasons despite his long-term American associations (he obtained a Ph.D. in political science under Woodrow Wilson at Princeton University). Furthermore, the intellectual resentment against American tutelage since the Korean War in the early 1950s is a constant undercurrent in contemporary Korean politics.

The quest for roots, as in Park's attempt to revitalize the spirit of loyalty and filial piety, was rejected outright by most liberal-minded intellectuals as ideological manipulation, but it nonetheless had educational value for the military establishment and the general populace. The original intention of establishing the Academy of Korean Studies (literally, the Academy for Korean Spiritual Culture) did not meet with approval from scholarly circles, but it served the function of offering ideological training to a cadre of government functionaries. Students who were trained as technocrats in the United States certainly played a significant role in developing the economy, but their impact on traditional Korean culture was limited. To them, Korean classics, history, thought, literature, and the arts had no more than antiquarian interest. The irony is that the military junta attempted to revitalize a sense of pride in the Korean past, whereas the cultural elite, the descendants of the *yangban* aristocracy as the modern counterparts of the traditional guardians of Confucian moral standards, became Westernized and iconoclastically anti-Confucian.

This observation is predicated on three assumptions. First, ideas of loyalty and filial piety, though not exclusively derived from Confucian sources, are rooted primarily in the Confucian tradition; it is inconceivable that they could be present in Korean culture independent of Confucian ethics. Second, the importance of the legacy of yangban to the power relationships of contemporary Korean society, as manifested in genealogy, local affiliation, marriage strategies and a host of other forms of human networking, is not an exaggeration; indeed, the term is still widely used, indicating its continuing significance in defining birth and status. Third, the split between the military establishment and the cultural elite, despite the power of the political center to co-opt leaders from business, academia, and the mass media to participate in a national effort to achieve economic goals, is a distinctive feature of the Korean intellectual ethos. The underlying value in this ethos is the Confucian belief in the moral influence of the educated, culturally articulate minority.

The irony is obvious: the cosmopolitan cultural elite, the traditional guardians of national identity, attacked the indigenous values of Korean society, whereas the military elite, partly motivated by extreme ethnocentrism, assigned themselves the task of reviving the national spirit. Under the influence of American-trained technocrats, the intellectual atmosphere in the institutes of higher learning was opposed to traditional Korean studies. The humanities, particularly those focusing on traditional Korean history and culture, received the least attention among aspirants for college education. The situation was compounded by the decision of the Ministry of Education in the 1960s to phase out "Chinese characters" *(hanmun)* from the print media so that *han'gul* (the native Korean syllabary) became the primary and in many cases the only available method of written communication. While the South Korean educational policy on language has been much gentler than the total abolition of "Chinese characters," ostensibly for the sake of educating the populace adopted in the North, it has fundamentally restructured the modern Korean writing system. Motivated by a strong desire to search for an independent cultural identity, this language revolution seemed both necessary and desirable. However, the price for immediate political gain was the expense of a loss of cultural continuity, and it was costly in the long run. For one thing, very few college students in the humanities trained in recent decades are equipped to read the writings of prewar Korean literati, let alone those of the scholar-officials in the Chosŏn dynasty (1392–1910).[53] This is in sharp contrast to the literary situation in Japan, where the end of the American occupation signaled a steady increase of the use of *kanji* (Chinese characters) in the mass media. Theoretically and practically, it seems that a mixture of hanmun and han'gul provides the best solution to the twin problem of cultural identity and linguistic flexibility, but the quest for an authentic Korean symbolic expression has been so powerful, as in the case of Professor Ch'oe Hon-bae at Yonsei University, that the vernacular script invented by King Sejong to promote popular education gradually evolved into an awe-inspiring national writing system charged with strong nativistic sentiments.

However, this seemingly peculiar phenomenon—those who were culturally the least sophisticated advocated a return to the traditional spiritual sources as a basis for national reconstruction, while those who were culturally the most articulate and refined became iconoclasts—is pervasive not only in Korea but in industrial East Asia as a whole. In the 1960s, the overwhelming majority of the interpreters of modernization took it for granted that the Confucian tradition was a major inhibiting factor in Korea's concerted effort to modernize. The incompatibility of the Confucian past and the Korean present was widely accepted as self-evident. Even though no drastic proposal advocating departure from Asia was suggested, the consensus was that unless Korea cut the umbilical cord of her Confucian past, she would never have a viable presence in the modern world. Speculation abounds in recent Korean historiography on what might have happened if the "practical learning" school had been successful in freeing itself from the moralism and ritualism of the mainline Confucian tradition: could Korea have developed her own form of industrialization, making her immune to Japanese imperialism?[54]

Chosŏn-dynasty Korea was a Confucianized society, and South Korea today is more Confucian than her East Asian neighbors in cultural orientation, social structure, political ideology, and economic strategy. As the longest dynasty in East Asian history in the last two millennia, Chosŏn rulership, with the full cooperation of the yangban, made a comprehensive and systematic effort to develop a civilization-state modeled on Confucian ideas. At least four features are noteworthy: (1) the central government is responsible for economic well-being, social stability, and universal education; (2) the family must be the basis of social solidarity; (3) the legitimacy of the government, though nominally based on hereditary kingship, is deeply rooted in the examination system, a meritocratic procedure of political leadership; (4) the cultural elite (the intelligentsia) should be the conscience of the people. It is not difficult to see the relevance of political centralism, familism, and intellectual populism to Korean society today. However, the matter is complicated by the fact that even though the underlying Confucian institutions and values are fully operative, the vitality of the Confucian persuasion has been seriously undermined by the government's single-minded attention to economic development and the iconoclastic mentality of the cultural elite. The birth of a "new" Korea, diametrically opposed to the feudal past symbolized by the Chosŏn dynasty, is so prominent in the self-consciousness of the Korean people that the Confucian legacy is often referred to in an apologetic tone if not with outright ridicule or impassioned denunciation.

The persuasive power of Korean feminists in condemning the male orientation of Confucian familism is perhaps the most outspoken,[55] but the liberal criticism of Confucian authoritarianism, hierarchy, and antidemocratic tendencies has become so much an integral part of the rhetoric of modernization that to characterize the Confucian legacy as a remnant of the stagnant past, a conservative stronghold against progress, or simply a reactionary ideology seems like a truism. The belief remains strong that the Confucian tradition, embodied in the modus operandi and modus vivendi of the Chosŏn dynasty, was mainly responsible for Korea's inability to modernize effectively in the nineteenth century and to withstand Japanese aggression. It is uncanny that Japanese scholarship on Korean culture has been instrumental in advancing this view.

The matter is further compounded by the new social forces unleashed in the twentieth century, in particular, Christian evangelism.[56] The Christianization of Korean society poses fascinating questions about the nature of Korean spirituality. Despite the domination of Confucian ideology for more than five hundred years, the nativistic religions of the "Hermit Kingdom," notably shamanism, have been full of vitality.[57] In fact, virtually all segments of Korean society, including many college students today, are attracted to shamanistic song, dance, and ritual. The impressive performance of Professor Lee Aejoo of the Seoul National University in transforming shamanist art into a powerful message of political protest through her graceful bodily movements is unique, but it also clearly indicates the explosive potential of the shamanist style of symbolic expression in the Korean body politic.[58] The moral fabric of the society, defined in Confucian terms, has a delicate texture of shamanistic sensitivity. Whether or not this is the main reason for Korea's receptivity to Christian evangelism, the shamanistic stratum in the Korean psyche seems well-disposed to mass emotional appeal. The emotional intensity in Korean religious life and political culture makes the Confucian heritage an integral part of the dynamism of meetings, rallies, campaigns, and demonstrations.

Actually the great success of Christian underground movements in sparking nationalist sentiments during Japanese colonization contributed to the power of Christian missions to generate enthusiasm for democracy in present-day Korea. The deliberate attempt by the Japanese colonizers to take advantage of Confucian values and institutions as mechanisms of ideological and political control must have dampened the effectiveness of the Confucian persuasion. Patriotic Christians played an important role in the underground movements against Japanese colonialism. Many of the leaders of the famous March First Movement (1919) were Christians. Whether or not the fear of international reprisals was the main reason, Japanese authorities, while continuing to jail and torture Korean Christians, were more tolerant of political activities undertaken by Christian organizations. On the contrary, they treated harshly any nationalistic endeavors inspired by nativistic sentiments. The abusive use of Confucian ethics, with emphasis on obedience and submission, may not have silenced the Confucian voice of protest but it did render much of the Confucian style of moral indignation ineffective. The politicization of Confucian values such as loyalty and filial piety by the Park regime to enhance its authority had the unintended consequence of the ideological bastardization of Confucian ethics and further alienated the intelligentsia from its Confucian roots.[59]

These inhibiting factors notwithstanding, the Confucian revival is clearly visible. The recognition that the overwhelming majority of the Korean literary and philosophical legacy is preserved in classical Chinese with a strong Confucian overtone has impelled the educational authorities to establish programs to train scholars to deal with primary sources. Scores of Chinese studies departments have been established throughout the country, making Chinese studies one of the fastest growing disciplines in Korean higher education in the last decade; the majority of the many newly established departments of Chinese studies came into existence in the last five years. The Confucian dimension in the curriculum is undeniable. Massive translation projects have been organized to make the literary and philosophical legacy of the Chosŏn dynasty accessible to the general public. The undertaking in the Academy of Korean Studies includes a complete translation with annotation of *The Great Norm in Man-*

aging the State (a thorough account of the imperial organizations, job descriptions, and codes of conduct of the Chosŏn court). By far the most comprehensive endeavor is the translation of the *Veritable Records of the Chosŏn Dynasty,* a chronological history of the major events of the state from the fourteenth to the twentieth century. While the claim that North Korean scholars have already completed the whole task has never been fully substantiated, South Korean scholars are still working on translating the chronicles of the seventeenth century into han'gul.

The nationwide scholarly attempt to confront the cultural heritage preserved in Chinese characters is a manifestation of the willingness of the intellectual community to reappropriate the forgotten tradition because of its perceived Confucian character. This seems closely connected with the perennial Korean concern for the proper way of dealing with her strong and often aggressive neighbors, namely, *sadaejuui,* literally "serving-the-greatism," but more dramatically rendered in North Korea nowadays as "flunkeyism." Indeed, the haunting question of how Korea can chart its own course of development independent of external forces, be they Chinese, Japanese, Russian, or, in recent years, American, without losing sight of its role as a communication center in a cosmopolitan universe has helped shaped Korean cultural identity for centuries. Korea's readiness to deal with China in this connection is a clear sign of a newly acquired self-confidence. A sort of China fervor is sweeping across the university campuses.[60] Reading material on contemporary China, in particular, on the literature, society, and politics of the People's Republic of China, has generated much excitement among college students. The diplomatic initiatives of President Noh, the *Nordpolitik,* to open dialogues with Moscow and Pyongyang as well as Beijing is certainly pertinent here, but in a deeper sense the dynamics have already been generated by a strong desire among Korean intellectuals to understand the modern transformation of the Chinese civilization-state as an integral part of their own search for cultural identity.

Surely the unprecedented growth of Christianity in South Korea raises challenging questions about the nature of Korean society: Will it remain the most Confucian of all East Asian societies? Will it become the first Christian nation in Asia? Will it achieve a new synthesis involving Christianity, Buddhism, Confucianism, and native shamanism in a distinctive Korean religion? It is highly unlikely that the Christianization of Korea will naturally lead to a de-Confucianization of Korea. An overwhelming majority of Korean Christians accept the solemn ritual of honoring deceased ancestors through the age-long practice of communal offering as the proper way of being Korean, not at all in conflict with the Christian doctrine forbidding idolatry. Korean Christians in this sense are also Confucians.

An extreme manifestation of the Korean search for cultural identity is the seemingly outrageous claim by a few reputable scholars that Korea is the "motherland of Confucianism."[61] This claim, though thoroughly disputed by the majority of East Asian intellectual historians working on the topic, evokes memories of one of the most powerful cultural symbols in Korea, namely Kija (Jizi). This legendary Shang minister who is said to have fled China to the East in the eleventh century B.C.E. has been worshiped as a patriarch of ancient Koreans. Together with the myth of Tan'gun, "born of a union between the son of the divine creator and a female bear,"[62] the legend of Kija provokes intense nationalist sentiments. Indeed it has deep roots in Korean archaeology, historiography, ethnology, and religious consciousness. The concerted scholarly effort to characterize Kija as a Confucian master before Confucius because he allegedly authored an important ancient classic which later became a source of inspiration for Confucian thinkers, and the deliberate academic attempt to make Kija the real founder of Confucianism, give us a glimpse of the fruitful ambiguity in the modern Korean search for originality and authenticity.[63] Despite the fact that Kija no longer attracts much attention among modern Korean intellectuals, it remains a potent idea for scholarly and ideological controversy.

A much more historically significant and intellectually consequential example of the Confucian revival is the movement commonly known as *T'oegyehak* (the Learning of Yi T'oegye [1501–70], one of the most influential thinkers in Korean history). Mobilized and organized by T'oegye's descendents, under the leadership of an extraordinarily inventive entrepreneur, Lee Dong-choon (1919–89), T'oegyehak has become an international phenomenon, with branches not only in East Asia but also in North America and Europe in less than two decades. Intent on presenting T'oegye's thought not only as a unique contribution to Korean culture but also as a manifestation of East Asian spirituality and indeed a humanist vision with heuristic value for the modern world, some of the most philosophical minds in Korea have made Yi T'oegye the research subject of a systematic, comprehensive, and long-term international scholarly endeavor. The ability of T'oegyehak to tap the best human resources in East Asian Confucian studies and to make a vast amount of the interpretive literature and the best editions of T'oegye's collected works available at modest cost helps to set new standards for Confucian studies throughout the world. T'oegye, the devoted follower and the creative transmitter of Zhu Xi's (1130–1200) teaching, is now the most studied Neo-Confucian thinker in East Asia. Since his portrait and his beloved Tosan Academy have appeared on the most frequently used thousand-won bill in South Korea for more than a decade, T'oegye is also the most widely circulated Confucian image in the twentieth century. T'oegyehak, which resulted from a combination of family honor, national pride, and financial resourcefulness, signals that the Confucian revival as a scholarly enterprise is well under way.[64]

Nevertheless, the Confucian revival as embodied in the movement to glorify T'oegyehak is seen as a mixed blessing. The participation of the Park regime and subsequent military establishments in promoting the Confucian cause tinged the public image of Master T'oegye with the shade of nonreflective conservatism, if not outright reactionary attachment to an outmoded way of life. Yet in a broader sense, partly because of the enduring legacy of yangban culture, Korean society has never lost its Confucian character. The Confucian presence in family rituals, moral education, marriage arrangements, political alliances, genealogical affiliations, and authority patterns is so conspicuous that Korea is more Confucian than Japan has ever become, and in many ways, than China wants to be. Despite conflict between the ruling minority and the cultural elite, there seems to be a consensus that for better or for worse, the Confucian tradition is a defining characteristic of Korean culture.

The Korean search for cultural roots is intimately connected with her sense that the hahn the Korean people experience is both a poignant reminder of her modern fate and a motivating force for realizing a future destiny. Confucian revivalism, together with Christian evangelism and shamanistic nativism, provides the Korean people, especially the articulate minority, with a prophetic vision: just as Korea historically served as an actual link between China and Japan, it will now become a true connection between East and West. The impressive effort to host the recent Olympiad as a demonstration of Korea's quest for international recognition is predicated on her heightened sense that the Koreanized Confucianism, and for that matter Koreanized Christianity, can and should become more original and more authentic.[65] The emotionality, sensitivity, commitment to principle, and sense of reverence for "things at hand" enable the Korean people to approach imported spiritual traditions (Buddhism as well as Confucianism and Christianity) with utter seriousness. It is not simply fervent culturalism or impassioned nativism but also a profound sense of mission laden with ethical and religious sentiments that empowers the Korean Confucians and/or Christians to acquire their chosen faith from the source; they are "essentialists" and "fundamentalists" in that they feel obligated to know and to interpret the true message in its genuine form.

The Confucian revival in South Korea is much more visible and better coordinated than its counterpart in Japan. It is a reflection of the Korean sense of destiny: she can become truly international by being authentically Korean; she wishes to be indisputably cosmopolitan through her genuine Koreanness. It seems that the Korean intelligentsia believes that the surest path toward a complete elimination of the psychopathology of hahn is to fully embody the hahn of the world—to domesticate it, digest it, absorb it, and internally transform it into an inexhaustible supply of energy for celebration.

Notwithstanding a fair amount of collective vainglory, as the Olympic extravaganza amply demonstrated,[66] the Korean claim that the seeming contradiction between particularism and universalism can be overcome is not unwarranted. Among the industrialized East Asian societies, the creative tension between internationalism and nationalism and between cosmopolitanism and nativism is most pronounced in South Korea. The generation of Korean scholars fluent in Japanese, Chinese, and English may be fading. The case of Professor Lee Sang-eun of Korea University, the dean of Confucian studies for three decades, is unique; as a graduate of Peking University, thoroughly familiar with Japanese Sinological scholarship and well-seasoned in American East Asian studies, Professor Lee trained a whole generation of Korean Confucians whose combination of classical education with modern consciousness enabled them to assume leadership positions in education, government, and industry.

The linguistic proficiency of the academic community in Korea is still awe-inspiring.[67] Comparable to the quadrilingualism at Dutch universities, Korean intellectuals manage to develop a global vision as a constitutive part of their higher learning. The ability of Korean scholars, students, officials, traders, and tourists to feel at home all over the world enhances the Korean sense of identity as a source of inspiration rather than a mere attachment to an outmoded form of life. Historically, Korea has an impressive track record of enabling borrowed cultural traditions to fare better there than they did in their original countries. Although it is still not known whether acculturated Korean Christianity will flourish better than most other Christian communities in the world, acculturated Korean Confucianism is indisputably the most authentic and the most fundamentalist in East Asia.

Like Dr. Okada, Professor Lee combined creative scholarship with administrative leadership. In his attempt to revive Confucian humanism as both an academic subject and an intellectual concern, he helped to develop an awareness among his colleagues and students that active participation in the affairs of the world does not mean that one needs to compromise one's ethical principles. His own involvement in leading demonstrations against Syngman Rhee's dictatorial regime was an eloquent argument for his personal integration of political activism and moral idealism. Thus, through exemplary teaching, he realized the possibility of being faithful to democratic ideas as a loyal Confucian. Like Okada, he investigated the relevance of the Confucian tradition for Korea's modernization; furthermore, he vigorously tapped Confucian spiritual resources for exploring a distinctive East Asian path to modernization. Under his directorship, the international conference on Asia and modernization held in Seoul in 1974 first raised the Weberian question about the role of Confucian ethics in East Asian economic development. In a deeper sense, what he envisioned then was the whole issue of tradition in modernity, specifically the desirability, if not necessity, of understanding the Confucian dimension in East Asian development.

Some of the Confucian values seem incompatible with, and even detrimental to, the modernizing process defined in contemporary Western terms. For example, the glorification of the amateur ideal is certainly at odds with the demand for professionalism in science and technology, and the belief in moral elitism is often in conflict with the idea of participatory democracy. Yet Professor Lee noted that since the Confucian tradition has become so much an integral part of the Korean form of life, Korean modernization, including its iconoclastic rejection of the Chosŏn dynasty, entails the modern transformation of Confucian humanism. At the same time the cultural form that Korean modernization assumes cannot be devoid of a Confucian character. Although Lee's message did not speak to those who took modernization to be a unilinear progression spearheaded by North America and Western Europe, it has shaped the context of Confucian revivalism in South Korea.[68] His assessment of the Confucian heritage set standards for appraising the positive and negative roles that Confucian ethics has played in the tradition and transformation of Korean political culture. Moreover, he was instrumental in establishing the Department of Philosophy at Korea University as a forum for the study of Confucian thought.

Lee struck a sympathetic cord among those who felt deeply that Confucian humanism as an ethics of responsibility must differentiate itself from political ideology couched in Confucian terminology in order to address the vital issue of cultural identity. The true Confucian may abdicate his duty as a servant of the state, but he is always obligated to look after the well-being of the people. Understandably, the nativistic power in contemporary Korean political culture, be it the catharsis of a shamanistic dance or the inflammatory rhetoric of a public speech, is often framed in the moral indignation of a Confucian discourse. Even the Marxist-inspired rhetoric that has become a major force in campus demonstrations is laden with Confucian symbolism: the public-spirited intelligentsia are presented as articulating the conscience of the people against a privatized and self-interested political faction corrupting the soul of the nation.[69]

The darker aspect of the Japanese Confucian revival—that it may use Shintoist ethnocentrism to fuel ultranationalist sentiments—is absent in South Korea. Deeply rooted in popular orthodoxy and orthopraxy as well as in elite culture, Korean Confucianism tends to be parochial, conservative, and anticommunist. However, the potential for Confucian thinkers to challenge Christian theologians and Westernized philosophers to participate in the development of a distinctive Korean mode of thought is great. The Korean Confucian revival may well become the model for similar efforts in the rest of East Asia.

Taiwan's Quest for Cultural Identity

Under Japanese occupation for fifty years (1895–1945) and American influence for a whole generation, Taiwan remains, nonetheless, Chinese to the core. Despite the rhetoric of the independence movement, which is predominantly a political protest against the discriminatory policy of the Nationalist government against native Taiwanese in high-level party and government appointments, Taiwan is ethnically, linguistically, and culturally Chinese. However, the heightened awareness that for better or for worse, Taiwan is fated to be Chinese has created in native Taiwanese as well as immigrant mainlanders a psychocultural syndrome commonly known in Taiwan's mass media as the "Chinese complex."[70]

The complex began when the ruling party (Guomindang/ Kuomintang/ KMT) made a concerted effort to style itself as the true inheritor of Chinese culture shortly after its total withdrawal from the mainland in 1949. For decades, Taiwan has prided herself on being "Free China," the real China, diametrically opposed to the Communists, who as the Taiwanese official interpretation would have it, abandoned Chinese cultural tradition and embraced a foreign ideology as its guiding principle in word and deed. The doctrine of the Three People's Principles, authored by Sun Yat-sen, who unequivocally identified himself with the Confucian tradition, is often contrasted with Marxism-Leninism to show that Mao Zedong's line of transmission (Marx, Engels, Lenin, and Stalin) is blatantly un-Chinese. The persistent and comprehensive policy of characterizing the Precious Island as the hope of Chinese culture drives home the point that Taiwan is not only an integral part of China but the base for the eventual restoration of Chinese culture on the mainland.

The liberal democrats, deeply worried about the political implications of the KMT's ideological manipulation of Chinese cultural values—notably loyalty and filial piety (comparable to the emphasis on national spirit by the Park regime in South Korea)—launched a frontal attack on the Confucian tradition in the 1960s. Their success in capturing the imagination of university students rekindled the enthusiasm for science and democracy in a way that was reminiscent of the anti-Confucian campaigns of the May Fourth generation. Criticism of Chinese culture became a code word for denouncing the authoritarianism of the KMT. The two-line struggle between the Westernizers and the traditionalists was helplessly entangled in heated political issues. The apparent triumph of the westernizers as liberal-democratic critics of the Nationalist government did not undermine the persuasive power of the traditionalists, especially those who were not official ideologues but cultural conservationists. A champion of the Confucian tradition, Xu Fuguan, emerged as the most influential intellectual both for his criticism of the KMT and his scathing attack on the policies of the Chinese Communist party. Even after his emigration to Hong Kong, his presence as the foremost political and cultural critic was still widely felt among college students in Taiwan. The works of the liberal professor at Taiwan University, Yin Haiguang, also inspired several generations of college students, but the inspiration was mainly due to his political protest rather than to his cultural iconoclasm.[71]

The KMT's official policy of transforming Confucian ethics into a political ideology made an indelible mark on moral education in primary and secondary schools, although it was never supported by the Western-minded technocratic intelligentsia. Chen Lifu, who returned to Taiwan after a sojourn in the United States in the late 1960s, engaged himself in an all-out effort to build a solid Confucian ideological basis for the KMT. As one of the most revered and feared political ideologists and party organizers in the KMT for decades prior to the Communist takeover, Chen was Chiang Kai-shek's right-hand man in developing an overall strategy for "national reconstruction." He also served as the minister of education during the Sino-Japanese War. Having been blamed for losing the mainland to the Communists, he committed himself to a voluntary exile in New Jersey for almost twenty years. Upon returning to Taiwan, he vowed never to enter practical politics again. Yet by reestablishing himself as a person of ideological influence with the government's blessing, he was able to lecture on Confucian ethics from the vantage of a senior statesman. His voice was heard not only in the schools but also in the army. Through television, radio, and the printed media, his ideas penetrated virtually every corner of the island country. Despite the resentment of liberal intellectuals, he was perhaps the best-known missionary for the Confucian faith. As a result, his interpretation of Confucian humanism as an integral part of moral education for primary and secondary schools was much more successful than it had been when he was the Minister of Education on the Mainland. The recent protest of teachers against the textbook based on his commentary on the Four Books demonstrated how extensive his influence has been in shaping the general direction of moral education in Taiwan.

The kind of Confucian message Chen Lifu delivered is a combination of cultural chauvinism, nationalism, ethnocentrism, anthropocentrism, and political conservatism. Chen believes that the continuous vitality of Chinese culture for more than five thousand years is firm proof that Confucianism, as the predominant intellectual tradition in China, is the superior ideology in human history. He also believes that humiliation, including a sense of "national humiliation" *(guochi)*, experienced by Chinese people in recent times was precipitated by anti-Confucian campaigns. Therefore the revitalization of Confucian ethics as a common creed is the proper way of restoring national self-respect and self-confidence. He further believes that Confucianism as rational humanism is compatible with science and technology. Trained as an engineer at the Pittsburgh Mining Institute, he is fond of using positivistic reasoning to show that as a political ideology, Confucianism has a bright future. At the same time, he also takes great pains to establish Confucian ethics as a "civil religion" in Taiwan. His strong faith in the Confucian tradition as a defining characteristic of Chinese culture enables him to assert repeatedly that the fate of Marxism-Leninism in China is sealed because it is incompatible with basic Confucian values such as family cohesiveness, social harmony, and political unity.[72]

Most recently, Chen Lifu authored a pronouncement which, under his influence, was signed by all members of the top senior advisory group to the KMT advocating the unification of the two Chinas on the basis of Chinese culture.[73] Specifically he recommended that neither Marxism-Leninism nor the Three People's Principles should be used as an ideological weapon for the purpose of United Front tactics. Instead, Chinese culture, articulated in terms of Confucian humanism, should serve as the common ground for the two sides of the Taiwan Straits to enter into mutually beneficial communication. He even recommended that once the Chinese Communist party openly acknowledges that the "Four Insistencies" (socialism, Marxism-Leninism, the thought of Mao Zedong, and one-party rule) are negotiable, the KMT should make a concrete proposal to use Taiwan's enormous foreign reserve for mainland China's economic development. As expected, the impassioned and yet well-reasoned pronouncement received much critical acclaim among overseas Chinese communities. Surprisingly, an editorial in the *People's Daily* fully endorsed the spirit of the pronouncement.[74] Whether or not it will lead to concrete results, Chen's Confucian revivalism scored a major victory in broadening the political discourse.

Chen has also been instrumental in establishing Confucian teaching *(Rujiao)* as a national religion. The persistent effort to revive the proper rituals of honoring Confucius is a case in point. The most important Confucian ceremony is now performed on 28 September, The Teacher's Day. With the encouragement of the government and financial support from groups sympathetic to Taiwan, the ceremony is also being performed by overseas Chinese communities throughout the world. Recently the ceremony has been revived in Qufu, Confucius's birthplace, as well. Still, the most authentic ceremony performed every year virtually without interruption for centuries, takes place in the Confucian temple in Seoul. There are reports that when Taiwan decided to revive the ceremony, they sent a delegation to South Korea to learn the music and dance accompanying the ritual. Despite Chen Lifu's indefatigable effort, the ceremony in Taiwan has never been officiated at by the top leadership of the KMT. Chiang Kai-shek and Chiang Ching-kuo (Jiang Jingguo) were both Christians. Many of their cabinet members were also Christians. However, the Confucian revival engineered by Chen Lifu, with the full support of the KMT, has been a major ideological force, though his deliberate attempt to make Sun Yat-sen and Chiang Kai-shek the perceived inheritors of the Confucian sage-kings was rejected by the intellectual community.[75]

The Confucius-Mencius Scholarly Society, directly under the ideological control of Chen, has among its numerous publications an annual journal and a monthly. With full financial support from the central government, the society has regularly sponsored conferences, seminars, and lectures. Despite its limited success in gaining respectability among serious scholars in the academic community, the society has been highly visible in its outreach activities in schools and adult education. The International Symposium on Confucianism and the Modern World, held in the opulent auditorium of the Central Library in November 1987, demonstrated that through Chen's influence, the society had the ear of official KMT circles. The presence of the premier, the minister of education, and several cabinet-level officials at the inaugural ceremony partly explained the ability of the society to put together an event much more elaborate than the Second International Sinological Conference organized by the Academia Sinica in the same year.

Significantly different from Chen Lifu's Confucian revival is the cultural movement of the "New Confucians," led by academicians first at Peking University (Xiong Shili and Liang Souming) in the 1920s, then at New Asia College (Tang Junyi) in Hong Kong in the 1940s, and finally at Tunghai University (Mou Zhongsan and Xu Fuguan) in Taiwan in the 1960s. Like the Confucian revival of the eleventh century, when scholars addressed perennial human concerns as a creative response to the challenge of Buddhism, the twentieth-century movement can be characterized as a collaborative effort to address vital issues in the twentieth century as a creative response to the impact of the modern West. "The impact of the modern West" in this sense refers to both the human condition in general and the Chinese predicament in particular. Broadly speaking, the movement is primarily concerned with culture and modernity and focuses on the modern transformation of Confucian humanism. Their movement's scholarly society, The Friends Association of Oriental Humanism *(Dongfang renwen youhui)*, and their journals, *Life (Rensheng)* and *Democratic Review (Minzhu pinglun)*, have served as an important source of inspiration for culturally concerned high school as well as college students in Hong Kong and Taiwan.[76]

To the leading philosophers of the movement, the vitality of the Confucian tradition lies first in its distinctly Chinese mode of understanding the dignity of the person as a center of relationships inextricably intertwined in an ever-expanding network of human communication involving the family, community, state, and world. Also, as a common heritage of East Asian humanism, the form of life it embodies allows the coexistence of a variety of cultural expressions; as a result, conflict in ethnicity, language, territoriality, class, gender, and religion is minimized, if not resolved. Furthermore, Confucian humanism, premised on an anthropocosmic vision which advocates harmony with nature and union with Heaven, is in a better position than the Enlightenment mentality to cope with issues in ecology, environment, and resources.

This seemingly idyllic portrayal of the Confucian tradition, sharply contrasted with the post-May Fourth Westernizers' depiction of it as feudalistic, authoritarian, patriarchal, and male chauvinist, is a deliberate attempt to underscore the moral idealism in the Confucian tradition as a manifestation of Chinese, East Asian, and indeed human spirituality. Despite wave after wave of iconoclastic attacks by the Westernizers on the detrimental effect of the Confucian habits of the heart on China's modernization, philosophers at New Asia College and Tunghai University insisted that the modernizing process in East Asia must address itself to the perennial humanistic values in the Confucian tradition. They argued that the strategy of either relegating Confucianism to a residual category or denouncing it as a dispensable psychopathological burden has not brought fruitful results. They further maintained that it is neither necessary nor desirable that cultural form in China be devoid of Confucian content. Indeed, they strongly believed that the spiritual resources in the Confucian tradition can and must be mobilized to serve as a powerful critique of the negative consequences of modernity defined in terms of the unique Western historical experience.

Underlying this mode of thought is a communal critical awareness that tradition is an integral part of the modernizing process, that modernity, properly understood, can assume a variety of cultural forms, and that the Western European and North American versions of modernity may not be the wave of the future for China. This awareness itself is both a realization of the authority of the past and a symbol of hope that the quest for a common ground in an increasingly pluralist global village need not take the self-destructive modern Western path. The significance of Confucian humanism, in light of this awareness, is not confined to its historicity. The Confucian form of life, to the extent that it locates ultimate human concerns in ordinary day-to-day existence, can continue to provide spiritual resources and standards of inspiration for the future.[77]

In the post-Cultural Revolution era (1976), mainland scholarship on the major Chinese intellectual trends since the May Fourth movement (1919) groups the New Confucians together with the socialists and the Westernizers as the most influential and significant philosophical voices. Fang Keli, a professor of Chinese philosophy at Nankai University and a committed guardian of the Marxist line among historians of thought in the People's Republic of China, has warned that it would be a grave mistake for the Marxists to underestimate the persuasive power of the New Confucians.[78] Jin Guantao, one of China's most articulate Westernizers, characterizes Chinese Communism, as sinicized by Mao Zedong and Liu Shaoqi, as a thoroughly Confucianized Marxism.[79] Although it is still uncertain whether the New Confucians will become a major intellectual force in the People's Republic of China, in the postwar era they have represented the preeminent Chinese style of philosophizing in Taiwan, Hong Kong, North America, and more recently, Singapore.

Despite strong tension and occasionally open conflict between the Confucian revival spearheaded by Chen Lifu and his KMT supporters and the cultural movement of the New Confucians (who are in general academic philosophers), both revivals have contributed to making Confucian discourse a defining characteristic of political culture in Taiwan.

A particularly noteworthy development in this connection is the emergence of a new generation of Christian interpreters of the Confucian tradition. Taiwan Catholics, centered around Fu Jen (Furen) University under the leadership of Archbishop Lo Guang, have made a concerted effort to present their understanding of what constituted the most authentic message of the Confucian tradition. Through book-length monographs, journal articles, public lectures, research seminars, international conferences, and appearances in the mass media, they have exerted a shaping influence on both the academic community and the general populace for more than two decades. Equipped with advanced degrees from European and American universities, the Fu Jen graduates have dominated the handful of departments of philosophy. Their conflict with the followers of the New Confucians, notably the Goose Lake circle, has become intensified in recent years. The acrimonious exchange between Mou Zhongsan and Lo Guang is more than episodic in this intriguing struggle for orthodoxy in Confucian discourse. While the New Confucians accuse the Catholics (a few of them are former Jesuit priests) of Christianizing the tradition, the Christian interpreters condemn Mou and his followers for couching the tradition in German idealism. Their scholarly debates are as much about hermeneutics in Western philosophy as about exegesis in Confucian thought. Since they are academic in orientation, they often find themselves at odds with Chen Lifu's attempt to provide the KMT official ideology, the Three People's Principles, with a Confucian justification. However, since both groups are far from immune to political pressure to render service to the KMT's anticommunist establishment, they cannot entirely distance themselves from the activities of Chen's Confucius-Mencius Scholarly Society.[80]

The vitality of Confucian discourse in Taiwan is marked, but for the last two decades, Taiwan's economy has been so fundamentally restructured that society and polity are undergoing convulsive ruptures as well. As a result, egoism, disintegration of the three-generation family, social conflict, political protest, and the vulgarization of culture have perhaps irreversibly changed the moral fabric of the island community. In this the Confucian discourse is also being transformed.[81] It will continue to serve as a frame of reference for adjudicating disputes, negotiating consensus, establishing communication, and identifying values.

Implications

The Confucian revival in industrial East Asia since the Second World War is by and large a cultural response to the modern West. It may have allied itself with nativistic sentiments such as Shintoism in Japan, shamanism in South Korea, and popular religion in Taiwan, but its overall posture is neither a yearning for the past nor an attachment to a threatened life-style. Rather, it is a deliberate attempt to mobilize traditional symbolic resources to bring them to bear on the critical issues generated by the modernizing process. It is therefore not an unreflective reaction against modernity but a critical understanding of some of the unintended consequences of industrialization, urbanization, bureaucratization, and the widespread influence of mass communication. In fact, there is strong evidence to show that the dynamic cultural forms enhancing economic productivity that industrial East Asian countries assumed have benefited from Confucian ethics.[82]

In a deeper sense, the core values in East Asia are still Confucian in nature. The majority of East Asian intellectuals embrace the ideas that the person is a center of human relationships, that family is an indispensable institution for human development, that society ought to be a fiduciary community, that politics should be characterized by exemplary leadership, and that cultural life should be shaped in part by the symbolic resources of the past.

The compatibility of Confucian humanism with modernity—defined in terms of science, democracy, liberties, human rights, and the dignity of the autonomous individual—remains a controversial issue.[83] Liberal thinkers in East Asia, under the influence of American social sciences of the 1960s, took it for granted that authoritarianism, familism, communion, and the demand for consensus are antagonistic to the modern mentality. However, nowadays there is strong reason to believe that government leadership based upon a pervasive sense of respect for authority, social solidarity as the result of family cohesiveness, communal participation, and elaborate efforts at consensus formation have made positive contributions to the economic dynamism of industrial East Asia. To cultural comparativists, the orienting question is not the compatibility with modernity of these typically East Asian habits of the heart informed by Confucian humanism but the variety of forms modernity must assume to make it universalizable.

This leads us to the intriguing problem of understanding the nature of the Confucian revival. Although it has not been seen as a coordinated effort, the international scholarly cooperation featuring New Confucians such as Tang Junyi (Hong Kong), Xu Fuguan (Taiwan), Lee Sang-eun (South Korea), and Okada Takehiko (Japan) certainly gives the impression of a cultural movement of transnational character. But the Confucian revival as a new phenomenon in East Asia involves so many isolated groups with their particular forms of local understanding that it remains an open question whether or not the New Confucians will be able to transform their scholarly joint venture into a broadly based cultural movement.

A salient feature of the Confucian revival is its critical spirit. Motivated by a profound sense of crisis, prompted by anxiety over national survival, ethnic pride, cultural identity, and even the human condition as a whole, the Confucian revivalists are forceful critics of modern Western culture.[84] However, even though they inevitably tap resources from Confucian classics, they are not at all interested in a literal interpretation of Confucian truth. Although some attempts have been made to identify the most authentic Confucian message for all ages, the general tendency is to take a highly pragmatic course of action by making the Confucian persuasion relevant to the modern world.

An excellent example of this is the famous 1958 manifesto on Chinese culture signed by Zhang Junmai, Tang Junyi, Mou Zongsan, and Xu Fuguan.[85] Intent on making known their collective judgment on the proper way of comprehending the relevance of the Confucian tradition to China and the world, they offered a holistic vision of the human condition from the Confucian perspective. Originally drafted by Tang in consultation with Zhang, the document was first circulated among a small coterie of like-minded scholars, then revised, enlarged, and finally redacted for the general public. A faith in the efficaciousness of the Confucian core curriculum and an assumption of the authentic transmission of the Confucian heritage throughout history are implicit in the manifesto, but the main thrust of the argument is to present a Confucian perspective on the human condition defined in terms of modern Western categories.

Between Mishima's ritual suicide as a denunciation of the sterility of modern commercial culture and the New Confucians' reconstruction of the meaning of the human "life world," the range of the Confucian revival is wide. However, despite its diversity, the emerging communal critical self-awareness among the Confucians in East Asia clearly indicates that for them, the search for cultural roots is an integral part of modern consciousness and indeed a persistent universal human concern.

Notes

The author wishes to express his deep appreciation to Ted de Bary, Chris Cleary, John Ewell, Rosanne Hall, and Milan Hitjmanek for their searching criticisms of the entire manuscript. He also wishes to acknowledge gratitude to Watanabe Hiroshi for his generous help in providing valuable sources on Japan.

1. Peter L. Berger, "An East Asian Development Model?" in Peter L. Berger and Hsin-huang Michael Hsiao, eds., *In Search of An East Asian Development Model* (New Brunswick, N.J.: Transaction Books, 1988), pp. 8–9.

2. For a brief description of this idea, see "The Philosophy of Change" and "Yin Yang Confucianism: Tung Chung-shu," in Wing-tsit Chan, trans. and comp., *A Source Book in Chinese Philosophy* (Princeton: Princeton University Press, 1963), pp. 262–88.

3. Cf. the essay by Winston Davis in this volume (chap. 14).

4. According to some scholars in mainland China, the date of Confucius's birth ought to have been 26 September 551 B.C.E.

5. *Encyclopaedia Britannica,* 17th ed., s. v. "Confucius and Confucianism."

6. Berger, "East Asian Development Model?" pp. 7–8.

7. Max Weber, *The Religion of China: Confucianism and Taoism,* trans. from German by Hans H. Gerth (New York, N.Y.: Free Press, 1951), p. 248.

8. For a general discussion on Weber in the context of rationalism, cf. Wolfgang Schluchter, *The Rise of Western Rationalism,* trans. and with introduction by Guenther Roth (Berkeley: University of California Press, 1981).

9. *Analects* 15, p. 23.

10. Tu Wei-ming, "Rise of East Asia: The Role of Confucian Values," *Copenhagen Papers in East and Southeast Asian Studies,* no. 4 (University of Copenhagen: Center for East and Southeast Asian Studies, 1989), pp. 81–97.

11. For a pioneering attempt to understand the cultural background of industrial East Asia, cf. Edwin O. Reischauer, "The Sinic World in Perspective," *Foreign Affairs* 52, no. 2 (1974): 341–48.

12. Tu Wei-ming, "A Confucian Perspective on the Rise of Industrial East Asia," *Bulletin of the American Academy of Arts and Sciences* 42, no. 1 (October 1988). For a general discussion of the cultural interaction of East Asia, cf. William T. de Bary, *East Asian Civilizations: A Dialogue in Five Stages* (Cambridge: Harvard University Press, 1988).

13. de Bary, *East Asian Civilizations.*

14. For a discussion on the Chinese case, see Tu Wei-ming, "The Enlightenment Mentality and the Chinese Intellectual Dilemma," paper presented to the Four Anniversaries Conference, Annapolis, Maryland, 11–14 September 1989. The proceedings, under the editorship of Kenneth Liberthal, are being published by M. E. Sharp in New York.

15. I am grateful to Robert Hewett,

senior fellow in charge of the U.S.-Japan News Project in the Institute of Cultural and Communication at the East-West Center in Honolulu, for this information.

16. For a thought-provoking, albeit somewhat outdated, attempt to address this issue, see Joseph Levenson, *Confucian China and Its Modern Fate: A Trilogy* (Berkeley: University of California Press, 1968).

17. Although there is a growing literature on this topic in Chinese and Japanese, the available material in English is extremely limited. See Tu Wei-ming, "Toward a 'Third Epoch' of Confucian Humanism: A Background Understanding," in Irene Eber, ed., *Confucianism: The Dynamics of Tradition*, (New York: Macmillan, 1986), pp. 3–21.

18. Tu, "Confucian Perspective."

19. Ibid.

20. Ibid.

21. For an account of Fukuzawa Yukichi's intellectual self-understanding, cf. Kiyoshi Yukichi, trans., *The Autobiography of Fukuzawa Yukichi* (Tokyo, 1934).

22. Nishida Kitarō, *Nihon bunka no mondai* (The problem of Japanese culture), based on lectures delivered at Kyoto University in 1938.

23. The publication of *Fundamentals of Our National Polity (Kokutai no hongi)* by the Ministry of Education in 1937 was a massive attempt to define Japan's unique polity based upon a divine emperor, Confucian ethics, and the samurai spirit. R. Tsunoda, William T. de Bary, and D. Keene, comps., *Sources of Japanese Tradition* (New York: Columbia University Press, 1958), pp. 785–95.

24. Ibid., pp. 759–805.

25. Ibid., pp. 603–8.

26. Ibid., p. 796.

27. For a general report on this issue, see *Far Eastern Economic Review,* 10 April 1986, pp. 22–23. A formal objection made by the Foreign Ministry of the People's Republic of China on 7 June 1986 said that the textbook contains serious historical distortions. A commentary of the *People's Daily* on 7 July 1986 criticized a proposed history textbook for whitewashing the infamous "Nanjing massacre" in 1937. It should also be noted in this connection that Prime Minister Nakasone dismissed the Education Minister Fujio Masayuki on 8 September 1986 "when South Korean outrage over remarks the outspoken Kujio made about Japan's colonial rule in Korea ignited a political firestorm which, for a time threatened to derail Nakasone's scheduled 20 September visit to Seoul." *Far Eastern Economic Review,* 18 September 1986, pp. 14–15. I am indebted to Dr. Kennon Breazeale of the East-West Center for this useful information.

28. For an account of this politically significant symbolic gesture, see n. 46.

29. The remark that Japan shares the common values of the modern West and participates in the security of the Western democratic and economic system, first expressed in the final communique of the Economic summit at Williamsburg, Virginia in 1983, was repeated in the Economic Summits of London (1984) and Bonn (1985). I am indebted to Dr. Manca Di Nissan of the United Nations University in Tokyo. Of course we could interpret the remark to mean that as an integral part of the industrialized world Japan is prepared to perform the role of an actively contributing member of the club.

30. Although analysis of this highly publicized discussion is scanty in English, it is unquestionably one of the most important and thought-provoking cultural phenomena in contemporary Japan. See Harumi Befu, "Cultural Construction and National Identity: The Japanese Case," a paper prepared for the Cultural Policy and National Identity Workshop, Institute of Culture and Communication, East-West Center, Honolulu, 19–22 June 1990.

31. For a provocative discussion on this issue, cf. Maruyama Masao, "Ansaigaku to Ansaigakuha," in Nishi Junzo et al., eds., *Nihon shiso taikei 31: Yamazaki Ansai gakuha* (Tokyo: Iwanami, 1980). Equally thought-provoking is Professor Maruyama's inquiry on the "*basso ostinato* of Japanese history." Cf. Maruyama Masao, "The Structure of Matsurigoto: The *baso ostinato* of Japanese Political Life," in Sue Henny and Jean-Pierre Lehmann, eds., *Themes and Theories in Modern Japanese History: Essays in Memory of Rich-*

ard Storry (London and Atlantic Heights, N.J.: Athlone Press, 1988), pp. 27–43. I am indebted to Professor Watanabe Hiroshi of Tokyo University for this information.

32. For an example of Motoori Norinaga's nativism, see excerpts from his *Tama kushiqe* (Precious combbox), in *Sources of Japanese Tradition,* pp. 520–23.

33. This is hardly the place to give an adequate account of this daunting scholarly intricacy, which has taken Japanese intellectual historians, such as H. D. Harootunian and Peter Nosco, much labor of love to unravel. Cf. H. D. Harootunian, *Things Seen and Unseen: Discourse and Ideology in Tokugawa Nativism* (Chicago: The University of Chicago Press, 1988). Also see his essay, "Disciplining Native Knowledge and Producing Place: Yanagita Kunio, Origuchi Shinobu, Takata Yasuma," in J. Thomas Rimer, ed., *Culture and Identity: Japanese Intellectual during the Interwar Period* (Princeton: Princeton University Press, 1990), pp. 99–132. Also, see Peter Nosco, "Masuho Zanko (1655–1742): A Shinto Popularizer between Nativism and National Learning," in Peter Nosco, ed., *Confucianism and Tokugawa Culture* (Princeton: Princeton University Press, 1984), pp. 166–187.

34. See excerpts from Hirata Atsutane's *Kodo Taii (Summary of the ancient way),* a "fundamentalist" assertion of the uniqueness of the Japanese mode of learning, in *Sources of Japanese Tradition,* pp. 542–47.

35. Also known as the "Three Imperial Regalia"; see Tsunoda et al., *Sources of Japanese Tradition,* pp. 19–20, 280–82.

36. For a discussion on the "I Novel," see Donald Keene, *Dawn to the West: Japanese Literature of the Modern Era* (Fiction) (New York: Holt, Rinehart, and Winston, 1983), pp. 4, 221, 506–55.

37. I am indebted to Dr. Darrell William Davis for this observation; see his "The Monumental Style: Film Form and National Identity in Prewar Japanese Cinema" (Ph.D. diss., University of Wisconsin, 1990).

38. Based on an oral presentation in Chinese by Professor Hayashi of Keio University presented to the Seminar on Chinese Religious Thought, Harvard University, 2 December 1988. The presentation is subsequently published in Chinese under the title, "The Possible Contribution of Japanese Modernism to 'The Third Stage of Development in Confucianism,'" *Kyoyo-Ronso* 84 (1990), pp. 23–37. For a thought-provoking analysis of the Tokugawa mentality and its relevance to modern Japanese ideology, see Herman Ooms, *Tokygawa Ideology: Early Constructs,* 1570–1680 (Princeton: Princeton University Press, 1985).

39. Cf. chap. 14.

40. Ibid.

41. Carefully chosen by a committee of elder statesmen and senior scholars, with speculation that the Confucian *doyen* Yasuoka Masahiro played a significant role in defining the parameters in the early stage of the process. The two characters—*hei* (peace) and *sei* (completion) are taken from perhaps the most archaic Confucian classic, *Book of Documents,* symbolizing the fruition of an age of peace and prosperity. However, the word *hei* used as a verb can also mean in a more active sense "to pacify," which is reminiscent of the expression "pax" in its more aggressive connotation. For a discussion of Yasuoka's role in this process, cf. articles in the *Asahi Shimbun* on 14 January 1989. I learned from scholars and officials knowledgeable about such matters that out of respect for the late Emperor Shōwa, prior to Emperor Akihito's accession, there was no official discussion of this matter. A consultation involving eight members on the appropriate name for the new reign was organized following the accession of Emperor Akihito. The name "Heisei" was officially reported to have been chosen selected by this consultation and was publicly announced on 7 January 1989. I am grateful to Ms. Sumiye Konoshima of the Institute of Culture and Communication at East-West Center and Mr. Shinichi Makatsugawa, vice-consul of the Consulate-General of Japan in Honolulu, for their help in providing me with valuable information on the subject. I am of course solely responsible for interpreting the role of Yasuoka Masahiro in this process. For a thorough scholarly discussion on *heisei* in Japanese, see Togawa Yoshio, *"Heisei toyu*

koto," in *UP,* nos. 203–4 (Tokyo University Publication Association, September–October 1989). I am indebted to Professor Watanabe Hiroshi for this information.

42. The common practice of rendering *heisei* as "achieving peace" is not adequate, for the whole idea is predicated on the belief that Japan has been blessed with the age of peace for decades.

43. The elaborate ritual involved in the inauguration of Emperor Heisei, which may turn out to be one of the most spectacular "semi-official" ceremonies of the twentieth century, clearly shows that emperorship as a symbolic universe is both relevant and significant in modern Japanese political culture.

44. Tsunoda et al., *Sources of the Japanese Tradition,* p. 646.

45. Ibid., p. 647.

46. Ibid.

47. Nagai Michio, "Education and Development," in the report on International Conference on Culture and Development in Asia and the Pacific, sponsored by United Nations University (5–7 March 1990), p. 123.

48. Suggestive readings on these subjects include E. Hamaguchi, *"Nihon rashisa" no saihakken* (Rediscovery of "Japaneseness") (Tokyo: Nihon Keizai Shinbunsha, 1982); R. Minamoto, *Giri to ninjō: Nihon-teki shinri no ichi kōsatsu* (Rightness principle and human feelings: considerations of the Japanese psychology) (Tokyo: Chūo Koronsha, 1969); E. O. Reischauer, *The Japanese* (Cambridge: Harvard University Press, 1977). 1977).

49. Cf. Okada Takehiko, *Seiza zazen* (Buddhist and Confucian meditation) (Tokyo, 1972). For an English translation and annotation of this book, see Rodney L. Taylor, *The Confucian Way of Contemplation: Okada Takehiko and the Tradition of Quiet-Sitting* (Columbia, S.C.: University of South Carolina Press, 1988). Also see his essay on "Modernity and Religion: A Contemporary Confucian Response," in Rodney L. Taylor, *The Religious Dimension of Confucian Humanism* (Albany, N.Y.: State University of New York Press, 1990), pp. 135–147.

50. Although Professor Okada is noted for his work on the Wang Yang-ming (1472–1529) tradition in Neo-Confucian thought, his work on the essence of Sung-Ming Confucian thought, on the modern significance of Confucius, on idealism and realism in Chinese intellectual history, and on the East Asian way of life have reached many audiences. Cf. Okada Takehiko, *O Yomei to Minmatsu no jugaku* (Wang Yang-ming and the Confucian Learning in Late Ming) (Tokyo: Mintoku, 1970).

51. The most dramatic recent event in the Korean-Japanese bilateral relationship was Emperor Akihito's formal apology "for Japan's brutal subjugation of Korea nearly a half century ago." This "unambiguous acceptance of responsibility for Japanese wartime aggression" was unprecedented. The choice of the expression "painful regret" and the specific acknowledgment of "the sufferings your people underwent during this unfortunate period, which was brought about by my country," at a state banquet in honor of the visiting South Korean president, Roh Tae Woo, contrasted sharply with Emperor Hirohito's "more circumscribed locutions" describing the war years as a "regrettable" period, without "acknowledging any specific Japanese responsibility." Cf. *The New York Times,* 25 May 1990. Cf. also the headline, editorial and background articles on the same subject in the *Asahi Simbun,* 5 May 1990, pp. 1–5.

52. For a general discussion of the relevance of Confucian ethics to South Korea's economic development, cf. R. P. Dore, "South Korean Development in Wider Perspective," in Chang Yunshik, ed., *Korea: A Decade of Development* (Seoul: Seoul National University Press, 1983), pp. 289–305.

53. For a focused investigation of a special linguistic issue in this connection, see Sim Jae-kee, "Chronological Study on the Assimilation of Chinese-Character Words in Korea," *Seoul Journal of Korean Studies* 2 (1989): 3–22.

54. For a focused investigation of this type of modernist thinking in Korea, see Vipan Chandra, *Imperialism, Resistance, and Reform in Late-Nineteenth-Century Korea:*

Enlightenment and the Independence Club (Berkeley: Center for Korean Studies, Institute of East Asian Studies, University of California, Berkeley, 1988). For a general discussion on "practical learning," see Michael Kalton, "An Introduction to Silhak," *Korean Journal* 15, no. 5 (July 1975), pp. 12–17.

55. See Chung Hee Soh, "Korean Women in Politics (1945–1985): A Study of the Dynamics of Gender Role Change" (Ph.D. diss., Department of Anthropology, University of Hawaii, 1987). For comparative purposes, see Mark Peterson, "Women without Sons: A Measure of Social Change in Yi Dynasty Korea," in L. Kendall and M. Peterson, eds., *Korean Women: View from the Inner Room* (New Haven: East Rock Press, 1983).

56. For a sociological analysis of this phenomenon, see Yong Choon Kim, "A Comparison of Korean and American Churches," *Journal of Social Sciences and Humanities* (Seoul: The Korean Research Center) 68 (June 1990): 55–70.

57. For a fascinating anthropological discussion on this intriguing issue, see Kwang-ok Kim, "Manipulation of Shamanism for Ritual of Resistance in Contemporary Korea, unpublished manuscript" (1990). For thought-provoking accounts of shamanism in contemporary Korean society, see L. Kendall, Shamans, Housewives, and Other Restless Spirits (Honolulu: University of Hawaii Press, 1985), and *The Life and Hard Times of a Korean Shaman* (Honolulu: University of Hawaii Press, 1988).

58. Kwang-ok Kim gives a moving account of Professor Lee's performance of "shamanistic ritual for Park Jong-chul" in May 1987; see Kim, "Manipulation of Shamanism."

59. Although no critical biography of General Park is available in English, his unusual background as a school teacher who later became a brilliant student in an elite Japanese military academy is known among scholars of modern Korea. I am grateful to Professor Carter Eckert and Mr. Milan Hetjmanek, both of Harvard University, for their insights into General Park's life history.

60. Although the term "China fervor" is used mainly by Chinese scholars who visited Korea to attend scholarly conferences, such as Zhang Liwen of the People's University, my own involvement in helping Korean scholars in the humanities to establish scholarly communication with their counterparts in the People's Republic of China has given me enough evidence to note that at least for the time being, China is a hot topic in the Korean academic community.

61. For example, Professor Yu Soonkuo, one of the leading scholars in Confucian studies in Korea, maintains that Korea is the "motherland" of the Confucian tradition. Cf. his article in *Essays in Commemoration of Professor Yu Soonkuo's Sixtieth Birthday* (Seoul: Korean Academy, 1985).

62. J. K. Fairbank, E. O. Reischauer, and A. M Craig, *East Asia: Tradition and Transformation* (Boston: Houghton Mifflin, 1973), p. 278.

63. It should be noted that the attempt by reputable historians to discredit or ignore the Kija legend does not at all undermine its symbolic significance in the formation of Korean cultural identity. Cf. Kibaik Lee, A *New History of Korea,* trans. Edward W. Wagner (Seoul, 1984), pp. 16, 330.

64. The career of Lee Dong-choon, a leading entrepreneur dedicated to the promotion of T'oegye study, is a fascinating case of Confucian revival in South Korea. Having established himself as a leading industrialist in steel, Mr. Lee then turned to the challenging enterprise of honoring his beloved ancestor, Master T'oegye, by establishing the International Society for T'oegye Studies. Through his political and business connections, he raised enough funds to host a series of international seminars since 1976. He was also instrumental in arranging some of the most ambitious publishing ventures to make original sources and interpretive literature in T'oegye studies available to scholarly communities all over the world. The most recent seminar was held in Moscow in August 1990 and was cosponsored by the Academy of Sciences of the USSR.

65. It is indicative that the theme of the international conference organized in con-

junction with the the Olympiad was "Man and Nature." The purpose was to identify "core values" for human survival; the underlying assumption is that true originality and authenticity in the spiritual quest must be universalizable. For an informative report on the underlying cultural issues concerning the Olympiad, see San-Chul Lee, "Seoul Olympics: Some Crossed Cultural Communications," *Media Asia* (Singapore) 16, no. 4 (1989): 193–97.

66. It should be noted that the Seoul Olympiad was the largest ever staged, with 13,674 athletes from 160 countries. It was "important in boosting Korea's international image and standing" (Lee, "Seoul Olympics," p. 194).

67. The case of Professor Kim Young-ok of Korea University is worth noting. With master's degrees from both National Taiwan University and Tokyo University and a Ph.D. from Harvard, he is thoroughly versed in Korean, Chinese, Japanese, and Western scholarship on East Asian thought. His approach to Confucian studies is global in perspective.

68. See his preface to Lee Sang-eun, ed., the *Report on the International Conference on the Problems of Modernization* (Seoul: Asiatic Research Center, Korea University, 1974).

69. On the surface, the political left may associate Confucianism with the political ideology of the conservative Liberal Democratic Party. In a deeper sense, however, the spiritual self-definition of the college student as the intellectual vanguard who must try to arouse the conscience of the nation is rooted in the *yangban* tradition defined in Confucian terms.

70. The term is widely used to designate not only a mind-set but also a process of political justification. It is often contrasted with the mental inclination of those who advocate the independence of Taiwan as both a political entity and a cultural system.

71. See Yin Haiguang, *Zhonguo wenhua di zhanwang* (The Reappraisals of Chinese culture) (Taipei: Wenxing Publishing Co., 1957).

72. The most representative work of Chen Lifu is *Sichu daoguan* (The Four Books through the unitary way) (Taipei: Sanmin, 1967).

73. It seems that Chen's declaration was drafted in response to the Party Congress of the KMT (July 1988). However, despite its obvious political motivation, the proposal that the two sides of the Taiwan Straits should be united on the grounds of shared cultural values has been widely accepted as a positive move by scholars, politicians, and the mass media on the mainland as well as in Taiwan.

74. Since only the overseas edition of the *People's Daily* fully endorsed Chen's proposal, it has been argued that it is basically a "united front" effort aimed at the overseas Chinese community. However, the very fact that the proposal generated much in-depth discussion on Chinese cultural identity suggests that it has raised an important question for concerned Chinese intellectuals throughout the world.

75. Although Sun and Chiang were Christians, they were both committed to the task of "cultural reconstruction" with particular emphasis on the revival of Confucianism as an integral part of their political ideology. Therefore, it is not farfetched for Chen Lifu to construct their public images as the true inheritors of the Confucian tradition.

76. A notable example of the continuous vitality of this movement is the so-called Goose Lake scholarly society in Taipei. Inspired by the philosophy of Mou Zongsan, Goose Lake academicians have made a significant contribution to keeping the Confucian discourse alive in the mass media.

77. For a general discussion on the relevance of Confucian thought to East Asian modernization, cf. Huang Guangguo, *Rujia shixianq yu tongya xiandaihua* (Confucianism and East Asian modernization) (Taipei: Chuliu, 1988).

78. Professor Fang Keli is currently directing a major research project on New Confucianism under the sponsorship of the Five-Year Plan of the Educational Commission of the State Council (1988–). The project involves a thirty-volume study of the principal figures, dominant themes, and

critical issues of the New Confucian movement since the May Fourth of 1919. Currently the project involves eighteen research units and forty-seven researchers throughout mainland China. It is one of the most ambitious intellectual undertakings since the Cultural Revolution (1976).

79. Cf. his article, "The Confucianization of Marxism," submitted to the Conference on the Prospects of the Third Epoch of Confucian Humanism, sponsored by the Institute of East Asian Philosophies, in Singapore, 27 August–3 September 1988.

80. As a response to the international conference on Confucius jointly organized by the Confucius Foundation in the People's Republic of China and the Institute of East Asian Philosophies in Singapore in the summer of 1987, the Confucius-Mencius Society, fully supported by the government, organized one of the most elaborate international conferences on Confucianism in Taipei in October 1988. The conference was cochaired by Chen Lifu and Archbishop Lo Guang, president of Furen (Catholic) University.

81. For a representative account of this new thinking in Taiwan, see Joseph P. L. Jiang, *Confucianism and Modernization* (Taipei: Freedom Council, 1987).

82. For an exploration of this issue, see Hung-chao Tai, ed., *Confucianism and Economic Development: An Oriental Alternative?* (Washington, D.C.: The Washington Institute Press, 1989).

83. The issue of human rights assumes a prominent position in this discussion; see R. Randle Edwards, Louis Henkin and Andrew J. Nathan, eds., *Human Rights in Contemporary China* (New York: Columbia University Press, 1986).

84. A philosophical argument for the relevance of Confucian humanism to modernity is formulated by Roger Ames and David Hall in *Thinking through Confucius* (Albany, N.Y.: State University of New York Press, 1988).

85. The declaration was first published in *Minzhu pinglun* (The Democratic review) 9, no. 1 (1958).

Select Bibliography

Berger, Peter L., and Hsin-huang Michael Hsiao, eds. *In Search of An East Asian Development Model.* New Brunswick, N.J.: Transaction Books, 1988.

Chen, Li-Fu. *The Confucian Way: A New and Systematic Study of the "Four Book."* Tai Pai National Chengchi University and New York: Saint John's University, Center of Asian Studies, 1972.

Chih, Andrew. *Chinese Humanism: A Religion beyond Religion*. Taiwan, Republic of China: Fu Jen Catholic University Press, 1981.

de Bary, William T. *Neo-Confucian Orthodoxy and the Learning of the Mind-Heart.* New York: Columbia University Press, 1981.

———. *East Asian Civilizations: A Dialogue in Five Stages*. Cambridge: Harvard University Press, 1988.

Edner, Mattias. *Chinese Religion*. Tokyo: Society for Asian Folklore, 1973.

Fairbank, J. K., E. O. Reischauer, and A. M. Craig. *East Asia: Tradition and Transformation*. Boston: Houghton Mifflin, 1973.

Gardner, Daniel K. *Chu Hsi and the Tahsueh: Neo-Confucian Reflection on the Confucian Canon.* Cambridge: Council on East Asian Studies, Harvard University Press, 1986.

Gernet, Jacques. *China and the Christian Impact: A Conflict of Cultures*. Trans. Janet Lloyd. New York: Cambridge University Press, 1985.

Hu, Shih. *The Chinese Renaissance*. 2d ed. New York: Paragon Book Reprint Co., 1963.

Lee, Kibaik. *A New History of Korea*. Trans. Edward W. Wagner, Seoul, 1984.

McNaughton, William., ed. *The Confucian*

Vision. Ann Arbor: University of Michigan Press, 1974.

Munro, Donald, ed. *Individualism and Holism: Studies in Confucian and Taoist Values*. Ann Arbor: Center for Chinese Studies, University of Michigan, 1985.

Schluchter, Wolfgang. *The Rise of Western Rationalism*. Translated and with introduction by Guenther Roth. Berkeley: University of California Press, 1981.

Thompson, Laurence G. *Chinese Religion: An Introduction*. 2d ed. Encino, Calif.: Dickenson, 1975.

Tsunoda, R., William T. de Bary, and D. Keene, comps. *Sources of Japanese Tradition*. New York: Columbia University Press, 1958.

Tu, Wei-ming. *Humanity and Self Cultivation: Essays in Confucian Thought*. Berkeley: Asian Humanities Press, 1979.

———. *Confucian Thought: Selfhood as Creative Transformation*. Albany: State University of New York Press, 1985.

———. *Centrality and Commonality: An Essay on Confucian Religiousness*. Albany: State University of New York Press, 1989.

Weber, Max. *The Religion of China: Confucianism and Taoism*. Translated and edited by Hans H. Gerth. New York: Free Press, 1968.

Yukichi, Kiyoshi, trans. *The Autobiography of Fukuzawa Yukichi*. Tokyo, 1934.

Yunshik, Chang, ed. *Korea: A Decade of Development*. Seoul: Seoul National University Press, 1983.

CHAPTER
14

Fundamentalism in Japan: Religious and Political

Winston Davis

Fundamentalism: Word and Theory

The Japanese are fond of saying that they are a uniquely group-oriented people. In Japan, group activity does indeed have an intensity which may astonish, offend, or frighten the foreign visitor. A visit (based on several personal experiences) to a generic Grand Festival of one of the country's New Religions will illustrate the point. We may call the group the "Church of Health and Happiness."

When we arrive at the "Tokyo Colosseum," we find the gigantic stadium already filled with tens of thousands of stalwart believers eagerly awaiting the arrival of their messiah. As we wait, we are serenaded by the brass bands of the National Health and Happiness Youth Corps. Scantily clad pom-pom girls twirling batons and doing other "routines" march by. Enormous banners, blaring trumpets, and Japanese *taiko* drums hail the grand entrance of the messiah himself. Balloons and live doves are released, bringing ecstatic cheers from the crowd. The chief ecclesiocrat of the Tokyo Central Church comes to the podium and officially announces the opening of the festival. The messiah solemnly proceeds to a gigantic, temporary altar and presents offerings of rice and *sake* before the *kami*. After this some popular entertainers, a well-known baseball player, and politicians from the Tokyo area take the stage. Following their greetings, lay members come to the microphone and in tear-filled voices offer their testimonies, telling of the innumerable miracles they have experienced as a result of the teachings of the Health and Happiness Church and the messiah's rite of healing. Each speech ends with exuberant expressions of thanks to the gods and the messiah for their blessings.[1]

Midway through the festival, the messiah, smiling broadly and waving to the crowd, retires to his backstage room, only to return to the podium a few speeches later to the stirring tune of a John Philip Sousa march, dressed this time in new green-and-gold robes. The people jump to their feet and clap and cheer for what seems to be a full five minutes. Finally the messianic sermon begins. A true raconteur, the messiah soon has the colosseum in the palm of his hand. In richly colloquial Japanese, he reminisces about the sicknesses and afflictions of the people who have come to him for help, about the decline of traditional Japanese morality since the war, and about various other evils of the day—money politics, pollution, and the threat of nuclear war. Finally he describes the Holy Nostrum: a simple amulet that will cure all illnesses, restore broken relations, revive the national spirit, and bring about world peace. Other ways to salvation will fail, he warns. The old religions—Christianity, Buddhism, Confucianism, and Shinto—are dead; their followers can't even perform miracles. The one and only way to health and happiness is the messiah's own Holy Nostrum. With this declaration, the sermon comes to an end. Again the faithful rise and cheer. Escorted by bands and banners the messiah, smiling, waving, and shaking hands, makes his way out of the colosseum to the black Cadillac waiting for him in the street.

The festival over, the faithful make their way through the crowded streets to their comfortable air-conditioned buses for the long trip back to the provinces. On the way back, a microphone is passed around the bus so that the pilgrims can express their gratitude to the messiah for "being allowed" to attend the festival. Each declares that from now on he will be more diligent in spreading the message of the Nostrum and will use it to perform more miracles than ever. Some use their turn at the mike to sing some of the charming old folk songs of the province. Beer and box lunches are passed out and before long many of the faithful are asleep.

As he watched a similar festival conducted by the Sōka Gakkai sect, Neil McFarland felt "almost frightened by the possible implications of these manifestations of mass energy and blind obedience. For one who remembers the World War II period, such a spectacle has a haunting effect. His mind flashes back to newsreel clips of Nazi youth rallies and other similar vignettes of the totalitarianism that once nearly destroyed civilization. Is the similarity here more than circumstantial? Is this fascism reborn?"[2]

In this context, fascism was too strong a term, an indictment rather than an explanation. If it was not fascism, what was it that McFarland saw? A highly mobilized kind of fundamentalism? The ritual equivalent of an American tent revival? An evangelistic campaign designed to energize, mobilize, or stabilize the working masses of Japan Incorporated?

The word *fundamentalism* seems a bit incongruous in the Japanese setting. If one were to ask a group of perceptive foreign visitors to describe the essence of Japanese life, the word "fundamentalist" probably would not even come to their minds. To most people, "fundamentalism" suggests an orientation which is the very opposite of the dynamic, flexible secularism that characterizes Japan today.[3] Specialists on Japanese religion and society seldom, if ever, use the word. The Japanese themselves usually reserve the words *konponshugi, genrishugi,* or the English loan-word *fuandamentarizumu* for Iranian or Protestant fundamentalism or for the Korean Unification

Church. This means that for most Japanese, to be a "fundamentalist" is to be a devotee of a *foreign* religion.[4]

If the word fundamentalist seems counter-intuitive as a label for Japan, can we, or should we, apply the word to this country and its religions in a theoretical or comparative way? If we do, will the Japanese recognize our designation as an appropriate description of movements in their country?

Although fundamentalism is usually applied as a descriptive term to specific historical religions or sects, it can also be used as a powerful theoretical concept in the comparative sociological study of religion and politics.[5] The following definition of fundamentalism is a heuristic distillation of the most important elements in the academic discussion of the subject today. It is not intended as a statement of the essence of the phenomenon as such but rather as a selection of those "family resemblances" (to use Wittgenstein's term) which seem most helpful in bringing the Japanese phenomenon into a comparative perspective.[6]

Since the time of Durkheim and Spencer, one of the basic theories of social science has been the notion that social development (or "modernization") can be gauged in terms of increasing levels of differentiation. Put simply, as a society develops, its various institutions and sub-systems become more clearly articulated.[7] Internally the developing society becomes more complex, its components increasingly interdependent. This is, however, only half of the story of development. If differentiation were a simple, undialectical process it would result in the complete atomization of society. From the point of view of social theory, the concept of differentiation must therefore be counterbalanced by an account of the reintegration of society.[8]

Although some describe developments of this sort rather glibly as sociocultural differentiation, society and culture do not always develop in tandem. On the contrary, social and cultural differentiation may get "out of sync." Take, for example, the social and existential suffering caused by rapid, unbalanced economic growth, or by catastrophic bouts of inflation or deflation. Society sometimes deals with such crises by deliberately imposing upon itself a simpler cultural system, represented in symbols harking back to earlier or more "primitive" levels of development, or by values believed to be better or more authentic because they originated "in the beginning" (or at least, long before "the trouble" began). "Fundamentalism" may be used, then, to indicate a pattern of coping with unbalanced social and cultural development by means of "symbolic regression." Fundamentalism therefore is by definition a reaction to modernization, although it is not necessarily a complete rejection of modernity as such.

Symbolic regression may be at the heart of all fundamentalist systems, but it is hardly a sufficient description of the phenomenon. Fundamentalists engage in symbolic regression with a certain animus against those who they think have misappropriated the cultural symbols of their tradition. This animus is often expressed in resentment, anger, distrust, coercion, and negative or hostile attitudes toward outsiders. Fundamentalism (though not necessarily the fundamentalist) is angry with the world—with highborn sinners who reap all of the world's benefits, with foreigners who exploit the fatherland, and with members of other races and religions who reject not only the Lord, but His elect. While the anger of some (contemporary Iranian Shi'ites, for example) seems to generate a collective, fundamentalist effervescence, that of others may be sublimated, institutionalized, or disguised as a prosaic, emotionally unflappable attitude toward the world. The fundamentalist does not trust others to find their own way back to the beginning, the truth, the text, or the Lord; and so fundamentalist groups keep close tabs on their own members. Talcott Parsons points out that fundamentalism imposes a "specificity of standards" on society and thus "narrows the range open to conscience. A member is not trusted to act conscientiously, in the light of moral principles. Rather, it is prescribed to him just what he must and must not do."[9]

One of the most seductive features of fundamentalism is its belief that a group can flourish only when it is "morally efficient," and that efficiency of this sort depends on direct control and supervision of members' personal lives by deacons, mullahs, or other commandants of the elect.[10] To ensure the moral efficiency of the group, fundamentalism turns first to the informal coercions of gossip and peer pressure. Ultimately it may resort to physical force to enforce its discipline. In the sociology of religion, morally efficient groups which maintain their purity in this way are called "sects." However, the fundamentalists' concern does not always end with the preservation of the purity of their own group. Those who see their country as a racial or religious extension of their own enclave are apt to believe that it is the nation itself which must be kept pure, not just the sect.

Fundamentalism manifests itself both religiously and politically.[11] Indeed, one of the distinct advantages of introducing the concept of fundamentalisms into the overall theory of social and cultural differentiation is that the structural relatedness of religious and political fundamentalism becomes all the more evident. For purposes of analysis, we must further divide fundamentalism into its institutional and diffuse forms. Institutional fundamentalism is that embodied in specific, organized religions or political parties. This manifestation of fundamentalism may be found among Japan's New Religions and in various political groups. Diffuse fundamentalism, on the other hand, is a "climate of opinion" spread less formally throughout the general culture, especially by the mass media. In what follows, I shall discuss Japan's prewar political fundamentalism in terms of "civil religion." As I use the term, civil religion is institutional whenever it takes the form of a cult established by the government or when it is promulgated by various organized religions. It assumes a para-institutional or diffuse form whenever it is spread by the media or "secondary institutions," to use Thomas Luckmann's term.[12]

Prewar Political Fundamentalism

Political fundamentalism was largely a reaction to the growing complexity, danger, and contradictions in Japanese life in the early twentieth century. The Meiji Restoration (1868) itself had been a reaction to the disintegration of the Tokugawa *bakufu* (or shogunate, 1600–1867) and its failure to deal with foreign challenges. The system of religious ideology and thought control that gradually came into being after 1868 was itself a response, or rather a series of responses, to various challenges to the authoritarian rule of oligarchs and landlords, to the system of military and industrial development they were promoting, and to traditional values. During and immediately after World War I, the young industrial nation was racked by inflation and labor unrest. In 1910 the government arrested several hundred anarchists and socialists, charging them with plotting against the life of the emperor. The execution of twelve of the suspects the following year marked the beginning of decades of harassment of the political left. Nevertheless, strikes and riots continued. University students and their teachers began to join the Communist Party. Demonstrators filled the streets demanding universal male suffrage. Young people began to espouse a hedonistic way of life that openly defied the traditional samurai ethic of self-sacrifice *(bushidō)*, a code which the government hoped to turn into a national ethic. "Too many young people appeared to be lost in a world of irresponsibility and self-centered existence. So-called *mobo* and *moga* ([Japanese-English for] modern boys and modern girls) dressed in Western clothes appeared, shocking many people. Much like today's hippies, the typical *moba* wore long hair and sometimes a beard and bell-bottomed pants. Coffee shops, dance halls, and other Western imports caused concern over the nation's future."[13]

The Japanese responded to this challenge by turning to an all-encompassing system of "symbolic regression." "Because of growing economic and social problems, plus the feuds and corruption rampant in parliamentary politics, people were inclined to turn their backs on the emerging political system in favor of *a return to the stability they imagined had existed earlier.* In other terms, Japan was suffering from a too rapid modernization which had led to a state of social disorganization, or anomie, in which large numbers of individuals felt that stable institutional patterns were crumbling and their own personal stability was in jeopardy."[14]

It seems indisputable that the period from 1930 to 1945 was a time of political fundamentalism as I have defined the term. It is imperative to understand how this came about. The Shinto myth of the divine descent of the Japanese emperors gave a religious flavor to Japanese nationalism in general and was especially prominent during those years. One does not, however, understand Japanese political fundamentalism simply by labelling it "Shinto Nationalism." It was more complicated and more comprehensive. Shinto itself was anything but a "militaristic religion." On the contrary, it was basically a simple peasant religion aiming at the fertility of the crops and at general well-being in this world. Its theology was generally of the simplest sort. Its ethics amounted to the cultivation of a "bright, pure, sincere heart" *(akaki, kiyoki, makoto na kokoro)*. Shinto took several forms, including the sectarian Shinto of the nineteeth and early twentieth centuries (sects with founders, later to be called *New Religions*) and the religion of the imperial household itself. While the latter was obviously connected with nationalism, it was not traditionally associated in the Japanese mind with ultra-nationalism or militarism.

We turn first to the institutional side of Japan's prewar civil religion. Nearly all of Japan's religions contributed to, or at least acquiesced in, the political fundamentalism of the state. Historically, Buddhism had done virtually nothing to thwart the authoritarianism of the state. Since the time of Shōtoku Taishi (573–621), it had offered its services as the palladium of the state. During the Nara period (710–784), Buddhism became the monopoly of the court, a powerful source of magic and religious legitimation. Throughout the middle ages, sect vied with sect for the patronage and protection of imperial court and shogun. In contrast to the churches of northern Europe and America, Japanese sects generally welcomed state control because it meant security. During the Tokugawa period (1600–1868), Buddhism, by now virtually a state church, was used by the shogunate to register, and thus control, the masses. To prove that they were not members of the forbidden Christian religion, families were made to enroll in specific Buddhist temples. (Before this it was possible for family members to belong to different temples.) As a result of this move, Buddhism became closely associated with the regime. Consequently, when the shogunate began to falter in the middle of the nineteenth century, Buddhism too seemed to be discredited. According to their critics, Buddhist priests had been totally corrupted by state patronage. Thus, the close association with the Tokugawa regime proved to be the undoing of the religion in the Meiji period. The syncretistic bonds which Buddhism had developed with Shinto during the course of the middle ages were officially severed. Following intense criticism by various scholars and government bureaucrats, Buddhism was severely persecuted in many parts of Japan from 1868 to 1871.

During this period, the government began a series of religiopatriotic experiments designed to unify the country. Through its Office of Propaganda (set up in the Department of Shinto), the government appointed priests, Confucian scholars, actors, professional storytellers and fortune-tellers as propagandists of a newly concocted national religion. The sermon topics assigned to the propagandists included patriotism, the benevolence of the gods and the emperors, belief that the gods gave birth to all things Japanese, and the importance of national wealth and armed strength. The propagandists met with little success, however, probably because their glib mixture of patriotism and Shinto seemed a mockery of traditional religion. "Members of the audience, when not observed, occasionally stuck out their tongues or ridiculed the sermons."[15] What is more, the heavy emphasis on Shinto alienated Buddhists who were already concerned about the destruction of temples going on around them. In the early 1870s, the Meiji oligarchs abandoned the Shinto-based Office of Propaganda in favor of a syncretistic state religion. In 1873, the new national priests were given the following doctrines to proclaim: respect for the gods and love for Japan, "heavenly reason" and the "way of humanity," and respect for the emperor and obedience to authorities. Even Buddhists petitioned the government to set up schools in which applicants for the national priesthood could be trained. In 1873, the government answered this request by establishing seminaries in the provinces called *Taikyōin* (Institutes of the Great Faith). But the Institutes also failed, probably because they too were ultimately dominated by Shintoists.

In 1868 the government constructed a "Place to Invite Souls" *(Shōkonsha)* in order to console the spirits of those who had died on behalf of the Meiji Restoration. When the government moved to Tokyo, one of the Shōkonsha was moved to Tokyo's Kudan area. In 1879, under the new name Yasukuni, the shrine was given the rank of a special government shrine under the direct control of the military.[16] Worshiped by the emperors themselves, the war dead enshrined at Yasukuni tragically increased from an original 3,588 in 1869 to 2.4 million by the end of 1945. As we shall see, the shrine has continued to be a focal point of Japanese nationalism to the present day.

In 1884, the national priesthood was discontinued. Soon the government turned to Shinto, but in a new format. From about 1897, government publications began to stress the "nonreligious" nature of Shinto. This ploy allowed the state to support major Shinto shrines throughout the country as a "patriotic cult" without seeming to violate the freedom of religion promised by the Meiji Constitution of 1899.[17] The government also hoped that its theory of the nonreligious nature of Shinto would mute criticism of its religious policies by Western missionaries and diplomats. Since neither the propagandists nor the national priests had been effective, the government was willing to settle for a state cult whose priests were actually forbidden to preach. In 1899, the Ministry of Education ruled that religion (Buddhism and Christianity in particular) should not be taught in the schools. From then on, the significance of "State Shinto" (as it was later called) would be made known by Imperial Rescripts, by orders issued by the Ministry of Education, and through the writings of official government scholars *(goyō gakusha)*.

In spite of the predominance of Shinto during those years, prewar political fundamentalism is not adequately explained in terms of "State Shinto" or "Shinto Nationalism." Buddhism, Christianity, and Confucianism, together with various popular religious movements, all made their contributions. As the persecution of Buddhism neared its end in 1871, the emperor himself had declared: "We should not only allow the people to believe elements of every religion. . . . To the extent that these religions do not violate the will of the Japanese gods, we should accept them without asking their nationality, master them, and put them to our own use."[18]

While Buddhism continued to come under attack for its "foreign origins," it had long acted as a national talisman. During the Meiji period, when peasants hesitated to take up sericulture for fear that killing silkworms would bring them bad karma, the government had dispatched Buddhist preachers to convince them that the work was in the national interest and religiously innocuous. Buddhists petitioned the government to be included in its new religiopatriotic experiments. During the ultranationalist period, Buddhist priests displayed their loyalty by worshiping at State Shinto shrines and going on pilgrimages to various national shrines. Temples reminded the people that Buddhist priests had founded Shinto studies and that Buddhism had originally been introduced to protect the nation. Buddhist literature during those years was replete with such patriotic slogans as *Kōkoku Bukkyō* (Buddhism protecting the nation).

Christianity was also part of the emerging prewar civil religion. While some Christians suffered for their faith, most could say with Uchimura Kanzō: "My Christianity is patriotic. . . . Patriotism means that one believes in the divine mission of the nation and devotes one's entire self in behalf of the mission."[19] Like Buddhists and the members of independent Shinto sects, Christians sought to avoid government persecution, hoping to gain official recognition by means of a strategy of accommodation with the government's program of industrial and military development. Thus Christians defended themselves in terms of their own good works. As Daniel Holtom put it, they could advertise their faith as "the faithful mongoose that killed the communist viper; it was the devoted watchdog that kept away the burglar of radicalism; it was the guardian angel that protected the citadel of the national life against the demons of unsocial license. It inspired a true religious faith that brought the blessings of God upon the soldiers that faced ungodly forces across the Siberian border."[20]

Sidney Mead points out that in democratic America, the public schools became virtually an "established religion."[21] The public schools played a similar role in the fundamentalist civil religion of prewar Japan. There, children were subjected to a steady diet of imperial ideology. The school day began with the children bowing in the direction of the imperial palace. Once a month the school became a virtual shrine for the veneration and recitation of the Imperial Rescript on Education.

> For a school's first reading of the rescript, the scroll had to be paraded to the school by teachers, pupils, local notables, the mayor, the post office chief, local people in government, and the area's eldest residents. A sacred space was prepared for the reading with fresh gravel and hung with red, white, and blue curtains. An offering of rice cakes was presented to the scroll as if it were a deity. The school principal assumed the priestly role, donning white gloves to intone the text. There were even cases of principals committing suicide to atone for mispronouncing a syllable.[22]

In spite of these school rituals, the imperial message did not always come across. When Tokutomi Sohō paid a visit to a third grade ethics class in the sea resort of Atami near Tokyo, he was astounded at the lack of knowledge about the emperor.

> "Why," the teacher asked, "must we be loyal to the Emperor?" A pupil stood up; "the Emperor . . . ," he began; but he stopped, tittering, unable to conclude. "Don't laugh," the teacher scolded . . . "Because we are indebted to the Emperor. Class," the teacher again asked, "why are we indebted?" The pupils stared in puzzled silence. "It is thanks to the Emperor," said the teacher, "that you come here and return home safely." To be sure the lesson was learned, the teacher continued: "To whom are we indebted that burglars don't enter our houses and that we have all come to school without meeting bullies?" A girl promptly spoke up: "The policeman." The teacher thought dejectedly for a time. "Of course that is true, but the policeman is ultimately the Emperor's. . . ." The innocent girl did not understand the teacher's purpose and only stared in mystified silence.[23]

Diffuse Political Fundamentalism

We turn now from institutional to para-institutional or diffuse forms of political fundamentalism. Since the Meiji Restoration, the principal agencies for the spread of diffuse political fundamentalism were the mass media. The role of the media in generating civil-religious sentiment was especially obvious in wartime. During the Sino-Japanese War, the *Yomiuri Shinbun* announced a prize competition for war songs which would "arouse feelings of hatred against our national enemy."[24] Diffuse political fundamentalism was often conveyed in the form of such patriotic slogans as "the eight corners of the world under one roof," "a National Essence standing foremost among the nations," "a hundred million hearts beating as one," "spreading the Great Cause throughout the world," "loyalty and patriotism," "the indestructibility of the Divine Land," "an imperial line unbroken for ages eternal," "Japan, flawless like a golden chalice," and "defending the Divine Land." Such slogans were liberally scattered throughout the political speeches, newspaper editorials, and sermons of the day. Each slogan had its own complicated history. Some were individually authored, such as the slogan "the imperial army will always win, and having won, will return alive." This was, in fact, the bon mot of Taniguchi Masaharu, the founder of a New Religion called Seichō no Ie.[25] Others appeared and spread anonymously.

Tsurumi Shunsuke points out that specific groups at various times tended to promote certain slogans instead of others. For example, the word *kōdō* (the Imperial Way) was used by younger officers, agrarian leaders, and the youth from about 1930 on. *Shindō* (proper behavior of subjects) was often used by high-ranking military men, new bureaucrats, and politicians. *Kokutai* (the National Essence) had a long history as a civil-religious slogan. In modern times, however, it belonged primarily to the rhetoric of aristocrats, older officers, and educators.[26] Above and beyond their political and military connotations, these slogans had a distinct religious flavor. According to Tsurumi, they even had an "amuletic effect." "The group of words *kokutai* (National Essence), *Nipponteki* (really Japanese), and *Kōdō* (Imperial Way), usually give anyone who used them the same feeling of security as an amulet. 'Provided I have this about me, I shall be able to keep myself safe from the malevolent, to escape accidental misfortune.' "[27]

Usually consisting of two to four characters read in the Chinese way *(onyomi)*, these slogans had the ponderous solemnity of the civil religious slogans on the American dollar, e.g., *annuit coeptis*, or *novus ordo seclorum*, Latin slogans which tendentiously proclaim that God "has favored our undertakings," or that "a new world order"—i.e., the United States itself—has been established. For Tsurumi, the slogans used by the Japanese before and during the war were both ambiguous and irrational:

> With the amuletic use . . . neither utterer nor recipient is clearly conscious that these amuletic words are employed only for luck or for reasons of courtesy, or are employed to foster and protect one's own political or social standpoint; that their use is not assertive; that they are, that is, non-cognitive. It is this lack of clarity which . . . has made the amuletic use harmful. If men had only had the wit to treat the various words they have used amuletically simply as ornaments, as symbols, they might not have been bemused by them and so have drifted unknowingly into war.[28]

So ambiguous were these notions that rival groups could, and in fact had to, use the same slogans. *Yokusan* (assisting the throne) was a slogan used both by those in favor of party government and by those opposed to parties. Originally nearly all politicians except the Communists indulged in their use. After about 1935 these slogans were monopolized by the most chauvinistic groups. Not all slogans were based on the "Way of the kami." Some Christian pastors, for example, explained the National Essence *(kokutai)* in terms of the Kingdom of God imagery more familiar to them. Buddhists contributed a number of their own slogans, such as *shinzoku nitai* ("undivided obedience to religious and political institutions"), *kōzen gokoku* ("protect the country by promoting Zen"), and *chingo kokka* ("pacify and preserve the country [through Buddhism]").[29] Tsurumi concludes that the mischief of these slogans was due to their "pseudo-assertive use and the habit of using words without properly understanding their meanings."[30]

While there is much to be said for Tsurumi's position—especially when one takes into account the seeming profundity of obscure-sounding Chinese compounds in Japanese—the function of the ambiguity and sacredness of these slogans is a more complicated matter. The amuletic nature of civil religious slogans makes it possible to use them to create a national consensus. Even in the 1930s, Japan still lacked the unity and "moral efficiency" yearned for by the political fundamentalist. As late as 1936, Prince Konoe was forced to admit: "Japanese public opinion is deeply divided; and there are many serious confrontations, including those existing between villages and cities, and army and the navy, and soldiers and diplomats. When I think of Germany before the Great War and examine the contemporary situation in Japan, no longer can I contain my profound sense of anxiety."[31]

Under such circumstances, the semantic obfuscation of civil religious slogans had a strategic role to play. The specific proposals of the politician are generally incapable of uniting or "de-differentiating" public opinion. Functioning as trump cards and not merely as amulets, patriotic slogans helped the politician play his hand. The skill of the politician could be measured by his ability to match policies with trumps. The trumps in this case were so ambiguous that the same card could actually be used to support contradictory policies. The trump-slogan "revere the emperor," for example, was first used to "play" the policy "support the shogunate." Later, however, anti-Tokugawa groups changed the slogan to read: "revere the emperor; overthrow the shogunate." While one usually thinks of such patriotic slogans as the monopoly of the loyalist, they were also used by rebels claiming to restore the National Essence. Rebels and assassins often prayed and bought amulets at the Yasukuni and Meiji shrines before setting out on their missions of mayhem and murder. What was constant in all cases was reverence for the throne; what was mutable was policy. By exploiting the prestige of nebulous Chinese compounds, policymakers were able to wrap their schemes in the numinous overtones of (what sounded like) scripture, thereby winning for themselves a far wider consensus than a purely rational examination of their policies would warrant. By creating an undialectical atmosphere around policy, civil religious slogans made political maneuvering easier. Even though they could facilitate change, once in place the same slogans encouraged a relentless drive toward political irrationality and inflexibility. The mythmakers began to believe in their own myths.

Enforcing Political Fundamentalism

The fundamentalist challenge was simple: it was to make Japan's complex society morally efficient by de-differentiating its social and cultural variations. Religious ideology was therefore applied to the task of submerging "the divisions of gender, class, and ethnicity in the cozy, penumbral illusion of spiritual unity."[32] In 1939, speaking in defense of the government's Religious Organizations Bill, Prime Minister Hiranuma Kiichirō said: "Let me emphasize that all religions must be one with the ideal of our national polity; they cannot be at odds with the spirit of our Imperial Way."[33] To achieve this end, more was needed than ritual and ideology. The state enforced its ideology and civil religion with law and physical force. The Newspaper and Publications Laws (1887), the Public Peace Police Law (1900), legislation creating the Higher Police (1904) and Special Higher Police (1911), and finally, the Peace Preservation Law of 1925 collectively created a system in which "thought criminals" were apprehended by "thought-control police" and judged by "thought procurators" for "dangerous thoughts"—usually, that is, for advocating trade unionism, socialism, or communism.

Religious groups also came under the control of the authoritarian state. To keep a closer eye on potential dissidents, the government forced Buddhist temples, Shinto shrines, and Christian churches to merge into larger collectivities. Physical attacks were made on the leaders of labor unions, political leftists, and religious dissenters. Among traditional religionists, Nichirenites and True Land Buddhists came under fire for fidelity to their own "single-practices."[34] The New Religions, however, were still more vulnerable. Their pantheons were sometimes different from the government's own approved list of *kami*. Their healing and liturgical practices were thought to be vulgar, primitive, and superstitious. And their eschatological visions—which sometimes included millenarian dreams about the "renewal of the world"—seemed at odds with the specific aspirations of the imperial system itself. It is most likely, however, that what the government feared about these groups was their independent, translocal social organization.[35]

Since True Pure Land Buddhism and other religious groups organized in this way had caused the former rulers of Japan so much trouble, the government was determined to root them out.[36] Beginning in the 1920s, the police periodically attacked such groups as Honmichi, Hitonomichi, Ōmoto, Sōka Gakkai, and Tenri Honmichi. It must be said that the government's policy of enforced moral efficiency worked. To "buy" protection, the independent Shinto sects submitted to regimentation by the state. Christian churches dismissed their missionary brethren (who had become an "embarrassment" to them) and enlisted in the nation's war effort. Christian universities obediently installed altars for the Shinto deities. The Buddhists, still badly shaken by the persecutions of 1868–71, did all in their power to show the "usefulness" of their faith in achieving the goals of "rich country, strong army."[37] The only serious protest came from such marginal groups as the Jehovah's Witnesses, the Holiness church, the Communists—and the fledgling Sōka Gakkai sect. Thus, in the end, only fundamentalists dared to oppose the fundamentalism of the state.

Contemporary Political Fundamentalism

As I have have contended, the clearest examples of Japanese fundamentalism assume a political character. In the period from 1930 to 1945, the ideologies of Meiji emperorism, State Shinto, National Morality, the family state, ultranationalism, and fascism gradually coalesced. Differences of political and ideological opinion persisted, of course, but were marginalized or disguised by the demands of the war itself. Images of family and village were used to de-differentiate symbolically a society which was being ravaged by the cultural and social "contradictions of capitalism." Hence, the ideal of unifying religion and government *(saisei-itchi)* played a central role in the rhetoric of national identity. The net outcome was a fascist state in which—to use Parsons's terminology—the range open to conscience was radically reduced. Conscience was restricted because the freedom to have opinions and make choices was curtailed in the service of other absolutes. As Maruyama Masao put it, fascism failed "to draw any clear line of demarcation between the public and the private domains."[38] The "inner" world of morality was forcefully subjugated to the all-encompassing "harmony" *(wa)* of the imperial system and the National Essence *(kokutai)*.

Political fundamentalism is by no means dead in Japan today. In the postwar era, as many as eight hundred right-wing organizations have sprung up throughout the country, with a total membership of about 120,000 and an active or extremist wing of some 20,000. Some of these groups are clones of the prewar reactionary movements and aim at the revival of emperor worship, the reestablishment of Shinto, and the restoration of the Yasukuni Shrine as the national palladium. With no regard for Japan's pluralist tradition, one leader remarked that "what our resource-poor country needs more than anything else right now is a spiritual mainstay. That is why we wish to see the emperor become the object of faith as a living god."[39]

The wrath of the extreme right was once directed against the "YP Structure" (the international status quo based on the Yalta and Potsdam accords), the "bogus MacArthur Constitution," and the clause in that Constitution prohibiting rearmament—all seen as foreign intrusions. The most disturbing feature of these groups has been the use of violence by some. This, of course, calls to mind the assassinations of political and industrial leaders during the fascist period. At various times, right-wing terrorists have killed the chairman of the Japan Socialist Party, stormed the homes and offices of publishers, and attacked a prime minister. Repeatedly they have disrupted the meetings of the left-of-center Japan Teachers Union. In Japan, acts of this sort are especially worrisome because of the perceived tendency of the Japanese to withdraw in the face of violence, or to placate the terrorist. In the 1970s, Japan's vacillating policy on international hijacking was defended in terms of the "spirit of compromise and forgiveness" which is "part of the national character."[40] There are, however, other ways of looking at the situation, and critics of the national character such as Van Wolferen have charged that in such instances, the Japanese simply lack "civil courage."[41]

While the conservative Liberal Democratic Party (LDP) has been the object of some right-wing terrorist attacks itself, it too has flirted with political fundamentalism—or at least with its symbols. Since 1973, the party has maintained that the emperor is the nation's "sovereign," not just its constitutional "symbol." It supports a religious interpretation of National Founding Day (11 February), the celebration of the enthronement of the first emperor, said to be the direct descendant of the sun goddess, Amaterasu. (This particular Shinto myth had provided a religious hue to earlier expressions of Japanese political fundamentalism.) Backed by various patriotic groups, the Association of Shinto Shrines, and such right-wing New Religions as Reiyūkai and Seichō no Ie, the party has relentlessly supported the nationalization of the Yasukuni Shrine. Five times between 1969 and 1974, the LDP presented bills in the Diet which would allow the state to give official support to the shrine. Even though these efforts were defeated, the party continues to push for an acceptance of the cabinet's worship at the shrine as an official act *(kōshiki sanpai),* in spite of the fact that the deities enshrined there include the spirits of Tōjō Hideki and other Class A war criminals.[42] In a country where ancestor worship is a living tradition, memorializing the war dead is an understandable practice. However, Yasukuni stands for more than ancestor worship. Japan's Asian neighbors naturally worry that the LDP's support of the shrine may portend the revival of more sinister, imperial ambitions. Japanese officials, however, seem remarkably inured to the sensitivities of these countries. One LDP dignitary, Okuno Seisuke, declared, at the Yasukuni Shrine itself, that Japan had not "invaded" China during the war but had acted merely to secure the "safety" of the Asian mainland. Although Okuno was forced to resign (May 1988), other LDP politicians defended him, saying that foreigners have "misinterpreted" Japan's wartime intentions.

Another important expression of political fundamentalism is textbook revision and the re-interpretation of history it entails. In spite of repeated protests from South Korea and China, LDP bureaucrats in the Ministry of Education continue to "revise" the textbooks of the nation's schools in order to de-emphasize, or obscure altogether, Japan's military aggressiveness during the war and to obliterate any reference to the barbaric brutality of its troops. These moves have also been justified in terms of "national character." The Japanese, say the LDP educators, naturally prefer "soft" language in contrast to the "harsh" tones of Western historiography.

Early in 1989, the Ministry ruled that the Rising Sun flag should be hoisted and that the national anthem, *"Kimigayo"* (long associated with emperor worship), should be sung at all school functions. Selections from Shinto mythology already are part of the standard curriculum.

Occasionally the rhetoric of the LDP sinks to the level of racism pure and simple. Ishihara Shintarō, former transportation minister, and Morita Akio, president of the Sony Corporation, have recently characterized all criticism of Japan's international trade policies as racial prejudice against the Japanese people.[43] In December 1986, former Prime Minister Nakasone Yasuhiro made a speech in which he blithely noted that the level of intelligence in America is "extremely low" because "there are many Blacks, Puerto Ricans and Mexicans" living here. Unfortunately, the LDP's racist sentiments do not exist in a vacuum. Throughout the country, economic recovery has bred not only a well-deserved sense of self-confidence but a new arrogance as well. An NHK poll taken in 1983 showed that 89 percent of all Japanese thought "they were superior to other races."[44]

Political fundamentalism has appeared as a tendency in the legal arena as well. Various decisions of the Japanese Supreme Court—which is largely the creature of the LDP and its bureaucracy—seemed consistently to disregard the principle of the separation of state and religion. In January 1965, the city of Tsu in Mie Prefecture paid 7,663 yen to Shinto priests for performing a ground-breaking ceremony. A member of the Tsu municipal assembly brought a suit against the mayor of the city, contending that he (the mayor) had violated the Constitution.[45] A regional court exonerated the mayor on the grounds that the ground-breaking ceremony was a "custom," not a religious service. In doing so, however, it resurrected the same argument the government had used before the war when it established Shinto, namely that Shinto is "not a religion." In 1971, the Nagoya Higher Court reversed the lower court's decision. The matter was finally brought to the Supreme Court which, agreeing with the first court, declared that the ground-breaking ceremony was a nonreligious "custom."

A later case involved the "enshrinement" in a Shinto shrine of the soul of Nakaya Takafumi, an officer killed in an auto crash while on duty in the Self Defense Force (SDF). The Friendship Association of the SDF enshrined Nakaya against the express wishes of his widow, who happened to be a Christian. The lower courts agreed with her that under these circumstances her husband should not have been enshrined. But on 1 June 1988 the Supreme Court, ruling in favor of the state, reversed these rulings.[46] These benchmark decisions caused many Japanese to fear that the courts were cooperating with the right wing of the LDP to re-create State Shinto. As in the struggle against the Yasukuni Shrine bills, some worried that giving official recognition to the Shrine was a step towards the revival of fascism itself.

If the LDP supports emperorism, the latter also comes to the aid of the LDP, sometimes in unexpected ways. Late in 1988, as the Showa emperor lay dying, the LDP and the press collaborated in promoting a "spirit of self-restraint" throughout the country. Concerts and cultural events were canceled. At athletic tournaments, officials starting races were asked to use whistles instead of pistols and to omit the traditional cries of "banzai." Sometimes, restraint took unexpected turns. At Tokyo's Disneyland, fireworks displays were called off. For several months nudes disappeared from the covers and centerfolds of popular magazines. Even managers of massage parlors rang up government offices to ask how they could exercise "self-restraint."

We must not allow the resurgence of nationalism to obscure the fact that all of these events—the Yasukuni bills, textbook revision, and ritual restraint—are taking place in an atmosphere which is significantly different from that of Japan in the 1930s. Groups opposed to the imperial system, for example, openly protested the "restraint" for the dying emperor, condemning it as "contrived respect." Many suspected, apparently with good reason, that restraint had been concocted to give the scandal-ridden LDP—not the emperor—a new lease on life and to tone down the uproar over a new, unpopular sales tax. Women's groups denounced the glorification of the Showa emperor on the grounds that the imperial system sanctifies the subordination of women.[47] Various individuals have defied resurgent nationalism, sometimes at considerable personal risk. One thinks in particular of Ienaga Saburō, who has fought textbook revision for decades, and of Motoshima Hitoshi, the mayor of Nagasaki, who recently raised the question of the emperor's responsibility for the war.[48] The campaign against the re-establishment of the Yasukuni Shrine has been spearheaded by Sōka Gakkai and the Union of New Religions (financed primarily by Risshō Kōseikai). The anti-Shrine campaign has also been supported by many Pure Land Buddhists and Christians, as well as by individuals like Nishikawa Shigenori, who has fought the Yasukuni Shrine bills for over twenty years. Democratic opposition of this sort was simply not possible before 1945.

Fundamentalism and Japan's New Religions

When one looks for fundamentalism in Japan, one is tempted to turn in the direction of the New Religions, organizations whose worldviews sometimes seem notoriously at odds with that of the modern world. In most of the New Religions there is virtually no difference between salvation and plain good luck. Toda Jōsei once even called his own sect, Sōka Gakkai, a "happiness manufacturing machine."[49] The chant used by the Agonshū sect nicely catches the spirit of this "inner-worldly" salvation: "Let's do it! I will certainly succeed! I am blessed with very good luck! I will certainly do well! I will definitely win!"[50]

Joseph M. Kitagawa describes the New Religions in the following way:

> These new religions present nothing new, as far as their religious contents are concerned. Many of them derived their doctrines from Shinto, Confucianism, Buddhism, or Christianity. Their teachings are eclectic and not well systematized, but their simple, direct, and practical beliefs and practices appeal to the masses who do not feel at home with the complex doctrines of established religions. . . . Most of them are highly centralized in their organizational structure, utilizing cell group systems as well as incentive plans. A few of them have semi-militaristic disciplines. All of them use modern mass media . . . and have efficient methods of tithing or its equivalent. What gives each of these new religions its distinctive character is the personality of the founder or organizers. Many of these boast unusual spiritual powers in divination, sorcery, incantation, fortune-telling, and healing which betray the shamanistic roots of their religious orientations. They also have the capacity to attract and maintain rapport with a large number of followers. For the most part, these new religions draw their adherents from the lower middle class, especially middle-aged and older women, although a few of them claim to have some followers among the upper middle class and young people as well.[51]

The Japanese term "New Religion" actually covers a broad spectrum of religious movements.[52] Basically they are alternatives or supplements to the Buddhist temple and Shinto shrine, Japan's "mainline denominations." Like political fundamentalism, the New Religions seem to have originated as a reaction to the growing complexity and frustration of Japanese life. The earliest nineteenth-century New Religions, for example, appeared in Kansai, the western part of the country where double cropping, advanced agricultural, and commercial techniques had resulted in an expansive, competitive economy. The spread of markets rocked the social order of towns and villages in the area. Economic monopolies *(za)* were destroyed and the nouveaux riches struggled to wrest power and status from declining families. Monopolistic religious cliques *(miyaza)* made up of the old established families disappeared, giving way to a new, more inclusive form of Shinto parish, the *ujiko*. The evangelistic, "whosoever will may come" attitude of the New Religions was congenial to the social and economic ambitions of up-and-coming families. As time went on, other New Religions arose in response to even greater upheavals—social, political, military and economic. While members of the New Religions seldom came from circles directly responsible for the new political fundamentalism, religion for them was often at least in part a reaction to the same crises.

Before we ask whether or not the New Religions are fundamentalist, we have to recognize the differences between them. In the West, vernacular religious movements often make their debuts as purveyors of magic or harbingers of eschatological utopias. As time goes on, they begin to attract more respectable clienteles. The charismatics and faith healers of the first generation give way to the theologians and ecclesiocrats of the second. Before long the sect becomes a church, or, to use the American term, a denomination. The instrumental motives that bound the first generation to the sect are replaced by social and familial obligations holding the second generation to its denomination.

Virtually the same "escalator" that elevates sects to the status of denominations in the West is at work in Japan's New Religions.[53] The first Japanese religions to ride the escalator were the sects of the late Tokugawa period: Kurozumi-kyō (1814), Tenri-kyō (1838), and Konkō-kyō (1859). Being the first to get on, they have been the first to get to the top, so that today they are among the more respectable of the New Religions. Hardacre has shown, for example, that in Okayama, Kurozumi-kyō now actually functions as a mainline Shinto shrine.[54] Likewise, Tenri-kyō, once a mere vernacular healing cult, today is part of the middle-class establishment of Kansai. Its founder, Nakayama Miki, after experiencing mediumistic trances, developed the healing powers of a traditional medium or shaman. Because she also criticized the government, she was repeatedly investigated and jailed by the authorities. Today, however, Tenri boasts a well-known university and library. Its hospital combines the best of Western medicine with the sect's traditional healing practices. And needless to say, its leaders are no longer at odds with the political establishment.

A second wave of New Religions—Ōmoto-kyō (1892), Honmichi (1913), Seichō no Ie (1930), Sōka Gakkai (1930), and Risshō Kōsei-kai (1938) among them—appeared after the establishment of the new Meiji regime. While claiming to heal the sick and improve the material life of their followers, these groups sought to induce in the faithful a Confucian-like sense of self-control. They promoted national, family, and religious identities, moral purpose, and a worldview which, apart from its archaic symbolism, was basically congruent with that of Japanese society in general.[55] Like Tenri-kyō, many have developed spiritual therapies designed to supplement, and not just replace, medical treatment. Today these groups (together with the pre-Meiji sects) are called the Older New Religions.

Let us take a closer look at one of these movements. Rishō Kōsei-kai was founded by Niwano Nikkyo, the one-time owner of a small pickle shop in Tokyo, and Naganuma Myoko, a sickly, shamanistic woman regarded by her followers as a "living Buddha." Originally, both were members of the Reiyūkai sect. The reason why they left Reiyūkai is obscure. Some say that it was because they were dissatisfied with the group's magical repetition of the Nichirenite chant, *Namu Myōhō Renge Kyō*. Others say, however, that Niwano was publicly chastised by the leader of Reiyūkai for his interest in divination and left in disgust. Whatever the cause of the schism, once the break was made, Naganuma became the charismatic leader of the new group, while Niwano played the classical Weberian role of the "routinizer" of his co-founder's charisma.

Most individuals join Risshō Kōsei-kai because of sickness or some other personal misfortune. Once a member, the individual is firmly tied to the organization in a variety of ways. Hierarchically, he becomes part of an ascending spiral of groups: a *han* (a group of seven families), a *kumi* (a group of fifty families), a *hōza* (three hundred families), and finally, a "church," or *kyōkai*. In addition, there are special groups of men, women, and young people designated for study and evangelism. What binds the individual most firmly to the group, however, is a personal relationship with, and sense of obligation to, the person who initially brought him into the church, namely, his "guiding parent" *(michibiki oya)*. Daily devotions in the local church, grand festivals (such as the Oeshiki, a day commemorating the death of the prophet Nichiren), and other meetings give the individual a collective setting in which to express and reaffirm his faith. Among these, the most important and effective is hōza. Not to be confused with the group of three hundred families just mentioned, this kind of hōza is sometimes called "group therapy." Small groups of ten to twenty people (mostly women) meet at various times throughout the day in their churches. McFarland describes the meetings in this way:

> Within an atmosphere of mutual trust and concern, troubled people reveal their difficulties to one another with a frankness that seems very un-Japanese. Problems that some more propriety-minded Japanese would die rather than reveal are laid out and explored with remarkable candor in these groups. Seemingly, nothing is too intimate or personal to be discussed. One's own illness or that of a family member, strained family relations, financial crises, behavior of children, juvenile delinquency, a philandering husband, and sexual incompatibility or inadequacy—all these and many other problems are eligible topics.[56]

While hōza is often called a "T group" or "group therapy," careful observers have noted some revealing differences. While Western group therapy tends to be open-ended, with all members of the group offering their advice and opinions, hōza is controlled by its clear-cut, well-defined religious framework. After the individual has revealed his or her personal problem, an official "theological" solution is suggested and the sect's Salvation Syndrome is directly applied to the case. This usually consists of advice to worship one's ancestors with greater devotion, observe proper "verbal, mental and bodily action," and follow the Bodhisattva Way no matter what the odds.

Over the years, Risshō Kōsei-kai has undergone a remarkable transformation, due in part, it seems, to the bad publicity the sect once received for miracle mongering. Whatever the ultimate reason, in recent decades Risshō Kōsei-kai has sought to distance itself from the fundamentalistic image of its archrival, Sōka Gakkai. It has done as much as possible to seem (and be) a reasonable, mainstream movement. However, as a vernacular religion, it naturally must continue to satisfy its members' needs for miracles and magic. This is provided largely by ancestor worship, divination (onomancy), and practices related to the idea of karma. Since the death of Naganuma in 1957, however, Niwano has tried to set the church on a more sophisticated course. As a practical organizer and teacher rather than a charismatic, he has called upon professional Buddhologists to provide the sect with doctrinal guidance. Some of these scholars (who often are not members of the sect themselves) are given an opportunity to write for church-sponsored publications. Others apparently have helped ghostwrite some of Niwano's own scholarly works. The process of the routinization of charisma has been accompanied to some degree by another socioreligious tendency, namely, the "disenchantment," or decline of magic (Max Weber's *Entzauberung der Welt*). Interest in the occult, geomancy, and shamanistic revelations is now played down. The period of Naganuma's ministry is now regarded, in Buddhist terminology, as the age or dispensation of "skillful means" *(hōben),* that is, a time when it was legitimate to appeal to the masses and spread the dharma by means of shamanism and charisma. Weaned away from magical practices, members nowadays are directed toward an ethical way of life based on repentance, personal purification, and the morality of the Bodhisattva. Nichiren himself is venerated not as a prophet (or the implacable monomaniac that he actually was) but simply as a teacher who underscored the importance of the *Lotus Sūtra*. At the popular level, many members probably continue to think that repetition of the Nichirenite chant is efficacious in and of itself, and that a pilgrimage to the church's Great Sacred Hall in Tokyo will cure any and all diseases. But a more sophisticated faith is now available, a worldview based on the Four Noble Truths and the Eightfold Path and other doctrines of classical Buddhism. Finally, like other mainline denominations, Risshō Kōsei-kai boasts a number of welfare institutions—hospitals, libraries, schools, and retirement homes—institutions established primarily for the benefit of its own members.

Immediately after World War II, the challenge of sheer physical survival left the Japanese little time for religion. Nevertheless hundreds of sects began to spring up around the country. The period of rapid economic growth from 1951 to 1972 was a time of winnowing and sifting for these movements. Some disappeared; others—like Sōka Gakkai, Risshō Kōsei-kai, and Reiyūkai—rode the wave of economic recovery to become enormously successful mass movements.

Getting on the escalator today are the so-called New New Religions—groups like Mahikari (1963), GLA (the "God Light Association") (1969), and Agonshū (1978). Some of these groups are virtual hothouses of magic and miracles. Their worldviews and practices are based not just on the Sino-Japanese tradition; they also draw from Western spiritualism, theosophy, and other occult sources. Sociologically the New New Religions are marked by rapid growth, high membership volatility, and the expansion of a cohort of very young believers.[57]

Most of the New Religions combine gospels of "saving luck" with a reaffirmation of traditional (i.e., prewar) values. This often translates into a conservative, indeed a reactionary, political ideology. Sūkyō Mahikari, one of Japan's New New Religions, for example, teaches that postwar democracy is merely a product of the "materialistic" culture of the West. Its imposition on Japan by the American Occupation caused many Japanese to be possessed by evil spirits—angered, apparently, by the corruption of the country by foreigners. Communism, on the other hand, was sent by the gods as an omen warning mankind of a coming eschatological ordeal known as the "Baptism by Fire." In the face of the double threats of democracy (from America) and communism (from China and Russia), Japan must quickly re-establish the "unity of religion and government" and the hierarchical relationships tradition had established between husbands and wives, parents and children. Likewise, the country must rediscover the ancient values of loyalty and patriotism.

Like other New Religions, the Mahikari sect has its own cosmogonic myth. The world, it teaches, was once ruled by the Japanese emperors from the "Continent of Mu," a land mass in the middle of the Pacific Ocean. After some time, the "spiritual" gods determined to speed up man's material civilization by retiring from the world and letting "materialistic" deities take over. The divine plan worked. But as man's material civilization improved, crime, wars, and human suffering also increased. To punish wayward humankind, the gods inflicted Mu with a series of devastating earthquakes and the continent finally sank beneath the ocean. Today, only the highest part of Mu, the Japanese archipelago, is left standing, a solitary witness to the continent which had once been the center of the world and the origin of the human race. If Japan heeds the call of the Savior, Okada Kōtama, the world in the twenty-first century will once again be reunited under her emperor and the glory of the ancient Muvian empire will be restored. The leaders of the new world will be the "Seed People" who support the Mahikari churches today. Thus, like other millenarian cults, Mahikari promises its humble followers that someday "the first will be last and the last first."[58]

The teachings of Mahikari's founder, Okada Kōtama, are not only ethnocentric; they are a religious sublimation of some of the values of Japanese fascism. Mahikari puts its neofascist ideas into practice in various ways. It uses an inverted form of the Buddhist swastika as one of its regalia. At festivals, Okada would mount a large dais to review his disciples marching before him in military formation. As they passed by, the troops smartly extended their arms to give their self-proclaimed messiah the Nazi salute. Today the impact of Okada's political views is reflected in the voting patterns of Mahikari members. About 54 percent claim to support the conservative, fervently anticommunist LDP. In an election in 1976, the LDP won only 26 percent of the Osaka vote in general. In contrast, Mahikari church in Osaka gave the Party 46 percent of its votes.[59]

With a membership of twelve to seventeen million, Sōka Gakkai is the largest of Japan's New Religions. Although its roots go back to the prewar writings of Makiguchi Tsunesaburō, the religion became a mass movement only in the postwar period under the leadership of Toda Jōsei and Ikeda Daisaku. Organized as a lay support group of the Nichiren Shō-shū sect of Buddhism, Sōka Gakkai teaches that it is the only true religion in Japan, or rather in the world, and that worship of a scroll bearing the name of the Lotus Sūtra and the recitation of the chant "Adoration to the Lotus of the Wonderful Law" *(Namu Myōhō Renge-kyō)* are the unique keys to human happiness.

Sōka Gakkai has shown itself to be the most aggressive of the forty-odd Nichiren sects, which in general have a well-deserved reputation for pugnacity. Gakkai members were once instructed to destroy the Shinto god shelves and Buddhist memorial tablets in their homes and to spit or make obscene gestures when passing buildings belonging to other sects. Most notorious of all was their practice of *shakubuku,* or evangelism by "breaking and subduing" the convert. In extreme cases, *shakubuku* was a euphemism for religious terrorism. Zealous evangelists invaded strangers' homes, refusing to leave until each member of the family converted. Some potential converts claim to have been blackmailed or even sexually abused. Such tactics have won the sect an enormous following, but also a bad reputation, especially in the eyes of the educated, secular segments of the population. As the religion neared the top of the sociological escalator, however, it became more sensitive to criticism. It developed a more subtle form of evangelism *(shoju),* refined its "theology," and in 1971 founded a university. President Ikeda Daisaku has raised his own stature considerably by means of well-publicized meetings with such luminaries as Henry Kissinger, Chou En Lai, and Arnold Toynbee.[60]

While Mahikari and many other New Religions throw their weight behind specific existing parties and candidates, Sōka Gakkai has spawned its own political organization, Kōmeitō, or the Clean Government Party. Although the Gakkai officially severed its ties with Kōmeitō in 1970, it is no secret that nearly all support for the party still comes from its religious parent. The Gakkai's original political aim was to offer an alternative to the established political parties, which it claimed were "controlled by foreign states."[61] Its ultimate goal was the "union of Buddhism and politics" *(ōbutsu-myōgō)* and the establishment of a "Buddhist democracy." While these notions are no more sinister than the Buddhocratic slogans of some of the mainline Buddhist denominations—e.g., "revere the emperor and serve the Buddha," or "protect the country by promoting Zen"—other Buddhist groups, having no political parties of their own, do not seem as capable of influencing political debate. While denying that the Gakkai was trying to restore the "unity of religion and government" of pre-1945 Japan, President Ikeda insisted that political thought and action always rest on religious principles. Since all religions but Sōka Gakkai are "false," the happiness of Japan—indeed, of the whole world—was thought to depend on the Gakkai and its political wing.

Sōka Gakkai's original political aims were naturally a source of concern to Japanese committed to the country's postwar Constitution. In 1967, one of the sect's directors announced: "Our purpose is to purify the world through the propagation of the teachings of the Nichiren Sho Denomination. Twenty years from now we will occupy the majority of seats in the National Diet and establish the Nichiren Sho Denomination as the national religion of Japan and construct a national altar at Mount Fuji."[62]

Twenty years have come and gone and only the "altar at Mount Fuji" has been built, but it is not a "national altar." However, Kōmeitō has now risen to be the second-largest opposition party, trailing only the Socialist Democratic party. Although its political fortunes have shifted time and again, it has nonetheless had about fifty-five representatives in the Diet since 1967. Twenty years ago James W. White found that apart from the construction of playgrounds, sewers, and highway guardrails, Kōmeitō's "substantive, autonomous achievements have been few."[63] This remains the case. Kōmeitō's original platform pledged the party to a "neo-" or "humanitarian socialism" (modeled after the British welfare state), to the "welfare of all people on a middle of the road *(chūdō)* basis," and to a "centralism beyond left-right conflict." With this platform Kōmeitō seems to have captured the middle of the political spectrum, which is nebulously anti-left, while Mahikari, Reiyūkai, Seichō no Ie, and other New Religions have appealed to the political instincts of the Tory proletariat and the conservative lower-middle classes. Historically, however, the political stands taken by Kōmeitō have shifted from the ambiguous platitudes of the 1950s to a de facto espousal of stands similar to those of the LDP. However, the Party has also dabbled in alliances with various other center parties, and even with the Communists.[64]

In 1980, the number of Kōmeitō Diet members was reduced from fifty-eight to thirty-four. This setback was explained largely in terms of popular discontent with the party's critical attitude toward the security treaty with the United States and its position that the Self-Defense Force was unconstitutional.[65] Kōmeitō responded to this stunning defeat the following year by "tilting to the right," proclaiming its support for both the security treaty and the SDF. For the first time its platform mentioned "the threat of the Soviet Union." Subsequently critics have accused Kōmeitō of having no genuine social or political commitments of its own. One must note, however, that Kōmeitō has never tried to put a religious (let alone a fundamentalist) payload into orbit. The reason is simple: in order to gain votes, the Party coveted broader popular support. This could only be obtained by getting aboard the escalator that magically transforms religious sects and political fringe groups into respectable mainline movements. Throughout the years, Kōmeitō has learned to compromise with the status quo—which in contemporary Japan is plutocratic, polyarchic, and generally respectful of civil rights. This in itself tends to curb the aspirations of the political fundamentalist.

Political respectability, however, has repeatedly eluded Sōka Gakkai and Kōmeitō, largely because of their leaders' poor judgment and (occasionally) personal corruption. In the 1950s, the Gakkai came under fire for conducting illegal house-to-house political campaigning under the guise of religious evangelism. In 1969 Kōmeitō and the Gakkai created a furor when they tried by all means, fair and foul, to prevent Fujiwara Hirotatsu from publishing his expose, *I Denounce Sōka Gakkai (Sōka Gakkai o kiru)*. The controversy over this book caused a precipitous loss of membership in both organizations and finally led to the official separation of the party and the Gakkai.

In recent years, the party has received even more bad press. In 1981 the Gakkai's legal advisor, Yamazaki Masatomo, was arrested on suspicion of receiving an enormous bribe from the Gakkai after promising not to divulge the group's secrets. Recently Ōhashi Toshio, a Kōmeitō member of the Lower House, was thrown out of the Party after he criticized the honorary Gakkai president, Ikeda Daisaku, for running both Sōka Gakkai and Kōmeitō for his own personal gain. In January 1989, Tashiro Fujio, Kōmeitō's only member in the Upper House, was indicted for bribery. On 21 May 1989, Yano Jun'ya resigned from Kōmeitō because of his involvement in the affairs of a scandal-ridden company. Finally, Kōmeitō's Ikeda Katsuya had the dubious distinction of being the first opposition member of the government to be indicted in connection with the Recruit scandal which brought down the government of Prime Minister Takeshita Noboru.[66]

New Religions as Fundamentalist Movements

The followers of the New Religions are fundamentalistic in some ways but not in others. One senses in their sermons and propaganda a keen resentment of the social elite and a frustration over the decline of traditional Japanese values. The anger of these groups is secondary, however, to a thirst for prestige and recognition that can be quenched only by assuming a deferential attitude toward the powers that be. The messiahs of the New Religions vent considerable anger and, in so doing, win the sympathy of those disturbed about and resentful of the direction of postwar Japan. Yet the aroused masses are seldom mobilized for direct social or political action. One might say that the attitude of the messiahs and the New Religions is a symbolic or dramaturgical anger. In most cases resentment and frustration are dealt with by means of symbolic regression. Some sects, such as Tenri-kyō and Mahikari, have their own cosmogonic myths. Others, like Sōka Gakkai, return to the exclusive, dogmatic message of a prophet of the past. All would like to return to the values of prewar Japan, and some, like Seichō no Ie and Reiyūkai, to some aspects of the imperial system itself.

Not all fundamentalists are fixated on the inerrancy of sacred texts. This, at least, is not generally a characteristic of Japan's New Religions, even though texts, such as the Lotus Sūtra, are venerated by some. The aggressiveness of the New Religions is seldom due to arguments over how rightly to "divide the Word of Truth." While factionalism is rife among the New Religions and in Japanese society in general, religious groups seldom break up over the interpretation of a text. Usually at issue are money, conflicting claims to leadership, and allegations of personal corruption. Furthermore, with the possible exceptions of Konkō-kyō and Risshō Kōsei-kai, most of the New Religions show little interest in systematic theology. The founder's own emotionally charged, religious bricolage seems perfectly suited to meet the needs of the masses coming to them in search of health, happiness, and good luck. The Protestant fundamentalist's habit of brandishing "proof texts" is thus quite rare in Japan's New Religions.

The New Religions also seem to deviate from a comparative definition of fundamentalism in that few of their followers are moral rigorists. Instead the morality of most New Religions finds its normative basis primarily in prewar popular national custom. While most instill in the faithful a spirit of self-mastery, some—Mahikari, for example—assume that there already are too many moral rules and principles in the world. What is important is to empower people to carry out existing precepts and live happy, healthy, and prosperous lives. This can be done only by providing them with the appropriate magicoreligious techniques, such as amulets, chants, prayer scrolls, and other nostrums.

Finally, most of the New Religions have had to compromise with their competitors, especially with Buddhist family temples and neighborhood Shinto shrines. For most Japanese, these institutions are objects of the *obligatory* religious affiliations of kith and kin.[67] Like cult movements in the West, the New New Religions pride themselves on open-ended membership practices. One is allowed to be a member of religions like Mahikari while simultaneously participating in the the activities of temples, shrines, and even Christian churches. Like Western cults, the New Religions show virtually no interest in disciplining wayward members. There is in fact almost no way to measure or define "waywardness." Thus the sociological profile of the New Religions differs in important ways from the exclusiveness and "moral efficiency" which we in the West associate with the fundamentalist movement.

Sōka Gakkai (especially in its period of unrestrained *shakubuku*) is the group most closely approximating fundamentalism. However, it too has begun to ascend the sociological escalator to positions of greater power and respectability. Compromising with the status quo, it has become increasingly mellow. Critics in Japan continue to worry about it, especially since its huge following still gives blind allegiance to Kōmeitō, a party whose political ideology is vague and unpredictable. The movement today is perhaps opportunistic rather than fundamentalistic. Its social stands apparently depend on its own self-interest and the opportunities afforded by each political situation. In the future its fundamentalism could become more adamant. For political reasons, however, it is likely to take a more moderate course.

Conclusions

The word *fundamentalism* has come to us primarily from the history of Judaism, Christianity, and Islam, religions based on monotheism, revelation, prophecy, and canons of written scripture. It may be that an extension of the term to the vastly different religions of East Asia will ultimately be deemed undesirable, even for analytical purposes. In this essay, however, I have defined fundamentalism in a way that avoids reference to the specific characteristics of these "Abrahamic" traditions. Nevertheless, I find in Japan a tendency to deal with complex social and political realities by withdrawing symbolically to the imagined simplicities of the past—a tendency that can be called fundamentalist. Although the Japanese have sometimes displayed an inclination to impose upon their society the cultural blueprints belonging to societies at "lower" levels of social and/or cultural differentiation, I do not believe fundamentalism of this sort is a necessary feature of Japanese culture.

It could be argued that Japanese culture by its nature discourages the growth of fundamentalism of a religious sort. The very "malleability, relativity and negotiability of truth in Japan" seem to make commitment to religious fundamentalism difficult to sustain.[68] Japan's long tradition of syncretism—or what could technically be called "centripetal religious differentiation"—has imposed an implicit civility on religious sects that makes the exclusive, dogmatic spirit of genuine fundamentalism difficult to maintain. In the past, only a few "single-practice" sects (such as the Nichirenites mentioned above) have dared to challenge the culture's syncretistic imperative. It may be that religions which entertain immanental concepts of the sacred (inspired, for example, by Mahayana Buddhism's emphasis on nondualism and the Original Awakening of all sentient beings) may simply be too relaxed about the human condition to succumb to the temptation of religious fundamentalism. In Japanese Buddhism there is no fall of man, Satan, or everlasting hell. Good and evil have not become the ontological dichotomy they are in the Abrahamic traditions. One is to cling to nothing, to no person, thing, or country—not even to religion, Buddha, or nirvana itself. Since salvation must be found in this illusory, samsaric world of flux, nothing is "fixed." Social and political agendas are legitimated not in terms of abstract principles (as in the West), but by projecting an image of benevolent paternalism.[69] One could argue that this highly fluid and absorbent worldview has been the foundation of Japan's protean culture, contextual values, and situational loyalties. One could therefore conclude that Japan's traditional culture may itself have kept religious fundamentalism in check.

The nationalism appearing in Japan today may be similar to that of the late 1930s, but it is forced to defend itself in a new, pluralistic climate. At several crucial points it has been checked by concerned groups of citizens (secular and religious) in ways made possible by the postwar constitutional order. Nevertheless, some scholars argue that the fascism of the period from 1930 to 1945 was not merely an "aberration in Japanese history."[70] In this view, the Occupation's achievements—far from the purge and reformation Americans like to think they were—were largely cosmetic. The Japanese system remained intact. The year 1945 therefore was not the watershed it is believed to have been. If these authorities are right, political fundamentalism may remain a latent structural element of Japanese culture. (Of course what is latent need not become manifest.)

What makes political fundamentalism of this sort seem so elusive is the fact that we in the West are used to a fundamentalism of a vastly different sort.[71] Some might argue that there can be no religious fundamentalism in a culture without universal principles, and that there can be no political fundamentalism without the traditional (Western) concept of the state. The experience of the Japanese seems to gainsay *both* of these presuppositions. What we seem to have in Japan is—and this *is* paradoxical—a kind of situational fundamentalism beholden to neither fixed principles nor the state.

In his book about what he considers the worrisome aspects of the modern Japanese "System," Karel Van Wolferen has written at great length about the underside of Japan's postwar success story—about an economy which routinely exploits foreign and domestic markets, a press that censors itself, movies that glorify war, allegations of police torture, and the underdevelopment (or underuse) of law. He points out that the Japanese Supreme Court refuses to exercise its constitutional role of judicial review, and that the LDP has plans to consolidate its (de facto) one-party rule by creating a complete political monopoly—the "mass inclusionary system" of the "new middle mass." Van Wolferen contends that unlike the Western democracies, the Japanese political System has internal "balances" but no real "checks."[72] Keenly aware of the power of their rivals, Japanese groups try to maintain a general equilibrium within the System. But, when the System loses its own balance, there is virtually no way to curb its own momentum from within.

Today the System's apparent inability to check its unlimited economic expansion lends considerable credibility to the Van Wolferen thesis.[73] While trade imbalances have already generated serious international friction, the greater fear is that, if thwarted, Japanese ambitions might assume the shape of an aggressive political fundamentalism once again. While militarism itself still seems a remote possibility, some Japanese intellectuals have already called for the development of a nuclear arsenal. More commonly—as in *The Japan That Can Say "No,"* by Ishihara Shintarō and Morita Akio—talk turns to how the country can use its formidable technological prowess to play off the United States against the Soviet Union and thereby pave the way for the "Century of Japan."

We have seen that institutionalized political fundamentalism seems to have been frustrated largely by the Constitution itself and by the determined efforts of various individuals and movements dedicated to democracy and civil liberties. The moral peccadillos and political misjudgments of the fundamentalists themselves have also contributed to fundamentalism's defeat. While social conformity is alive and well in postmodern Japan, blatant fanaticism and coercion are limited to the underworld and to a few religious and political sects. Nevertheless, the fear, anger, and resentment that nourish fundamentalism around the globe can be sensed in Japan's reaction to the constant hectoring by the West over unfair trade practices. The distrust one senses in fundamentalism in the West is also well entrenched in Japanese institutions. One wonders, for example, whether the omnipresence of the group is just a fact of Japanese culture, or whether the leaders of Japanese schools, businesses, and other institutions simply do not trust individuals to study and work on their own. Many of the same institutions also make use of coercion, another characteristic often associated with fundamentalism. "In Japan, far from being abhorred, intimidation is accepted as an inevitable aspect of social and political life; inevitable because the informal, non-legal relations that characterize the System lead very naturally to dependence on informal coercion (i.e., intimidation) to maintain order and safeguard the power of power-holders."[74]

In conclusion, it seems to me that religious fundamentalism (as we use the term in the Western academic world) has not generally prospered in Japan. Single-practice sects and fanatical New Religions ultimately tend to be reabsorbed by a generally tolerant and syncretistic pattern of religious affiliations. Nevertheless, the memory of the religiopolitical fundamentalism that swept the country in the thirties and forties continues to influence the perception of Japan both in the West and in the rest of East Asia. The recent tendency of Japanese politicians and intellectuals to reject criticism of Japan as "Japan bashing" only strengthens the foreigner's anxiety that once again the country might try to cope with external pressure by narcissistically withdrawing to the myths of cultural and racial homogeneity. Thus political fundamentalism (informed by civil-religious symbolism and slogans) is a more significant possibility for contemporary Japan than strictly religious fundamentalism. Yet although nationalism and self-confidence are on the rise, genuine political fundamentalism remains only a minority position. Nevertheless, dealing with international confrontations and complex domestic issues by symbolically de-differentiating society, regressing to the myth of racial purity, and re-creating a culturally united and morally efficient family-state is certainly not without precedent in recent Japanese history.

Whether political fundamentalism ever again becomes more than a possibility depends, then, on the situation. The conditions that led to the situational fundamentalism of the past include the threat of foreign domination and recurring bouts of inflation, deflation, and unemployment, economic events usually followed by protests against the political and economic leadership of the country. In the future, similar situations might result in similar patterns of reaction. The future course of Japanese fundamentalism may well be determined by the international ramifications of the economic unification of Europe in 1992. If the economic unification leads to the erection of new trade barriers and the partition of the globe into exclusive trade zones, the establishment of a new Greater East Asia Co-Prosperity Sphere might seem to be an attractive—indeed, a realistic—alternative for Japan. This in turn could lead to the spread of new forms of political and religious fundamentalism not only in Japan but also in the United States.

Notes

1. To one familiar with such scenes, the sentiments expressed by the speakers are quite predictable, each speech having been cast in the invisible mold of the church's own Salvation Syndrome. Perhaps more important is the fact that the speeches are carefully read and censored by church officials before the festival begins.

2. H. Neill McFarland, *The Rush Hour of the Gods: A Study of New Religious Movements in Japan* (New York: Harper Colophon Books, 1970), p. 195.

3. One-fourth to one-third of Japanese families have members active in the New Religions.

4. On Japanese television, after reporting an act of terrorism inspired by religious fundamentalists abroad, the anchor will often pause and say something like, "We Japanese can hardly imagine people who take their religion so seriously."

5. I must say at the outset, however, that I realize that this endeavor may prompt some Japanese to accuse me of the kind of Japan bashing *(Nihon tataki)* which unfortunately has become common in recent years. While I wish to assure Japanese readers that such is not my intention, I must admit that there are some aspects of contemporary Japanese life which do cause me deep concern. The reasons for the opprobrium attached to the term *fundamentalism* in Japan and elsewhere lie in its history. Fundamentalism was initially the self-designation of conservative Protestant groups at loggerheads with biblical scholarship and some aspects of modern science (the theory of evolution in particular). Equally important is the fundamentalists' reputation for rancorous particularism, a partisan spirit that questions the religious credentials of all outside their own sect. Journalism has applied the fundamentalist label to Shi'ite Iran, a country which is the declared enemy of the United States and a known source of terrorism around the globe. Since these two cases—the Protestant and the Islamic—constitute the classical types of fundamentalism in the popular and academic mind, it is probably impossible to expunge all negative connotations from the term. Thus, the history of the word itself inevitably raises the problem of the fairness and/or bias of scholars who use it. But this is not necessarily grounds for eschewing fundamentalism as a term in religious research. To appreciate a religion is not necessarily the best or only way to understand it. Indeed, those who espouse a studied "non-judgmental" approach to religious studies often seem to miss what to the casual observer is most obvious about religion. In religious studies, as in the rest of the humanities, scholars who come to their work without values or commitments of their own seldom understand or appreciate the significance of their own subject matter. I do believe that fundamentalism in its pure form is a potential threat to the kind of open, democratic society in which I hope to live and raise my children. Nevertheless, my purpose here is to understand and explain fundamentalism, not to criticize or belittle it.

6. Cf. Martin E. Marty, "Fundamentalism as a Social Phenomenon," *Bulletin of the American Academy of Arts and Sciences.* 42, no. 2 (November 1988): 15–29.

7. S. N. Eisenstadt describes the notion more technically as "the ways through which the main social functions or the major institutional spheres of society become disassociated from one another, attached to specialized collectivities and roles, and organized in relatively specific and autonomous symbolic and organizational frameworks within the confines of the same institutionalized system." S. N. Eisenstadt, "Social Change, Differentiation, and Evolution," *American Sociological Review* 29 (1964): 376.

8. As Talcott Parsons put it, "differentiation processes also pose new problems of integration." *Societies: Evolutionary and Comparative Perspectives* (Englewood Cliffs: Prentice-Hall, 1966), p. 22.

9. Talcott Parsons, "Religion in a Modern Pluralistic Society," *Review of Religious Research* 7, no. 3 (Spring 1966):139.

10. Parsons (ibid.) argues that, contrary to what the fundamentalist believes, liberalism (or modernism) is not without its own fundamental beliefs and values. Ideally, liberalism is a system which trusts the individual to put those fundamentals into practice and does not keep him under surveillance while he tries. Insofar as there is no conscience without freedom and trust, liberalism can be said to presuppose and even create conscience. When liberalism fails to generate conscience in this way, or when in spite of its idealism, the economic institu-

tions associated with it run amok, liberalism may create a crisis, making the more efficient moral and political solutions of fundamentalism extremely attractive.

11. Although the political fundamentalism dealt with in this paper happens to be a fundamentalism of the right, the concept of fundamentalism can also be applied to the left. The primary difference is that in the latter case, symbolic regression is replaced by an equally audacious reduction of complex reality to a yet-to-be-realized utopia or system. In both kinds of fundamentalism, anger, distrust, coercion, and the restriction and manipulation of conscience seem to be essential ingredients.

12. Luckmann says that in America, for example, secondary institutions include "syndicated advice columns, 'inspiration' literature ranging from tracts on positive thinking to *Playboy* magazine, *Reader's Digest* versions of popular psychology, the lyrics of popular hits." Thomas Luckmann, *The Invisible Religion: The Problem of Religion in Modern Society* (New York: Macmillan, 1968), p. 104. A putative case of diffuse fundamentalism is called "Japan Theory." A recent media phenomenon, Japan Theory in some ways seems to be the secularization of the country's prewar civil religion.

13. Richard H. Mitchell, *Thought Control in Prewar Japan* (Ithaca: Cornell University Press, 1976), p. 30. The atmosphere in Japan during these years was probably not unlike that of Iran under the late shah. Coffee shops and bell-bottomed pants were just as offensive to traditional Japanese as wineshops and Western hats were to Iran's Shi'ites. Both countries were responding in "fundamentalist" ways to rapid, unbalanced growth and the careless distortion of tradition. In both cases, massive attempts were made to de-differentiate complex societies and force upon them "morally efficient" regimes. The major difference in the two cases was that in Japan political fundamentalism was largely the work of the government and its official scholars *(goyō gakusha)*. Japanese political fundamentalism was therefore imposed from above. In Iran, on the other hand, fundamentalism came from the alienated mullahs and the masses and was therefore generated from below. Cf. Edward Mortimer, *Faith and Power: The Politics of Islam* (New York: Vintage Books, 1982), pp. 322–29.

14. Mitchell, *Thought Control,* p. 32. Emphasis mine.

15. Hideo Kishimoto, *Japanese Religion in the Meiji Era* (Tokyo: Toyo Bunka, 1969), pp. 133–34.

16. The military also controlled Shinto shrines set up in Korea, Taiwan and the other parts of Japanese-occupied East Asia.

17. Actually, the Constitution had not separated religion and state. It had merely provided for freedom of religion "within limits not prejudicial to peace and order, and not antagonistic to their [the people's] duties as subject" (article 28).

18. Kishimoto, *Japanese Religion in the Meiji Era,* p. 88.

19. Cited in Tetsuo Arima, *The Failure of Freedom: A Portrait of Modern Japanese Intellectuals* (Cambridge: Harvard University Press, 1969), p. 19.

20. Daniel C. Holtom, *The National Faith of Japan* (New York: E. P. Dutton, 1938), p. 84.

21. Sidney Mead, *The Lively Experiment* (New York: Harper, 1963), p. 68.

22. Helen Hardacre, *Shinto and the State, 1868–1988* (Princeton: Princeton University Press, 1989), p. 109.

23. *Kokumin Shinbun* (The People's Newspaper), 7 April 1893, cited in Kenneth B. Pyle, *The New Generation in Meiji Japan: The Problem of Cultural Identity, 1885–1895* (Stanford: Stanford University Press, 1969), p. 133.

24. Donald Keene, *Landscapes and Portraits: Appreciations of Japanese Culture* (Tokyo and Palo Alto: Kodansha, 1971), p. 267.

25. McFarland, *Rush Hour of the Gods* (1970), p. 155.

26. See Shunsuke Tsurumi, "Kotoba no omamoriteki shiyōhō ni tsuite," in *Nichijōteki shisō no kanōsei* (The possibility of everyday thought) (Tokyo: Chikuma Shobō,

1967); Richard H. Minear, *Japanese Tradition and Western Law: Emperor, State, and Law in the Thought of Hozumi Yatsuka* (Cambridge: Harvard University Press, 1970), pp. 57–68 on *kokutai.*

27. Tsurumi, "Kotoba no," p. 38.

28. Ibid., pp. 34–35.

29. Winston Davis, "Buddhism and the Modernization of Japan," *History of Religions* 28, no. 4 (May 1989): 306–8.

30. Tsurumi, "Kotoba no," p. 33.

31. Cited in R. P. Dore and Tsutomu Ōuchi, "Rural Origins of Japanese Fascism," in James W. Morley, ed., *Dilemmas of Growth in Prewar Japan* (Princeton: Princeton University Press, 1971), p. 323.

32. Hardacre, *Shinto and the State,* p. 9.

33. Cited in Sheldon M. Garon, "State and Religion in Imperial Japan, 1912–1945," *Journal of Japanese Studies* 12, no. 2 (1986): 301.

34. The "single practice" sects of the Late Heian and Kamakura Buddhism were in effect dramatic reductions of the multifaceted, balanced, and comprehensive nature of traditional Buddhism to one, simple religious discipline. The Zen master Dōgen (1200–1253), for example, made meditation *(zazen)* itself his "single practice." The fiercely intolerant prophet—"shaman" might be a more appropriate word—Nichiren (1222–1282) declared that the *Lotus Sūtra* and the chant *Namu Myōhō Renge Kyō* were keys to salvation. The True Pure Land sect, founded by Shinran Shōnin (1173–1262), was devoted to the worship of Amida Buddha and the chanting of his name (Namu Amida Butsu). In all these cases, the single-practice sects displayed an exclusive, sectarian tendency which defied other religious obligations, a tendency some historians have imprecisely called "monotheistic." Because the religious life of most of Japan was explicitly syncretistic, the Nichirenites and, to a lesser extent, the True Pure Land Buddhists, repeatedly found themselves at odds with their communities.

35. Ibid., p. 299.

36. Confraternities which were translocal and based on an exclusive, single practice had long been the source of resistance and rebellion. The Honganji Pure Land Movement is a good example. During the fifteenth and sixteenth centuries, confraternities of this sect (also called the Ikkō sect) became involved in violent uprisings called Ikkō-ikki. In the 1440s, members of the Ikkō sect seized control of Kaga and Noto provinces and ruled them until Honganji was brought to its knees by Oda Nobunaga in the sixteenth century. Nichirenites also offered resistance to the government at various times.

37. Cf. Winston Davis, "Buddhism and the Modernization of Japan."

38. Masao Maruyama, *Thought and Behaviour in Modern Japanese Politics,* ed. Ivan Morris (London: Oxford University Press, 1969), p. 6.

39. Masayuki Takagi, "Right Wing Draws Public Attention," *Japan Quarterly* 27, no. 4 (Oct.–Dec. 1980), p. 484.

40. Winston Davis, "The Hollow Onion: The Secularization of Japanese Civil Religion," in Hiroshi Mannari and Harumi Befu, eds., *The Challenge of Japan's Internationalization: Organization and Structure* (Tokyo: Kodansha, 1983), pp. 221–22.

41. Karel Van Wolferen, *The Enigma of Japanese Power: People and Politics in a Stateless Nation* (New York: Alfred A. Knopf, 1989), p. 211.

42. Cf. Hardacre, *Shinto and the State,* p. 145–49.

43. Recently Ishihara, the popular LDP politician, has called for the development of a Japanese version of Star Wars, or what he calls "air mines" (devices that would work like sea mines, but in outer space). Seeing high tech as Japan's ultimate weapon, Ishihara advocates a strategic control of the flow of advanced technology to other countries. Recently in *A Japan That Can Say No,* a book co-authored with Morita Akio, Ishihara calls for an autonomous Japanese foreign policy that would distance Japan from the United States. A deal could be made with the Soviets whereby Japan would transfer technology (at least computer chips) to the Russians in return for the recovery of her northern territories (held by the USSR since

the end of World War II) and for the rights to develop Siberia. Many believe that the only thing that prevents Ishihara from moving into the prime minister's office is the fear of other LDP politicians that he might prove to be a loose cannon. If prime ministers were chosen by popular vote, Ishihara might already be the head of the government. Cf. "A Japanese Nationalist Finds a Wide Audience for His Racial Theory," *The Wall Street Journal* (7 November 1989); "Land of Rising Sun Turns the Heat on America," (London) *Sunday Times* (29 October 1989), B6–7; and Ian Buruma, "Just Say Noh," *New York Review of Books* (7 December 1989), pp. 19–20.

44. *The Japan Times* (overseas weekly edition, 23 January 1988), p. 4.

45. At issue was article 20 of the Constitution, which stipulates that "no religious organization shall receive any privileges from the state," and article 89, which says that "No public money or other property shall be expended or appropriated for the use, benefit or maintenance of any religious institution." Cf. Hardacre, *Shinto and the State,* pp. 138 and 149–50.

46. It is difficult to fault the court in any simple way, especially since Mr. Nakaya and his parents were not Christians, and since it was possible to differentiate between the action taken by the Friendship Association and that of the Self-Defense Force itself.

47. While seven women have sat on the Chrysanthemum Throne, a law made in the Meiji period limits succession to the male descendants of the sun goddess. Asked recently whether the Meiji law violates the UN convention on women's rights, Foreign Minister Abe Shintarō had to remind his interrogators that imperial succession is not a basic human right.

48. Soon after he made his statement about the emperor's responsibility for the war, right-wing groups began to harass Mayor Motoshima. A man was arrested while trying to set the mayor's office on fire, and sound trucks encircled City Hall blaring rightist slogans. Finally, on 18 January 1990, the mayor was shot and nearly killed by the sub-chief of a small right-wing sect called the Spiritual Justice School. Motoshima's opinion, while controversial, was not exceptional. While there was much heartfelt grief at the death of the emperor, a poll released in February 1989 showed that approximately 60 percent of the Japanese people believe the emperor was "somewhat" responsible for World War II. *Japan Times* (11 March 1989), p. 3.

49. MacFarland, *Rush Hour* (1970), p. 79.

50. Ian Reader, "The Rise of a Japanese 'New New Religion': Themes in the Development of Agonsū," *Japanese Journal of Religious Studies* 15, no. 4 (December 1988): 244.

51. Joseph M. Kitagawa, *Religion in Japanese History* (New York: Columbia University Press, 1966), p. 333.

52. The term *shinkō shūkyō* (New Religion), coined in the early 1920s, was modeled after the expression *shinkō narikin* (nouveaux riches) and had the same negative connotations.

53. Winston Davis, "Japanese Religious Affiliations: Motives and Obligations," *Sociological Analysis* 44, no. 2 (Summer 1983).

54. Helen Hardacre, *Kurozumikyō and the New Religions of Japan* (Princeton: Princeton University Press, 1986), pp. 106–8.

55. Hardacre, *Kurozumikyō,* pp. 7ff.

56. H. Neil McFarland, *The Rush Hour of the Gods: A Study of New Religious Movements in Japan* (New York: Macmillan, 1967), p. 174.

57. It is estimated that as much as 60 percent of the membership of Sekai Mahikari Bunmei Kyōdan is made up of teenagers and that 40 percent of Ōyama Nezumi no Mikoto Shinjikyōkai are under thirty years of age. Yokoyama Michiyoshi and Nishiyama Shigeru, "Shin-shinshūkyō būmu: sono shōtai" (The New New Religions Boom: Its Real Nature), *Chūō Kōron* 103, no. 4 (1988): 134.

58. Winston Davis, *Dojo: Magic and Exorcism in Modern Japan* (Stanford: Stanford University Press, 1980), pp. 64–72.

59. Ibid., pp. 255–70. Hardacre found that 81.4 percent of the conservative Rei-

yūkai sect supports the LDP. *Lay Buddhism in Contemporary Japan: Reiyūkai Kyōdan* (Princeton: Princeton University Press, 1984), p. 252. ("Support" and "voting," of course, are two different things.)

60. Meeting foreign dignitaries up to and including the Pope seems to be an essential part of the legitimation process of the leaders of Japan's New Religions. The conversations with Toynbee (who was given a sizable honorarium) were especially useful to the sect since the illustrious British historian seemed to treat Ikeda as an equal, lavished praise on Sōka Gakkai, and extolled its place in world history. In this way then, Western clerics and academics unwittingly help to keep the escalator of respectability running (and well oiled) for the leaders of Japan's New Religions.

61. Ikeda Daisaku, *Seiji to shūkyō,* (Tokyo: Hōshōin, 1964), pp. 262–64.

62. Noah S. Brannen, *Sōka Gakkai* (Richmond, Va.: John Knox Press, 1968), p. 127.

63. James W. White, *The Sōka Gakkai and Mass Society* (Stanford: Stanford University Press, 1970), p. 154.

64. In 1975 it was learned that the Gakkai had entered into a secret ten-year entente cordial with the Japan Communist Party, a party which in public it routinely castigates. Word also got out that Ikeda Daisaku had been meeting secretly with Communist chief, Miyamoto Kenji, since the beginning of the year. In 1980 these scandals and other personal ones forced Ikeda to step down from the Gakkai's presidency to become "honorary president." Since this time he has continued to rule both organizations as an éminence grise.

65. Since the postwar Constitution forbids the development of armed forces, Japan is said to have a "Self-Defense Force," not an army, navy, or air force. This verbal sleight of hand has been upheld by the country's courts, but it is still regarded as unconstitutional by many. Although government spending on the SDF has been limited to about 1 percent of GNP, the phenomenal growth of the Japanese economy in recent years has already enabled the Japanese to build the world's third-largest military machine.

66. The Takeshita cabinet fell apart in 1989 after it was learned that the Recruit Company, an information and real estate firm, had given more than nine million dollars in political contributions to forty-four politicians, most of them members of the ruling LDP.

67. Cf. Winston Davis, "Japanese Religious Affiliations," *Sociological Analysis* 44, no. 2 (Summer 1983).

68. Van Wolferen, *Enigma,* p. 241.

69. Ibid., p. 202.

70. Ibid., pp. 347ff.

71. In the same way, it could be said that the reason why we have not been able to respond to the economic challenge posed by Japanese capitalism is that we are blinkered by a vastly different concept of capitalism.

72. Van Wolferen, *Enigma,* p. 340.

73. Here the political ideology of the Cold War seems to color our understanding of Japan as an economic competitor. The argument that the Soviet Union was a system unable to check its aggressive appetites from within was often used during the postwar years by those who advocated "containing" Communism. For an application of a significantly similar argument to Japan, see James Fallows's influential essay, "Containing Japan," *The Atlantic Monthly,* May 1989, pp. 40–54.

74. Van Wolferen, *Enigma,* p. 342. Even though "inevitable" is too strong a word, this is an important insight. For other examples of the coercive and manipulative side of Japan's success story, see Patricia Tsurumi, *The Other Japan: Postwar Realities* (Armonk, N.Y.: M. E. Sharpe, 1988); Satoshi Kamata, *Japan in the Passing Lane: An Insider's Account of Life in a Japanese Auto Factory* (New York: Pantheon Books, 1982); and Mikiso Hane, *Peasants, Rebels, and Outcastes* (New York: Pantheon, 1982).

Select Bibliography

Arima, Tetsuo. *The Failure of Freedom: A Portrait of Modern Japanese Intellectuals.* Cambridge: Harvard University Press, 1969.

Brannen, Noah S. *Sōka Gakkai.* Richmond, Va.: John Knox Press, 1968.

Davis, Winston. *Dojo: Magic and Exorcism in Modern Japan.* Stanford: Stanford University Press, 1980.

———. "The Hollow Onion." In Hiroshi Mannari and Harumi Befu, eds., *The Challenge of Japan's Internationalization.* Tokyo: Kodansha, 1983.

———. "Japanese Religious Affiliations: Motives and Obligations." *Sociological Analysis* 44. no. 2 (Summer 1983).

———. "Buddhism and the Modernization of Japan." *History of Religions* 28, no. 4 (May 1989).

Eisenstadt, S. N. "Social Change, Differentiation, and Evolution." *American Sociological Review* 29 (1964).

Hane, Mikiso. *Peasants, Rebels, and Outcastes.* New York: Pantheon, 1982.

Hardacre, Helen. *Lay Buddhism in Contemporary Japan: Reiyūkai Kyōdan.* Princeton: Princeton University Press, 1984.

———. *Kurozumikyō and the New Religions of Japan.* Princeton: Princeton University Press, 1986.

———. *Shinto and the State 1868–1988.* Princeton: Princeton University Press, 1989.

Holtom, Daniel C.*The National Faith of Japan.* New York: E. P. Dutton, 1938.

Kamata, Satoshi. *Japan in the Passing Lane: An Insider's Account of Life in a Japanese Auto Factory.* New York: Pantheon, 1982.

Keene, Donald. *Landscapes and Portraits: Appreciations of Japanese Culture.* Tokyo and Palo Alto: Kodansha, 1971.

Kishimoto, Hideo. *Japanese Religion in the Meiji Era.* Tokyo: Toyo Bunka, 1969.

McFarland, H. Neil. *The Rush Hour of the Gods: A Study of New Religious Movements in Japan.* New York: Macmillan, 1967.

Mead, Sidney. *The Lively Experiment.* New York: Harper, 1963.

Michiyoshi, Yokoyama and Nishiyama Shigeru. "Shin-shinshūkyō būmu: sono shōtai" (The New New Religions Boom: Its Real Nature). *Chūō Kōron* 103, no. 4 (1988).

Minear, Richard H. *Japanese Tradition and Western Law: Emperor, State, and Law in the Thought of Hozumi Yatsuka.* Cambridge: Harvard University Press, 1970.

Morley, James W., ed., *Dilemmas of Growth in Prewar Japan.* Princeton: Princeton University Press, 1971.

Mortimer, Edward. *Faith and Power: The Politics of Islam.* New York: Vintage Books, 1982.

Parsons, Talcott. *Societies: Evolutionary and Comparative Perspectives.* Englewood Cliffs: Prentice-Hall, 1966.

———. "Religion in a Modern Pluralistic Society." *Review of Religious Research* 7, no. 3 (Spring 1966).

Pyle, Kenneth B. *The New Generation in Meiji Japan: The Problem of Cultural Identity 1885–1895.* Stanford: Stanford University Press, 1969.

Tsurumi, Patricia. *The Other Japan: Postwar Realities.* Armonk, N.Y.: M. E. Sharpe, 1988.

Van Wolferen, Karel. *The Enigma of Japanese Power: People and Politics in a Stateless Nation.* New York: Alfred A. Knopf, 1989.

White, James W. *The Sokagakkai and Mass Society.* Stanford: Stanford University Press, 1970.

CHAPTER
15

Conclusion: An Interim Report on a Hypothetical Family

Martin E. Marty and R. Scott Appleby

As we mentioned in the introduction, the preceding essays taken together are in no sense exhaustive of the phenomena under consideration in this series of volumes. One could continue almost indefinitely with examples of fundamentalist or fundamentalist-like movements simply by scanning any day's headlines from Afghanistan, Soviet Central Asia, Algeria, sub-Saharan Africa, Northern Ireland, and dozens of other flash points around the world where religion forms at least the ideological basis, and often the cultural and social context, for complex and highly sophisticated movements of reaction against threatening features of the contemporary world. The first book to appear placing movements in comparative focus featured, for example, eleven contributors examining, among other cases, Wahhabism in West Africa, "incipient fundamentalism" among Sri Lankan Hindus in England, Christian fundamentalism as a counterculture in urban south India, and aspects of fundamentalism in a Turkish town.[1]

The recent comparative study by Bruce Lawrence, *Defenders of God: The Fundamentalist Revolt Against the Modern Age,* develops five traits that distinguish fundamentalists of many traditions from both their modernist opponents and their pious coreligionists. Among these is the contemporaneity of their enterprise: fundamentalism is primarily a twentieth-century phenomenon, with "historical antecedents, but no ideological precursors." For example, in Islam, the tradition in which Lawrence has specialized, fundamentalism represents "a delayed reaction to the psychological hegemony of European colonial rule." Thus it could occur in majoritarian Muslim countries only "after they had become independent nation-states, that is, in most instances, after World War II."[2]

These two comparative and definitional volumes represented the first scholarly assault upon what had become a common practice of clustering unique cases under the general inclusive term "fundamentalism" without sufficient nuancing of that term—a tendency of journalists and scholars alike which has led to misperceptions, misunderstanding, and in many cases, to the exacerbation of tension and ill will either by those who have been labeled fundamentalists or by those who wish to categorize, objectify, and thus reduce and dismiss their opponents by imposing the word as a term of opprobrium. Clustering is not a good idea in any comparative study or analysis that aims at genuine understanding, whose authors hope that each group described therein would recognize itself in its distinctiveness. To flash a series of images taken from the headlines and to present these as episodes of an integrated or coordinated global phenomenon does not serve such understanding. Indeed, as the essays in this volume have demonstrated, those people and groups now known as "fundamentalists" emerge from different regions of the world, cite different holy books, or have different interpretations of the same holy book, or follow no holy book at all but a venerable tradition instead. Some movements have resorted to violent means, while others assemble and proselytize within the limits of the law. Obviously the movements studied here under the banner "fundamentalism" are not in conspiracy globally and would be bitterly opposed one to another on most central religious issues (while forming some interesting political coalitions on others—American Christian fundamentalists and the Gush Emunim, for example, each wishing, for different reasons, that the Holy Land be returned to the Jews).

Moreover, the images of violence on the West Bank and Gaza, of revolution in the streets of Iran, of assassinations and massacres in the Punjab, are misleading if they are not balanced with images of moderate Sikhs eschewing violence and condemning extremism, of Shi'ite refugees pinned helplessly in the Lebanese crossfire, and of observant Jews in Israel calling for negotiations with Palestinian Arabs. And such qualifications do not begin to account for the fact that fundamentalists themselves are not, as individuals or as groups, undifferentiated in motives and strategies. Nor is truth served if fundamentalists are portrayed, in headlines or studies, as in every case committed to violence, as obstructionists, as unthinking foes of progress, or as inherently representative of a regressive trend in religion and in human civilization.

Fundamentalism seemed an appropriate subject for an interdisciplinary public policy study in part because it inspires the effort to create structures and institutions comprehending every aspect of human existence. As movements of sustained opposition to the secularist attempt to position religion alongside other ideologies and value systems competing for a hearing in the public forum, fundamentalisms resist, at least in principle, the reduction of religion to ideology alone and attempt to provide a thoroughgoing and integrated system that does not readily yield to the compartmentalizing tendencies of the modern social sciences. Accordingly, economists, social theorists, political scientists, cultural historians, anthropologists, legal scholars, and social psychologists must collaborate if the phenomenon is to be analyzed in all of its dimensions. And despite the obvious centrality of religion in the recent emergence of movements of radical reaction to postcolonial modernity, scholars of religion have been overlooked, by and large, in policy analysis and formulation, with undesirable results.[3]

Thus this first of six volumes of essays is in part an attempt to describe the *religious character* of various fundamentalist movements within the context of the particular social, political, religious, and economic conditions in which they emerged or came to prominence in this century. Accordingly, the list of authors includes historians of religion, cultural anthropologists, and sociologists of religion, several of whom have been participant-observers in the movements under consideration. The essays were intended to be both ambitious and modest: ambitious in that authors were asked to cover large regions and summarize decades or centuries of historical background; modest in that this exercise was to be at the service of one goal, namely, the examination of movements in light of possible traits of the hypothetical "family of fundamentalisms," as presented in an earlier communication to the authors.[4]

Our own caution about applying the term "fundamentalism" beyond its original historical context would be supplanted by reluctance were we to allow the Protestant Christian case, for which the term was coined, to dictate the content of the term. Instead, in this volume we have begun by emptying the term of its culture-specific and tradition-specific content and context before examining cases across the board to see if there are in fact "family resemblances" among movements commonly perceived as "fundamentalist."

One promising way to stretch the parameters of the study is to explore cases that do not seem to belong but come close enough to shed light on those that do. For example, Tu Wei-ming describes the Confucian revival in East Asia without feeling obliged to make it fit into the hypothetical family of fundamentalisms. Tu's reading of neo-Confucianism does evoke certain family traits, in that he presents the phenomenon as (1) a revival drawing upon what are perceived to be fundamentals of a religious tradition which has suffered erosion, or direct cultural ban, or manipulation, by secular forces in the modern age. Furthermore (2) these fundamentals are retrieved, privileged, and sanctioned (3) as a means of protecting or forging anew an ethnic or national identity seeking validation in the postcolonial era. In this connection Tu writes of the complex feeling of "humiliation, remorse, regret, and bitterness" shared by Koreans *(hahn)* and Chinese *(chi)* because of "their sense of crisis at confronting the West combined with a profound fear of annihilation and a powerful feeling of destiny." He sees the renewed religious impulse as offering a common ideological and cultural basis for the shaping of a reformed social or political order through a possible Japanese-Korean-Chinese alliance leading to a united East Asia.

On the other hand, it is not clear that the Confucian revivalists—primarily intellectual elites and presumably in small numbers—enjoy either an institutional base of their own or an identifiable following. Their political and social program remains skeletal, and its coherence with the retrieved Confucianism seems unclear. These missing elements seem crucial to the common fundamentalist enterprise of transforming the world in light of, and by application of, the retrieved fundamentals. Thus the East Asian case provides both a fertile comparison and a contrast to other movements of religious reaction in our era.

Constructing A "Pure" Fundamentalism

What have the various authors concluded in fulfilling their assignment? The following summary and review does not treat of scholars, theories, and movements other than those featured in these pages; that broader task will be part of the burden of a later volume. Nor will this summary dwell on the unique elements in each of the preceding cases: their distinctiveness will be apparent upon a close reading. Rather, these concluding paragraphs strive simply to highlight some of the apparent family traits of fundamentalism that recur in these pages.

It is difficult if not impossible to isolate for definitional purposes any pure form of religious extremism. The precondition for the existence of a pure form of the religious extremism called fundamentalism would be a movement totally differentiated from other forms of culture and independent of all social institutions. Extremism, then, "might be best described as an ideal typical impulse rather than as objectified in individuals or institutions," for "once extremism or extremists organize to attain their goals, the process of organization introduces the very communal type constraints from which extremism initially freed itself."[5]

With this qualification in mind, it is possible to offer, on the basis of the essays in this volume, a brief description of the "ideal typical impulse" of fundamentalism, accompanied by selected examples of its occurrence in particular movements and institutions.

In delineating this pure form of fundamentalism *religious idealism* is a central category of analysis, for the transcendent realm of the divine, as revealed and made normative for the religious community, alone provides *an irreducible basis for communal and personal identity*. Only an identity thus rooted is guaranteed to remain free from erosion, impenetrable, immune to substantial change, aloof from the vicissitudes of history and human reason. In this regard Abdulaziz Sachedina contends that the core of Islamic fundamentalism is "the religious idealism that promises its adherents that once the Islamic norm is applied, it will effect dramatic change and vanquish the manifold sociopolitical and moral problems afflicting the Muslim peoples." Because they are "an inseparable part of the divinely originated cosmos," humans aim at implementing God's will as expressed in the religious-moral law, the Shari'a. "In this sense," Sachedina writes, "secularism, which in the context of modern Western civilization signifies a movement away from God, will inherently remain alien to Islam's theocentric emphasis." Despite a radically different cosmology and theology, Theravada Buddhist "fundamentalists," Donald Swearer contends, also "understand identity as *ontological*—as rooted in the very nature of being and the cosmos and thus beyond the reach of human temporal and spatial considerations and the relativizing force of history." Similarly, born-again Christians see themselves as participants in "a new creation": having escaped the sinful world, they "put on Christ," and enjoy the benefits of a new status as righteous servants of their Lord.

Because the integrity of religious identity depends on the intelligibility and reliability of divine revelation—whether the proximate source of that revelation be the

Qur'an, the Bible, or the Granth Sahib—fundamentalists tend to depict revealed truth as *whole, unified, and undifferentiated.*

In describing the Roman Catholic candidate for the fundamentalist family, William Dinges demonstrates the importance of *integralism* for Catholics who have bitterly opposed the modernist appropriation of historical consciousness and neo-Kantian epistemologies threatening the religious world view upon which Catholicism rests. Because the Roman Catholic neoscholastic system is so delicately coordinated, so tightly woven, to loosen even one strand by obstreperous criticism is to threaten the cohesion of the whole—and thus to undermine the institutionalized authority of Catholic religious elites.

The reliance on religion as a source for identity explains a good deal about the *intentionally scandalous* aspects of fundamentalism. Lacking this redemptive identification with the transcendent Other, outsiders would not be expected to accept the transrational claims of the true believer; indeed, they would find in them a trip wire, a stumbling block (Greek *scandalon*). Common to most of the movements portrayed in these pages are beliefs and behaviors that violate the canons of the post-Enlightenment secular rationality that has characterized Western thought over the course of the past three centuries. In securing an identity and a role in the cosmos immune to absorption, fundamentalists oppose "historical consciousness," especially as it is interpreted and translated by modernists into the foundational principles of relativism. Thus fundamentalists reject the notion that we know and believe and have our being within time and space as the sole arena of human agency; that belief and practice is therefore historically conditioned and contingent; and that, accordingly, as all belief systems and religions are thus bound, no one of them holds an a priori advantage over any other in terms of cognitive truth claims. Such assumptions threaten fundamentalist purchase on unassailable identity, as would any sociomoral system based on the post-Enlightenment notion that we cannot know revelation from a transcendent God, if such a God exists, except and only through the radically limited capacities of the human mind. Were fundamentalists to concede these points—which they do not—religious identity would lose its transcendent, erosion-free source; and the ethos and behaviors which proceed from that identity would seem suddenly susceptible to tests of relative adequacy and to "foreign" criteria of evaluation. To be thus comprehended by outsiders would be to suffer reduction to the social, economic, or psychological categories of credentialed unbelievers disrespectful or ignorant of the "sacred spark" (a concept shared by Sikh, Jewish, and Hindu radicals) which animates and brings meaning to human existence.

Thus fundamentalist beliefs and behaviors remain inherently scandalous to outsiders. As we shall see when we move from the consideration of an ideal type to actual behavior, fundamentalists may gradually modify or deemphasize extreme doctrines or practices. *But extremism, rhetorical or actual, serves a number of purposes, among them the posing of a litmus test separating true believers from outsiders,* who betray their true colors by their refusal to accept literally doctrines such as the Virgin Birth, or the return of the Hidden Imam, or the healing and magical powers of the messiahs of the Japanese New Religions. Thus fundamentalists celebrate their distinctiveness as they reject in principle all forms of hermeneutics and insist that theirs is the correct (because literalist and thus self-evident) rendering of sacred texts and myths; as they claim privileged access to absolute truth; as they divide the world into kingdoms or provinces of light and darkness, elect and reprobate; or as they insist on the purity and integrity of their doctrine and practice and stridently resist compromise of either for the sake of the greater good.

Repudiating secular-scientific notions of progress and gradual historical evolution, for example, fundamentalists often see themselves as actors in an eschatological drama unfolding in the mind of God and directing the course of human history. Indeed, *dramatic eschatologies* shape fundamentalist identity and inform action in many, if not all, cases.[6] Shi'ites endure the injustice of the temporal order as they await the appearance of the just ruler, the Hidden Imam, at the end of time; or in his absence they follow a divinely designated successor into militant activism. In either case, identity is provisional. Suffering does, and ought to, characterize Shi'ite earthly life until the day of vindication. Haredi Jews are also long-suffering devotees of a messiah to come; until the day when the messiah comes, they consider themselves "in exile" in this world and eschew human efforts to hasten the final redemption. Christian fundamentalists have justified various programs of action by invoking their own scenarios of the apocalypse.

In this eschatological mode, *fundamentalisms seize upon particular historical moments, matched to sacred texts and traditions, and interpreted according to an uncanny calculation of time and space.* For most Israelis the Yom Kippur War of 1973 was a humiliating setback. "Proud Zionism" suffered a mighty blow: failures in the battlefield were perceived as the result of ideological and moral decay. Among the apparent losers, ideologically speaking, were the activists of the radical movement Gush Emunim, who had tied their messianic prophecies to specific geopolitical events such as the stunning Israeli victory over Egypt in the 1967 Six Day War. However, instead of feeling disappointment and abandoning their messianic and strategic conceptions, the activist-believers emerged with a greater confidence in their arcane method of reading history. Why? As Gideon Aran explains: "The success of religion in such cases depends on its ability to supply the faithful with an explanation of the frustrating incident in terms of the faith itself, an interpretation corroborating belief with events ostensibly contradicting it. The 'embarrassing blunder' is integrated into the overall scheme of things so that it becomes the axis of a new phase of religion. A complex theology developed surrounding those historical episodes, rendering their crisis potential a source of inspiration for religious revival." Thus the decline of secular Zionism was interpreted as compatible with the loftiest messianic expectations. According to Gush Emunim, Aran writes, "secular Zionism has a function in the messianic plan and is therefore vital and sacred. There is a Jewish mission which only Zionism can fulfill, but once it realizes its destiny and exhausts itself and its secularity, its latent religiosity will come to light. In the final accounting, modern secular Judaism will be exposed as episodic, exactly like Orthodox Judaism." Both will yield to religious-national revolutionary Judaism. "Thus the perceived post-1973 decline of classic Zionism reinforces faith and impels believers to activism."

From the symbolic repertoire of messianism the believers also retrieve concepts and prophecies that sustain the group during moments of crisis. Particularly relevant in the days of the Intifada, for example, is the teaching that "withdrawal from the territories in the wake of a cruel war is a crucible, a trial in which God tests Israel . . . these are the 'pangs of the messiah,' the trials and tribulations which emerge before redemption, heralding and conditioning its fulfillment." By such interpretations, apparent defeat may be understood as a vindication of righteousness.

Some of the traits of fundamentalism examined here are more accurately attributed to the "People of the Book," Jews, Christians, and Muslims, than to their first, or distant, cousins in the fundamentalist family: Hindus, Sikhs, Buddhists, and Confucians. Sacred texts do not play the same constitutive role in South Asian and Far Eastern traditions as they do in the Abrahamic faiths, nor is history conceived of as a structured drama proceeding inexorably to a climactic final act. And as Winston Davis writes of Japanese Buddhism, "there is no Fall of man, Satan, or everlasting hell. Good and evil have not become the ontological dichotomy they are in the Abrahamic traditions." Thus it is particularly noteworthy that at least four of the six South Asian or Far Eastern fundamentalist-like movements examined in these pages do in fact privilege a sacred text and presume to draw certain fundamentals—beliefs and behaviors—from it. And, absent the end-time dualistic eschatologies inherent in the Abrahamic traditions, there are nonetheless references to a coming cosmic upheaval in the rhetoric of these groups. For example, Sukyo Mahikari, one of Japan's New New Religions, rejects postwar democracy and communism alike and depicts the latter as "sent by the gods as an omen warning mankind of a coming eschatological ordeal known as the Baptism by Fire." Charismatic leaders of these New Religions are indeed called "Messiahs," and in the cosmogonic myth of the Mahikari, "If Japan heeds the call of the Savior, Okada Kotama, the world in the twenty-first century will once again be reunited under her emperor and the glory of the ancient Muvian empire will be restored. The leaders of the new world will be the 'Seed People' who support the Mahikari churches today. Thus, like other millenarian cults, Mahikari promises its humble followers that someday 'the first will be last and the last first.' "

Such dramatic and dualistic readings of sacred texts and renderings of metahistory provide fundamentalists with a cosmic enemy, imbue fundamentalist boundary-setting and purity-preserving activities with an apocalyptic urgency, and foster a crisis mentality that serves both to intensify missionary efforts and to justify extremism.

Because confrontation and opposition are essential to the dynamic of reaction, radical fundamentalism requires a worthy adversary. Thus the temporal antagonist is enhanced and enlarged no less than the protagonist. *Fundamentalists name, dramatize, and even mythologize their enemies,* situating oppressive dictators or Westernized elites or compromising coreligionists within the same eschatological or mythic structure in which they see themselves. The West is "the Great Satan"; the American Occupation caused many Japanese to be possessed by "evil spirits"; secular Zionism is a cosmic precursor to revolutionary messianic Judaism. Samuel Heilman and Menachem Friedman point out that "many of the 'heroes' of moderated acculturationists—people like the maskil Moses Mendelssohn and chief rabbi Abraham I. Kook of Palestine, or most of the leaders of religious Zionist parties—became *antiheroes* for the haredim. Haredi Judaism portrayed these Jews as creating an ideology of mediocrity in which failure to struggle against the eroding effects of contemporary culture was the greatest sin."

Indeed, the identification and elaboration of the enemy is often the initial step in the fundamentalist rhetoric of negation and the development of a *contra-acculturative orientation.*[7] In the Nasser-era prison writings of the radical ideologue of Egypt's Muslim Brotherhood, Sayyid Qutb, *jahiliyyah* society (the pre-Islamic or non-Islamic population ignorant of the Prophet and his message) assumed the intentionality and deviance of those who would willfully oppose God's rule. As John Voll writes, "this jahiliyyah is rebellion against God and results in the oppression and exploitation of humanity. In Qutb's analysis nationalism imparted sovereignty to the Arab nation rather than to God." Hence, the obligation of the "true Muslim" was to "combat this satanic form of unbelief." Given such identification, extremist measures were justified: the unbeliever *(kafir)* was to be identified and exposed *(takfir)*, and the devout were to withdraw from the jahiliyyah society to form an activist core dedicated to the Islamization of society. "In this view," Voll points out, "Islam and jahiliyyah cannot coexist, and the prevailing social order must be overturned." Similarly, during the Cold War era in Latin America, Pablo Deiros writes, fundamentalist faith missions and fledgling indigenous evangelical churches with a "fundamentalist impulse" were "anti" movements: they defined themselves in opposition to both the ancient Hispanidad culture and to creeping secularism, and their proselytizing appeal turned on anti-Communist, anti-Catholic, and anti-ecumenical polemics.

Whether the outsider is simply an indifferent infidel or is instead in conspiracy with other unbelievers, or linked with satanic forces, *fundamentalists set boundaries, protect the group from contamination, and preserve purity.* Boundary setting takes many forms. One is to delineate and rename a sacred space—for radical Sikhs, the Punjab is Khalistan (the land of purity); for Gush Emunim activists, the West Bank and Gaza are the biblical Judea and Samaria. Another is to adopt distinctive, symbolic dress—for Sikhs, unshorn hair and short pants; for the Gush Emunim, prayer shawls and long beards combined with jeans or military fatigues. The haredim are unparalleled boundary setters and purity preservers. In attempting to recreate "the Eastern Europe of the orthodox imagination . . . an idealized image of a perfectly Jewish world" before erosion and acculturation sullied it, these Jews continue to demarcate their neighborhoods in Israel, New York, and elsewhere by their distinctive dress (the long black caftans and broad-brimmed black hats, knickers, and white shirts), language (Yiddish), and a variety of customs reminiscent of pre-Holocaust Eastern European Jewry.[8]

The need for purity, for escape from the contamination of the unbeliever, is evident in the conversion rites of some of the groups portrayed herein. In the fundamentalist attempt to "reorganize" Hinduism, Arya Samaj rites of initiation ensured the purity of turn-of-the-century recruits. Ancient rites of purification revived by Aryas to reclaim Indians lost to Islam or Christianity were later used to purify the status of low-caste Hindu groups. "Mass ceremonies were performed on large groups of outcastes and aboriginals. . . . The rituals were simple, often comprising a bath, a shave of the head, and initiation into simple ritual formulae. Nevertheless, their grandiose scale could make them seem impressive to those who witnessed them," Daniel Gold writes. "Arya Samaj preachers were thus often successful when they exhorted villagers to accept the efficacy of the rites and receive the newly purified as people whose touch no longer pollutes. Accordingly, the ceremony might be concluded by a caste Hindu taking food from the hand of a former untouchable, or with a newly purified person drawing water from the village well—neither of which acts would have been tolerated before."

Missionary zeal is indeed characteristic of many of the groups profiled in this volume. Believers who would relax the guard, form coalitions with nonfundamentalists, and deemphasize the importance of conversion, are often the first to arouse fundamentalist ire. Thus Christian fundamentalists set themselves apart from their ecumenically minded liberal co-religionists who, out of respect for the integrity of other faith traditions, have abandoned this traditional practice. "When fundamentalists left other denominations in the early twentieth century," Nancy Ammerman writes, "they took missionary zeal with them and invested in missionary agencies throughout the world. Denominations struggled with stay-at-homers, but fundamentalists' mission efforts around the world grew by leaps and bounds." Meanwhile, on the Indian subcontinent, a distinctive Sikh identity was formed in reaction to the aggressive attempts at "reconversion" by Hindu revivalists.

Indeed, "fundamentalists" East and West have updated and modified traditional forms of proselytism. Rather than devote its energies to the sizable non-Muslim population of Malaysia, the dakwah movement directs "the call" to lax members of the Muslim community. By arousing this dormant population, dakwah leaders intend to rededicate the entire umma to a more strict observance of the faith. Thai Buddhism is experiencing a similar revival. In a departure from the practice of traditional Thai monastic centers, the Dhammakaya actively recruits members and buses them to the thousand-acre headquarters outside of Bangkok for activities ranging from the celebration of major Buddhist holy days to the practice of meditation. The movement has been particularly aggressive in recruiting members from secondary schools and institutions of higher learning and has also been successful in building support among the military, government officials, and the members of the royal family. "Hence its constituency comes from a wide range of youth, college-educated young adults, and leaders in the economic and political sectors."

Thus far, in reviewing "family traits" that recur frequently in these historical and phenomenological essays, we have observed the fundamentalist quest for an irreducible basis for personal and communal identity—a quest that takes place within a theocentric and/or dualistic view of history in which enemies must be opposed, converts purified from contamination, litmus tests given, time and space renamed and reinterpreted, the cosmos reordered. The ingredient which lends urgency to the quest and finally inspires the "world-conquering" activism of our imagined "pure fundamentalism" is a heightened sense of immediate danger. *Fundamentalisms arise or come to prominence in times of crisis, actual or perceived.* The sense of danger may be keyed to oppressive and threatening social, economic, or political conditions, but the ensuing crisis is perceived as a *crisis of identity* by those who fear extinction as a people or absorption into an overarching syncretistic culture to such a degree that their distinctiveness is undermined in the rush to homogeneity.

Fundamentalists and would-be fundamentalists around the world have certainly suffered no dearth of crisis situations during the late nineteenth and twentieth centuries—an unstable era in which rapid urbanization, modernization, and uneven rates of development occurred during the withdrawal of Western colonial forces—if not Western administrative, judicial, educational, and political structures and philosophies—from much of the third world. The vulnerability of masses of people to totalitarian dictators and military regimes in this era, the social and economic dislocation and deprivation attendant upon migration to the cities, the conditions of misery and exploitation experienced by millions of subject peoples—these have been copiously documented in our generation and are dutifully reported and summarized by the authors of these essays. In tracking the emergence of fundamentalisms the authors find most salient in these reports the ways in which these conditions of upheaval and disorientation have provided an opening, an undeniable aggregate need, for alternative philosophies, structures, and institutions that would retain certain traditional values even as they reflected adjustments to the potentially overwhelming pace and shape of change. Pablo Deiros describes the plight of the rural migrants in Latin American cities after World War II: "Uprooted from families and religious traditions, living in slums at the mercy of criminals and, at times, governmental predators, the urban poor became a fertile seedbed for evangelical proselytism. The weakening of traditional social controls, the sense of confusion and helplessness in the anonymity of city life, the shock of new social values accompanying the adaptation to industrial work, the absence of familiar community loyalties and of the encompassing paternalism characteristic of rural employment: all these conditions led to an acute crisis of personal identity for the migrants. Under such conditions the exchange of old religious values for new ones was, and remains, likely to occur."

The dimensions and locus of the crisis varied in different settings. North American Protestant fundamentalism did in fact emerge in sectors of the nation undergoing rapid urbanization and industrialization—the Northeast at the beginning of the century; the South and Southeast during the second half. However, as Nancy Ammerman points out, fundamentalists north and south were mobilized in the 1970s not only in reaction to cultural displacement by secular elites, but out of a conviction that these elites had effectively taken possession of national institutions and symbols and were threatening to unravel "the moral fabric" of the country. This threat became palpable in the decade of crisis from 1963 (following the Supreme Court ban on prayer in public schools) to 1973 (the year of the Supreme Court decision permitting abortion on demand). To fundamentalists fuming on the margins, secular humanism seemed to infiltrate the public school curriculum; the "new morality" led to sexual promiscuity and a culture of pornography and drugs; the nation endured a failure of self-confidence in the controversy over the Vietnam war; the corruption of political institutions culminated in, and was epitomized by, the Watergate scandal. The crisis was not simply personal or professional or regional; it was a moment of decision, a battle between secular humanists and the Judeo-Christian tradition for cultural hegemony over the interpretation of the founding documents and principles of the nation. The call to mobilize in political action groups proceeded from the fundamentalist rhetoric of crisis and from the conviction that, absent alternative institutions and a wholesale assault on the emergent cultural mainstream, "traditional American values" would not survive the generation. Fundamentalists must organize "to turn the nation around."

In the eighty-four new nations that emerged in the wake of the global realignment after World War II, such personal and cultural crises occurred in the context of a quest for a formula for national identity that would allow rival ethnic and religious blocs to exist peacefully within the same borders and under the same constitution. Fundamentalists leaders, among others, called attention to the repeated failures of national elites to ensure a secure identity for these competing factions. For example, when postcolonial liberal nationalism and later, Arab socialism, failed to lift the Egyptian masses out of poverty and to defeat the Israeli army, Islamic fundamentalists, who had been providing alternative institutions and messages since the 1930s, explained the failures of governmental policies by pointing to (neglected) Islam as the one indigenous Arab glory not shared with the West. The fundamentalist implementation of the Shari'a was the only authentic basis for a true Islamic state; varieties of Islamic modernism, more congenial to the regimes of Nasser, Sadat, and Mubarak, had led to sterile compromises and ineffective imitation of the West.

In the rhetoric of crisis is often embedded a justification and apologetic for extreme measures: *fundamentalists seek to replace existing structures with a comprehensive system* emanating from religious principles and embracing law, polity, society, economy, and culture. In this, as both Winston Davis and T. N. Madan suggest, fundamentalism contains within it a totalitarian impulse. This *totalitarian impulse* has been in evidence in the political and religious manifestations of fundamentalism in Japan, in the efforts of radical Shi'ite and Sunni groups to implement Shari'a across the board, and in the dramatic struggles to achieve integrated nationhood in India. There the attempt to rally diverse ethnic and religious communities under one national banner led to crises of identity for segments of the Sikh population, the Muslim population, and the Hindu population, each of which organized to defend turf and to attenuate erosion. In recounting the development of the Muslim state of Pakistan, Mumtaz Ahmad notes that the interests of the conservative ulama and the fundamentalists converged on most issues: both groups demanded the abolition of bank interest, the introduction of the Zakat system, the implementation of Islamic penal and family laws, the enforcement of a strict sociomoral code in sex roles, the prohibition of birth control, and the state suppression of heretical groups. However, the Jamaat-i-Islami and other fundamentalist movements characterize Islam as a *deen*—a comprehensive way of life which covers the entire spectrum of human activity, be it individual, social, economic or political—while the conservative ulama confine Islam to the five pillars (profession of faith, prayer, fasting, alms-giving, and pilgrimage). For the Jamaat-i-Islami, Islam means the total commitment and subordination of all aspects of human life to the will of God. "They present Islam as a dynamic and activist political ideology which must acquire state power in order to implement its social, economic, and political agenda."

Fundamentalist movements of this type deem political activism the necessary expression of socioreligious concerns. While both the ulama and the modernists seek influence in policy-making circles, Ahmad notes, "the fundamentalists aspire to *capture* political power and establish an Islamic state on the prophetic model. They are not content to act as pressure groups, as are the ulama and the modernists. They want political power because they believe that Islam cannot be implemented without the power of the state." As lay scholars of Islam, leaders of such fundamentalist movements are not theologians but social thinkers and political activists. They are least interested in doctrinal, philosophical, and theological controversies associated with the classical and medieval Islamic thinkers. The main thrust of their intellectual efforts is the articulation of the socioeconomic and political aspects of Islam. Out of his more than 120 publications, for example, the Jamaat-i-Islami's founder, Maulana Maududi, has only one title on a purely theological issue. His entire commentary on the Qur'an reads like an Islamic legal-political text, providing guidance in the fields of constitutional, social, civil, criminal, commercial, and international law. By providing Islamic discourse with a political vocabulary, Maududi's influence on contemporary Islamic fundamentalist groups has been pervasive. In employing terms and phrases such as "the Islamic system of life," "Islamic ideology," "Islamic politics," "the Islamic constitution," "the economic system of Islam" and "the political system of Islam," Maududi elaborated the core concept *iqamat-i-deen* (the establishment of religion), i.e., the total subordination of the institutions of civil society and the state to the authority of divine law. While the Jamaat-i-Islami defined and formulated the goal of the newly born state in terms of Islamic revivalism, Ahmad points out, very few secular politicians and administrators saw the goal as anything other than social and economic development.

In developing these comprehensive systems fundamentalism has proven itself *selectively traditional and selectively modern*. Fundamentalists are not simply traditionalists or conservatives. In fact, they reject the clinging to tradition and the uncritical conservation of all that has emerged in the tradition, for they view tradition as a mosaic of compromises, as the body of accumulated adaptations to the demands of specific historical, and thus contingent, circumstances. Fundamentalists do not object to innovation or adaptation in itself but to the elevation of these adaptations to a privileged status which in turn precludes the flexibility required in crafting a comprehensive response to contemporary challenges. Unlike traditionalists, fundamentalists view traditions thus canonized as little more than accretions—casuistic means, often, of softening the fervor and modifying the pristine vision of the founder or the charismatic leader who realized the founder's dream.

This is not to suggest that fundamentalists reject traditional elements altogether, for as we shall see, they select carefully from among the plethora of doctrines, practices, and interpretations available in the tradition. However, the privileged past is defined with a keen eye on the particular challenges of the present and the opportunities of the future. Abdulaziz Sachedina demonstrates that Ali Shari'ati and Ayatollah Khomeini were brilliant innovators who reinterpreted and developed the Shiʿite doctrine of the "Guardianship of the Jurist" so as to support absolutist, theocratic rule in Iran. In this way, Sachedina writes of the charismatic leaders of Shiʿites in Iran, Iraq, and Lebanon, "their return to Islamic fundamentals is based on the acceptance of the linear notion of development of an Islamic society. As such, their retrieval of relevant teachings that would enable them to build an Islamic system adaptable to modern circumstances is selective . . . their fundamentalism can be designated as an activist type of reaction involving creative interpretation of religious ideas and symbols to render them applicable to contemporary Muslim history."

Thus fundamentalists do not simply reaffirm the old doctrines; they subtly lift them from their original context, embellish and institutionalize them, and employ them as *ideological weapons against a hostile world*. The Christian fundamentalist doctrine of biblical inerrancy is the nineteenth-century innovation of Princeton theologians who deemed its formulation and development necessary, given the advent of the Higher Criticism, in order to preserve the traditional Christian belief in the divine origins of the Bible. Similarly, the Roman Catholic definition of papal infallibility was deemed a necessary "development of doctrine" given the European Kulturkampf against the church and the virulent strains of atheism and materialism threatening its institutional life. And, in traditions in which orthopraxis counts for more than orthodoxy, fundamentalist-like movements reinvigorate traditional practice with a puritanical discipline. In practice, the traditional Thai moral ethos "has been characterized by a nuanced and nonjudgmental stance toward violations of this code." However, the Santi Asoka movement rejects this traditional stance as unsuitable, given widespread "drinking, smoking, gambling, prostitution, and the dissemination of a hedonistic ethos via cinema and television . . . in a social environment the movement judges to be immoral." Accordingly, lay disciples and monks congregate for intensive training sessions governed by a strict set of rules for personal behavior and interaction. Santi Asoka deems the restoration of the traditional ideals of Thai Buddhist identity impossible "without a prior radical transformation of [contemporary] Thai belief and practice."

In the process of interpreting the tradition, evaluating modernity, and selectively retrieving salient elements of both, *charismatic and authoritarian male leaders* play a central role. Gideon Aran captures the charismatic intensity of the Gush Emunim visionary Moshe Levinger, who "bears the torch so far ahead of the camp that he often detaches himself from the rest." As have other fundamentalist leaders, Levinger has successfully equated his way with the revealed or "official" way. "Even Gush Emunim members who oppose Rabbi Levinger are greatly impressed with his consistency, dedication, and self-sacrificing manner," Aran writes. "They find it difficult to withstand his enthusiastic demands, original interpretations, far-reaching forecasts, and heroic personal example." By Pablo Deiros's account, the fortunes of Christian fundamentalism in Latin America turn on the persuasive abilities of the male authority figure, be he the local pastor or the mass evangelist such as the charismatic Luis Palau.

Similarly, the critical role of Shiʿite religious leaders in inspiring and sustaining movements of reaction is documented in Abdulaziz Sachedina's essay; as he points out, the charismatic leader is invested with the final authority in retrieving and interpreting the sacred past, and thus controls the course of the (movement's) future. And while Sunni Muslim fundamentalists have not relied as heavily on the leadership of clerics (ulama), they have nonetheless reaffirmed the practice of independent reasoning (ijtihad) in place of reliance on the copious and rigid opinions of the medieval commentators. The impact of an authoritarian leader in reshaping religious ideals and practice is also evident in the history of Hindu revivalism. K. B. Hedgewar, the founder of the RSS, looked not to Vedic scripture but to the legends of Shivaji, the seventeenth-century Maharashtrian hero who led a successful revolt against the Mogul empire. Shivaji's success derived from both spiritual and practical virtues: on the one hand, martial valor and support for Brahmanical institutions; on the other, worldly wisdom and an organizational talent that gave him the ability to forge an effective fighting force out of soldiers from diverse peasant castes. "Loyalty, discipline, reverence for one's heritage, and skill in effectively rousing ordinary people: these were the virtues Hedgewar admired. Around quasi-military ideals and a philosophy of Hindu Nation, then, he attempted to shape an organization that would have broad popular support."

A recurrent theme of these essays is that, in the strategies and methods these leaders adopt in remaking the world, fundamentalists demonstrate *a closer affinity to modernism than to traditionalism.* Although they reject the secularist shaping of modernity, they are envious of what they perceive as modernist cultural, political, and religious hegemony. In short, they wish to best modernists at their own game of adaptation—but without the identity-eroding consequences of such adaptation. "Possessed of a naive, intense enthusiasm for traditional religious Judaism, coupled with feelings of inferiority and envy in regard to the modern, secular Zionist world," Gideon Aran writes of the hard-core members of the Gush Emunim, "these young people sought to participate in the dynamics and achievements of that world. Thus, they developed a strikingly original and ambitious worldview that differed significantly from both religious and secular national perspectives, and they sought religious validation for their initiative." This mix of envy and appreciation of modern means cloaks a resentment of modern ends that characterizes fundamentalist critiques, as in Jerry Falwell's description of a secularized America as "a society today that is quite sophisticated and very educated . . . a clever generation . . . but one that is suffering because men are doing what is right in their own eyes and disregarding God's immutable laws. If a person is not a Christian, he is inherently a failure."

Coupled with this envy and resentment of modernity is a shrewd exploitation of its processes and instrumentalities. Several of the fundamentalist movements which arose during or immediately after the colonial period organized in conscious imitation of the West. Indian groups, for example, adopted Western organizational models, and Western-educated members of all communities began organizing themselves along broader religious lines. For the Hindus especially this meant delineating a broad-based communal identity beyond caste that had not been emphasized strongly before. "Movements of organized Hinduism thus give expression to problems of pluralism long familiar to India, but which have become transformed and exacerbated in modern contexts of colonialism, nationhood, and democracy," Gold writes. "For at the same time that Hindus organized against British political and cultural imperialism, organized groups of educated Hindus, Muslims, and Sikhs competed against each other for a privileged position in colonial society." The adoption of Western models entailed substantial transformations of the structures of traditional religion. For example, the importance of committee membership in the revivalist groups often overshadowed caste. "Where once people found religious authority in their family priest or a lineage of gurus, they may now find it in a formalized organizational hierarchy." With structural innovations come changes in ideas about Hindu community itself: questions arise about both its external boundaries and the traditional socioreligious divisions within it. Revivalists believe that a new socioreligious order among Hindus is crucial for the vitality—if not the very survival—of Hinduism in the modern world. Both to effect these internal reforms within and to ward off external threats, Hindus must organize. "If fundamentalist religion implies a resolute religious reaction to forces of modernity, then fundamentalist Hinduism is necessarily organized Hinduism."

A similar imitation of modern systems took place among Islamic movements during the period of Westernization. In the process of formulating his ideas on Islamic ideology, for example, Maududi was greatly impressed by the then-emerging ideologies of communism and fascism. However, he found most useful for his own purposes, not the ideals of the communists and fascists, but their methods and organizational strategies. His frequent references in his writings to the ideological purity, organizational discipline, and ascetic character of the communist and fascist movements foreshadowed his later organization of the Jamaat-i-Islami. "Maududi came to the conclusion that the best way to transform a society was to create a small, informed, dedicated, and highly disciplined group which would work to assume social and political leadership," Mumtaz Ahmad writes. Eventually, in order to communicate with a generation of Muslim youth trained in Western-style educational systems, fundamentalists in Pakistan and elsewhere in the Muslim world "adopted Western ideas of organization, made full use of modern publishing technology, and accepted the Western premise of instrumental, if not substantive, rationality." To this generation of Muslims they presented a goal of equality with and independence from the West, based on appropriating the technological benefits the West had to offer, without, however, adopting a Western ethos. "The fundamentalist organizations became popular because they offered an authentic Islamic cultural identity during a period of Muslim identity crisis," Ahmad explains, "yet they also effectively articulated in Islamic idioms the socioeconomic and political concerns of social strata that were faring poorly under the Western system."

Not only did fundamentalists draw upon modern organizational methods and structures; they also benefited from the encouragement or direct support of colonial powers and later took advantage of the openness of secular democracies. Exploitation of modern systems includes a striking number of instances in these pages alone, in which fundamentalists have acquired and enjoyed various forms of support by governments and administrations they might ultimately oppose. In an example of a pattern of colonial policy in which the weaker of competing ethnic groups was privileged to offset majoritarian indigenous groups, the British in India, concerned about Hindu uprisings, were early accomplices in the development of a distinctive Sikh identity and helped shape the notions of the Sikhs as a martial race. They encouraged baptized Sikhs to adhere to their code of conduct and disallowed the abandonment of the conventional marks of Sikh identity. In order to counterbalance the influence of potential socialist activists, Egyptian president Anwar Sadat pardoned and released Islamic fundamentalists imprisoned under Nasser and lifted the ban on campus organizations devoted to the Islamic movement. The momentum for Islamization thereby established eventually led to his assassination at the hands of disgruntled Islamic radicals. Similarly, authoritarian military regimes which came to power in Latin America in the wake of the economic depression of the 1930s offered concessions and privileges to independent fundamentalist mission churches and groups considered hostile to counterrevolutionary communists.

Fundamentalists have also sought and taken advantage of openings or inconsistencies in the articulation of postcolonial national identities and platforms. When India became a secular state by constitutional proclamation, it guaranteed the fundamental rights of freedom of conscience, free profession, practice, and propagation of religion, and freedom to manage religious affairs. Radical Sikhs subsequently called upon the Indian government to honor its own constitutional principles by recognizing their religious right to *repudiate* the separation of religion and politics in the conduct of their own community life, and in fact to establish a separate state on this basis. In similar fashion, the Gush Emunim has deftly seized on a crisis in Israeli identity by appealing to the nationalism of right-wing members of the Likud party. Gideon Aran reports that in the late 1980s, Gush Emunim activists could be found on the government payroll as rabbis, teachers, students, soldiers, Interior and Defense Ministry officials, and even as functionaries of the Ministry of Religious Affairs. "Ironically, in the new reality of the territories, much of the institutional antiestablishment activism is essentially financed by the government itself—a situation defined as scandalous by critics of the Gush Emunim," Aran writes. "The [movement's] institutionalization over the past decade extends to both the administrative sphere (for example, the movement has a proper headquarters, with a permanent staff, representatives abroad, etc.) and to the political sphere (personalities identified with the movement can be found in various parliamentary factions, such as the NRP, Tehiya, and Morasha) . . . so much so that the movement's cadres are often perceived as civil servants." By exempting yeshiva and kollel students from the military draft, the secular government of Israel has also, perhaps inadvertently, provided the conditions by which haredi society has developed its own alternative institutions, all the while inculcating an anti-Zionist ethos among its adherents.

Rather than complicity with fundamentalisms, one observes in Malaysia the government's inability to stem the tide. A coalition of ethnic groups, the government has failed to provide an effective rival to Islam's pervasive symbol system of meaning and legitimacy. Manning Nash notes the contrast to the situation of Indonesia, where the military fought a war of independence and on many occasions has defended the nation against "extremists"—earning it a national position and legitimacy that the Malaysian military does not have. Supported by the nonfundamentalist ideology of the Panca Sila, the strong central Indonesian government enforces the cooperation of ethnic blocs and inhibits the eruption of religious and ethnic insurgence. Malaysia's ethnic turmoil had a different outcome: following the 1969 riots, the central government, the elite, and the military "had no alternative other than to renegotiate the compact of 1952 along the lines of a movement toward greater Malay privileges and consequent openings to a more militant Islam," Nash explains. "The open system of Malaysia is thus more vulnerable to fundamentalism in the political arena than is the highly controlled government in Indonesia."

Fundamentalist ideology and programs have received an additional boost from the failed policies of secular regimes and from the unpopular or esoteric teachings of religious liberals and modernists. For example, the failure of both liberal and socialist paths to development, as pursued by Kemal Atatürk of Turkey, Reza Shah of Iran, Ayub Khan of Pakistan, Nasser of Egypt, and Sukarno of Indonesia, strengthened the appeal of Islamic fundamentalists. Islamic modernists have been the fundamentalists' chief rivals in devising a modern response to these failures of secular regimes. What differentiated the two, however, was the *mass appeal of fundamentalism*. "The modernist writings were addressed primarily to Westerners and those Muslims who had acquired Western education; the fundamentalists, on the other hand, addressed the Muslim masses," Ahmad writes. "The former were mostly academic and scholastic, the latter inspirational and devotional. With the expansion of education, the development of a vernacular press, the opening up of new occupational opportunities, and the emergence of new social groups by the middle of the twentieth century, fundamentalist Muslim thinking became more appealing to certain segments of the Islamic populations than either secular or modernist thought." Sachedina attributes the success of certain contemporary Shi'ite revolutionary movements to the prior dissemination of the activist interpretations of ayatollahs Khomeini (Iran), Baqir Sadr (Iraq), Musa Sadr (Lebanon), and others through tracts read aloud, or written in the simple language of rural Shi'ites, during the commemorative rituals of 'Ashura. In similar fashion, Christian fundamentalists pride themselves on their populist appeal: preachers evoke "traditional American values" in straightforward, colloquial English, and present a religiopolitical message by careful identification of doctrines with mainstream values of an American society which, as Nancy Ammerman points out, remains strikingly conservative in its beliefs about the Bible, divine revelation, and the importance of a born-again experience. Winston Davis explains the appeal of New Religions to Japanese overwhelmed by the rapid but uneven pace of modernization in part by their retrieval of simple if elaborate myths from the imperial past; such "symbolic regression," he argues, is one effective way in which these groups strive to "dedifferentiate" society.

Pablo Deiros makes the point that fundamentalist and Pentecostalist success in Latin America has come at the expense of a Roman Catholic church perceived as elitist not only in political identification but in style of worship. He also notes that "the average meeting of historic Protestant churches is often described as colorless, tasteless, and boring. The sermon too often deals not with religious expression and life but with the 'grammar of religion,' namely, the doctrines which are not infrequently a verbal substitute for the real-life experience. Similarly, the hymns are many times foreign importations, in which the words are didactic rather than lyric. The utter lack of group pageantry, drama, and participation make these services seem more like a session in a lecture hall than a corporate worship of the Most High." On the other hand, in place of the Catholic church's technical-theological language, "Pentecostals have a highly significant system of communication. All may receive the gift of tongues—a more ecstatic experience than reciting the abstract phrases of a specialized language. Much of Pentecostal liturgical dancing and group participation in prayer is a form of folk drama. . . . There is great emphasis upon group participation in prayer and singing, and the sermons are generally on the intellectual level of the people, with plenty of opportunities for men and women to respond not only verbally but by signs of the indwelling of the Spirit." The strength of the structure of Pentecostalist and fundamentalist churches, Deiros continues, is that it "allows the full participation of almost everyone and a gradation which depends largely on function rather than background."

Perhaps even more important in explaining the popular appeal of various fundamentalisms has been the seeming authentication of their religious claims and political solutions by their consistent service to populations displaced or ill-served by modern secular governments. As noted above, "pure" fundamentalists are institution builders with a comprehensive plan for society; absent the political or military might to implement the entire program, they do not shrink from accomplishing piecemeal the desired regeneration of society. Nor are the schools, hospitals, medical clinics, and orphanages they fund and staff anything less than centers for the propagation of the fundamentalist faith and worldview. By meeting unmet needs, fundamentalist social networks, alternate institutions, and welfare programs are also a way of recruiting members, of building sympathy in the larger community, and of fighting back against godless regimes.

Indeed fundamentalist institutions play a variety of roles. These pages abound with examples, including John Voll's description of the Muslim Brotherhood, both at its time of origin sixty years ago and today, as established in and through a network of social service institutions crisscrossing Egypt. These agencies served as a safety net of sorts for thousands of displaced migrants to Cairo and other cities. Originally conceived as Hasan al-Banna's response to a perceived lack of leadership on the part of the ulama, the Brotherhood has entered the mainstream of Egyptian life through the social outreach provided by these agencies, even as it has spawned radical splinter groups which eschew conventional and gradualist means of social transformation. "Fundamentalist activism is the pioneer movement," Voll writes, "but there is also a dynamic spirit involving a growing numbers of people in social political activism of nonmilitant style in Egypt." Fundamentalist institutions also offer an extraordinary religious canopy under which people can congregate. Thus social agencies have been breeding grounds not only for radical activists but more often for fundamentalist missionaries within Sikhism, haredi Judaism, and Theravada Buddhism, for example. Finally, in lieu of the ideal (and rare) situation in which fundamentalists have assumed control of a state (as in Iran), these social institutions function as "worlds within the world," controlled environments in which the fundamentalist plan is realized in microcosm.

This spectrum of functions is represented within North American Christian fundamentalism. Alternate institutions were formed by incipient fundamentalists in the 1930s on the heels of embarrassing public defeats at the hands of liberals. Thereafter, independent denominational agencies thus became the organizational replacement for (ineffective) denominational affiliation. This phase of fundamentalist institution building was also characterized by service to thousands of alienated Americans "on the margins"—economically, socially, culturally, and emotionally. Thousands of independent fundamentalist churches sprang up in rural and urban areas alike and sponsored group activities for every night of the week. Meanwhile, the broad-based appeal of Charles Fuller's popular old-fashioned revival hour was revealed in "the many letters he had received from heartbroken, heart-hungry humanity, contemplating suicide," for whom Fuller's reassuring message of purpose and hope made a difference. As Ammerman summarizes the import of these various networks, agencies, and institutions: "To become a fundamentalist was to join a group—a local, visible, supportive community. Living in a hostile world required nothing less." Another brand of alternate institution which began to thrive in the "hostile world" of the 1960s and 1970s is the Christian school. Christian academies and day schools have tripled in number during the past twenty years. They attempt to provide a "total world" encompassing every aspect of students' lives, with a pedagogy and curriculum rooted in the "Christian" worldview: fundamentalist history is *His* story; fundamentalist math, an entrée to the ordered and dependable processes of creation; fundamentalist science, a lens by which to view an enchanted universe sustained at every moment by divine providence. Although the primary goal of these academies is to train Christian preachers and missionaries, many of their graduates will matriculate at one of the new Christian universities and colleges that are preparing students for entry into the mainstream of American life.

Many of the traits of our hypothetical aggregate "pure fundamentalism"—the envy of the modern; the tendency to foster a sense of crisis and urgency; the flair for the dramatic and symbolic act; the shrewd, popular, and effective adaptations to modernity—converge in fundamentalism's seemingly innate understanding of, and effortless manipulation of, modern mass media of communication (and propaganda). As many of these authors note, as the twentieth century wore on, the new center for the celebration, elaboration, and reinforcement of religious and communal identity was increasingly the television set (or radio) rather than the local synagogue, church, or mosque. Modern media are ideal for those who wish to reach the outsider, the marginalized. Through the media, the margin may become the center, or one of many centers. North and South American Christian televangelism (and mass outdoor rallies by televangelists promoted on the airwaves) provide the obvious examples of the canny use of communications technology. Perhaps more striking to the American reader are Donald Swearer's description of the "skillful use of the media and the lavish productions" at the Prathum Thani headquarters of the Wat Dhammakaya; or Aran's recounting of the ways in which members of the Gush Emunim, sensitive to the need to shape the sensibilities of fence-sitting Israelis unconvinced about the wisdom of the occupation, "staged" the planting of settlements in the territories for the Israeli media, which were "enamored of them from the beginning." Swearer notes that the broad-based popular support for the Dhammakaya movement "stems from an astute (media) packaging of a fundamentalistic form of Thai Buddhism that offers a way of embracing a secular modern life-style while retaining the communal identity once offered by traditional Buddhism—all the while maintaining that it is 'authentic' or 'true' Buddhism in contrast to its competitors." In this regard Pablo Deiros's description of fundamentalism as an "impulse" within Latin American evangelicalism might help to explain why the fundamentalist ethos is spread through the images and sound bites of modern media, as well as through the organizations and structures of a mass movement.

"Pure" Fundamentalism: A Final Example and Definition

Radical Sikhism provides a vivid example of many of the traits and the dynamics outlined above: a people fearing extinction under the conditions of a modernizing, westernizing, postcolonial, newly independent nation-state express their economic and political grievances through a communal reassertion of religious identity. This linkage is promoted by a number of charismatic leaders, the most prominent of which (in recent times) creates a new-old "pure" Sikh identity from a selective retrieval of traditional precepts and symbols. This retrieval is determined, at least in part, by a measure of political calculation.

As T. N. Madan points out, historically there have been many sources of Sikhism and several definitions of who is a Sikh. Yet the Singh Sabha movement, led by Sikh cultural elites at the turn of the century who feared assimilation into a syncretistic Hindu society, narrowed the definitions to one and excluded those who did not conform to it. Prior to this time, "Sikhs and Hindus not only lived together in Punjab but also shared a common cultural life, with common symbols and common cognitive and affective orientations." Sikhs had identified themselves in terms of village, cult, lineage, or caste, and did not project a single Sikh identity. But this sense of threat, due to the upsurge of Hindu communalism represented by the Arya Samaj, forced the polarization of the Sikh community and the forging of a new identity. The Arya Samajists denied the autonomy of the Sikhs as a sociocultural community and launched a purificatory movement, aimed first at preventing the conversion of Hindus to Islam and Christianity, later at "reconverting" Sikhs. Inevitably, the Singh Sabhas retaliated and attempted to win latitudinarian Sikhs and Hindu admirers of the faith into the fold of the baptized and the unshorn. Boundaries were set in "the demarcation of Sikh sacred space by clearing holy shrines of Hindu icons and idols, the cultivation of Punjabi as the sacred language of the Sikhs, [and] the foundation of cultural bodies exclusively for youth."

Meanwhile, the Singh Sabhas exemplified the institution-building side of fundamentalism as well by establishing schools and a college, opening orphanages, founding archives and historical societies, and producing a flood of polemical and scholarly literature on Sikh tradition. Significantly, the movement made the Granth Sahib freely available in printed editions. By the close of the century, Madan continues, there were over a hundred Sabhas all over Punjab, together contributing to the tide of Sikh separatism.

Instead of asserting a lost orthodoxy, these early radicals combined elements from diverse and often conflicting Sikh traditions so as to enhance the distinct nature of the religion—a move which resulted in a new and different Sikh identity, complete with ideology and practices commonly associated with Sikhism today. The contemporary heirs of the Singh Sabha movement have adopted the sense of threat and the crisis mentality. They consider themselves "pure Sikhs," defenders of the basic teachings of the Sikh gurus and the economic interests of the community. Their reaction has been directed not only at Hindus and Muslims but at those within Sikhism who violate their prescriptions for authentic Sikh practice (and thus identity), such as the Nirankari sect.

The charismatic leader of the Sikh radicals, Jarnail Bhindranwale, taught that in the pluralist environs of northern India, Sikhs require the protection of their own separate state in order to maintain their religious beliefs and practices without hindrance. He appropriated to his own purposes the slogan "The community of baptized Sikhs will rule." Like many fundamentalist leaders, Bhindranwale used the language of religion to give utterance to genuine and widespread economic grievances of both rural and urban believers. The Indian government's ineptitude and indifference to the Sikh plight "opened the way for Bhindranwale to present the issue of center-state relations in a religious framework—as discriminatory treatment of a religious minority by the government and as a threat to cultural identity." It was therefore a matter of general concern to the entire Sikh community.

In such a situation, Bhindranwale argued, "pure" Sikhs must reconvert the lapsed and resist external enemies, such as Hindus who denied Sikhs a separate socioreligious identity and the central and state governments which gave protection to apostates and other enemies of the Sikhs. In support of his advocacy of militancy as righteous action, Bhindranwale selected two precepts from the rich and diverse praxis and teachings of the ten Sikh gurus: the inseparability of religion and the state, or politics; and the indivisible or corporate character of the Sikh community. He also devoted a great deal of energy and rhetoric to defining both "a good Sikh," one who adheres to eighteenth- and nineteenth-century codes of conduct, and his enemies, those who have modernized or secularized their life-style. For his Sikh warriors Bhindranwale stressed the importance of remaining unshorn: a scandalous appearance would invite hostility and breed courage to resist it. To the traditional symbols of Sikh identity, the beard, the sword, and the short pants, Bhindranwale added two modern symbols, the motorcycle and the revolver.

Having thus dramatized the conditions facing Sikhs in the Punjab, Bhindranwale could pursue his reading of Sikh tradition to its inexorable end. Neither the people of the Punjab nor the precepts of the Sikh religion condone murder, but Bhindranwale's followers took arms, attacked several hundred innocent Hindus, and dared the opposition and the government to take the temple and defile sacred land. These were the typically confrontational actions of a fundamentalist leader who sought to foster a crisis, a time of decision, in order to force believers to choose between two worldviews in direct contradiction with each other. There was a certain logic, however disagreeable, to Bhindranwale's progression to violence. As Madan demonstrates, a careful consideration of the tradition indicates that militancy is advocated only as a last resort; however, radical or pure fundamentalists such as Bhindranwale are convinced that they have reached their last resort in their pursuit of a fundamentalist state—a pursuit untainted by compromise.

In these pages, then, fundamentalism has appeared as a tendency, a habit of mind, found within religious communities and paradigmatically embodied in certain representative individuals and movements, which manifests itself as a strategy, or set of strategies, by which beleaguered believers attempt to preserve their distinctive identity as a people or group. Feeling this identity to be at risk in the contemporary era, they fortify it by a selective retrieval of doctrines, beliefs, and practices from a sacred past. These retrieved "fundamentals" are refined, modified, and sanctioned in a spirit of shrewd pragmatism: they are to serve as a bulwark against the encroachment of outsiders who threaten to draw the believers into a syncretistic, areligious, or irreligious cultural milieu. Moreover, these fundamentals are accompanied in the new religious portfolio by unprecedented claims and doctrinal innovations. By the strength of these innovations and the new supporting doctrines, the retrieved and updated fundamentals are meant to regain the same charismatic intensity today by which they originally forged communal identity from the formative revelatory religious experiences long ago.

In this sense contemporary fundamentalism is at once both derivative and vitally original. In the effort to reclaim the efficacy of religious life, fundamentalists have more in common than not with other religious revivalists of past centuries. But fundamentalism intends neither an artificial imposition of archaic practices and life-styles nor a simple return to a golden era, a sacred past, a bygone time of origins—although nostalgia for such an era is a hallmark of fundamentalist rhetoric. Instead, religious identity thus renewed becomes the exclusive and absolute basis for a recreated political and social order that is oriented to the future rather than the past. By selecting elements of tradition and modernity, fundamentalists seek to remake the world in the service of a dual commitment to the unfolding eschatological drama (by returning all things in submission to the divine) and to self-preservation (by neutralizing the threatening "Other"). Such an endeavor often requires charismatic and authoritarian leadership, depends upon a disciplined inner core of adherents, and promotes a rigorous sociomoral code for all followers. Boundaries are set, the enemy identified, converts sought, and institutions created and sustained in pursuit of a comprehensive reconstruction of society.

Deconstructing Pure Fundamentalism

This definition of "pure fundamentalism," a synthesis of extremes to which certain movements tend, hardly provides an adequate guide to, or reflection of, the complexity and variety of the global phenomena portrayed in this volume. At best it perhaps provides a point of departure for subsequent investigations that, in exploring violations and modifications of this type, will likely render this early description obsolete. Such "violations of type" are indeed numerous in this volume, and it is worth briefly sketching some of them, not only to demonstrate the complexity of the fundamentalist phenomena but also to indicate some measure of the work that lies ahead in accounting for the almost endless variations on the central themes.

First, to assert that religious idealism is a central category of analysis for these movements is neither to isolate it from other categories nor to suggest that such idealism, or religious character, is determinative of particular kinds of fundamentalist behavior. In most cases the religious symbols, rituals, and concepts available to a charismatic leader come from a vast repertoire of possibilities within the tradition. The prevalence of eschatological scenarios does not, for example, guarantee that such scenarios will be interpreted in a consistent or predictable pattern within the fundamentalisms of a given tradition—or even within a given fundamentalism over time. Premillennialist Christians save souls, preserve moral and religious purity, create alternate rather than competing structures, and as a rule shun political activism in deference to the Coming Lord; while postmillennialist reconstructionists seek to topple humanistic governments, even if by lawful means and under the aegis of divine power. There is, then, no simple identification of messianic vision and sociopolitical program: the activist fundamentalists of the 1970s and 1980s, for example, fall somewhere between the premillennial and postmillennial extremes. Similarly, haredi Jews wait anxiously upon the Lord, eschewing reform by human hands. If they organize politically or engage in violence, it is less to establish a new order and more to preserve their threatened niche in the current one. Meanwhile, activist-believers of Gush Emunim also expect a messianic age, but their particular blend of magic and mysticism, coupled with their esoteric doctrine of the sacred spark embedded in even the most secularized hearts of Zionism, leads them to usher in the messianic age through particular sociopolitical acts designed to nudge the secularists toward their ultimate religious destiny (the most prominent of which has been the establishment of pioneering settlements in the disputed territories). And, despite the persistent expectation of the return of the Hidden Imam among Shiʿites, the same threefold religious experience—martyrdom, occultation, and precautionary dissimulation—has been invoked by different Shiʿite religious leaders to promote programs of activism under certain sociopolitical circumstances and of passive withdrawal under others.

Furthermore, although fundamentalisms have a religious basis—and in fact claim to represent the pristine and most authentic religious impulses of the tradition—the authors of this volume consistently question that very authenticity. Even while giving movements their due for compassionate and effective responses to social needs, they point out that fundamentalists narrow and rationalize the rich historic tradition at their disposal, often robbing it of its mysteries, mysticism, magical qualities, complexities, ambiguities, and situational character. For example, the richly symbolic and connotative scriptural descriptions of the Final Age are often reduced by fundamentalists to denotative blueprints of the order to come, demystified in the service of detailing the concrete plan of action required for sociopolitical ends. In this and other examples of the "objectification" of revelation, there is a curious and perhaps awkward imitation of the perceived empiricism of the enemy (secular rationality).

Donald Swearer is most direct in charging that "the absolutism of fundamentalism stems from this basic transformation of the religious worldview. The narrowly ideological nature of fundamentalism means that it is not 'religious' in the classical sense of that term but rather a variant of a secular faith couched in religious language and elevating traditional religious symbols stripped of their symbolic power to evoke a multiplicity of meanings." Swearer recalls the claim that Dharmapala's "intellectualist" view of Sinhalese Buddhism was derived from agnostic Westerners who used Buddhism as a foil against Christianity. Furthermore, according to Swearer, "the primary 'fundamentalism' extracted from the sacred 'source texts' of Sri Lanka (the myths and legends) is properly speaking more reflective of, and at the service of, the nationalist rather than the Buddhist worldview—although the two are inseparable in the rhetoric of the charismatic fundamentalist leaders." Religions thus harnessed to nationalism are often regarded as more pure and orthodox than the traditional forms they seek to supplant; in turn, nationalism readily takes on the character of a fervid, absolutistic revival of religion. "In the case of Sri Lanka, as elsewhere, the search for national identity is prior and conditions the fundamentalism of the religion(s) incorporated into nationalism." When fundamentalists give myths and legends a narrow, political interpretation, "they assume a totalitarian, highly ideological form, redundant in meaning."

Among the qualifications about the religious character of "pure fundamentalism" is the awareness that religion, culture, and economic interests have all been emphasized as the key element or elements in the fundamentalist demand for autonomy or independence. "The face is the same," T. N. Madan writes, "but the masks worn over it have been various." In this regard, a corollary to the variety of religious interpretations and blueprints for action available within the fundamentalist repertoire is *the variety of political alliances and platforms congenial to fundamentalism*. Fundamentalisms have both supported and opposed nationalist movements; have participated in democratic processes in some cases, but have favored authoritarian regimes or modified theocracies in others; have forged alliances with communists and socialists in order to form ruling coalitions in some nations, while bitterly opposing them in others. Although "pure fundamentalists," shrewd and media-savvy in their courting of public support, were described as enjoying in many instances a broad-based popular appeal, the hard core of that support has time and again proved to be statistically insignificant. Winston Davis has described the appeal of political and religious fundamentalism in Japan as situational; this can be said, with only slight qualification, of Sikh, Christian, and Jewish fundamentalisms as well. This is to suggest that fundamentalist elites or hard-core members working within a political system are *potentially* influential; that potential is activated when, and to the extent that, the statistically significant fringe, or soft-core, members or sympathizers rally around the leadership on a particular issue or issues. Thus the Moral Majority's success in the 1970s, such as it was, is attributable to the fact that "the New Christian Right convinced enormous numbers of voters that involvement was important through the intense commitment of a relatively small number of supporters."

The Jamaat-i-Islami of Pakistan provides an example of a movement that failed to mobilize the anticipated soft-core support, despite massive publicity and public contact campaigns. The Jamaat had since 1948 aspired to an Islamic "theodemocracy" in order to transform the entire spectrum of collective life in accordance with the teachings of the Qur'an and Sunna. "Hamara Mutalaba: Islami Dastur" ("We want an Islamic constitution") became a popular slogan throughout the country. For twenty years the Jamaat organized and lobbied for democratic elections on the assumption that given a free choice, the overwhelming majority of the people of Pakistan would vote for an Islamic constitution based on the Shari'a. In December 1970 a fair election was held, and the expectations of twenty years were shattered. The electorate's rejection of the Jamaat's goals undermined the movement's waning commitment to democracy and led to a new political strategy based on street power rather than number of seats in parliament. The Jamaat began to seek influence and power through nondemocratic means, including collaboration with the military regimes. "The facility and ease with which the Jamaat joined hands with the martial law regime of General Zia-ul-Haq in 1977 can be explained with reference to their disenchantment with the democratic process which they had experienced in 1970," Mumtaz Ahmad writes.

The contrast between the methods and goals of the Jamaat-i-Islami and its chief rival for recruits and influence on the Indian subcontinent, the Tablighi Jamaat, illustrates the diversity of patterns within fundamentalism and underscores the desirability of constructing a typology of fundamentalist and fundamentalist-like movements. The Jamaat-i-Islami is dedicated to the resacralization of political life and the establishment of an Islamic state with the Qur'an and Sunna as its constitution and the Shari'a as its basic law; the Tabligh movement is dedicated to the moral and spiritual renewal of individual believers, expected to fulfill their religious obligations even in the absence of an Islamic state. Yet Mumtaz Ahmad describes both as fundamentalist movements in view of their literalist interpretation of the Qur'an and the Sunna and in view of their common hostility toward, and reaction against, Islamic liberalism and their shared dedication to restore pristine Islam. Both of the movements enjoy enormous support in certain important sectors of Indian, Pakistani, and Bangladeshi societies. Apart from these similarities, however, there are important differences in their ideologies, organizations, and methods of *da'wa* (call). While the Tablighi Jamaat is a grassroots movement with followers from all sections of society, the Jamaat-i-Islami's support base consists mainly of educated, lower-middle-class Muslims from both the traditional and modern sectors of society. The Jamaat-i-Islami's emphasis on Islamization of politics and state has tended to transform the movement into a modern cadre-type political party, while the Tablighi Jamaat's program of strengthening the spiritual moorings of individual believers has helped it retain its character as a da'wa movement. The Jamaat-i-Islami is a highly structured, hierarchically organized, bureaucratic-type organization that has established a clear line of authority and a huge network of functional departments and nationwide branches; the Tablighi Jamaat, on the other hand, is a free-floating religious movement with minimal dependence on hierarchy, leadership positions, and decision-making procedures. Although both are primarily lay movements with minimal participation by the ulama, the Tablighi Jamaat is definitely closer to traditional forms of Islam than is the Jamaat-i-Islami, which in its own self-perception represents a synthesis of tradition and modernity. The Tablighi movement, moreover, shuns political involvement, because "those who are engaged in politics, whether they call themselves Islamic or secular, are always ready to compromise on their principles and values in the name of pragmatism, political strategy, tactics, or whatever."

The Tablighi Jamaat believes that political power does not in itself ensure the effective organization of an Islamic social order; political change must be preceded by the moral transformation of individuals and society. The policy implication of the Tablighi position for Indian Muslims is obvious: since Muslims in India are neither in possession of political power nor in a position to achieve it in the foreseeable future, those portions of the Qur'anic teachings that deal with government, state, and politics do not apply to them and will remain suspended. The Jamaat-i-Islami, whose ideology is based on the concept of Islam as a "complete way of life," considers the Tablighi Jamaat as a "pocket edition" of Islam and accuses it of making an un-Islamic distinction between religion and politics. The political neutrality of the Tabligh workers is interpreted by the Jamaat-i-Islami as their willingness not only to operate within the existing socioeconomic and political conditions but by acquiescing to help perpetuate and strengthen, if not legitimize, them.

This striking variance in Islamic movements in the same region is not unusual and raises a number of questions: Are both movements indeed fundamentalist? Which movement achieves the greater impact on outsiders? What are the political and social consequences of these varying approaches to religious revival?

Authors of the current volume have made a tentative beginning in charting varieties of fundamentalism, a task that will continue in later volumes. John Voll, for example, identifies discrete historical phases in which fundamentalism has been in dialectical relationship with trends in Egyptian society and government. Contemporary fundamentalism, he demonstrates, is manifested at four levels—in the widespread popular "return to religion" of the 1970s and 1980s; in the official state support of moderate Islamic institutions and policies; in the "mainstream" fundamentalism of the Muslim Brotherhood's social and political organizations; and in the militancy of radical activists, some of them splinter groups once identified with the Muslim Brotherhood. Similarly, Nancy Ammerman judges it necessary to distinguish between the radical Christian Reconstructionists, or members of Operation Rescue who go to jail, and "mainstream fundamentalists" like Jerry Falwell, who prefer to work within the law.

Other kinds of distinctions must be made among fundamentalist movements. In Israel, members of the Gush Emunim have grown up together in the same neighborhood schools, summer camps, and army units, and share songs, jokes, and newsletters. Women and children are an integral part of the movement. Their language is a "distinctive inflection and vocabulary: a rare mixture of Talmudic-based Yiddish expressions uttered with an Askenazic-Diaspora accent and a native Israeli vernacular borrowed from the IDF's lexicon and from the jargon of advanced technology, peppered with expressions of heroism and characterized by a congenial simplicity." Thus Aran describes the Gush Emunim as closer to "sectarian variation of fundamentalism than the mass anonymous type." And as mentioned above, the "situational fundamentalisms" of Buddhist and Confucian traditions warrant further scrutiny in terms of a typology of fundamentalism.

Such a typology must account, then, for the patterns of passive withdrawal from, and active engagement with, the outside world, both among movements and within the same movement over time. These patterns are observed in each essay in this volume, in the "exile politics" and "defensive engagement" of the haredi Jews, the "oppressed conscience" of Latin American fundamentalist churches, and the bursts of activist energy, followed by periods of enervation, in the rhythms of Gush Emunim life. This volume has also provided documentation of changes in fundamentalist strategy *over time* within an activist orientation: at a certain point, fundamentalists may be forced to form coalitions and to adopt tactics previously deemed unsuitable or foreign. For example, Abdulaziz Sachedina writes that "in their accommodation with modernity and in their efforts to provide a viable Islamic alternative ideology in a modern nation-state, jurists such as Khomeini and Sadr had to make meaningful choices of their own, which included accepting some elements of modern secular political culture like nationalism and even popular political participation—an anomaly to the traditional conceptualization of political authority. By the mid-1970s, Khomeini had provided the Iranians an innovative but authentically traditional alternative to the "colonizing culture" of the West. Daniel Gold, writing of the elections in India in 1989, describes the stunning victory of the political party backed by the Hindu revivalists and comments on the coalitions necessary to form and sustain the victorious alliance.

Also to be charted are the progressions within fundamentalism from "insider" to "outsider" status within a pluralist culture—or vice versa. In the case of Christian fundamentalism, for example, the movement remained alive and began to thrive because its institutional structure was so strong in spite of its outsider status. Periods of public prominence and prosperity in turn have provided the economic and social foundations for new phases of institution building. The demands of institutionalization and the consequences of success further compromise pure fundamentalism. The difficulty of maintaining ideological consistency is underscored by the fact that once established, institutions tend to have a life and momentum of their own, shaping the actions of those who serve them. Self-perpetuation, even at the cost of compromise, becomes a priority. The millennialism of the Christian Reconstructionists, for example, holds that the Bible will eventually become the dominant force in the culture, and that Christians will come to power without resorting to political or military coercion to restrict nonbelievers: they will participate with God in a victory God has

ly at the defi-
tory volume—
rich tapestry

d clerical manage-
ons according to
pected, so alien to
that it was less a
ssment. The par-
n a revolutionary
w nor particularly
of a popular revo-
tablishment of a
unlikely as to be
ll Down: America's
Iran [New York:
paperback edition,

ty, "Fundamental-
on," *Bulletin of the*
ts and Sciences 42
9.
, "Extremism as a
al for the Scientific
3): 79.
i fundamentalism,
dramatic eschato-
muted eschatology
mainstrean Sunni
sm and forceful in-
he individual Mus-
ous self-fulfillment"
ndence to authors,

cked in Samuel C.
n Friedman's essay

ys a less prominent
ntalism, so too are
demarcated; they
istinctiveness of the
establish barriers
environment.

utional base, reconstructionists find them-
hat will reduce taxes or erode the govern-
s that enforce Christian moral norms. And
e and visibility, a new generation of leaders
ask-oriented . . . in response to this pro-
no less radical, they seem much more prac-
unim has suffered from success, especially
's role in inciting the Intifada.

portrayed in this volume both as angry
amuel Heilman's term, and as creators of
proven themselves able to enter and leave
nd of course the circumstances change at
s of the various movements and individ-
ere asked to bring their historical essays
ssible, but that "moment" has changed
these essays to be copyedited. During
Iraq invaded Kuwait and Saddam Hus-
ly suppressed Shi'ite opposition to his
Western forces in Saudi Arabia and
ament was assassinated, reportedly by
sraeli riot police killed twenty-one Pal-
f in Jerusalem, sparking new and un-
sm on the part of Jewish and Islamic
dical Rabbi Meir Kahane was assassi-
Muslims died in India during weeks of
of the Babri mosque/the birthplace of
s barred from the presidential election
on enough votes to qualify for a run-
ditors to ask readers immediately to
at remains in the present tense.

of scholars will examine the various
ty. Tentatively entitled *Remaking the*
mine the points of disagreement be-
orldviews, with particular attention
on of technologies. The inquiry then
imate to the most public, beginning
ly and interpersonal relationships.
ories informed by fundamentalists'
development of educational systems
smitting fundamentalists' message;
legal reform, political activism, and
itancy when polities break down or
conomists, military experts, anthro-
litical scientists, and sociologists of

education. In these and subsequent volumes, scholars will tug vigor
nitional and descriptive threads woven together in this initial, explora
and discover whether they unravel or instead form the fabric for
depicting various manifestations and forms of "fundamentalism."

Notes

1. Lionel Caplan, ed., *Studies in Religious Fundamentalism* (Albany: State University of New York Press, 1987).

2. Bruce B. Lawrence, *Defenders of God: The Fundamentalist Revolt Against the Modern Age* (San Francisco: Harper and Row, 1989), pp. 100–101.

3. Gary Sick, the principal White House aide for Iran on the National Security Council staff during the revolution and the Iranian hostage crisis laments the failure of American policymakers to comprehend the enduring appeal and motivational force of radical religion in the Third World: "[There are] contradictions between Khomeini's Islamic, theocratic revolution and the Western tradition of secularizing revolutions. In my view, this tension between the secular and the religious was a major contributing factor to the failure of both Iranians and Westerners to recognize the revolution in its early stages and to gauge properly its actual course and eventual outcome. We are all prisoners of our own cultural assumptions, more than we care to admit. Those of us who are products of Western cultural tradition—even if our national origins are in Africa or Asia—share certain assumptions that are so firmly ingrained that they no longer require discussion but are regarded almost as natural law—inevitable and irrevocable. It is now two centuries since the first modern revolution in 1776, and over that span of time the world has grown accustomed to the most outlandish proposals for the revolutionary change of political, social and economic conditions. We may be difficult to persuade, but we are no longer easily surprised. Nevertheless, Khomeini's call for the establishment of a religious philosopher-king, the *vilayat-i faqih,* an
ment of political instituti
religious law was so unexp
existing political traditions
surprise than an embarra
ticipation of the church i
movement was neither ne
disturbing, but the notion
lution leading to the e
theocratic state seemed s
absurd" (Gary Sick, *All F*
Tragic Encounter With
Viking Penguin, 1985;
1986], pp. 192–93).

4. Cf. Martin E. Mar
ism as a Social Phenome
American Academy of A
(November 1988): 15–2

5. Charles S. Liebma
Religious Norm," *Journ*
Study of Religion 22 (198

6. "The case of Sun
for example, displays le
logical tendencies. The
stems in part from th
component of voluntar
clination to encourage
lim to strive for relig
(Gehad Auda, corresp
1 May 1990).

7. The term is unp
Heilman and Menache
(chap. 4).

8. If eschatology pl
role in Sunni fundam
boundaries less sharp
serve to identify the
group rather than t
against the surroundin

GLOSSARY

Aḥmadiyya. A Mahdist sect founded in 1882 by the Punjabi Mirzā Ghulām Aḥmad (1835–1908). Declaring the West to be a form of the Antichrist, Aḥmad urged his followers to concentrate on the quietist path of Islamic renewal rather than to actively confront Western power. Ahmad in his later years would claim to be the Mahdī, the Second Coming of Jesus, and the last avatar of the Hindu god Vishnu.

Anabaptist. From the Greek *ana* (again) and *baptizo* (literally, to rebaptize), this movement rose to prominence in the sixteenth century by virtue of its extreme position in denying the validity of infant baptism. The term came to be loosely applied to a variety of small Protestant sects, of which the Mennonites and the Hutterites survive to this day.

Ashkenazic Jews. European Jewry, most often associated with Germany and Yiddish language and culture. The term is used in contrast to "Sephardic Jews," those of Spanish origin, although the latter term is often used for Jews from Middle Eastern countries as well.

ʿAshura. The tenth day of the month of Muḥarram; the date of Ḥusayn's death in Kerbala in modern-day Iraq, which is the occasion throughout the Shiʿite world for intensely emotional commemoration ceremonies, often characterized by the performance of passion plays reenacting the martyrdom of Ḥusayn and self-flagellation to mourn the failure of the people to provide the promised support of Ḥusayn.

Autochthonous. An autochthonous church is one that is local in terms of membership, inspiration, and finance and control. The term is most often used in connection with Latin American Protestantism to distinguish those churches which spring from the local community from those whose roots are North American.

Ayatollah. From the Arabic *Āyat Āllah* (literally, "sign of God"), this title, which came into vogue in Iran only in the twentieth century, is an honorific indicating a leading *mujtahid* (q.v.), or Islamic jurisprudent in Twelver Shiʿism.

Bhikku. A member of the sangha, the Buddhist order of monks.

B'nai Brith. The Anti-Defamation League of the B'nai Brith, or "Sons of the Covenant" in literal Hebrew, was founded in Chicago in 1913 by attorney Samuel Livingston to fight anti-Semitism. It is the world's largest Jewish service organization.

Bushidō. The traditional samurai code of ethics, which combined an idealized view of Japanese feudalism with elements of Shinto, Confucian ethical teachings, and Zen Buddhism into a comprehensive code of conduct: "The Way of the Warrior."

Charismatic Movement. A twentieth-century movement which has swept a number of Protestant denominations and independent churches, and which since the late 1960s has become influential in the Roman Catholic Church as well. The movement centers on ecstatic forms of worship, most notably speaking in tongues and healing through faith, which are considered to be the gifts of the Holy Spirit.

Creationism. Or Scientific Creationism. Belief, first published by Charles Hodge in

What Is Darwinism? (1874), that the account of the world's origin in the biblical book of Genesis is literally true and historically accurate.

Denominationalism. By strict definition, "denominationalism" describes the organizational shape of American Protestantism, with denominations whose arenas of competition range far beyond abstract points of theology. The term in this sense has often been misleadingly applied to competitive sects (q.v.) in such religious traditions as Buddhism or Judaism. Among some Protestant fundamentalists, denominationalism has come to have a pejorative connotation and may even be used as an epithet for Protestants who remain attached to the mainline denominations.

Dhamma. (Sanskrit Dharma) Dhamma has a number of meanings which coalesce on two different but interrelated levels. As the *law*, it is the ordering principle of the cosmos, governing all forms of existence. It is therefore also the necessary *path* for the human to follow, both to escape from the chain of existence through serial incarnations and to improve the conditions of existence in this world by harmonizing that existence with the cosmic order.

Dispensationalist. One who adheres to the doctrine that history is divided into "dispensations," the last of which will be the reign of Christ. There are a variety of interpretations of these dispensations and especially of the sequence of Final Things. Most common is the teaching that there are seven such ways in which God has dealt with or will deal with the world, and that the millennial (*see* millenarianism) reign will be preceded by the Rapture (q.v.).

Druze. A secretive sect of Ismā'īli Shi'ites who broke away from the Fāṭimid caliphate in Egypt, accepting the claim of the Fāṭimid Caliph al-Ḥākim to be an incarnation of the divinity in 1017 C.E.

Ecumenism. A movement which arose early in the twentieth century and sought to increase cooperation among the Christian denominations of the world. The movement coalesced at a 1910 gathering of Protestant missionary churches in Edinburgh, Scotland. World War I gave it impetus. Highpoints include the 1927 World Conference on Faith and Order in Lausanne, Switzerland, which concentrated on joint social action, and the 1948 formation of the the World Council of Churches at Amsterdam, Holland. The WCC initially consisted of 148 Protestant and exile Eastern Orthodox denominations, with the Russian Orthodox church joining later and bringing with it several Eastern European denominations.

Epistemology. From the Greek *episteme* (knowledge or science). Epistemology is the philosophical science which may be considered a theory of knowledge. It is concerned with understanding all facets of human knowledge, from its origins to its nature, and extends to the theoretical limits of human knowledge.

Eschatology. From the Greek *eschatos* (last things) and *logos* (knowledge of). The eschatological interests of postexilic Judaism, Christianity, and Islam center on a number of often related doctrines concerning the final things or the end of history. These include messianism, resurrection and subsequent immortality, and a final judgment and triumph of the faithful.

Etiology. From the Greek term *aitia* (cause). Etiology is the study of causation and can be applied to any branch of knowledge or inquiry.

Faqīh. A practitioner of *fiqh* (q.v.).

Fiqh. Jurisprudence. It is the study and application of the religious *Shari'a* (q.v.) law. Considered the "Queen of Islamic Sciences."

Guru. A Sanskrit term translating literally as "heavy." A guru in Hinduism is primarily a teacher, although in the Indian sense the guru is expected to provide a model for all phases of life. In popular modern Hindu parlance, the guru is considered to be an individual with a deep, mystical connection to the deity. The term has been borrowed by a variety of cultures and religious traditions, for example, the *tok guru* of Malaysian popular Islam, without substantial changes of connotation.

Hadith. The documented reports of the sayings and actions of the Prophet Muhammad which do not appear directly in the Qur'an, as reported by his close companions *(anṣār)* and family members *(ahl al-bayt)*. The most reliable collections of hadith, those of al-Bukhārī (d. 870) and al-Muslim (d.875), serve with the Qur'an as the basis of every school of Islamic law.

Ḥajj. The pilgrimage to Mecca to be undertaken, if humanly possible, at least once in the life of each Muslim. One of the "Five Pillars of Islam," the Ḥajj is today televised throughout the Islamic world and was the occasion for violent clashes between Saudi forces and Iranian pilgrims in the 1980s.

Halakha. The Jewish legal system, based on the Talmudic compendium of 613 divinely ordained commandments.

Haskala. A Hebrew term meaning "enlightenment." This movement was especially active in late-eighteenth-century Germany, and under the intellectual influence of Moses Mendelssohn (d. 1786), it sought to promote within Judaism secular education and the values of the European Enlightenment as a method of integrating Jewry into the mainstream of European culture.

Hermeneutics. From the Greek *hermeneutikos* (interpretation). It refers to the interpretation of texts.

Hijrah. In its original sense, the term refers to the flight of the Prophet Muhammad from Mecca to Medina in 622 C.E. (the year 1 in the Islamic Hijrah calendar). The term has been adopted by Islamic fundamentalist groups to signify a termporary escape from societies deemed by them to have abandoned Islam.

Inerrancy. The term was originally associated with fundamentalist Protestantism, which held the text of the Bible to be the Word of God, revealed without error, although later transcriptions or translations did introduce some errors. This is the source of the Protestant fundamentalist emphasis on finding the "original autographs" of biblical text.

Ijtihad. The use of reason to interpret Shariʿa (q.v.) in the light of present-day circumstances. Shiʿite Islam enshrines this function as the prerogative of senior *mujtahids* (q.v.), while for all practical purposes Sunni Islam gradually abandoned the practice through the teaching of al-Ghazali (d. 1111) and others who "closed the gates of ijtihad." A key demand of many Sunnī fundamentalists is to reopen the practice of ijtihad.

Imam. A highly emotive word carrying several meanings. For Sunnis, an imam is a prayer leader. For Shiʿites, an Imam is one of the historical leaders of the Shiʿite community (numbering either five, six, or twelve in different Shiʿite sects). These leaders have over time taken on messianic aspects which preclude anyone now living from adopting the title in this sense. However, the term is applied in the sense of an honorific to outstanding Shiʿite religious leaders, most recently to Ayatollah Khomeini of Iran and Musa Sadr of Lebanon.

Integralism. This conservative movement within Roman Catholicism in the late nineteenth and twentieth centuries was so named for its position that each and every tenet of the Catholic tradition descended from the medieval scholastic theologians must be upheld as integral to the seamless perfection of the whole of Roman Catholic doctrine.

Intifada. Literally, in Arabic, "to shake off." "Intifada" has been adopted as the name for the Arab uprising against the Israeli occupation of the West Bank and Gaza Strip which began in late 1987 in the Gaza Strip and rapidly spread throughout the occupied territories.

Jainism. A nondeistic religion which arose between the sixth and eighth centuries B.C.E., Jainism is a system based on the doctrines of a series of great teachers with the early seventh century figure of Mahāvīra as the most important for his systemization of the Jain canon. Jainism, like Buddhism and Hinduism, is a karmic religion whose practicers seek escape from the cycle of rebirth through the Three Jewels (right belief, right knowledge, and right conduct).

Jihad. Struggle, usually an internal process against bad habits or irreligious behavior. The term also denotes war ordained as in the service of religion, although the circumstances justifying such a struggle are the subject of considerable debate.

Kabbalistic. An adjective derived from the rich and complex traditions of Jewish mysticism, popularly grouped together as "the Kabbala," which stood in opposition to the legalistic doctrine of the Talmudists (*see* halakha). In general, the kabbala's development may be traced to approximately two centuries before Christ, and reached its fullest flowering by the fourteenth century. "Kabbalistic" in current usage indicates that a particular idea or doctrine originates in the literature of kabbala, with the work of Isaac Luria (d. 1572) of primary importance. Hasidic Jews look to the kabbalistic work of the Besht (Israel ben Eliezer, d. 1760).

Kami. Primarily a term for Shinto (i.e., The Way of the *Kami*), the word itself refers loosely to supernatural beings, gods and goddesses, and spirits of every sort, as well as to the awesome power of nature and to the certain great men of the past. It has been adopted by a number of Japanese religious traditions.

Karma. (Sanskrit) A complex doctrine, originating in early Hinduism and subsequently adopted by Buddhism and Jainism, which holds that all human actions, positive and negative, have effects which determine the cycle of birth and death.

Kerygma. Literally, "good news," in Greek; refers to the New Testament message of salvation in Jesus Christ.

Kashrut. More commonly, "kosher" (acceptable). Jewish dietary laws describe the requirements for acceptable food.

Madrasah. The traditional educational institution of the Islamic world. The curriculum centers on religious subjects, particularly Islamic law, with literature, Arabic grammar, and history also taught. In recent years some madrasah have also incorporated modern, Western learning. The madrasah carries on the tradition of resident study along the lines of a boarding school.

Mahdi. A messianic figure in Islam, the mahdi in Islamic eschatology (q.v.) will be sent by God to defeat the enemies of Islam and establish a universal realm of perfect peace which will culminate in the Final Judgment. The appearances of false Mahdis have not been infrequent in Islamic history, however, with the last well-known example being Muḥammad bin 'Abd Allāh al-Qahtani, who in 1979 attempted to seize the Grand Mosque in Mecca.

Manichaeism. In its original sense the religion of Mani, a third-century C.E. sage or prophet of Babylonian origin, Manichaeism posited a stark, strongly dualistic view of the cosmos serving as the battleground between the Kingdom of Light, identified with God, and the Kingdom of Darkness, which came to be identified with Satan. Also indicates a dichotomy between spirit and matter. From the European Middle Ages to this day, the term has been applied to describe a number of religious groups or doctrines holding a strongly dualist worldview.

Marja' al-Taqlīd. Literally "model of imitation," this title is bestowed on the highest-ranking *mujtahids* (q.v.) of Shi'ite Islam. The rulings of the *marja'* are authoritative and binding on all who voluntarily acknowledge his authority. In some historical periods there is a sole *marja'*, in other times there is a "circle of marja's," while occasionally no one is so recognized.

Millenarianism. For Christians, millenarianism is centered on the New Testament Book of Revelation, holding the promise of Christ's establishment of a thousand-year reign of perfect peace and justice on this earth, followed by a general resurrection and judgment of the dead. The oral traditions of Islam hold out a similar promise, although the thousand-year period is not in all sources.

Missiology. A term associated most often with Roman Catholicism. Missiology is the study of the church's mission of evangelization, both in historical terms and in the present context. Protestantism utilizes the term too. One who specializes in the outreach and conversion activities of various Protestant churches is often styled a missiologist.

Mujtahid. A senior Shi'ite who is entrusted with the exercise of *ijtihād* (q.v.).

Modernism. For Roman Catholics the term denotes a primarily clerical movement of the late nineteenth and early twentieth centuries which was strongest in Europe. Condemned by Pope Pius X in 1907, Catholic modernism tried to integrate church doctrine with modern scientific thought, including biblical criticism. Among Protestants, modernism was associated with higher biblical criticism, as well as with an emphasis on ethics and works over theological speculation and dogma.

Nirvana. (Sanskrit) The term means literally "blown out" or extinguished. Nirvana is the escape or salvation from the karmic cycle of reincarnation.

Ontology. From the Greek *ontos* (being), "ontology" means literally the "knowledge of being." It is the branch of philosophy seeking to comprehend all aspects of the nature of being, ranging from the nature of God to human nature.

Pali Canon. So named for the language in which it is written, the Pali Canon contains the oldest-known collection of Buddhist texts. The originals, all now lost, are believed to have been written within 500 years of Buddha's death. The canon covers a vast range of subjects, including religious doctrine, history and royal lineage, and rules of monastic discipline.

Pentecostal Sects. A number of Protestant sects, centered in the United States but with a worldwide appeal, which put primary emphasis on the charismatic (*see* Charismatic Movement) gifts of the Holy Spirit, particularly glossolalia (speaking in tongues) associated with the day of Pentecost recounted in the New Testament.

Pietism. A movement originating in the Lutheran church and based originally on the teachings of Philip J. Spener (d. 1705), which combined a highly emotive, participatory form of community-based worship.

Purāṇa. One of the four classes of Hindu scripture known as the Shāstras (q.v.), the Purana is in essence a book of eighteen extended religious poems which were gathered and codified in the fourth century C.E.

Praxis. From the Greek meaning deed or action, praxis refers to the practical application of philosophical or theological doctrine or theory.

Presbyterians. Deriving its forms of organization, as well as much of its doctrine, from John Calvin, the Presbyterian church is noted for leadership invested in a "presbyter," or elder, rather than exclusively under the control of ordained clergy. Above the local level are regional organizations of member congregations governed by representatives of ministers and lay elders, in equal numbers.

Rapture. Christian doctrine based on I Thessalonians 4:17, holding that the horrors of the tribulation (q.v.) will be avoided by the elect as they will be raised into the air with Christ to await the millenial kingdom (*see* Millenarianism).

Salaf. An Arabic term whose literal meaning is "ancestors," *salaf* in Islamic parlance refers to the the first generation of Muslims, under the guidance of the Prophet Muhammad, whose example is considered to be the most authoritative source of guidance for Muslims today on questions ranging from religion and ethics to, for many fundamentalists, law and government (*see* Salafiyyah Movement).

Salafiyyah Movement. An early-twentieth-century Islamic movement founded by the Islamic modernist thinkers Jamāl ad-Dīn al-Afghānī and Mohammad 'Abduh. The name of the movement somewhat misleadingly means the "way of the pious ancestors." In fact, the movement aimed at a synthesis of Islamic beliefs with modern Western learning (*see* Salaf, Ijtihād).

Samsara. A Hindu and later a Buddhist term referring, in the most general terms, to the cycle of rebirth. It is thus closely related to the doctrine of karma (q.v.). Ignorance is traditionally considered to be the root cause of samsara, yet samsara is often considered in positive terms, in that it encourages man to adopt the rigorous path to liberation.

Sangha. The community or class of Buddhist monks. Along with the Buddha and the dhamma (q.v.), the sangha is one of the Three Jewels in which Buddhists seek refuge and ultimate liberation from the karmic cycle of rebirth and the unhappiness of life.

Sannyāsin. A renunciate, literally, "one who renounces," in Sanskrit. The *sannyāsin* is one who has reached the fourth and highest stage of the Brahman religious life by renouncing caste, giving up all material considerations of the householder, and living the mendicant life.

Sects. "Sects" is related in meaning to "denominations" (*see* Denominationalism), save that adherents of sects are seen as deviating in some way from the doctrinal or behavioral norms of the denominational group. Sects therefore tend to be small and cohesive and are often held together by some form of charismatic leadership.

Shamanism. A term originally associated with the peoples of Siberia and Central Asia and used to refer to a set group of magical and cosmological rituals. The term *shaman* has come in recent years to be loosely applied to figures as disparate as Christian charismatic preachers, faith healers and specialists in miracle cures, spiritualists of various sorts, and most accurately, American Indian tribal medicine men. In all of these forms, the central function of the shaman is to mediate between the spiritual and physical worlds so as to achieve a balance which followers of such a figure may find comforting, or even profitable.

Shari'a. The body of Islamic sacred or "canon" law. Derived primarily from the Qur'an and secondarily from the Sunna, or Oral Traditions of the Prophet, these immutable laws are held to be the basis of a divinely ordained pattern of life and are believed to regulate every aspect of life. There are today four major schools of Shariʿa among Sunnīs and one Shiʿite school.

Shāstras. Literally "Sacred Book" in Sanskrit, *shāstras* is the general term for the four classes of Hindu scriptures: *shruti, smṛti, purāṇa* (q.v.), and *tantra.*

Sit Shiva. The Jewish rite of mourning, somewhat analogous to the Roman Catholic wake, in which the bereaved family hosts a gathering with both religious and social dimensions.

Soteriological. In its original sense, the *soter* or savior is the hero of a struggle for knowledge (gnosis) or liberation whose victory is seen to extend beyond himself to the whole body of his followers, or gnostic initiates in this sense.

Sufism. A term applied to the rich but highly eclectic mystical tradition of Islam. Sufis sought a mystical union with Allah through love and renunciation. Sufis came over time to be identified with Shiʿism and were of key importance in the conversion to Islam of successive waves of tribal invaders into the lands of Islam.

Sunna. Literally "custom" in Arabic, the term refers to the customs and habits of the Prophet Muhammad, which are in the ideal normative and binding on Muslims. Drawn from the Qur'an and the *hadith* (q.v.), the Sunna provides a model of all phases of life to which, by imitation, the Muslim is enjoined to aspire.

Sūtra. (Pali Sutta). A distinct, terse, literary form in which the ancient Hindu Vedas (q.v.) and the later works of Mahayana Buddhism are cast. In the form of aphorism, which is the literal Sanskrit meaning of the term, these verses transmit the rules governing the correct forms of ritual, grammar, philosophy, and the like.

Taqiyya. Dissimulation as a protective Shiʿite doctrine which allows the believer to conceal his real beliefs whenever his life might be endangered by those beliefs.

Tariqah. A term which is used both to indicate the Sufi tradition (*see* Sufism) and to designate individual Sufi brotherhoods, or "lodges."

Theravada. The oldest of the three main schools of Hinayana Buddhism. Theravada Buddhists produced the Pali canon.

Tribulation. Series of events following the Rapture (q.v.) and ending with the final battle against the Antichrist and the establishment of the millennial kingdom by Christ.

Ultramontanism. In its strongest form, ultramontanism reflects the claim of Roman Catholicism and the papacy to dominance over the temporal and ecclesiastical order. Developed in reaction to the winds of modernity sweeping Europe in the latter eighteenth century, ultramontanism contributed to the strongly conservative cast of the nineteenth-century papacy, culminating in Pope Pius IX's pontificate and the First Vatican Council (1869–70), at which the doctrine of papal infallibility was adopted (*see* Integralism).

'Ushr. The Islamic tithe on a Muslim's property, which is intended to support the needy. *'Ushr* is not to be confused with *Zakat,* a tithe on income which is one of the "five pillars" of Islam.

Vedas. Literally, "knowledge," in Sanskrit. The Vedas are a wide-ranging collection of Indian sacred texts, composed 1400 B.C.E.–400 B.C.E. While there remains little scholarly agreement on the precise nature of this body of knowledge, it may be possible to discern four basic divisions. The Brāhmaṇas contain the rites of sacrifice. The Āraṇyakas are speculative treatises interpreting the Brañhmaṇas. The four-part Saṃhitās are Vedic hymns used in connection with the sacrifices. The Upaniṣads, also known as the Vedāntas (lit. "end of Vedās," in Sanskrit), are a collection of some two hundred texts which contain the full flowering of Hindu philosophy.

Yeshiva. A Jewish religious academy whose exclusively male student body undertakes extensive study of the Talmud and other rabbinic literature. In addition to training students for careers in religion, the Yeshiva may offer courses to Jews from all walks of life seeking to enrich their knowledge of Judaism.

Yishuv. The Jewish community in Israel. The yishuv consists of the "old yishuv," the pre-Zionist Jewish population of Palestine, and the "new yishuv," the Zionist immigrants.

CONTRIBUTORS

Mumtaz Ahmad
Associate Professor of Political Science
Hampton University

Nancy T. Ammerman
Associate Professor of the Sociology of Religion
Candler School of Theology, Emory University

R. Scott Appleby
Associate Director
The Fundamentalism Project
American Academy of Arts and Sciences

Gideon Aran
Lecturer in Sociology and Anthropology
Hebrew University, Jerusalem

Winston Davis
Wilson-Craven Professor of Religion
Southwestern University

Pablo A. Deiros
Professor of History
Seminario Internacional Teológico Bautista, Buenos Aires

William D. Dinges
Associate Professor of Religion and Religious Education
Catholic University of America

Menachem Friedman
Associate Professor of Sociology
Bar-Ilan University, Ramat-Gan

Daniel Gold
Associate Professor of South Asian Religions
Cornell University

Samuel C. Heilman
Professor of Sociology
Queens College, City University of New York

James Hitchcock
Professor of History
St. Louis University

T. N. Madan
Professor of Sociology
Institute of Economic Growth
University of Delhi

Martin E. Marty
Fairfax M. Cone Distinguished Service Professor of the History of Modern Christianity
University of Chicago

Manning Nash
Professor of Anthropology
University of Chicago

Abdulaziz A. Sachedina
Professor of Religious Studies and Oriental Languages
University of Virginia

Donald K. Swearer
Eugene M. Lang Research Professor of Religion
Swarthmore College

Tu Wei-ming
Professor of Chinese History and Philosophy
Harvard University

John O. Voll
Professor of History
University of New Hampshire

INDEX